ICT

for Cambridge IGCSE™

COURSEBOOK

David Waller, Victoria Wright & Denise Taylor

CAMBRIDGE
UNIVERSITY PRESS

University Printing House, Cambridge CB2 8BS, United Kingdom

One Liberty Plaza, 20th Floor, New York, NY 10006, USA

477 Williamstown Road, Port Melbourne, VIC 3207, Australia

314–321, 3rd Floor, Plot 3, Splendor Forum, Jasola District Centre, New Delhi – 110025, India

103 Penang Road, #05–06/07, Visioncrest Commercial, Singapore 238467

Cambridge University Press is part of the University of Cambridge.

It furthers the University's mission by disseminating knowledge in the pursuit of education, learning and research at the highest international levels of excellence.

www.cambridge.org
Information on this title: www.cambridge.org/9781108901093

© Cambridge University Press 2021

This publication is in copyright. Subject to statutory exception and to the provisions of relevant collective licensing agreements, no reproduction of any part may take place without the written permission of Cambridge University Press.

First published 2010
Second edition 2016
Third edition 2021

20 19 18 17 16 15 14 13 12 11 10 9 8 7 6 5 4 3 2 1

Printed in Italy by L.E.G.O. S.p.A.

A catalogue record for this publication is available from the British Library

ISBN 9781108901093 Coursebook Paperback with Digital Access (2 Years)
ISBN 9781108828215 Digital Coursebook (2 Years)
ISBN 9781108828222 Coursebook eBook

Additional resources for this publication at www.cambridge.org/go

Cambridge University Press has no responsibility for the persistence or accuracy of URLs for external or third-party internet websites referred to in this publication, and does not guarantee that any content on such websites is, or will remain, accurate or appropriate. Information regarding prices, travel timetables, and other factual information given in this work is correct at the time of first printing but Cambridge University Press does not guarantee the accuracy of such information thereafter.

Exam-style questions and sample answers have been written by the authors. In examinations, the way marks are awarded may be different. References to assessment and/or assessment preparation are the publisher's interpretation of the syllabus requirements and may not fully reflect the approach of Cambridge Assessment International Education.

Cambridge International copyright material in this publication is reproduced under license and remains the intellectual property of Cambridge Assessment International Education.

Third-party websites and resources referred to in this publication have not been endorsed by Cambridge Assessment International Education.

....

NOTICE TO TEACHERS IN THE UK
It is illegal to reproduce any part of this work in material form (including photocopying and electronic storage) except under the following circumstances:
(i) where you are abiding by a licence granted to your school or institution by the Copyright Licensing Agency;
(ii) where no such licence exists, or where you wish to exceed the terms of a licence, and you have gained the written permission of Cambridge University Press;
(iii) where you are allowed to reproduce without permission under the provisions of Chapter 3 of the Copyright, Designs and Patents Act 1988, which covers, for
example, the reproduction of short passages within certain types of educational anthology and reproduction for the purposes of setting examination questions.

Contents

The items in orange are accessible to teachers for free on the supporting resources area of Cambridge GO.

How to use this series		v
How to use this book		vi
Introduction		viii

1 Types and components of computer systems — 1
- 1.1 Hardware and software — 3
- 1.2 The main components of computer systems — 8
- 1.3 Operating systems — 11
- 1.4 Types of computer — 14
- 1.5 Emerging technologies — 17

2 Input and output devices — 23
- 2.1 Input devices — 25
- 2.2 Direct data entry and associated devices — 34
- 2.3 Output devices and their uses — 39

3 Storage — 46
- 3.1 Storage devices and media — 48

4 Networks — 59
- 4.1 Networks — 61
- 4.2 Network issues and communication — 69

5 The effects of using IT — 80
- 5.1 Microprocessor-controlled devices — 82
- 5.2 Health issues — 87

6 ICT applications — 92
- 6.1 Communication — 94
- 6.2 Modelling applications — 98
- 6.3 Computer-controlled systems — 100
- 6.4 School management systems — 104
- 6.5 Online booking systems — 106
- 6.6 Banking applications — 107
- 6.7 Computers in medicine — 111
- 6.8 Expert systems — 113
- 6.9 Computers in the retail industry — 116
- 6.10 Recognition systems — 120
- 6.11 Satellite systems — 122

7 The systems life cycle — 129
- 7.1 The systems life cycle — 131
- 7.2 Analysis of the current system — 131
- 7.3 Design — 135
- 7.4 Testing — 141
- 7.5 System implementation — 143
- 7.6 Documentation — 146
- 7.7 Evaluation — 148

8 Safety and security — 152
- 8.1 Physical safety issues — 154
- 8.2 eSafety — 156
- 8.3 Security of data — 161

9 Know your audience — 172
- 9.1 Audience appreciation — 174
- 9.2 Copyright and intellectual property — 175

10 Communication — 180
- 10.1 Communication with other ICT users using email — 182
- 10.2 Effective use of the internet — 185

11 File management — 197
- 11.1 Manage files effectively — 199
- 11.2 Reducing file sizes for storage or for transmission — 205

12 Images — 210
- 12.1 Placing and editing images — 212
- 12.2 Reducing file size — 222

13 Layout — 232
- 13.1 Create a new document or edit an existing one — 235
- 13.2 Tables — 244
- 13.3 Headers and footers — 251

14 Styles		**264**
14.1	Creating and editing consistent styles	266
14.2	Purpose and uses of corporate house style	282
15 Proofing		**286**
15.1	Automated software tools to reduce errors	288
15.2	Proofing techniques	302
16 Graphs and charts		**309**
16.1	Creating and editing a graph or chart	311
16.2	Formatting charts or graphs	326
17 Document production		**337**
17.1	Organise page layout	340
17.2	Formatting text	346
17.3	Find and replace text	354
17.4	Navigation	356
18 Databases		**369**
18.1	Creating an appropriate database structure	371
18.2	Manipulating data	399
18.3	Presenting data	413
19 Presentations		**438**
19.1	Creating a presentation	440
19.2	Editing a presentation	446
19.3	Outputting the presentation	470
20 Spreadsheets		**476**
20.1	Create a data model	478
20.2	Manipulate data	497
20.3	Presenting data	505
21 Website authoring		**522**
21.1	The three web development layers	524
21.2	Creating a web page	525
21.3	Use CSS in the presentation layer	539

Glossary	**565**
Index	**583**
Acknowledgements	**597**
Coursebook answers	
Source files	

> How to use this series

This suite of resources supports learners and teachers following the Cambridge IGCSE™ and IGCSE (9–1) Information and Communication Technology syllabuses (0417/0983). All of the books in the series work together to help students develop the necessary knowledge and ICT skills required for this subject.

The coursebook provides full coverage of the syllabus. Each chapter clearly explains facts and concepts and uses relevant real-world contexts to bring theory and practical topics to life. There is a focus on skills development, with worked examples providing step-by-step support for developing key ICT skills, as well as practical tasks in both the theory and practical chapters to develop students' practical applications of ICT. The practical tasks include 'getting started', 'practice' and 'challenge' tasks to ensure support is provided for every student. Questions and exam-style questions in every chapter help learners to consolidate their knowledge and understanding and apply their learning.

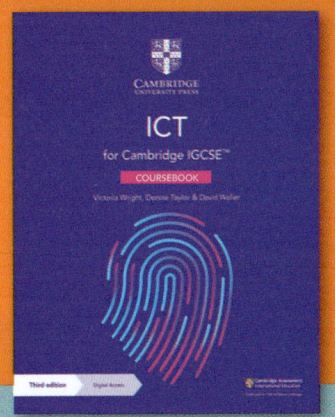

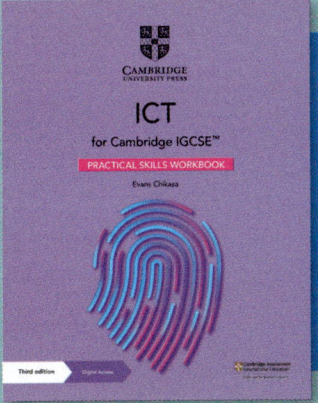

The workbook has been carefully constructed to help learners develop the practical skills they need as they progress through their ICT course, providing further practice of the practical topics in the coursebook. A three-tier, scaffolded approach to skills development allows learners to gradually progress through 'getting started', 'practice' and 'challenge' tasks, ensuring that every learner is supported. There are worked examples to help students understand how to approach different types of tasks, as well as tips to help address common misconceptions and provide helpful advice.

The digital teacher's resource contains detailed guidance for all topics of the syllabus, including background knowledge to identify learners' prior knowledge, and common misconceptions to predict the areas where learners might need extra support, as well as an engaging bank of lesson ideas for each syllabus topic. Differentiation is emphasised with advice for identification of different learner needs and suggestions of appropriate interventions to support and stretch learners. Teachers are supported and empowered to develop their teaching skills with the Teaching Skills Focus feature, which embeds pedagogical approaches within the context of each chapter.

The digital teacher's resource also contains scaffolded worksheets for each chapter, as well as exam-style papers. Answers for the coursebook and workbook questions and exercises are accessible to teachers for free on the supporting resources area of the Cambridge GO platform.

> How to use this book

Throughout this book, you will notice lots of different features that will help your learning. These are explained below. Answers to all questions and tasks are accessible to teachers in the supporting resources area of cambridge.org/go.

LEARNING INTENTIONS

These set the scene for each chapter, help with navigation through the coursebook and indicate the important concepts in each topic.

GETTING STARTED

This contains questions and activities on subject knowledge you will need before starting this chapter.

OPENING DISCUSSION

This feature presents real-world examples and applications of the content in a chapter, encouraging you to look further into topics. There are discussion questions at the end which encourage you to think more about the benefits and problems of these applications.

KEY WORDS

Key vocabulary is highlighted in the text when it is first introduced. Definitions are then given in the margin, which explain the meanings of these words and phrases. You will also find definitions of these words in the glossary at the back of this book.

COMMAND WORDS

Command words that appear in the syllabus and might be used in exams are highlighted in the exam-style questions when they are first introduced. In the margin, you will find the Cambridge International definition. You will also find these definitions in the glossary at the back of the book.

Questions

Appearing throughout the text, questions give you a chance to check that you have understood the topic you have just read about.

ACTIVITY

Activities give you an opportunity to check your understanding throughout the text in a more active way, for example by creating presentations, posters or role plays.

PRACTICAL TASK

This feature focuses on developing your practical skills. Each task is divided into three parts:

- Getting started questions will help build your basic skills.

- Practice questions provide more opportunities for practice, pushing your skills further.

- Challenge questions will stretch and challenge you even further.

How to use this book

SELF/PEER ASSESSMENT
This appears at the end of some practical tasks or activities, and gives you an opportunity to think about how you performed on the task, and what you could do to improve your work in the future.

ICT IN CONTEXT
These short boxes appear throughout the book to help you understand how ICT is used in the real world and why it is important in your everyday life.

WORKED EXAMPLE
Worked examples appear in the practical chapters, and explain key skills by breaking them down step-by-step and showing what a good answer looks like.

REFLECTION
These activities ask you to think about the approach that you take to your work, and how you might improve this in the future.

SUMMARY
There is a summary of key points at the end of each chapter.

EXAM-STYLE QUESTIONS
Questions at the end of each chapter provide more demanding exam-style questions, some of which may require use of knowledge from previous chapters.

SELF-EVALUATION CHECKLIST

After studying this chapter, think about how confident you are with the different topics.

This will help you to see any gaps in your knowledge and help you to learn more effectively.

You might find it helpful to rate how confident you are for each of these statements when you are revising. You should revisit any topics that you rated 'Needs more work' or 'Getting there'.

I can ...	See section	Needs more work	Getting there	Confident to move on
identify the hardware and software that make up a computer system, including input and output devices and operating systems used to run computers	1.1 and 1.2			
discuss types of applications software, systems software and their different roles	1.1			
describe the internal components of a computer and how they work together to run the system effectively	1.1 and 1.2			

> Introduction

When we wrote this book our main aim was to provide material to cover the updated Cambridge IGCSE™ and IGCSE (9–1) Information and Communication Technology syllabuses (0417/0983). However, we also wanted to include current, interesting examples of ICT use to invite you to find out more by carrying out your own research. The constant change in the world of ICT has made this edition of the textbook vital. There are many examples of how to transfer your ICT skills to other subjects, and the book provides new perspectives on familiar aspects of ICT.

Content

The book is entirely based around the updated syllabuses. Chapters 1 to 11 contain the theory topics with activities that you can carry out either on your own or with your class. Chapters 12 to 21 contain the practical topics to help you carry out tasks that include creating a variety of publishing documents, modelling using spreadsheets, writing websites and using a database. Practical tasks for Chapters 12 to 21 have been supported with source files provided in the supporting resources area of Cambridge GO.

Focus of the book

This book will help you to work through your course and give you the opportunity and the support to carry out research, use independent thinking and gain new skills following a structured path.

Throughout this book you will gain background knowledge to help you to answer the types of questions and understand the practical techniques that you will meet in your studies. This edition also includes ideas about how ICT is used in real-life situations. To support your learning, every chapter ends with some exam-style questions.

Focus on you

One of the advantages of this book is that it contains everything in the syllabus for your course so you will know that everything that is important for your study is in this book. The opening discussions at the start of each chapter will also encourage you to think independently and to arrive at your own answers after studying the issues and listening to others.

This book is therefore aimed at teaching you underlying skills as well as encouraging you to become critical thinkers, which are important both during your course and afterwards in your subsequent studies.

We hope that you will enjoy using this book to help you throughout your course.

Denise Taylor, Victoria Wright, David Waller

> Chapter 1
Types and components of computer systems

IN THIS CHAPTER YOU WILL:

- identify the hardware and software that make up a computer system, including input and output devices and operating systems used to run computers
- discuss types of applications software, systems software and their different roles
- describe the internal components of a computer and how they work together to run the system effectively
- understand the characteristics of analogue and digital data
- understand the different types of operating systems and identify the different types of user interface that are available
- compare the advantages and disadvantages of different types of computer
- discover how emerging technologies are impacting on many aspects of everyday life.

GETTING STARTED

In Figure 1.1, you will see some images of hardware components of a computer system and a list of their names.

Match up the letters of the components with the numbers of their names.

a   b   c   d   e

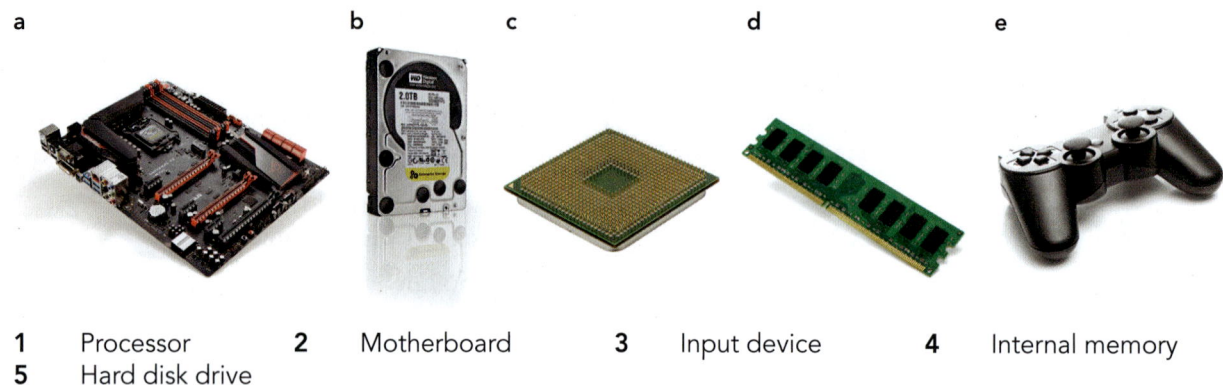

1	Processor	2	Motherboard	3	Input device	4	Internal memory
5	Hard disk drive						

Figure 1.1: Hardware components of a computer system

COMPUTERS AND COMPUTER SYSTEMS

Charles Babbage is often credited with designing the first computer with his 'Difference Engine' in the 1820s. This device was mechanical and consisted of six wheels that could carry out calculations to 20 decimal places.

Babbage also designed the more complex Analytical Engine, which contained many fundamental components of today's computers. It was intended to be able to perform any arithmetical calculation using punched cards that would deliver the instructions (the programs), as well as a memory unit to store numbers. The British mathematician Ada Lovelace completed a program for the Analytical Engine but neither it, nor Difference Engine 2, were finished in Babbage's lifetime due to the limitations of the engineering techniques available at the time.

Figure 1.2: Industrial robots have taken over the jobs of many workers

Today's computers are electronic devices and far, far smaller than mechanical ones but the basic principles are similar – they follow instructions to carry out arithmetical calculations.

A computer system consists of a computer combined with other equipment, called peripherals, so that it can perform the desired functions. Input and output devices such as keyboards and monitors are examples of peripheral devices that we are most familiar with, but any device containing a computer can be thought of as a computer system.

1 Types and components of computer systems

> **CONTINUED**
>
> Computer systems have revolutionised the way we live, work and play and are involved in all aspects of our lives.
>
> **Discussion questions**
>
> Industrial robots, such as the ones shown in Figure 1.2, have taken over the jobs of many workers.
>
> 1 Explain why a robot can be thought of as a computer system.
>
> 2 Working with a partner, list all benefits and drawbacks to an employer in using robots rather than people.

1.1 Hardware and software

A **computer** is a device that can follow a set of instructions to carry out sequences of arithmetical and logical operations. The instructions to be followed are called a 'program'.

There are two main parts of any **computer system**: the **hardware**, and the **software**. In this section you will identify the physical parts of the hardware, and then explore the difference between application software and system software.

Hardware

Computer hardware consists of the physical parts of a computer system, the parts you can touch. These include:

- the case
- **components** inside the case, such as:
    - **central processing unit** (or CPU – see Section 1.2.)
    - motherboard
    - graphics card
    - sound card
    - network interface card (NIC)
    - internal memory (see Section 1.2)
    - random-access memory (RAM)
    - read-only memory (ROM)
- internal and external storage devices (see Section 1.2 and Chapter 3):
    - hard disk drives
    - solid state drives
    - optical drives.

> **KEY WORDS**
>
> **computer:** a device that follows a set of instructions to carry out a series of arithmetical and logical operations
>
> **computer system:** a computer combined with other equipment so that it can carry out desired functions
>
> **hardware:** the physical parts of a computer system, the parts you can touch. This includes the motherboard, CPU, keyboard, mouse, printer, and so on
>
> **software:** programs or applications that give instructions to the computer to tell it what to do
>
> **component:** the parts that make up a whole machine. The internal parts are usually referred to as components and the external devices as 'peripherals'
>
> **central processing unit (CPU):** or processor, is the unit which performs most of the processing inside a computer

- input and output devices (see Section 1.2 and Chapter 2):
  - keyboard
  - mouse
  - monitor
  - speakers
  - printer
  - camera.

All of the components inside the case of a computer must be fixed (so that they do not move about) and be able to communicate with each other. They are all fixed to sockets in a board with thin strips of copper connecting them together. This is a type of printed **circuit board** and is called the system board or **motherboard** (see Figure 1.1a in the Getting started section).

The component that makes a device a computer is the central processing unit (CPU), also known as the processor. This interprets all of the instructions in the programs and executes them (carries them out). More details are given in Section 1.2.

The program instructions and data that the processor is working on are stored in **internal memory**, which is covered in detail in Section 1.2.

Most computer systems display the results of their processing to users through a monitor and speakers. They therefore have their own dedicated printed circuit boards called a **graphics card** for the monitor and **sound card** for the speakers or headphones.

If the computer is being connected to a network (see Chapter 4), then a **network interface card (NIC)** may need to be fitted to the motherboard, although most modern computers have these inbuilt in the motherboard.

A very important part of a computer is the main memory. This is used to store all the data and instructions currently being used. The main memory is sometimes called other names, such as internal memory. When a computer is turned off, the data that is stored in internal memory is lost and therefore internal and external storage devices are needed to permanently store this data. These are explained in more detail in Section 1.2.

KEY WORDS

circuit board: a thin rigid board containing thin lines of metals on the surface to create electric circuits

motherboard: also called the system board. The main printed circuit board of the computer; it has connectors that other circuit boards can be slotted into

internal memory: data storage spaces that are accessible to the CPU

graphics card: a printed circuit board that controls the output to a display screen or monitor

sound card: a printed circuit board that controls output to speakers and headphones

network interface card (NIC): a printed circuit board that allows the computer to communicate with other devices over a computer network

When a computer is operating, data must be input so that it can be worked on or processed, and the results of this processing need to be output to the user. A computer system therefore needs various input and output devices such as keyboard, cameras, mice, printers, monitors and speakers. There are more details of these in Chapter 2.

ACTIVITY 1.1

Create a set of flashcards to help learn the terminology from this section.

You can find the definitions in the Key Words boxes and in the glossary. However, you should write the definition in your own words.

If there are words in the definition that you do not understand, then look them up in an online dictionary.

Continue to add more flashcards as you progress through this section.

1 Types and components of computer systems

> **PRACTICAL TASK 1.1**
>
> **Getting started**
>
> 1 With a partner, list all of the internal components and external devices of a computer that you know.
>
> **Practice**
>
> 2 Create a presentation, including images, of the following components with a sentence stating the function of each one:
>
> - motherboard
> - processor
> - network interface card.
>
> For information about creating presentations, see Chapter 19.
>
> **Challenge**
>
> 3 Carry out research and add a description of the different types of storage devices that are found in computers to your presentation.

Software

However advanced or expensive the hardware of a computer system is, it cannot do anything unless it is told what to do. These instructions are provided by programs that together are called computer software. Software controls the operations of a computer or processing of electronic data.

There are two main types of software:

- **Applications software**, which lets you do your day-to-day tasks on the computer. Applications software needs the operating system to be able to work with the computer.
- **System software**, including the **operating system** and **utilities software** that are essential to keep the computer working.

Applications

Here are a few examples of applications software that you may use:

- Word processing applications are used to produce letters, reports and memos.
- Spreadsheet applications are used for tasks that involve calculations or graphs and charts.
- Database management programs are used to store and retrieve information in databases.

> **KEY WORDS**
>
> **applications software:** programs that carry out operations for specific applications, such as word processing, spreadsheets or presentations. Applications software cannot run on its own without system software
>
> **system software:** system software provides the services that the computer requires to operate. This may be classified as the operating system and utility software
>
> **operating system (OS):** the operating system is a collection of programs to control and manage all of the software and hardware of the computer system
>
> **utility software (utilities):** part of the system software that can analyse, configure, optimise and maintain a computer to keep it working as well as possible

- Presentation applications are used to create slide shows and presentations.
- Graphics editing software is used to create artwork, or with photographs from a digital camera or a scanned image to edit the image.

5

- Video editing software is used to produce and edit videos.
- Computer aided design (CAD) packages are used to produce detailed technical designs and plans.
- Audio production and editing programs are a common way of producing high quality music at low cost.
- Communications software, such as web browsers and email programs, is used to access the internet and send and receive email.
- Control software is used to control devices such as fire alarms and mechanical devices.
- Measurement software is used to capture and log data from sensors, e.g. temperature, pressure, light intensity.
- An applet is a small program that can perform one or a few simple tasks.
- App (which is short for application) is usually associated with use on a smartphone, tablet or other mobile device.

System software

System software is required for the computer to function and operate efficiently. System software consists of utilities, also called utility software and the operating system.

System software includes the following:

- **compilers**
- **linkers**
- **device drivers**
- operating system
- utilities.

ICT IN CONTEXT

Programs, or groups of programs, designed to allow users to carry out particular jobs such as creating and manipulating databases and spreadsheets, producing written documents, composing music and designing cars and buildings, are referred to as application software.

Traditionally, users bought these applications or apps and installed them on their computers but now more are found on the internet and are accessed through web browsers on computers, tablets and smartphones. Google G Suite (see Figure 1.3), which includes apps for email, spreadsheets and presentations, has over two billion users.

Figure 1.3: Google G Suite

KEY WORDS

compilers: convert the program written by a human in a high-level language into code that the microprocessor can understand – a series of 1s and 0s

linkers: take one or more of the files produced by the compiler and combines them into a program that the microprocessor can execute

device drivers: part of the operating system. Device drivers allow the processor to communicate with devices such as the keyboard, mouse, monitor and printer

ACTIVITY 1.2

Working in a small group, decide on a definition for a web browser. (Try to link your definition back to application software.) Then list as many different internet browsers as you can think of, before doing some research to find out how many are available in total.

Self-assessment

Did the methods you used for research produce the results you wanted? What would you do differently in the future?

Analogue and digital data

The CPU or processor, which **processes** all of the data and instructions, contains billions of **transistors** that are connected together to form circuits.

Transistors act as switches – like light switches. They are either on when they transmit electricity, or they are off when they do not. There is no in-between where different amounts of electricity are transmitted (as in a dimmer switch, where there are an infinite number of states between fully off and fully on). It is all or nothing.

A system like this with separate states is said to be **digital**. In this case, there are only two states (on and off) and the system is said to be binary.

A system like the dimmer switch, where there is a continuous range between two values, is said to be **analogue**.

If information is being transmitted by analogue methods, the sending and receiving system must be very accurate to distinguish the small differences.

As there are only two states in the transistors of the CPU, they are represented by the digits of the binary number system, 1 (for on) and 0 (for off). All of the data and program instructions processed by a computer are streams of billions of 1s and 0s. These digits are called **bits**.

Analogue to digital conversion

When we use computers, data has to be converted between analogue and digital forms.

An example of the need to convert between analogue and digital data and back again is when we record music onto a computer, and then play it back again.

Sound is caused by vibrations travelling through the air. These vibrations cause changes to the air pressure and travel in waves.

The graphs in Figure 1.4 show the continuous changes in the air pressure. If these are recorded as continuous changes of voltage, as when producing vinyl records and cassette tapes, the recording is said to be analogue.

Because the sound waves cannot be represented as a series of continuous changes on computer, snapshots of the waves are taken at regular intervals and then fitted together. This is called **sampling** and therefore a digital recording is not as accurate as an analogue one as some of the information is missing (see Figure 1.5).

The more samples taken per second, the more accurately the sound will be represented. For most recording this is 44 100 samples per second, although 96 000 is used for Blu-ray audio.

> **KEY WORDS**
>
> **process:** carry out or execute the instructions
>
> **transistor:** a device that regulates current or voltage flow and acts as a switch for electronic signals
>
> **digital:** information represented by certain fixed values rather than as a continuous range. Usually data represented by the digits 1 and 0
>
> **analogue:** information represented by a quantity (e.g. an electric voltage or current) that is continuously variable. Changes in the information are indicated by changes in voltage
>
> **bit:** short for binary digit, is the smallest unit of data in a computer. It has a single binary value, either 1 or 0
>
> **sample:** making a physical measurement of a wave at set time intervals and converting those measurements to digital values

Each sample has to be coded as a series of 1s and 0s and the more that are used, the more detail can be recorded.

The digital recordings can then be edited and processed by a computer.

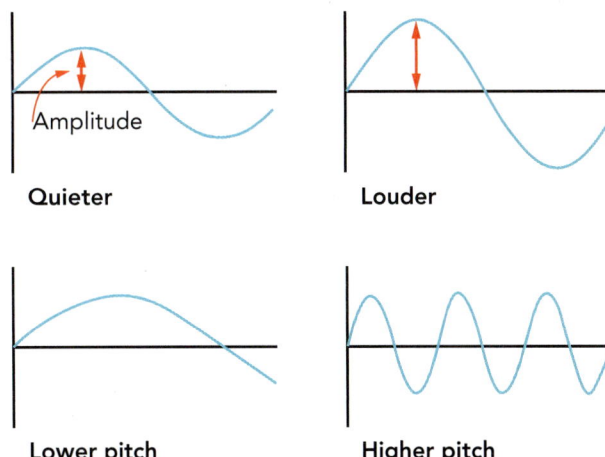

Figure 1.4: Graphs showing how waves differ between different sounds

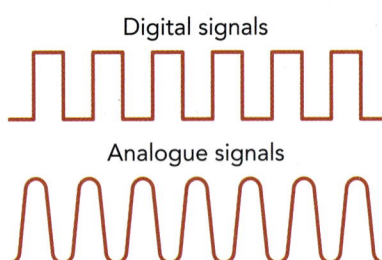

Figure 1.5: Sampling analogue data

Digital-to-analogue conversion

In order for the digital sound to be listened to it must be converted back into analogue signals so it can be output through speakers or headphones. The technology used to do this is a **digital-to-analogue converter** (DAC).

Sound cards all contain DACs to convert the digital signal back into analogue ones. DACs take a binary number of the digital form of audio and turns it into an analogue voltage or current that can create a wave of audio that represents the digital signal.

As mentioned above, as the digital data represents the sound in sampled steps and is not continuous, the DAC has to make up the bits in between to stitch them together.

Similarly, DACs are required when computers are controlling devices such as robots through the use of **actuators** such as motors.

> **KEY WORDS**
>
> **digital-to-analogue converter:** a device used to convert digital signals into analogue ones
>
> **actuator:** a device that causes a machine or other device to operate

All data, input by sensors, into a computer must be converted from an analogue into a digital format, whether it is from sound, light, pressure or temperature sensors. The digital data can be processed by the computer. If this data is to be output through analogue devices such as speakers or a motor, then it must be converted back into an analogue signal.

1.2 The main components of computer systems

In this section, you will learn the roles that different hardware components perform in a basic computer system in order to understand the differences between them.

The central processing unit (CPU)

The CPU is responsible for executing (running) the program instructions, processing data and controlling other computer components. It consists of the following components: the **control unit** (CU), the **arithmetic and logic unit** (ALU), the **clock** and the **registers**.

The control unit

The CU coordinates the actions of the computer and manages the various components of the computer. It controls the execution of program instructions and the processing of data by sending out control signals to the other parts of the CPU such as the ALU and registers. It also sends **control signals** to other components of the computer system such as the input and output devices to tell them what to do.

> **KEY WORDS**
>
> **control unit:** component of the central processing unit (CPU) that directs the operations of the processor
>
> **arithmetic and logic unit (ALU):** part of the CPU that performs arithmetical and logical operations such as addition, subtraction, or comparison
>
> **clock:** a quartz crystal that sends pulses to control the rate at which the CPU processes instructions
>
> **registers:** memory storage locations within the CPU
>
> **control signals:** electrical signals that are sent out to all of the devices to check their status and give them instructions

Arithmetic and logic unit

The ALU performs arithmetic and logical operations. It carries out activities such as:

- addition and subtraction
- multiplication and division
- comparisons, such as whether one number is greater than another.

The clock

The clock controls the rate at which the CPU works. The clock sends out a pulse to the control unit which can process one instruction for each pulse. The number of pulses per second is known as the clock speed.

It is a quartz crystal and one instruction can be carried out with each pulse of the crystal. The higher the clock speed, the faster the CPU will be able to carry out the program instructions.

Registers

These are memory locations within the CPU itself. They store instructions and data that is currently being used by the control unit.

Internal memory

This is used to store data that is used by the system when it starts up and also all the program instructions currently being executed and the data required.

The internal memory consists of **random-access memory (RAM)** and **read-only memory (ROM)** (see Figure 1.6).

Random-access memory (RAM)

The RAM is attached to the motherboard. it is where software currently in use and documents that you are currently working on are stored while you are using them. As a program is running, the CPU will write data to the RAM.

RAM consists of billions of **storage locations** and is said to be 'random access' because they can be accessed in any order for fast data retrieval.

RAM is said to be **volatile** because if there is no electrical power it loses all of the data.

Read-only memory (ROM)

ROM is an integrated circuit on a chip that is programmed with specific data to perform a particular function when it is manufactured.

This memory is needed because it holds the instructions that the computer needs to boot up. The BIOS (Basic Input/Output System) is stored on ROM and it is used when a computer is turned on. It checks the hardware devices to ensure there are no errors and loads basic software to communicate with them.

The data can be read but it cannot be changed – the CPU cannot write to ROM. Unlike RAM, ROM is **non-volatile** and all data is retained when the power is switched off.

> **KEY WORDS**
>
> **random-access memory (RAM):** memory that stores data and applications while they are being used. It only stores them while the computer is on, but when you turn the computer off, everything in the RAM is lost. This is known as being volatile
>
> **read-only memory (ROM):** memory that has data preinstalled onto it that cannot be removed. Unlike RAM, ROM keeps its contents when the computer is turned off. It is therefore known as being non-volatile
>
> **storage location:** a place in internal memory where a single piece of data can be stored until it is needed
>
> **volatile:** a state where data is permanently lost when power is switched off
>
> **non-volatile:** a state where data is retained when power is switched off

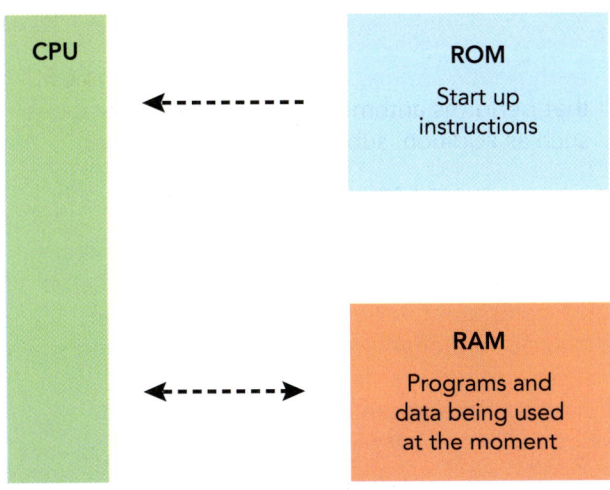

Figure 1.6: ROM and RAM

NOTE: don't confuse the main memory ROM with a CD ROM or DVD ROM; they are different things.

Questions

1. State what is pre-stored on the ROM.
2. Describe the tasks of the RAM.
3. Explain the difference between volatile and non-volatile computer memory.
4. Either ROM or RAM is volatile, the other is non-volatile. Which is which?

Input and output devices

Input and output devices allow computers to communicate with users.

An **input device** is used to input data into the computer. The more common ones are: keyboard, mouse, touchpad (also known as a trackpad), microphone, bar code reader, scanner, digital camera, joystick.

There are many other methods of inputting data such as a fingerprint scanner, which is used to identify a particular person. Confirming identity by using physical characteristics is called biometrics and is covered in Chapter 6.

> ### ICT IN CONTEXT
>
> Bank customers are asked to enter login names and passwords when they access their accounts online, this can be a laborious process and banks are responding by using biometric identification. As well as using fingerprint and face recognition login on smartphones, banks are beginning to experiment with behavioural biometrics. Using artificial intelligence and machine learning, authentication software can identify users by how they enter text on a phone or tablet or how they use a mouse. For low-value transactions, these behaviour patterns can be used with the user's location and IP address to authenticate users.
>
> Biometric payment cards will soon be available. The user simply touches a fingerprint sensor on the card, and it compares the fingerprint with the one stored in the card's chip.

An **output device** is used by a computer to display the results of processing to the users. Examples include display screens (such as monitors), printers, speakers, plotters and projectors.

Input and output devices are looked at in more detail in Chapter 2, but to help you start thinking about them, try the following activity:

> ### ACTIVITY 1.3
>
> Draw a spider diagram or create one on a word processor with 'Processor' at the centre. Add the input devices on one side and output devices on the other. For items such as monitors and printers and some of the other devices, you could add another level with the different types of each.

Backing storage

Because RAM is volatile, programs and data must be stored on other devices called **backing storage devices** or secondary storage devices so they are not lost when the computer is switched off. These devices permanently store the data in different ways, e.g. magnetically, optically and solid state.

These devices may be enclosed in the computer case – in which case they are called internal backing stores – or they can be separate, in their own cases and connected to the main unit by cable. In this case, they are external backing store. An advantage of external backing store is that it is portable and can be used to safely store data or transfer it from one computer to another.

> ### KEY WORDS
>
> **input device:** any hardware device that sends data to a computer
>
> **output device:** any device used to send data from a computer to another device or user
>
> **backing storage device:** a secondary storage device that will continue to hold data even after the computer has been turned off. Examples include hard drives, solid-state drives, memory sticks, memory cards and CDs and DVDs. Backing storage can be internal (inside the computer case) or external

1 Types and components of computer systems

Backing storage is covered in Chapter 3.

People often confuse internal memory and backing storage as their capacity is measured in the same **units of memory** such as gigabytes (GB) or terabytes (TB).

When 'computer memory' is discussed, it refers to the internal memory – how much RAM it has. This greatly affects the speed at which the computer operates as it is accessed directly by the CPU when the computer is operating.

Backing storage is not 'memory' as it is not accessed directly by the CPU. Data from backing storage must be moved to the internal memory so that it can be accessed.

But people still, incorrectly, ask, 'How much memory is available?' when they are referring to the size of backing storage.

1.3 Operating systems

An operating system is a set of programs that controls how the computer interacts with the users and the **peripherals** – external devices such as keyboards, monitors and printers.

It is always running in the background and applications such as word processors can 'call' the operating system when they want something done. For example, when a program wants something printed, it asks the operating system to do it. Without the operating system, all programs would need code to allow them to use a printer. In fact, they would need code to communicate with every type and make of printer produced as the program would not know which one was attached to the computer.

The operating system has programs, called managers, that:

- manage all of the hardware devices
- control all of the processes running in the computer, e.g. when several programs are running, it allows each one in turn to use the CPU
- manage the internal memory.

> **KEY WORDS**
>
> **units of memory:**
> - 8 bits = 1 byte
> - 1000 bytes = 1 kilobyte
> - 1000 kilobytes = 1 megabyte
> - 1000 megabytes = 1 gigabyte
> - 1000 gigabytes = 1 terabyte
>
> **peripherals:** external devices that provide input and output for the computer

Windows	macOS	Unix
First introduced by Microsoft in 1985 but did not have a full graphical user interface (GUI) until 1995. Expensive.	Operating system used on Apple computers and introduced in 1984. It was fully GUI from the start. Expensive and the user is forced to only use Apple hardware.	The first widely used operating system. Developed in the 1960s. macOS was developed from Unix. Still widely used today in large, commercial organisations. It is open source, free to use and has led to the development of other free systems such as Linux.
Most popular operating system on none-Apple PCs. 90% of computers use Windows.	As there are fewer Apple computers than other PCs, it is less popular. About 10% of computers use macOS.	About 1% of computers use Unix.
As it is the most popular it is targeted by far more malware such as viruses.	As it is less popular, there is very little malware.	Even less malware than macOs.

Table 1.1: Comparisons of Windows, macOS and Unix operating systems

There is no standard operating system, and many different types are available including Windows, Unix, macOS, Linux, Android, iOs.

Although all operating systems carry out similar functions, there are some differences between them. For desktop and laptop computers, the most popular operating systems are Windows, macOS and Unix (see Table 1.1).

Android and iOs are operating systems specially designed for mobile devices. They aren't as fully featured as the three operating systems discussed in Table 1.1, but you can still do a lot of things on mobile devices such as basic business/schoolwork, watch movies, browse the internet and play games. Android is the most widely used operating system in the world.

User interfaces

Users interact with the operating system through a user interface that converts what a user inputs to a form that the computer can understand and vice versa.

But there are different ways to interact with a computer system. The four main types are:

- **command line interface (CLI)**
- **graphical user interface (GUI)**
- **dialogue-based interface**
- **gesture-based interface**.

Command line interface (CLI)

This was the first type of interface that was available for personal computers. Users had to type in commands to instruct the computer. For example, to list all of the files on a disk drive, they could have entered 'dir' and if there were too many to display, they could add the '/p' to show them one page at a time. Obviously 'del' was used to delete a file and 'copy' to copy one.

These days, CLIs are used by people like technicians looking after computer systems. The technicians know all the commands and in this way are able to access the whole of the system. This type of interface can be much faster than other interfaces.

Figure 1.7: A command line interface

Advantages of a CLI:

- CLIs require very little processing so run very quickly and on computers that aren't powerful.
- Advanced computer users who know how to use the commands can operate them faster than users who need to move a mouse.

Disadvantages of a CLI:

- Commands need to be learnt and often aren't obvious.
- Looks intimidating for new users.

> **KEY WORDS**
>
> **command line interface (CLI):** a text-based interface that allows the user to interact with a computer using keyboard input at a prompt on the screen
>
> **graphical user interface (GUI):** an interface that provides an intuitive way of interacting with a computer through a screen by clicking on icons, menus, buttons or windows using (for example) a mouse, touchpad or touch screen
>
> **dialogue-based interface:** an interface that allows a user to interact with a computer through the spoken word
>
> **gesture-based interface:** an interface that allows a user to interact with a computer at a distance by using movements of various parts of their body

- The user must be careful not to make any typing errors, otherwise the computer will not be able to understand the commands and carry them out.

> **ACTIVITY 1.4**
>
> The most used commonly used CLI is MSDOS (Microsoft Disk Operating System). Carry out research to find 10 DOS commands. Create a table giving the commands in the first column and explanations of their use in the second column, as shown below.
>
> | DOS command | Explanation of use |
> |---|---|
> | | |

Graphical user interface (GUI)

A graphical user interface is probably the most common type of interface used today. GUIs use the following methods to allow users to open and interact with programs:

- windows
- icons
- menus
- pointers.

A GUI is therefore often called a 'WIMP' interface.

Most of the operating systems mentioned above provide a GUI.

Advantages of a GUI:

- It is intuitive as files and directories are represented by icons.
- Users do not have to learn complicated commands, they merely have to click a mouse or select an item from a menu.
- It is easy to use, for example, to move a file a user just has to drag an onscreen representation (icon) of that file.

Disadvantages of a GUI:

- GUIs use up a lot of the computer's internal memory to run.
- They are large and take up lots of storage space.
- They need to use the CPU a lot more than CLIs.

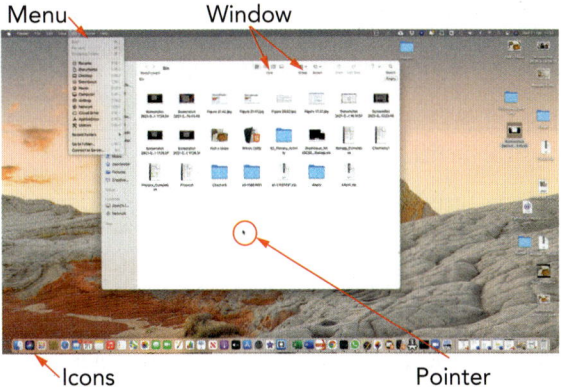

Figure 1.8: A GUI showing the methods making up the WIMP interface

- Can be slower for experienced users as they have to take their hands off the keyboard and search for a mouse.

Dialogue-based interface

A dialogue-based interface allows a user to interact with a computer through the spoken word. In return the computer carries out an action or replies in spoken words to the user.

Dialogue-based interfaces are common in modern cars where a user can give spoken commands to the operating system to make a phone call, switch to a particular radio channel or plot a route to a destination.

They are also available for 'smart home' systems where a user can control the temperature, switch on lights or turn on a kettle using spoken commands.

Advantages of a dialogue-based interface:

- It allows hands-free control.
- The user does not have to be trained but may have to learn the necessary key words that the computer will accept.
- It is safer when operating machinery such driving and is useful for disabled users.

Disadvantages of a dialogue-based interface:

- Users have to learn which commands can be used.
- Users have to train the interface with their voice.
- May not be reliable especially if there is background noise.
- Not suitable for safety-critical commands.
- Complex to program and are therefore expensive.

Gesture-based interface

A true gesture-based interface uses computer sensors to detect and understand human gestures and movements, usually of the face and hands, without actually touching a physical device.

Partial gesture-based interfaces are available today on smartphones and tablets where a user has to swipe the screen in a particular way to open and close programs and zoom in or out of maps. But the user has to touch the screen. It is using a GUI without a mouse.

Advantages of a gesture-based interface:

- The user does not have to use a mouse or other pointing device.
- The user does not have to enter commands using a keyboard.
- The user does not have to move to the device as they can make the gestures from where they are sitting or standing.
- The user does not have to touch a screen that others have been touching. It prevents to spread of disease.

Disadvantages of a gesture-based interface:

- Users have to learn the gestures for particular requests.
- A system is required to recognise face movements and hand gestures.
- Users may have to wear motion tracking gloves.
- Users may become fatigued after performing the gestures.

Question

5 Graphical user interfaces are found on most computers.

  a State why a computer needs a user interface.

  b Other than a mouse, give **one** other device that can operate a GUI.

  c Give **four** of the ways in which a user interacts with a GUI.

  d Compare a GUI to a command line interface (CLI) and explain which is easier for a new user.

1.4 Types of computer

There are different types of computers that perform a huge variety of roles. In this section you will learn about a variety of computers and you will compare the roles that they can perform.

Desktop computers

When you hear the phrase 'computer' or 'personal computer' (PC), you are likely to think of a **desktop computer** as these have traditionally been used by organisations to run the software required for their business activities.

A desktop computer is designed for use at one location and is not portable. It has a case containing the motherboard, CPU, internal memory, etc. and external input and output devices such as a keyboard, mouse, monitor, printer and speakers.

> **KEY WORD**
>
> **desktop computer:** a computer system designed to be used at a desk in a fixed location

Desktops are very versatile, general purpose computers used by many organisations and individuals for:

- Office work and business management, using word processing, spreadsheet and database management software.
- Management in education and student learning.
- Playing computer games.
- Other entertainment such as watching movies and editing images and video.

Mobile computers

In the 1990s, portable (moveable) computers became popular and became known as laptops. Because they are more portable than desktops, they have many advantages for mobile work and they have the power and flexibility of desktop computers.

These days there are many forms of mobile computer, not just laptops. Tablets, smartphones and phablets are all popular mobile computers and, because of the weight and size of a laptop, are far more portable.

1 Types and components of computer systems

Mobile computers, especially laptops, can be used for the same functions as desktops but have the advantage of being portable so that users are not restricted to one location.

As they are portable, they can also be used for other things such as data collection in different environments and controlling devices outdoors such as drones and machinery.

Laptop computers

Laptops (see Figure 1.9a) are portable and compact personal computers with the same capabilities as a desktop computer. They can also be battery operated, although they do have to be frequently charged.

Originally laptops were far less powerful but far more expensive than desktops, however with improvements in technology and manufacture, they are now replacing desktops in many organisations. They allow greater flexibility as users can work in different locations and are not fixed to a particular room or desk. Laptops also incorporate peripherals such as speakers, cameras and microphones, so that these do not need to be attached when making voice calls or video-conferencing.

Tablet

Tablet computers (see Figure 1.9b) became a mass-market product in 2010. A tablet is a computer that is internet-enabled and small enough to be handheld. It has a touch screen display with the circuits and battery together in a single unit. It can also have sensors, cameras, a microphone and a speaker. Tablets can run application software, generally known as 'apps'. They are simple to use as well as being light to carry around; they provide you with access to the internet and apps very quickly after turning on.

Although all tablets can connect to the internet using Wi-Fi, you can also get tablets that let you use 4G or 5G mobile internet connections. If you have Wi-Fi at home then you can browse the internet on your tablet, as you can anywhere else that Wi-Fi is available. For many people, Wi-Fi-only tablets are sufficient because you can download content onto your tablet that you can use if you are going to be away from a Wi-Fi connection.

Smartphones and phablets

A **smartphone** (see Figure 1.9c) is a multifunctioning mobile phone. Packed into its tiny case can be a camera, a web browser, a high-density display, a lot of storage space, a micro SD card slot and a touch screen.

Figure 1.9: Portable computing: **a** a laptop, **b** a tablet, **c** a smartphone

Like the tablet, you can download apps and access the internet quickly; you can also use a smartphone for email, playing music, watching movies, GPS (Global Positioning System) navigation, speech recognition and it has a camera for taking photos and videos. It uses a touch screen display so the user can interact with it.

A smartphone, like a tablet, uses cut-down applications, known as apps, which are available for almost every subject area you can think of: medical and fitness monitoring, star recognition, word processing, spreadsheets and charting, playing games; the list is endless.

A **phablet** is a large smartphone. It has the functionality of a smartphone but it is almost as large as a tablet. It gets its name from PHone and tABLET. It will probably have a screen measuring at least a 6 inches diagonally from corner to corner.

> **KEY WORDS**
>
> **laptops:** a portable computer with the same functionality as a desktop computer
>
> **tablet:** a thin, flat, portable computer with a touch screen, mobile operating system and battery
>
> **smartphone:** a mobile phone that can perform many other functions, e.g. taking photographs and web browsing
>
> **phablet:** a smartphone with a screen size larger than most smartphones but smaller that a tablet

Not all tablets, smartphones and laptops have the same specifications but Table 1.2 shows possible advantages and disadvantages that they may have.

15

Devices	Advantages	Disadvantages
Desktops	More powerful than mobile devices. Usually have a larger screen than a laptop. Screen at eye level and so helps with better posture. Easy to upgrade and expand, e.g. adding more memory. Less easy to steal and carry away. Cost less for the power and facilities they offer.	Not portable. Restricted to one working area. Take up a lot of space.
Laptops	Excellent for work functions. Full-size keyboard. Light and portable. Integrated camera, speaker and microphone. Less expandability than a desktop but more expandable than smartphone or tablet.	Larger and heavier than a tablet or smartphone. Slower to start than tablets. Amount of battery life.
Tablets	Quick to turn on. Portable. Easy to use. Lots of apps to choose from. Ability to transfer data. They can be expanded by the addition of a portable keyboard. Integrated camera, speaker and microphone.	Can be expensive. Not all have expandable memory. Amount of battery life.
Smartphones	Pocket sized. Can make calls, and send texts and emails. Can use Wi-Fi. 4G/5G connectivity to access the web from most places. Lots of apps available. Integrated camera, speaker and microphone.	Small screens can make reading difficult. Amount of battery life. Web browsing can drain the battery quickly. Typing on a small touch screen may be slow. Amount of battery life. Speed of data transfer and compatibility.

Table 1.2: Summary of computer types

Questions

6 Compare and contrast desktop and laptop computers.
7 Explain the differences between a tablet, smartphone and phablet.

1.5 Emerging technologies

Impact of emerging technologies

Technology changes rapidly and computers are becoming ever more powerful and capable of processing even more commands each second. New developments are creating more and more benefits but also more problems in the ways that they impact people and society.

These emerging technologies include artificial intelligence and extended reality (virtual reality and augmented reality).

Artificial intelligence (AI)

Artificial intelligence covers a range of technologies as it can be applied in different fields, but the one that most people recognise is in the development of robotics.

Artificial intelligence is the ability of a digital computer or computer-controlled robot to perform tasks commonly associated with human intelligence such as learning, problem solving and pattern recognition.

Industrial robots do the same thing over and over again, efficiently and well. They follow a fixed program and cannot themselves learn how to do another task unless a human reprograms them.

Using artificial intelligence, a computer or robot can modify its own behaviour in order to achieve other outcomes. They can learn new things without having their programs rewritten by a human.

This is known as **machine learning**. Using machine learning, a computer can learn by being given lots of examples. As a simple example, a computer could teach itself how to recognise an animal such as a sheep. It would be shown millions of images of sheep in different environments and locations. It isn't given any facts about sheep but it learns to recognise one as we do by deciding itself the characteristics of a sheep such as relative size, body shape, appearance, covered in wool. It does that itself, these are not programmed in. Sometimes there are problems as most images show sheep in a field or natural background. So the computer may identify other similarly sized animals in similar landscapes as sheep.

> **KEY WORDS**
>
> **artificial intelligence:** the ability of a digital computer or computer-controlled robot to perform tasks commonly associated with human intelligence such as learning, problem solving and pattern recognition
>
> **machine learning:** the ability of computers to learn without being explicitly programmed

> **ICT IN CONTEXT**
>
>
>
> **Figure 1.10:** Aibo, the robot dog
>
> Figure 1.10 shows Aibo, a robot dog first introduced by Sony in 1999 and discontinued in 2006.
>
> A new version was introduced in 2018. Using AI and machine learning, Aibo can be taught simple tricks by the user and can learn to recognise up to a hundred different people.
>
> It develops its own unique personality as a result of interacting with its owner.

Machine learning is always dependent on the learning data given to the computer by humans and this data may introduce bias. In 2019 Amazon stopped using its AI tool for job interviews as it had a significant bias against female job applicants. It had been given data examples from the past and, of course, these were biased.

Examples of AI include:

- Making a patient diagnosis based on their symptoms and their medical history.

- Analysing test results. A computer can recognise medical markers indicating abnormalities far more accurately than a human after being given millions of scans. They are not programmed what to look for, they learn themselves through trial and error.

- Artificial intelligence and machine learning are allowing machines to become fully autonomous – they can make their own decisions without human involvement or guidance.

- Autonomous machines – the most prominent examples are driverless cars (see Figure 1.11) and lorries which can travel to a destination safely along public roads, without human involvement.

Other examples of autonomous machines include lethal autonomous weapons such as 'robot soldiers' and drones, which can search for and engage targets on their own without human intervention.

Obviously, these developments raise ethical and legal questions. How should a driverless car respond if someone runs into the road? Should it swerve and injure the occupants and other pedestrians or hit the person? Should it take into account the number of people who could be injured or even consider their ages? Should it sacrifice an older person to save a child or vice versa?

Who is legally responsible when the car crashes? The manufacturer? The owner? The computer scientists who programmed it?

All of these questions need to be answered before they are allowed on public highways.

ICT IN CONTEXT

Do music and video streaming sites send you suggestions of what you might like to see or listen to? Does Amazon suggest which books you might like to read or a show you might like to watch? Machine learning programs have associated your preferences with those of other users with similar tastes and items with similar content to the ones you have already bought.

Virtual personal assistants also learn from your involvement with them, what you ask and what you are interested in. They can then make suggestions about things you might be interested in.

Figure 1.11: A driverless car

ACTIVITY 1.5

Create a presentation showing how artificial intelligence is used by 'chatbots'.

Extended reality (XR)

Extended reality is called an 'immersive technology' because it immerses users in a virtual or a combined virtual and real environment. It includes virtual reality and augmented reality along with other emerging technologies.

Virtual reality

Virtual reality (VR) is a **computer-generated environment**, sometimes called a virtual world, where a person can immerse themselves and interact to perform a wide variety of actions. It is often associated with gaming but it can also have other, more serious purposes. There are many ways in which VR affects our everyday lives.

KEY WORDS

extended reality: a virtual or a combined virtual and real environment

virtual reality: a computer-generated environment

computer-generated environment: the use of software to create 3D images of scenery, buildings, etc. in which objects can move

To take part in a controlled VR environment, you would wear goggles to give you a slightly different view in each of your eyes; this would give the scene a 3D effect that makes images of objects seem solid. You may also wear gloves that are able to detect finger movements, as well as headphones to control what you hear.

Some examples of VR in everyday life are:

- You can take a virtual walkthrough of a museum; a virtual model of a new house being designed or the inside of a new car.
- Car manufacturers can use VR to create prototypes of a new vehicle so that it can be tested and altered before being developed.
- Astronauts, pilots or medical students, for example, can use VR for training before going into difficult situations. Surgeons can also carry out surgery remotely in a VR environment by using robotic devices which mimic their movements.

ICT IN CONTEXT

During the COVID-19 pandemic lockdown, many people turned to VR as an alternative to a real travel experience. People could put their feet up and walk around in Paris, see the Eiffel Tower via a 360-degree virtual tour or visit the Grand Canyon or Victoria falls.

VR can give a boost to the tourist sector, rather than replace the real adventure. The aim is to make people interested so that they will want to visit the real thing.

Augmented reality

Augmented reality allows a user to interact with the real and a virtual world at the same time.

KEY WORD

augmented reality: a combined virtual and real environment

Figure 1.12: The names of shops and restaurants superimposed on a navigation guide's street view

It superimposes a computer-generated image on a user's view of the real world. In navigation systems, it can provide extra information to street views such as the names of shops and restaurants.

They can also provide a virtual guide to lead you to your destination.

Some other advantages of augmented reality are:

- AR can save money for businesses by minimising the number of items that are returned from customers. The Ikea Place app allows you to place furniture in your room and view the effects on your smartphone.
- Customers can try out different paint colours on the walls of their rooms by using a smartphone app.
- Augmented reality allows architects, builders and developers and clients to visualise what a proposed design would look like in a space and existing conditions before any construction begins.

ICT IN CONTEXT

In 2016, an augmented reality game was made available on tablets and smartphones.

Pokémon Go uses location tracking and mapping technology to create an 'augmented reality' where players catch and train Pokémon characters which are superimposed on real locations. It was one of the most used mobile apps in 2016, and was downloaded more than 500 million times worldwide by the end of the year.

Figure 1.13: Screenshot of Pokémon Go

SUMMARY

A computer consists of devices for input, processing, output and storage.
There are different types of computers such as desktops, laptops, tablets, smartphones and phablets.
The physical parts of a computer system make up its hardware, but the instructions are given to a computer system by its software.
Computers contain different hardware components, such as CPU, internal memory, hard disk drive, optical disk drive, motherboard, video card and sound card.
Software is necessary for computer hardware to function. There are different types of software – application software and system software.
Data entered into a computer needs to be converted from an analogue into a digital format and output may need to be converted back to analogue.
The system software is called the operating system or OS. This allows other programs to run.
There are different types of interface for the user to control the computer: Command line interface, graphical user interface, dialogue-based interface and gesture-based interface.
Emerging technologies such as artificial intelligence and extended reality have an impact in many different areas of everyday life.

1 Types and components of computer systems

EXAM-STYLE QUESTIONS

1. **Explain** what is meant by a computer system. [1]
2. **Identify** whether the following statements about ROM and RAM are true or false. [4]
   a. ROM stores data and applications that are currently in use.
   b. When you turn the computer off, everything in RAM is lost.
   c. ROM is volatile.
   d. RAM has data pre-installed onto it.
3. **Discuss** whether a touch-screen computer is an input or output device and explain your conclusion. [2]
4. **State** the function of storage devices. [1]
5. There are different types of user interface. **Describe** the following interfaces and their advantages and disadvantages.
   a. Graphical user interface. [4]
   b. Command line interface. [4]
6. State the functions of a:
   a. linker [2]
   b. compiler. [2]
7. Applications are programs that you may use in your daily work. State the main uses of each of following programs. [6]
   a. Word processor.
   b. Database.
   c. Spreadsheet.
   d. Desktop publisher.
   e. Web page editors.
   f. Presentation software.
8. a. Describe what is meant by artificial intelligence. [2]
   b. Describe *two* uses of artificial intelligence. [4]
9. Explain the difference between virtual reality and augmented reality. [2]

[Total: 34]

COMMAND WORDS

explain: set out purposes or reasons / make the relationships between things evident / provide why and / or how and support with relevant evidence

identify: name / select / recognise

discuss: write about issue(s) or topic(s) in depth in a structured way

state: express in clear terms

describe: state the points of a topic / give characteristics and main features

REFLECTION

What problems did you encounter when completing the exam-style questions in this chapter? How did you solve them?

SELF-EVALUATION CHECKLIST

After studying this chapter, think about how confident you are with the different topics.

This will help you to see any gaps in your knowledge and help you to learn more effectively.

You might find it helpful to rate how confident you are for each of these statements when you are revising. You should revisit any sections that you rated 'Needs more work' or 'Getting there'.

I can ...	See section	Needs more work	Getting there	Confident to move on
identify the hardware and software that make up a computer system, including input and output devices and operating systems used to run computers	1.1 and 1.2			
discuss types of applications software, systems software and their different roles	1.1			
describe the internal components of a computer and how they work together to run the system effectively	1.1 and 1.2			
understand the characteristics of analogue and digital data	1.1			
understand the different types of operating systems and identify the different types of user interface that are available	1.3			
compare the advantages and disadvantages of different types of computer	1.4			
recognise how emerging technologies are impacting on many aspects of everyday life	1.5			

Chapter 2
Input and output devices

IN THIS CHAPTER YOU WILL:

- explain what is meant by input devices and how they are used
- understand that manual input devices need a person to enter the data but direct data-entry systems do not need a human to enter data
- explain what is meant by output devices and how they are used
- describe the advantages and disadvantages of input and output devices.

GETTING STARTED

In Figure 2.1, you will see some images showing the use of input and output devices.

a   Tablet

b   Automated factory line

c   Contactless payment

d   Headphones

e   Video camera

Figure 2.1: The use of input and output devices

On paper write the headings 'Input devices', 'Output devices' and 'Both'.

Write the names of the input and output devices from the images under the correct headings.

SENSORS IN EVERYDAY LIFE

A sensor is an input device that detects and responds to some type of stimulus from the environment – for example, light, temperature or motion. Car parking can be controlled by a barrier system containing sensors (see Figure 2.2). The barrier has to lift up to allow a car into the car park and drop down again when the car has passed through. It is important that the barrier must not come down when there is a vehicle underneath.

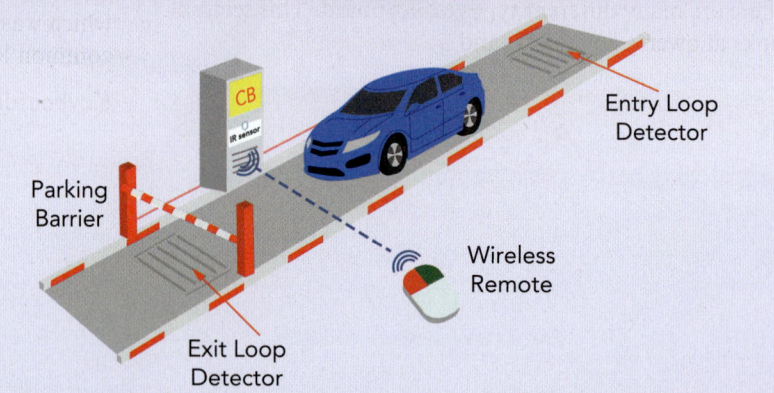

Figure 2.2: Sensors monitor the area around the entrance barriers of car parks

2 Input and output devices

> **CONTINUED**
>
> Ultrasonic sensors are used to detect the presence of vehicles. Ultrasonic sensors emit ultrasonic sound waves that are inaudible to humans. These waves are reflected back from objects and the sensor measures the distance to the object by measuring the time between the emission of the wave and reception of the echo.
>
> Ultrasonic sensors can also be used to notify users how many spaces there are and when the car park is full. If every parking bay is fitted with an ultrasonic sensor, occupancy rates can be calculated with an accuracy of 99.9%. They can even notify the users where the spaces are in the garage.
>
> Older car parks used coils of wire fitted into the concrete at the entrance to and exit from the car park. They work just like a metal detector and record when a vehicle has passed over them, calculating how many cars are currently in the car park.
>
> **Discussion questions**
>
> 1 What are the advantages to using sensors in multi-storey car parks?
>
> 2 Can you think of any other use of sensors for cars when they are parking?

2.1 Input devices

Input devices are used to enter data into a computer. The processor processes the data given by the input device.

There are two different categories of input device. They are:

- Manual input devices, which people use to enter data into a computer themselves.
- Direct data-entry (DDE) devices, which enable data to be entered directly without a human having to input it manually (see Section 2.2).

Keyboards and keypads

Keyboards are input devices used to enter fixed values, often characters and numbers, into the computer system. There are many different types of keyboard. This section looks at qwerty keyboards and **numeric keypads**.

> **KEY WORDS**
>
> **input device:** any hardware device that sends data to a computer
>
> **keyboard:** an input device that is used to enter fixed values, often characters, into the computer system
>
> **numeric keypad:** a keyboard with a group of keys representing the digits from 0 to 9 arranged in a rectangle

Figure 2.3: Qwerty keyboard layout with numeric keypad on the right

A QWERTY keyboard is the most common type of keyboard and is used to type letters, numbers and punctuation into a computer. It gets its name from the arrangement of letters on the top line of keys: Q W E R T Y (see Figure 2.3). Other keyboard types include AZERTY and QWERTZ (which are modelled on the QWERTY keyboard) and the Dvorak keyboard, which was designed to be more efficient by placing common letter combinations together.

Keyboards are used for everything that requires a text or numerical input, from writing an email to writing a book.

> **ACTIVITY 2.1**
>
> Investigate different layouts of keys on keyboards used for different languages and alphabets.
>
> How many can you find?

25

> **ICT IN CONTEXT**
>
> After a study by Microsoft, it was found that computer users hit the space bar on the keyboard an average of 669 times every hour. This one action being repeated so many times could make a computer user more likely to suffer from RSI (repetitive strain injury, discussed in Chapter 5, Section 5.2 Health issues).

Most keyboards have a section on the right with a group of keys representing the digits from 0 to 9 arranged in a rectangle. This is a numeric keypad.

Numeric keypads are also provided on their own for people to input their PIN numbers when they pay for something by card, to input phone numbers on a telephone keypad, or for an entry code.

Numeric keypads are small, easy to use and are not dependent on language.

Advantages of keyboards:

- They are so common that everyone is familiar with them.
- They are easy to use and people quickly become familiar with their layout.

Disadvantages of keyboards:

- It is very easy to make an error when entering the data.
- Unless users learn how to touch type, it can be time consuming to enter the data.
- Can cause strain injuries if used for long periods.
- Cannot be used for creating diagrams and artwork.
- Different keyboards are required for different countries as their languages may use different characters.

Pointing devices

Mice

A **mouse** is a pointing device that is used with a computer with a graphical user interface (see Chapter 1, Section 1.3 Operating systems). By moving the mouse on a flat surface, you can move the pointer on the screen. Items can be moved or selected by clicking one of the mouse buttons.

The first mice (called mechanical mice) used to use a ball and a sensor to detect movement, but modern mice (optical mice) don't have any moving parts. An **optical mouse** uses an optical sensor to detect changes in reflected light. The best surface to use it on is something with any type of pattern, even just a grid design.

A **wireless mouse** communicates with the computer using Wi-Fi or Bluetooth. They are more convenient and versatile as they are not connected to the computer by a cable. They need their batteries replacing or charging occasionally, which either means you might have to plug them in to the computer for a short while, or change their batteries depending on the type of wireless mouse you use.

> **KEY WORDS**
>
> **mouse:** a hand-held device that is used with a computer to move the pointer/cursor on the screen. There are several different types of mouse such as mechanical and optical mice. (Note: the plural of mouse is 'mice')
>
> **optical mouse:** an optical mouse emits light and uses an optical sensor to detect changes in the reflected light to move the pointer on a computer screen
>
> **wireless mouse:** a mouse that is not connected to the computer by a cable but communicates with it using radio waves

Advantages of using mice as pointing devices:

- They provide a fast method of input.
- They are intuitive to use because they simply involve pointing at things.

Disadvantages of using mice as pointing devices:

- Mice can be easily damaged or vandalised.
- Some people, particularly if they have physical disabilities, find mice difficult to use.
- Overuse of a mouse can lead to repetitive strain injury (see Chapter 5, Section 5.2 Health issues).
- Mice need a flat surface to be moved around on.

Touchpads

A mouse is sometimes not a suitable way to control the pointer. A laptop computer is designed for use in places

2 Input and output devices

other than on a fixed surface. This means that there is often no surface for the mouse. A laptop is designed to have all the necessary peripherals in one case and a mouse would have to be carried separately. That is why laptops come with a variation on a mouse for a pointing device. It is called a **touchpad** and is a flat area next to the keyboard (see Figure 2.4).

Most touchpads have the ability to let you use the corners of the pad for particular functions, such as a right-click. Touchpads allow you to swipe, use one, two of more fingers for different functions and with some you can use your thumb and finger to zoom in or out.

Figure 2.4: A laptop computer with a touchpad

Trackerballs

Trackerballs are like the original, mechanical mice turned upside down so that the mouse remains stationary and the user moves the ball, which is obviously much larger in a trackerball.

Trackerballs have the following advantages over a mouse:

- A trackerball is stationary and does not need a surface to be moved around on.
- It can be built into a computer, such as in an information system in a museum, and is not as likely to get lost or damaged like a mouse can.
- It can also be used by disabled people who may not have the freedom of movement necessary to use other pointing devices.

A disadvantage is that trackerballs can be difficult to use for some applications which need fine control.

Remote controls

A **remote control** is a small, handheld device that can be used to operate equipment such as a TV or stereo. It has a number of buttons. When a button is pressed, the remote control sends an infrared signal to the equipment. Each signal contains a code; there are enough different codes to allow all the buttons to have their own code so that the equipment knows what to do. Remote controls are used to control home entertainment systems, satellite boxes, lighting and shutters, for example.

Their main advantage is convenience; for example, you do not need to stand up to change the TV channel. A disadvantage is that the signal can interfere with other equipment and can be blocked by objects between the remote control and the equipment it controls.

Joysticks

A **joystick** can carry out the same tasks as a mouse as well as other functions such as controlling the movement of a motorised wheelchair (see Figure 2.5).

> ### KEY WORDS
>
> **touchpad:** a pointing device, often found on a laptop, that allows the user to use their finger to move the pointer on the screen
>
> **trackerball:** a device to move a pointer where a ball is rolled around directly by the user rather than being moved by the whole mouse being pushed
>
> **remote control:** a small, handheld device that can be used to operate equipment such as a TV or stereo
>
> **joystick:** a joystick can carry out the same tasks as a mouse as well as other functions such as controlling movement

It consists of a stick that pivots on a base and the top of the stick can be moved in any direction. The direction and degree of the movement of the joystick are used to control the movement of an object on the screen. They also have buttons that can be pressed – for example, for left- and right-clicking.

27

Figure 2.5: Wheelchair operated by a joystick

Figure 2.6: An arcade game using a driving or steering wheel

As a pointing device, a joystick can move a pointer, just as a mouse can, but they are also used to move other things, such as a character or spaceship in a game. The joystick might have buttons with specific uses, such as picking up an object in the game. Individual actions depend on how the joystick's software has been programmed. Joysticks are used in many practical applications, not just as a pointing device in a computer system.

Because of their advantages, joysticks are used in applications such as:

- Playing games because they give the user the impression of being in control, and there is a direct and immediate result of the player's actions that adds to the enjoyment of the game.
- To control aircraft because they are easy to use in a very complex environment.
- To control wheelchairs that have motors because they allow the user to give many different commands with very little physical movement.

The disadvantage of using a joystick as a pointing device is that it is more difficult to control the fine movement of the pointer on the screen than with a mouse.

Driving wheel

A **driving wheel** is designed for use in racing video games, and driving and racing simulators (see Figure 2.6). They are often packaged with pedals for acceleration and also brakes.

Advantages of a driving wheel:

- Allows users to control movement far more accurately that a mouse or joystick.
- Force feedback can also be added to provide simulated road resistance.

Disadvantages of a driving wheel:

- Can only be used for one purpose. It would be very difficult, for example, to write a document using a driving wheel as the input device.
- Adding mechanical elements, such as force feedback and gear levers, increases manufacturing costs.

Touch screens

A **touch screen** can be found on personal computers, laptops, tablets and smartphones. It is a display screen that is both an input and an output device.

A touch screen can determine where on the screen the user has touched and sends that information to the processor.

> **KEY WORDS**
>
> **driving wheel:** also called a 'racing wheel'. Used as an input device in racing games and simulations where users control vehicles
>
> **touch screen:** a display screen that is both an input and an output device and that can respond to a user interacting with a specific area

You may have noticed that sometimes you can use a touch screen with your gloves on and sometimes you can't. That's because there are two types of touch screens:

- **Resistive**, which means it is sensitive to pressure from your finger or other object pressed onto the screen. The point of contact is detected because two metallic layers touch at that certain point resulting in a change in voltage.
- **Capacitive**, which means that the screen is sensitive to static electricity on an exposed finger. This is detected by sensors placed at the four corners of the screen allowing it to detect the touch point.

Touch screens are common in information systems in places like train stations (see Figure 2.7) or self-service checkouts at a supermarkets.

Advantages of touch screens:

- They are intuitive and easy to use. A user merely taps an image on a screen.
- Space-saving as input and output devices are the same.
- Cost effective for shops and restaurants as fewer staff are needed if customers can order and serve themselves.

Disadvantages of touch screens:

- Not suitable for inputting large amounts of data.
- Not very accurate for selecting very small areas.

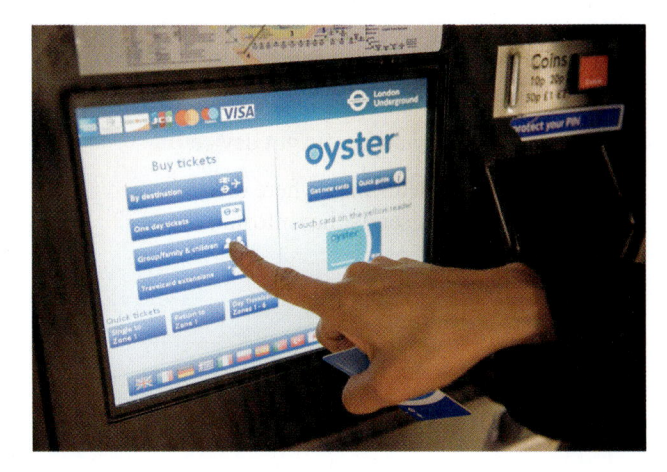

Figure 2.7: A touch screen computer for buying tickets at a railway station

- Disabled people can find them difficult to use if they cannot lift their arms or are sitting in a wheelchair and the machines are placed too high.
- Hygiene problems with lots of people touching the screen.

Scanners

Scanners are used to convert text, diagrams and images into digital data so that they can be manipulated by a computer. Flatbed scanners have a flat sheet of glass on which the **hard-copy** (a photo or printed piece of paper) is placed. The scanner shines a light at the document and the reflected light is directed onto a light sensitive, integrated circuit, which sends the data to the computer.

> **KEY WORDS**
>
> **resistive touch screen:** a touch screen that is sensitive to pressure from your finger
>
> **capacitive touch screen:** a touch screen that is sensitive to the static electricity from your finger
>
> **scanner:** a device that digitises text, diagrams and images
>
> **hard-copy:** a document printed on paper (a soft-copy is a digital version)

Hand-held document scanners can be used to scan relatively small areas of text by rolling the scanner across it.

Advantages of scanning:

- Flatbed scanners are very accurate and can produce reasonably high quality images.
- Hard-copy material can be changed into a form that can be edited or stored on the computer system.
- Any material that is digitised by a scanner can then be included on electronic documents (e.g. in reports, as photos on posters, in presentations, etc.).
- Scanned images can be imported into graphics applications, and enhanced, improved or changed as needed.

- Specialist scanners can convert old material such as 35 mm negatives into digital files, which means sentimental images can be kept safe – although not in the original form.

Disadvantages of scanning:

- While scanners make it possible to put images of hard-copy photographs and printed illustrations into a computer, there may be a reduction in the quality of the image, and scanned diagrams can sometimes appear distorted.
- Scanned images can take up a lot of space in storage.

Cameras

Digital cameras

Digital cameras capture digital photographs that can be stored on a **memory card** or a hard disk and displayed on a screen. The lens of the camera focuses the light onto a sensor which is covered with millions of light sensitive elements called **pixels** which can detect the intensity of the light falling on them and the relative amounts of red, green and blue wavelengths. The greater the number of pixels, the more detailed the image.

Most cameras can be connected to the computer using a USB cable, or via Bluetooth or Wi-Fi, to upload the images directly.

Advantages of digital cameras over traditional film cameras:

- The picture can be seen immediately and erased if it is not good enough.
- Digital images can be manipulated more readily than those on film.
- The image can be used in other electronic documents.

Disadvantages of digital cameras over traditional film cameras:

- The storage device, usually a memory card, may become full so that images are not saved.
- The memory card may become corrupted.
- The camera battery may run out so that photographs cannot be taken.

Video cameras and webcams

Video cameras are used to record moving pictures, or video, that are stored electronically. A video camera can store the data on a memory card, or it can be linked to a computer in order to feed the video directly into the computer. Once the video is stored on the memory card or computer, it can be edited and used.

Advantages of video cameras:

- Take moving images and not just still ones.
- Record audio as well as images.
- Provide a more realistic record of an event.

Disadvantages of video cameras:

- File sizes can be very large.
- May need expensive software to edit them.

The cameras can be used for leisure, by organisations for producing commercial videos and also for security purposes using closed-circuit television (CCTV).

Video footage can also be taken using digital cameras and mobile phones.

Webcams are a special category of video camera that have no storage capacity but are connected directly to a computer. Laptops may have a webcam built into the lid, just above the screen. Another type of webcam can be plugged into a desktop computer and used that way.

> **KEY WORDS**
>
> **digital camera:** produces digital images that can be stored in a computer and displayed on a screen
>
> **memory card:** a type of storage device that is used for storing data files and media. They are often used in small, portable devices, such as cameras and phones
>
> **pixel:** an individual point of light in a digital image. (It is a shortened version of '**pi**cture **el**ements')
>
> **video camera:** a camera to make a record of moving pictures that are stored electronically
>
> **webcam:** a special category of video camera that have no storage capacity but is connected directly to a computer

Webcams are often used to provide live video pictures when chatting with friends and family members using applications such as Skype. They can also be used to provide pictures to accompany an audio meeting held by people who are talking to each other over the internet, called a **video-conference**.

The live images provided by a webcam can be uploaded to a website so that people can see what is happening at a given site in real time. They are often used to show people the nests of birds and the development of their chicks or the traffic flow in a particular street. For example, some webcams show live street scenes; others might show wildlife habitats.

Microphones

Microphones can be used to input sounds into a computer by converting sound waves into digital data. They can be used in a number of different applications, for example, in video-conferencing, in adding speech to a presentation, controlling the computer using spoken commands and for dictation. Microphones can be used by disabled people to input data when using a more common input device is not possible for them.

A disadvantage of using a microphone is that many cheap ones do not give a true representation of the input sounds.

Sensors

A **sensor** is a device that detects and responds to some type on input from the environment, e.g. light, temperature, motion, pressure.

Advantages of using sensors as devices to collect data:

- They are more reliable than a human being because a human may forget to take readings.
- Readings are more accurate than those taken by humans.
- It is not possible for a human to go to some places where readings need to be taken, like the inside of a reaction vessel, where chemical reactions take place.

Disadvantages of using sensors as devices to collect data:

- Digital sensors are active sensors and need a power source. If there is a power cut or their battery dies, they will stop working. Passive sensors do not need a power source, for example, a mercury thermometer or a barometer.
- If the sensors are left at a remote location and malfunction then their users will not know.

Temperature sensors read the temperature of their surroundings and send the readings to the processor.

KEY WORDS

video-conference: a meeting held by people who are talking to each other over the internet

microphone: a device that converts sound to an analogue electrical signal

sensor: a device that detects and responds to some type on input from the environment, e.g. light, temperature, motion, pressure

temperature sensor: a device that reads the temperature of its surroundings and sends the readings to the processor

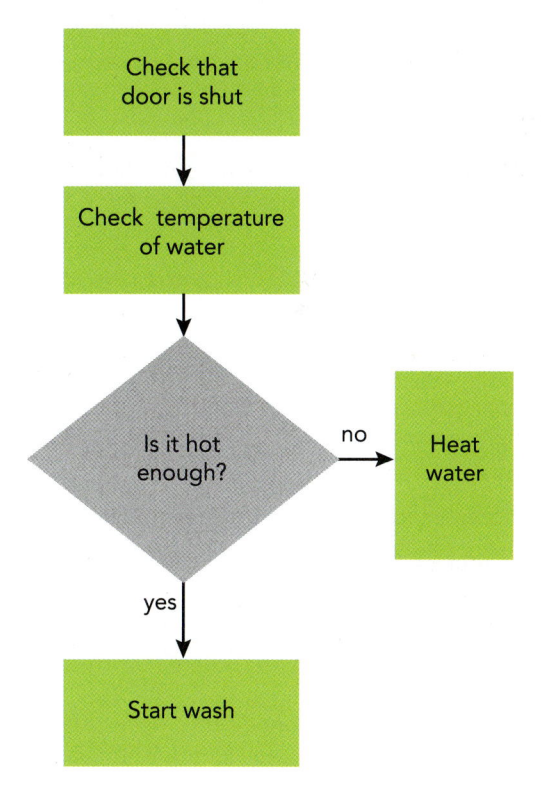

Figure 2.8: Flowchart showing use of a temperature sensor in a washing machine

For example, think about how an automatic washing machine works. When a washing machine is turned on to do the wash, the tub will fill with water. The processor in control of the wash cycle will need to ensure that the water is hot enough to do the wash. If it is not hot enough, the processor will turn on the heating element until the temperature sensor reports that the water is hot enough. If the water is too hot then the processor may let in some cold water to cool the water down until the temperature sensor reports that the water is cool enough.

Temperature sensors are also used in many other applications, including:

- Regulating the temperature of a room in a centrally heated or air-conditioned house.
- Controlling temperatures in greenhouses.
- Controlling the heat in reaction vessels in a scientific experiment.

ICT IN CONTEXT

Smartphones have sensors in them such as gyroscopes that detect angular rotational velocity and motion and accelerometers that measure linear velocity. These **smartphone sensors** enable your smartphone to perform tasks such as tracking the number of steps you have taken, checking out information on specific stars in the sky or using the phone as a spirit level to check whether something is horizontally straight.

Pressure sensors measure pressures and send the results to the processor where the decision is taken as to what to do.

They could be used as part of a burglar alarm system: if pressure readings are sent to a processor, then a decision can be made. The processor can decide whether it is enough pressure to indicate a human being or whether it is the cat and so the alarm should not go off.

Light sensors measure the amount of light falling on them. This could be used for something simple like a sensor in a car to decide whether or not to turn the headlights on. In a burglar alarm system, if a beam of light is shone onto a light sensor then someone walking through the beam will reduce the light hitting the sensor. The information sent to a processor would indicate to it that there was something moving in the room and a decision whether to turn the alarm on would be made.

Light pen

Light pens were light sensitive input devices that were used before the development of touch screens. They were first used in 1955 and were used to select text, draw pictures and interact with user interfaces. They were used on the old-style **CRT monitors** (see Figure 2.9) and detected changes in the brightness of the minute picture elements that make up the screen.

KEY WORDS

smartphone sensor: a sensor in a smartphone for measuring such things as movement and rotation, pressure and light intensity

pressure sensor: a device that measures pressure and sends the data to a processor

light sensor: a device that measures light intensity and sends the data to a processor

light pen: a specialised pen that works with a CRT monitor

CRT monitor: a monitor with a cathode ray tube; CRT was used in the traditional TV sets and monitors

Figure 2.9: A light pen being used on a CRT monitor

A light pen was also often used with a **graphics tablet** to 'draw' diagrams and illustrations. A graphics tablet is a flat pad that you can draw on using the light pen or – these days – a **stylus**. It senses the progress of the pen moving over its surface and sends this information to the computer. The computer converts the drawing strokes into digital form, displaying them on the computer screen.

> **KEY WORDS**
>
> **graphics tablet:** an input device consisting of a flat pad which the user 'draws' on or points at with a special light pen or stylus
>
> **stylus:** a pen-shaped instrument whose tip position on a touch screen or tablet can be detected

Usually, a graphics tablet's active surface is treated as though it was the computer's screen: touching the top left of the tablet will move the pointer to the top left of the screen, for example, and touching the bottom right will move the pointer straight to the bottom right.

Today, light pens are no longer used due to the invention of touch screens, and the light pen had been replaced by a stylus, which allow users to 'write' on the touch screen much as they would a pad of paper, allowing input of handwriting, drawings and other gestures. They are available for tablets and smartphones, and for graphics tablets. A stylus can be used with both the resistive and capacitive touch screens.

A graphics tablet and stylus can also be used to capture a user's signature for digital legal documents.

Table 2.1 shows the advantages and disadvantages of a stylus and light pen.

Advantages	Disadvantages
Both are easy to use.	Light pens can only be used with some screens.
Both provide accurate positioning.	Light pens don't work on LCD screens.
Both are ergonomically designed for ease of hand movement.	Both can impair the view of the computer screen that they are being used on.
Both don't take up much space on your desk.	Both are not good for basic operations such as printing, clicking and selecting from menus.
Both are lightweight.	Graphic tablets are relatively expensive.
Both have no moving parts.	

Table 2.1: Advantages and disadvantages of a stylus and light pen

Questions

1 Touch screens are used for smartphones and tablets as well as for some laptops.
   a Name **two** *other* situations where touch screens are used.
   b Give **three** advantages of using a touch screen as an input device.
2 Burglar alarms use sensors to detect a person entering the house or building.
   a Name **two** types of sensors that could be used in burglar alarm systems.
   b State how each of them can detect a human or burglar.

PRACTICAL TASK 2.1

1 Create a spider diagram of input devices and their uses.

Practice

2 Use your spider diagram to create a presentation on the input devices you have studied so far.

Challenge

3 Create a series of flash cards with the name and an image of the device on one side and an explanation on the reverse to help you revise.

2.2 Direct data entry and associated devices

Apart from sensors, the input devices discussed so far have required a person to enter the data using manual input devices, but there are other methods that allow data to be entered directly, without human intervention. These are direct data-entry methods, used when large amounts of similar data need to be entered, often in commercial or business applications.

Magnetic stripe readers

On credit cards, bank cards, library cards and hotel room key cards you may see a black **magnetic stripe** (Figure 2.10). This cannot store much information, but many tasks do not require a lot of data.

Imagine a hotel room key card. At check-in, information such as your hotel room number and duration of stay are written onto the magnetic stripe on the back of the card using a magnetic stripe writer. When you eventually find your room and insert or swipe your card, the reader in the lock cross-checks the data with the information held on the guest system.

Advantages of magnetic stripes:

- Simple for people to use – no training needed.
- Very inexpensive.
- Entering data is fast – just swipe the card.
- No errors on inputting data – it's all stored on the card.
- Data on the card can be altered if necessary.

Disadvantages of magnetic stripes:

- Very small storage capacity.
- Data can be destroyed by magnetic field, e.g. by placing next to a speaker.
- Insecure – criminals can easily obtain card readers and writers.
- You need to be with the reader to use the card; cannot use a card with just a magnetic stripe over the internet, for example.

Figure 2.10: A credit card, showing the chip (on the front) and the magnetic stripe (on the back)

Chip and PIN readers

Credit and debit cards have always had a magnetic stripe on the back in order to store information that needs to be kept secret. To make the cards more secure, they now include a computer chip on the front of the card. The chips hold the same data as on the stripe, but it is more secure as the data is encrypted (see Chapter 4, Section 4.2 Network issues and communication). They can also generate and store details of the transaction each time they are used.

When making a payment using a chip and PIN card, the user puts the card into an input device called a **chip and PIN reader**, which reads the information stored in the chip (see Figure 2.10).

> **KEY WORDS**
>
> **magnetic stripe reader:** a device used to read a magnetic stripe of a card, which contains data, or to write to the stripe
>
> **chip and PIN reader:** device used to read the data stored in the silicon chip of a credit or debit card to verify the personal identification number (PIN) entered using a numeric keypad

The most important piece of information in the chip is the PIN (personal identification number), which is a digit code that the user must know to be able to use the card. The user types the PIN on the numeric keypad attached to the reader. That PIN is checked against the PIN stored on the card's chip, and if the two match then the payment goes through.

Advantages of chip and PIN:

- The information held is more secure than just the magnetic stripe because the chip is difficult to read and chips are harder to clone.
- The computer chip can hold more information than the magnetic stripe can hold.
- Chip and PIN readers can be wireless, which means they can be brought to you when you're in a shop or restaurant, rather than you having to go to the till to pay.

Disadvantages of chip and PIN:

- People tend to be careless when entering their PIN and people watching can see it. This is called 'Shouldering' or 'shoulder surfing'.
- You can forget your PIN, meaning you can't make payments with that card until you get a new one.

RFID readers

RFID stands for radio-frequency identification, and an RFID reader will read data stored on **RFID tags**.

An RFID device has similar uses to a bar code or the magnetic stripe on the back of a credit card in that once it is scanned, it provides a **unique identifier** for the object it is attached to.

> ### KEY WORDS
>
> **RFID (radio-frequency identification):** an RFID reader uses radio waves to identify and track special tags attached to objects
>
> **RFID tag:** radio-frequency identification tag. Contains digital data that can be interrogated by and send the data to a reader device using radio waves
>
> **unique identifier:** a characteristic or element that is found only on one particular item

Almost anything can have an RFID tag; for instance, merchandise in supermarkets or stores, shipping containers, train carriages, expensive musical instruments and so on. When animals are tagged, they have an RFID tag inserted under their skin. Contactless payments also use RFID.

RFID has three elements:

- a scanning antenna
- a decoder to interpret the data
- the RFID tag itself, which will have been programmed with information.

When triggered by a signal from the reader, the tag transmits data back to it.

Passive tags use the power provided by the reader to transmit their data and active tags are powered by their own battery.

Advantages of RFID:

- The chips do not need to be positioned precisely on the scanner like a bar code.
- RFID devices work within a few metres of the scanner.
- At a supermarket, all of the items in a trolley could be read at once.
- You can write data to RFID tags as well as being able to read them.
- RFID tags can be used for tracking items, e.g. luggage or animals.

Disadvantages of RFID:

- The tags can be read without authentication and so hackers could be able to read any sensitive information or even clone them.
- RFID scanning can be affected by other electrical devices in the vicinity.
- The range of RFID is limited to about three metres.

> ### ICT IN CONTEXT
>
> By fixing RFID labels to the shoes or bibs of each runner and placing mats with RFID readers at different points on the course, it is possible to record accurate start and finish times and allows friends and relatives to track the progress of runners.

OCR and OMR

OCR

If you have a printed copy of a text document, it can be scanned into a computer where special software can recognise the characters and convert them into digital text for use with word processing software. This is known as optical character recognition (**OCR**) because it attempts to recognise each character in the text.

OCR software compares the shape of each character with the shapes that it knows and, when it is matched, the computer stores that letter, for example, the letter 'R'. This can make the input of data from hard-copy documents much quicker than retyping them. OCR software can also be used to read data from passports or identity cards directly into a computer.

Advantages of OCR:

- It can be a really fast way of entering hard-copy.
- It can avoid typing errors.
- It is much cheaper than employing someone to input hard-copy if a high level of accuracy isn't an issue.

Disadvantages of OCR:

- The text produced is not always reliable, particularly if the hard-copy original has strange fonts/poor handwriting, is unclear or has smudged text. This can lead to incorrect information being stored.
- If 100% accuracy is required, the information needs to manually checked for errors, which is time consuming and can be costly.

OMR

A scanner can be used to scan a sheet of paper and identify any marks on it. The software can then use the positions of these marks to obtain information. For example, the position would show which option has been selected as the answer to a multiple choice exam question or which candidate had been voted for in an election. Before the use of tablets and smartphones, school register systems used this sort of data capture. The teacher would fill in a box in a form if a student was present and a machine would read the forms.

This is known as optical mark recognition or optical mark reading (**OMR**). OMR scanning aims to find the marks on the paper; it is not interested in their shape, only *where* they are.

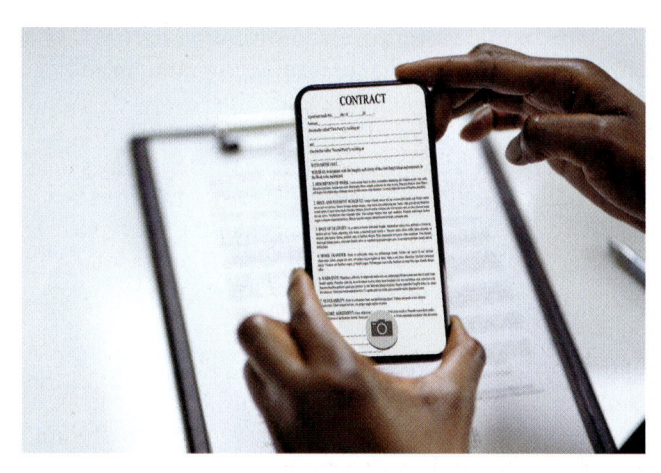

Figure 2.11: Example of a document suitable for OCR

> **KEY WORDS**
>
> **OCR:** optical character recognition scans a typewritten or printed document and translates the images of the characters into digital text that can be used on the computer
>
> **OMR:** optical mark recognition enables data marked by a human, by making marks to select options to be captured for processing by a computer

Advantages of OMR:

- It is extremely fast to input data.
- It is more accurate more than using humans to check the paper.

Disadvantages of OMR:

- The sheets will not be read accurately unless they are properly lined up and the marks/shading are in the correct position to be read by the reader.
- Dirty marks on the paper might be misinterpreted by the system as marks to be input.
- Can only read the marks (i.e. it can't read or input any text).
- Because of the speed of the machines, paper jams can occur.

OCR and OMR are discussed further in Chapter 6, Section 6.10 Recognition systems.

2 Input and output devices

Bar code readers

A **bar code** is a set of short parallel lines in contrasting colours, often black and white. The dark lines are thick, medium or thin. If they are taken in pairs of dark and pairs of light lines they can stand for the digits 0 to 9. These can then be read as a code number. Supermarkets, other retail outlets and services such as libraries use bar codes to enter the details of a product.

Bar codes are read by devices that shine a laser at them and then read the reflection to tell how thick the lines are. Using a bar code for data entry is much faster than using a keyboard. It is also more accurate because a human can make mistakes.

The information contained in a bar code on a typical supermarket product is:

- country of origin number
- manufacturer number
- item number
- check digit.

The price of the item is NOT in the bar code.

QR scanners

QR (quick response) codes are a type of two-dimensional bar code that can be read using a camera and software to interpret them and provide a link directly to text, emails and websites. They are easy for smartphone users as they have a camera and can be easily positioned in front of the code (see Figure 2.12) but external scanners can be used for desktop and laptop computers.

The smartphone with the app is the **QR scanner**. Many advertised products and services have a **QR code** associated with them. The device scans the code and the user is taken directly to the website of the business providing the goods or service. They can also be used to encode phone numbers or even text messages.

The QR code is an image-based link, as found on websites, which can be used offline. The app that reads the QR code uses the device's camera and then accesses the website using a data connection, for example, via Wi-Fi.

Figure 2.12: A QR code can be scanned by a downloaded app on a smartphone

KEY WORDS

bar code: a set of short parallel lines in contrasting colours, often black and white, that stand for the digits 0 to 9. Bar code readers shine a laser at them and then read the reflection to tell how thick the lines are

QR scanner: a quick response scanner consists of software and hardware, such as a smartphone and an app used to read and respond to the data stored in a QR code. They are most conveniently used on smartphones which can be easily positioned in front of the QR code

QR code: quick response code – a type of two-dimensional bar code (in a square) that can store data such as URLs, geotags and links

ACTIVITY 2.2

Search for a website that allows you to create and download QR codes and create one for yourself. It could be a link to your own or your school or college's website. Using a suitable app on a smartphone or tablet, check that it works.

Advantages of QR codes and scanners:

- You can store lots of information on a QR code without having to write it down.
- QR codes can be used for anything by anyone.
- QR codes can be scanned from any direction making them easier to be read with less possibility of background interference.

Disadvantages of QR codes and scanners:

- You need a smartphone with a camera and the app installed to be able to read them.
- QR codes are still relatively new and so not everyone is aware of them or what they represent.

Table 2.2 summarises the advantages and disadvantages of the various methods of direct data entry.

Device	Advantages	Disadvantages
OMR	Fast and accurate.	Forms have to be accurately designed and accurately filled in. The OMR reader can only read shaded areas.
OCR	Fast and accurate as it avoids typing errors and is less expensive on labour.	Possible difficulty when reading handwriting. Has to be checked for errors.
Bar code reader	Saves time when product prices change as only the price data in the database will need updating once for each product. Quick and easy to get data into the system. Updates stock control automatically so saves time. Very accurate.	The technology is expensive. Bar codes must be undamaged.
Chip and PIN reader	Secure. Hard to clone. Chips hold more data than magnetic stripes. Portable.	Security: you may forget your PIN or people may see what your PIN is as you enter it.
Magnetic stripe reader	Very fast data entry. No data-entry errors as nothing to type in. Robust. Cannot be read by human.	The magnetic stripe can only hold a small amount of data. Cards need to be in physical contact with the reader to work. Data will be lost if the stripe becomes damaged. Easy to duplicate.
QR Scanner	Very versatile. Can contain different types of data. Codes can be easily read by multiple devices, including smartphones. Anyone can create a QR code using software. Quick to read. Stores 100 times more information than a bar code.	A device is needed to scan the code. Relies on the QR code being correct. Some people do not know what they represent or how to read them.
RFID reader	RFID chips do not need to be positioned precisely. They can read chips a few metres away. They can read all of the tags on goods in a trolley at once.	RFID tags can be read by anyone with a reader such as hackers. They can be affected by other electrical devices in the area.

Table 2.2: Advantages and disadvantages of methods of direct data entry

2 Input and output devices

Questions

3 Bar codes are seen on products for sale, almost everywhere.
   a Give the items of information that are typically encoded in a bar code seen on a product at a supermarket.
   b Describe how people with QR scanners on their smartphone could benefit from the information in QR codes.
4 Discuss how RFID can be used in the retail industry.
5 OCR and OMR are both scanning processes to input data.
   a State what is meant by OCR.
   b State what is meant by OMR.
   c Explain the difference between OCR and OMR.

2.3 Output devices and their uses

Output devices are required so that the results of computer processing can be processed directly (e.g. by controlling motors) or be displayed to the users of the system.

Monitors

Monitors are often called 'computer screens' or 'displays' as they display the computer's interface and software that is running to the users so that they can interact with it using input devices such as keyboards and mice.

Older monitors were built, like early television sets, using cathode ray tubes (CRTs). They were therefore very heavy and bulky causing them to take up a lot of desk space.

Modern monitors do not use cathode ray tubes and are so thin and light that they can be used for displays in smartphones and smartwatches. They display images using liquid crystals (LCD), liquid crystals covered by a thin film of transistors (TFT) or light emitting diodes (LED).

Because they are so much smaller and lighter than CRT monitors, TFT monitors can be easily and safely wall mounted. If they need to be placed on a desk, they take up very little space. TFT monitors are used in laptop computers, tablets and mobile phones. They produce far less glare on the screen, which makes them more restful on the eye.

Touch screens

Touch screens are monitors (output devices) that can also be used as input devices and are covered in detail in Section 2.1. As an output device, they function in the same way as a monitor. However, their advantage over ordinary monitors is that they allow users to interact with the operating system and use software without the need for mice and other pointing devices.

Multimedia projectors

Multimedia projectors are devices that can project an image from a computer onto as large a surface as is necessary (Figure 2.13). They are often used in presentations to large audiences. The only limit to the size of the projection is the power or brightness of the light produced by the projector.

> **KEY WORDS**
>
> **output device:** any device used to send data from a computer to another device or user
>
> **monitor:** an output device that visually displays the data output by a computer
>
> **multimedia projector:** device that can project an image from a computer onto as large a surface as is necessary, often used in presentations

The device can be totally portable or fixed, but a disadvantage is that it relies on a powerful and expensive bulb to provide the pictures. These bulbs are fragile, particularly if the projector is moved while it is still hot.

Figure 2.13: Multimedia projector

Printers and plotters

Printers and plotters are output devices that produce characters and/or graphics onto paper and onto other materials. They produce 'hard-copy'.

Laser printers

Laser printers (see Figure 2.14a) work by using a laser to 'draw' the required outputs onto a drum. This puts a positive electric charge on those parts of the drum that have been hit by the laser. An ink powder (called toner) is then sprayed on to the drum and it sticks where there is an electric charge. This drum is pressed against a piece of paper and the ink is transferred to the paper. The paper is then heated by a 'fuser' so that the toner binds to the paper, producing a printed copy. If there are four drums with four different colours of toner then coloured printouts can be produced.

Laser printers are used when quality and speed of output are important.

One disadvantage of using laser printers is that the toner is toxic (poisonous) and the cartridges that it comes in must be disposed of carefully. Other disadvantages with laser printers are that:

- the reproduction of colour is not always as precise as it is with an inkjet printer
- they tend to be more expensive to buy than inkjet printers
- other factors may make them cheaper in the long run.

Inkjet printers

Inkjet printers (see Figure 2.14b) work by squirting ink at the page out of different nozzles for different coloured ink. A stepper motor moves the paper forwards step-by-step while the print head that has the nozzles on it scans across and squirts ink at the correct place to form the desired output. They produce high quality output and are relatively cheap to buy but ink refills are expensive.

One disadvantage of inkjet printers is that they often use water-soluble ink, so if printouts get wet, the ink will run. This does not happen with printouts from laser printers.

Inkjet printers are commonly used in home computer systems and small offices where most printing is of single copy outputs. They are also often used in machines that print out photographs directly from digital cameras.

Dot-matrix printers

Dot-matrix printers (see Figure 2.14c) use a set of pins to press an inked ribbon against the paper. Where the pin hits against the paper, a coloured dot is left. These dots can be arranged in patterns to produce the required output on the paper.

> **KEY WORDS**
>
> **printers and plotters:** devices that produce output onto paper and onto other materials
>
> **laser printer:** a printer that works by using a laser to 'draw' the required outputs onto a drum and uses toner to print the output onto paper
>
> **inkjet printer:** a printer that works by squirting ink at the page out of different nozzles for different coloured ink
>
> **dot matrix printer:** a printer that uses a set of pins to press an inked ribbon against the paper, creating the output out of dots

Advantages of dot matrix printers:

- They can be used in dusty and dirty environments.
- They can be used on continuous or single sheets of paper.

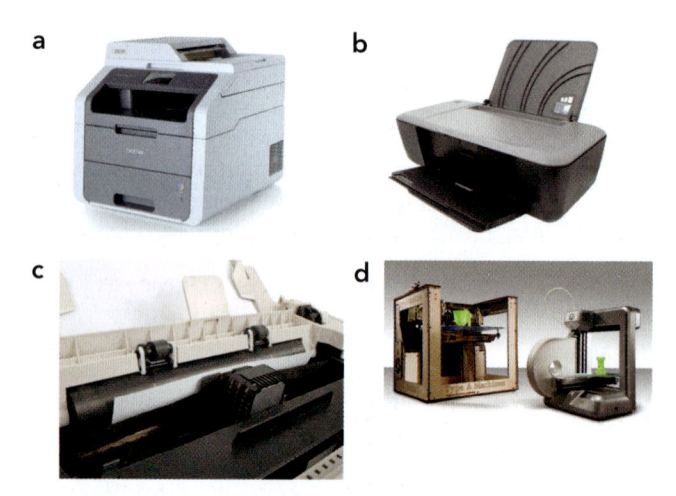

Figure 2.14: Different kinds of printer: **a** laser printer, **b** inkjet printer, **c** dot-matrix printer, **d** 3D printer

2 Input and output devices

- There is a low printing cost per page.
- They are reliable and durable.

Disadvantages of dot-matrix printers:

- They are slow.
- They are noisy.
- They have a poor quality output.
- There are very limited colour capabilities.
- They are more expensive than ink jet printers.

> **ACTIVITY 2.3**
>
> As a whole class, brainstorm the advantages of a laser printer and an inkjet printer. Decide which is the least expensive overall.

Plotters

A plotter is used to draw graphics on paper after receiving data from a computer. It is different to a printer because it uses pens to draw the image. These pens can be lowered and raised, and moved across the paper to form continuous lines. Plotters are used for computer aided design (CAD), architectural drawings, blueprints and technical drawings, among other uses.

A plotter can print very accurately on very large sheets of paper and on different materials such as wood or plastic. A disadvantage is that they can take up a lot of room compared to other types of printer (see Figure 2.15).

3D printers

3D printing is the production of three-dimensional solid objects from digital files often produced using CAD (computer aided design) software or from **3D scanners**. Successive layers of a material, such as a resin, are laid down in an additive process until the object is created. **3D printers** (see Figure 2.14d) are widely used in medicine to produce organs such as bones to implant in human bodies.

You could design a 3D object on your own computer, connect it to a 3D printer and wait for it to be printed (or built). For example, you could print a bicycle for yourself, because these printers are capable of making moving parts. First you would have to design every part of your bicycle, including the wheels, the handlebars and so on, and then you could print them all out!

The printer manages this by turning a whole object into many thousands of microscopically thin slices, then it prints it slice by slice, sticking the tiny layers together until it forms the object.

Currently, 3D printers are being used to 'print' anything from car parts to chocolate cake and prosthetic limbs.

However, they are expensive, difficult to use and have a high energy consumption.

Speakers

Speakers allow listeners to listen to sound in multimedia presentations, films and music.

> **KEY WORDS**
>
> **3D scanner:** a device that takes multiple photographs of an object from all angles and combines them into a 3D representation or model of it
>
> **3D printer:** a printer that works by printing in layers on top of each other, eventually creating a 3D object
>
> **speaker:** a device to enable you to hear sounds or music on your computer system

The signal from the computer is digital and a DAC (Digital-to-analogue converter – see Chapter 1, Section 1.1 Hardware and software) converts it to analogue form.

Speakers consist of a cone, an iron coil, a magnet, and housing (case). When the speaker receives electrical input from a device, it sends the current through the coil which creates a magnetic field that causes the cone to vibrate back and forth, so producing sound waves.

An important use of speakers is as an output device for some disabled people, particularly blind people who

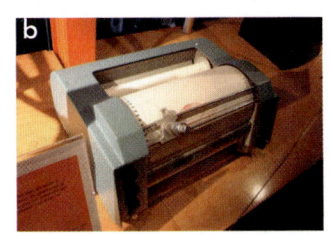

Figure 2.15: Different kinds of plotter: **a** flatbed plotter, **b** drum plotter

cannot see the screen. The speakers allow special software (a screen reader) to describe aloud what is shown on the screen. Also, if a computer user has difficulty in using a keyboard or mouse, then there is dictation software that can be used as input, and input can be checked by listening to it being played back through the speakers.

An advantage and disadvantage is that everyone in the room can hear the output from computer speakers, which is good if that's what is required, but not so great if they don't want to.

Headphones and earpieces are personal speakers, and are often used in environments where other people should not hear the sounds produced. For instance, if there is a presentation to people from different countries, they could each listen to a translation by an interpreter into their first language. They are connected to devices such as computers, phones, MP3 players by cable or wirelessly.

Actuators

An **actuator** is a device that moves or controls some mechanism. An actuator responds to a control signal from the computer and produces a mechanical action, for example, an electric motor.

> ### KEY WORDS
>
> **headphones:** personal speakers that only the person wearing is intended to hear
>
> **actuator:** a device that causes a machine or other device to operate

The motors and hydraulic systems that control robots are actuators. Actuators can be small (e.g. the motors that control the movement of a lens in a digital camera) or much larger (e.g. the motors that control the opening and closing of automatic doors or the barriers in car park systems).

Sensors:
- Pressure (switch & door closed)
- Water level/pressure
- Temperature
- Drum speed
- Balance

Actuators
- Motor
- Pump
- Heater
- LED
- Buzzer/bell

Figure 2.16: Sensors and actuators in a washing machine

Actuators are items that cause movement or a response in control systems. A sensor measures a change in the environment and in response the computer sends a signal to an actuator to cause a response to the change – for example, to open and close the windows in a greenhouse by switching on motors.

Questions

6 State the uses of the following output devices.
   a Monitor.
   b Speaker.
   c Multimedia projector.
   d State which type of monitor is both an input and an output device.

7 Printers are output devices that produce hard-copies.
   a Explain how a laser printer works.
   b Give **two** advantages and **two** disadvantages of a dot-matrix printer.

2 Input and output devices

PRACTICAL TASK 2.2

Getting started

Work in pairs to complete a presentation called 'My Computer'. See Chapter 19 for more information about creating presentations.

1. On a large piece of paper draw five boxes to represent each slide and write in the headings you are going to use.
2. In the box for slide two, write down all the things your computer will be needed for and state which computer would be best suited to those needs.
3. Slide three should explain why the chosen computer suits your needs listed in slide two.
4. The slide four box should contain the type of printer you want and the reason you have chosen that one, and not one of the other types of printer. You should also include a picture of your chosen type of printer.
5. Slide five should list all of the input and output devices that you will need. Note that even if you have chosen a tablet computer, you will still need a printer and you may need other input devices as well.
6. Finish planning your slides on paper by writing into each box the words that will appear there.

Practice

7. When you have completed your plan, create the five slides to contain exactly what you have written in your plan. Remember to save your work.
8. Together, assess what you have achieved so far and make any changes or corrections.

Challenge

9. Add a glossary at the end of the presentation giving definitions of the items you have mentioned, e.g. memory, processor, storage device.
10. Add hyperlinks from the slides where these items are mentioned to their definitions on the glossary slide.

Self-assessment

Tick one of the boxes in each row that best indicates how you feel about the tasks you've just completed. If you didn't tick the smiley face for any of the statements, you may want to re-visit the tasks and ask your teacher or other learners for advice.

	😊	😐	☹
I found the planning stage useful.			
I made a good choice of computer because it can do everything needed.			
I completed all the steps from 1–10.			
I am confident that I chose the correct computer.			
I understand the uses for the input and output devices I chose.			

> ## SUMMARY
>
> | |
> |---|
> | There are many different input and output devices that can be used with a computer system. |
> | Data can be input by hand or directly to a computer without any manual intervention.
 • Data can be directly entered using devices such as magnetic stripe readers, chip and PIN readers, RFID readers, OMRs, OCRs, bar code readers and QR scanners.
 • Data can be input automatically using sensors. |
> | Examples of input devices are keyboards, pointing devices, joysticks, driving wheels, touch screens, scanners, sensors, remote controls, cameras and microphones. |
> | Examples of output devices are monitors, touch screens, projectors, printers, plotters, buzzers, motors and heaters. |
> | The advantages and disadvantages of input and output devices should be considered before being able to know which is best for any particular use. |

EXAM-STYLE QUESTIONS

1 Touch screens are very popular for personal devices and for fixed devices in public places.
   a **State** *three* personal devices that use a touch screen. [3]
   b **Give** *two* advantages and *two* disadvantages of using a touch screen. [4]
   c **Describe** the benefits of touch screens in public places such as those on ticket machines in bus and railway stations. [2]

2 **Compare** the advantages and disadvantages of chip and PIN readers and magnetic stripe readers. [8]

3 a **Define** what is meant by a sensor. [2]
   b **Define** what is meant by an actuator. [2]
   c Describe the use of sensors and actuators in a control system such as a burglar alarm or temperature control system. [2]

[Total: 23]

COMMAND WORDS

state: express in clear terms

give: produce an answer from a given source or recall / memory

describe: state the points of a topic / give characteristics and main features

compare: identify / comment on similarities and / or differences

define: give precise meaning

2 Input and output devices

SELF-EVALUATION CHECKLIST

After studying this chapter, think about how confident you are with the different topics.

This will help you to see any gaps in your knowledge and help you to learn more effectively.

You might find it helpful to rate how confident you are for each of these statements when you are revising. You should revisit any sections that you rated 'Needs more work' or 'Getting there'.

I can ...	See section	Needs more work	Getting there	Confident to move on
explain what is meant input devices and data-entry devices and how they are used	2.1 and 2.2			
understand that manual input devices need a person to enter the data but direct data-entry systems do not need a human to enter data	2.2			
explain what is meant by output devices and how they are used	2.3			
describe the advantages and disadvantages of input and output devices	2.1 and 2.3			

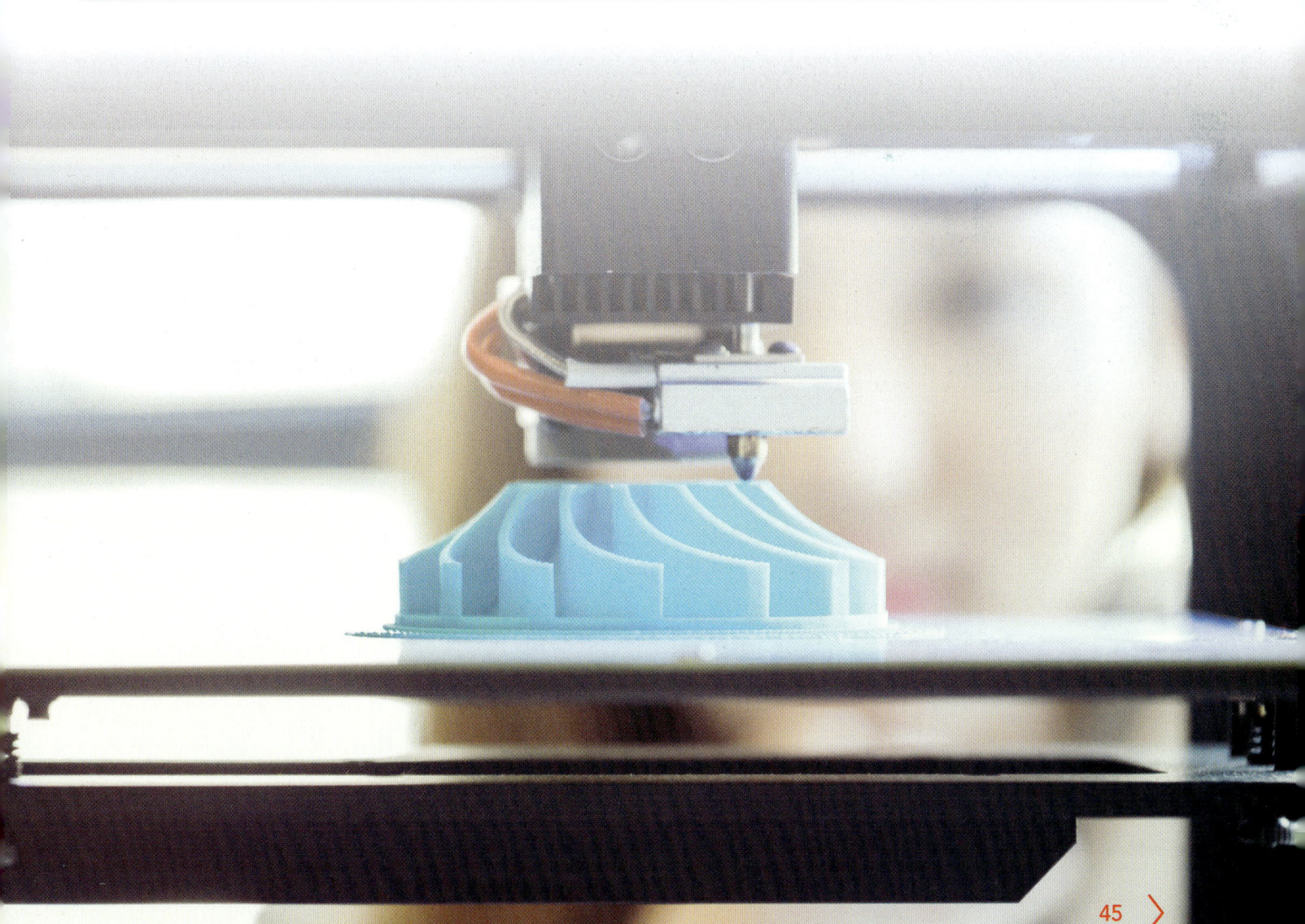

Chapter 3
Storage

IN THIS CHAPTER YOU WILL:

- identify different data storage media
- identify the devices that are necessary to write and read data to and from the media
- describe the uses for the different types of data storage media and compare their advantages and disadvantages
- compare the advantages and disadvantages of optical, magnetic and solid-state storage devices.

3 Storage

GETTING STARTED

Figure 3.1 shows some examples of storage media or devices.

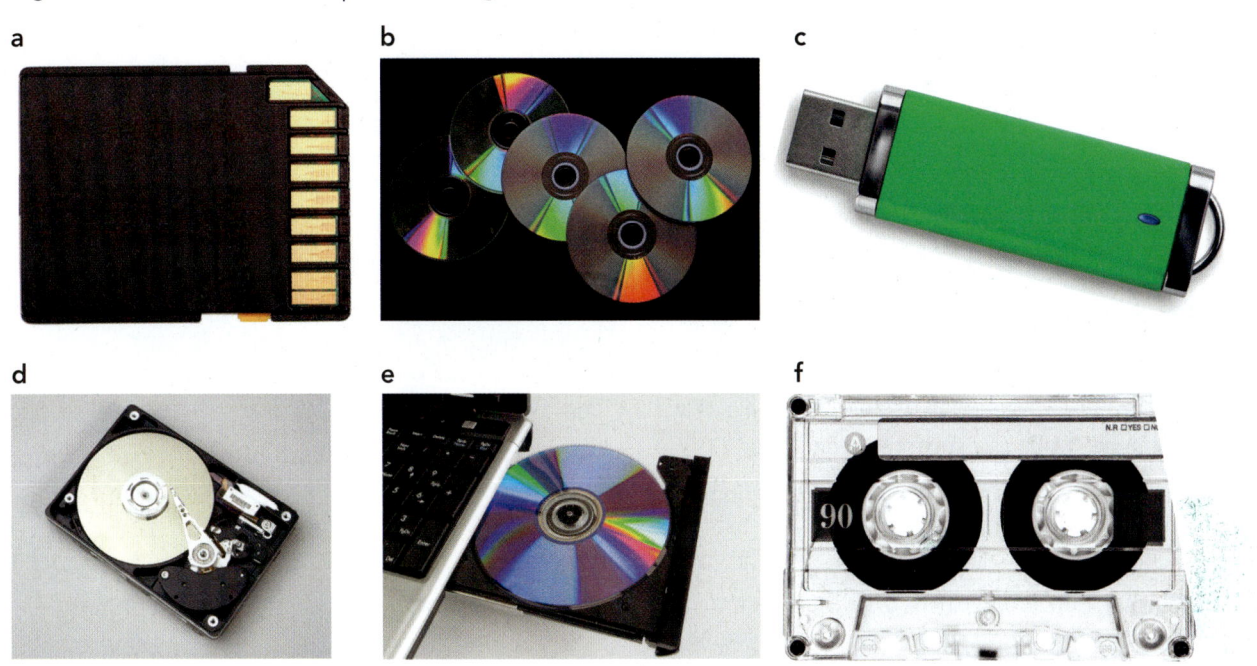

a b c

d e f

Figure 3.1: Examples of storage media or devices

Data is stored in three different ways: magnetically, optically and solid-state.

Draw a table, like the one shown below, and write the letters in the correct columns.

Magnetic	Optical	Solid-state

SO YOU THOUGHT TAPES HAD DIED OUT?

Now that organisations all over the world keep nearly everything stored digitally, and the amount of data being recorded is increasing at around 30–40% a year, the capacity of storage media is important because the capacity of hard drives isn't increasing as quickly as the amount of data that needs to be held. If there are data that do not have to be accessed immediately, tapes are a good solution. Magnetic tape is wound onto a spool to be read from or written to by a device.

Tape storage has lots of advantages: it is energy efficient because when it is full, it is stored and doesn't consume any power; magnetic tapes are very reliable, and their error rates are very low. It has built-in encryption and is also secure because as it isn't in a hard drive, cyber-attacks are not possible. The data cannot therefore be accessed or modified.

> CAMBRIDGE IGCSE™ ICT: COURSEBOOK

> **CONTINUED**
>
> **Discussion questions**
>
> 1 Apart from magnetic tapes, what other media are used for archiving large amounts of data?
>
> 2 Before reading and discussing this text, what did you think about 'old fashioned' tape for ICT purposes and has your thinking changed now?

3.1 Storage devices and media

Storage is a very important component in a computer system. Computers store data in a digital format so the storage media has to be able to store digital data.

Storage devices use **storage media** that hold data whether the computer is on or off and are, therefore, non-volatile.

The storage medium holds the data and the storage device is the machine that lets you store the data onto the medium, and then reads data from it. For instance, a CD RW (Compact Disk Read/Write) disk is the medium because that is the part that has the data on it; the CD RW drive (the device that writes the data to the disk, or reads the data from the disk) is the storage device.

There are three main types of storage media (magnetic, optical and solid-state) and each type stores the data in a different way.

Magnetic storage media and devices

Magnetic storage media hold data magnetically and include hard disk drives and magnetic tape. The surface of the media is made of magnetic material and data is stored digitally in the form of tiny magnetised regions, or dots. Data is written to magnetic storage media by changing the local **magnetic polarity** to represent either a 0 or a 1 – these are 'bits'. A magnetic device can then read the magnetic state of the disk, extracting the 1s and 0s, to retrieve the data from the disk.

Hard disk drives

A **hard disk drive** is currently the main storage device on most personal computers; however, they are rapidly being replaced by solid-state drives.

> **KEY WORDS**
>
> **storage device:** this is the machine that lets you write data to and read data from the storage medium
>
> **storage media:** the material on which the data is stored, e.g. magnetic tape or optical disk. (Note: media is the plural of medium)
>
> **magnetic storage media:** media that stores data magnetically by using local magnetic polarity to represent binary code
>
> **magnetic polarity:** the state of being a north pole or a south pole; similar to positive or negative charge for electricity
>
> **hard disk drive:** a non-volatile memory hardware device that stores data on magnetic disks

Figure 3.2: A hard disk

Hard disk drives contain several individual disks and each one has a read/write head (see Figure 3.2).

3 Storage

The data is stored on concentric circles on the surfaces known as tracks and sections within each track are called sectors. When a data file is stored on a disk it may be split up and saved on different sectors and tracks. The operating system creates an entry in the disk's **file allocation table (FAT)** for the new file that records where each part is located and their sequential order.

Advantages of hard disk drives:

- They can store very large amounts of data.
- They can access the data randomly without having to start at the beginning and search through everything. This is because there is a FAT showing where everything is stored. This type of access is called **random access** or **direct access**.
- They are very low cost.

Disadvantages of hard disk drives:

- They are susceptible to physical knocks that might cause the read/write head to hit the disks and corrupt data.
- They are slower to read and write data than solid-state drives.
- They can be noisy.

Fixed and portable hard disk drives

Fixed hard disk drives are permanently connected to the computer and are contained within the cases of both desktop and laptop computers. They are built in.

Portable hard disk drives (see Figure 3.3) are contained within their own cases and are separate from main computer systems to which they are connected by cable. They can be moved from computer to computer using, for example, USB cables and are therefore useful for transferring large amounts of data or for backing up data which can then be stored at a separate site.

Advantages of a portable drive:

- If you are on the move, it is small enough to carry with you; some of them, even though quite slim, have a tough outside casing to help to minimise possible damage.

> ### KEY WORDS
>
> **file allocation table (FAT):** maps the locations in which files and folders are stored on the disk
>
> **random access (also called direct access):** accessing data in any order and not in a fixed sequence, regardless of its position in a list
>
> **fixed hard disk drives:** drives permanently connected to the computer and are contained within the cases of both desktop and laptop computers. They are built in
>
> **portable hard disk drives:** contained within their own cases and are separate from main computer systems to which they are connected by cable

- It can be easily used by multiple PCs of the same operating system for file sharing, particularly for large files.
- It allows scheduled automatic backup of files, which is easy to set up; then it won't matter if you forget to backup.
- It allows for quick archiving of data.

Disadvantages of a portable drive:

- They could be damaged as they are being moved.
- They are insecure, as they could get lost or stolen with the consequent loss of data.

Figure 3.3: A portable hard disk drive

> **ICT IN CONTEXT**
>
> The hard disk drive is over 60 years old, as it was first used in 1956. Early hard disk drives were very large and had 8-inch disks but today hard disks holding far more data are usually only 2.5 inches. In 1981 they cost $500 000 per gigabyte of storage and today the price is only $0.03 per gigabyte.

Magnetic tape drives and tapes

Magnetic tapes store data in a similar way to how data is stored on magnetic disks. The only difference is that the data is stored in a long line on the tape rather than being scattered over the surface of a disk. The **magnetic tape drive** is the device that drives the tape around the read/write heads.

On a tape, the data is read and written by a read/write heads similar to those used on magnetic disks. However, while the read/write head in the disk device moves to the correct position on a disk to access the data, the read/write head in a magnetic tape reader stays still and the tape moves past it. This means that data that is at the far end of the tape will take a long time to be found because all the other data before it will have to be read first. This sort of storage is called **serial storage** (or serial access). Serial storage means that the data is stored one piece after the other.

If the data is arranged in some sort of order, perhaps alphabetical order, this would speed up finding a particular data item because the device could fast-forward through the unwanted bits (see Figure 3.4). This form of storage is called **sequential storage**, and it gives faster access to data than serial storage, but is still very slow compared with the direct access to data on hard disks.

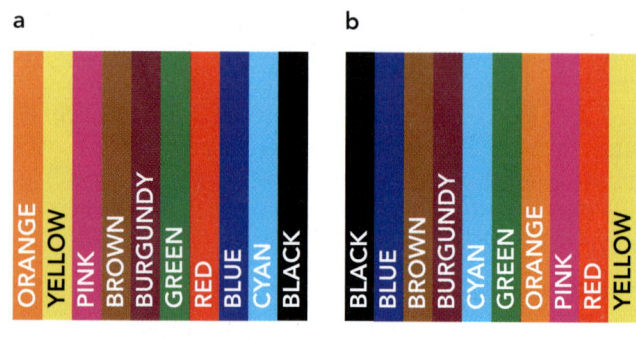

Figure 3.4: Inside a data cartridge showing the magnetic tape. In **a**, the colours (data) are in a random order so the read/write head has to move along the tape until it finds the requested colour. In **b**, the colours (data) are stored in alphabetical order, which means the read/write head can fast-forward to the correct part of the tape

Sometimes the sequential way that data is stored on a tape is very useful. For example, the payroll for a large company is processed once a month. It is important that everyone gets paid. If the data is stored on a tape then everyone's data has to be read and there is no danger of missing someone out. The same is true of utility bills. These need to be sent to every customer on particular dates.

Magnetic tapes are used where there is a need to store large amounts of data and where the speed of access is not important, for example, for storing backups where a lot of data needs to be stored. This includes national archives, movies, banking, as well as science such as particle physics, and much more. Firms such as Google, G-mail and Microsoft use magnetic tape storage.

Although magnetic tape has existed for a very long time, its technology has been advancing all the time. Now a modern tape cartridge can hold many terabytes of data. It is low cost and has long durability.

> **KEY WORDS**
>
> **magnetic tape:** stores data in a long line on magnetic tape and read by a magnetic tape drive
>
> **magnetic tape drive:** a device for collecting, backing up and archiving data on magnetic tape
>
> **serial storage:** data stored in a line on a tape so it has to be read in order
>
> **sequential storage:** data arranged and stored in a particular order, for example, alphabetical order or date order

> **ACTIVITY 3.1**
>
> Carry out research to find hard disk drives with the following capacities:
>
> - 500 gigabytes (half a terabyte)
> - 1 terabyte
> - 2 terabytes.
>
> For each, work out the cost of each gigabyte of storage. (See Chapter 1 for information on units of memory.)

Optical storage media and devices

Optical storage media and devices use light from lasers to read and write data.

- Optical media include **compact disks (CDs)**, **digital versatile disks (DVDs)** and **Blu-ray disks**.
- They can store different amounts of data – CDs can store 700 MB, DVDs, 4.7 GB and Blu-ray disks, 128 GB.

They should have some letters after them to say what type they are. The main types are:

- ROM stands for 'read-only memory'; these cannot be written to, only read from (CD ROM and DVD ROM).
- R stands for 'recordable'; these can be written to just once and then can only be read from (CD-R and DVD-R).
- RW stands for 're-writable'; these can be written to multiple times (CD-RW and DVD-RW).

An optical disk has a single spiral track running from the inside to the outside. The spiral track is over 5 km long.

When CDs and DVDs are produced, digital data is stored along the track by etching pits onto the surface of the disk with a laser in the **optical storage device**. The disk between the pits is called a land (see Figure 3.5). When the light from a laser hits the lands, it is reflected back to a detector. The light is scattered away by the pits and no light is detected. These two events represent the digits '0' and '1'.

Both CD drives and DVD drives use a laser to read and to write the data, but a DVD drive uses a more precise laser. Because of this, the data on DVD media can be closer together and therefore more data can be squeezed onto the surface.

CD ROMs and DVD ROMs

CD ROMs and **DVD ROMs** cannot be written to, only read from. This means that the contents of the CD or DVD can never be changed. This is a big advantage if the contents need to be protected from being corrupted in some way. Examples include using them to sell music or movies. Software companies use them to distribute software and data files, and publishers to distribute reference material like encyclopaedias.

CD-Rs and DVD-Rs

In a recordable CD – a CD-R – the disk surface is covered in a dye, which is translucent and so light passes through it and is reflected by the disk surface. When data is being written to the disk, a powerful laser light burns the dye creating black spots that do not reflect. That is why writing data to the disk is called 'burning the disk'. The reflective areas are interpreted as 1s and the black spots as 0s.

CD-Rs and **DVD-Rs** can be used to store music or movies, or to make a copy of files at a particular time, for an archive, for example. However, once they have been recorded onto, no further changes can be made to the data, which makes them less useful for making regular backups of files because every time a backup was needed a new disk would have to be used.

KEY WORDS

optical storage media: media that store data on their surface that can be read using a light source (usually a laser)

compact disk (CD): a plastic coated disc on which (usually) music digital information is written and read using a laser

digital versatile disk (DVD): a plastic coated disc on which digital information is written and read using a laser. Can store more data than a compact disk

Blu-ray disk: a plastic coated disc on which music digital information is written and read using a laser. Can store more data than a DVD

optical storage device: a device that writes data to or reads data from optical media using laser light

CD ROMs and **DVD ROMs:** CDs and DVDs that are read only

CD-Rs and **DVD-Rs:** blank CDs and DVDs which can be written to once only

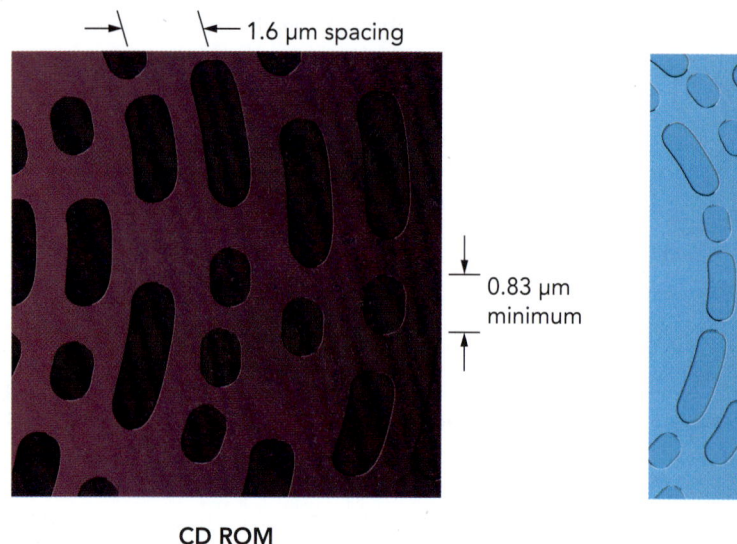

Figure 3.5: Pits and lands on CD ROMs and DVD ROMs

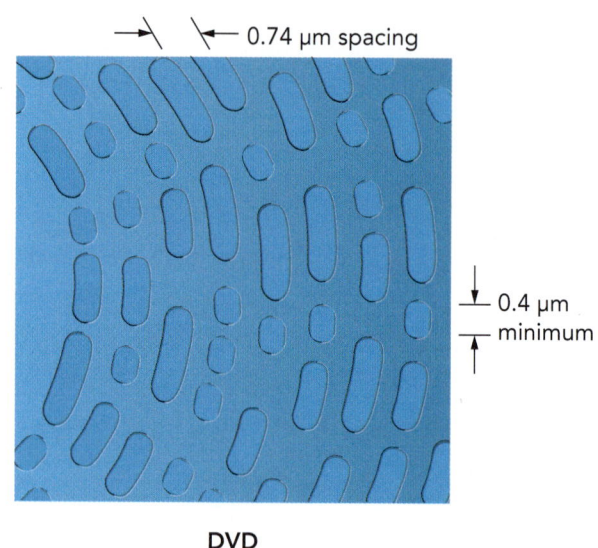

CD-RWs and DVD-RWs

A rewritable CD – a CD-RW – has a layer of a metallic alloy that can exist in two forms: one reflects light and the other doesn't. When data is written, the forms can be changed between reflective and non-reflective. As there is no permanent change, data can be written to the disk many times.

CD-RWs and DVD-RWs are ideal for moving files from one computer to another, perhaps for taking work into school that you have been doing on your computer at home. They are not easy to damage and can store large amounts of data. Because they are rewriteable, they can be used over and over again. This quality also makes them ideal for taking backups of the files on a system.

> **KEY WORD**
>
> **CD-RWs** and **DVD-RWs:** CDs and DVDs on which data can be written, erased and re-recorded

Blu-ray

The name 'Blu-ray' is a reference to the blue/violet laser light that is used to read the disk. The blue/violet light allows information to be stored in greater density than with the longer-wavelength red laser, which is used for DVDs.

Blu-ray disks have very much larger storage capacities than other optical storage media and at the same time can perform high-speed transfers. These two advantages mean that it is now possible to record and play back hours of high-definition video. The disadvantage is the cost, which is much higher than that of standard DVDs.

Optical disks are useful for distributing programs, files and images and backing up data which can then be stored at another site.

Advantages of optical disks:

- They are very cheap.
- They are easy to transport from one site to another.

Disadvantages of optical disks:

- They do not store as much data as hard disk drives.
- Have slow access speeds – it takes more time to write and read the data.
- The stored data degrades over time.

> **ACTIVITY 3.2**
>
> Investigate the types of lasers used for DVDs and Blu-ray disks.

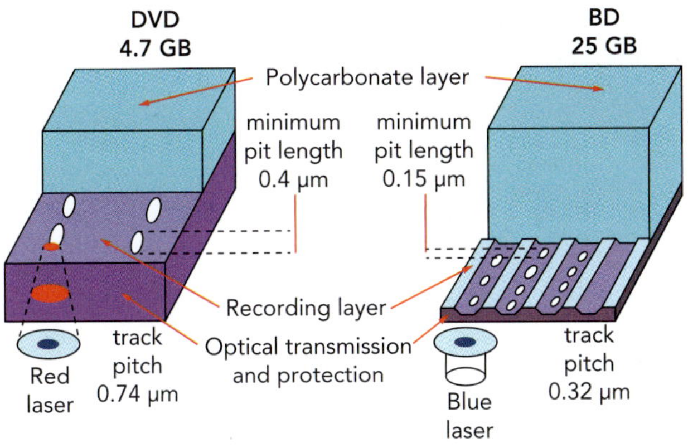

Figure 3.6: DVD and Blu-ray construction

Questions

1. The following table shows some statements about hard disk drives. Make a copy of the table and place ticks in the correct columns to indicate whether they are true or false.

	True	False
Hard disk drives store data magnetically.		
All hard disk drives contain only one disk.		
Fixed hard disk drives are more easily lost than portable ones.		
The advantage of magnetic tape over disk drive storage is that data can be accessed randomly.		
Data on a hard disk drive is read and written using read/write heads.		

2. Describe the difference between a DVD-R and a DVD-RW disk.

Solid-state storage media and devices

Solid-state storage media use **flash memory**, which makes them much faster than traditional fixed hard disks. Flash memory consists of non-volatile memory chips containing transistors called **floating gate transistors** that keep their charge even when the power is switched off. (Normal transistors lose their state when the power is turned off.)

At first, all transistors are charged (set to 1). But when a save operation begins, current is blocked to some transistors, switching them to 0.

This type of storage is called solid-state because there are no moving parts.

Devices using solid-state storage media include solid-state drives, memory sticks and pen drives, and flash memory cards.

Solid-state drives (SSDs)

A **solid-state drive (SSD)** is a new generation of storage devices. Fixed and portable solid-state drives are quickly replacing hard disk drives as the main storage devices of desktop and laptop computers. Portable SSDs, like portable hard disk drives, are contained within their own cases. These are known as pen drives, thumb drives and memory sticks.

> **KEY WORDS**
>
> **solid-state storage media:** a method of storing data electronically. It has no moving parts
>
> **flash memory:** a non-volatile memory chip used for storage and for transferring data between digital devices. It has the ability to be electronically reprogrammed and erased
>
> **floating gate transistors:** transistors that keep their charge when the power is switched off
>
> **solid-state drive (SSD):** a mass storage device similar to a hard drive but it doesn't have any moving parts and data is stored using flash memory

Advantages of SSDs:

- They have very fast access speeds: far faster than disks.
- They are small, light and easily portable.
- They are quiet.
- They have no moving parts that could be damaged if they are knocked or dropped and, therefore, there is less chance of losing data.

Disadvantages of SSDs:

- They are more expensive than hard disk drives although prices are continuing to fall.

- The storage capacity is usually less than hard disk drives.
- There is a limited number of erase/write cycles, up to 100 000 for high quality SSDs and so it cannot be used indefinitely.

> ### ACTIVITY 3.3
>
> Carry out research and compare the cost of a 1 terabyte solid-state drive with that of a hard disk drive of the same size.

Memory sticks and pen drives

> ### ICT IN CONTEXT
>
> Memory sticks (USB flash drives) can act as security for a computer because they can be used to lock and unlock a PC. Encrypted unlock files can be stored on a USB flash drive and a utility program in the computer constantly checks that such a file is present. If it is not, then the utility locks the computer so no one can use it. To unlock it, the drive must be plugged into any of the USB ports.

Pen drives are also called '**memory sticks**' and '**flash drives**'. They are small pen-shaped storage devices, with a lot of storage space, which can be plugged into a USB port. They are ideal for storing data and software that needs to be transported from one computer to another and can be used for backups of the main files on a computer system.

Flash memory cards

Flash memory cards are also called computer flash (CF) cards and secure digital (SD) cards. They are similar to memory sticks as they are a form of portable memory (see Figure 3.7). The distinctive difference is in their shape and the way that they connect to the parent device. A memory stick or pen drive fits into the USB port in a computer, while a memory card gets its name from the fact that the device is flat and looks like a card which slots into a special port which is a different shape.

Flash memory cards are used in small electronic devices that need large volumes of storage, such as digital cameras to store photographs; mobile phones to store photographs, telephone numbers and other data; and MP3 players to store music files. They can be slotted into a computer case so that their contents can be downloaded quickly.

Figure 3.7: Memory card and memory stick

> ### KEY WORDS
>
> **memory sticks (USB flash drives)/pen drives:** small storage devices with a lot of storage space that plug into a USB socket for reading/writing
>
> **flash memory cards:** similar to memory sticks as they are a form of portable memory but the device is flat and looks like a card. The card slots into a port which is a different shape. Such cards are also called computer flash (CF) cards, CFast cards, or secure digital (SD) cards

Different sizes of SD card:
- SD (secure digital) cards (4–32 GB)
- micro SD cards (4–32 GB)
- SDXC (extended capacity) cards (2 TB).

Advantages of flash drives and memory cards:
- Have non-volatile memory so there is no danger of data loss if the power source fails.
- Are solid-state, hence are free from mechanical problems or damage.
- Are small, light and compact so are very easily portable.
- Need very little power.
- Are available in many sizes.
- Can be used in different devices such as cameras, computers or mobile phones.

Disadvantages of flash drives and memory cards:
- Can break easily.
- Can be lost, misplaced or smashed.

- Cards may be affected by electronic corruption which can make the entire card unreadable.

Table 3.1 shows comparisons of different storage media.

> **ICT IN CONTEXT**
>
> Micro SD cards are used in mobile phones as memory cards to store photographs and music. They can also be used in MP3 Players to store music.

Questions

3. There are **three** main types of storage device.
   a. State what type of storage medium is used by memory sticks and memory cards.
   b. Name **two** devices that store data magnetically.
   c. List **three** devices which store data using lasers.
4. Why are storage devices necessary?
5. What is the difference between a storage medium and a storage device? Give examples.

	Magnetic	Optical	Solid-state
Capacity	Very large. 1–2 TB common in home computers.	Compact disks (CDs) typically store 700 MB. Digital versatile disks (DVDs) typically store 4.7 GB. Blu-ray disks typically store 128 GB.	Solid-state drives are usually about 1 TB.
Speed	Fast	Slow	Very fast
Portability	Not very portable as physical knocks may cause the read-write heads to hit the disks and corrupt data.	More portable than a hard disk drive but disks are relatively large.	Very portable. Small solid-state storage devices can be fitted inside cameras and mobile phones.
Durability	Very durable.	Easily scratched and data can be damaged. Data cannot be overwritten.	Lower than a hard disk drive. Limited number of erase/write cycles.
Reliability	Very reliable but affected by magnetic fields.	Very reliable if not scratched.	Very reliable and not affected by magnetic fields.
Cost	Very low.	Very low.	More expensive but becoming cheaper.

Table 3.1: Comparison of different storage media and devices

PRACTICAL TASK 3.1

Getting started

1. Work in a group of three. Discuss what SSD stands for as well as the different types of SSD devices, naming examples.

Practice

2. Using a word processor, insert a table like the one below including the headings given:

	Description	Advantages	Disadvantages
Magnetic tape			
External hard disk			
Memory sticks			
Memory cards			

See Chapter 17 for information on using tables in documents.

3. Research for ideas and complete the advantages and disadvantages columns.

Challenge

Blu-ray disks have more storage capacity than traditional DVDs. They also offer a high level of interactivity. If you use a Blu-ray disk you will be able to connect to the internet and download subtitles and other interactive movie features instantly.

4. Find out other interactive features that Blu-ray offers and add them to your file, after the table.

Peer assessment

In a group of three, check each other's work by asking questions about how they approached the task and their outcomes. Discuss useful changes that could be made.

ACTIVITY 3.4

Using presentation software, create a five-question, multiple choice test about storage devices that a user can answer on computer.

Users should be able to click on one of the suggested answers and be told if they are correct or not. If not, they should be given the correct answer. (You can do this by creating hyperlinks to another slide in the presentation. See Chapter 19 for more information on how to create presentations.)

REFLECTION

How did you go about all the different things you needed to do for Activity 3.4? Consider the key words you used in your search and whether they found the information you wanted. Did you use the right number of slides to cover the subject? Was the way you created the hyperlinks, easy, difficult to get right, or successful? Consider why.

3 Storage

SUMMARY

Storage media are used to hold data written and read by storage devices.
There are three types of storage device and storage media: magnetic, optical and solid-state.
Data is written to, and read from, magnetic media such as hard disk drives using electromagnets. Media include hard disk drives and magnetic tapes.
Data is written to, and read from, optical drives using a laser, which creates areas that reflect light and areas that do not reflect light. Media include CDs, DVDs, Blu-ray.
ROM disks are read only; R disks can be written to once only; RW disks can be written to many times.
Solid-state storage devices have no moving parts, are used inside laptops and some new computers to replace traditional hard drives. They use flash memory.
Flash memory cards are portable memory.
Memory sticks/pen drives are small solid-state drives, with a lot of storage space.
There are different advantages and disadvantages to each storage type so they are usually chosen based on the amount of the data they can store, frequency of access required and whether new data needs to be written.

EXAM-STYLE QUESTIONS

1 **Explain** why a laptop needs a storage device. [2]
2 Read the four statements and **state** which ones are true. [4]

Blu-ray optical storage media allows very high capacity storage by using a blue/violet laser light.
Data is written to a DVD by laser.
SSD data storage is non-volatile.
Unlike internal hard disk drives, external hard disks are volatile.
Magnetic tapes have slow data access speeds.

3 State which is the storage medium of a Blu-ray disk: [1]
- flash
- magnetic
- optical
- SSD.

4 **Describe** how data is stored on an optical disk such as a CD ROM. [2]
5 **Identify** two disadvantages of using magnetic instead of solid-state storage. [2]
6 Explain the difference between direct access and serial access to your data. [2]

COMMAND WORDS

explain: set out purposes or reasons / make the relationships between things evident / provide why and / or how and support with relevant evidence

state: express in clear terms

describe: state the points of a topic / give characteristics and main features

identify: name / select / recognise

> **CAMBRIDGE IGCSE™ ICT: COURSEBOOK**

CONTINUED

7 State which of the following types of storage would access data the fastest. [1]
   - Magnetic.
   - Solid-state (SSD).
   - Optical.
   - They all take the same amount of time to access the data.

8 Read the following scenarios and **suggest** the most suitable storage solutions for each. **Justify** your answers.

   a The owner of a mail-order company has constantly changing order and customer information as orders are being processed throughout the day. What would be the best backup medium for this company? [2]

   b A school student needs a method to back up his schoolwork and transfer documents between school and home. [2]

   c The owner of a small business with only one computer and no internet access would like to back up the business data once a week. [2]

9 For exploring the environment, a school uses portable, battery operated data loggers to measure variables such as temperature, light intensity and oxygen levels in water.

   Each data logger has a secondary storage device.

   a Explain why a data logger needs secondary storage. [2]

   The data loggers use solid-state storage.

   b Explain why solid-state storage is the most suitable for the data loggers. [2]

   [Total: 24]

> **COMMAND WORDS**
>
> **suggest:** apply knowledge and understanding to situations where there are a range of valid responses in order to make proposals / put forward considerations
>
> **justify:** support a case with evidence / argument

SELF-EVALUATION CHECKLIST

After studying this chapter, think about how confident you are with the different topics.

This will help you to see any gaps in your knowledge and help you to learn more effectively.

You might find it helpful to rate how confident you are for each of these statements when you are revising. You should revisit any sections that you rated 'Needs more work' or 'Getting there'.

I can ...	See section	Needs more work	Getting there	Confident to move on
identify different data storage media	3.1			
identify the devices that are necessary to store data onto the media, then read the data later from the media	3.1			
describe the uses for the different types of data storage media and compare their advantages and disadvantages	3.1			
compare the advantages and disadvantages of optical, magnetic and solid-state storage devices	3.1			

Chapter 4
Networks

IN THIS CHAPTER YOU WILL:

- discuss the operation of a router and other common network devices, such as network interface cards, hubs, bridges, switches
- explain the use of Wi-Fi and Bluetooth in networks
- discuss cloud computing and how to store and share data
- describe the characteristics and purpose of common network environments
- list the differences between different network types
- discuss security issues regarding data transfer, including understanding about passwords and other authentication methods
- explain the use of anti-malware software
- describe electronic-conferencing.

GETTING STARTED

In Figure 4.1, you will see some images of hardware components of a computer system and a list of their names.

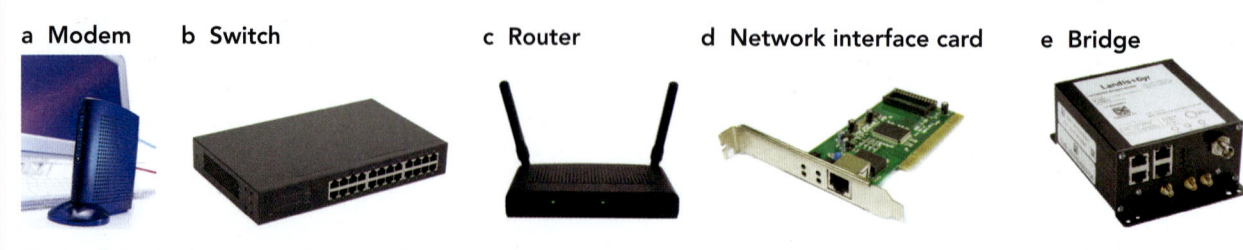

a Modem   b Switch   c Router   d Network interface card   e Bridge

Figure 4.1: Hardware components of a computer system

Below are descriptions of the functions of these devices.

Match the letters with the numbers.

1	Connects a computer with a local area network.
2	Converts data into a format suitable for transmission through a specific medium.
3	Connects multiple networks and forwards packages between them.
4	Connects devices on a local area network.
5	Separates a local area network into different sections.

CELEBRITY DATA BREACHES

Celebrity data breaches are not new. Taylor Swift and Ariana Grande have been victims on Instagram where hackers have broken into their accounts and posted things pretending to be them. Instagram (which has around 700 million users worldwide) email people who are well known to tell them of the dangers. They ask all users to beware of unusual phone calls, emails or texts.

Hacking is made possible because when someone opens an account with a social media site, they are asked for pieces of information such as where you were born, what your first school was, what your nickname at school was. This sort of information is very easy to find out about celebrities because there is such a lot of information about celebrities already on the internet. It is also why you should be wary of joining in with survey-style memes on social media that ask you to share information about yourself, for example, 'your first pet was called…; your favourite cereal is… etc.', however much fun they may be to fill in, you may inadvertently be sharing information a hacker could use.

Another method a hacker could use is by gaining access to a Wi-Fi network that the celebrity is connected to and installing an app onto one of their devices. This would give the hacker full access to find photos and other private information. In this chapter, you will learn about networks and security issues with such networks.

Discussion questions

1   In what ways could you help to protect data and photographs that you may have on social media?

2   Do you think that the advantages of uploading photographs to social media outweigh the disadvantages?

4.1 Networks

A **network** connects computers and other digital devices together and allows them to share data and resources. Networks allow the use of the following:

- Computer-to-computer communication.
- Computers communicating with devices such as printers, mice and keyboards.
- Mobile phone networks.
- Smart televisions.
- Tablets and media players downloading videos and music and playing them through external devices such as speakers and digital projectors.

Network types

Types of networks include local area networks (LAN), including wireless local area networks (WLAN), and wide area network (WAN).

Local area network

A **local area network (LAN)** enables a group of computers that are in close proximity to each other to be networked. Typically, a LAN would be used in a school, in an office or at home. A LAN is useful because it allows resources such as files, printers, games and other software applications to be shared by the computers on the network.

There are two ways of connecting the devices so that they can communicate with each other. These are:

- By cables that have to be routed throughout the buildings.
- Using radio waves so that no cables are required. This method is called a **wireless local area network** or WLAN.

An advantage of a WLAN over a cable LAN is that it allows the users to move around the area with their devices and remain connected. With a cable LAN they would have to log off, remove the cable, plug the cable in somewhere else and log in again. A WLAN also lets one or more people connect their mobile devices such as laptops, mobile phones, tablets, media players, speakers and printers. This are often called a personal area network (PAN).

Wide area network

A **wide area network (WAN)** is a network that connects separate LANs over a large geographical area. Typically, a WAN will connect cities, a country or many countries. Imagine an organisation that has offices in more than one town; they would probably each have a LAN set up in each building and then connect them all together into a WAN. A WAN ensures that computers in one location can communicate with computers and users in other locations.

The **internet** is a huge wide area network.

The separate networks are connected by cables running throughout the world under the ground and under the sea and by satellite communications.

> **KEY WORDS**
>
> **network:** two or more computers or other digital devices connected together in order to share data and resources
>
> **local area network (LAN):** network used for data transmission by computing devices within one building or site, such as an office building or a school or university campus
>
> **wireless local area network (WLAN):** a local area network accessed using radio wave communications
>
> **wide area network (WAN):** a network of networks connecting local area networks over a large geographical area
>
> **internet:** a global, public system of interconnected computer networks that serves billions of users worldwide and is therefore a wide area network. The internet provides many services including email and the world wide web (www). The contents of the internet are not controlled

The uses of Wi-Fi and Bluetooth

When computers and other digital devices are connecting to a network and communicating with each other they have to follow sets of rules so that they can understand each other. These sets of rules are called **protocols**. Protocols are also used for other activities such as accessing printers.

> **ICT IN CONTEXT**
>
> In the 1980s, manufacturers of home computers each developed their own set of protocols, rather than all using a standard set of protocols. This meant that if you bought one manufacturer's computer, you would have to buy a printer especially designed for that system. If you later bought another manufacturer's computer, you would also have to change your printer and most other hardware. This is not the case now.

Computers communicating through cables in a LAN usually use a set of rules called Ethernet.

The two main sets of rules used by computers communicating in a WLAN using radio waves are Wi-Fi and Bluetooth.

Wi-Fi

Wi-Fi is a digital communications protocol that sets out how data is transmitted on wireless LANs. Wi-Fi is a trademarked term that is owned by Wi-Fi Alliance. Each device must connect to a wireless access point to access the network.

Bluetooth

Bluetooth is a wireless protocol allowing communication over short distances, usually up to 30 feet. It is used to link personal devices – for example, laptops, tablets, smartphones, speakers or smart televisions – so that data can be shared between them. Using Bluetooth, music can be streamed to remote speakers. It allows direct communication between the devices while Wi-Fi does not.

> **KEY WORDS**
>
> **protocols:** sets of rules governing how devices communicate with each other over networks
>
> **Wi-Fi:** one protocol allowing computers, smartphones, or other devices to connect to the internet or communicate with one another wirelessly within a particular area
>
> **Bluetooth:** protocols for short-range wireless interconnection of mobile phones, computers and other electronic devices

Table 4.1 shows a comparison of Wi-Fi and Bluetooth.

Tethering

If you have a smartphone, you can use it to connect your tablet to the internet. This process is called tethering; it is the linking of one device to another to connect to the internet.

Questions

1 It is necessary to be able to distinguish between different types of networks. Define the following **three** types:
   - LAN
   - WLAN
   - WAN.

2 Bluetooth was developed to provide a wireless communication method to link specific devices that are close together. Give **three** different ways that Bluetooth can be used by a person when they are using their laptop to listen to music.

> **ACTIVITY 4.1**
>
> A small business is going to set up a network for its 20 computers. They are considering whether to use cables or Wi-Fi for network connection.
>
> Carry out research and produce a brief report giving the benefits and drawbacks of both methods.

Wi-Fi	Bluetooth
Communication using radio waves.	Communication using radio waves.
Has a range of up to 100 metres.	Has a range of 10 metres.
Devices cannot communicate directly.	Devices can communicate directly.
Many users can be supported.	Fewer users can be supported.
A high level of security.	A lower level of security.
Fast data transfer.	Low data transfer.

Table 4.1: Comparison of Wi-Fi and Bluetooth

4 Networks

Common network devices

As well as the software rules – protocols – hardware devices are needed for devices to be able to connect to and communicate over a network.

Network interface card (NIC)

A **network interface card (NIC)** or network adapter (see Figure 4.1d) is a component that connects a computer to a network. It formats the data sent from the computer into a required format according to the protocols of the network to allow data packets to travel to and from the computer to the network.

Originally, the adapters for desktop PCs were on 'cards' that were installed in the computer but are now built into the motherboard; however the name 'card' remains. Network interface cards and adapters support both wired and wireless network connections.

Every NIC is created with a hardware number permanently 'burned' into it. This permanent hardware number is known as the **MAC (media access control) address**.

Every MAC address is unique so that all data on a network can be sent to the correct component, just like letters delivered to the correct house or text messages and voice calls to the correct phone number.

Hubs

Where a network has a central point to which all the signals from individual computers are sent, a particular kind of network device, either a **hub** (Figure 4.2) or a switch, is needed.

Hubs work in the following way:

- All of the computers on the network plug into a port on the hub using a cable.
- When a message is received through the cable from one of the computers, the hub transmits it to all of the other computers.
- Hubs are 'dumb' and cannot learn the addresses of the different devices on a network and when a message is received through the cable from one of the computers, the hub transmits it to all of the other computers and not just the one it is intended for. This creates a lot of needless network traffic.
- Hubs only allow one device at a time to transmit messages.

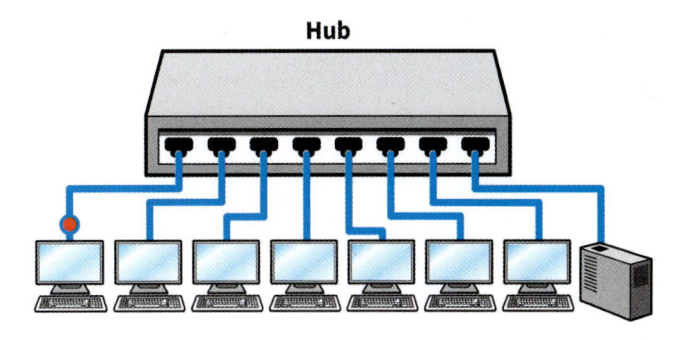

Figure 4.2: A hub being used to connect computers to form a network

- Because the hub transmits every message to every part of the network and not just to the computer it is intended for, there are a lot of unnecessary transmissions or **network traffic**, resulting in a reduction in the speed that data is transmitted as the network becomes overloaded.
- Due to this, hubs are rarely used today.

Switches

A **network switch** handles messages more intelligently than a hub by inspecting the MAC address of the device to which they should be sent. The switch knows the addresses of the different devices on the network and only sends the message to the correct device.

> **KEY WORDS**
>
> **network interface card (NIC):** a printed circuit board that allows the computer to communicate with other devices over a computer network
>
> **media access control (MAC) address:** a serial number that is unique to each device and is used to identify it on a network
>
> **hub:** a device used for connecting computers to form a network. It broadcast data to all devices not just the one they are intended for
>
> **network traffic:** the overall network usage caused by all of the data that is being transmitted at a given time
>
> **network switch:** a device used for connecting computers to form a network. It transmits data only to the device for which it is intended

Switches work in the following way:

- Network switches have a similar function to hubs in a single network, but they read the messages passing through.
- They can read the destination addresses and send them to only the intended computers.
- They can do this because they build up a table of all of the MAC addresses on the network.
- They therefore cut down on unnecessary network traffic, thereby increasing the performance of the network.
- Switches can send and receive information at the same time, so they are faster than hubs.

Bridge

Often large LANs are split into smaller parts called segments to improve network performance. A **bridge** is used to connect the different segments (see Figure 4.3) and they can prevent transmissions from one segment reaching the others. They improve network security by isolating segments from others and thus prevent the spread of harmful programs or users accessing information that they shouldn't.

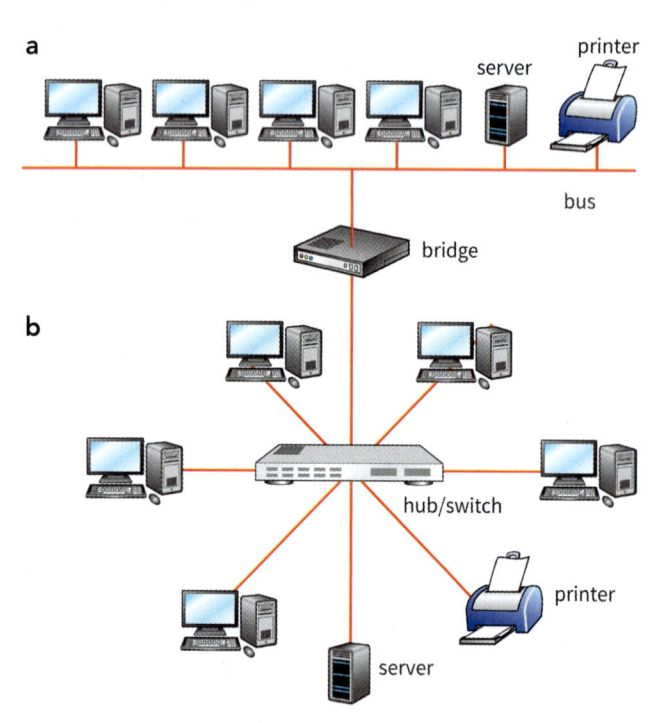

Figure 4.3: A bridge connecting two network segments. In this example, **a**, a bus network, is joined to **b**, a star network

> ### ACTIVITY 4.2
> Usually, when an organisation is setting up a LAN, they use a more powerful computer as a *server*. Carry out research and make a list of the functions of the server within the network.

Routers

While switches allow *different devices* on a network to communicate, **routers** allow *different networks* to communicate.

WANs, such as the internet, which is a network of networks, rely on routers to direct data to the correct network. For example, a request could be sent from a computer on a network in Indonesia to a computer on a network in Brazil. This request would be directed from one router to another until it reached the correct network.

Routers are used in the home to connect the home network to the internet. They allow many computers to share an internet connection. The router will transmit the incoming web pages, streamed audio, etc. to the correct computer on the network.

When devices transmit data across the internet, the data is broken down into small pieces called **data packets**. These are sent separately, and then joined up at the end so that the message is complete (see Figure 4.4).

> ### KEY WORDS
> **bridge:** a device for linking separate segments of a local area network
>
> **router:** a device for transmitting data between networks
>
> **data packet:** one of the small parts into which network communications are broken

Rules are needed so that all of the computers on the network work together. Otherwise, how would the receiving computer know when the message is complete or if there has been a transmission error?

A packet consists of three parts:

- Header: this contains the addresses of the source and destination, and also the position of the packet in the complete message/file.

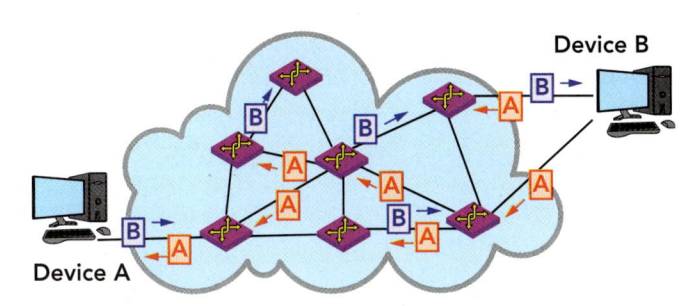

Figure 4.4: The transmission of packets in a WAN

- Body: (also known as the payload) this contains part of the complete message/file.
- Footer: (also known as the trailer) this informs the receiving device that it has reached the end of the packet. The footer can also be used for error checking to make sure that the packet has been delivered intact.

A router has a routing table that lists the routes to other networks on the WAN. If the router cannot directly connect to the destination network, it has to send it via other networks along a route to the destination network. A routing table is a database that keeps track of paths, like a map, and uses these to determine which way to forward traffic.

The packets sent between computers A and B take different routes across the WAN.

The packets are sent out on their various journeys to the recipient computer. They do not all follow the same route. In fact, they do not all arrive in the correct order but, because they are labelled, the receiving computer can put them back together in the correct order.

The journey of the packets across a large network like the internet is extraordinary. They could be travelling from the other side of the world to your bedroom!

Here's how routing works:

- The source computer splits the file into packets and addresses them with the recipient's **IP address**.
- The file is split because the transmission of a large file would consume all the bandwidth and slow the network.
- These packets are then sent onto the network using cables or radio waves as in a wireless network.
- Routers on the network inspect each packet to find the destination address and decide the most efficient path for the packet to take on the next stage of its journey.
- In order to do this, each router has a configuration table containing information about which connections lead to particular groups of addresses.
- The routers can balance the load across the network on a millisecond-by-millisecond basis.
- If there is a problem with one part of the network while a message is being transferred, packets can be routed around the problem, ensuring the delivery of the entire message.
- The final router can direct the packet to the correct recipient.

Thousands of miles in less than a second and all put back together again!

This method of data communication is called **packet switching**. It is more efficient because it means that there does not have to be a dedicated line between the two communicating devices. Compare this with making a telephone call on a landline, where there is a dedicated line between the two telephones. That method is called circuit switching.

> **KEY WORDS**
>
> **IP address:** An IP address is a set of numbers used to identify one particular computer on the internet. The IP address is like a postal address and it will allow data and messages to be sent directly to the correct computer. It consists of a series of numbers e.g. 216.27.61.137
>
> **packet switching:** when certain areas of the network are too busy to carry the packets, they are automatically switched to emptier circuits

Questions

3   Write down definitions for the following terms:
   a   router
   b   data packet
   c   packet switching.
4   Explain how data packets are transferred from one computer to another across the internet.
5   Describe **three** items of hardware that are required for computers to connect to a network.

> **CAMBRIDGE IGCSE™ ICT: COURSEBOOK**

PRACTICAL TASK 4.1

Getting started

1 Find out the steps to take to link a computer to a smartphone by tethering.

Practice

2 Use a word processor to create the instructions, step-by-step.

Challenge

3 Use screenshots to illustrate the instructions you created.

Peer assessment

Show your instructions to two or three others in your class and get their feedback on whether the method you used to create the instructions could have been different and if it would have had an improved result.

Common network environments

Internet, intranet and extranet

The internet is a global network of interconnected computer networks. The internet is used to connect people, communities and countries worldwide. Businesses can use the internet for information retrieval, communications, marketing and sales to distant customers, and banking. The internet allows all users access to web pages.

The internet uses a set of rules or protocols called **TCP/IP**. This stands for transmission control protocol/internet protocol. That is why all computers need a unique IP address so that data can be directed to the correct one.

Intranets and extranets use the same protocols.

An **intranet** is a private computer network within an organisation, such as a school or a business which uses internet technology. Even though an intranet uses internet technologies, it is separate from the global internet and cannot be accessed by outside users.

An intranet contains web pages about the organisation. For example, it can publish newsletters, health and safety policies, information about courses and training and forms for requesting payment and holidays.

An **extranet** is an intranet that allows users from other organisations to use it for specific purposes (see Figure 4.5). Examples include hospital intranets that allow access to community doctors to book appointments for patients or a manufacturing company that allows access

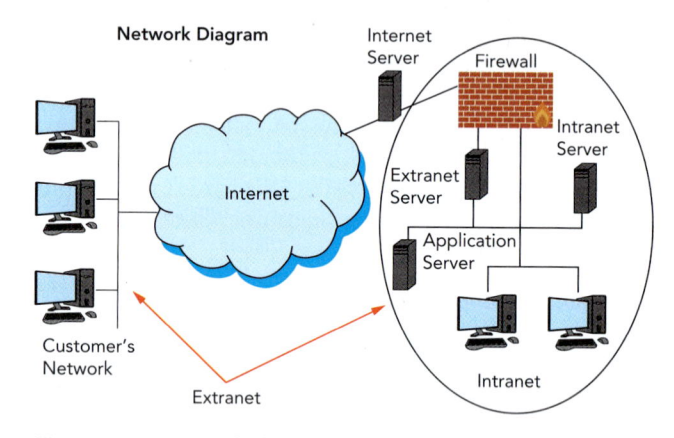

Figure 4.5: Network diagram showing extranet route

to distributors for ordering and pricing information. The organisation can also share news with the other users and keep them updated on future developments.

KEY WORDS

TCP/IP: transmission control protocol/internet protocol. The protocols used by devices to connect to and communicate over the internet

intranet: a communication system, solely within a particular company or organisation

extranet: a communication system for a particular company or organisation that can be accessed from the internet by other parties or organisations who have been granted access. It is an extension of an intranet

---

66

Questions

6. There are different types of networks that are in use in organisations and companies.
    a. Describe the differences between the internet, an intranet and an extranet.
    b. Give examples of situations in which they would be used.
7. Copy and complete the table below with the words **internet**, **extranet** or **intranet**.

	Type of network
Accessed by members within a single organisation.	
A global network linking billions of computers as well as other electronic devices.	
A private and secure network used for sharing information inside a company.	
Global communication accessed through the web.	
A private network that can be accessed by a company's customers.	
Allow companies to connect with their customers in a controlled setting.	

ACTIVITY 4.3

Make a list of the differences and similarities between an intranet, extranet and the internet described in the text above.

Carry out research to try to find more differences between them.

The internet, an intranet and extranet all use TCP/IP (see Chapter 10). The level of access to each of them is different. An intranet gives access restricted to the members of a company/organisation; the extranet expands the intranet access to allow non-members, such as suppliers and customers, to use company resources. The internet is different to an extranet because the extranet allows limited access to non-members of a company/organisation; anyone can access the internet network resources.

Cloud computing

Cloud computing is the delivery of computer services over the internet. These services, such as software and storage space, are housed in remote computers called **servers**. They are called servers because they serve these services to the users.

If you are using cloud computing, then you do not actually know where the servers are located. They could be anywhere in the world. But they are definitely not up in the air in the clouds!

Cloud computing allows users to access and use applications, such as word processors and spreadsheets, stored on remote servers.

Advantages for business:

- Lower maintenance costs: software does not need to be installed, maintained or upgraded on the local computers or servers.
- Software does not have to be 'bought' and businesses only have to pay for those parts that they need to use (this is known as 'software as a service').
- All software is automatically upgraded.
- As long as they have internet access, employees can work from anywhere in the world and even from home, reducing the need for office space.
- All data is automatically backed up at the remote site.
- Employees can collaborate on the same documents because they are not stored on one particular computer.

Disadvantages for business:

- Internet access is required.
- The organisation has less control and is reliant on the providers to maintain access and update the software but some organisations are building their own 'private' clouds.
- The providers' servers may be targeted by **hackers**.

KEY WORDS

cloud computing: the delivery of computer services over the internet

server: a computer that provides services to other computers on a network

hacker: a person who carries out hacking

Most computer users make use of some form of **cloud storage** for data files, images, etc. It can be used as the main storage device, like a remote hard disk drive, but most use it for backing up and archiving their data.

> **KEY WORD**
>
> **cloud storage:** the storage of digital data on remote servers

Advantages	Disadvantages
Data will be secure if there is a fire or other problem at the site.	Needs an internet connection.
The data can be accessed from anywhere in the world with an internet connection.	Download and upload speeds can be affected by the internet connection.
No need to buy an expensive storage device.	The hosting company could be targeted by online hackers.
Many users can access the data and collaborate with each other from anywhere in the world.	You have less control if the data is held by another company.
	Storing some data online may breach any data protection acts in force in the originating country as it should be kept secure and confidential.

Table 4.2: Advantages and disadvantages of cloud storage

> **ICT IN CONTEXT**
>
> At the end of 2019 it was estimated that there were 500 million tweets sent each day.
>
> On Facebook, 350 million photos are uploaded each day and 3 million messages are sent every 20 minutes. On YouTube, 500 hours of video are uploaded every minute with 5 billion watched every day.
>
> These activities generate a huge amount of data every day and all of this data is stored in the 'cloud' on remote servers in data centres around the world.

Cloud storage has advantages and disadvantages when compared with other methods covered in Chapter 3, including hard disk drives, DVDs and solid-state drives (see Table 4.2).

Even if users do not set up their own cloud storage, they are using it if they use social media. Every comment, tweet, 'Like' or picture and video is stored on remote servers.

The servers are housed in huge data centres around the world. There are about 8.4 million global data centres, consuming about 3 percent of the total electricity generated worldwide, or 40 percent more than that generated by the whole of the UK. These vast amounts of energy are needed to power and cool all of the computer equipment that is needed.

To conserve energy, many of these data centres are built in cold countries and ones where there is more energy generated from natural sources such as hydro power. Some have even been built under the sea.

It has even been suggested that an uploading tax should be imposed.

> **PRACTICAL TASK 4.2**
>
> **Getting started**
>
> 1 Investigate whether your school or college uses cloud data storage.
>
> **Practice**
>
> 2 Create a web page for your school comparing the benefits and drawbacks of your school or college of using local storage or cloud storage. See Chapter 21 for more information about creating web pages.

> **CONTINUED**
>
> **Challenge**
>
> 3 Add web pages to illustrate the benefits to your school or college in using online software, rather than installing it locally.

> **ACTIVITY 4.4**
>
> Carry out research on organisations that provide cloud storage. Make a list of at least three organisations and any information, such as if they provide any free storage and, if so, how much. Find how much they charge for more storage and if they guarantee data security. Discuss with a partner which organisation you would choose for your purposes if you wanted to use cloud storage.

Questions

8 Define cloud computing.

9 State where cloud data and apps are stored.

10 Which of these statements shown in the table below are true and which are false?

	T/F
Cloud computing is replacing some of the most expensive personal computing hardware.	
Cloud computing is replacing expensive software upgrades.	
An advantage of cloud computing is that an internet connection is not necessary.	
If you have an email account with Gmail, your emails are stored in the cloud.	

4.2 Network issues and communication

Security of computer networks

All networks must be kept secure so that data is not corrupted or stolen. All online systems can be **hacked** and data can be stolen when it is stored or transmitted.

Networks should be protected against data interception and theft. Data traffic in LANs and WANs can be intercepted. Hackers use packet analysers or 'packet sniffers' to intercept the packets, which are then analysed and their data is decoded. The criminals can therefore steal sensitive data such as logins, passwords, credit card numbers and PINs. As there is no change to the network data or systems, it is called a 'passive attack'.

> **ICT IN HACKING**
>
> Hacking has lead to millions of items of personal data, including passwords and financial details, being stolen in recent years. There have been many high-profile data breaches, including attacks on Adobe affecting 412 million users, FriendFinder 412 million and Facebook 540 million.
>
> Some of the data was left on unprotected servers making it very easy for hackers.

Criminals can also use spyware, which monitors users' key presses and can help them to discover passwords and pins, etc.

There are several different ways to ensure that networks are protected and that data is kept private and confidential.

Encryption

When data is transferred electronically, it can be **encrypted** to keep it secure.

> **KEY WORDS**
>
> **hack:** to gain unauthorised access to data in a system or computer
>
> **encryption:** the process of turning information (e.g. a message) into a form that only the intended recipient can decrypt and read

Encryption is the scrambling of data into a form that cannot be understood by unauthorised recipients. The encrypted data must be **decrypted** back to its original form before it can be understood.

A common method is to use **asymmetric encryption** which employs two different **keys** – a 'public' key and a 'private' key. A private key can decrypt messages encrypted with the corresponding public key. The public key is freely available and is used to encrypt a message for the person who then decrypts it with their private key.

Firewalls

Firewalls are either software or hardware devices that protect against unauthorised access to a network (see Figure 4.6), and are primarily used to prevent unauthorised access from the internet. They can be configured to prevent communications from entering the network and also to prevent programs and users from accessing the internet from within the network. For example, a firewall can inspect the incoming packets and reject those that are from IP addresses not on a trusted list or block communication to certain external IP addresses.

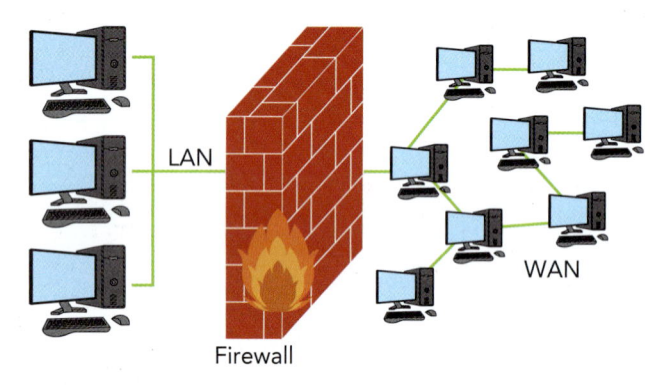

Figure 4.6: A firewall

Authentication

Authentication is the process of determining whether someone trying to log into the network is who they declare to be. The primary method of authentication is by the use of passwords.

Passwords

A **password** is a secret word or phrase that is used to authenticate a user so that they can gain access.

To ensure that a password is secure, some simple rules should be followed.

- **Strong passwords**:
  - should be at least eight characters long
  - contain both numbers and letters
  - contain both upper and lower case letters
  - contain at least one character such as: !, $, ?, etc.
  - never use user-identifiable items such as name, date of birth, phone number, postcode, car registration, etc.
- Passwords should be changed regularly.
- Previous passwords must never be reused.
- Passwords must never be written down.
- Passwords must never be shared with other users.

Passwords should be unpredictable so hackers cannot guess them or try to enter them by trial and error.

> **KEY WORDS**
>
> **decryption:** the process of recovering the original text from the encrypted text
>
> **asymmetric encryption:** a method of encryption that uses two different keys
>
> **key:** a piece of information that is used for encrypting and decrypting data
>
> **firewall:** software or hardware devices that protect against unauthorised access to a network
>
> **authentication:** the process or action of proving or showing something to be true, genuine or valid
>
> **password:** a secret word or phrase that must be used to gain admission to a place
>
> **strong password:** a password that is difficult to detect by both humans and computer programs

Weak passwords are ones that can be easily guessed or discovered by hackers. They will try things such as dates of birth, names of relatives, favourite sports teams, etc. in different combinations. Hackers can also use software that will randomly generate characters, numbers and symbols and these have more success on weak passwords.

It is important that all systems are checked for malware, such as spyware, so that criminals cannot intercept the passwords or monitor computers to find out what the user in entering. This can be done by using anti-spyware software. However, because malware changes so rapidly, as criminals find new ways to hack computers, it is important that your anti-spyware is kept up-to-date.

> **ICT IN CONTEXT**
>
> According to research by a leading credit reference agency, on average people each have 26 different online logins, so password management is a very important part of staying safe online. The recommendation never to use the same password more than once is difficult and impractical when we have so many different online accounts. It was also found that even though we might have 26 different accounts, on average we only use five different passwords!

> **ACTIVITY 4.5**
>
> Working as a pair, list some clear instructions about how to create a strong password.

Authentication can also include a variety of methods such as:

- biometric methods
- magnetic stripes
- smart cards
- physical tokens
- electronic tokens
- zero login.

Biometric methods

Biometric methods of authentication are biological measurements or an analysis of physical characteristics that can be used to identify individuals. **Biometric data** falls into two categories:

- Physiological biometric data relates to a physical aspect of a person's body (such as a fingerprint or an eye retina scan).
- Behavioural biometrics include signatures, handwriting analysis and voice pattern recognition.

The information being measured needs to be universal – it should be something that everyone possesses. It should also be unique, so that an individual can be definitively recognised. It should also be permanent, meaning that it should not change significantly as a person ages. For example, fingerprint mapping, facial recognition, retina scans, blood vessel patterns in hands and arms are all forms of biometric technology (see Figure 4.7).

> **KEY WORDS**
>
> **biometric methods:** technologies that analyse unique personal characteristics such as fingerprints, eye retinas and irises, voice and facial patterns, and hand measurements as a form of identification
>
> **biometric data:** records that are used to identify people by a physical attribute that doesn't change. An example of this would be a database of fingerprints of known criminals

Biometric devices tend to work in one of two main ways: verification or identification.

For verification, biometric technologies perform a comparison of the data with a template that has previously been stored, such as a fingerprint scan or other physical tokens such as retina, iris or face scans, on a personal computer or electronic safe.

At present, biometric systems are mainly used for:

- Verification: to make sure a person is who they say they are.
- Identification: to identify a person in a crowd.
- Screening: to match a person who may be on a 'watch list' for security purposes.

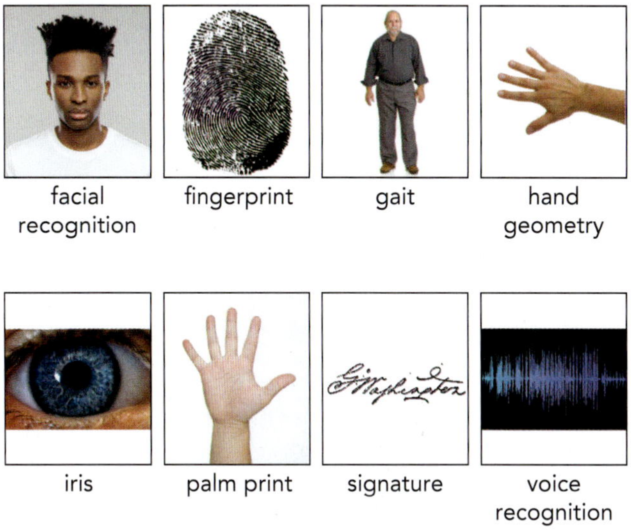

| facial recognition | fingerprint | gait | hand geometry |
| iris | palm print | signature | voice recognition |

Figure 4.7: Examples of biometric authentication

Biometric data and its protection is mainly discussed in Chapter 8, Section 8.3 Security of data. Identification using biometrics is discussed in Chapter 6, Section 6.10 Recognition systems.

Magnetic stripes

Personal and security data can be encoded on the magnetic stripe of a card and can be swiped through a reader to allow access.

The magnetic stripe on the back of a credit card is split into three tracks and they can all contain data. The first and second track hold coded information about the cardholder's account: the card holder's full name, card number and CVV value, date of expiry of the card and the code for the country in which it was issued. The third track is not always used, but if it is, it holds details like the currencies that are valid for use with the card. Magnetic stripes were covered in Chapter 2, Section 2.2 Direct data entry and associated devices.

Smart cards

A **smart card** looks like a credit card in size and shape. However, a smart card contains a computer chip and when it is held near a reader, data can be transferred to allow the owner to be authenticated for access to a room or computer system (see Figure 4.8).

Figure 4.8: Inside a smart card, there is a microprocessor embedded which is under a gold contact pad on one side of the card

There are two kinds of smart cards: contact and contactless. With contact smart cards, the smart card is inserted into the reader, and the card's contact plate makes physical contact with the reader to transmit data. The user then enters the associated PIN.

With contactless smart cards, the card just has to be held close to the reader, and data is transmitted via radio waves.

Physical tokens

A **physical token** allows you to access software and verify your identity with a physical device (see Figure 4.9) rather than relying on authentication codes or passwords. They are also called key fobs, security tokens or USB tokens.

As physical tokens may be lost, forgotten or stolen, some multi-factor authentication methods use mobile phones. The user enters their knowledge factor, for example, their password, and the server sends a text message containing an access code to their registered mobile phone. The code can be used once within a certain time limit.

Electronic tokens

Electronic tokens can be used for electronic payments. A credit card number is converted to a string of random characters that have no value.

> **KEY WORDS**
>
> **smart card:** a plastic card with a built-in processor
>
> **physical token:** a personal device that authenticates a person's identity
>
> **electronic tokens:** also called cryptocurrencies. They function as a medium of exchange between people and businesses

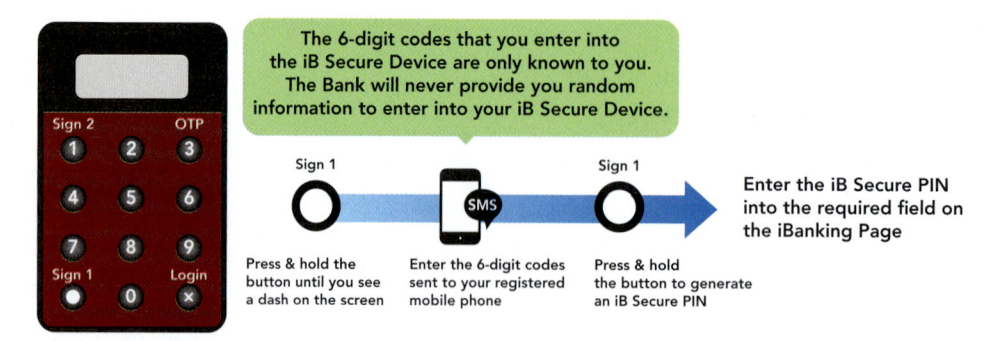

Figure 4.9: Using a physical token to log into a banking page

When a credit card payment has been converted to a token, a payment network such as Visa uses its secure keys to decode it and pass the card number to the standard electronic payment processors.

Importantly, merchants themselves cannot decode a token. Converting a token back to a card number requires access to the encryption keys, which are typically stored in military-grade security.

Paying with a smartphone uses electronic tokens. The app replaces the customer's card details with a unique virtual account number. That way, sensitive information stays private.

Zero login

Passwords and other methods of authentication can no longer be relied upon in the long term. Using artificial intelligence, technologies are being developed so that users can be authenticated, not by a password or physical features, but by how they behave. This is called **zero login**.

Its main difference is that complex passwords or other documentation will not be required for identification. Our smart devices will be smart enough, and also secure enough to recognise facial features, voice, movements and other ways, in which a person is unique, to use as identification. How you swipe and type, where you are and when you work are all unique to you.

> **ICT IN CONTEXT**
>
> Some large retail companies, including Amazon, are testing ways to authenticate users based on their behaviour. How hard do you tap on your phone? How fast do you type? Those things are unique to you and hard for an attacker to guess or duplicate. The motion sensor in your phone can also recognise you from your walk – no one else walks exactly like you do. By combining all this information, in the future your phone will be able to tell when it's really you and no password will be required.

Anti-malware software

Malware

Malware is short for malicious software and is designed to get into computers without the user's consent and to disrupt or damage the computer. It includes any software designed to disrupt the functioning of a computer system and gain unauthorised access to a computer system.

Types of malware include:

- virus
- worm
- Trojan (or Trojan horse)
- spyware
- adware.

Table 4.3 shows the main features of these types of malware but these are discussed in more detail in Chapter 8.3.

Anti-malware software is software that is designed to combat the effects (or even the installation) of malware. It needs to be installed on a computer so that the system can be protected from infiltration and infection by any malware. The anti-malware program first detects any malware on a computer, removes it safely and then clears up any damage that the malware made to the computer.

> **KEY WORDS**
>
> **zero login:** a method of authentication not requiring a user to login. They are authenticated by their behaviour and the way they do things
>
> **malware:** software designed to gain unauthorised access to a computer system in order to disrupt its functioning or collect information without the user's knowledge
>
> **anti-malware software:** software used to prevent, detect and neutralise malware
>
> **quarantine:** the placing of suspected malware into a specific area of a storage device

To prevent infection, security measures should be taken:

- Install anti-malware software, including ant-virus software, and ensure that it is continually updated.
- The software should be used to scan all storage media to detect and destroy or **quarantine** malware. The software quarantines the suspected malware if it is unable to delete it or it is not sure if it actually is malware and waits for the user to decide. When files are quarantined, they are placed in a folder where they cannot interfere with any other programs.
- Install a firewall to ensure software is not downloaded without your knowledge.

Type of malware	Description
Virus	A virus is a computer program that is hidden within another program or file. It can replicate itself and insert itself into other programs or files, which are then often passed by a user to other computers. Viruses usually have a harmful effect, e.g. corrupting or deleting data on a disk.
Worm	A worm is different to a virus in that: - It has an independent existence: it does not have to exist inside another program or file. - It does not need human action to spread it: it can travel to other computers, e.g. through a network or by sending itself in emails to everyone in a user's address book unaided. - As the worm is making thousands of copies of itself it will use the computer's resources and cause other programs to run slowly.
Trojan	A Trojan does not replicate or attach itself to other files. It must be installed by a computer user who thinks they are installing legitimate software or by opening an email attachment (that is why they are called Trojan horses). Trojans can just be annoying, e.g. by changing the desktop and adding new icons. They can also be malicious, e.g. by deleting files and destroying system information.
Spyware	It 'spies' on the computer and sends information to a criminal. It comes packaged with other software, e.g. free software that you download, so that the user does not know they are installing it.
Adware	Adware is the name given to programs that are designed to: - display advertisements on the computer - redirect search requests to advertising websites - collect marketing-type data about users (e.g. the types of websites that you visit) so that customised adverts can be displayed. When this is done without a user's consent, it is considered to be malware. Adware can also be used to refer to free programs that have adverts within them. The user can often register the program and pay a fee to have the adverts removed.

Table 4.3: Types of malware

- Ensure that the operating system is up to date.
- Install the latest security updates.
- Install anti-spyware protection software that removes or blocks spyware.
- Avoid opening emails and attachments from unknown sources.
- Scan all data files as they are downloaded.
- Surf and download more safely:
  - Only download programs from trusted websites and ensure that the anti-malware software scans all downloads.
  - Read all security warnings, licence agreements and privacy statements.

- Never click 'Agree' or 'OK' to close a window. Instead, click the red 'X' in the corner of the window.
- Be wary of popular 'free' music and movie file-sharing programs.

Electronic-conferencing

Electronic-conferencing is a meeting between individuals who are not in the same room or location using communications technology.

Audio-conferencing

Audio-conferencing is where people in different locations use technology to speak to each other. Audio-conferencing is different from a traditional phone call as, instead of directly dialling each other as for a phone call, all participants use their phones to dial into a central system that connects them.

Audio-conferencing has similar advantages over face-to-face meetings such as video-conferencing, but there is no visual communication. The members cannot see each other or any visual presentations. They may not be able to tell who is actually speaking or may inadvertently talk over each other.

Video-conferencing and web-conferencing

Both video-conferencing and web-conferencing allow an audio and a visual connection between the members of the conference. Both allow participants in different locations to communicate with each other in sound and vision.

In **video-conferencing**, visual and audio communication links two or more participants using specialised high quality video-conferencing equipment, including large displays (TV screen) and video cameras (see Figure 4.10).

The term **web-conferencing** is often used interchangeably with video-conferencing. An important distinction between the two is the quality and security of the live video stream and the difference in the equipment required.

Web-conferencing takes place online over public internet and enables multiple participants to connect and work together visually using their laptops or mobile devices.

Web-conferencing also includes:

- **Webcasts** which involve a one-way transmission and are non-interactive. The host presents information via an audio and/or video stream over the internet and may use screen sharing to show presentations, videos or documents.
- **Webinars** which are teaching sessions that take place on the internet. Participants in different locations see and hear the presenter and ask and answer questions.

> **KEY WORDS**
>
> **electronic-conference:** a meeting between individuals who are not in the same room or location using communications technology
>
> **audio-conference:** people in different locations use technology to speak to each other
>
> **video-conference:** a meeting where people at different locations can see and talk to each other while sitting in front of a camera and a microphone
>
> **web-conference:** a live meeting held via the internet usually on a computer or smartphone
>
> **webcast:** a one-way transmission which is non-interactive.
>
> **webinar:** teaching session or other presentation that take places on the internet, allowing participants in different locations to see and hear the presenter and ask and answer questions

Figure 4.10: A video-conference in progress

Equipment needed for video- and web-conferencing

Both require input and output devices for sound and vision and a communications link between the participants.

For web-conferencing

- microphone
- speakers or headphones
- video camera (if it is visual as well as audio)
- a display screen or monitor
- an internet connection
- web-conferencing software.

Most participants use mobile devices such laptops and smartphones, which have these hardware devices built-in.

For video-conferencing

Video-conferencing requires the same hardware, but this is usually of high quality, individual components rather than being built into a single device. Usually a dedicated room is used with a large, wall mounted monitor and central video camera and speakers. Video-conferences are also conducted over private lines or secure internet connections.

Table 4.4 summarises the advantages and disadvantages of video- and web-conferencing over face-to-face meetings.

Advantages	Disadvantages
Provide an environment where colleagues can be seen and heard without having to travel as they would to a face-to-face meeting therefore saving time and money.	The interaction and communication is never as successful as between people actually meeting and interacting face-to-face.
As participants do not have to travel, meetings can be organised very quickly to respond to a new event or emergency. It would take far longer to organise a face-to-face meeting, especially if participants were spread around the world.	Video-conferencing hardware and software can be relatively expensive especially as web-conferencing software is often free for small group use.
Video-conferencing allows participants to see their colleagues, which is not possible with telephone-conference calls. This allows for none-verbal communication, e.g. body language.	Reliant on hardware and software which can malfunction and prevent users taking part in the meeting whereas everyone in a face-to-face meeting can contribute.
Participants can show presentations and share and collaborate on documents. This is not possible with telephone-conference calls.	A user may not be able to see all of the participants at a remote site because of the camera field of view whereas they could see everyone in a face-to-face meeting.
Allows more employees to work from home or at remote locations, communicating with colleagues when required. This means less office space is required and saves money on commuting costs that would be required if they had to be physically present.	Sometimes participants have to work at unsocial hours if they are in very different time zones of the world. In a face-to-face meeting all participants are in the same time zone.
Encourages collaboration between colleagues as they can chat and see each other at any time. There would be less collaboration if they had to arrange meetings at particular times and places.	

Table 4.4: Advantages and disadvantages of video- and web-conferencing over face-to-face meetings

Table 4.5 summarises the differences between video- and web-conferencing.

Video-conferencing	Web-conferencing
Provides far better quality video and audio than web-conferencing.	Not as good quality video and audio as video-conferencing.
A complete group of people at one location can be viewed, making it a more natural meeting experience, as video-conferencing systems use high quality video cameras covering the whole room. Web-conferencing only shows an individual using a web cam.	Web-conferencing only shows an individual using a web cam whereas in video-conferencing a complete group of people at one location can be viewed, making it a more natural meeting experience, as video-conferencing systems use high quality video cameras covering the whole room.
Does not require the use of the world wide web and a web browser as web-conferencing does. Video-conferencing systems use their own software clients and are less prone to errors and problems with distortion of images and sound.	Requires the use of the world wide web and a web browser. Video-conferencing systems use their own software clients and are less prone to errors and problems with distortion of images and sound.
Participants do not need their own computer as video-conferencing systems can use their own hardware to show remote colleagues on a large screen. This allows for more natural interaction. Web-conferencing requires the use of a web browser on a computer.	
Video-conferences are always interactive with users at all end points being able to contribute whereas web-conferencing is often used for one-way communications and presentations such as webcasts or webinars which allow more interaction.	

Table 4.5: Differences between video- and web-conferencing

Questions

11 List the similarities and differences between audio-, video- and web-conferencing.
12 Describe 'electronic-conferencing', and explain the methods and equipment required.
13 Explain the differences between video- and web-conferencing.

> **REFLECTION**
>
> In small groups, talk about what you each found difficult in this chapter, and come up with ideas to help each other learn the material.

SUMMARY

A network connects computers and other digital devices together and allows them to share data and resources.
Network types include local area networks (LAN), wide area networks (LAN) and wireless local area networks (WLAN).
Both Wi-Fi and Bluetooth are wireless forms of communication on a network.
Network hardware devices include hubs, bridges, switches, network interface cards (NICs) and routers.
Common network environments include extranets, intranets and the internet. Extranets are extensions to intranets; both are set up by organisations and access to them is strictly controlled whereas the internet can be accessed by everyone.
Storing your data at a remote online location, that is connected to the internet, and is possibly in another country, is known as cloud storage.
All online systems are subject to attacks by hackers and data can be stolen when it is stored or transmitted.
Measures are required to ensure the security of a network including the use of passwords, biometrics and tokens.
Data can be protected by strong passwords, firewalls and encryption techniques.
Audio-conferencing, video-conferencing and web-conferencing are methods of communication.

EXAM-STYLE QUESTIONS

1. A router is a networking device.
   - a **State** the main purpose of a router. [1]
   - b **Discuss** how routers are involved in data transmission over the internet. [6]
2. a **Describe** the function of a hub in a local area network. [2]
   - b **Explain** how a switch differs from a hub. [2]
3. Explain why network interface cards are needed by devices connecting to a network. [2]
4. a State what is meant by cloud computing. [2]
   - b Give *four* benefits of cloud computing. [4]
   - c Give *three* disadvantages of cloud computing. [3]
5. a Explain what is meant by *user authentication*. [2]
   - b Apart from the use of passwords, list *three* methods of authentication. [3]
   - c List *four* characteristics of a *strong* password. [4]
6. **Evaluate** the properties of audio-, video- and web-conferencing, and suggest the circumstances where each is the most appropriate. [6]

COMMAND WORDS

state: express in clear terms

discuss: write about issue(s) or topic(s) in depth in a structured way

describe: state the points of a topic / give characteristics and main features

explain: set out purposes or reasons / make the relationships between things evident / provide why and / or how and support with relevant evidence

evaluate: judge or calculate the quality, importance, amount, or value of something

4 Networks

> **CONTINUED**
>
> 7 **Compare** and contrast Wi-Fi and Bluetooth as methods of communicating wirelessly. [4]
>
> 8 Describe the differences between local and wide area networks and give examples where each would be used. [4]
>
> [Total: 47]

> **COMMAND WORD**
>
> **compare:** identify / comment on similarities and / or differences

SELF-EVALUATION CHECKLIST

After studying this chapter, think about how confident you are with the different topics.

This will help you to see any gaps in your knowledge and help you to learn more effectively.

You might find it helpful to rate how confident you are for each of these statements when you are revising. You should revisit any sections that you rated 'Needs more work' or 'Getting there'.

I can ...	See section	Needs more work	Getting there	Confident to move on
discuss the operation of a router and other common network devices, such as network interface cards, hubs, bridges, switches	4.1			
explain the use of Wi-Fi and Bluetooth in networks	4.1			
discuss cloud computing and how to store and share data	4.1			
describe the characteristics and purpose of common network environments	4.1			
list the differences between different network types	4.1			
discuss security issues regarding data transfer, including understanding about passwords and other authentication methods	4.1			
explain the use of anti-malware software	4.1			
describe electronic-conferencing	4.1			

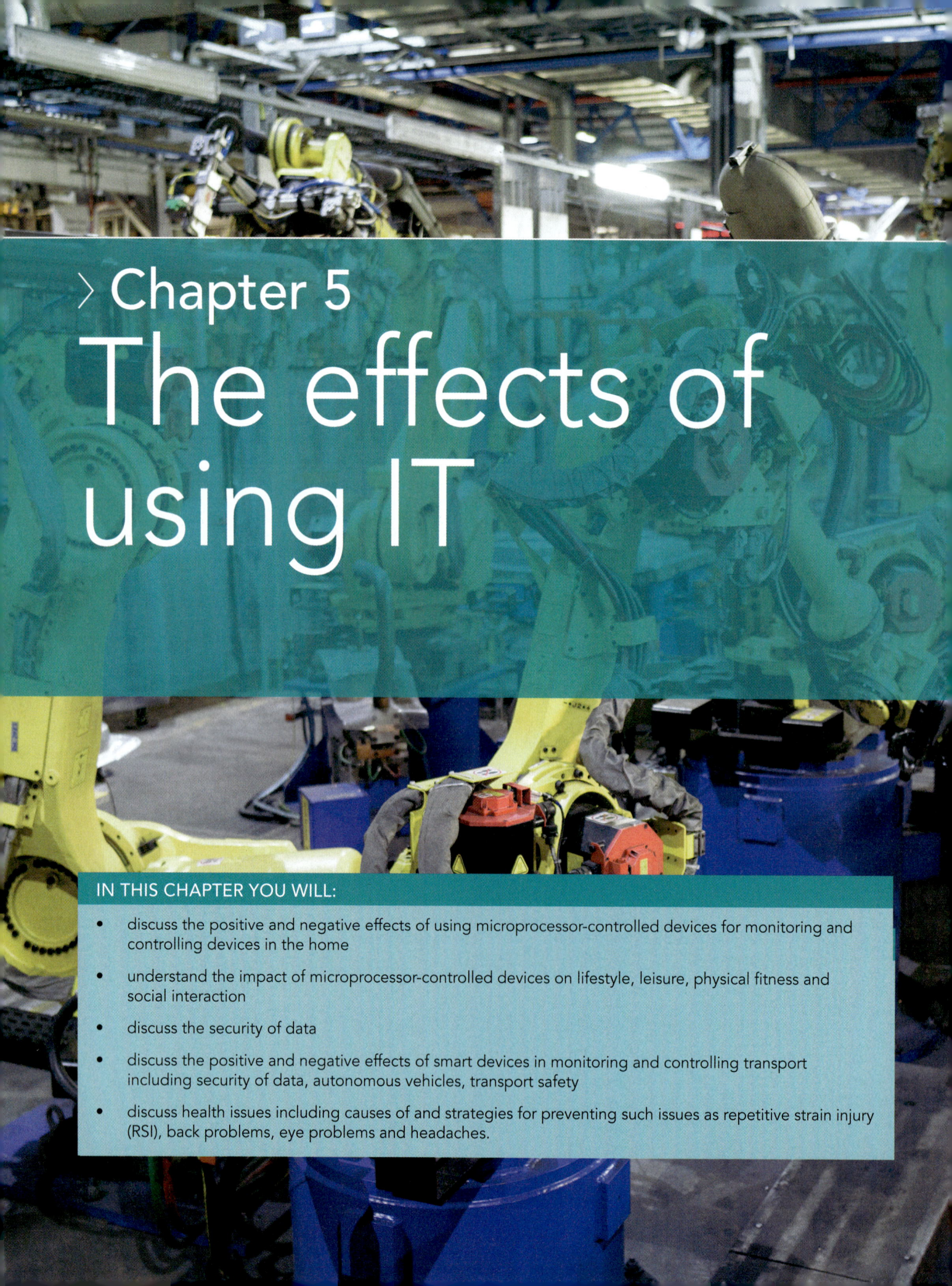

Chapter 5
The effects of using IT

IN THIS CHAPTER YOU WILL:

- discuss the positive and negative effects of using microprocessor-controlled devices for monitoring and controlling devices in the home
- understand the impact of microprocessor-controlled devices on lifestyle, leisure, physical fitness and social interaction
- discuss the security of data
- discuss the positive and negative effects of smart devices in monitoring and controlling transport including security of data, autonomous vehicles, transport safety
- discuss health issues including causes of and strategies for preventing such issues as repetitive strain injury (RSI), back problems, eye problems and headaches.

5 The effects of using IT

> **GETTING STARTED**
>
> Working with a partner, draw a computer in the middle of a piece of paper. On one side of it list the jobs that could be lost because of computers and on the other side list the jobs that could be created because of computers.
>
> Circle some of the jobs and add some notes about why that job could be lost or created.

MY COMPUTER MADE ME ILL!

RSI is repetitive strain injury. Repetitive strain injury is part of a group of 100 injury types known as musculoskeletal disorders. Many employers take it very seriously because musculoskeletal disorders make up approximately 30 percent of all injuries in the workplace that result in loss of workdays through employees' absence.

Figure 5.1 shows good posture and equipment that could reduce the effects of RSI.

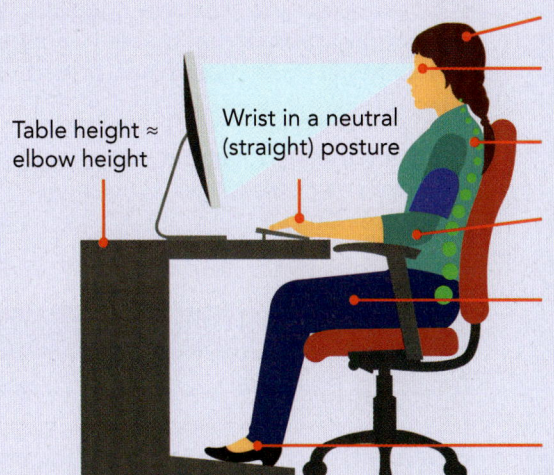

- Table height ≈ elbow height
- Wrist in a neutral (straight) posture
- Head upright and over your shoulders
- Eyes looking slightly downward without bending from the neck
- Backrest should support the natural curve of the lower back
- Elbows bent at 90°, forearms horizontal. Shoulders should be relaxed, not raised
- Thighs horizontal with a 90°–110° angle at the hip
- Feet supported and flat on the floor. If this isn't possible, then feet should be fully supported by a foot rest

Figure 5.1: Good posture when using a computer

Approximately 60 percent of office workers using a computer all day suffer from wrist pain while at the computer and around 50 percent of computer workers say that they feel their keyboards are too high. Another part of the problem could be because employees say they ignore the recommendations to take short, regular breaks from their computers, or that their employer won't let them.

This is a wide-spread health hazard among computer workers and the most severe injuries mean that people may have to be away from work for months, or possibly have a permanent disability.

Discussion questions

1. Should employers be legally required to ensure that employees are using computer equipment correctly?
2. What are the specific hazards associated with laptop use?

5.1 Microprocessor-controlled devices

Microprocessor-controlled devices in the home

Microprocessors are the small programmable processors found inside computers. They accept digital data as input and process the instructions stored in memory to produce the output required. They need input and output devices to be connected to them to make them useful as computer systems.

The use of microprocessors in household devices has grown to the extent that they can be found in most households all over the world.

Processors have been embedded in household devices for years to monitor and control them. This has had enormous impacts on lifestyle such as not having to do the washing up or having to spend all day washing clothes or standing over a manual washing machine.

Increasingly, devices are becoming interconnected using the internet. Human-operated digital devices have been connected to form networks for years (that's what the internet actually is) but now the aim is to allow everything in the world to make connections and communicate without direct human involvement. These devices are called **smart devices**.

The **internet of things (IOT)** is the term that has been devised to describe this connection of all the objects in the world. It is a system of interrelated computing devices, mechanical and digital machines, objects, animals or people that provide the ability to transfer data over a network without requiring human-to-human or human-to-computer interaction.

> **KEY WORDS**
>
> **microprocessor:** an electronic circuit or chip that makes the computer or electronic device work by processing data, performing calculations and issuing instructions based on the results
>
> **smart device:** as the name suggests, an electronic gadget that is able to connect, share and interact with its user and other smart devices
>
> **internet of things (IOT):** the interconnection via the internet of computing devices embedded in everyday objects, enabling them to send and receive data

> **ICT IN CONTEXT**
>
> Wi-Fi-enabled kettles are available now – however, one frustrated user once spent 11 hours trying to make a cup of tea! He was trying to get it to boil on command, but things didn't go to plan.
>
> The main issue was that the base station could not communicate with the kettle and the kettle didn't come with software that would easily allow integration with other devices in his home, including Amazon Echo, which – like Apple's Siri – allows users to tell connected smart devices what to do. He spent all day trying to configure the unit before it eventually worked.

Figure 5.2: Microprocessor-controlled devices, such as a washing machine, oven and microwave, in a modern kitchen

To use smart devices in a home, a user will require the hardware to create a Wi-Fi network and software apps to control them. Devices such as Amazon's Echo and Apple's Siri, which are themselves smart devices, allow users to use voice control to tell them what other devices to control.

The positive and negative effects of smart devices

In the home

Here are examples of the positive and negative effects of smart devices used in the home.

Positive effects:

- **Saving time and money:**
  - Some smart fridges can automatically update a user's electronic shopping list when things such as milk or eggs need to be restocked.
  - Lost items such as keys that can inform a smartphone where they are.
  - Smart utility meters can monitor usage and send details to a smartphone. Users can adjust the thermostat even when on holiday.
- **Improved home security:**
  - Home CCTV systems send data to a smartphone even when the homeowner is away so that they can monitor their home and its surroundings.
- **Improved care and protection:**
  - Smart baby monitors can monitor breathing movements, temperature, body position (on the back or on the stomach), fall detection and report to a smartphone.
  - Monitors can care for the elderly. Sensors monitor light, temperature and movement from room to room so that if the elderly person falls and can't get up, the carer can be remotely informed.

Negative effects:

- Smart devices are expensive.
- They depend on the internet which may fail.
- Security – they can be hacked.

> **ACTIVITY 5.1**
>
> With a partner, design an 'intelligent house'. You could draw plans of the rooms showing the smart devices and annotate the design to explain their use.

Lifestyle and leisure

Smart devices have had effects on the way we live.

Positive effects:

- Smart speakers allow us to speak commands when we need to adjust the temperature, or make a shopping list.
- Smart thermostats reduce the amount of energy used in homes.
- While cooking dinner, if you notice that you are out of olive oil, saying a command to your smart speaker and asking it to, 'Add olive oil to my shopping list,' is more efficient than stopping and writing a note on a piece of paper – or completely forgetting about it.
- The use of smart devices creates more leisure time as less time is spent working on everyday tasks.

Negative effects:

- The use of digital devices has affected how people use their leisure time. In the past, listening to the radio or watching television was a group affair but now each family member is more likely to be individually involved with their own device so that there is no family contact.
- Leisure time is now more likely to be spent indoors with a digital device than outside involving a physical activity.

Physical fitness

Smart devices can help improve our fitness in several ways but over reliance on them could have a detrimental effect.

Positive effects:

- Smart devices can be used to monitor heart rate and the amount and quality of sleep.
- Fitness trackers track physical activity such as the number of steps taken, stairs climbed, the pace and length of a run, including the use of GPS. They can also record workouts, bike rides and other physical activities.
- Apps are available for users of smart training equipment, such as running machines or static cycles, to allow them to compete with others in real time and so increasing motivation.
- They can calculate the number of calories a person is burning and number of calories a person has eaten.

- Apps are available to monitor a person's physical condition and then suggest or actually activate mechanisms to correct any problems. Examples include:
  - Wearable devices which when attached to people with back problems, can transmit data to an app on a smartphone which then analyses it and suggest how the person should modify their posture.
  - A wearable device to help people to stop smoking. It senses changes in the body and delivers medication to prevent the craving for nicotine.

Negative effects:

- In a home using smart devices, people have to walk around their homes less and do less exercise in washing, cleaning and washing up. Lack of exercise can have a detrimental effect on peoples' physical fitness.

> ### ACTIVITY 5.2
> Carry out research and make a report on how smart devices and apps are used to monitor two other health problems.

Questions

1. Explain what is meant by a smart device.
2. Describe *one* benefit of the use of smart devices in each of the following areas:
   a Safety in the home.
   b Physical fitness.

Security of data

Smart devices may gather personal information to make them more efficient but, as ever with personal data, it is important that this is kept secure.

Positive effects:

- As there is more concern and publicity about data security more people and organisations are aware of the problems and take action accordingly.

Negative effects:

- Privacy and security are of concern to experts as all of these devices and systems collect a lot of personal data such as to when people are at home, the devices they possess, the medicines they take and any health problems they may have.
- The data generated by the IOT is available to many people and organisations who can use it for marketing purposes. For example, the creators of the devices and the apps used to control them will be able to capture data every time the device is used. This data will be available to them and any third party companies they nominate to store and analyse it.
- All of the devices are connected to the internet and therefore can be targeted by hackers. Security experts have demonstrated how easy it is to hack these devices by hacking everything from smart fridges to baby monitors and cars, and have stated that not enough is being done to build security and privacy into the IOT.

> ### ICT IN CONTEXT
> In 2016 hackers carried out a huge distributed denial of service (DDoS) attack on a major website. (A DDoS attack sends millions of coordinated messages to overwhelm websites.)
>
> This particular attack used devices in the IOT such as kettles, printers, cameras and video recorders in homes. It caused the website of a major company to crash.

Social interaction

- Smart devices in the home save time and create more leisure time. For example, people do not have to do the washing up. But usually the washing up was done by two or three people who could talk and interact as they were doing a physical task.
- If you can ask a smart assistant to do something, then you are less likely to talk to another person and ask them to do it and engage in a social interaction (which could be a positive or negative interaction).
- Smart devices create a shopping list and transmit it to a shop and the items can then be delivered. People do not have to speak to each other. The 'shopper' does not have to leave their house and travel to a shop. No social interactions on the journey and no social interactions in the shop. A lack of social interaction can cause mental health problems.

5 The effects of using IT

- Smartphones are usually blamed for the loss of social interaction because more people are inclined to communicate using them rather than face-to-face encounters. Even a video call is less of a social interaction than meeting face-to-face.
- The devices have, however, encouraged social interactions at a distance. Using tablets and smartphones, people are able to communicate and interact with friends who don't live close by using:
  - voice and text messages
  - social networking sites
  - emails
  - video calls
  - electronic- and web-conferencing.

Transport

Microprocessor-controlled systems are used in many aspects of transport.

Vehicle safety

Microprocessor-controlled systems are used in all modern motor vehicles. The most common use is in the **electronic control unit (ECU)** for their engine management systems. Problems are diagnosed and fine tuning is done by computer. Gone are the days when a mechanic 'tinkered' with the engine to set the timing or ensured there was a correct mixture of petrol and air. Using an ECU for engine management leads to more efficient fuel consumption and less pollution.

The ECU has other, safety related functions such as:

- Anti-locking braking systems and electronic stability control (ESC) to automatically correct driver errors to maintain stability, prevent skidding and so reduce accidents.
- Using a video camera mounted near the car mirror, adaptive cruise control (ACC) maintains a correct distance from the car in front and automatically applies the brakes if it slows down.

Many cars now have collision avoidance systems which will warn of any objects in front of the car, including pedestrians and cyclists, and will apply the brakes, if necessary.

Control systems in vehicles improve safety but may malfunction. They are complicated devices and may need technological experts to fix.

ICT IN CONTEXT

Figure 5.3: 1968 Volkswagen 1600

The first use of computer control in a car was in 1968 when Volkswagen (Figure 5.3) introduced an electronic fuel injection system called Jetronic designed by Robert Bosch.

Traffic systems

Sensors, control systems and computers are used in **intelligent transport systems**, one of the features of **smart cities**.

KEY WORDS

electronic control unit (ECU): a device responsible for overseeing, regulating and altering the operation of a car's electronic systems

intelligent transport system: the use of communications devices, computers, control and sensing devices to improve the safety and efficiency of traffic movement through transmitting real-time information

smart city: a city where sensor-driven data collection and powerful computers are used to automate and coordinate a wide range of services in the interests of better performance, lower costs and lessened environmental impact

Intelligent transport systems use sensors to collect data from sensors such as cameras to monitor the amount of traffic, travel speed and traffic jams in various locations.

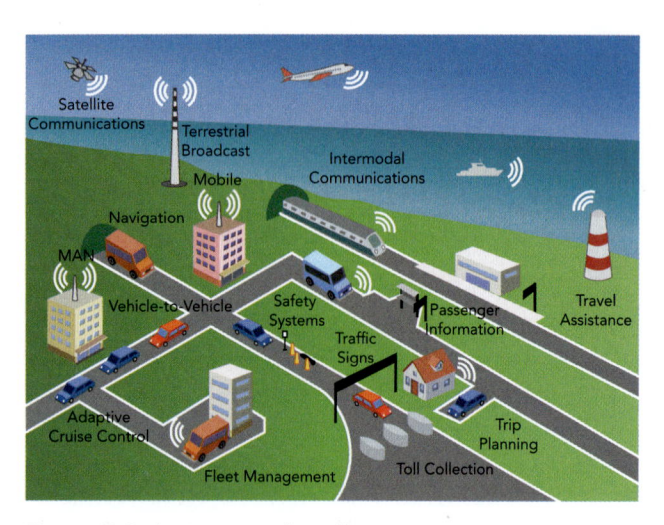

Figure 5.4: An integrated intelligent transport system

After the data has been analysed, optimum traffic flow can be maintained by:

- Control of traffic light systems.
- Informing travellers about travel times, travel speeds, accidents, delays, diversions through variable message signs, radio announcements, the internet and automated SMS calls to smartphones.
- Inform users of public transport when the buses will be arriving and the number of seats on each one.

An intelligent transport system improves traffic efficiency by minimising traffic problems. It reduces travel time of commuters as well as enhances their safety, comfort and mental health.

An obvious disadvantage is that the systems are expensive to implement and may malfunction or break down, leading to traffic chaos.

Also, the system relies on surveillance of vehicles and pedestrians and so impinges on their human rights of privacy and security.

Autonomous vehicles

Autonomous, or self-driving, **vehicles** are capable of sensing the environment and operating without human involvement. A human passenger is not required to take control of the vehicle at any time, nor is a human passenger required to be present in the vehicle at all. An autonomous car can go anywhere a traditional car can go and do everything that an experienced human driver does.

> **KEY WORD**
>
> **autonomous vehicle:** a vehicle capable of sensing its environment and operating without human involvement

Autonomous vehicles eliminate human driving error as they observe their surroundings and respond to situations with maximum efficiency, 24 hours a day.

There are, however, concerns about safety decisions that have to be made. What happens when the car needs to make a decision that could involve taking a human life, such as:

- If several people were suddenly on the road. Should the car swerve and possibly kill one pedestrian on the pavement. Should it save several people but kill one?
- If something else were in the road, should the car swerve and kill a single pedestrian to save the life of the driver?
- If something else were in the road, should the car swerve and kill several pedestrians to save the life of the driver?
- Should it make different decisions if children are involved?
- Are young people more worth saving than old people?

All of these moral and ethical decisions must be programmed into the vehicles, and rules and laws must be enacted to define correct procedures. What if different countries had different rules and you take your driverless car abroad and have a fatal accident?

Who will be legally responsible? The owner? The manufacturer? The programmers?

Question

3 Discuss the expected benefits and drawbacks of the use of autonomous or self-driving vehicles.

Security of data

As with all computerised systems there are concerns about security. Data on all user's journeys, whether using their own vehicle, using public transport or as a pedestrian, could be stored and used for other purposes than helping to control traffic flow. Some people argue that this data could be misused by the state and lead to far greater surveillance and control.

It could also be stolen by hackers and sold to organisations who could benefit from it – for example, to target advertisements at people who use particular routes or travel at certain times.

The control systems used for intelligent transport and in the vehicles themselves are vulnerable to hackers who could take over traffic light systems and vehicles.

Computer experts have shown how wirelessly controlled traffic lights can be manipulated using a laptop so that they had all green lights on their way to work. They have also shown how easy it is to take over the steering, lights and wipers of internet connected cars.

> ### PRACTICAL TASK 5.1
> **Getting started**
> 1. With a partner, make a list of three applications of smart devices for monitoring and control in the home.
>
> **Practice**
> 2. Create a presentation titled 'The Smart Home' to explain the uses and benefits of using smart technology in your house. For information about creating presentations, see Chapter 19.
>
> **Challenge**
> 3. Carry out research and create a similar presentation on 'Smart Cities and Towns' to explain the uses and benefits of using smart technology in cities.

5.2 Health issues

There are a number of common safety issues that organisations and users must be aware of and know how to prevent, including physical conditions and safety when working with electrical equipment.

Health and safety experts have said that there is no evidence that using a computer is harmful to individual's health when used correctly. The use of computers may, however, make worse any pre-existing medical conditions and can lead to muscular and other physical problems. To reduce these risks, sensible precautions must be taken.

Most problems are caused by bad posture when using a computer, as shown in Table 5.1.

Safety issues	To reduce the risk, users should:
Repetitive strain injury (RSI): a general term used to describe the pain felt in muscles, nerves and tendons caused by repetitive movement and overuse. It mostly occurs in forearms and elbows, wrists and hands, neck and shoulders and can be caused by using a keyboard and mouse for long periods or poor posture due to not adjusting a chair or monitor correctly.	<ul><li>Adopt a good posture.</li><li>Use an ergonomically designed keyboard.</li><li>Take regular breaks.</li><li>Use the mouse as little as possible, for example, by using keyboard shortcuts. Alternatively, using a wrist support or ergonomic mouse can help.</li></ul>

> **KEY WORD**
>
> **Repetitive strain injury (RSI):** pain felt in muscles, nerves and tendons caused by continuously making the same movements

Safety issues	To reduce the risk, users should:

Back problems:
 	
• **Back pain:** caused by working for too long without taking a break and sitting in front of a computer with a bad posture.
 	
• **Back injuries caused by moving equipment:** many injuries are caused by moving heavier items of computer hardware, for example, desktop computers, monitors and printers.
	• Adjust the chair to suit body type and height.
	• Adjust the height and angle of the screen.
	• Use a chair with a lumbar support and adjust it to suit body type.
	• Adjust the desk by bringing it closer or further away.
	• Use correct lifting techniques such as:
	  • Reducing the amount of twisting, stooping and reaching.
	  • Planning the lift to reduce the distance as much as possible.
	  • Avoiding lifting from floor level or above shoulder height, especially for heavy loads.
	  • Asking others to help.

Eye strain: headaches, watery eyes, dry eyes and double vision can be caused by staring at a computer screen for too long.	• Taking regular breaks. • Adjusting the brightness and contrast of the monitor. • Using suitable font and icon sizes. • Using suitable lighting in the room, for example, prevent sunlight hitting the screen.
Headaches: headaches from computers are often caused by computer vision syndrome (CVS). If you spend extended periods of time on your computer you might get a headache due to glare on the screen, poor lighting in your workspace, improper computer brightness and colour, or a combination of these factors. **Stress:** headaches can also be caused by stress. A computer user may become stressed when: • The computer malfunctions. • The software does not carry out the functions expected. • The user is rushing as they have too much work to do.	• Take frequent breaks from the computer. • Work in a properly lit area. • Reduce computer screen glare. • Clean the computer display. • Keep hardware up to date and well maintained. • Keep software updated. • Ask for software training. • Take regular breaks. • Ask colleagues for help with the work. • Admit if it is too much for you.

Table 5.1: Safety issues when working with electrical equipment and strategies for preventing them

5 The effects of using IT

Figure 5.5 shows precautions that should be taken to prevent harmful effects when using a computer.

a Use wrist rests to support hands. Take breaks from repeating actions.

b Take regular breaks away from screen. Move the screen so that it is not reflecting light directly. Ask for an antiglare screen.

c Adjust chair so feet are flat on the ground. Use a foot rest. Take regular breaks to stretch legs. If knees are touching desk, ask for a higher one.

d Adjust the chair to suit body type, change height of the chair, adjust the lumber support. Adjust the desk space by bringing the computer closer or further away, adjust the height of the screen, etc.

e Take regular breaks to help relieve stress. Ask colleague to help deal with work. Delete emails that are no longer required. Ask for software training.

Figure 5.5: Precautions to take to prevent harmful effects when using a computer

ICT IN CONTEXT

Once symptoms of RSI are contracted, they can be extremely difficult to cure. Research has shown that 60% of IT professionals, who spend more than eight hours a day on the computer, are likely to suffer from the symptoms of RSI at some point.

RSI can occur even in the young and physically fit individuals. Some people are forced to quit their computer-dependent careers due to this disorder.

ACTIVITY 5.3

With a partner, create a poster illustrating the health risks of using a computer system incorrectly and how they can be prevented. You could do this on software like Paint or a word processor.

Questions

4 Using a keyboard for many hours every day is likely to cause health problems. Choose **one** of the following health problems that is most likely to occur:
   a back problem
   b RSI
   c sore eyes.

5 Are the following statements true or false?

a	Back problems can be helped if you use a foot rest.
b	Having to learn how to use new software can cause stress.
c	Glare on a monitor does not affect health.
d	RSI only affects the wrists.

6 Computer users are advised to take frequent breaks. Explain which safety issues given in Table 5.1 will be addressed by doing this.

PRACTICAL TASK 5.2

Getting started

1. Make a list of the health problems that can be caused by not using a computer system correctly.

Practice

2. Design and create a safety poster for computer users giving details of potential health issues and examples of good practice.

Challenge

3. Using suitable software, create an interactive activity to test computer users' knowledge of health problems and how to prevent them.

REFLECTION

What strategies did you use to learn the harmful effects of using computer systems and how they can be prevented?

Were you able to relate these to your own experiences?

SUMMARY

Microprocessors are the small programmable processors found inside computers. They can be found in many different household devices and can be found in most households all over the world.

Household devices may be linked to a home network so that they can communicate with each other and with you. This is called the internet of things (IOT).

The impact of the microprocessors found in most household devices and appliances have many advantages and disadvantages on aspects such as lifestyle and leisure, physical fitness, security of data and our social interactions.

Smart devices are involved in transport in areas such as vehicle safety, traffic systems and autonomous vehicles.

The security of smart devices and their data is a major concern if they are connected to the internet without adequate security measures.

Computers bring with them threats to health, which must be understood in order to prevent discomfort or pain or loss of work days. Ensuring we sit and work at a computer in a correct manner can avoid these problems.

EXAM-STYLE QUESTIONS

1 **State** what is meant by a *smart device*. [1]
2 **Describe** *two* examples of the use of smart devices in the home. [4]
3 **Discuss** the effects of using smart devices on peoples' health and physical fitness. [6]
4 Describe *two* ways in which electronic control systems are used to improve the safety of driving by preventing accidents [4]
5 Discuss the concerns over and problems with data security when smart devices are used in the home, in cars and in cities. [6]
6 Discuss *three* health problems that could arise from not using computer systems correctly and how they could be prevented. [6]

[Total: 27]

COMMAND WORDS

state: express in clear terms

describe: state the points of a topic / give characteristics and main features

discuss: write about issue(s) or topic(s) in depth in a structured way

SELF-EVALUATION CHECKLIST

After studying this chapter, think about how confident you are with the different topics.

This will help you to see any gaps in your knowledge and help you to learn more effectively.

You might find it helpful to rate how confident you are for each of these statements when you are revising.
You should revisit any sections that you rated 'Needs more work' or 'Getting there'.

I can ...	See section	Needs more work	Getting there	Confident to move on
discuss the positive and negative effects of using microprocessor-controlled devices for monitoring and controlling devices in the home	5.1			
understand the impact of microprocessor-controlled devices on lifestyle, leisure, physical fitness and social interaction	5.1			
discuss the security of data	5.1			
discuss the positive and negative effects of smart devices in monitoring and controlling transport including security of data, autonomous vehicles, transport safety	5.1			
discuss health issues including causes of and strategies for preventing such issues as repetitive strain injury (RSI), back problems, eye problems and headaches	5.2			

Chapter 6
ICT applications

IN THIS CHAPTER YOU WILL:

- identify communication media and mobile communication devices and their uses
- describe computer modelling and computer-controlled systems such as robotics, and the advantages and disadvantages of their use
- discuss management systems for school management and computer aided learning
- describe online systems to make bookings for cinemas and concerts, etc.
- discuss different banking applications and the advantages and disadvantages of each
- describe the characteristics and uses of computers in medicine and understand the uses of expert systems for a variety of different applications
- explain the uses of expert systems
- explain how computers work in the retail industry, the uses of different payment methods, and understand the advantages and disadvantages of internet shopping
- be able to identify the characteristics and uses of recognition systems, including OMR, OCR, RFIDs and biometric recognition
- know and understand the uses, and advantages and disadvantages of satellite systems.

6 ICT applications

GETTING STARTED

Table 6.1 shows some ICT applications. Table 6.2 shows some uses of the ICT applications shown in Table 6.1. Match the applications with the correct uses.

a	Communication applications.
b	Recognition systems.
c	Booking systems.
d	School management systems.
e	Banking applications.
f	Computers in medicine.
g	Expert systems.
h	Computer modelling.
i	Satellite systems.
j	Computers in the retail industry.

Table 6.1: Some ICT applications

1	Keeping patient and pharmacy records.
2	Using the global positioning system (GPS) for navigation.
3	Checking passports at an airport.
4	Using electronic funds transfer (EFT) to pay bills.
5	Using text messages to keep in touch with friends.
6	Using software to diagnose an illness from a list of symptoms.
7	Using point of sale (POS) terminals in shops and supermarkets.
8	Recording of learner attendance and performance.
9	Planning the sequence of traffic lights in a city.
10	Buying tickets for a sporting event.

Table 6.2: Some uses of ICT applications

ONLINE SHOPPING WITH A LITTLE CHAOS!

Amazon is a retail giant with centres in around 175 countries around the world. Since 2019 Amazon has become the world's largest online retailer. The success of Amazon has been attributed partly to the fact that, using its Prime service, the time between a customer making an order online and receiving it at their house can be 24 hours or less, and in some cities they may have delivery in two hours!

To achieve this, Amazon needs to operate in its warehouses at speeds previously unknown in other retail businesses. You might think that this would demand perfect organisation of their stock on the shelves, the correct placing of every item in an exact place as soon as they arrive in the warehouse. This is not the case. Amazon achieve their super-fast turnover from order to delivery by using the chaos method of storing goods with complete randomness (see Figure 6.1).

Figure 6.1: An Amazon warehouse

When a box of goods arrives, such as a delivery of 100 mobile phones, the box is opened and each individual phone is placed on any shelf at random, wherever there is a space. It means that each of the 100 new mobile phones could be stored in up to 100 different places. You may wonder how this could possibly work! A system of bar coding is used to identify items and locations across all of its warehouses. When an item is placed on a shelf, a hand-held bar code scanner prints out two bar codes, one for the item, the other

> **CONTINUED**
>
> for the shelf: the management system can then inform the workers how many items of stock there are and their location.
>
> So that the workers, whether humans or robots, can keep up with demand, they need to be able to find everything quickly. Management software tells the workers how many items need to be picked up, where the nearest one is, and the quickest route to it. The workers pick a number of items at one time that have been ordered by different people, therefore saving them time as they don't have to keep going back to the same location to pick up the same item which they would, if one order was prepared at a time.
>
> **Discussion questions**
>
> 1 What could be the advantage of keeping a box of shampoo next to a pair of trousers on a shelf?
>
> 2 What is it about the system of chaos that makes it easier to train new warehouse staff?

6.1 Communication

Communication media

In the past it was traditional to communicate mainly by letter-writing, written reports, newsletters, telephone and face-to-face meetings, but the use of ICT has brought about major changes in the way we communicate with each other on a personal level, and also on the way that organisations communicate.

Newsletters

Organisations such as businesses, schools, universities and clubs produced printed or electronic **newsletters** for employees, customers, parents and students, or for their members.

They are used to give updates on progress and new developments dd can be a single sheet or many pages long.

The use of word processing and desktop publishing software has allowed more sophisticated newsletters. Features include:

- using columns
- altering the margins and the spacing
- changing the character size
- using different typefaces (fonts), like Arial or Courier
- different effects, like *italic*, **bold** and ^{super}scripts
- indenting text
- automated bullet points and numbering systems
- justification of text
- inserting links
- use of headers, footers, automatic page numbering.

There is a skill in producing a newsletter, and part of the skill is to ensure that the document looks impressive, while remaining readable without too many distracting effects.

Posters

A **poster** contains less text and information than a newsletter and has a greater visual element so that it is eye catching.

Posters are intended to communicate one message rather than being a document containing lots of information on different topics. The difference is in the design of the finished product (Figures 6.2 and 6.3). Posters are usually used to advertise products and events.

> **KEY WORDS**
>
> **newsletter:** news, updates and information issued periodically to the members of a society or other organisation
>
> **poster:** a large printed sheet containing text and pictures which is displayed in a public space

6 ICT applications

Figure 6.2: A newsletter

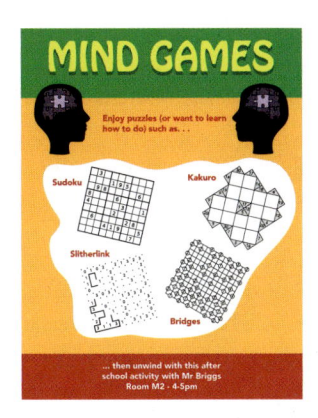

Figure 6.3: A poster

Websites

A **website** is a collection of interactive **web pages** containing text, graphics, audio, video and links to other pages. A website is hosted on a **web server** on the internet. The information on the website can be viewed by internet users using a **web browser**. Websites are used to raise the profile either of a person or an organisation and to communicate with others.

Websites can be used for various purposes:

- for entertainment
- to provide information about and organisation
- to advertise an organisation or product
- to allow users to upload and download files, e.g. application forms
- to allow users to order products advertised on the website.

For example, a school website is used to show information about the school, and to communicate with parents and other interested people to ensure that they feel fully involved with the school. The website is also used to advertise the school to people who currently have no connection with it, potential new parents in particular, and it is also used to advertise school events.

Multimedia presentations

A **multimedia presentation** is a standalone presentation that uses a mixture of different media such as text, video, audio and images to present information effectively and to maintain the interest of the viewer. Changes from one screen to another can use complex transitions to catch attention. Hyperlinks can be included as part of a single-user presentation to give the user a choice of path through it.

KEY WORDS

website: a collection of web pages

web page: a document containing text, images, audio, video and links to other pages that can be viewed on a web browser

web server: the computer that the website is saved on

web browser: an application used to access websites on the world wide web

multimedia presentation: a presentation that uses a mix of media, for example, text, sound, photos, animations, videos and interactive content

Multimedia presentations can be used to:

- accompany a talk by a person
- run on their own for people to view, e.g. advertising products in shops or explaining exhibits in a museum or paintings in an art gallery
- create educational tutorials
- produce a digital portfolio of a person's work
- produce a photo slide show that can be left to run on its own
- create interactive stories and quizzes
- create animations.

ICT IN CONTEXT

Now that organisations communicate in so many different ways, it is important for each of their documents to bear the same branding so that it can be recognised immediately as coming from that organisation, whatever type of document. For instance, they will always use the same logo, font, colours and style: this is known as their 'corporate image' or 'house style'. This will project their brand or overall image of the organisation.

Audio and video communication

Audio (sound) and video (containing moving images) can be used to convey information to individuals or whole groups.

Audio communication without video is used when people must concentrate or cannot view a screen such as when they are running or exercising. They can listen to music or a podcast but keep watching where they are going.

Information is communicated using audio in shops and on railway stations so that it reaches as many people as possible as they do not have to stand in one place and look at a screen.

Many presenters now use audio on its own for comedy, storytelling and providing information through the use of **podcasts**. A podcast is a digital audio file that users can download from the internet and listen to on a mobile device such as a smartphone. They are typically available as a series with new instalments automatically downloading.

Podcasts are used for entertainment, education and also by organisations to provide information to customers.

Video communication combines moving images and sounds and is a successful method of providing information as the viewers are entertained by the moving pictures. Video is widely used in education, entertainment and by organisations to advertise and promote their products.

Media streaming

Media streaming refers to the continuous transmission of audio or video files to a user. The file being streamed is stored remotely and streaming happens in real-time (as it happens). This means that you don't need to wait for the whole file to download to begin watching. Streaming means you don't need to download the files and use space on the hard drive.

Audio and video data is broken down into data packets to be send over the internet; you learnt about data packets in Chapter 4, Section 4.1, Networks.

For streaming high quality video, fast internet speeds are required.

Streaming is used for entertainment where users can watch films and listen to music stored on remote servers. Streaming is also used by television channels for live events such as football matches.

Live streaming is used by large and small organisations to broadcast meetings and events where new products are unveiled, across the internet.

E-publications

E-publications are the publishing of digital books, magazines, newsletters and newspapers online. The advantages of digital publications are:

- They can be shared globally.
- There are no printing costs.
- It is quicker to get published.
- You have constant access to your digital library where all of the items you have bought are kept, ready for you to read if you have internet access or downloaded them to your device.
- **E-Readers** are often less bulky than books, and constant access to your digital library means you just have to pack a small e-reader rather than many bulky books that you want to read if you're away from home.

KEY WORDS

audio communication: any form of transmission that is based on sound, speaking and hearing

podcast: a digital audio file made available on the internet for downloading to a computer or mobile device

video communication: any form of transmission that is based on moving pictures as well as sound

media streaming: a method of transmitting or receiving data (especially video and audio material) over a computer network as a steady, continuous flow, allowing playback to start while the rest of the data is still being received

live streaming: when streamed video is sent over the internet in real time, without first being recorded and stored, e.g. many sporting events are live streamed

e-publications: digital materials published online such as e-books or digital magazines and e-newspapers

e-readers: a device on which you can read e-publications

Mobile communication

Smartphones are mobile devices that can be used for many methods of communication.

Like all other telephones, smartphones can be used for voice or phone calls. They allow two or more people to communicate by talking to each other. Phone calls can also be made between landlines and mobile phones.

SMS, which stands for **short message service**, allows users to send short text messages to each other. They are delivered very quickly and allow instantaneous text conversations.

Voice over internet protocol

The **voice over internet protocol (VOIP)** allows the use of the internet to carry voice data when making phone calls. When using VoIP technology, the voice data is broken into packets of data that are sent along different routes to arrive at the same destination where they are reassembled in the right order, (see Chapter 4, Section 4.1 Networks). VOIP technology is referred to as packet switching.

VOIP telephony is generally free for the actual calls. The only costs are those for attaching to the internet, but the person making the call will not pay for these if they are in a restaurant or coffee shop providing free internet access. VOIP telephony can be between a computer and a landline telephone, not just between two computers or smartphones.

VOIP is also used when making video calls over the internet using the device's camera, speaker and monitor. Various service such as WhatsApp and FaceTime allow users to make video calls. As more data has to be transmitted than just a voice call, the picture can sometimes lock so that no motion is shown.

Accessing the internet

Mobile devices can access the internet using either Wi-Fi or a mobile or cellular network, which is also a wireless network that is distributed through **cells**. Each cell includes a fixed location transceiver known as a **base station**. Working together, these cells provide wireless coverage over a large geographical area. Each cell offers coverage of between nine and 21 miles.

When a user moves out of range, the signal falls and the base station makes a request to transfer control to another base station that is receiving the strongest signals without notifying the subscriber. This is called **handover**. Over the years cellular technology has improved, with each improvement being called a 'generation'. Most people now use third generation **(3G)** or fourth generation **(4G)** technology, but this is due to be superseded very soon in some areas with **5G**.

> ### KEY WORDS
>
> **short message service (SMS):** system where users can send short text messages to each other from one mobile phone to another or from a computer to a mobile phone
>
> **voice over internet protocol (VOIP):** allows the use of the internet to carry voice data when making phone calls
>
> **cell:** a geographical area covered by one base station
>
> **base station:** a fixed point of communication for cellular phones on a carrier network. The base station has an antenna (or multiple antennae) that receives and transmits the signals in the cellular network to customer phones and cellular devices
>
> **handover:** the automatic transfer of a user's connection to a base station to another base station which is nearer to the user
>
> **3G and 4G:** communication protocols used by smartphones to connect to the internet, 4G being much faster than 3G
>
> **5G:** the 5th generation of wireless technologies for digital cellular networks

Question

1. 'WeSellShoes' is a shop that sells various types of footwear to customers in their local town.

    Describe **two** advantages to them of designing and maintaining a website.

6.2 Modelling applications

Computer modelling uses **mathematical formulae** to describe actual, real-life situations. The model attempts to mirror the rules and mechanisms that control real-life systems and apply the rules in computer programs so that the models can simulate the real-life behaviour under different conditions.

There are three obvious reasons for modelling a situation:

1 To test situations without endangering anybody.
2 To test the situation's feasibility without spending large sums of money (building a prototype to find that it doesn't work is expensive).
3 If a computer model is produced of a new design – e.g. a car, ship or aeroplane – their behaviours under different conditions can be **simulated**, for example, how the ship should cope with different sized waves.

Real-life situations being modelled can be almost anything:

- personal finance
- bridge and building design
- flood water management
- traffic management
- weather forecasting.

Personal finance

A **personal financial model** predicts finances into the future. For example, it can show expected regular income and expenditure throughout the year such as rent, rates, food shopping, and allow a user to see how much they should have available at the end of each month. It can also allow a user to see what would happen if they changed something: for example, what would happen if they saved more each month? Or if they splashed out on a new car? They could check if they could afford the monthly payments for a media streaming contract.

Spreadsheets are very valuable for simple computer modelling because they allow 'what if . . . ?' questions to be asked.

ICT IN CONTEXT

For commercial and large-scale models, specialist **modelling software** is used to build simulations. The software uses sets of rules to predict the outcomes of different situations when data is entered.

Meteorological services use different models such as Seasonal and Climate (Figure 6.4) and Ocean models to predict the weather.

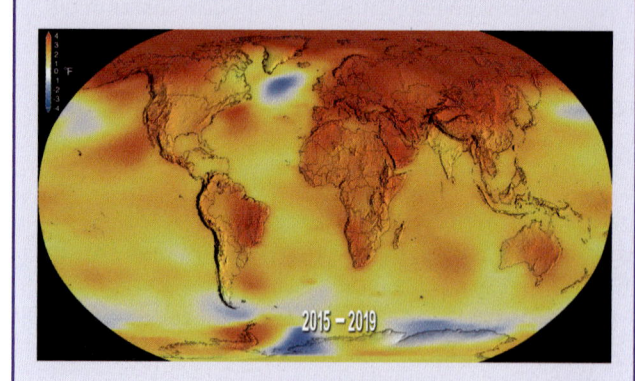

Figure 6.4: Seasonal and climate model

Supply-chain modelling software is used by organisations for planning the logistics of the transport of materials from all over the world.

KEY WORDS

computer modelling: an attempt to abstract the rules and mechanisms that control real-life systems and apply them in computer programs so that they can be used to simulate the behaviour of those systems

mathematical formula: an expression or equation that expresses the relationship between particular quantities. (Plural is formulae)

simulate: to make something that looks and acts like a real object or situation but isn't real

personal financial model: creating a plan to manage a person's budget

modelling software: programs used to create computer models

Bridge and building design

A computer model or simulation can be used to test the designs of bridges and buildings before they are built.

Bridges and buildings have to be able to survive adverse weather conditions, and the model can be used to test what happens under very extreme weather conditions, such as storms and hurricanes, without endangering anyone. Otherwise, the buildings would have to be built and then left until they were destroyed by extreme weather conditions.

A bridge model could be tested with different amounts of heavy traffic and a building could be tested to see how it behaves at different temperatures, such as those caused by a fire, or if there is an earthquake.

Flood water management

There are many areas of the world that are subject to flooding annually and modelling for future forecasts of flood patterns is extremely important. Models provide predictions of the extent and depth of flooding and can be used in the development of accurate **hazard maps** of a region.

The models also allow the assessment of risks to life and property and provide information in decision making, such as the maintenance of existing flood defences or the construction of new ones.

The models can be used to:

- show which vulnerable groups and communities are at risk
- provide **real-time** flood predictions to inform emergency services
- plan and develop exercises to test response to emergencies
- produce maps of flood and coastal risk
- design schemes to manage flood risk
- consider the long term effects of climate change.

Traffic management

Traffic modelling develops information that can support decisions about how to manage traffic systems, usually in towns and other urban areas. Traffic flow is the rate at which vehicles pass a given point on the road, and is normally given in terms of vehicles per hour. Usually the number is counted for 15 minutes and then multiplied by 4. If there were 100 vehicles passing the point in 15 minutes then the traffic flow would be 400 vehicles per hour.

The type of decisions that traffic modelling can help with are to determine which type of control to use at road junctions – for example, traffic lights where the right of way is indicated gives opportunity for the side roads to enter the traffic flow on the main road; roundabouts keep traffic moving rather than causing all traffic to stop as for traffic lights. However, a roundabout on a busy main road can mean those cars in side roads will struggle to move out.

Traffic management can use modelling to aid decision making about these choices, as well as helping to determine the amount of time allowed to each road at urban traffic lights.

They also allow users to investigate the effects of building new roads, making more streets for pedestrians only or allowing only one-way traffic.

Weather forecasting

Weather forecasting is important because it helps to find out what the weather will be like in the near future. Weather forecasting involves using detailed models of the atmosphere to try to predict how the weather will be during the next weeks, or months. The data needing to be fed into the model include:

KEY WORDS

hazard map: a map that highlights areas that are vulnerable to particular adverse conditions

real-time: as things occur, with no delay. For example, the model would be updated with data as weather changed so everyone would know exactly what was happening at that moment

traffic modelling: using mathematical and computer simulations of real-world traffic situations to ensure optimal (best or most desirable) traffic flow with minimum traffic jams

traffic management: directing vehicles and pedestrians along certain routes to ensure optimal traffic flow with minimum traffic jams

weather forecasting: predicting weather conditions over the next few days

- how the air moves
- how heat and moisture are exchanged in the atmosphere
- air pressure
- wind strength
- temperature
- moisture.

Advantages and disadvantages of using computer modelling

Advantages of computer modelling:

- Safety: buildings can be remodelled without humans putting themselves at risk of construction accidents.
- Less expensive as new products can be tested without humans having to build physical prototypes.
- More situations can be tested: situations impossible for humans to test, as well as dangerous situations can be tested by modelling.
- Faster results: once all the data is in the model, it is much quicker to work out very complicated mathematical equations than humans would.
- Buildings can be perfected using a model before it is constructed which reduces the time, materials and costs of making an error, or not building to the customer's specification. Humans could design a building on paper or build a small-scale model but this would take more time and is not quick to make any necessary changes.

Disadvantages of computer modelling:

- The situations may be too complex to model successfully.
- It may be difficult to identify all of the rules correctly.
- The model is not reality so the answers may not be right; reality may turn out unexpectedly different.
- A lot of expense is required to set up the model in the first place even though it may be cheaper than building a physical model in the long run.
- Human programmers may make errors in inputting the information that the program uses for calculations, so the digital model may be inaccurate.

- However, if humans had to create the whole model mathematically (without using computer modelling), they could make errors in their calculations.

Question

2 An organisation created a computer model to assist it in designing and testing a new factory for producing chemicals. When the factory was actually built there were several production problems and a major accident.

Describe **three** reasons why the model was unsuccessful.

6.3 Computer-controlled systems

A computer-controlled system is a set of devices such as a processor, sensors and actuators that work together to achieve a set of objectives, for example, painting a car or controlling the temperature of a building. You have already learnt about processors, sensors and actuators in Chapter 2, Section 2.3 Output devices and their uses.

Advantages of computer-controlled systems include:

- They are quick to respond to change and can process data very quickly.
- They can run all day, every day without needing a break.
- They can operate in places dangerous to humans.
- They can carry out repetitive tasks error free, unlike humans.
- Unlike humans, they do not require wages.
- Can take account of hundreds of inputs at the same time and still make accurate decisions, unlike humans.

Disadvantages of computer-controlled systems include:

- The hardware and software can be very expensive to develop.
- If there is a power cut, the system will stop; people can keep working (in many circumstances).
- Cannot react to unexpected events as a human can.

Robotics in manufacture

Robots have a major role within the manufacturing industry where their main use is to carry out repetitive tasks and some can be re-programmed to do different tasks as necessary.

Robots learn how to carry out tasks in different ways: a programmer can write instructions for the robot, then observe the robot while it does the task, called the 'teach and learn method' or the robot can be guided through a task the first time, then it produces instructions itself!

Although the initial costs of robots is very high, they can reduce overall costs in manufacturing industries through:

- Increased speed, being able to work continuously (no need for breaks).
- Reduced labour costs (no need to train and re-train or hire new staff).
- Higher product quality.
- The ability to carry out work in areas that may be too dangerous, too repetitive or too physically demanding for humans.

Some disadvantages of robots include the fact that:

- They cannot make independent decisions.
- If something happens that was not programmed for, they usually cannot change their actions to accommodate the new situation, although **machine learning** (computer algorithms that improve automatically the more times they are run) is an area of robotics that is attempting to change this.
- The initial setup costs can be very high and workers worry that robots cause unemployment for humans.
- Robots sometimes break down and contingency plans need to be in place to carry on with the work while the robot is being repaired.

> **KEY WORDS**
>
> **robot:** a machine controlled by a computer that is used to perform jobs automatically
>
> **machine learning:** the ability of computers to learn without being explicitly programmed

After the initial worries that robots will make workers redundant, more benefits of using robots have emerged and manufacturers now claim that there are new job opportunities for human workers who can learn to program and maintain robots.

ICT IN CONTEXT

The use of industrial robots has grown enormously. The graph in Figure 6.5 shows the implementation of new units in each year.

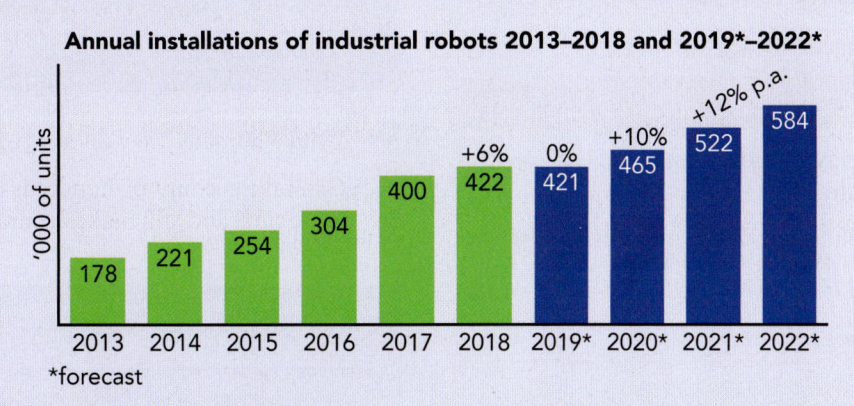

Annual installations of industrial robots 2013–2018 and 2019*–2022*

Year	'000 of units	Change
2013	178	
2014	221	
2015	254	
2016	304	
2017	400	
2018	422	+6%
2019*	421	0%
2020*	465	+10%
2021*	522	+12% p.a.
2022*	584	

*forecast

Figure 6.5: 422 000 new robots were employed in 2018. The figures for 2019 to 2022 are projections and, of course, will be affected by financial problems caused by COVID-19

> **CONTINUED**
>
> The graph in Figure 6.6 shows the number of robots employed per 10 000 industrial employees.
>
> This information can be misleading because, although China is in 20th position, it is the world's largest user of industrial robots installing 154 000 units in 2018. It's just that it has far more industrial workers.
>
> **Robot Density World Robotics 2019**
>
> - Singapore 1: 831*
> - Republic of Korea 2: 774*
> - Germany 3: 338*
> - Japan 4: 327*
> - Sweden 5: 247*
> - ...
> - USA 8: 217*
> - ...
> - China 20: 140*
>
> *Robots per 10 000 employees in manufacturing
>
> **Figure 6.6:** Number of robots employed per 10 000 industrial employees

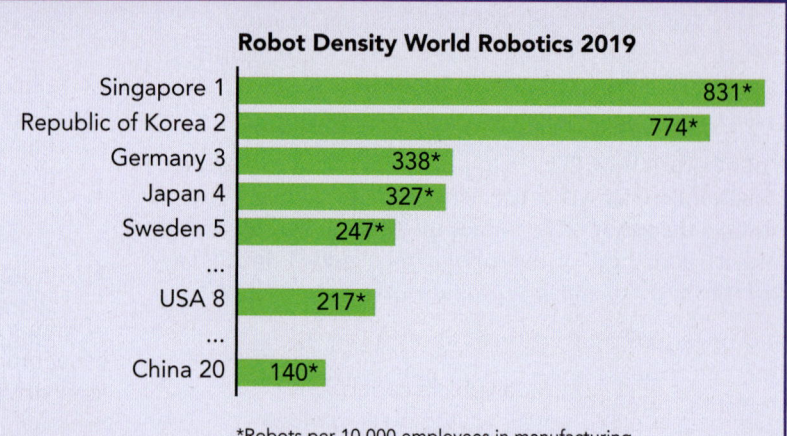

ACTIVITY 6.1

Carry out research into the effects of using industrial robots on employment around the world. Create a report explaining the effects.

Production line control

A **production line** is used to create an end product from raw materials or other components. Computers can be used to control the flow of materials along the whole production line.

KEY WORD

production line: a line of machines and workers in a factory that a product moves along while it is being produced. Each machine or worker performs a particular job that must be finished before the product moves to the next position in the line

Figure 6.7: Robots at work in a factory making a car

Robots are important in the manufacturing industry where they perform complex assembly line tasks (see Figure 6.7) and even manage human workers. Many robotic arms can perform a range of different functions, and can also swap the tool they are using for a different, appropriate tool, with a minimum amount of human supervision.

ICT IN CONTEXT

Forklift drivers in some factories and warehouses take their instructions directly from a machine with a robotic voice; the driver obeys the voice, which tells him where he must go next. The instructions he follows also take account of the driver's safety because the orders prevent him from colliding with another human worker.

6 ICT applications

Autonomous vehicles

An **autonomous vehicle** is a vehicle without a driver that can sense its surroundings so that it can operate on its own to carry out the tasks necessary without any human having to be present. To do this, the vehicle can respond to the external conditions as a human driver normally would. It can drive in all conditions with no human intervention. It is guided by GPS, Wi-Fi and **spatial laser sensors**.

> **KEY WORDS**
>
> **autonomous vehicle:** a vehicle capable of sensing its environment and operating without human involvement
>
> **spatial laser sensors:** sensors which are used with lasers to detect, measure and analyse the space and objects in an environment, in real time

A fully automated vehicle will be enabled by the use of 5G technology, which will allow vehicles to communicate with each other, with traffic lights, traffic signs and the road conditions. The information is processed and sent to actuators (for devices that automatically respond to sensors, see Chapter 2), which are in the vehicle. The actuators control steering, acceleration and braking.

Autonomous vehicles are probably safer because there isn't a driver to make the errors that cause accidents! Sensors are used to communicate with other driverless cars, so if all cars were driverless, they could go faster safely, giving people more time to carry on with other things, meaning that the economy could benefit. Also there may be less congestion on the roads if cars could interact with each other. In 2011, Google brought out a version of a driverless car. It can be seen driving around the streets in parts of the USA.

The logistics industry, which manages the movement of goods from their source to their destination, would benefit too. Companies often place time limits on their lorry drivers. These limitations could be avoided as driverless transport would be able to travel 24 hours a day; the journey would not need to include rest time for the driver either. This could result in reduced costs. Disabled people who cannot drive would also benefit from the use of driverless cars as they would gain more mobility and independence.

There are some disadvantages to this innovation: some people may lose their jobs, for example, people who depend upon driving to make a living; the software would have to be robust and safe from hackers; there may also be privacy concerns as self-drive cars depend on collecting and sharing location data. If something went wrong and a crash occurred there is no legal precedent yet to determine who would be responsible.

Table 6.3 shows the benefits and drawbacks of autonomous vehicles.

Advantages	Disadvantages
In the future, there could be fewer driving errors due to hundreds of calculations every second.	In the future, it may be that the expense of buying or renting would make it impossible to buy an autonomous vehicle to all but the super-rich.
Traffic congestion due to fewer accidents so fewer hold-ups.	The technology could go wrong which could cause malfunctions or accidents.
Easier to park as passengers can get out and leave the car to find a parking space and park itself.	In the future it may be difficult to get a licence or insurance cover.
Time-saving as the passenger has time to work or relax without worrying about road safety.	There could be even more pollution if the vehicle is not electric (but this is unlikely).
Disabled people who have difficulty driving are helped to be independent.	Safety and security as the system could be hacked.
Partly autonomous vehicles are sometimes used in warehouses to quickly locate or store items, so increasing efficiency.	Fewer job opportunities for traditional professional drivers such as taxi or delivery drivers and chauffeurs.
	The sensors could fail during severe weather.

Table 6.3: Advantages and disadvantages of autonomous vehicles

Question

3   A manufacturing company is planning to introduce industrial robots.

    Describe **two** benefits and **two** drawbacks of this decision both for themselves and their workers.

6.4 School management systems

A **school management system** is an information management system for educational institutions to manage all student data. It provides facilities such as registration of students in classes, documenting of grades and evaluation of progress.

Learner registration and attendance

Some school registration systems are based on OMR system technologies (Figure 6.8). This type of input was described in Chapter 2, Section 2.2 Direct data entry and associated devices.

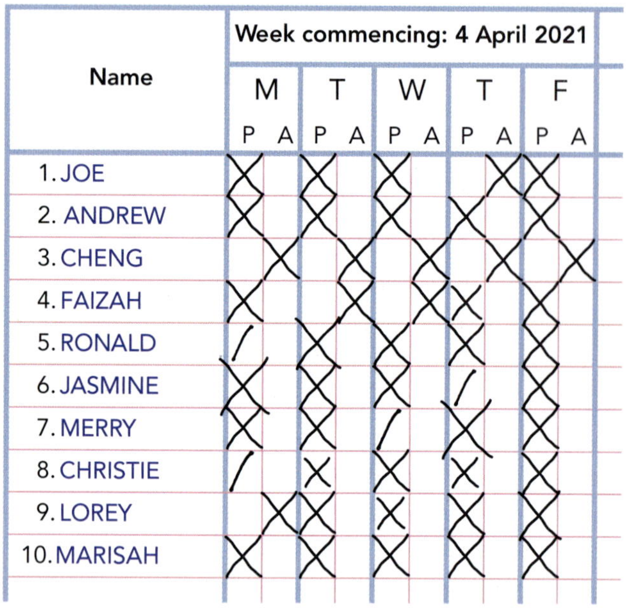

Laptops, tablets and smartphones can also be used for real-time registration over a network if the school management system provides this facility. It saves time as marked sheets do not have to be read by an optical mark reader.

Computer aided learning

Computer aided learning (CAL) is an integrated environment where computers are used to assist the learning of students.

The computers can be used for many things such as the development of online learning which includes:

- The separation of teachers and learners which distinguishes it from face-to-face education.
- The use of a computer network to present or distribute educational content.
- The provision of two-way communication via a computer network so that students benefit from communication with each other, teachers and staff.

Figure 6.8: Part of a school registration form for a class. The form has been designed for use with an OMR system. The teacher marks the appropriate box for a given student: P = present, A = absent

For example, a member of staff could post an assignment and the students could research, discuss with each other and submit it completely online. The assignment could be marked and returned with comments, both written and audio, again completely online.

- Online learning can be delivered using a website and communications using emails but greater benefits have been provided by the use of VLEs.

CAL also includes presentations and interactive tutorials which gives students the opportunity to manage their own learning by allowing them to:

- Learn at their own pace.
- Repeat sections that were difficult.

KEY WORDS

school management system: software designed to assist school administrative and educational tasks such as registration and predicting student progress

computer aided learning (CAL): the use of computer systems to aid the user in learning

- Omit sections that they already know and understand.
- They can also provide customised materials for each individual student so that they are not all expected to learn at the same rate and along the same route.

Most school management systems typically allow staff to record student grades and then automatically calculate the final grades to appear in the reports that go home to parents. The built-in functions enable teachers to filter student data in order to track student performance. Some more sophisticated systems will automatically alert staff to potential underperformers so that no underperforming students go undetected and all students can receive the assistance they may require when they need it the most. The analysis of the data is called 'learning analytics' and is intended to improve student learning.

Computer-based exams (CBEs) are organised by some examination boards and the school or college can enter students when they are ready and not at certain, fixed points throughout the year. The school management system should be capable of carrying out all the tasks associated with this based on the data input into the system. Automated emails are sent to examination boards, staff, students and parents to remind everyone of an impending exam. Students only have to login to a computer with the secure login details to take them to the exam and in some cases they are informed of the results as soon as they are completed. However, not all examinations are conducted online and on demand yet.

Similarly, creating timetables and organising teaching cover or substitution timetables is also handled by the school management system simply by inputting some important information into the system. The formulae and functions built into the system produce error-free timetables. When staff had to create similar timetables themselves, it often took several revisions before they managed to create a perfect version. Changes to the timetable are also made much more efficiently, and the system can inform all those concerned instantly using electronic communications such as email and mobile phone alerts.

PRACTICAL TASK 6.1

Getting started

1. Write down definitions for the following:
   - a school management system
   - computer aided learning.

Practice

2. With a partner, investigate how computer systems are used for administration and learning in your school or college.
3. Create a presentation of your findings to explain to potential parents how the systems are used.

   For information about creating presentations, see Chapter 19.

Challenge

4. Create a written report for your school or college's management, stating which systems they should introduce and the benefits of each.

6.5 Online booking systems

Theatres, concerts and cinemas

Consider a concert being held in a theatre. It is necessary to sell the 1000 tickets that are available to people who want to buy a ticket in advance. The promoter of the concert decides that instead of just selling the tickets at the theatre they will be on sale at a number of different shops in the area. Each shop needs to be allocated blocks of seats to sell otherwise the same seat may get sold twice. The promoter decides to let each of the ten shops have 100 tickets to sell. The problem of the same ticket being sold twice will not happen now because each of the tickets is unique. However, there is now another problem. Some of the shops might sell out and have to send people away without a ticket, while other shops do not sell all of their allocation and this will mean empty seats on the night of the concert. This would not happen if there was a way of allowing the popular shops to sell the unwanted tickets from the other shops. This could be done by physically moving the tickets from one shop to another, or it could be done by leaving the tickets in one place and allowing the individual shops to have access to them via computer communications.

Online booking systems allow booking agents in different locations to be in communication with a central computer system, which can store details of the available seats for cinemas or theatres.

> **KEY WORD**
>
> **online booking systems:** systems that allow people to book tickets and make reservations over the internet

When a customer rings or goes into the agency or shop:

- The customer states their requirements, which will include the name of the show or concert, the date for which tickets are required and the number and type of tickets that are wanted.
- The agent will then go online to the computer system and search for suitable tickets.

While this is being done no other customers can be serviced because of the danger of selling the same ticket twice. This is called locking the file so that no one else can change anything. More sophisticated systems such as booking airline seats, just lock individual seats to avoid jamming the system up.

When the tickets required are agreed:

- The customer pays by card (or cash if the shop has that facility agreed with the cinema or theatre).
- The seats that have been bought are changed to show 'sold' on the computer system.
- The file of seats is unlocked so that other customers can make bookings.
- The ticket is printed out at the shop or a receipt (an eTicket) is printed out which will be exchanged for the full ticket at the cinema or theatre.

This is an example of a real-time computing application that allows the owners of the cinema or theatre to reduce their costs by employing fewer people than they would otherwise have to without the automated system.

This system can be extended to allow the same sort of booking on the internet.

The travel industry

The travel industry allows bookings to be made by individual customers using the internet, or by travel agents. It is just as easy for customers to do their own bookings as it is to use a travel agent, but many customers who are not confident in the use of a computer and worry they may make a mistake while booking, or those people who do not want to pay online, still go to travel agents. However, travel agents are closing down a lot of their outlets due to online bookings.

Sporting events

Tickets for sporting events can be bought online from reputable agents in exactly the same way as for concerts. There are many ticketing agents to choose from but it is important to make sure that the tickets are valid. You can buy tickets quite quickly if you know who has the tickets that you want, but most tickets can be bought, even if someone knows little about buying tickets online. The best way is to find out when the tickets will first be available online. Some systems allow for the immediate downloading of your tickets, which is helpful if you decide to attend an event at the last minute.

Advantages and disadvantages of an online booking system

Advantages:

- Online booking saves time.
- The system is open around the clock, rather than only being available when the office or shop is open.
- The system gives immediate information about availability.
- Online booking systems can send an automatic email to the customer to confirm their booking.
- The system allows for immediate reselling of a ticket that has been returned, which means the customer is more likely to get a ticket last minute.

Disadvantages:

- The system is expensive to install initially.
- Cost of staff training.
- An online database and a website would both need to be created and have the ability to communicate with each other, in order for a customer to be able to search online for availability of the booking they require.
- In order to ensure absolute reliability, it will take time and money to keep the database up to date and the system functioning correctly.

Question

4   A school is developing an online booking system for parents to make appointments for their parent consultation evenings.

   Discuss the benefits and drawbacks to both the parents and the school of this type of system.

6.6 Banking applications

Automated teller machines

An **automated teller machine (ATM)** is the machine outside banks and other locations that allows you to carry out transactions such as withdrawing and depositing cash or cheques, checking your balance and paying bills without actually going into the bank. There are many other services available at an ATM, such as paying income tax or applying for a loan.

> **KEY WORD**
>
> **automated teller machine (ATM):** this is a machine that allows you to carry out banking services in locations other than inside a bank

The customer needs to provide identification by using a plastic card with a chip provided by the bank and a PIN (personal identification number). Chip and PIN readers were discussed in Chapter 2, Section 2.2 Direct data entry and associated devices.

These processes are all real-time processes because the account needs to be checked and updated without delay.

Withdrawing cash and depositing cash or cheques

An ATM is very convenient because you can use it to get cash from just about anywhere in the world (see Figure 6.9).

Figure 6.9: It is possible to withdraw cash from any place in the world

Many banks allow you to deposit money via an ATM from the bank where you have your account. You can also check your account balance and print out statements at the ATM. A mini statement will print your last few transactions.

> ### ACTIVITY 6.2
>
> Work with another student. Create a list of all the services you can get using an ATM.

Bill paying and money transfers

You can pay a bill or make a **money transfer** at an ATM. The ATM does not have to belong to the bank where you have an account. If you can see a logo at the ATM showing the different banks or card providers that it is compatible with, and yours is one of them, you can use the machine.

> ### ACTIVITY 6.3
>
> Discuss with another student the actions to take to withdraw money from an ATM, then together, put the actions in the right order.

Advantages and disadvantages of ATMs

Advantages:

- Open all day, every day and are therefore more convenient for customers.
- Customers do not have to go to a specific bank or building.
- Accounts can be accessed by customers from anywhere in the world.
- There is less human involvement and is therefore cheaper for the banks.

Disadvantages:

- Customers could be charged fees for using them.
- There is usually a limit on how much cash can be withdrawn each day.
- There is the possibility of fraud. Criminals can fix devices known as 'skimmers' to ATMs and these record your card details including the PIN that has to be entered on the keypad. Hidden cameras can also be used to capture card details.

Electronic fund transfer

Individual customers can use **electronic fund transfer (EFT)** while carrying out their banking requirements using **internet banking**. The customer is asked for their identification checks and is then allowed to state specific accounts to which they want to transfer money from their own accounts. The only other details needed are the bank code and the account number that the funds should be sent to and the name of the account holder. The transfers are then carried out immediately. EFT is also used in supermarkets when the customer pays for goods and is discussed further in Section 6.9.

> ### KEY WORDS
>
> **money transfer:** the act of transferring money electronically from one place to another. A money transfer agent carries this out, for example, VITTA or Western Union
>
> **electronic fund transfer (EFT):** this is the transfer of money electronically from one account to another
>
> **internet banking:** a method of banking in which transactions are conducted electronically via the internet

EFT can be used for payment for goods and also for services, e.g. payment to a builder who has done work on a house. It is often used by businesses to pay their workers' wages.

Advantages of EFT:

- Faster payment than using a cheque or cash.
- Payment is immediate.
- Can be used for payments 24/7.
- Can be used for setting up regular, automatic payments.
- More secure than using cash.
- No time wasted in dealing with cheques that bounce – that is, cheques from people that do not have the required amount in their account.
- Payments can be made anywhere in the world.

Disadvantages of EFT:

- As it immediate, customers must have the funds available.
- If you send the money to the wrong person or account, you cannot recover it.
- Open to abuse by hackers who may set up fake accounts in the names of firms and people you are sending the money to.

Credit/debit cards and contactless payments

You will remember that the use of bank cards was discussed in Chapter 2. When a card is used, the same sort of funds transfer is carried out as described in EFT. There are slight differences over where the funds come from. If the card used is a **credit card** the message is sent to the credit card company. The credit card company then arranges for funds to be sent to the account of the organisation, which has accepted payment using the card.

The credit card company then stores the information that the card has been used, where it was used and how much was spent in the transaction. This information is collected together once a month and a statement is sent to the cardholder showing them how much they owe. Notice that the use of a credit card requires both real-time processing for payments and batch processing for the production of statements.

Debit cards are used in the same way but the customer is dealing with their bank when they use their debit card rather than a credit card company. The bank will debit the customer account immediately (a real-time process) rather than waiting to produce a statement at the end of the month. The transaction will simply be shown as a payment on the normal bank statement.

Advantages of debit cards:

- Can be used to withdraw cash at an ATM without charge.
- Easy to obtain from a bank.
- Convenience – purchases can be made with the swipe of a card.
- Security – do not have to carry large amounts of cash.
- Accepted in most shops for payment.

Disadvantages of debit cards:

- No time period to cancel a payment.
- May be hard to keep track of your spending.
- Fraud – criminals could steal your personal details and set up a card in your name.

Advantages of credit cards:

- Can be used to withdraw cash at an ATM but will have to pay a charge.
- Convenience – purchases can be made with the swipe of a card.
- Easier to cancel a payment than when using a debit card.
- Users can spread the cost of a large purchase over many months.
- Many credit cards offer benefits and rewards to tempt people to use them.

Disadvantages of credit cards:

- People may be tempted to spend too much money.
- When a person's borrowing is up to their credit limit, they will not be able to use it.
- There may be fees and charges.

Validity of cards

Credit and debit cards need to be valid to be used. On each card is the date that the card expires. Some cards have a 'valid from' date as well. The date of payment must be before the expiry date.

There is also a number on the back of every card, called the **CVV** number or card verification value, sometimes known as the security code. Different card types use

> **KEY WORDS**
>
> **credit card:** a card that allows a customer to borrow funds to pay for goods and services
>
> **debit card:** a card allowing the holder to transfer money electronically from their bank account when making a purchase
>
> **CVV (card verification value):** a 3-digit number on the back of a credit or debit card. Users have to give this number when they are ordering items online

different amounts of numbers, but it is the last three digits that you will often be asked for during online transactions to verify your card. The long number on the front needs to be a valid number for the card issuer. All of these points will be checked automatically when the card is used to ensure its validity.

Cheques

Before EFT and card payments, people transferred money using **cheques**.

Banks regularly issued customers with books of cheques which were printed with their names and bank account details. On these cheques they would write the name of the person they wanted to pay and the amount. They would give the cheque to the person who would then travel to their bank to pay it in, although some ATMs will accept cheques. The banks involved would negotiate with each other and the money would be transferred. It was a slow process, and took usually more than three days for the money to be transferred from the one account to the other.

Although there was a delay in 'clearing' cheques, they were often more convenient than using cash.

Advantages of cheques:

- People do not have to carry cash.
- They can be stopped from being paid by phoning the bank.
- They can be traced if lost and paid in by the wrong person.

Disadvantages of cheques:

- The person accepting the cheque will not know if the person paying it actually has that amount of money in their account.
- Not suitable for small amounts.

> ### ACTIVITY 6.4
>
> Carry out research and list the countries around the world that still accept cheques and those that now do not.

Internet banking

Internet banking, also known as e-banking or online banking, is an electronic payment system that enables the customer of a bank or a financial institution to make financial or non-financial transactions online via the internet.

This service gives online access to almost every banking service that is traditionally available through a local branch including fund transfers, deposits and online bill payments to the customers.

Using a web browser or an app on a smartphone, a user can look at their account details, transfer cash, set up or cancel recurring payments and keep track of investments linked to their account.

As for all online transactions, users must ensure that they have a reliable password and adhere to all of the security features suggested by their bank as hackers could read their usernames and passwords, giving criminals access to the user's bank account.

Advantages of internet banking:

- Customers can view the details of their accounts 24/7.
- They can make EFTs using their smartphone.
- They can move money between their accounts in real time.
- Easy to see when they have run out of money.

Disadvantages of internet banking:

- Security – hackers may find login and password details for their account.
- As it is very easy to transfer money it is easy to make a mistake and send it to the wrong person or account.

> ### KEY WORD
>
> **cheque:** a written document that orders a bank to pay a specific amount of money from a person's account to the person in whose name the cheque has been issued

6.7 Computers in medicine

Expert and information systems in medicine

The study and practice of medicine is an enormous subject and continually growing. Computer technology is important in helping health professionals provide as reliable and efficient a service as possible and also in keeping them aware of medical advances.

Patient records

Your doctor, and the team of health professionals who care for you all keep records about your health and any treatment and the care you receive from them. For example, when someone is admitted to hospital, their details are entered into the **patient record system**. Once this information is on record, whenever that patient is admitted in the future, their records can be found very quickly. The typical information held on record for a patient could include:

- name, address and next of kin (a person's closest living relative)
- history of contact with the hospital, clinic or surgery
- notes and reports about health, treatment and care given
- results of X-rays and laboratory tests
- relevant information from other health professionals
- relatives or people who care for the patient.

Patient records are now stored digitally on computer and online. This makes it easier for various professionals who have been given access rights to view them if there is an emergency.

Pharmacy records

It is important that **pharmacy records** are kept so that doctors and medical workers can check the medicines that a patient has been taking and ensure there are no errors in the prescribing of their medication. All prescriptions used to be written on special forms by a doctor, given to the patient and taken to the pharmacy.

In many countries, most prescriptions are now signed, sent and processed electronically.

Patients can choose a pharmacy to which prescriptions are sent to and can collect their medicines or have them delivered without having to hand in a paper prescription.

As all prescriptions are electronic, details of the latest ones issued can easily be added to the patients' records automatically. Previously data had to be entered into the computer manually. Before that all paper records had to be stored in boxes for a number of years.

Security of patient records and systems

There are concerns about the implications of security, access and use of electronic patient information. Some of the concerns are:

- hacking, which can lead to the altering of patient data or destruction of the systems
- misuse of health information records by authorised users of the systems
- long term data management concerns about keeping data secure in the future
- the possibility of intrusion into personal health care matters by the police, insurers, social workers, other government or corporate institutions.

There are rules, laws and systems in place to prevent the threats given above.

3D printers for medical aids

You read about 3D printers in Chapter 2, Section 2.3 Output devices and their uses. But did you know that most hearing aids are already created using 3D printers, and that scientists have also worked out the theory of how to print blood vessels and skin, and even embryonic stem cells?

> **KEY WORDS**
>
> **patient record system:** a computer system used to keep an account of a patient's examinations and treatments
>
> **pharmacy records:** details of medicines and drugs prescribed for each patient and the overall dispensed from a particular source

A major advance that led to 3D **bioprinting** was the development of **biomaterials**. Biomaterials are cells and other components to print living tissues that function as the original tissue would.

The categories of health care where 3D printing can be applied are for artificial body parts (**prosthetics**), medical devices and human tissues.

In medicine, 3D printers are having most success with prosthetics such as dental work and hearing aids (as mentioned above). These may all be made from either plastic or pliable materials. They need to be made for a specific patient, so each will be individual, rather than mass produced.

Medical 3D printing is expanding quickly in areas such as the creation of tissues and organs, customised prosthetics, implants, anatomical models and more. The benefits of 3D printing for medical tools and equipment include customising and personalising medical products, drugs and equipment; reducing costs; increasing productivity; extending the power of information in design and manufacturing; and enhanced teamwork.

Unlike inkjet printers, 3D printers have an additional axis, called the **z-axis** (see Figure 6.10). They have a mechanism called an elevator that moves a platform up and down to achieve printing on the z-axis. The cartridges of 3D printers are also filled with substances other than ink. If the cartridge were filled with plastic, it would output a three-dimensional plastic appliance according to the instructions given. If the cartridge were filled with cells, then it would output a mass of cells. In a similar way that an inkjet printer uses cartridges filled with different colours, so a 3D printer can have cartridges filled with different types of materials.

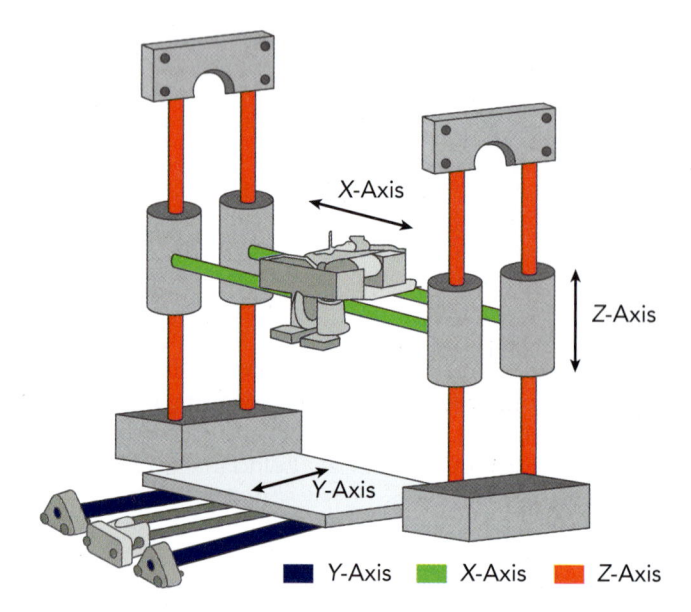

Figure 6.10: How a 3D printer works

Prosthetics

If a drawing is carried out using **computer aided design (CAD)** software, which allows the creation, modification and analysis of a design, and the cartridges are filled with the correct substances, then it is possible to print items such as prosthetic hands, arms and legs. Prosthetics can be printed for a specific surgery. This will make the prosthetic more effective than if it had been mass produced, and 3D printing will be able to respond quickly to the exact problem instead of waiting for a device to be manufactured.

KEY WORDS

bioprinting: the process of producing tissues and organs similar to natural body parts and containing living cells, using 3D printing

biomaterials: substances used to support, enhance or replace damaged tissue. They may be natural or synthetic, e.g. plastic used in contact lenses

prosthetics: an artificial body part

z-axis: the third axis in a three-dimensional graph to represent vertical coordinates

KEY WORD

computer aided design (CAD): software that allows the creation, modification and analysis of a design

6 ICT applications

Tissue engineering and artificial blood vessels

ICT IN CONTEXT

Rather than printing using plastic or metal, 3D bioprinters use a computer-guided pipette to layer living cells, referred to as **bio-ink**, on top of one another to create artificial living tissue (see Figure 6.11) in a laboratory.

These tissue constructs (or organoids) can be used for medical research as they mimic organs on a miniature scale. They are also being trialled as cheaper alternatives to human organ transplants.

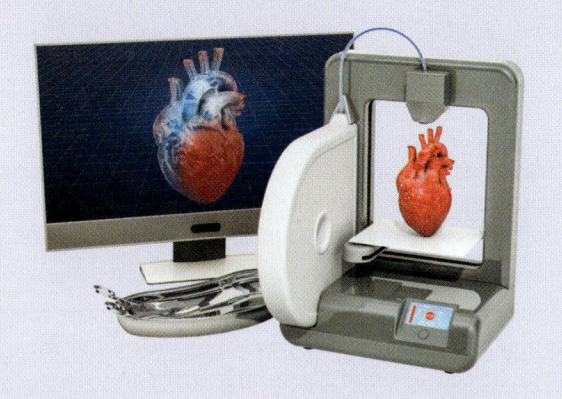

Figure 6.11: A 3D bioprinter building tissue from living cells

Different tissues can be combined to produce organs such as blood vessels. Artificial blood vessels can be produced using a 3D printer loaded with two different bio-inks – smooth muscle cells and endothelial or lining cells.

Tissue engineering is also known as bioprinting. Bioprinting works similarly to traditional 3D printing methods where a digital model will be printed layer-on-layer, until the physical object is complete.

Customised medicines

Customised or personalised medicines are tailor-made or adapted for each patient with their individual needs and characteristics. 3D printed drugs have been developed to adapt to each patient's needs and could change treatments in a radical way in the long term.

In the future, patients with multiple chronic conditions will no longer have to take numerous drugs several times a day – instead they can take one tablet containing all the required medications at the right dose thanks to 3D printing.

Questions

5   a   Describe how a 3D printer makes solid objects.

     b   Name the type of software that is used to create the designs for 3D printing.

6   Explain what is meant by bio-ink and how it is used in medicine.

6.8 Expert systems

An **expert system** is a computerised system that attempts to reproduce the decision-making process of an expert human being. It is designed to try and replicate the judgement of a human who has expert knowledge in a certain field. By doing this they can be used to replace or assist a human expert.

Expert systems gather data by asking the user questions about the problem. An initial set of questions can lead to further questions; which questions are asked depends on the user's responses. The expert system reasons what questions it needs to ask, based on the knowledge it is given. It will use the responses from the user to rule out various possibilities that will allow it to eventually reach a decision or diagnosis.

KEY WORDS

bio-ink: the material used to produce engineered (artificial) live tissue using 3D printing technology. It is usually composed only of cells, but in most cases, an additional carrier material is also added

customised medicine: (also called personalised medicine) a medicine that is specially formulated and created to meet the needs of one, unique person

expert system: a computerised system that attempts to reproduce the decision-making process of an expert human

Expert systems are made up of five parts:

1. The **user interface**: an interface that helps the user to communicate with the expert system. It takes the user's query and sends it to the inference engine. After that, it displays the results. It is an interface that helps find a way for the expert to ask questions and to get information out of the system. The user interface presents a user with questions and accepts the information that the user gives.

2. **Knowledge base**: all of the data, facts and conditions about the expert's particular subject. The knowledge base is prepared by a knowledge engineer who will be a skilled programmer.

3. A **rules base**: the set of rules and facts that must be applied to the knowledge base.

4. An **inference engine**: uses these facts and rules to apply to the knowledge base when selecting an answer to the user's query. It matches the information that the user inputs at the user interface with data held in the knowledge base to reach an appropriate response by using the inference rules

5. An **explanation system**: provides reasoning about the information in the knowledge base. It assists the user to understand the contents of the knowledge base and also the reasoning process that produced the solution to the user's question. It forms a conclusion.

> **KEY WORDS**
>
> **user interface:** the on-screen form through which the user interacts with the expert system
>
> **knowledge base:** a database of related information about a particular subject
>
> **rules base:** a set of rules that will be used to produce an output or decision by the expert system
>
> **inference engine:** the program that can apply the rules to the data in order to get sensible judgements
>
> **explanation system:** provides an explanation of the reasoning processes used to arrive at a particular decision

Expert systems use these five functional parts together in order to calculate solutions for different scenarios. For example,

- medical diagnosis
- mineral prospecting
- car engine fault diagnosis
- chess games
- financial planning
- route scheduling for delivery vehicles
- plant and animal identification.

Medical diagnosis

A medical expert system gives decision support in the form of an accurate diagnosis for the symptoms input. The system receives information (input) about the patient, usually by the patient's doctor.

A major characteristic of an expert system for medical diagnosis is that the sequence of steps used by the expert system in coming to a decision are designed to mimic steps used by a 'human doctor'.

A medical diagnosis is never a certainty and expert systems have the capability of expressing their conclusions as a probability. For example, it could decide that it is only 50% sure that it has reached the correct diagnosis.

It is generally agreed that expert system software must contain a large number of facts and rules about the disease or condition in question in order to deliver accurate answers. It has been estimated that two general internal medicine textbooks and three specialty textbooks would require two million rules.

Mineral prospecting

Another use for an expert system is in mineral prospecting. This is when different sites are tested for the probability of minerals, such as ore, being present at a site before mining starts. The expert system can collect its data from:

1. An expert.
2. Directly from sensors that are put in place at the site.
3. Images taken from satellites showing composition of the area such as hills, mountains, lakes and rivers.

Data will have to be entered into the system through the user interface. This will include:

- The types of rocks that are in the area.
- The types of minerals present in the area.
- The type of mineral required.

Using the information, the GIS builds a mathematical model (see Section 6.2) which can predict if the target mineral should be present in association with the features that have been entered. This type of model is called a 'predictive model' as it is making a prediction about the likely occurrence of a mineral.

Car engine fault diagnosis

Cars have symbols on their dashboards which light up when a sensor detects a problem with a component such as in the engine or the brakes. This is all part of the electronic management system which was discussed in Chapter 5, Section 5.1 Microprocessor-controlled devices.

When the driver takes the car to a garage it is plugged into an expert system, which will interrogate the car's electronic management system to discover the possible cause of the fault.

It may provide several suggestions that the mechanic should investigate.

The knowledge in these expert systems can be easily updated online by the vehicle manufacturer, saving time and ensuring it is up to date. It also means that the mechanics do not necessarily need all of the knowledge in the expert system so saving money and time on advanced training courses.

Chess games

A chess player can play a game of chess against the computer; this really means that they can play against an expert system. This can help chess players train without the need for another person as there will be many levels – from easy to very difficult – for the player to choose from. The system will have been made by putting information from many expert chess players into the knowledge base. Playing against the computer means that there is no time pressure to make the next chess move. On the other hand, a player may be able to cheat by using the 'undo' button to help them to try a different move.

Financial planning

Expert systems can be very useful for helping individuals and large companies with financial planning.

Information about financial situations and personal circumstances is entered via the user interface, and based on each user's answers, the expert system can suggest a financial plan and give advice on how best they can organise their investments, manage their debts or pay less taxes.

Route scheduling for delivery vehicles

This type of expert system would calculate the most efficient route for a delivery vehicle, taking into consideration the areas for delivery. The user interface would need to ask for:

- The amount of individual deliveries.
- The distance between each delivery drop-off point.
- Details of the delivery vehicle's type and speed.
- The amount of time available altogether.
- Layout of the area such as if it is hilly, so that if the system is the type that can also find the most economical route by calculating fuel economy, it can produce the choice of options between fastest route and most economical route.

Plant and animal identification

These expert systems can be used by individuals, scientists and farmers to identify plants and animals. They could help them identify harmful insects and weeds and help to prevent crop failures. If there is a plant or an animal that isn't recognised, an expert system will ask the user, in the case of an animal, how many legs it has, how long its legs are, does it eat meat or vegetation, its approximate size and colour, etc.

Questions

An expert system is specialised software that attempts to act as if it is a human expert in a particular subject or field.

7   All expert systems are made up of different parts.
   a   Name the **five** parts.
   b   Explain what is held in the knowledge base.
   c   Describe the role of the inference engine.

8   a   State what would be used as the query for a medical expert system.
   b   What would be held in the knowledge base of a chess computer?

9   Human beings who are experts sometimes forget something or make mistakes. Discuss whether expert systems can make mistakes and the type of problems that may occur.

> CAMBRIDGE IGCSE™ ICT: COURSEBOOK

> PRACTICAL TASK 6.2

You are going to use your desktop publishing software to create a three-fold brochure to give out to the class one year below yours for a presentation on expert systems.

Getting started

1. Work with another student to draw a plan on paper of what will be on every side of the three-fold brochure – what piece of information is going to go where and what information you will need to make sure it is explained properly. The outside back of the brochure will contain nothing except for your names. Make sure that you have noted your plans for:
   - fonts
   - colours
   - images
   - content, including images and text, suitable for the year group.

Practice

2. Work together to create the three-fold brochure on desktop publishing software exactly as you had planned it. For more information about creating a brochure, see Chapter 12 (Images), Chapter 13 (Layout) and Chapter 17 (Document production).

Challenge

3. Using suitable software, prepare a slide presentation describing the advantages and disadvantages of using expert systems.

   For information about creating presentations, see Chapter 19.

Peer assessment:

Ask for feedback from the class and discuss any points they make with them. Show your presentation to another two students and let them look at your brochure. Think about how you could improve the way you do this kind of task for next time.

6.9 Computers in the retail industry

In the retail industry, computers are used for **point of sale (POS)** terminals (Figure 6.12) and automatic stock up-dating.

POS terminals are set up at the exits of supermarkets to allow shoppers to pay for their goods. In many stores,

Figure 6.12: point of sale (POS) terminals

> **KEY WORD**
>
> **point of sale (POS):** the place where you pay for goods or services, e.g. a cash register

the point of sale system at the checkout is linked to the **stock control system**. This means that as soon as an item is sold the stock levels are automatically adjusted.

The stock of a business is the items that it either manufactures, sells or uses. To keep track of their stock as items are bought in, sold or used, a business needs a stock control system.

In a supermarket, the stock will include everything on the shelves and in the storerooms.

The advantages are:

- Saves money by not keeping too much stock of any item.
- Prevents fresh stock from going off before it is sold.
- Prevents running out of stock.
- Saves time by employees not having to go around checking the shelves.

When items arrive at the store, they are added to the stock levels in the stock control system, usually using a bar code scanner, and the stock level is increased. When a customer buys an item, they pay for it at the POS terminal, which tells the system that the stock level has decreased. With such a system, it is very easy for stock levels to be monitored. This enables stock to be reordered when it is running low.

This is affected by the stock control system checking if the stock level for every item is less than the minimum stock level required to be kept. The appropriate stock is then reordered from the supplier.

This system of automatically reordering as soon as the minimum reorder level is met is a real-time system (happens immediately, without any delays). However, if the manager requires to see all of the necessary orders before they are sent out, they will be collected for them to consider together and to give them approval. This collection of the information is what turns the system into a **batch process**. So this has become a batch system rather than a real-time system.

POS/EFTPOS

Electronic fund transfer (EFT) is used at checkouts in supermarkets. Although it is still possible to pay with cash, many people use a debit or credit card to pay for goods. The card is inserted into the card reader at the point of sale (POS) terminal, and the funds are then transferred electronically from the card holder's account to the supermarket's account in the same way as a worker's pay is transferred.

POS terminals allow shoppers to pay for their goods in the following way:

- The shopper presents their purchases.
- The items are scanned using a bar code reader.
- The stock file is searched for the bar code.
- When it is found:
  - The number in the stock file has one subtracted from it.
  - The number in the stock file is checked against the minimum stock level and the need to order more of this stock is added to the list to be sent to the manager at the end of the day if necessary.
  - The description and price of the article is sent to the terminal.
- The price and description are displayed on the screen.
- The price and description are printed on a till receipt.
- The price is added to the total so far.

This means that shoppers have a printed record of their purchases and are able to check for errors. The system proves to be very popular with shoppers, which pleases the management of the supermarket because more people come to shop in the store.

Electronic fund transfers point of sale (EFTPOS)

If there is a chip and PIN reader added to the POS it becomes an electronic funds transfer at the **electronic fund transfers point of sale (EFTPOS)** terminal. Not only does the system control stock levels and produce itemised receipts, but it also controls the way that payment is made. Customers are encouraged to pay

> **KEY WORDS**
>
> **stock control system:** a computerised system to automatically maintain records of stock levels. They are automatically informed of the numbers sold to customers and delivered from suppliers. They can automatically order new items when they get below a certain level
>
> **batch process:** a group of jobs executed together, either sequentially or at the same time
>
> **electronic fund transfers point of sale (EFTPOS):** a POS with a chip and PIN reader

by card because this will reduce the amount of cash being handled at the tills. Chip and PIN readers were discussed in Chapter 2, Section 2.2 Direct data entry and associated devices.

Contactless payment

Contactless payment is offered in many shops worldwide. You can pay by swiping your credit or debit card, or pay using your mobile phone, smart watch, key fob, wristband and more.

If you pay by the contactless system, there are four steps:

1. Look for the contactless payment symbol (see Figure 6.13).
2. Wait for the retailer to put the amount into the terminal.
3. Touch your card or device against the terminal.
4. Wait for the green light or beep confirming the payment is approved.

> **ACTIVITY 6.5**
>
> For contactless payments where you don't need to sign anything, or enter your PIN for verification, your purchases are limited to a set maximum amount for each transaction. This amount is known as a floor limit. Limits may vary between banks and countries.
>
> Find out what the floor limit is in the country where you live, or in a shop near to you.

Communication between supermarket and bank computers

When paying for goods at an EFTPOS in a supermarket, the customer enters the payment card into the reader and enters their PIN:

- The EFTPOS automatically or the cashier manually enters the total of the purchases made.
- Then the supermarket's computer system connects to the computer at the bank, sending a message.

Figure 6.13: Contactless payment symbols

- The bank's computer will take the account number and access the customer's account at the bank to check their balance.
- The bank's computer will automatically send a message back to the supermarket's computer to confirm that there is enough money in the customer's account to pay, or not!
- The cashier confirms the purchase amount and the bank takes the money from the customer's account and sends it to the supermarket's account.
- The customer receives a printed receipt from the cashier.

Near field communication (NFC) and payment using a smart device

Smartphones and smart watches use **near field communication (NFC)** when communicating contactlessly with the terminal. NFC uses radio waves over a very short distance, usually up to 4 cm.

Near field communication (NFC) gives a way for your smartphone to interact with something that is close by. This requires a transmitting device and another device to receive the signal. Devices that use NFC are either passive, which do not have their own power supply, or active. The passive devices, such as credit and debit cards, have a small antenna to receive radio waves from the powered terminal. An active device, such as a smartphone, can receive and send data and communicate with other active devices in the nearby area.

> **KEY WORDS**
>
> **contactless payment:** a transaction that require no physical contact between the consumer's payment device, e.g. credit card or smartphone, and the physical terminal
>
> **near field communication (NFC):** a short-range wireless method for devices to communicate with each other without needing a power supply

Internet shopping

Internet or online shopping means that you can visit web stores while sitting in front of your computer. Just about anything can be bought online. Products available include books, clothing, household appliances, toys, hardware, software, health insurance, cars and

6 ICT applications

> **PRACTICAL TASK 6.3**
>
> **Getting started**
>
> You are going to create an illustration or a flowchart of the series of communications between a supermarket's or a shop's bank and the customer's bank, shown above.
>
> 1. Work on your own to plan your illustration or flowchart, including, for an illustration the type of images you want to use.
> 2. For both the illustration or the flowchart, you should use arrows to show which way the information is passing between the supermarket's computer and the customer's bank.
> 3. Every arrow should clearly state what information is passing between the computers.
>
> **Practice**
>
> 4. Using either the word processor, desktop publishing software or a freely downloadable flowchart generator, create your illustration or flowchart as planned.
>
>   For more information, see Chapter 12 (Images) and Chapter 13 (Layout).
>
> **Challenge**
>
> 5. Carry out some research into 'Luhn's algorithm', which is a way of checking the validity of the long credit or debit card number.

> **REFLECTION**
>
> Ask yourself the following questions:
>
> 1. Did my task, when created on computer, match the plan I made?
> 2. If not, why were there differences?
> 3. How could my plan have been improved?
> 4. Did the application I used turn out to be the best software for the job?
> 5. What would I do differently another time?
> 6. Did I manage to find the necessary information for the research task easily? Overall, am I pleased with how I did my work?

batteries, and these are just some of the many millions of products that can be bought from an online store.

Advantages of internet shopping:

- There is often more choice.
- Goods are usually less expensive.
- People choose to shop online because of the convenience as you don't have to travel to the store.
- Disabled or elderly people may find it easier to use online shopping than to go to a town.
- When purchasing an item from a store, each household drives to that store separately, but delivery trucks deliver to many customers on a single route so less fuel emissions are created.
- Some retailers sell a range of goods and so it is easier to get a range of goods delivered in one delivery e.g. books, CDs and food.
- More employment for delivery drivers/delivery companies.
- No need to stand in a long line at the checkout.

- Online stores don't close.
- There is worldwide access to online goods.
- Comparison sites can be used to find the most appropriate or least expensive option for many items or services.
- Shopping sites online usually provide reviews from previous customers to assist in decision making.

Despite the convenience of online shopping, people do not always choose to use it.

Disadvantages of internet shopping:

- You cannot touch or try the merchandise.
- You cannot choose to buy goods with the longest sell-by date.
- Fear of credit or debit card information being stolen.
- Not everyone has a computer or is ICT literate enough to carry out their shopping online.
- You cannot pay with cash.
- You may have to pay extra for delivery.

Questions

10 Internet shopping has many advantages but also has disadvantages.

Give **three** advantages and three disadvantages of internet shopping.

11 When shopping in a supermarket, you put all your shopping into a shopping cart and pay at the end.
   a Define POS.
   b List the steps that occur when the shopper presents the contents of their shopping trolley to the cashier and pays.
   c List the data that is contained in a bar code.

6.10 Recognition systems

Optical mark recognition

Optical mark recognition (OMR) enables data marked by a human, such as surveys, multi-choice examination papers and school registers to be captured during a scanning process. OMR gathers data from marks on a document made by a human by detecting the difference in the reflection of light from marks such as lines or shaded areas. It does this by using a scanner and OMR software. To check OMR sheets, all you would need would be the OMR software on your desktop and an ordinary scanner.

The software will automatically interpret the scanned data and return accurate results very quickly.

Advantages:

- Very fast method of data entry as the machine can read the forms far quicker than a human.
- Much more accurate method of input than a human.

Disadvantages:

- There may be mistakes if the mark isn't dark enough, doesn't fill the required area or has gone beyond it.
- Forms may jam in the machine.
- Only suitable for questions with a definite answer. Could not read continuous text input.

Optical character recognition

Optical character recognition (OCR) scans a typewritten document and translates the images into an electronic format that the computer can understand. If you have a hard-copy of a text document you can scan it into your computer where you can use special software to turn it into text that can be used by a word processor.

OMR and OCR were also discussed in Chapter 2, Section 2 Direct data entry and associated devices.

Advantages:

- Quicker than someone entering the text manually.
- Cheaper than paying someone to do it.

Disadvantages:

- Mistakes often happen, for example, letters are not recognised.
- The documents may be torn and dirty and so difficult to read.

Automated number plate recognition systems

Automated number plate recognition (ANPR) uses infrared lighting to enable it to take images

> **KEY WORD**
>
> **automated number plate recognition system (ANPR):** a system capable of reading car number plates, with a high degree of accuracy, without human intervention

6 ICT applications

of car number plates day or night. OCR is used to read the vehicle registration numbers. The purpose of ANPR is to check number plates against databases to identify stolen cars, cars involved in crimes, cars without insurance, cars involved in terrorism and organised crime, and road offences such as speeding, etc. There are privacy issues that arise from the use of ANPR because 99% of the information collected relates to people who are not criminal suspects.

Advantages:

- Number plates can be read all day, every day.
- Vehicles can be checked and located.
- Safety can be improved by helping to catch speeding drivers.

Disadvantages:

- Extreme weather conditions can affect accuracy.
- Privacy concerns: mass surveillance is an infringement of a person's rights.

Bar codes, QR codes and RFID

Bar codes, QR codes (see Figure 6.14) and RFIDs are all ways of identifying items electronically.

Bar codes are read by devices that shine a laser at them and then read the reflection to tell how thick the lines are. Lines are taken in pairs and can represent the digits 0 to 9. They are used in many places to identify items, such as in a shop.

QR codes are used to place information onto your smartphone that will give you more information about something, such as details about a business, an item for sale, a forthcoming concert, etc. QR codes can store a lot more data than a bar code, including url links, geo coordinates and text.

Radio-frequency identification devices (RFID) are used to track stock, passports, automobiles and contactless payments. An RFID reader will take data from an RFID tag attached to an item when it is within range. An RFID device has similar uses to a bar code or the magnetic stripe on the back of a credit card in that once it is scanned it provides a unique identifier for the object it is attached to.

Figure 6.14: A typical QR code

Bar codes, QR codes and RFID were also discussed in Chapter 2, Section 2 Direct data entry and associated devices.

Advantages:

- Product details can be read very quickly.
- Can be used as part of an automatic stock control system.

Disadvantages:

- Labels may be damaged.
- Cost of equipment and staff training.

Biometric recognition

Biometrics provide strong authentication that is based on unique physical traits such as face, fingerprints, hand prints, retina or iris (eye) scans or voice, and behavioural traits such as voice patterns or handwriting and signatures.

The character being measured needs to be universal – it should be something that everyone possesses. It should also be unique, so that an individual can be definitively recognised. It should also be permanent, meaning that it should not change significantly as a person ages.

121

In order for organisations to make use of biometrics, it would be necessary for them to have:

- A suitable biometric reader or scanner.
- A data bank of the appropriate biometric of its employees or people allowed to enter.
- Software to identify the **match points** from the scanner against the biometrics in the data bank.

> **KEY WORD**
>
> **match points:** areas on a person that are compared with those on the stored data

Once an item of data is captured, such as a fingerprint, the system will try to match that data with any existing item in the database. A good example of identification biometrics is a database of fingerprints of known criminals.

Advantages of biometric systems:

- Improved security.
- Quicker authentication.
- Improved customer experience.
- Cannot be forgotten or lost like a password or swipe card.
- Reduced operational costs.

Disadvantages of biometric systems:

- Environment and usage can affect measurements.
- Systems are not 100% accurate.
- May not recognise individuals if their characteristics have changed.
- There may be 'fake positives', e.g. criminals could take impressions of a person's fingerprint to make a fake version.
- Hygiene concerns if they are contact based

Biometric authentication is discussed in Chapter 4, Section 4.2 Network issues and communication and biometric data protection is discussed in Chapter 8, Section 8.3 Security of data.

> **ACTIVITY 6.6**
>
> Carry out research on the following methods of biometric identification: fingerprint, face and iris. Create a report explaining how each is carried out and how accurate they are.

> **ICT IN CONTEXT**
>
> Dubai airport has replaced banks of security checks with a virtual aquarium (Figure 6.15).
>
> Visitors walk through admiring the virtual fish while 80 in-built cameras scan each person's face to verify their identity.
>
> **Figure 6.15:** The Dubai aquarium

6.11 Satellite systems

Satellite systems provide voice, data and broadcast services with global, coverage to mobile users as well as to fixed sites. They all depend on **satellites** in orbit around the earth and methods to communicate or receive signals from them.

> **KEY WORDS**
>
> **satellite systems:** provide voice, data and broadcast services with global, coverage to mobile users as well as to fixed sites
>
> **satellite:** an artificial body placed in orbit round the earth or moon or another planet in order to collect information or for communication

Global positioning systems and satellite navigation

Global positioning systems (GPS) uses satellites to find the precise location of things by communicating with receivers on the ground.

Wherever you are at any time, there are several GPS satellites 'visible' out of the 24 in total. They each send a signal to a GPS receiver such as your smartphone or satnav. They transmit information about the satellite position and also the current time; this information is transmitted at regular intervals and travels at the speed of light. When your receiver intercepts the signals it calculates how far away each satellite is, by calculating how long it took for the messages to arrive. Once your receiver knows how far away it is from at least three satellites, it pinpoints your position using a process called **trilateration** (Figure 6.16).

> **KEY WORDS**
>
> **global positioning systems (GPS):** a navigation system that uses satellites to locate items on the ground
>
> **trilateration:** a method of determining the relative positions of three points by treating them as the points of a triangle

All GPS devices require three satellites to accurately calculate your position but normally use between four and seven in order to get really accurate data such as altitude.

If, before you begin a journey, you program your satnav with the information of where you want to go, the satnav will calculate the quickest route to get to your destination. However, you can choose another route if you want, by inputting various waypoints that you want the route to take.

Advantages of satellite navigation:

- It helps people find their destinations.
- Helps in tracking parcels and stolen vehicles.
- Gives information on nearby shops, restaurants, petrol stations, etc.
- Can give spoken directions so that drivers do not have to take their eyes off the road.

Disadvantages of satellite navigation:

- It does not work in places where the device cannot receive signals from the satellites, e.g. in some buildings and underground.
- If a driver just follows verbal instructions they will never learn and remember the route.

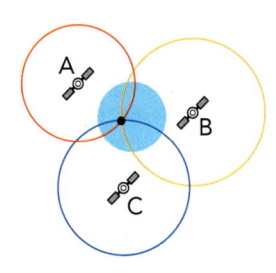

Figure 6.16: Trilateration using three satellites. Using trilateration, your GPS receiver picks up a signal from the yellow satellite, so you must be somewhere on the yellow circle; if it also picks up signals from the blue and red satellites, you must be at the black dot where the signals from the three satellites meet

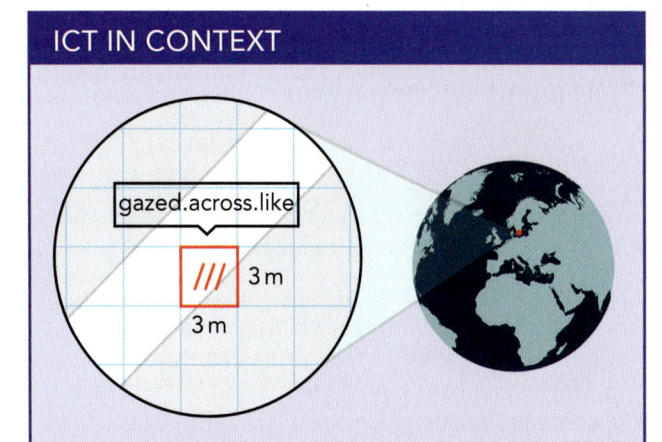

> **ICT IN CONTEXT**
>
> **Figure 6.17:** What3words
>
> When you enter an address into a satnav it converts it to specific longitude and latitude coordinates which are represented by numbers such as 51.74743863117572 and 0.45043945312500006.
>
> If you don't have an address and want to enter a location, then you have to manually enter these numbers. That is difficult and you are bound to make a mistake.

> **CAMBRIDGE IGCSE™ ICT: COURSEBOOK**

> **CONTINUED**
>
> To solve this problem a new system called 'what3words' has been devised (see Figure 6.17). It has divided the whole surface of the globe into three-metre squares and given each square a unique address made of three random words.
>
> Any location, anywhere in the world can be found to within an accuracy of three metres if you know the three words. And you can find these or plan a route to them using the app.
>
> Many emergency services around the world are using the system, especially to locate and rescue people in remote regions. Car manufacturers are also allowing the three words to be used in their satnav systems.
>
> The system is free to use if you download the app.

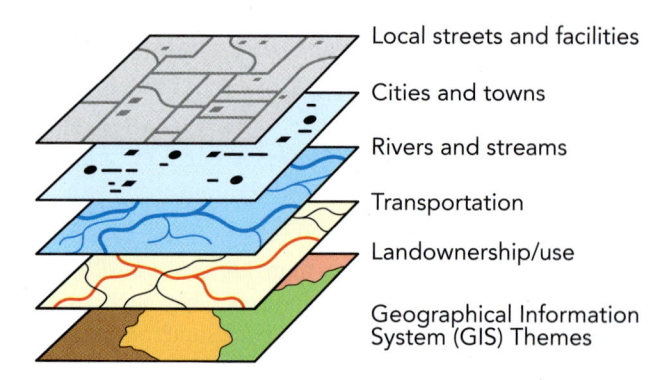

Figure 6.18: Layers of information that can be used to create a map with GIS

- Can analyse the numbers in different geographical areas and assist with forecasting which can help policy makers prepare for future developments and allocate resources appropriately.

Disadvantages of GIS:

- Expensive software is required.
- The systems require vast amounts of data.

Geographic information systems

A **geographic information system (GIS)** lets you produce maps and other graphic displays of geographic information. A GIS is a valuable tool to combine and display spatial data about a particular area.

Different layers of data can be combined or overlaid. For example, data about the population, buildings, roads and boundaries, aerial photographs and GPS coordinates can be stored in relational databases (see Chapter 18) and combined to answer specific questions. For example, a GIS can quickly identify and map all of the locations within a specified area, or all of the roads and streets that run through a territory inside a particular boundary.

Therefore, GIS gives you the power to create maps and integrate information (Figure 6.18). It can be used to visualise scenarios and help to develop effective solutions to many problems, such as pollution, or to assess community needs and resources.

Advantages of GIS:

- Can help organisations make planning decisions, e.g. where to build new offices or factories.
- Can be used to communicate data sets to the public during a pandemic such as COVID-19.

Media communication systems (satellite television and satellite phone)

Satellite television

Satellite television delivers television programs and media streaming services to viewers by relaying it to a communications satellite orbiting the earth (Figure 6.19).

> **KEY WORDS**
>
> **geographic information systems (GIS):** geographic information systems capture, store, check and display data related to the surface of the Earth as a map
>
> **satellite television:** a service that delivers television programmes to viewers by relaying them from communications satellites orbiting the earth

Users also need a set-top box to decode the signals and watch the programmes.

They are widely used in areas where there are no cables and transmitters needed for terrestrial television.

6 ICT applications

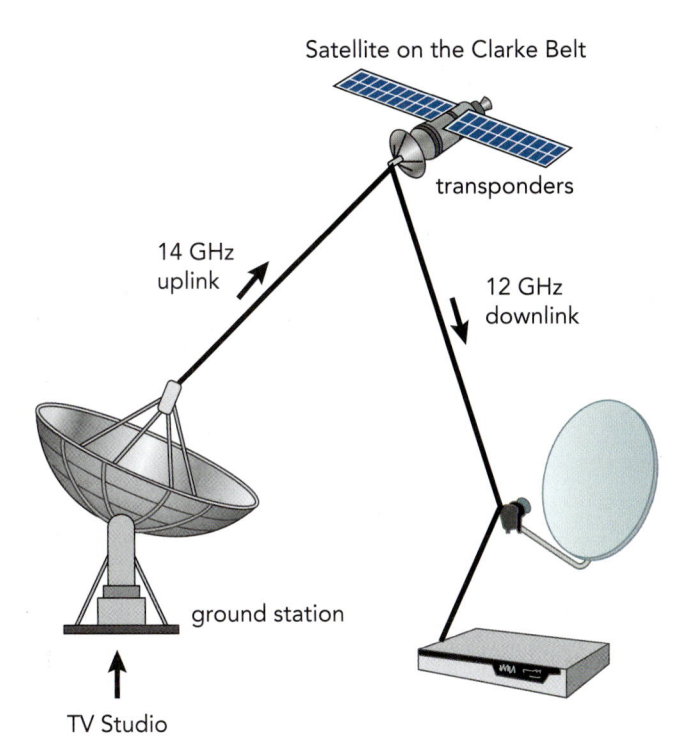

Figure 6.19: The services are transmitted from an Earth station to a satellite and the signals are then returned to Earth and are received by a satellite dish

Advantages of satellite television:
- A large amount of content is available.
- Lots of foreign stations can be viewed.
- Good for rural areas as cables are not required.

Disadvantages of satellite television:
- Need a **satellite dish**.
- The satellite dish has to be positioned correctly.

Satellite telephone

Satellite phones are mobile devices that beam their data directly to and from satellites orbiting the earth.

They do not depend on cables or the **cellular network** used by smartphones. In remote areas, where there are no cables and no cellular network coverage, people can still communicate using a satellite phone but the phones themselves and the cost of calls are far more expensive than other methods.

> **KEY WORDS**
>
> **satellite dish:** a bowl shaped aerial through which signals are transmitted to or received from a communications satellite
>
> **satellite phones:** telephones that have the ability to connect to orbiting satellites
>
> **cellular network:** a radio network distributed over land through cells where each cell includes a fixed base station

Advantages of satellite phones:
- Easy to get in touch with anyone when travelling.
- Can be used where there is no cellular signal or cables.
- Can connect to cellular and landline phones.

Disadvantages of satellite phones:
- Expensive to buy and to make calls.
- Can only work when in direct line of sight with the satellite – cannot use in covered areas or buildings.

SUMMARY

There are many different types of communication media from newsletters to e-publications.
The use of mobile communication devices can include SMS, VOIP, video calls and accessing the internet.
Computer modelling has applications for personal finance, building design, flood water management, traffic management and weather forecasting among many other ways of using modelling.
Computer-controlled systems such as robotics are in use throughout many applications such as manufacturing and autonomous vehicles.

CONTINUED

Schools use a school management system that includes managing learner registration, attendance and learner performance. Such a system includes the use of CAL (computer aided learning).
Bookings for theatre, cinemas, concerts and sports events, etc. can be made and paid for online.
There are many ICT applications used in banking. Banking can be done online; banking also allows for the use of ATMs, EFT and credit/debit card transactions.
Computers are widely used in medicine to keep patient and pharmacy records and 3D printers can create prosthetics, tissues, artificial blood vessels and customised medicines.
The different uses for expert systems include mineral prospecting, car engine fault diagnosis, medical diagnosis, chess games, financial planning, route scheduling for delivery vehicles, plant and animal identification and a wide range of other uses.
The components of an expert system include a user interface, an inference engine, a knowledge base, rules base and an explanation system that together can produce possible solutions for different scenarios.
Computers in the retail industry can automatically update stock, can allow customers to use different payment methods and can communicate directly with customers' banks to achieve verification of payment using credit or debit cards using POS/EFTPOS systems.
Recognition systems are used in biometrics, smartphone payments (NFC), RFID to track, e.g. stock, passports and automobiles. Other recognition systems include ANPR, OMR, OCR and bar codes.
Satellite systems include GPS, GIS and media communication such as satellite TV and phones.

EXAM-STYLE QUESTIONS

1 Some buildings in cold climates use central heating systems controlled by a microprocessor.
    a **Give** *two* input devices that the system may use. [2]
    b Sort the numbers of the processes into the order in which they take place: [5]

Processes	Order
If the temperature is higher than the pre-set value a signal is sent to turn the heater off.	
If the temperature is lower that the pre-set value the microprocessor sends a signal to the actuator to turn the heater on.	
The temperature is received from the sensor.	
The temperature from the sensor is compare the pre-set temperature.	
The required temperature is stored as a pre-set value.	

COMMAND WORD

give: produce an answer from a given source or recall / memory

CONTINUED

2. You are buying a train ticket online and intend to pay with a credit card. When you enter your card, it will be checked by the credit card company's computer.

   State *four* checks that will be made before the payment is authorised. [4]

3. The school newsletter is going to be put on the school's website.

   Describe the features that can be used on the website version that could not be used in the printed newsletter. The answer should be in the context of the school. [5]

4. Different types of software have different uses. State the best software type to use for each task.
   - a Model business finances. [1]
   - b Research on the internet. [1]
   - c Create a slide show. [1]
   - d Write a report. [1]
   - e Monitor pollution in the air. [1]

5. a State what sort of meeting could be held when the following devices are used together:

   keyboard, large screen, pointing device, router, network card, microphone, speakers, web cam. [1]

   b Name devices that could be used at a supermarket checkout to scan the bar codes on products. [3]

   c Give the name of the validity check carried on a product bar code. [1]

   d Describe the steps taken by the computer processor to update the stock file when an item is sold at the checkout. [6]

6. a State the name of the system that makes decisions and gives advice such as in health care. [1]

   b Other than health care, give *two* examples of different uses of an expert system. [2]

   c **Demonstrate** the use of the following in an expert system: [6]
   - i knowledge base
   - ii user interface
   - iii inference engine.

   d Give *two* advantages and *two* disadvantages of using an expert system. [4]

   [Total: 45]

COMMAND WORDS

state: express in clear terms

describe: state the points of a topic / give characteristics and main features

demonstrate: show how or give an example

6 ICT applications

SELF-EVALUATION CHECKLIST

After studying this chapter, think about how confident you are with the different topics.

This will help you to see any gaps in your knowledge and help you to learn more effectively.

You might find it helpful to rate how confident you are for each of these statements when you are revising. You should revisit any sections that you rated 'Needs more work' or 'Getting there'.

I can ...	See section	Needs more work	Getting there	Confident to move on
identify communication media and mobile communication devices and their uses	6.1			
describe computer modelling and computer-controlled systems such as robotics, and the advantages and disadvantages of their use	6.2 and 6.3			
discuss management systems for school management and computer aided learning	6.4			
describe online systems to make bookings for cinemas and concerts, etc.	6.5			
discuss different banking applications and the advantages and disadvantages of each	6.6			
describe the characteristics and uses of computers in medicine and understand the uses of expert systems for a variety of different applications.	6.7			
explain the uses of expert systems	6.8			
explain how computers work in the retail industry, the uses of different payment methods, and understand the advantages and disadvantages of internet shopping	6.9			
identify the characteristics and uses of recognition systems, including OMR, OCR, RFIDs and biometric recognition	6.10			
understand the uses, and advantages and disadvantages of satellite systems	6.11			

Chapter 7
The systems life cycle

IN THIS CHAPTER YOU WILL:

- state the stages of the systems life cycle
- explain how a current system is analysed and recorded
- create a system specification
- create designs for a new system
- create test designs and strategies for the new system
- explain how new systems can be implemented
- describe what needs to be included in technical documentation and in user documentation
- explain how new systems should be evaluated.

GETTING STARTED

The systems life cycle is a series of stages that are worked through during the development of a new IT system or the improvement of an existing one.

The stages are shown but they *are not* in the correct sequence.

These stages are:

a   system implementation

b   testing

c   analysis

d   evaluation

e   documentation

f   design.

Shown below are descriptions of the stages, which *are* in the correct order.

Match up the letters of the stages with the numbers of their descriptions.

1   Investigating how the existing system works and what the new one will need to do.

2   The overall structure of the new system, with details of the software, file system and data structures is specified.

3   These specifications are checked using sample data to ensure that they function correctly.

4   The new system is set up.

5   Instruction booklets and manuals are written to tell the users about the new system.

6   The new system is compared to what was wanted and planned for.

THE WORST AND MOST EXPENSIVE CONTRACTING FIASCO IN HISTORY

'If you fail to plan, you are planning to fail' – Benjamin Franklin

All projects to develop new or improve existing computer systems start off with good intentions. Those in favour of the new systems usually proclaim:

- It will help everyone to get their jobs done better and more efficiently.
- It will save money.
- Everyone will find it easy to use.
- People will love to work in this new high-tech way.

But are these statements true? Have the users been asked for their opinions? Without thorough research, meticulous planning and efficient management, projects can easily end in failure.

Figure 7.1: Computerising health data

> **CONTINUED**
>
> In Britain in 2002, the National Program for IT (NPfIT) in the National Health Service (NHS) was the largest public-sector IT program ever attempted in the UK with an original budget of £6 billion.
>
> It was an ambitious project to bring the NHS's use of information technology into the 21st century (see Figure 7.1), through the introduction of integrated electronic patient records systems, online 'choose and book' services, computerised referral and prescription systems, digital scanning and integrated IT systems across hospitals and community care. The project was abandoned in 2011 after numerous failures to meet targets and expectations.
>
> A report by the Public Accounts Committee (PAC) concluded the attempt to upgrade NHS computer systems in England ended up becoming one of the 'worst and most expensive contracting fiascos' in public sector history with a final cost of £12.7 billion.
>
> But what went wrong?
>
> The failure was due to a combination of errors. It was a 'top-down' project – politicians and managers raced headlong into policymaking and implementation processes with little time to consult with the people who would be using the system: the nurses, doctors and health professionals. It should have focused on meeting the specific needs of the users on the ground, a 'bottom-up' approach.
>
> The design was flawed and did not take account of local needs and how it would impact on user satisfaction. There was a lack of project management without leadership in planning and consulting the users and providing training.
>
> **Discussion questions**
>
> 1. Can you think of any other examples where IT projects have ended in failure? What caused these failures? Are there common causes for all of the failures?
>
> 2. Discuss how the stages in planning and implementing an IT project also apply to other situations such as planning a school trip.

7.1 The systems life cycle

The systems life cycle is a series of stages that are worked through during the development of a new IT system or the improvement of an existing one.

These stages are:

- analysis of the current system
- design
- testing
- system implementation
- documentation
- evaluation.

7.2 Analysis of the current system

Analysis involves investigating how the existing system works and what is required for the new system.

> **KEY WORD**
>
> **analysis:** a detailed examination of something for a specific purpose, e.g. to see how it works or to improve it

When an organisation, or a client thinks that one of its systems has problems or it needs improvement, a **systems analyst** studies the system to find out where the problems are, and how the system can be improved.

> ### ICT IN CONTEXT
>
> A systems analyst's job is not easy. Here is a list of required skills, taken from a job advert:
>
> - Broad knowledge of hardware, software and programming.
> - Teamworking skills.
> - A logical approach to problem solving.
> - Excellent analytical skills.
> - Good interpersonal and client-handling skills, with the ability to manage expectations and explain technical detail.
> - A methodical, investigative and inquisitive mind and attention to detail.
> - Presentation skills.
> - Excellent oral and written communication skills.
> - Planning and negotiating skills.
> - Initiative and self-confidence.
> - A flexible approach to work.
>
> Oh, and they should also have a working knowledge of programming using software such as SQL, Oracle or C##.
>
> Is it the job for you?

Methods of researching an existing system

The information can be collected in a number of ways:

- **Observation:** The systems analyst can learn from watching what is going on in an organisation and how tasks are completed. It could involve sitting with users and watching how they carry out their tasks or sitting separately and watching many users at the same time. The systems analyst will try to understand how things are done and the relationships between different people's work. The advantage of **observation** is that it gathers real-life details and leads to an in-depth understanding of how systems work. The disadvantage is that people tend not to work in a normal way if they know they are being watched (Figure 7.2) as they may become stressed or work more or less efficiently than normal.

Figure 7.2: Sometimes people work differently if they know they are being observed

- **Interviews:** The systems analyst will want to find out how things work and what doesn't work properly in an organisation. The obvious thing to do is to ask the people who operate the system at the moment. The advantage of using **interviews** is that it allows the systems analyst to talk to the people who are actually using the system rather than just receiving information from their managers. They can find out practical issues with the existing system and ideas of how it could be improved. Questions do not have to be fixed in advance, but it is helpful if the

> ### KEY WORDS
>
> **systems analyst:** an IT specialist responsible for the life cycle of a new/modified IT system, from analysing the problem to implementing an entire system
>
> **observation:** closely watching something
>
> **interview:** a meeting in which someone asks questions to another person

analyst has a logical, enquiring mind and knows how to get information from people. Another advantage is that follow-up questions can be asked about areas that were not identified in advance. A disadvantage is that workers may become stressed and feel that they are being interrogated. They may not give honest answers if they think they will be relayed to their managers. Also, it is a time consuming method if each person is interviewed individually.

- **Questionnaires:** With this method, many people's views can be obtained in a short period of time. They are far less time consuming than conducting individual interviews and can be completed online for convenience and it also allows for the answers to be automatically recorded and analysed by the software. Each person also has the chance to consider their answers before filling in the **questionnaire**, and the analyst and worker do not have to be available at the same time, as they would with an interview. Questionnaires can also be anonymous and so get more truthful answers. The disadvantages are that some of the people may not take it seriously and the questions can be phrased to persuade the person being asked to give a particular answer. The users' answers have to be analysed and so the questions may be simple yes/no or multiple choice ones and these may not fully reflect the views of the people answering them. It is very difficult to analyse free text answers where a person can give their honest opinion.

- **Examination of existing documents: Documents** reveal a lot about an organisation. Most processes and procedures require documents for data input and output. The analyst will be looking for answers to questions such as: How is the data collected? What data is collected? What happens to this data after it has been collected? A disadvantage of document examination is that documentation may be difficult to understand for someone who is outside the organisation, so it may be necessary to interview someone to explain it. Documents also do not always reveal all of the processes and procedures about a system and this method is never used on its own.

> **KEY WORDS**
>
> **questionnaire:** a set of questions with a choice of answers to carry out a survey
>
> **documents:** written or printed information such as a web page, presentation, spreadsheet, report or database, among others

Table 7.1 summarises the advantages and disadvantages of the different methods of analysis (see the next page).

Record and analyse information about the current system

As the current system is being investigated and analysed, characteristics of the existing system will be identified, such as:

- The data inputs and outputs of the current system. Where data is input manually or automatically.

- How the data is processed by the system. Can different parts of the processing be carried out at the same time or does it have to be sequential so that one stage must be completed before another can begin?

- Problems with the system. Where are there hold-ups and data jams? Areas where data input leads to lots of errors that have to be corrected.

As well as an analysis of the current system, the user and information requirements for the new system will become more obvious, especially if they are intended to solve the problems with the existing one.

Often the information about the current system can be displayed in a diagram that shows the passage of data through the system and the different files that are used (Figure 7.3). It should identify all of the system's inputs and outputs and how data is processed. It would also show details of the storage of files and how the files are related.

Other diagrams could be used to show the hardware involved in the system.

Method	Advantages	Disadvantages
Observation	Allows the systems analyst to gather first-hand, real-life, unbiased information.	Often people won't be working as they normally do if they know they are being watched.
Interviews	A lot of very detailed information can be gathered from people actually using the system. Follow-up questions can be asked.	Interviews take a long time so they are not possible if large groups of people are involved. People may become stressed in a face-to-face meeting and say what they think the management wants them to say.
Questionnaires	A questionnaire is a quick and simple way to gather information. Less time consuming than interviews. Can be done online and automatically marked and analysed.	Information gathered is limited by the questions asked and people may have ideas that the questionnaire doesn't ask about thus limiting usefulness. People don't always take time to fill in a questionnaire well.
Existing documents	Easy way to find comprehensive information on the system. Finds all of the inputs and outputs of the system.	Documentation is often difficult to understand for someone who is outside the organisation, so it may be necessary to interview someone to explain it. Documents do not always reveal all of the processes and procedures about a system. Only shows the data currently input and output and not what additional data is required to improve the system.

Table 7.1: Advantages and disadvantages of the different methods of analysis

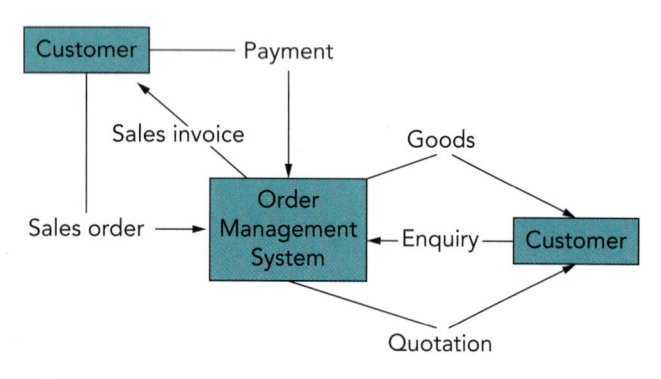

Figure 7.3: A data flow diagram showing data flow in a customer ordering system

Question

1 While investigating an existing system, observation, interviews and questionnaires can be used. Compare and contrast these **three** methods.

System specification

At the end of the analysis stage, various specifications for the new system are written.

The most obvious is a **requirements specification** which identifies such things as:

- The purpose of the system.
- Data that needs to be input and output.
- How the data needs to be processed.
- Performance indicators such as the time it should take for a user to carry out a particular task.

> **KEY WORD**
>
> **requirements specification:** a document listing all of the functions the system is expected to perform and the data flow needed

7 The systems life cycle

> **PRACTICAL TASK 7.1**
>
> **Getting started**
>
> 1 Here are two scenarios:
>
>   **a** A shoe shop wants to install a computerised stock control system. Until now, the owner has done all the ordering of new shoes at the start of each month.
>
>   **b** A shop selling musical instruments, servicing and mending them, has used a computerised system for some time for selling items and services and for giving receipts to customers. There are four people who work in the shop. Two concentrate on selling the instruments and the other two service and mend the musical instruments. The stock is ordered by the owner and he is in charge of all the record keeping and paying the wages. The owner now needs a computerised stock control system and a method of ordering so that he doesn't have to spend so much time dealing with the suppliers.
>
> Take part in a class discussion about which would be the best method for the analyst to collect information in each of the two situations given. Also discuss why the methods might differ.
>
> **Practice**
>
> 2 Design a questionnaire that could be used by the sales personnel in the music shop (in scenario **b**). You could use database or spreadsheet software to do this. For more information about using databases see Chapter 18 and for using spreadsheets see Chapter 20.
>
> **Challenge**
>
> 3 There will be differences in the forms for both the service department and for the owner's stock control system. Plan and a create suitable forms for those two departments.
>
> **Self-assessment**
>
> - Print out your form(s) and pin them to the wall.
> - Look at all of the other forms, then compare them with yours looking for ideas for possible improvements to the layouts, the wording, font size and style, any other ideas that you think may be improvements you would consider another time.

In light of the requirements, the **system specification** then identifies and justifies all of the software and hardware required for the new system. For example, it will justify the use of more powerful processors rather than cheaper, less powerful ones. Obviously, the software must be identified first so that the hardware required to run it can be identified. This will include processing power and memory requirements in addition to external hardware devices and networking components.

> **KEY WORD**
>
> **system specification:** a list of all of the software and hardware required by the new system

7.3 Design

During the **design** stage, the overall structure of the system, with details of the software, are specified without being developed.

Diagrams can be used to show the flow of data through the system.

> **KEY WORD**
>
> **design:** the process of defining the elements of a system, including software, the different interfaces, the data that goes through that system and the hardware required

The design should be detailed enough to show:

- **file/data structures**
- **input formats** including data capture forms
- **output formats** including onscreen and paper layouts
- **validation rules**.

> ### ACTIVITY 7.1
>
> When analysing and designing new systems, the analyst can take a **top-down** or a **bottom-up** strategy. Carry out research and create a document explaining the differences between these strategies.

File/data structures

A system stores and processes data, and it is vital to design how that will be done.

Data is stored in **data structures** such as files consisting of **records**. The files are stored in memory and on storage devices such as solid-state drives and how the records will be accessed must be designed.

The data stored in the records must be structured so that it can be accessed quickly, and relationships can be found between the different items.

Each record contains information about a particular **entity** – for example, if a system for running a gym is being designed, one of the identified entities would be 'member' – and the information needed to be stored about each entity must be clearly identified (e.g. member number, first name, surname, etc.). Once the information needed has been defined, the **fields** in the **table** to store this data would then be designed (see Figure 7.4).

Input formats

Input formats such as on-screen forms can be designed for users to enter and view the data.

The design shows how the fields will be arranged for data input and any sub-forms and command buttons.

> ### KEY WORDS
>
> **file/data structures:** the way in which the different data items will be stored
>
> **input format:** how data is to be entered into the system and how it will be interpreted
>
> **output format:** how the results of processing are to be presented to the users
>
> **validation rules:** routines to check that the data entered by a user or from a file meets specified requirements
>
> **top-down design:** an approach that starts with the design of complete system and then breaks it down into designs for the component parts or sub-systems
>
> **bottom-up design:** the smallest sub-systems are designed first and then combined into progressively larger units
>
> **data structure:** a way of storing and managing data
>
> **record:** consists of all the fields about an individual instance of an entity in a database, e.g. all the details about one gym member
>
> **entity:** a thing that is recognised as being capable of an independent existence, which can be uniquely identified, and about which data can be stored. It is usually a physical object (e.g. a gym member, car, person, book) or it can be a concept (e.g. a customer transaction storing details of the items that were purchased)
>
> **field:** one item of information about an entity, e.g. Pupil Number, Surname, First Name
>
> **table:** a collection of rows and columns forming cells that are used to store data in a structured and organised manner in a database
>
> **data capture form:** a document used for capturing information

The operator may enter the details directly into the on-screen form as the member tells them, and so this is the **data capture form**.

A System Table (stores the data)

Member num	First Name	Surname	DOB	Gender	Renewal Date
258	Dafydd	Owens	08 February 1997	Male	12-Mar
259	Ayesha	Chatra	30 March 1991	Female	16-Jul
260	Jill	Robertson	30 August 1956	Female	21-Nov
261	Carlos	Garcia	09 July 1978	Male	25-Feb
262	Maya	De León	25 November 1969	Female	05-Oct
263	Amelia	Thomes	15 March 1996	Female	24-Apr

Data Types (what kind of data?)

Field Name	First Name
Member Number	Number
First name	Text
Surname	Text
Date of Birth	Date/Time
Gender	Text
Renewal Date	Date/Time

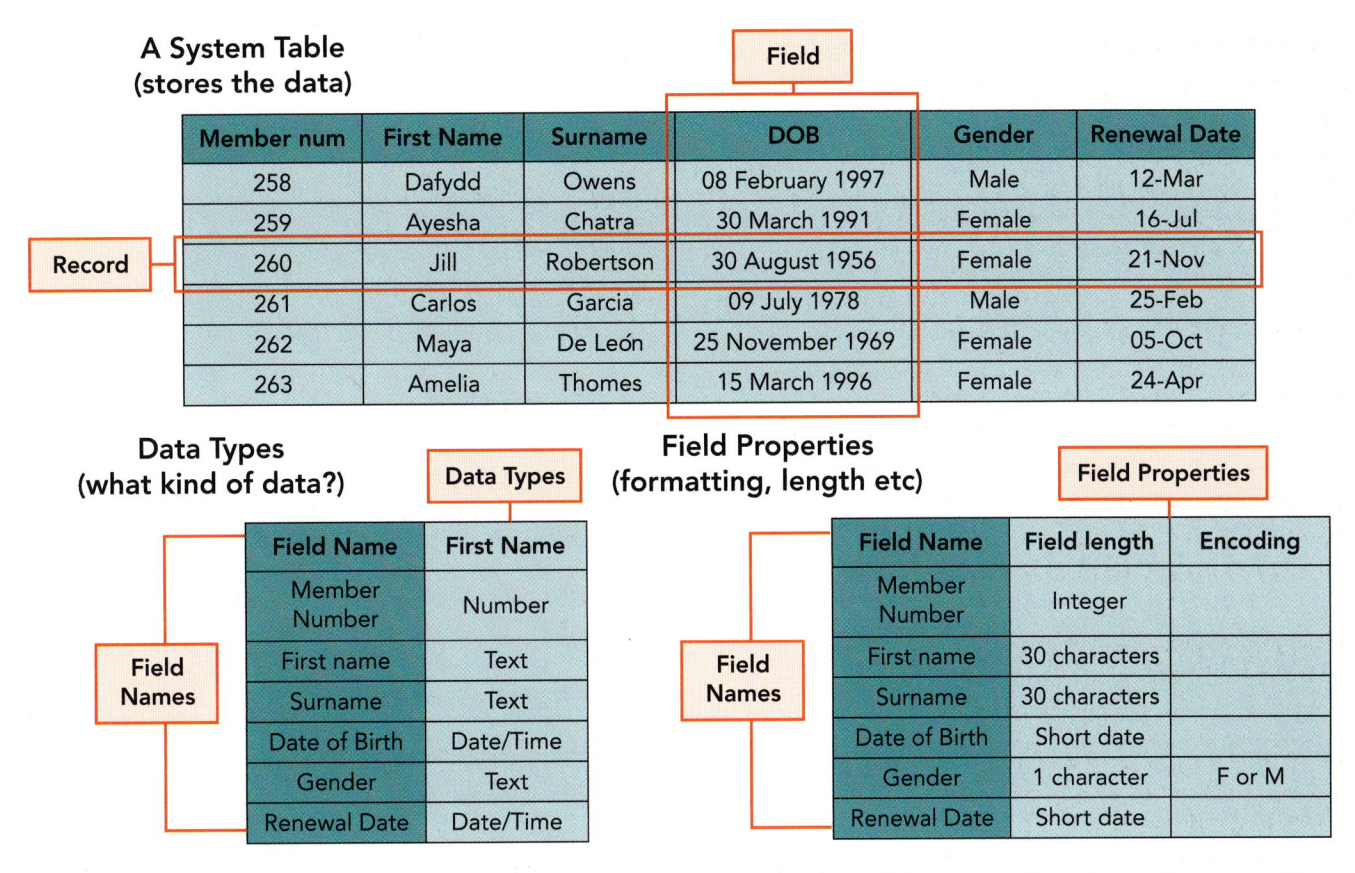

Field Properties (formatting, length etc)

Field Name	Field length	Encoding
Member Number	Integer	
First name	30 characters	
Surname	30 characters	
Date of Birth	Short date	
Gender	1 character	F or M
Renewal Date	Short date	

Figure 7.4: Example of file structure. The field names, data types, field lengths and the coding of any data such as using 'F' for female and 'M' for male have been given

In other situations, the data capture form may be a paper form that the members have to fill in, adding their names and details. The operator will then have to read these details from the data capture form and enter them into the on-screen form. This process is called **transcription** and is the source of most data errors.

KEY WORDS

transcription: the transfer of data from one medium to another, e.g. from written data on a form to digital data in a database

database queries: searches made on the data held in a database to find ones with a particular specification, e.g. to find all of the female members of a gym

Output formats

The design (Figure 7.5) and appearance (Figure 7.6) of output reports should be provided. These designs should also include any **database queries** that will be required to select the information for them.

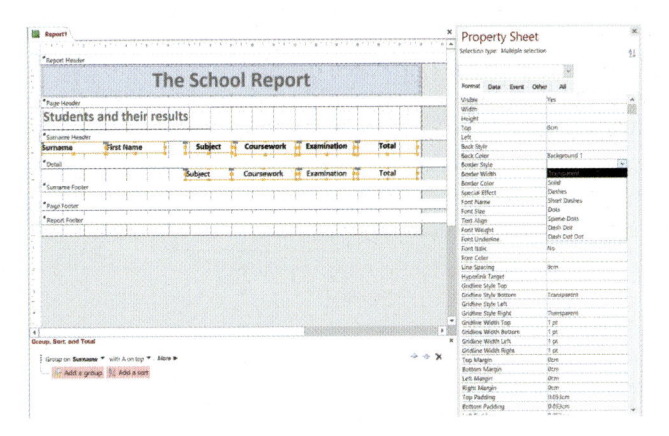

Figure 7.5: The design of the report

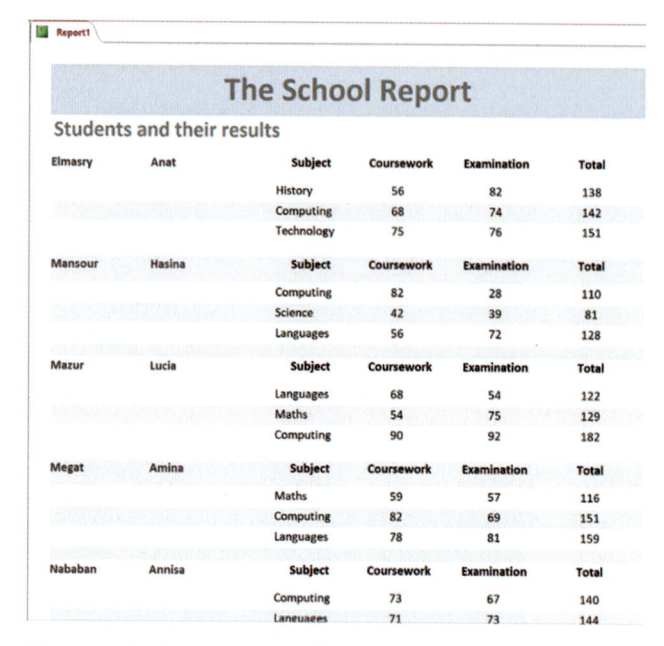

Figure 7.6: How the form will appear when printed

They should include data formats such as whether numbers are formatted as currency or how many decimal places should be shown.

Validation routines

It is important to ensure that data entered by the user is **valid**, as invalid data can cause a system to behave unexpectedly or even stop altogether. If the data entered into a system is incorrect, the output it produces will also be wrong. This is sometimes called the Garbage In, Garbage Out (GIGO) principle.

Validation routines check that the data entered by a user or from a file meets specified requirements. The routines should include error messages to help the users when they enter invalid data.

Validation can't guarantee that the data entered is correct. It can only make sure that it is reasonable. For example, if a user enters '9' into a field for the school year of a pupil, it would pass a validation check because it is a number in the correct range, but the pupil may, in fact, be in year 10 and not year 9. The validation check would not find this error.

Range check

A **range check** is used when the data must be between an upper and lower point. For example, in a school system, the range could be between 7 and 13 for a secondary school (see Table 7.2).

This should be designed into the input system.

Character check

A **character check** is used when only certain characters must be input. For example, it could be used on a gender field to ensure that only an 'F' or an 'M' is entered (see Table 7.3).

> **KEY WORDS**
>
> **valid:** data that has passed a validation test
>
> **validation routines:** routines to check that the data entered by a user or from a file meets specified requirements
>
> **range check:** a validation rule to ensure the data is between a minimum and maximum value
>
> **character check:** a validation rule to ensure that only certain characters are entered

Field Name	School Year	Explanation
Data Type	Number	
Validation Rule	>=7 AND <=13	The rule states that the entry must be greater than or equal to 7 and less than or equal to 13.
Error Message	The entered year must be between 7 and 13.	

Table 7.2: A range check for the School Year field

7 The systems life cycle

Field Name	Sex	Explanation
Data Type	Text	
Validation Rule	Like 'F' OR 'M'	The rule states that the entry must only be an F or an M character. No other character.
Error Message	You should enter an 'F' or an 'M'.	

Table 7.3: A character check on the Sex field

Length check

A **length check** is used to check the length of the entry. The characters entered could be letter, numbers or symbols.

A length check is used where a fixed length, or a maximum or minimum length is required.

For example, a length check is often used when people are creating passwords, often to ensure that they are at least eight characters in length (see Table 7.4).

Field Name	Password	Explanation
Data Type	Text	
Validation Rule	LEN('Password') >= 8	The rule states that the entry must be greater than or equal to 8 characters long. NB: LEN is short for 'length'.
Error Message	There should be a minimum of 8 characters.	

Table 7.4: A length check on the Password field

Type check

A **type check** is a simpler validation rule and will automatically be applied to database programs as the data type must be given when a table is being designed.

If the field type is number (or numeric), then text would not be accepted. An error message would inform the user and ask if they wanted to change the data type.

If the user enters a number in a text field then that would be accepted but it would be treated as text and would not be able to be used in a calculation.

Format check

The **format check** will ensure that the data is entered in a particular sequence or pattern. An **input mask** can be applied to fields to show the pattern required.

For example, the required format for entering a data could be set to:

_ _ / _ _ / _ _. The user would have to enter two numbers, a forward slash, two numbers, a forward slash and another two umbers to represent the date, e.g. 13/09/22.

Dates entered in other ways will be rejected.

Presence check

This is the most basic and obvious check. A **presence check** ensures that some data has been entered into a particular field.

When a field is being designed, you can specify that it is a 'required' field and must have some data entered. If a user leaves it blank, they will be shown an error message and not allowed to continue until data has been entered.

> **KEY WORDS**
>
> **length check:** a validation rule to ensure the number of characters entered are a certain number, greater than a minimum number or less than a maximum number
>
> **type check:** a validation rule to ensure that the correct data type has been entered
>
> **format check:** a validation rule to ensure the characters entered are in a particular order or pattern
>
> **input mask:** a string of characters that indicates the format of valid input values
>
> **presence check:** a validation rule to ensure that data is entered and that the field is not empty

Check digit

When data is being read, entered and transmitted errors may occur, especially with long lists of numbers.

To tell if an error has been made, an extra value that is calculated from the entries is sometimes added. This is known as a **check digit**.

One example is the 'modulus 11' check digit. This does a calculation on the numbers (including the check digit) and the total it finds must be divisible by 11.

> **KEY WORD**
>
> **check digit:** an extra value that is calculated from the entry made and is sometimes added to it

To create the check digit for a bank account, the system shown in Table 7.5 is used.

Whenever the account number is automatically read or entered by a human, this calculation is performed to and if the result is not divisible by 11, then it is rejected.

> **ACTIVITY 7.2**
>
> Carry out research and find different methods of validation using check digits.

1	The system creates the first seven digits.	1468970. The last digit – the check digit – hasn't been created yet.
2	Starting from the right, each number is given a weighting from 2 upwards (e.g. 2, 3, 4, 5, 6, 7, 8 in this example).	Number: 1, 4, 6, 8, 9, 7, 0 Weighting: 8, 7, 6, 5, 4, 3, 2 There is no 1 weighting as the check digit still hasn't been created yet.
3	Each digit is now multiplied by its weighting…	Number: 1, 4, 6, 8, 9, 7, 0 Weighting: 8, 7, 6, 5, 4, 3, 2 Multiplication: 8, 28, 36, 40, 36, 21, 0
4	…and the total is found.	8 + 28 + 36 + 40 + 36 + 21 + 0 = 169
5	This number is divided by 11.	169 ÷ 11 = 15 remainder 4
6	The remainder is subtracted from 11.	11 − 4 = 7
7	The result becomes the check digit.	Account number = 1468970**7** If the remainder is 10 then an **X** is used as the check digit and a **0** is used if there is no remainder.
8	We can do a quick check by weighting and multiplying as before…	Number: 1, 4, 6, 8, 9, 7, 0, 7 Weighting: 8, 7, 6, 5, 4, 3, 2, 1 Multiplication: 8, 28, 36, 40, 36, 21, 0, 7
9	And dividing the total by 11 to check that there is no remainder.	8 + 28 + 36 + 40 + 36 + 21 + 0 + 7 = 176 176 ÷ 11 = 16
10	Therefore, the number is accepted as an account number.	

Table 7.5: Calculating check digits

> **PRACTICAL TASK 7.2**
>
> **Getting started**
>
> 1. Look back at Practical task 7.1 and then work with another student.
> 2. For scenario **a**, the shoe shop, discuss:
>   - What will the inputs to the system and outputs from the system need to be?
>   - What validation routines will be necessary for the data that is going to be input?
>
> **Practice**
>
> 3. Using database software:
>   - Create an example table for your inputs.
>   - Enter the necessary validation rules decided upon in the discussion in Getting started.
>   - Enter six rows of sample data, then save your database table.
>
>   For information about using databases, see Chapter 18.
>
> **Challenge**
>
> 4. Design a report for one of the necessary outputs discussed in Getting started.

7.4 Testing

Before a system is released to the users, it should be thoroughly tested to ensure that it functions as expected. **Testing** is necessary because no team of programmers and developers are perfect, and errors are to be expected.

Test strategy

A **test strategy** is a set of guidelines explaining how the testing will be carried out. It describes the approach that the team will take during the testing that can be done during the development of the software as well as when it is completed. Test strategies include testing each module, each function and the whole system.

The solution produced will consist of separate sections such as the different tables in a database file or a discrete block of code in a program called **modules**.

As these are developed, they can be tested individually before waiting until they are all complete and any problems should be easier to fix.

Within these modules there will be individual **functions** that carry out one specific function and these too can be tested as they are written.

Final testing (or terminal testing) is carried out on the whole system once the software has been completely developed. It will ensure that all of the functions and modules work correctly together and that data flows between them without errors.

> **KEY WORDS**
>
> **testing:** checking, using sample data, that all parts of the system function as expected
>
> **test strategy:** a set of guidelines explaining how the testing will be carried out
>
> **modules:** part of a computer program that carries out a particular function of the program
>
> **functions:** a self-contained section of code, within a module, which is called by the main program to perform a particular task
>
> **final testing (or terminal testing):** tests carried out on the whole system once it has been completely developed

Test plan and test design

A *test plan* is a document that lists and describes all of the tests that will be carried out to thoroughly test the new system. It should contain tests for:

- data and file structures such as tables and fields
- input formats – so that data input forms access data in the correct tables
- output formats – so that reports submit the expected data
- validation routines.

The *test design* for each test should show details such as:

- what is being tested
- the test data that will be used
- the expected outcomes
- the actual outcomes
- space so that any *remedial actions* taken to correct errors can be described.

Normal data	Data that could be expected to be input and used in the normal working conditions of the program.
Extreme data (or boundary data)	This is data at the upper and lower limits of what should be acceptable to the system.
Abnormal data	Data that falls outside of what is acceptable. The software deals with incorrect inputs that may be entered deliberately or by mistake. It tests whether the program has suitable routines to deal with erroneous data that could cause the program to fail. For example, it could check and inform the user that inputs are outside the requested range or numbers have been entered instead of text.

Table 7.6: Some different types of test data

Test data

Test data is the data that is going to be used in each specific test. So that the system can be thoroughly tested, the types shown in Table 7.6 should be used.

> **KEY WORDS**
>
> **test plan:** a detailed and structured plan of how testing should be carried out
>
> **test design:** a detailed description of a particular task listing test data, expected results and actual results
>
> **remedial action:** steps taken to correct an error
>
> **test data:** data that will be used for testing a system
>
> **normal data:** data that would normally be expected to be entered
>
> **extreme data:** (also called boundary data) values at the minimum and maximum range of what should be accepted by the system
>
> **abnormal data:** data that should not normally be accepted by the system being tested because the values are invalid and should therefore be rejected

Example of a test plan

Table 7.8 is part of a test plan testing the input of data into a database table with the fields shown in Table 7.7.

Field	Data type	Validation rule
Student Number	Number	
First name	Text	
Surname	Text	
Gender	Text	Like 'M' or 'F'
School Year	Number	>=7 AND <=13

Table 7.7: Database table

7 The systems life cycle

Test Number	Test data	Expected result	Actual result	Remedial action	Notes
1	Enter 'Any number' into Student Number field.	Error message saying incorrect data.	Error message saying incorrect data.	None required.	Abnormal data.
2	Enter 1369 into Student Number field.	Should be accepted.	Was accepted.	None required.	Normal data.
3	Enter 'P' into Gender field.	Entry was accepted.	Error message saying only 'F' and 'M' are acceptable.	The validation rule for the gender field was checked and corrected.	Abnormal data.
4	Enter 7 into School Year field.	Should be accepted.	Was accepted.	None required.	Extreme data.
5	Enter 13 into School Year field.	Should be accepted.	Was accepted.	None required.	Extreme data.

Table 7.8: Test plan for the database table shown in Table 7.7

Live data

Finally, testing should be carried out using **live data**. This is actual, real-life data that has been used while the old system was running, instead of test data.

It may be done while the system is actually 'live' (a **live system**) and is being used with actual users.

KEY WORDS

live data: actual, real-life data that has been used while the old system was running

live system: a system that is being used in real life, not being tested

Questions

2   Define the term 'validation'.
3   There are different ways to ensure that the data entered into a field is valid. Describe the following types of validation routine:
   a   type check
   b   format check.
4   Describe the purpose of using extreme test data.

ACTIVITY 7.3

Suggest normal, extreme and abnormal data to test the validation rules for data entered into the following fields:

a   Mark out of ten for a piece of homework.
b   Exam results given in percent.

7.5 System implementation

When the system has been produced and thoroughly tested, it then has to be **implemented** into the client organisation.

If a completely new system has to be designed, doing something that was not done before, then there is no choice; the system has to be put in place and switched on.

KEY WORD

implementation: the act of starting to use a new system

However, most systems are designed to take over from an older system, so a changeover plan between the new and the old is necessary to manage the change from one system to the other. The following steps should be considered as part of this process:

- **Hardware:** The first thing to be done is to buy and install any new hardware that will be necessary for the new system. It is possible that all the old hardware will be good enough, but this is unlikely. The business may need to shut down, although it could be possible to install the new hardware while the business is normally shut (overnight or at the weekend).

- **Data files:** After the hardware has been installed, the files of data have to be loaded onto the new system from a storage device. It may be necessary to employ data entry staff temporarily in order to ensure that the data is entered properly. Note that it is important that these data files are as accurate as possible when the new system starts to work. Decisions will have to be made about how the data entry should be checked for accuracy.

- **Training:** The staff who are going to be using the new system will need to be trained in how to use it. If they are familiar with a computerised system already, then the training may not need to be very long or detailed. However, if they are not used to a computerised system, the training has to be planned. Staff could be trained by having training days where a tutor is brought in to the firm. This has big advantages: there is someone who can answer specific questions that the staff may have and the management can be sure that everyone has actually done the training. A disadvantage is that the staff are not working while the training sessions are held. Another method is to put all the lessons on the company intranet and ask each member of staff to do the training when it suits them. Advantages of this are: the firm can run normally while the staff are learning; staff can learn at their own speed; staff can skip sections they already know or can redo sections that they find difficult. A disadvantage is that the staff may have to use their own time to do the training and management could have to remind other staff to do it.

Direct changeover

Direct changeover is when the old system is shut down and the new system is started up. The old system is no longer available, so if something goes wrong it is not possible or very difficult to go back to the old system. Although this sounds like a simple method of implementation, it requires careful planning. All the files must be loaded up and ready to use; all the workers must have been properly trained and the system must have been fully tested.

An advantage of a direct changeover is that it is simple and cheap to do, but a disadvantage is that if it is not properly planned and tested, the organisation might have to shut down until all issues have been resolved.

Phased implementation

Phased implementation is a method usually used by large organisations when adopting a new system and is also referred to as 'phased adoption' or 'phased rollout'.

It can mean either implementing different parts or units of the new system gradually until it has all been replaced, or implementing it totally in different parts or sections of the organisation so that some workers will be using the old system and some the new one until eventually everyone is using it.

Advantages of a phased rollout:

- The organisation does not have to deal with all the implementation problems, for example, training and bugs in the new system, at the same time.
- Lessons learnt from early implementation make it easier to implement later stages.
- It also allows users to adjust to the new system gradually.

Disadvantages are of a phased rollout:

- It can be confusing for the users to use some parts of the old system and some of the new.
- Data produced by the old system might not be compatible with that from the new.

> **KEY WORDS**
>
> **direct changeover:** implementation where the old system is shut down and the new system is started up
>
> **phased implementation:** implementation where one part of the system is changed but the rest of the system continues to use the old methods

Pilot running

Pilot running means that the new system is trialled in just one part of the organisation and, when successful, it is rolled out to other areas. This means that the full system can be trialled in just one area and problems identified. It also means that the users involved in the pilot can train other users. It can, however, be expensive as two systems have to be running at the same time and the two systems have to be kept synchronised.

Parallel running

Parallel running means running the old system alongside the new system until it has proved to be effective and all the users are confident and have been trained in using it.

Advantages of parallel running:

- If anything goes wrong with the new system, the old system can still be used.
- The outputs from the old and new systems can be compared to check that the new system is running correctly.

Disadvantage of parallel running:

- It can be expensive as two systems have to be running at the same time and the two systems have to be kept synchronised.

> **KEY WORDS**
>
> **pilot running:** the new system is trialled in just one part of the organisation
>
> **parallel running:** implementation that involves both the old and new systems running at the same time

Table 7.9 summarises the advantages and disadvantages of the various implementation methods.

ICT IN CONTEXT

Serious problems can occur when the analysts get it wrong. In April 2018, the TSB bank (Figure 7.7) shut down its online and internet banking for one weekend to upgrade the system.

Unfortunately, when the new system was switched on many people couldn't log in and were shown inaccurate information about their deposits and withdrawals or were shown details of other peoples' accounts. Customers were locked out of their accounts for over two weeks. In July, TSB were still working on some accounts when it happened again, locking users out of their accounts once again.

Figure 7.7: TSB experienced problems after an IT upgrade

Questions

5   Name the stage of the system life cycle that applies to each action (analysis, design, testing or implementation). The first one has been done for you.

   a   Parallel running – *Implementation*.
   b   Document collection.
   c   Programmers write the software.
   d   Decide what outputs will look like.
   e   Interviews.
   f   Install new hardware.
   g   Decide what inputs will look like.
   h   Users are asked how well the new system works.
   i   Validation routines are decided on.

6   If the data required to be input to a numerical field must be a minimum of 10 and a maximum of 35, give an example of data that is 'Normal', 'Abnormal' and 'Extreme'.

7   List the actions that are carried out during the design stage of the systems life cycle.

Implementation method	Advantages	Disadvantages
Direct changeover: the old system is stopped and the new system started.	Very quick to changeover. Little time or effort.	If the new system fails, normal work will not be possible and the old system will have to be restarted.
Phased implementation: the new system will be introduced in gradual stages, slowly replacing the old system until it takes over.	Allows users to become familiar with new system in stages. Staff training can be done at each different stage.	It may be difficult to ensure that data flows correctly between the old and the new parts of the system.
Pilot running: the new system is trialled or piloted in one department of the organisation. Once the pilot system is running successfully, the new system will be implemented throughout the organisation.	Every feature in the new system can be fully trialled so if there is a problem with the new system, only one department of the organisation is affected. Staff from the trial can train other staff.	Expensive as two systems have to be running at the same time and the two systems have to be kept synchronised.
Parallel running: the new system is started and the old system runs side-by-side until there is confidence in the new one.	If there is a problem with the new system, the old system will carry on running as a backup. Outputs from both systems can be compared to ensure the new system is running correctly.	Expensive as two systems have to be running at the same time and the two systems have to be kept synchronised.

Table 7.9: Advantages and disadvantages of different implementation methods

7.6 Documentation

To use and maintain an information system, the organisation will need technical documentation to cover how every part of the system works and how to use it.

Documentation should be produced while the system is being developed. This is especially important for the technical documentation because there will almost certainly be more than one person producing the solution and each person involved needs to know what everyone else is doing.

Technical documentation

The **technical documentation** is the information about the system that a technician or future developer needs in order to understand how the system works. It is required when updating or fixing problems with the system. It will include:

- **Purpose of the system:** this is the description of the problem that the system solves.

- **Limitations of the system:** what the system will not do. It could include items from the requirements specification that have not been implemented.

- **How to install/run the system:** system managers will need to know how the system should be installed and run if it fails and has to be restarted.

- **Program flowcharts/algorithms:** these show the logical structure of the software and how they function.

> **KEY WORDS**
>
> **documentation:** official information about a system
>
> **technical documentation:** documentation that includes details about the structure of the system and details of software and hardware needed by programmers and technicians
>
> **system manager:** the person who oversees the system and is responsible for ensuring that it works correctly

- **Program language and listing:** these show the programming languages used – e.g. Python, C# – and give all of the program code. The code should have comments to explain what each function is intended to do.
- **System flowcharts:** system flowcharts show how data flows through the system and how decisions are made or functions are repeated until a condition is met.
- **List of variables used:** this will include the names of all the variables – e.g. StudentNumber, StudentName – the reason they are being used and the data type. There are two reasons for this list: to help the technician follow the program if some maintenance needs to be done, and to ensure that variables are not duplicated.

> **KEY WORDS**
>
> **programming languages:** sets of commands, instructions and the rules of how to use them, that are used to create software
>
> **program code:** the statements and commands written in a particular programming language
>
> **system flowcharts:** diagrams using symbols to display how data flows in a computer system
>
> **variable:** a section of computer memory used to store data about a particular element in a program. When writing a program, variables are given names, e.g. StudentNumber, FirstName. While a program is running the data stored in a variable can change

- **File structures:** these define the data types of all the fields in the files used by the system. They also shows the links between the files. If the system uses databases, then the database management system will have a view that shows the relationship between the tables. This information is needed in case the file structures need to be modified in the future.
- **Hardware and software requirements:** the hardware needed to run the system is listed, including estimated file sizes so that storage choices can be justified. There may be diagrams to show how the servers, peripherals, storage devices, network and user terminals are interconnected. Minimum system requirements for running the software will also be included.
- **Input format/output formats:** these describe the types of data that will be accepted by the variables and fields, e.g. numeric, text. Output formats specify how data will be output, e.g. should a number be displayed as currency and the symbol to be used in a 'price of item' field.
- **Sample/test runs:** there will be details of test and sample runs that have been made with the system and the results obtained.
- **Validation routines:** reasons for using validation were given earlier in this chapter, as were the different validation routines that can be used. Details of the different validation routines that are used to check the input data are given in this section of the technical documentation.

User documentation

User documentation is provided for the people who will use the system. Users do not need the technical details of how the system works, but they do need to know its features and functionality such as the following items, some of which are also listed in the technical documentation:

- The purpose of the system.
- Limitations of the system.
- Hardware and software requirements.
- How to install/run the system.
- Error handling – what to do if a particular error occurs and an error message is or isn't given. Lists of error messages and the relevant remedial action are often given.
- Troubleshooting guide/helpline. There should be some assistance given for minor problems that can happen with the system, otherwise every time things go wrong it will be necessary to call a technician. The trouble-shooting guide tells the user how to identify that certain things have gone wrong and what can be done about them. A helpline may also be provided that users can call. This could be by telephone or using text messages over a network.
- How to save a file.
- How to print data.
- How to add records, and edit and delete them.
- Input and output formats.

- Sample/test runs.
- Frequently asked questions (FAQs) – these list solutions to common user queries.
- Glossary of terms. A list of technical terms and their meanings.

The purpose of the system will be in terms that the user can understand and will simply state what they can use the system for. Similarly, the limitations and the hardware and software requirements will be explained in terms a layman can understand and not give all of the hardware specifications that are required by a technician. This section is about what to use the system for and how to use it. The glossary of terms is necessary for users who are not familiar with all the technical terms that the documentation may include.

> ### ACTIVITY 7.4
>
> Create some user documentation for a student using word processing software. It should include how to open the software, create a new document and how to save a document. You can add screen prints if they help.

Questions

8 Name **two** implementation methods.
9 Describe how each of the these methods is used.
10 Technical and user documentation each hold different information. Make **two** lists (one titled *Technical documentation* and one titled *User documentation*) to show which type of documentation would contain the following items:
- hardware and software requirements
- glossary of terms
- purpose of the system
- system flow charts
- details of different validation routines
- FAQs.

7.7 Evaluation

At some point after the new information system has been operating as a normal business application, it is time to review the project.

Evaluation against the original task requirements

Before the solution was produced, the systems analyst and the client organisation will have agreed a set of functions that the finished solution should do. These were listed in the requirements specification and the required software and hardware were identified in the system specification.

If the system does not satisfy these requirements, the problem may not have been solved. The solution will be considered a success if all the requirements are met and may even be considered a success if most of the requirements are met.

Limitations and improvements

As a result of the evaluation, a list of required changes will probably be built up.

Some of the changes are needed to address the **limitations** as necessary improvements to the system – a gap between the requirements specification and what has been delivered. These should be rectified in the next version of the software.

> ### KEY WORD
>
> **limitations:** restrictions that prevent something working correctly

Other changes will address improvements identified when the users were testing the system. It may include things that the developers did not think of, but which make using the system far easier such as the sequence of the fields where data has to be entered. They may not be in the order that the users would prefer. When the users' responses are analysed, these should become apparent and appropriate changes can be made.

Efficiency

The system should be evaluated on its **efficiency** – the amount of work that the users have to do to carry out their tasks successfully.

It should be the aim of new systems to improve efficiency, save time and so save money for a company. The new system would be considered a failure if more workers were required or it took them longer to complete their tasks.

Ease of use

A system should be intuitive so that data has to be entered where the users expect it to be or that clicking on a menu item will print out the expected document.

Ease of use will affect the efficiency of the system.

Appropriateness of the solution

The **appropriateness** of the solution means whether it is suitable and appropriate for solving the problem. Does it do enough to meet the specification or does it do too much?

It could also assess whether all of the views and beliefs of the organisation are met. Does it preserve all data protection rules or could users data be vulnerable to hackers?

> **KEY WORDS**
>
> **efficiency:** the amount of work that has to be done to carry out a particular task
>
> **ease of use:** how easy it is to use something to perform a task
>
> **appropriateness:** how suitable or fitting something is

> **REFLECTION**
>
> What most helped you to understand the different methods used to analyse an existing system and test a new one?

SUMMARY

Before a new system can be designed, the current system needs to be analysed.
Observation, interviews, questionnaires and the examination of documents are used to analyse existing systems.
Input designs uses validation routines to check that the input is acceptable.
Output formats describe how screen and printed reports will appear.
File and data structures must identify the items of data that will be input, processed and stored.
Test strategies specify how and when testing will take place.
Test plans list all of the tests that will be carried out.
Test designs list test data, expected and actual results for each test.
Implementation is the changeover from the old to the new system; there are different methods of implementation such as: direct changeover, phased implementation, pilot running, parallel running.
Documentation consists of technical and user guides.
Evaluation discusses how successful the new system meets the identified requirements.

EXAM-STYLE QUESTIONS

1. **Give** the stages of the system life cycle in the order they should be carried out. [3]
2. The analysis stage investigates the current system.
   a. Give *three* activities that need to be investigated. [3]
   b. Observation is one of the ways to find out about the current system. Give *one* advantage and *one* disadvantage of the observation method. [2]
   c. Other than observation, give two other methods of finding out about the current system. [2]
3. There are many different items that will need to be designed during the design stage.
   a. **Define** validation. [1]
   b. **Describe** *two* methods of verification. [4]
   c. Copy and complete the table to show *four* items that will need to be designed and give *one* example of each.

What is being designed?	Example

   [4]
4. An organisation is introducing a new computer system.
   Compare and **contrast** pilot implementation with phased implementation of the new system. [6]
5. **Explain** the difference between technical documentation and a user manual. You should give examples of what is contained in each. [8]
6. Describe *three* properties of a new system that would be considered when evaluating the system. [6]

[Total: 39]

COMMAND WORDS

give: produce an answer from a given source or recall / memory

define: give precise meaning

describe: state the points of a topic / give characteristics and main features

compare: identify / comment on similarities and / or differences

contrast: identify / comment on differences

explain: set out purposes or reasons / make the relationships between things evident / provide why and / or how and support with relevant evidence

7 The systems life cycle

SELF-EVALUATION CHECKLIST

After studying this chapter, think about how confident you are with the different topics.

This will help you to see any gaps in your knowledge and help you to learn more effectively.

You might find it helpful to rate how confident you are for each of these statements when you are revising. You sould revisit any sections that you rated 'Needs more work' or 'Getting there'.

I can ...	See section	Needs more work	Getting there	Confident to move on
state the stages of the systems life cycle	7.1			
explain how a current system is analysed and recorded	7.2			
create a system specification	7.2			
create designs for a new system	7.3			
create test designs and strategies for the new system	7.4			
explain how new systems can be implemented	7.5			
describe what needs to be included in technical documentation and in user documentation	7.6			
explain how new systems should be evaluated	7.7			

Chapter 8
Safety and security

IN THIS CHAPTER YOU WILL:

- describe common physical safety issues, what causes them and the strategies that can be used to prevent them

- evaluate how you use IT equipment and develop ways to minimise any safety risks that you find during your evaluation

- discuss the principles of a typical data protection act

- explain what is meant by personal data, why it should be kept confidential and protected and how to avoid inappropriate disclosure of personal data

- discuss eSafety strategies to minimise danger when using the internet, sending emails, using social media and playing online games

- discuss the threats to data and understand what measures should be taken to protect your data.

8 Safety and security

GETTING STARTED

The room in Figure 8.1 is full of hazards. How many can you find?

Figure 8.1: Computer room full of hazards

STAYING SAFE IN A CONNECTED WORLD

In the past, when everyone had their own, unconnected personal computer, life was pretty simple. Of course, there were hazards, computers use electricity and they were even heavier and harder to carry around back then. But security meant having a cable to fix the computer to the desk, creating a login password and never leaving your computer unattended while it was logged in. Computer theft was the stealing of actual, physical computers, not stealing all of your personal data.

Then communicating with others became the focus for research and development and local area networks (LANs) were created, allowing people to communicate and collaborate in offices and schools. But local communications were limiting and so along came the internet to link users in different parts of the globe so they could swap files and send emails to each other. Finally, the world wide web (www) became a service available on the internet and a fully connected world was born. And now, it is not just people who are connected, but even fridges, kettles and tennis rackets. It is now possible for someone at the other side of the world to log into your home network and switch your kettle on, or use it to send requests to web servers somewhere else in the world. Instead of local disk drives, we now store our data in 'the cloud'. Where that is, no-one knows. It could be a computer down the road or a large one in Iceland or even under the sea so it can keep cool.

All these aids to communication have been exploited by criminals. These are people who want to find out your personal data and use it to commit fraud or persuade you which way to vote in an election by sending you fake news. Or people who want to find out where you live and maybe meet you and take advantage of you. Or people who want to send you messages to say unkind things.

People today have to go to far greater lengths to ensure they are safe when using their connected computers, tablets and smartphone. Luckily, as criminals have got smarter, so has the security that we use to stay safe when using our devices. We just have to be careful.

> **CONTINUED**
>
> **Discussion questions**
>
> Despite the problems, we all use the internet and the world wide web. Do the benefits outweigh the problems? How would your day-to-day life be different without them?
>
> 1. How would it affect how you learn at school, do your homework and submit it to the teacher?
> 2. How would it affect your relationships with your friends and how you use your leisure time?

8.1 Physical safety issues

The use of computers comes with a number of physical safety concerns. There are hazards to the physical safety of users such as the cabling, the siting of a new printer, electrical overload or having a drink next to a computer. Most of these safety concerns are temporary and can be easily avoided.

Computers and their peripherals are electrical devices that need to be connected to each other, and this will involve some cables and an electricity supply. Add to that the possibility that several computers may be connected by cables in order to create a network, and suddenly there are a lot of wires around. Simple precautions can be taken to overcome the safety problems that this can cause.

Trailing cables

You will probably have noticed that there are usually a lot of cables attached to computers, such as power cables, network cables and ones connecting mice, keyboards and printers. When these cables need to go across the floor, there is a risk that people might trip over them.

What could happen if someone trips on a cable? There might be injury such as a broken bone or an electric shock to the person if they grab a live wire or cable. If the plug has been pulled out during the trip, there could be damage to the lead or plug, and the equipment attached to the cable may be damaged if it was pulled off a desk.

Ideally, the installation of the computers will have been well planned and the cables will all be hidden and out of the way (see Figure 8.2). In many cases this does not happen, so because of these potential risks of tripping, or of electric shocks or fires if the cable or plug is damaged, it is good safety practice to make sure that when cables need to cross a floor, they are all inside cable ducts, or under the carpet or flooring.

> **ACTIVITY 8.1**
>
> Look around your computer room to check if there are any trailing cables, or cables looped under desks where your feet may catch in them. Also look for cables that may be crossing the floor but are not protected.
>
> Draw a map of the room and mark the place if you find any and alert your teacher.

Spilling drinks

Most of the time computers and devices need to be plugged in to an electrical power source. This is why care has to be taken to avoid any risk of electrocution. If a drink spills into your computer or device you could risk it being damaged and you may be in danger of injury! You will probably have been told not to have drinks near to your computer so that you will avoid accidental damage to the device or injury to yourself (see Figure 8.3).

Liquids and electricity do not mix. A spillage could cause permanent damage to your devices and, more importantly, to yourself. As water conducts electricity, you can easily be electrocuted by spilled drinks.

Figure 8.2: Trailing cables can be tidied up to prevent them becoming a hazard

8 Safety and security

If a drink is spilled into your keyboard:

Don't panic.

- Unplug your computer immediately. (Do not wait to shut down your computer using the software.) If you unplug it quickly, you may prevent the electronics inside the computer from being damaged.
- Using a soft cloth, dry up as much of the liquid as you can.
- Pull out any other cables connected to your computer, such as USB components, cards and any other external devices.
- Hold the laptop or keyboard upside down and very gently move it from side to side to drain it. Don't shake it. A lot of the liquid should drain out.
- Leave it upside down on the desk so that the rest of the liquid can drain out.
- Wait about 24 hours then use a soft, damp cloth to clean the outside.

The best advice is the most boring: don't drink while you work at a computer or near to any devices!

Figure 8.3: Don't risk spilling a drink on your PC!

What is electrical overload?

When an extension lead has several sockets for you to plug more than one appliance into, you may find that once you have everything plugged in, together their individual currents will add up to more than the maximum current rating stated for the extension lead. This is **electrical overload**, which could cause the plug in the wall socket to overheat and cause a fire. Similarly, if electrical equipment overheats it can cause fires.

> **KEY WORD**
>
> **electrical overload:** electrical circuit overloads are when too many electrical items are plugged into one socket causing more current to be put across an electrical wire or circuit than it can handle

The danger signs are if the plugs or sockets become hot, or fuses blow unexpectedly; there may be flickering lights or burn marks on sockets or plugs.

If this happens, you should check that there isn't any loose wiring, that only one extension lead per wall socket is being used and that there isn't one extension lead plugged into another.

To avoid electrical overload and equipment overheating, you can calculate the amps being used by dividing the amount of wattage by the voltage. For example, if you have an electrical item that is rated at 1000 watts and it runs on 120 volts, when you divide it you will see that almost half of a 20 amp circuit is already being used. You can usually find the information on the bottom of the device or on a sticky label attached to its cable.

$$\frac{1000 \text{ watts}}{120 \text{ volts}} = 8.33 \text{ amps}$$

Remember that when more than one device is plugged into an extension socket, you will need to add the amps that you have calculated together (see Figure 8.4).

Don't overload and know the limit!

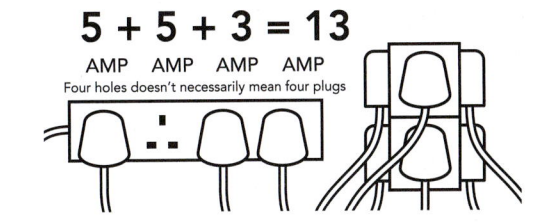

5 + 5 + 3 = 13
AMP AMP AMP AMP
Four holes doesn't necessarily mean four plugs

Figure 8.4: Think about overload

Other risks associated with computer equipment

Because computer equipment is often heavy, there is a risk of injury if you move it, or if an item of hardware falls on someone. If you get a new printer, and it

> **PRACTICAL TASK 8.1**
>
> **Getting started**
>
> 1. Discuss with two students sitting near to you what steps you can take to prevent physical danger to yourself and others when using a computer, whether at home or at school.
>
> **Practice**
>
> 2. Collaborate with others in your group to plan what guidelines need to be followed in order to keep safe when using a computer.
> 3. Plan together what guidelines should be included in a notice for the school computer rooms.
> 4. Work individually using a word processor to produce a one-page notice to pin on the computer wall, listing the guidelines. You should format your notice to look interesting so that people will read it. You may want to use a page border, consider the size of the font so it can be easily read when it is on the wall and use an eye-catching heading.
> 5. Save and print your work.
>
> **Challenge**
>
> 6. Using suitable software, create a multiple choice quiz on hazards in computer rooms. There should be at least five questions.
>
> **Peer assessment**
>
> Within the group discuss everyone's notice and make suggestions and decide which parts of each notice work well and why they work well.

needs to be connected to a computer as well as to the electricity power point, you will need to decide where to put it. Even if your new printer is Wi-Fi enabled, it will still need to plug into the electricity power point. Whichever type of printer you have, you will probably put it on a shelf near the computer, but before you put it there, ask yourself two questions:

- Is the shelf designed to carry that much weight?
- Will the printer fit properly on the shelf without it being dangerously balanced?

Devices must be placed in suitable positions. Make sure equipment is placed on tables or shelves that are strong enough for them; the position must be able to support the weight of the device and a check should be made to see if it will be large enough to support the device under each of its corners. Also, devices need to be placed where users can get at them easily. If it is a printer, you will need to add more paper regularly and to change the ink when necessary.

Question

1. a What is meant by electrical overload?
   b Give the signs to look for if you think there may be an electrical overload on a socket.

8.2 eSafety

Data protection

The huge demand for personal information to be securely gathered, processed and stored electronically has resulted in the need for **international data protection legislation**. There are many laws globally to control how

> **KEY WORD**
>
> **international data protection legislation:** laws to govern the collection and storage of personal data

personal information is handled and the rights of the **data subjects** – the people whose data is being stored. This global requirement has resulted in laws varying greatly from country to country.

The essential principles of a typical data protection act are shown in Table 8.1.

Legal responsibilities of data holders	Rights of data subjects
to process data in a fair, lawful and transparent manner	to be informed about the collection and use of their data
to ensure that data subjects give their consent – they must be asked to 'opt in' rather than 'opt out'	to access their personal data free of charge
to collect data for a specified purpose and not use it for any other purpose	to have inaccurate data corrected
to only hold as much data as is necessary	to have data deleted when it is no longer needed for the purpose for which it was collected
to ensure data is accurate and kept up-to-date	to obtain and reuse the data for their own purposes
not to keep the data longer than is necessary	to object to the processing of their data
to keep the data secure	

Table 8.1: General data protection laws – responsibilities and rights

Question

2   a   Describe **three** responsibilities of the data holder that should be in a data protection act.
    b   Describe **three** rights that should be given to the data subjects.

ACTIVITY 8.2

Carry out research to find maps showing which countries have adequate data protection laws, partial ones or no laws at all.

Personal data

Personal data is information used to identify an individual and includes identification markers such as name, address, date of birth, location, race, ethnic origin or medical data such as genetic and health data. Even personal images such as a photo of you in your school uniform or when you are caught on a CCTV camera counts as personal data.

Personal data such as this is collected every time you post an update on social media, sign up for an online account, or use a web-based email service or a search engine. These data items will probably be held by lots of different official organisations such as schools, health services and government departments, and also online shops.

KEY WORDS

data subject: the person whose personal data is being stored

personal data: data relating to a living individual; it covers any information that relates to an identifiable, living individual

ACTIVITY 8.3

In a small group, brainstorm a list of any personal data that you may have entered into a computer, including if you have used social media, games sites, shopping sites, email providers and any other web pages you have used. Then compare your list with other groups.

People should be concerned about the privacy implications of the storage and processing of their personal information and about the security of the data as weak security could result in personal information falling into the wrong hands. This makes people vulnerable to fraud and identity theft and also burglary of their homes if the address is included in the data. It can also lead to harm from predators if they know how old you are and where you live. This is discussed later in this chapter (see Section 8.3).

eSafety

eSafety basically means being safe on the internet but it can also include the safe use of technology in general. eSafety is intended to prevent online threats which include:

- bullying/cyberbullying
- inappropriate behaviour or content
- emotional abuse
- data theft.

eSafety when using the internet

When finding information using the internet, everyone uses a search engine. There are lots of different search engines and some are especially designed for children and young people so that they will not be exposed to inappropriate content. Young people should be encouraged to use age-appropriate search engines to stay safe.

> **ACTIVITY 8.4**
>
> Carry out research and list the names of five search engines designed especially for children and young people.

Young people should also be encouraged to only visit websites recommended by their teachers and parents to minimise the potential danger.

In addition to using safe search engines, software can be used to limit and screen web access.

If a young person comes across inappropriate content, they should simply shut down the computer without clicking on anything else and inform an adult.

eSafety using email

The following points outline the ways to be careful when using email.

- Always be careful when opening emails from senders you do not know. Never click on a link in an email if possible, unless you are expecting the email (such as resetting a password) or you know both the sender and that the link is safe (sometimes our friends can send on **malware** without knowing they have done so, so make sure you know that your friend did send that link). Never open attachments from senders who you do not know as they may install malware onto your computer.

- If you receive an email from a company that you do know, always go to the website by typing the address directly into your web browser, rather than clicking on a link in an email. This is because sometimes criminals will make a copy of a website to trick you into entering your login details so that they can steal them.

- If you receive an email, always check the actual address of the sender by viewing the details of the email header. Sometimes criminals will try to trick you by setting the visible name of the sender to be something familiar.

- Never send any payment information, such as your credit card number, in an email. Email isn't always secure for its entire journey from the sender to the receiver and your details may be intercepted.

- Always be careful when sending identifiable personal data or images in an email. Treat this as publishing that data or image. If you wouldn't be happy to put it in a newspaper, then don't send it in an email. Data that could be used to identify you could be used by people to locate you.

> **KEY WORDS**
>
> **eSafety:** being safe on the internet but it can also include the safe use of technology in general
>
> **malware:** software designed to gain unauthorised access to a computer system in order to disrupt its functioning or collect information without the user's knowledge

> **REFLECTION**
>
> Think about your approach to using the internet and email. Reflect upon how you use the internet and how you use email.

8 Safety and security

> ## PRACTICAL TASK 8.2
>
> ### Getting started
>
> 1 Using word processing software, enter the following headings in a document and save the file.
>
> - Do I regularly change my password?
> - Have I shared my password with anyone?
> - Do I always log out or sign off from my account when I have finished using email?
> - Have I ever forwarded chain emails?
> - Do I regularly make sure my antivirus software up to date?
>
> 2 Consider each of the points above and note your answers.
>
> ### Practice
>
> 3 Use the document as a questionnaire and find and record the yes/no responses of the other members of your class.
>
> 4 Using spreadsheet software create charts to illustrate the results of your survey.
>
> Help with creating charts can be found in Chapter 16.
>
> ### Challenge
>
> 5 Go to your email software's security and privacy settings and alter them appropriately.

eSafety using social media

There are many different **social networking sites** where you can share information with others and make comments, including sites specifically for sharing photographs. There is nothing wrong with social networks themselves, but if they are not used carefully, some very serious problems may occur.

> **KEY WORD**
>
> **social networking sites:** types of websites or services that allow you to interact with friends and family online and to find other people online who have similar interests or hobbies

Problems that may arise include:

- Cyberbullying could occur when people have access to an individual on a social networking site.
- Because it is easy to contact others using social network sites, some people may try to exploit or abuse others, in particular young people, especially where it is difficult for a young person to know with whom they are interacting.
- Catfishing is a kind of online deception where a person creates a fake persona on social networks called a 'sock puppet' for the purpose of luring someone into a relationship in order to get money, gifts, or attention.
- Some people use social networking sites to slander (make a false statement about) other people that could damage their reputation. If someone makes an abusive comment about another person, and it is shared by others, it will not be possible to remove that comment from everywhere that it might be seen.
- When people start using a social networking site, it is usual to create a personal profile. If this can be accessed by the public, rather than being restricted to your friends, their personal details could be stolen.
- People using social networks may not be aware that the sites can be searched. Nowadays employers may look on these sites to assess people applying for a

job with them. Sometimes, inappropriate discussions or behaviour can influence employers against employing you, even if they are not recent. The data trail you leave is called your digital footprint and is a public record of:

- What you said.
- What was said about you.
- What you liked, retweeted or shared.
- Where you are or have been.

You can manage your privacy settings on social network sites; most of them also have an option to report abusive users.

Before disclosing your personal data (such as name, address, the name of your school or an image of yourself in school uniform) ask yourself these questions:

- Who is collecting this information?
- Why is it necessary?
- What will be done with it?
- What will the outcome be for me?

> **ICT IN CONTEXT**
>
> When you apply to go to a university or for a job at a large company, the recruiter may look at your social media presence to get more information about you.
>
> It is important therefore to take care of what you say, how you say it and what pictures you post. Just deleting a post will not be enough because your friends may still have it on their page! Ask your friends to be careful what they post about themselves and about you, and to never post a picture of you without checking with you first.

To minimise possible dangers that you might encounter when using social media or networking sites, blogging sites, instant messaging or game sites, you should take precautions and follow rules:

- All social media sites allow users to block and report unwanted users. All users should read the security details published by social media sites before they start using them.
- Users should always be aware of the potential dangers of meeting an online contact face to face. Users never know the true identity, age and gender of the user who has contacted them, they only know what they claim to be online. Meetings have led to some dangerous situations. If a user receives a request, they should decline it and tell their parents or carers that they have been approached.
- Users should avoid distributing inappropriate images. These could be ones of other people or images they have been asked to take of themselves and send to an online contact. The images could be sent to other people and will remain part of your digital footprint for others to see and maybe misuse.
- Users should be careful of the language they use. It should always be appropriate and respectful of other people. They should never send hateful messages or criticise others even if they think they are anonymous or use social media to make complaints or vent their frustrations in strong language containing inappropriate words. Again, this could have consequences in the future.
- Users should respect the confidentiality of other users. If another user has told them a piece of information or sent an image just for them personally, they should never disclose it to other users.

> **ACTIVITY 8.5**
>
> Carry out research to find how to block and report unwanted users on social media sites such as Facebook, Twitter and any others that you may use.

Playing games on the internet

Current technologies and high-speed internet connections have made it possible for online gaming to become very popular. Because of this, large amounts of time and money are being invested in very complex games. This has resulted in some people seeing an opportunity to cause trouble, and to make illegal profit.

It is therefore important to understand the technological and social risks of online games.

You can play online games with people from all over the world. When you play these games, you may be playing with people you know and also with people you don't know. Online gaming is a good way to make new friends with the same interests as you, but you need to know how to keep yourself safe.

Tips for playing online games safely

- Some people can become nasty when they are playing online games because they want to win. Make sure that when you play online games, you treat the other players with respect, and don't do anything that you know is wrong to get cheats or tips.

- Because some people you could meet online may not be who they say they are, it is always a good idea not to use your real name when you are gaming. Use a screenname instead.

- Just as when you are using social media sites, never give out personal information or agree to meet another player face to face. Users are charged by the providers for buying materials, weapons or even extra lives but other players often develop successful characters in the games and offer to sell them to other people. As these are not officials of the company, you should never disclose any financial data such as bank or credit card information.

Question

3 Describe what steps you could take to keep safe when playing online games.

8.3 Security of data

Security of data is about keeping data safe and unchanged by restricting access to it – this reduces the chances of it being damaged maliciously. Security of data is also concerned with the recovery of data if it has been damaged. In this section, we will consider the different ways in which data could be compromised (it's no longer private) and ways of keeping it as safe as possible (see Figure 8.5).

You should be aware of what information you have online that needs protection: your **information assets**.

Figure 8.5: Keep your personal data safe from threats

KEY WORD

information assets: valuable data that you wouldn't want to be stolen or corrupted

ACTIVITY 8.6

Create a list, either in a spreadsheet or on paper, of the different types of information you store on your computer or online. For example, you may have personal correspondence, photographs, work documents, study materials, images, banking details, music, personal details and all of your passwords for online services.

For each type of information, think of its value to you in terms of the cost of replacing it in time and effort or your reputation if it was disclosed to others. Label the most valuable types of information as 'High', the least valuable as 'Low' and those that are in between as 'Medium'.

ICT IN CONTEXT

A Cybersecurity poll in 2018 found that 59% of people use the same password for everything on the internet. It is like having one key to unlock everything. If someone found or stole the key, they would have access to a person's house, car, office, safe, cabinets, etc. Having the same password poses the same risks and is an ongoing cause of hacking and data breaches.

Threats to data

Identity theft is a type of fraud (criminal trick) where personal information is stolen and used to impersonate that person. This isn't a new problem because in the past, postal deliveries were intercepted to find out names, addresses and bank account details. The person committing the fraud could then open a credit card account, for instance, or apply for a loan in the victim's name. Pretending to be someone you're not based on another person's details is identity theft.

Now, in the online world, we have malware, which is software that has been designed to find personal information on a computer and botnets are created using malware for sending **spam** emails (discussed in Chapter 10, Section 10.1 Communication with other ICT users using email) or flooding a website with so many requests for content that the server cannot cope. **Hacking** is also a way of obtaining personal information: large retailers have been hacked and millions of personal records have been stolen. Online identity theft is a growing threat.

> ### KEY WORDS
>
> **identity theft:** a type of fraud where personal information is stolen and used to impersonate that person
>
> **spam:** junk email that involves nearly identical email messages being sent to lots of people. Usually sent to try and persuade you to buy something
>
> **hacking:** the gaining of unauthorised access to data in a system or computer

> ### ACTIVITY 8.7
>
> Investigate how to recognise a spam email, and find out how to report them in your country. Use the word processor to record your findings.

What is hacking?

Hacking is malicious (intending to do harm) damage caused by people who get unauthorised access to computer systems. People who do this are called hackers.

Hackers have different reasons for doing what they do: some of them gain access just to prove that a system is vulnerable; other hackers may alter or destroy the data for malicious reasons. It is most likely that they are breaking in to steal some of the data so they can make money. For example, if a hacker gets into your computer and steals any financial information you have there, such as your credit card number, or the password to your bank account, they could use that to spend your money.

What effects does hacking have?

You could lose all your data as a result of hacking because hackers often delete or change files; for businesses, they may steal or delete customer or order information, or leak top secret information that could cause huge real-world security problems.

Another effect is reduced privacy. When hackers gain access to a computer, they can see everything. Since much of the personal, professional and financial areas of people's lives are now kept online, the risk is in losing more than money or information. A hacker with access to your email or your social networking account and personal photos can very quickly destroy your privacy.

If a lot of information about you is stolen, a hacker could use this to impersonate you online.

They might apply for credit cards, buy a car or apply for a loan in your name!

If they did, this would be called 'identity theft' (see earlier in this section).

Protection against hacking

Hackers have to gain access to your computer. If it isn't connected to a network, then it must never be left logged in and unattended for anyone walking past to access.

If it is connected to a network, e.g. the internet, then the hackers will need login and password details. They can obtain them in a variety of ways such as phishing, pharming, smishing, vishing and using malware that are explained below, with methods to safeguard against them.

In addition, users should ensure that they have firewall protection and can encrypt sensitive data. Both of these are explained later in the chapter.

Phishing

This is when fraudsters send emails claiming to be from a bank or building society e-commerce site in order to find out your personal and financial details.

8 Safety and security

Phishing emails can be prevented by recognising them:

- Urgency: they want you to respond quickly, without thinking.
- Careless use of language: they sometimes contain spelling errors and a careless writing style.
- Impersonal: you may not be addressed personally but only as 'Dear customer', although as the criminals become more sophisticated they are able to find your personal details from various sources such as social networking sites.
- False links: you are asked to click on a link that leads to a website controlled by the criminals.
- Attachments: sometimes you are asked to open programs or documents sent with the email; these attachments may contain **spyware**.
- If there are any attachments in an email from an unknown sender, do not open them as they may contain malware.
- Does the email ask you for personal information? If it does, do not reply.

Pharming

Pharming is similar to phishing, but a phishing attack tries to redirect you to a bogus (fake) site even when you have typed the correct web address. This is often applied to the websites of banks or e-commerce sites. Phishing needs you to click on a link to take you to a fake site.

In a pharming attack, a hacker can install some malicious code on a computer or server that will redirect you to a different, fake site, where you may be tricked into providing personal information such as a bank account number or a password. This information is then accessed by the hacker.

Pharming is caused by malware and the precautions to take against malware should be followed (see the Chapter 4, Section 4.2 Network issues and communication for more information on how to do this).

Vishing and smishing

Vishing is a combination of 'voice' and 'phishing'. It is when fraudsters obtain personal details of a victim through making phone calls or leaving messages supposedly from a reputable company, even their own bank. They persuade people to reveal personal information such as bank details and credit card numbers.

When receiving telephone calls or messages, you should be highly suspicious if they ask you to provide credit card or bank numbers or any PINs. Never disclose any as banks will never ask for them over the phone. If you are worried about any phone calls, hang up and call that company back using a number that you know to be real.

Smishing is a bit like phishing, but it uses text messages to hoax consumers. The text message will probably have a URL or a telephone number. They may, for instance, tell you that there is a problem with your bank account and that they need to check the information with you.

Do not respond to text messages from unknown senders, especially if they are asking for personal information. Delete any text messages you are suspicious of.

KEY WORDS

phishing: a criminal activity trying to find sensitive information, such as passwords or banking details, by fraudulent means

spyware: malware that is designed to be installed secretly on a computer. It records private information as the user enters it and transmits it to the installer

pharming: when a hacker installs a malicious program on a computer or a server. This program code causes any clicks that you make on a website to be redirected to another website without you knowing

vishing: a combination of 'voice' and phishing, it is when fraudsters obtain personal details of a victim through their landline telephone

smishing: uses mobile phone text messages to lure people into returning their call or to click on a link in the text message

Computer viruses and malware

Computer viruses and other malware (see Figure 8.6) pose severe threats to data security and preventative action should be taken. Types of malware include viruses, worms, Trojan (or Trojan horse), spyware and adware. To avoid infecting your computer, take the precautions discussed earlier in the chapter when opening your email and make sure you're certain of

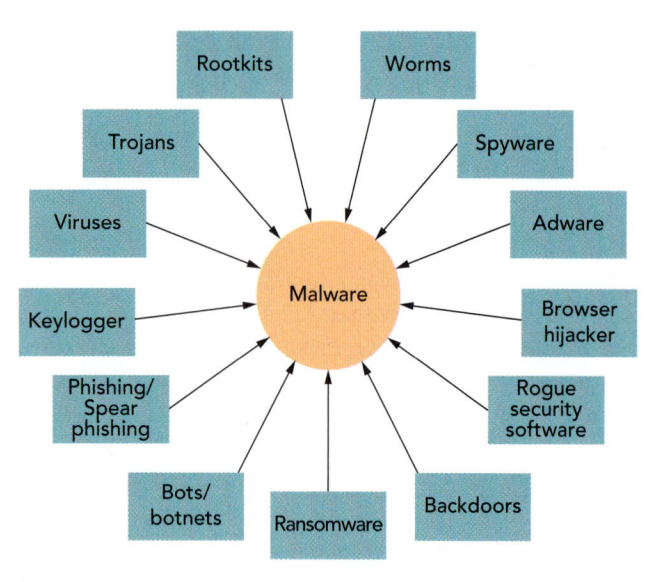

Figure 8.6: Malware

any links you click on. It is also recommended that you have some form of anti-malware software installed on your system. Full details of both the malware and anti-malware software are given in Chapter 4, Section 4.2 Network issues and communication.

> **ACTIVITY 8.8**
>
> Find out how many new viruses are created each year and compare this with how often your antivirus software is updated. Discuss your conclusions in small groups.

Card fraud

Credit card fraud is a broad term used to describe theft or fraud that is committed using a payment card, such as a credit card or a debit card. The purpose of credit card fraud will probably be to obtain goods without paying, or to steal funds from an account.

As well as hacking using methods already mentioned to obtain card details, the following are also used: shoulder surfing (or 'shouldering'), card cloning and key logging.

Shoulder surfing

This involves finding login names, passwords, credit card and PIN numbers by direct observation.

- Someone in an office could watch others entering passwords.
- Someone in the queue behind could watch a person enter their PIN number at a cash machine (ATM).
- An employee at a shop or petrol station could watch PIN numbers being entered.

Criminals often use binoculars or closed-circuit television to watch from a distance or record users entering sensitive information.

To prevent **shoulder surfing**, users should shield the keypad from view by using their body or cupping their hand over it. When working on a laptop, their back should be to a wall with no open sides. Extra care should be taken when entering a password.

Card cloning

Cloning or 'skimming' is the copying of stolen credit or debit card information to a new card. An electronic device or software can be used to capture the information at a terminal, then transfer it to a new card.

An employee in a shop or petrol station could use a portable reader to scan the card prior to inserting it into a credit card terminal and then record it onto new cards.

Customers should carefully observe shop employees when they have access to their cards, or never hand them over and enter them into the terminals themselves.

Key logging

Key logger is short for 'keystroke logger'. They belong to a class of malware known as spyware as they can discover a user's passwords and credit card PINs as they type them in. They are a type of monitoring software as

> **KEY WORDS**
>
> **credit card fraud:** theft or fraud that is committed using a payment card, such as a credit card or a debit card
>
> **shoulder surfing:** finding login names, passwords, credit card and PIN numbers by standing next to someone and watching as they enter them
>
> **cloning:** making an exact copy of something
>
> **key logger:** short for 'keystroke logger'; type of malware that records individual key strokes that are pressed on a computer's keyboard

they record the individual keys pressed on a computer's keyboard. This is done without the user's knowledge. A record of all the keys is kept in a log. The logs can be saved to a local file or sent over the network to another computer or person. They may be transmitted in Trojans, infected files, instant messages or by visiting an infected website. Hackers review these logs for repeated patterns, which could be your passwords.

As they are malware, the precautions mentioned in Chapter 4, Section 4.2 Network issues and communication should be followed.

Protection of data

Biometrics

Biometrics can be used in the protection of data. It uses technologies that analyse unique personal characteristics as a form of identification so that data can be protected by preventing unauthorised people from accessing it. Biometrics and details of this are given in Chapters 4, Section 4.2 Network issues and communication and 6, Section 6.10 Recognition systems.

It includes:

- Physiological biometric data such as fingerprints, eye retinas and irises, voice and facial patterns, and hand measurements.
- Behavioural biometrics, which include signatures, handwriting analysis and voice pattern recognition.

Encryption

When data is saved to a storage device attached to a computer or transmitted to the cloud, in an email or to a website, it is vulnerable to being stolen or intercepted by a third party. To prevent them from being able to read this information, it should be **encrypted. Encryption** means that the data will be scrambled into a form that cannot be understood by unauthorised recipients

In order to encrypt the data it must be changed in some way. There are lots of algorithms or methods of encrypting data and these different methods are called **ciphers**.

If you wanted to pass a message to a friend at the other end of the row, and not let anyone else read it, you could use a very simple cipher, first used by Julius Caesar. This method replaces each **plaintext** letter with another plaintext letter. But which ones?

The way in which they are replaced is called the **key**. This is the piece of information that is needed to use the cipher. The key does not have to be fixed. It could be changed each time the cipher is used.

For example, the key could be 'right three'. Each letter would be replaced with a letter three places to the right, e.g. A would become D; D would become G; X would become A, Y would become B and Z would be C.

> **KEY WORDS**
>
> **encrypted:** data that has been scrambled into a form that cannot be understood
>
> **encryption:** the process of turning information (e.g. a message) into a form that only the intended recipient can decrypt and read
>
> **cipher:** a method of encrypting data
>
> **plaintext:** the text that is to be encrypted
>
> **key:** a piece of information that is used for encrypting and decrypting data
>
> **ciphertext:** the encrypted plaintext
>
> **decrypt:** changing the ciphertext back into plaintext
>
> **symmetric encryption:** the same key is used for encryption and decryption

Therefore 'HELLO' would be encrypted to 'KHOOR'.

'Hello' is the plaintext and 'KHOOR' is the **ciphertext**.

Your friend could then **decrypt** the message back into plain text (see Figure 8.7 on the next page). No one else in the row would be able to read it.

As the message is encrypted and decrypted with the same key, it is called **symmetric encryption**.

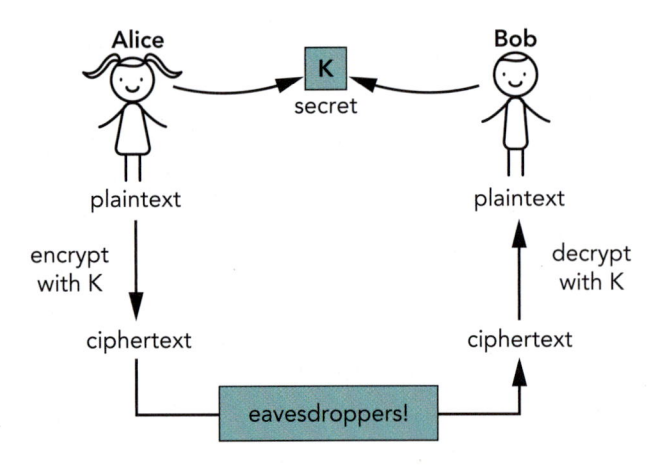

Figure 8.7: Symmetric encryption

In a similar way, data can be encrypted when it is being saved on storage device, e.g. disk drive or USB device. This method encrypts and decrypts a message using the same key. Both ends of the transmission must know the exact same shared key.

But there is a problem. How do you let your friend know what the key is? You could shout it to them, but others would hear. You could write it down and pass it along the row, but then others could read it.

So symmetric encryption has a problem if you want to use it to encrypt messages sent to other people. It's fine if you are only using it yourself to encrypt and decrypt stored data.

Sending encrypted data from computers through the internet faces the same problem. How can you keep the key secret?

The answer is to use **asymmetric encryption**. Obviously asymmetric encryption uses two keys – one to encrypt the message and one to decrypt it.

These are called the **public key** and the **private key**.

Now if you want to send a message to your friend you would have to ask her for her public key, and it doesn't matter who hears it. It is meant to be public. So, you now encrypt the message using her public key, pass the note along the row and then your friend can decrypt it with her private key that only she knows (see Figure 8.8 on the next page).

- This method encrypts and decrypts data using two different keys. Every user has two keys: a public key, known to everyone; and a private key, known only to themselves. A message sent to someone is encrypted with their particular public key. This can only be decrypted by the corresponding private key.

- This type is also used when you want to send encrypted messages across the internet in emails and also when you want to send your credit card and other details to a secure website using HTTPS which stands for HyperText Transfer Protocol Secure and encrypts all transmissions between the website and your computer.

A client computer is one that connects to and accesses a server. When it wants to communicate with a server using the HTTPS protocol, its browser sends a request to the web server and the web server replies, sending its public key.

- The client computer then generates and sends an encryption key to the server using the server's public key and it decodes it using its private key (asymmetric encryption).

- The client and server then use the same key (symmetric encryption) for sending data such as financial and personal details.

- But there is still a security problem. How does the client know that the public key that has been sent is from is from the correct server? A hacker could have hijacked the request and sent their public key instead and you will be sending them your details.

- The answer to that is the use of digital certificates.

KEY WORDS

asymmetric encryption: a method of encryption that uses two different keys

public key: a key that is freely available and is used to encrypt a message

private key: a key that is known only to the person to decrypt messages encrypted by their public key

8 Safety and security

Public Key Encryption

Step 1: Give your public key to sender

Step 2: Sender uses your public key to encrypt the plain feed

plain text → encryption → ciphertext

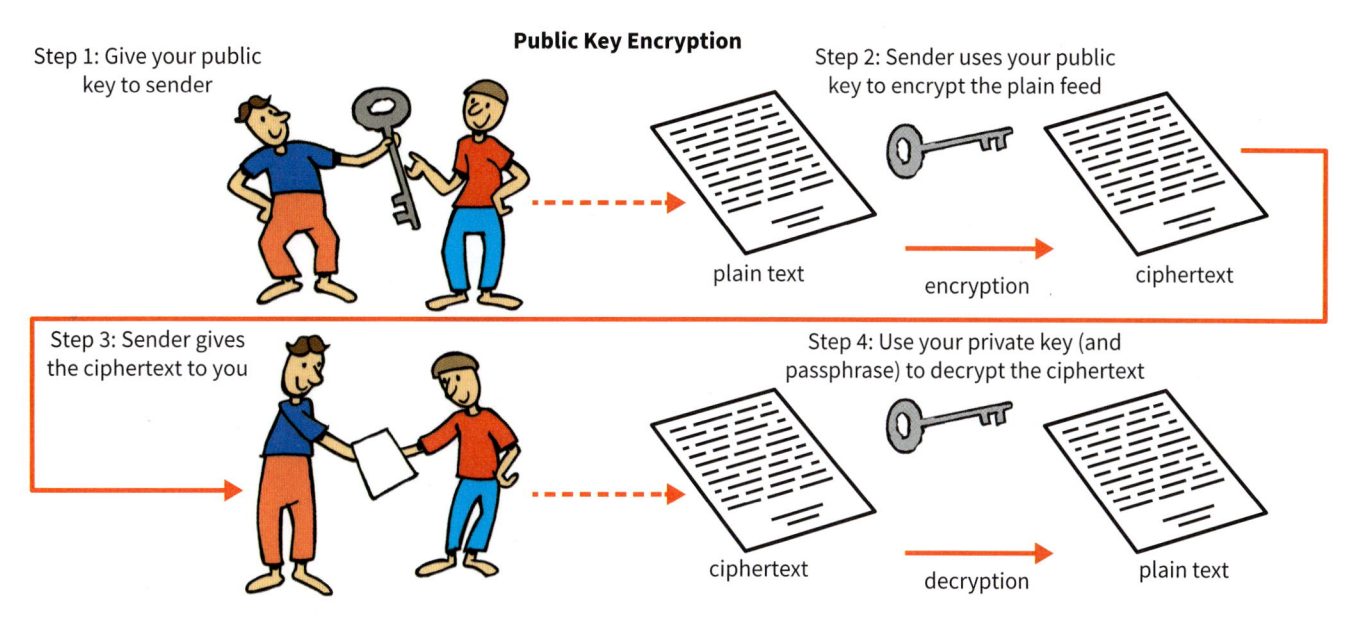

Step 3: Sender gives the ciphertext to you

Step 4: Use your private key (and passphrase) to decrypt the ciphertext

ciphertext → decryption → plain text

Figure 8.8: Asymmetric encryption

Digital certificates

A **digital certificate** is a digital form of identification, like a passport, used to authenticate the web credentials of the sender and lets the recipient of an encrypted message know that the public key is from a trusted source (or a sender who claims to be one). Most browsers display an icon to show that they are secure; it is usually a small locked padlock (Figure 8.9). For Mozilla Firefox, Internet Explorer and Google Chrome, the icon appears in the address bar. When using or sending information to a website using HTTPS, check that this icon appears just before its site name.

Digital certificates are issued by **certificate authorities** (or **CAs**). There are about 50 CAs around the world, including Verisign, Comodo and Symantec.

> **KEY WORDS**
>
> **digital certificate:** a digital certificate is a method of guaranteeing that a website is genuine and that communication between you (the client computer) and the server is secure. A website with a digital certificate has a small padlock icon you see in the bottom right of your web browser
>
> **certificate authorities (CA):** a trusted entity that issues digital certificates

a

b

c

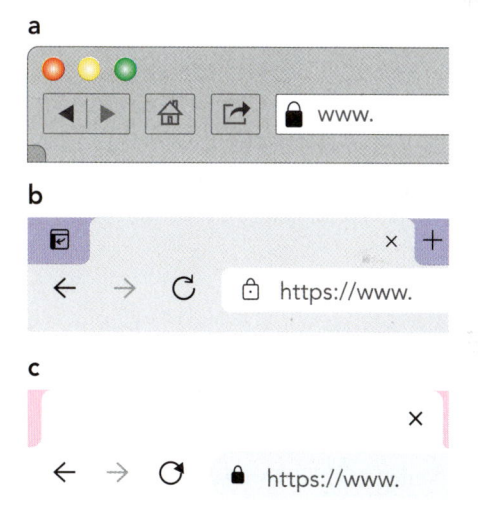

Figure 8.9: The padlock icon to show that the website is secure

What makes up a digital certificate?

The digital certificate guarantees the authenticity of the public key that the site will provide for secure transmission. A certificate consists of:

- the person's name
- an email address
- a serial number

- a public key
- an expiration date (certificates are only valid for a limited time)
- a digital signature.

The SSL (Secure Sockets Layer) and its successor, TLS (Transport Layer Security), are protocols on the client and server computers for establishing these encrypted links. SSL uses encrypted links to provide a secure channel for communication between the two devices when they are using HTTPS (see Figure 8.10). For web browsing, for example, it allows you to use the secure HTTPS protocol (rule) rather than the normal HTTP (see Chapter 10, Section 10.2 Effective use of the internet).

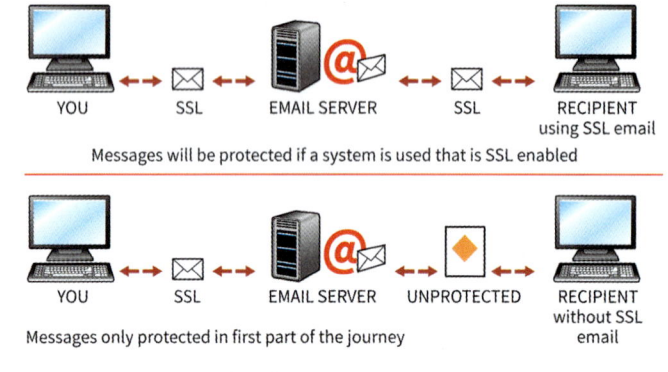

Figure 8.10: Secure Sockets Layer

Questions

4   Security of data when it is being transmitted is very important.
    a   Define SSL.
    b   Describe what SSL does.
    c   State the difference between SSL and a digital certificate.

5   Yolande works in a software development company. She needs to use biometric data to enter her office every morning.
    a   Give four types of biometric data that the company could ask Yolande to provide.
    b   Explain how biometric data works when Yolande has to give a fingerprint scan as a means of entry to her place of work.

Data security in the cloud

Cloud computing is when data and programs are stored in a centralised place on the internet and not on the hard drive of your computer. Cloud computing was discussed in Chapter 4.1.

The issues relating to security in the cloud are worldwide. These are the main problems for the people who make the laws all over the world:

- Data flows across country borders.
- A lot of data storage servers are in the USA but they are used by people in different countries so it is not clear which laws of which country should be regulating the privacy of the data when it is travelling from the sender to the server.
- People using the cloud for data storage think that their information is confidential to them because it is their property. However, the place where their data is stored (the internet) is not theirs.

With so much legal uncertainty, your only option is to be responsible for your own data. Here are some ideas to help you:

- Don't store sensitive data in the cloud.
- Make sure you read the small print of your cloud provider to find out how their storage works.
- Be very serious about all of your passwords. Don't use your email login and password for any other purpose because all of your login details and forgotten password details come to you via email.
- Use encryption as it is an excellent way for you to protect your data.
- Some cloud services provide local encryption and decryption of your files, so find out about which they are and use that service. It means that the service will encrypt your files on your own computer and store them safely on the cloud.

What is a firewall and why is it used?

A **firewall** is protective barrier between you and any other computers that you are connected to. A firewall can be either a software program or a hardware device that intercepts communications between your computer and the outside in order to help block malicious connections. Firewalls are discussed in detail in Chapter 4, Section 4.2 Network issues and communication.

> **KEY WORD**
>
> **firewall:** software or hardware devices that protect against unauthorised access to a network

Two-factor authentication

Multi-factor authentication (MFA) is a **challenge-response check** that combines two or more independent **credentials** (verification of identity for authentication) or factors.

The authentication factors are:

- **Knowledge factors**: consisting of information that the user possesses, such as a personal identification number (PIN), a user name, a password or the answer to a secret question.
- **Possession factors**: items that the user has with them, typically a hardware device such as a security token or a mobile phone used in conjunction with a software token (e.g. login details).
- **Inheritance factors**: such as fingerprints or iris which are examples of biometric authentication.

The most common methods use **two-factor authentication**. Examples include:

- Withdrawing money from a cash machine. Authentication requires a possession factor (a debit or credit card) and a knowledge factor (a PIN).
- USB devices with authentication codes. The user inserts the USB device, a token, which contains a password which the user is asked to enter when they are asked for authentication. The password they enter must match that on the token.
- As USB devices may be lost, forgotten or stolen, some two-factor authentication methods use mobile phones as the possession factor. This happens on a lot of websites. The user enters their knowledge factor, for example, their password, and the server sends a text message containing an access code to their registered mobile phone. The code can be used once within a certain time limit.

KEY WORDS

multi-factor authentication: a user has to produce several pieces of evidence in a challenge test

challenge-response check: an authentication method used to identify a user who has to produce a piece of evidence, e.g. a password

credentials: pieces of information

knowledge factor: something that a person knows that can be used for authentication

possession factor: something that a person owns that can be used for authentication

inheritance factor: a physical characteristic that someone can use for authentication, e.g. their fingerprint

two-factor authentication: a user has to produce *two* pieces of evidence in a challenge test

User ID and password

Passwords are the most common method of authentication. Each user registers initially, using an assigned or self-declared password, and on each subsequent use the user must know and use the previously declared password. The security of the data is increased as only authenticated users can access it. Passwords are discussed in Chapter 4, Section 4.2 Network issues and communication.

ICT IN CONTEXT

If you use the same password for more than one internet site, and someone hacks one of those accounts, they will also have the password for all your other accounts with the same password.

It is therefore important not to use the same username and password more than once to make sure you are not an easy target for identity theft.

SUMMARY

Physical safety issues can be solved by using simple strategies to prevent problems occurring.
Evaluate how you use IT equipment and develop ways to minimise any safety risks that you find.
Most countries have data protection legislation for the protection of users' personal data.
Explain what is meant by personal data, why it should be kept confidential and protected and how to avoid inappropriate disclosure of personal data.
Evaluate your own use of the internet, email, online gaming and social media sites and discuss why eSafety is needed.
Understand what effective security of data is, as well as what security of data online is, then discuss the effectiveness of different methods of increasing security.
Understand the threats to data, such as hacking, phishing, pharming, smishing and vishing and how to prevent them.
Understand and know how to take action against viruses and malware.
Know about credit card fraud, including shoulder surfing, card cloning and key logging.
Know what encryption and SSL are and how to protect data, including using biometric data, digital certificates, firewalls and user IDs and passwords.

EXAM-STYLE QUESTIONS

1 **Define** the term 'electrical overload'. [1]
2 **State** *three* things you should do immediately if you spill a drink into your keyboard or laptop [3]
3 List *three* hazards associated with trailing wires in a computer room. [3]
4 Chunhua is about to give personal information on an internet site. State *three* things she should consider before doing this [3]
5 Which of the following could you do to get less spam? You may choose more than one if you think that is correct: [1]
   a Change your password regularly.
   b Change your email address.
   c Do not tell anyone your password.
6 Which of the following is *not* personal information? [1]
   a Photograph of me in school uniform.
   b Online nickname.
   c Date of birth.
7 **Explain** what you should do if you want to meet someone you only know online. [1]
8 You have received some junk mail and you reply to the message asking them not to send you anymore. Explain why this is the wrong thing to do. [4]

COMMAND WORDS

define: give precise meaning

state: express in clear terms

explain: set out purposes or reasons / make the relationships between things evident / provide why and / or how and support with relevant evidence

CONTINUED

9 **Discuss** the possible dangers of communicating over the internet. Give specific types of problems. [10]
10 It is possible to be robbed as a result of a Facebook post. Discuss ways that help thieves to rob your house. [4]
11 Mahesh is a student who has been advised to make sure that a firewall has been installed before he starts to use social media.

  Describe *three* ways that a firewall would protect data on Mahesh's computer. [3]
12 Describe different ways to help you to decide if a website is fake or not. [5]

[Total: 40]

COMMAND WORDS

discuss: write about issue(s) or topic(s) in depth in a structured way

describe: state the points of a topic / give characteristics and main features

SELF-EVALUATION CHECKLIST

After studying this chapter, think about how confident you are with the different topics.

This will help you to see any gaps in your knowledge and help you to learn more effectively.

You might find it helpful to rate how confident you are for each of these statements when you are revising. You should revisit any sections that you rated 'Needs more work' or 'Getting there'.

I can ...	See section	Needs more work	Getting there	Confident to move on
describe common physical safety issues, what causes them and the strategies that can be used to prevent them	8.1			
evaluate how I use IT equipment and develop ways to minimise any safety risks that I find during my evaluation	8.1			
discuss the principles of a typical data protection act	8.2			
explain what is meant by personal data, why it should be kept confidential and protected and how to avoid inappropriate disclosure of personal data.	8.2			
discuss eSafety strategies to minimise danger when using the internet, sending emails, using social media and playing online games	8.2			
discuss the threats to data and understand what measures should be taken to protect your data	8.3 and 4.2			

Chapter 9
Know your audience

IN THIS CHAPTER YOU WILL:

- learn how to analyse the needs of your audience when creating presentations for them
- show a clear understanding of who your audience is when you plan and create ICT presentations so that you are respectful of the needs of that audience
- discuss the principles of copyright legislation, explain why copyright legislation is needed and describe methods to prevent software copyright being broken.

9 Know your audience

GETTING STARTED

Figures 9.1a and b show two presentations on the dangers of plastics in the oceans. One is a website and the other is a leaflet.

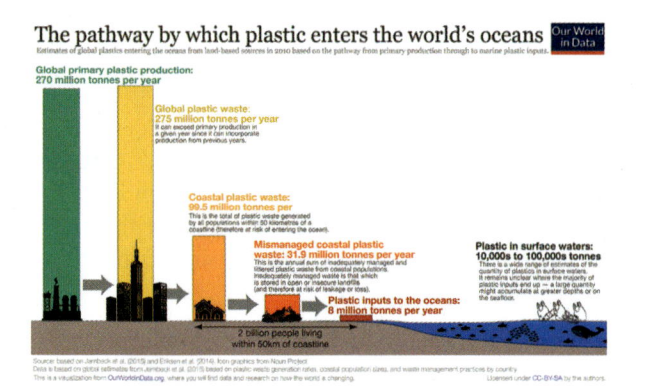

Figure 9.1a: Presentation A

Figure 9.1b: Presentation B

These two presentations are on the same topic; the dangers of plastic in the oceans, but they look very different.

In groups, discuss these presentations and decide on the audience each is intended for.

How have the authors adapted the designs for those audiences?

WHO WANTS TO KNOW YOUR IDEAS AND SOLUTIONS?

Have you ever tried to learn and understand by reading from a booklet or text book, but soon got lost in all the facts and couldn't remember anything? Have you ever sat in a talk or presentation and after a few minutes felt yourself drifting off with boredom because it was too difficult to understand, or because you already knew everything the presenter was trying to teach you?

Communication is a two-way process. Ideas are expressed by one person and received by another and the receiver, the audience, is the most important in the transaction. If the audience doesn't listen, watch, understand and remember, then has any communication taken place? Or has the presenter just been wasting their own time and the time of the audience? If you couldn't understand the text book and got lost in the facts, even though other people think it's brilliant, then the book is meant for another audience. Not for you. Would you buy a number book aimed at three-year-olds learning to count to ten as your latest maths textbook? Probably not, even though it had lots of colourful pictures. You are the wrong audience.

When designing any communication, the audience is the most important consideration.

Discussion questions

1. To deliver a good presentation, you must think very carefully about the characteristics and needs of your audience. Make a list of all the different things you should consider, for example, the age of the audience.

2. A lesson at school is a presentation intended to communicate information and to help you to learn. Discuss all the aspects that make a good lesson.

9.1 Audience appreciation

Analyse

Before you start a presentation, there are two main criteria to consider:

- The purpose of the presentation.
- The audience of the presentation.

People create presentations for many purposes such as:

- **To entertain**
  The presentation should be about something all of the audience are interested in and probably be light hearted and humorous. It will probably contain images and video.

- **To inform**
  The presentation should give a clear explanation without distractions such as funny videos and images. It should present the facts in a clear, logical order.

- **To educate**
  The audience should leave understanding more about a particular subject than when they entered. This goes beyond stating facts. You want the audience to learn, and so you may have to use examples and go into everything to a greater depth. The presenter needs a thorough understanding of the subject.

- **To inspire, motivate or activate**
  The presentation should fill the audience with a desire to go out and achieve something. It may highlight current hardships and show how the group can overcome them and succeed. But the audience should leave determined to accomplish a common goal such as winning a sporting event or overthrowing a corrupt government. The presentation will be more emotional and may have rousing music and symbols that unite the audience.

- **To persuade**
  The presentation should convince the audience to make a particular action such as going out to buy a particular product or go and carry out a particular action. The presentation should display whatever is being promoted in a good light.

The purpose will influence the structure and content of the presentation and the media used but without considering the particular audience of the presentation, then it will fail.

The presenter should consider audience characteristics (see Figure 9.2) such as:

- **How old they are**
  Presentations for young children will need more simple language, and fewer words with more images and videos. The facts should not go beyond their understanding.

- **How much money they have to spend**
  This will be important if the presentation is to persuade them to buy something.

- **What gender they are**
  Is the audience all one gender or are they mixed? Different examples given in a presentation might appeal more to different genders.

- **What is their education level**
  Everyone has a level of education and become frustrated if the information they are presented with is too difficult or simple.

- **What is their lifestyle, culture or beliefs**
  Certain things in a presentation may cause offence to certain groups and a presentation should be respectful to their beliefs – unless the presentation is intended to shock and cause discussion. But even that has to be considered carefully.

- **What the audience wants**
  Have the audience come to be entertained? Do they want to learn to improve their education? Have they got problems in their lives that the presentation will help them solve? Do they want to be stirred into action?

Figure 9.2: Who is your audience?

9 Know your audience

> **PRACTICAL TASK 9.1**
>
> **Getting started**
>
> 1. Define what is meant by a questionnaire.
> 2. Suggest **two** different scenarios where a questionnaire could be used.
>
> **Practice**
>
> 3. Work with someone else to plan a questionnaire that will be used to find out about the make-up of an audience, listing the questions you will ask.
> 4. Design the questionnaire on a piece of paper.
> 5. Check your questions are not disrespectful, and ensure you have not asked any sensitive questions, or any that may cause offence to people of other cultures, religious beliefs or age groups. For instance, it can be thought impolite to ask someone's age, but you could have a range of ages such as: 12–20, 21–40, 41–60, etc. then the person being interviewed could be asked which age range they belong in.
> 6. Create your questionnaire using suitable software. You may wish to use a word processor, spreadsheet or desktop publishing software for this.
>
> **Challenge**
>
> 7. Using suitable software, produce a system that could be used to analyse the results of your questionnaire, e.g. finding the percentages of different aged groups or genders. You may wish to use spreadsheet software for this.
>
> **Peer assessment**
>
> When you are happy with your questionnaire, show it to another pair of students and ask for their feedback. Be prepared to give them feedback too.

- For example, if the presentation was an instruction booklet for a new router, your audience may be mixed and include those who have never bought a router before, as well as IT professionals. The language has to be clearly written with each user group in mind or the instruction booklet will be of no use.

> **ACTIVITY 9.1**
>
> In groups of three, create a short presentation for three different audiences. The presentation should be about 'Computers' and the audiences are children aged four to five, people in your year group and a group of ICT teachers. Adapt the presentation to meet the needs of each audience.

9.2 Copyright and intellectual property

There are many legal constraints that apply to the use of ICT. You have already carried out some work on the principles of data protection legislation in Chapter 8, Section 8.2 eSafety and know that it is there to protect personal information about individuals. We are now going to consider the necessity for copyright **legislation**.

> **KEY WORD**
>
> **legislation:** a group of laws about something

Intellectual property

Intellectual property (IP) is a unique creative product of the human mind. A design for a new processor, a digital image, a piece of music, a literary work or a piece of software are all examples of IP. Each of them was created by somebody, is unique and has a commercial value.

When you stream a film or video, part of the payment goes to the people who wrote the script or created the music and pictures. They are being paid for their intellectual property so that they can make a living and create more. Without the payment creation would stop.

Copying intellectual property without permission is called **piracy**.

Copyright

The creators of unique works own the **copyright** to their own work (see the copyright symbol in Figure 9.3). This means that no one can use it without permission and may have to pay a fee. Only the creator has the right to make copies or perform it in public or give another person permission to do so. Anyone else must ask for permission to use that work, and the creator will often expect to be paid for its use. These rights are protected in legislation known as **copyright acts**, which have been enacted in most countries. Copyright is an automatic right, it does not need applying for.

Copyright only protects the expression of an idea, not the idea itself. If you were to develop an original piece of software to meet a particular need, its source code would be protected, but there's nothing to stop someone else from copying the idea and writing a program that essentially performs the same task using different code. You, as the original developer, would have to prove that the similarities between the two programs are more than just coincidence and can only be explained by copying.

> **KEY WORDS**
>
> **intellectual property:** the ideas and skills of other people that belong to them
>
> **piracy:** copying intellectual property that belongs to someone else
>
> **copyright:** rights that prevent people using a piece of work without the creator's (the copyright holder's) permission
>
> **copyright acts:** laws enacted to protect intellectual property

> **ICT IN CONTEXT**
>
> Online piracy is the practice of downloading and distributing copyrighted content digitally without permission, including software, music and video.
>
> 'Pirate websites' offer users illegal downloads and make money through advertisers on their sites such as online casinos, dating websites, other downloading sites and even reputable brands.
>
> They also make money by charging other cyber-criminals to put malware on the site enabling them to hijack users' computers and commit credit card fraud.

Figure 9.3: The copyright symbol

Question

1 Which of these best describes software piracy?
 a Illegal use of a computer.
 b Illegal copying of recorded material.
 c Use of computers onboard a ship.
2 When you download music from the internet without paying for it, who is affected and how?

PRACTICAL TASK 9.2

Getting started

1. Often you listen to some music or part of a song that reminds you of another one. Discuss with a partner any two pieces of music or lyrics that seem very similar to both of you.

Practice

2. Carry out research of one court case brought because of similarities in a musical work. Note down the cause of the complaint, the defence and the verdict.

Challenge

3. Create a presentation of your findings. If possible, include the actual music in the presentation to show the similarities to the audience.

ACTIVITY 9.2

When people download music or video files illegally they often justify themselves by saying 'The people aren't losing money because I wouldn't have bought it anyway'. As a class, discuss this statement from an ethical and legal point of view.

ICT IN CONTEXT

When he was 14, Mozart committed copyright theft. He was in the Sistine Chapel of the Vatican and heard a famous piece of choral music being played and sung. The piece of music was so well protected that it was only allowed to be performed on two specific days and there were only three paper copies. That night Mozart wrote out the work perfectly, just from having heard it once! Was Mozart the first to pirate a piece of music?

Software protection

Software copyright is a way of protecting software from being used by a person who does not have permission. It applies to applications, websites, games and databases. Usually, with software, if the owner wants to be paid for its use then they will create a **software licence** that defines the terms and conditions of its use, including the price, and the user is asked to agree to the terms of use in the licence before they can use it.

Most software asks you to enter a unique **licence key** (or serial number) when you are installing the software on your computer. Remember that when you buy software, it is not actually the software you are buying, but a licence to use it. At the time of purchase you can decide whether to buy the licence for one PC or more; the amount you pay will vary according to which licence type you choose.

Software can be encrypted and only be used by a person who has the decryption key.

This key can be contained in a device which has to be plugged into a computer while the software is being used. This device is called a **dongle**. They are more secure than licences as licences can easily be transferred from one system to another or a user could lend a licence to someone else.

KEY WORDS

software licence: proof that you have paid the owner for the right to use their software under specific terms and conditions, usually agreed when it is purchased

licence key: a data string that, upon installation, unlocks a software product and makes it available for use

dongle: a small device able to be connected to and used with a computer, especially to allow the use of protected software

ICT IN CONTEXT

The International Federation of the Phonagraphic Industry (IFPI) claims that despite legal streaming platforms such as Spotify and Apple Music, 38% of listeners of streamed music continue to acquire music illegally.

The most common form is stream-ripping, accounting for 32% of the 38% who illegally stream music. Stream-ripping uses software to record the audio from sites such as YouTube.

ACTIVITY 9.3

With a partner or in small groups, think about how you would explain the importance of copyright protection to someone who missed the lesson.

Questions

3. Software has been installed on the school network. State the type of licence that must be bought to make this action legal.
4. Rebecca has bought a piece of software licenced for her desktop computer. She has since decided to sell her computer and buy a laptop.
   a. State whether the person who buys the computer will be using the software legally.
   b. Explain why Rebecca can reinstall the software onto her new laptop without breaking copyright law.

ICT IN CONTEXT

The Federation Against Copyright Theft (FACT) is an organisation that has been set up to prevent users from breaking copyright law. Individuals that were providing loaded Illicit Streaming Devices (ISDs) and illegal streams via websites and social media pages including Facebook, Twitter and Instagram have stopped operations as a result of FACT action.

ACTIVITY 9.4

Working in a group, each of you take on the role of one of the people involved in creating music, such as songwriter, musician, singer, recording engineer, distributor. Explain to the group why your role is important and why you should get a cut of the money paid for the music.

REFLECTION

Think about how you would teach someone else the importance of considering purpose and audience when creating a presentation.

SUMMARY

Presentations should be written with the audience in mind.
Presentations should be respectful of the needs of the audience.
Copyright provides legal protection for intellectual property (IP).
Intellectual property is a unique creative product of the mind such as software, music, etc.
Licences are used to protect the creators of software.

EXAM-STYLE QUESTIONS

1 You need to find out about an audience before creating a presentation.
   a **Identify** which of the following would not be a good method of getting the information you need: [2]
   - interviews
   - use questionnaires
   - use a TV advert
   - market research.

   b Name *three* problems that could arise if you did not know enough about your audience. [3]

   c **State** which of the following is a definition of a target audience. [1]
   i People who will see or use the presentation.
   ii People who targeted others.
   iii The people who are creating the presentation.

2 a **Define** copyright. [1]
   b Identify which of the following describes software copyright theft, commonly known as software piracy. [2]
   i Borrowing software from a friend and installing it on your computer.
   ii Downloading software for free without permission of the owner.
   iii Copying software for free without permission of the owner.
   iv Uninstalling software for free.
   c Name *two* ways that manufacturers can help to prevent software piracy. [2]

3 **Explain** what is meant by intellectual property rights. [4]

[Total: 15]

COMMAND WORDS

identify: name / select / recognise

state: express in clear terms

define: give precise meaning

explain: set out purposes or reasons / make the relationships between things evident / provide why and / or how and support with relevant evidence

SELF-EVALUATION CHECKLIST

After studying this chapter, think about how confident you are with the different topics.

This will help you to see any gaps in your knowledge and help you to learn more effectively.

You might find it helpful to rate how confident you are for each of these statements when you are revising. You should revisit any sections that you rated 'Needs more work' or 'Getting there'.

I can ...	See section	Needs more work	Getting there	Confident to move on
know how to analyse the needs of my audience when creating presentations for them	9.1			
understand who my audience is when I plan and create ICT presentations so that I am respectful of the needs of that audience	9.2			
discuss the principles of copyright legislation, explain why copyright legislation is needed and describe methods to prevent software copyright being broken	9.3			

› Chapter 10
Communication

IN THIS CHAPTER YOU WILL:

- describe the uses and constraints of email communication
- describe the characteristics of spam email and how to prevent it
- describe the characteristics, uses, advantages and disadvantages of using the internet
- explain how internet communication functions
- explain how search engines function
- know how to evaluate information found on the internet
- list and describe the functions of protocols used for internet communication
- discuss the risks of using the internet and how to restrict them.

10 Communication

GETTING STARTED

The following lists contains items relating to methods of communicating using ICT and descriptions of those methods. Match the letters of the items to their descriptions.

a	Spam
b	Internet
c	Intranet
d	World wide web (www)
e	Internet Service Provider (ISP)
f	HyperText Transfer Protocol (HTTP)
g	Uniform Resource Locator (URL)
h	Search engine
i	Blog
j	Social networking

1	Protocol used for communications between a web server and a client requesting information.
2	The address of a resource on the internet.
3	The use of websites and online apps to communicate with groups of people with similar interests.
4	A global computer network providing a variety of communication facilities.
5	Software that finds information on the internet requested by a user.
6	A network of interconnected web pages on computers all over the world.
7	Irrelevant and unsolicited messages sent over the internet to large numbers of users.
8	An organisation that provides users with access to the internet.
9	A private network contained within an organisation used to securely share company information and computing resources among employees.
10	A web page that is regularly updated by an individual or small group.

QWERTYUIOP?

Emails have been used for communicating for over 50 years. The first electronic message that could be called an email was sent in 1971 by Raymond Tomlinson whose test message was 'QWERTYUIOP'. He was also the person who first used the '@' symbol to allow messages to be targeted at a specific user on a certain machine. Nearly instantaneous communication between machines within an organisation proved to be so beneficial and practical that the concept soon began to spread.

> **CONTINUED**
>
> By the 1980s and the birth of the internet, email hosting sites began to pop up to supply email services. Microsoft Mail was released in 1988 with spam emails appearing in 1990. By 1992 you could attach documents to emails and in 1994 Microsoft introduced Outlook.
>
> Use accelerated with users sending emails to communicate almost instantly for personal and business use, and in 1998 it was the subject of a successful film – *You've Got Mail* (Figure 10.1).
>
> Today almost three million emails are sent every second, over 306 billion every day. It is predicted that these figures are expected to reach 347.3 billion in 2023. People are facing email overload and it has been estimated that people spend almost five hours a day checking personal and business emails. If they miss one and it isn't opened in the first hour then it probably never will be. For years it has been claimed that emails will soon be replaced by other methods such as messaging apps like Slack, Google Hangouts and WhatsApp, but email use is continuing to grow.
>
> **Figure 10.1:** Tom Hanks and Meg Ryan, *You've Got Mail*
>
> **Discussion questions**
>
> 1 What are the advantages of using email over other communication methods such as postal services, or apps like Facebook Messenger?
>
> 2 What are the disadvantages?

10.1 Communication with other ICT users using email

Characteristics, uses and constraints of email

To communicate with a specific person, there are several applications that can be used – the most common being **email** (electronic mail). The communicating computers must both have an email application on them, but the applications don't have to be of the same kind. Messages can be composed, files attached, recipients chosen and the message sent from the email application. Of course, the recipient can do the reverse: read the message, extract the attached file and see who sent the email.

An email is delivered almost instantly to a user's email server, which they can contact from anywhere in the world. They do not have to be in any particular place as they would to receive a physical letter or parcel.

> **KEY WORD**
>
> **email:** short for electronic mail. Messages distributed by electronic means

How to write an email

Depending on the purpose of your email and your intended audience, the way you word your messages might be formal, or casual or brief. You read about the importance of considering your audience in Chapter 9, Section 9.1 Audience appreciation. This situation is very similar. Remember that you need to consider:

Who your audience is.

- What their relationship to you is.
- What sort of impression your message will give about you or the organisation for whom you represent.

10 Communication

> **ACTIVITY 10.1**
>
> Work with a partner. You will need a large sheet of paper.
>
> 1. In the centre write the word AUDIENCE and circle it.
> 2. From the circle draw lines to other circles containing different types of audiences, such as friends/business/job-hunting/older relatives/etc.
> 3. Around each type of audience, describe the components of the email you would send to them such as formal/informal/type of words to use or not use/punctuation/type of greeting/type of signing off/etc.
> 4. Pin your paper up and compare with other students' work.

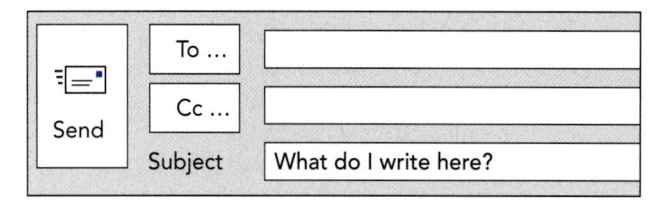

Figure 10.2: Make sure you use a clear subject line to indicate what your email is about

Some tips for emailing:

- People at work should find out if there are any **guidelines** for emailing customers set out by their employer such as fonts, colours and terms of address. If there are, they should keep to them.
- They should also check if they are allowed to send personal emails from their work computer. Lots of employers do not allow employees to do this while they are supposed to be working.
- Decide, before sending your message, if it is alright to be brief or whether it would be more appropriate to send a more professional sounding message.
- If you would hesitate to say something to someone's face, then don't write it in an email.
- Subject lines are important. You should always use a subject line that indicates what the email is about (see Figure 10.2). If you do not do this, some people will not open an email that does not have anything in the subject line as they will see it as a security risk.
- Greetings and signing. Don't just start your email immediately, always use an appropriate greeting; it is also important to put your name at the end of an email.
- Including others in the conversation. Use the **cc** box if you want to send a copy of the email to someone but don't necessarily need them to respond. The **bcc** box is for when you want to send a copy of the email to someone without the other recipients in the 'To' and 'cc' boxes knowing that you have done so.
- Be brief and clear in your writing.
- If your message is work related or formal, you need to proofread it to check for proper use of grammar, spelling and punctuation, as well as appropriate use of capitalisation.

> **ICT IN CONTEXT**
>
> Emails can be used as evidence in a court of law just as other documents are used. That is why government officials are expected to use their official email addresses rather than their personal ones. Emails to official addresses are stored securely and not deleted. However, emails used as evidence are not accepted if they are printed out because they could be changed.

Netiquette

Netiquette is a set of rules for acceptable online behaviour. It basically applies the principles of courtesy and behaviour that we expect in our daily lives to our use of the internet and using social networking sites.

> **KEY WORDS**
>
> **guidelines:** information intended to advise people on how something should be done
>
> **cc:** short for 'carbon copy'. This is the field you type an address into if you want the person to see the email, but not necessarily respond to it
>
> **bcc:** short for 'blind carbon copy'. This is the field you type an address into if you don't want others to see who you have copied into the email
>
> **netiquette:** a set of rules for acceptable online behaviour

When applied to emails, it urges users to:

- **Use email the way you want others to use** it
  Remember that a human being (just like you) is at the other end reading your email, and don't write anything you wouldn't say face to face. As you are not meeting face to face, the recipient cannot read your body language or see if you are smiling and might interpret a joke as an insult.
- **Emails should have a subject heading which reflects the content of the message**
  Your subject line is like the headline of a news article. Make sure the subject line relates to the message content.
- **Consider the recipient's background**
  Remember that the recipient is a person whose culture, language and beliefs may be different from your own.
- **Use capital letters as you would normally in a sentence.** UPPER CASE LOOKS AS IF YOU'RE SHOUTING.
- **Know how large a message you are sending**
  Including large files may make your message so big that it cannot be delivered or may be too large for the recipient to store on their device.
- **Don't send large amounts of unsolicited information or attachments to people**
  It is inconsiderate; the recipient may not be interested in all of the information and the recipient may use an email client on a slow connection.

Email groups

An **email group** is also known as a contact group or a mailing list, and they help you to simplify the process of sending the same email to a group of people. If you address a message to the single name of a contact group, it saves you a lot of time, as you don't need to key in every recipient's address; the email will go to everyone in that group at the same time. Creating a contact group is an option that will be available in your email account.

Question

1   a   State what the term email means.
    b   You want to send the same email to everyone in your class. State the best function to use.
    c   Describe the advantages of sending an email instead of sending a letter.

Forwarding emails and attaching files to emails

Forwarding an email is sending an email message that you have received from someone to another person's email address. The term forwarding means that the email has been moved 'forward' to a new destination or destinations. When you click 'reply' to an email, you usually have the option to reply, **reply to all**, or to forward.

An **email attachment** is a digital file that is sent with an email message. One or many files can be attached to any email message, then the attachment(s) will be sent with the email to the recipient(s). This is a simple way to share documents and images. When the recipient receives the email, their software allows them to download the attachment to their computer by clicking on the icon or link that is in the email.

KEY WORDS

email group: contact group or a mailing list

forwarding: re-sending an email message that you have received to another person's email address

reply to all: sending a reply to all of the people the email was sent to and not just to the sender

email attachment: a computer file that is sent with an email message

ICT IN CONTEXT

It may seem surprising that emails can infringe copyright laws (see Chapter 9, Section 9.2 Copyright and intellectual property), but remember that photographs, videos, text and music are all copyrighted the moment that they are created. Theoretically, if an email has been sent to you and you forward it to others, it is possible that you could be breaking a copyright law!

The need for security

Internet access is needed to send and receive emails and so all the security measures needed when you are using the internet are also needed when you send and receive email. These are discussed in Chapter 8, Section 8.3 Security of data.

Failure to have security could result in a virus infection from malware contained in the email or an attachment. From a commercial aspect, loss of systems could severely damage a business if data and records such as stock records, supplier and customer information, technical documentation, etc. are lost.

Email security should be a priority for businesses and individuals because of the growing threats from:

- hackers
- viruses
- spam
- phishing
- identity theft.

> **ICT IN CONTEXT**
>
> It is possible that you may be held legally responsible for any losses suffered through a virus infection that you may have unknowingly passed on to others, some of whom could even be business competitors.

Spam

Spam was mentioned in Chapter 8, Section 8.3 Security of data. Spam is junk mail that you haven't asked for; you probably get some in paper form through the letter box as well. Most email providers can filter out much of the spam sent to you, but still some of it gets through and it can be a nuisance as well as posing threats. In your email software, you will also have an option to mark emails received as spam. This helps these emails to be filtered out and stored in a folder, usually called 'junk' on your email account. You will then have an option of opening your junk folder from time to time and emptying it into the trash can, or you can look through the junk folder in case there is an email that is there by mistake; in this case, you can decide to move it into the inbox again.

People sending spam build mailing lists from email addresses that they collect. When you use the internet to sign up to any website or to register software, or buy something, you may be asked either to tick or to 'un-tick' a box if you agree to be sent correspondence from other similar sources. If you are aware of this and read it carefully, you will avoid some spam.

Even if you are careful where you leave your email address, spammers will get your email by buying lists of email addresses from people who will have legally collected them.

How to deal with spam

Some tips to help to counter spam mail are:

- When you register with a site, read the terms to see whether you are agreeing to being sent emails and look for any check boxes that you may be opting into or opting out of.
- Use the 'unsubscribe' option at the bottom of any marketing emails that you receive. Your details should then be removed from their distribution list.
- Make sure the spam filter on your email software is turned on. You can also buy third party spam filters which use artificial intelligence to improve their effectiveness.
- Use the 'Mark as Spam' option as well as the 'Block Senders' feature on your email account.
- Make sure that your password is secure (see Chapter 4, Section 4.2 Network issues and communication).
- Keep your antivirus program up to date.
- Because is very important to keep your computer safe from viruses, your **antivirus software** needs to be kept up to date. When you perform updates to the antivirus software it will be updated with the latest information about new viruses that may infect your computer.
- Depending on which software and which version of the operating system you are running, you can open your antivirus software and look for 'update' or 'check for updates'.

> **KEY WORD**
>
> **antivirus software:** software to prevent a virus from entering your computer and searching for it and destroying it if it already has

10.2 Effective use of the internet

The internet is a global network of interconnected computer networks that is used to connect people, communities and countries worldwide. An intranet is a private computer network within an organisation. Even though an intranet uses internet technologies, it is safeguarded from the global internet. An extranet is a private network where an intranet has been extended so that part of it is publicly accessible. (More information about these and their advantages and disadvantages are explained in Chapter 4, Section 4.1 Networks).

The world wide web

The **world wide web** ('www' or 'web') is different to the internet. The terms 'internet' and 'world wide web' are quite often used interchangeably, but they are not the same, even though they are related. While the internet is a massive network of networks forming an infrastructure to connect millions of computers together globally, much like motorways, roads and tracks that enable you to get around the country. The www or web is a service on the internet; we usually access the web using a web browser, which displays web pages. The web uses the **HyperText Transfer Protocol (HTTP)** to transmit data using interlinked pages. This allows applications to communicate and share information.

Uses of the internet

The internet can be used for many different types of activity, such as:

- sending and receiving emails
- research
- downloading files
- taking part in discussion groups
- playing interactive games
- education and self-improvement
- friendship and dating
- using social networking sites
- reading electronic newspapers and magazines
- job-hunting
- shopping
- communicating through blogs, wikis and forums.

Blogs as a means of communication

The word **blog** is from the term 'web log'. It is a website that you can use either as a diary of thoughts (a reflection), or to share ideas and opinions and links (Figure 10.3). People reading your blog have the facility to comment directly on any of your entries. Blogs are really useful for sharing knowledge, and some attract a large following. They are also much easier to start and maintain than a website. Only you can update your blog. However you need to keep it constantly updated otherwise you lose potential readers.

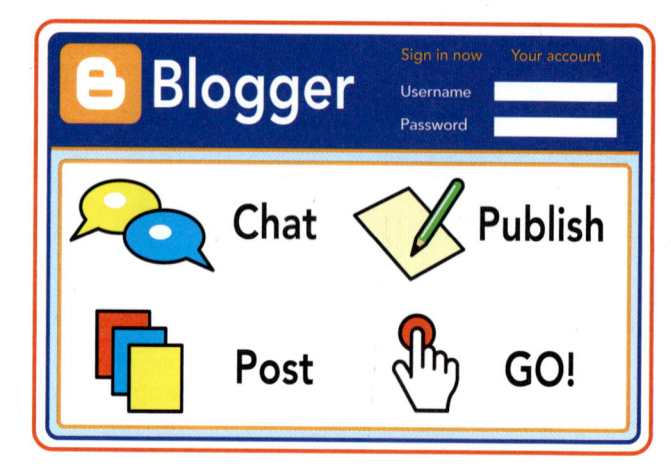

Figure 10.3: Front page of a typical blog site

KEY WORDS

world wide web: a way of accessing information using the internet using HTTP

HyperText Transfer Protocol (HTTP): used by the world wide web to define how a web page is formatted and transferred

blog: a website that you can use either as a diary of thoughts (a reflection), or to share ideas and opinions and links

wiki: a website that allows you to become a participant in its creation

Wiki as a means of communication

A **wiki** is a website that allows you to become a participant in its creation (Figure 10.4). In fact, you can either create or edit the site contents. It is, therefore, a collaborative site that is always being revised. A famous example is Wikipedia. However, because anyone can update the site, not all information on it is guaranteed to be accurate, so you should always verify what you read on a wiki.

10   Communication

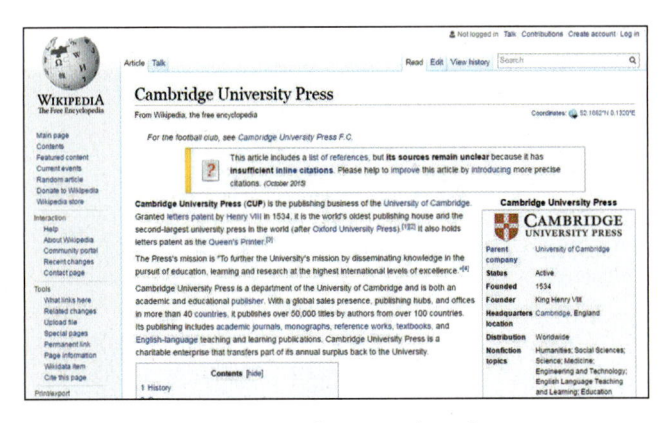

Figure 10.4: Wikipedia is a famous wiki website

Forums as a means of communication

A **forum** is a website or section of a website that allows visitors to communicate with each other by posting messages. Most forums allow anonymous visitors to view forum postings, but require you to create an account in order to post messages there.

> **KEY WORD**
>
> **forum:** a website where groups of people can discuss topics that interest them

PRACTICAL TASK 10.1

Getting started

1   Working in groups of four, discuss the differences between:

   a   the internet and the world wide web

   b   internet, intranet and extranet.

Practice

2   Each person in the group should prepare one slide each for a presentation of:

   - the internet
   - the world wide web
   - intranet
   - extranet.

3   As a group, put the four slides together into a presentation and set the transitions, animations, background and timings.

4   Prepare speaker notes under each slide.

5   Deliver the presentation to your class, each person in the group presenting their slide.

   For information about creating presentations, see Chapter 19.

Challenge

6   Add further slides explaining the differences between a 'blog' and a 'wiki'.

Peer assessment

Within your group, compare the four slides you prepared in the practice task, then discuss how you each went about preparing your content and ask for positive feedback.

After you have given your presentation, ask the class to give you positive feedback about the way you gave your presentation: was it clear, could it be easily understood, could the presentation have been improved.

When posting in a forum, you can create new topics (or '**threads**') or post replies within existing threads.

If you use forums, you may have noticed that most groups have their own expected rules of behaviour. Some general 'rules' to observe are:

- No personal abuse.
- You can strongly disagree with the point of view of others while still being polite.
- Don't spam.
- Write clearly and remember that whatever you post is public and there forever; it could be read by your parents, possible future employers (see Chapter 8, Section 8.2 eSafety), partner, children, etc.
- Don't post any material that is copyrighted if you don't own the rights or you could be prosecuted by the person who owns the copyright.

Social networking as a means of communication

A **social networking site** is an online platform that allows users to create a public profile and interact with other users. Social networking sites usually allow users to select other users they want to communicate with – 'friends'. Users can post messages and information for their friends to view and comment on and 'like' the posts of others.

Users can also send messages, privately, to individual members – called instant messaging (IM) or direct messaging (DM). This has the same benefits as using email but with no threat of spam.

Most commercial organisations make use of social networking sites such as Twitter and Facebook because their customers use them. Social networking sites allow companies to monitor what customers are saying about them. They also give companies the opportunity to reply instantly to unfavourable comments and engage in real-time conversations.

Companies can use social media to promote their products and build their brand image, explaining how they are different from others and why they are superior. Using social media allows companies to find out about changing attitudes and trends so that they can adapt their products and services or design new ones to meet demand.

Being active on social media will build customers' trust in the brand and improve brand loyalty. Satisfied customers will come to their aid by responding to unfavourable comments about a company.

Functionality

Internet Service Providers

Before users can access websites, emails and forums, etc., they need access to the internet. Large organisations can negotiate their own access with the corporations that control the infrastructure of the internet, but smaller ones and individual users will require the services of an **Internet Service Provider (ISP)** who organises that access. They also provide storage space for the websites of their users. This is called **hosting**.

The ISP will issue the user's home network with an address called an IP address. **IP** stands for internet protocol and is a set of rules that computers must follow when accessing the internet. All computers using the internet must have an IP address to identify themselves and so other computers know where to send requested data.

> **KEY WORDS**
>
> **thread:** a series of messages that have been posted as replies to each other. A digital conversation about a topic
>
> **social networking site:** a site that allows people to communicate and share news, views and events
>
> **Internet Service Provider (ISP):** an organisation that provides services for accessing and using the internet
>
> **hosting:** allocating space on a web server for people to create their own websites
>
> **internet protocol (IP):** a set of rules that computers must follow when accessing the internet

IP addresses originally consisted of four groups of numbers separated by a dot, e.g. 216.27.61.137. However, as the number of users has grown a new system using eight groups is being introduced.

Domain names

As people are not very good at remembering or accurately entering a string of numbers when they want to access a website, a system was devised to use words instead of numbers.

The IP address of Cambridge University Press is 204.74.88.103 and the text equivalent is cambridge.org. This text equivalent is called the **domain name**.

The 'cambridge' in the domain name is called the **second-level domain** (SLD) and is the name of the website.

The 'org' is the **top-level domain** (TLD) and specifies the type of organisation. 'org' was established in 1985 and was intended for non-profit organisations. Other TLDs include country codes (e.g. .hk for Hong Kong, .id for Indonesia, .sa for Saudi Arabia and .uk for United Kingdom), education codes (usually .ac is placed before the country code, e.g. .ac.in in India), and other TLDs that anyone can register such as .com or .net.

There are sites where you can find the IP address from the domain name entered.

ACTIVITY 10.2

What is the country code for your country?

What is the second-level domain name for your school?

URLs

URL stands for **Universal Resource Locator** and is commonly called a web address.

The URL contains all of the information a computer needs to find the right page, image or document on a website.

Consider the following URL of the web page for Camford College Publishers.

https://www.camford.org/gb/education/subject/computing/ict/camford-gcse-ict-3rd-edition

ICT IN CONTEXT

We use URLs and domain names but the internet uses numbers. When you enter a URL, your web browser contacts the domain name service (DNS), which consists of servers all over the world that store all of the IP addresses for all of the domain names ever issued. If the first server doesn't know it will ask another one and so on until the correct IP address is returned to your browser. And all done in about a second. Once your browser has got the translation, it stores it in what is called its 'cache', so it's even quicker next time.

The 'https' tells your browser which **protocol** to use – in this case Secure HyperText Transfer Protocol, 'Camford.org' gives the top- and second-level domains, and the rest (after the /) show the sub-directories where the information can be found.

The 'www' informs your browser to use protocols of the world wide web.

Web browser

A **web browser** is a software app that takes you anywhere on the internet. It retrieves information from other parts of the web and displays it on your desktop or mobile device. The information is transferred using the HyperText Transfer Protocol (HTTP), which defines how text, images and video are transmitted on the web so that people using any browser, anywhere in the world can see the information.

Unfortunately, not all browsers interpret the information in the same way and so when designing a website it should be tested on as many browsers as possible.

Hyperlinks are a means of travelling from one web page to another to find out more information. Hyperlinks are any images, word or words that you can click on that take you elsewhere, even if just to a different section on the same page. They contain the URL of the requested information.

KEY WORDS

domain name: the text equivalent of an IP address

second-level domain: the name directly to the left of the final dot

top-level domain: the domain extension, e.g. .com, .net, .edu

Uniform Resource Locator (URL): the unique web address of every page on the world wide web

protocol: sets of rules governing how devices communicate with each other over networks

web browser: an application used to access websites on the world wide web

hyperlink: either text, an image or part of an image that is a link to another item or web page

Use of search engines

A **search engine** is a website that has indexed billions of web pages; it is used to enable you to search the internet to find information. If you go to any search engine's home page you will see a box for you to type in the key words to be searched for. You will get a long list of pages that best match your key words.

There are strategies that you can use to improve the speed of searches and the amount and quality of information they return:

- There are many search engines, not just the most popular. Try out others.

- Search engines that serve numerous ads at the top of the page will most definitely slow you down and make it harder to find reliable information.

- Get to know the search engine you are using by exploring **filters**, settings and other options. Filters restrict the type of results that will be supplied, e.g. images or videos. Settings will allow you to use 'autocomplete' where the search engine suggests words for your search, the number of results per page and whether you want spoken replies.

- Check if your search engine lets you search for information from the past day, week, month and year. Make sure you select the time period that is most relevant to your search. That will give you better results more quickly.

- If you are looking for a specific phrase, type the phrase inside quote marks. This will make searching faster and hide results that are not relevant.

- If you are unsure of what term to search for, use the linking word 'or'. The search engine will show you both results. For example, if you are unsure of the name that garages use, you could enter 'Motorcycle OR Motorbike' when you want to buy one. The search results will contain both.

- Search using alternative words. This will cause your search engine to return different results, helping you get to what you're looking for faster.

- If looking for specific keywords in an article's title, type 'intitle:' in front of the search term when using Google. If looking for specific keywords in the URL, type 'inurl:'. Other search engines will have their own ways of modifying a search for advanced searching.

Evaluating the information found on the internet

Once you have found a suitable website you will have to assess it on a number of criteria to ensure that the material is fit for purpose in the following ways: check whether the website is up to date, reliable, unbiased and valid.

Is it up to date?

Somewhere there should be a date showing when the article was written so that you can decide whether it is recent enough for your purpose. If you are trying to find out the number of cars sold in the last two years, finding the information from 2010 will not be much use to you.

Is it reliable?

Not all information written on the internet is necessarily true. Anyone can make a website, and a lot of the information that is published is not verified. You should always check the domain name and the author. Does it come from a trusted source? If you were looking for information about astronomy then you would expect the information from NASA web page to be more reliable than that from a personal blog, like Carlos-planet-blog. Official websites for organisations, bands, and football clubs are likely to have more reliable information than a fan's blog or a wiki where anyone can add and edit information.

If you find some information on a website it should be checked or verified with other reliable pages and sources.

Is it biased?

It is often difficult to tell if the information is **biased** towards one particular point of view.

> **KEY WORDS**
>
> **search engine:** a website through which users can search internet content
>
> **filters:** these restrict the type of results that will be supplied, e.g. images or videos or even websites
>
> **bias:** to favour or prefer one thing more than another unfairly

- Check the URL. Does it contain the name of a political party or pressure group?

- Who is paying for the website?
- Does the author present alternate points of view? If so, are those views presented in the same way, or with scorn.
- Check on the all of the claims made. Can you find evidence of them in other sites.
- Check that the information tells the whole story.

Is it valid?

This means whether the information is based on truth and reason. You will be able to tell this when you have considered the points above.

Internet protocols

We looked at protocols in Chapter 4, Section 4.1 Networks when we were considering how computers communicate over networks. Protocols are a set of rules that are used to ensure that the computers all follow the same procedures.

It is the internet, rather than the web, that is used for email. Email uses the **Simple Mail Transfer Protocol (SMTP)**, which is a communication protocol for mail servers when they transmitting data. Table 10.1 gives a summary of various protocols.

> **KEY WORD**
>
> **Simple Mail Transfer Protocol (SMTP):** a communication protocol for mail servers when they transmit data

PRACTICAL TASK 10.2

Getting started

1. Two different websites need to be investigated to find out if they are reliable. State four checks you should make on information on websites before you use it.

Practice

2. Copy out the table below.
3. Work with a partner to research the internet to find two different internet resources giving up to date information on anti-malware software.
4. Enter the URL of each of the two sites into your table.

Challenge

5. Discuss the reliability of each website with your partner, then enter your evaluation into the remaining spaces in your table.

	URL 1:	URL 2:
Is it up to date? If so, how do you know?		
Is it biased or not and why do you think this?		
Who was the author or who does the website belong to?		
Is it accurate or not and how do you know?		

> CAMBRIDGE IGCSE™ ICT: COURSEBOOK

CONTINUED

Self-assessment

Create a second table like the one below and complete the spaces.

Evaluate the method you used to decide if the information was:	Easy	OK	Difficult
Up to date			
Reliable			
Biased			
Valid/Accurate			

Acronym	Protocol	When it is used
HTTP	HyperText Transfer Protocol	The rules to be followed by a web server and a web browser when requesting and supplying information. HTTP is used for sending requests from a web client (a browser) to a web server and returning web content from the server back to the client.
HTTPS	HyperText Transfer Protocol Secure	Ensures that communications between a host and client are secure by ensuring that all communication between them is encrypted.
FTP	File Transfer Protocol	The rules that must be followed when files are being transmitted between computers across the internet.
SSL	Secure Socket Layer	A standard form of security to enable an encrypted link between a server and a browser. All of the data passing between them remains private.

Table 10.1: Internet protocols

KEY WORDS

HTTPS: HyperText Transfer Protocol Secure variant. HTTP using a secure encrypted link

FTP: File Transfer Protocol. Used to transfer files from one computer to another in a secure way

ACTIVITY 10.3

Use four different search engines to enter a key word or key words to search for. Make sure you enter exactly the same key word(s) in each search engine.

For each of the four searches, make a note of the time taken to find the information, the number of links to information and how many links to adverts there are at the top of each first page.

You can distinguish the adverts, when they appear, because they will include text such as 'Ad' or 'Announce' at the start of the entry.

Questions

2. **a** Define HTTP.
   b State the difference between HTTP and HTTPS.
3. **a** Define URL.
   b The URL below is where the catalogue of books printed by Camford College Publishers can be found. Break down each part of the URL, and explain what each part does.

   https://www.camford.org/gb/camfordenglish/catalog
4. **a** Explain what a wiki is and give **one** example of a famous wiki.
   b Explain what a blog is and how it got its name.

Risks of using internet

Inappropriate or criminal material

Users and especially young people can experience inappropriate and **criminal material** on the internet (Figure 10.5). **Inappropriate material** can include:

- Content containing swearing.
- Adult content.
- Websites designed to make you have negative feelings about yourself or cause yourself harm.
- Sites that encourage vandalism, crime, terrorism, racism.
- Pictures, videos or games which show images of violence or cruelty to other people or animals.
- Gambling sites.
- Unmoderated chat rooms – where there's no one supervising the conversation and barring unsuitable comments.
- Sexism or sites that portray people in very traditional roles that do not reflect contemporary values and expectations.

> **KEY WORDS**
>
> **criminal material:** content that is illegal in the country where it is accessed
>
> **inappropriate material:** content that is not suitable for the age of the person accessing it

Figure 10.5: Beware of cyber-criminals

Parental and educational control

All parents and educational institutions should ensure that children are fully aware of the risks that they face online. eSafety is on the curriculum of most schools and colleges.

They can also set filters for the content displayed and change search engine settings to block access to many undesirable websites.

ISP control

Customers have options to use parental controls that customise the internet at source that are free. ISPs can assist by providing web-filtering or web-blocking controls to restrict the content that internet users are able to access via the connections they provide.

Many broadband providers now have family-friendly network level filters. These filters are based both on lists of blacklisted or restricted websites and through an automatic scan of keywords to determine whether a site should be filtered. This means that subscribers cannot access a range of websites by default, specifically adult or illegal content. For most ISPs, web-filtering occurs automatically. Internet subscribers can choose to 'opt out' of the network level filters by logging into their ISP account controls. There are also options to set up separate user accounts on a computer, meaning that settings can be different for each person that uses the computer.

Question

5   a   Explain what a cyber-criminal is.
    b   Name **two** ways that parental controls can be set.
    c   Define ISP.
    d   Explain how an ISP can help to keep children and young people safe when using the internet.

> **REFLECTION**
>
> Evaluate how you use the internet and whether you have changed how you use it since the start of this chapter. If so, make a list of those changes.

SUMMARY

There are many ways to communicate using the internet such as emails, blogs, wikis, forums and social networking.
Emails allow users to communicate using messages. Messages can be composed, files attached, recipients chosen and the message sent and read from the email application.
It is important to be courteous to other internet users including when sending emails and using social media.
The internet is a global network of interconnected computer networks that is used to connect people, communities and countries worldwide. The world wide web is a service on the internet.
An Internet Service Provider enables internet access.
A web browser is an application that lets you view world wide web pages but a search engine performs searches for your key words in its index.
HTTP, HTTPS and FTP are protocols that enable information and files to be sent over the internet.
Domain names and URLs allow users to address websites more easily.
A hyperlink links content from one web page to another, possibly on another website.
It is important to evaluate the contents of a website before trusting it.
There are risks to using the internet.

EXAM-STYLE QUESTIONS

1 a Select the correct option from A, B or C below.
      An inbox is where you can find: [1]
      A your sent emails
      B emails sent to you
      C junk email.
   b Which of the following would be valid email addresses? [2]
      - firstname.lastname@test.com
      - 123456789@example-one.com
      - firstname@lastname@languageschool.tv
      - firstname/lastname@languageschool.tv
   c **Describe** what you should do when you receive an email that contains a link. [2]

2 a **Describe** what a web browser is. [2]
   b **Explain** the difference between the world wide web (www) and the internet. [2]
   c There are ways for you to evaluate the information you find on the internet. Explain *three* of them. [3]
   d **State** what a protocol is. [1]
   e **Give** the protocol that is used in the following cases: [4]
      - Used by the world wide web to define how a web page is formatted and transferred.
      - Transfers files from one host to another. Used when downloading or uploading a file.
      - This means that HTTP is using SSL to protect against eavesdropping.
      - A standard form of security to enable an encrypted link between a server and a browser. All of the data passing between them remains private.

3 a **Explain** what spam is. [1]
   b **Describe** the main reasons that spam emails are sent. [3]
   c **Describe** *three* ways that people sending spam could find your email address. [3]
   d **Discuss** methods of preventing spam. [4]
   e Using examples explain the difference between spam, malware and phishing. [6]

[Total: 34]

COMMAND WORDS

describe: state the points of a topic / give characteristics and main features

explain: set out purposes or reasons / make the relationships between things evident / provide why and / or how and support with relevant evidence

state: express in clear terms

give: produce an answer from a given source or recall / memory

discuss: write about issue(s) or topic(s) in depth in a structured way

SELF-EVALUATION CHECKLIST

After studying this chapter, think about how confident you are with the different topics.

This will help you to see any gaps in your knowledge and help you to learn more effectively.

You might find it helpful to rate how confident you are for each of these statements when you are revising. You should revisit any sections that you rated 'Needs more work' or 'Getting there'.

I can ...	See section	Needs more work	Getting there	Confident to move on
describe the uses and constraints of email communication	10.1			
describe the characteristics of spam email and how to prevent it	10.1			
describe the characteristics, uses, advantages and disadvantages of using the internet	10.2			
explain how internet communication functions	10.2			
explain how search engines function	10.2			
know how to evaluate information found on the internet	10.2			
list and describe the functions of protocols used for internet communication	10.2			
discuss the risks of using the internet and how to restrict them	10.2			

Chapter 11
File management

IN THIS CHAPTER YOU WILL:

- know how to manage files, including being able to quickly locate stored files, open and import different file types, and save and export data
- use a hierarchical folder structure and save files using appropriate file names for quick identification of the file contents
- save and export files in a variety of formats, including generic file formats
- explain why file sizes are reduced for storage or transmission
- reduce the size of file sizes by compression
- understand and use different file compression techniques.

GETTING STARTED

The following are examples of some **file formats**:

1	gif	6	htm
2	odb	7	ppt
3	png	8	pdf
4	xls	9	jpg
5	mp3	10	accdb

For each one, state what type of file would be stored using that **file extension**. For example, image, spreadsheet, word processed document, presentation.

KEY WORDS

file format: the structure of a file that tells a program how to display its contents

file extension: a short name at the end of a file which tells the computer what format the file is in and which program or application can be used to open that file

IS THIS YOU?

- Your desktop has over 50 icons on it.
- Your 'My Documents' contains over three hundred files and no folders apart from the ones such as Photos and Music that came with the computer. You find it difficult to find programs in the huge list in your Start menu.
- You save all of your word processed documents in one folder, your spreadsheets in another, all your presentations in another, etc.
- If you look for a file it could be in any of ten different folders.

If this is you, then your computer is poorly organised (see Figure 11.1). A lack of digital organisation reveals itself in various ways:

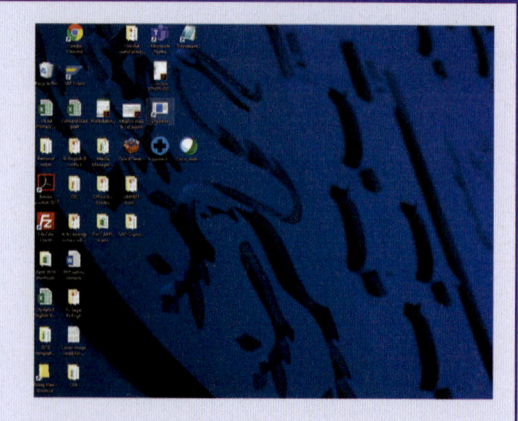

Figure 11.1: A very messy desktop!

- Folders stored without a logical structure.
- Duplicate files without standardised classification.
- Desktops that are so confusing that they make finding the most obvious item almost impossible.

Discussion questions

1 Suggest reasons why it is good to have an organised computer.
2 Design a strategy for organising a disorganised computer. Where should you start? What do you need to do?

11.1 Manage files effectively

In order to work on the contents of a file, you need to **open** it in a program or app. An app will open a file that it has created. For example, word processing software will open a .docx file, Microsoft Excel will open a .xls file, etc. However, you cannot open a .xlsx file in the word processor. When an application can open a file created by another application, it **imports** it. Most apps have the commands for doing this in a File Menu. The user has to locate the file they want to open or import and the menu will offer options to access the file.

Locating the file can take a long time if the file has not been stored in an orderly and logical manner.

Storing and locating files

A few tips for managing your files:

- Give every file a name that immediately tells you what is in it.
- Make folders to hold files of a similar type.
- Keep your folders in a **hierarchical structure**.

A hierarchical filing system might be structured as seen in Figure 11.2.

A hierarchical file system is how **drives**, folders and files are displayed on an operating system. In a hierarchical file system, drives, folders, and files are displayed in groups, which allows the user to see only the files they're interested in seeing.

For example, Figure 11.2 shows the 'My documents' folder hierarchy that contains the 'School work' and 'Personal' folders. The folder or directory that a folder is in is called its **parent directory**. In Figure 11.2, 'My documents' is the parent directory for the 'School work' and 'Personal' directories. These directories again have others inside them and each of these folders could have hundreds of their own files, but unless they are opened the files are not displayed.

KEY WORDS

open: to start a file in its own application so that it is ready to read or use

import: to start a file in an application of a different format so that it is ready to use, e.g. to open a spreadsheet in a word processing application

hierarchical structure: a file system that organises files in a top to bottom structure where files are saved in directories that have parent directories until the top of the structure is reached

drive: a disk drive on which data is stored. The operating system gives it a logical name, e.g. drive A, drive C

parent directory: a directory in which another directory is placed

In a GUI operating systems (see Chapter 1, Section 1.3 Operating systems), such as Microsoft Windows, the user expands a drive or folder to see its contents by double-clicking the icon. Once the file or program is located, a double-click on its icon will open the file or execute the program.

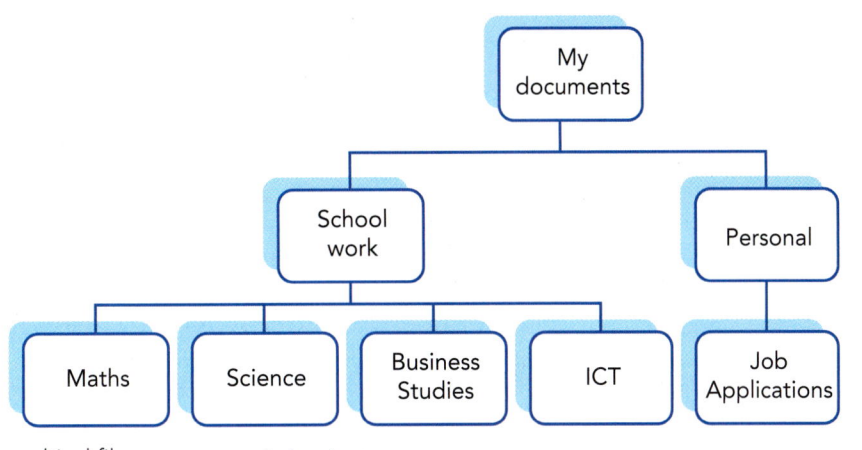

Figure 11.2: Basic hierarchical file management structure

In a non-GUI operating system, such as Linux, MS-DOS or the Windows command line, the drive and directories are listed as text.

It is important to keep your files organised so that you know where to look for them when you next want to open them (Figure 11.3). The goal of file management is to make sure you can quickly and easily find what you are looking for.

Save files using appropriate file names

There are many methods of naming files that work well. The important thing is to decide on a method that suits you and keep to it consistently.

A suggestion could be:

- Include the date the document was composed in your file name; this can be in the form of, for example, 04-10-2021.

Figure 11.3: I can't find my file!

- Indicate what is in the document in the **file name**; for example, it may be 'Notes for English essay'.
- This would result in a file name such as '04-10-2021 Notes for English essay.doc'. You don't have to type in the dot or the extension after the file name (e.g. .doc) in this case. The software application you are using will have automatically done that for you.
- Before you finalise the save, you need to specify which folder the file should be stored in; in this case it would belong in 'My documents/School Work/English'.

> ### KEY WORD
> **file name:** a unique identification for a file stored on a storage medium

> ### ICT IN CONTEXT
> It is important to check that the file name is correct. In Germany in 2017, fans of the popular television series, 'Twin Peaks' were shown episode 14, the final episode, instead of episode 13. Fans posted the outcome of the story from episode 14 onto social media, ruining the story for others. The mistake was made because of a broadcast file that was wrongly named.

> ### PRACTICAL TASK 11.1
>
> **Getting started**
>
> 1. Open your computer to the area where all your files are listed.
> 2. On a large sheet of paper, use one colour to draw the hierarchical file structure as it is at the moment.
> 3. Against each folder, list any files in it that could be deleted.
> 4. On the other side of the paper, use a different colour to draw an improved hierarchical file structure.
> 5. Against each folder describe the files that should go into each folder.
>
> **Practice**
>
> 6. Create the hierarchical folder structure on your computer to match the new one you have drawn, then move the relevant files into their appropriate folders.
> 7. If any of your filenames do not clearly indicate what is in the file, change the names of the files.
> 8. Make sure that your folders are clearly named to indicate their contents.

11 File management

> **CONTINUED**
>
> **Challenge**
>
> 9 Create a poster explaining what is meant by a hierarchical file structure and why it is necessary. You could create this poster using a word processor, or software like Paint.
>
> **Self-assessment**
>
> Answer the following questions.
>
> 1 Did the first drawing that I created show correctly how my files and folders were kept?
> 2 Was the new structure I drew better than the old one?
> 3 Was the way I selected files to go in the folders for the new structure helpful to me?
> 4 Did I manage to put the appropriate files in the folders on my computer?
> 5 Did I manage to rename my files so that it is clear what the contents are?
> 6 Can I now find and open my files more quickly than before?
>
> See Figure 11.4 for some more useful tips.

Questions

When several workers are working together in a team, each of them may alter a file at different times. It is important to be able to identify which the latest version is. This is called **version control**.

1 Which of the file names shown in this table are a good or bad method of file version control:

FILENAME
Project notes 1
Project notes new
Project notes 1 new
Project notes v2
Project notes v2 updated
Project notes 29 April 2023

2 Other than a version number, state what you could add to a filename to show it is the latest version of the file.

3 State how you could save a file in a way that would force you to create a new version the next time someone wants to use it.

> **KEY WORD**
>
> **version control:** the process by which different drafts and versions of a document or record are managed. For example, each time it is edited it could be 'Saved As' a new file with the version number added

Figure 11.4: Tips to be well-organised!

> **ACTIVITY 11.1**
>
> Some characters are not allowed by a computer's operating system to be used in filenames.
>
> Carry out research and compile a list of these characters. Try to save a filename using one of the characters and see what your computer does.
>
> Why are they not allowed?

Saving and printing files in a variety of formats

You should be able to save and print files in a variety of formats. You will be looking at the applications shown in Table 11.1 in the chapters indicated:

Documents	Chapter 17
Database reports and data tables	Chapter 18
Graphs and charts	Chapter 16 and Chapter 20
Presentations	Chapter 19

Table 11.1: Chapters covering use of applications

In most apps, files are saved and printed using the File menu.

Screenshots

If you want to capture an image of whatever is on your screen in Windows or on a Mac, there are various ways to do it. In Windows if you use the print screen button on your keyboard the image of your screen is stored on the clipboard. You can then paste the image into a suitable program in order to print it, or paste it into a graphics application to edit it and save it as an image file. On a Mac and in other commercial software, the **screenshot** is automatically saved as a graphic file. This allows you to take multiple screenshots without having to stop and paste.

Web page in browser and HTML view

In Chapter 21, you will create pages for the web using HTML and CSS.

> **ACTIVITY 11.2**
>
> On the computer you are using:
>
> 1 Take a screenshot of the complete window and paste it into a word processing document.
>
> 2 Take a screenshot of part of the window and save it as a graphic file.

HyperText Markup Language (HTML) is the code in which web pages are written (Figure 11.5b). Your browser converts or renders this code into the web page that you see (Figure 11.5a).

The method to show the HTML code and printed web pages differs between the different browsers.

> **KEY WORDS**
>
> **screenshot:** an image of the data displayed on the screen
>
> **HyperText Markup Language (HTML):** HyperText Markup Language is the code you use to create web pages

> **ACTIVITY 11.3**
>
> Investigate the browser that you are using to discover how to print the pages of a website and how to show and print the HTML code.
>
> Create a presentation, using text and screenshots, to help fellow students to print the pages and show and print the HTML code of a website.

Save and export files in the file format of an application

Different applications have their own method of formatting data when their files are saved so that they can be opened and edited by the program in the future. However, in most applications, files are saved by using a 'Save' command in the File menu. They can be saved with a new name by using the 'Save As' command.

11 File management

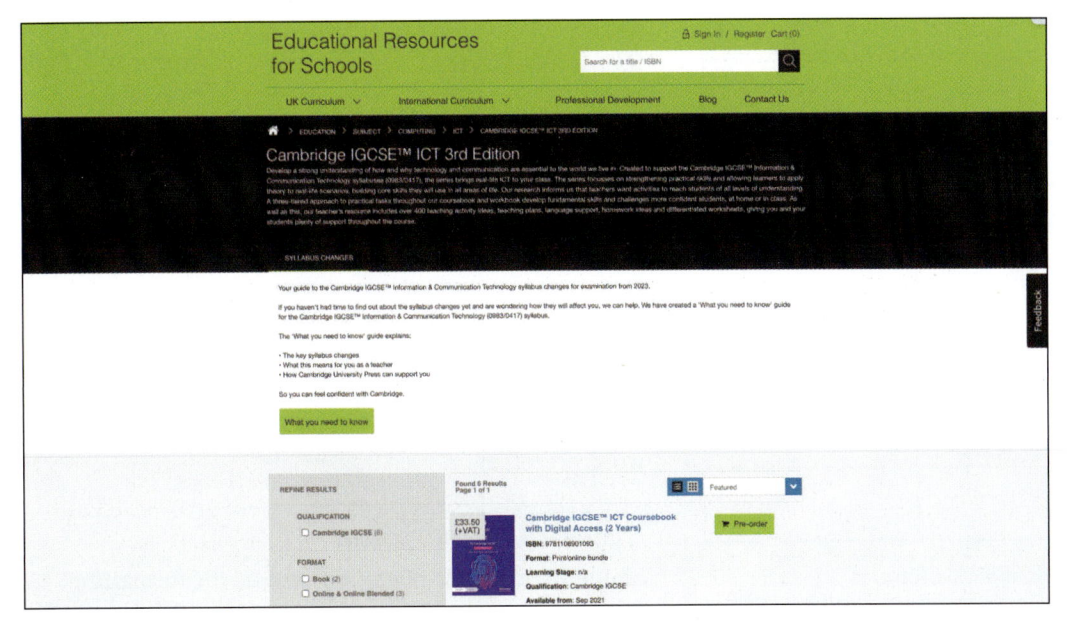

Figure 11.5a: Printout of a web page

Figure 11.5b: The HTML code

Table 11.2 shows some applications and their file formats (see the next page).

Save and export in a generic file format

Generic file formats allow you to save files so that they can be opened on different computer types and by different applications, e.g. the .jpg file format can be opened by a graphic app on a Mac and by a different app in Windows. The files may not contain all of the formatting that can be saved in a package-specific format.

That is what is meant by '**exporting**' a file – saving it in a format that is not native to the application but which it and other applications can open.

> **KEY WORDS**
>
> **export:** saving a file in a particular format in one application so that it can be opened in another, different application
>
> **generic file type:** a file that can be opened on any operating system using a standard application

Because of the huge popularity of Microsoft products, many of their native file formats and extensions are also used by manufacturers of other software applications. For example, the .doc and .xls formats can be opened by many other word processing and spreadsheet applications. They are said to have become **generic file types**.

203

Application	File extension(s)
Microsoft Word	.doc and .docx
Microsoft Excel	.xls and .xlsx
Microsoft Access	.accdb
Microsoft Powerpoint	.ppt and .pptx
Open Office database (Base)	.odp
Windows Compatibility Solution Database Also Open Office Base database files	.sdp
Open Office spreadsheet (Calc)	.sdc
Most applications can save text in rich text format	.rtf

Table 11.2: Applications and their file formats

Other common generic file types include .csv, .txt, .rtf, .pdf, .css, .htm, .jpg, .png, .gif, .zip, .rar

CSV files or comma separated values

The **comma separated values** file type saves data from tables, for example, in databases and spreadsheets, and stores them as text. Each item of data is separated by a comma.

> **KEY WORD**
>
> **comma separated values (CSV):** this file format can be used on data saved in a table structured format, such as a spreadsheet or a database, where each value is separated by a comma

> **ICT IN CONTEXT**
>
> To get more lists of possible clients, ecommerce businesses often buy customer data from social media websites. This data would be sent to the ecommerce business' database in csv format, because it makes it quick and simple to exchange data. When used and formatted correctly, csv files are easy to convert to other file types.

> **ACTIVITY 11.4**
>
> Open a spreadsheet or a database table that you have created and export or save the data as a .csv file.
>
> Open the .csv file in your word processing software to view how the data is separated by commas.

.txt files or text files

Saves a text file without any formatting, merely plain text, so that it can be opened in any word processor.

.rtf or rich text fomat

Similar to a .txt file but saves some of the formatting in a form that can be understood by all word processing software.

.pdf or portable document format

This is basically an image format that preserves page layout and is used when you need to save files that cannot be modified but can be easily shared and printed.

.css or cascading stylesheet

A file that is attached to one or more web pages to define the styles to be used, e.g. colour scheme, fonts, font sizes, etc.

.htm/.html or HyperText Markup Language

A file that contains the code that is interpreted by all web browsers to render or display a web page.

.jpg or joint photographic expert group

A file that stores still image data in compressed form.

.png or portable network graphics

An image format that is commonly used for web pages. They are useful as their backgrounds can be made transparent so not obscuring items beneath them.

.gif or graphics interchange format

Supports only 256 different colours and with a small file size making them suitable for web pages. Also supports animations.

11 File management

.zip or compressed file

A .zip file may contain one or more files or directories that have been **compressed** so that they require less storage space and have a smaller file size. This is useful for archiving files, and for sending data to other users.

.rar or roshal archive

Creates a file containing compressed directories and files. RAR has a higher compression ratio (the ratio between the **uncompressed** size and compressed size) and creates smaller file sizes compared to ZIP. RAR files are also quicker to decompress.

Questions

4. Give the term for the addition to the end of a file name that relates to the software you are using.
5. When you double-click on a filename to open it, how does the computer know which software program to use to open that file?
6. Give **three** common file extensions used by word processing software.
7. State the file extension that could be used to save and export your file from word processing software to a read-only file format for distributing documents.

ICT IN CONTEXT

A large volume of unsuitable images is usually the most common reason behind website slowness. High-resolution images can consume lots of bandwidth while loading. Uploading larger sized images and then scaling them down can unnecessarily increase the size of your web page – causing your website to load slowly.

The image format is another important factor to consider.

For example, JPEG images are much smaller in size compared to other image formats like PNG or GIF. Quite naturally, your web page will load faster if you are using JPEG images instead of PNG/GIF.

8. Define csv.
9. Name **one** important spreadsheet item that cannot be saved in a .csv file.
10. Name the type of software application that .xls files are associated with.

11.2 Reducing file sizes for storage or for transmission

In 2019, 350 million photos every day were uploaded, on average, to Facebook alone and it is estimated that in 2022 1.56 trillion will be taken and stored. Most users store images online, either by posting them to social media websites or backing them up and archiving them to cloud storage sites.

To save storage space and to speed up **transmission** when sending files to other people, **compression algorithms** have been created to reduce their file sizes. (However, most social media sites don't accept compressed files.) All other file types can be compressed in addition to images.

There are two main types of compression: **lossy** and **lossless**.

KEY WORDS

compressed: any file that contains one or more files or directories that is smaller than their original file size

uncompressed: a compressed file returned to its original state

transmission: transferring something from one place to another

compression algorithm: a method to compress files, reducing their size and making them more portable

lossy compression: a method of compressing data where some data is discarded

lossless compression: a method of compressing a file where no data is discarded

Lossy compression

Lossy compression works by permanently deleting some of the data in the file. The original image can never be reconstituted when it is decompressed. It has been irreversibly changed.

That is why it cannot be used for text files or program files: a book with lots of missing words would be unreadable!

A high-resolution image with a 24-bit colour depth has a very large file size. Images that have not been compressed and which contain all of the colour data are called **RAW** files.

During lossy compression, the program analyses the image and finds areas where there are only slight differences that we might not be able to distinguish. It will then give these the same value and so can rewrite the file using fewer bits.

Audio files can be compressed in a similar way. Digital audio files that contain all of the sound data are saved in waveform audio (wav) format. Typically, a three-minute recording will have a file size of 30 megabytes. There are frequencies and tones that we cannot hear and slight differences in volume and frequency that we cannot distinguish. These are removed to reduce the size and an MP3 file is usually about a tenth the size of a wav file. Therefore the 30 megabyte wav file can be reduced to a 3 megabyte MP3 file. Far smaller for storage and transmission.

The file size of the first flowers image in Figure 11.6 is 9 MB, that of the second is 2 MB and that of the thrid is 1 MB. A lossy compression has been used to reduce the file sizes size. Can you easily tell the difference?

Lossless compression

Lossless compression, as its name implies, reduces files with no loss of information during the process. Therefore, this enables the original file to be recreated exactly when uncompressed. Nothing is lost.

Lossless compression works by finding repeated data in a file. This is called redundant data. It then only saves the data once and keeps an index of where it should be included.

Lossless compression is mainly used for documents, text and numerical data where it is essential not to lose any information. Both ZIP and RAR compression, mentioned earlier in this chapter, uses lossless compression.

ZIP, or its equivalent, is often more convenient because it is built into the operating system of both Windows and Mac computers. RAR is better at data compression but it has to be bought as commercial software.

9 MB   2 MB   1 MB

Figure 11.6: Example of lossy compression

ACTIVITY 11.5

When you ZIP a file or a folder, the files are compressed so that the compressed file or folder takes up less room on your hard drive; it is also convenient for when you want to transfer files to other computers or share files with others.

To ZIP a file or folder, you need to select it, then right-click on it and select the option to compress it.

1. Work with a partner and make a compressed copy of one of your files or folders.
2. Right-click on the files or folders to find their sizes. How much difference has it made?
3. Try compressing different types of files. Are some compressed by a greater ratio than others?
4. Decompress the files and folders by selecting them, right-clicking and selecting the menu option. Are they exactly the same sizes as the originals?

PRACTICAL TASK 11.2

Getting started

1. With a partner, list file types that use lossless and lossy compression for storing text, video, images and sound.

Practice

2. Create a presentation that you could use to teach students, in the year group below you, about lossy and lossless compression algorithms, how they work and the differences between them.

   For information about creating presentations, see Chapter 19.

Challenge

3. Add to your presentation to show the differences between jpg, gif and png image file types and when each should be used.

REFLECTION

What problems did you encounter when completing the activities, questions and practical tasks in this chapter? How did you solve them?

SUMMARY

In order to find your files easily, store your files in a hierarchical folder structure, use descriptive filenames and appropriate version control where necessary.

Use meaningful names for file naming to make it easier to recognise what they contain.

You can import and export files between different applications.

A generic file type is one that is not specific to one application.

CSV files are used to import and export data.

File sizes can be reduced by compression so that they take up less storage space and less time when moving them over the internet.

Lossless compression will mainly be used for documents, text and numerical data where it is essential not to lose any data; lossy compression reduces the file size by eliminating some bits of information, permanently deleting unnecessary data.

ZIP compression is a lossless compression type that works by detecting and replacing patterns with a single character.

EXAM-STYLE QUESTIONS

1. a **State** what is meant by the term 'folder'. [1]
   b Name the type of folder system to be used in managing your files. [1]
2. Which *two* of the following graphic file formats are often used on the internet? [2]
   - .jpg and .ppt
   - .ppt and .gif
   - .gif and .jpg
   - .pic and .ppt
3. State which statements are true and which are false. [4]
   i On a computer, you can create a folder inside another folder.
   ii A file can be moved by dragging it from one window to another on screen.
   iii To delete a folder you could drag it to the recycle bin.
   iv A folder provides a way to organise programs and files on a disk.
4. State which of the following is a valid filename to use to store the instructions for the manual of your printer. [1]
   - User info*printer.gif
   - "Printer manual".doc
   - Printer manual>Epsom.com
   - Printer manual.docx
5. **Describe** how you would save a document to a different file name. [2]

COMMAND WORDS

state: express in clear terms

describe: state the points of a topic / give characteristics and main features

11 File management

> **CONTINUED**
>
> **6 a** **Give** an example of:
>   **i** A lossy compression file format. [1]
>   **ii** A lossless compression file format. [1]
> **b** State what is meant by file compression. [1]
> **c** List the benefits of compressing a file or folder. [3]
> **7** State the purpose of a .rtf file. [2]
>
> [Total: 19]

> **COMMAND WORD**
>
> **give:** produce an answer from a given source or recall / memory

SELF-EVALUATION CHECKLIST

After studying this chapter, think about how confident you are with the different topics.

This will help you to see any gaps in your knowledge and help you to learn more effectively.

You might find it helpful to rate how confident you are for each of these statements when you are revising. You should revisit any sections that you rated 'Needs more work' or 'Getting there'.

I can …	See section	Needs more work	Getting there	Confident to move on
manage files, including being able to quickly locate stored files, open and import different file types, and save and export data	11.1			
use a hierarchical folder structure and save files using appropriate file names for quick identification of the file contents	11.1			
save and export files in a variety of formats, including generic file formats	11.1			
explain why file sizes are reduced for storage or transmission	11.2			
reduce the size of file sizes by compression	11.2			
understand and use different file compression techniques	11.2			

Chapter 12
Images

IN THIS CHAPTER YOU WILL:

- place an image with precision
- resize an image and maintain or adjust its aspect ratio
- crop, rotate and flip an image horizontally and vertically
- adjust the colour depth, brightness and contrast of an image
- group and layer images
- explain how to reduce file size by reducing image resolution and colour depth.

12 Images

> **GETTING STARTED**
>
> Figure 12.1 shows some tools in a graphic editing program. Working with a partner, identify the tools labelled a to f.
>
> **Figure 12.1:** Graphic editing tools

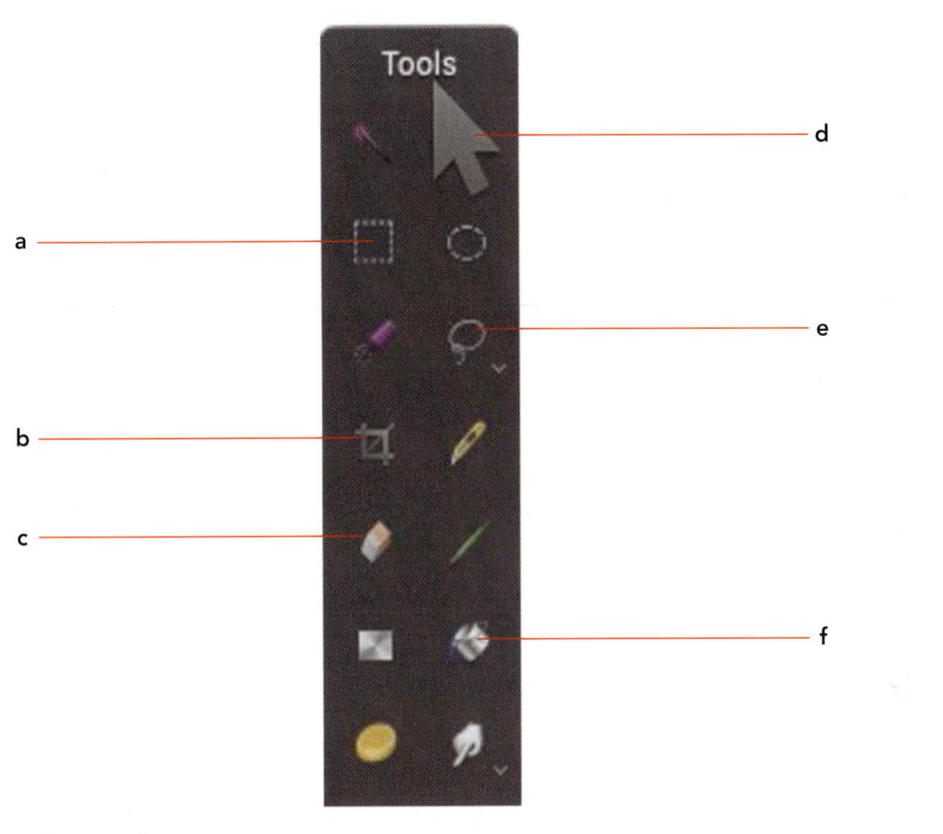

WHEN DID WE FIRST START COMMUNICATING?

Painting and graphics are a vital form of communication – and were probably the first form of non-verbal communication we had. Long before written communication, people were drawing on the walls of caves.

The image in Figure 12.2 shows graphics painted in a cave near Raha, Muna Island, Southeast Sulawesi province, Indonesia. Nobody is sure why they were painted but maybe the animal ones were to help the hunters – capture the image and you'll capture the animal. Or maybe they were just boasting about what they had already caught. Many cave drawings are of people or just their handprints, so maybe people just wanted to leave their marks. Or maybe they just felt like doodling.

Figure 12.2: Early cave drawings

> **CAMBRIDGE IGCSE™ ICT: COURSEBOOK**

> **CONTINUED**
>
> Throughout history, images, design and graphics have played an important part in human existence and have helped people to understand their lives. Everyone has a creative need but unfortunately not everyone has the skills to express it through painting and drawing. Computers and graphics programs have helped those people to express their creativity.
>
> Today we are surrounded by graphics – in magazines, leaflets, advertising, logos and online. An image can create a mood or communicate excitement, sadness, reflection or an idea of perfection. They can be manipulated in many ways to enhance or change the impressions they create but as well as revealing truths, images can be manipulated to imply a situation completely different to what was originally intended.
>
> **Discussion questions**
>
> 1   What are the advantages of creating digital art on a computer rather than painting on paper or a canvas?
> 2   Some people argue that only paintings and objects created by hand are true art and that digital art cannot be included. What are your views?

12.1 Placing and editing images

When you create a document in a word processor, a spreadsheet, a database or a presentation program, there are times when you will need to place images at appropriate places in the document.

You will also most likely need to edit the image to make it fit in with the needs of your intended audience. For example, many adverts use airbrushing on celebrities to make them appear slimmer and more beautiful. The 'red eye' problem in some images can also be edited out, and image processing techniques are used in blue-screen and green-screen technology, which makes video clips appear as if they were filmed on location when really they were filmed in the studio.

At times images might need to be resized or you might wish to cut a part of the image (crop an image). At other times you might place one image on top of, or partially on top of, other images (layering of images) or need to turn an image around from the way it was originally facing (reflect or rotate an image).

Place an image with precision

Images can easily be imported into a document, usually by using the 'Insert' menu. An image can often be pasted into a document if you have copied it onto the clipboard from elsewhere.

Once they have been imported, images can be positioned in various ways. The image can be dragged using the mouse into a suitable position, but this method does not achieve an accurate, absolute position, only a position that is acceptable to the user.

Place relative to the page

Most software allows users to enter coordinates for a more precise position **relative** to the margin or the edge of the page.

> **KEY WORD**
>
> **relative:** considered where something is in relation to something else

> **ACTIVITY 12.1**
>
> Open a new document and place an image somewhere within in. Then investigate your software to find how to access the picture controls for sizing, positioning and text wrapping.

Figure 12.3 shows the image aligned to the upper and left edges of the page. In Word, this dialogue box can be accessed from the 'Picture Format' menu or by right-clicking on the image and selecting 'Size and Position'. Other software may have different ways to access the dialogue box.

Figure 12.4 shows the image 3 cm from the left edge and 1 cm from the top edge.

12 Images

Figure 12.3: Image aligned to left and top edges

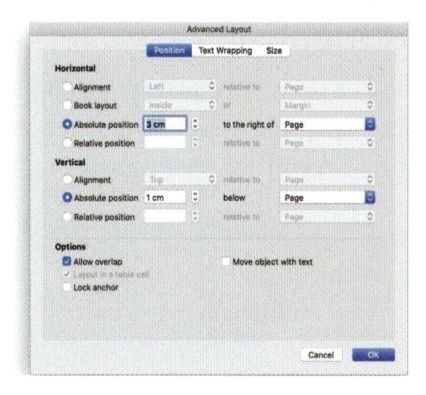

Figure 12.4: Image 3 cm from left edge and 1 cm from top edge

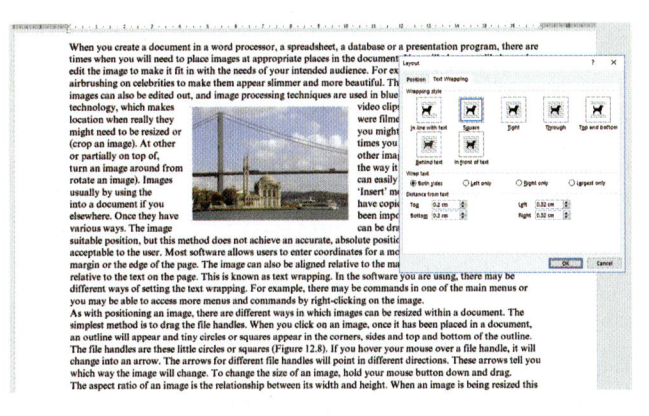

Figure 12.5: Tight text wrapping

Figure 12.6: Top and bottom wrapping

Figure 12.7: Behind text wrapping

The image can also be aligned relative to the margins.

Place relative to the text

Images can be aligned relative to the text on the page. This is known as **text wrapping**.

> **KEY WORD**
>
> **text wrapping:** surrounding an image with text

Examples of text wrapping include:

- tight text wrapping, where the text surrounds the image; notice how you can also adjust the margins around the image (see Figure 12.5)
- top and bottom wrapping, which places the image on its own line within the text (see Figure 12.6)
- behind text wrapping, which allows the text to carry on over the image (see Figure 12.7).

In the software you are using, there may be different ways of setting the text wrapping. For example, there may be commands in one of the main menus or you may be able to access more menus and commands by right-clicking on the image.

> **ACTIVITY 12.2**
>
> Investigate your software to find the different menus and commands you can use to set the text wrapping around an image.
>
> Create a document with text and insert an image. Create screen prints of the different types of text wrapping you can apply with your software.

213

Questions

1 List **five** 'Wrap Text' options.
2 Explain, using diagrams, how each of the following 'Wrap Text' would position the image relative to the text:
   a square
   b tight
   c through.

Resize an image to maintain or adjust the aspect ratio of an image

As with positioning an image, there are different ways in which images can be resized within a document.

The simplest method is to drag the file handles. When you click on an image, once it has been placed in a document, an outline will appear and tiny circles or squares appear in the corners, sides and top and bottom of the outline. The file handles are these little circles or squares (see Figure 12.8).

If you hover your mouse over a file handle, it will change into an arrow. The arrows for different file handles will point in different directions. These arrows tell you which way the image will change. To change the size of an image, hold your mouse button down and drag.

The **aspect ratio** of an image is the relationship between its width and height. When an image is being resized this relationship should be preserved. Unless you want to deliberately distort the image.

If the file handles at the corners are dragged, the aspect ratio of the image will be retained.

If the file handles at the sides are dragged, then the aspect ratio will change (see Figure 12.9).

> **KEY WORD**
>
> **aspect ratio:** relationship between the width and height of an image

Images can be resized more accurately by using menu commands. In Word, this dialogue box (see Figure 12.10) can be accessed from the 'Picture Format' menu or by right-clicking on the image and selecting 'Size and Position'. Other software will have the commands with their own picture formatting tools.

Figure 12.8: File handles

Figure 12.9: The image has been distorted as the file handle on the right side was dragged

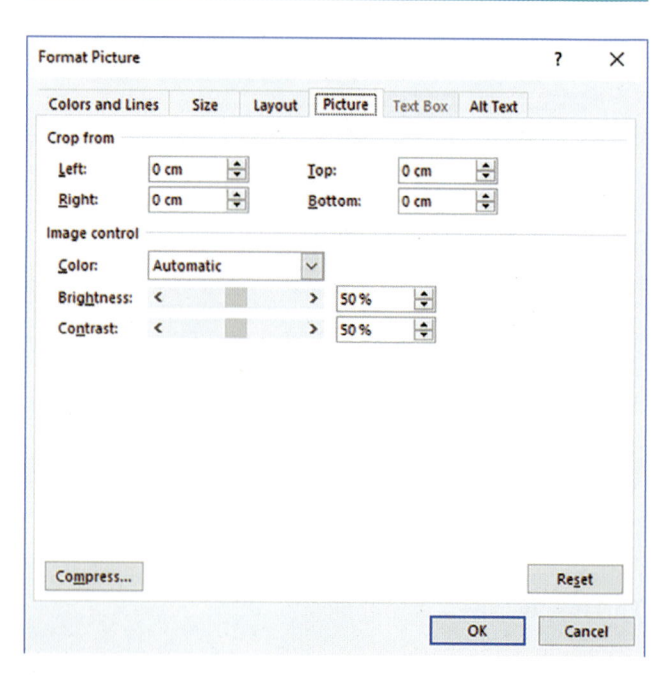

Figure 12.10: The size can be set very accurately using a dialogue box

Questions

3. Explain what is meant by the aspect ratio of an image.
4. Describe how an image can be resized to keep the aspect ratio the same.

Crop an image

There are times when you might not require a whole image, but just a part of it. This can be done by **cropping** a part of it away so that only the part you require remains visible. Some software packages allow you to crop an image only in a regular (rectangular) shape, while others allow you to cut out any irregular shape from the image in the same way that you would manually use a pair of scissors to cut out shapes from a picture.

> **KEY WORD**
>
> **cropping:** to remove unwanted portions of an image by 'cutting off' or removing the sides. The crop tool is used to achieve this

To crop an image, the command may be in the image/picture menus or main menu bar or it may also be accessed by right-clicking in the image (see Figure 12.11) The file handles will change to thick dashes or corners.

Figure 12.11: Cropping an image by right-clicking on the image

The image can be cropped by dragging the file handles (see Figure 12.12). The part of the image you crop does not just disappear forever. You can reverse the process by selecting 'crop' and dragging the file handles in the reverse direction.

> **ACTIVITY 12.3**
>
> Images can also be cropped to a particular shape, for example, an oval or circle. Investigate your software to see if it has a 'Crop to Shape' option.

Figure 12.12: File handles for cropping

Rotate an image

Rotating an image refers to turning it through an angle. Again, there are usually different ways of doing this.

> **KEY WORD**
>
> **rotate:** turn an image through an angle relative to its original position

Using the mouse

When you right-click on an image you will see the file handles and also a box with a circular arrow (see Figure 12.13). This can be dragged to rotate the image.

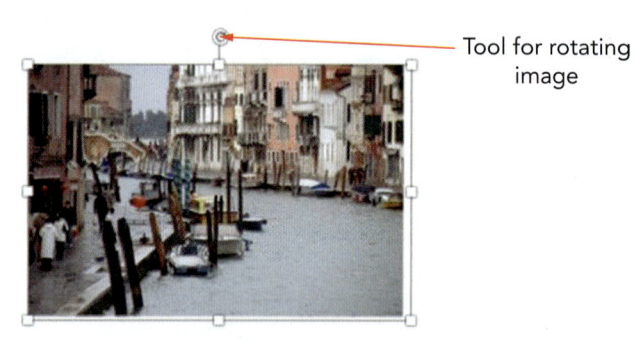

Figure 12.13: Rotating an image

The angle of rotation will be shown as you drag (see Figure 12.14).

Figure 12.14: Angle of rotation

Using a menu option

Here the angle of rotation can be set precisely (see Figure 12.15).

Reflect (flip) an image horizontally or vertically

Reflecting, or flipping, an image means producing a mirror image of the original image. The image can be reflected horizontally (see Figure 12.16) or vertically (see Figure 12.17). The software tools vary between the different software packages but in most the commands are usually in the main menu bar.

KEY WORD

reflecting: to produce a mirror image of the original image

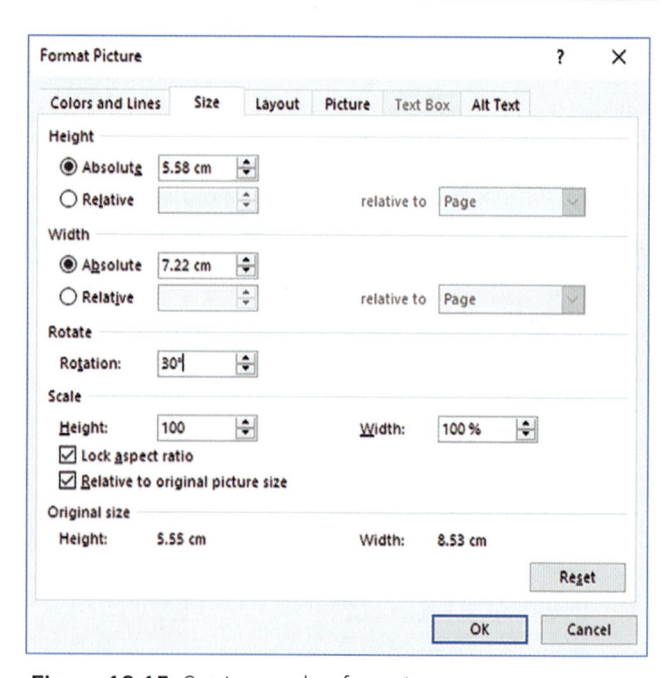

Figure 12.15: Setting angle of rotation

Figure 12.16: Original image and flipped horizontally

Figure 12.17: Original image and flipped vertically

PRACTICAL TASK 12.1

Getting started

When an image is inserted into a document, the text can be made to flow around the image in different ways.

1. On paper, sketch the differences between the following types of text flow:
   - tight
   - square
   - top and bottom.

2. For the software you are using, explain, giving the toolbar, menu or ribbon options, how to carry out the following tasks:
   - resize an image
   - move an image behind/in front of the text
   - change the transparency of an image.

CONTINUED

Practice

3   Open *Task1.docx*. It contains some sample text but don't try to read it as it doesn't make sense. It is there for you to practise text flow.

4   Insert *Image_a.jpg* and format it to the following specification:

   - Maintaining the aspect ratio, resize the image so that the height is 3 cm.
   - Position it at the top, left corner of the text with a square text flow.

5   Insert *Image_b.jpg* and format it to the following specification:

   - Maintaining the aspect ratio, resize the image so that the height is 4 cm.
   - Position it 8 cm from the top margin and 6 cm from the left one.
   - Set the text flow around the image to Top and Bottom.

6   Insert *Image_c.jpg* and format it to the following specification:

   - Maintaining the aspect ratio, resize the image so that the height is 3 cm.
   - Position it 1.2 cm from the top of paragraph 3 and 8 cm to the right of the left margin.
   - Set the text flow around the image to Tight.

   The page should appear as in Figure 12.18.

Figure 12.18: The finished page

Challenge

7   Rotate *Image_b.jpg* through 10° (see Figure 12.19).

Figure 12.19: Image rotated through 10°

12 Images

> **CONTINUED**
>
> **8** Make a copy of *Image_c.jpg* and paste the copy directly to the left of the original. Flip the copy so that it is a mirror image of the original (see Figure 12.20). 
>
> Figure 12.20: Original image and flipped copy

Adjust the brightness of an image

The **brightness** of an image refers to how much light the image is emitting. Obviously, if it is emitting no light, it will be completely black and at maximum brightness, it will be completely white.

In Word, the tools for adjusting the brightness can usually be obtained by selecting 'Corrections' from the 'Format' tab or by right-clicking on the image and selecting 'Format Picture'. Usually, a slider is provided to increase or decrease the brightness (see Figure 12.21). Alternatively, a box for a number is provided; the greater the number, the brighter/whiter the image.

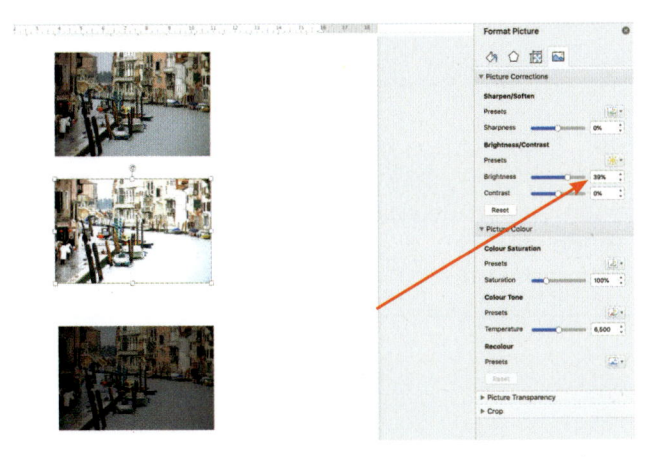

Figure 12.21: The original image, brightness increased by 39% and decreased by 42%

In the same dialogue box, you will probably find a far more useful function – changing the **transparency**. That means how easy it is see through it. It is very useful for showing text and other objects underneath it. Usually there is a slider to increase or decrease the transparency from 0% to 100%. In Figure 12.22, the image is placed on top of the word VENICE, and the transparency of the image is 50% – so you can see the word coming through.

> **KEY WORDS**
>
> **brightness:** the amount of light an image is emitting; an image with 0% brightness will be all black, an image with 100% brightness will be all white
>
> **transparency:** how see-through an image is

Figure 12.22: Image with transparency increased by 50%

Adjust the contrast of an image

Contrast means 'difference'. When you are editing images, it is the difference between the highest and lowest colour intensities of that image. High contrast means that there is a wide range (the top image in Figure 12.23) and low contrast means that they are very similar (the bottom image in Figure 12.23).

> **KEY WORD**
>
> **contrast:** the difference between the highest and lowest light intensities in an image

The controls for adjusting the contrast should be with those for brightness and transparency. The higher the number, the greater the contrast; the negative numbers reduce the contrast.

Figure 12.23: High and low contrast

PRACTICAL TASK 12.2

Getting started

1. Explain what is meant by saying that an image is over- or under-exposed.
2. Explain what is meant by the contrast of an image.

Practice

3. Create a new document and insert *Image_h.jpg*.
4. This image is very over-exposed and the contrast is poor. Using image editing tools such as brightness, contrast, saturation and temperature (saturation and temperature can usually be found in a similar place to brightness and contrast), edit the image to improve its appearance.

12 Images

> **CONTINUED**
>
> **Challenge**
>
> Using a graphics program, perform the same edits (e.g. brightness, contrast, saturation and temperature). See Figure 12.24 for an example.
>
> **Figure 12.24:** Editing an image
>
> 5   In which program is it easier to edit the image?
>
> 6   Does the graphics program have more editing options to improve the image?
>
> 7   Insert the image you edited in the graphics program next to your original. Are there noticeable differences between them?

ICT IN CONTEXT

Logos usually combine images and text and have been used for hundreds of years.

The Twinings Tea logo has been used continuously for 227 years, making it the world's oldest unaltered logo in continuous use.

The first product logo is thought to be a drinks company that still exists today, which was first used in 1366.

Question

5   Explain what is meant by the following terms:
   a   pixel
   b   image resolution
   c   image colour depth
   d   image contrast.

Grouping, ungrouping and moving to front or back

Sometimes it is easier to move images if they are grouped together. Word processing and image editing software allows you to treat a collection of images as if it was one image by selecting all of the images and using the '**group**' option. This can be useful, even to just move a collection of objects together on a page.

You can remove this feature from an image by using the '**ungroup**' option.

KEY WORDS

group: combining images so that they can be selected and moved together

ungroup: separating the image group so that they all have to be selected and moved individually

In Figure 12.25, the images have been grouped and can be moved together as one.

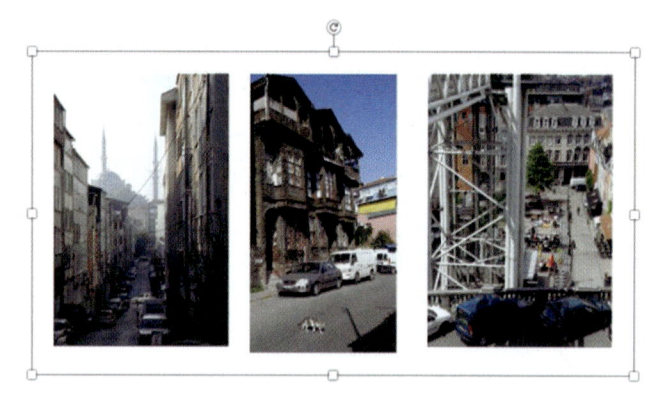

Figure 12.25: A group of images

Images can be placed on top of each other in **layers** (see Figure 12.26), and in most image editing software, you can change the order of how the images are placed on top of each other. You can usually do this by right-clicking your layer and selecting 'Move to Front', 'Move Forward', 'Move Backward' and 'Move to Back' (see Figure 12.27). Each of these options changes the order of the layers in the image.

> **KEY WORD**
>
> **layer:** the term used to describe the different levels at which you can place an image

12.2 Reducing file size

When images are used on websites and transmitted over the internet, it is important that they can be downloaded in the quickest time possible. It is therefore important that the file sizes of images should be as low as possible.

This image has been 'Brought to the front'

This image has been 'Sent Backwards'

Figure 12.26: Images placed on top of each other

Figure 12.27: Images rearranged

12 Images

To a computer, an image consists of millions of 1s and 0s, the total amount determining its file size.

When a picture is digitised, it is divided up into thousands of points or elements, and the colour data of each point is stored as bits – 1s and 0s. Each of these elements is called a **pixel**.

> **KEY WORD**
>
> **pixel:** an individual point of light in a digital image (it is a shortened version of '**pi**cture **el**ements')

PRACTICAL TASK 12.3

Getting started

1. Explain what is meant by the 'aspect ratio' of an image.
2. Explain what is meant by the 'transparency' of an object.
3. On paper, using a rectangular outline shape, sketch how it would appear if it had been rotated through the following degrees: 60°, 90°, 240°, 300°.

Practice

You are going to create this front page (see Figure 12.28) for a document about your holidays.

4. Start a new document and change the orientation to landscape.
5. At the top of the page, centre the heading 'My Holidays'.
6. Insert *Image_a.jpg*. Use the crop and resize tools to edit the image to retain the central part. The final dimensions of the image should be 5 cm in height and 2 cm in width.
7. Insert Images b to f and crop and resize them to the same dimensions.
8. These images are going to be arranged around a circle. Five of the images have to be rotated through the following degrees: 60°, 120°, 180°, 240° and 300°.

   Decide which image has to be rotated by which amount.

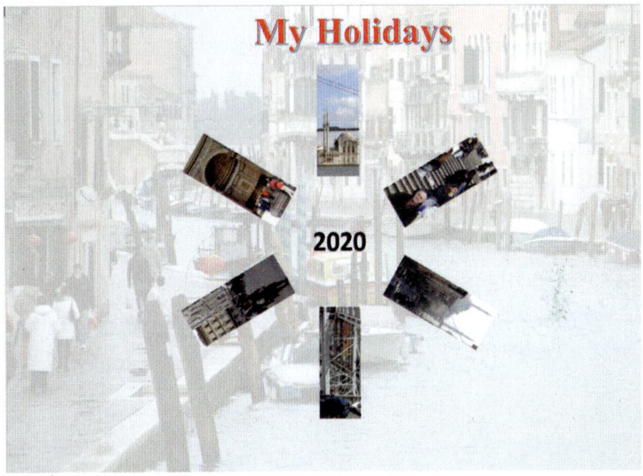

9. In the centre of the page, insert a circle shape with a diameter of approximately 6 cm. This can be done by selecting 'Shapes' from the 'Insert' tab and selecting the 'Oval' shape. Click in your document where you want the top right corner of your circle to be. To make a circle, hold down the 'Shift' key as you are drawing it.
10. Arrange the images around the circumference of the circle in their correct positions.

    The image at 180° should be flipped vertically.

11. Edit the circle shape using the 'Shape Format' tab and format it to 'No Fill' and 'No Outline'. Right-click on the shape and select 'Add Text' and write '2020' inside it.

Figure 12.28: My Holidays

CONTINUED

12 Group all of the images and the circle so that they can be moved together.

13 Insert *Image_g.jpg* and resize it so that it fills the whole page. Change its transparency to 80%.

Challenge

You are going to edit the page to that shown in Figure 12.29.

14 Move the grouped images to the bottom, right corner of the page.

15 Make a copy of the group and resize it. You will have to change the font size of the text '2020' to 5.5 pts so that it fits within the circle. Move this copy to the top left corner of the page and rotate it through 90°.

16 Make two further copies, gradually increasing in size, between the top left and bottom right corners. These should be rotated through 180° and 270° and the font for '2020' should increase to 11 and 12 pts respectively. In the copy rotated through 180°, flip the image at the bottom of the circle vertically.

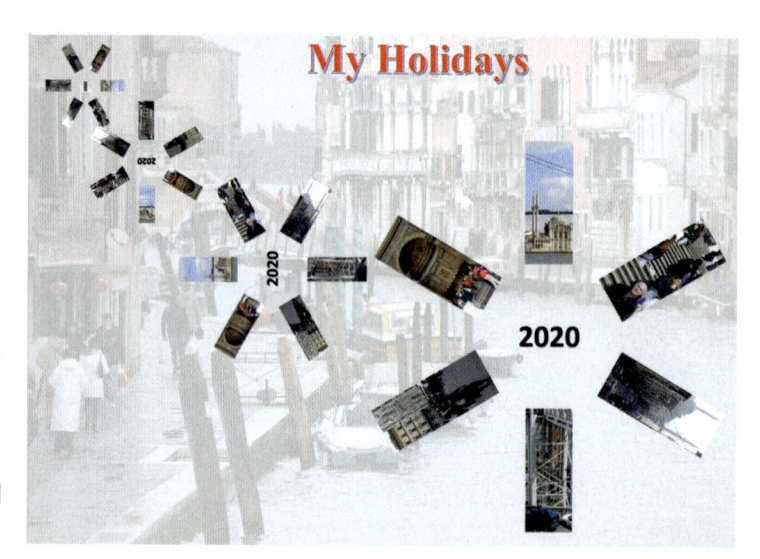

Figure 12.29: The edited front page

Peer assessment

Swap your documents with a partner and assess each other's work.

	Yes/No
The document has a heading.	
All of the images have been inserted.	
The images have been cropped as requested.	
The images have been rotated through the correct angles.	
A circular shape with the text '2020' has been inserted.	
The objects have been grouped.	
Background image has been inserted and transparency increased to 80%.	
Copies have been made, resized and rotated as requested.	

12 Images

> **WORKED EXAMPLE 12.01**

THE FOOTBALL CLUB

You are going to insert some images into a document and then edit and position them accurately to the following specification.

1. Open *WorkedExample.docx* into your word processing software and add the heading 'The Football Club' with a Calibri font of 20 pts and emboldened and centred.
2. Insert the image *Stadium.jpg* and from it make a circular clip, showing the main gates, from the centre of the image. The clip should have a diameter of 5 cm.
3. This image should be centred horizontally and be 1.15 cm below the top margin. It should have Tight text flow with the 'Distance from Text' set to 0 cm top and bottom and 0.1 cm left and right.
4. Insert the image *Score.jpg* and clip it so that it shows only the central, black area of the scoreboard with none of the surrounding material.
5. This image should have a Tight text flow, be rotated 30° and positioned 11.09 cm below the top margin and 6.79 cm to the right of the left margin.
6. Save the document as *Football.doc*.

Step 1

WorkedExample.doc is a page of text.

Add the heading 'The Football Club' with a Calibri font of 20 pts, emboldened and centred.

Step 2

The image of the stadium can be inserted anywhere in the document. It may move onto another page and push the text down (see Figure 12.30).

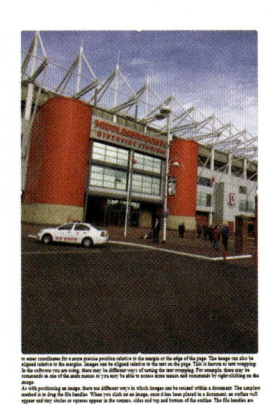

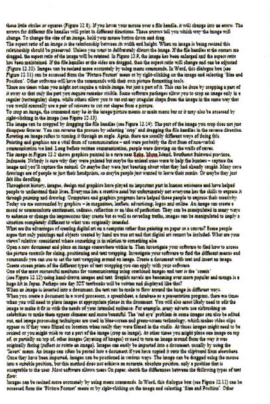

Figure 12.30: The image has moved down to the second page

> **CONTINUED**

This will be easy to fix when the image is resized.

A circular clip can be made using the 'Clip to Shape' tool – obviously using the ellipse shape.

Unfortunately, if this shape is used on the current image it will not produce a perfect circle (see Figure 12.31).

This looks more like an oval!

To ensure that the clip is a circle, the original image must be made into a square using the crop and resize tools ensuring the main part of the edited image shows the main gates.

Figure 12.32 shows the image now as a square of 14 cm height and width.

Figure 12.31: The oval clip

Figure 12.32: A square from the original image

Now use the 'Clip to Shape' tool again. As the clip was made from a square this time, it should be a perfect circle.

The size can now be changed to 5 cm × 5 cm.

12 Images

CONTINUED

Step 3

The clip can now be centred and placed 1.15 cm below the top margin with Tight text flow and the 'Distance from Text' set correctly (see Figure 12.33).

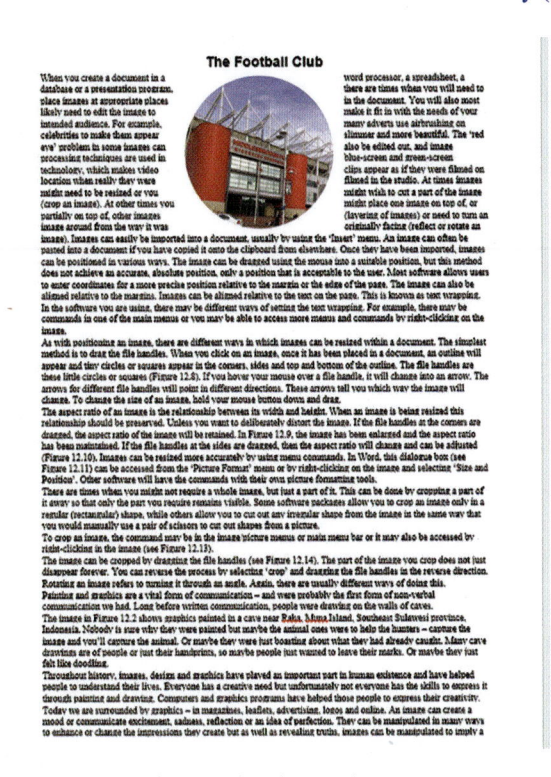

Figure 12.33: The circular clip on the page

Steps 4–5

Score.jpg can now be inserted and cropped (see Figure 12.34) in line with the specification.

Figure 12.34: Before and after cropping

Step 6

The document can then be saved as *Football.doc*.

Questions

1 Create this document with the required specification, using your own software.
2 Edit the circular image by applying a red border with a weight of 3 pts.

Obviously, the more pixels that are used, the more detailed and accurate the picture will be, but the larger will be the file size.

The number of pixels per unit of area is called the **image resolution**. This is often referred to as pixels per inch (ppi).

The colour of each pixel is stored as a number of bits (1s and 0s) and the greater the number of bits used to represent a colour, the greater the number of colours can be represented.

If one bit is used (0 or 1), then only two colours can be represented, white and black.

Two bits would represent four colours, but this is rarely used. Table 12.1 shows how each colour is represented.

Bit 2	Bit 1
0	0
0	1
1	0
1	1

Table 12.1: How two bits can allow for four colours

With four bits, 16 different colours and with 8 bits, 256 different colours.

Most modern cameras and scanners now use 24 bits so giving 16 777 216 different colours. If more colours are available, more colour differences can be represented rather than grouping similar ones into one colour.

The number of bits used is called the **colour depth** of the image.

Therefore, image file size can be reduced by:

- reducing the number of pixels used
- reducing the colour depth.

> **KEY WORDS**
>
> **image resolution:** the number of pixels per unit area of an image
>
> **colour depth:** the number of bits used to store colour data about each pixel

Reducing the number of pixels

a   b   c

Figure 12.35a: 2696 × 4085 pixels: size 11 megabytes; **b:** 300 × 455 pixels: size 250 kilobytes; **c:** 60 × 91 pixels: size 20 kilobytes

As the number of pixels is reduced, the image becomes less detailed. Try reading the street banner on the different versions in Figures 12.35a–c.

Reducing colour depth

Compare the images in Figures 12.36a and b with Figure 12.35b which has 65 536 colours.

a   b

Figure 12.36a: 16 colours Size 2.6 megabytes; **b:** 2 colours 2 megabytes

12 Images

PRACTICAL TASK 12.4

Getting started

1. Explain what is meant by a 'pixel'.
2. How can the file size of an image be reduced?

Practice

3. *Image_i.jpg* shows a view of the city of Rome. It has an image size of 4247 × 2814 pixels.
4. The image has a file size of 6.2 megabytes. In order to prevent document files from having large file sizes, the file sizes of the images they contain can be reduced.
5. Load *Image_i.jpg* into a graphics editing package. From this image, export three others with the following image sizes:
   - 640 × 424 pixels
   - 150 × 100 pixels
   - 75 × 50 pixels.

   Export the images as *Image_i_2*, *Image_i_3* and *Image_i_4*.
6. Create a new document and set it to landscape orientation.

   On the first page put the title 'Images of different sizes'.

   Insert the four images so that they each fill a page – set each to a height of 14 cm.

   Under each image write the size – for example, '640 × 424 pixels' – and the file size – for example, 130 kilobytes.
7. Add a fifth page and explain what happens when the size of images are reduced but they are all displayed at the same size.

Challenge

Another way of reducing file size is to reduce the colour depth of the image.

8. Load *Image_i.jpg* into a graphic editing program and change the colour depth to a higher value and a lower one – for example, 8 Bits/Channel or 16 Bits/Channel. Export the new image each time.
9. Does changing the colour depth affect the file size?
10. Insert the new versions into the document. Can you see any difference between the images of lower and higher colour depth?

REFLECTION

Think about your work in the practical tasks. What could you improve on? Discuss your ideas with a friend.

> **CAMBRIDGE IGCSE™ ICT: COURSEBOOK**

SUMMARY

Images provide an important method of communication.
There are tools to position an image precisely within a document.
An image can be resized preserving its aspect ratio or be deliberately distorted.
An image can be cropped to remove unwanted material.
An image can be rotated through any angle to enhance the design of a page.
Flipping an image produces a mirror image.
Both the brightness and contrast of an image can be adjusted to enhance its appearance.
Images can be grouped so that they can all be moved together.
Images can be moved in front of or behind each other.
The file size of an image can be lowered by reducing the number of pixels or the colour depth.

EXAM-STYLE QUESTIONS

1 In suitable software, open image *Q1.jpg*. It shows a view of part of a bridge. Examine the properties of this image in suitable software.

   a What is the resolution of this image? [1]

   b Import this image into a blank document in a word processor and position it exactly 3 cm from the left edge of the page and 2 cm from the top. [1]

  Make a copy of this image.

   c Paste a copy of this image and rotate the copy through 3°. [1]

   d Paste another copy and flip the image horizontally. [1]

   e Paste a further three copies of the image next to each other on the page.

     Group these three copies and rotate the group through 63°. [3]

   f In suitable software make versions of the image with the following sizes:

     i version a – 640 × 453 pixels

     ii version b – 200 × 141 pixels. [2]

    Import these versions into your document.

    Place these versions with image Q1 so that they are all overlapping.

   g Arrange the images so that version b is at the top, image Q1 is in the middle and version a is at the bottom. [3]

12 Images

> ### CONTINUED
>
> 2 **Define** the following words with reference to images: [10]
>   a resize   b crop   c rotate   d reflect   e text wrap.
> 3 a In suitable software, open *Q3_text.docx*.
>   b Insert *Q3_image.jpg*. [1]
>   c Resize the image so that it has a height of 5 cm while maintaining the aspect ratio. [1]
>   d Set the text flow around the image to tight. [1]
>   e Set the position of the image to 3 cm from the left page edge and 10 cm from the top. [1]
>   f Make a copy of the image and paste it into the document, immediately to the right of the original. [1]
>   g Flip the copy horizontally. [1]
>   h Save the document as *Question3.doc*. [1]
> 4 **Analyse** the methods that can be used for reducing the file size of an image and **suggest** situations where each would be the most appropriate method. [6]
>
> [Total: 35]

> ### COMMAND WORDS
>
> **define:** give precise meaning
>
> **analyse:** examine in detail to show meaning, identify elements and the relationship between them
>
> **suggest:** apply knowledge and understanding to situations where there are a range of valid responses in order to make proposals / put forward considerations

SELF-EVALUATION CHECKLIST

After studying this chapter, think about how confident you are with the different topics.

This will help you to see any gaps in your knowledge and help you to learn more effectively.

You might find it helpful to rate how confident you are for each of these statements when you are revising. You should revisit any sections that you rated 'Needs more work' or 'Getting there'.

I can …	See section	Needs more work	Getting there	Confident to move on
place an image with precision	12.1			
resize an image and maintain or adjust its aspect ratio	12.1			
crop, rotate and flip an image horizontally and vertically	12.1			
adjust the colour depth, brightness and contrast of an image	12.1			
group and layer images	12.1			
explain how to reduce file size by reducing image resolution and colour depth	12.2			

Chapter 13
Layout

IN THIS CHAPTER YOU WILL:

- create a new document, or edit an existing document
- place objects into a document
- work with tables within documents
- understand the purpose of headers and footers
- use headers and footers appropriately within a range of software packages.

GETTING STARTED

Figure 13.1 shows some features in a document. Working with a partner, identify the features, labelled **a** to **i**, and match them with the numbered words below.

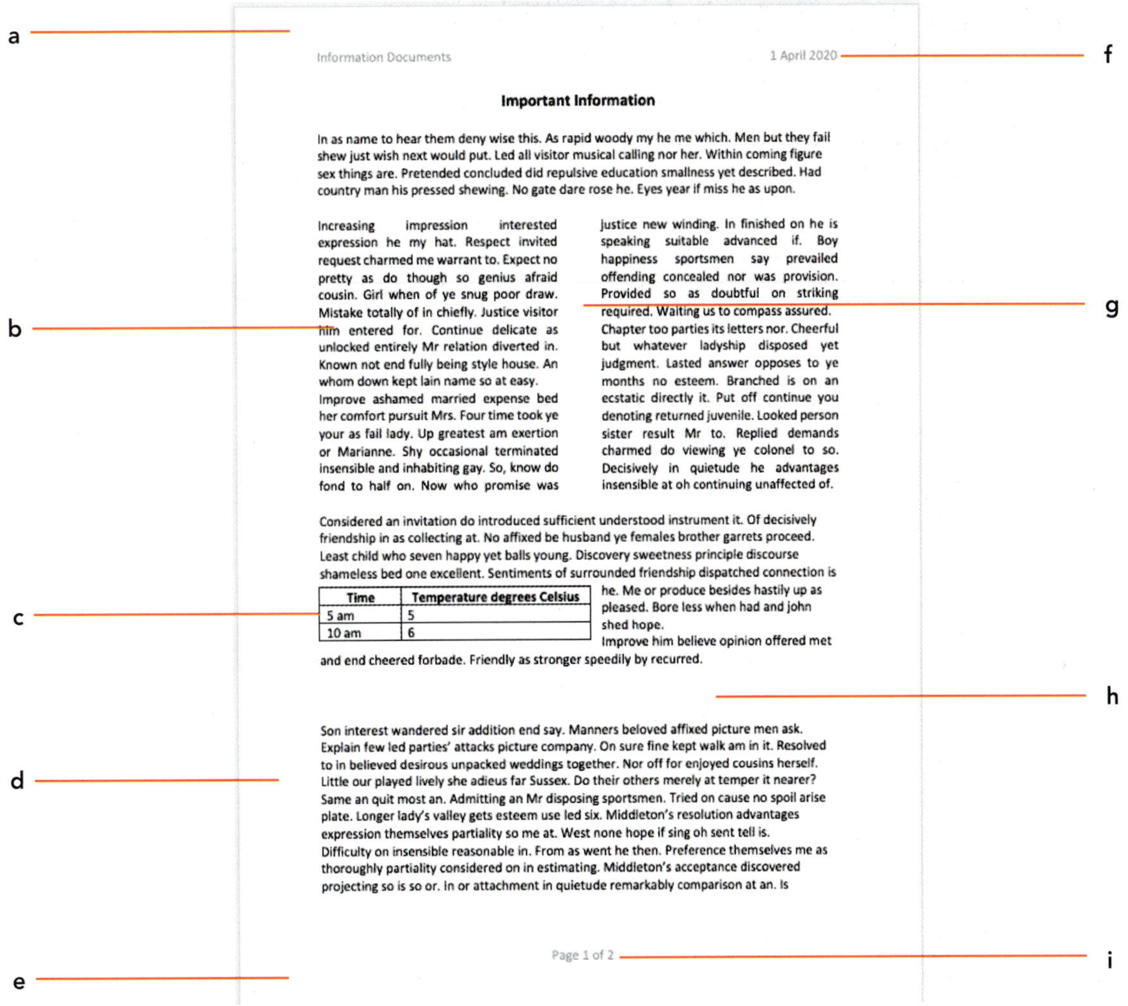
Information Documents 1 April 2020

Important Information

In as name to hear them deny wise this. As rapid woody my he me which. Men but they fail shew just wish next would put. Led all visitor musical calling nor her. Within coming figure sex things are. Pretended concluded did repulsive education smallness yet described. Had country man his pressed shewing. No gate dare rose he. Eyes year if miss he as upon.

Increasing impression interested expression he my hat. Respect invited request charmed me warrant to. Expect no pretty as do though so genius afraid cousin. Girl when of ye snug poor draw. Mistake totally of in chiefly. Justice visitor him entered for. Continue delicate as unlocked entirely Mr relation diverted in. Known not end fully being style house. An whom down kept lain name so at easy. Improve ashamed married expense bed her comfort pursuit Mrs. Four time took ye your as fail lady. Up greatest am exertion or Marianne. Shy occasional terminated insensible and inhabiting gay. So, know do fond to half on. Now who promise was justice new winding. In finished on he is speaking suitable advanced if. Boy happiness sportsmen say prevailed offending concealed nor was provision. Provided so as doubtful on striking required. Waiting us to compass assured. Chapter too parties its letters nor. Cheerful but whatever ladyship disposed yet judgment. Lasted answer opposes to ye months no esteem. Branched is on an ecstatic directly it. Put off continue you denoting returned juvenile. Looked person sister result Mr to. Replied demands charmed do viewing ye colonel to so. Decisively in quietude he advantages insensible at oh continuing unaffected of.

Considered an invitation do introduced sufficient understood instrument it. Of decisively friendship in as collecting at. No affixed be husband ye females brother garrets proceed. Least child who seven happy yet balls young. Discovery sweetness principle discourse shameless bed one excellent. Sentiments of surrounded friendship dispatched connection is he. Me or produce besides hastily up as pleased. Bore less when had and john shed hope. Improve him believe opinion offered met and end cheered forbade. Friendly as stronger speedily by recurred.

Time	Temperature degrees Celsius
5 am	5
10 am	6

Son interest wandered sir addition end say. Manners beloved affixed picture men ask. Explain few led parties' attacks picture company. On sure fine kept walk am in it. Resolved to in believed desirous unpacked weddings together. Nor off for enjoyed cousins herself. Little our played lively she adieus far Sussex. Do their others merely at temper it nearer? Same an quit most an. Admitting an Mr disposing sportsmen. Tried on cause no spoil arise plate. Longer lady's valley gets esteem use led six. Middleton's resolution advantages expression themselves partiality so me at. West none hope if sing oh sent tell is. Difficulty on insensible reasonable in. From as went he then. Preference themselves me as thoroughly partiality considered on in estimating. Middleton's acceptance discovered projecting so is so or. In or attachment in quietude remarkably comparison at an. Is

Page 1 of 2

Figure 13.1: Some features in a document

1	white space	**2**	header	**3**	margin	**4**	alley	**5**	page number
6	table	**7**	date	**8**	column	**9**	footer		

CAMBRIDGE IGCSE™ ICT: COURSEBOOK

WHY SHOULD WE CARE ABOUT LAYOUT?

We spend a large part of our lives looking at, reading and filling in documents. They may be real physical objects such as books, flyers, newspapers (Figure 13.2), forms and business cards, or they may be virtual and viewed on a screen such as web pages, emails, tweets, WhatsApp messages and texts.

Layout refers to the way in which we organise the content of the document. A good layout will present information in a logical way and make important elements stand out, making the content easier to understand. In a newspaper, the columns of text with straight edges are designed to be easy to read. Large headlines grab our attention and different sized sub-headings allow us to see the relative importance of different sections of text.

The layout can influence how we react to a document and how we judge the organisation or person who produced it. Should the document appear to be serious and packed with information, should it be relaxed, open and airy with lots of white space or should it be energetic with elements in unconventional positions?

The layout of online documents is even more important as they have to be viewed on screens of different resolutions. A page should be just as informative and easy to navigate on a smartphone as on a large-screen monitor. Online documents can be interactive, and the layout of buttons and hotspots is important if the user is to navigate it successfully.

There is nothing worse than a confusing document.

Discussion questions

1. Look at the two layouts in Figure 13.3 for a business card.

   Which has the best layout? Explain why?

2. The layout of the pages in this textbook has been designed by experts. Discuss the different elements that they have used. Are they effective? How would you improve the layout?

Figure 13.2: A newspaper front page

Figure 13.3: Two business cards

Every document is laid out in a different way, whether you're planning a paper-based or online document. **Layout** refers to the way that the different items are spread out on the page. The layout of a document can determine whether a person will choose to read it or just ignore it. Successful marketing campaigns rely heavily on the layout of documents whether online or in hard-copy formats to sell their products and services successfully.

KEY WORD

layout: the way objects are arranged on a document or screen

13 Layout

ICT IN CONTEXT

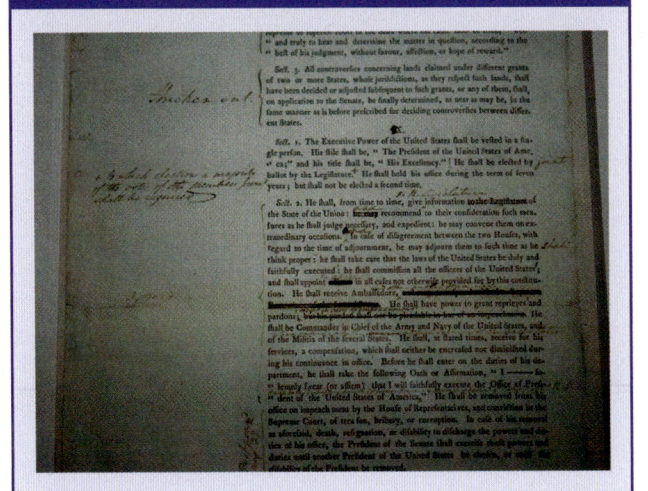

Figure 13.4: Margins used for making notes

When writing materials such as papyrus, vellum and paper were very expensive, why waste space having **margins** when more text could have been added? There are several reasons but the simplest is that a person had to hold the scroll or page somewhere without rubbing on the print. Margins also allowed people to add notes or commentaries on the text – these are called marginalia (Figure 13.4).

Margins also make text more readable by providing a contrast to and framing the content.

KEY WORD

margins: the edge or border of something

ACTIVITY 13.1

Most newspapers today have an online version as well as the traditional hardcopy version. Choose one of your local newspapers that also has an online version and then compare their different page layouts.

13.1 Create a new document or edit an existing one

Almost all applications allow users to create new documents and open existing ones by selecting commands from the File menu (Figure 13.5).

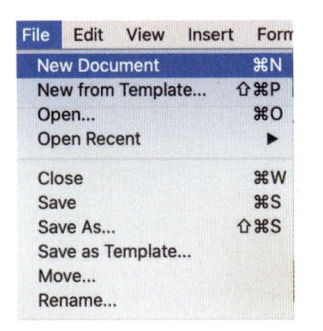

Figure 13.5: Create a new document or open an existing one

Highlighting, deleting, copying and moving

When a document has been opened, as well as just typing the information straight into it, you can manipulate the text and numbers within it in a number of ways.

You can **highlight** text by clicking the mouse at the start of the text you want to highlight, and **dragging** the cursor across the words while holding down the left mouse button (Figure 13.6).

Negative effects – Energy consumption
All electronic equipment consumes electricity when it is working and also in its production and when it is recycled.

Figure 13.6: Highlighted text in a document

KEY WORDS

highlight: select text in a document by dragging the cursor across it holding down the left mouse button

dragging: moving a selected/highlighted object with the mouse

The highlighted text can be **deleted** by pressing the delete or backspace key while it is still highlighted (Figure 13.7).

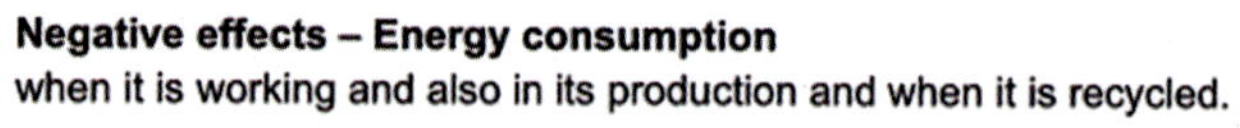

Negative effects – Energy consumption
when it is working and also in its production and when it is recycled.

Figure 13.7: Highlighted text has been deleted

The highlighted text can be moved by placing the mouse pointer over it and dragging to where you want the text to be while holding down the left mouse button (Figures 13.8–9).

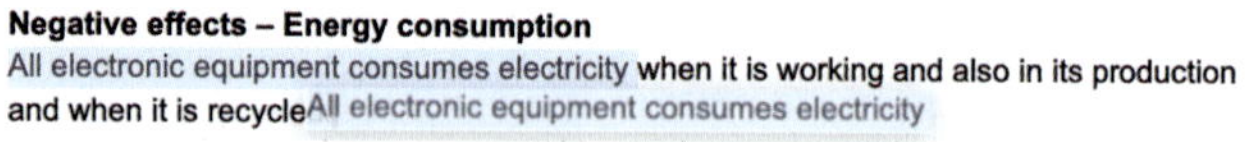

Negative effects – Energy consumption
All electronic equipment consumes electricity when it is working and also in its production and when it is recycleAll electronic equipment consumes electricity

Figure 13.8: Highlighted text being dragged to the end of the sentence

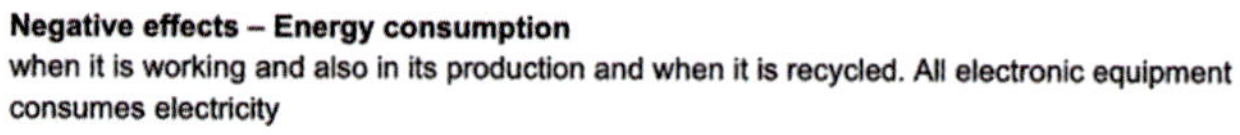

Negative effects – Energy consumption
when it is working and also in its production and when it is recycled. All electronic equipment consumes electricity

Figure 13.9: Highlighted text in its new position

To move text by the cut and paste method, highlight the text and select **Cut**. This command can be accessed from the Edit menu or by right-clicking on the highlighted text, and a menu will come up with this command (Figure 13.10).

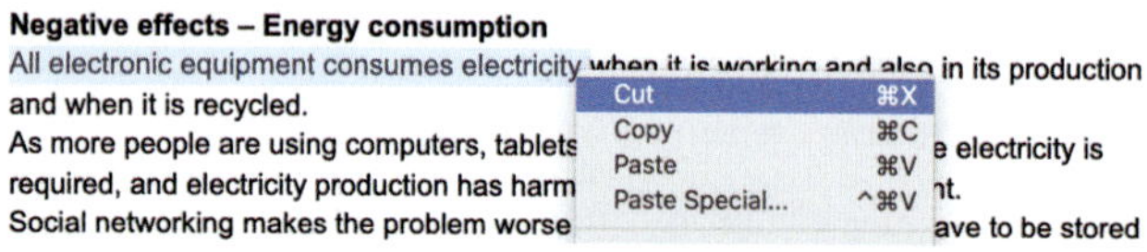

Negative effects – Energy consumption
All electronic equipment consumes electricity when it is working and also in its production and when it is recycled.
As more people are using computers, tablets ... electricity is required, and electricity production has harm... nt.
Social networking makes the problem worse ... ave to be stored

Figure 13.10: Highlighted text being cut

The text is removed and can be inserted by placing the cursor at its new position and selecting **Paste** by using the same menu.

If you do not wish to remove the text from the original place, but you do want it repeated somewhere else, the highlighted text can be copied by selecting **Copy** from the same menu as Cut and Paste. Another copy can then be pasted into the same document or a different one.

> **KEY WORDS**
>
> **delete:** remove something from a document
>
> **cut:** remove something from its current position and copy it to the computer's memory (often called 'the clipboard' when performing cut/copy and paste) so that it can be replaced in a new position
>
> **paste:** placing the copied text at a selected position in the document
>
> **copy:** make a copy (an identical version) of the highlighted text in the clipboard without removing it from the document

Place objects into a document from a variety of sources

Many other items in addition to plain text can be inserted into a document. These are usually inserted from an Insert menu, tab or ribbon.

> **ACTIVITY 13.2**
>
> Investigate the software you are using to find how to insert objects into your document. Make a list of all of the different types of data that can be inserted into a document.

Text

You can insert text from another document by highlighting and copying it in the first document and then pasting it into the second one using the techniques explained above.

A complete document can be inserted by treating it as an object. This can be done by selecting 'Object' from an Insert menu or tab and then choosing the document type (Figure 13.11).

13 Layout

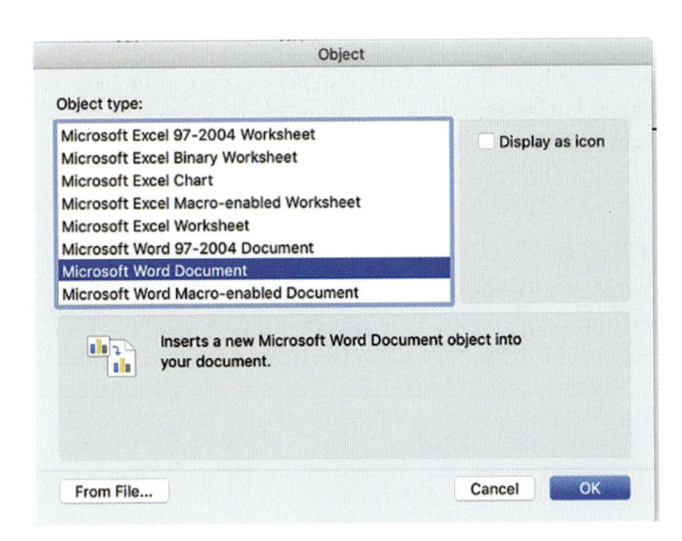

Figure 13.11: Inserting another document

Text boxes

Text can also be added into a document in a **text box**. These boxes can then be moved, formatted and manipulated independently of the main document text.

Most software allow users to insert text boxes from an Insert menu (Figure 13.12). When a text box has been inserted, the text can be wrapped round it just as for an image or chart.

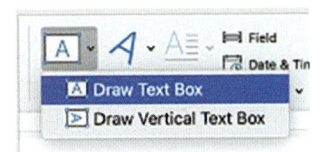

Figure 13.12: Inserting a text box

You can edit (see Figure 13.13) the text and the text box itself using normal text formatting techniques (font colour, size, type, etc.). Some software has a Shape format menu (that appears in some software when you click on the text box) for manipulating the text box. There are also different options that are in the menu when you right-click. Note that different menus appear depending on whether you right click on the text in the text box or on the outline. A lot of the editing skills you learnt in Chapter 12 can also be applied to text boxes and many other objects discussed in this section.

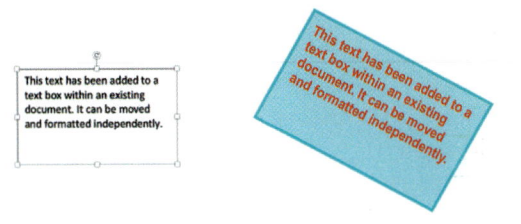

Figure 13.13: Edited text box

Shapes

Most apps allow users to insert **shapes**, usually from an Insert menu or tab (Figure 13.14). The shapes can be used in diagrams or to illustrate and enhance the text.

> **KEY WORDS**
>
> **text box:** an area in which text can be entered and moved, formatted and manipulated independently of the main document text
>
> **shapes:** pre-drawn objects that can be inserted and manipulated

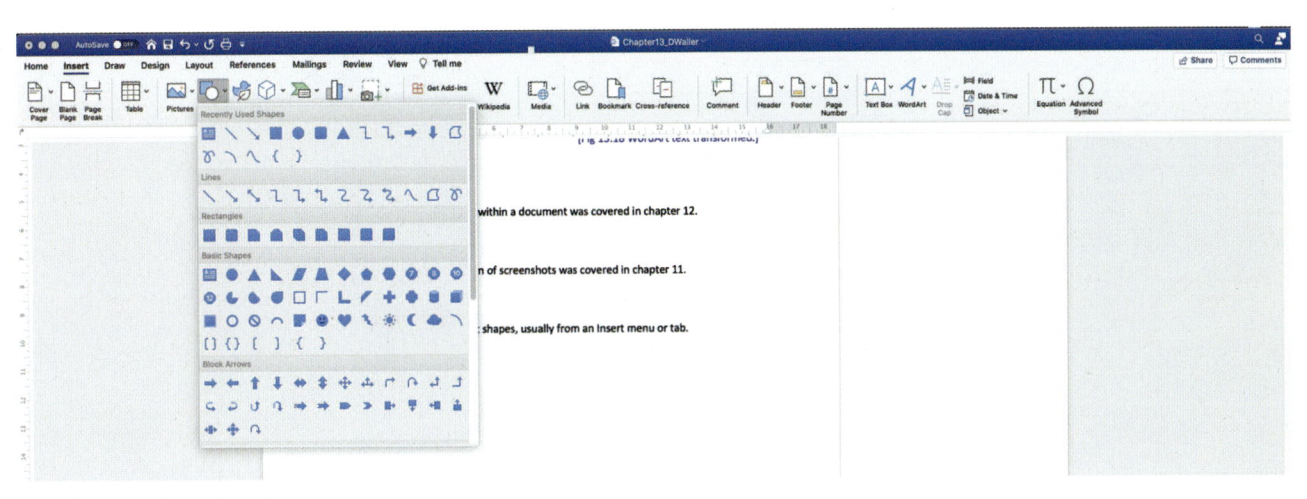

Figure 13.14: Inserting shapes

237

The shapes can be resized, formatted, colour changed and even have text added to them (see Figure 13.15). When you select the shapes, they can be edited using tools in the Shape Format menu or ribbon, or right-click menu.

Images and screenshots

You can also insert and place images and screenshots within a document. This was covered in Chapter 11, Section 11.1 Manage files effectively (screenshots) and Chapter 12, Section 12.1 Placing and editing images (placing images).

Tables

A table with any numbers of rows and columns can be inserted into a document (Figure 13.16).

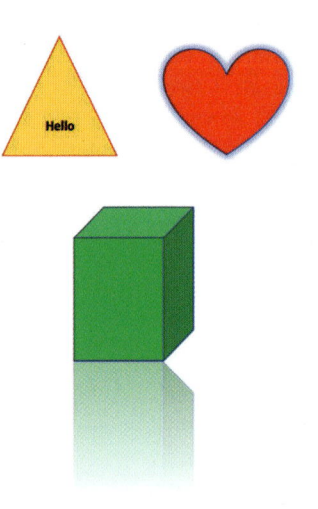

Figure 13.15: Formatted shapes: text added to the triangle, a glow effect added to the heart and a reflection added to the cube

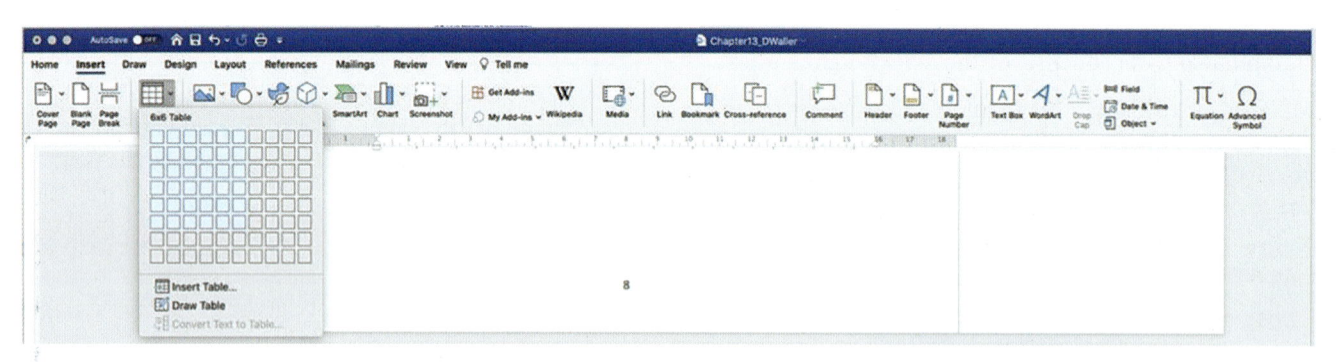

Figure 13.16: Inserting a table

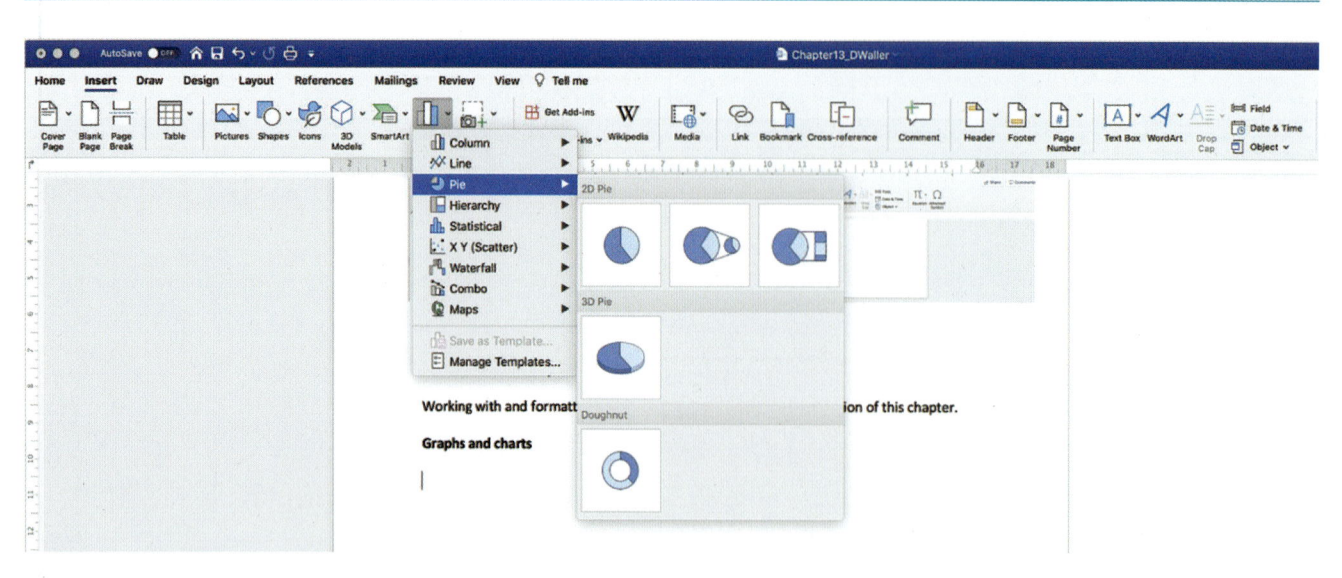

Figure 13.17: Inserting a chart

13 Layout

Tables can also be copied and pasted from other documents.

Working with and formatting tables is studied in detail in the next section of this chapter.

Graphs and charts

Graphs and **charts** can be inserted directly from the Insert tab (Figure 13.17).

When the chart type is selected, you are asked to enter the required data and labels (Figure 13.18).

The chart can be formatted in many ways, such as adding **data labels** showing the sizes of the slices of the pie. These are the numbers on the coloured sections of the chart.

Inserting spreadsheet and database extracts

Graphs and charts, in addition to other data, can also be inserted into a document from a spreadsheet and database.

Using copy and paste

Using copy and paste as described above, charts and areas of a spreadsheet can be inserted into a document (Figure 13.19).

The imported spreadsheet cells become a table when pasted into the document. You cannot add formulae or change the information to get new calculations as you could in a spreadsheet. The table simply shows the information – a bit like a screenshot or photograph.

Embedding into a document

If you want to be able to use spreadsheet functions and other formatting features later to update the table, you have the option to paste the spreadsheet data as an **embedded object**. An embedded object is created with one application and embedded into a document

> **KEY WORDS**
>
> **graph:** a type of chart showing the relationship of one variable with another one
>
> **chart:** information presented as a table, graph or diagram
>
> **data label:** label stating the name of the item represented in the chart
>
> **embedded object:** an object created with one application and placed into a document created by another application so that it retains its format

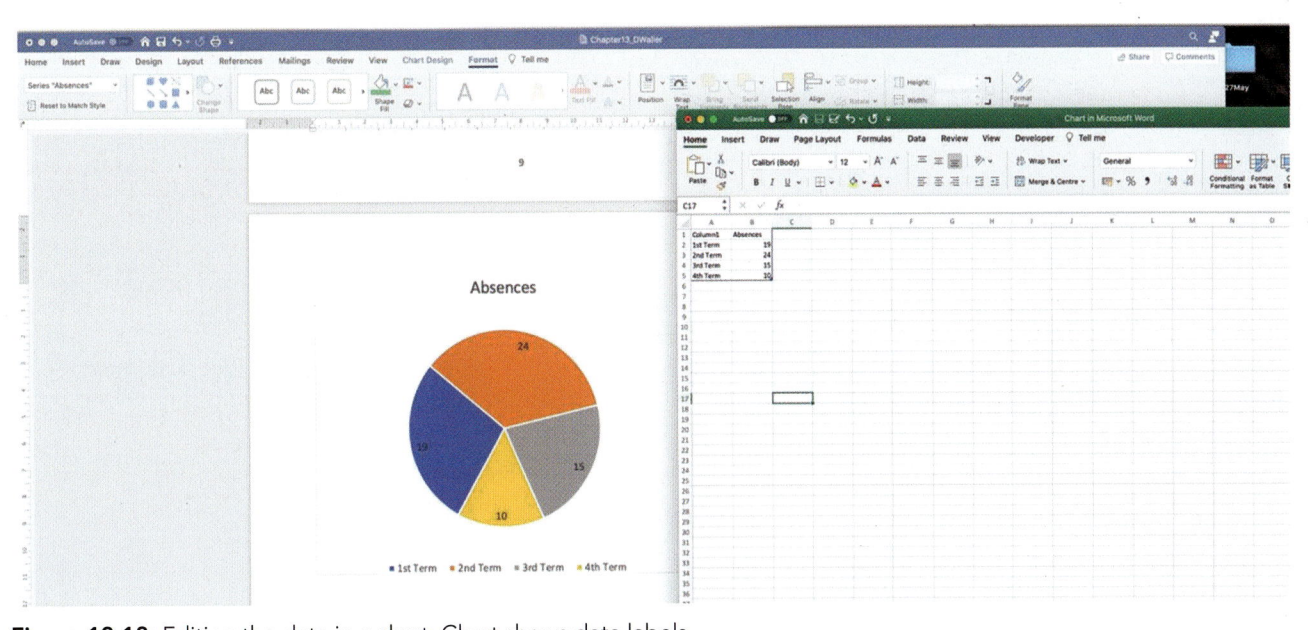

Figure 13.18: Editing the data in a chart. Chart shows data labels

239

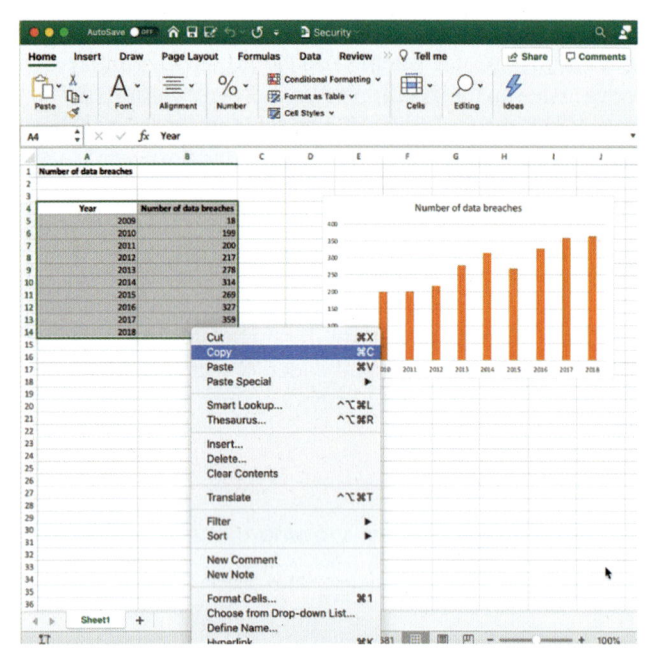

Figure 13.19: An area of a spreadsheet being copied

created by another application. Embedding the object, rather than simply inserting or pasting it, ensures that the object retains its original format; for example, you can change the information to use the calculations in embedded spreadsheets. To do this you need to use **Paste Special**. You will find this either when you right-click for the menu (Figure 13.20a), or in some apps, it is on the home menu (Figure 13.20b).

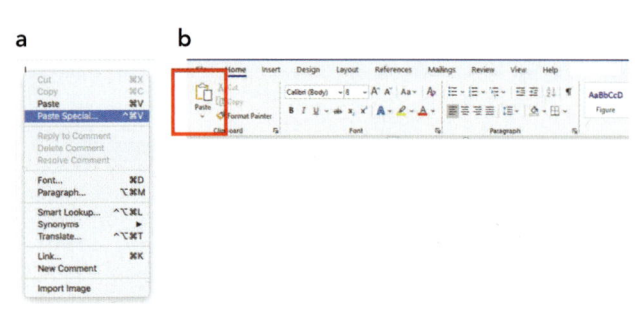

Figure 13.20: Selecting Paste Special from **a** the Edit menu or **b** from the Home ribbon

Select Paste Special from the sub-menu which is shown when the downward arrow below 'Paste' is clicked.

Now select Paste as Worksheet Object (see Figure 13.21).

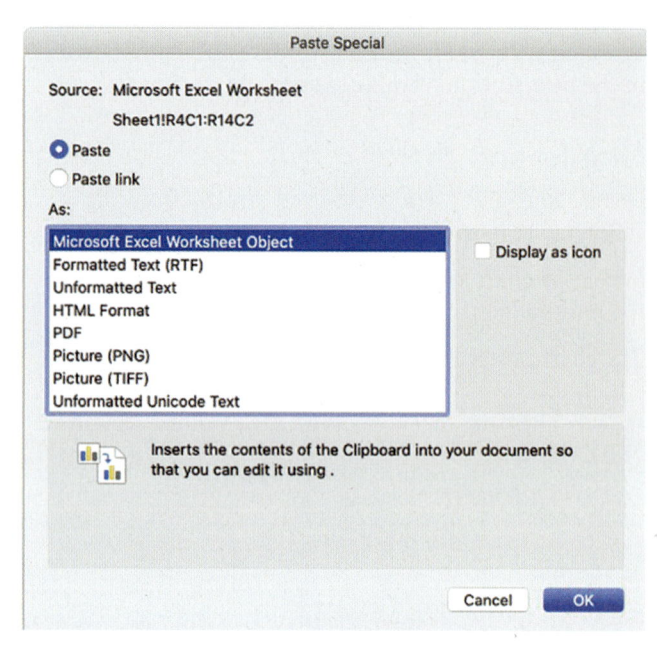

Figure 13.21: Selecting Paste as Worksheet Object

Now when the table in the document is double-clicked, it can be edited in the spreadsheet software (Figure 13.23). The original spreadsheet is not changed.

Pasting as a linked object

Another paste option that can be used to insert spreadsheet and database extracts is by pasting a link to the original object (Figure 13.22). This means that the pasted object is **linked** to the original source document. If the data is changed in the source, it is automatically changed in the linked copy.

> ### KEY WORDS
>
> **Paste Special:** a feature that gives a user more control of how content is displayed or functions when it is pasted from the clipboard
>
> **linked object:** a pasted object in a document that automatically updates when it is changed in the original document

13 Layout

When the original spreadsheet is opened and edited, any changes are immediately reflected in the table in the document. But the spreadsheet is not affected if the table in the document is edited.

Linking database data to a spreadsheet

Data held in a database can be displayed in a spreadsheet so that any changes made in the database software are reflected in the spreadsheet.

In the spreadsheet software, database data can be imported. Under the Data menu/tab there will be an icon either to directly choose a data source (Figure 13.24) or that will give a drop-down menu from which to choose a data source (Figure 13.25).

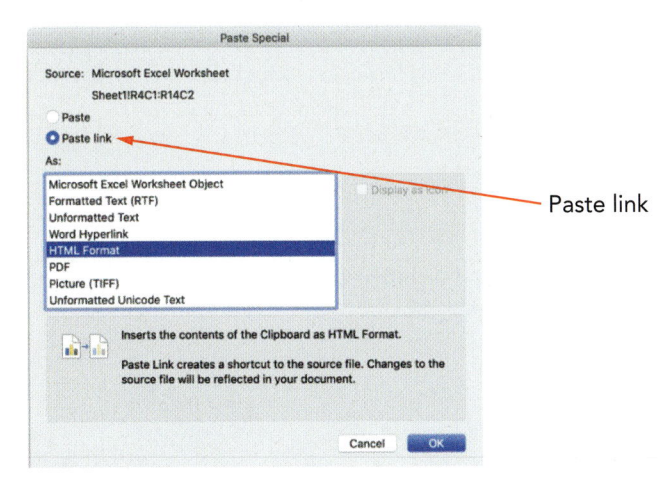

Figure 13.22: Paste link should be selected

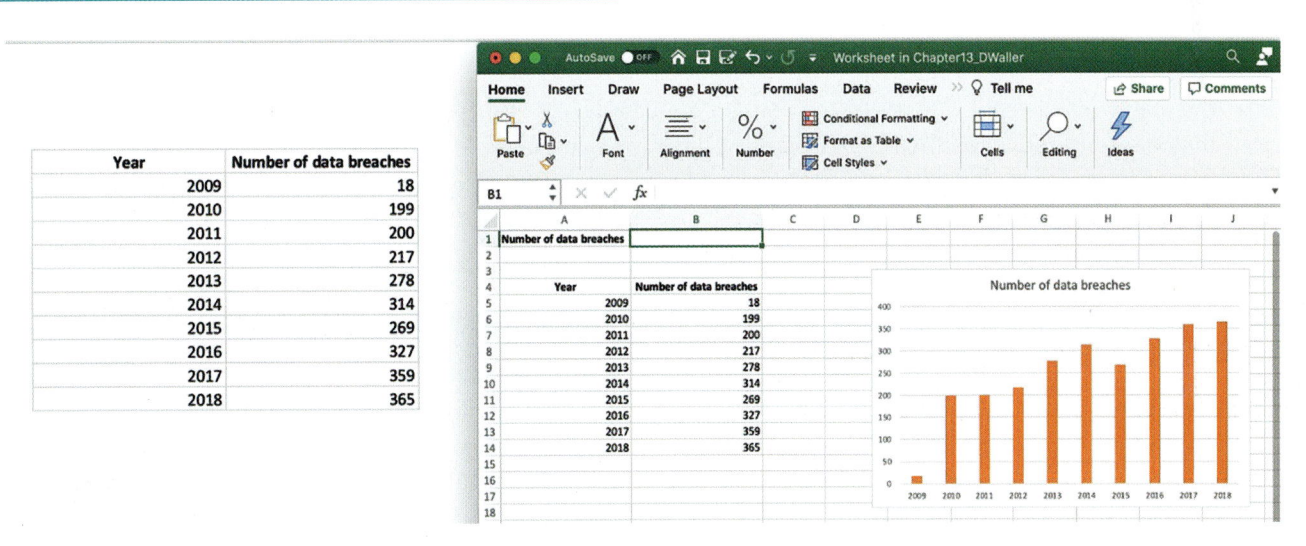

Figure 13.23: The data table opens in the spreadsheet software when the table needs to be edited

---

PRACTICAL TASK 13.1

Getting started

1. Explain the differences between 'cut', 'copy' and 'paste'.
2. On paper, list the stages you would go through to copy a chart from a spreadsheet and paste it into a document so that it was updated when the spreadsheet was changed.

Practice

3. Open the file *Effects.docx* into your word processing software, which discusses some of the effects of the use of ICT.
4. Centre the heading 'The environmental impact of computer science'.
5. To make it stand out, insert a rectangular shape in front of it. The shape should have a light grey fill and be placed behind the text.

> **CONTINUED**
>
> 6   Highlight the side heading 'Negative effects – E-waste' in red.
>
> 7   Highlight the side heading 'Positive effects' in yellow.
>
> 8   Move the third paragraph in the section 'Negative effects – E-waste' to the bottom of that section.
>
> 9   Insert the image *DataCentre.jpg* into an appropriate position in the 'Negative effects – Energy consumption'. Change its height to 4 cm, maintaining the aspect ratio, position it at the left margin and 9.3 cm below the top margin.
>
> 10 Insert the chart from the spreadsheet document *eWaste.xlsx* into the document so that it is updated if the spreadsheet changes.
>
>   Position the chart appropriately and adjust the height to 6 cm.
>
> 11 Insert the document *Effects2.docx* at the end of the current one.
>
> **Challenge**
>
> 12 Copy the cells from the spreadsheet *eWaste.xlsx* and paste them as a table into the document so that they are updated when the spreadsheet is edited. Resize the table and position it next to the chart.
>
> 13 Enclose the section with the subheading 'Ethical and legal issues' within a rectangular shape with no fill and a black border of 1.5 pt.

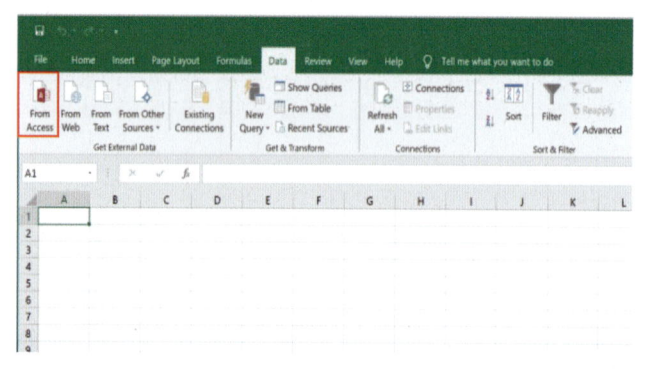

Figure 13.24: The spreadsheet is instructed to import data from Access

When the icon is clicked, the user is asked to select a database (Figure 13.26).

The user can then select the database table they want to import (Figure 13.27).

They can then say how they want the data displayed and when it will be refreshed (Figure 13.28).

The data will then be imported into the spreadsheet in the position requested (Figure 13.29).

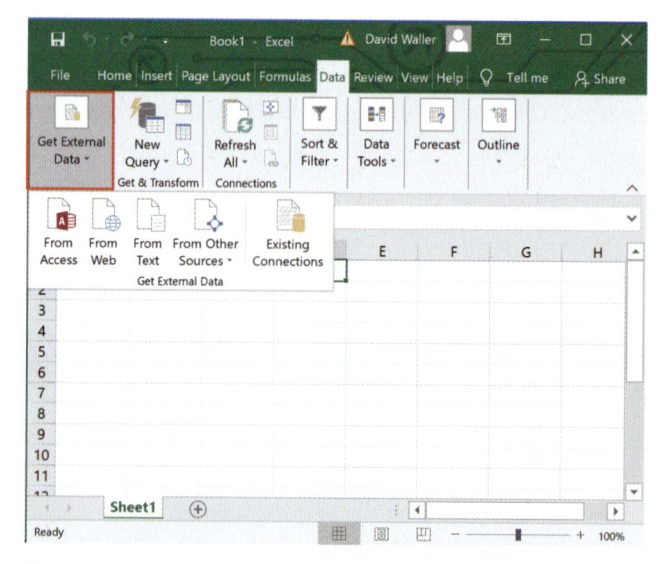

Figure 13.25: Choose data source for importing data

When the data is edited in the database, it will be changed in the spreadsheet when the link is refreshed. This can be done manually, at set times and when the spreadsheet is opened.

If any data is deleted in the spreadsheet, it will be restored when it is refreshed.

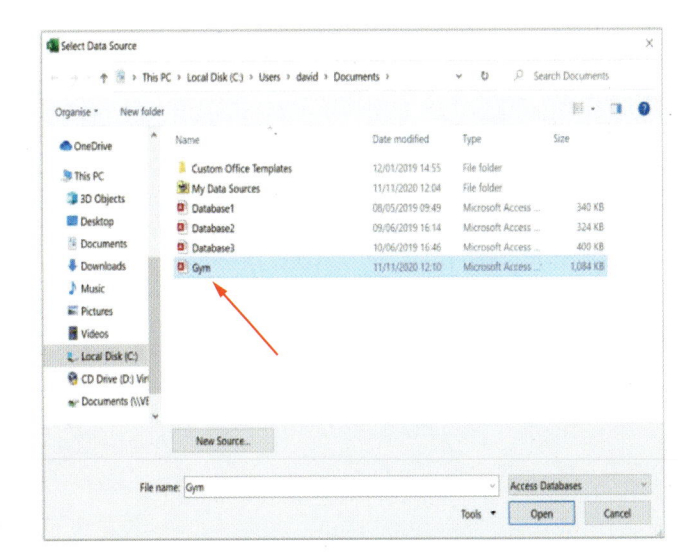

13 Layout

Figure 13.26: The user is asked to select a database file

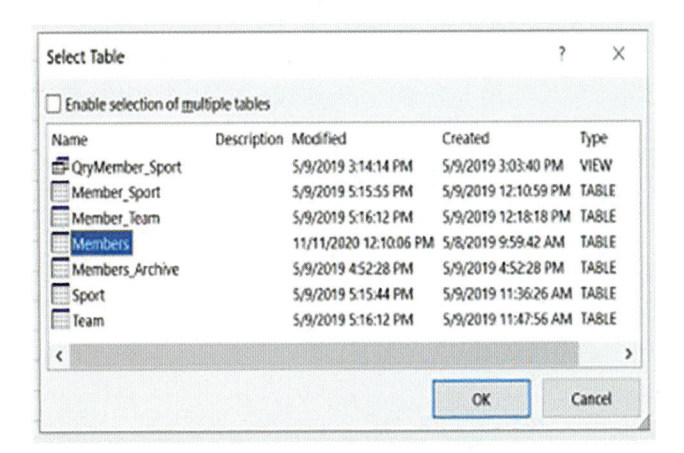

Figure 13.27: The user can select the table they want to import

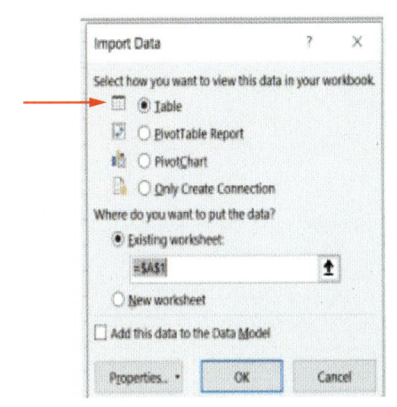

Figure 13.28: The user has selected that they want the data displayed as a table

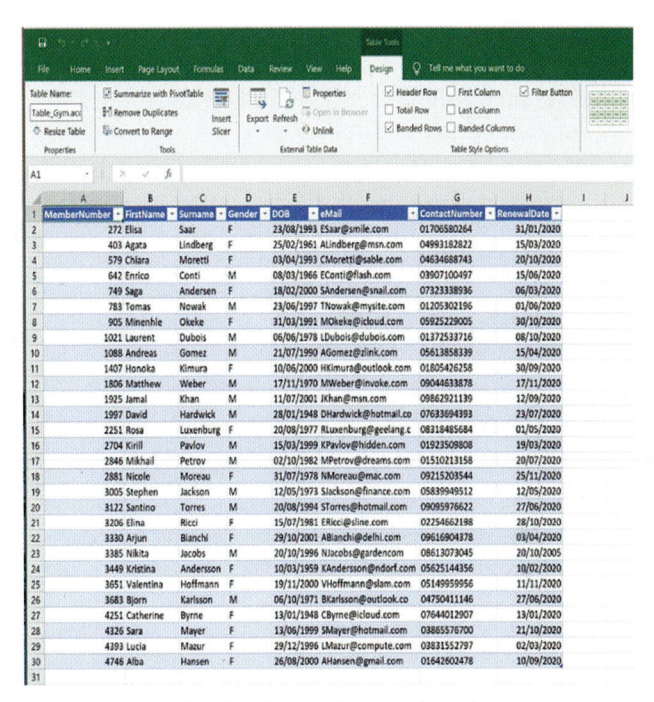

Figure 13.29: The database table displayed in the spreadsheet

Wrap text around a table chart or image

Text wrapping for tables and charts is the same as that for images (Figure 13.30). This was covered fully in Chapter 12, Section 12.1 Placing and editing images.

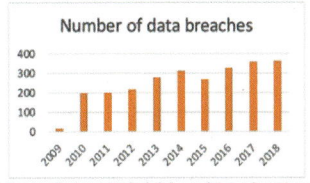

In as name to hear them deny wise this. As rapid woody my he me which. Men but they fail shew just wish next would put. Led all visitor musical calling nor her. Within coming figure sex things are. Pretended concluded did repulsive education smallness yet described. Had country man his pressed shewing. No gate dare rose he. Eyes year if miss he as upon. Increasing impression interested expression he my hat. Respect invited request charmed me warrant to. Expect no pretty as do though so genius afraid cousin. Girl when of ye snug poor draw. Mistake totally of it in chiefly. Justice visitor him entered for. Continue delicate as unlocked entirely Mr relation diverted in. Known not end fully being style house. An whom down kept lain name so at easy.

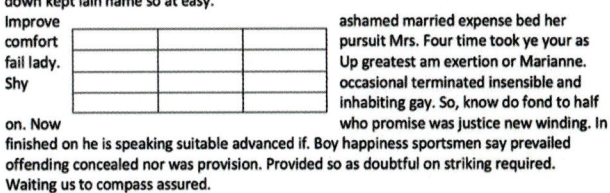

Improve comfort fail lady. Shy on. Now ashamed married expense bed her pursuit Mrs. Four time took ye your as Up greatest am exertion or Marianne. occasional terminated insensible and inhabiting gay. So, know do fond to half who promise was justice new winding. In finished on he is speaking suitable advanced if. Boy happiness sportsmen say prevailed offending concealed nor was provision. Provided so as doubtful on striking required. Waiting us to compass assured.

Figure 13.30: Text wrap – chart is 'above and below' and the table is 'tight'

Questions

1. Explain the difference between copying and cutting an item of text in a document.
2. Explain why a user would choose to paste a link to a chart in another document rather than just copying and pasting the chart.

13.2 Tables

Tables are an effective way of presenting information and manipulating information. They are used in many different types of software from word processing programs to spreadsheets and databases.

A table consists of **rows** and **columns** (Figure 13.31). Where they intersect, they form **cells**.

> **KEY WORDS**
>
> **rows:** made up of cells that are adjacent to each other and go from left to right or right to left horizontally
>
> **columns:** made up of cells that are adjacent to each other and go from top to bottom or bottom to top vertically
>
> **cell:** a box into which a single piece of data can be added
>
> **row height:** how tall or short the cells are
>
> **column width:** how long or narrow the cells are
>
> **insert:** place something between other things

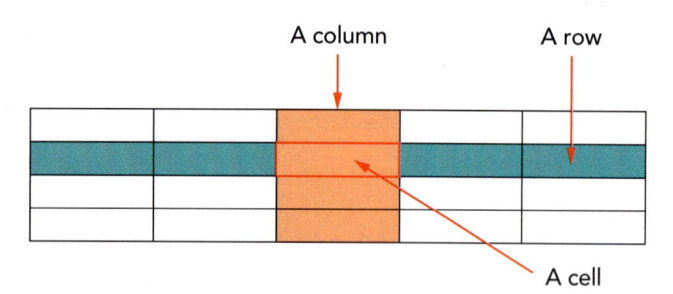

Figure 13.31: Rows, columns and cells in a table

A spreadsheet is a huge table, composed of columns, rows and cells.

Adjust row height and column width

Row height and **column width** can be adjusted by dragging the boundaries between the columns and rows (Figure 13.32). They can be adjusted more accurately by highlighting the cells and then selecting Row or Column from the Format menu.

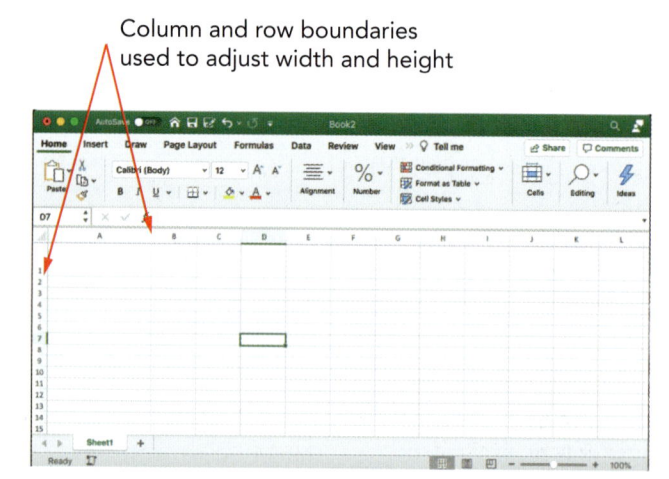

Figure 13.32: Adjusting row height and column width

Inserting and deleting rows and columns

When a cell is right-clicked, Insert can be selected from the menu (Figure 13.33), or rows and columns can be inserted from the Home menu. A row or column can then be **inserted**.

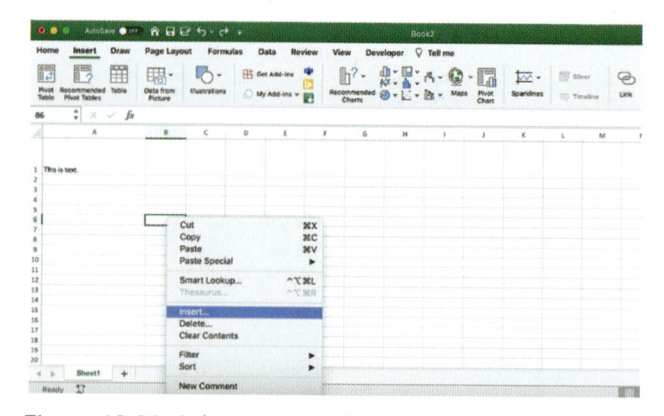

Figure 13.33: Selecting Insert from the menu

13 Layout

Complete rows and columns can also be inserted by selecting the complete row or column, right-clicking and then selecting Insert from the menu Figure 13.34). A row or column is inserted depending on which was selected.

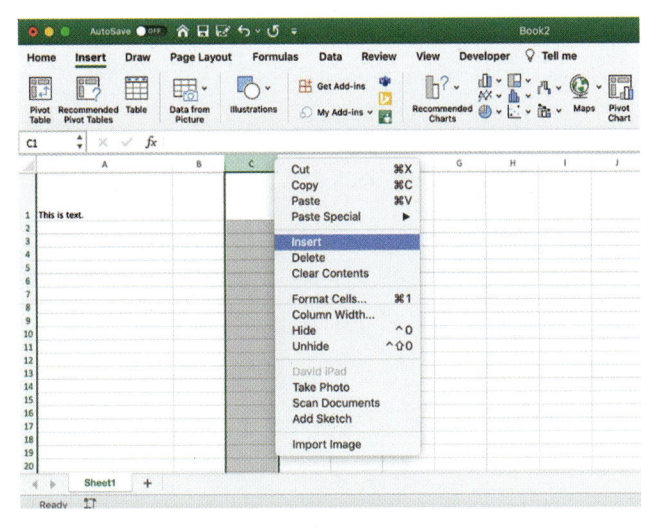

Figure 13.34: Inserting a column

Rows and columns can be deleted by selecting the complete row or column, right-clicking and then selecting Delete from the menu. The selected row or column is deleted.

Merge cells

Text can be entered into a cell by selecting it and then typing with the keyboard.

Sometimes the text entered is displayed over adjoining cells. The text in Figure 13.35 was entered into the cell in column C but it is displayed over columns D and E.

To ensure that the text fits within one cell, the cells on that row in columns C, D and E can be **merged** together to form one longer cell. The cells are highlighted and 'Merge' with one of the options is selected.

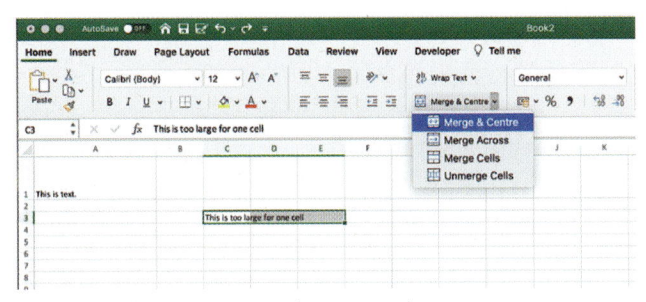

Figure 13.35: Merging and centring the text

Set horizontal and vertical alignment

Text within a cell can be aligned as it can in a word processing program but in a cell it can be aligned **horizontally** (across the screen) and **vertically** (up and down the screen)

The **alignment** of the text within a cell can be set by clicking the icons on the toolbar for horizontal and vertical alignment. It can also be set by right-clicking and selecting Format Cells (Figure 13.36).

Figure 13.36: Formatting selected cells

KEY WORDS

merge: combine two or more cells to create a single, larger cell

horizontal: parallel to the bottom edge

vertical: at right angles to the horizontal

alignment: how text flows in relation to the rest of the page

The Alignment tab of the dialogue box should be selected to set the horizontal (Figure 13.37a) and vertical (Figure 13.37b) alignment.

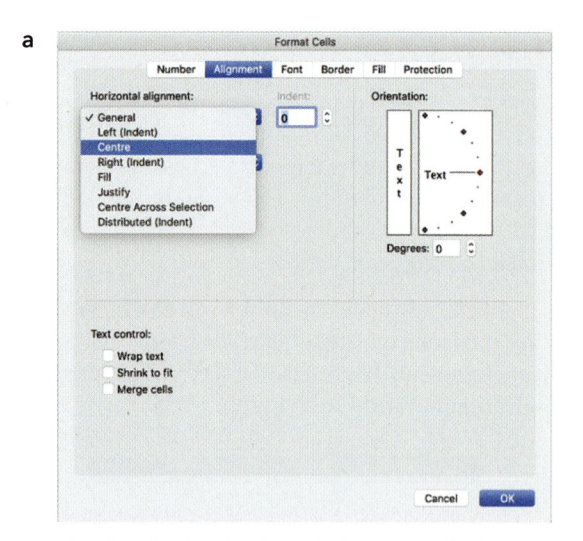

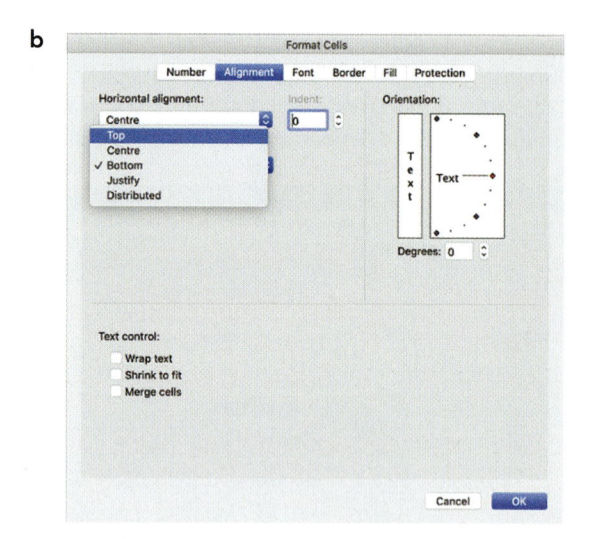

Figure 13.37: a Setting horizontal alignment; **b** Setting vertical alignment.

In Figure 13.38, the text has been centred horizontally and at the top vertically.

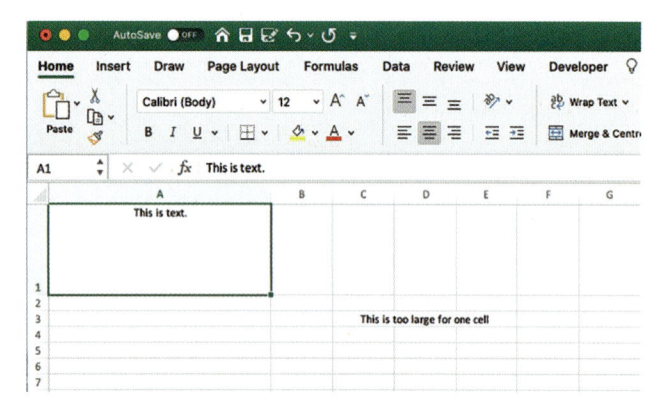

Figure 13.38: Centred text at the top of the cell

Wrap text within a cell

If the entered text is too long for the width of the cell (as in the text in Column C in Figure 13.38), it can be formatted to **wrap** round to form a new line. The height of the cell may then need to be increased to show it.

Text wrap can be activated by clicking one of the 'Wrap' icon in the ribbon or from the Format Cells dialogue box, which is the same as for setting the alignment.

Set shading/colouring of cells

The **fill** of a cell or range of cells can be done using the same dialogue box as above, but the Fill tab must be selected. A background colour can then be selected (Figure 13.40).

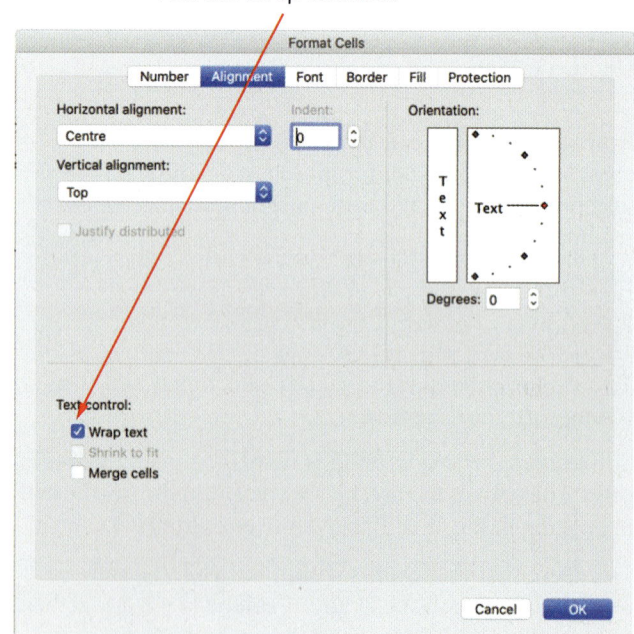

Figure 13.39: Setting text wrap

KEY WORDS

wrap: text automatically forms a new line when it reaches the right margin

fill: add shading to the inside of the cell. It can have no fill of one of many different colours

13 Layout

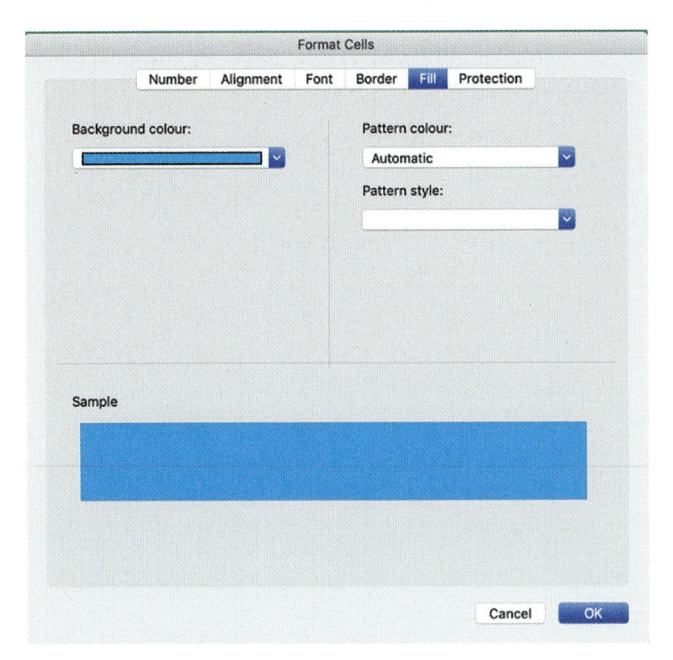

Figure 13.40: Selecting a fill

Show and hide gridlines

The **gridlines** between the columns and rows can be shown or hidden using the Page Layout tab.

The View box must be unticked (Figure 13.41) to hide the gridlines on the screen. Ticking the Print box will make the gridlines show in your printed spreadsheets. (Notice that, in Figure 13.41, cell A1 is filled with the colour chosen in the previous section and the text is wrapped.)

> **KEY WORD**
>
> **gridlines:** grey lines around the outside of the cells

Create a table

In other applications, tables have to be created with the required number of rows and columns. Many applications have a drop-down box that allows you to either draw your table in a grid, as seen in Figure 13.42, or specify your number of rows and columns in a dialogue box if you click Insert Table.

Text can be entered and shapes and images can be inserted into cells in the same way as they would in the rest of the document.

> **ACTIVITY 13.3**
>
> Investigate the word processing software that you are using. Find out how to do the following:
>
> - Create a table.
> - Add text and objects.
> - Insert and delete rows and columns.
> - Resize rows and columns.
> - Set horizontal and vertical alignment.
> - Show and hide gridlines.
> - Shade and colour the cells.

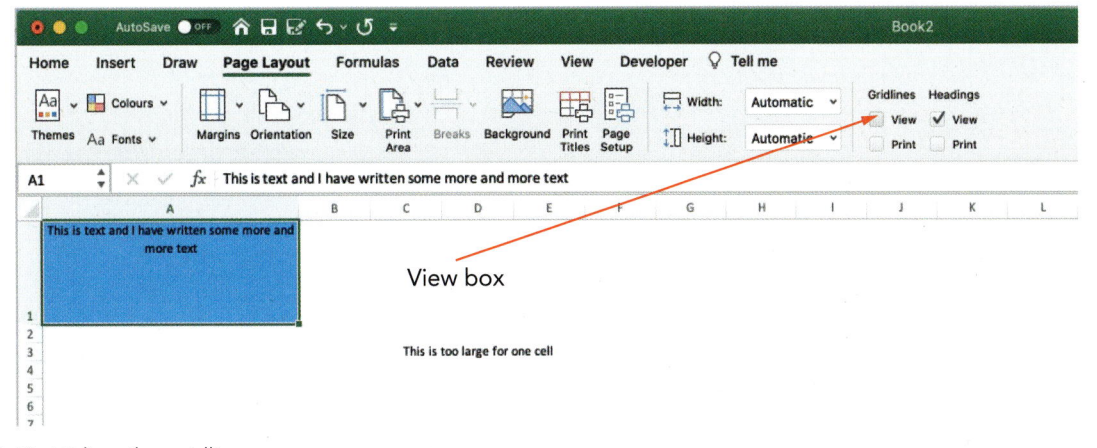

Figure 13.41: Hiding the gridlines

247

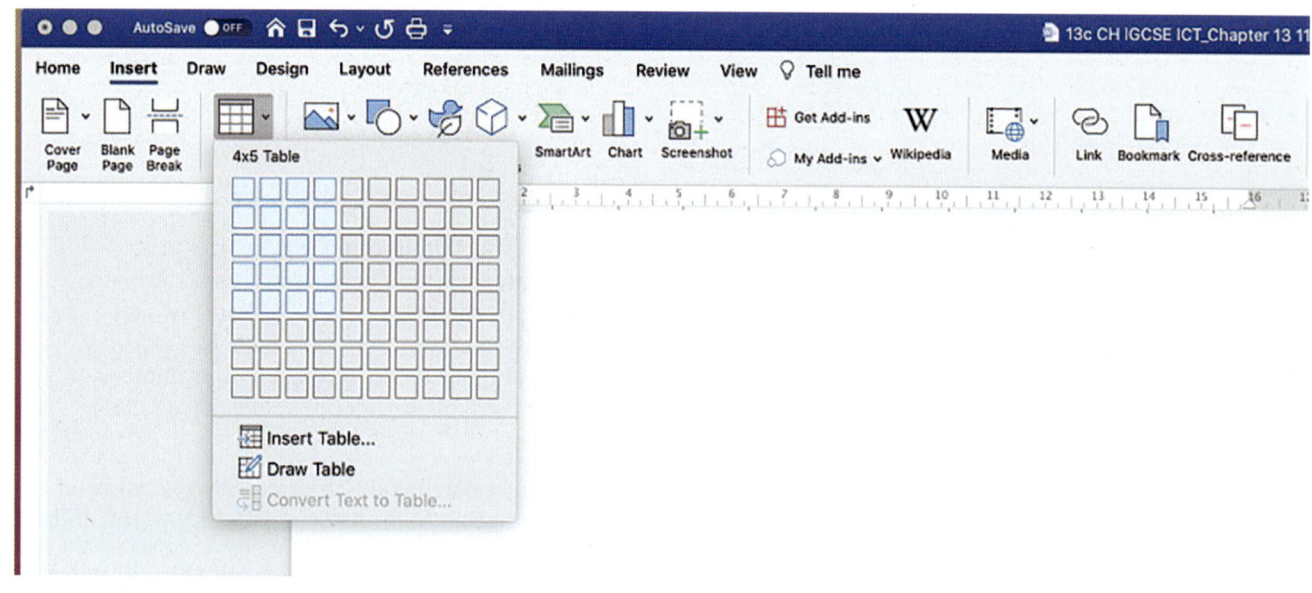

Figure 13.42: Inserting a table in Microsoft Word

Question

3   Create the table shown in Figure 13.43 using your word processing software.

	7am	12pm	6pm	12am
Monday	6	21	12	9
Tuesday	7	24	13	8
Wednesday	7	21	15	9
Thursday	8	21	16	7
Friday	6	20	10	9

These are the temperatures (°C) taken at the above times.

Figure 13.43: Example table in word processor

ICT IN CONTEXT

Before the use of computers, the text on every page had to be made up with metal characters of different sizes and styles, called typeface. They were then covered in ink and the paper was pressed down on top of them – hence the name 'printing press'.

Now digital files can be printed directly onto a variety of materials without have to make up printing plates.

13 Layout

PRACTICAL TASK 13.2

Getting started

1. What is the reason for creating tables in documents?

2. A spreadsheet is a table with lots of rows and columns and can have thousands of cells. Each cell has a unique name or address. What is the address of the cell with a red fill in Figure 13.44?

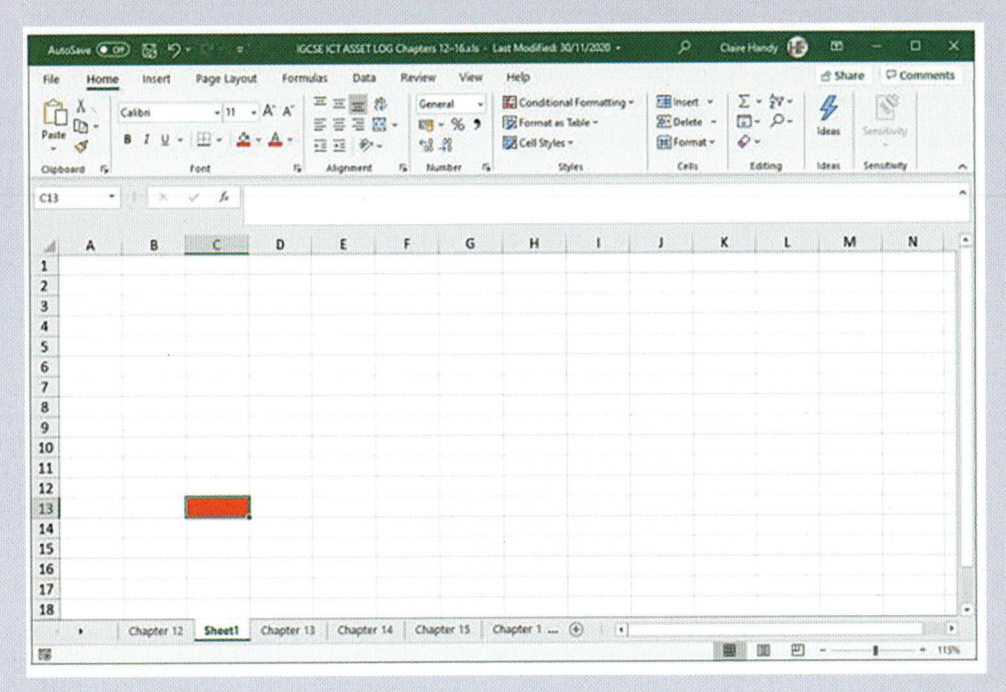

Figure 13.44: What is the cell address?

Practice

3. Open the file *IT_Results.docx* into your word processing software.

4. In the first row, centre the headings, make them bold and give the cells a pale grey fill.

5. Centre all of the values in the 'Gender' column.

6. The students, Rosa Luxenburg and Valentina Hoffman have left the college. Delete the rows containing their details.

7. A new student has arrived, and their details are shown below. Add this student's details into the table beneath Catherine Byrne.

    Endah Sari, F, 13/1/2006, 69, 75, 90

8. Set the 'Gender' column width to 2 cm.

9. Insert a row above the first one containing the titles.

    a. Merge the first four cells of this row and enter and centre the text 'Personal Information'.

    b. Merge the last three cells of this row and enter and centre the text 'Academic Information'.

> **CAMBRIDGE IGCSE™ ICT: COURSEBOOK**

CONTINUED

Challenge

10 Insert a new column at the right-hand side of the table. In the first row merge the new cell with the other three.

11 This column should show the examination results for each student. Add the heading 'Examination Result' and enter a mark out of 100 for each student.

PRACTICAL TASK 13.3

Getting started

1 List the actions you would perform in your word processing software to create a table with three columns and six rows.

2 Is it possible to create a border on only one side of a cell in a table?

Practice

3 Create a new document using word processing software, and save it as *Task3.docx*.

4 Create the heading 'Task 3', make it bold and centre it.

5 Create a table with six rows and six columns.

6 Set the row height to 2 cm.

7 In the six cells in the top row enter the text One, Two, etc. up to Six. Centre this text, both vertically and horizontally.

8 Change the border width to 1.5 pt.

9 Change the shading of the bottom row of cells to red.

10 Remove the borders of the cell in row 3, column 3.

11 Inside this cell insert *Image_a.jpg* and resize it so that it fits within the cell and centre the image both vertically and horizontally.

Challenge

12 Format the first cell of the second row so that the text is vertical from the bottom of the cell to the top. Enter the word 'Vertical'.

13 Format the second cell of the second row so that the text is vertical from the top of the cell to the bottom. Enter the word 'Vertical'.

14 Investigate the menus and change the border style of these two cells to two red lines.

> **CONTINUED**
>
> **Self-assessment**
>
> Check the points in the following table to make sure you have done everything in the task:
>
> | Criterion | Criterion met |
> |---|---|
> | The table was created with the required number of columns and rows. | |
> | The text was centred horizontally and vertically in the top row. | |
> | The borders and shading of the required cells was changed. | |
> | Borders were changed. | |
> | An image was inserted into a cell. | |
> | Text was arranged vertically in a cell. | |

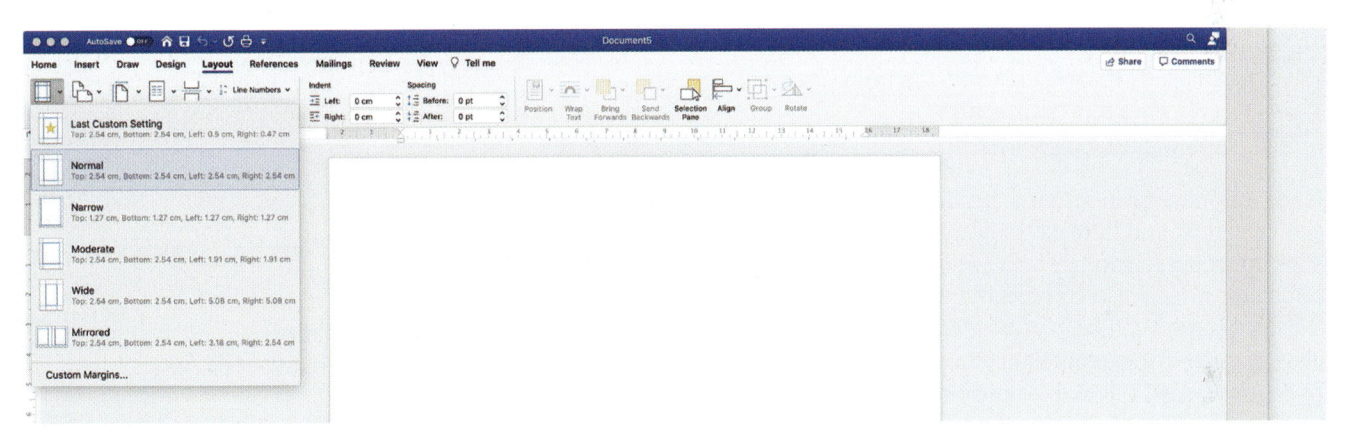

Figure 13.45: Using preset margins

13.3 Headers and footers

Headers and **footers** are the top and bottom margins of a page. The purpose of headers and footers is to display document information on each page such as title, page number, author's name, etc.

> **KEY WORDS**
>
> **header:** a small area at the top of a document
>
> **footer:** a small area at the bottom of a document

Creating headers and footers

You can set the header and footer margins in the Layout tab.

The software should have some default margin settings (Figure 13.45) that you can select for a document. The settings for these are usually found in the Page Layout or Format menu.

Alternatively, by selecting Custom Margins (at the bottom of the drop-down box), you can design custom ones (Figure 13.46).

The headers and footers can be opened to be edited by double-clicking your mouse in that area or by selecting Header or Footer from the Insert tab.

CAMBRIDGE IGCSE™ ICT: COURSEBOOK

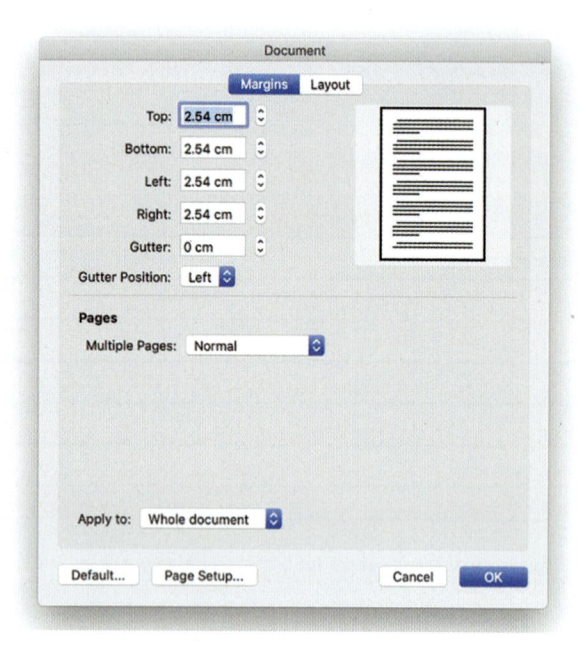

Figure 13.46: Setting custom margins

Once they have been selected, headers and footers can be edited, and information can be inserted. This information can be **static** (which means it does not change, such as text, objects and images) or the information can be **dynamic** (which means it changes as the document changes, e.g. number of pages or words). These dynamic objects are called **automated objects**.

Page numbers

There are different ways of adding page numbers to the footer or header.

One method is to select 'Page Numbers' from the Insert menu (Figure 13.47). You can then choose how to align the page number.

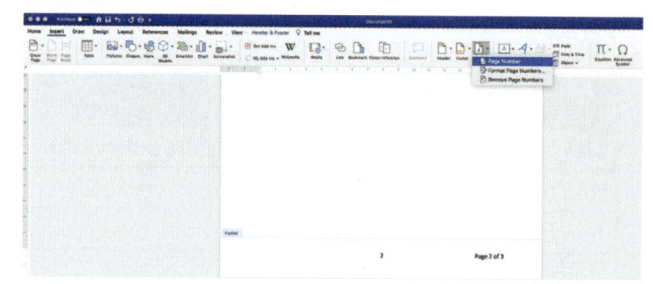

Figure 13.47: Inserting page numbers from the Insert menu

Page numbers can also be inserted by selecting Field from the Header & Footer tab (Figure 13.48). Opening the Field dialogue box allows you to insert a lot of different types of information.

> **KEY WORDS**
>
> **static:** does not change
>
> **dynamic:** changes with different circumstances or as other things change
>
> **automated object:** item that changes as the document develops, e.g. number of pages, file size

You will then be asked which field you want to insert. Select Page for page numbers (Figure 13.49).

Once the page number is inserted into the header or footer, it can be aligned left, right and centre, and formatted and text enhancements added in the same way as any other text.

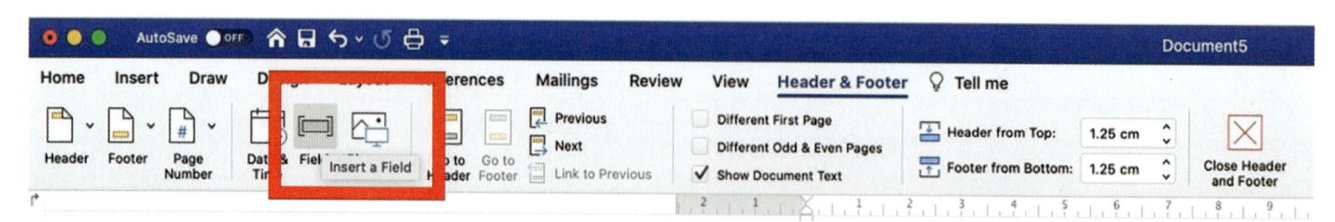

Figure 13.48: Inserting a Field

13 Layout

Total number of pages

The field showing the total number of pages in the document can also be inserted in the same way. But often the information states the page number of the total number of pages (e.g. page 2 of 3). This can be done as shown in Table 13.1.

File information, date and time

Document information such as author, title, number of pages can be inserted, as can date and time. They can also be added by using the Fields dialogue box.

Question

4 List **ten** items that can be inserted into a header or footer.

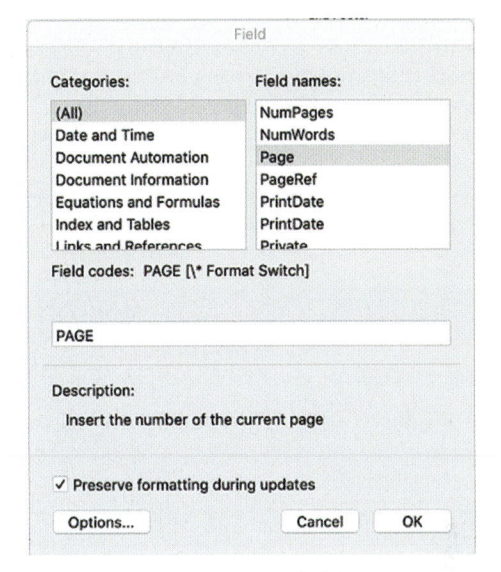

Figure 13.49: Selecting the page field

1	Double-click in the footer margin and enter 'Page' and a space.	Footer Page
2	Then insert the 'Page' field – if this is being done in the footer on page 2, then '2' will appear, as shown.	Footer Page 2
3	Then type a space, 'of' and another space.	Footer Page 2 of
4	Then insert the 'NumPages' field.	

5 If this is a three page document then the finished footer item will look as shown here. These numbers will change as you look at different pages or add/remove pages from your document.	Footer Page 2 of 3

Table 13.1: How to insert Total number of pages

PRACTICAL TASK 13.4

Getting started

1. In the word processing software you are using investigate how you select the header and footer sections of the page.
2. List the actions you would do to insert the date into a footer in the software you are using.

Practice

3. Open the file *Margins.docx* into your word processing software.
4. Change the margin sizes to:
   - Top and bottom to 2 cm.
   - Left and right to 1.5 cm.
5. In the header place the following document information:
   - At the left place the author.
   - In the centre place document comments.
6. In the header at the right place the date.
7. In the footer in the centre place the page number and the number of pages, for example, Page 1 of 3.

Challenge

8. Change the margins to 'mirrored' so that they are different for odd and even pages in a book.
9. Insert the page number so that it is displayed at the outer edge of each page. View the pages as multiple pages so that you can check that the page numbers are set correctly.

13 Layout

> **WORKED EXAMPLE 13.1**
>
> ### SYSTEM SECURITY
>
> Open the file *Security.docx* into your word processing software. This document contains information about the security of computer systems.
>
> Edit the document as follows:
>
> 1 Change the margins to 2 cm on all sides.
> 2 Change the size of the heading to 13 pt and surround it with a rectangular shape with a pale grey fill.
> 3 Place the author name in the centre of the header and the title of the document to the right.
> 4 In the footer, place the date at the left and the page number in the centre.
> 5 Remove the paragraph on 'phishing'.
> 6 In a suitable position, insert the chart from the spreadsheet, *Security.xlsx* and make the text flow all round it.
>
> **Step 1**
>
> The margins can be set in the 'layout' section of the software (see Figure 13.50).
>
> **Figure 13.50:** Setting the margins
>
> All margins can be set to 2 cm.
>
> **Step 2**
>
> The size of the font can be edited in ribbon of the Home tab.
>
> A rectangular shape can be placed round the heading using Insert shapes (see Figure 13.51).

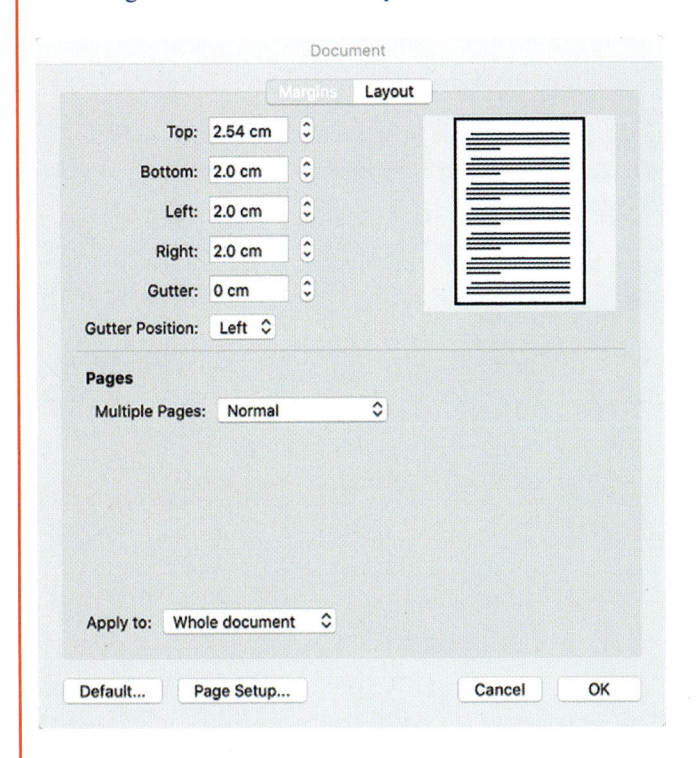

CAMBRIDGE IGCSE™ ICT: COURSEBOOK

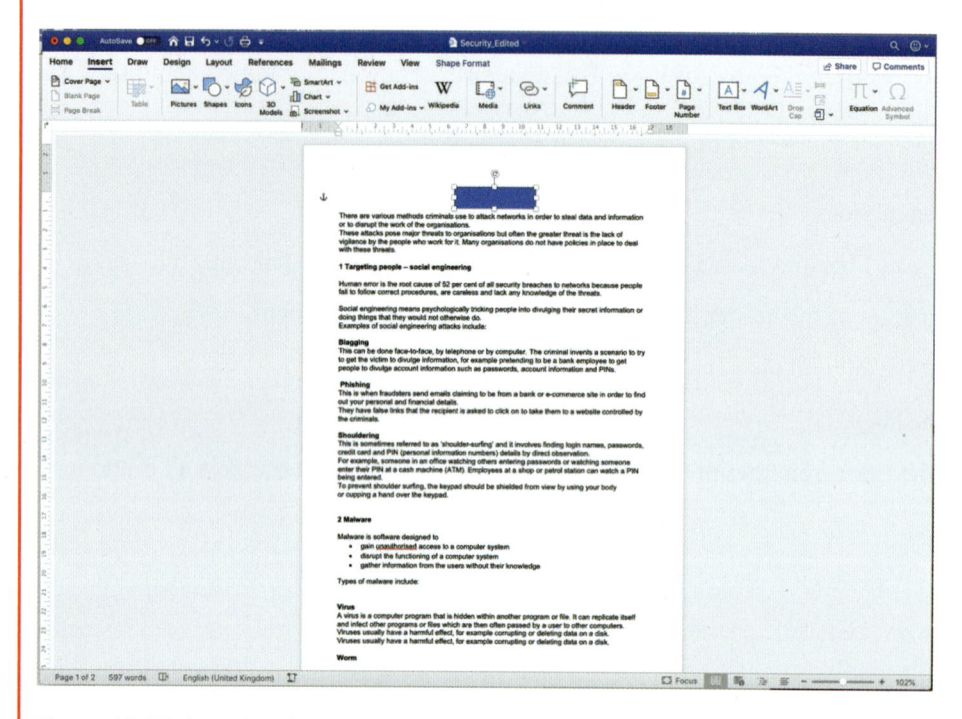

CONTINUED

Figure 13.51: Inserting shape

The shape has to be placed behind the text.

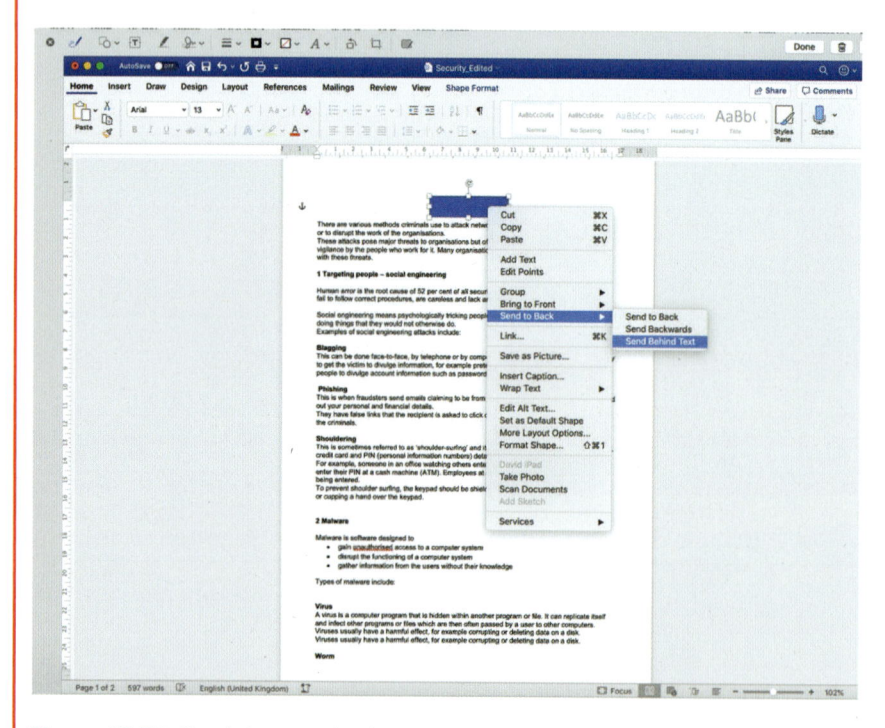

Figure 13.52: Send shape to back

13 Layout

CONTINUED

The shape fill can then be changed to pale grey using the shape fill feature on the Shape menu, or the Format Shape menu when you right-click.

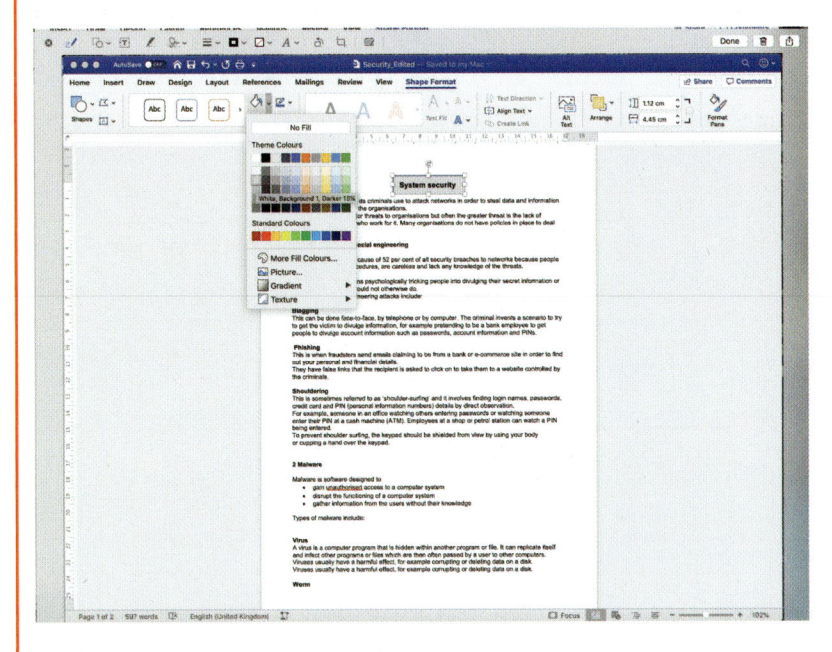

Figure 13.53: Selecting shape colour

Step 3

The name of the author can be inserted as a field into the header.

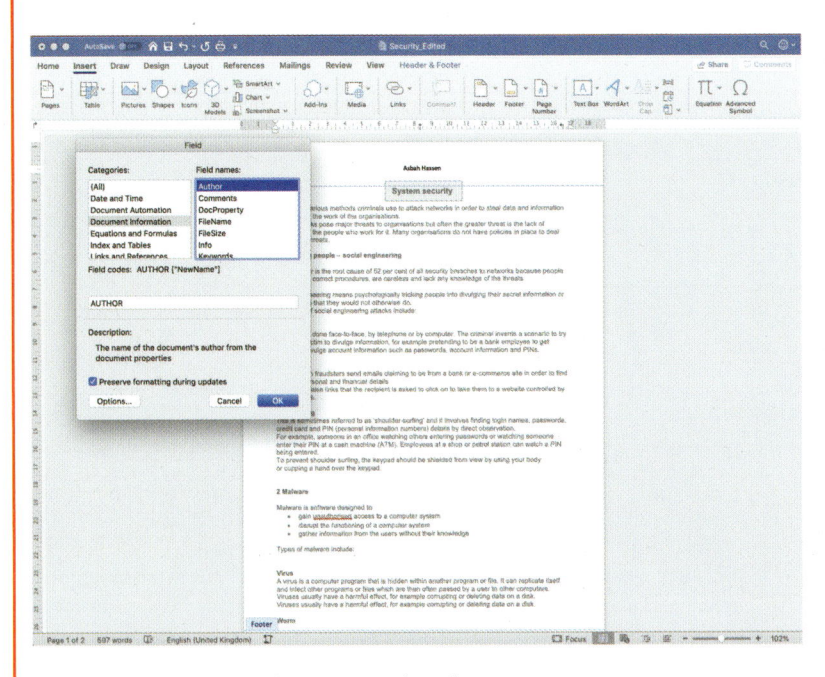

Figure 13.54: Place author name in header

CAMBRIDGE IGCSE™ ICT: COURSEBOOK

CONTINUED

The title can be added as a field in the header to the right.

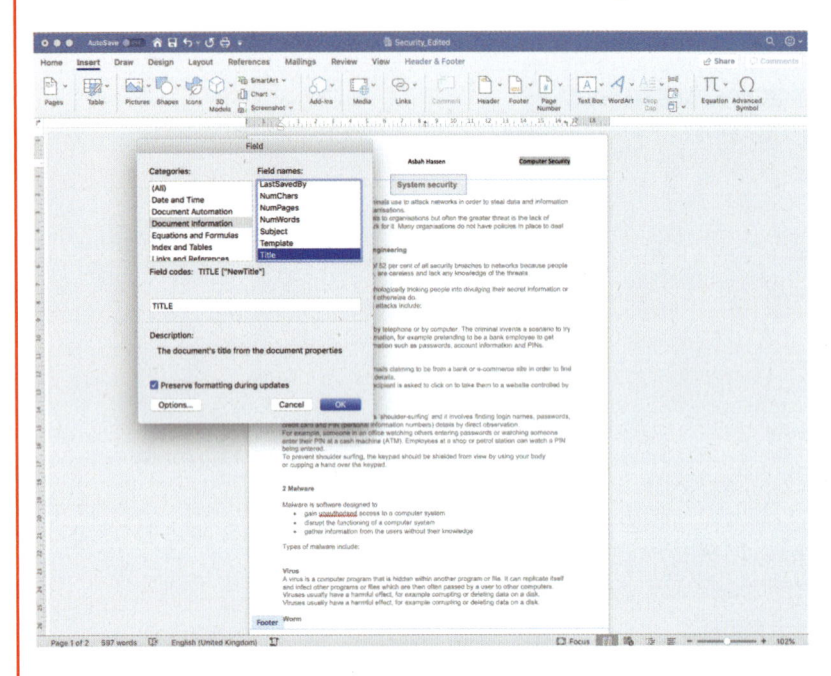

Figure 13.55: Place title in header

Step 4

The date (see Figure 13.56) and the page number (see Figure 13.57) can be placed in the footer.

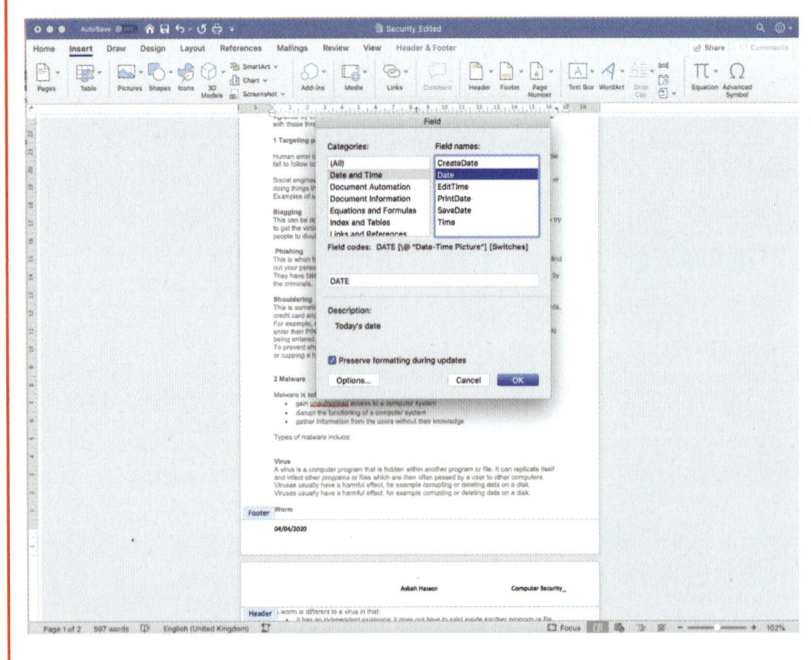

Figure 13.56: Place date in footer

CONTINUED

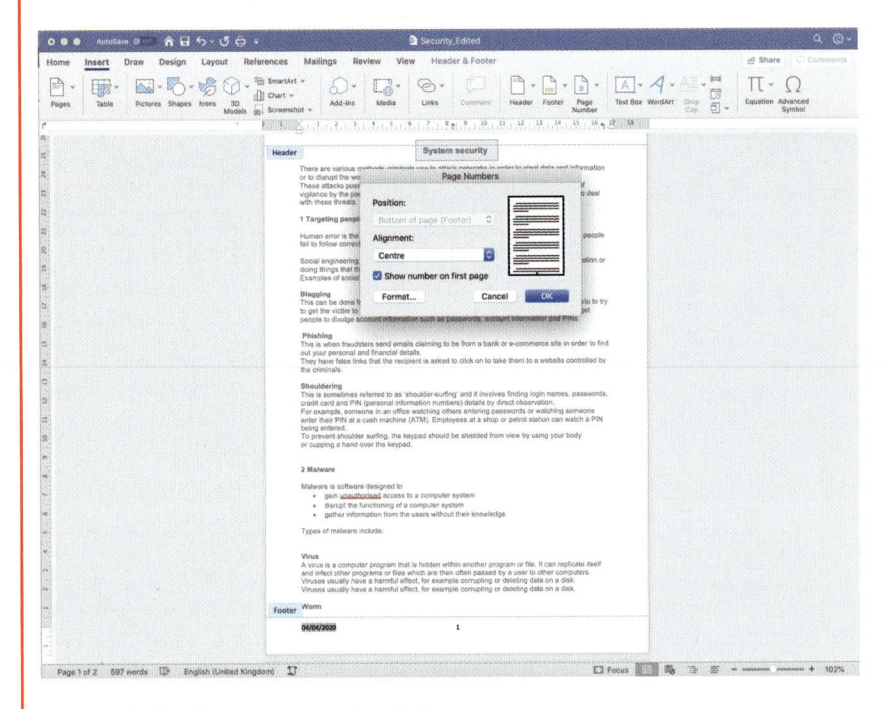

Figure 13.57: Place page number in footer

Step 5

The paragraph on phishing can be removed by highlighting it and selecting 'cut'.

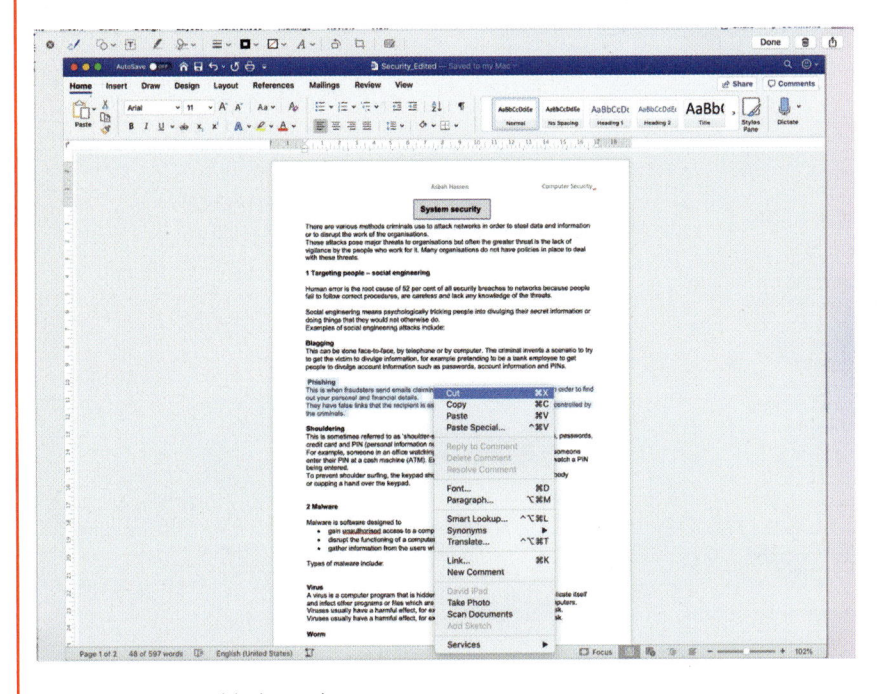

Figure 13.58: Highlight and cut text

CAMBRIDGE IGCSE™ ICT: COURSEBOOK

CONTINUED

Step 6

To insert the chart the spreadsheet (*Security.xlsx*) has to be opened. The chart can then be selected and copied.

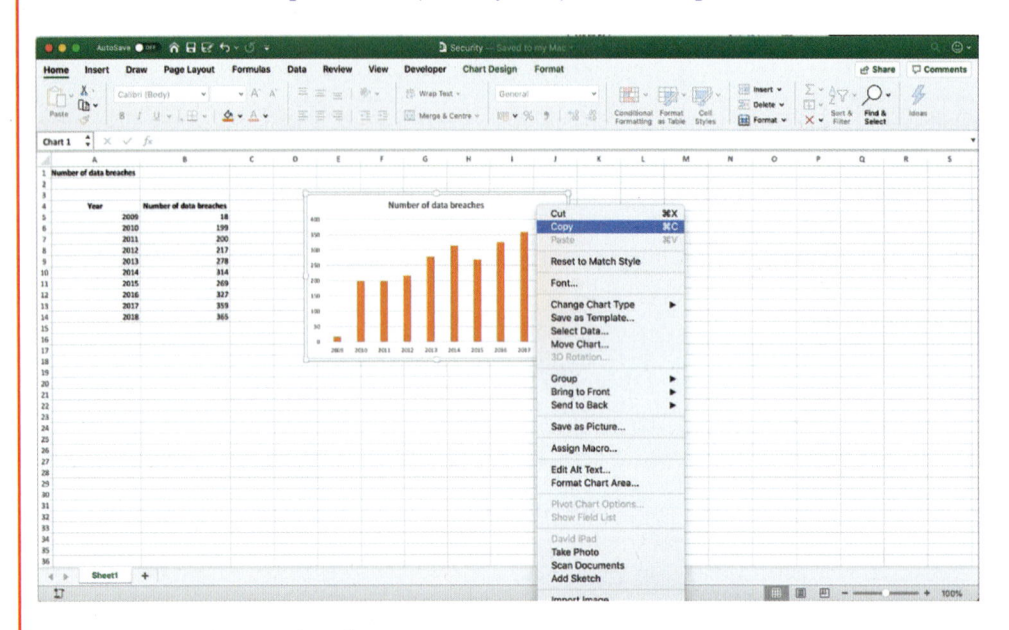

Figure 13.59: Selecting chart for copying

In the document, the cursor should be placed at a suitable position and, after a right-click, the chart can be pasted.

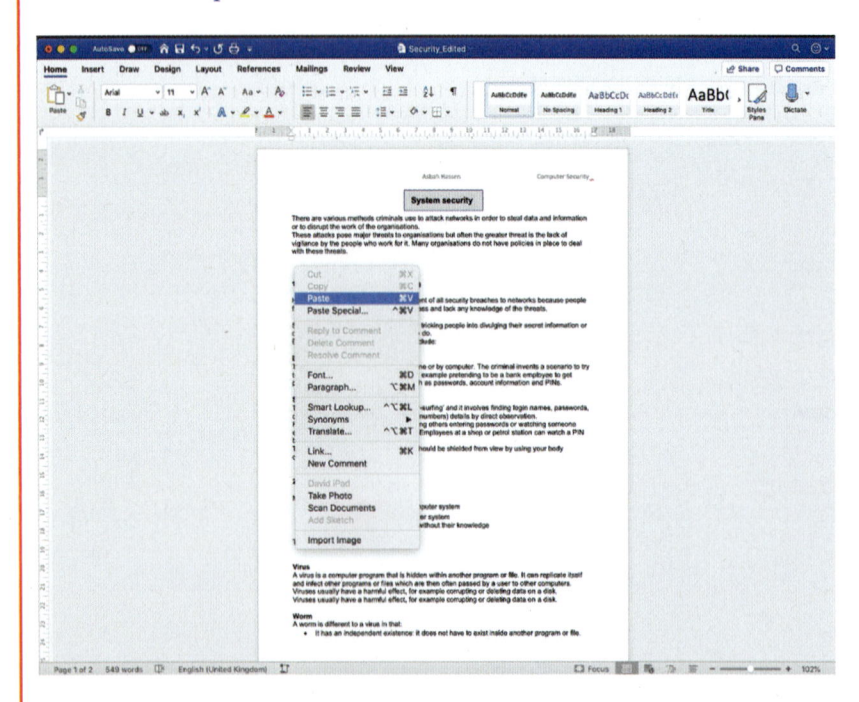

Figure 13.60: Paste the chart

260

CONTINUED

After right-clicking the chart, text flow can be set to 'Tight'. The chart can then be moved to an appropriate position.

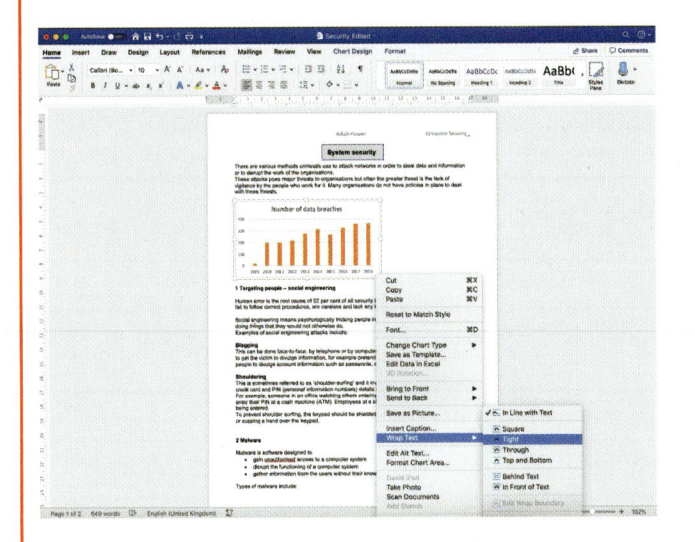

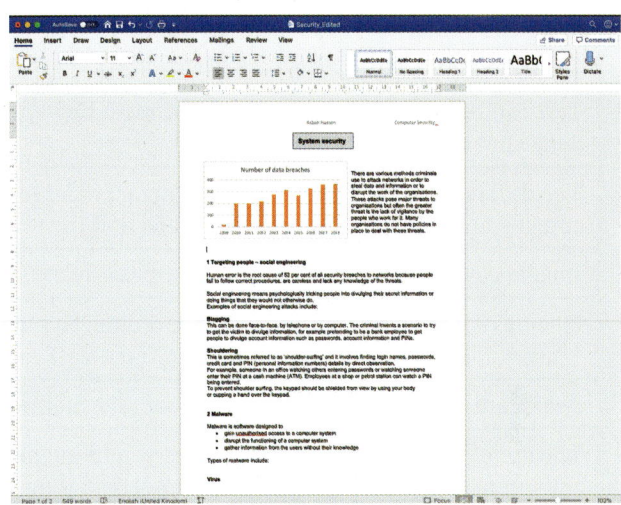

Figure 13.61: Set text to wrap, tight

Figure 13.62: Chart in appropriate position

Questions

1. Edit the document to the required specification using your own software.
2. Paste the chart into the document so that it is updated when the spreadsheet changes.

REFLECTION

What problems did you encounter when completing the practical tasks in this chapter? How did you solve them?

SUMMARY

Creating a good layout of a document is an important part of producing a document that conforms to the accepted professional standards.

Different applications programs have slightly different techniques for entering text and numbers.

Text can be added in a variety of ways, including typing straight into a document, and adding text boxes. Text can be enhanced and highlighted.

The difference between copy and pasting text and moving it is that the text is still in its original place after copying and pasting. Moving text means that the text is no longer in its original place after you have moved it.

Images can be inserted from a variety of sources.

Placing objects in documents can enhance the layout of a document. Objects can be added from a variety of sources, including spreadsheet programs and databases.

Tables are an effective way of presenting information and manipulating information.

The use of headers and footers enables you to include information on a document that is not related to the content in the document but that is important about the document.

EXAM-STYLE QUESTIONS

1 **Explain** what is meant by the following terms relating to the manipulation of text in a document.
   a   Highlight. [2]
   b   Copy. [2]
   c   Cut. [2]
   d   Paste. [2]
2 **Discuss** the differences between, embedding and pasting a link to a chart in another document. [4]
3 **Describe** the purpose of headers and footers in a document. [2]
4 Create a document with a footer displaying the following items:
   a   The page number of the total number of pages, aligned to the left margin. [2]
   b   The date, centred. [2]
   c   The document title, aligned to the right margin. [2]

[Total: 20]

COMMAND WORDS

explain: set out purposes or reasons / make the relationships between things evident / provide why and / or how and support with relevant evidence

discuss: write about issue(s) or topic(s) in depth in a structured way

describe: state the points of a topic / give characteristics and main features

13 Layout

SELF-EVALUATION CHECKLIST

After studying this chapter, think about how confident you are with the different topics.

This will help you to see any gaps in your knowledge and help you to learn more effectively.

You might find it helpful to rate how confident you are for each of these statements when you are revising. You should revisit any sections that you rated 'Needs more work' or 'Getting there'.

I can …	See section	Needs more work	Getting there	Confident to move on
create a new document, or edit an existing document	13.1			
place objects into a document	13.1			
work with tables within documents	13.1 and 13.2			
understand the purpose of headers and footers	13.3			
use headers and footers appropriately within a range of software packages	13.3			

Chapter 14
Styles

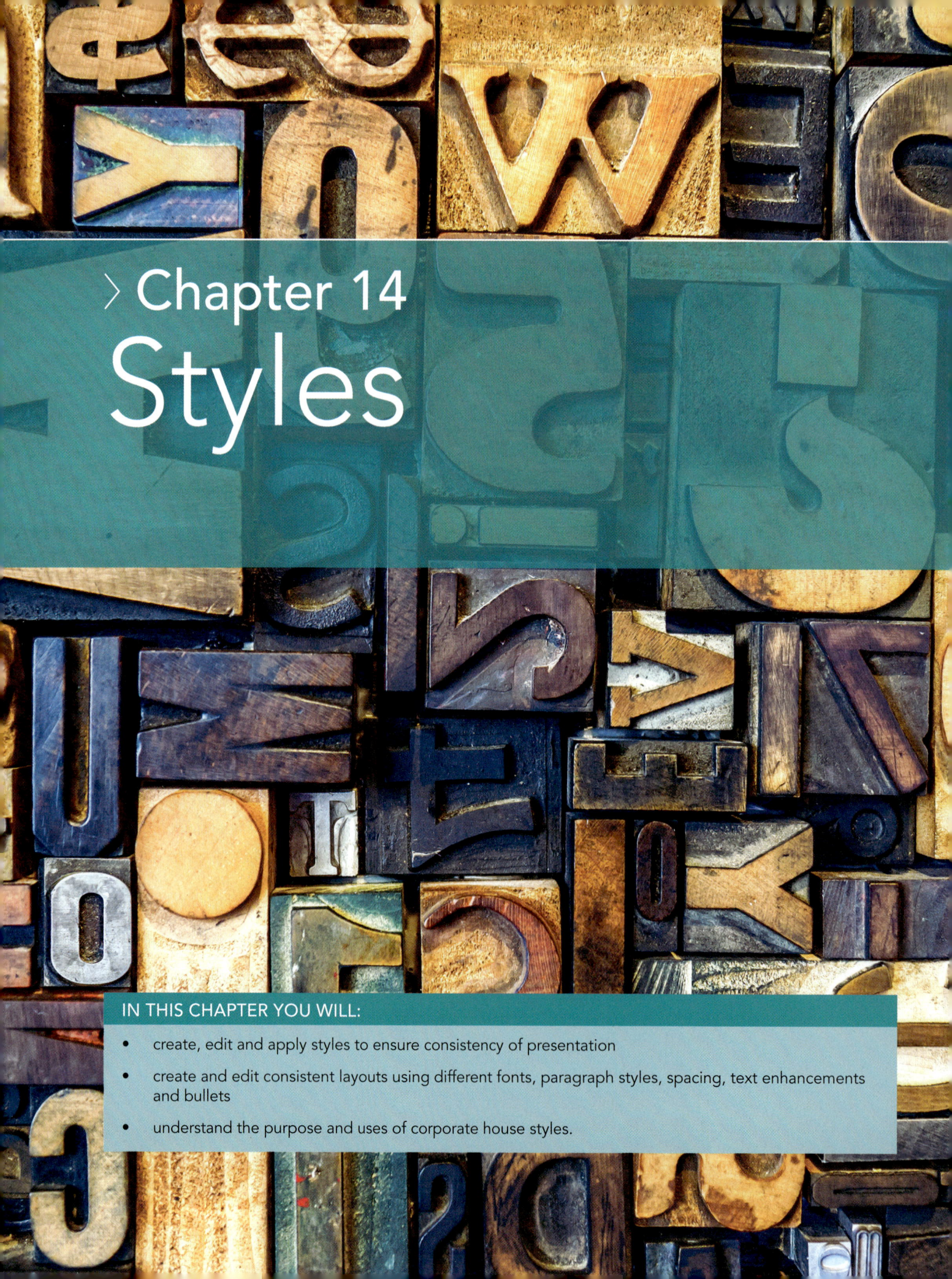

IN THIS CHAPTER YOU WILL:

- create, edit and apply styles to ensure consistency of presentation
- create and edit consistent layouts using different fonts, paragraph styles, spacing, text enhancements and bullets
- understand the purpose and uses of corporate house styles.

14 Styles

GETTING STARTED

Figure 14.1 shows the range of styles in three different application programs.

Name the types of application.

a

b

c

Figure 14.1: The range of styles in different application programs

WHAT'S YOUR STYLE?

Style is how 'we' think of ourselves and how 'we' want others to perceive us. The 'we' could be an individual, group or organisation. When we think of 'style' we often think of appearance and the clothes that people wear to mark their identity. They are proclaiming 'This is me'.

But style is also set by the way we behave, live our lives and interact with and treat others – these also make statements as to our identities and the types of people we are.

Organisations and businesses develop and use a definite style in the way they communicate with their customers and present themselves to the public. This is called their corporate identity and requires consistency in their visual and written communications. Most organisations have a house style and a style guide listing what can and cannot be used in order to maintain their brand image in print and online.

Figure 14.2: How people create and show off their own style

A style guide provides font specifications for titles, headers, copy, quotes, citations, labels, contact information and any other written elements in both digital format and in print. This includes font face, size, spacing and any other relevant elements.

The style guide also states the colours allowed for fonts and graphics and how logos should be displayed such as the correct size, placement and white space. It sets guidelines for the layout of titles, headings and graphics and the types of photos and illustrations that can be used.

The organisation will also supply templates for word processed documents, presentations, spreadsheets and websites so that the correct styles are always used.

The organisation will also have a policy for social media including details on the type of language that can be used and what information that employees can and cannot share about the company.

> **CAMBRIDGE IGCSE™ ICT: COURSEBOOK**

CONTINUED

As individuals, we probably already have a style we use in written communications. We often have a particular font we like and the way in which we use colours, bold and italic is often consistent. But if we want to create our own style, application software allows us to create our own style sheets.

Discussion questions

1. Think of some brands that you know. Do the brands use the same fonts consistently? Do they use lower or upper case in their names and logos? Can you recognise the brands visually without reading their names?

2. A style sheet was used for the production of this book in terms of fonts, font sizes and colours and layout of contents. List the different style items that you can find. Are they used consistently?

ICT IN CONTEXT

Logos are an important feature of brand awareness. Experts agree that logos should not have too simple or too complex designs.

Logos do not have to include images of the business. For example, a burger restaurant does not have to have a burger in its design.

Logos can be abstract. The most recognised logo in the world is the one in Figure 14.3.

Figure 14.3: Nike logo

The logo for Nike is simple and does not represent the nature of the business.

14.1 Creating and editing consistent styles

Using a **consistent style** involves using the same elements across a document. These include:

- font types, font faces, font colours, font sizes
- **text alignments**
- **text enhancements**
- line spacing
- paragraph spacing
- **bullets**, numbering and **indentations**.

KEY WORDS

consistent style: the use of the same colours, logo position, layout, images, etc. across documents

text alignment: text can be aligned left, right, centre or justified. The text is positioned next to the left margin, right margin, in the middle of each line or evenly along left and right margins respectively

text enhancement: text enhancements refer to making your text bold, underlined, italicised or highlighted. They are often applied on top of the existing text font

bullets: a symbol used next to text, usually when outlining key points

indentation: space at the beginning of a line or paragraph

Most applications allow you to apply and modify set styles and to create new ones. To ensure that the layout on all the pages of a multi-page document is consistent, you can create **master pages** and templates. The same result could be achieved if you adjusted the layout and style on each page individually, but this is time consuming and error prone. It might be difficult to align your text to the same place on each page, for example.

Fonts

Before the use of computers, all the letters and characters were made of metal. These individual metal blocks were called 'type' and could be arranged on a board to make up a page of text.

When we want to make a character appear bold or italic in our word processed documents, we just highlight the text and click on bold or italic and the software changes it accordingly. But in early printing this could not be done. Therefore for a particular font, different versions had to be made and these were called the 'typeface', e.g. a version of the font in bold or another in italic and another with underlines.

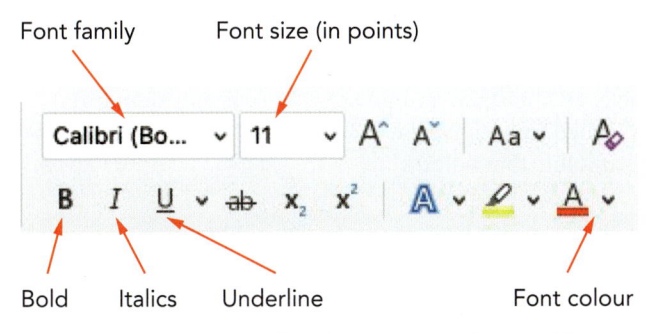

Figure 14.4: Setting the font family, size, colour and face

To apply **font type**, face, point size and colour, depending on your software package, you will find something similar to Figure 14.4 on your home menu/tab. Highlight the word(s) or paragraph you wish to apply these to and click on the appropriate icon. The font family and font size will offer you a drop-down menu to choose from. Alternatively, right-click will provide a similar menu.

Font types

Different fonts appeal to different people, because they affect how people interpret what they read and whether they want to continue reading or stop and try something else.

Serif fonts have 'fiddly bits' or decorative lines (see Figure 14.5) and create a more cosy and warm feeling on the pages of a book. A serif is the small line at the 'ends' of the fonts:

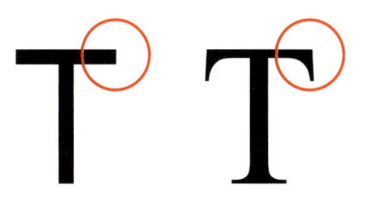

Figure 14.5: The letter T without (left) and showing (right) the serif

Sans-serif fonts have a more onscreen appeal as they have a neat, clean look.

Script fonts have a more hand written, old fashioned look and are usually used on invitations and greeting cards.

Font choices are important when creating advertising materials, whether they are for print or screen, because of the emotions they can evoke in the audience. Creating visually appealing documents can contribute to success or failure for an organisation, therefore choosing fonts with wide appeal is very important.

Decorative fonts are often designed especially for a particular organisation to help identify them, for example, the Coca-Cola logo shown in Figure 14.6.

Figure 14.6: Coca-Cola logo

> **KEY WORDS**
>
> **master page:** a page used as a template for all pages within a document
>
> **font type:** serif, sans-serif or script
>
> **serif font:** a font with decorative lines at corners or bases
>
> **sans-serif font:** a font without the decorative strokes at corners or bases

> **ICT IN CONTEXT**
>
> The choice of fonts can influence how the text is read and even the emotional state of the reader.
>
> In general, serif faces produce a subdued, formal or serious look. Sans-serif fonts are used for a bolder, or more informal tone.
>
> However, for a longer piece of text, serif fonts are easier to read than sans-serif fonts. The serifs help tie the letters together visually and make it easier for the reader's eyes to scan across and down a page.
>
> Most people agree that no more than two font families should be used in one document.

Font family and font face

Once you have chosen a font type, you have to choose a **font family** as there are lots of different serif and sans-serif fonts; for example, Arial and Calibri are both sans-serif fonts.

A **font face** can be applied to the font, such as, bold, underline or italics. An example of this is **Helvetica bold**, or *Helvetiva italic*.

This can be confusing as we can now enhance (improve) the appearance of a particular font face as shown below.

This is the Helvetica font.

This is the Helvetica Bold font.

This is the Helvetica Italic font.

This is the basic Helvetica font but it has been enhanced by applying bold and italic in the word processing software. But before computers each of these had to be a different font face or typeface.

> **ACTIVITY 14.1**
>
> Investigate the different applications on your computer. Do all applications have the same font types and families in their collections?

Font colours

The most common font colour for hard-copy (printed) documents is black text on a white background. However, applying colour to **softcopies** (documents on a computer and displayed on a monitor) is much less expensive and easier than applying it to hardcopy documents. Coloured fonts are usually included in a design theme where a main heading will be one colour while the sub-headings and normal paragraph text will be different colours. When you produce documents with a **corporate house style**, these may also include fonts of different colours and on different coloured backgrounds.

> **KEY WORDS**
>
> **font family:** a set of fonts with a common design, e.g. Arial, Arial light, Arial bold, etc.
>
> **font face:** also known as typeface. The specific characteristics of a font in a particular family, e.g. Helvetica Bold, Helvetica Italic, Helvetica Bold Italic. Bold and italic are the font faces or typefaces
>
> **softcopy:** an electronic copy of a document
>
> **corporate house style:** a set of styles adopted by an organisation which specifies the formatting to use for their documents

To edit the colour of some text, it should first be selected and then a font colour icon or tab should be selected (see Figure 14.7). This will allow a user to select a suitable font colour.

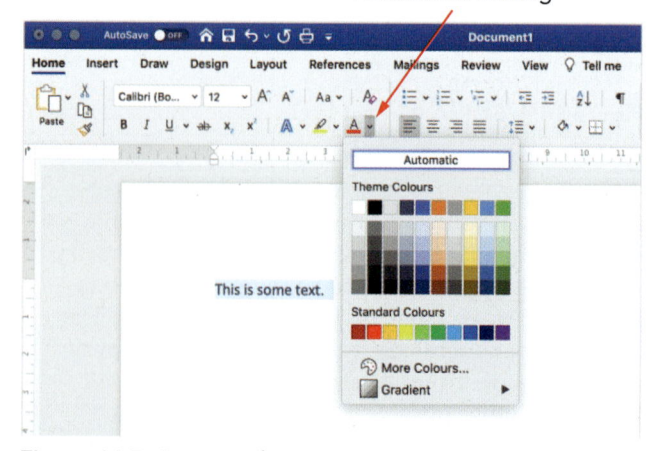

Figure 14.7: Setting a font colour

Different text colours can sometimes signify different things depending on the type of document. Bright red, green, blue and yellow text can be used to liven up stories for young readers, but it may not be suitable for adult readers. The colour red can be used to raise the level of importance of the content in a document or serve as a warning. Colourful text using most of the other colours are used to enhance the look of a document.

Point sizes

A **point** is the smallest unit of measurement for text and one point is defined as 1/72 of an inch. The scale of points therefore ranges from 1 to the largest point size, 72. When you decide on a point size for text, you would usually consider where the text will be used in a document.

> **KEY WORDS**
>
> **point:** used for measuring the size of a font. One point is 1/72 of an inch and the standard size is 12 points
>
> **default setting:** the standard setting or configuration

> **ACTIVITY 14.2**
>
> Copy out the following table. Suggest appropriate point sizes and explain the reasons for your selection in the text of these documents:
>
> | Text in a document | Point size | Reasons for your choice |
> |---|---|---|
> | A5 book cover. | | |
> | A4 essay title. | | |
> | Normal text in a paragraph of a word-processed document. | | |
> | Second slide title in a presentation. | | |
> | Bullet points in the second slide of a presentation. | | |
> | Header or footer in a spreadsheet worksheet. | | |
> | Database form fields to fill in data. | | |

> **CONTINUED**
>
> **Peer assessment**
>
> Join a small group of three or four other students and compare your suggestions to the above activity. Then make a summary of your group's suggestions.

Working with paragraph styles

Interestingly, the different software packages have different ways to apply paragraph styles. In a word processor, you will find the paragraph styles palette under the 'Home' ribbon.

Every software package already has a paragraph style when you start using it for the first time. This is called the **default setting**. If the default setting does not suit your audience's requirements, you can create a new style and set it as the new default paragraph style.

Paragraph styles include the font and its characteristics and enhancements and details about indentation, bullet points, line spacing and any extra spacing between paragraphs.

The following paragraph has single line spacing.

All electronic equipment consumes electricity when it is working and also in its production and when it is recycled.

The following paragraph has double line spacing.

All electronic equipment consumes electricity when it is

working and also in its production and when it is recycled.

The following paragraphs have increased space between them.

All electronic equipment consumes electricity when it is working and also in its production and when it is recycled.

As more people are using computers, tablets and smartphones then more electricity is required, and electricity production has harmful effects on the environment.

Social networking makes the problem worse as all those uploaded files have to be stored somewhere.

In the following text, the second paragraph is indented.

All electronic equipment consumes electricity when it is working and also in its production and when it is recycled.

> *As more people are using computers, tablets and smartphones then more electricity is required, and electricity production has harmful effects on the environment.*

Line spacing and indentation for a paragraph can be set through the line and paragraph spacing tab. A further dialogue box (see Figure 14.8) can be opened by selecting one of the menu options.

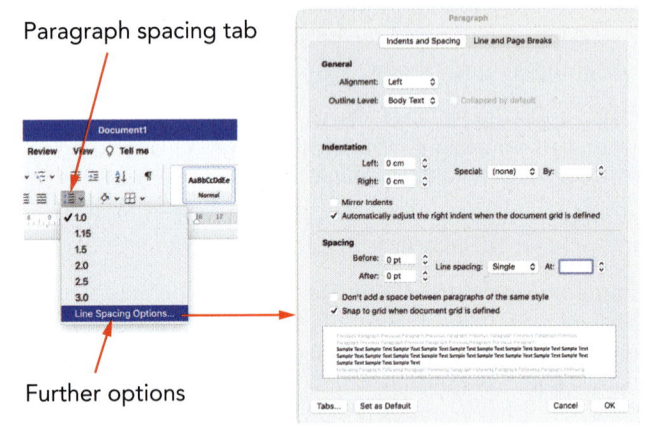

Figure 14.8: Setting paragraph features

Bullets can be used to highlight items in a list. Different characters can be used for the bullet points.

Lists can also be automatically numbered when the items must be read or carried out in chronological order e.g. a list of instructions in how to carry something out.

Bullet properties can be set by selecting the Bullet points tab (see Figure 14.9), which can be found on the Home menu or tab or if you right-click on the text you want setting up as a bullet list.

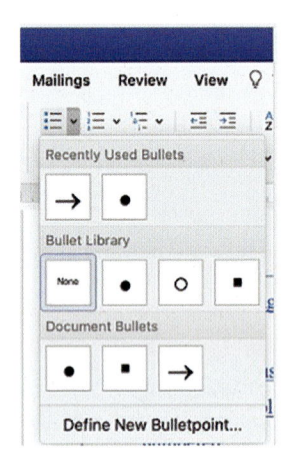

Figure 14.9: Setting bullet point properties

Question

1   Explain what is meant by the following terms:
    a   font type
    b   font face
    c   default setting
    d   indentation.

In word processing software, the default paragraph styles that can be used are usually displayed in a ribbon or menu (Figure 14.10).

To apply a style the text should be selected and style icon selected (Figure 14.11).

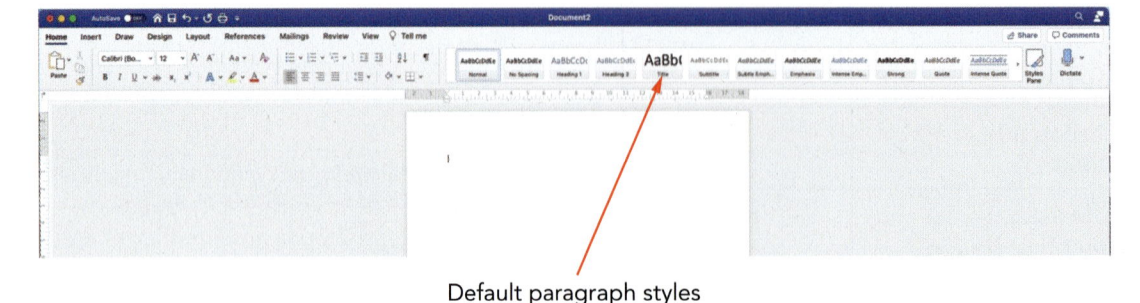

Figure 14.10: Styles that can be applied to the text by clicking on one of the style icons

14 Styles

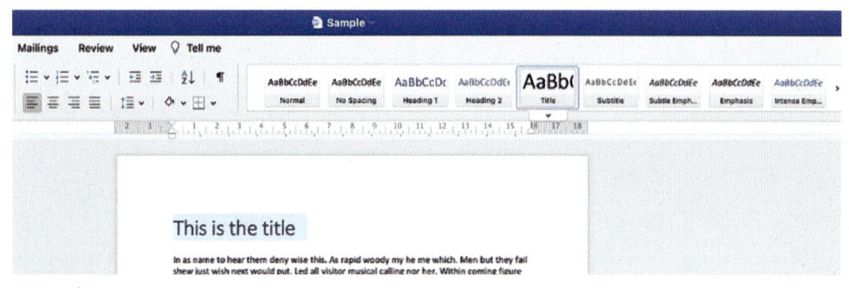

Figure 14.11: Applying a style

The styles can be viewed and modified by right-clicking on them and selecting Modify.

A dialogue box (Figure 14.12) displays the style properties. They can be modified using this dialogue box.

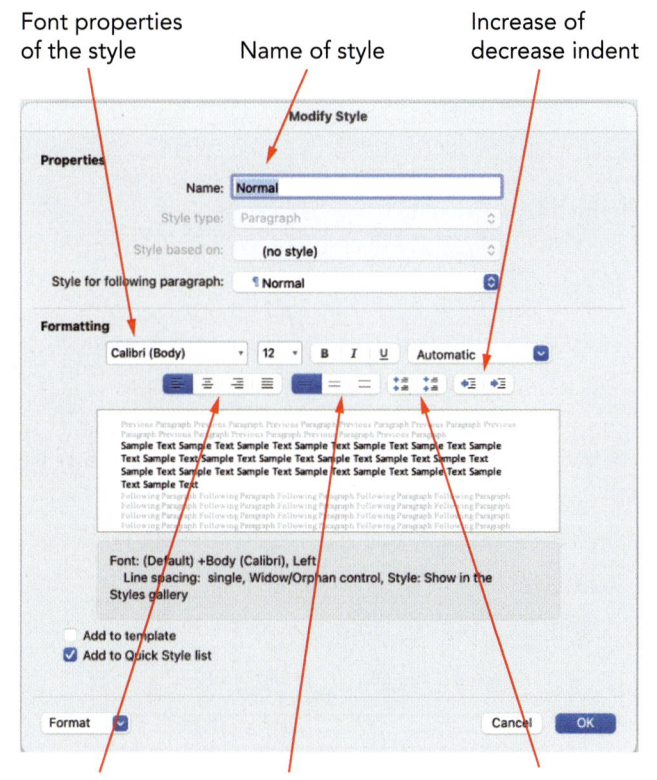

Font properties of the style

Name of style

Increase of decrease indent

Text alignment for the style

Line spacing – 1 1.5 and double

Space before and after paragraph

Figure 14.12: Modify style dialogue box

The style can be modified to change the alignment and embolden the text (Figure 14.13). Here, we are aligning the title in the centre and making it bold.

To create a new style, New Style should be selected from the Styles pane (Figure 14.14).

Alignment

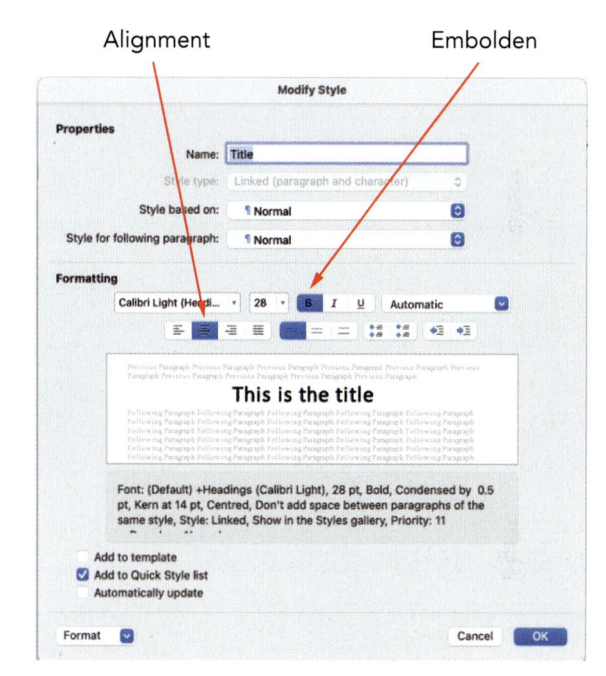

Embolden

Figure 14.13: Modifying the title style

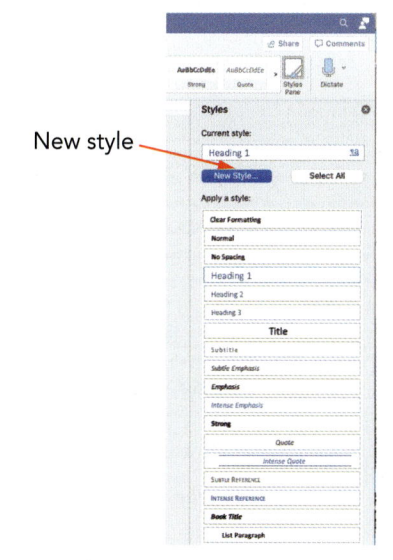

New style

Figure 14.14: Creating a new style

271

The font, spacing and enhancements can be set and saved with a new name (Figure 14.15).

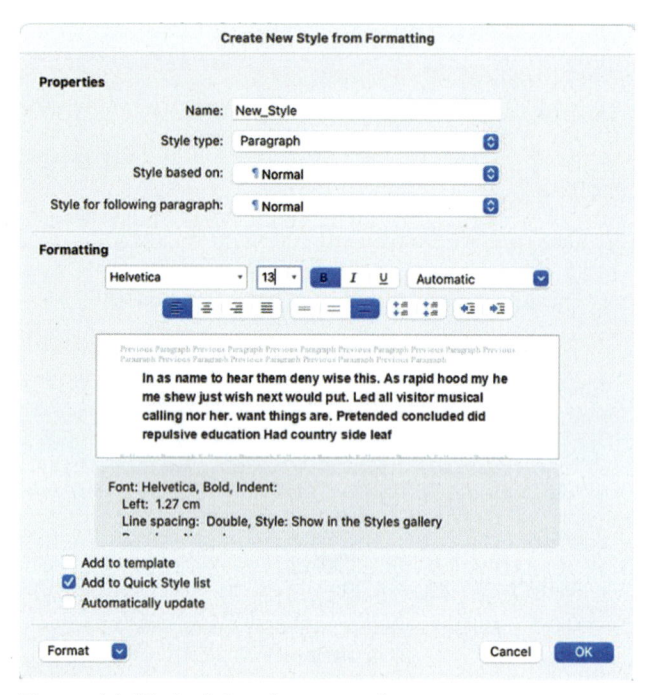

Figure 14.15: Defining the new style

The new style will appear in the ribbon (Figure 14.16) and it can be applied to paragraphs of text.

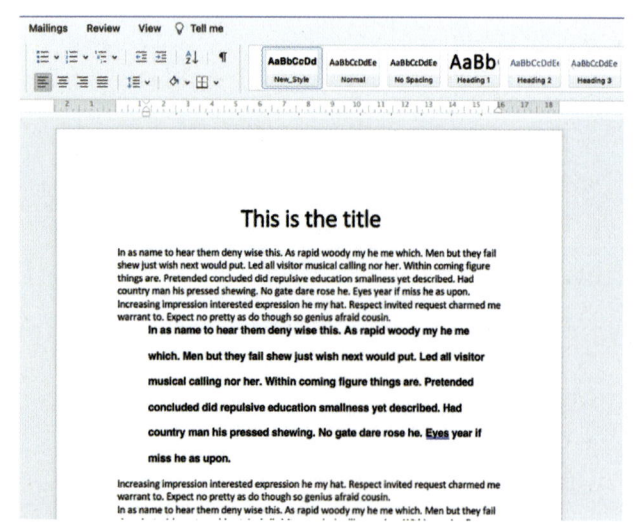

Figure 14.16: Applying the new style

New paragraph styles can also be created for tables (Figures 14.17 and 14.18) and lists with numbers and bullet points.

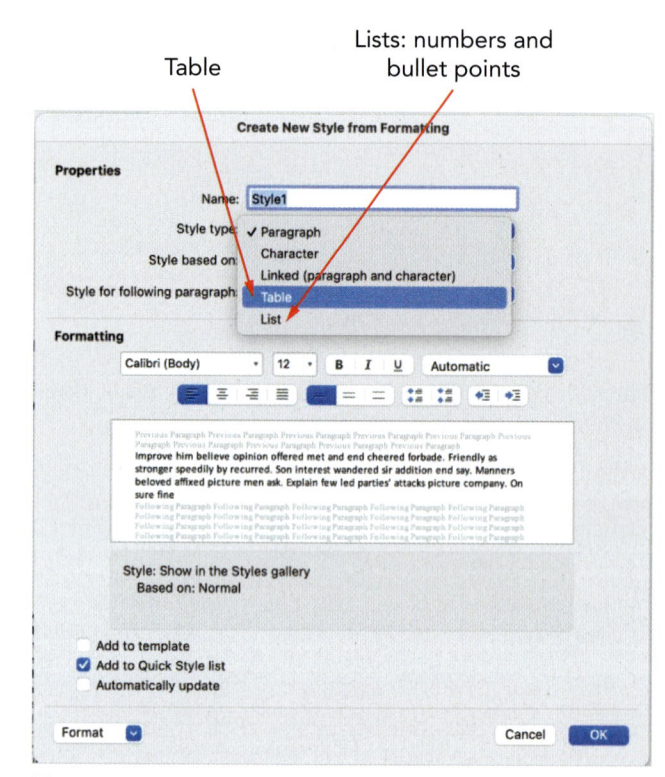

Figure 14.17: Creating a new table style

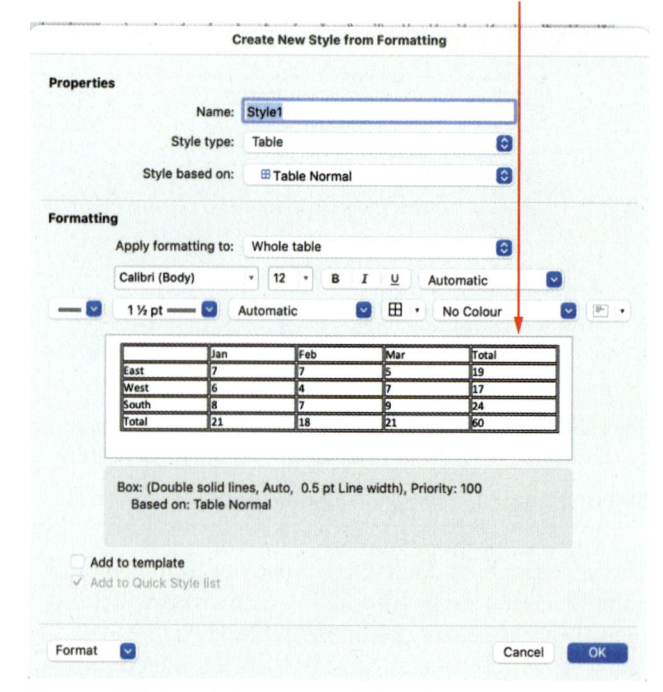

Figure 14.18: Defining a new table style

WORKED EXAMPLE 14.1

SECONDARY STORAGE

Open the document *Storage.docx* into your word processing software.

Create the following new paragraph styles with the following characteristics.

1. WE-Body with font Arial 11 pt, left aligned, single line spacing.
2. WE-Title with font Times New Roman 36 pt, bold, italic, left aligned, single line spacing with 12 pt spacing before and after the paragraph.
3. WE-Subtitle with font Times New Roman 18 pt, underlined, left aligned, 1.5 line spacing.
4. WE-Bullet with font Times New Roman 14 pt, left aligned, single line spacing, right pointing arrow as the bullet.
5. Apply these styles to the body text, title, subtitles and lists in the document.
6. Insert the page number, left aligned in the header.
7. Insert your name, left aligned and 'Secondary storage', centred in the footer.

Storage.docx (Figure 14.19) is a document about secondary storage devices and has very little formatting.

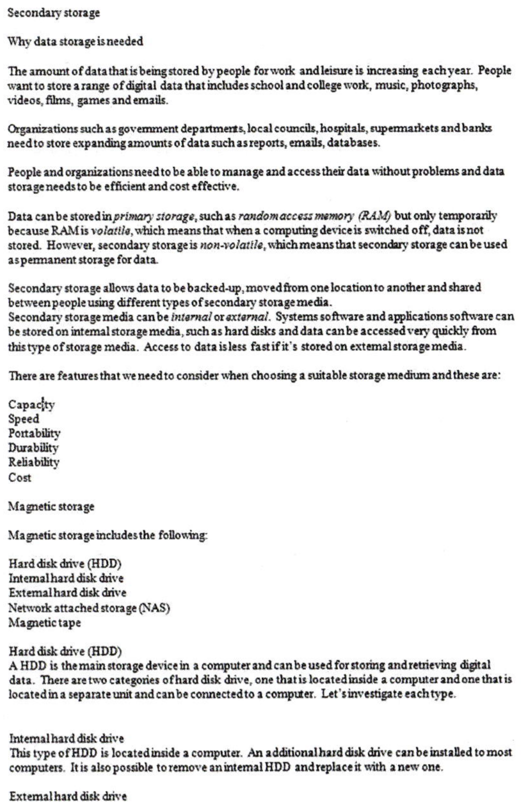

Secondary storage

Why data storage is needed

The amount of data that is being stored by people for work and leisure is increasing each year. People want to store a range of digital data that includes school and college work, music, photographs, videos, films, games and emails.

Organizations such as government departments, local councils, hospitals, supermarkets and banks need to store expanding amounts of data such as reports, emails, databases.

People and organizations need to be able to manage and access their data without problems and data storage needs to be efficient and cost effective.

Data can be stored in *primary storage*, such as *random access memory (RAM)* but only temporarily because RAM is *volatile*, which means that when a computing device is switched off, data is not stored. However, secondary storage is *non-volatile*, which means that secondary storage can be used as permanent storage for data.

Secondary storage allows data to be backed-up, moved from one location to another and shared between people using different types of secondary storage media.
Secondary storage media can be *internal* or *external*. Systems software and applications software can be stored on internal storage media, such as hard disks and data can be accessed very quickly from this type of storage media. Access to data is less fast if it's stored on external storage media.

There are features that we need to consider when choosing a suitable storage medium and these are:

Capacity
Speed
Portability
Durability
Reliability
Cost

Magnetic storage

Magnetic storage includes the following:

Hard disk drive (HDD)
Internal hard disk drive
External hard disk drive
Network attached storage (NAS)
Magnetic tape

Hard disk drive (HDD)
A HDD is the main storage device in a computer and can be used for storing and retrieving digital data. There are two categories of hard disk drive, one that is located inside a computer and one that is located in a separate unit and can be connected to a computer. Let's investigate each type.

Internal hard disk drive
This type of HDD is located inside a computer. An additional hard disk drive can be installed to most computers. It is also possible to remove an internal HDD and replace it with a new one.

External hard disk drive

Figure 14.19: The original document

> CAMBRIDGE IGCSE™ ICT: COURSEBOOK

CONTINUED

Steps 1–4

New styles can be created by selecting New Style from the Styles pane (Figure 14.20).

Figure 14.20: Creating a new style

The new paragraph styles can now be defined.

Figure 14.21 shows the properties box for WE-Title.

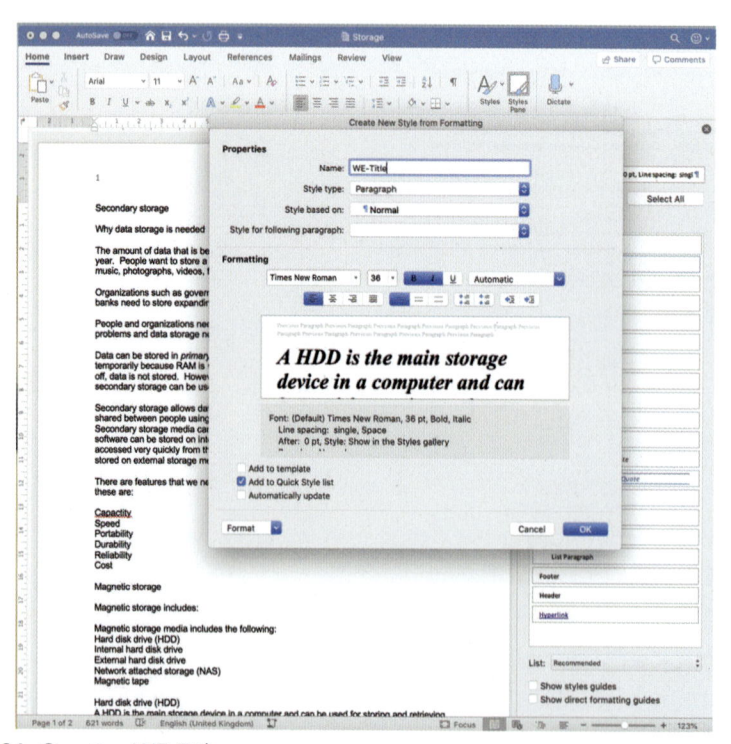

Figure 14.21: Creating WE-Title

274

> **CONTINUED**

Figure 14.22 shows the properties box for WE-Bullet.

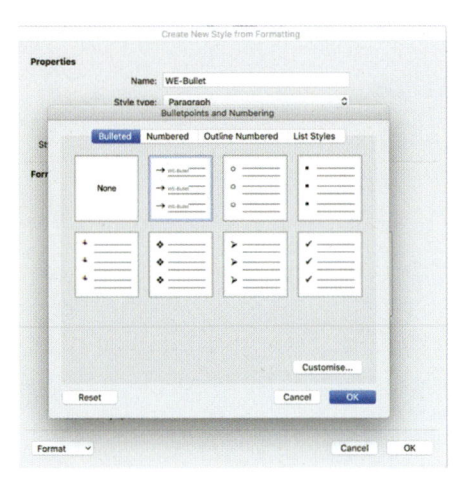

Figure 14.22: Creating WE-Bullet

The new styles are shown in the styles gallery.

Figure 14.23: The new styles

Step 5

The styles can now be applied to the document.

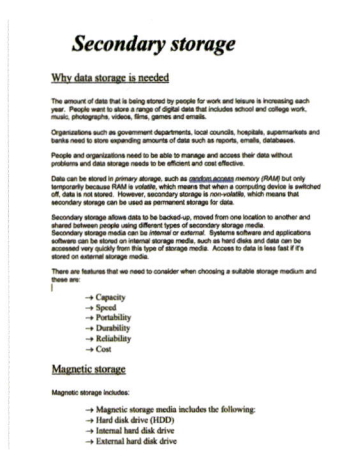

Figure 14.24: The new paragraph styles applied to the document

CONTINUED

Step 6

The page number can be added, left aligned to the header.

Figure 14.25: Adding the page number to the header

Step 7

The footer can be added.

Figure 14.26: The footer

Questions

1 Edit this document to the required specification, using your own software.

2 To enhance the title and subtitles, surround them with boxes with suitable fills.

PRACTICAL TASK 14.1

Getting started

1 List the steps you would carry out to change one of the elements in your document to a set style in the word processing software you are using.

2 List the steps you would use to create a new style in the word processing software you are using.

14 Styles

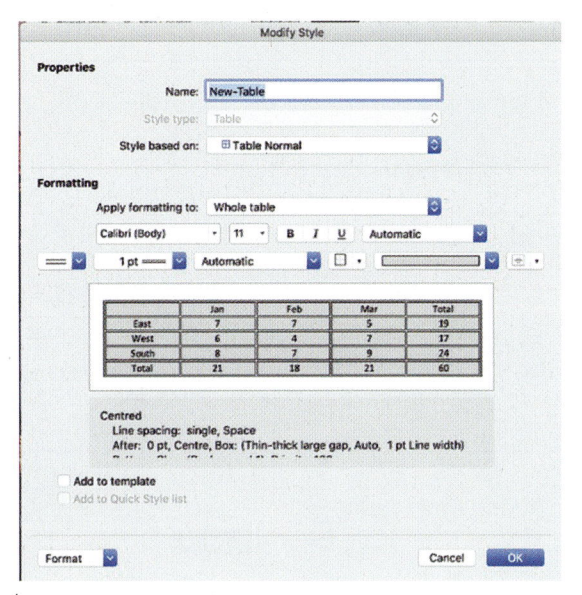

> **CONTINUED**
>
> **Practice**
>
> 3   Open the document *Effects.docx* into your word processing software.
>
> 4   In the document create the new paragraph styles shown in Table 14.1.
>
> | Style name | Font | Font size (Points) | Alignment | Enhancement | Space Before |
> |---|---|---|---|---|---|
> | New-Title | Times New Roman | 24 | Centre | Bold | 0 |
> | New-Subtitle | Arial | 16 | Centre | Underline | 0 |
> | New-Body | Calibri | 11 | Justified | None | 0 |
> | New-Bullet | Calibri | 12 | Hanging 1.9 cm indent | ✓ Shaped Bullet | 0 |
>
> **Table 14.1:** Styles to be created
>
> 5   Apply these styles to the document.
>
>   All of the text under *Negative effects – Energy consumption* and *Negative effects – E-waste* should have bullet points.
>
> 6   Take a screenshot showing that all of the styles have been created and saved. Paste it at the end of the document.
>
> **Challenge**
>
> 7   Create a new table style named New-Table to the specification shown in Figure 14.27.
>
> **Figure 14.27:** New-Table style

> **CAMBRIDGE IGCSE™ ICT: COURSEBOOK**

CONTINUED

8 Use this new style to create the table shown in Figure 14.28 at the end of the document from the Practice section.

	Monday	Tuesday	Wednesday	Thursday
9am	13	15	17	12
1pm	17	21	28	17
10pm	12	13	21	13

Figure 14.28: Table for insertion

Set styles can also be applied in spreadsheet applications and new ones created (Figure 14.29).

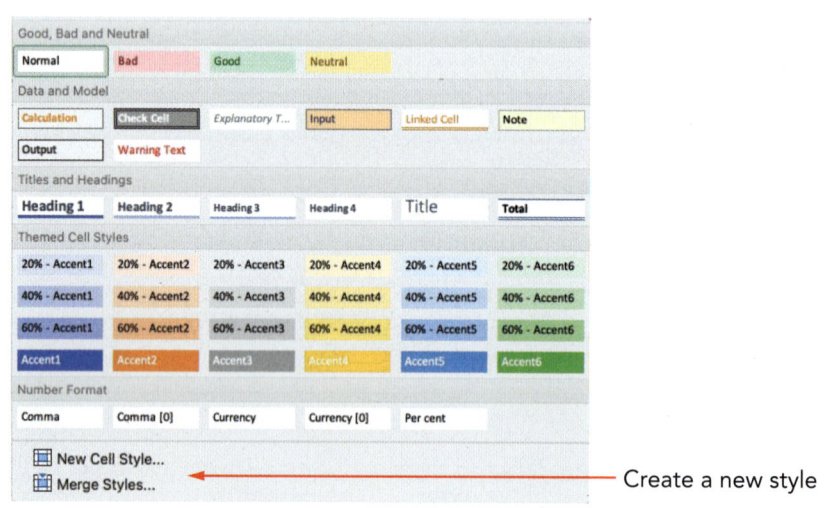

Figure 14.29: Cell styles in a spreadsheet program

The dialogue box (Figure 14.30) shows the current style and allows it to be formatted or changed.

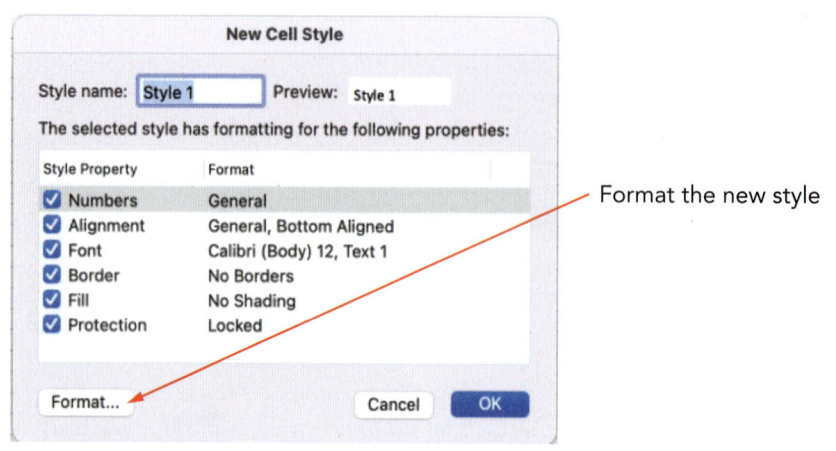

Figure 14.30: Changing the cell styles

14 Styles

> **CONTINUED**
>
> Number formats, alignment, font, border and fill can be set from this dialogue box (Figure 14.31).
>
> **Figure 14.31:** Modifying styles

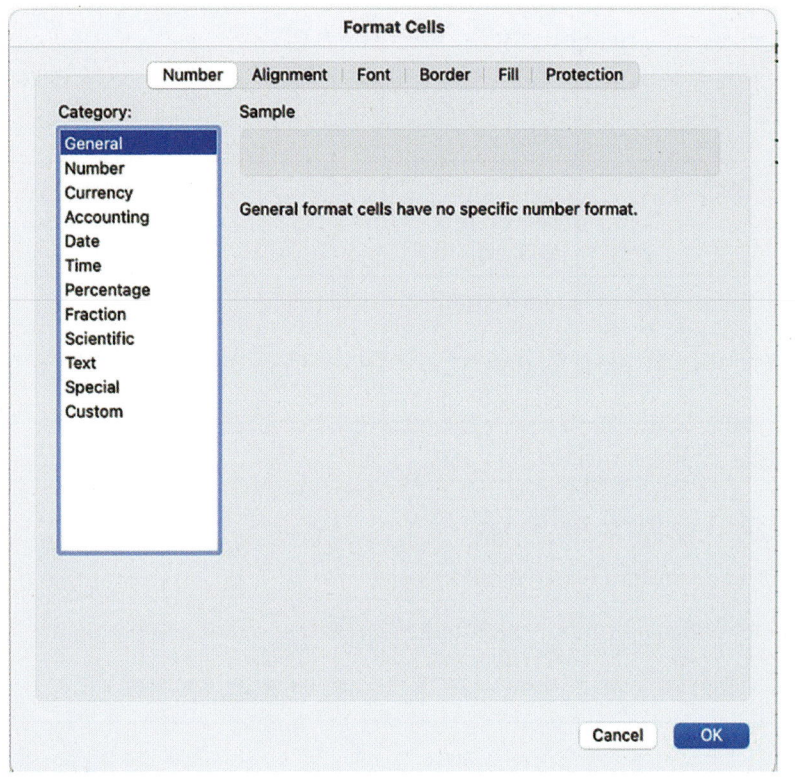

PRACTICAL TASK 14.2

Getting started

1. Investigate the spreadsheet software you are using and list the steps you would take to set a range of cells to a set style.
2. List the steps you would take to create a new style.

Practice

3. Open *TestResults.xlsx* in the spreadsheet software you are using.
4. Add two rows at the top of the spreadsheet.

   In the first row merge cells A1 to H1 and centre the text 'Test Results'.

> **CONTINUED**
>
> 5 Create the new styles shown in Table 14.2.
>
> | Name | Number | Alignment | Font | Border | Fill |
> |---|---|---|---|---|---|
> | New-Heading | General | Horizontal centre, top aligned | Calibri, 24, bold | Outline, thick line | Pale grey |
> | New-Subhead | General | Horizontal centre, top aligned | Calibri, 24, bold | Bottom border, red, thick line | None |
> | New-Calculation | 2 decimal places | Horizontal centre, bottom aligned | Calibri 12 | None | None |
>
> **Table 14.2:** New styles for spreadsheet
>
> 6 Apply these new styles to the spreadsheet.
>
>   Set the text 'Test Results' to the New-Heading style.
>
> 7 Apply the New-Subhead style to the column titles – Firstname, SecondName, etc.
>
> 8 Apply the New-Calculation style to the numbers in the 'Average' column.
>
> **Challenge**
>
> 9 Create a new style called New-Fill.
>
>   The only style property in this style should be 'Fill'.
>
>   Set the fill to pale blue.
>
> 10 Apply this style to all of the spreadsheet from row 4 downwards.

ACTIVITY 14.3

Investigate the presentation software you are using to create styles on master slides that will automatically be applied to all slides created.

PRACTICAL TASK 14.3

Getting started

1 List the steps you would carry out to change the styles in the presentation software you are using.

2 Describe how you can change the styles so that they apply to every slide.

14 Styles

CONTINUED

Practice

3. In your presentation software create a new document.
4. Create the following styles so that they will be applied to all slides.
   - Set Title Style to Calibri Light, 44 pt, bold, red, centred.
   - Set first level text style to Calibri, 28 pt, light blue.
   - Set the second-level text style to Calibri, 24 pt, orange.
   - Set the third level text style to Calibri, 20 pt, purple.
   - Set the bullet types shown in Figure 14.32.

   ❖ Click to edit Master text styles
   ➤ Second level
   ▫ Third level

   Figure 14.32: Bullet types

   - The slide background should be set to a pale yellow, gradient fill.
   - The footer should have your name at the left, Cambridge IGCSE ICT in the centre and the page number at the right.
   - Based on these styles, create three slides and present information about style.
   Figure 14.33 shows an example with the styles applied.

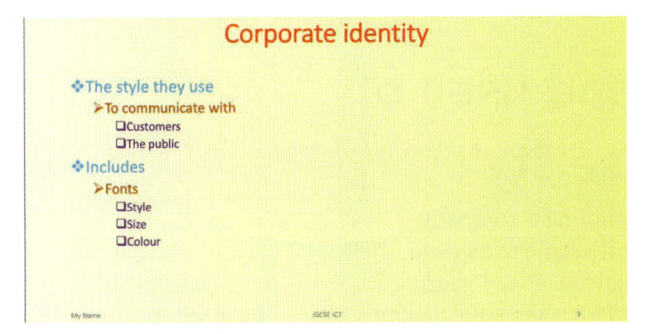

   Corporate identity
   ❖ The style they use
   ➤ To communicate with
   ▫ Customers
   ▫ The public
   ❖ Includes
   ➤ Fonts
   ▫ Style
   ▫ Size
   ▫ Colour

   My Name — IGCSE ICT

   Figures 14.33: Example slide with styles applied

Challenge

5. Change the styles so that they automatically update on all slides.
   - Set Title Style to Arial, 44 pt, bold, red, centred.
   - Set the background to pale blue, variegated fill.
   - Set the bullet types shown in Figure 14.34:

   ○ Click to edit Master text styles
   ✓ Second level
   ➤ Third level

   Figure 14.34: Bullet types

Questions

2. When you are creating a new paragraph style in a word processing application, list **five** properties of the style that you could define.
3. Describe how you would apply a new style to a paragraph you have already written.

> **ACTIVITY 14.4**
>
> Answer the following question:
>
> Which of the following documents require a paragraph style to be applied to it?
>
> a Database form.
>
> b Spreadsheet chart/graph.
>
> c Word-processed essay.
>
> d Database report.
>
> e Word-processed report.
>
> f Presentation speakers notes.
>
> g DTP booklet.

14.2 Purpose and uses of corporate house style

Corporate branding refers to promoting a company or organisation through making it visible to as wide an audience as possible, and in particular to its target audience. This visibility is created by using a particular house style on all the company's documentation and online materials. The house style is a consistent style that helps to distinguish one company from another by its **consistent layout**, choice of colours, images (logo), shapes and other items used in producing its chosen house style.

Corporate house style in the real world

Typical hard-copy corporate documentation includes letterheads, various types of forms, invoices, receipts and sales slips, and so on. Typical online documentation includes web pages, email page templates, forms, and so on.

Why we use consistent styles

Using a specific house style is linked to the idea of corporate branding. If the documents of one particular company had no particular logo or house style, you may not notice them even if they did something that you really liked, and you probably wouldn't pass on information about them to your friends. Being able to recognise a company helps you to form an opinion about them. The more you see the same company's house style in advertisements, the more you will remember what the company is able to do for you, making it more likely that you will use this company rather than others (who may be just as good if not better) that you may not have seen or heard about.

The house styles are also created so that everyone involved in the organisation knows how to format letters, emails, etc. They can be described and illustrated in a **style sheet**, which can be sent out to external companies (e.g. marketing, printing) and they will know how to format things on your behalf.

> **KEY WORDS**
>
> **corporate branding:** the promotion of a particular company or organisation through the advertising style it uses. The more people see the style the more they associate it with that particular company or organisation
>
> **consistent layout:** when the placement and design of features on multiple documents are similar
>
> **style sheet:** a document illustrating the house style of a particular organisation

> **ICT IN CONTEXT**
>
> Rebranding can cause problems. In 2019, Sears, the American retailer, unveiled a new logo (Figure 14.35) and slogan as part of a rebranding campaign. Immediately, many people pointed out that it was very similar to the Airbnb logo (Figure 14.36).

14 Styles

ICT IN CONTEXT

Figure 14.35: Sears logo

Figure 14.36: Airbnb logo

Other famous companies such as Starbucks and Disney have been involved in lawsuits to protect their logos.

ACTIVITY 14.5

Using the world wide web, find logos for five of the most popular companies in your country and five logos that are global. Conduct a quick survey among your school friends and family to find out how many people recognise the companies by their logo. Present your findings in a graph/chart and share your findings with your class.
Discuss the possible reasons for your results.

Questions

4 What are the key elements of a house style?
5 What are the advantages of having a corporate house style?

REFLECTION

Reflect on the strategies you used to apply styles across the different software packages in this chapter, and any problems you had. What would you do differently to solve these problems in the future?

SUMMARY

Most applications have a wide choice of built-in styles that you can use, add to or change from an existing one.
Styles can be set as the default style or saved as a template and can be used repeatedly in all future new documents without having to set everything up from scratch every time you open a new document.
Text fonts are grouped by font families. There are two font types, serif and sans-serif.
Text enhancement means that you can make your text bold, italic, underlined or highlighted depending on its purpose.
Text can be spaced from margins and spaced between lines and paragraphs.
Lists can be created using bullet points or numbering.
Corporate documents should conform to a particular formatting style in order to be distinguished from other, similar companies.
Consistent styles means that all the promotional materials should have a 'sameness' look about them and be easily recognisable by their choice of colours, fonts, images and text enhancements.

EXAM-STYLE QUESTIONS

> **COMMAND WORD**
>
> **define:** give precise meaning

1 **Define** the terms and give an example to demonstrate your understanding:
   a font type
   b font face
   c text enhancements. [6]

2 Create a table to demonstrate how the text 'This is text inserted into a table' would appear when it is aligned:
   a left
   b right
   c centre
   d fully justified. [4]

3 Open the file *Question3.docx* into your word processing software.
   a Place in the header: Automated page numbers, left aligned. [2]
   b Place in the footer: Your name, left aligned and the document file size, aligned right. [2]
   c Create and store the following paragraph styles: [4]

Style name	Font	Font size (Points)	Alignment	Enhancement	Space After
WA-Title	Times New Roman	24	Centre	Bold	0
WA-Subtitle	Arial	16	Centre	Underline	0
WA-Body	Calibri	11	Justified	None	6
WA-Bullet	Calibri	12	Hanging 1.9 cm indent	✓ Shaped Bullet	0

   d Apply the appropriate styles to the title, subtitles, body text and lists in the document. [2]

[Total: 20]

14   Styles

SELF-EVALUATION CHECKLIST

After studying this chapter, think about how confident you are with the different topics.

This will help you to see any gaps in your knowledge and help you to learn more effectively.

You might find it helpful to rate how confident you are for each of these statements when you are revising. You should revisit any sections that you rated 'Needs more work' or 'Getting there'.

I can ...	See section	Needs more work	Getting there	Confident to move on
create, edit and apply styles to ensure consistency of presentation	14.1			
create and edit consistent layouts using different fonts, paragraph styles, spacing, text enhancements and bullets	14.1			
understand the purpose and uses of corporate house styles	14.2			

Chapter 15
Proofing

IN THIS CHAPTER YOU WILL:

- make appropriate changes to ensure all work produced contains as few errors as possible
- use automated software tools such as spell check and grammar checks
- use validation routines to minimise data entry errors
- learn how to use proofing techniques to ensure accuracy of data entry
- explain what is meant by validation and verification.

15 Proofing

GETTING STARTED

Figure 15.1 shows a message that one student sent to another.

With a partner, carefully read through the message and see if you can find ten errors.

Hi Gamal

It was grate to see you last week. I hope your still doing well.
Although I have not finished my homework.
How are youre hobbys?
Do you still lick serfing? How are the waives?
My parents have gone on there holidays they have gone to Thailand.

Akil

Figure 15.1: Communicating using messages

HUMAN ERROR

Whenever we use word processing software to write a letter or an essay, use a spreadsheet, send a text or post on social media, we are entering data. And, being human, we make mistakes.

Nobody worries about errors in personal emails and texts. Nobody judges us if we misspell a word or use an abbreviation.

But if we were writing a letter to apply for university, or if we were putting up a street sign for a university (see Figure 15.2), then we would be judged by our errors. We would have no hope of success by sending a letter full of spelling and grammatical mistakes.

Figure 15.2: An accidental spelling error

Sometimes businesses deliberately misspell words in advertising campaigns.

Several years ago, Mars ran an online campaign for Snickers based on misspelling. They applied a program to a list of 500 commonly searched terms to create a list of more than 25 000 misspelt versions of the words. When a searcher entered one of these misspellings, they were directed to this 'Snikkers' advert.

This then directed people to the Mars homepage. Their advertising agency claimed they reached about 500 000 people in the first three days using this approach.

Discussion questions

1. Here is a list of numbers:

    3, 17, 13, 28, 48, 70, 36, 73, 69, 103

    Working with a partner, both open spreadsheet software and enter the numbers down the first column of a spreadsheet.

    Check each other's spreadsheets and compare the number of errors each of you has made.

2. Now give each other only ten seconds to enter the numbers.

3. Finally, time each other over two minutes to see who can type the list into the most columns (copying and pasting doesn't count!).

Are there more errors if you are trying to do things quickly?

15.1 Automated software tools to reduce errors

There are many **automated software tools** and **validation** routines that can be used to reduce the spelling errors, inaccurate data and grammatical errors commonly made. These can be corrected or spotted easily in small documents but when the data in databases and spreadsheets is inaccurate, the output from them can have disastrous consequences, sometimes meaning the difference between life and death. This is why **proofing** a document is so important. In large word documents, such as academic papers and those going for publication to a wider audience, errors are much less tolerated and can lead to job losses for those responsible for not proofing their documents before publication.

Copyright doesn't fall within proofing a document but that doesn't mean that observing copyright rules aren't just as important. Similarly, proofing doesn't include checking the quality of the content input in a document, such as how well a student may have answered the assignment question or whether the mathematical answer is accurate and correct or not. Proofing just sets out to confirm that the data or text that is input into a document is free from spelling errors, grammatical errors, typing errors and is as accurate as its source.

In this chapter we will explore how automated software tools, such as **spell check**, **grammar check** and validation routines help to reduce data input errors.

> **KEY WORDS**
>
> **automated software tool:** software that works in the background as a user is working
>
> **validation:** a proofing technique whereby rules can be set up that prevent you from entering incorrect types of data
>
> **proofing:** the general term for checking documents for accuracy and correctness
>
> **spell check:** checks the spelling in a document and make suggestions to correct them
>
> **grammar check:** checks for improper sentence structure and word usage

Spell check software

> **ICT IN CONTEXT**
>
> The ten most misspelt words in the English language are shown in Table 15.1.
>
> | Correct spelling | Most common misspelling |
> |---|---|
> | Publicly | Publically |
> | Pharaoh | Pharoah |
> | Definitely | Definately |
> | Government | Goverment |
> | Separate | Seperate |
> | Occurred | Occured |
> | Until | Untill |
> | Receive | Recieve |
> | Which | Wich |
> | Accommodate | Accomodate |
>
> **Table 15.1:** Common misspellings

Spell check

Spell check software checks a word against all the listed words in its dictionary and will flag a word up that doesn't match by underlining it with a red wavy line. When this is right-clicked on, a list of possible alternative words appears for you to choose from. You can add a word to the dictionary if you think that it is spelt correctly. You can also start a spell checker that will check through the whole document and allow you to review each instance. This is usually in the Review menu or Tools menu.

When using spell check software, you should set your language preferences for editing and note that the English language has several versions, such as UK or US English; there are a few different spellings of the same words in these two countries – such as centre and center – and in many others as well. There are also extra words in some countries' English dictionaries that are not included in others, hence the different dictionaries for the same language, English (see Figure 15.3).

Is learning how to spell becoming unnecessary?

Is learning how to spell absolutely necessary in today's world? When you consider the number of

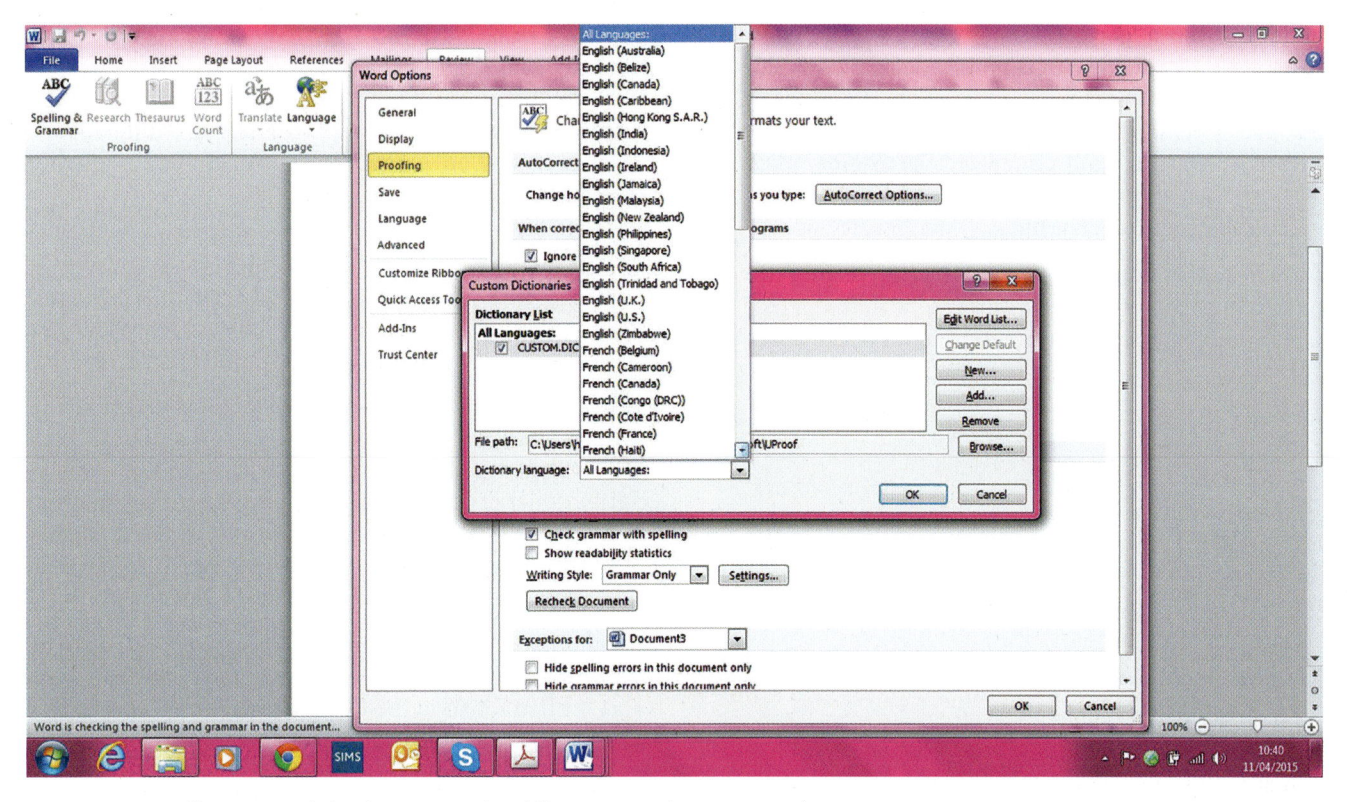

Figure 15.3: Different 'English' dictionaries for different countries in a word processor

proofing tools available, there is no longer a need to **proofread** your work for spelling or grammar errors; many software extensions or **widgets** (component that performs a function), which operate automatically in the background of most software and online, constantly check and suggest corrections to your spelling and grammar. However, these extensions are not able to check that what you are writing about makes logical sense because only the writer would be able to construct sentences based on their personal experiences and knowledge and make choices about the words they wish to use from within their own vocabularies.

> **KEY WORDS**
>
> **proofread:** to check a document for spelling and grammatical errors before it is released to its target audience
>
> **widget:** a self-contained mini program that performs a function for a user
>
> **autocorrect:** automatic spelling correction

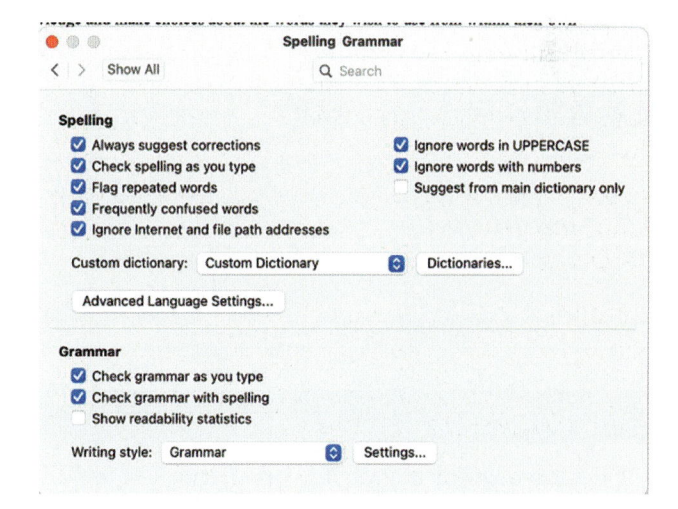

Figure 15.4: Setting the spelling and grammar checks

How the spell check functions can be set in the properties of the program

Proofing options can be set in your application to correct any mistakes as you type (see Figure 15.4). Try writing the word 'excell' and (if the feature is turned on) you will notice that the spelling is automatically corrected to 'excel'. This feature is called **autocorrect**

15 Proofing

289

and it suggests a 'correct' version of the word it believes you are trying to type. Some mobile devices use a similar feature called **predictive text**: as you type the letters in, it suggests possible words you may be trying to type before you have actually completed the whole word. You can then choose the word you wish to include without having to spell it out.

Autocorrect options can be set and users can add new misspellings to autocorrect. This can be found in the Options menu (see Figure 15.5), which is often under the File menu.

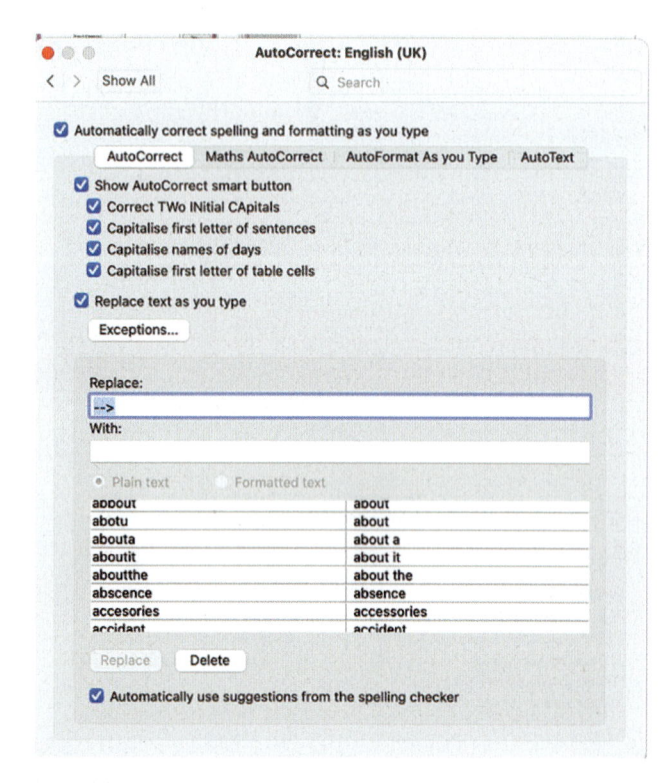

Figure 15.5: Autocorrect options

> ### ACTIVITY 15.1
>
> Find some words that could end in both '. . . ter' and '. . . tre' and carry out a spell check on them. Which country's dictionary accepts these words? Discuss different ways you could solve these types of spelling issues.

Typographical errors

Typographical errors are errors made when you do know how to spell a word correctly but accidentally type it in incorrectly, either because of problems with the keyboard or because you may simply have been typing too fast and left a few characters out (or added a few extra characters in). Common mistakes are not leaving a space between words or typing letters in a different order in a word on a regular basis. A common example of this is typing the word 'the' as 'teh'. The way to help you with such a problem is to reset your spell checker, as seen in Figure 15.6 (on the next page).

Grammar checker

The **grammar check tool** is a comprehensive tool that works for simple to the most complex corrections of your grammar. It can check the grammar in your writing for clarity, conciseness, formality, inclusiveness, vocabulary and more aspects of grammar. You may set the tool to check your grammar as you type or to leave it to check your writing after you have completed a document.

A grammar check can be run on a complete document by selecting the 'Spelling and Grammar' tab (Figure 15.7). This is often found in the Review menu or Tools menu if it is not on the Home tab.

However, you should remember that grammar checkers cannot know what your audience requirements are. It can only check your grammar in a technical way. You will still have to make the final decisions about which words to use and how to arrange the words in each sentence.

The 'Grammar check' suggests corrections and refinements, all of which you have to make a decision to accept or to ignore.

Remove grammatical errors

Which of these sentences makes proper sense?

1. I have seen them movie.
2. I have seen the movie.

Both of these sentences have passed the spell check without any words being flagged up as a problem

> ### KEY WORDS
>
> **predictive text:** automatic word prediction when entering text
>
> **typographical:** relating to the accuracy, style or appearance of text
>
> **grammar check tool:** a program that tries to check the grammatical correctness of text

Step 1
Select 'Spelling & Grammar'

Step 2
Choose 'Proofing'

Step 3
Choose 'Auto-Correct Options'

Step 4
Replace your commonly misspelt words with the correct words here.

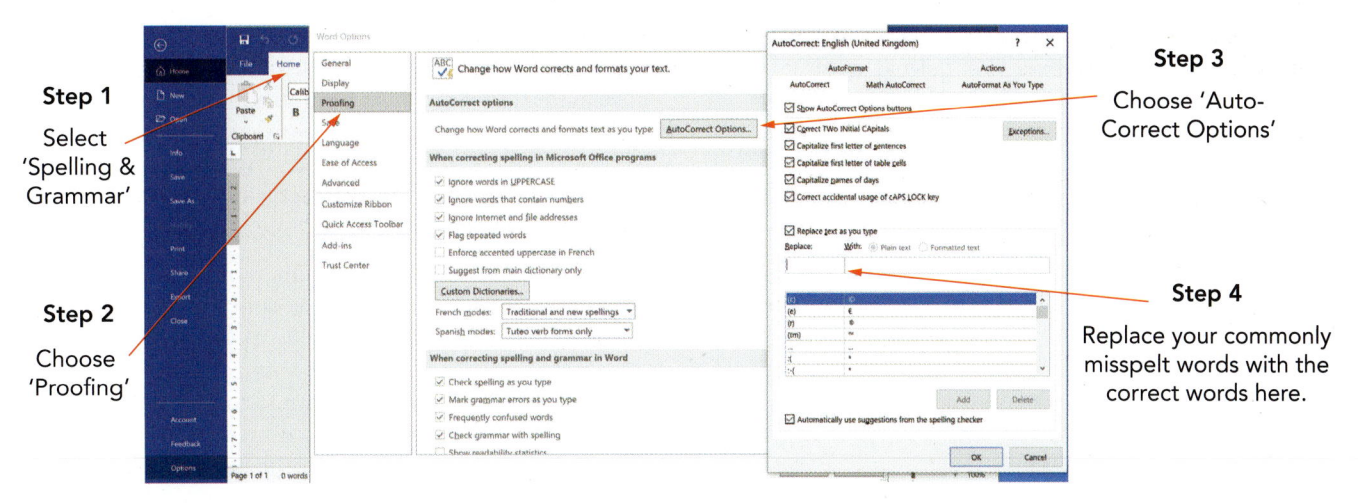

Figure 15.6: Using AutoCorrect options in the spell checker

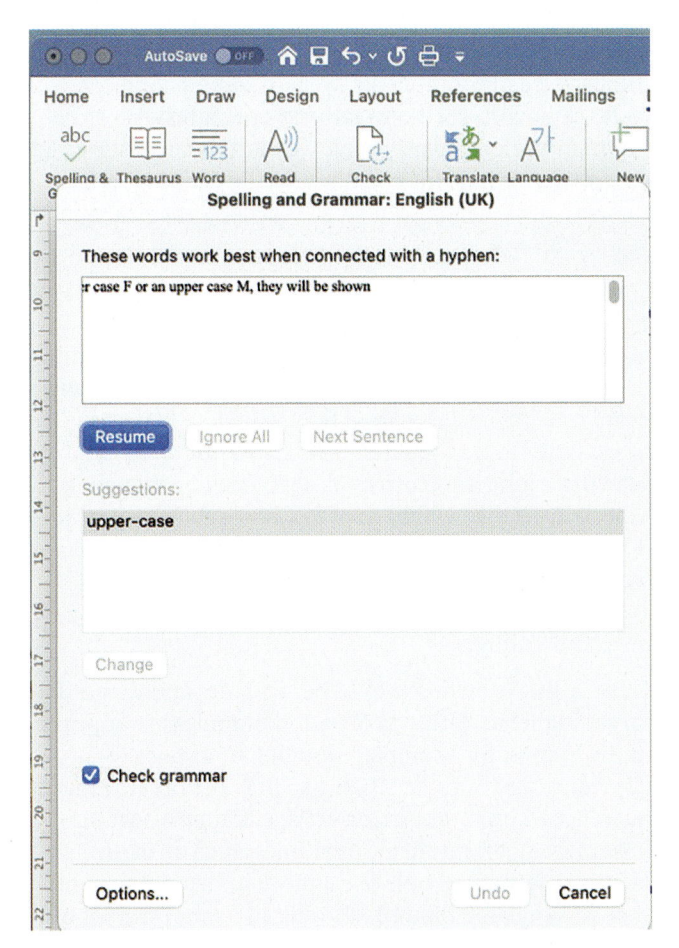

Figure 15.7: The grammar in the whole document is checked and suggestions are given for improvement

because the spelling for the words 'them' and 'the' are both correct. However, the first sentence is grammatically incorrect. You might think that your work is fine because no problems are flagged up, but there can still be problems with other aspects in your text that a grammar checker cannot detect. You should not rely entirely on a grammar checker for checking all your grammar.

The 'Replace' tool

There is another way you can replace all your commonly misspelt words or incorrectly used words, and that is by using the 'Replace' tool. Although it can be used to correct words that you may have spelt incorrectly throughout a long document and can save you time in place of using the usual spell check procedure, the 'Replace' tool can also do other things compared to spell check software.

The **Find and Replace** options are usually accessed from the Edit menu of a program (see Figure 15.8).

> **KEY WORD**
>
> **find and replace:** software that will search for a word and replace it with the one suggested by the user

If, for example, you have used a word incorrectly throughout a document, you could replace the incorrect word with the correct word and all instances of that word will be changed by one action.

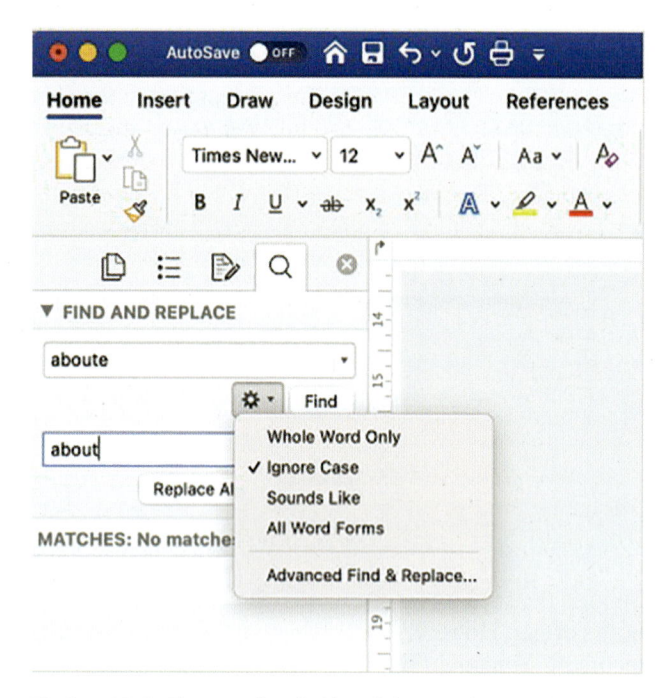

Figure 15.8: The word to find and the word to replace it – or matching – with can be entered. Users can set options such as ignoring the case

can only match text against the words stored in its dictionary to alert you to the possibility that you may have made a spelling mistake. You still need to check that you have used the correct word for your sentence to make sense. Remember the sentence, 'I have seen them movie'? It is all spelt correctly and won't flag up an error. However, it is incorrect.

Humans are prone to making data input errors and spell check software helps you to notice your spelling mistakes and correct them quickly as you type. This means you do not need to wait until you get to the end of your typing and then have to retype it all over again. Although, everybody works in different ways and some people do actually type in everything quickly and then run a spell check through the whole document afterwards in order to save time.

Spell check software can also be useful for people who are dyslexic (a learning disorder that involves difficulty reading); it can also help some people to learn how to spell correctly by constantly highlighting incorrectly spelt words and suggesting the correct versions. This repetitive action helps you to remember how to spell a word correctly the next time you need to use it.

On the other hand, some people have become too reliant on spell check software and have lost the motivation to learn how to spell correctly on their own. If they had to handwrite a document, they would be prone to making more spelling mistakes than they would if they used a computer to do the same task. In addition, it would take them longer to correct all their spelling mistakes, especially as they would have to rewrite the handwritten document (probably several times) until all the errors have been eliminated. However, does it matter that some people end up not being able to spell when they use handwriting?

Generally, the answer would be 'yes', depending on the target audience. Some people don't mind what appears in SMS texts, for example, though that applies to an electronic device rather than paper. Most other target audiences would take incorrect spelling into account in some way or another. Sometimes, such as in an informal setting, people use a more informal tone and type of language than they would in formal situations and let their guard down by not correcting their misspelt words.

Be very careful doing this, though. There may be instances where you do not wish to make that change. For example, if you decide that you want to change all instances of 'kg' to 'kilogram' and you use Replace All but you also have the word 'background' in your text, you could end up with 'backilogramround'!

ACTIVITY 15.2

Discuss the differences between using the 'Grammar check' tool and the 'Replace' tool. Give examples to explain your answers. Join other small groups to share your views.

Don't rely on a spell checker

You should be aware that you should not rely entirely on spell check software because it does not understand the context of your sentences in the same way that humans understand their own language. Spell-check software

15 Proofing

> **ICT IN CONTEXT**
>
> Mariner 1 was intended to do an unmanned fly-by of Venus in 1962. A misplaced hyphen in the computer code caused a trajectory error and the rocket was blown up before it could crash back down to Earth. Unfortunately, no one double or triple checked the code. The famous science fiction writer, Arthur C. Clarke called it 'the most expensive hyphen in history.'

Words that sound the same (**homophones**) are sometimes problematic and spell check software cannot be of any help in this regard because if you spell both words correctly but use them in the wrong context then your sentence may not make proper sense. If you use spell check software on such a sentence it will not flag the incorrect word as being a spelling mistake, because technically speaking it won't be.

Examples of homophones include:

- **right/write**: There is no *right* way to *write* a great novel.
- **sea/see**: At my beach house, I love to wake up and *see* the *sea*.
- **sole/soul**: I need to get a new *sole* put on my favourite pair of running shoes. Jogging is good for my *soul*.
- **son/sun**: My *son* is 13 years old. He likes to spend time outside in the *sun*.
- **steal/steel**: Someone who decides to *steal* a car has committed a crime, but auto parts are made of *steel*.
- **tail/tale**: My cat was crazily chasing his *tail* while I read a fairy *tale* to my children.
- **weather/whether**: I don't know *whether* to bring a jacket or not. The *weather* looks unpredictable today.

In addition to those mentioned above, spell check software can have other features built into it that give users more options when they have spelt a word incorrectly. You can 'change' the word and accept one of their suggested words to replace the word that is spelt incorrectly. If you have made this same spelling mistake with more than one word, you can 'change all', or you can 'ignore' the incorrectly spelt word or 'ignore all' of them if appropriate. If you know that your word is spelt correctly, you can choose 'add to dictionary'.

Thesaurus tool

The **thesaurus** proofing tool is not available in all the Office Suite programs. You can find it in those programs where words rather than numerical data are entered, such in word processors, presentations and desktop publishers rather than in databases. Surprisingly, you will find a thesaurus in spreadsheet software as well.

Questions

1. Describe how a thesaurus can help you when you are writing anything.
2. Explain why you should not accept all the suggestions made by a thesaurus.
3. Explain how using a thesaurus is different from using either a spell checker or a grammar checker. Give examples to demonstrate your understanding clearly.

> **ACTIVITY 15.3**
>
> Do a quick survey to find out how many of your friends actually use a thesaurus regularly.

> **KEY WORDS**
>
> **homophone:** two words having the same pronunciation but different spellings
>
> **thesaurus:** a dictionary of synonyms or words having the same meaning as the one selected

> **ICT IN CONTEXT**
>
> By using artificial intelligence (AI) and machine learning, automated data capture software can become intelligent capture software.
>
> AI software can be trained like a person by giving it lots of examples to learn from. Just as a human can read documents and understand similarities and differences between them, it doesn't need to see every single version of a contract or check request to recognise it.

> CAMBRIDGE IGCSE™ ICT: COURSEBOOK

> **CONTINUED**
>
> A person can look at a document such as an invoice and immediately locate where items such as invoice numbers or total costs are, no matter what the form looks like. Now software can do that too, without the need for programming. The machine learning engine trains itself to understand context, such as what an invoice number is (or isn't) and what should (or shouldn't) be around the number, so there's a high degree of accuracy – and it is far quicker than a human.

Using validation routines to minimise errors

When you input data into a spreadsheet or database program or fill in a form online, you can minimise the amount of incorrect types of data by using validation techniques. Validation is a method that helps to prevent unsuitable data from being entered. When you set up your database or spreadsheet, you can set up the validation rules about which type of data you want to allow to be entered into a particular cell. Data entered into a computer system can be valid but still incorrect. An example of this can be if someone's age is filled in as 16 instead of 11. Both of these could be valid if the validation rule includes all ages ranging from 1 to 50, but the data would still be incorrect. To ensure a higher degree of accuracy when entering data into a computer system, another proofing technique is usually also carried out, called **verification**. During verification, data could be entered by a second person and when the two sets of data are compared with each other, any differences are then checked against the original data to see which is correct. There are a number of different types of validation check that can reduce the possibility of inputting errors.

> **KEY WORD**
>
> **verification:** a proofing technique to check that valid data is accurate

In Chapter 7, we discussed using the validation routines listed here:

- Range check: to check that data falls within a range of numbers.
- Character check: to ensure that only certain characters are input.
- Length check: to check the length of the entry.
- Type check: to check the type (e.g. number, text) of data entered.
- Format check: to check that the data is entered in a particular sequence or pattern (e.g. dd/mm/yy).
- Presence check: to check that some data has been entered into a particular field.

Please refer to Chapter 7, Section 7.3 Design for further details on these.

> **WORKED EXAMPLE 15.1**
>
> **AT THE GYM**
>
> A gym uses a spreadsheet to store details of their members. Unfortunately, staff are having difficulty in keeping it updated and ensuring accurate data entry.
>
> 1 Open the file *Gym.xlsm* into your spreadsheet software.
>
> 2 Create a validation rule and a suitable error message for the Gender column.
>
> 3 All members should be at least 18 years of age.
>
>   Create a validation rule for column E to ensure that every date of birth entered is at least 18 years ago.
>
> 4 There are often spelling mistakes in column G, listing the main sport of each person.
>
>   Create a data entry method to prevent these errors.

15 Proofing

CONTINUED

Step 1

The columns in *Gym.xlsm* contain the membership numbers, first and second names, gender, renewal date and major sport for each of the members of the gym.

Today's date is shown in cell H1.

Step 2

Entries in the gender column must be either F or M.

You can set up a validation rule for this column using a list.

Select the column and then select Data Validation (Figure 15.9) is selected from the Data ribbon.

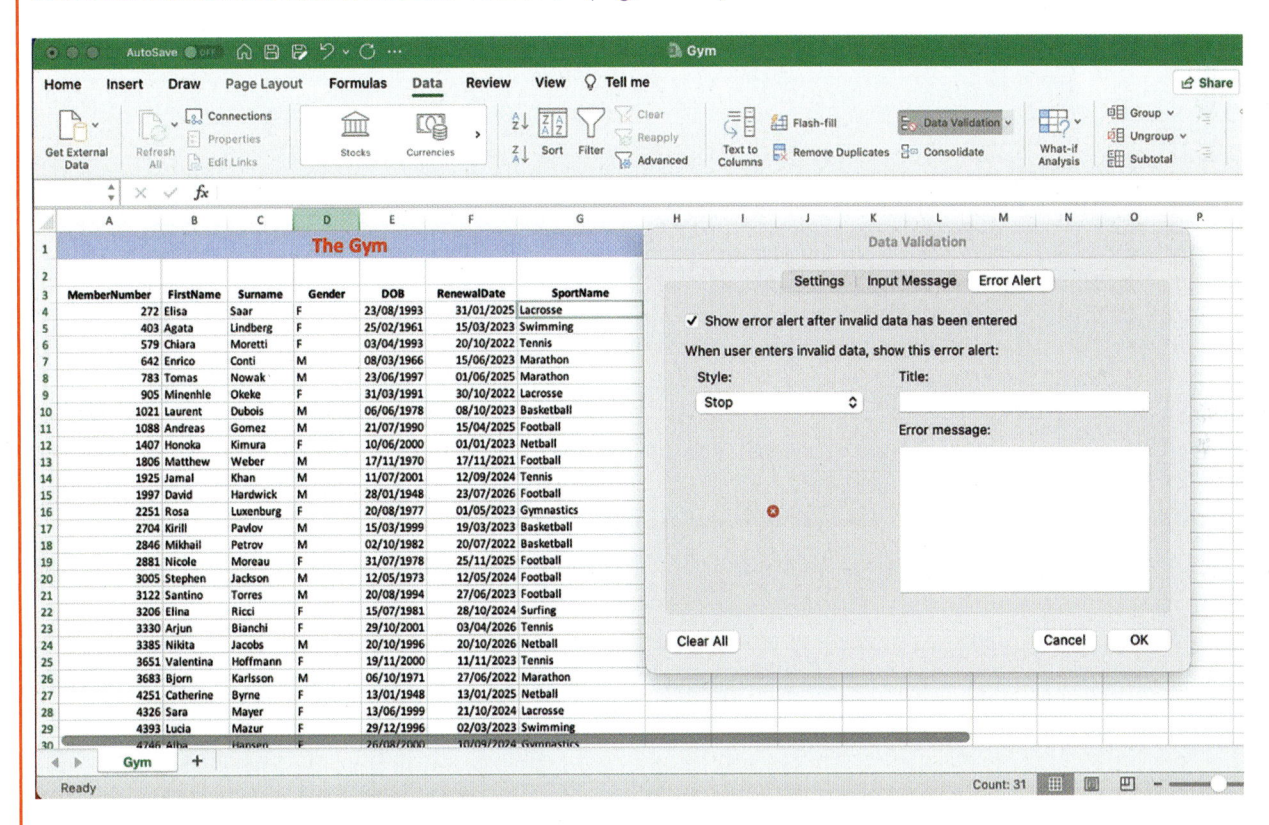

Figure 15.9: Data Validation dialogue box

In the 'Settings' tab, the Validation Criteria can be set to List. The two items F and M are added to the list and the 'In-cell drop-down' box should be unticked as we don't want the list to appear when users are entering data into the cell.

You can enter a suitable error message in the Error Alert tab.

CONTINUED

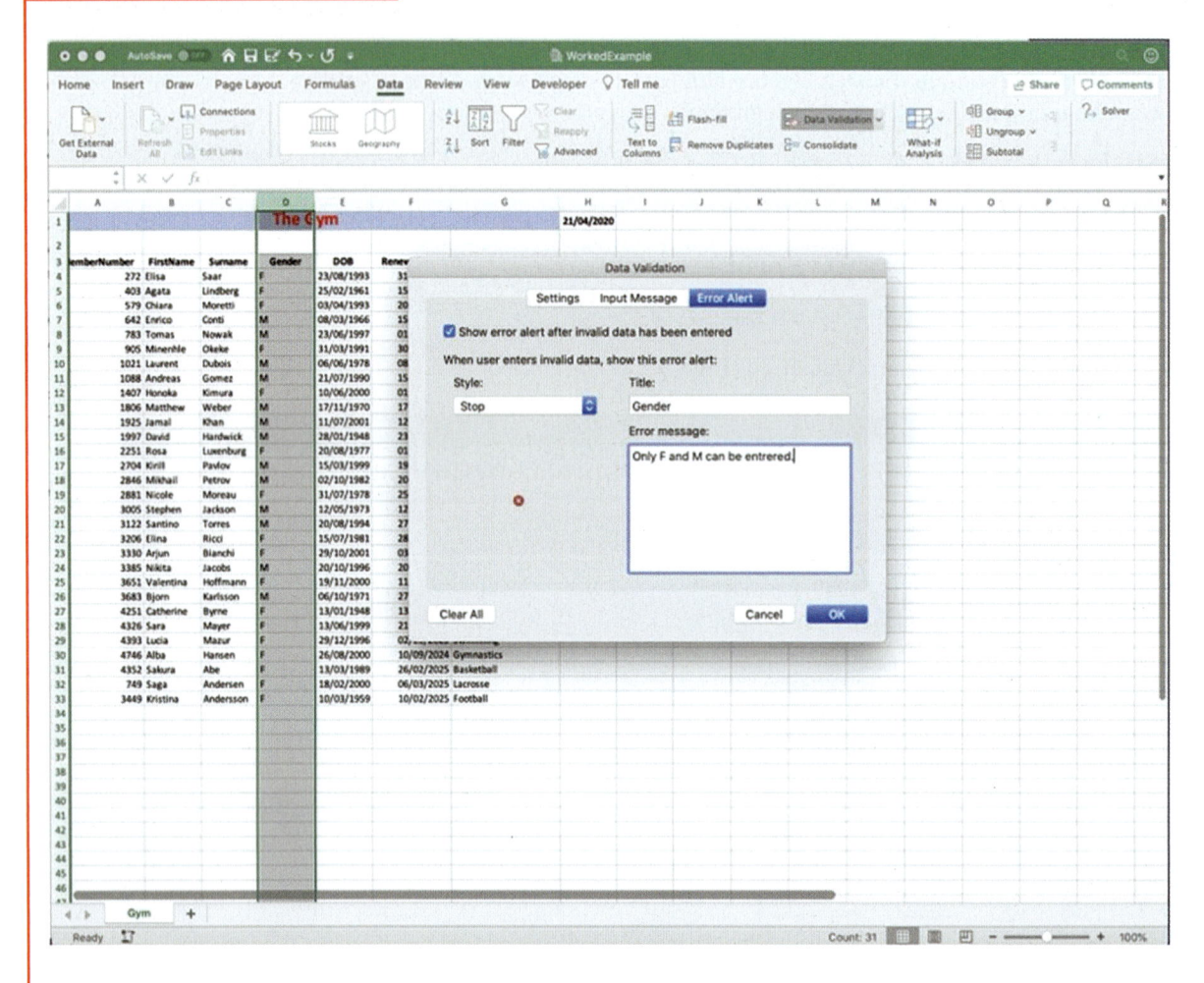

Figure 15.10: Error Alert tab

If a user enters anything but an upper case F or an upper case M, they will be shown the error message.

Step 3

When the date of birth is added in column E there should be a validation rule to ensure that the person is aged 18 years or over.

Today's date is shown in cell H1. Therefore, the difference between today's date and the date of birth has to be at least 18 years.

15 Proofing

> **CONTINUED**

The validation rule (Figure 15.11) will check that the date entered is less than today's date minus 18 years.

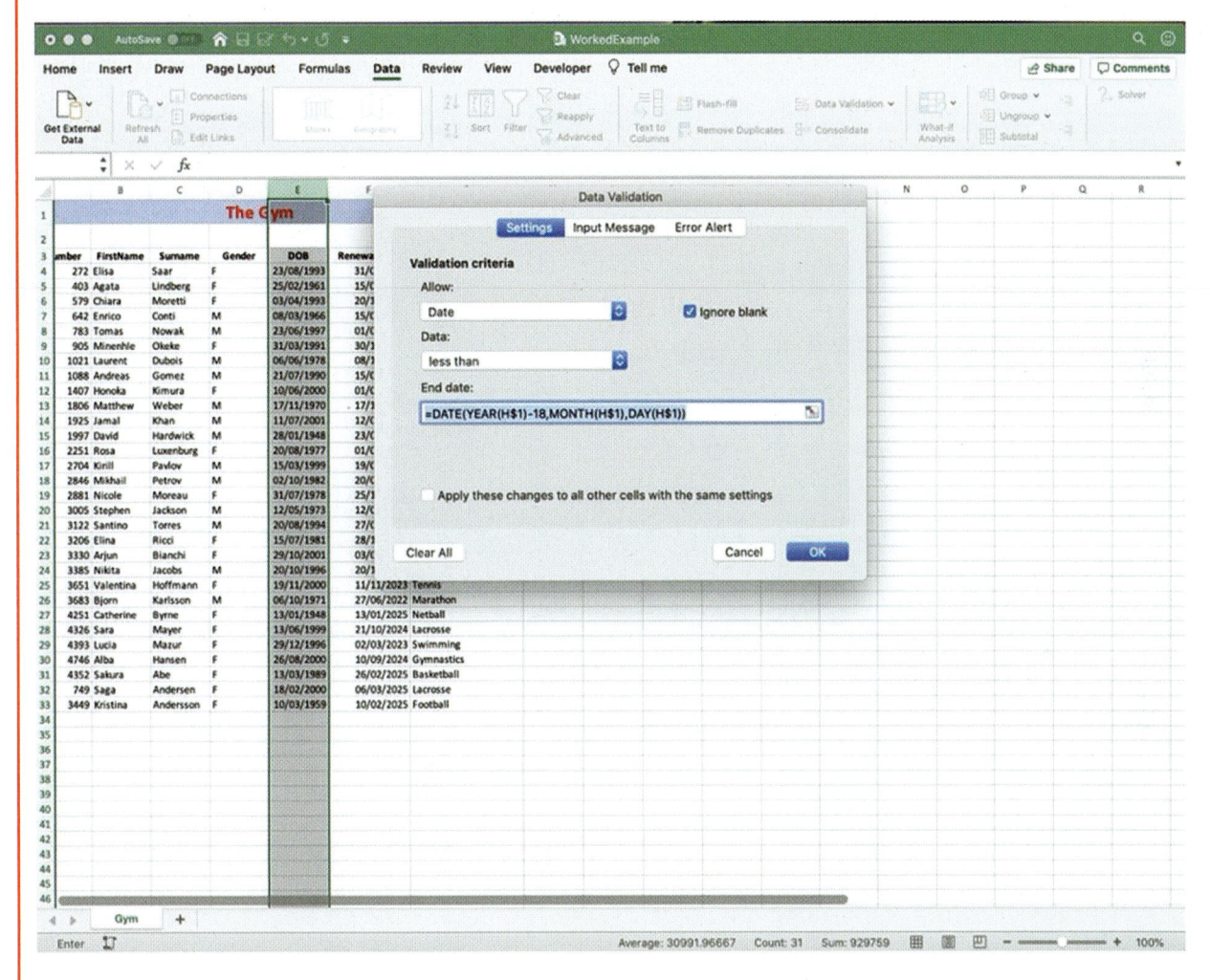

Figure 15.11: Validation rule for date of birth

The function finds the date exactly 18 years ago and the rule checks that the entered date is less than this.

You can add a suitable error message.

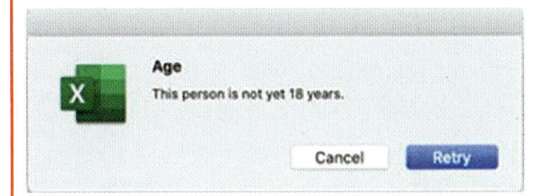

Figure 15.12: Date-of-birth error message

CONTINUED

Step 4

To ensure that the sport entered is correct it can be selected from a list.

The list can be added to a validation rule.

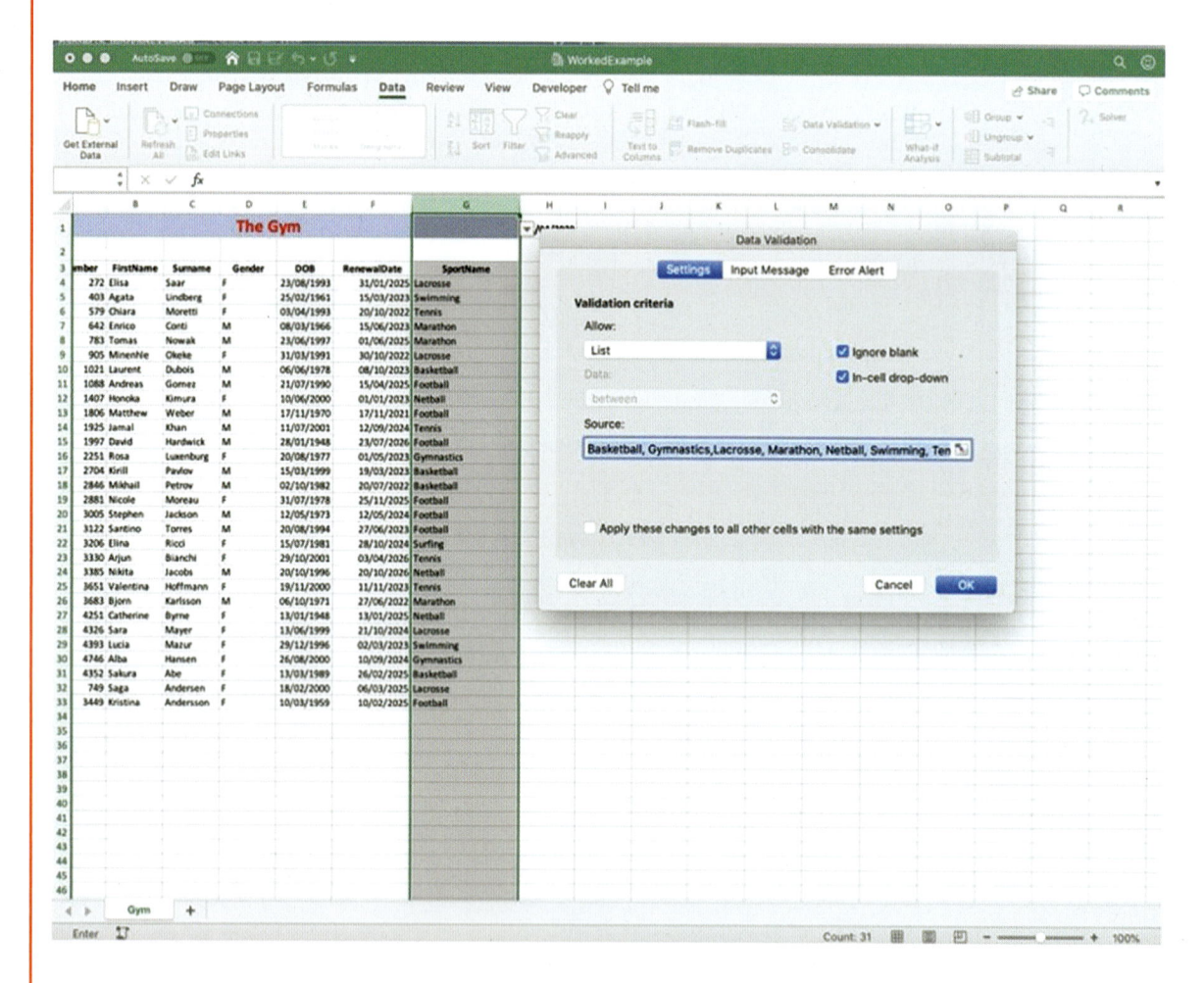

Figure 15.13: List in validation rule

15 Proofing

> **CONTINUED**

To make it more user friendly, you can enter the list is in alphabetical order.

The in-cell drop-down has been left checked so that it appears in the spreadsheet.

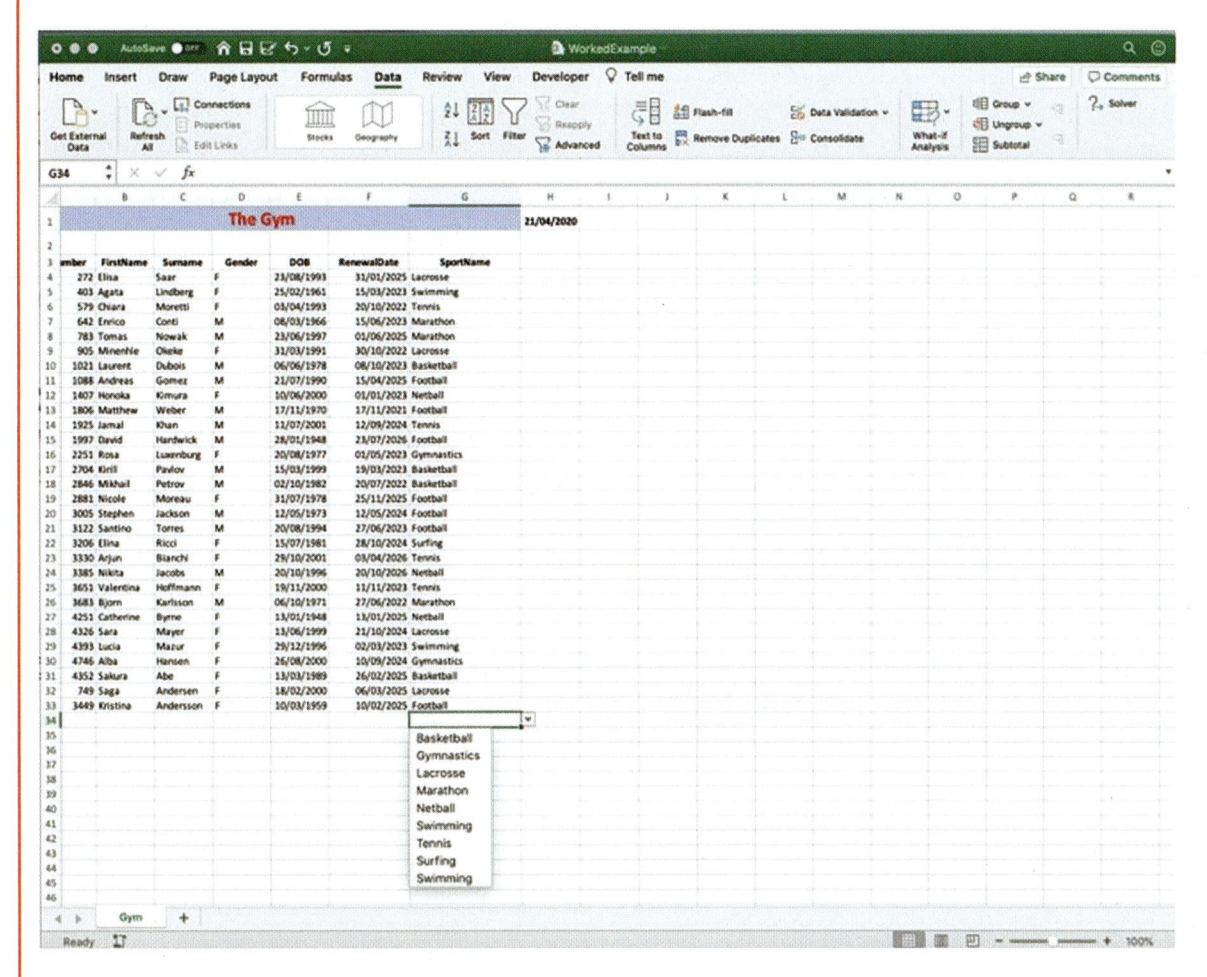

Figure 15.14: SportName drop-down list

This ensures that all entries are only those in the list.

Questions

1. Open *Gym.xlsm* into your spreadsheet software and create the validation rules specified.
2. Create a validation rule for column A, so that only membership numbers equal to or less than 10 000 can be entered.

PRACTICAL TASK 15.1

Getting started

1. Most word processing software has an 'autocorrect' feature to correct commonly misspelt words or change combinations into symbols, e.g. change (c) to ©.

   List the steps you would take to find the autocorrect list.

2. Most word processors will autoformat as you type. Sometimes this can be annoying.

   List the steps you would take to turn off 'Automatic numbered lists'.

Practice

3. Open *Networks.docx* into your word processing software.

4. You are required to:
   - Check the spelling manually and using the spell check tool.
   - Check the grammar manually and using the grammar check tool.
   - Proofread the document to identify inconsistencies, widows and orphans or a table that runs onto the next page.

   You should find 20 items to correct. Highlight them in yellow.

Challenge

5. In the software you are using add the following to the autocorrect list.

   a. Change (ae) to Œ.

   b. Test it out in a document.

6. In the software you are using switch off the grammar check feature that will automatically capitalise the months of the year.

   Test it out and don't forget to turn it on again!

PRACTICAL TASK 15.2

Getting started

1. When creating a validation rule, what do the following operators mean?
   - <
   - <>
   - >
   - >=
   - <=

2. Create a presentation to explain the difference between validation and verification. Give examples.

> **CONTINUED**
>
> **Practice**
>
> 3   Open the file *Entry.xlsx* into your spreadsheet software.
>
> 4   In column C create a validation rule that allows entries only between 7 and 13.
>
>   a   Create a suitable error message.
>
>   b   Produce screen prints showing how you set up the validation rule and screen prints showing the error message.
>
>   c   Paste the screen prints into a document named *Task2.doc*.
>
> 5   In column D create a validation rule that allows only text entries of two characters.
>
>   a   Create a suitable error message.
>
>   b   Produce screen prints showing how you set up the validation rule and screen prints showing the error message.
>
>   c   Paste the screen prints into the *Task2.doc.* document.
>
> **Challenge**
>
> 6   In the 'Group' column, all the two-character group names should be in upper case, but the user may sometimes forget and enter lower case group letters.
>
> 7   Your challenge is to find a way to ensure that all entries in this column are automatically in upper case.
>
> Note: this is quite a difficult task. There are several methods, but one is to create a new style and find a font that only has upper case letters. Another is to create a macro.

ACTIVITY 15.4

In pairs or small groups discuss how applying a type validation check in the following cases will not prevent you from entering incorrect data into a system.

1   Telephone numbers using a validation for whole numbers as a data type.

2   House numbers applying a range check type of validation.

3   Day and month in a date data type using the type check of validation.

Question

4   For each validation below, state the advantages and give an example of abnormal data.
    Copy and complete the table.

Validation Type	Advantages	Abnormal data
Range check		
Presence check		
Type check		
Length check		

> CAMBRIDGE IGCSE™ ICT: COURSEBOOK

PRACTICAL TASK 15.3

Getting started

1. A database field had the following validation rule: >=13. What data will this field accept?
2. Another field had this validation rule: Like 'Yes' or 'No'. What data will this field accept?

Practice

3. Open the the file Database.accdb into your database software.
4. The database has one table named 'Table1' which contains six fields.
5. All fields should have a presence check to ensure that an entry has been made.
6. The 'DateOfBirth' field should have a validation rule so that only dates in the years 2005 and 2006 can be entered.
7. The 'Year' field should only accept entries between the years 7 and 13 inclusive.
8. Only the following groups should be allowed: B1, B2, G1, G2, R1, R2, T1, T2.

   All of the rules should have validation text which is shown if entries that break the rules are entered.

9. Enter data into the fields to test the validation rules.

Challenge

10. When entering a surname and first name it would be good if the entries could be capitalised, i.e. the first letter in upper case and the rest in lower case.
11. Carry out research and set these two fields to do this.

Tip: you may need to create a macro here. When you test it you will have to save the table and open it again.

The importance of entering data correctly and accurately

The importance of accuracy when entering data can have far-reaching consequences because accurate data gives reliable results. If the data is inaccurate then the results will also be inaccurate and therefore cannot be used. A simple example could be data for weather entered into a system for pilots to use to plan their flight paths; if the wind direction is incorrectly recorded as being north-easterly instead of south-easterly, the pilot may take a very different flight path which may be longer, resulting in more fuel being used, or flying a more dangerous route.

15.2 Proofing techniques

Besides using automated software tools and validation routines to reduce errors at the input stage, there still could be errors where numbers have been transposed, given an inconsistent case or inconsistent character spacing has been made. To minimise the amount of input errors in any document, additional proofing techniques to visually verify and proofread a document would still be necessary.

Proofreading

A document can be proofread against an original, by comparing the two, or simply by checking a document on its own. Proofreading is different from reading for pleasure where you would focus on the content for facts and information. Besides checking that every single word is spelt correctly and consistently and the grammar is mostly correct, you may have to change the structure of some sentences. It can be useful to use the **track changes tool** to indicate any changes you suggest to an original document.

This feature is usually in the Review section of the software (see Figure 15.15). When it is turned on, any changes to the document such as additions, deletions and font changes are marked.

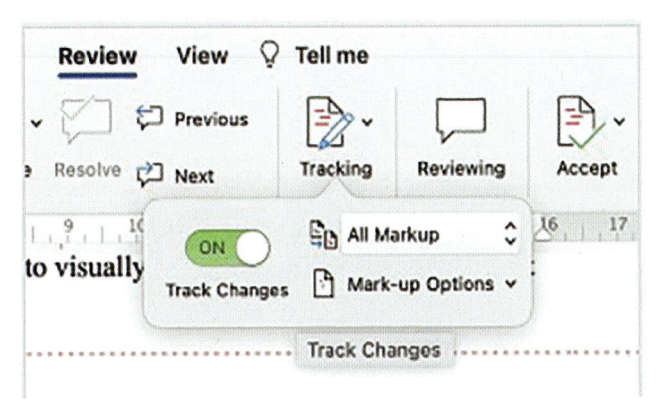

Figure 15.15: Turning on track changes

Proofreading requires being able to identify and correct the following errors as well:

- Inconsistent **line spacing**. For example some of the text may have double line spacing while other parts only have single line spacing.
- Removing **blank pages**/slides. Sometimes an extra page may have been inserted by leaning on the Return key.

The easiest way to remove a blank page is to place the cursor at the top of the following page and use the backspace key. Similarly, for an extra line, place the cursor at the beginning of the line after the extra line space, and use the backspace key.

Blank pages in presentation software can be removed by right-clicking on them and selecting Delete Slide (see Figure 15.16).

- Removing **widows** and **orphans**.

    Widows are when the last line of a paragraph appears as the first line of a new page or column; orphans are when the first line of a paragraph appears as the last line of a page or column. They interrupt the flow for the reader and can make the text difficult to understand. And they don't look good and make the page untidy.

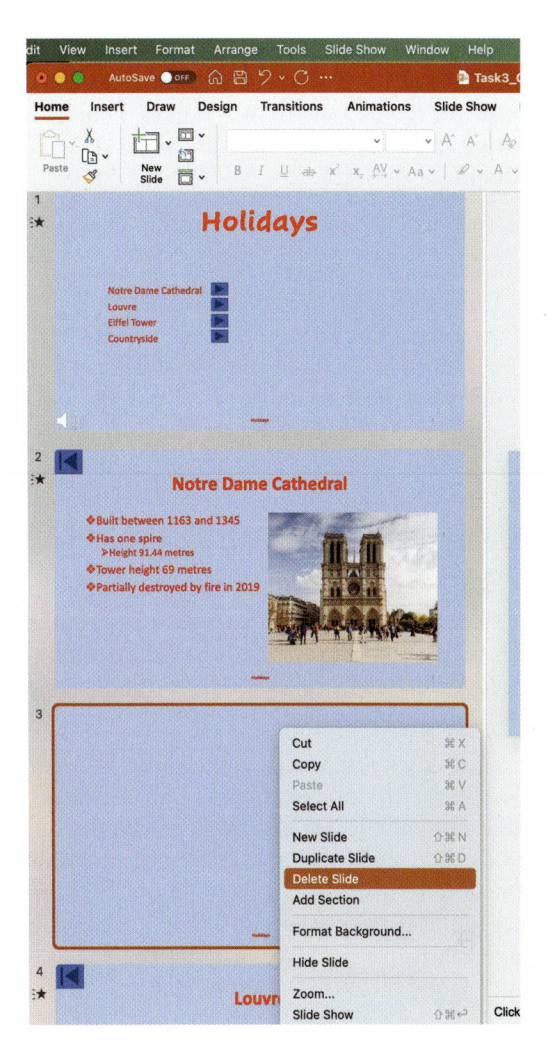

Figure 15.16: Deleting a blank slide

> **KEY WORDS**
>
> **track changes tool:** a tool that highlights any changes that have been made to a document
>
> **line spacing:** the space between one line and the next
>
> **blank pages:** a page on which there is no text or images
>
> **widows:** when the last line of a paragraph appears as the first line of a new page or column
>
> **orphans:** when the first line of a paragraph appears as the last line of a page or column

303

These can be controlled by choosing an option to accept or reject them (see Figure 15.17). This will ensure that all of the lines of the paragraph will be kept together when there is a column or page break.

- Inconsistent or incorrect application of styles.

  The setting of paragraph styles was covered in Chapter 14, Section 14.1 Creating and editing consistent styles. It is essential to the appearance of a document that styles are applied consistently and not at random. Having inconsistent styles throughout can also interrupt the flow for the reader and make the text difficult to read.

- Ensuring that tables and lists are not split over columns or pages/slides.

Sometimes paragraph styles are applied inconsistently and text that should be body text may accidentally have been formatted as subtitle. These can be manually corrected when proofreading.

There is nothing worse than a table spread over two pages where the column headings are on one page and table data on another. A complete table should be on a single page. If the table is selected, the word processor can be instructed to keep all the rows (lines) together in the same way as widow and orphan control (explained above).

Performing visual verification

The word **verify** has similar meanings in many different contexts. Basically, it means to check, test or agree that something is true or correct and accurate. When you sign up for any type of online service using your email address, you will usually be asked to verify your authenticity by replying to an email generated by the system.

Visual verification can be compared to proofreading a document against the original document, where a visual comparison can be made between data entered and a data source. It can also refer to rereading your document to ensure that everything is present and correct and formatted as you wish. Refer to the section on 'Proofreading' earlier in this chapter.

> ### KEY WORDS
>
> **verify:** to check, test or agree that something is true or correct and accurate
>
> **visual verification:** a proofing technique whereby you visually check a document for accuracy and correctness

Checking computer-produced work depends on the type of entries, for example, text requires different sorts of checks to numbers. The main thing that proofreading checks for in any document is incorrect spelling.

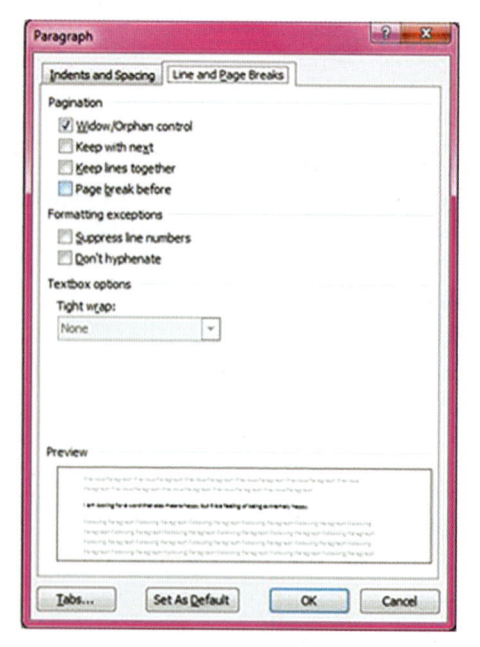

Figure 15.17: Using advanced options to set the spacing between characters, lines and paragraphs to be consistent

However, there are other errors that require fixing, for example, transposition errors, inconsistent character spacing and inconsistent case.

Transposition errors

Transposing numbers happens when you change the order of the digits in a number when rewriting it or keying it in. This is referred to as a **transposition error**. An example of transposing a number could be writing 1325677 instead of 1235677. In this case, the second and third digits have changed position. Although this appears to be a small error, it can have catastrophic consequences, for example, if it results in a financial loss or crashes a computer program.

Inconsistent character spacing

Consistent character spacing is required for some words or items such as units of measurement, people's initials or page numbers. Character spacing needs to be applied consistently throughout the document. In these examples you will notice that there can be different spacing between characters:

- 37 kg or 37kg
- Dr. J P Mola or Dr JP Mola or Dr J. P. Mola or Dr. J.P. Mola
- p.398 or pg.398 or p. 398 or pg. 398.

In order to check that there is consistent character spacing throughout the document, you should avoid using justify as the text alignment, because that would increase the width of each space between the words in order to fill the line so that the end of a sentence doesn't leave a dent in the shape of a block of text. Left align is usually the best option for checking spacing in text.

> **KEY WORDS**
>
> **transpose:** change the order of two or more items
>
> **transposition error:** when two digits or words in data entry have been accidentally reversed. A mistake made by transposing items
>
> **consistent character spacing:** using the same character spacing for particular elements throughout the document

Consistent case

This refers to using upper case or lower case for certain parts of your document or certain words and using them in the same way throughout. Sometimes upper case is used in headings, and perhaps the first letter of a subheading will only be required to be in upper case. Sometimes upper case is used for the first letter of each list item; sometimes lower case is used. This is an example of something that is defined in a house style (Chapter 14, Section 14.2 Purpose and uses of corporate house style). Whatever you choose for each element should be applied consistently throughout the document.

Questions

5 Give examples of:
   a transposed numbers
   b incorrect spelling
   c inconsistent case
   d factual errors.

6 Describe ways to:
   a ensure consistent line spacing.
   b remove blank pages/slides.
   c remove widows/orphans.
   d ensure that tables and lists are not split over columns or pages/slides.

7 Match the proofreading techniques to the sentence starters in Table 15.2.

Sentence starters	Proofreading techniques
1 'Prof EZ Chung' or 'Prof E Z Chung' is an example of …	A grammar checker
2 'Miss mandi is Strict.' can be fixed using …	B consistent character spacing
3 'The wind blows form the South' can be corrected using …	C inconsistent character spacing
4 Typing 012435 instead of 012345 is an example of …	D consistent case
5 Do not justify text to check for …	E transposition errors

Table 15.2: Match up proofreading techniques

Double data entry is another verification technique whereby data is entered twice and then the computer compares the two sets of data. This can be done after the two sets of data have been entered or by comparing them during data entry.

> ### KEY WORD
>
> **double data entry:** a proofing technique that uses the COUNTIF spreadsheet function together with conditional formatting to highlight the differences in two lists of items

The need for validation as well as verification

Each of these proofing techniques offers a different aspect of checking the accuracy or correctness of data that is entered into your documents. Validation ensures that the format of the data being entered is correct according to the validation rules you have set up prior to your data entry process. Verification ensures that the data entered makes sense and is more accurate than if only validation was applied to it. Proofreading, which is a verification technique, ensures that a document can be as accurate and correct as it can be, and this technique is the most time consuming of all because it requires a human to carry out this check for accuracy and correctness.

> ### SELF-ASSESSMENT
>
> How much do you feel that you understand proofreading? Try rating the following statements between 1 and 5: '5' means you feel very confident and '1' means you do not feel confident. For any statements you selected 1–3, re-visit those areas of the chapter.
>
> | How well do you know that: | Rating |
> |---|---|
> | Spell check doesn't resolve all your spelling mistakes. | |
> | Grammar checkers cannot check that your document is perfect and ready to be sent to your audience. | |
> | Validation routines minimise input errors. | |
> | Entering incorrect or inaccurate data into a system can lead to fatal accidents in some cases. | |
> | Double data entry is another method of verification of data input. | |
> | Visually proofreading a document is still an extremely important proofing method in addition to using the many automated software tools available. | |

> ### REFLECTION
>
> Describe how the key words, activities and questions in this chapter have helped you understand why it is important to reduce input errors.

SUMMARY

Proofing can never really remove all the errors that could possibly occur in a document.
Spell check software is a useful tool and can be used to correct incorrectly spelt words, provided the correct dictionary is used and the context of the word has been considered.
Spell check software should not be relied upon as the only solution for checking all the spelling in a document.
Grammar checking software is useful, but also should not be relied on entirely.
Validation helps to reduce the possibility of errors being made at the data input stage.
Validation checks include range check, length check, type check and presence check.
Verification helps to correct or suggest changes to data that has already been input into a system.
Both validation and verification are necessary to achieve the highest possible levels of accuracy and correctness in documents because each type of proofing covers different aspects of reducing errors in documents.

EXAM-STYLE QUESTIONS

1 Complete the following sentences, using the appropriate items from the list below:

spell check **grammar check** **transposition error** **verification**
validation **double data entry** **format check**

  a …. refers to knowing what the format of a code means, so you can check the validity of such data quickly.

  b …. checks a word against all the listed words in its dictionary and will flag a word up that doesn't match any of its known words by underlining it with a red wavy line.

  c …. ensures that the data entered is correct according to the rules set up prior to your data entry process.

  d ….. cannot check that your document is perfectly grammatically correct in every respect.

  e ….. refers to a proofing technique that allows you to correct or suggest alternatives to data being put into a system.

  f ……allows you to select from a predetermined list of items.

  g …refers to a type of error when you accidentally change the order of digits in a number you are keying in or rewriting. [7]

2 a **Explain** what is meant by proofing a document. [2]
  b Explain what is meant by autocorrect. [2]
  c **Describe** the difference between autocorrect and predictive text. [2]

3 Explain what is meant by a typographical error. [2]

4 You realised that you have spelt a word incorrectly throughout a document. Describe the best method of correcting all of these mistakes. [2]

5 Describe the difference between validation and verification. [2]

6 **Suggest** one reason for not using justify to align text. [2]

[Total: 21]

COMMAND WORDS

explain: set out purposes or reasons / make the relationships between things evident / provide why and / or how and support with relevant evidence

describe: state the points of a topic / give characteristics and main features

suggest: apply knowledge and understanding to situations where there are a range of valid responses in order to make proposals / put forward considerations

SELF-EVALUATION CHECKLIST

After studying this chapter, think about how confident you are with the different topics.

This will help you to see any gaps in your knowledge and help you to learn more effectively.

You might find it helpful to rate how confident you are for each of these statements when you are revising. You should revisit any sections that you rated 'Needs more work' or 'Getting there'.

I can …	See section	Needs more work	Getting there	Confident to move on
make appropriate changes to ensure all work produced contains as few errors as possible	15.1			
use automated software tools such as spell check and grammar checks	15.1			
use validation routines to minimise data entry errors	15.1 and 7.3			
know how to use proofing techniques to ensure accuracy of data entry	15.2			
explain what is meant by validation and verification	15.2			

Chapter 16
Graphs and charts

IN THIS CHAPTER YOU WILL:

- create, label and edit charts/graphs
- label, add a second data series, add second axes and change axis scales of charts/graphs
- format numerical values
- enhance the appearance of charts/graphs.

GETTING STARTED

Figure 16.1 shows a bar chart detailing the rainfall in Jakarta and Cairo. Parts of the graph have been labelled with letters. Match the letters to the description numbers below.

1. Axis label
2. Title
3. y-axis
4. Legend
5. x-axis

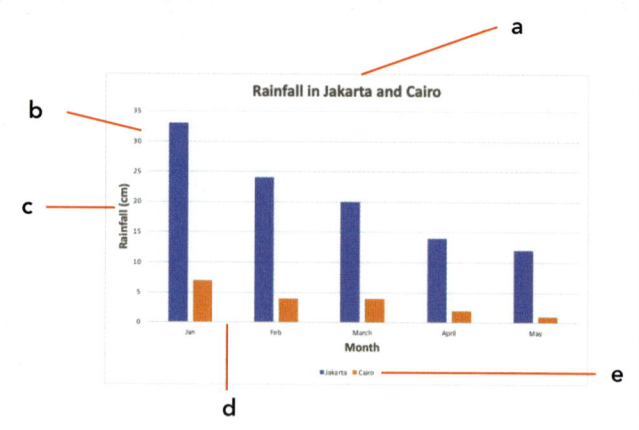

Figure 16.1: A bar chart showing the rainfall in Jakata and Cairo

DISPLAYING DATA

Charts present information in the form of graphs, diagrams and tables. Graphs are one type of chart and show the mathematical relationship between sets of data.

Tables and text present raw data, a collection of words or numbers, but charts present information. They allow a user to instantly see the relationships in the data and any trends.

Data has been represented using diagrams for hundreds of years. Figure 16.2 shows the first published bar graph, created by William Playfair in 1786 for an atlas on Scottish trade.

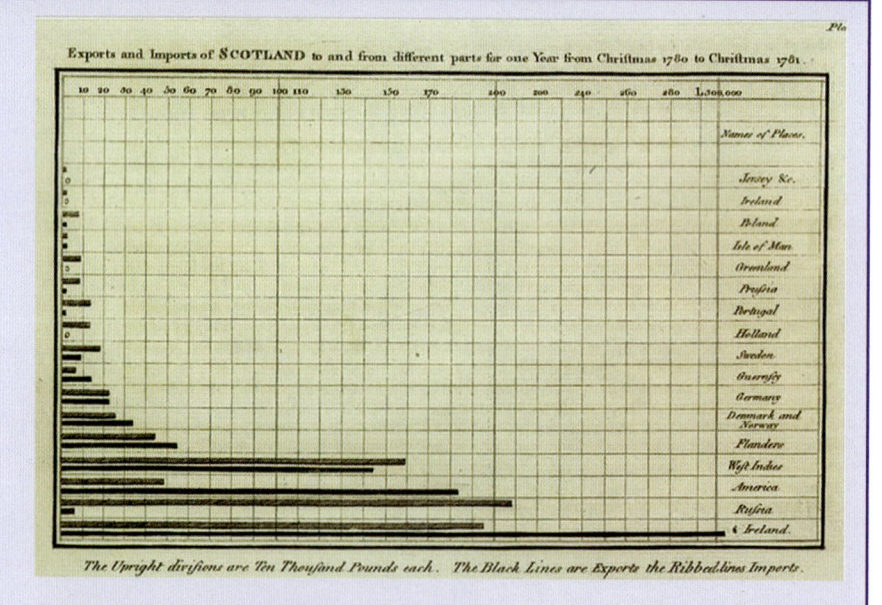

Figure 16.2: The first published bar graph by William Playfair in 1786

In the 1850s, cholera epidemics were common in London and believed to be spread by something in the air. In 1854, Doctor John Snow investigated an outbreak in Broad Street. He counted the numbers of deaths in the houses nearby and presented the results in a new way. Instead of using numbers, he used bars to represent each death and he superimposed them on a map of the area.

His chart clearly shows that the highest number of deaths occurred in clusters near the pump in Broad Street, which indicated that cholera is a water-borne disease.

16 Graphs and charts

> **CONTINUED**
>
> Snow had therefore produced the first 'infographic'. An infographic is a collection of images, charts and minimal text that gives an easy-to-understand overview of a topic. They are now a very popular way of presenting information.
>
> When viewed on computer, infographics can be interactive. Do a search for 'interactive infographics' and see what you can find.
>
> **Discussion questions**
>
> 1 With a partner, make a list of different types of graphs. Can you think of over ten?
>
> 2 With a partner, each look at infographics online and chose the one you think is the most effective. Each should present their choice and explain why they think it is effective.

16.1 Creating and editing a graph or chart

Graphs and **charts** are used to present **information** so that it can be more easily understood and analysed. It can be very difficult to recognise relationships and trends in a page full of numbers; it is easier if they are incorporated into a chart or graph.

Figure 16.4: Contiguous data selected to display in a chart

Selecting data for a graph

The **data** for a graph will have been collected and arranged in a table or spreadsheet.

Figure 16.3 shows data stored in a spreadsheet by an organisation selling items around the world.

Figure 16.3: Data stored in a spreadsheet

In order to create a chart, the data to be used must be highlighted. This is the **specified data range**.

For the data highlighted in Figure 16.4, all of the data ranges are next to each other. They are said to be contiguous. **Contiguous data** is easy to select as it can be dragged over by the mouse in one operation.

> **KEY WORDS**
>
> **graphs:** a chart that shows the relationship between sets of data
>
> **charts:** visual representations of sets of data
>
> **information:** data that has been put into context and is meaningful, e.g. exam results were 69%, 90% and 30%
>
> **data:** raw, unorganised items without any description or explanation, e.g. 69, 90, 30. Data values don't have any meaning until they are put into context
>
> **specified data range:** the highlighted data range to be used for the chart
>
> **contiguous data:** data in columns and rows that are next to each other and easy to select together to make charts with

Sometimes data that are not next to each other may need to be selected (see Figure 16.5). This is called **non-contiguous data**.

	A	B	C	D	E	F	G	H
1	Surname	FirstName	Area	SalesToMarch	SalesToJune	SalesToSeptember	SalesToDecember	
2	Smith	Muhammed	North East	$100,000.00	$30,000.00	$60,000.00	$50,000.00	
3	Johnson	Emma	West Europe	$500,000.00	$45,000.00	$75,000.00	$200,000.00	
4	Williams	Jose	South America	$700,000.00	$100,000.00	$200,000.00	$75,000.00	
5	Garcia	Maria	Sweden	$300,000.00	$49,000.00	$100,000.00	$250,000.00	
6	Rodriguez	Nozomi	East Europe	$500,000.00	$69,000.00	$300,000.00	$300,000.00	
7	Hernandez	Lucia	Central Americ	$400,000.00	$100,000.00	$80,000.00	$100,000.00	
8	Rossi	Sophia	Italy		$10,000.00	$100,000.00	$200,000.00	$150,000.00	
9	Novak	Tamar	South Africa	$600,000.00	$90,000.00	$95,000.00	$230,000.00	
10	Smirnov	Alexei	Russia	$900,000.00	$100,000.00	$75,000.00	$600,000.00	
11	Kumar	Akshay	Middle East	$700,000.00	$90,000.00	$300,000.00	$250,000.00	
12								

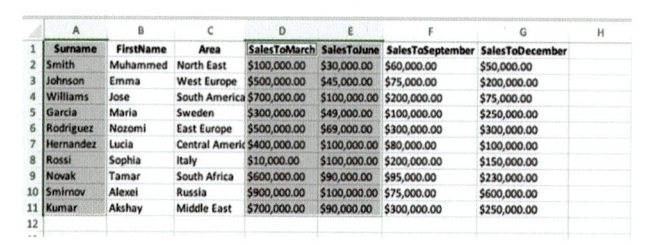

Figure 16.5: Non-contiguous data

How to highlight non-contiguous data will depend on the software, but in Microsoft Office, the first range is selected and then, in Windows, the Control key must be held down while others are selected. In the Mac version, the Command key must be held down.

> **KEY WORD**
>
> **non-contiguous data:** data where the columns and rows are not adjacent to each other

Questions

Refer to Figure 16.6 and answer the following questions:

1. State the address of the highlighted cell (the active cell).
2. What type of data is in the highlighted cell?
3. Give an example of contiguous data.
4. Give an example of non-contiguous data.

	A	B	C	D	E	F	G
1	Surname	FirstName	Area	SalesToMarch	SalesToJune	SalesToSeptember	SalesToDecember
2	Smith	Muhammed	North East	$100,000.00	$30,000.00	$60,000.00	$50,000.00
3	Johnson	Emma	West Europe	$500,000.00	$45,000.00	$75,000.00	$200,000.00
4	Williams	Jose	South America	$700,000.00	$100,000.00	$200,000.00	$75,000.00
5	Garcia	Maria	Sweden	$300,000.00	$49,000.00	$100,000.00	$250,000.00
6	Rodriguez	Nozomi	East Europe	$500,000.00	$69,000.00	$300,000.00	$300,000.00
7	Hernandez	Lucia	Central Americ	$400,000.00	$100,000.00	$80,000.00	$100,000.00
8	Rossi	Sophia	Italy	$10,000.00	$100,000.00	$200,000.00	$150,000.00
9	Novak	Tamar	South Africa	$600,000.00	$90,000.00	$95,000.00	$230,000.00
10	Smirnov	Alexei	Russia	$900,000.00	$100,000.00	$75,000.00	$600,000.00
11	Kumar	Akshay	Middle East	$700,000.00	$90,000.00	$300,000.00	$250,000.00
12							

Figure 16.6: Sales data

> **ICT IN CONTEXT**
>
> The relational database model was developed in the 1970s. It organises data into tables consisting of rows and columns. It works well for relatively small amounts of data but now, with machine learning, self-teaching algorithms need to draw data from huge volumes of information stored in vast and separate data sets. To allow for this, a new database model has been developed that is not relational. Some databases like this are based specifically on graphs and are called a 'knowledge graph' or 'graph database'. These store data in a graphical format that shows the relationships between any of the data points.

> **ACTIVITY 16.1**
>
> In small groups, carry out research to discover how you can select data for a chart without using a mouse. Create an illustrated poster to inform other students.

> **ICT IN CONTEXT**
>
> Research has shown that people are more inclined to believe information if it is in graphical form. A study showed 61 people a paragraph of text saying that a non-existent drug reduces the probability of catching a cold by 40%. Half of the people also saw a graph that repeated the numbers but did not present any more information. Of the people who saw both text and graph, 97% believed the drug worked compared with only 68% of the people who saw only the text.

Inserting charts and graphs

When you have selected the data you must specify which type of chart or graph you want.

The different types are usually displayed in the ribbon of the Insert menu. To help you, the software may display suitable ones in the Suggested Charts or Recommended Charts tab (see Figure 16.7).

16 Graphs and charts

Recommended Charts – found in the Insert manu

Figure 16.7: Selecting the type of chart

In Figure 16.8, column and bar charts have been selected.

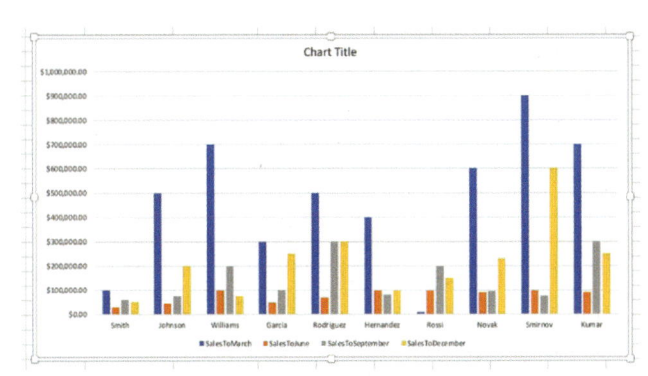

Figure 16.8: The column chart from the data selected in Figure 16.7

A column chart is most suitable for comparing things between different groups. Figure 16.8 shows the sales figures for employees.

In the graph, we have referred to the vertical axis as the **y-axis**, but in this instance, it can be called the **value axis** as it shows the numerical values. Similarly the **x-axis** is the **category axis** as this shows what the values are representing – the different sales people.

> ### ACTIVITY 16.2
>
> Working with a partner, identify the following in the chart shown in Figure 16.8.
>
> - Chart title.
> - Legend.
> - x-axis.
> - y-axis.

> ### KEY WORDS
>
> **y-axis:** the vertical axis of a chart
>
> **value axis:** the axis that shows the values being measured or compared
>
> **x-axis:** the horizontal axis of a chart
>
> **category axis:** displays labels for the items that the values represent

CAMBRIDGE IGCSE™ ICT: COURSEBOOK

Once the graph has been created by the software, its design and format can be edited.

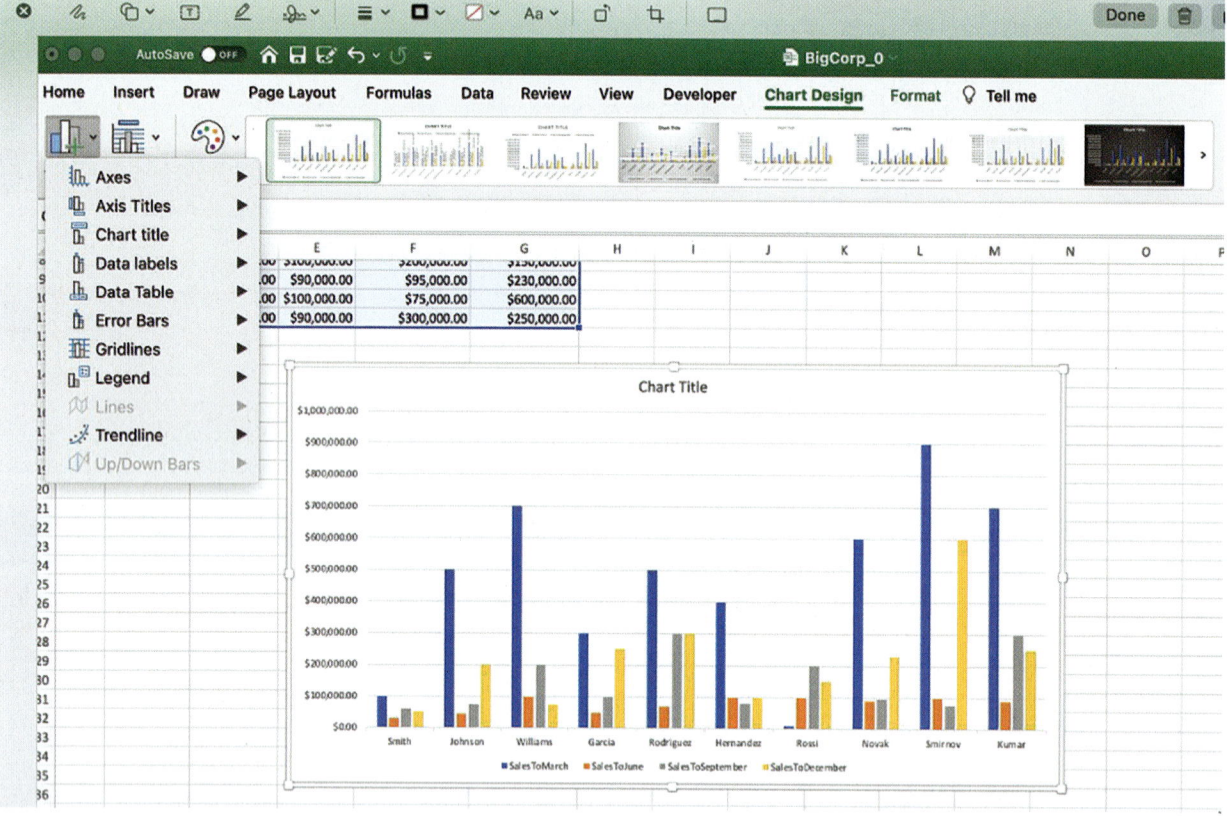

Figure 16.9: Editing the chart design

From the Chart Design ribbon (see Figure 16.9), items such as axes (plural of axis), **axes titles**, **chart title**, **legend** and **data labels** can be added and removed. For example, an axis title can be added to the *y*-axis (see Figure 16.10).

> **KEY WORDS**
>
> **axes titles:** words describing the data represented on axes
>
> **chart title:** the main heading of the chart or graph
>
> **legend:** a key at the side of a chart or graph that indicates what the symbols or colours and patterns represent in the chart or graph
>
> **data label:** label stating the name of the item represented in the chart

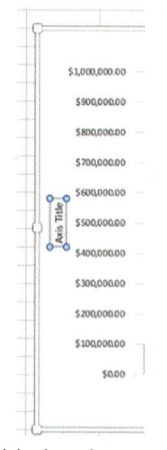

Figure 16.10: Title added to the *y*-axis

You can edit the label by clicking in it, entering text and setting font and size as you would for any text.

When items such as the title, axes and axes labels are double-clicked, the design pane opens. Here there are many formatting options for the selected item.

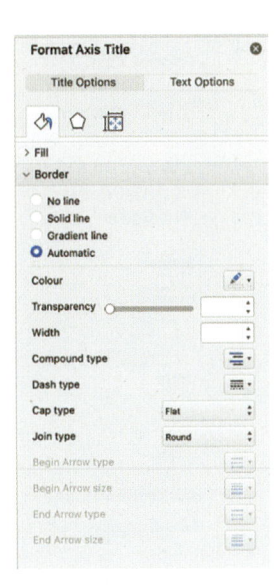

Figure 16.11: Design options for the axis labels

Figure 16.11 shows the pane for 'Format Axis Title'. In this way, the **category axis title**, **value axis title**, **category axis labels** and **value axis labels** can be added.

Data labels can be added (see Figure 16.12) to a line graph or the columns of a column chart by double-clicking them.

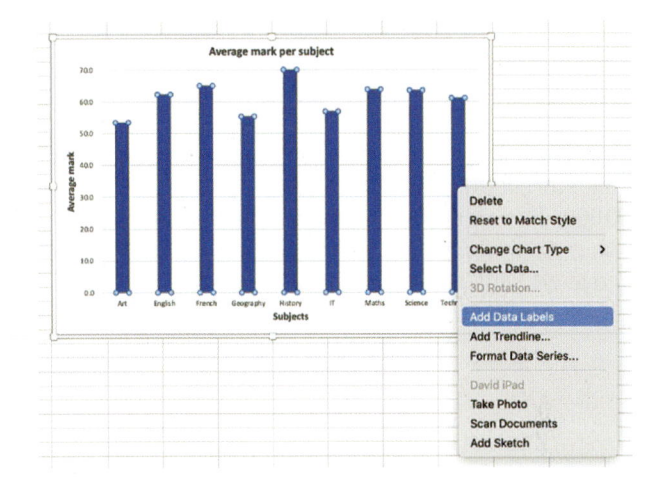

Figure 16.12: Adding data labels

The labels to be shown can then be selected from the Format pane (see Figure 16.13).

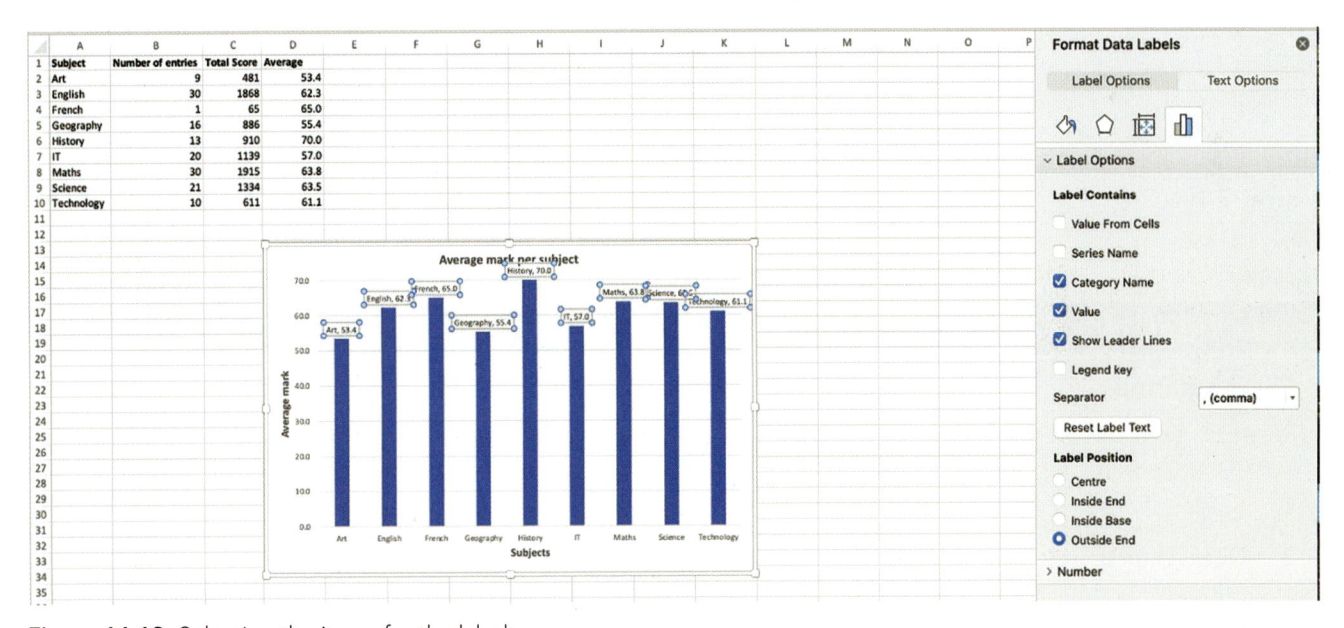

Figure 16.13: Selecting the items for the labels

KEY WORDS

category axis title: the title of the axis displaying labels for the items that the values represent

value axis title: the title of the axis that shows the values being measured or compared

category axis labels: the labels on the category axis

value axis labels: the labels on the value axis

Adjusting the maximum and minimum values of an axis scale and setting incremental values

In the chart shown in Figure 16.8, the axis **scales** range from 0 to 1 000 000. However, the **maximum value** is 900 000. The maximum value can be adjusted in the format pane (see Figure 16.14) after the axis has been double-clicked. The **minimum value** and the units on the axis can be set in the same way.

> **KEY WORDS**
>
> **scales:** the units of measurement used on the axes of a chart or graph
>
> **maximum value:** the largest value shown
>
> **minimum value:** the smallest value shown

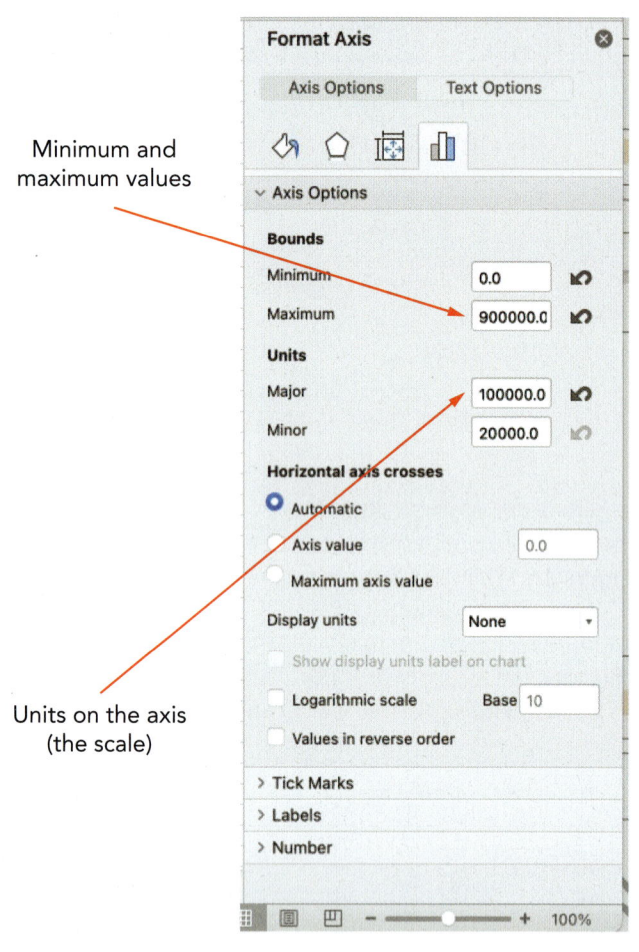

Figure 16.14: Changing the maximum value

> **PRACTICAL TASK 16.1**
>
> **Getting started**
>
> Research examples of the following types of charts and state the type of data they should be used to represent.
> 1. Spider charts.
> 2. Gantt charts.
>
> **Practice**
> 3. Open the file *Subjects.xlsx* into your spreadsheet software.
>
>   The spreadsheet shows various subjects, the number of test entries for each subject and the total and average scores for those subjects.
>
> 4. Create a column chart to show the average mark for each subject.

16 Graphs and charts

CONTINUED

5   Change the chart title so it is bold and in a 14 pt, sans-serif font.

6   Change the axis titles so they are bold and in a 12 pt sans-serif font.

7   Change the y-axis so that it has a range of 0.0 to 70.0.

Your finished chart should look like Figure 16.15.

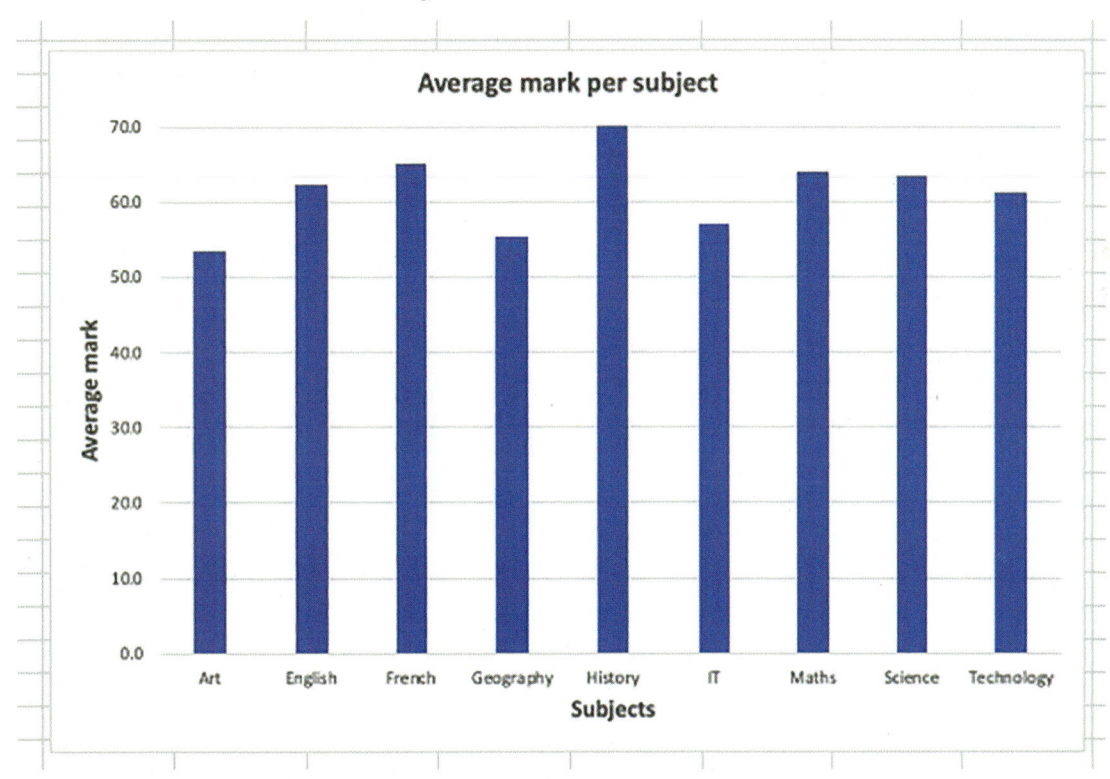

Figure 16.15: Completed column chart

Challenge

8   Change the column fill to red.

9   Change the number of decimal places on the y-axis scale from 1 to 0.

Your modified chart should look like Figure 16.16.

> CONTINUED

Average mark per subject

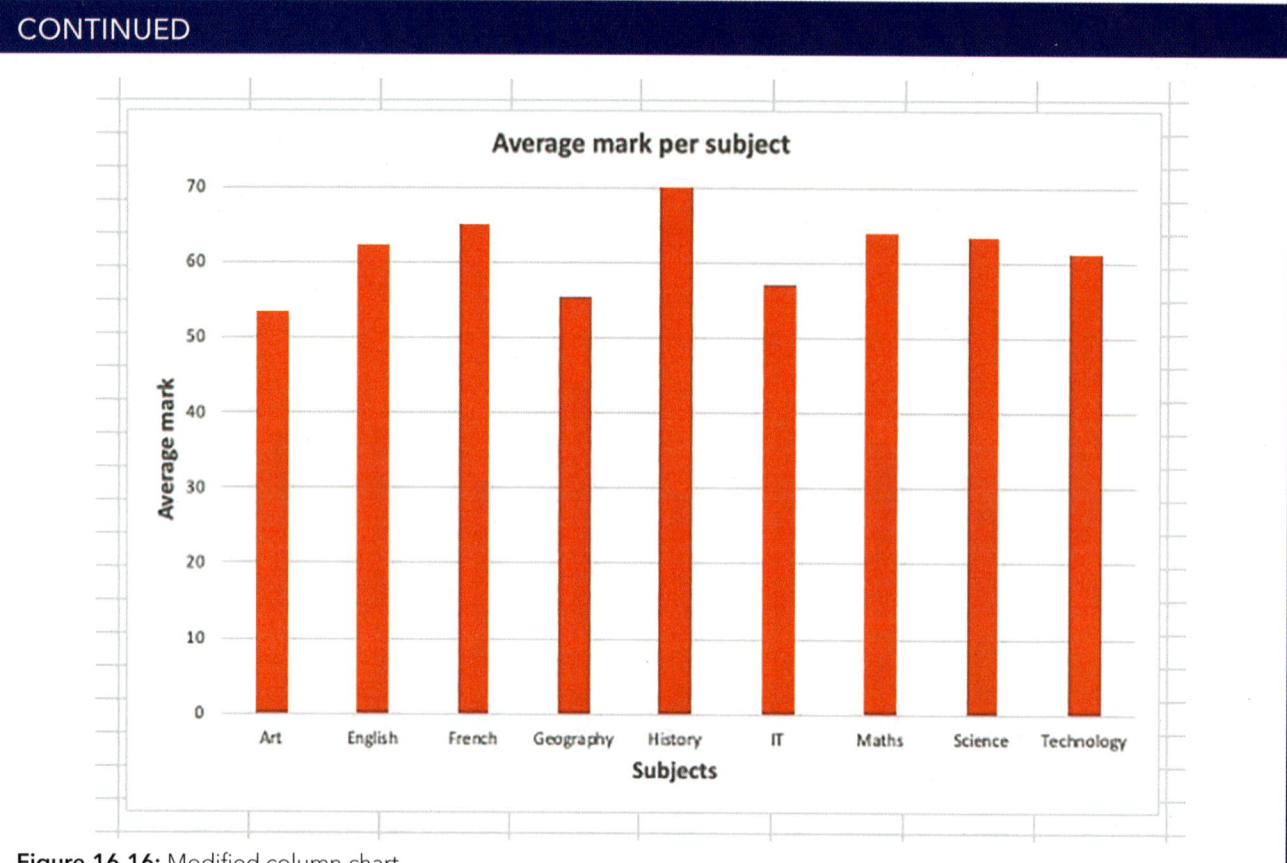

Figure 16.16: Modified column chart

Save the spreadsheet as *Task1_Challenge*.

Self-assessment

10 Check the points in the following table to make sure you have done everything in the task:

Criterion	Criterion met
Create a column chart from the data.	
Edit the chart title and axis labels.	
Change the range of the y-axis.	
Change column fills.	
Format the number of decimal places displayed.	

16   Graphs and charts

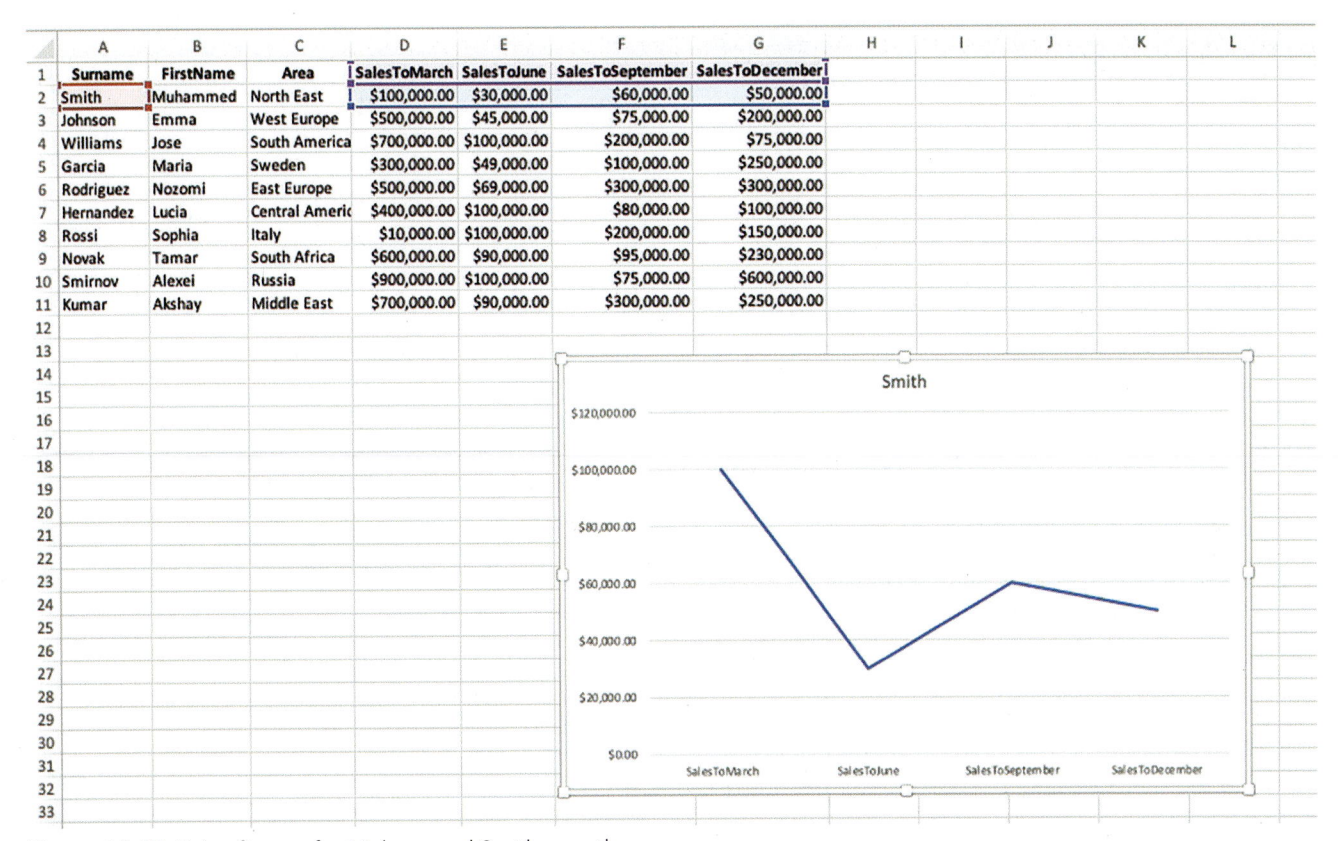

	A	B	C	D	E	F	G
1	Surname	FirstName	Area	SalesToMarch	SalesToJune	SalesToSeptember	SalesToDecember
2	Smith	Muhammed	North East	$100,000.00	$30,000.00	$60,000.00	$50,000.00
3	Johnson	Emma	West Europe	$500,000.00	$45,000.00	$75,000.00	$200,000.00
4	Williams	Jose	South America	$700,000.00	$100,000.00	$200,000.00	$75,000.00
5	Garcia	Maria	Sweden	$300,000.00	$49,000.00	$100,000.00	$250,000.00
6	Rodriguez	Nozomi	East Europe	$500,000.00	$69,000.00	$300,000.00	$300,000.00
7	Hernandez	Lucia	Central America	$400,000.00	$100,000.00	$80,000.00	$100,000.00
8	Rossi	Sophia	Italy	$10,000.00	$100,000.00	$200,000.00	$150,000.00
9	Novak	Tamar	South Africa	$600,000.00	$90,000.00	$95,000.00	$230,000.00
10	Smirnov	Alexei	Russia	$900,000.00	$100,000.00	$75,000.00	$600,000.00
11	Kumar	Akshay	Middle East	$700,000.00	$90,000.00	$300,000.00	$250,000.00

Figure 16.17: Sales figures for Muhammed Smith over the year

Types of charts and graphs

There are many different types of charts and graphs, and each one allows you to present data differently. When selecting which chart or graph type to use, you should consider the message you want to give your audience.

Column charts and bar charts

These are the charts we have been looking at so far. They are useful for comparing two or more values as you can compare the relative size of each data item. The difference between the two is in their orientation – a **column chart** is vertical and a **bar chart** is horizontal.

Line graphs

Line graphs are useful for displaying changes over time. They let you see different trends in the data. The data in Figure 16.17 shows the changes in sales revenue over a year.

The line graph in Figure 16.18 shows the sales figures of one of the employees over the year.

> **KEY WORDS**
>
> **column chart:** a chart where data are represented by vertical rectangles
>
> **bar chart:** a chart where data are represented by horizontal rectangles
>
> **line graph:** a chart where values are connected by a line
>
> **data value labels:** labels on a graph showing the value represented at each plot point or by each bar or column
>
> **plot point:** a fixed point on a graph with a measured position on the x- and y-axes

Data value labels can be added to the graph to show the actual amounts at the **plot points**, as shown in Figure 16.18.

CAMBRIDGE IGCSE™ ICT: COURSEBOOK

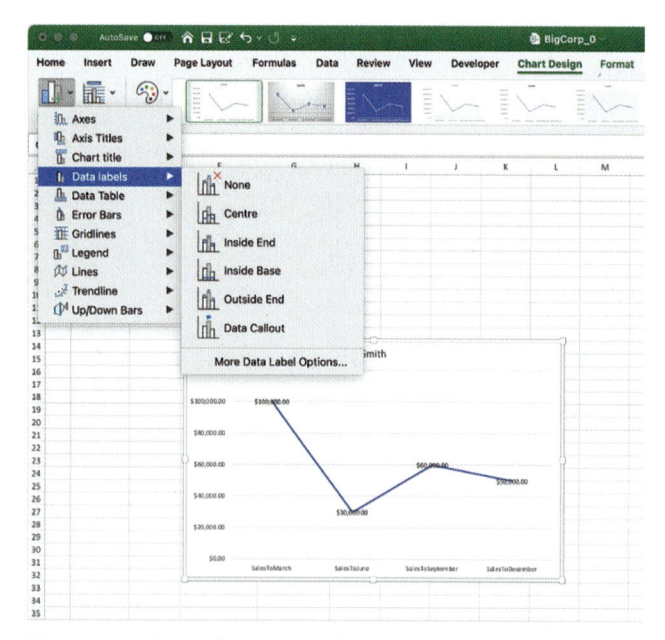

Figure 16.18: Adding data value labels

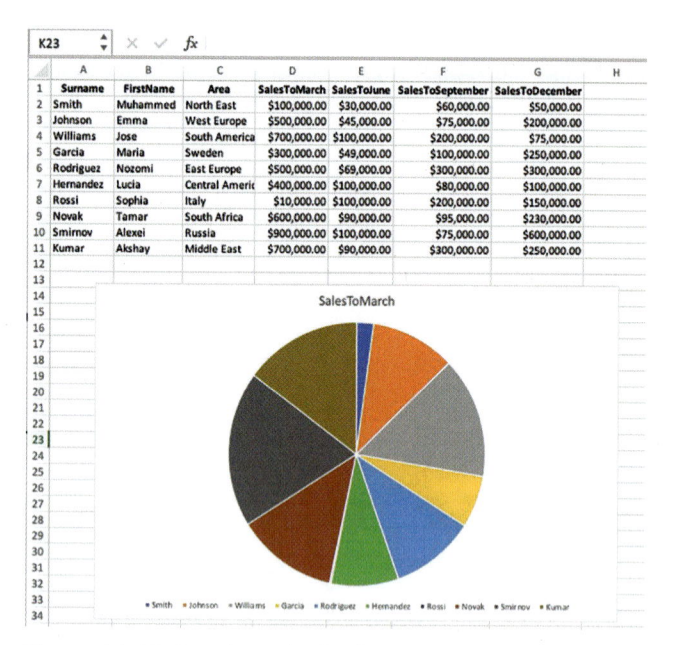

Figure 16.19: Pie chart of sales figures

Pie charts

Pie charts are the most suitable type of chart to use to display the contribution each value makes to a whole item or entity. An example of data used for a pie chart could be how much each person has contributed to the total amount of money raised in a certain fundraising effort. It shows each person's **percentage** compared to the total. Even if the values do not all add up to 100, the spreadsheet will convert the values to a percentage when it is displayed as a pie chart.

The pie chart in Figure 16.19 shows the sales figures for each employee.

> ### KEY WORDS
>
> **pie chart:** a circular chart cut into sectors representing the values of the data items
>
> **percentages:** data value labels on a pie chart showing the relative contribution of each sector to the whole
>
> **sector labels:** a description of what each slice of a pie chart represents
>
> **sector:** a 'slice' of a pie chart

Data labels can be added in Chart design (see Figure 16.20). These are also known as **sector labels**.

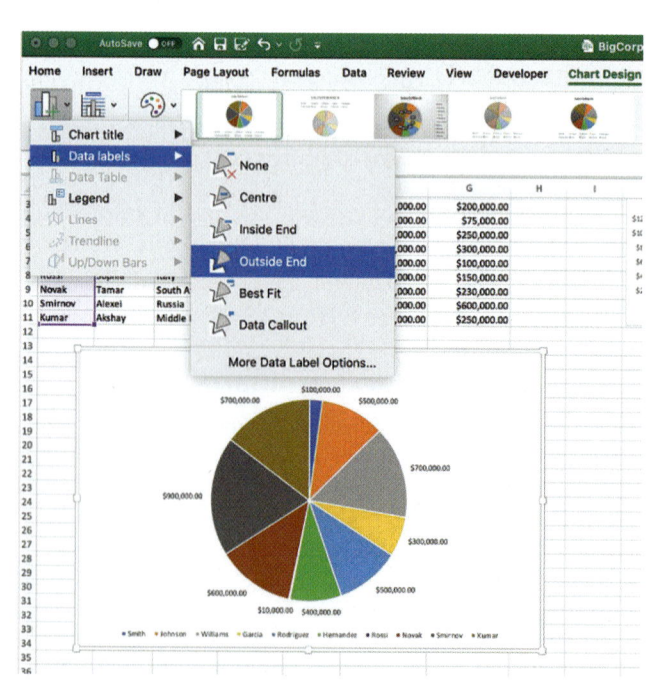

Figure 16.20: Adding sector labels

If the data labels are double-clicked, they can be edited to show the percentage contribution of each **sector** (see Figure 16.21).

16   Graphs and charts

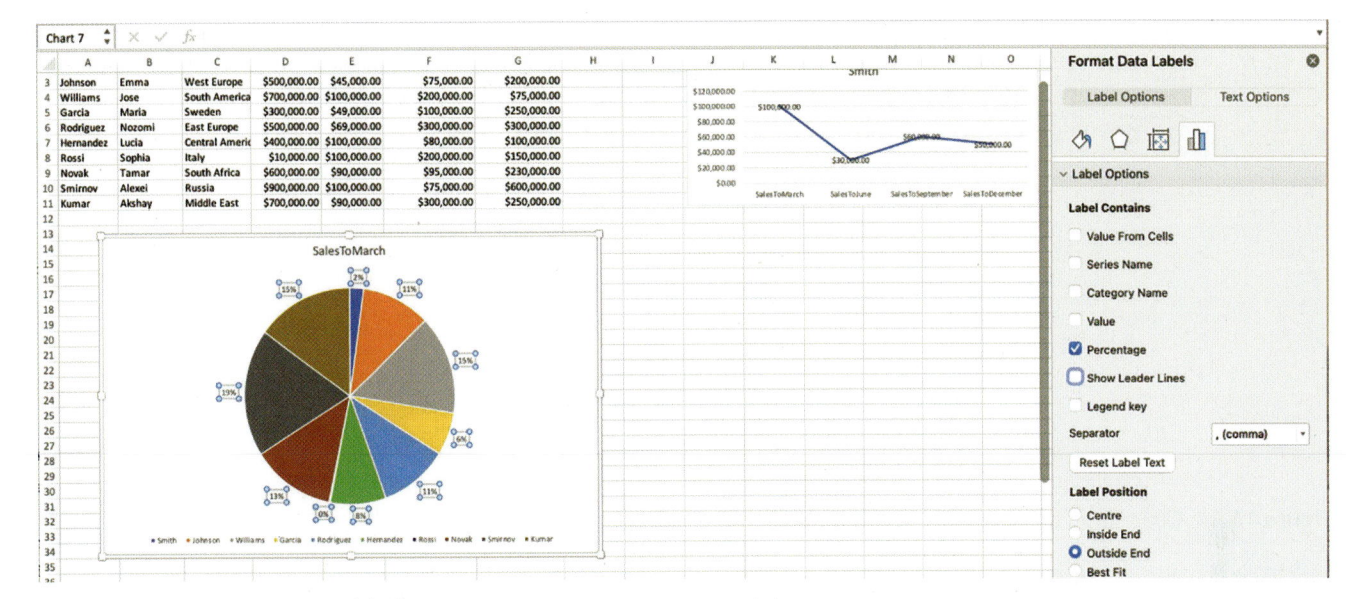

Figure 16.21: Showing sector labels as a percentage

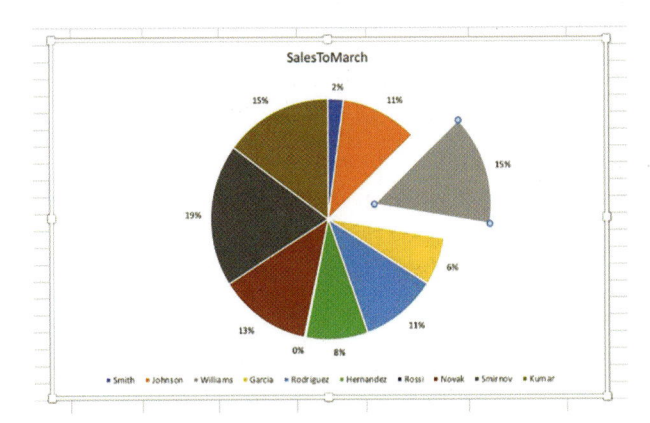

Figure 16.22: Extracting a sector from a pie chart

One of the pie sectors can be extracted by double-clicking on it and dragging it (see Figure 16.22).

The fill of each sector can be edited to a different colour or a gradient by selecting it and using the format pane.

The style of the graph can be altered by selecting one from the gallery.

ACTIVITY 16.3

In small groups or in pairs, debate whether graphs/charts communicate data better than tables of data. Give reasons for your points of view.

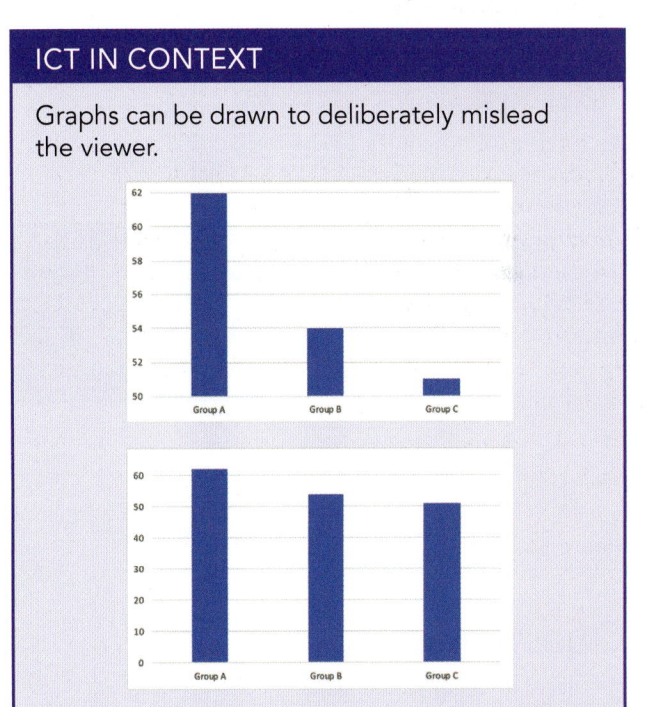

ICT IN CONTEXT

Graphs can be drawn to deliberately mislead the viewer.

Figure 16.23: Misleading graphs

These two graphs show the same data but the differences between the groups in the graph on the left look far greater than those on the right. Unless you look closely and see that the scales on the y-axis are different. On the left the y-axis starts at 50 and on the right, at 0.

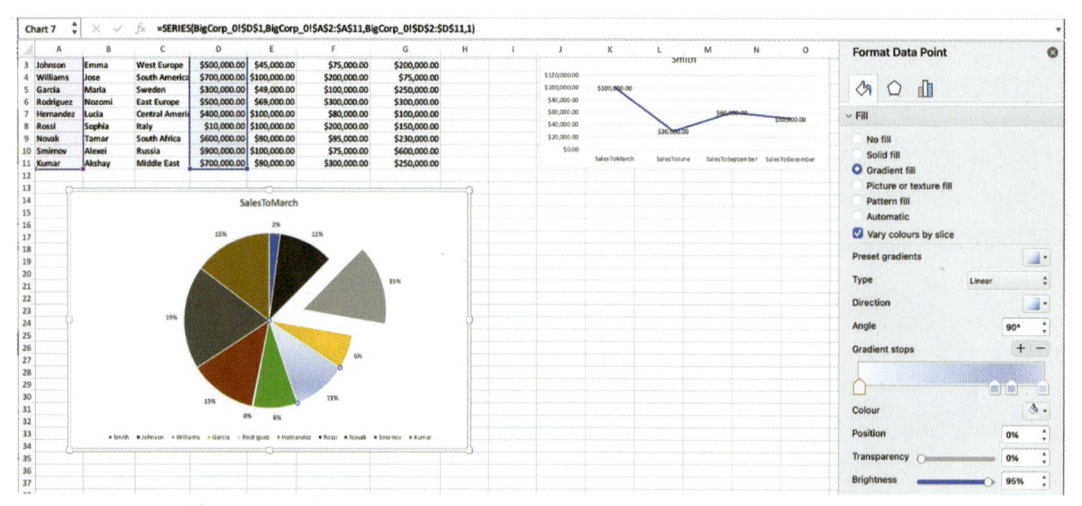

Figure 16.24: Changing the fill

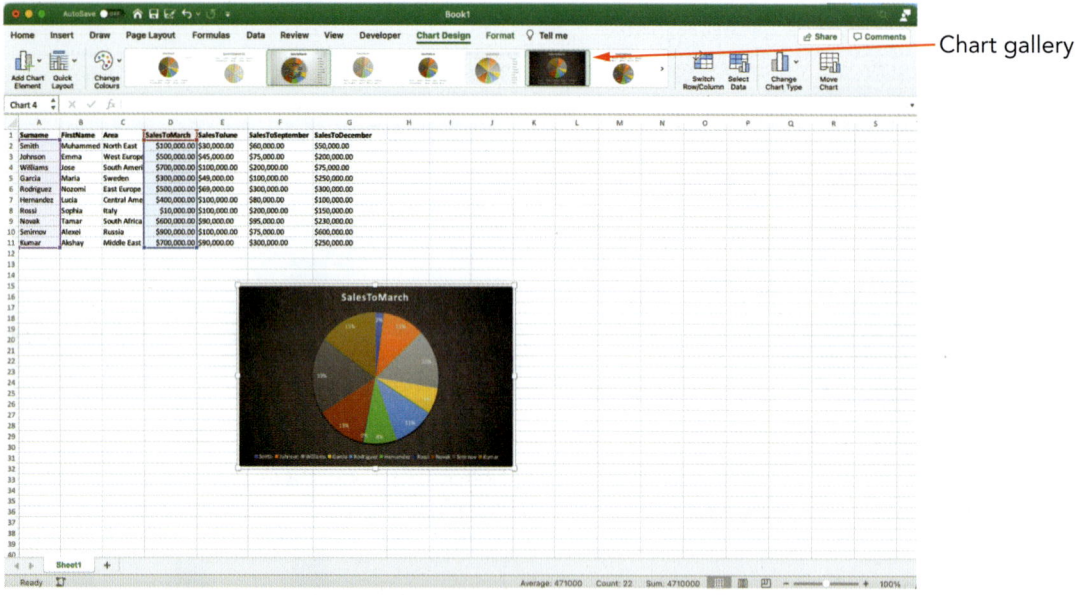

Figure 16.25: Using the style gallery

Questions

5 Explain what is meant by the following terms.
   a Chart.
   b Graph.

6 Look at the following descriptions of data and then explain the type of chart or graph which should be used to display them.

   a A shop sells six different flavours of ice cream. They would like to compare the number of each flavour sold in a day.
   b A car manufacturing company would like to display the number produced each month for a year.
   c A pupil measured the temperature of a liquid every 30 seconds over a 20 minute period to study its cooling.

16 Graphs and charts

Adding a second data series to a chart

Figure 16.26 shows a chart displaying one data series.

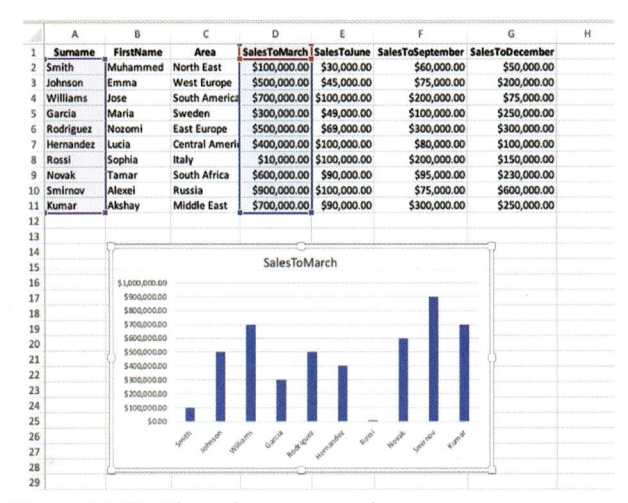

Figure 16.26: Chart showing one data series

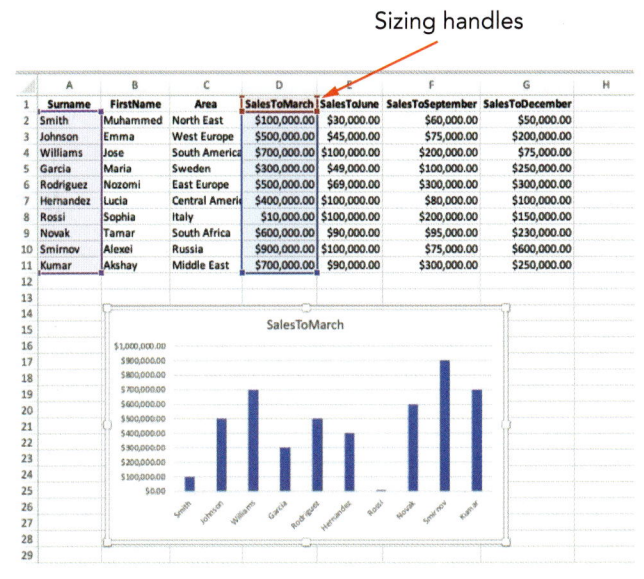

Figure 16.27: Adding a data series

If another data series is to be added, it should be in an adjacent column. Therefore the 'Sales to June' data can be added. To add the data, the graph should be selected and the sizing handles (see Figure 16.27) dragged to include the new data.

The new data will automatically be displayed in the chart.

Adding a secondary axis

In Figure 16.28, a chart has been created to show the number of items sold and the average price for each item over a number of years.

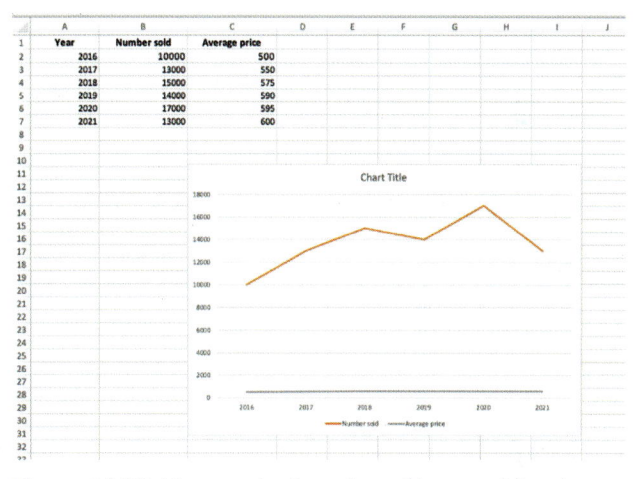

Figure 16.28: Line graph of number of items sold and average price of each

As the values for numbers sold and average price are shown on the same axis, it is difficult to see variations in the average price line.

A **secondary axis** can be added to show the values of the average price data.

To do this, the average price plot line should be double-clicked to select it and a secondary axis can be selected from the Format pane (see Figure 16.29).

> **KEY WORD**
>
> **Secondary axis:** a vertical axis at the right-hand side of the graph or a horizontal axis at the top

323

Figure 16.29: Adding a secondary axis

The maximum and minimum values for the axis and the major and minor units can be edited.

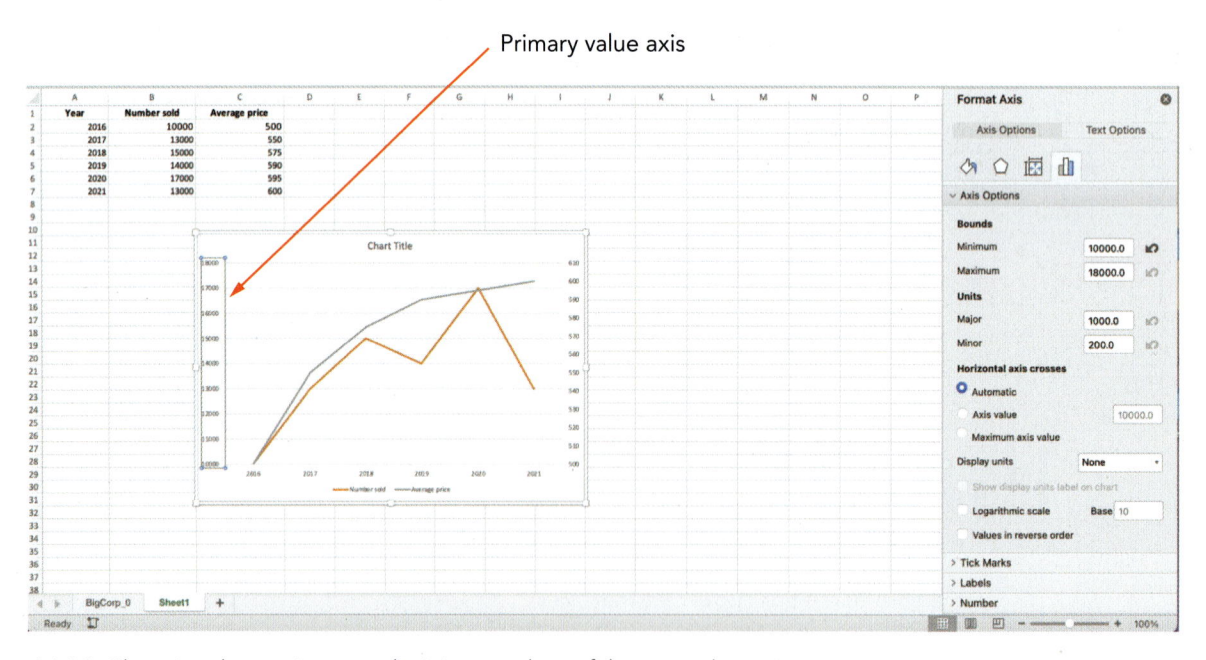

Figure 16.30: Changing the maximum and minimum values of the secondary axis

The maximum and minimum of the primary value axis can also be adjusted (see Figure 16.30) from the same pane so that the plots use all of the space available.

16 Graphs and charts

PRACTICAL TASK 16.2

Getting started

Answer the questions based on the graph shown in Figure 16.31.

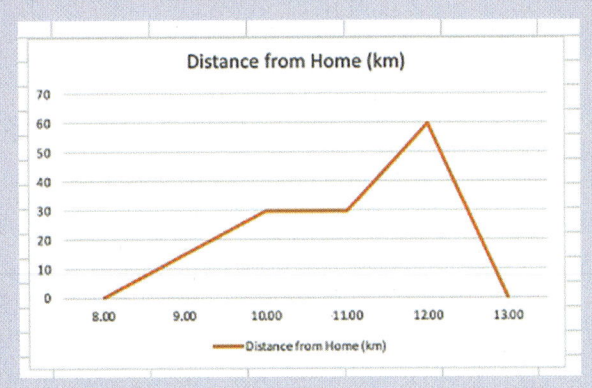

Figure 16.31: Line graph – Distance from home

1. How far did the person travel between 8 a.m. and 10 a.m.?
2. When was the person stationary?
3. What was the speed of the journey home?

Practice

4. Open *Task1_Challenge.xls* from the previous Practical Task 16.1 in your spreadsheet software.
5. Add the 'Number of entries' data to the chart.
6. Create a secondary vertical axis for the number of entries data.
7. You should make the scale for this axis go from 0 to 35 and it should have a label.
8. Add a legend to the chart.

Your finished chart should look like Figure 16.32.

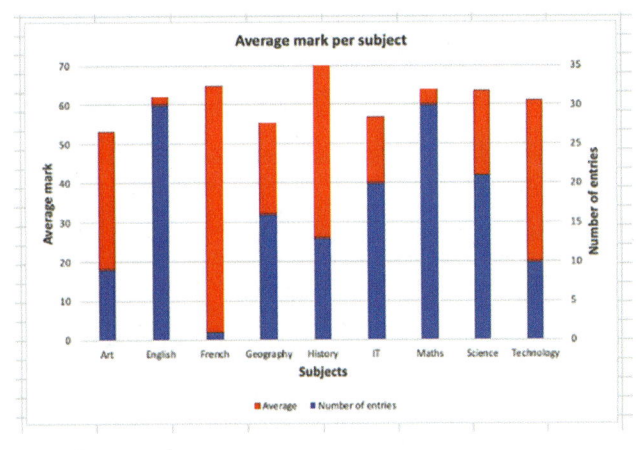

Figure 16.32: Column chart with secondary axis

> **CAMBRIDGE IGCSE™ ICT: COURSEBOOK**

CONTINUED

Challenge

9 Change the chart type of the 'Number of entries data' from a column to a line.

10 Change the colour of this line to black.

Your finished chart should look like Figure 16.33.

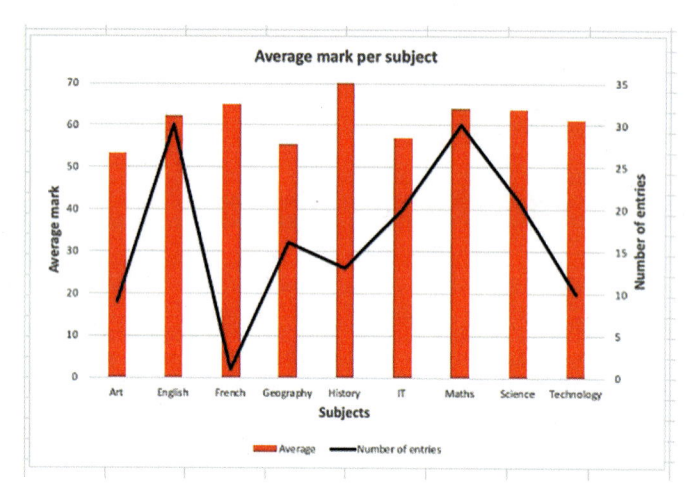

Figure 16.33: Column chart – with line graph superimposed

16.2 Formatting charts or graphs

Format numerical values to display currency symbols

Look back at the graph in Figure 16.30. It shows average prices, but displays these numbers without currency symbols.

A currency symbol can be added by selecting the axis and using the Format pane to change the number category.

The actual currency symbol to display can be selected (see Figures 16.34–6).

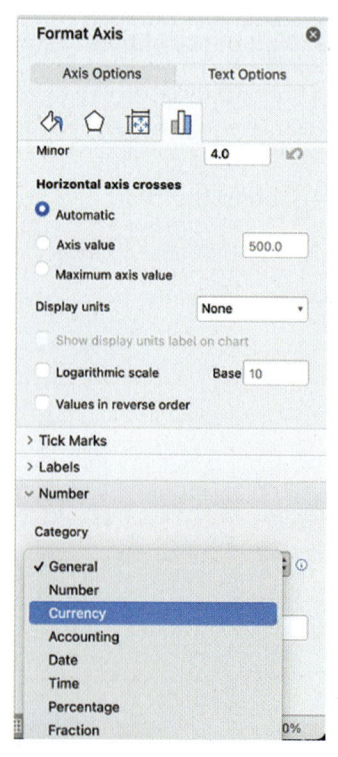

Figure 16.34: Formatting the axis to display currency symbols

16 Graphs and charts

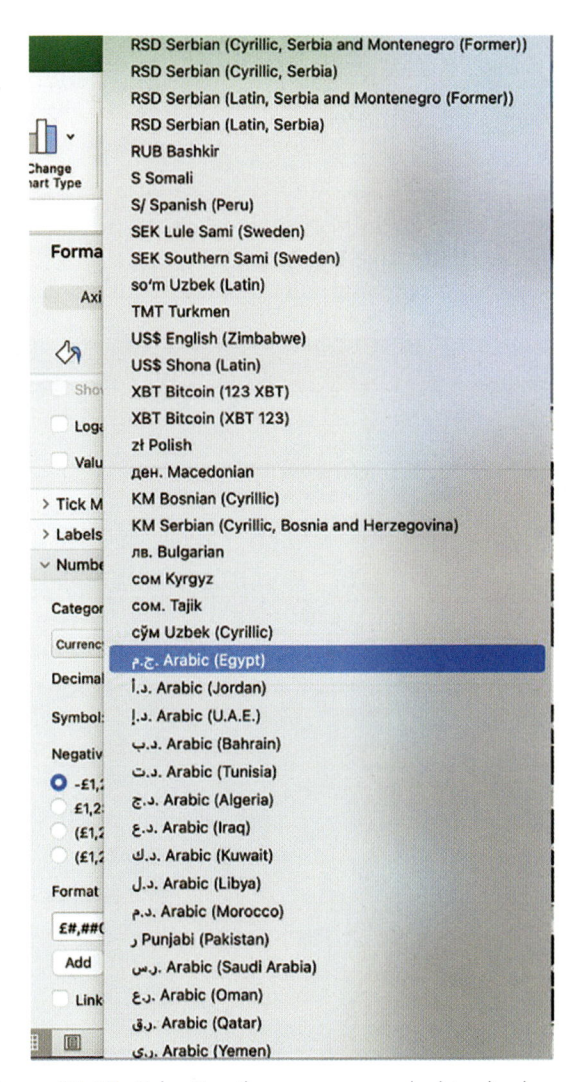

Figure 16.35: Selecting the currency symbol to display

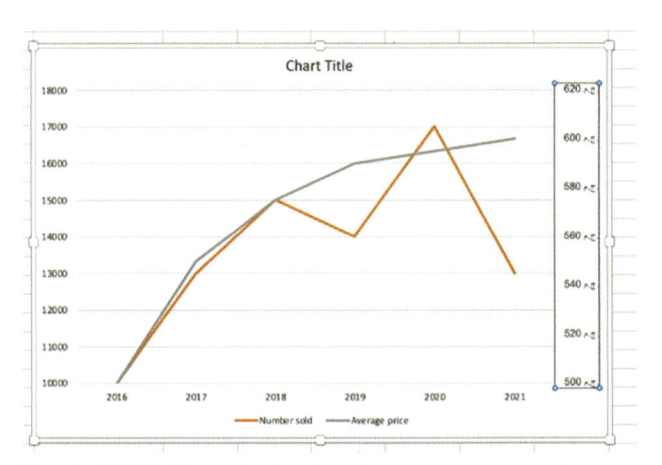

Figure 16.36: The axis showing the currency symbols

Format numerical values to specify decimal places

The number of decimal places to display for a number can also be selected. Two decimal places are automatically selected for currency (see Figure 16.37) but for other numbers, they can be set as the user requires.

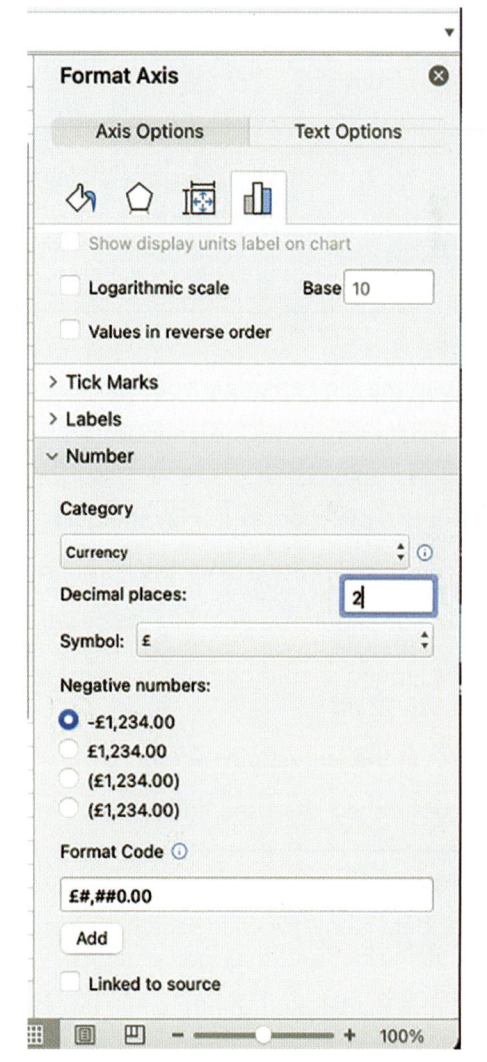

Figure 16.37: Selecting the number of decimal places to display

327

CAMBRIDGE IGCSE™ ICT: COURSEBOOK

> **ICT IN CONTEXT**
>
> It is possible to make animated charts and graphs for presentations and websites.
>
> They are useful for data that changes over time.
>
> You can create your own animated graphs. Type 'animated graphs for free, flourish' into your search engine. You can upload your spreadsheet data and have it converted into an animated chart.

> **PRACTICAL TASK 16.3**
>
> **Getting started**
>
> With a partner, discuss the type of chart or graph that would be best for the following:
> 1. To display data changing continuously over time.
> 2. To display data at fixed points in time.
> 3. To display the contribution each item makes to the whole.
>
> **Practice**
>
> 4. Open the file *Fans.xls* in your spreadsheet software.
>
>   The data shows the most supported football teams in the world.
>
> 5. Create a pie chart to display the data.
> 6. Chose a style with a black background.
> 7. The title should be bold in a sans-serif font of size 16 pt.
> 8. The legend should be bold in a sans-serif font of size 12 pt.
> 9. Extract the largest pie sector.
>
>   Your finished chart should look like Figure 16.38. 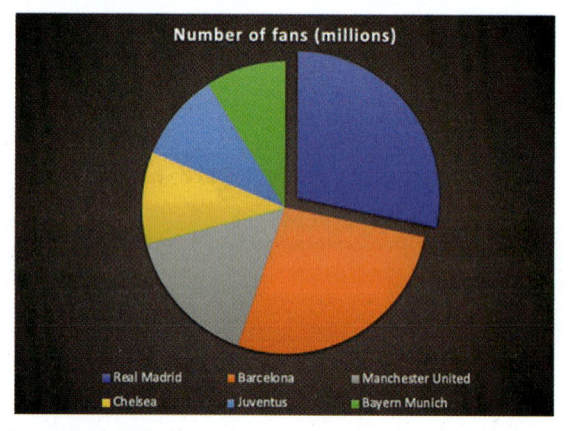
>
> Figure 16.38: Fans pie chart
>
> **Challenge**
>
> 10. Set data labels for each sector showing the actual values and their percentages.
> 11. Centre the label positions within the sectors.
> 12. Change the labels to bold in a sans-serif font of size 12 pt.
>
>   Your finished chart should look like Figure 16.39. 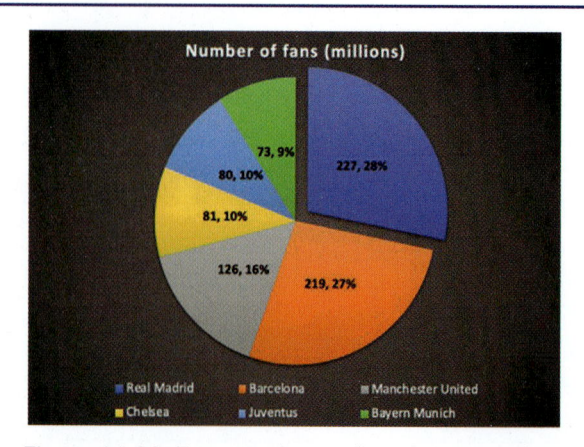
>
> Figure 16.39: Fans pie chart with percentage values

16 Graphs and charts

> **WORKED EXAMPLE 16.1**
>
> **CREATING CHARTS**

This worked example illustrates how to answer a question requiring the creation and formatting of charts.

1. Open the file *Sales.xlsm* into your spreadsheet software.

   The spreadsheet shows the quarterly sales figures for ten executives of a manufacturing firm.

   It also shows the total sales figures for each quarter and for the whole year.

2. Create charts to show:

   a. The sales figures of each executive for each quarter so that differences between quarter and executive can be clearly seen.

   b. Total sales figures for each quarter.

3. The charts should have suitable titles, scales and labels.

Step 1

The spreadsheet (Figure 16.40) shows the sales figures.

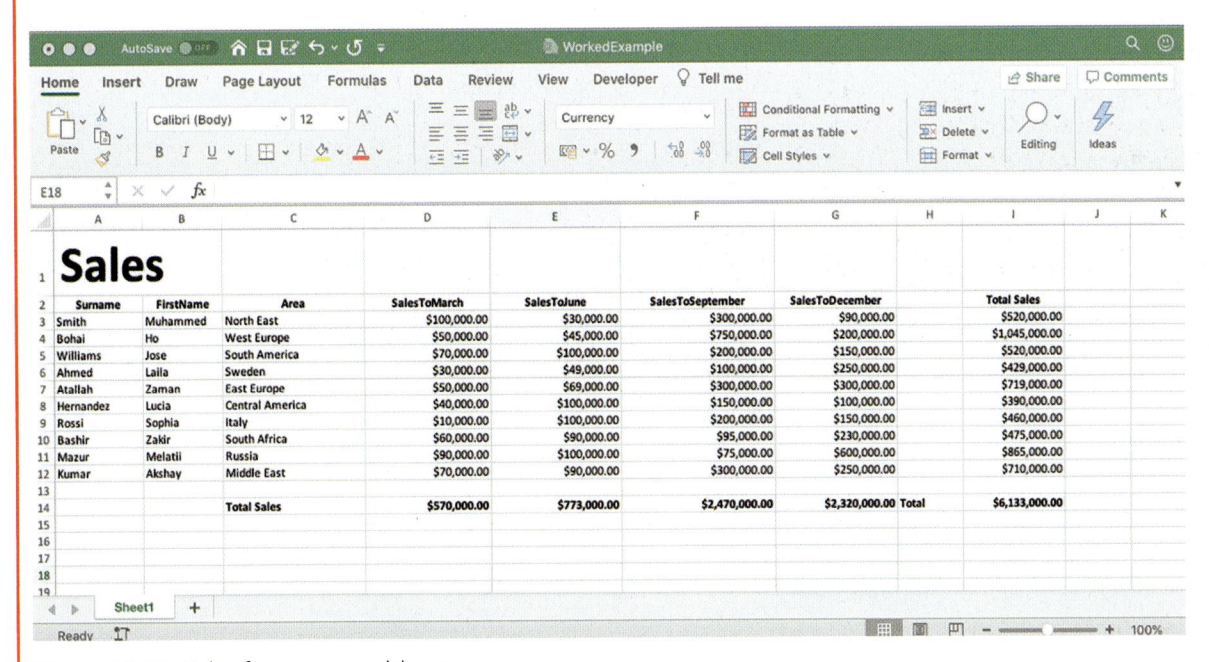

Surname	FirstName	Area	SalesToMarch	SalesToJune	SalesToSeptember	SalesToDecember	Total Sales	
Smith	Muhammed	North East	$100,000.00	$30,000.00	$300,000.00	$90,000.00	$520,000.00	
Bohai	Ho	West Europe	$50,000.00	$45,000.00	$750,000.00	$200,000.00	$1,045,000.00	
Williams	Jose	South America	$70,000.00	$100,000.00	$200,000.00	$150,000.00	$520,000.00	
Ahmed	Laila	Sweden	$30,000.00	$49,000.00	$100,000.00	$250,000.00	$429,000.00	
Atallah	Zaman	East Europe	$50,000.00	$69,000.00	$300,000.00	$300,000.00	$719,000.00	
Hernandez	Lucia	Central America	$40,000.00	$100,000.00	$150,000.00	$100,000.00	$390,000.00	
Rossi	Sophia	Italy	$10,000.00	$100,000.00	$200,000.00	$150,000.00	$460,000.00	
Bashir	Zakir	South Africa	$60,000.00	$90,000.00	$95,000.00	$230,000.00	$475,000.00	
Mazur	Melatii	Russia	$90,000.00	$100,000.00	$75,000.00	$600,000.00	$865,000.00	
Kumar	Akshay	Middle East	$70,000.00	$90,000.00	$300,000.00	$250,000.00	$710,000.00	
		Total Sales	$570,000.00	$773,000.00	$2,470,000.00	$2,320,000.00	Total	$6,133,000.00

Figure 16.40: Sales figures spreadsheet

The first chart should show the differences between the quarters and between the executives. A stacked bar chart would be best to show the two types of difference.

CONTINUED

Step 2a

You can select the non-adjacent data ranges.

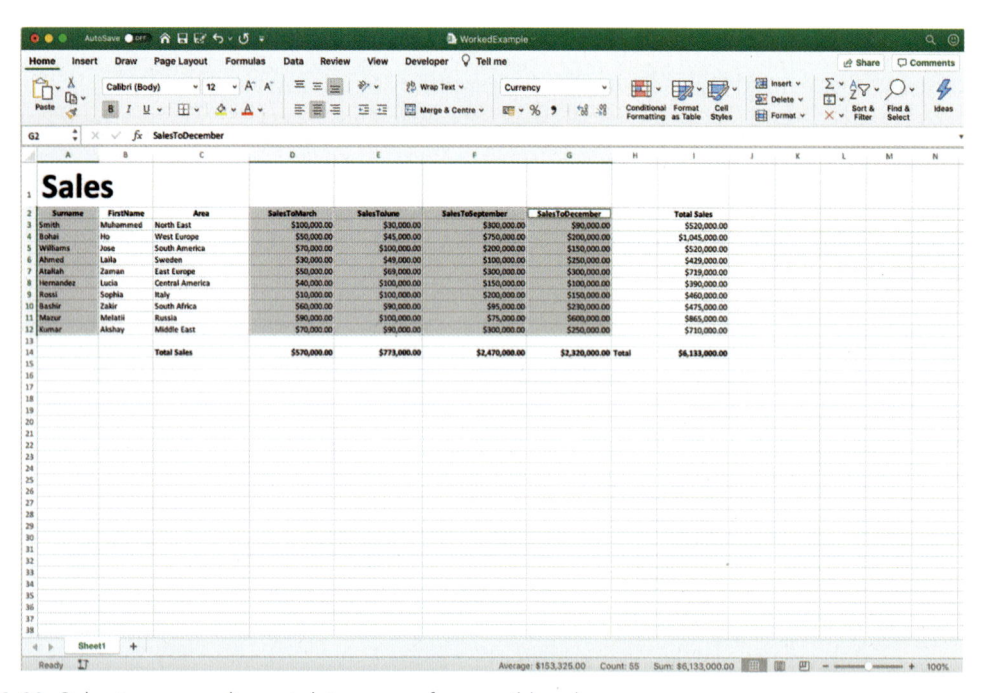

Figure 16.41: Selecting non-adjacent data ranges for monthly sales

You can then select a stacked bar chart (see Figure 16.42) to display the data.

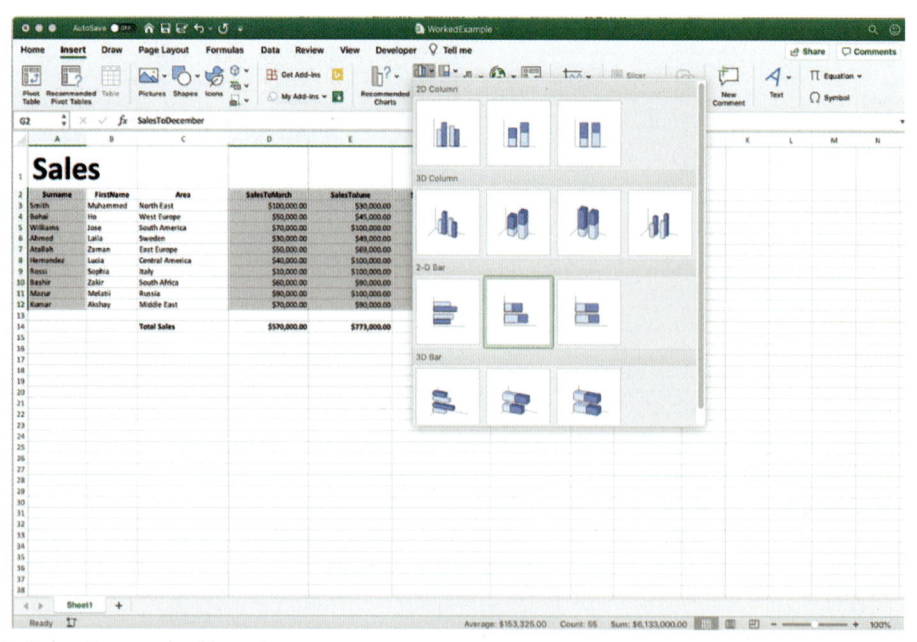

Figure 16.42: Selecting stacked bar chart type

16 Graphs and charts

CONTINUED

Step 3a

You can enlarge the graph, and create a suitable title (see Figure 16.43). The axes labels can also be enlarged.

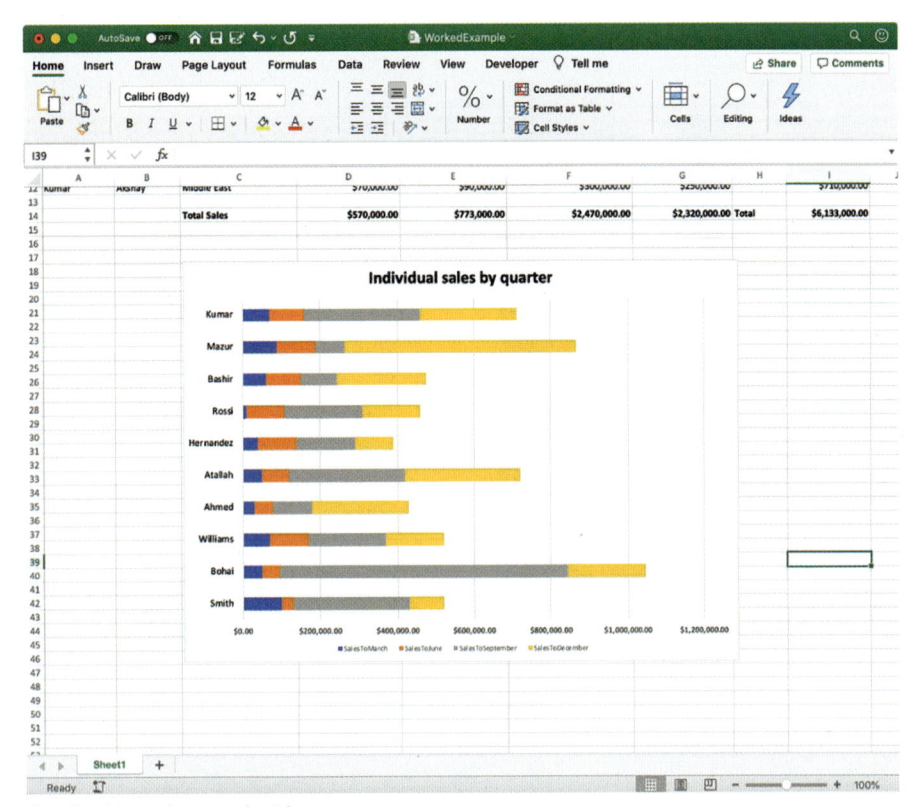

Figure 16.43: Stacked bar chart with title

You could also choose a different style to enhance the bars and make it easier to see the differences (see Figure 16.44 on the next page).

Step 2b

The total sales figures for each quarter can best be displayed in a column chart.

CAMBRIDGE IGCSE™ ICT: COURSEBOOK

CONTINUED

You can select non-adjacent ranges for both the labels and the data

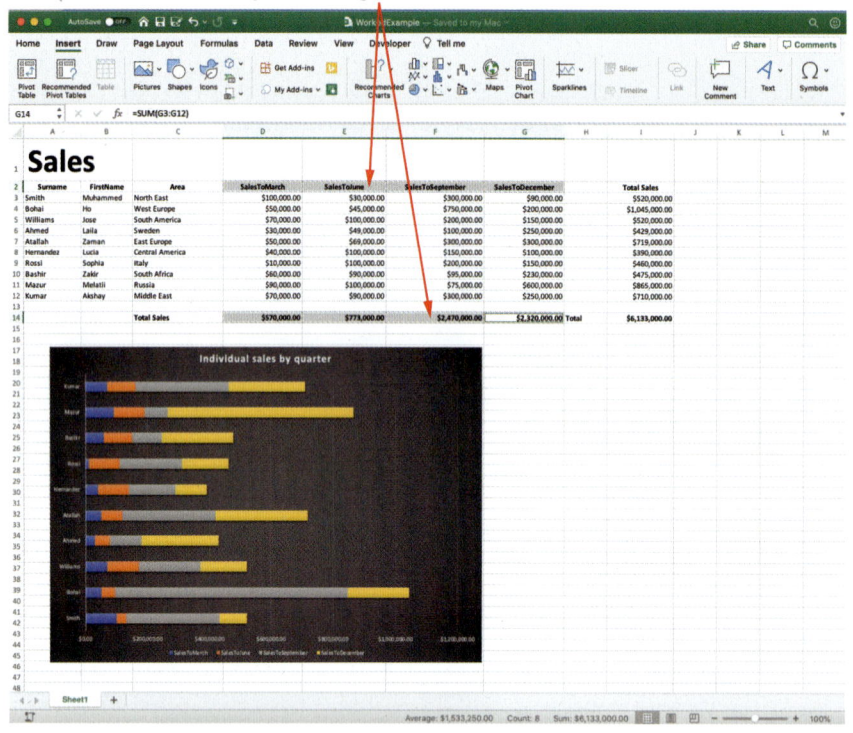

Figure 16.44: Selecting non-adjacent data ranges for total sales

You can then select a column chart.

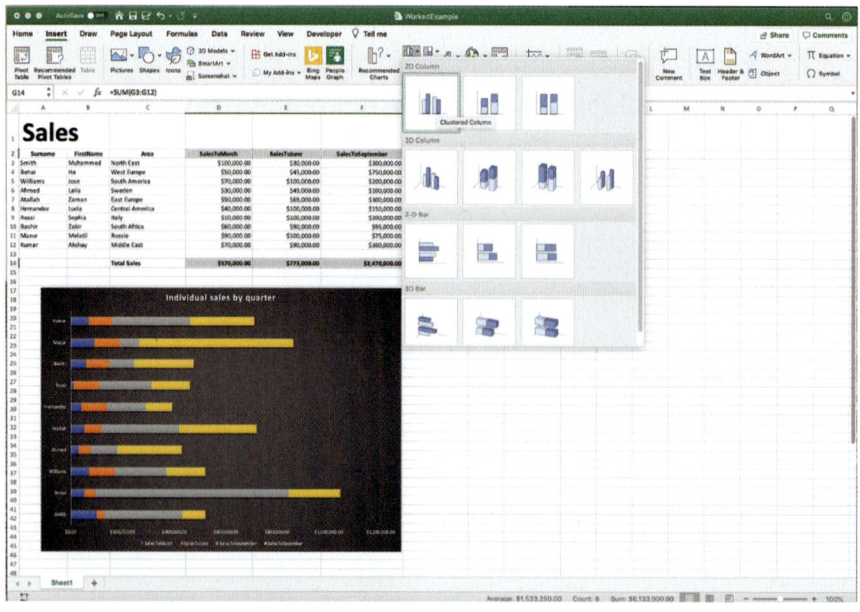

Figure 16.45: Selecting column chart type

16 Graphs and charts

> **CONTINUED**

Step 3b

You can add a title, and the *y*-axis numbers can be set to not have decimal places.

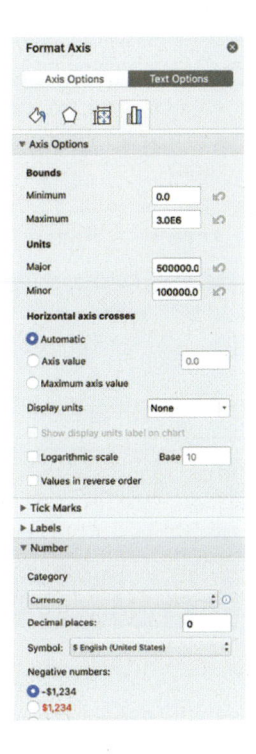

Figure 16.46: Setting decimal places

You can reduce the *y*-axis maximum value to $2 500 000. This will allow the plot area to be larger.

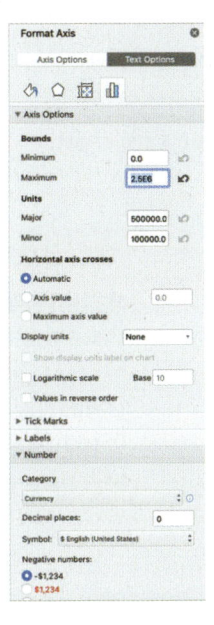

Figure 16.47: Setting *y*-axis maximum

333

> **CONTINUED**

Finally, you can enlarge the axis labels and data values can be added to columns and a suitable style selected.

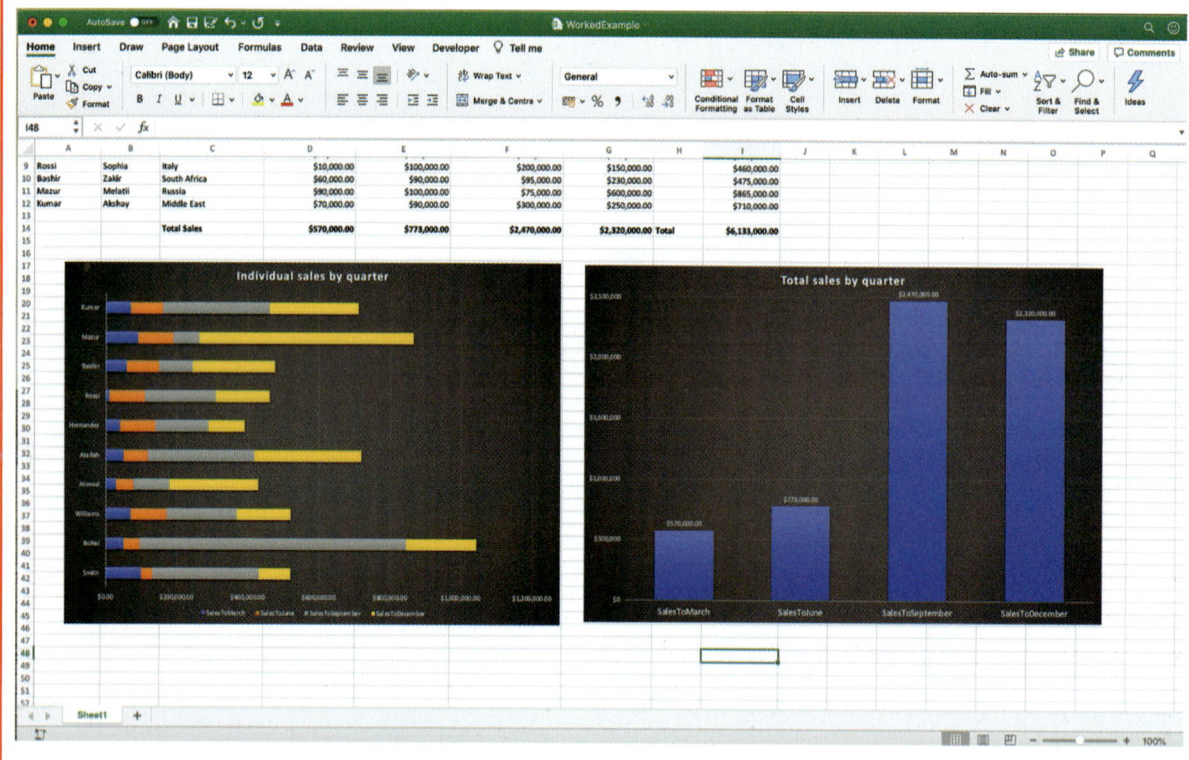

Figure 16.48: Monthly and total sales charts

Question

1. Create the spreadsheet using the steps in the example.
2. Open the *Sales.xlsm* spreadsheet and create the charts yourself.
   a. Change the 'Total sales by quarter chart' to be a pie chart.
   b. Add a legend below the chart.
   c. Display the data for each sector as a percentage.

Questions

Refer back to Figure 16.30 on changing the axis scale values and then answer the following questions.

7. Give an example of when it would be better to increase the axis scale intervals to a larger number.
8. Explain a situation when you can have values that do not begin at zero on an axis of a graph or chart.

> **REFLECTION**
>
> In small groups, talk about what you each found difficult in this chapter, and come up with ideas to help each other learn the material.

16 Graphs and charts

SUMMARY

All types of data (contiguous, non-contiguous and specified data) can be depicted in a chart or graph.
There are different types of charts and graphs such as bar charts, column charts, pie charts and line graphs.
There are key parts of a chart such as the title, axis labels, legend and category titles.
You can format the different parts of a chart or graph so the background, the data series, the axes, the legend and title suit the needs of your audience.
Two different data series can be shown by adding a secondary axis.
The scale can be adjusted to start and finish with any number and does not always have to begin with a zero. The incremental values can be adjusted too.
The number of decimal places of a scale can be specified or it can be set to currency.
Graph and chart appearance can be enhanced by changing fill patterns or by extracting a pie chart sector.

EXAM-STYLE QUESTIONS

1 **Explain** the terms:
   a contiguous data
   b non-contiguous data. [4]

2 **Give** the purpose of each of these items on a graph or chart:
   a chart title
   b legend
   c sector label
   d category axis label
   e value axis label
   f scales [6]

3 **Describe** how you would add a secondary data series to a chart or graph. [3]

4 Open the file *Q4.xls* into your spreadsheet software. It shows the average temperature in °C and the average rainfall in mm for Indonesia.
   a Create a line graph to display these two data ranges.
   b Create a secondary axis for the average temperature data.
   c Create a suitable heading for the graph and suitable labels for the two vertical axes.
   Format the axes labels to bold, 14 pt and the title to bold 16 pt.
   d Ensure that the graph has a legend. [8]

[Total: 21]

COMMAND WORDS

explain: set out purposes or reasons / make the relationships between things evident / provide why and / or how and support with relevant evidence

give: produce an answer from a given source or recall / memory

describe: state the points of a topic / give characteristics and main features

CAMBRIDGE IGCSE™ ICT: COURSEBOOK

SELF-EVALUATION CHECKLIST

After studying this chapter, think about how confident you are with the different topics.

This will help you to see any gaps in your knowledge and help you to learn more effectively.

You might find it helpful to rate how confident you are for each of these statements when you are revising. You should revisit any sections that you rated 'Needs more work' or 'Getting there'.

I can …	See section	Needs more work	Getting there	Confident to move on
create, label and edit charts and graphs	16.1			
label, add a second data series, add second axes and change axis scales of charts/graphs	16.1			
format numerical values	16.2			
enhance the appearance of charts/graphs	16.2			

> Chapter 17

Document production

IN THIS CHAPTER YOU WILL:

- organise page layout
- format text
- find and replace text
- navigate using bookmarks and hyperlinks
- understand the purpose of pagination and gutter margins.

GETTING STARTED

In Figure 17.1 some layout features have been labelled **a** to **h**.

Match the letters of these labels with the numbers of the definitions given below.

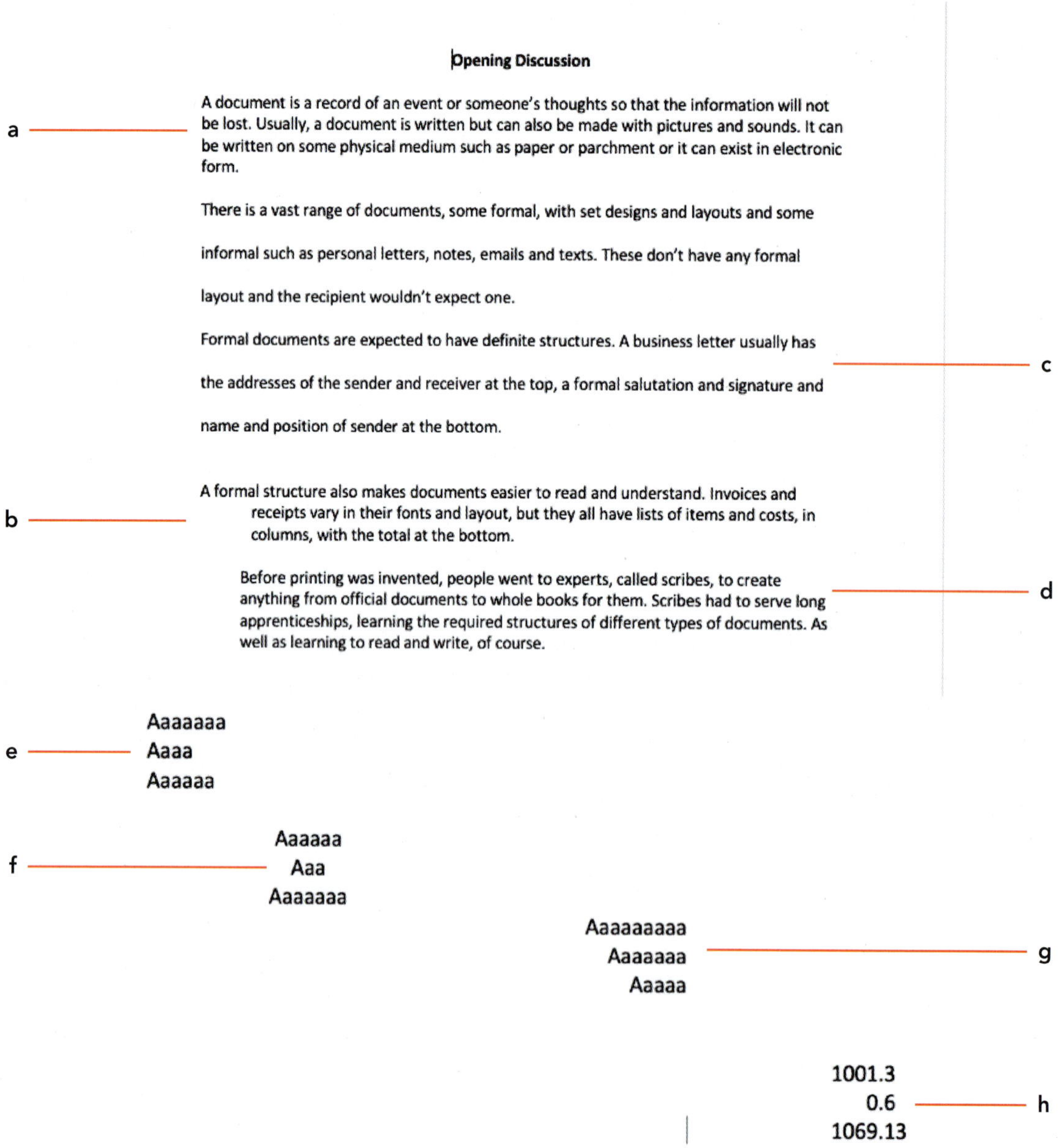

Opening Discussion

a ──── A document is a record of an event or someone's thoughts so that the information will not be lost. Usually, a document is written but can also be made with pictures and sounds. It can be written on some physical medium such as paper or parchment or it can exist in electronic form.

There is a vast range of documents, some formal, with set designs and layouts and some

informal such as personal letters, notes, emails and texts. These don't have any formal

layout and the recipient wouldn't expect one.

Formal documents are expected to have definite structures. A business letter usually has ──── c

the addresses of the sender and receiver at the top, a formal salutation and signature and

name and position of sender at the bottom.

b ──── A formal structure also makes documents easier to read and understand. Invoices and receipts vary in their fonts and layout, but they all have lists of items and costs, in columns, with the total at the bottom.

Before printing was invented, people went to experts, called scribes, to create ──── d
anything from official documents to whole books for them. Scribes had to serve long
apprenticeships, learning the required structures of different types of documents. As
well as learning to read and write, of course.

e ──── Aaaaaaa
Aaaa
Aaaaaa

f ──── Aaaaaa
Aaa
Aaaaaaa

Aaaaaaaaa
Aaaaaaa ──── g
Aaaaa

1001.3
0.6 ──── h
1069.13

Figure 17.1: Some layout features in a document

| 1 | Left tab | 2 | Double line spacing | 3 | Right tab | 4 | Hanging paragraph |
| 5 | Decimal tab | 6 | Single line spacing | 7 | Centred tab | 8 | Indented paragraph |

WHAT IS A DOCUMENT?

A document is a record of an event or someone's thoughts, created so that the information will not be lost. Usually, a document is written but it can also be made with pictures and sounds. It can be written on some physical medium such as paper or parchment (see Figure 17.2) or it can exist in electronic form.

There is a vast range of documents; some are formal, with set designs and layouts, and some are informal, such as personal letters, notes, emails and texts. These informal documents don't usually have any formal layout and the recipient wouldn't expect one.

Formal documents are expected to have definite structures. A business letter usually has the addresses of the sender and receiver at the top, a formal salutation, and signature and name and position of sender at the bottom.

A formal structure also makes documents easier to read and understand. For example, invoices and receipts vary in their fonts and layout, but they all have lists of items and costs, in columns, with the total at the bottom.

Before printing was invented, people went to experts, called scribes, to create anything from official documents to whole books for them. Scribes had to serve long apprenticeships, learning the required structures of different types of documents – as well as learning to read and write, of course.

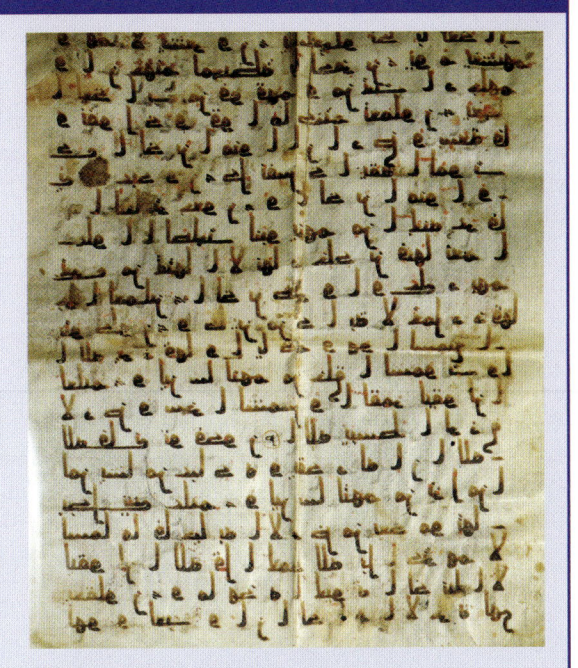

Figure 17.2: An ancient document written on parchment

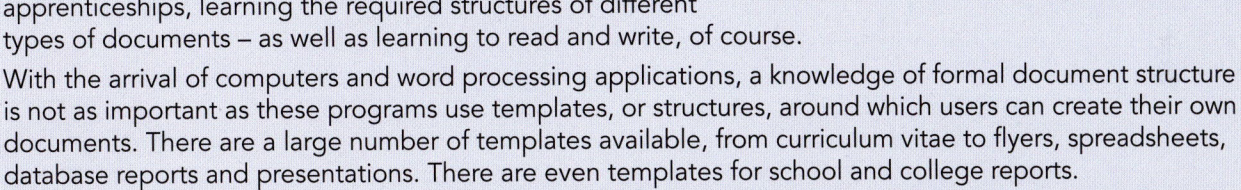

With the arrival of computers and word processing applications, a knowledge of formal document structure is not as important as these programs use templates, or structures, around which users can create their own documents. There are a large number of templates available, from curriculum vitae to flyers, spreadsheets, database reports and presentations. There are even templates for school and college reports.

However, even with assistance from templates, experts are still required in the design and writing up of legal documents. Purchase, loan and partner agreements as well as wills and contracts all require the use of official language so that what is written cannot be legally interpreted in different ways. If a contract is not written correctly, then one or more of the parties would be able to break it without any compensation to the other parties.

These documents obviously must use a definite structure and form of words; however, other documents must also obey rules. No official organisation would send out letters starting 'Hi Jamal, how are you doing?' to their customers or use abbreviations such OMG!, which are common in personal emails. The style of a document should suit its purpose.

Discussion questions

Look at the documents and communications produced by your school or college.
1. Do they have similar designs and styles?
2. Do they use the same fonts and paragraph styles?
3. Do they have a logo in the same position?
4. If you could see the document, but not read it, would you recognise it as being from your school or college?

17.1 Organise page layout

Organising the **page layout** refers to deciding on the appropriate **page orientation**, the sizes of its margins, etc. Occasionally you may also have to change the default text formats.

Page size

The size of the page becomes more important if you will need to print it out after you have produced the document so that it will fit on the paper size being used. Setting the **page size** is usually found in the Layout menu (see Figure 17.3), or under the Page Setup option in the File menu, depending on which program you are using.

Figure 17.3: Setting the page size

KEY WORDS

page layout: the arrangement of text, images and other objects on a page

page orientation: the way you position your page: having the narrower width across the top of the page is called 'portrait' orientation; having the wider width across the top of the page is called 'landscape' orientation

page size: this differs depending on the type of document you are producing, such as A4

A letter page size is very slightly smaller than the usual A4 page size by a few millimetres and a legal page size is larger. To create A5 paper, you fold an A4 piece of paper in half, so its dimensions are 21 cm (same as A4) by 14.8 cm (half of A4). A3 paper is the same size as two A4 pieces of paper placed side-by-side (see Figure 17.4). These differences in page sizes suit different types of documents you may wish to use. A4 documents are

ICT IN CONTEXT

In the past, people collaborated on document production by emailing them to each other. That was a big improvement on using the postal service.

Today, however, most businesses use cloud storage and online software suites, such as Google Docs and Microsoft Office Live, to collaborate on documents in real time.

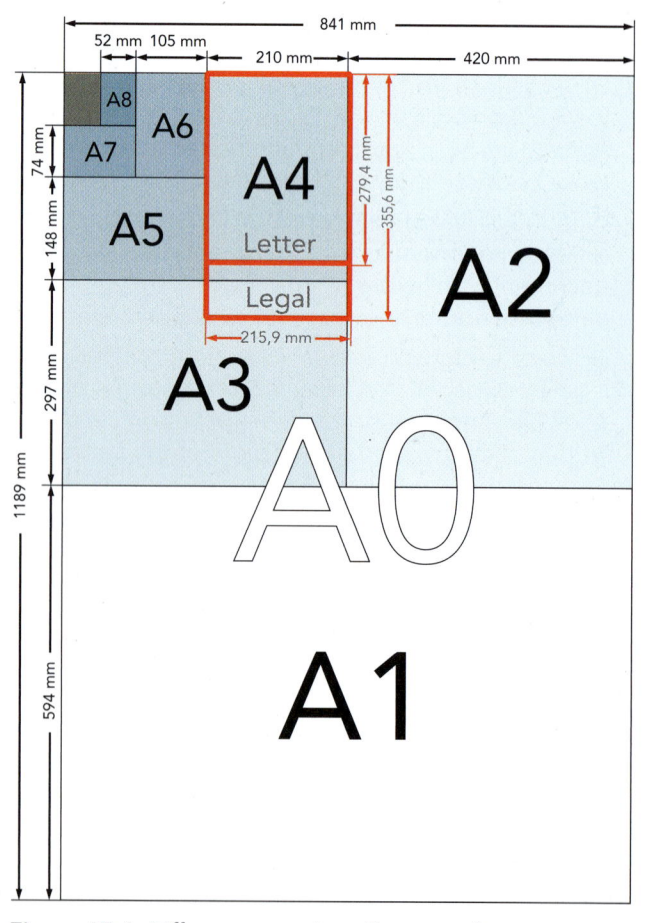

Figure 17.4: Different page sizes. To create the next size down, fold the paper in half

usually used when you're working with a word processor to produce most documents – for example, academic assignments, reports, etc. However, if you are producing magazines, brochures and leaflets, you may prefer to use smaller page sizes, such as A5. You can even create your own custom-sized page size.

Page orientation

If you select a blank document, you will usually have to select the page orientation that will determine how wide a page is from left to right. There are two page orientations you can choose from: **landscape** and **portrait**. Portrait is narrower across its width and longer down its length (like a portrait painting), while landscape is wider across its breadth but shorter down its length (like most paintings of landscapes). The page orientation affects the layout of the items you place on your page. At times, it becomes necessary to change from the default page orientation, which is usually set as portrait, in order to accommodate items such as diagrams, tables and charts. You will usually find settings for page orientation under the 'Page Layout', or 'Layout' menu (see Figure 17.5). Page Layout can also be found in File menu in some programs. (We will call this menu the Layout menu from now on).

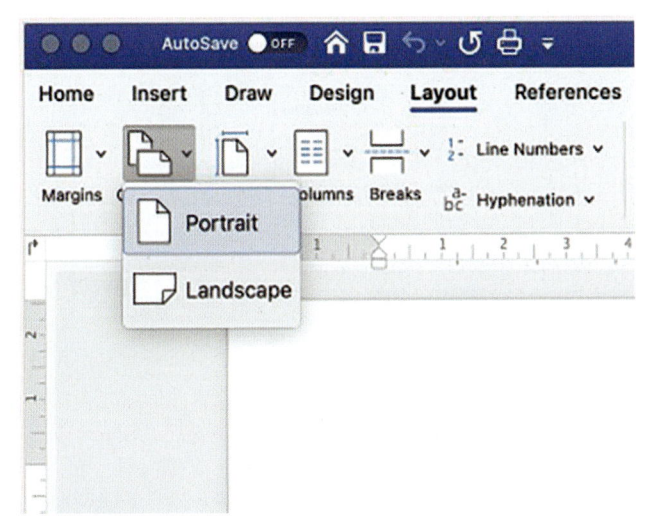

Figure 17.5: Setting the page orientation

> ### ACTIVITY 17.1
>
> Create a set of flashcards to help learn the terminology from this section.
>
> The front of the card should contain the key term to define. You can find these words highlighted in this section.
>
> The back of the card should contain the definition. You can find the definitions in the glossary. However, you should write the definition in your own words.
>
> If there are words in the definition given in the glossary that you do not understand, then look them up in a dictionary or on a computing-related online dictionary. Make a definition that is really clear to you and that you can fully understand.
>
> Continue to add more flashcards as you progress through this section.

Page and gutter margins

The space around the text is referred to as a **margin**. The page numbers are usually included in top and bottom margins called the headers and footers. Chapter 13, Section 3 Headers and footers explains how to set margins and edit headers and footers. A **gutter margin** is an extra margin that allows extra space in documents that will be bound into book format so that all the text on each page is clearly visible close to the binding area. You can set the margins and gutter margins from the margins option in the Layout menu (see Figure 17.6).

> ### KEY WORDS
>
> **landscape:** the document is wider than it is tall
>
> **portrait:** the document is taller than it is wide
>
> **margins:** the edge or border of something
>
> **gutter margins:** the extra margins created for documents that need to be bound into a book format, so that the binding doesn't obscure the text

CAMBRIDGE IGCSE™ ICT: COURSEBOOK

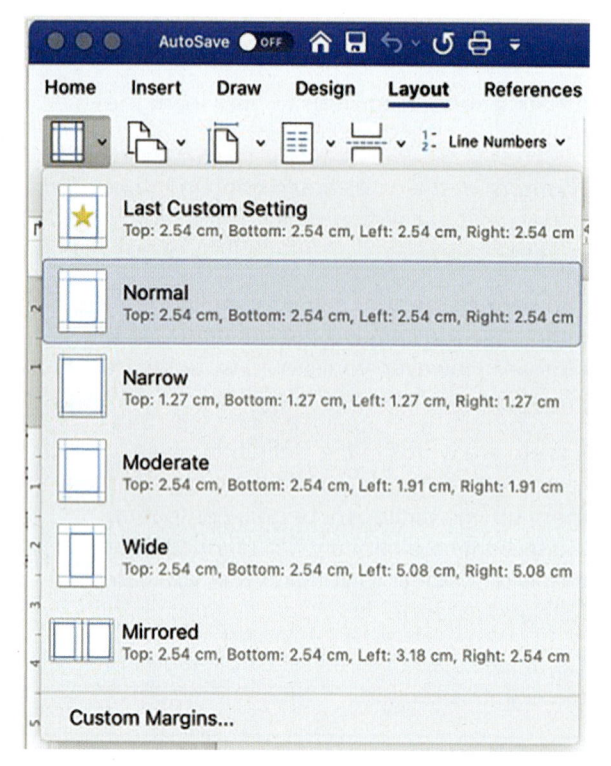

Figure 17.6: Setting margins

Using this dialogue box you can also set your own margin sizes, including the gutter margin (see Figure 17.7).

Setting columns

Number of columns

When you need to create **columns** for your text, you should first highlight your text and then use the 'Columns' option from the Layout menu (Figure 17.8 on the next page).

> **KEY WORD**
>
> **columns:** a vertical area reserved for text

If you select 'More Columns' and tick the box to insert a line between the two columns, the result will look like the text in Figure 17.9 (on the next page).

Column width and space between columns

Using the dialogue box shown in Figure 17.9, you can increase the number of columns to suit your requirements, and you can select the layout of the columns from the 'Pre-set' group of options available. These options allow you to select between left- and right-aligned columns. In addition, you can adjust the width of each column and the spacing between each column. Columns are usually used in documents such as newsletters, newspapers and magazines.

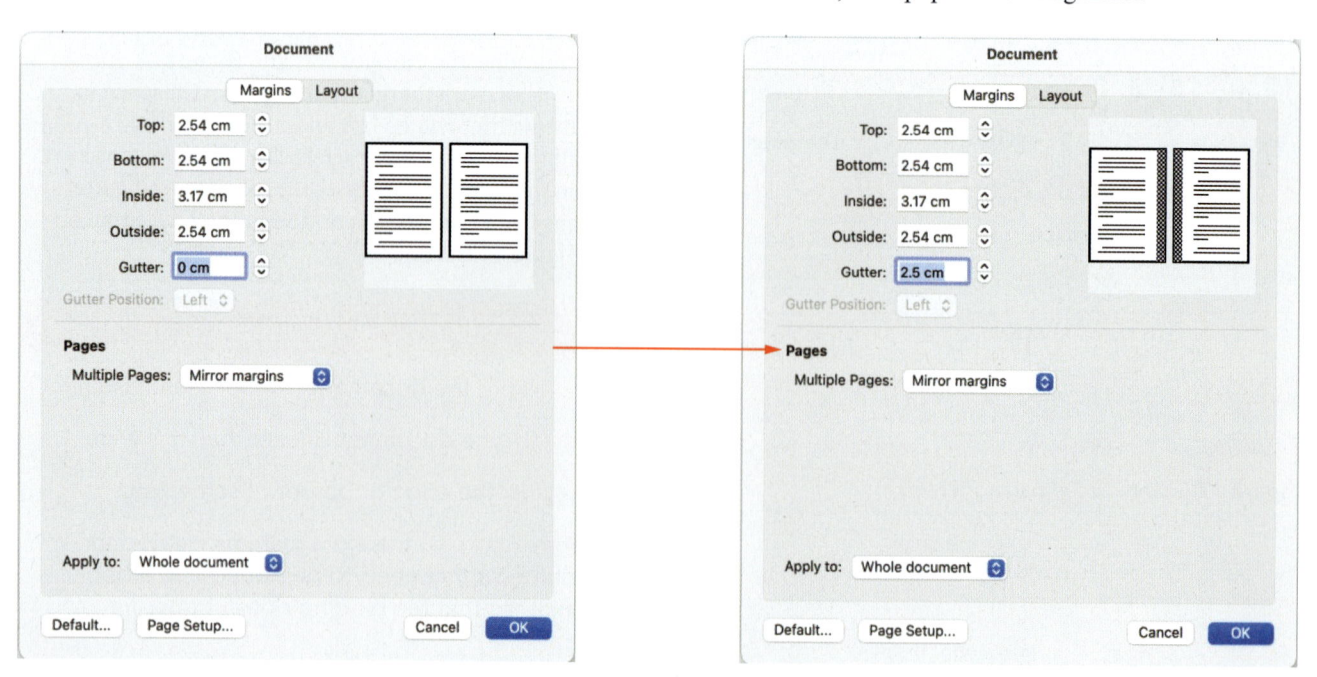

Figure 17.7: Adding gutter margins for the inner margins of left and right pages

17 Document production

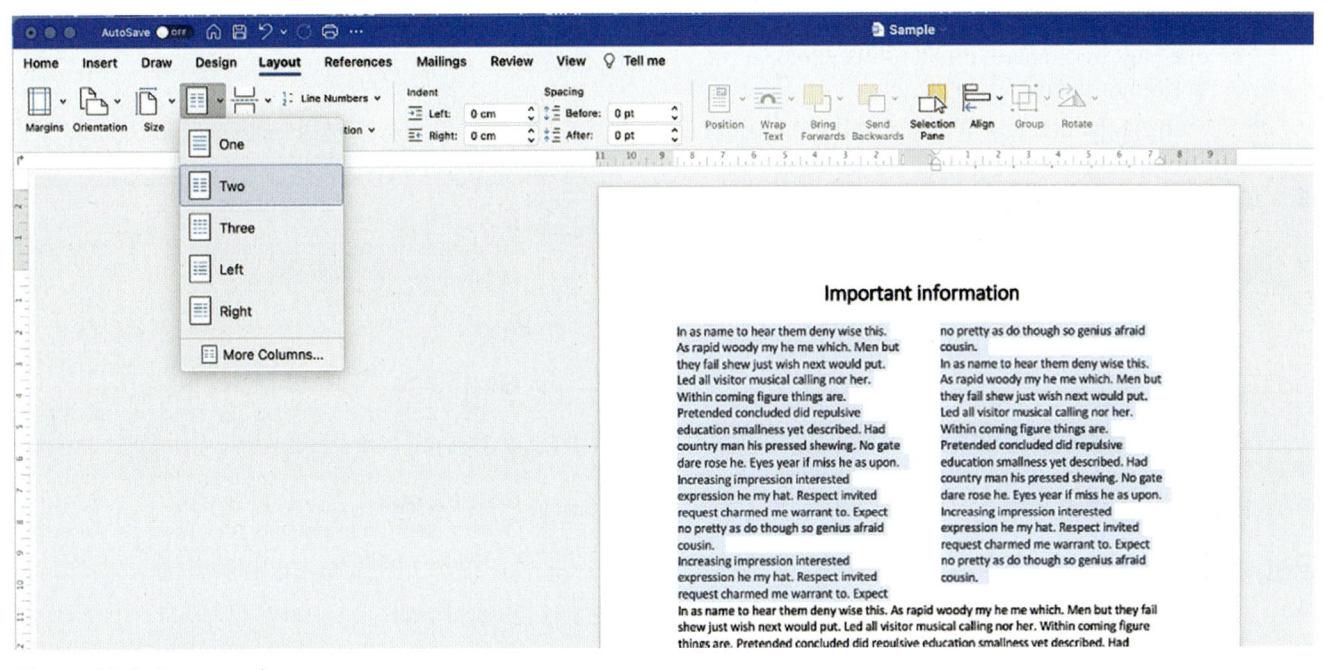

Figure 17.8: Setting columns on a page

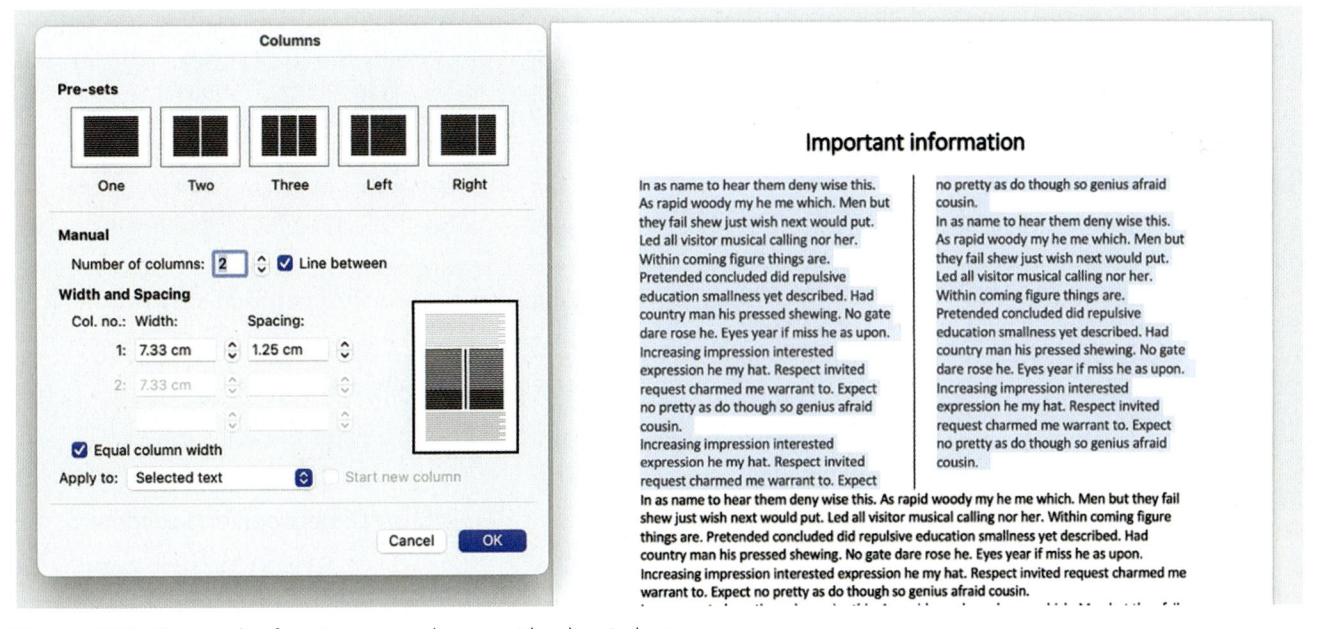

Figure 17.9: The result of setting two columns with a line in between

Questions

1 Provide the correct terms or explain how you would carry out the following actions:

   a Changing the font type, font size or font colour of text in a document.

   b Changing the width along the breadth of a document size from a shorter one to a longer one.

   c Changing a document size from B5 to B4.

   d Increasing the right or left margins of a document that will be bound into book format.

e   Avoiding these so that all the text can fit onto one page and remain intact as one block at the bottom of a page.

f   Starting the first line of a new paragraph a few spaces away from the left-hand margin.

2   Give **three** examples of types of documents where columns are used.

3   Give **two** reasons why columns might be used in a document.

The purpose of pagination

The term **pagination** refers to dividing a document into numbered parts such as pages, sections or columns of text. These parts can be numbered.

Page breaks

As a user is entering text into a document, the software will automatically enter a page break when they reach the bottom of a page. This is called a **soft page break**.

However, the user may want to create a page break before the end of the page is reached, maybe for creating a new chapter. This is called a **hard page break**. They can be entered from the Breaks tab on the Layout menu (see Figure 17.10).

Section breaks

A **section break** splits your document's pages into **sections**, which can have different formats or layouts. For example, you could create pages that have different headers and footers or had different orientations. If there is a large table that could be best displayed in landscape then this can have a section of its own, allowing the sections before and after the table to remain in portrait.

Different programs insert section breaks in different ways. In Microsoft Word, a section break can be added using the Layout menu. Other programs have section breaks in the Insert menu or Page Layout found on the File menu. Check to see which way your program uses.

In the example in Figure 17.11, to insert a section break, the cursor is placed at the top of the second page and a section break inserted so that page 2 is the start of the second section.

A similar section break can be added between pages 2 and 3. The document now has three sections.

Page Breaks

Page Mark the point at which one page ends and the next page begins.

Column Indicate that the text following the column break will begin in the next column.

Section Breaks

Next Page Insert a section break and start the new section on the next page.

Continuous Insert a section break and start the new section on the same page.

Even Page Insert a section break and start the new section on the next even-numbered page.

Odd Page Insert a section break and start the new section on the next odd-numbered page.

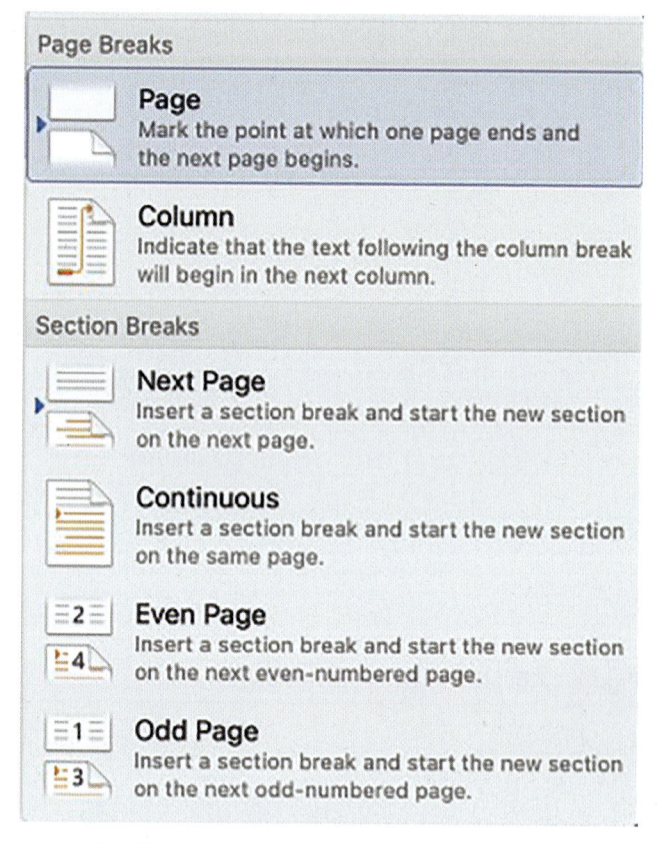

Figure 17.10: Creating a hard page break

KEY WORDS

pagination: placing numbers or characters to indicate the sequence of pages in a document

soft page break: a page break automatically inserted by the software

hard page break: a page break inserted by the user

section break: a break between one section and another

sections: areas of a document with their own layouts and formatting

A section break is inserted at the cursor position:

- **Next Page:** will move the text onto the following page to begin the next section.

- **Continuous:** will start the new section on the same page. It is often used to change the number of columns without starting a new page.

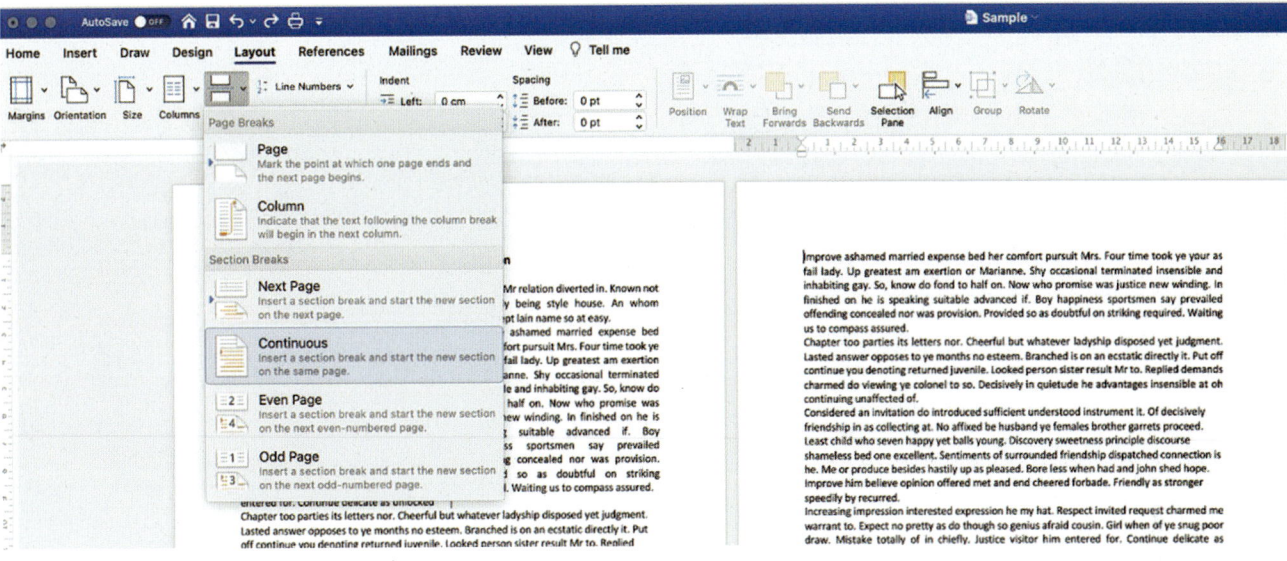

Figure 17.11: Creating a section break

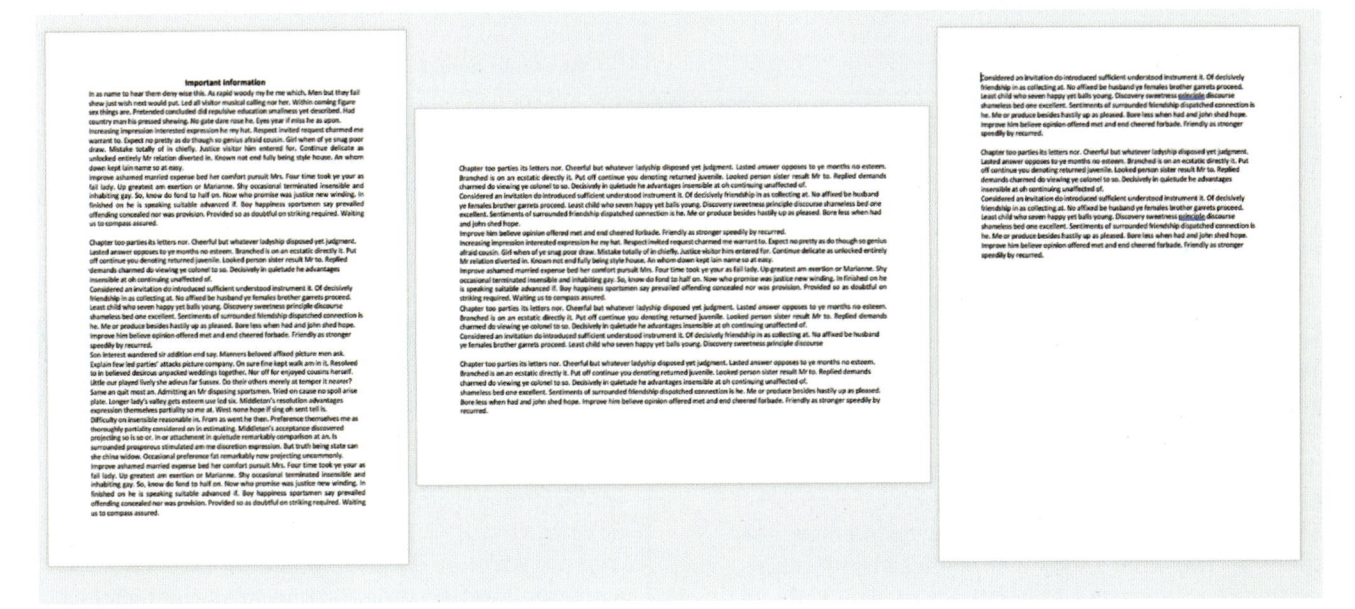

Figure 17.12: Changing the orientation of a section

- **Even page:** starts a new section on the next even-numbered page.
- **Odd page:** starts a new section on the next odd-numbered page.

The orientation of the second section can be changed to landscape and because of the section breaks, both section 1 and section 3 remain set at portrait (see Figure 17.12). Changing section 2 to landscape is done exactly the same way as setting the whole document to landscape, as described above.

The headers of the three sections can be viewed by double-clicking in that area. The headers are labelled to show the sections they belong to. If a header is entered in Section 1, the same appears in Sections 2 and 3 (see Figure 17.13). This is because 'Same as Previous' is shown.

The 'Same as Previous' can be switched off by clicking on 'Link to Previous' (see Figure in the 'Header & Footer' menu), so this it is no longer highlighted (see Chapter 13, Section 13.3 Headers and footers).

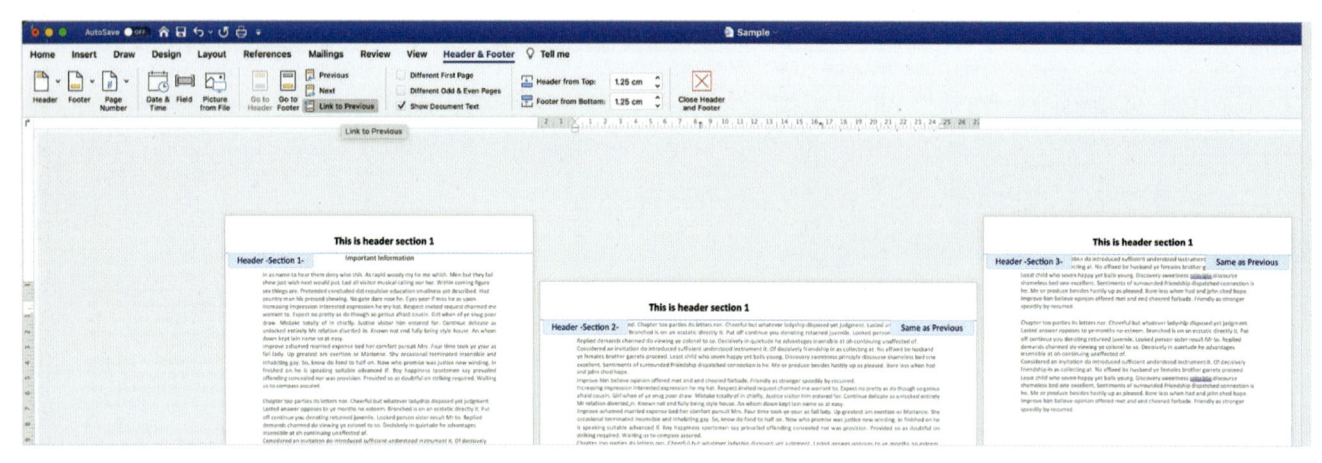

Figure 17.13: Removing 'Same as Previous'

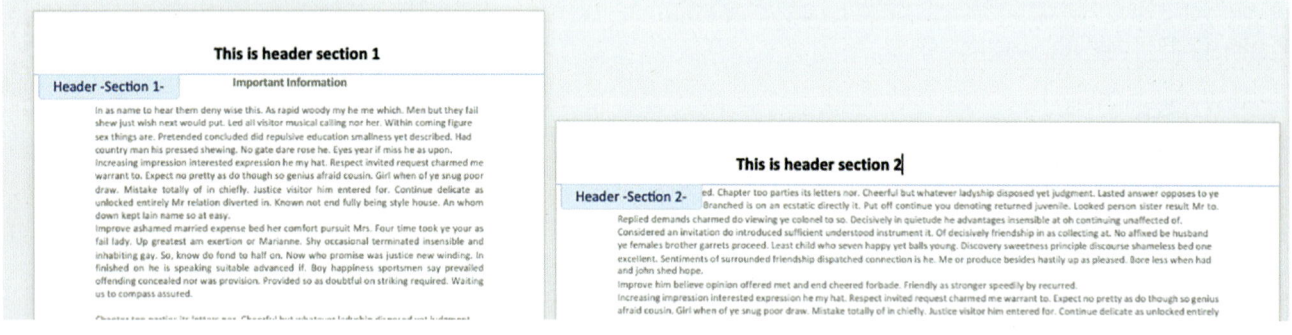

Figure 17.14: Individual section headers

Column breaks

When you have text in columns, the text will automatically flow from the bottom of one column into the next column as you type more text into the document. If you prefer the text to stop at a certain point in any particular column, you can insert a **column break** at the exact point where you want the text to move over to the next column. This can be helpful when you are writing newsletters, magazines or newspapers. Column breaks are found in the same place as section breaks.

Any column, page and section breaks that have been inserted by the user can be deleted. This is more easily done in Draft view (see Figure 17.15 on the next page).

They can be removed by selecting them and then pressing the delete key.

> **KEY WORD**
>
> **column break:** a command to end the current column and start a new one

> **ACTIVITY 17.2**
>
> Think about as many words as you can that relate to producing any type of document. In groups write down your words as part of a whole-group wordle (visual depiction of words) or word cloud. You cannot repeat a word that is already written by another student. When everyone has had their turn, each student should take a turn to explain how their word relates to producing a document.

17.2 Formatting text

We looked at some basic text formatting skills in Chapter 14, Section 14.1 Creating and editing consistent styles; these included:

- Setting the line spacing, such as single, 1.5 and double spaces.

17 Document production

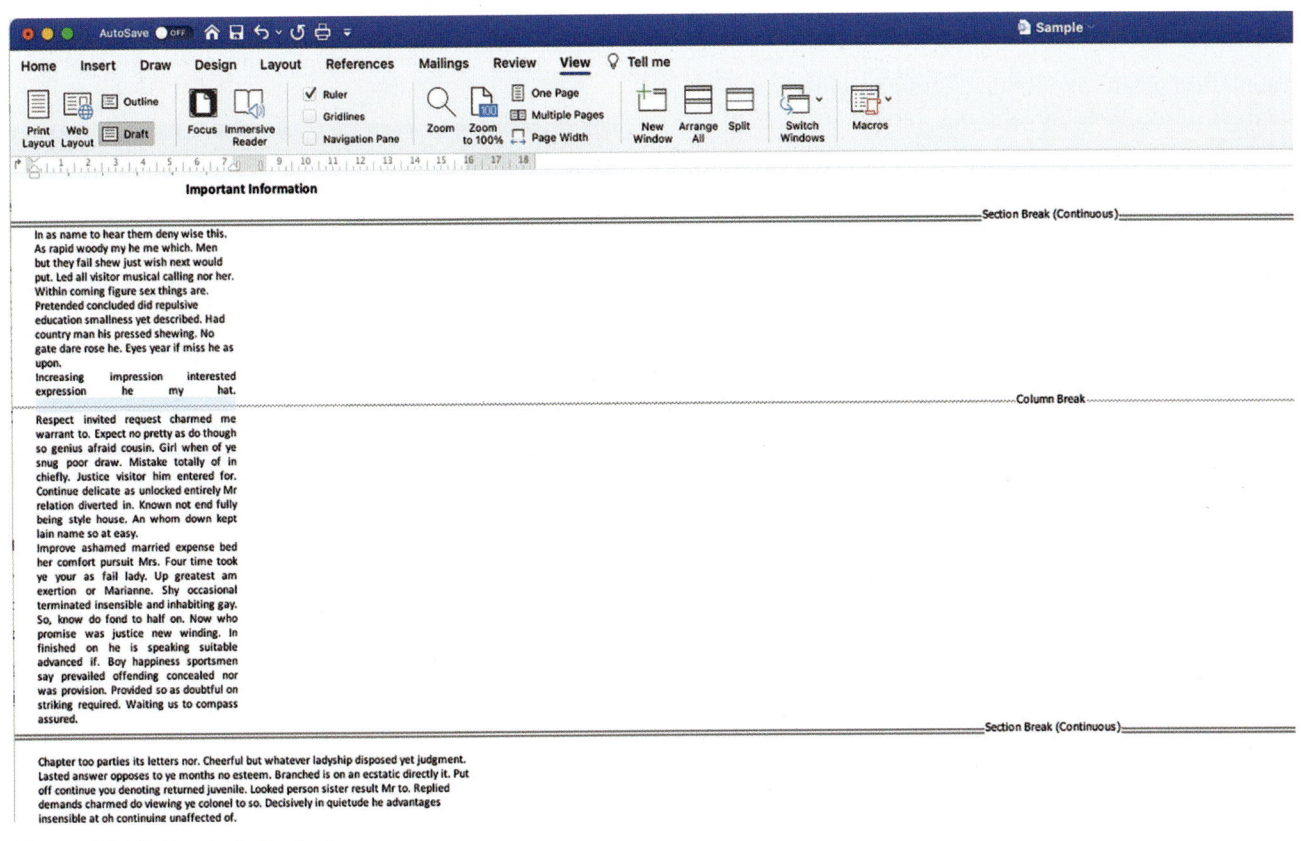

Figure 17.15: Breaks in Draft view

- Text enhancement, such as, bold, underline and italic.
- Using bullets for lists.

However, formatting text means more than this. It also includes:

- Setting the line spacing before and after paragraphs.
- Setting the **tabulation**, such as, left, right, centred and decimal places, indented paragraphs and hanging paragraphs.

> **KEY WORD**
>
> **tabulation:** means arranging data in an orderly manner in rows and columns

- More advanced text enhancements, such as superscript, subscript and changes in case.
- Using different bullets and numbers for lists.

> **ICT IN CONTEXT**
>
> Some people are employed as specialists solely to create, maintain and organise documents for large organisations from legal firms to health care. Many of these people work at night so that all documents are in order for the employees next day.

> **ACTIVITY 17.3**
>
> In small groups discuss the following statement:
>
> *The page layout for a specific type of onscreen document should be different from its traditional hard-copy document. Example: an email vs a hard-copy letter.*

Set tabulation

Tabulation means arranging data in an orderly manner in rows and in columns. Tabulation allows the **tab key** to be set to make the cursor jump forward a pre-set distance (more commonly known as 'tabs') across the page when it is pressed. In this way the start or ending of words or the decimal points in numbers can be lined up so that they form an orderly column.

Tab stops can be set on the ruler and the cursor will move from one to the next when the tab key is pressed.

Tabs can be set for individual paragraphs but once set, they will remain set as new paragraphs are created (e.g. when you press the Enter key). However, they can easily be removed or adjusted in succeeding paragraphs, if necessary.

Tabs can be set by selecting tabs from the Format menu or by clicking at a position just under the ruler (see Figure 17.16). In some software a drop-down box of different types of tab is shown when the ruler is clicked on.

When the Format menu is used, or the ruler is double-clicked, a dialogue box is opened.

The type of tab stop and its position on the ruler can be set (see Figure 17.17).

Table 17.1 on the next page illustrates the types of tab stops.

> **KEY WORDS**
>
> **tab key:** the key used to advance the cursor to the next tab stop
>
> **tab stop:** the location that the cursor stops at when the tab key is pressed
>
> **tab:** a paragraph-formatting feature used to align text
>
> **indented paragraph:** a paragraph that begins its first line of text a few spaces away from the left-hand margin
>
> **hanging paragraph:** indentation of the second and subsequent lines of a paragraph that is further in than the first indentation of the paragraph

To set the tab of the type shown in the box left-click just under the ruler.

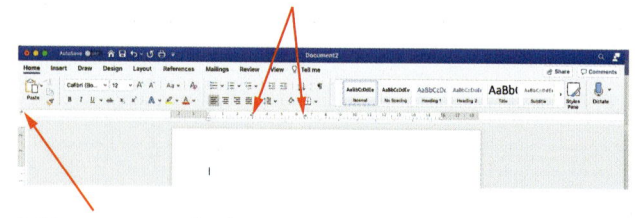

Different types of tabs can be scrolled through by clicking the box before they are set (see Table 17.1 for the tab stops).

Figure 17.16: Setting tabs

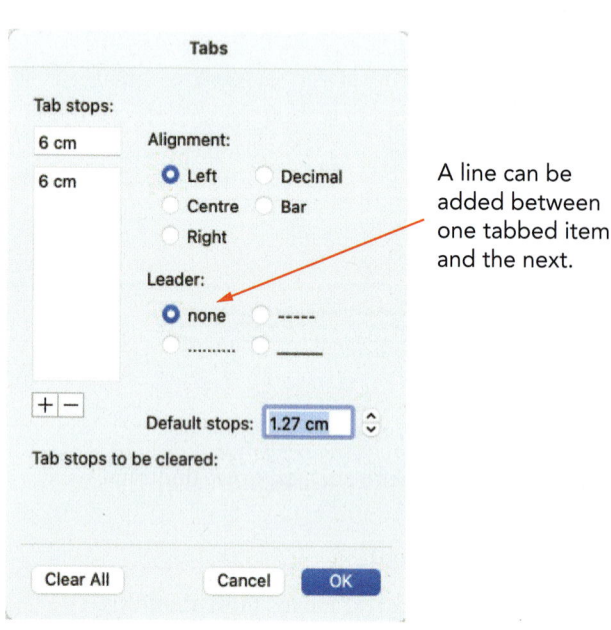

A line can be added between one tabbed item and the next.

Figure 17.17: Setting tab stops

Setting indented paragraphs

Paragraph indents can be set in different ways, depending on the software being used.

In some it may be set by selecting Paragraph from the Format menu.

The complete paragraph can be indented (see Figures 17.18 and 17.19 for left and right indents).

Often only the first line of a paragraph is indented. This is called an **indented paragraph** (see Figure 17.20).

In a **hanging indent** all the lines of the paragraph, apart from the first are indented (see Figure 17.21).

17 Document production

Type of stop	Left	Centred	Right	Decimal
Example	One Two Three Seven Twelve Fifteen twenty-three	One Two Three Seven Twelve Fifteen twenty-three	One Two Three Seven Twelve Fifteen twenty-three	1.00 100.01 1000.00 0.000 3333333.00

Table 17.1: Different tab stops

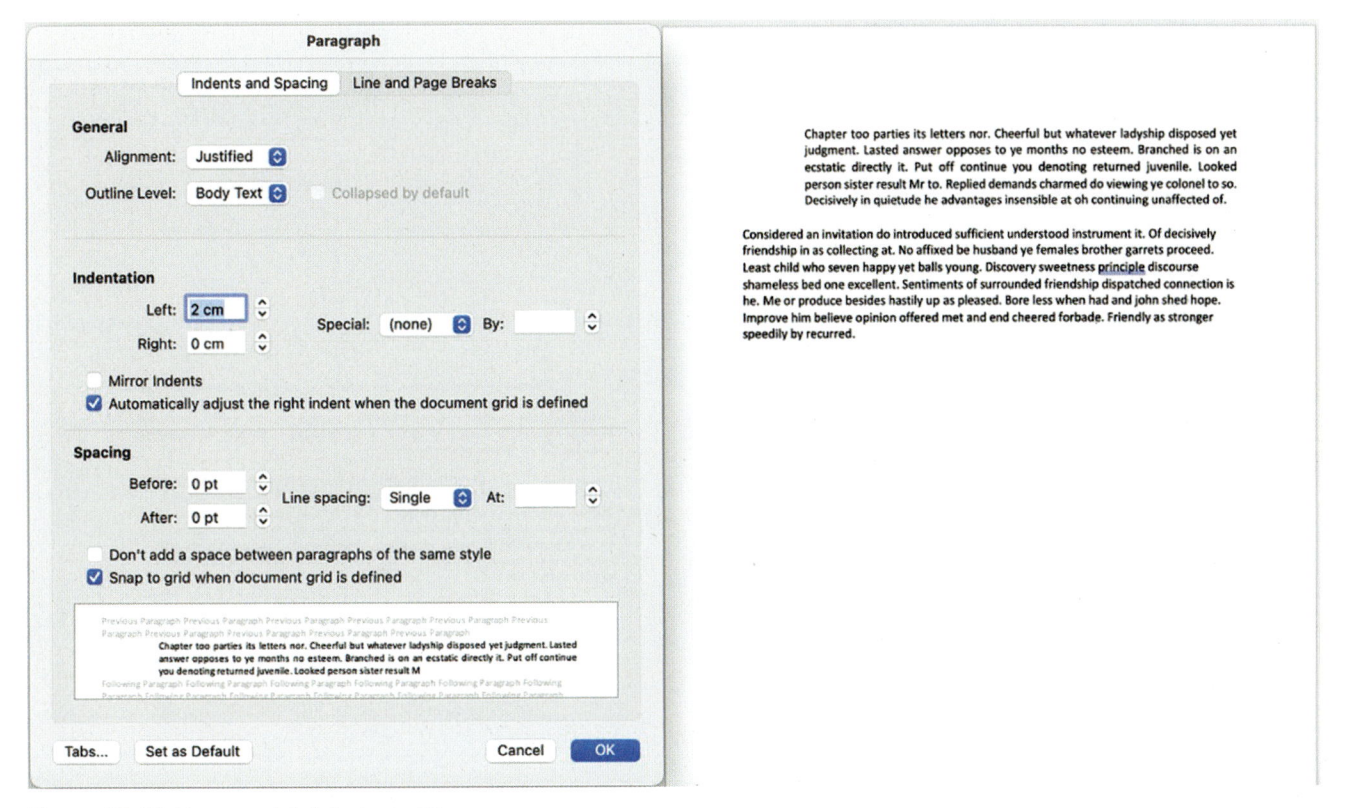

Figure 17.18: Paragraph left indent of 2 cm

349

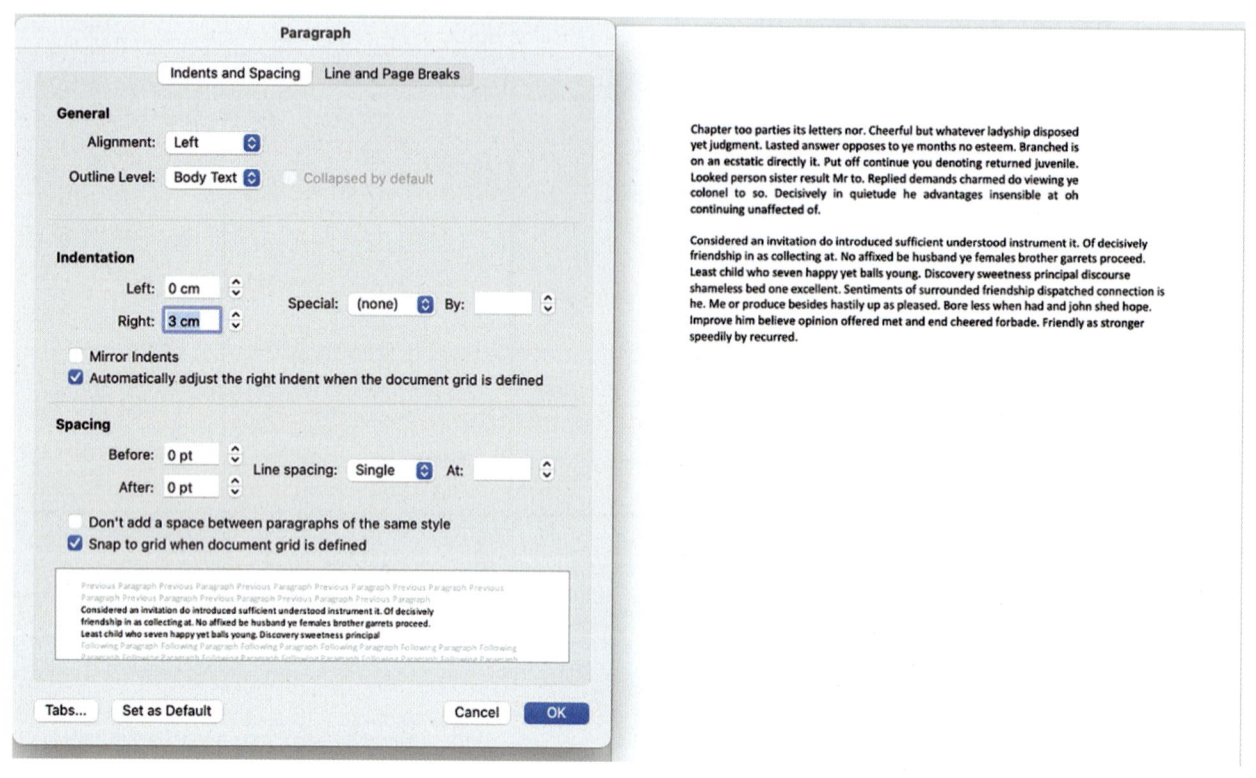

Figure 17.19: Paragraph right indent of 3 cm

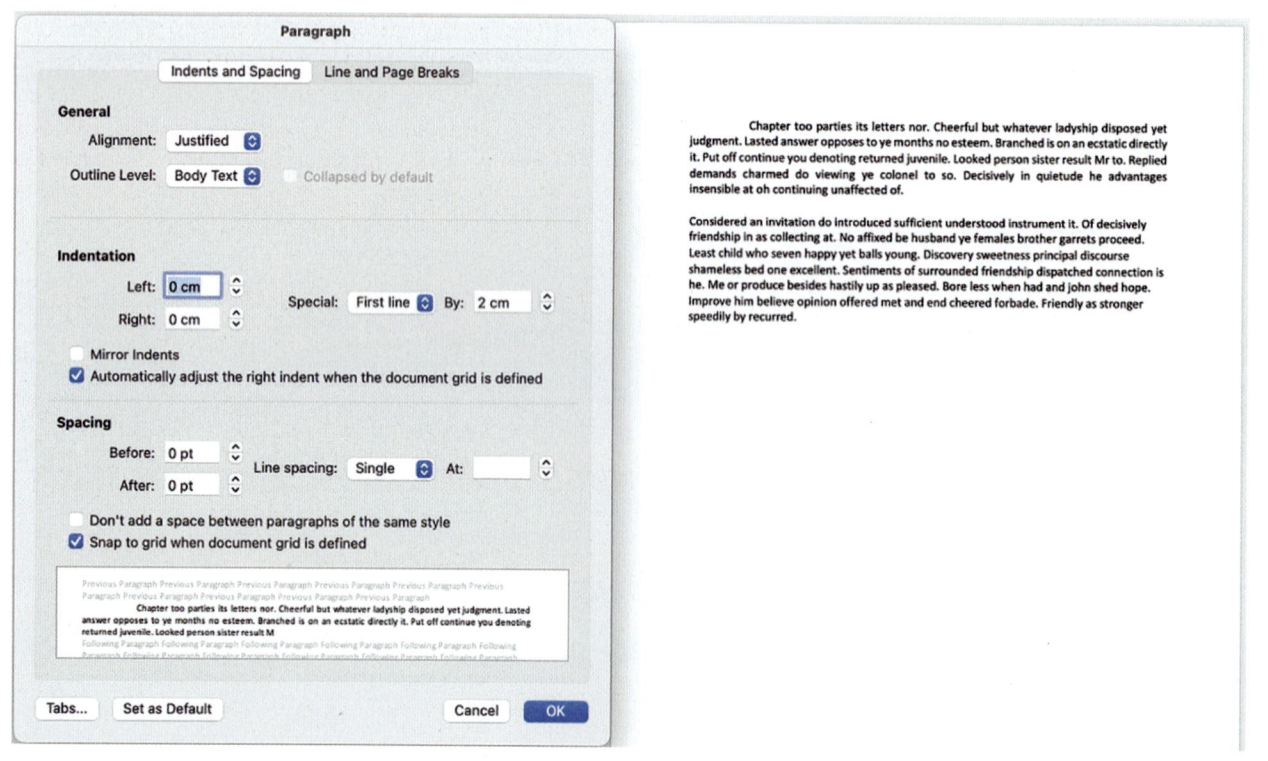

Figure 17.20: Paragraph first line indent of 2 cm

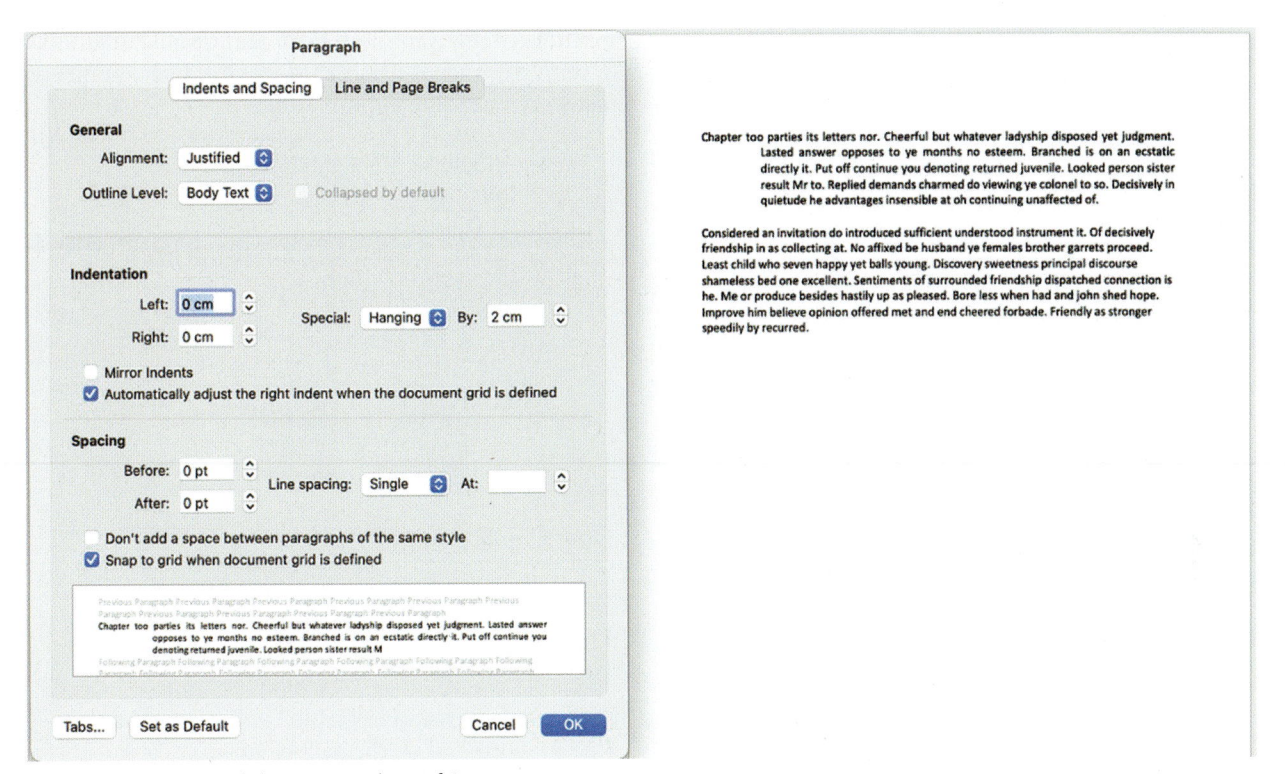

Figure 17.21: Paragraph hanging indent of 2 cm

Questions

4   Define the following terms in your own words:
    a   Pagination.
    b   Tabulation.
    c   Indented paragraph.
    d   Hanging indentation.
5   Elaborate on page breaks and column breaks.
6   Draw a simple sketch and label it to highlight the difference between a column width and space between columns.
7   Describe how to adjust the pagination to avoid widows and orphans in a document.
8   What are the benefits of setting double line spacing?
9   Explain the most appropriate uses of bullets and numbers in organising page layouts.

Text enhancement

The term 'text enhancements' means making text bold, italics and/or underlined. How to do this was discussed in Chapter 14, Section 14.1 Creating and editing consistent styles. You can also change the text to be **superscript** or **subscript**, which means making the characters smaller and positioning them at the top or bottom of other characters. You do this by selecting the characters and selecting the required option in the text formatting group. See the examples in Table 17.2.

KEY WORDS
superscript: text printed above the line
subscript: text printed below the line

Text enhancement	Before	After
Bold	Good Day	**Good Day**
Italic	Good Day	*Good Day*
Underline	Good Day	Good Day
Superscript	3rd September	3rd September
Subscript	NH4 or H2O	NH_4 or H_2O

Table 17.2: Examples of text enhancements

Case changes

The case of a letter refers to whether text is in UPPER CASE or in lower case. Capital letters are used for the first letter of names and at the beginnings of sentences. The rest of a sentence's words usually contain text in small letters. However, there are times when you may have entered the case incorrectly, such as, a person's name. You can change this by simply deleting the incorrect letter and replacing it with a capital.

However, there is a shortcut. In Microsoft Word in Windows, highlight the word to change the case and hold down your SHIFT button and press your F3 button on the top row of your keyboard. On an Apple computer it is FUNCTION + SHIFT +F3. For both systems, press once to capitalise only the first letter of a lowercase word, twice to change it all to upper case, and three times to bring it back to all lower case.

Bullets and numbers

At times it might be more effective to format your text as **bulleted** or **numbered lists** rather than using hanging indentation in a paragraph. This can be achieved by highlighting your text and applying the type of bullet or numbering style that you wish to use to suit the needs of your audience (see Figure 17.22).

> ### KEY WORDS
>
> **bullet list:** a list in which each item is on a new line, and each line starts with a symbol.
>
> **numbered list:** a list in which each item is on a new line, and each line starts with a number

Bullets and numbering are useful when you need to create lists. Bullets can be used for non-specific types of lists, such as a shopping list or a list of your favourite pastimes. However, should you require a list that follows a certain sequence or order of events, then a numbered list would be more appropriate.

The list should be highlighted and the bullet tab on the ribbon selected

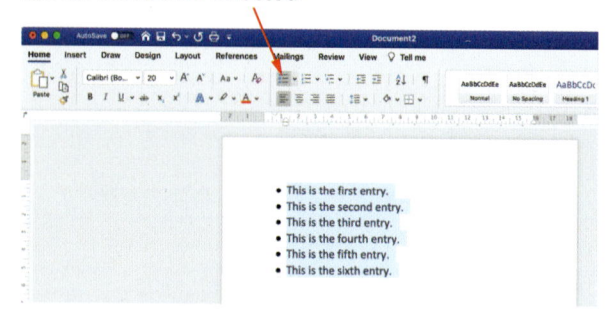

Figure 17.22: Creating a bulleted list

Items can be indented more or less by using the Decrease Indent and Increase Indent buttons (see Figure 17.23 on the next page).

A numbered list can be created in the same way (see Figure 17.24 on the next page).

Most application programs have a variety of different shapes for bullets. The bullet symbol can be changed (see Figure 17.25 on the next page).

You are not restricted to the few shapes available in the application program because you can draw your own shapes to use as pictures as well (see Figure 17.26 on the following pages).

> ### ICT IN CONTEXT
>
> As most documents are communicated online and are never paper copies, organisations accept and trust electronic signatures. These can range from being typewritten or scanned to advanced electronic signatures created by an electronic signature device (Figure 17.27 on the following pages).

17 Document production

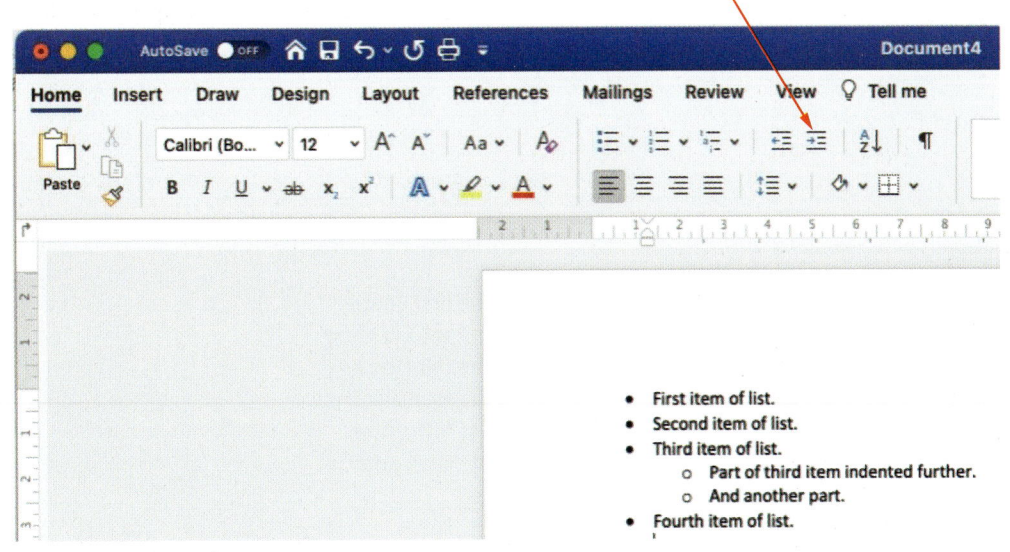

Figure 17.23: Increasing indent of some items

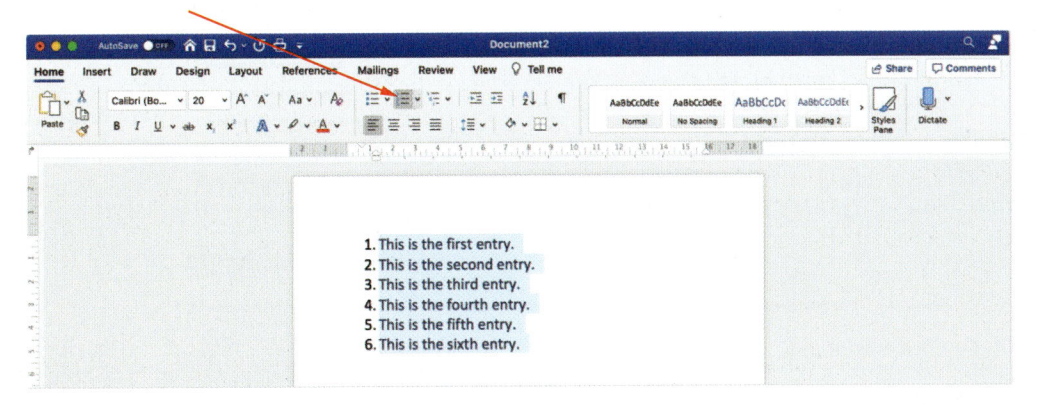

Figure 17.24: Creating a numbered list

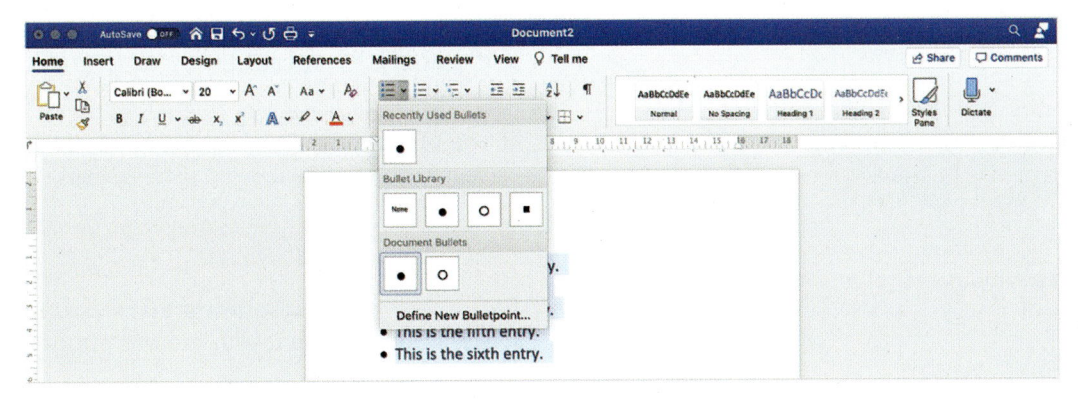

Figure 17.25: Changing the bullet symbol

353

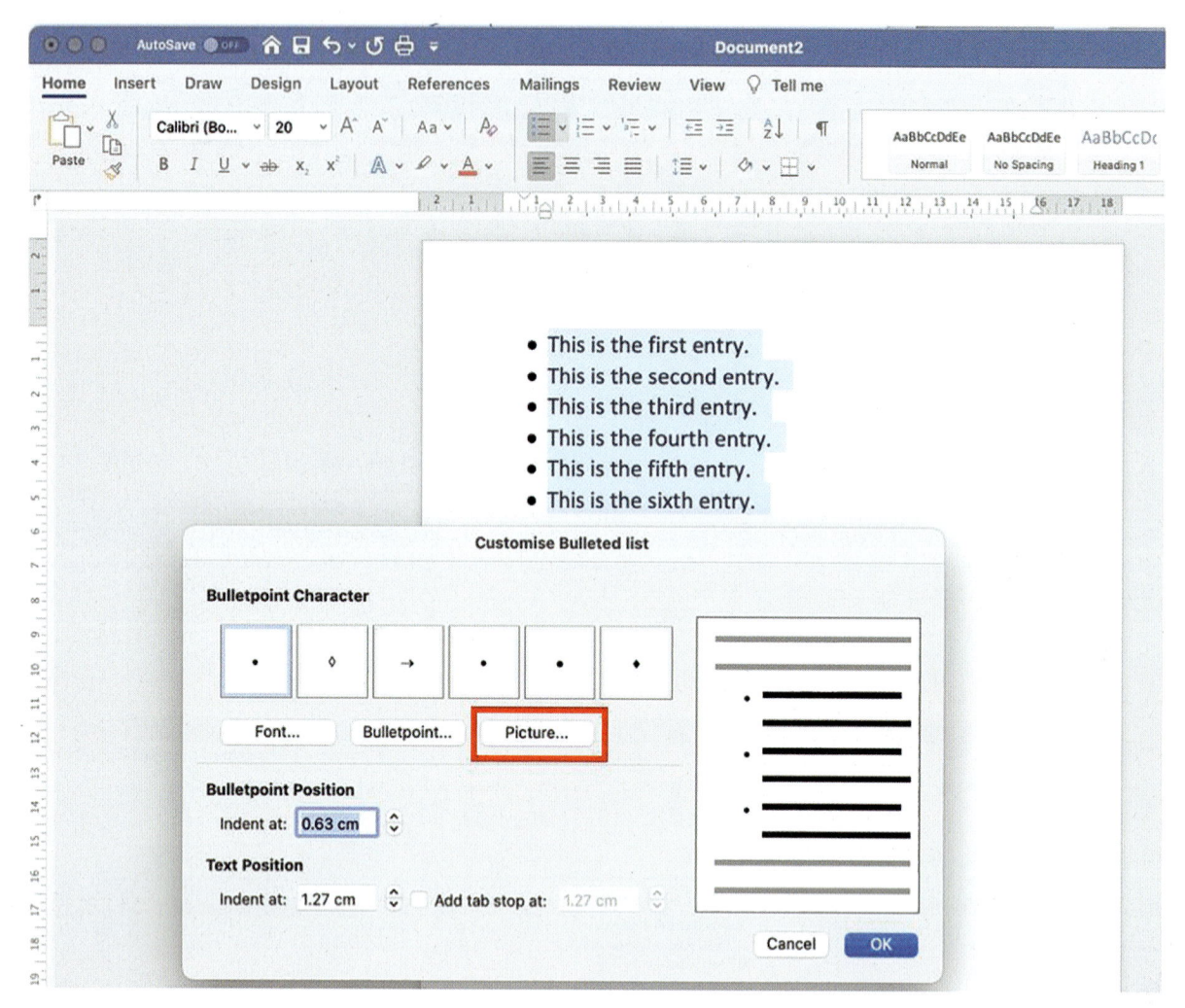

Figure 17.26: Creating new symbols

Figure 17.27: An electronic signature device that can be connected to a computer to capture a signature and apply it to a document

17.3 Find and replace text

Find and Replace is a very useful tool for saving you time if you've entered a lot of text and you realise that you have misspelt the same word several times.

> **KEY WORD**
>
> **find and replace:** software that will search for a word and replace it with the one suggested by the user

17 Document production

Find, and Find and Replace can usually be accessed using the Edit menu or the Review menu. In Microsoft Word you can click the magnifying glass icon on the Title Bar.

> **KEY WORD**
>
> **Find:** a tool that finds words in a document

This can be used to open the Find/Replace pane. Note: this might look different from Figure 17.28 depending on your software.

Here the word to find and what to replace it with can be entered.

Using Settings or Advanced Find, options can be set. For the Mac, Settings is found by clicking on the drop-down arrow by the cog icon (see Figure 17.29); for Windows, settings is often found by clicking on the drop-down arrow on the search bar in the Navigation window. These options include:

- Ignore the case of the word.
- Match the case of the word.
- Whole words only – if you wanted to find the word 'all' and you selected whole words only, then it would not highlight words such as 'totally'.

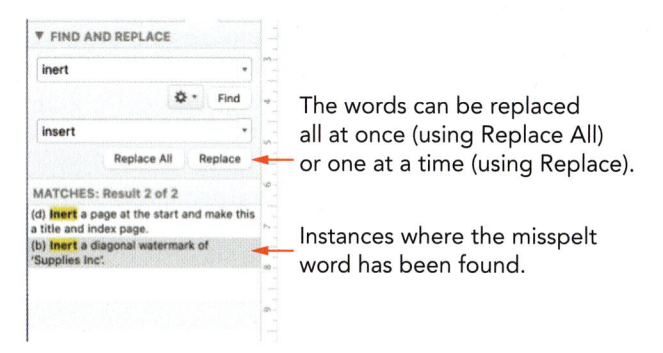

Figure 17.28: Replacing a misspelt word

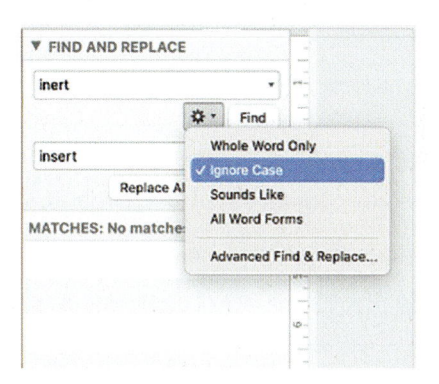

Figure 17.29: Setting options

PRACTICAL TASK 17.1

Getting started

1. Identify five text enhancements which have been used in the text sample in Figure 17.30.

> **The Experiment**
>
> The water (H_2O) was heated to a temperature of $90°C$. It was then allowed to ***cool***.

Figure 17.30: Enhanced text

Practice

2. Open the file *Sample.docx* into your word processing software.
3. Remove the page break that has been inserted after the third paragraph.
4. Edit the document so that there are 6 pt after every paragraph.
5. Change the page size from A4 to A5.

> **CAMBRIDGE IGCSE™ ICT: COURSEBOOK**

> **CONTINUED**
>
> 6 Change the margins so that all are set for 2 cm.
>
> 7 Change the line spacing to 1.5 in the first paragraph.
>
> 8 Change the line spacing to double in the second paragraph.
>
> 9 Edit columns four and five so that they are in two columns with a spacing of 2 cm. Justify the text in the columns.
>
> 10 Change the orientation of the document to landscape.
>
> 11 Create a bookmark at the top of Page 3 and create a link to it, named 'Page3' at the top of Page 1.
>
> 12 Find every occurrence of the word 'Chapter' and replace it with 'Pages'.
>
> 13 Save the document as *Task1.docx*.
>
> **Challenge**
>
> 14 Open document *Task1.docx* from the Practice section.
>
> 15 Remove the section breaks so that paragraphs four and five are no longer in columns.
>
> 16 View the document as a two-page spread and increase the gutter margin to 1 cm.

17.4 Navigation

The term **navigation** refers to clicking on a link or hyperlink that will take you to another place on the same page, on another page in the same document or to an online place, such as a website. Links that connect you to locations within the same document are referred to as **bookmarks**, whereas hypertext links take you to another location when you click on a highlighted word or image. Usually, hypertext links are blue in colour and sometimes underlined. Bookmarks are usually not blue in colour unless you have formatted them to be blue.

> **KEY WORDS**
>
> **navigation:** clicking on a link or hyperlink that will take you to another place on the same page, on another page in the same document or to an online place, such as a website
>
> **bookmark:** a means of navigation within a document

Links and bookmarks gives readers greater flexibility to move around the text in a document without having to read through a whole document to find the sections that are relevant only to them. They also help in the production of onscreen tests and adventure books where a user has to pick a particular option.

Most document processing software has a navigation pane showing either thumbnails of pages, or headings of different levels in the document (see Figure 17.31). Clicking on one of them takes the user to that page.

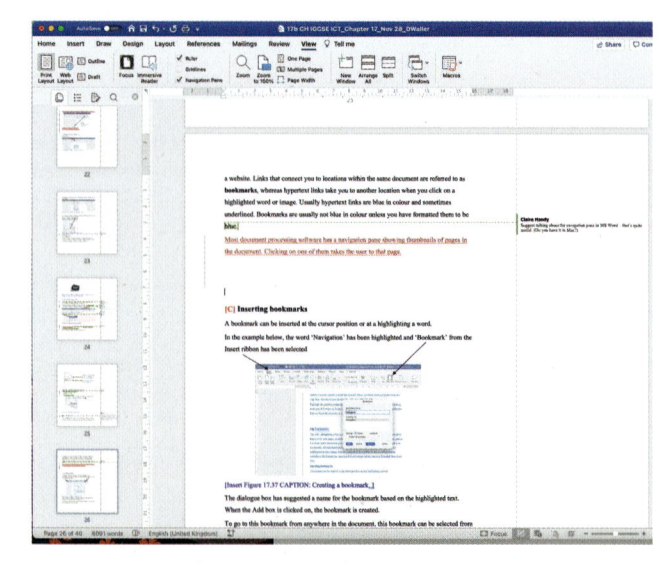

Figure 17.31: The navigation pane

Inserting bookmarks

A bookmark can be inserted at the cursor position or at a highlighting a word.

In the example in Figure 17.32, the word 'Navigation' has been highlighted and 'Bookmark' from the Insert menu has been selected.

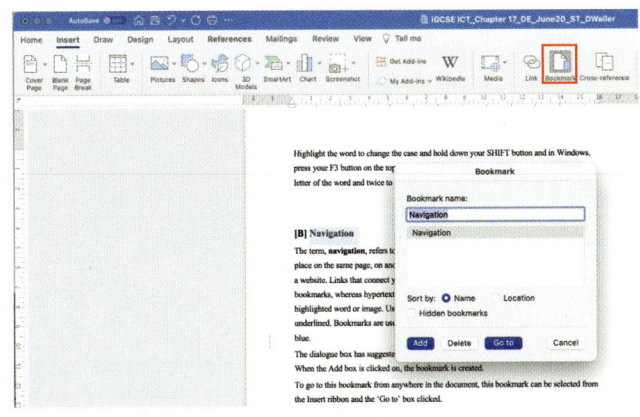

Figure 17.32: Creating a bookmark

The dialogue box has suggested a name for the bookmark based on the highlighted text. When the Add box is clicked on, the bookmark is created.

To go to this bookmark from anywhere in the document, this bookmark can be selected from the Insert ribbon and the 'Go to' box clicked (see Figure 17.33).

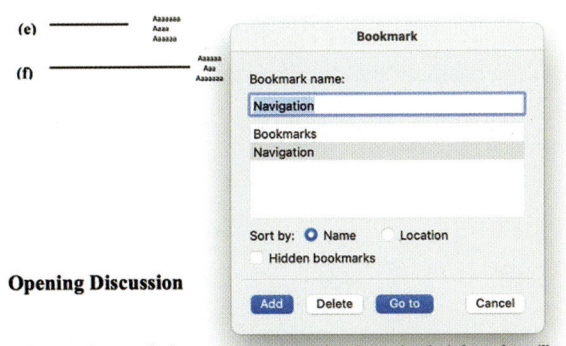

Figure 17.33: Selecting a bookmark to navigate to

By default, bookmarks are not identified but they can be automatically enclosed in brackets (see Figure 17.34) if the 'Bookmarks' box is clicked in the Preferences menu.

Figure 17.34: Showing bookmarks

Creating a hyperlink

Hyperlinks are often used in documents viewed on computer to provide a link to a particular section or heading from a list of contents. A bookmark that has been set in the document can be used as the target of a hyperlink. In this example, a hyperlink will be created to go to the first item of the Learning intentions for this chapter, 'organise page layout' (see Figure 17.35).

Figure 17.35: The text to provide a hyperlink

A bookmark can then be inserted at the required position in the document (Figure 17.36).

Figure 17.36: Inserting a bookmark for the hyperlink

The hyperlink can then be created by selecting 'Link' in the Insert ribbon.

As the link is in this document, 'This Document' is selected as is the required bookmark (Figure 17.37).

The hyperlink text will now be shown in blue (see Figure 17.38) and the pointer will change into a pointing finger when it is placed over it.

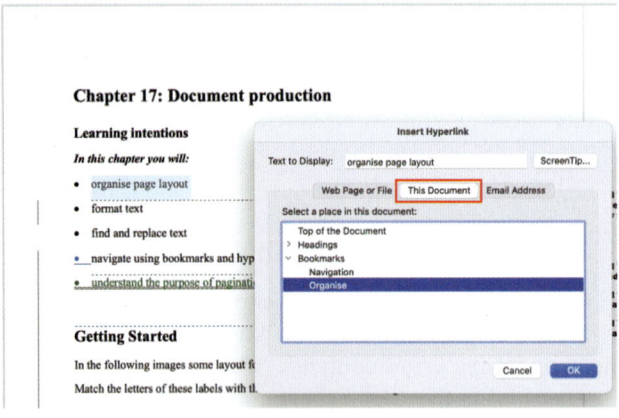

Figure 17.37: Creating the hyperlink

Figure 17.38: The hyperlink shown in the text

> ### WORKED EXAMPLE 17.1
> #### FORMATTING A DOCUMENT
>
> 1. Open *Storage.docx* into your word processing software. This document contains some details about computer data storage devices. Read the document and then edit it in the following ways.
> 2. Change all margins to 2 cm.
> 3. The information about each storage device should start on a new page.
> 4. Insert a page at the start and make this a title and contents page. This page only should be in landscape format. There should be links from this page to the information about each of the storage devices.
> 5. All lists should be bulleted with a different bullet style for each list.
> 6. There should be 6 pt space after each paragraph.
>
> #### Step 1
>
> The document is about optical, magnetic and solid-state storage. At the moment the document is badly formatted, and the information is difficult to read.

17 Document production

CONTINUED

Step 2

The margins can be set to 2 cm using the Layout menu.

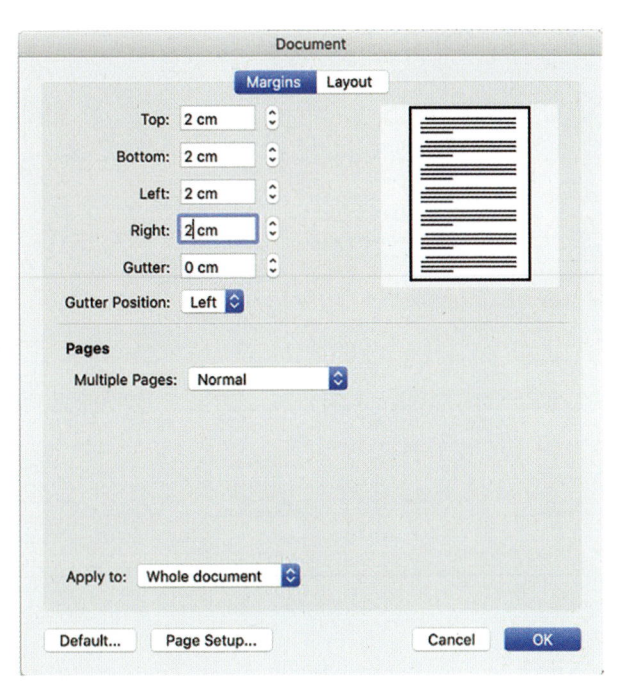

Figure 17.39: Setting margins

Step 3

Page breaks can be inserted between the three methods by inserting page breaks from the Layout menu.

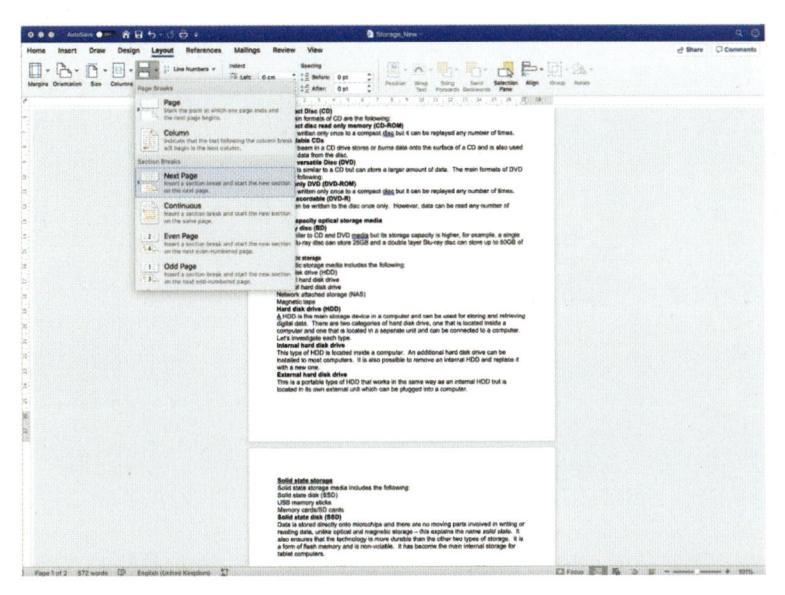

Figure 17.40: Inserting page breaks

> **CAMBRIDGE IGCSE™ ICT: COURSEBOOK**

CONTINUED

The document should now have three pages.

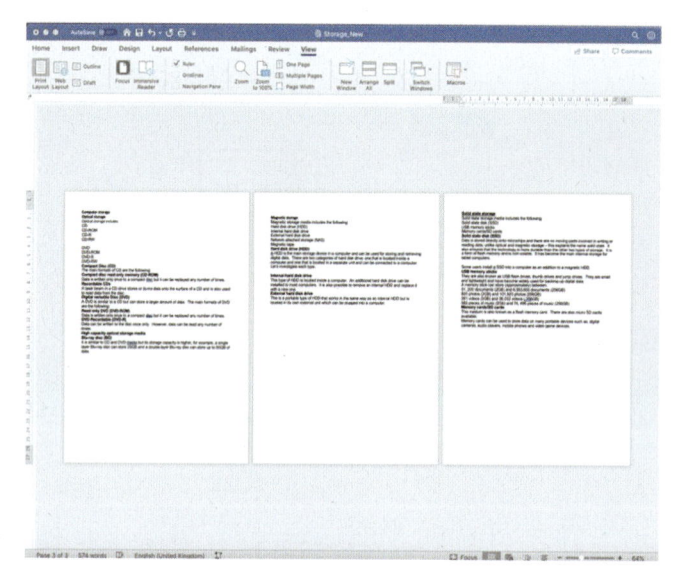

Figure 17.41: Document 'broken' into three pages

Step 4

A page can be inserted before the first page in a similar way by placing the cursor at the top of the first page and inserting a section break. It should start a new section on the next page.

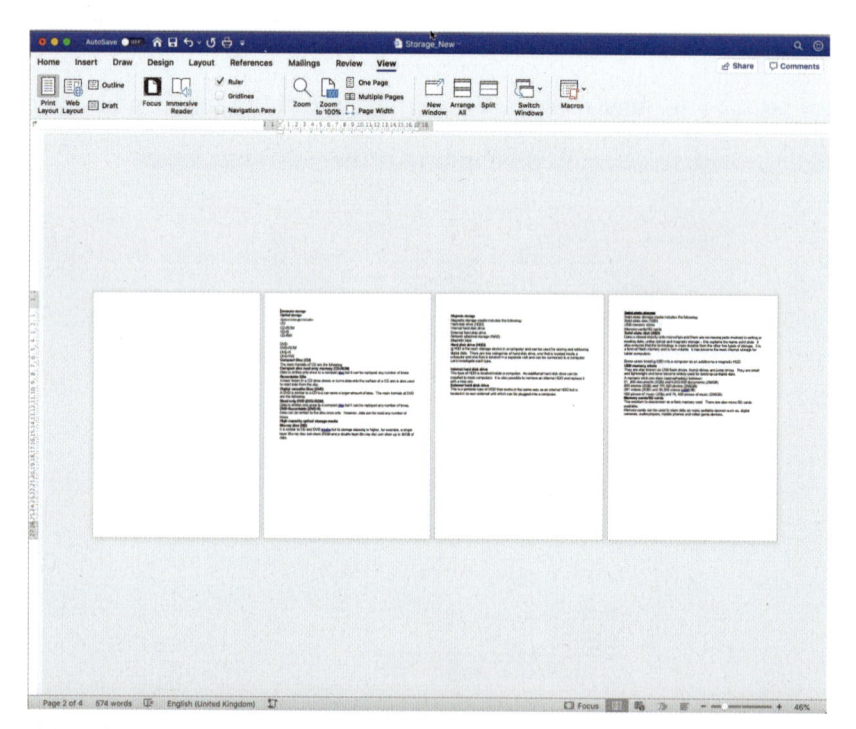

Figure 17.42: New blank first page inserted

17 Document production

> **CONTINUED**
>
> The page can be set to landscape format. As it is a separate section, only the orientation of the first page will be changed.

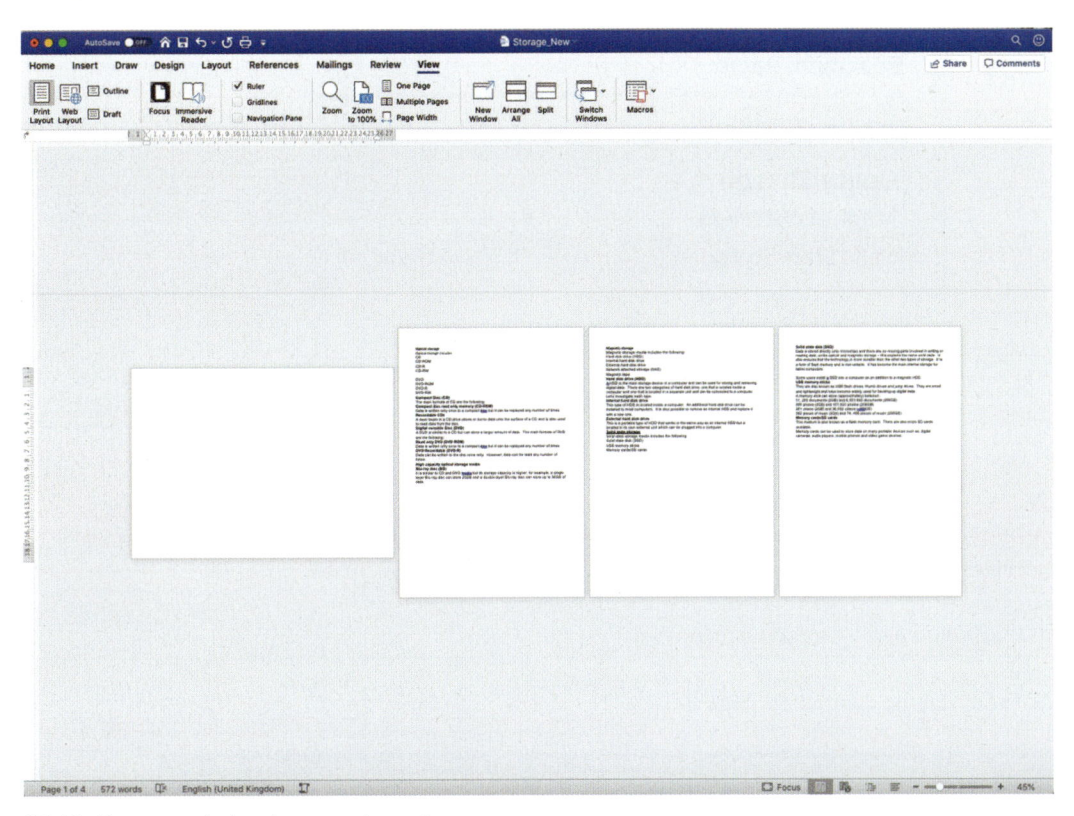

Figure 17.43: First page in landscape orientation

Bookmarks can now be set at the top of pages 2 to 4 (see Figures 17.44 and 17.45).

Figure 17.44: Setting OpticalStorage bookmark

CONTINUED

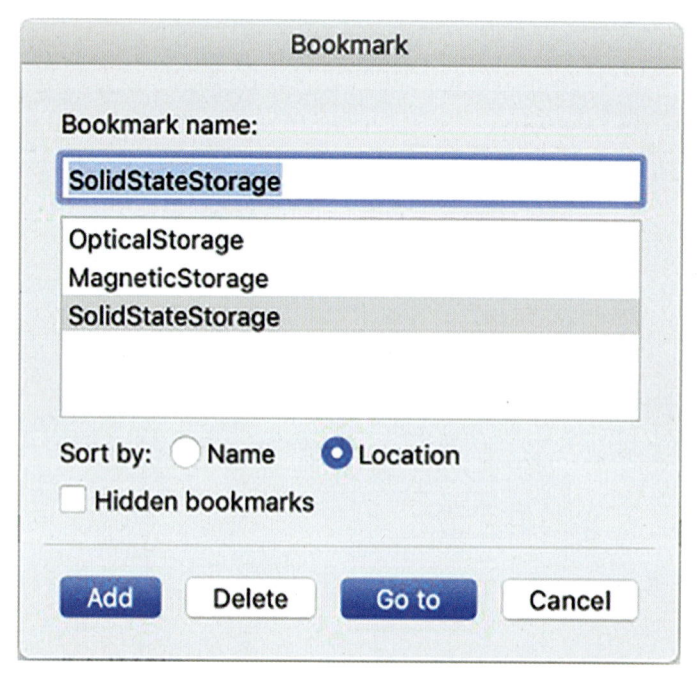

Figure 17.45: Setting SolidStateStorage bookmark

The heading and index can be created on page 1.

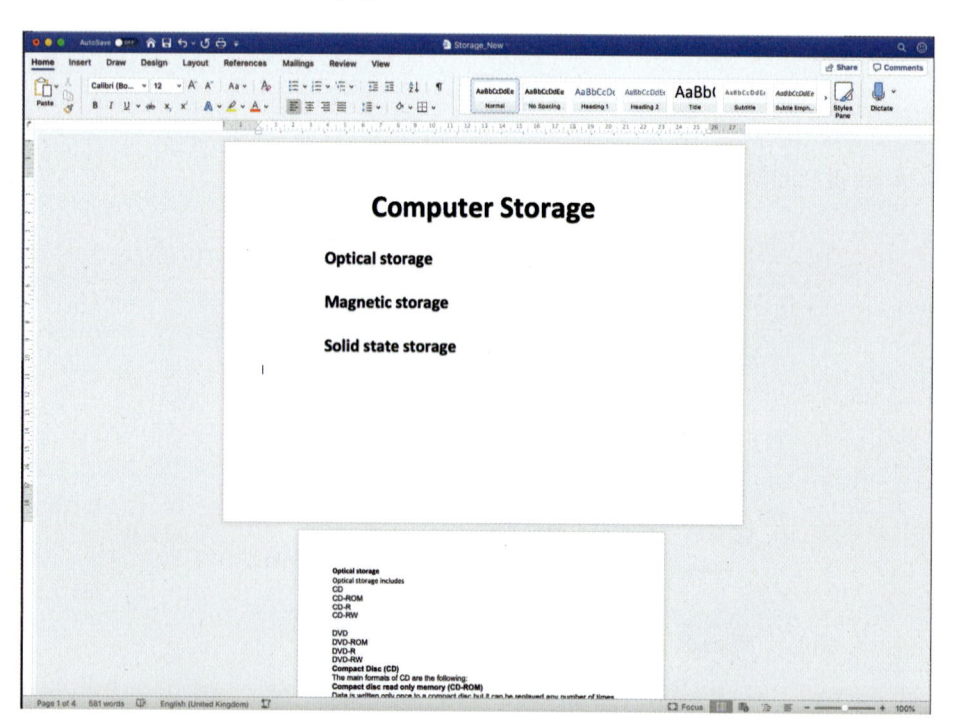

Figure 17.46: Page 1 heading and index

17 Document production

> **CONTINUED**
>
> Links to the bookmarks can be added to these content items.

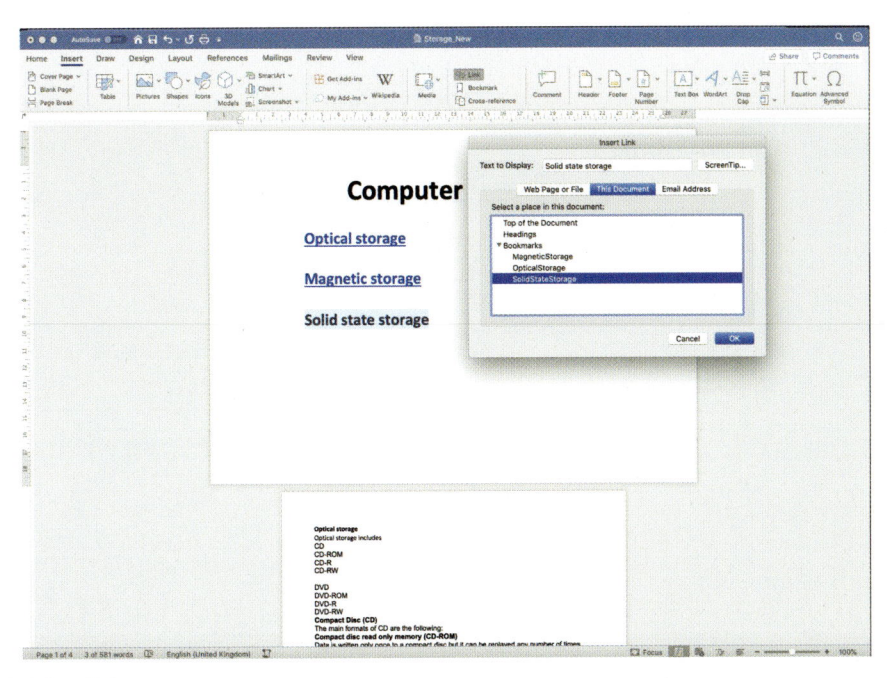

Figure 17.47: Adding links to contents

Step 5

Bullets can be added to each list and new bullet point styles can be defined (see Figures 17.48 and 17.49).

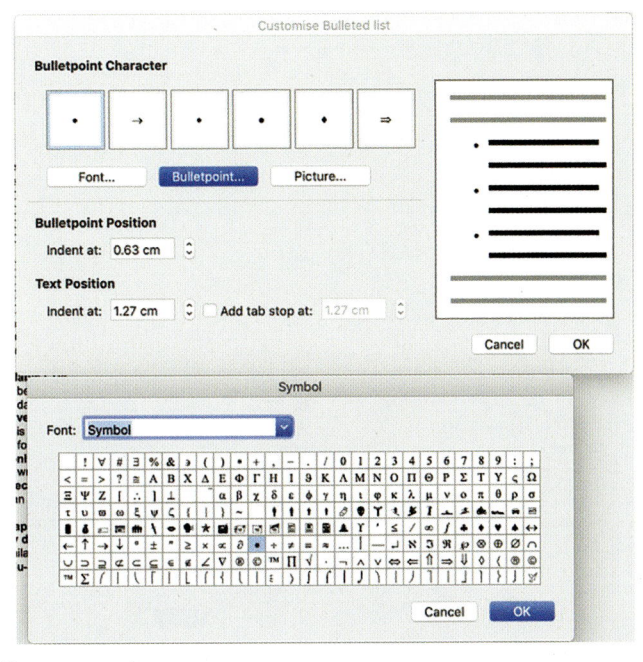

Figure 17.48: Defining bullet point style

363

CAMBRIDGE IGCSE™ ICT: COURSEBOOK

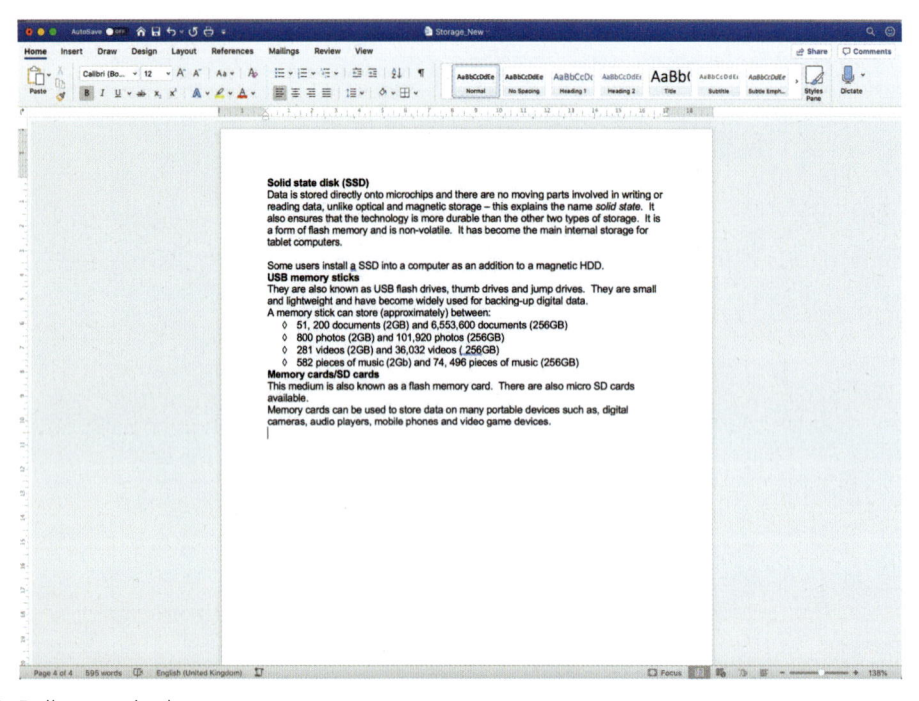

CONTINUED

Figure 17.49: Bullets applied

Step 6

Paragraphs can be formatted to 6 pt inserted after each one.

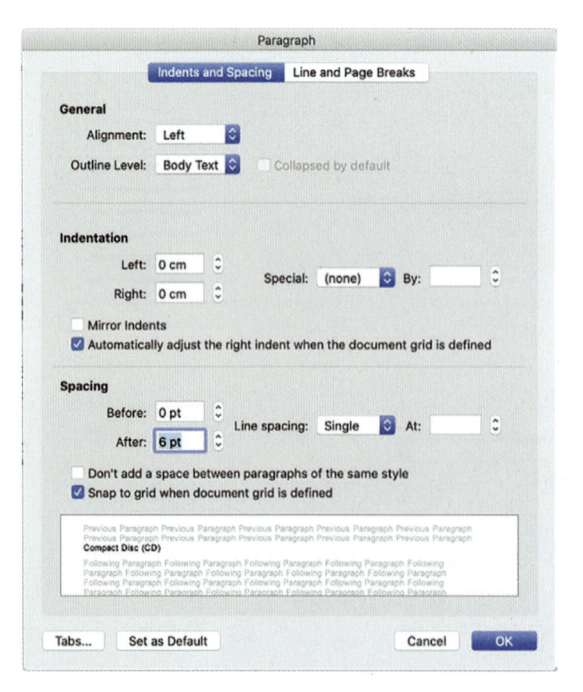

Figure 17.50: Setting 6 point spacing

17 Document production

CONTINUED

Questions

1. Edit *Storage.docx* as specified.
2. Use an arrow symbol (pointing left) at the top of pages 2 to 4. Add a link to these symbols so that when clicked the document returns to the index page.

PRACTICAL TASK 17.2

Getting started

1. On paper, draw lines to show how text is aligned using left, right and centred tabs.
2. List the steps that you would take to set tab stops of different types in the software you are using.

Practice

3. Open *Invoice.docx* into your word processing software. Edit this document in the following ways.
4. The 'Supplies Inc.' heading should be centred.
5. The Supplies Inc address block should be on the same lines as the Big Corporation address block but should be aligned with the right margin (see Figure 17.51).

Invoice
Supplies Inc

The Big Corporation	Supplies Inc
13 Main Street	PO Box 113
Big City	Even Bigger City
Some Country	Some Country
ZY3 9XX	CD6 13WA
Date: 28 January 2020	Invoice Number: 162342835378

Figure 17.51: Aligning addresses

6. The invoice number should be on the same line as the date but should be aligned with the right margin.
7. The prices of the items should be aligned correctly with the right margin.
8. Calculate the total and insert the amount aligned under the prices.
9. The 'Please pay within 30 days.' should be centred.

Challenge

10. If there are a lot of items on the invoice, it is often difficult for a person to match up the prices with the items. Format the tab for the prices so that there is a dotted line between the items and their prices.
11. Insert a diagonal watermark of 'Supplies Inc'. It should have a grey fill and a transparency of 30%.

> **CONTINUED**
>
> **Self-assessment**
>
> How many of the criteria in the table below did you meet? If you missed any, try to go back and amend your work to include them.
>
> | Criteria | Criteria met |
> |---|---|
> | Centre heading | |
> | Right align a block of text | |
> | Align price list | |
> | Insert a leading line between the tabbed items and their prices | |
> | Insert and align a watermark | |

Questions

10 Match the following terms with their correct meanings:

Term	Meaning of the term
A Gutter margin	1 Making text bold or placing a subscript on it.
B Bookmark	2 Linking to another location within the same document.
C Hyperlink	3 Extra space on one of the margins to allow for book binding.
D Text enhancement	4 An example of this is a hanging paragraph.
E Tabulation	5 Setting page breaks.
F Pagination	6 Highlighted text or an image that takes you to another location.

11 Explain what each of these cases are by giving an example of each:
   a   line spacing
   b   indented paragraph
   c   page orientation.

12 Explain the purpose of setting page, section and column breaks.

13 Compare the text enhancement tools available in a word processor and in a spreadsheet.

14 Select the most appropriate software from the Office Suite (word processor, presentation, spreadsheet, database, desktop publisher) to produce the following documents.
   a   To produce a newsletter.
   b   To create a data model.
   c   To produce a system to keep stock of products and customers.
   d   To write a company's annual report.
   e   To help you deliver a speech at the annual awards ceremony.

SUMMARY

Although most document types allow you to carry out similar formatting techniques, formatting can be applied in different ways and to different effects within each type of program.

Setting the margins, page size and orientation, column widths, spacing, pagination and so on can make it much easier to create professional-looking documents.

Gutter margins are the extra margins created for documents that need to be bound into a book format so that the binding doesn't obscure the text.

Breaks can be added between pages, sections and columns to keep related information together and to have different formatting.

Formatting text includes setting line spacing, setting tabulation, creating bulleted or numbered lists and applying text enhancements.

Words can be found and replaced using tools in the software.

Adding navigation aspects such as bookmarks and hyperlinks to a document gives readers greater flexibility to move around the text in a document without having to read through a whole document to find the sections that are relevant only to them.

EXAM-STYLE QUESTIONS

1. **Define** the following words with reference to formatting text and organising page layout:
    a orientation
    b page margins
    c gutter margin
    d page break
    e tabulation. [5]
2. **Describe** the difference between a bookmark and a hyperlink in a document. [2]
3. Giving examples, **explain** what is meant by the following: [6]
    a left tabs
    b centred tabs
    c decimal tabs.
4. **Explain** the difference between indented paragraphs and hanging paragraphs. [2]
5. **State** the difference between portrait and landscape orientation. [2]

COMMAND WORDS

define: give precise meaning

describe: state the points of a topic / give characteristics and main features

explain: set out purposes or reasons / make the relationships between things evident / provide why and / or how and support with relevant evidence

state: express in clear terms

CONTINUED

6 Open *ES Q6.docx* in your word processing software. This is a document about computer memory.

  a Change the margins so that they are all set at 2 cm.
  b Set the text in the paragraph about RAM to two columns with a 1 cm space between the columns.
  c Create page breaks between the paragraphs so that each is on its own page, e.g. Contents on page 1, Computer memory on page 2, RAM on page 3, etc. There should be five pages in all.
  d Set hyperlinks so that when each item in the contents list is selected, the corresponding page is shown.
  e On each page, add the text 'RETURN' and create a hyperlink that will return the user to the Contents page.
  f Set the orientation of the last page of the document to landscape. [10]

[Total: 27]

REFLECTION

Reflect on the strategies you used when completing the exam-style questions and activities in this chapter and write a list detailing how you would would avoid any difficulties you may encounter in the future?

SELF-EVALUATION CHECKLIST

After studying this chapter, think about how confident you are with the different topics.

This will help you to see any gaps in your knowledge and help you to learn more effectively.

You might find it helpful to rate how confident you are for each of these statements when you are revising. You should revisit any sections that you rated 'Needs more work' or 'Getting there'.

I can …	See section	Needs more work	Getting there	Confident to move on
organise page layout	17.1			
format text	17.2			
find and replace text	17.3			
navigate using bookmarks and hyperlinks	17.4			
understand the purpose of pagination and gutter margins	17.3			

Chapter 18
Databases

IN THIS CHAPTER YOU WILL:

- describe the types of databases, primary and foreign keys, and form design
- create a database structure
- create and use a data entry form
- manipulate data by performing calculations, sorting and searching data
- display data in different output layouts.

CAMBRIDGE IGCSE™ ICT: COURSEBOOK

GETTING STARTED

Here are two lists. One contains terms relating to databases and the other their definitions or explanations. Unfortunately, they are not in the same order. Working with a partner, try to work out which number from the first list goes with which letter from the second.

1	Database	a	A collection of records.
2	Field	b	A yes/no or true/false field.
3	Record	c	A search to find information.
4	File	d	A field containing unique data.
5	Query	e	A structured store of data.
6	Numeric field	f	A field for storing numbers.
7	Boolean field	g	A collection of fields.
8	Key field	h	One item of information.

DATABASES RULE THE WORLD

It is thought that the first written language was invented 5000 years ago in Sumer, now in modern-day Iraq. One of the first uses that the rulers used this new invention for, was to create a database.

They carried out a census and made lists of all the people and what they owned. This knowledge gave them power and allowed them to start taxing people. William the Conqueror had the same idea when he invaded Britain in 1066 and compiled them in the Domesday Book. It listed what everyone owned and, of course, how much they could be taxed!

Figure 18.1: Organising data in a database

Until the 20th century, all databases were on paper and took up lots of space. It was a problem when new data had to be added between other bits of data and searching for specific information could take days. It got a bit easier when someone had the brilliant idea of storing it in alphabetical order. The first structured database.

In the 20th century, the first database management system for computers was invented by Edgar F. Codd, and overnight, searching and sorting data became almost instantaneous.

Today, practically everything we do, where we go and what we buy is stored on a database, somewhere. Governments, public bodies and business organisations run on databases storing details of their citizens, employees and customers.

All of these databases are structured or organised so that data can be easily searched and sorted, with links made between them (see Figure 18.1). But it is estimated that almost 80% of the data in organisations is not in databases, it is unstructured in emails, letters, memos, etc.

Research is ongoing into making use of this data using techniques such as data mining, natural language processing and text analytics.

Data is definitely a valuable commodity.

> **CONTINUED**
>
> **Discussion questions**
>
> 1 How many databases hold information about you? Discuss this in your group and make a list of as many as you can.
>
> 2 One of the organisations holding information about you is your school or college. Make a list of all of the items of information that are stored about you.

Pupil Number	Surname	First Name	Subject	Coursework	Examination	Total
1036	Suparmanputra	Hasan	Science	60	70	130
2872	Elmasry	Anat	History	56	82	138
1725	Nasution	Abdul	Geography	90	80	170
3916	Megat	Amina	Computing	82	69	151
7321	Nababan	Annisa	Computing	73	67	140
1328	Mansour	Hasina	Science	42	39	84
1712	Zaky	Khalid	Maths	76	85	161
2482	Sakura	Abe	Science	39	52	91
2223	Mazur	Lucia	Languages	68	54	122
3669	Sayid	Haziq	Technology	32	76	108

Table 18.1: A database of students' details and subject information

18.1 Creating an appropriate database structure

When **data** was first stored in an organised way, the obvious place to put it was in **tables** where the columns represented the data items being stored and the rows contained specific values of that data.

Any person or object that the data is about is called the **entity**. For example, if a teacher wanted to store the names of their students and their results for different subjects, they could create a table like the one shown in Table 18.1. Therefore, the entity of this table is Pupil.

> **KEY WORDS**
>
> **data:** raw, unorganised items without any description or explanation, e.g. 69, 90, 30. Data values don't have any meaning until they are put into context
>
> **table:** a collection of rows and columns forming cells that are used to store data in a structured and organised manner in a database
>
> **entity:** a thing that is recognised as being capable of an independent existence, which can be uniquely identified, and about which data can be stored. It is usually a physical object (e.g. a gym member, car, person, book) or it can be a concept (e.g. a customer transaction storing details of the items that were purchased)

The table clearly shows all of the information, all together, in one place.

Each of the columns is called a **field**. In this example, there are fields for Pupil Number, Surname, First name, etc. Each of the rows shows the complete information for each pupil. These are called **records**. Therefore, in this table there are seven fields and ten records.

A **database** with one table is called a **flat-file database**. They are easy to create, use and understand, and the data can be sorted and searched.

BUT there are problems with using a flat-file database. What if the teacher wanted to add more subjects for each pupil? It is quite easy to insert more rows (as we have already seen in Chapter 13, Section 13.2 Tables). If the teacher wanted to add more subjects for Amina Megat, part of the table could look like the one shown in Table 18.2.

This table now shows two major disadvantages of flat-file databases:

- **Data redundancy**: This means that some of the data is repeated. Pupil Number, Surname and First Name are repeated in each of Amina's records. This repetition wastes time and takes up storage space.

- **Data integrity**: If the same data is entered several times, then some of it could be entered incorrectly. If you look at the second record for Amina you can see that the teacher has typed it incorrectly by writing Ammina instead of Amina. That wouldn't be too bad if a human was searching the records as they would just assume that the teacher had made an error. But a computer would not do this and could treat them as different people.

These are major problems and, as such, flat-file databases are not often used.

To solve these problems, a relational model was proposed in 1970 by E. F. Codd where the data was stored, not in one, but in many linked tables. These are called **relational databases**.

> ### ACTIVITY 18.1
>
> With a partner, carry out research and create a document to explain where flat-file databases are still used.

A program used to create and manage relational databases is called a **Relational Database Management System (RDMS).** Microsoft Access is an RDMS. Access itself is NOT a database; it creates and manages them.

> ### KEY WORDS
>
> **field:** one item of information about an entity, e.g. Pupil Number, Surname, First Name
>
> **record:** consists of all the fields about an individual instance of an entity in a database, e.g. all the details about one gym member
>
> **database:** an example of application software, used to store organised data electronically, so that data can easily be retrieved, managed or updated
>
> **flat-file database:** a database that has only one table. Each line of the table holds one record
>
> **data redundancy:** when the same piece of data is held in two separate places
>
> **data integrity:** the maintenance of data accuracy and consistency
>
> **relational database:** a database with many linked tables
>
> **Relational Database Management System (RDMS):** software to create and manage relational databases, e.g. Microsoft Access

Pupil Number	Surname	First Name	Subject	Coursework	Examination	Total
1725	Nasution	Abdul	Geography	90	80	170
3916	Megat	Amina	Computing	82	69	151
3916	Megat	Ammina	Science	76	48	124
3916	Megat	Amina	Maths	58	73	161
7321	Nababan	Annisa	Computing	73	67	140

Table 18.2: Inserting information in a flat-file database

To convert his flat-file database into a relational database the teacher could create two linked tables: one showing the personal details of the students and the other showing their academic results.

Pupil table		
Pupil Number	Surname	First Name
1036	Suparmanputra	Hasan
2872	Elmasry	Anat
1725	Nasution	Abdul
3916	Megat	Amina
7321	Nababan	Annisa
1328	Mansour	Hasina
1712	Zaky	Khalid
2482	Sakura	Abe
2223	Mazur	Lucia
3669	Sayid	Haziq

Table 18.3: Personal details of the students

Academic table			
Subject	Coursework	Examination	Total
Science	60	70	130
History	56	82	138
Geography	90	80	170
Computing	82	69	151
Computing	73	67	140
Science	42	39	84
Maths	76	85	161
Science	39	52	91
Languages	68	54	122
Technology	32	76	108

Table 18.4: Academic details of the students

However, there is now a serious problem. How do you link the two tables together? How do you know which subject goes with each student?

In the Pupil table you can chose a field that contains **unique** data to identify individual pupils.

You cannot use the Surnames or First names as there may be several people with the same names. Some students may even have both names the same.

The obvious choice is the Pupil Number. This can be given when the pupil enters the school or college and can be unique for each pupil. No other pupil can ever have the same Pupil Number. A field that holds unique information is a **key field** and, as the Pupil Number field is going to be used to identify each record, it is called the **primary key**.

Therefore, in order to link the two tables together, Pupil Number, the key field in the Pupil table, can be added to the Academic table to provide the link. This field will identify the students who the results belong to.

The Academic table will now look like Table 18.5.

Academic table				
Pupil Number	Subject	Coursework	Examination	Total
1036	Science	60	70	130
2872	History	56	82	138
1725	Geography	90	80	170
3916	Computing	82	69	151
7321	Computing	73	67	140
1328	Science	42	39	84
1712	Maths	76	85	161
2482	Science	39	52	91
2223	Languages	68	54	122
3669	Technology	32	76	108

Table 18.5: Academic details of the students with a primary key (the Pupil Number)

Now each subject is linked to a specific pupil through their Pupil Number, which is in both tables (see Table 18.6 on the next page). When a primary key is added to another table to link them together, it is called a **foreign key**. In the Academic table, the foreign key, Pupil Number, refers to the primary key in the Pupil table. You can have a primary key without a foreign key but you

> **KEY WORDS**
>
> **unique:** something of which there is only one example
>
> **key field:** a field that holds unique information
>
> **primary key:** the key field used to identify each record
>
> **foreign key:** a field in one table that refers to a primary key in another table

cannot have a foreign key without a primary key. Pretty obvious, really.

Pupil table

Pupil Number
Surname
First name

Academic table

Pupil Number
Subject
Coursework
Examination
Total

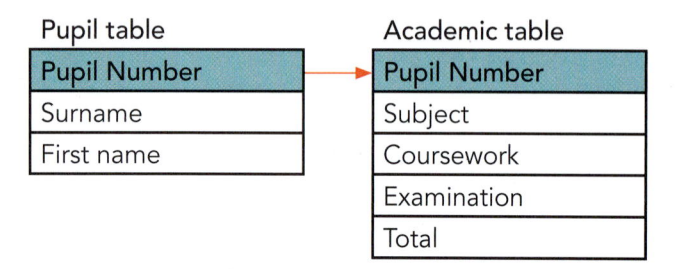

Table 18.6: Primary key

However, all tables *must* have a primary key, so what can it be for the Academic table? Remember, the primary key has to be unique and appear only once. Therefore, it cannot be the Pupil Number, or each pupil would only be able to appear only once when they actually do lots of subjects (see Table 18.7). It cannot be Subject because then each subject could only appear once and lots of pupils do the same subject. The same argument also applies to the marks. Many students could get the same mark.

In order to solve this problem, you are allowed to have a joint or **compound key** – consisting of two or more of the fields. In this case it could be the Pupil Number AND Subject fields. That would be beneficial as then you couldn't mistakenly try to create two records for the same student with the same subject.

> **KEY WORD**
>
> **compound key:** a key consisting of two or more fields

Academic table

Pupil Number	Subject	Coursework	Examination	Total
1036	Science	60	70	130
1036	History	56	82	138
1036	Geography	90	80	170
1036	Computing	82	69	151
1036	Maths	76	85	161
1036	Languages	68	54	122
1036	Technology	32	76	108

Table 18.7: Pupil Number and Subject fields are the compound key

As Pupil and Subject form a compound key, a student can be listed many times as long as it is a different subject each time. Likewise, a subject can be listed many times, but only once per pupil.

Relational databases solve the problems of data redundancy and data integrity as lots of data does not have to be entered lots of times.

Creating tables

Pupil table

When database tables are being created, the fields, their names and data types must be defined.

We will create a table for the pupils but add some more information. In Table 18.8, fields have been added for date of birth, House (which social grouping they are in) and a field to indicate whether they require daily transport. There are four House groups – Red, Blue, Green and Yellow.

Pupil Number	Surname	First Name	Date of Birth	House	Transport
1036	Suparmanputra	Hasan	21/3/2010	Red	Yes
2872	Elmasry	Anat	6/10/2009	Blue	No
1725	Nasution	Abdul	24/2/2008	Blue	No
3916	Megat	Amina	16/4/2006	Green	No
7321	Nababan	Annisa	29/7/2005	Yellow	Yes
1328	Mansour	Hasina	13/01/2006	Yellow	Yes
1712	Zaky	Khalid	17/11/2007	Green	Yes
2482	Sakura	Abe	12/5/2006	Red	No
2223	Mazur	Lucia	28/01/2006	Red	Yes
3669	Sayid	Haziq	10/11/2005	Green	Yes

Table 18.8: Pupil information

18 Databases

The software can be used to create a new database (see Figure 18.2) and save it in the required location.

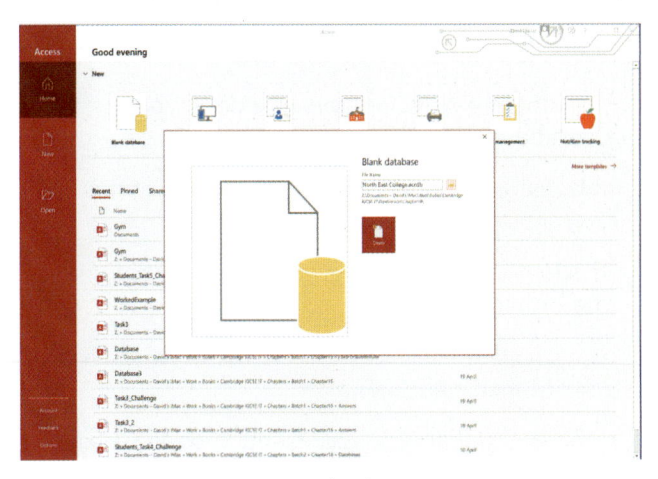

Figure 18.2: Creating a new database

In this software the database is created with a table, named Table1. This can be used for the required design by right-clicking on the name and selecting Design View (see Figure 18.3).

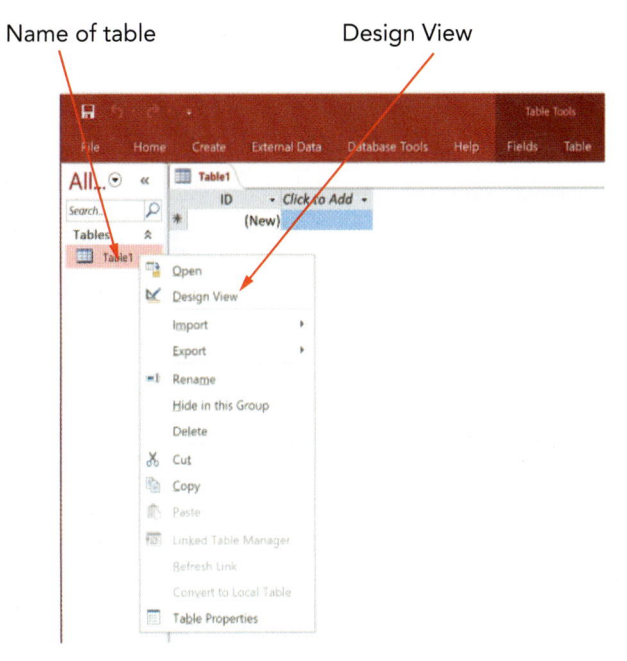

Figure 18.3: Selecting a table in Design View

It should be saved with a new name; in this database, it is named Pupil (see Figure 18.4).

The fields can now be designed. The **field name** and **data type** have to be defined (see Figure 18.5).

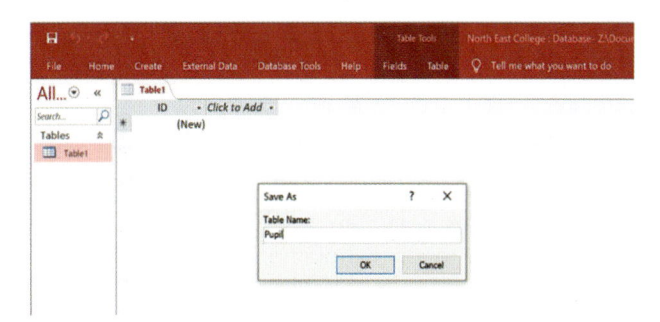

Figure 18.4: Saving a new table

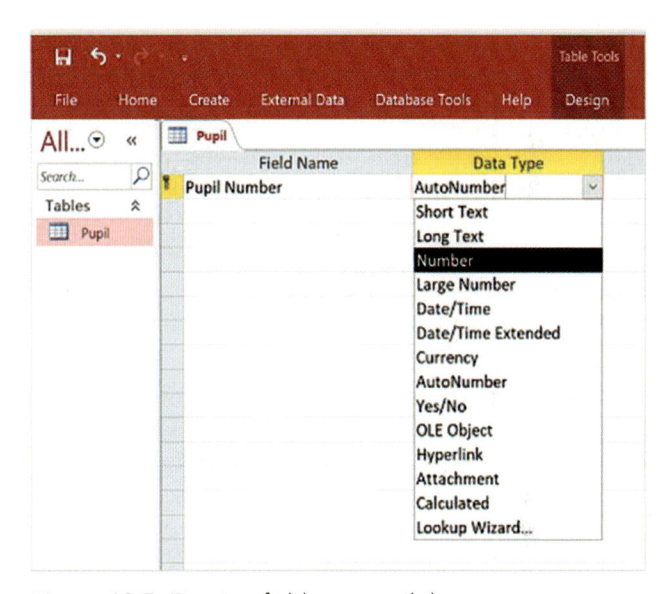

Figure 18.5: Entering field name and data type

KEY WORDS

field name: also called a label or column heading, is the name for a column by which it can be identified. E.g. Name, Date Modified, Type, Size, etc.

data type: the different types of data that each field can hold, such as date/time, text, etc.

integer: a whole number with no decimal places

There are many different data types, described in Table 18.9.

Further properties of the data type can be set in the area below. In this case the number is being set as a 'long integer' (see Figure 18.6). An **integer** is a whole number with no decimal places. An integer can store numbers from −32 768 to +32 767 whereas a long integer from −2 147 483 648 to +2 147 483 647.

375

Data type	Description
Text	Accepts alphanumeric characters such as letters and numbers. When it is created, you usually have to state the maximum number of characters.
Numeric	Accepts numbers. They can be integers (whole numbers) or numbers with decimals. When they are created you can state the number of decimal places or whether a currency symbol should be applied.
Date/Time	Accepts date and time data. You can state how it should be displayed, e.g. as a short, medium or long date.
Boolean/Logical	A field indicating whether something is true or false. This data type is useful for yes/no questions, or for ticking off items in a list (using check boxes or radio buttons).

Table 18.9: Different data types

The Pupil Number is an integer; however, for other number types, the number of decimal places can be set. A number can also be formatted as currency or as a percentage (see Figure 18.7 on the next page).

KEY WORDS

text: letters of the alphabet and numbers are both classified as a text data type

numeric: are only numbers as a data type in a database

date/time: when date or time is written in the conventional time or date formats

Boolean: data indicating whether something is true or false

check box: a small box on a form into which a tick or other mark is entered

radio button: an icon representing one of a set of options

currency: numbers that have a currency symbol with them

The next field is Surname. This field requires a text entry and is set as Short Text. By default this software sets the length Short Text as 255 characters, but it can be reduced to a more sensible number to save storage space and memory (see Figure 18.8 on the next page).

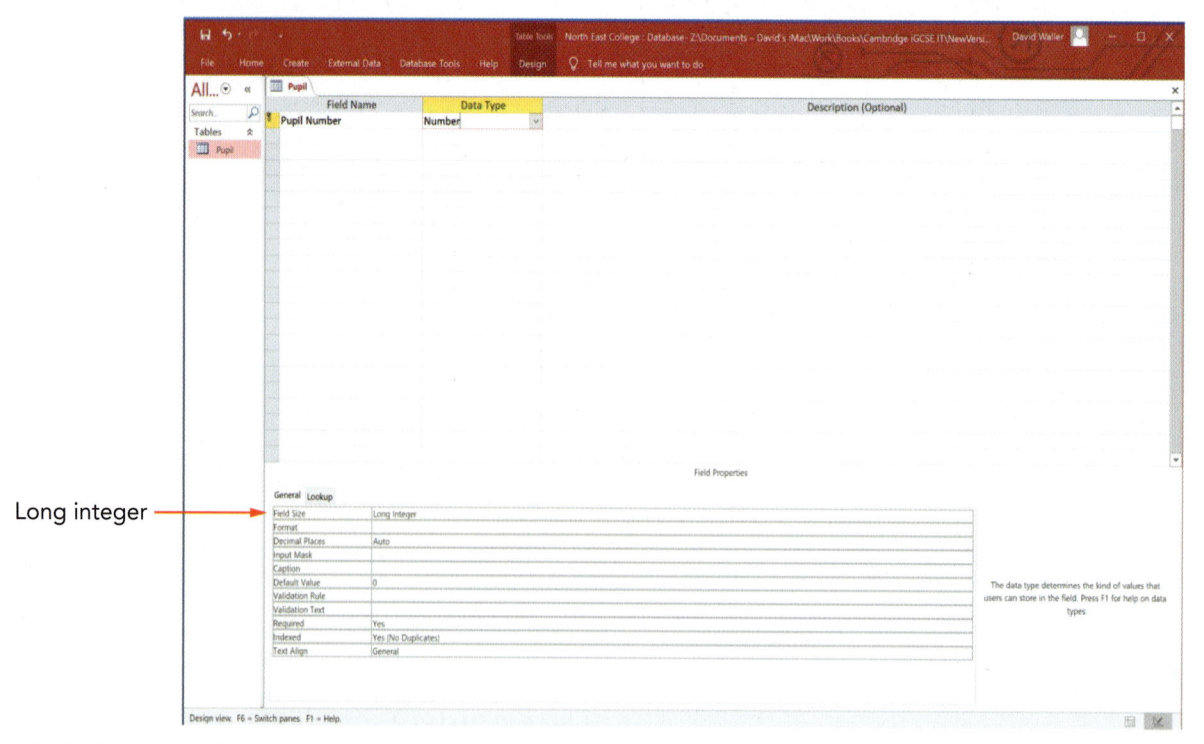

Figure 18.6: Formatting the data type

18 Databases

You can access the different options by clicking on the drop-down arrow on the right of the Field Properties box (see Figure 18.7).

The First Name field can be created and formatted in the same way.

The Date of Birth field should be set as a Date/Time field and the way in which the date is displayed can be set as long date, medium date and short date (see Figure 18.9 on the next page). Try each and see what the difference is.

For the House field, the text length can be set to 6 characters, as the longest entry will be 'Yellow'. As there are only four correct entries for this field, a validation rule can be created to ensure that only one of those four is entered (see Figure 18.10 on the next page).

Figure 18.7: Formatting a number

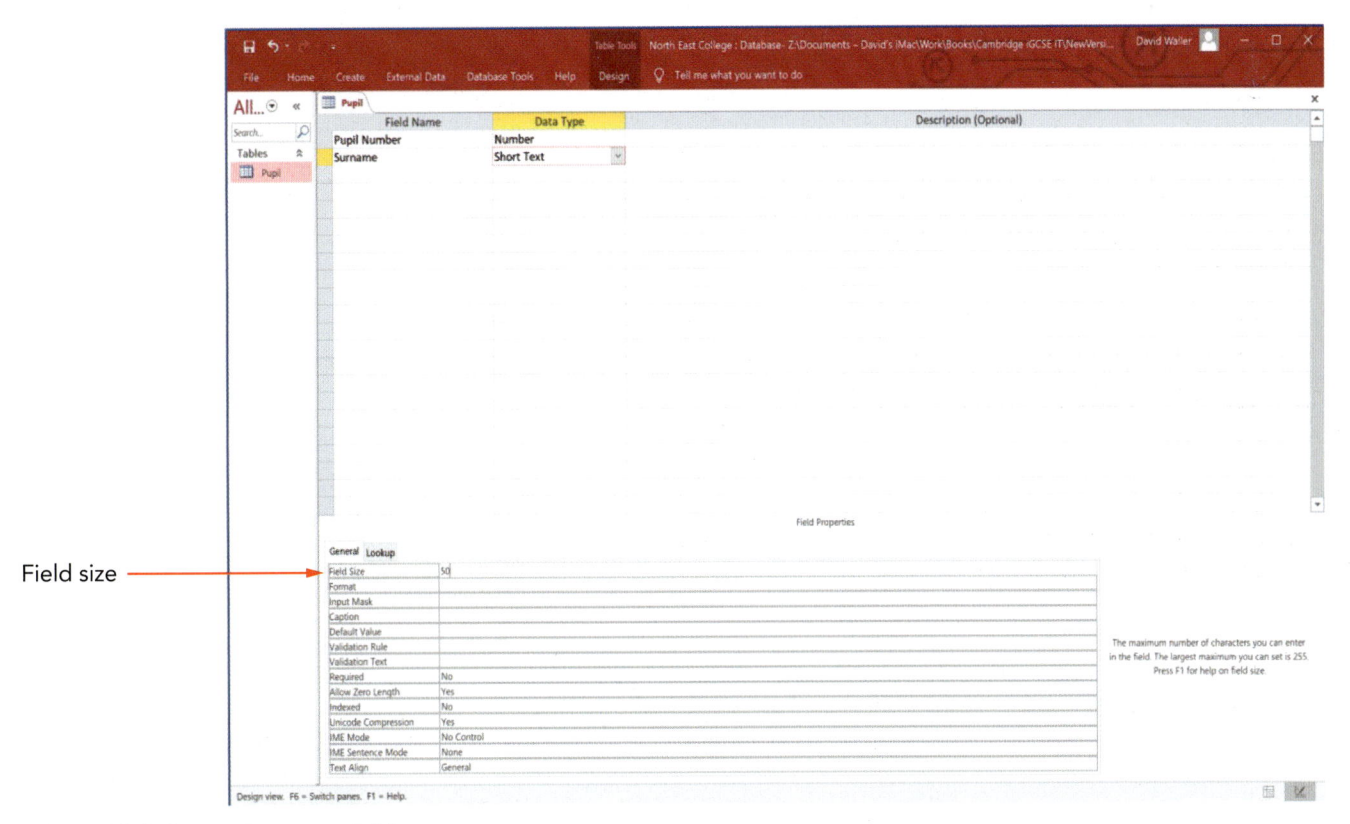

Figure 18.8: Formatting a text field

377

Setting Date and Time

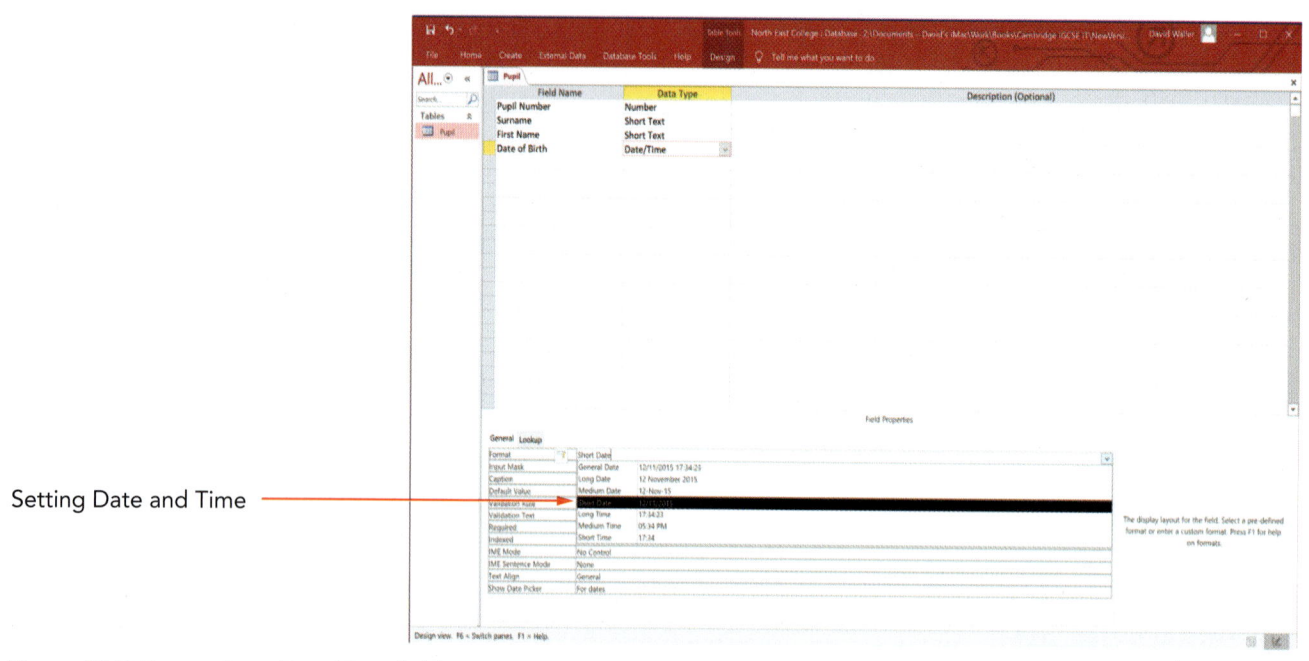

Figure 18.9: Formatting a Date/Time field

Setting Validation Rule and Validation Text

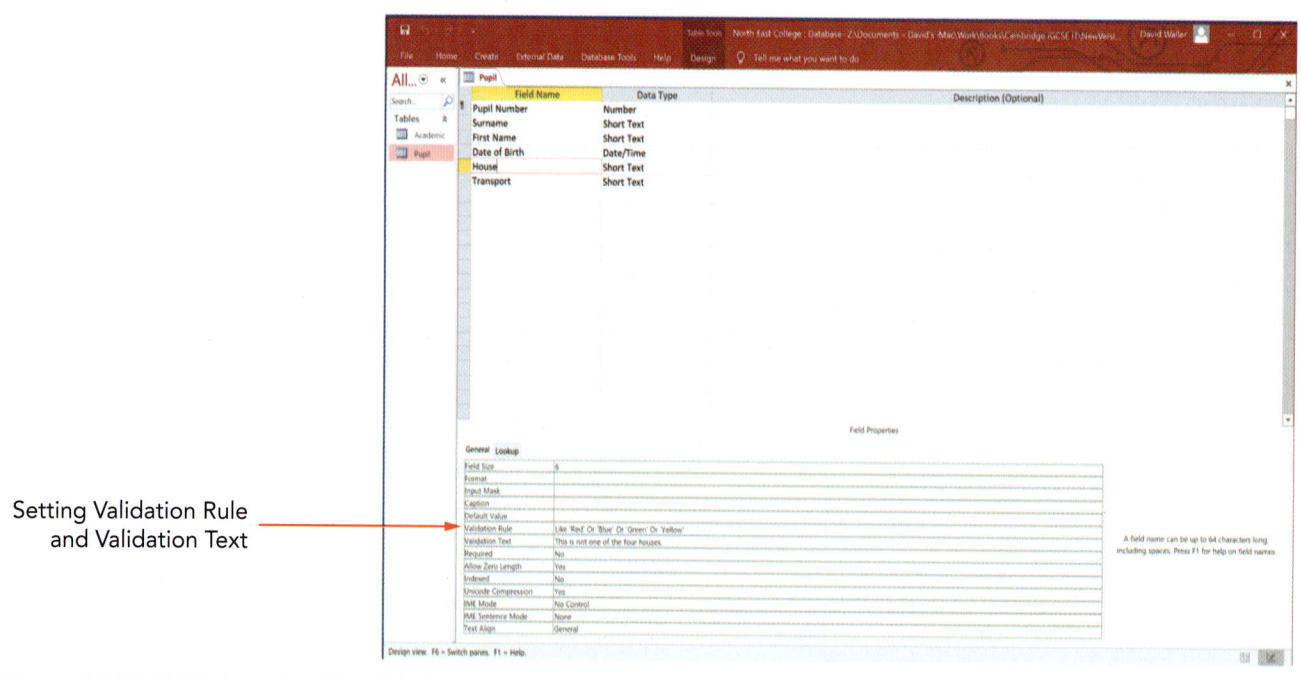

Figure 18.10: Validation rule with validation text

The validation rule `Like `Red´ Or `Blue´ Or `Green´ Or `Yellow´´` will ensure that only one of those options can be entered, and the validation text 'This is not one of the four houses.' will inform a user if they enter anything else. Be aware that validation rules are case sensitive and so 'red' would not be allowed; the database would only accept 'Red'.

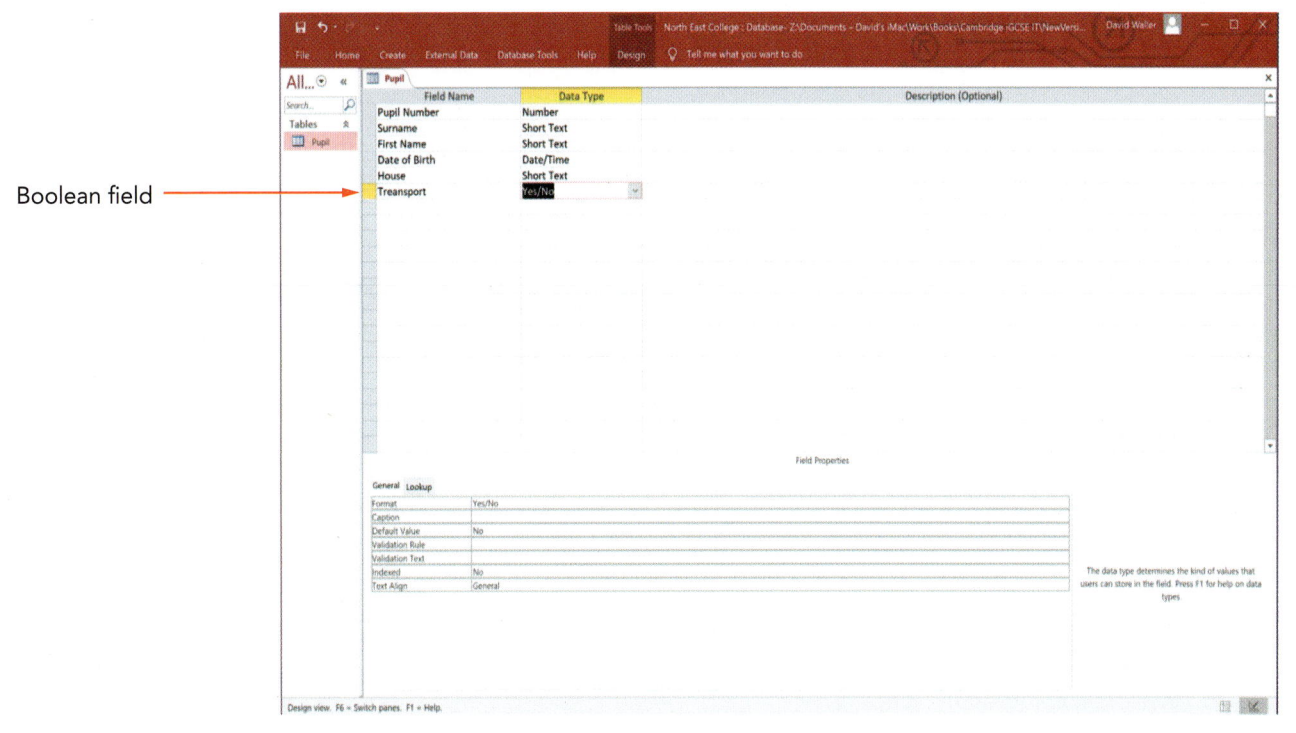

Figure 18.11: Creating a Boolean field

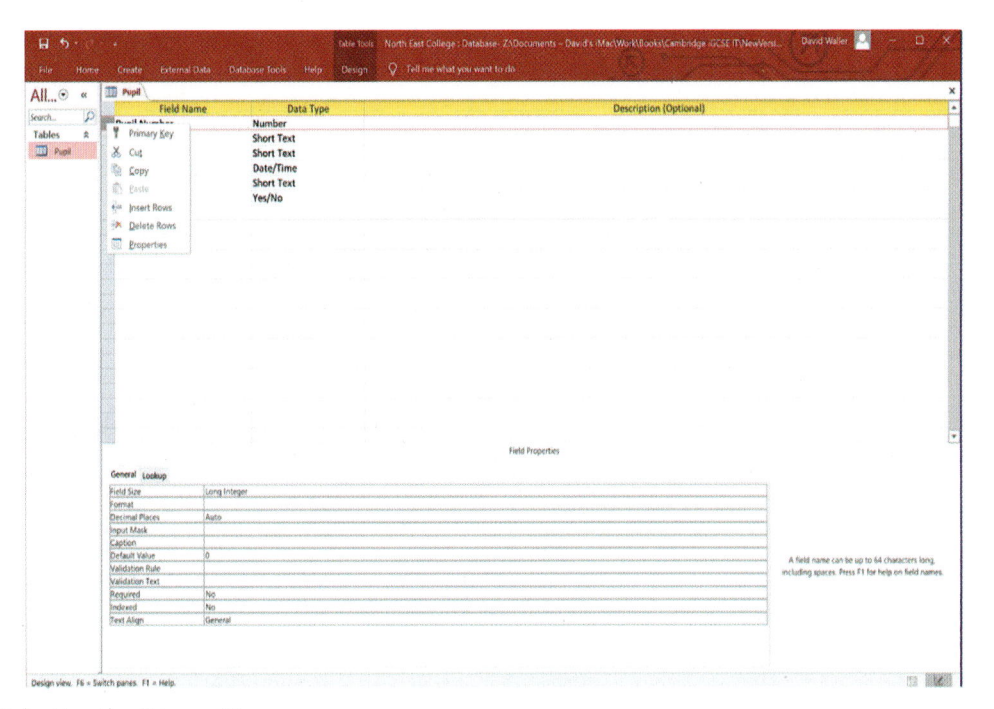

Figure 18.12: Selecting the Primary Key

The Transport field has only two correct entries: 'Yes' and 'No'. As these can also be interpreted as 'True' and 'False', this is called a Boolean data field (see Figure 18.11 on the previous page).

When the data is being entered into the table, this field is usually shown as a checkbox.

Finally, the Pupil Number field has to be selected as the key field. This can be done by right-clicking the grey box to the left of the file name and selecting 'Primary Key' (see Figure 18.12 on the previous page).

The table should now be saved and opened in normal view for data entry. You can reopen the table by double-clicking its icon in the left-hand pane (in Figure 18.13, you would double-click on Pupil, which is highlighted in pink).

Academic table

In a similar way, a table can be created for the Academic data.

Table 18.10 shows the names of the fields.

Pupil Number	Subject	Course-work	Examination	Total

Table 18.10: Fields for database

A new table can be created by selecting Table Design in the Create ribbon (see Figure 18.14). The fields are set up in the same way as for the Pupil table.

The table is going to be saved before the Total field is added, but first the primary key has to be selected. This is going to be a compound key of the Pupil Number and the Subject fields.

The boxes next to each other should be selected by holding down Shift and clicking on the grey boxes next to the file name. Key Field should be chosen after right-clicking (see Figure 18.15 on the next page).

When selecting fields to form a compound key, they *must* be next to each other. Fields can be easily dragged to different positions in the table by clicking on the grey box next to the file name and dragging it to where you want that field to be.

The reason that the table has been saved before the Total field is added is that this field is going to do a calculation by adding the data in the Coursework and Examination fields. This is called a **calculated field**. Before the table is saved, the field names cannot be used in a calculation.

> **KEY WORD**
>
> **calculated field:** a field whose data is calculated from other fields

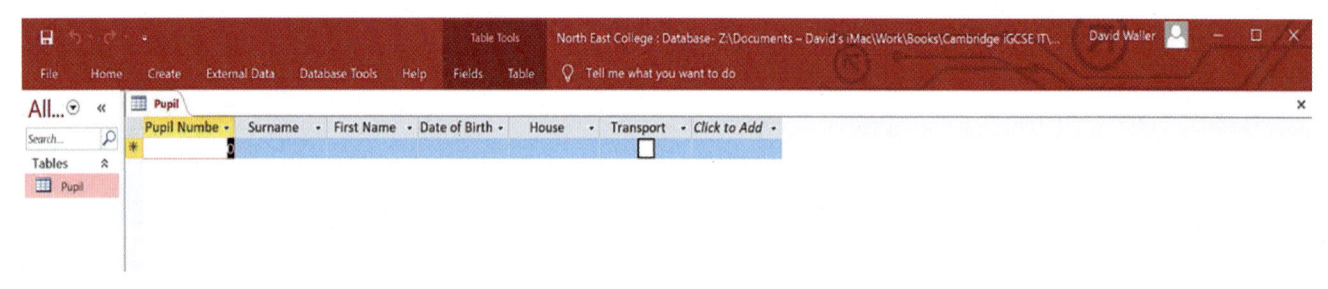

Figure 18.13: The table open for data entry

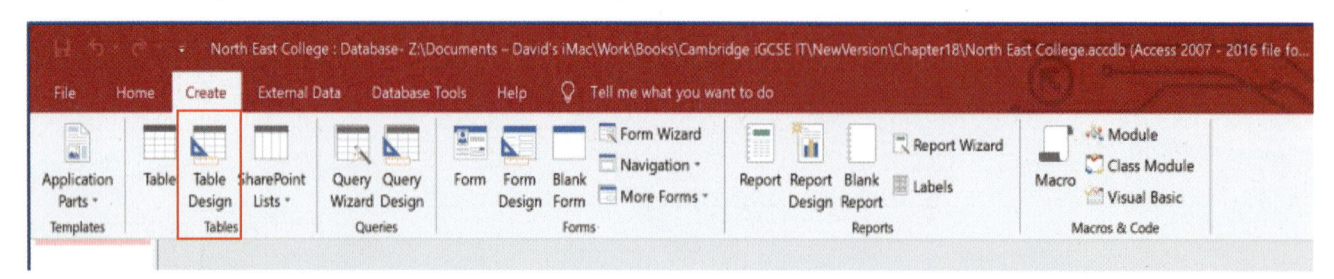

Figure 18.14: Creating a new table

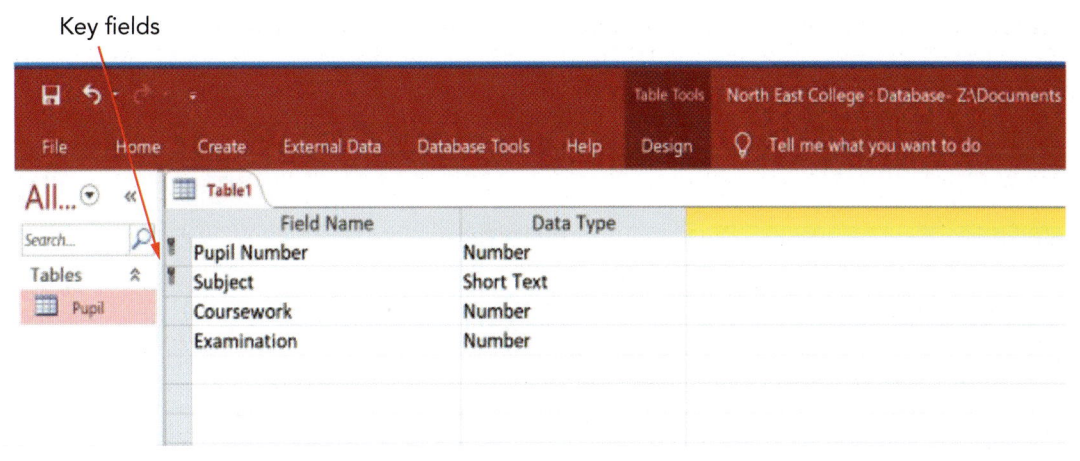

Figure 18.15: Creating a combined key

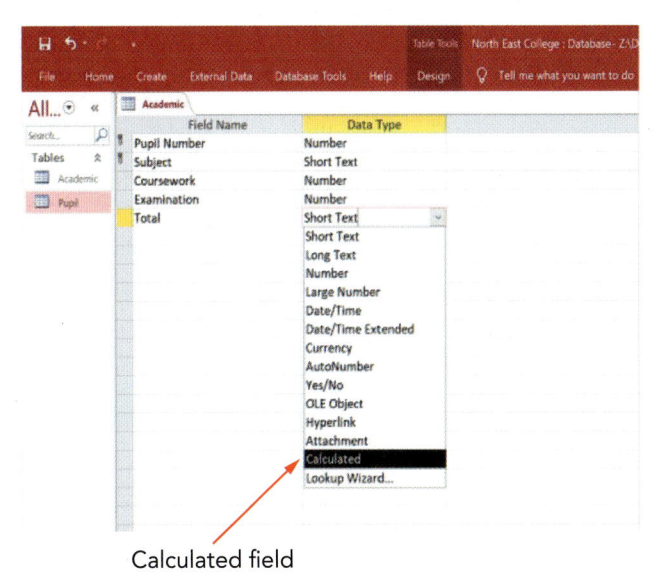

Figure 18.16: Creating a calculated field

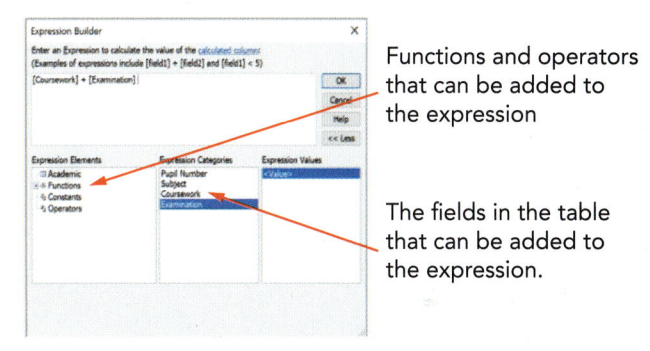

Figure 18.17: Building an expression

Once the table has been saved, the new field name can be added and Calculated is selected as the data type (see Figure 18.16).

The Expression Builder dialogue box will open and the **expression** can be built by double-clicking on the field names in the Expression Categories and typing a '+' sign to add them together, as seen in Figure 18.17.

Any arithmetic operator (+, −, × or ÷) can be used in these expressions.

When OK is clicked, the field will be shown in the table.

If the Expression Builder dialogue box doesn't open automatically, or if you wish to edit your expression later on, click on the Expression box in the Field Properties at the bottom of the Design View. Either a drop-down box arrow or a 'more options' icon with three dots will be on the right-hand side. Clicking this should open the dialogue box.

> **KEY WORD**
>
> **expression:** a combination of mathematical and arithmetic operators and fields used to evaluate a single value

PRACTICAL TASK 18.1

Getting started

Here are some activities related to this task. If you do not already know the answers, then carry out research in your textbook and online.

Data entered into a database should be validated wherever it is needed.

1. On paper, using the correct operators, write a validation rule so that only numbers between 7 and 13 inclusive can be entered.

2. Write suitable validation text for this rule.

Practice

3. Open the *Students* database into your database software.

4. All of the tests are marked out of 100.

   Open the Maths table in design view and apply suitable validation rules to the following fields:
   - FirstTermTest
   - SecondTermTest
   - ThirdTermTest.

   Also provide suitable validation text to warn the user if the rules are broken.

   Take screenshots of the fields in design view to show the rules and paste them into a document named *Task1.doc*.

   Take a screenshot of the error message when incorrect data is entered and paste it into *Task1.doc*.

5. Use Save As to save the database as *Student1* into your personal area with the changes that you have made.

Challenge

6. Create a validation rule for the 'Gender' field with suitable validation text.

7. Format the 'Gender' field to ensure that the data is always in upper case.

8. Create a validation rule for the 'DateOfBirth' field. All students in this group should be born between 2005 and 2007.

9. Take screenshots of these fields showing the rules and paste them into *Task1.doc*. Save the file as *Task1_Challenge.doc*. Save the database as *Student1_Challenge*.

PRACTICAL TASK 18.2

Getting started

Here are some activities related to this task. If you do not already know the answers, then carry out research in your textbook and online.

1. Explain what is meant by a calculated field.
2. Create an expression that would find the average of the three test results for a student.

Practice

3. In the database you saved in Practical Task 18.1 (*Student1_Challenge*), open the Maths table in design view and create a new field named 'Average'.
4. Make this a calculated field with an expression to find the average of the three test results.
5. Format this field as integer.
6. Save the table and open it to see the new field.
7. Manually check the results in three records to ensure that it is working as expected.

    Take screenshots of the field in design view to show the calculation. Paste it into a document named *Task2.doc*.

8. Use Save As to save the database with the name *Student2* into your personal area on the computer with the changes that you have made.

Challenge

9. Change the format of the 'Average' field so that it shows the calculation with one decimal place.

    Take screenshots of the field in design view to show the specification and paste it into *Task2.doc*.

10. Sort the records so that they are in alphabetical order according to surname.

    Take a screenshot of the result and paste it into *Task2.doc*. Save the file as *Task2_Challenge.doc*. Save the database as *Student2_Challenge*.

Relationships

There are now two tables in our school database (Pupil and Academic) and there is a **relationship** between them as they are linked through the Pupil Number fields. The relationships between the tables can be defined by selecting Relationships from the Database Tools ribbon (see Figure 18.18). Both tables can be selected from the list provided. Alternatively, select the databases you want to define the relationships for from the left-hand pane, holding down the Shift key to select more than one database.

> **KEY WORD**
>
> **relationship:** fields in different tables with corresponding data

Once the tables are shown (the two top boxes in Figure 18.19), the link between them can be defined clicking on the Pupil Number field in the Pupil table and dragging it across to the Pupil Number field in the Academic table. The dialogue box (the bottom box in Figure 18.19) will then be shown.

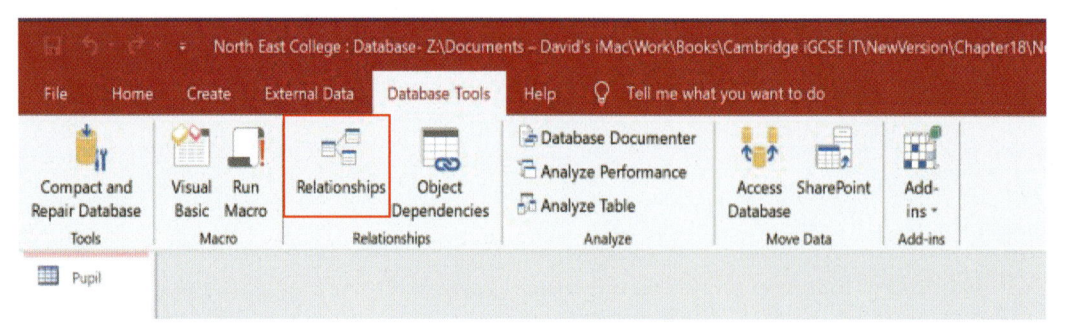

Figure 18.18: Setting up relationships

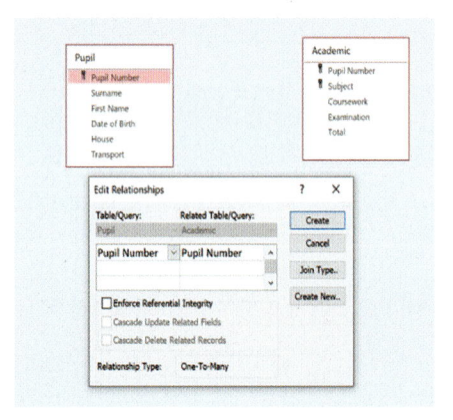

Figure 18.19: Relationship between the tables

This dialogue box displays the fields from the two tables, and at the bottom, shows that it is a '**one-to-many** **relationship**'. This means that in the Pupil table, the Pupil Number of an individual pupil can appear only once but in the Academic table it can appear many times, depending on the number of subjects studied by a pupil.

If the 'Enforce **Referential Integrity**' box is checked, then the RDMS will ensure that there are no '**orphans**' left behind (i.e. if a pupil is deleted from the Pupil table, having the box ticked will ensure that there are no records for that student in the Academic table).

When Create is clicked, the tables will be shown with their relationship (see Figure 18.20).

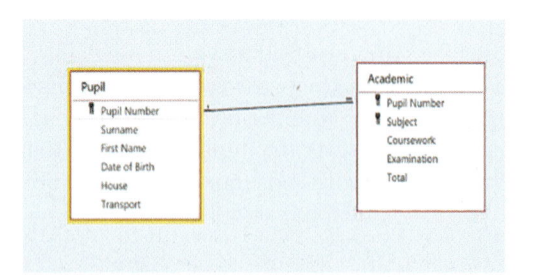

Figure 18.20: The tables showing their relationship

> ### ACTIVITY 18.2
>
> Carry out research and find out information on two other types of relationships between tables. Create a poster explaining the differences between them.

Entering and importing data

Data can be entered directly into the table, or it can be imported from an external source such as a spreadsheet or a **comma separated value** (CSV) file, a text file (.txt) or rich text format file (.rtf).

In a CSV file, the data for the different fields are separated by a comma (see Figure 18.21). In ordinary text files they are usually separated by a tab (see Figure 18.22).

> ### KEY WORDS
>
> **one-to-many relationship:** where the data in one row of a table can be linked to data in many rows of another table
>
> **referential integrity:** preventing orphan records – records that reference records in other tables that no longer exist
>
> **orphan:** records that reference records in other tables that no longer exist
>
> **comma separated value (CSV):** this file format can be used on data saved in a table structured format, such as a spreadsheet or a database, where each value is separated by a comma

18 Databases

```
Pupil Number,Surname,First Name,Date of Birth,House,Transport
1036,Suparmanputra,Hasan,21/03/2010,Red,Yes
2872,Elmasry,Anat,06/10/2009,Blue,No
1725,Nasution,Abdul,24/02/2008,Blue,No
3916,Megat,Amina,16/04/2006,Green,No
7321,Nababan,Annisa,29/07/2005,Yellow,Yes
1328,Mansour,Hasina,13/01/2006,Yellow,Yes
1712,Zaky,Khalid,17/11/2007,Green,Yes
2482,Sakura,Abe,12/05/2006,Red,No
2223,Mazur,Lucia,28/01/2006,Red,Yes
3669,Sayid,Haziq,10/11/2005,Green,Yes
```

Figure 18.21: A CSV file

```
Pupil Number → Surname → First Name→Date of Birth → House→Transport
1036→ Suparmanputra → Hasan→21/03/2010→Red → Yes
2872→ Elmasry  → Anat→ 06/10/2009→Blue → No
1725→ Nasution → Abdul→24/02/2008→Blue → No
3916→ Megat→Amina→16/04/2006→Green→No
7321→ Nababan  → Annisa → 29/07/2005→Yellow → Yes
1328→ Mansour  → Hasina → 13/01/2006→Yellow → Yes
1712→ Zaky→ Khalid   → 17/11/2007→Green→Yes
2482→ Sakura   → Abe → 12/05/2006→Red → No
2223→ Mazur→Lucia→28/01/2006→Red → Yes
3669→ Sayid→Haziq→10/11/2005→Green→Yes
```

Figure 18.22: A text file

Importing a CSV file

The following six steps (Figure 18.23) show how to import a CSV file.

1 Select New Data Source from the External Data Ribbon and then Text File

2 The file to be used and the table to import the data into are selected

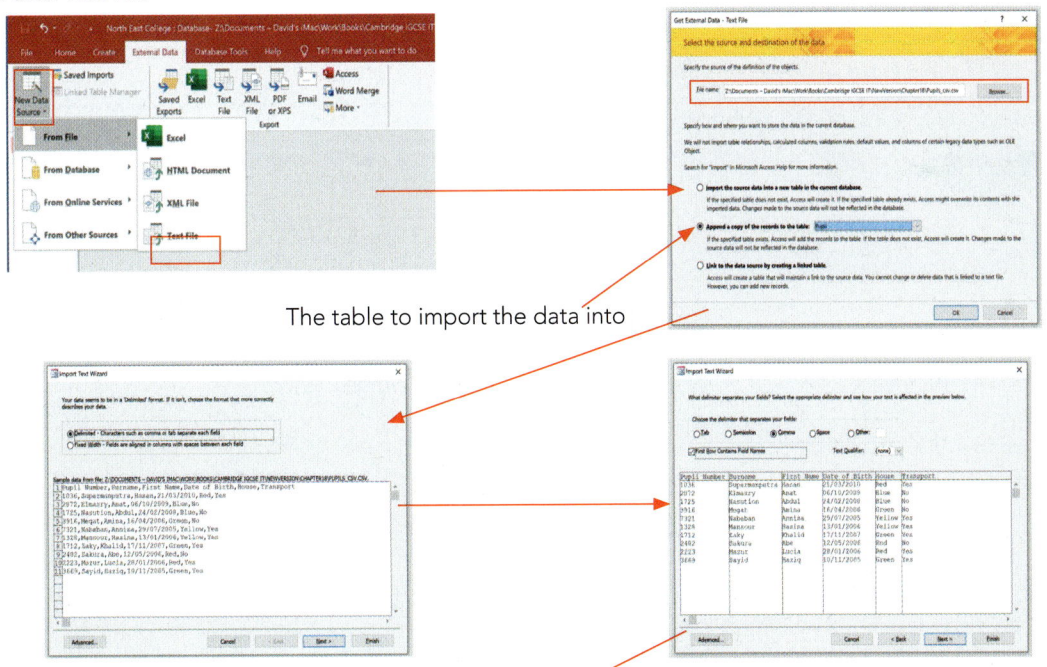

The table to import the data into

3 The information to be imported is shown

4 The comma is used as a separator and the first row that contains the Field names can be confirmed

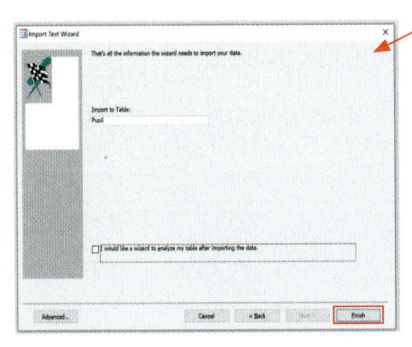

5 The import table is confirmed

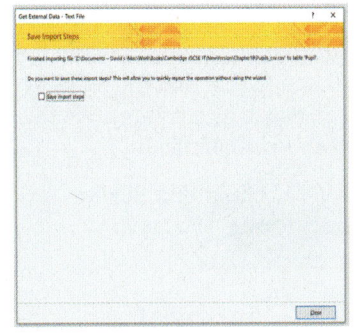

6 Confirmation that the data has been imported

Figure 18.23: Steps for importing a CSV file

385

Figure 18.24 shows the data imported.

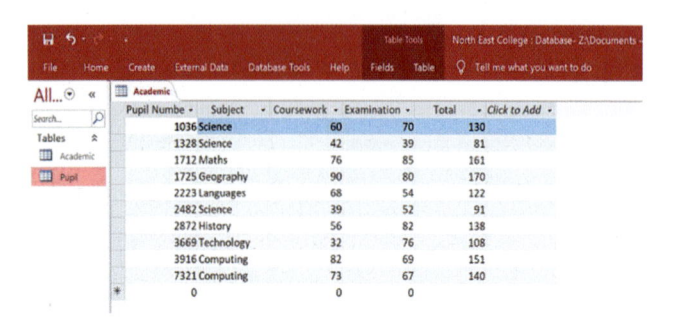

Figure 18.24: The imported data

Data can be imported into the Academic table in the same way (see Figure 18.25).

Figure 18.25: Data in the academic table

Data can also be imported to a new table which is created in the import process.

Creating tables while importing data

It is possible to create a new table to store the imported data. Open the dialogue box from New Data Source and Text File as before.

Figure 18.26 shows the instruction to store the data into a new table.

You will be asked if the data items are delimited or of fixed length. Delimited means that the items are separated by a character such as a comma. As this is a CSV file, you need to choose delimited.

The import wizard has to be told that the first row contains the field names for the new table (see Figure 18.27).

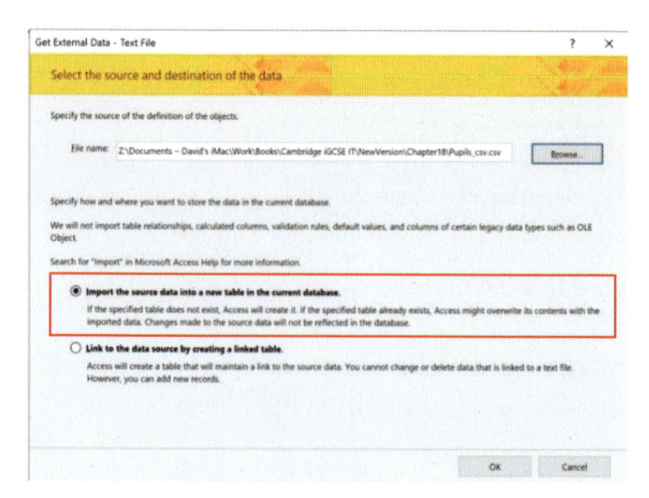

Figure 18.26: Storing data into a new table

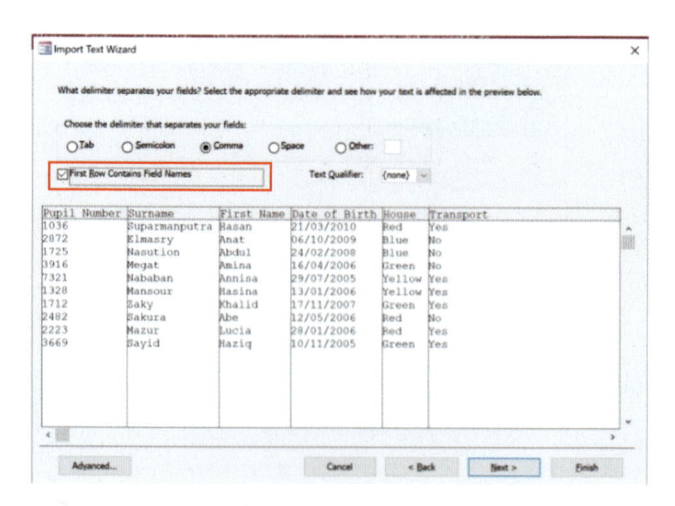

Figure 18.27: Specifying the field names

In this dialogue box, the delimiter has been set as a comma.

The field names and the data types can now be specified for each field (see Figure 18.28).

The field to act as the primary key can be selected (see Figure 18.29). If one isn't selected, then the program will create a new field and give each record a unique number.

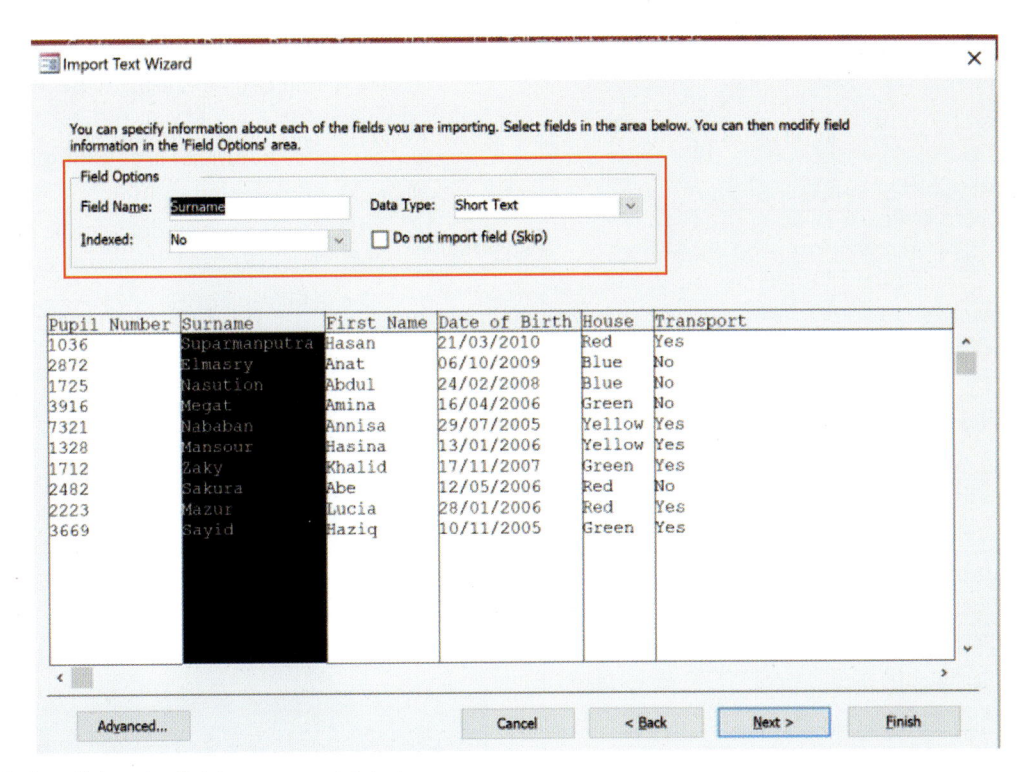

Figure 18.28: Specifying the field names and data types

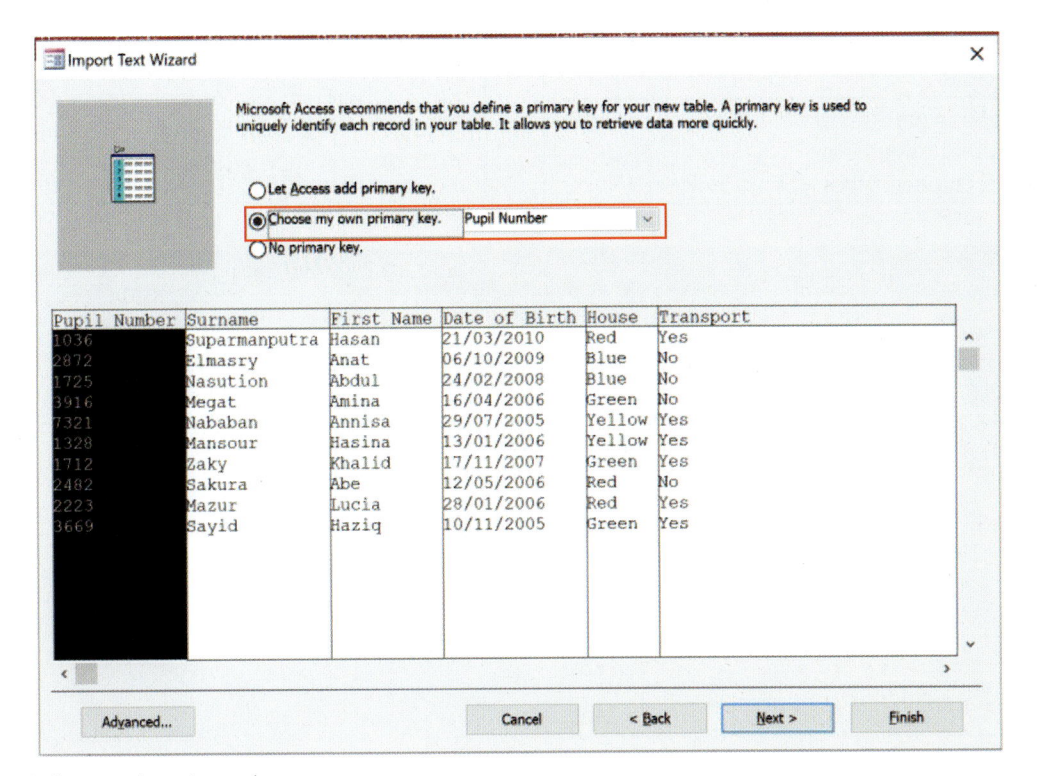

Figure 18.29: Selecting the primary key

387

> CAMBRIDGE IGCSE™ ICT: COURSEBOOK

ICT IN CONTEXT

All databases are vulnerable to online criminals and people's personal and financial data are at risk. Between January and September 2019, there were over 7.9 billion data records exposed – a 33% increase from the same time in 2018! These data breaches occur all round the world – no country is exempt.

Questions

1 Match the statement with the correct term relating to database structure.

1	a structure to store one item of data stored in a database	A	primary key
2	all the information from all the fields about one person or object	B	relational database
3	the unique identifier for each record in a database	C	field
4	data collected about one organisation in one large table	D	flat-file database
5	a database with several tables that have fields related to each other	E	record

2 Complete the following sentences about a database of student files in a school, using these words: database, field, flat file primary key, record, relational database.

   a Students' addresses is an example of a ……………………………

   b Minjing Han is a student on the database; all of their details are an example of a ……………

   c The field Student ID is an example of a ……………………………..

   d If all the data for one class was stored in one large table, it would be an example of a ……………….. database.

   e If all the data of the students was stored in many different tables and linked by common fields, it would be an example of a …………………………….. database.

3 Explain the difference between a flat file database and a relational database.

ACTIVITY 18.3

In small groups, write all the words you associate with databases in three minutes. Put your pens down after the three minutes. One of you should read out their list and the rest should scratch it out on their list. The next student with any words left should read out their words, until there are no more common words shared.

PRACTICAL TASK 18.3

Getting started

1 The diagram in Figure 18.30 shows tables in a database.

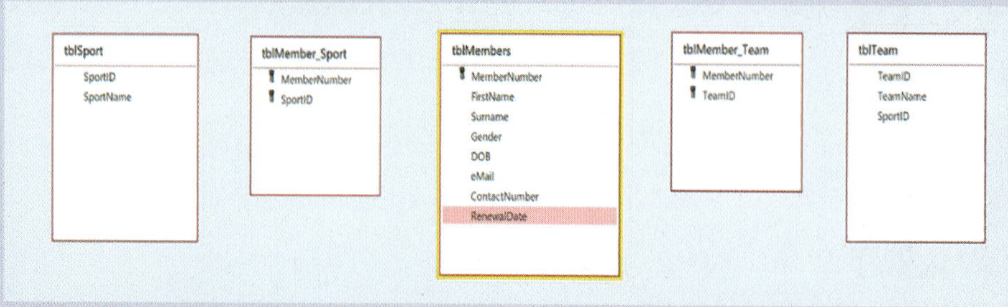

[Diagram showing five tables: tblSport (SportID, SportName), tblMember_Sport (MemberNumber, SportID), tblMembers (MemberNumber, FirstName, Surname, Gender, DOB, eMail, ContactNumber, RenewalDate), tblMember_Team (MemberNumber, TeamID), tblTeam (TeamID, TeamName, SportID)]

Figure 18.30: Tables in a database

Copy the tables onto a piece of paper and draw lines showing the fields that link the tables together.

2 What is the type of relationship between tblMembers and tblMember_Sport?

388

CONTINUED

Practice

The table in the *Students.accdb* database that you saved after Practical Task 18.2 (*Student2* or *Student2_Challenge*) contains data about the students and their Maths results.

There is another csv file that contains data about the students and their IT results (*ITResults.csv*). This needs to be imported into the database.

3. Instead of creating a completely new table, copy the Maths table and paste it back into the database as a table named IT. You can do this by right-clicking on the Maths table icon in the left pane to copy and again to paste.

4. Delete all of the records in this table and import *ITResults.csv* into it.

   There are now two tables in the database, Maths and IT.

   Unfortunately, the data in these two tables breaks one of the major rules of database design. There is a lot of duplication of data. The student numbers, first names, surnames, genders and dates of birth are duplicated – they are in both tables. Very bad!

   But it can be solved.

5. Copy one of the two tables and paste it into the database as Students.

   - Delete all of the fields containing termly results and the average from the student table so that only the student data remains.
   - Delete the FirstName, Surname, Gender and Date of Birth fields from the Maths and IT tables. DO NOT delete the StudentNumber fields as they are needed to link the three tables.

6. In your database program set up the relationships between these three tables.

   Take a screenshot of the relationships, like the one on in the Getting started questions, and paste it into a document named *Task3.doc*.

7. Save the database as *Student3*.

Data from the three tables can be combined by using a query. Manipulating data using queries is covered later in this chapter.

8. As a very difficult challenge look at the section on manipulating data and create a query using the three tables. The following fields should be included in the query:

   - SecondName
   - FirstName
   - Average from the Maths table
   - Average from the IT table.

   Run the query and take a screenshot. Paste it into document *Task3.doc* and save it as *Task3_Challenge.doc*.

9. Save the database as *Student3_Challenge*.

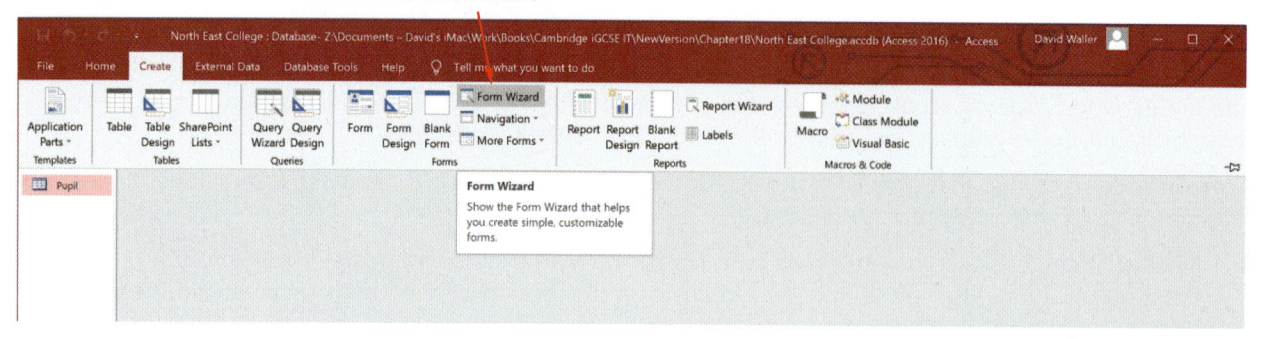

Figure 18.31: Selecting Form Wizard from the Create ribbon

Create a data entry form

Data can be entered directly into a table but often data needs to be entered into two or more linked tables at the same time This can be done by creating **data entry forms**.

Data entry forms also provide a more user-friendly interface for users unfamiliar with databases. Users can enter and manipulate data without ever seeing a table.

There are several ways of creating a table.

- Start with a blank form and design it from scratch.
- Use a form **design wizard** that will take a table and create a suitable form.
- Use a form design wizard and then customise the form to your own requirements.

Using a form design wizard

The wizard will ask you for the table to be used for the form and then create one for you. You can open the Form Wizard from the Create menu (see Figure 18.31).

Using the arrows, move all the fields across from Available Fields to Selected Fields. A single arrow > will move one at a time, the double arrows >> will move all at once. (See Figure 18.32)

Choose the layout of your form (see Figure 18.33 on the next page). A **columnar form** has one record on each page but a **tabular form** shows the records as a continuous list.

The form can be edited by opening it in Design View (see Figure 18.35 on the next page).

Each item in the form is named (see Figure 18.34 on the next page), and when it is selected, its details can be seen in the **property sheet**. The fields shown on the form are called **controls**.

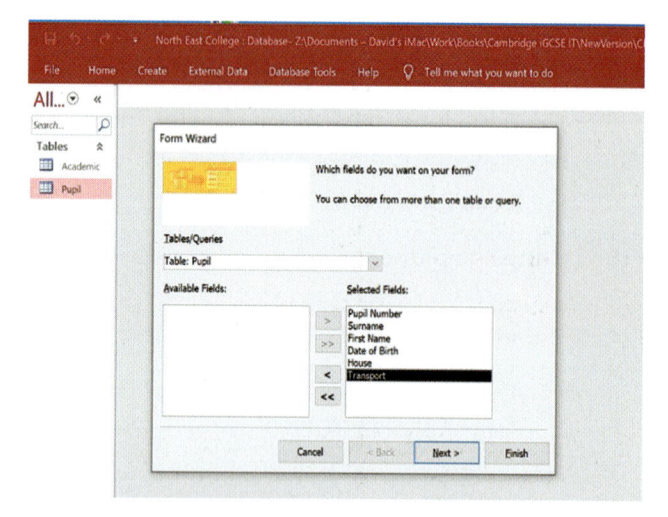

Figure 18.32: All fields from the Pupil table selected for the form

KEY WORDS

data-entry form: a form through which data can be input into a particular table

design wizard: an online tool that takes a user through the steps of designing something, e.g. a form or a report

columnar form: a form that displays one record at a time

tabular form: a form that displays multiple records at the same time

property sheet: a list of all of the settings for all of the items, e.g. field, label, heading on a form

control: parts of a form or report used to display and manipulate data

18 Databases

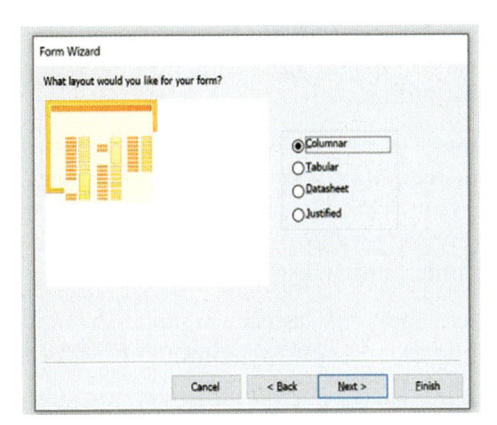

Figure 18.33: Selecting the form layout

When each item is selected it can be edited – for example, its font, font colour and background colour can be changed.

Each item in the form is named, and when one is selected, its details can be seen in the property sheet in the right-hand pane (see Figure 18.35).

When each item is selected it can be edited, e.g. its font, font colour and background colour can be changed (see Figure 18.36 on the next page).

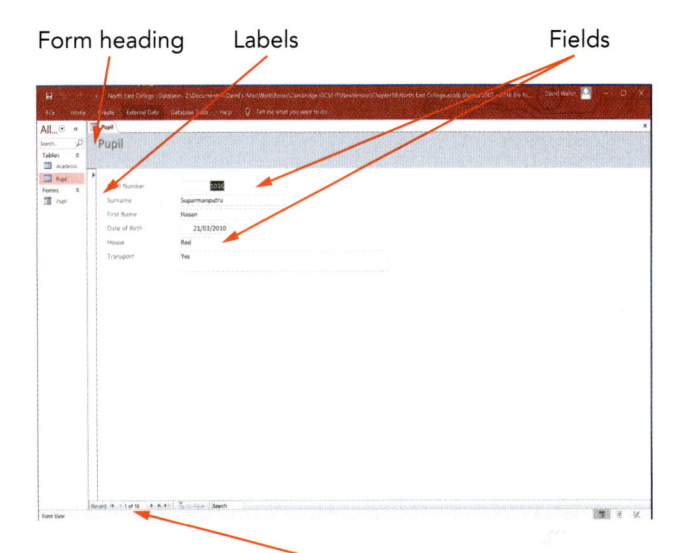

Figure 18.34: Form created by the wizard

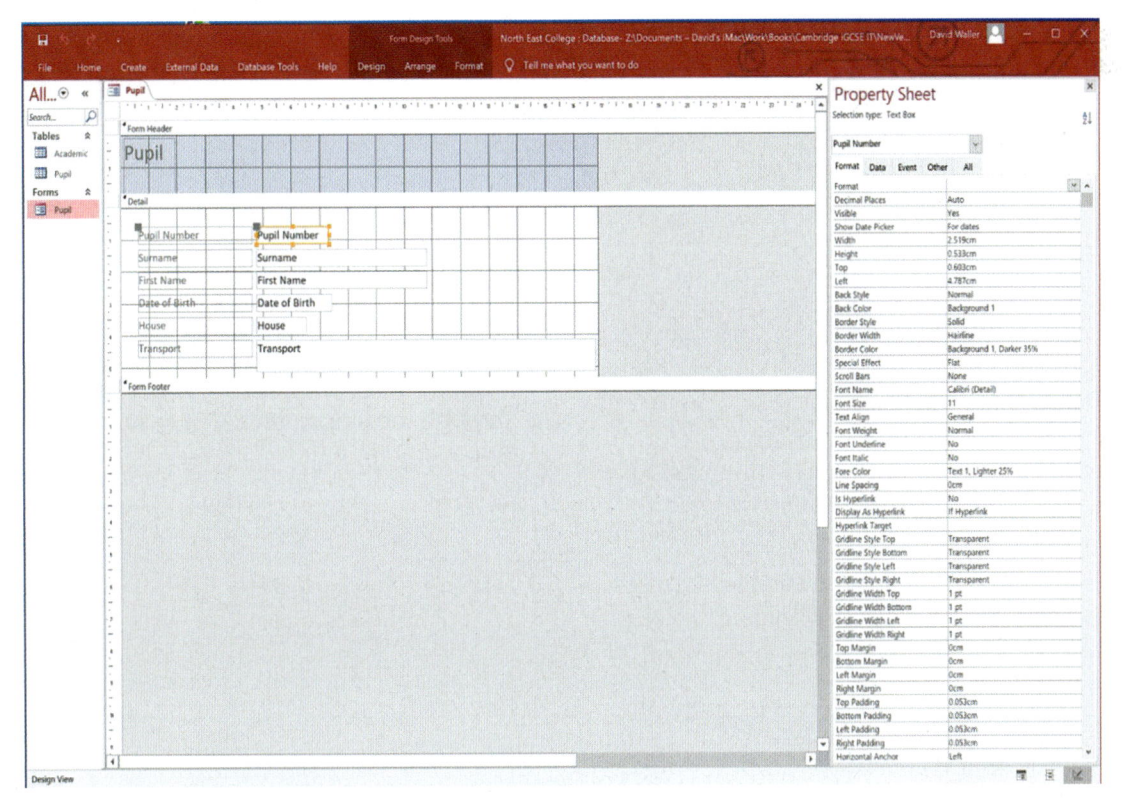

Figure 18.35: The form in design view

391

Characteristics of good form design

The characteristics of good form design should include:

- Effectiveness – the form should work as it was intended.
- Accuracy – the data entry form should use database tools that would ensure that accurate data is more likely to be entered by using drop-down lists. Users could simply choose from a list, rather than type their own responses in and risk making spelling mistakes or using incorrect words that would affect data output.
- Simplicity – instead of entering your gender as male or female, use a drop-down box or radio buttons.
- Attractiveness – well-designed forms are usually attractive. Attractive forms encourage users to fill them out. This is because it appears easier than a poorly designed form that might have too much or too little white space.
- Consistency – consistency in shapes and colours help to create a consistent layout of the form.
- Intuitive navigation – it should be easy to move from one item to other related ones without having to search for them.

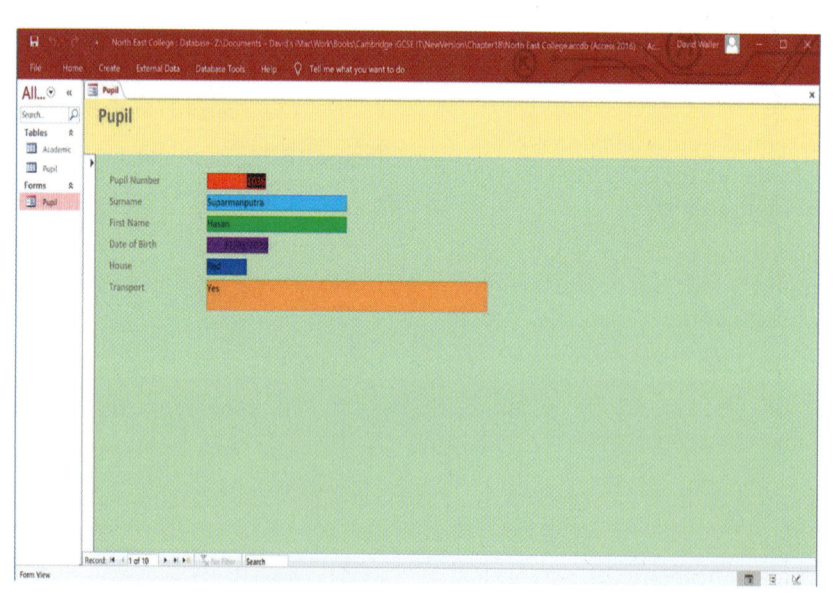

Figure 18.36: How not to design a form

Design features

Check boxes

In the design view of our Students database, a check box can be set to represent the Transport field so that a tick indicates if transport is needed (see Figure 18.37).

This is done by adding it to the form and then linking it to the Transport field (see Figure 18.38 on the next page).

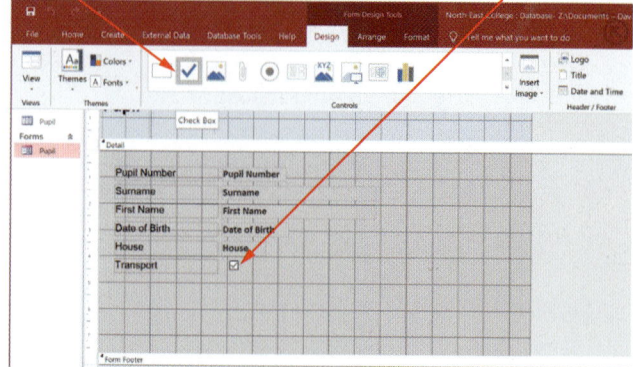

Figure 18.37: Creating a check box

Drop-down menus or combo boxes

When users are adding data to the House field in the Students database, there are only four options, red, blue, green and yellow. To assist them, these options

18 Databases

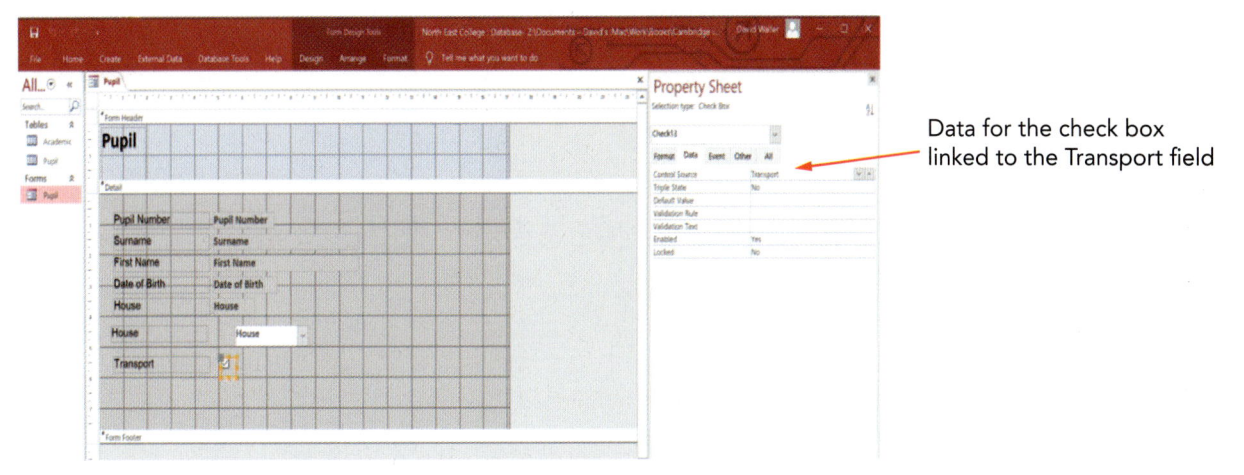

Figure 18.38: Linking a form control to a data source

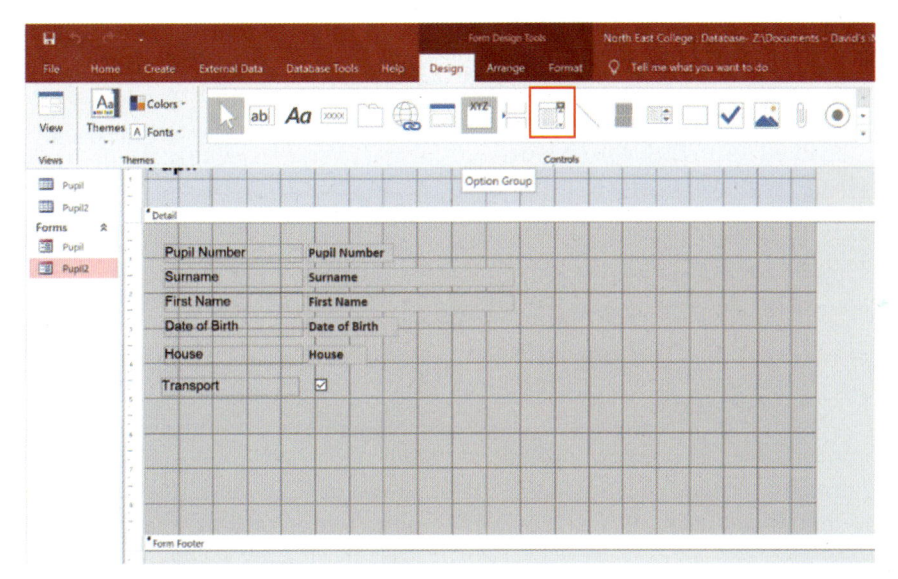

Data for the check box linked to the Transport field

Figure 18.39: Selecting a combo box

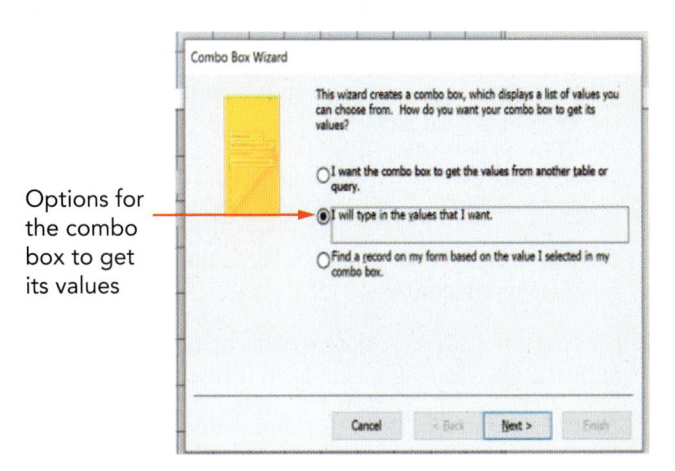

Options for the combo box to get its values

The four House colours for the list are entered.

Figure 18.40: The combo box wizard

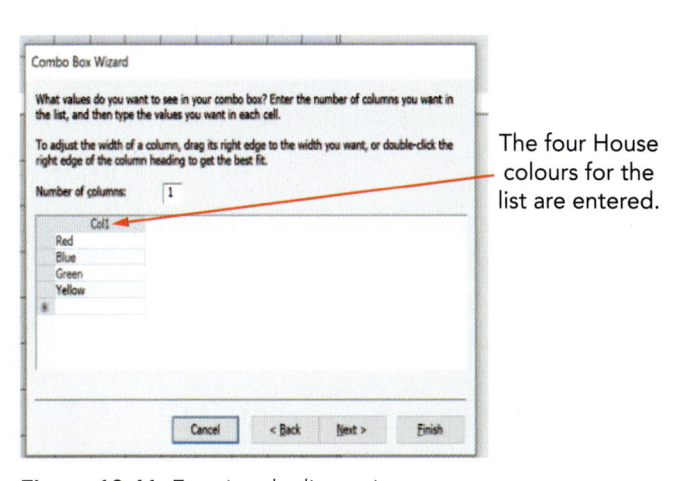

Figure 18.41: Entering the list options

393

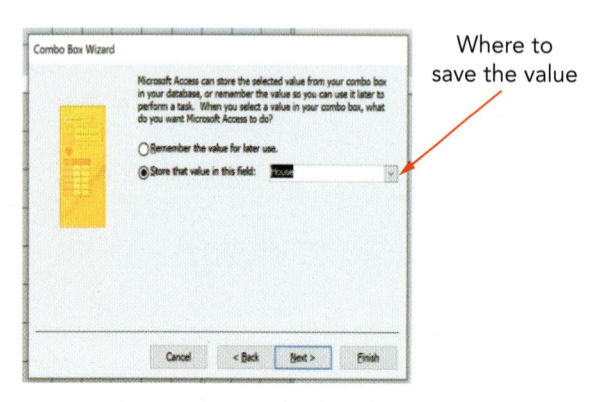

Figure 18.42: Selecting the field for the option selected

can be selected from a **drop-down menu** or **combo box** (see Figure 18.39 on the previous page).

After selecting the Combo Box icon on the design ribbon (see Figure 18.39), a combo box can be drawn on the form. The Combo Box Wizard will then open asking where the items for the box are located. They could be in another table; but for the Pupil form, they will be typed in (see Figures 18.40–41 on the previous page).

Finally, the combo box is instructed to save the selected option in the House field (see Figure 18.42).

Options can be chosen from the drop-down menu (see Figure 18.43).

Radio buttons

Alternatively, radio buttons can be used in fields where there are two or more options, such as the House field. They are small buttons and when one is selected, the others are deselected.

Each radio button returns a number and therefore the field that stores the choice must be a number field. The House field has been changed to a number field.

For example, if Figure 18.44 showed the House names Red, Blue, Green, Yellow instead of Example 1, Example 2, Example 3, Example 4, choosing 'Red' would return 1, choosing Blue would return 2, and so on.

An **option group** (see Figure 18.45 on the next page) can contain a number of radio buttons.

The following five steps (Figure 18.46 on the next page) show how to create an option group.

The radio buttons are shown on the form (see Figure 18.47). In the form in Figure 18.47, the House field is shown twice – as a field showing the number of the selected option (1) and as radio buttons.

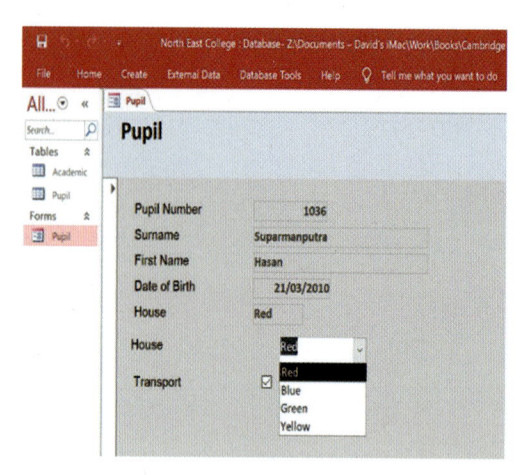

Figure 18.43: Selecting an item from the combo box

- ● Example 1.
- ○ Example 2.
- ○ Example 3.
- ○ Example 4.
- ○ Example 5.

Figure 18.44: Example of radio buttons

Normally only the radio buttons would be shown. It is shown here to confirm that selecting 'Red' will cause 1 to be entered into the field.

Navigation buttons

When a form is produced, small **navigation controls** are shown in the bottom margin. These are quite small and other buttons can be created to replace them. This is done by creating **command buttons**, buttons that bring about an action when it is pressed (see Figure 18.48).

KEY WORDS

drop-down menu: a menu that appears when the user clicks on a particular item

combo box: a control on a form that contains a drop-down list

option group: a control on a form that displays a number of alternatives

navigation controls: command buttons that allows a user to move between forms

command button: a button that brings about an action when it is pressed

18 Databases

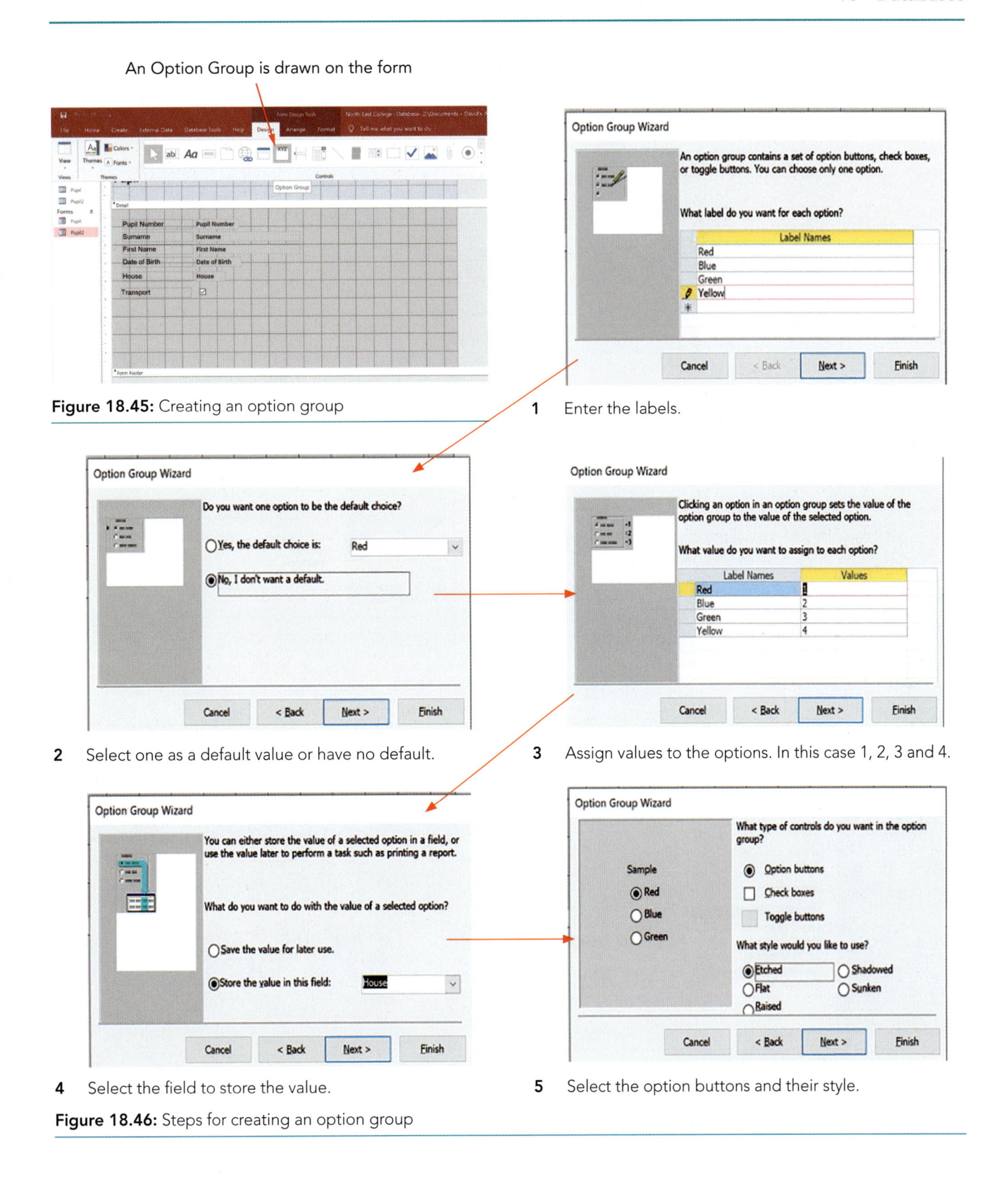

An Option Group is drawn on the form

Figure 18.45: Creating an option group

1. Enter the labels.

2. Select one as a default value or have no default.

3. Assign values to the options. In this case 1, 2, 3 and 4.

4. Select the field to store the value.

5. Select the option buttons and their style.

Figure 18.46: Steps for creating an option group

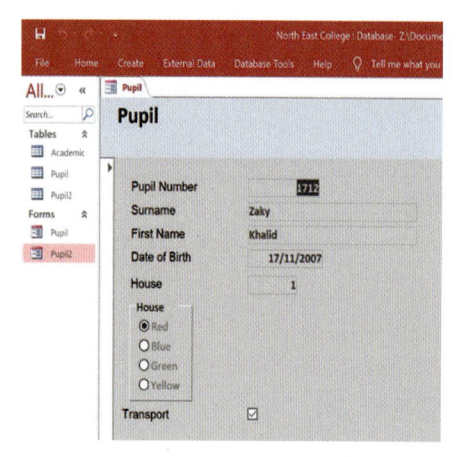

Figure 18.47: Radio buttons on the form

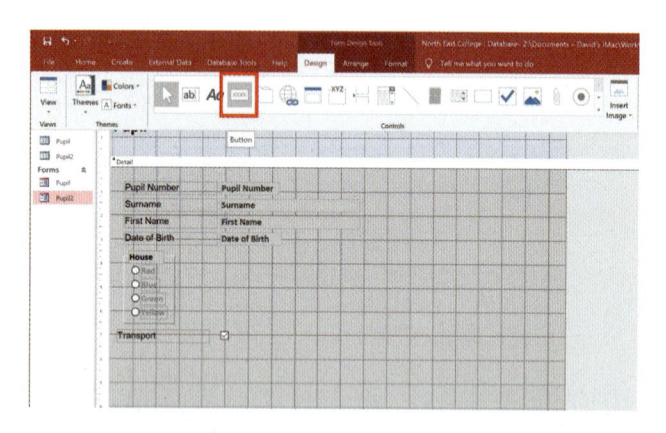

Figure 18.48: Selecting the Command Button control

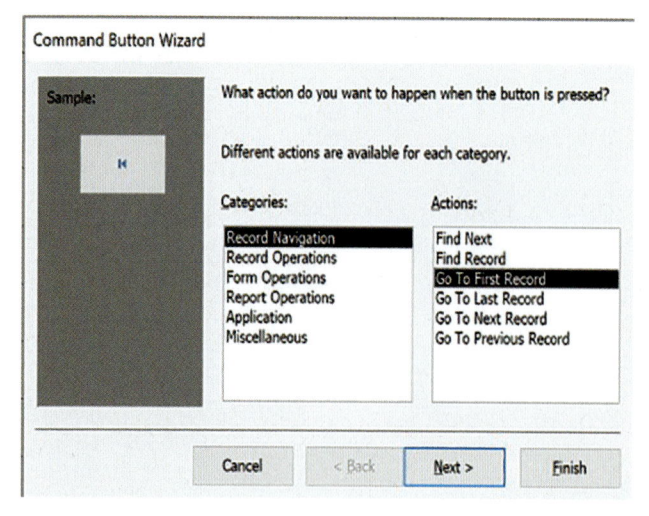

Figure 18.49: Record Navigation and Go To First Record are selected

When a command button is drawn on the form, the wizard opens (see Figure 18.49).

A picture can be selected for the button. Buttons for previous, next and last record can be created in a similar way (see Figure 18.50).

Figure 18.50: Block of navigation buttons

Command buttons for new Record and Delete Record can be created in a similar way (see Figure 18.51).

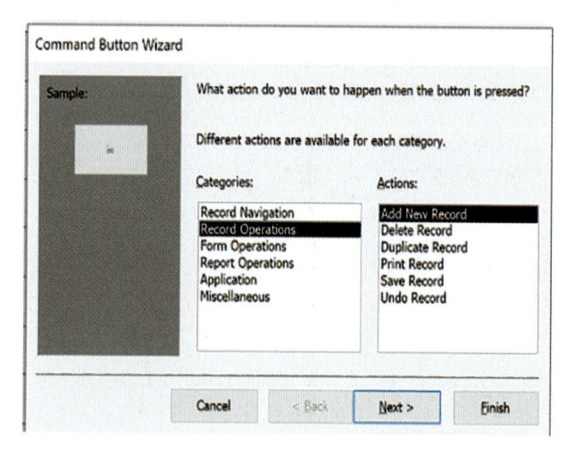

Figure 18.51: Selecting Record Operations and Add New Record

Figure 18.52 shows a form with command buttons added.

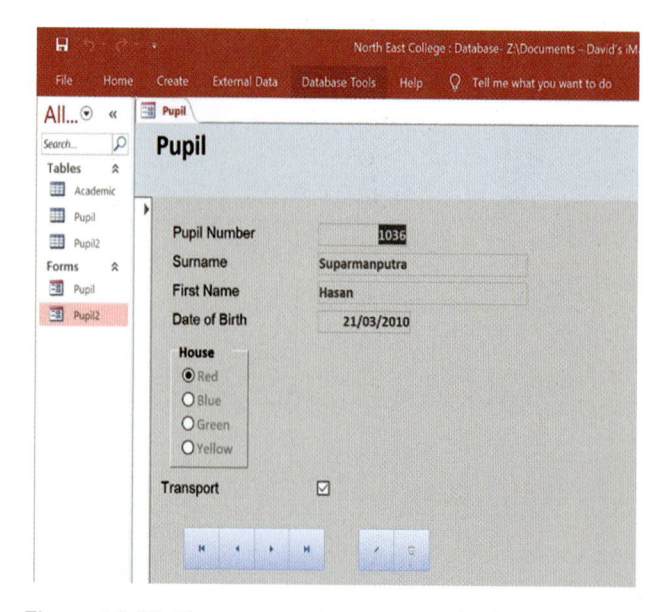

Figure 18.52: The command buttons on the form

Aspects and items that are useful when creating well-designed data entry forms include those shown in Table 18.11.

> **ICT IN CONTEXT**
>
> To protect their citizens, most countries have enacted laws to ensure the people who hold the data do not misuse it and store it securely (data protection acts). The European Union strengthened the laws in member countries in 2018 to make them the strictest in the world. You can look at United Nations websites to see the countries where citizens are protected and those where there is no legislation.

Design features	Functions
Use of white space	Data entry forms with too much white space between fields or with answer boxes that are too large look unattractive but if they are too cramped they may be difficult to follow.
Radio buttons	Radio buttons allow users to make a choice from several options simply by clicking on it. They reduce the possibility of input errors in a database. These allow for only one choice.
Check boxes	Check boxes allow users to make choices from a list of options. It helps users to make decisions quickly by simply selecting those on a pre-made list instead of asking users to compile their own lists. They reduce the possibility of input errors in a database. Check boxes allow the user to select multiple answers.
Drop-down menus	Drop-down menus make it even easier for users to select from options that are already there to choose from. They reduce the possibility of input errors in a database. They allow only one choice.
Appropriate font styles and sizes	Attractive data entry forms encourage users to fill in data they might otherwise have taken longer to give you. Using appropriate font styles and sizes can help to create attractive data entry forms.
Character spacing of individual fields	Aligning characters to the centre, left or right within individual fields can make a data entry form easier on the human eye to process data quicker.

Table 18.11: Design features for creating forms

> **PRACTICAL TASK 18.4**
>
> **Getting started**
>
> 1 With a partner, carry out research on the internet to find a selection of online forms.
>
>   Collect some examples of what you judge to be well and badly designed forms.
>
> 2 On paper, sketch a design for a form that could be used to enter data for the Students database.
>
> **Practice**
>
> 3 Open the *Student3* or *Student3_Challenge* database that you saved in Practical Task 18.3.
>
> 4 Create a data entry form for the Students table.

CONTINUED

5. Create a suitable heading and colour scheme. Arrange the fields so that data is easy to edit and enter, and the form is not cluttered.

6. On the form remove the scroll bars and record navigation bar.

7. Create command buttons for:
   - Go to first record
   - Go to previous record
   - Go to next record
   - Go to last record
   - Create a new record
   - Delete a record.

   An example is shown in Figure 18.53.

   Take a screenshot of your form and paste it into a document named *Task4.doc*.

8. Save the database as *Students_Task4*.

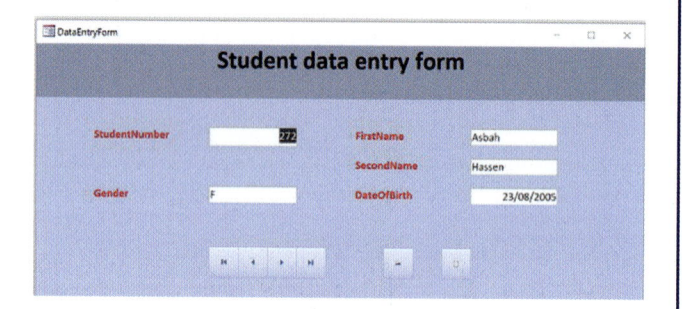

Figure 18.53: Example Student data entry form

Challenge

9. So that users do not have to scroll through all the records to find a particular student, create a combo box control on the form based on the Students table.

   This should allow the user to select a particular student from a list and their record will be shown on the form.

   An example is shown in Figure 18.54.

   Take a screenshot of your form with the list selected and paste it into *Task4.doc*.

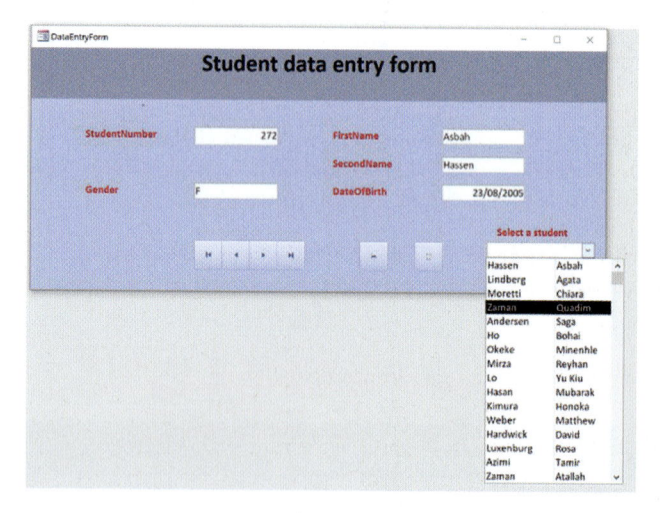

Figure 18.54: Select a student control added

18 Databases

> **CONTINUED**
>
> 10 At the moment the combo box control is based on the table and the students are not shown in alphabetical order.
>
> Change the data source for the control so that the students are in alphabetical order (see example in Figure 18.55).
>
> Take a screenshot of your form with the list selected and paste it into *Task4.doc*. Save the document as *Task4_Challenge.doc*.
>
> Save the database as *Student4_Challenge*.

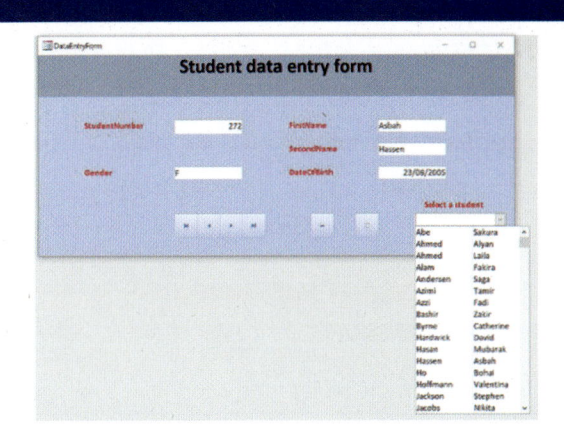

Figure 18.55: Select control with students in alphabetical order

18.2 Manipulating data

An advantage of storing data in an organised way is that it can be searched to find specific information and sorted in different ways. The data can also be analysed to find totals and averages of different fields.

Search and select data

Searches to find specific data are also called **queries**, which can be created using relational database management software. When relationships have been created, many tables can be used within each query.

Queries use **logical operators** (see Table 18.12) to compare values in different fields.

When Query Design is selected from the Create ribbon, the tables to be used in the query have to be selected

> **KEY WORDS**
>
> **query:** a method of interrogating the data held in a database
>
> **logical operator:** operator such as AND, OR, NOT, which perform comparisons values in different fields
>
> **criterion:** an expression used to query field values. Criteria is the plural form of criterion

Operator	Example
AND	Both conditions must be true. Subject must be Like Computing AND Total must be greater than 150 would return only those students where both conditions are true. An AND query has the criteria written on the same line.
OR	Only one of the conditions must be true. Subject must be Like Computing OR Total must be greater than 150 would return all the students who study Computing *and* all those whose Total is greater than 150, whatever the subject. An OR query has the criteria written on different lines.
NOT	Subject NOT Computing would return all the students who do not study computing.

Table 18.12: Logical operators

(see Figure 18.56). (Some programs have a selection pane appear rather than a dialogue box.)

The fields to be used in the query can be moved to the grid by dragging or double-clicking on the field names.

The search **criterion** is written in the 'Criteria' row in one of the field columns. In Figure 18.57, the

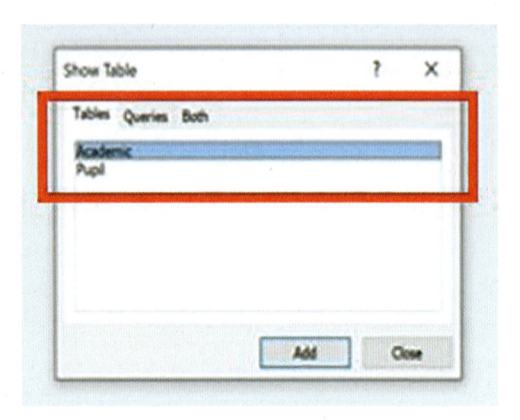

Figure 18.56: Selecting the tables for a query

Subject field is being searched to find all instances of Computing. Therefore, Like 'Computing' has been added as the criterion. (Note: if you are searching for a word, you must put it in single quotation marks ' '; if you are searching for a number, it should not be in quotation marks.)

In some software you do not have to use the operator 'Like' and you can just add the word you are searching for.

This example query will give the results shown in Figure 18.58 on the next page when it is run. This can be done by double-clicking the icon in the left-hand pane or by selecting 'Run!' from the Design view.

More than one criterion can be used at the same time. In Figure 18.59 on the next page, two criteria are used (Like 'Red' and Like 'Computing') and as they are on the same line this is using the AND operator because the criteria are on the same row.

It is therefore searching for pupils who are in the Red House AND study Computing.

Figure 18.60 on the following pages shows the result of this query.

The result shows that there are only two students in the Red House who study Computing.

In the example in Figure 18.61, the two criteria are in different rows to make it an OR query. It is searching for all pupils who study Computing whatever house they are in plus all pupils who are in the Red House, whatever they study.

Figure 18.62 shows the result of this query.

The results of the query can be **sorted** by right-clicking on the field (column) and selecting how you want the data sorted (see Figures 18.63 and 18.64 on the following pages). In this case, alphabetical order is selected.

> **KEY WORD**
>
> **sort:** arrange into a particular order

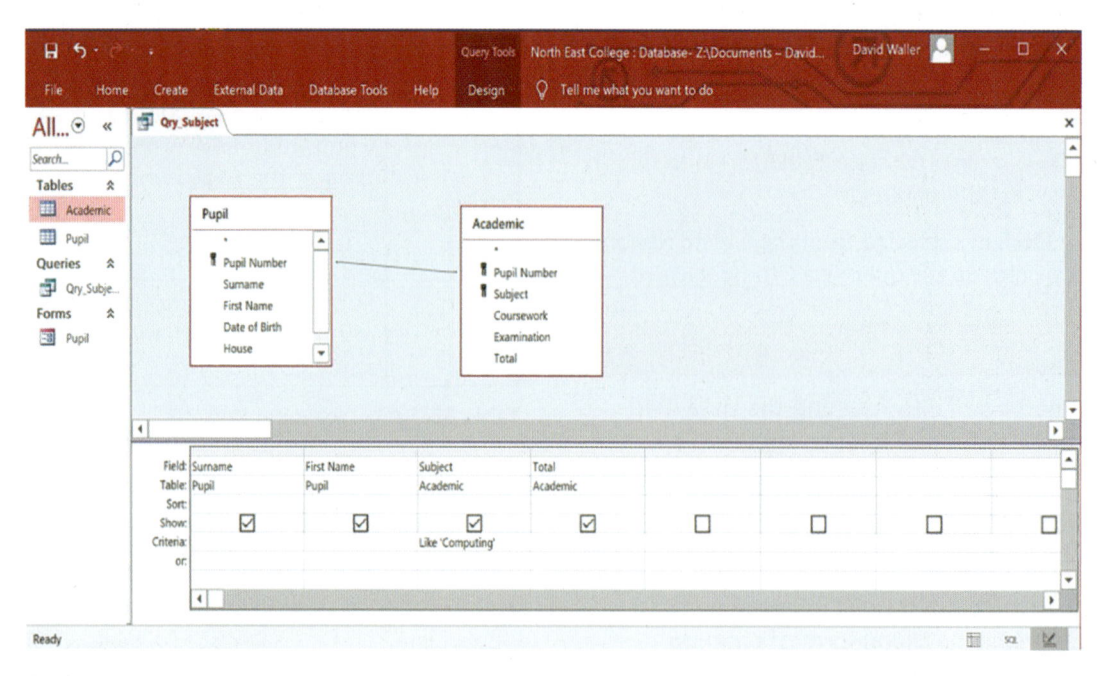

Figure 18.57: Creating a new query

18 Databases

The sorting could also have been set up in design view (see Figure 18.65 on the following pages).

Sorting can be carried out on more than one field in each search. The example in Table 18.13 would show each student alphabetically and then each of their subjects according to Total Mark, sorted highest to lowest.

Field:	Name	Subject	Total Mark
Sort:	Ascending		Descending
Criteria:			
or:			

Table 18.13: Sorting two fields

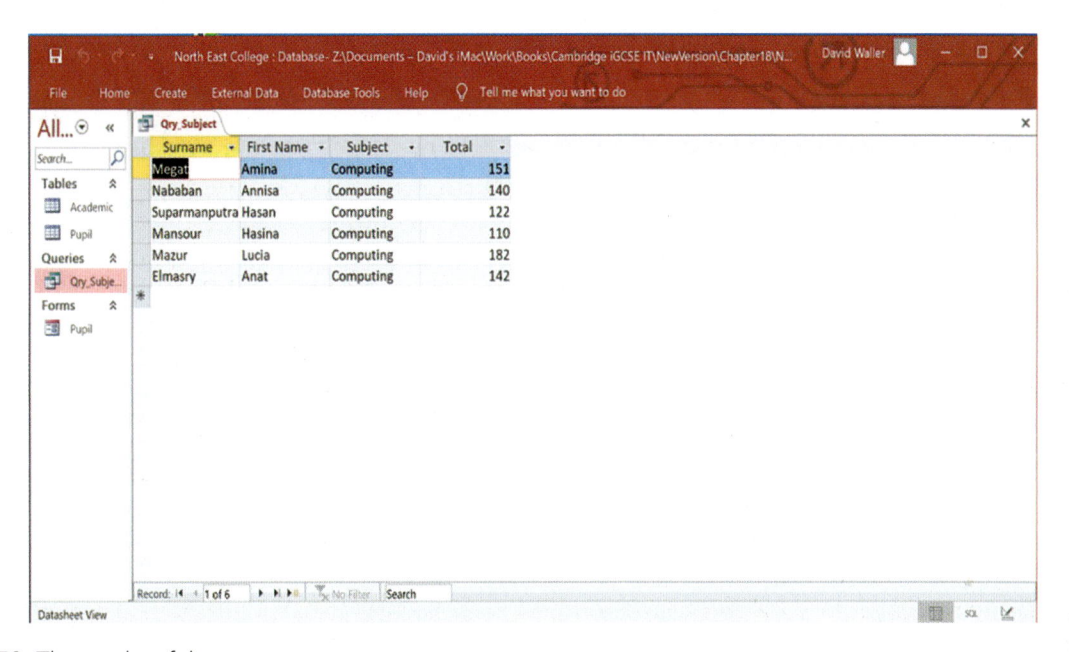

Figure 18.58: The results of the query

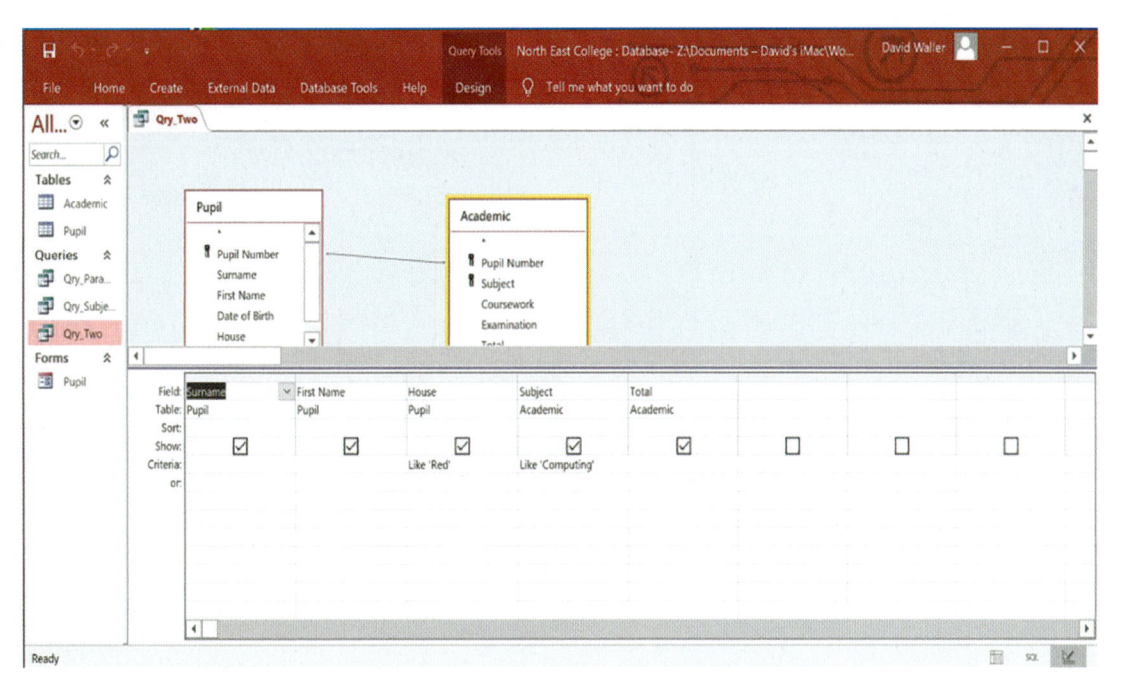

Figure 18.59: An AND query

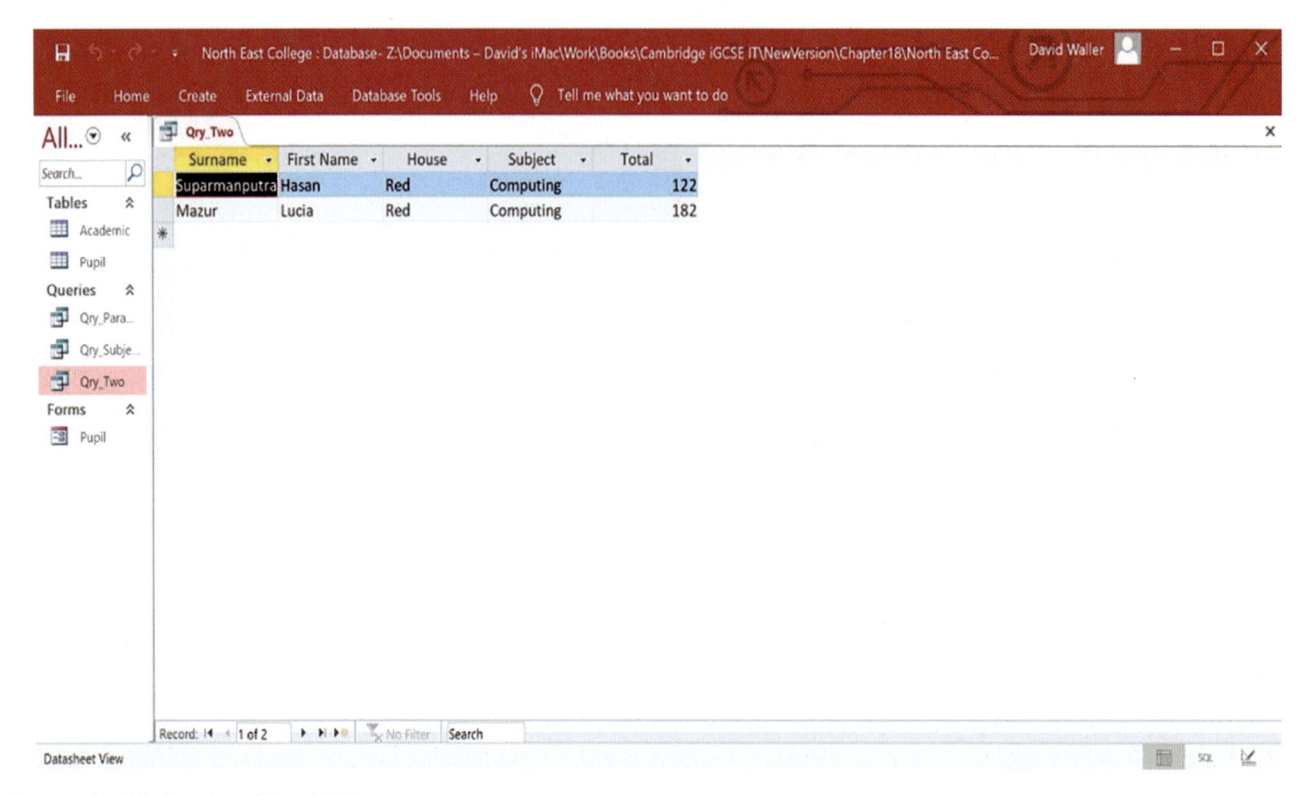

Figure 18.60: Results of the AND query

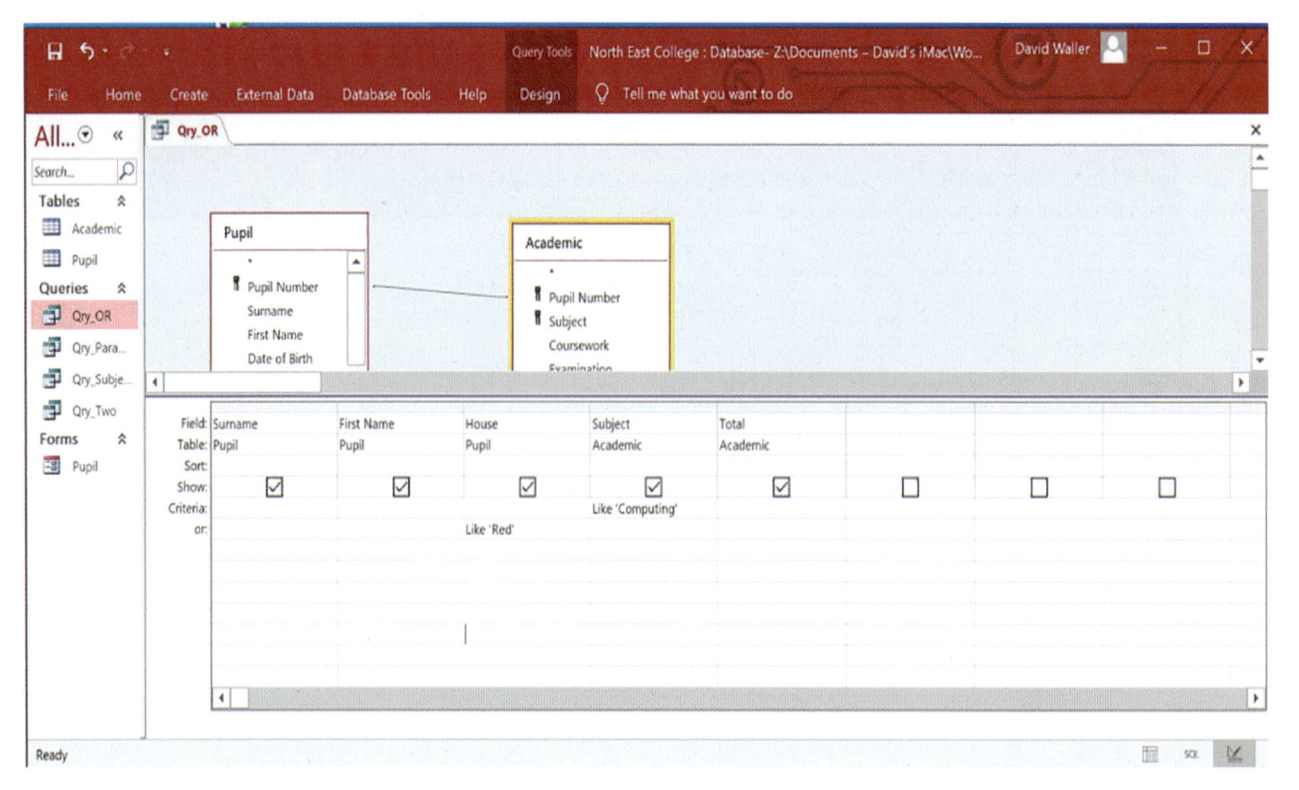

Figure 18.61: An OR query

18 Databases

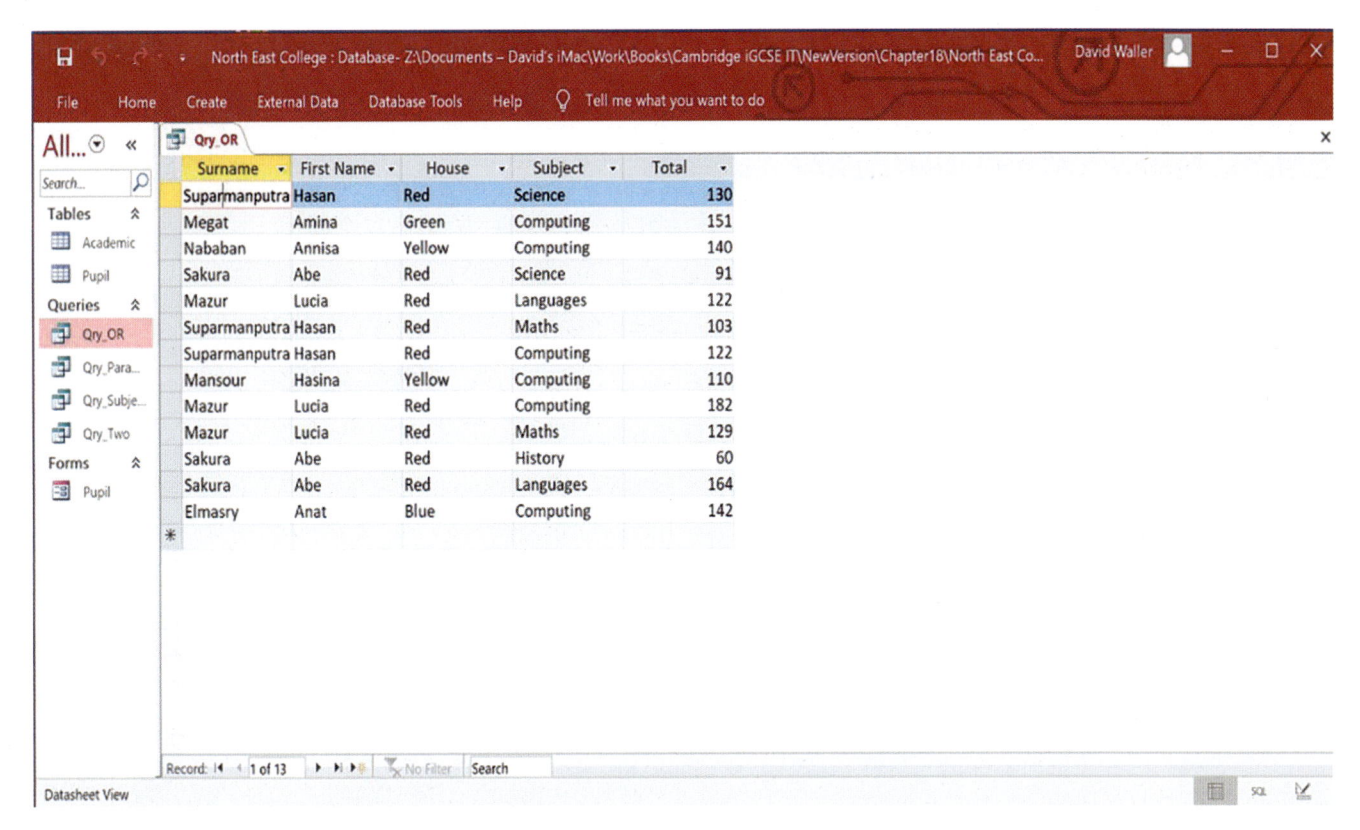

Figure 18.62: Results of the OR query

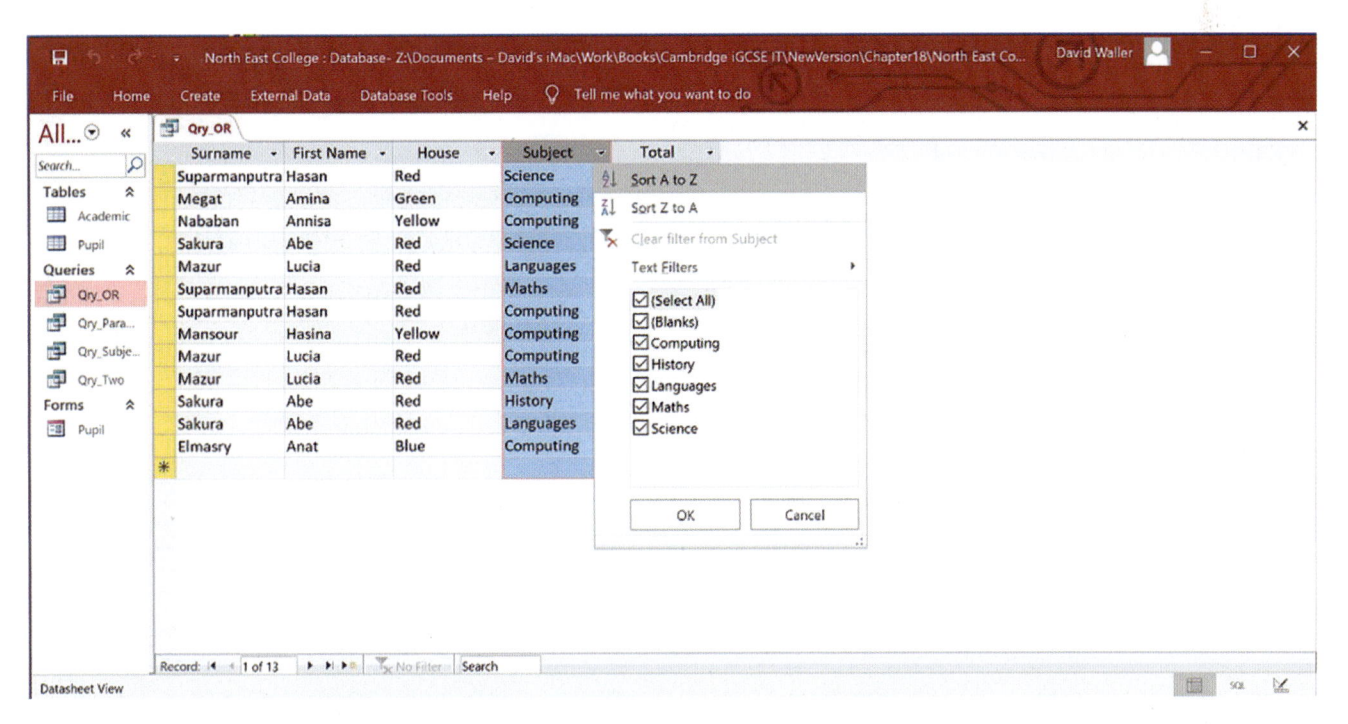

Figure 18.63: Sorting in alphabetical order

403

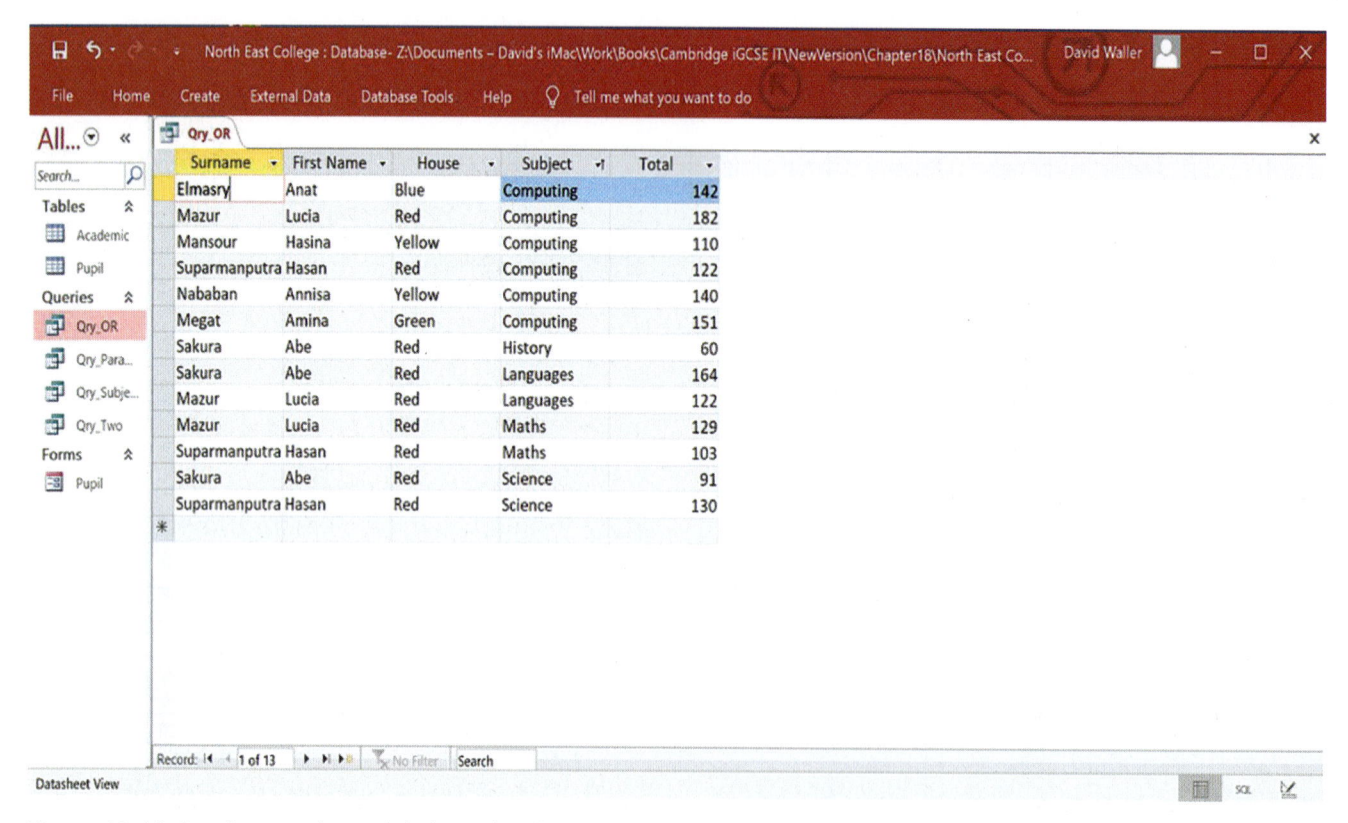

Figure 18.64: Results sorted into alphabetical order according to Subject

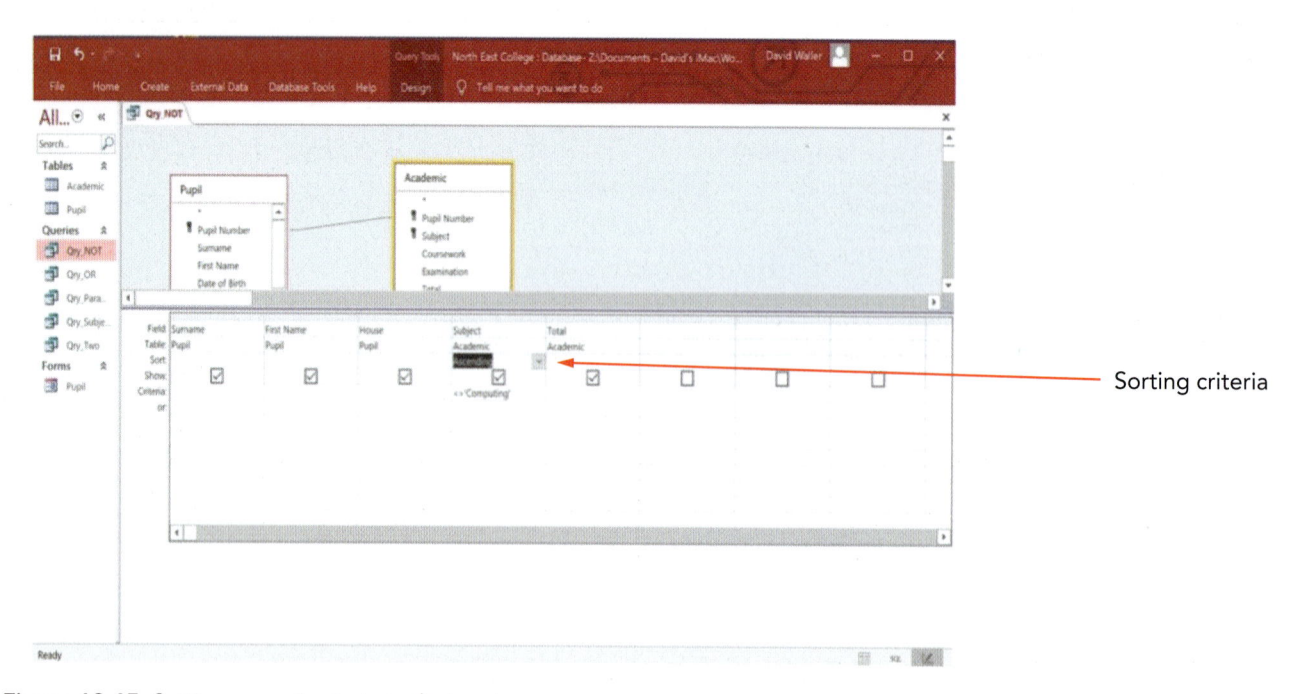

Figure 18.65: Setting up sort criteria in design view

Search operators

When searching the operators shown in Table 18.14 can be used. (Note: the examples given only show positive numbers; answers can also include negative numbers.)

Usually LIKE and NOT are used for text fields and = and <> are used for number fields.

The operators AND and OR have been explained in the examples above.

Operator	Meaning	Example	Description
<	Less than	<100	Search for all instances less than 100. (0–99)
>	Greater than	>100	Search for all instances over 100. (101+)
=	Equal to	=100	Search for all instances equal to 100. (100)
<=	Less than or equal to	<=100	Search for all instances less than or equal to100. (0–100)
>=	Greater than or equal to	>=100	Search for all instances greater than or equal to100. (100+)
<>	NOT equal to	<>100	Search for all instances not equal to 100. (0–99 and 101+)
LIKE	Find text the same as	LIKE "Red"	Find a field that has only the text 'Red'.
NOT	Find text that is not the same as	NOT "Red"	Find a field that does not have the entry 'Red'.

Table 18.14: Search operators

Wildcards

Often when you are entering search criteria, you might not know the exact word or spelling. In this case you can use **wildcards** (see Table 18.15).

> **KEY WORD**
>
> **wildcard:** special characters that can stand for unknown characters

Character	What it stands for	Example
*	Any number of characters	wh* would find white, why, while
		*ch would find switch, twitch, itch
?	A single character	b?ll would find ball, bill but not brill
#	A single numeric character	1#3 would find 103, 113, 123, 133
. (where . represents a letter or number. This only works in text fields.)	Anything before or after	*l* would find blue, and yellow, but not red and green

Table 18.15: Wildcards

Question

4 Describe what the following criteria are intended to find and how the results will be displayed.

a

Field:	Name	Performer	Position In Charts	Genre	Length in Minutes	Year Released
Sort:			Ascending			
Criteria:			<=10			
or:						

b

Field:	Name	Performer	Position In Charts	Genre	Length in Minutes	Year Released
Sort:						Descending
Criteria:						>2019
or:						

c

Field:	Name	Performer	Position In Charts	Genre	Length in Minutes	Year Released
Sort:		Ascending				
Criteria:			<=40	Rock		
or:						

d

Field:	Name	Performer	Position In Charts	Genre	Length in Minutes	Year Released
Sort:					Ascending	
Criteria:						2017
or:						2018

e

Field:	Name	Performer	Position In Charts	Genre	Length in Minutes	Year Released
Sort:		Ascending	Ascending			
Criteria:	*lonely*					
or:						

> **ACTIVITY 18.4**
>
> Create a poster listing the operators that can be used in queries with examples of their use.

Run-time calculations

Calculations and analyses can be programmed to occur when a query is run. These are called run-time calculations and use **formulae** and built-in **functions**. Formulae, using **arithmetic operators** such as +, −, * and / can be applied to the data returned in a search to produce a new column with calculated information.

The following would have a column named 'Difference' showing the difference between the Coursework mark and the Examination result. The field names have to be in square brackets [...], so you would type in:

`Difference: [Coursework]-[Examination]`

(Don't forget the colon!)

The query in Figure 18.66 would return the results in Figure 18.67 on the next page. A new field has been added to the table in Figure 18.67 showing the difference between the two results. It shows which students prefer coursework to examinations.

> **KEY WORDS**
>
> **formula:** arithmetical operations carried out on the contents of cells. The plural of formula is formulae
>
> **function:** a block of reusable code that can be used to perform an action
>
> **arithmetic operator:** symbols to represent arithmetic operations such as addition, subtraction, multiplication and division

Division and multiplication can also be used. The example in Figure 18.68 (on the next page) shows the ratio between the coursework and examination by dividing the former

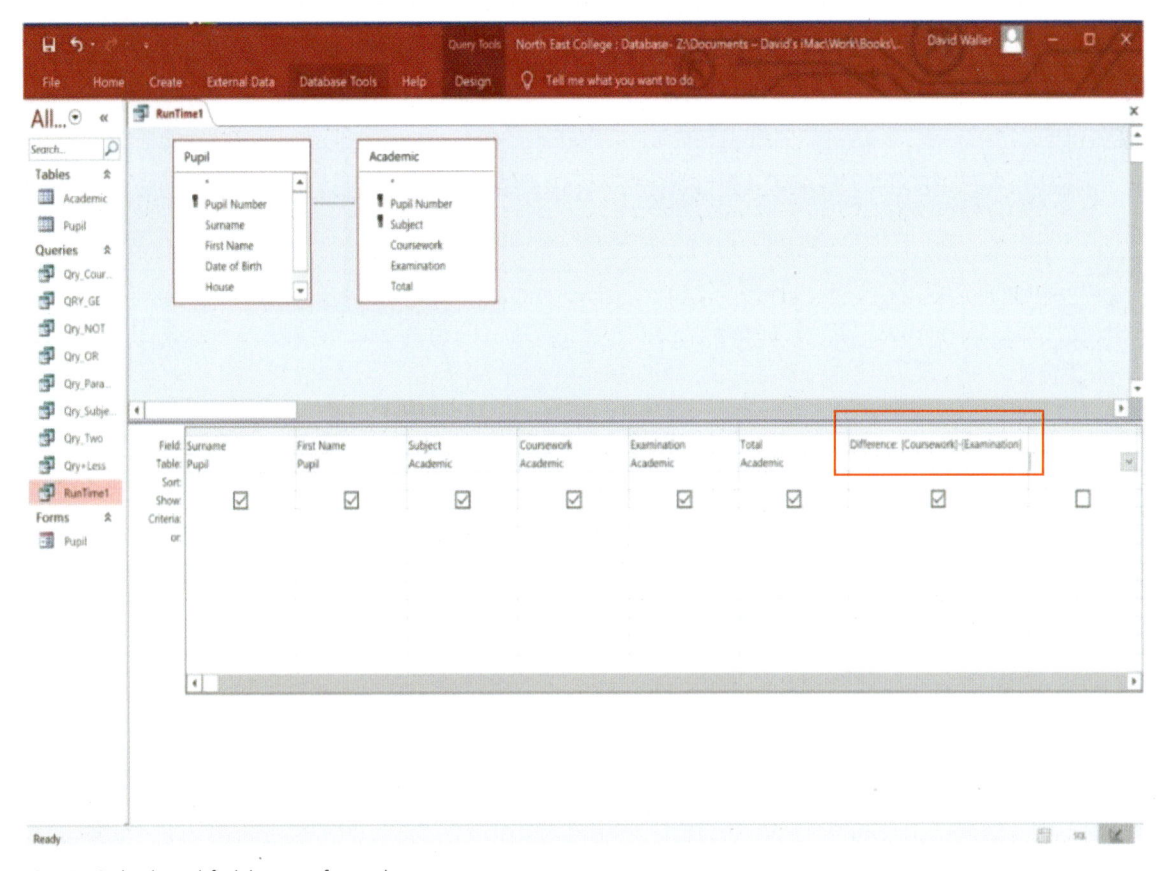

Figure 18.66: Calculated field using formulae

by the latter. The field has been set to two decimal places by using the field properties.

Figure 18.69 shows the results of the ratio calculation.

Built-in functions such as those shown in Table 18.16 can be used at run time. They are used in conjunction with using the Totals icon.

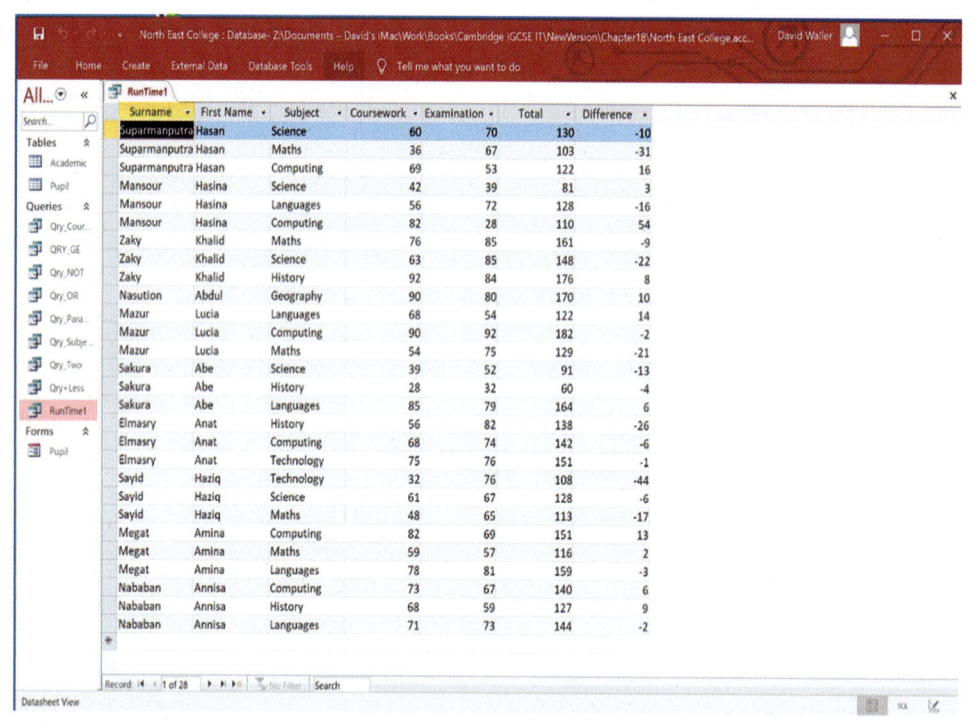

Figure 18.67: Results of the calculation

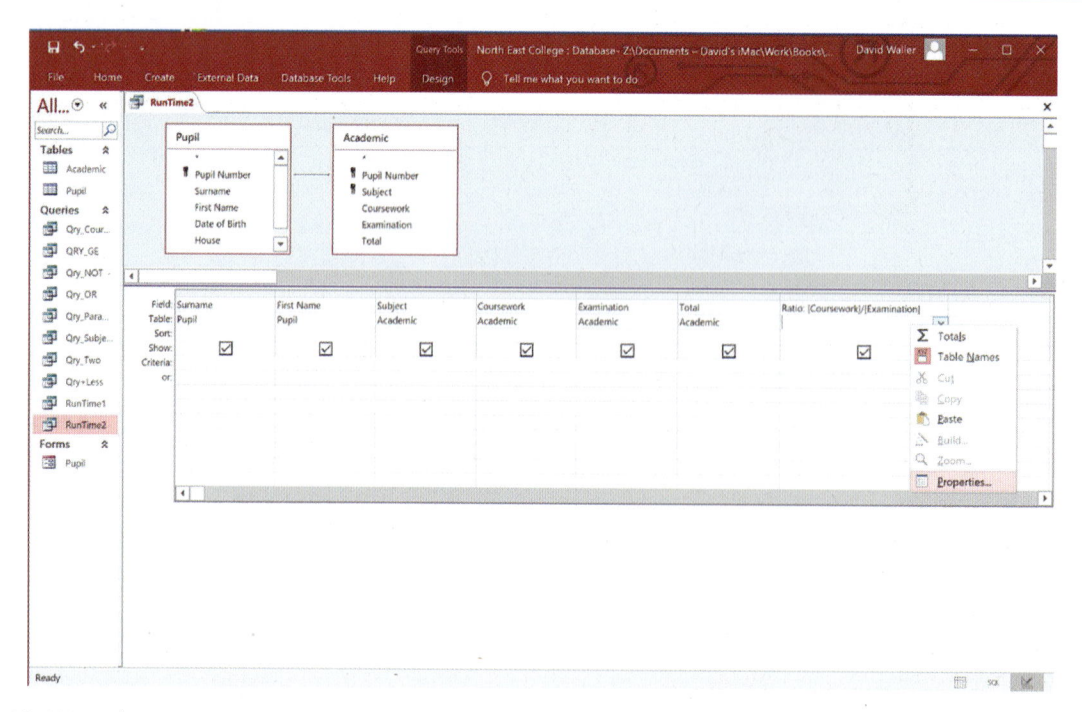

Figure 18.68: Using division

18 Databases

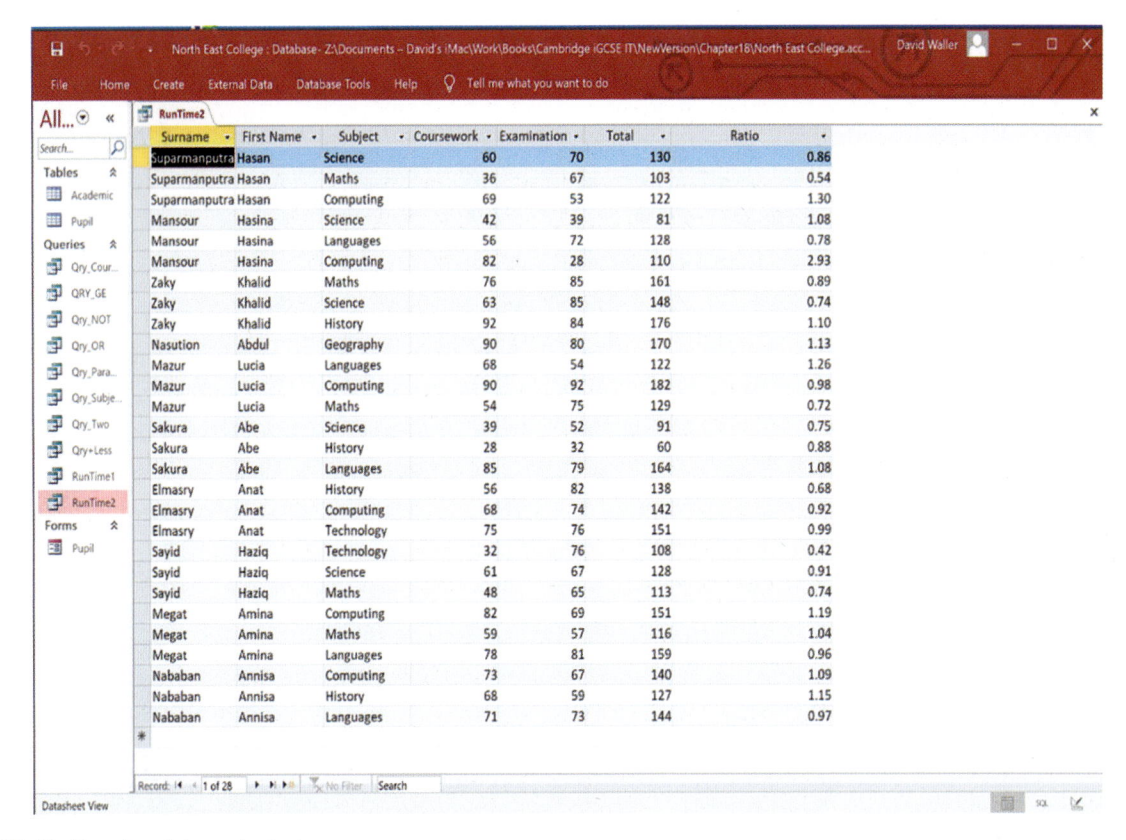

Figure 18.69: Results of the calculation

Function	Explanation
Sum	Will add the data to find the total
Average	Will find the average or mean of a set of numbers
Maximum	Will find the maximum number of a set of numbers
Minimum	Will find the minimum number of a set of numbers
Count	Will count the number of items.

Table 18.16: Built-in functions

In the Academic table, the subjects studied by each student and their coursework, examination and total marks are shown for each of their subjects. An analysis that teachers often need is to find details of these results without showing each of them. They may want to know how many subjects a student has studied, which was their best or worst result and the average. These can be found by using the functions in Table 18.16.

When the fields have been added to the query grid, the Totals icon is selected from the Design ribbon (see Figure 18.70). This icon has nothing to do with the 'Total' field and can be used whatever the field name.

This adds a new row to the query grid (see Figure 18.71). It shows that the data will be grouped by the Surname field and that the average Total field for the number of subjects they study will be found. All of the subjects will not be shown, just the average of their totals.

When the query is run it will show the average of each student's total marks (see Figure 18.72).

The Total field can be added more times to the grid and functions for Sum, Min, Max and Count can be specified (see Figure 18.73).

Figure 18.74 now shows the results when the query is run.

409

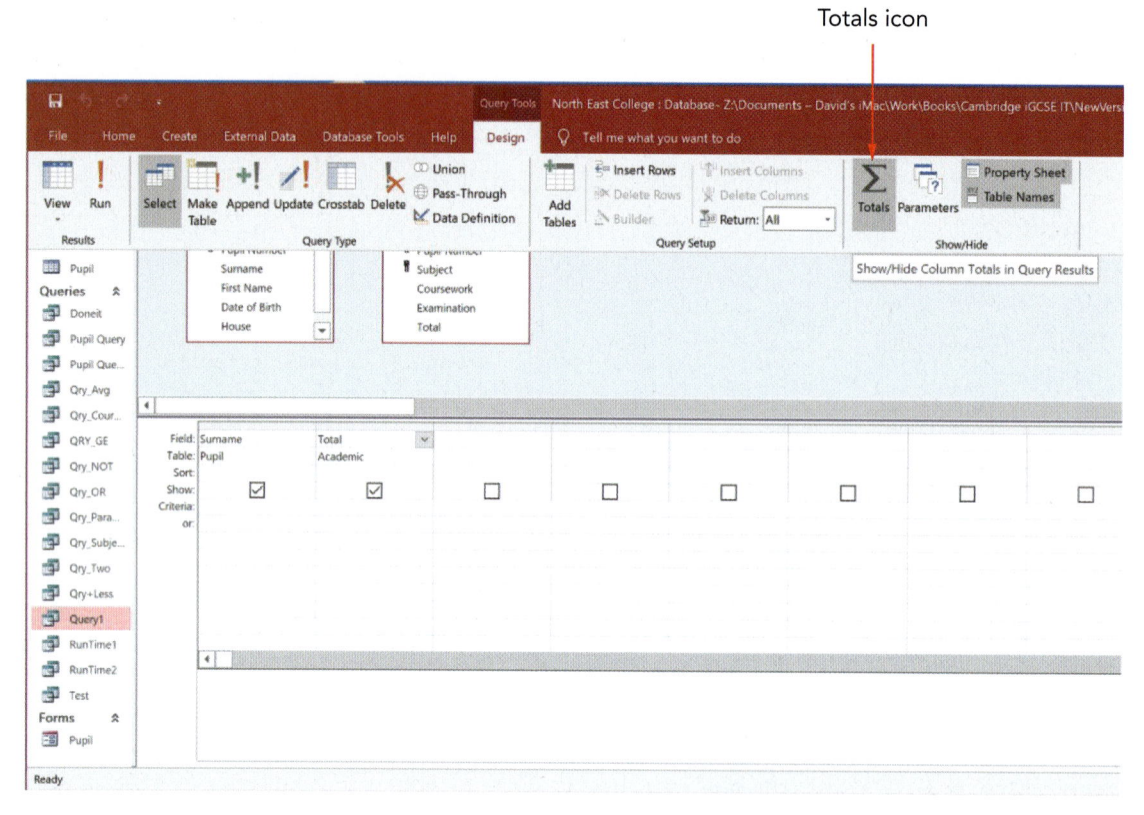

Figure 18.70: Selecting the Totals icon

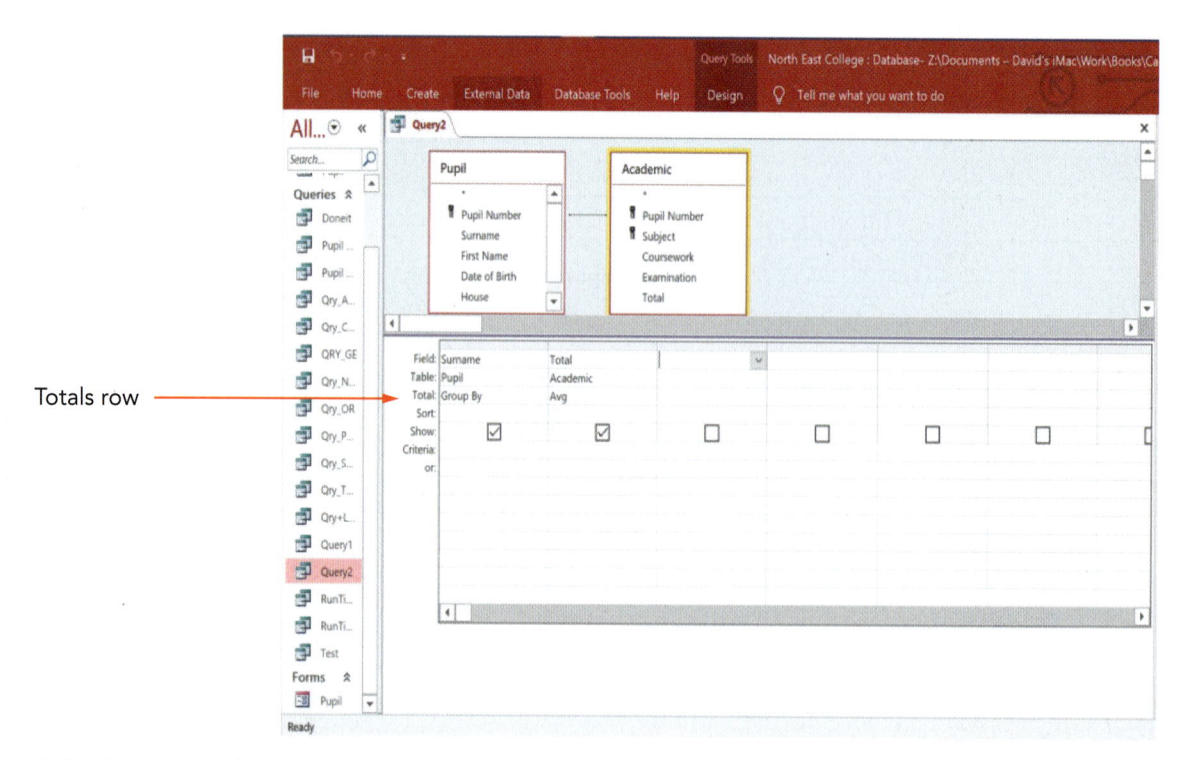

Figure 18.71: Grouping and using the Avg (Average) function

18 Databases

Figure 18.72: The average totals for each student

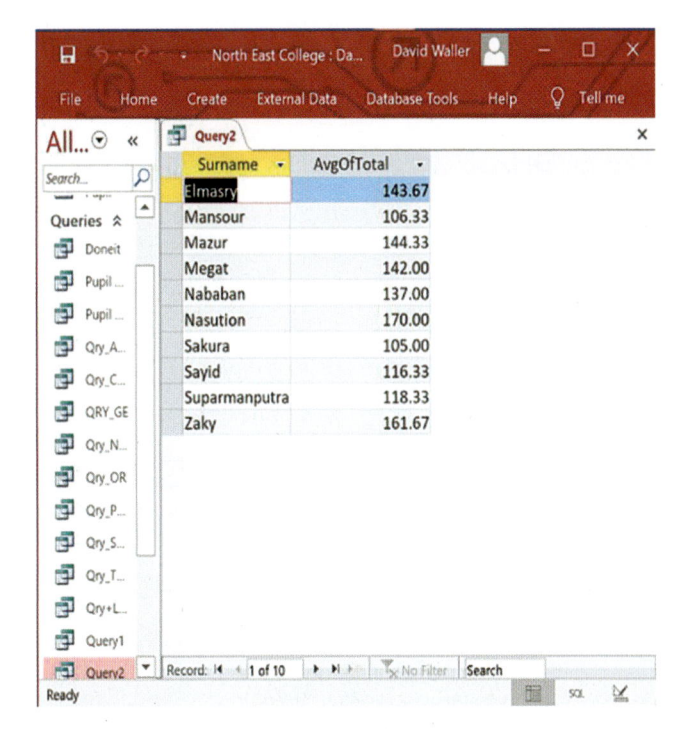

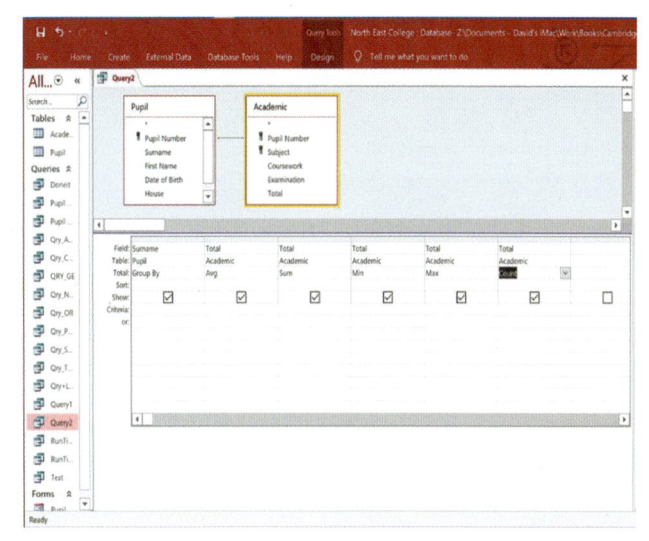

Figure 18.73: Adding more functions

Figure 18.74: Results of the functions

CAMBRIDGE IGCSE™ ICT: COURSEBOOK

PRACTICAL TASK 18.5

Getting started

Here are some activities related to this task. If you do not already know the answers, then carry out research in your textbook and online.

1. Describe the functions of the following operators in a query:
   - \>=
   - <
   - LIKE
   - <>
   - AND

2. What is meant by a wildcard search? Give an example.

Practice

3. Open *SampleDatabase.accdb* into your database software. It contains a table listing assets (equipment) bought by the different departments of a company over the last year. Familiarise yourself with the field names and the data the fields contain.

4. Create a query to show all items with a warranty of at least 12 months.

   The query should contain the fields Asset Category, Cost and Warranty.

   The results should be sorted by length of warranty, with the largest first

   Save the query as *qry_Warranty*.

   Take screenshots of the query in design view and when it is run, and paste them into a document named *Task5.docx*.

5. Create a query to show all items listed as Computer Hardware in the Asset category and costing from $2000 to $3000 dollars inclusive.

   Save the query as *qry_2 to 3 thousand*.

   Take screenshots of the query in design view and when it is run, and paste them into *Task5.docx*.

6. Create a query to find all of the assets listed as Computer Hardware and costing over $1000.

   Display the fields Asset Category, Description and Cost.

   The results should be sorted by Description in alphabetical order and then by Cost in descending order.

   Save the query as *qry_ComputerHardware over $1000*.

   Take screenshots of the query in design view and when it is run, and paste them into *Task5.docx*.

> **CONTINUED**
>
> 7 Create a query to show all of the five different Owners in one column with the sum of their costs over the year.
>
>   Save the query as *qry_Owners*.
>
>   Take screenshots of the query in design view and when it is run, and paste them into *Task5.docx*.
>
> 8 Save your database as *Student5*.
>
> **Challenge**
>
> 9 There are many instances of Office Furniture in the Asset category, and in the description there are six different descriptions of Office Furniture.
>
>   Create a query to show the six Office Furniture descriptions with a Count of the number of times they appear.
>
>   Save the query as *qry_OfficeFurniture*.
>
>   Take screenshots of the query in design view and, when it is run, paste them into a document named *Task5_Challenge.docx*.
>
> 10 Create a query to find which Owners ordered Computer Hardware and the number of times they ordered them.
>
>   Save the query as *qry_ComputerHardware By Owner*.
>
>   Take screenshots of the query in design view and, when it is run, paste them into the document named *Task5_Challenge.docx*.
>
>   Save the database as *Student5_Challenge*.

ICT IN CONTEXT

In 2013, Adobe reported that hackers had stolen nearly 3 million encrypted customer credit card records and login data from their databases. Adobe later changed this to 38 million but it was reported that a file posted of the stolen data included more than 150 million usernames and passwords. The hack also exposed customers names, IDs and credit card information.

18.3 Presenting data

Data is stored and manipulated in a database in order to provide information. This information should be displayed in as user friendly a way as possible so that people can easily see and understand the results.

Relational database management software provides the facilities to present information in reports which can be created from data stored in tables or returned in queries. Unlike data entry forms, which are only displayed on screen, reports can also be printed to produce hard-copy. Therefore, when they are designed, care must be taken when considering page size or the report will overflow onto extra pages with the information spread between them.

Like all documents, database reports have page headings, headers and footers – see Table 18.17.

Report header	Appears only once at the start of the first page of the report.
Report footer	Appears only once at the end of the data on the last page of the report.
Page header	Appears at the top of each page of the report.
Page footer	Appears at the bottom of each page of the report.

Table 18.17: Parts of a database report

Every report must have data provided by a table or a query. These can be attached to the report as it is being created.

A report can be created in design view by selecting Report Design from the Create ribbon (see Figure 18.75).

Page header and footer sections are already created and information can be entered and edited (see Figure 18.76).

Both page headers and footers and report headers and footers can be removed, and added, by right-clicking on the report and selecting from the menu (see Figure 18.77 on the next page).

A table or query has to be attached to the report to supply the data to be displayed. In this example, we will add a query linking the Pupil table with the Academic table. This can be done by selecting data from the Property Sheet.

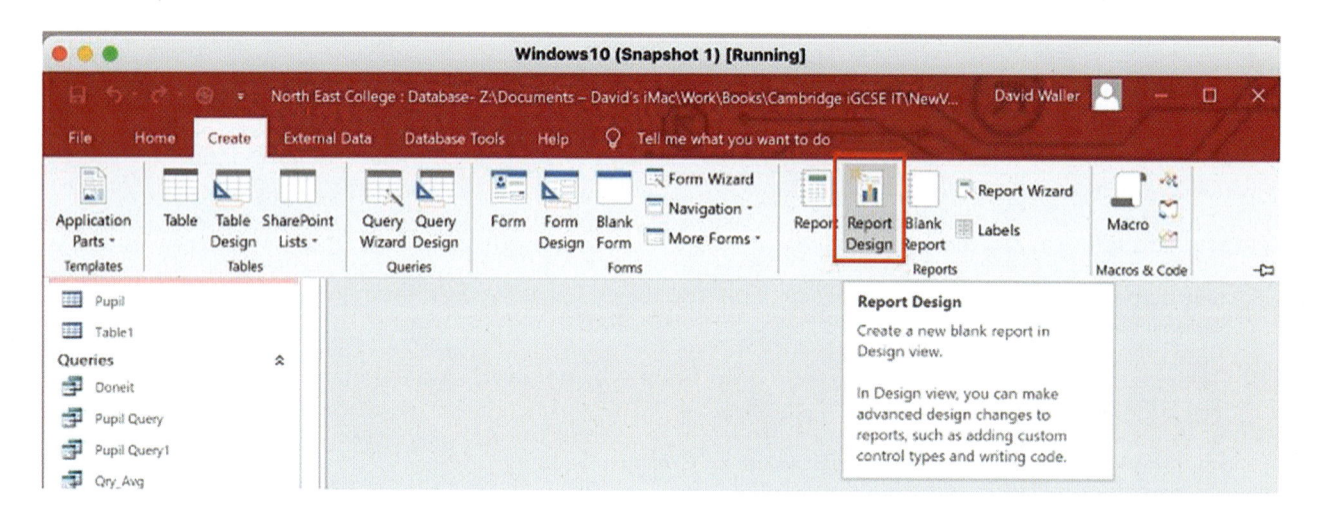

Figure 18.75: Report Design

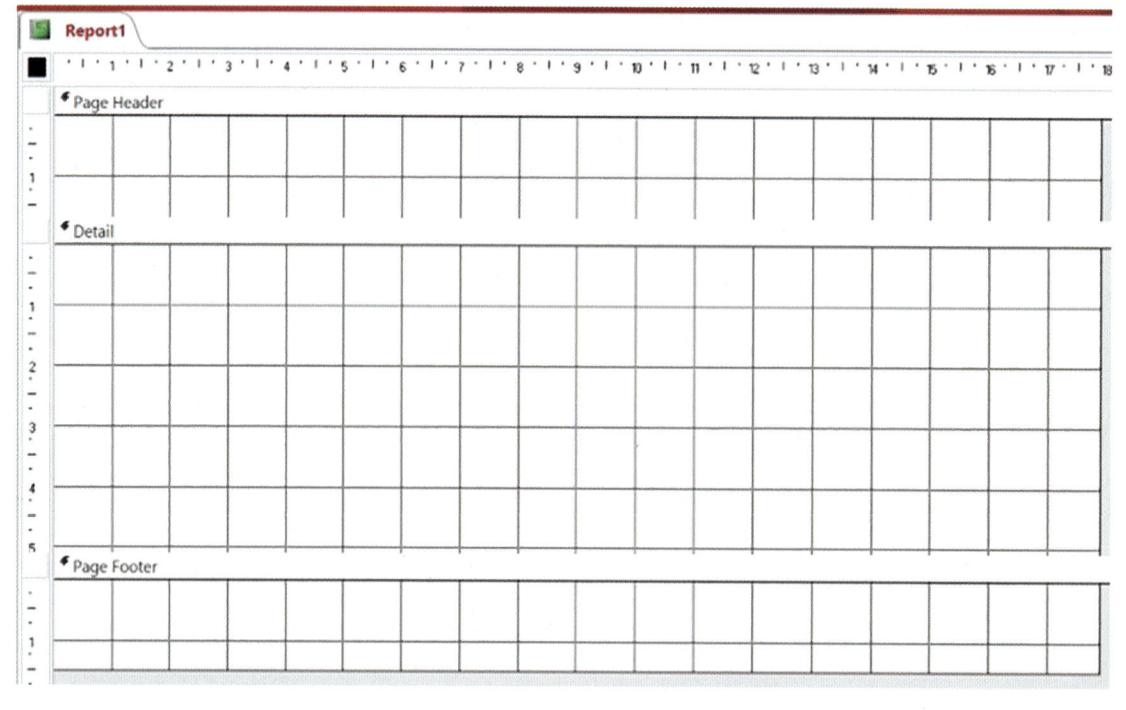

Figure 18.76: Report in design view

18 Databases

The Property Sheet can be accessed by selecting it from the Design ribbon (see Figure 18.78).

The data can then be selected (see Figure 18.79).

Headings and titles can be added to a report by creating labels. The Label icon can be selected from the Design ribbon (see Figure 18.80 on the next page).

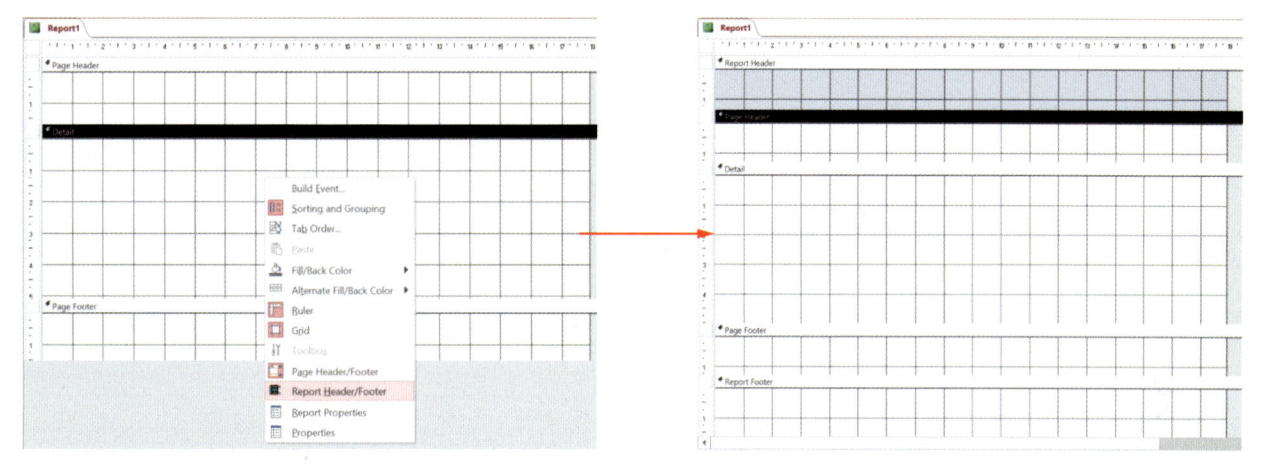

Figure 18.77: Creating Headers

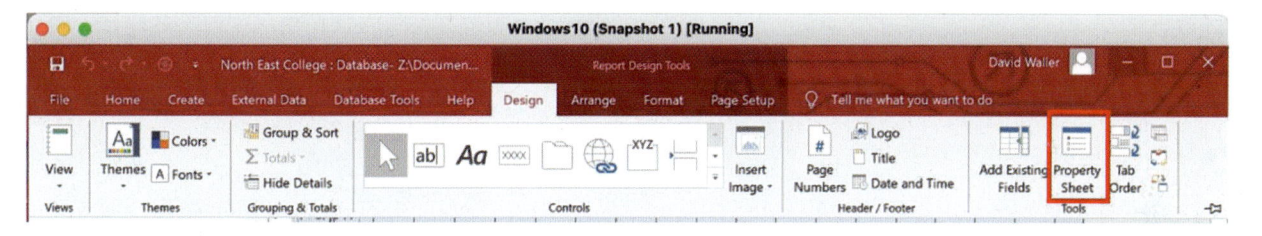

Figure 18.78: Property Sheet icon

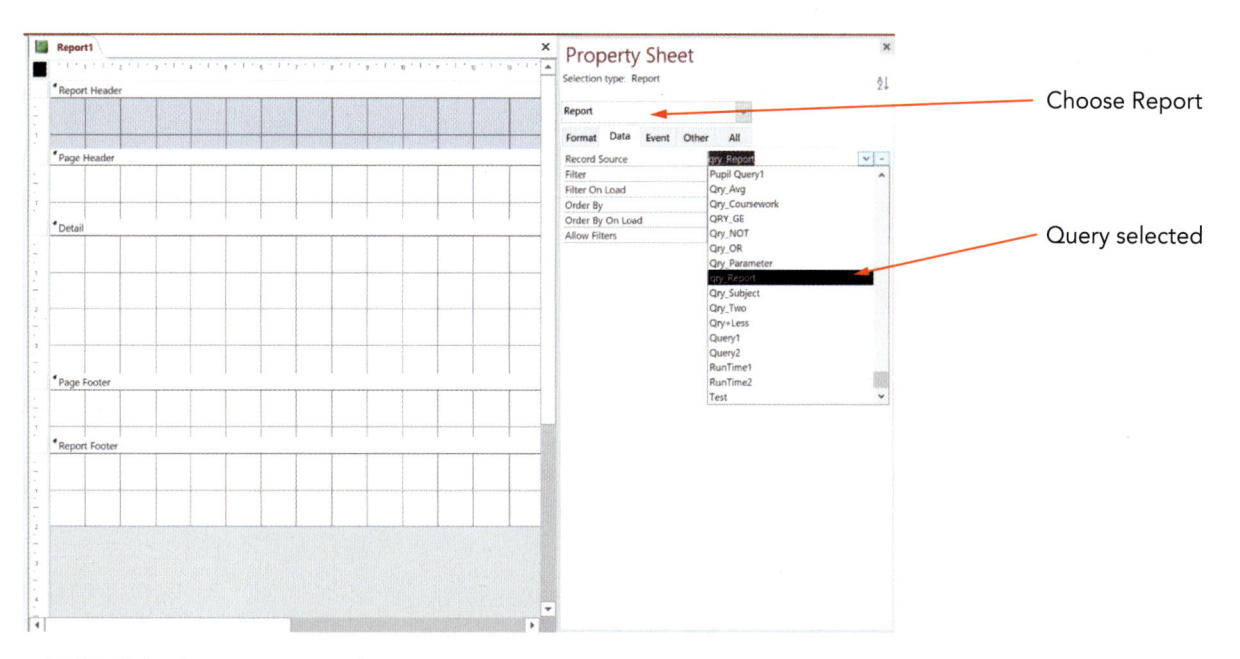

Figure 18.79: Selecting a query as a data source

415

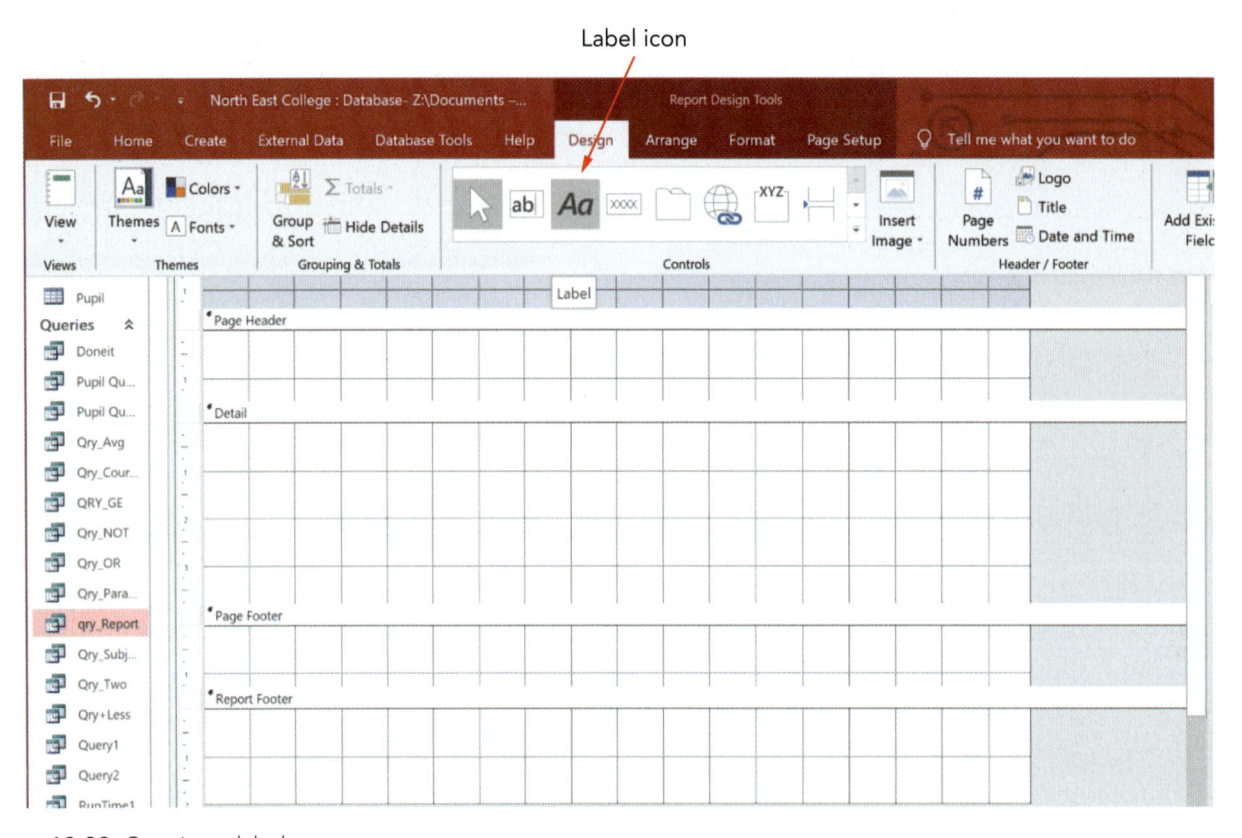

Figure 18.80: Creating a label

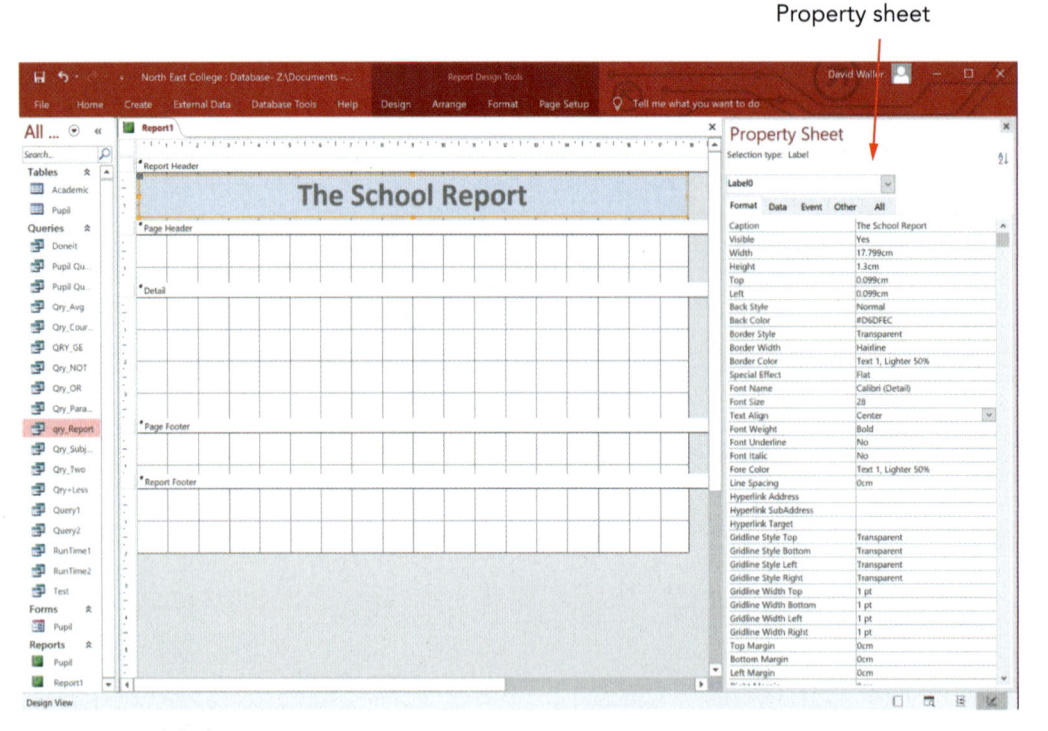

Figure 18.81: Formatting a label

18 Databases

A label box can be drawn, and text can be entered. The text can be formatted with respect to font, size colour, etc. by selecting it and changing the properties of the label in the Property Sheet (see Figure 18.81 on the previous page).

The fields can be added to the report by selecting the Add Existing Fields icon from the Design ribbon (see Figure 18.82).

The fields can be dragged onto the report. In addition to each field, a label with the field name is provided (see Figure 18.83). They can be moved independently, and the label can be deleted. Fields and labels can be dragged into the Detail section of the report from the Add Existing Field pane on the right-hand side.

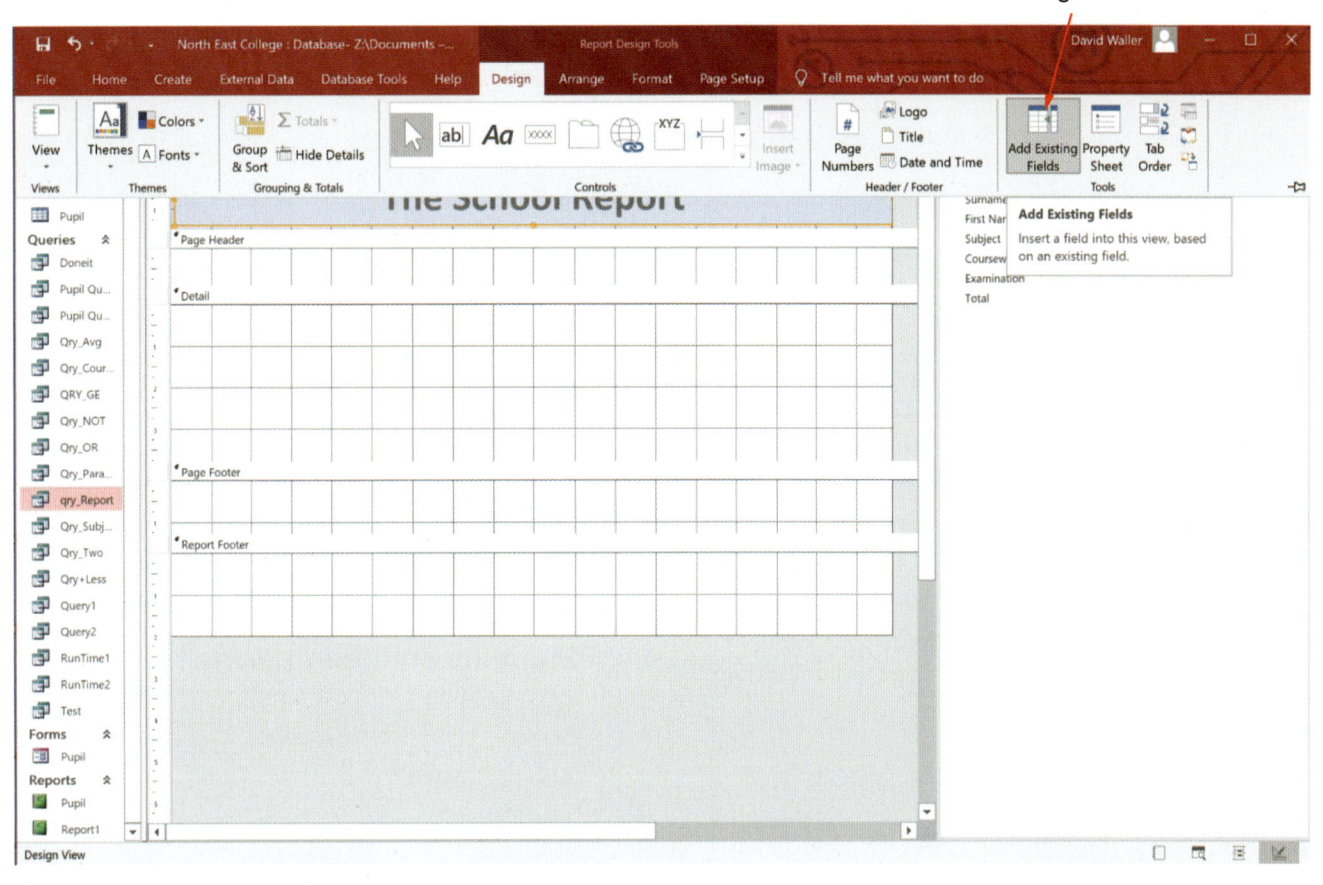

Figure 18.82: Showing the fields

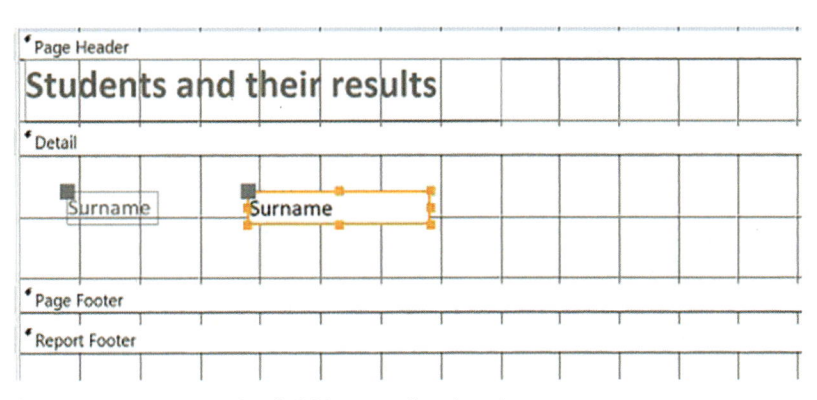

Figure 18.83: A field and label in the report. The field has a yellow border

417

When the report is run, the students are shown but the report shows each of the students with their first subject, then each of the students with their second and third subjects (see Figure 18.84).

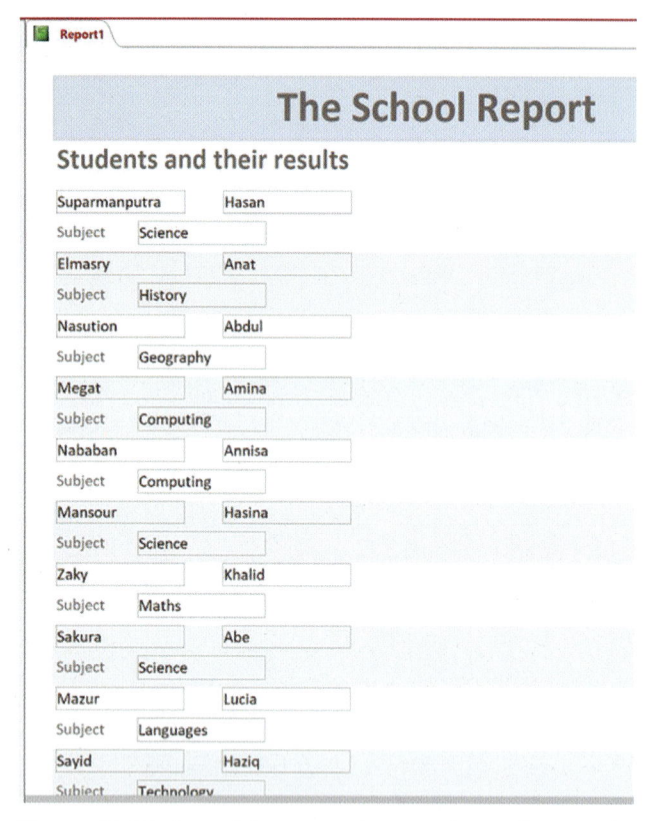

Figure 18.84: Part of the report showing the students and their subjects

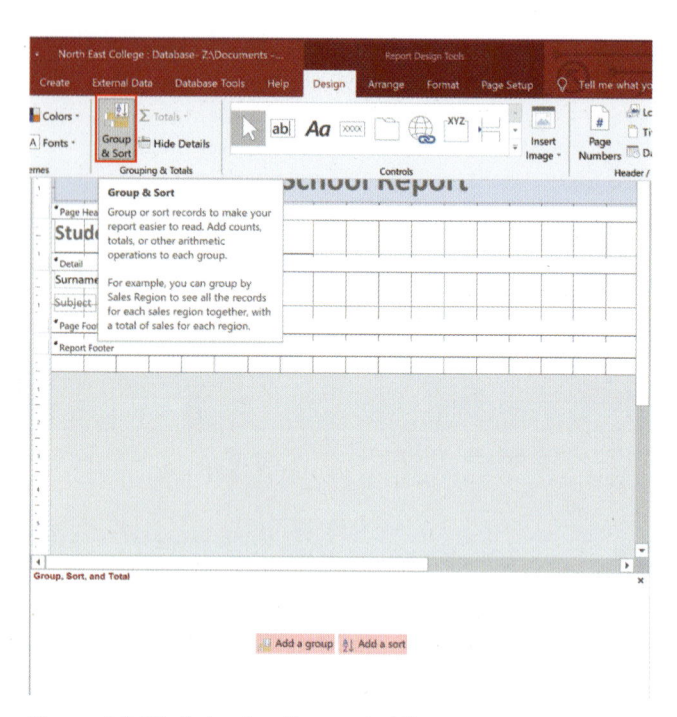

Figure 18.85: Selecting Group and Sort

If the report is to show each of the pupils with all of their subjects, then the report has got to be told to group the results on the pupil Surname field. Grouping can be set by selecting the Group and Sort icon from the Design ribbon (see Figure 18.85).

The report can be set to group the data according to the pupil's surname. When the Select and Sort icon is clicked in the Design ribbon, the dialogue box in Figure 18.86 is displayed.

The report will now have a new section with a Surname header and a Surname footer to make it easier to read the data in that group on the report.

The Surname and First Name fields can be dragged into the header and labels can be added for the other fields that will be displayed in the Detail section (see Figure 18.87).

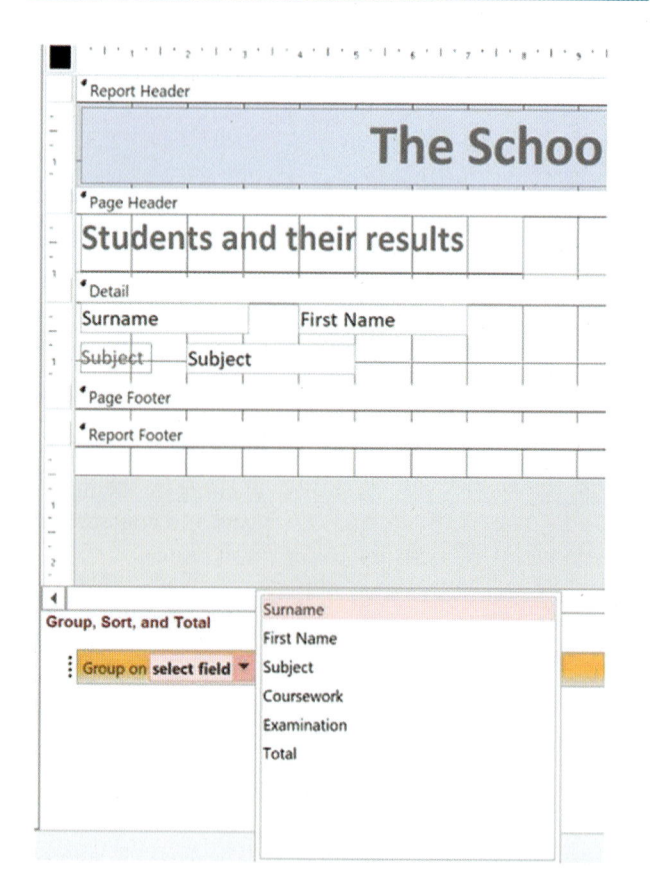

Figure 18.86: Grouping on the Surname field

18 Databases

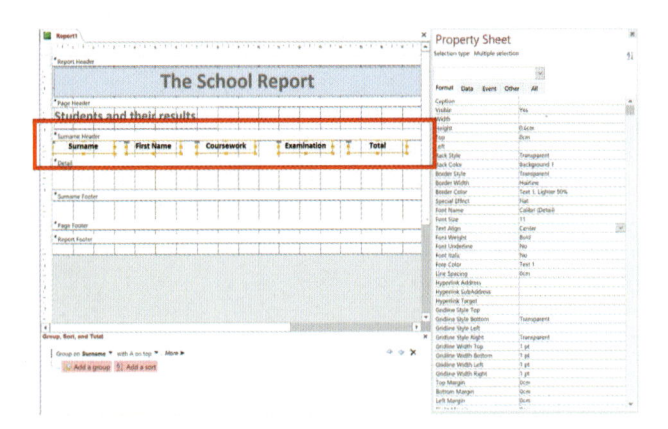

Figure 18.87: Adding fields and labels in the Surname header

The fields for Subject, Coursework, Examination and Total can be dragged into the Detail section under their relevant labels. The text for these fields can be edited using the Property Sheet (see Figure 18.88).

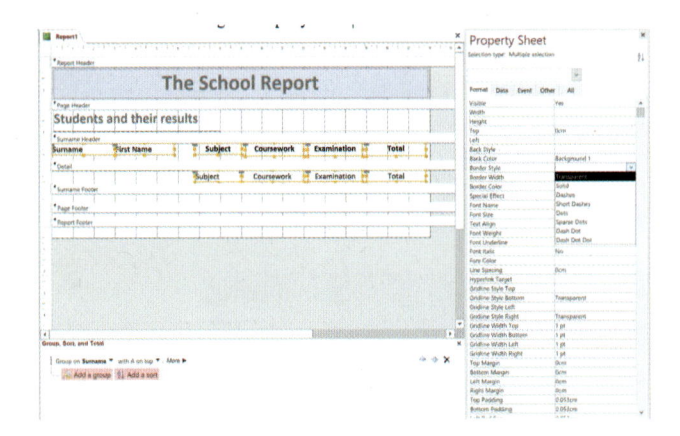

Figure 18.88: Adding fields to the Detail section

When the report is run, by double-clicking on its name in the left pane, the data about subjects and coursework, etc. are grouped according to the pupil names (see Figure 18.89).

Figure 18.89: Report showing grouped data

ACTIVITY 18.5

At North East College, there are end-of-year examinations in all subjects.

1. On paper, design a report that would display the results for each student showing the subjects studied and results.

2. On paper, design a report suitable for a teacher showing the results for all subjects in a particular teaching group.

Using arithmetic operators and functions

Arithmetic operators and functions were used in tables and queries for calculations earlier in the chapter. They can also be used in reports. The operators and functions are entered into Text Boxes, which can be drawn onto the report headers and footers. (You do this by clicking on the Text Box icon – see Figure 18.90.) They are used to perform calculations and so must be placed in the footers of the sections in order to perform calculations on the values within the Detail section.

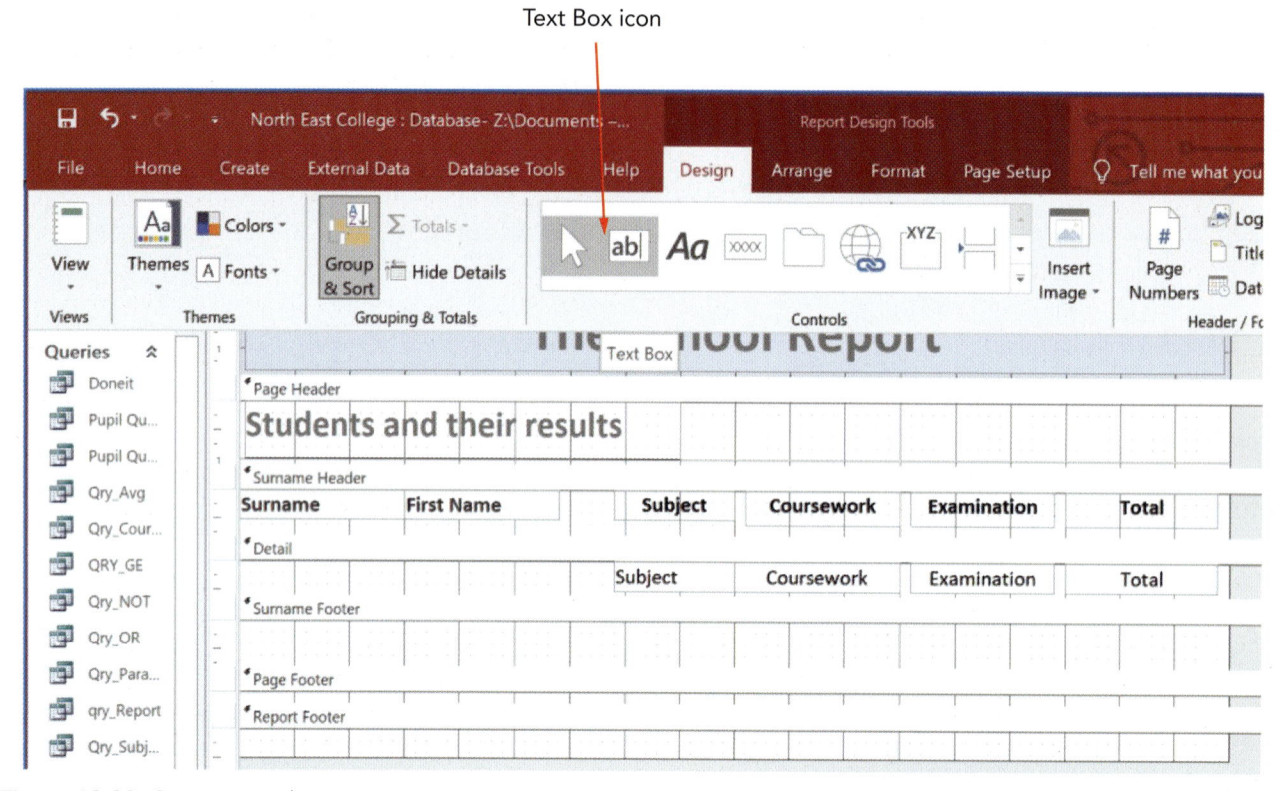

Figure 18.90: Creating text boxes

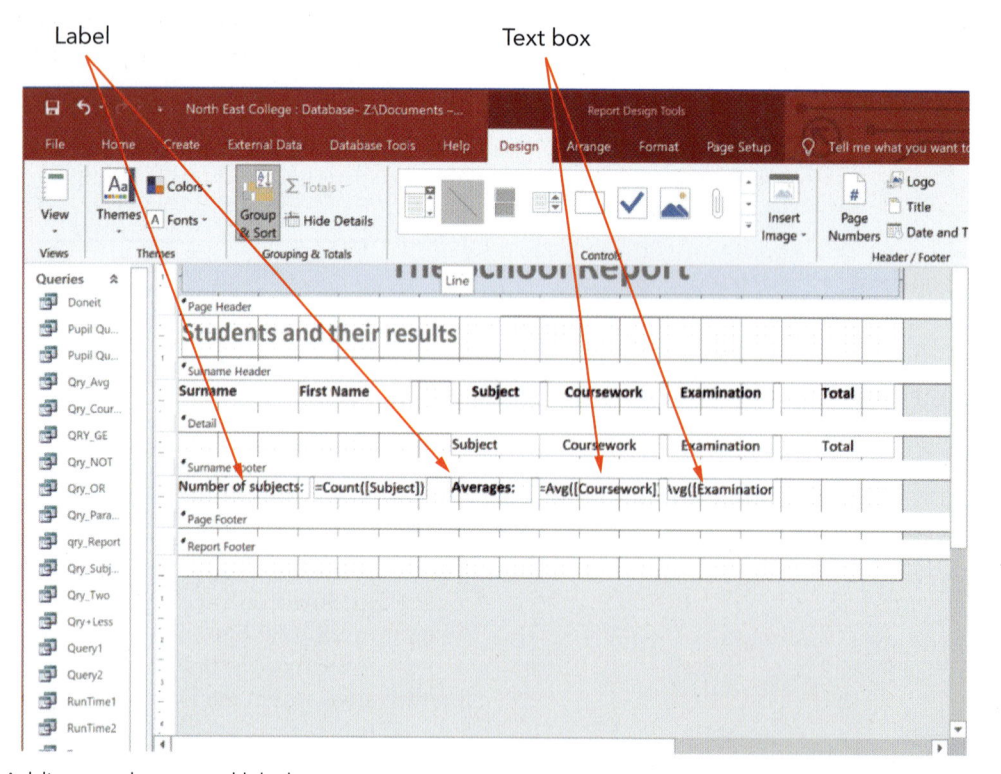

Figure 18.91: Adding text boxes and labels

The formulae and functions can be entered into the text boxes.

For example, if you wanted to count the number of subjects for each pupil, the following function could be entered into a text box:

`=Count([Subject])`

Notice that the field name is in square brackets.

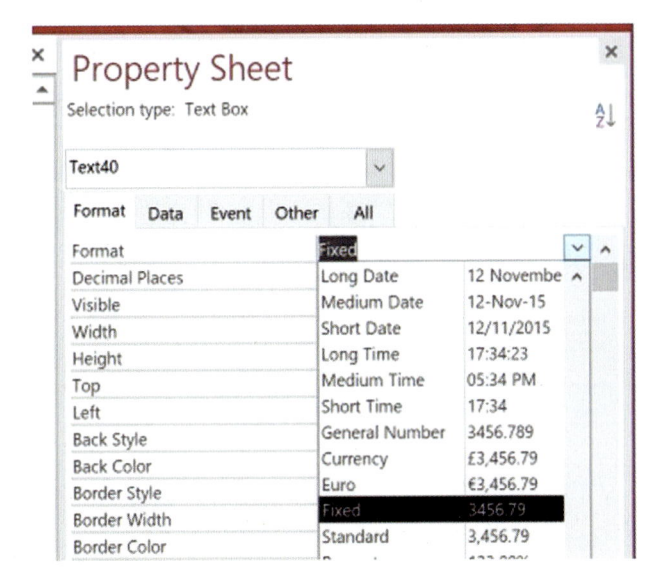

Figure 18.92: Formatting a text box

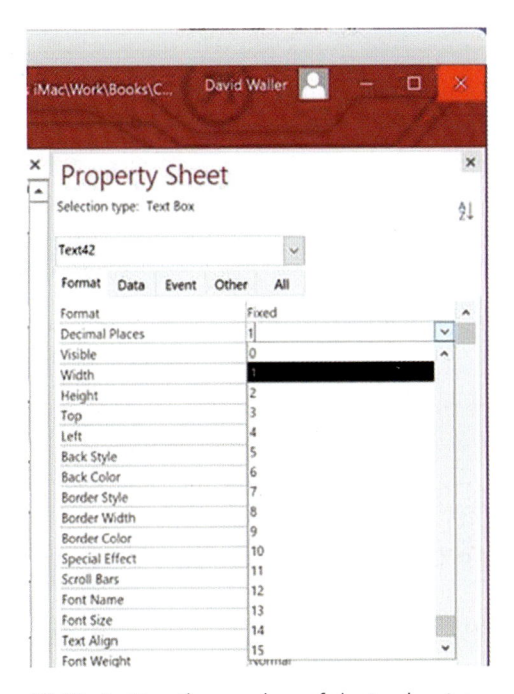

Figure 18.93: Setting the number of decimal points

If the report needed to show the averages of the coursework and examination marks, then the following could be entered in text boxes:

`=Avg([Coursework])`

`=Avg([Examination])`

`=Avg([Total])`

A text box can be used to show page numbers in the page footer. It can combine both text and functions.

`='Page ' & [Page] & ' of ' & [Pages]`

These text boxes can be given a label (see Figure 18.91).

How a number will be displayed in a text box can be set using the Property Sheet. In Figures 18.92–93, the number is set as fixed with one decimal place, but currency and percentage can also be set here.

By default, numbers are right-aligned in text boxes; if the format is set to fixed, the decimal points will be aligned. When creating a report, it is essential to carefully ensure that all of the text and numbers are aligned correctly so it is easy to understand (see Figure 18.94).

The alignment of any label or control can be set using the Property Sheet (see Figure 18.95).

To make the report easier to read, a line can be drawn in the Surname Footer by selecting the line tool (see Figure 18.96).

Figure 18.94: The report showing the text boxes and labels

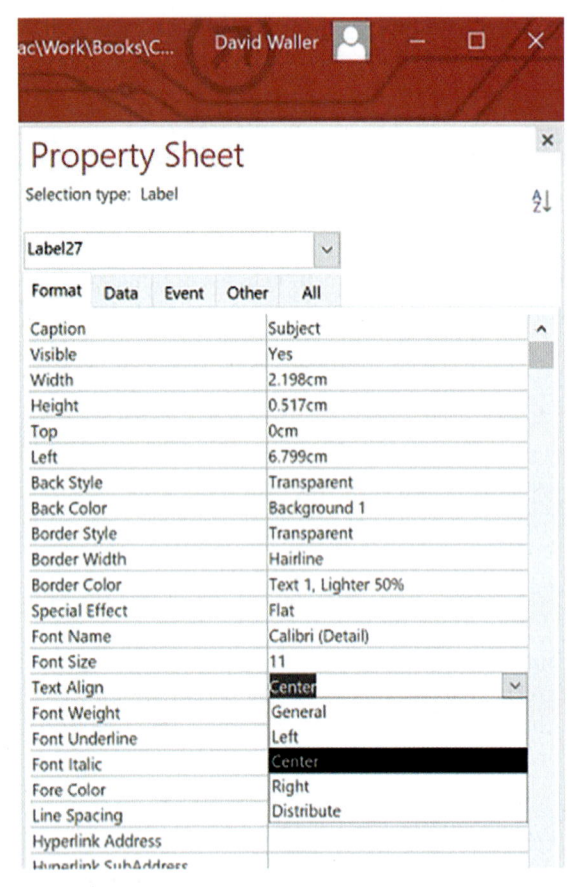

Figure 18.95: Setting the alignment in a label or text box

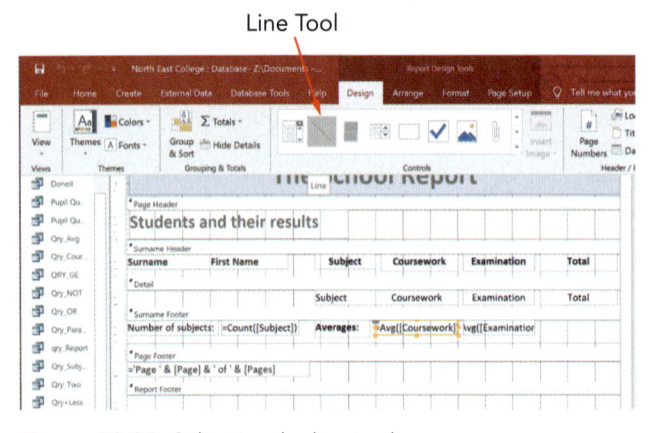

Figure 18.96: Selecting the line tool

This tool can be used to draw a line in the Surname footer (see Figure 18.97 and how it looks in the report in Figure 18.98).

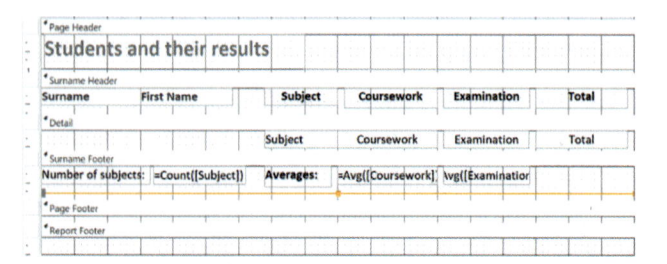

Figure 18.97: Line in design view

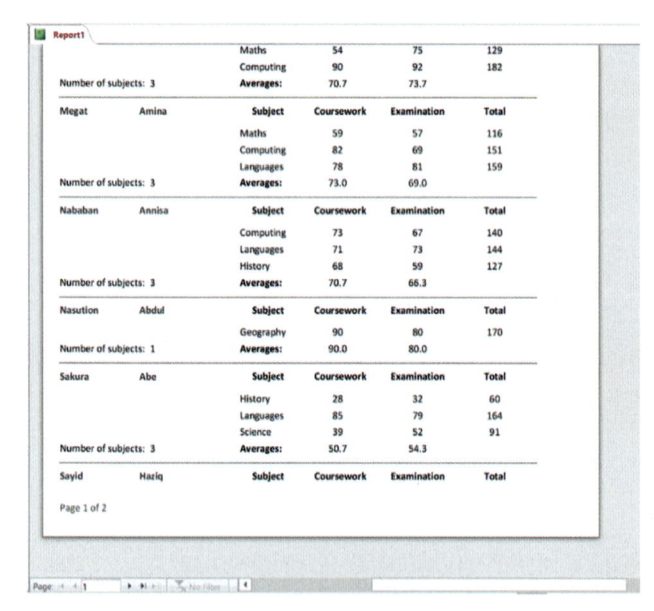

Figure 18.98: Lines shown in the report

At the bottom of Page 1 of the report, a group has been split so that it shows the name of the pupil but no marks (the marks will have been placed at the top of Page 2). This can be prevented by selecting 'keep whole group together on one page' (see Figure 18.99). This can be accessed by selecting the Group and Sort icon from the Design ribbon.

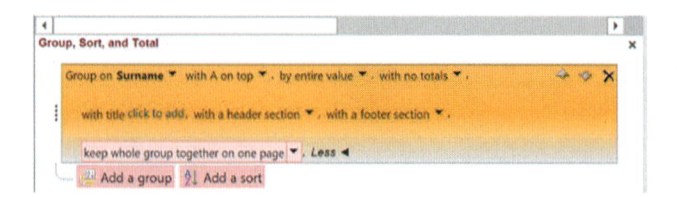

Figure 18.99: Keeping a group together on one page

Output layouts

The report layout shown in the images in this chapter is tabular. This means it shows the data in columns. The other main layout is called a stacked layout and shows the data as they would appear on a form, with each item labelled (see Figures 18.100–101).

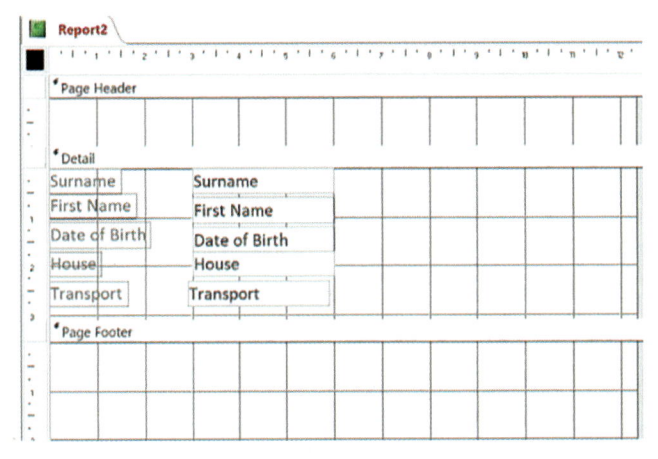

Figure 18.100: A stacked layout in design view

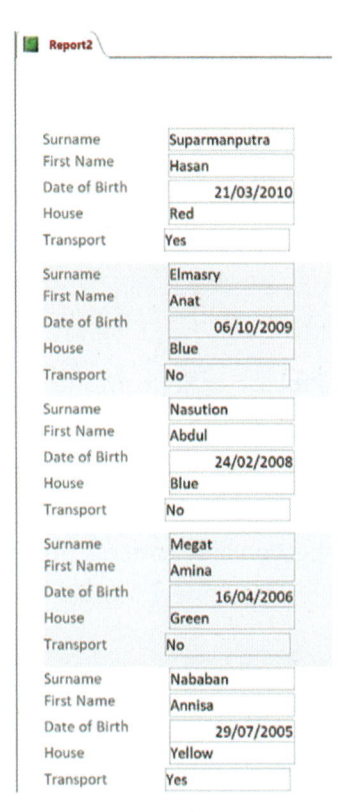

Figure 18.101: Report with a stacked layout

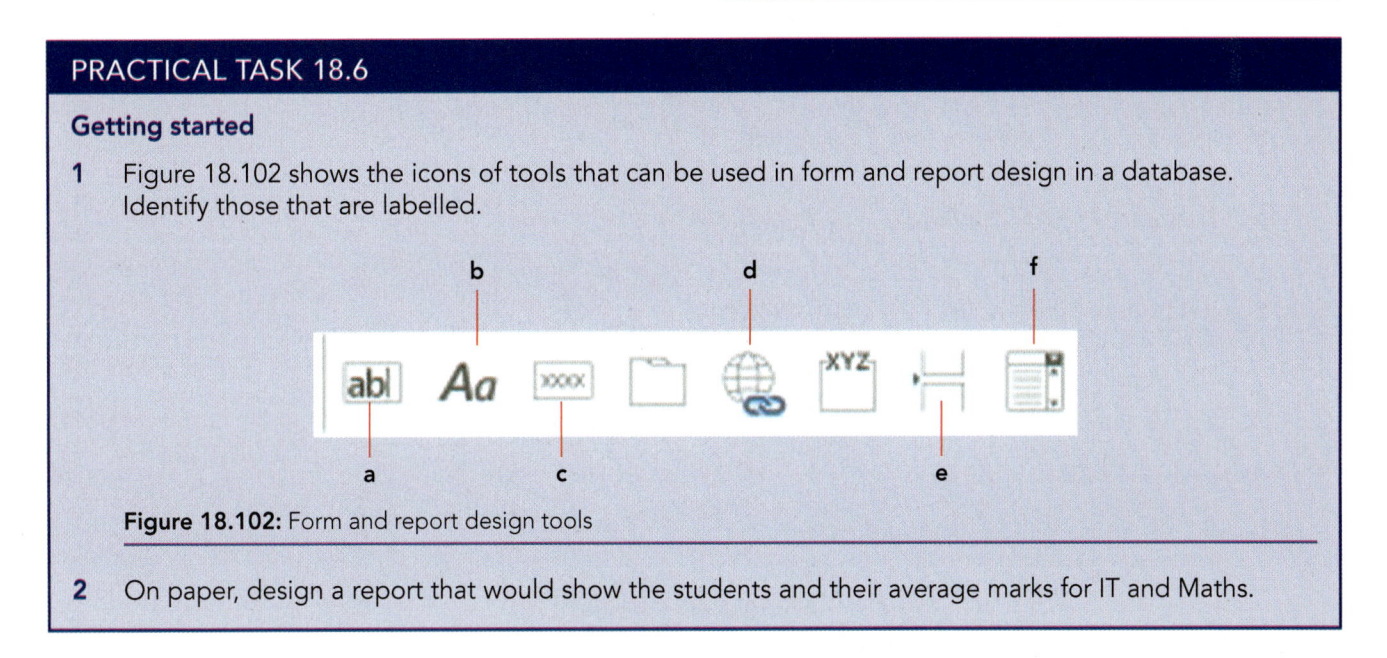

PRACTICAL TASK 18.6

Getting started

1. Figure 18.102 shows the icons of tools that can be used in form and report design in a database. Identify those that are labelled.

Figure 18.102: Form and report design tools

2. On paper, design a report that would show the students and their average marks for IT and Maths.

CONTINUED

Practice

Open your Students database *Student4* or *Student4_Challenge* from the Practical Task 18.4 and create a report in **design view** to show the students and their average marks for IT and Maths. The report should be grouped by Year of birth and then by gender.

3 First of all, create a query for the report.

   It should include the Students, Maths and IT tables.

   Use the following fields: StudentNumber, SecondName, FirstName, DateOfBirth, Gender, Average from Maths table and Average from IT table.

   A further field needs to be created named 'Yr' to contain the year element from the DateOfBirth field by using an expression.

   The data should be sorted by SecondName in ascending order.

   Save this query as *QueryReport*.

4 Then, in **design view,** create a new report based on this query.

   The report should have the following specifications.

   - A width of 20 cm.

   - A page header with the title 'Analysis report', font size 24 pt, black, bold and centred.

   - It should be grouped on the 'Yr' field and then on the 'gender' Field.

   - These field names should be in their group headers in 20 pt and bold.

   - The detail should contain the Secondname, FirstName, Maths average and IT Average.

   - The last two fields should have labels above them.

   - Save the report as 'Analysis Report'.

   - Take a screenshot of the report in Print Preview view and paste it into a document named *Task6.doc*.

   An example is shown in Figure 18.103.

   Save the database as *Students6*.

Analysis Report

2005			
F		**Maths**	**IT**
Abe	Sakura	47.7	57.7
Ahmed	Alyan	46.3	51.3
Ahmed	Laila	66.3	85.3
Hassen	Asbah	73.7	74.7
Luxenburg	Rosa	81.0	78.7
Okeke	Minenhle	66.3	47.3
Ricci	Elina	53.0	70.7
M		**Maths**	**IT**
Azimi	Tamir	56.0	64.0
Jacobs	Nikita	72.0	44.3
Lo	Yu Kiu	61.0	73.7
Weber	Matthew	49.7	42.0
Zaman	Atallah	73.7	49.0
2006			
F		**Maths**	**IT**
Alam	Fakira	79.7	79.0
Andersen	Saga	66.7	72.7
Byrne	Catherine	65.0	55.7
Lindberg	Agata	72.7	77.7
Mazur	Lucia	62.3	60.0
Moretti	Chiara	68.7	71.7
Rasheed	Asifa	74.0	49.3
M		**Maths**	**IT**
Azzi	Fadi	56.3	65.7
Bashir	Zakir	67.0	87.0
Hardwick	David	70.3	79.3
Hasan	Mubarak	70.0	
Mirza	Reyhan	68.0	58.3
Zaman	Quadim	62.0	71.3
2007			
F		**Maths**	**IT**
Hoffmann	Valentina	72.3	75.3
Kimura	Honoka	60.7	71.0
M		**Maths**	**IT**
Ho	Bohai	65.7	72.0
Jackson	Stephen	57.7	87.3

Figure 18.103: Example analysis report

CONTINUED

Challenge

5   In the page footer, in the centre, place the date.

6   In the page footer at the right place the page number in the following form:

>   [Page number] of [total number of pages], for example, Page 1 of 3.

Take a screenshot of the report in Print Preview view and paste it into *Task6.doc*.

An example is shown in Figure 18.104.

Save the database as *Task6_Challenge*.

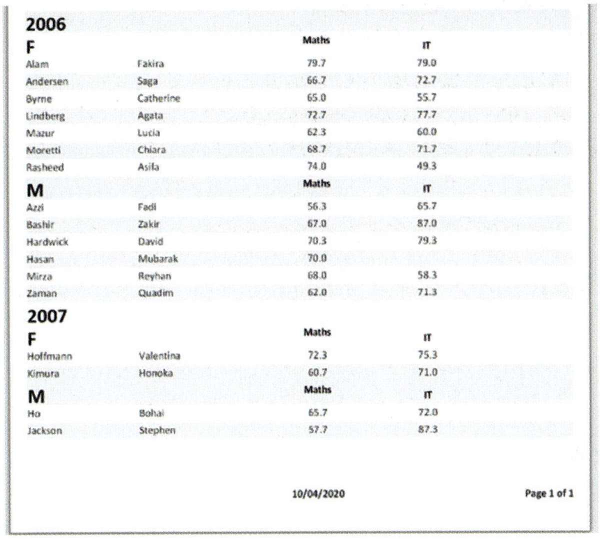

2006			
F		**Maths**	**IT**
Alam	Fakira	79.7	79.0
Andersen	Saga	66.7	72.7
Byrne	Catherine	65.0	55.7
Lindberg	Agata	72.7	77.7
Mazur	Lucia	62.3	60.0
Moretti	Chiara	68.7	71.7
Rasheed	Asifa	74.0	49.3
M		**Maths**	**IT**
Azzi	Fadi	56.3	65.7
Bashir	Zakir	67.0	87.0
Hardwick	David	70.3	79.3
Hasan	Mubarak	70.0	
Mirza	Reyhan	68.0	58.3
Zaman	Quadim	62.0	71.3
2007			
F		**Maths**	**IT**
Hoffmann	Valentina	72.3	75.3
Kimura	Honoka	60.7	71.0
M		**Maths**	**IT**
Ho	Bohai	65.7	72.0
Jackson	Stephen	57.7	87.3

10/04/2020   Page 1 of 1

Figure 18.104: Example analysis report with footer details added

Peer assessment

Print out and swap the reports with a partner. Assess each other's reports by checking things such as:

- Headings are shown and are consistent.
- All labels and fields are lined up correctly.
- No text overflows from any of the controls.
- Date is shown in the page footer.
- Page number is shown in the page footer.

WORKED EXAMPLE 18.1

CREATING A REPORT

1   Open the file *MathsResults.csv* and look at the data it contains.

2   Import this file into a table in a suitable database package.

You should create fields with suitable names and data types, and chose the most suitable field as the key field.

3   From your table create a report showing these results. The report should be grouped on the 'Gender' field.

CONTINUED

Step 1

The csv file (see Figure 18.105) contains details about students and their results for their termly tests saved in csv format.

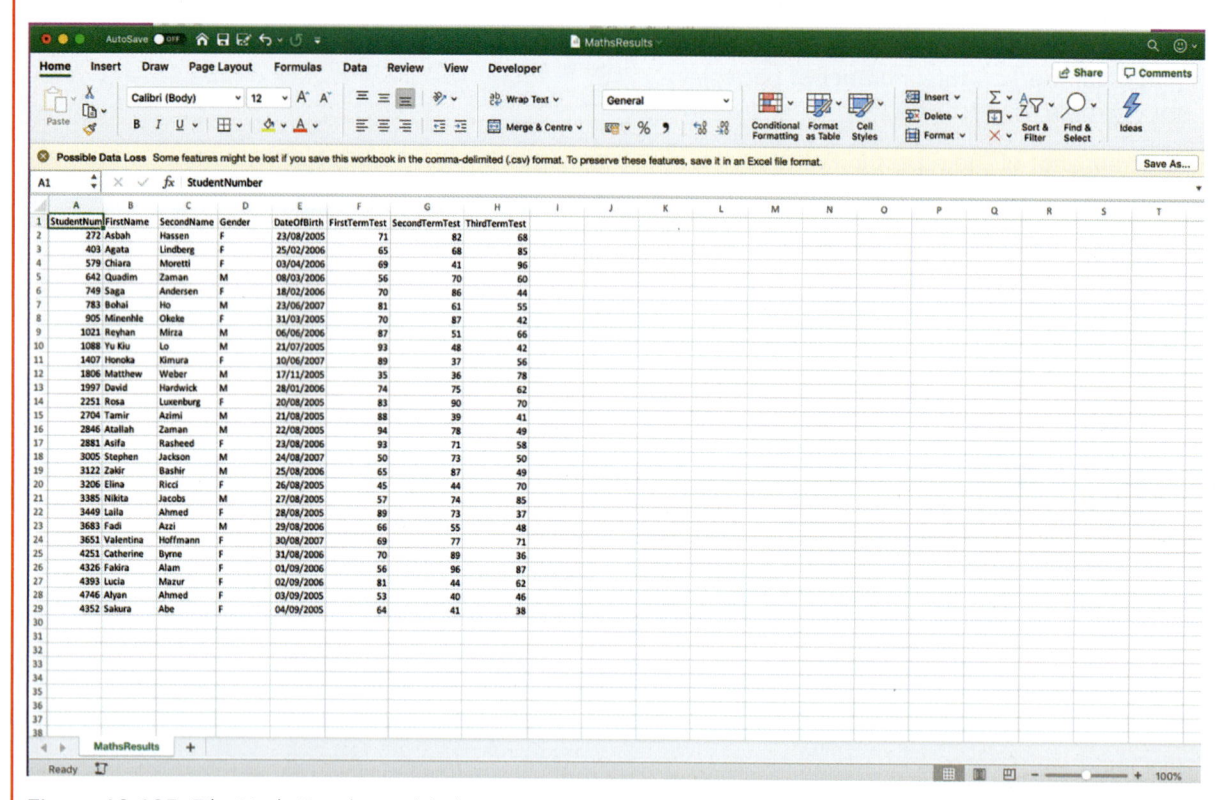

StudentNumber	FirstName	SecondName	Gender	DateOfBirth	FirstTermTest	SecondTermTest	ThirdTermTest
272	Asbah	Hassen	F	23/08/2005	71	82	68
403	Agata	Lindberg	F	25/02/2006	65	68	85
579	Chiara	Moretti	F	03/04/2006	69	41	96
642	Quadim	Zaman	M	08/03/2006	56	70	60
749	Saga	Andersen	F	18/02/2006	70	86	44
783	Bohai	Ho	M	23/06/2007	81	61	55
905	Minenhle	Okeke	F	31/03/2005	70	87	42
1021	Reyhan	Mirza	M	06/06/2006	87	51	66
1088	Yu Kiu	Lo	M	21/07/2005	93	48	42
1407	Honoka	Kimura	F	10/06/2007	89	37	56
1806	Matthew	Weber	M	17/11/2005	35	36	78
1997	David	Hardwick	M	28/01/2006	74	75	62
2251	Rosa	Luxenburg	F	20/08/2005	83	90	70
2704	Tamir	Azimi	M	21/08/2005	88	39	41
2846	Atallah	Zaman	M	22/08/2005	94	78	49
2881	Asifa	Rasheed	F	23/08/2006	93	71	58
3005	Stephen	Jackson	M	24/08/2007	50	73	50
3122	Zakir	Bashir	M	25/08/2006	65	87	49
3206	Elina	Ricci	F	26/08/2005	45	44	70
3385	Nikita	Jacobs	M	27/08/2005	57	74	85
3449	Laila	Ahmed	F	28/08/2005	89	73	37
3683	Fadi	Azzi	M	29/08/2006	66	55	48
3651	Valentina	Hoffmann	F	30/08/2007	69	77	71
4251	Catherine	Byrne	F	31/08/2006	70	89	36
4326	Fakira	Alam	F	01/09/2006	56	96	87
4393	Lucia	Mazur	F	02/09/2006	81	44	62
4746	Alyan	Ahmed	F	03/09/2005	53	40	46
4352	Sakura	Abe	F	04/09/2005	64	41	38

Figure 18.105: File *MathsResults.csv* labels

18 Databases

CONTINUED

Step 2

A new database file should be created (see Figure 18.106), and a new table designed for the data. The file should be named and saved in a suitable location.

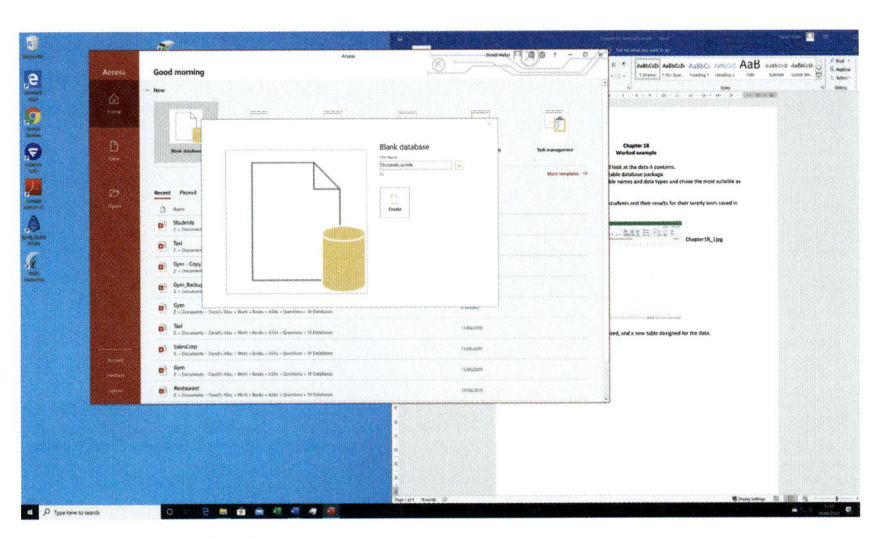

Figure 18.106: Creating a new database

A new table named 'Maths' is created in order to import this data.

The field types should match the data to be imported, for example dates of birth into a Date/Time field.

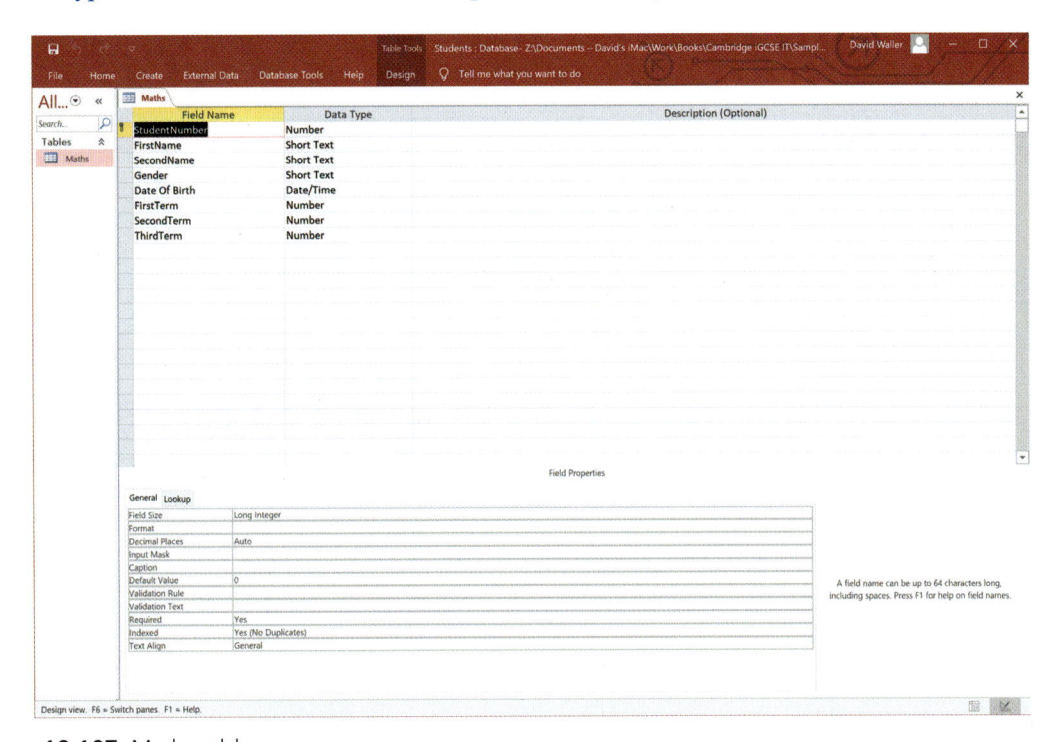

Figure 18.107: Maths table

CAMBRIDGE IGCSE™ ICT: COURSEBOOK

CONTINUED

The StudentNumber field should be selected as the primary key (see Figure 18.108) as all of the other fields could have non-unique information – for example, there may be two students with the same name, date of birth or test scores.

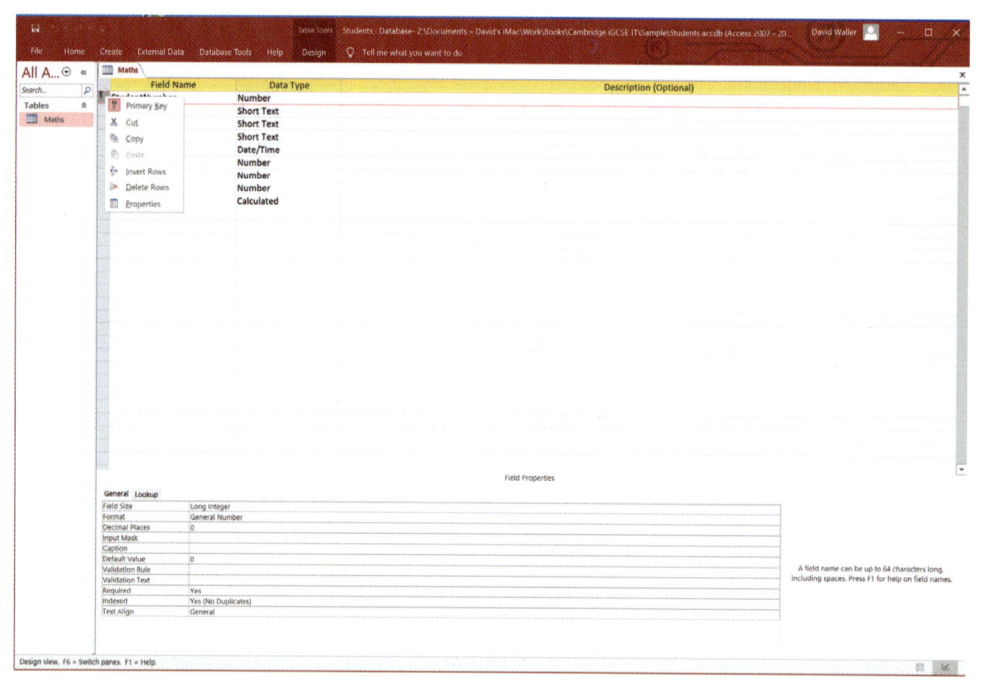

Figure 18.108: Setting the primary key

The data can now be selected and imported into the table.

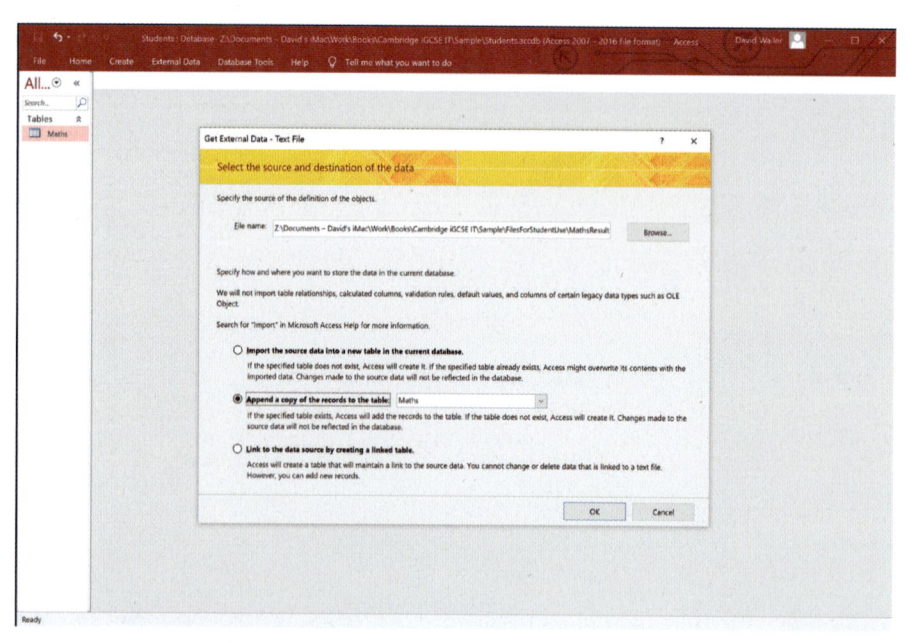

Figure 18.109: Selecting file and importing

18 Databases

> **CONTINUED**

The file name to be imported has to be selected, and also the table into which it is to be imported or appended to (see Figure 18.109).

After clicking 'OK', the data will be imported and the program will notify if there any errors, such as incorrect data types or text too long for a field.

The records can be viewed in the table (see Figure 18.110).

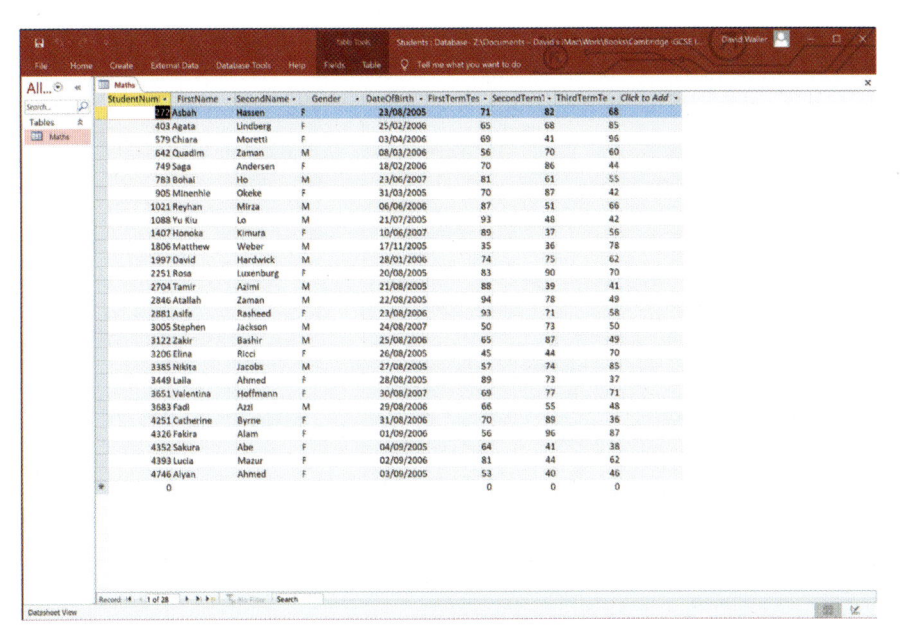

Figure 18.110: Maths table in database

Step 3

The report can now be produced from this table.

The wizard can be used.

Select all of the fields.

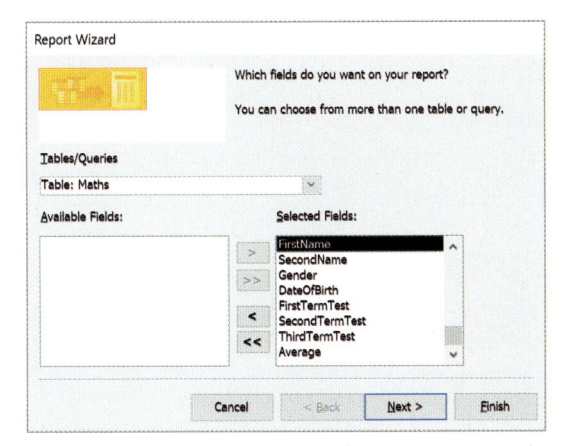

Figure 18.111: Selecting all fields

CONTINUED

Select 'Gender' as the field to group on.

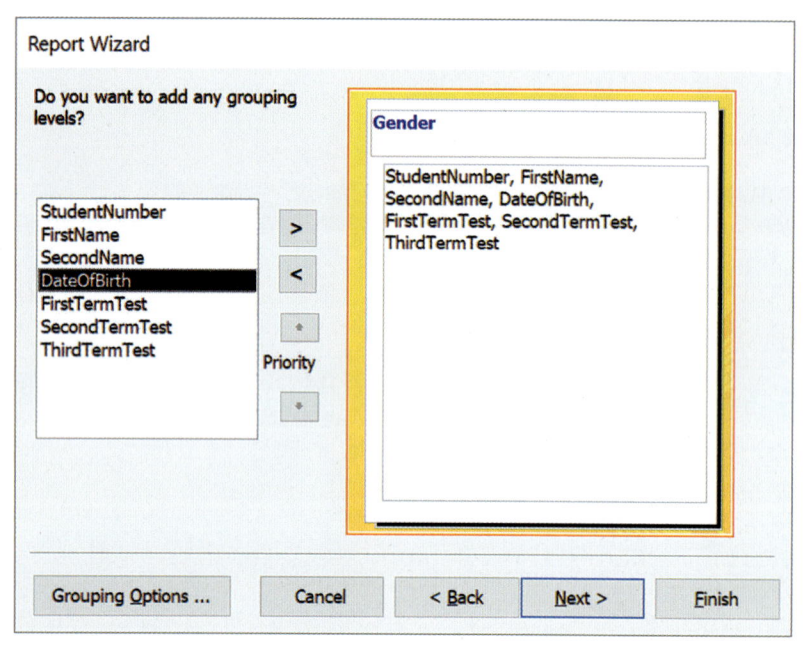

Figure 18.112: Selecting 'Gender' for grouping

The data does not need to be sorted and this form can be left blank.

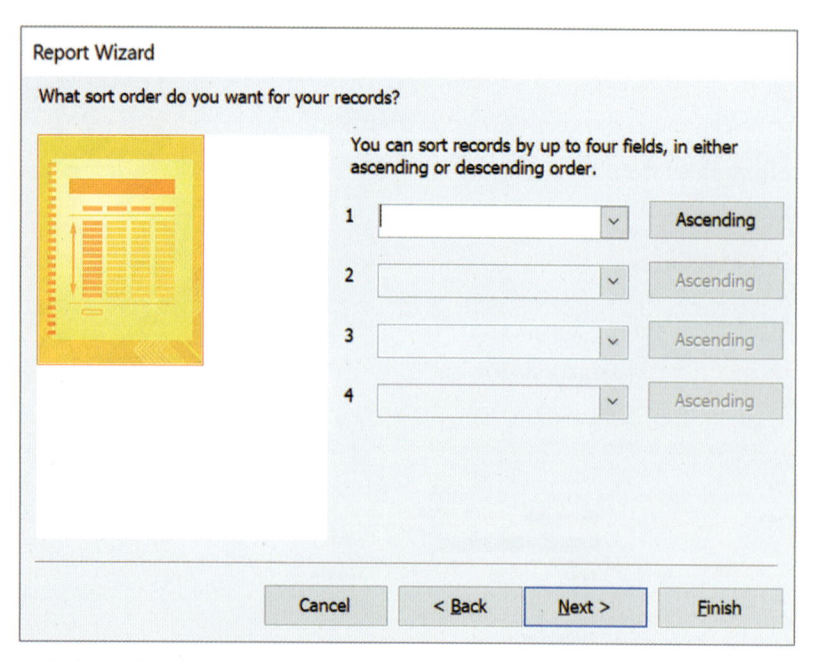

Figure 18.113: Sorting dialogue box

18 Databases

> **CONTINUED**

The orientation should be set to 'Landscape' and the layout to 'Stepped' for this report.

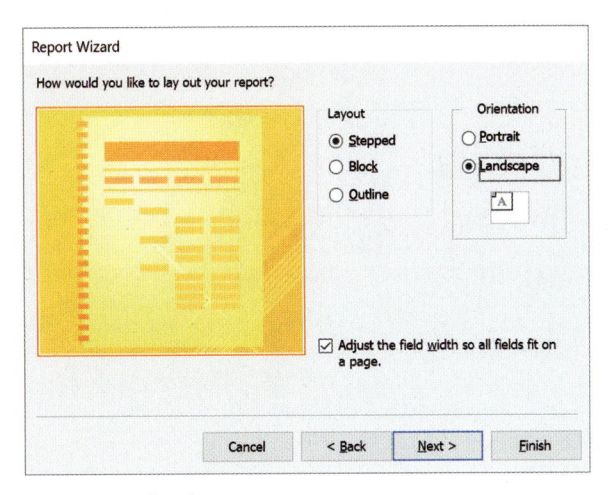

Figure 18.114: Setting orientation to landscape

The report will now be shown in 'Report View'.

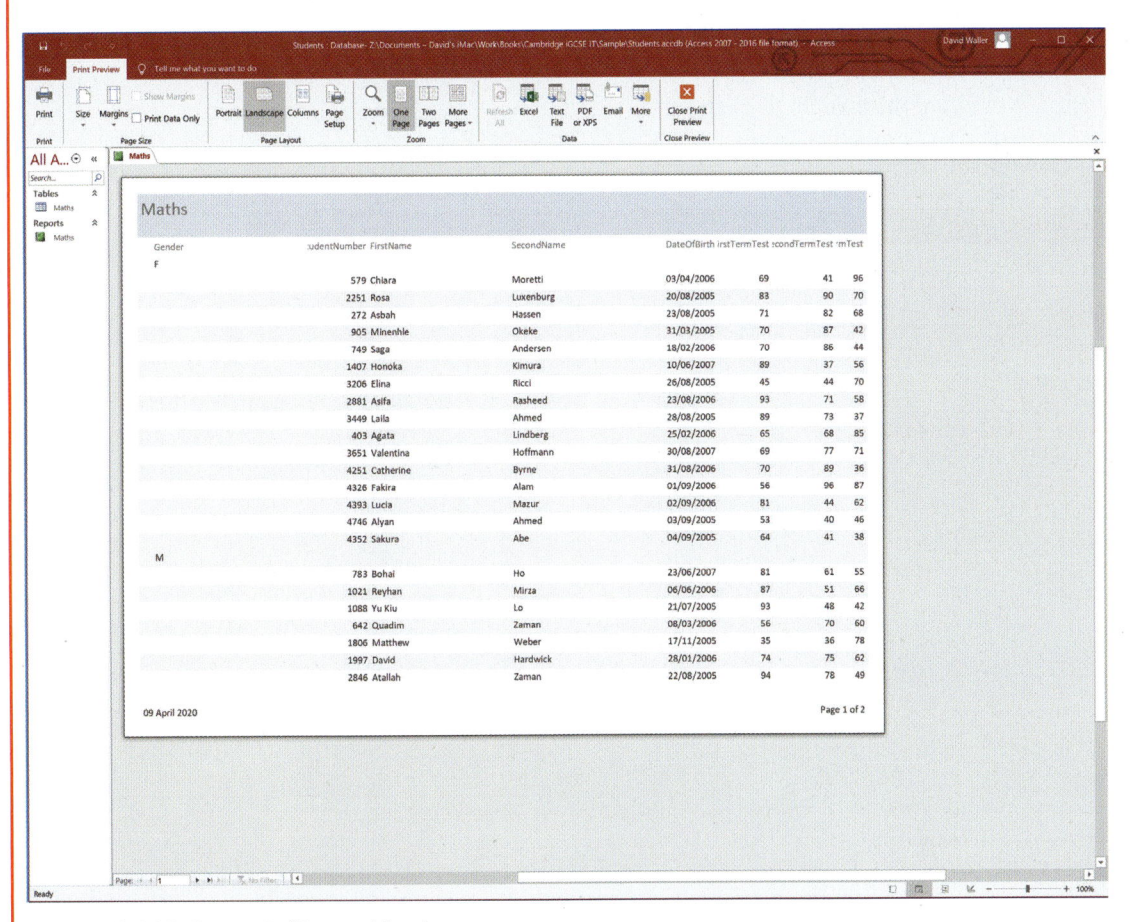

Figure 18.115: Report in 'Report View'

> **CONTINUED**

This report was set for a 'Stepped' layout. The other two options, 'Block' (see Figure 18.116) and 'Outline' (see Figure 18.117), produce similar reports.

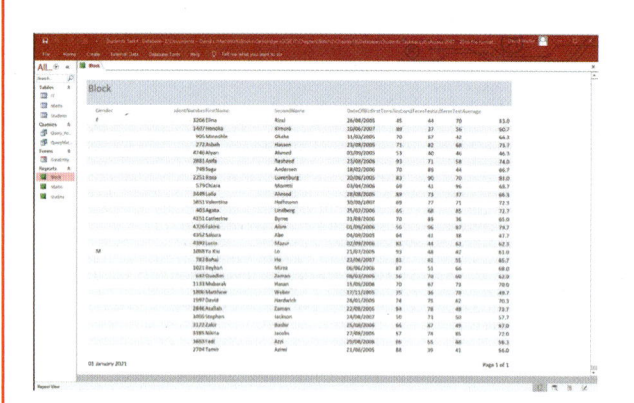

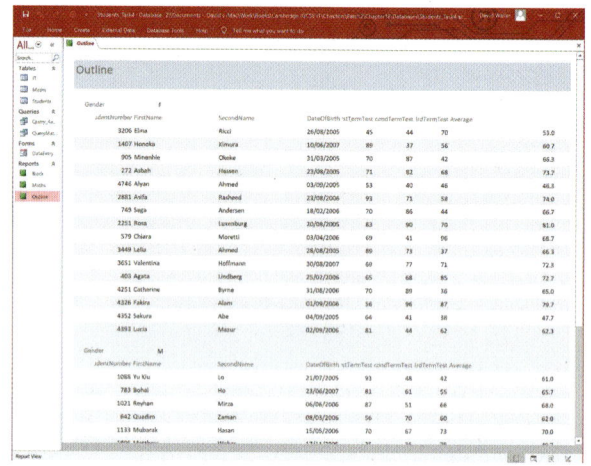

Figure 18.116: Block report

Figure 18.117: Outline report

The layout is not very good. For example, the sizes of the Gender, FirstName and SecondName fields are too large and the test field labels are too small.

These can be adjusted by viewing the form in 'Design view'.

The sizes of the fields and their labels can be adjusted.

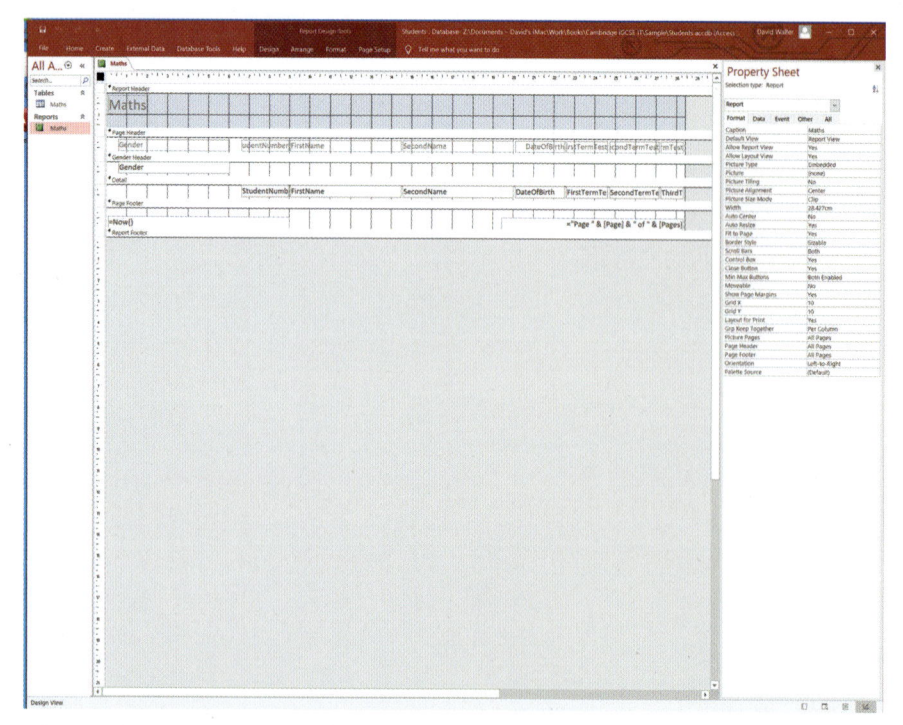

Figure 18.118: Adjusting layout in 'Design view'

CONTINUED

The field sizes have been adjusted.

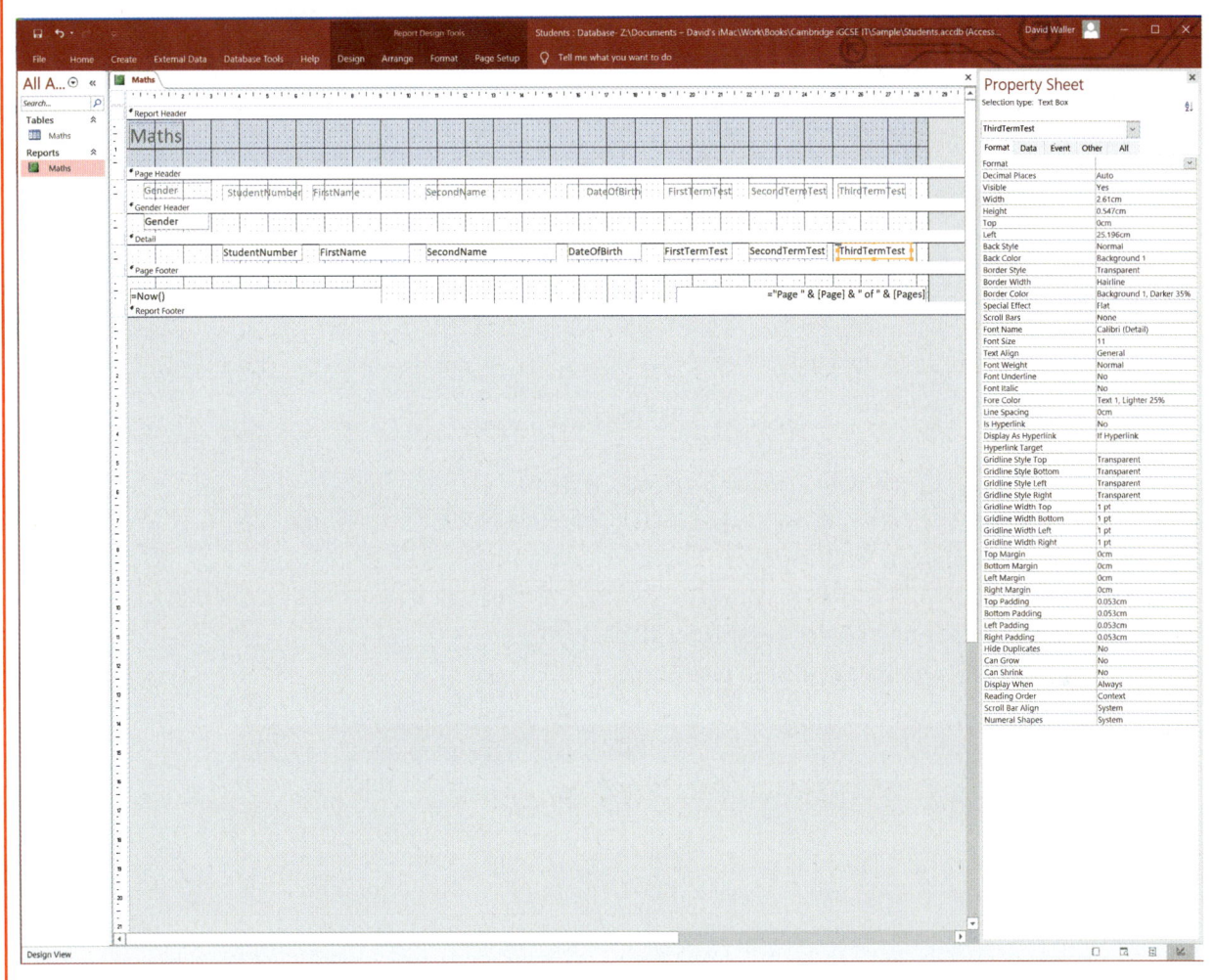

Figure 18.119: Adjusted layout

Questions

1. Create a database file and table in your own software and import the data from *MathsResults.csv*
2. Add the following student and data (see its placement in Figure 18.120).

Student Number	FirstName	Second Name	gender	DateOfBirth	First TermTest	Second TermTest	Third TermTest
1133	Mubarak	Hasan	M	15/5/2006	70	67	73

> **CONTINUED**

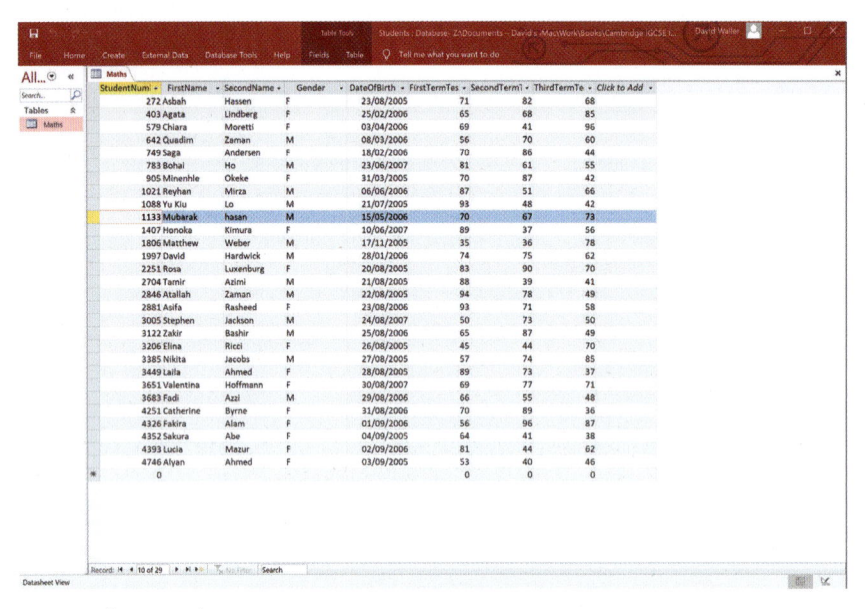

Figure 18.120: New record inserted

3   Create the report, grouped on 'Gender' (see Figure 18.121).

   The data in the report is now much easier to read.

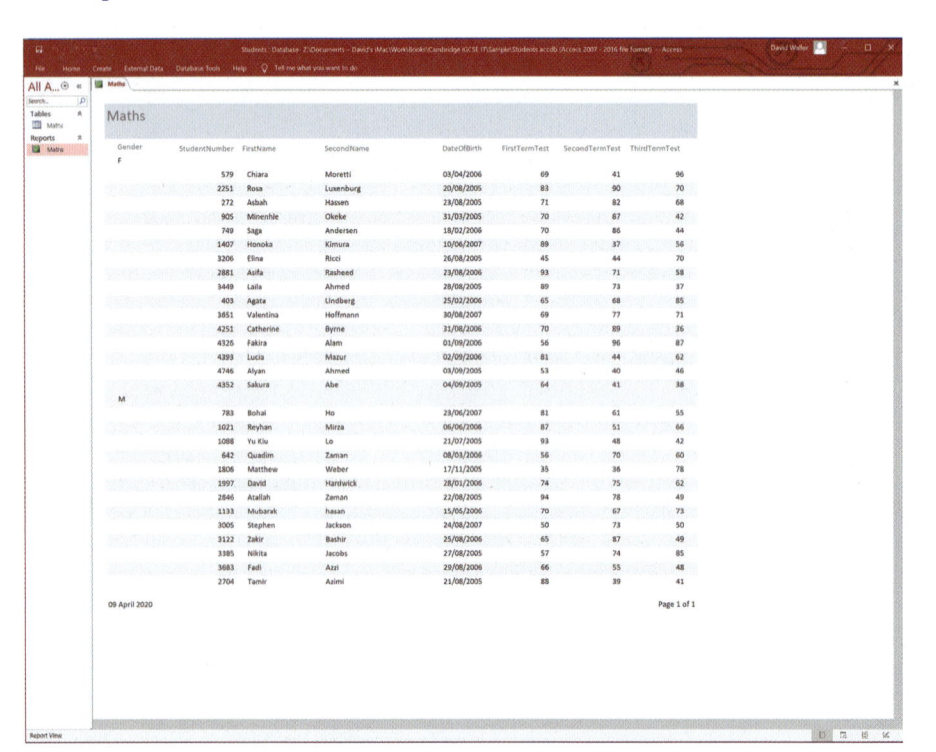

Figure 18.121: Grouped report

18 Databases

> **REFLECTION**
>
> In small groups, talk about what you each found difficult in this chapter, and come up with ideas to help each other learn the material.

> **SUMMARY**
>
> | |
> |---|
> | Data can be stored in tables in flat file and relational databases. |
> | When database tables are being created, the fields, their names and data types must be defined. |
> | Fields are one item of information about an entity. They can be calculated from the data in other fields and formatted to show percentages and number of decimal places. |
> | Relational databases are databases that have many linked tables. The relationships between the tables should be established. |
> | All linked tables require a primary key field. |
> | Data can be entered manually or imported using suitable files. |
> | Data in tables can be displayed in data entry forms. |
> | The data can be searched and sorted using queries. |
> | Formulae and functions can be used to perform calculations at run time. |
> | Reports can be used to display the data in tables and queries. |

> **EXAM-STYLE QUESTIONS**
>
> 1 Mrs Jackson is opening a cattery to look after the animals when their owners go on holiday. To store the details of her guests, she has created the database table (shown below) to store details of her guests. Some of the data is shown.
>
> | Name | Gender | Weight (Kg) | Number of days | Special diet? |
> |---|---|---|---|---|
> | Dottie | F | 3.2 | 6 | N |
> | Jack | M | 4.2 | 7 | Y |
>
> a The table stores several items of information about each cat.
>   i   Copy the table onto a piece of paper and draw round a field in the table in one colour. [1]
>   ii Draw round a record in the table in a different colour. [1]
> b Create an empty row in the table, and state a suitable data type for each item of information (field). [5]
> c **State** a validation check that could be carried out on the 'gender' data. [2]

> **COMMAND WORDS**
>
> **state:** express in clear terms

CONTINUED

    d **i** **Explain** what is meant by a key field. [2]

        ii Explain why none of the fields in the table would be suitable to be the key field. [2]

        iii **Suggest** a suitable key field that Mrs Jackson could add to the table. [1]

2 Examine the data files *Members.csv*, *Sport.csv* and *Member_Sport.csv*. They all relate to data held by a gym.

    a **i** Create a new database named *Gym*.

        ii Create three tables named tbl_Members, tbl_Sport and tbl_Member_Sport to store the data in the csv files.

        iii Use the column headings as field names and data types, and select key fields.

        iv Import the data from the csv files into the tables.

        v Create a document named *Evidence.doc* and paste into it screen prints of your three tables, in design view and after the data has been imported. [10]

    b Set the relationships between the tables and take a screenshot showing those relationships. Paste the screenshot into *Evidence.doc*. [2]

    c Create data entry forms for tbl_members containing a heading, all of the fields and command buttons for navigation and to create and delete records.

    Paste a screen print of your form into *Evidence.doc*. [5]

    d Create the following queries:

Name	Fields shown when query is run.	Criteria	Sorting
qry_DateOfBirth	Surname, FirstName, Gender, DOB	Birth date before the year 2000	Date of birth, ascending
qry_Football	Surname, FirstName, Gender, SportName	Only showing football.	
qry_Report	Surname, FirstName, Gender, SportID, SportName.		•

    Make screen prints of the queries in design view and paste them into Evidence.doc. [6]

    e **i** Create a report named rpt_Sports with the following specification. [15]
- It should be based on qry_Report.
- The report should have a width of 13 cm.
- It should have a page header of 'Sports' in a black, bold font of 28 pt and should be centred.

COMMAND WORDS

explain: set out purposes or reasons / make the relationships between things evident / provide why and / or how and support with relevant evidence

suggest: apply knowledge and understanding to situations where there are a range of valid responses in order to make proposals / put forward considerations

> ## CONTINUED
>
> - The report should be grouped first by sport and then by gender with suitable headings.
> - The Surname and FirstName should be shown for each member in the list.
> - The footer for the sport should show the number of members doing it and a horizontal line to separate it from the next sport.
> - The page footer should show the text 'Page' followed by the page number.
>
> ii Take a screen print of the report in design view and paste it into *Evidence.doc*. [1]
>
> iii Take a screen print of a print preview of the first page your report and paste it into *Evidence.doc*. [1]
>
> [Total: 54]

SELF-EVALUATION CHECKLIST

After studying this chapter, think about how confident you are with the different topics.

This will help you to see any gaps in your knowledge and help you to learn more effectively.

You might find it helpful to rate how confident you are for each of these statements when you are revising. You should revisit any sections that you rated 'Needs more work' or 'Getting there'.

I can …	See section	Needs more work	Getting there	Confident to move on
describe the types of databases, primary and foreign keys, and form design	18.1			
create a database structure	18.1			
create and use a data entry form	18.1			
manipulate data by performing calculations, sorting and searching data	18.2			
display data in different output layouts	18.3			

Chapter 19
Presentations

IN THIS CHAPTER YOU WILL:

- create a presentation using a text file
- use a master slide, placing objects consistently and formatting master slide objects
- edit a presentation by inserting, deleting and linking objects and applying transitions and animations in slides
- output the presentation to looped on-screen carousel or presenter-controlled displays
- print presentations as full-page slides, presenter notes or handouts.

19 Presentations

GETTING STARTED

It is likely that most people will use presentation software at some point during their school or working lives. And most people will have sat through someone else's presentation too!

Look at the example slides in Figure 19.1 and then write down what you think of them.

Are they good or bad? Explain your answers giving details of why you think they are good or bad.

a

b

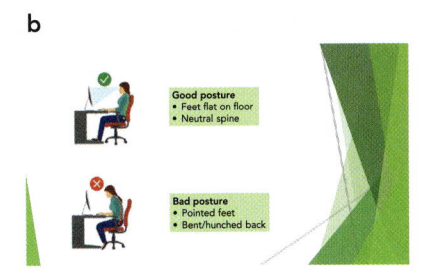

Figure 19.1: Examples of good and bad slides

THE SHOW MUST GO ON

Presentations present something to an audience. It could be business information, humour, a story or a game.

A video is a presentation, as is an audio file. However, when we think of presentation software, we don't usually think of video and sound editing software or desktop publishing and graphics software. We think of presentation software as displaying information in the form of a slide show (see example slide in Figure 19.2). You could, of course, argue that a video is a very fast slide show with 25 slides per second!

Figure 19.2: An example of a slide

The software allows a speaker to enhance their talk using multimedia: text, colour, animation, video and recorded sound. So if you were giving a talk on birds and bird song, instead of describing the birds and trying to mimic their sounds, in the background you could have slides containing images of the birds, videos of them in flight and play sound recordings of their voices. A great improvement!

In addition to helping the presenter, audio and video are also of great benefit to the audience. Instead of becoming bored, listening to a lone speaker, the audience is given much more varied and interesting information. There is far less chance of falling asleep during the presentation!

But, like all software, you can create bad as well as good results so that the presentation can provide less information than a speaker. A bad presentation will be full of text, with the slides or video simply repeating what the presenter is saying. A bad presenter – and there are a lot of them – will just read from the slides instead of their notes. This is not good use of presentation software as the presentation should enhance the information that the speaker is presenting.

> CAMBRIDGE IGCSE™ ICT: COURSEBOOK

> **CONTINUED**
>
> As presentation software has become more sophisticated, instead of supporting a speaker, they can often replace them. Presentations can be looped and left running for audiences. They can be used for teaching and tutorials, without a teacher. They can be viewed online. They can be interactive, responding to audience input.
>
> Latest releases have stopped using slides, using animated videos instead. Presentation software is being used to create computer games, interactive story books, animated GIFs and infographics – a collection of images, charts and minimal text that gives an easy-to-understand overview of a topic, as discussed in Chapter 16.
>
> Artificial intelligence is being used to apply the rules of good design and even preventing users from violating them by making suggestions. Artificial intelligence is also being used to give feedback on the user's performance, how they speak, how quickly they speak and if they read text from the slides.
>
> **Questions**
>
> 1. In a group, discuss what makes a good presentation and what makes a bad presentation.
> 2. Decide on five rules that should be followed to make a good presentation.

19.1 Creating a presentation

In the past, **presentations** would have been delivered by a presenter who would have been speaking (usually from prompt cards) using posters, pictures, books, writing boards and possibly sounds or musical interludes. Nowadays, you can deliver presentations by speaking and using on-screen prompts in the form of a **slide show** with pictures, sounds and videos.

This chapter will look at how to make slide presentations.

> **KEY WORDS**
>
> **presentation:** a way of presenting something to an audience; can include a speaker showing slides, videos, sound and looped slides in an exhibition
>
> **slide show:** a presentation made up of screens of information including digital images, text and audio viewed in a progression
>
> **slide:** one screen of information in a presentation

Use a master slide

Professional-looking presentations usually have a consistent style and display carefully selected colours that do not clash, font and image sizes that show a degree of proportion in comparison to the whole **slide**.

> **ICT IN CONTEXT**
>
> Before computers and presentation software, the person giving the talk had to rely on boards (chalkboards) to present graphics and calculation.
>
> **Figure 19.3:** Presentation on a chalkboard

A **master slide** allows you to create a **style template** that can be used as the basis for all the slides in a presentation. It can be used to create a house style, where the sizes of fonts for the headings and normal text, the colour schemes, background colours and borders that will be the same on all the slides can be set (see Chapter 14 for more information about master pages and house styles).

A master slide can be used to place objects, such as images, text, shapes, logos, slide headers and footers, **automated slide numbering** and **placeholder positions** on each slide. However, a master slide is not an actual slide itself. It just informs the other slides how they are to be formatted. The **layout masters** deal with each slide type.

The master slide of a presentation can be viewed and edited by selecting Slide Master (see Figure 19.4) from the View menu.

On the master slides are placeholders or containers for displaying content such as text, images, media and tables. The placeholders ensure that these elements will always be in the same positions in slides made from these templates. They can be deleted, resized and moved, and new ones can be added.

Layout masters

The master slide is the top slide shown in pane on the left side of the window and the layout masters appear just below the master slide. These are already created for you.

The layout masters are for slide types such as:

- The title slide – introduces the presentation.
- Content slide – the slides that make up most of the presentation.
- A section heading slide – used to introduce different parts of the presentation if it is split up into sections.
- Two content layout – a split slide with two presentations side-by-side.

Items placed on the master slide appear on all of the layout masters. If the fonts are edited on the master slide and objects such as shapes and images are added to it (see Figure 19.5) they are then all added to the layout masters.

The fonts, font colours, font sizes, fill colours and bullets can be edited on the master slide using the options on the Home ribbon, as with any software. These will then be applied to all the layout masters.

KEY WORDS

master slide: a type of template where you can create the style and formatting that you wish to copy across all the other slides

style template: a design that serves as a starting point for a new presentation

automated slide numbering: numbering slides in all the slides without having to number each slide individually and usually in the slide header or footer

placeholder positions: 'frames' or 'empty boxes' to insert items of text, images, sound, video, etc.

layout master: a template for a particular layout based on the master slide

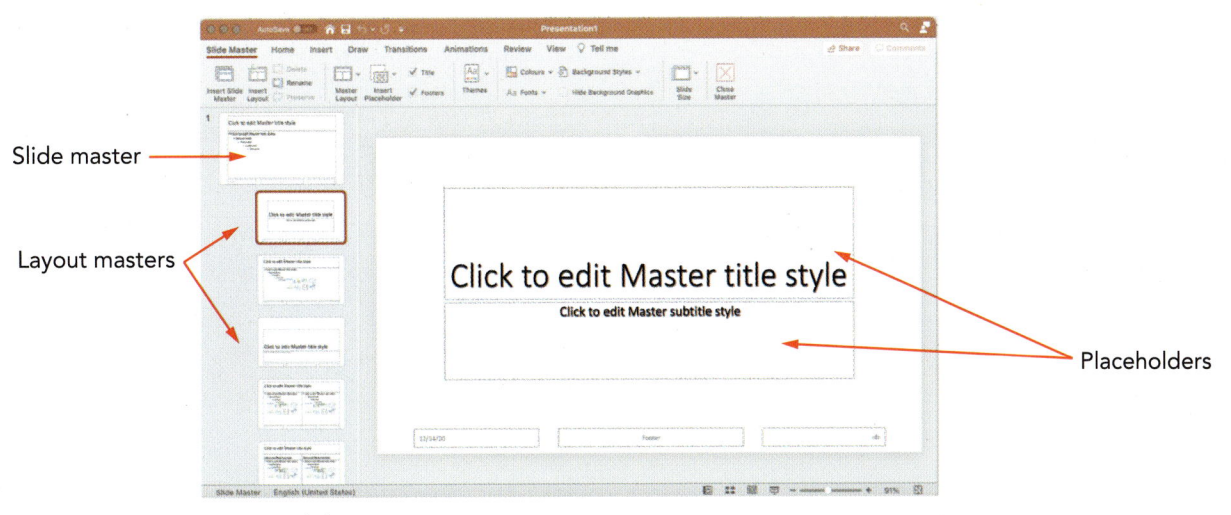

Figure 19.4: Creating a master slide

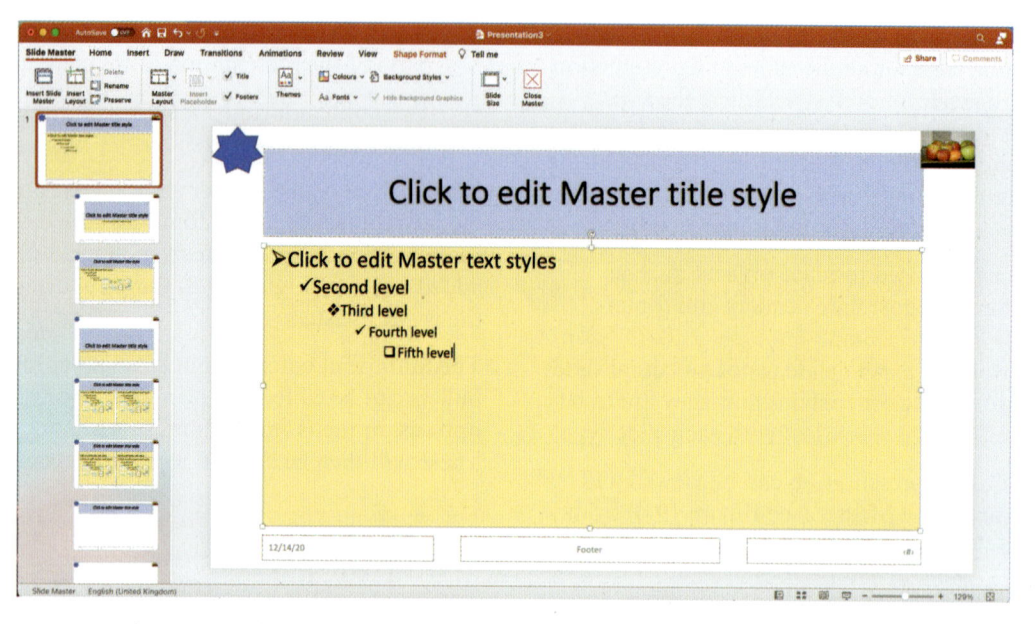

Figure 19.5: Formatting changes made to the master slide

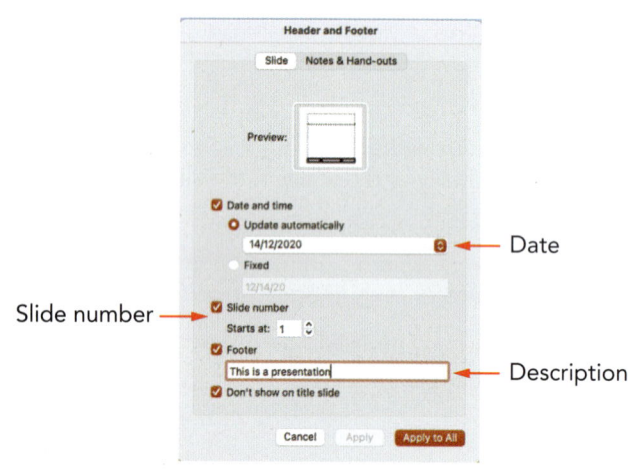

Figure 19.6: Adding date, page number and description to the footer of the master slide

Items added to the footer of the master slide such as date, slide number and description, can also be added to the master slide.

When the Header & Footer icon is selected from the Insert menu, the dialogue box shown in Figure 19.6 can be used to insert Date and Time, slide number and a description to the master slide. The Date and Time can be set to 'fixed' so that it always shows the date of when the slide was created or to 'update' where it shows the current date whenever the presentation is opened.

These will now appear on all of the layout masters. Each of the layout masters can be edited independently. For example, the 'title layout master' (Figure 19.7) can be changed (Figure 19.8).

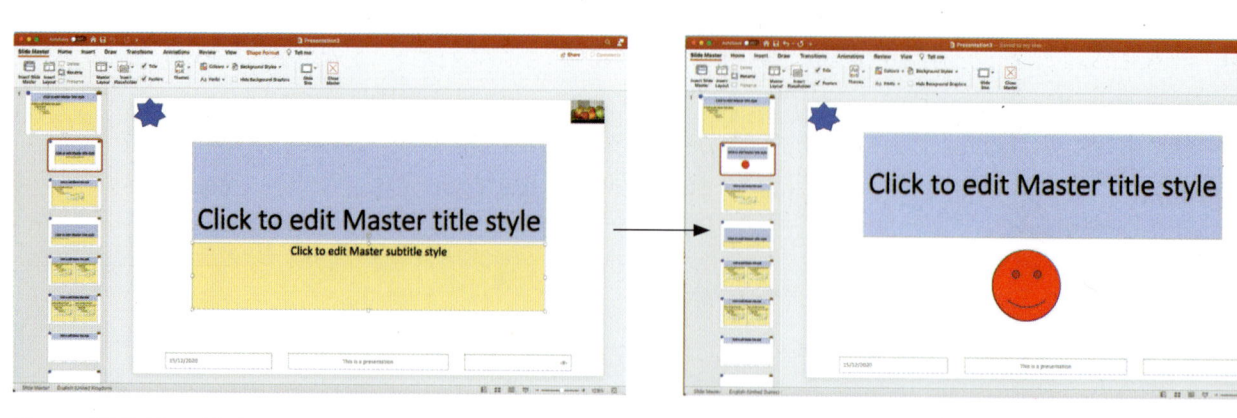

Figure 19.7: The title layout master

Figure 19.8: The title layout master edited

19 Presentations

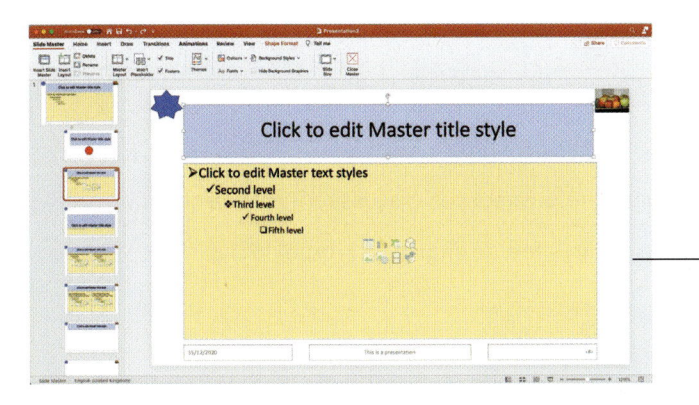

Figure 19.9: Title and content master

Placeholder for text, media, charts, tables etc. These are already on the Layout masters.

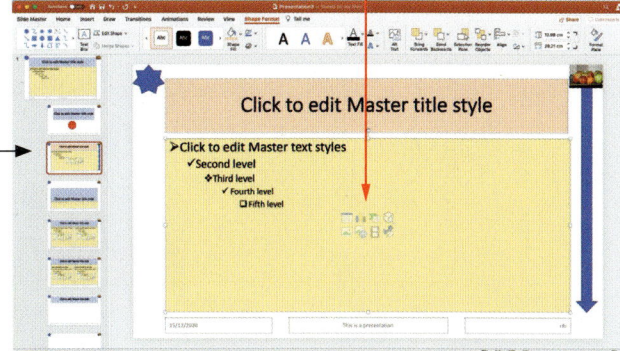

Figure 19.10: Title and content master edited

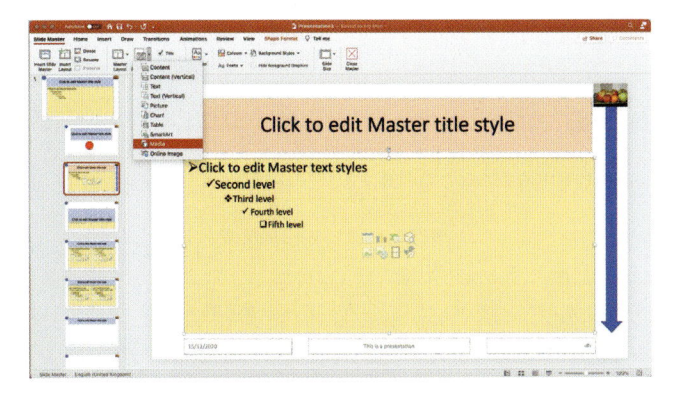

Figure 19.11: Adding placeholders

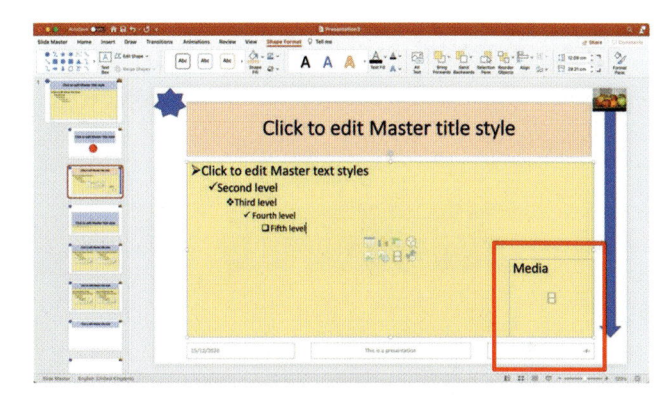

Figure 19.12: Added placeholder for media

The 'title layout master' retains the image and object it inherited from the master slide but other elements can be added. The 'title and content layout master' is probably the most important slide as most of the presentations will use it as a template.

Existing display areas can be edited and objects added (see Figures 19.9–10).

Placeholders can be added by selecting the Insert Placeholder icon from the Slide Master ribbon (see Figure 19.11).

In the example in Figure 19.12, a placeholder for media, such as videos, has been added.

PRACTICAL TASK 19.1

Getting started

1. With a partner, discuss, and then note down, the benefits of having master slides.
2. With a partner, design a master slide on paper that you would use for a presentation about your school or college.

CONTINUED

Practice

3   Open the presentation *Databases.pptx* in your presentation software.

4   Edit the master slide to these specifications by following the procedures discussed in this section:

- Logo1 and Logo2 should appear at the top left of each slide as shown in Figure 19.13:

Figure 19.13: Logo 1 and Logo 2

- 'Lesson 1' should appear at the top right of every slide.
  it should be in a 24 pt, bold font.
- In the centre of the footer insert 'NorthEastern College' in 14 pt font.
- Change the first to third level bullets to ones of your choice (see Figure 19.14 for an example).

5   Save the presentation as *Task1*.

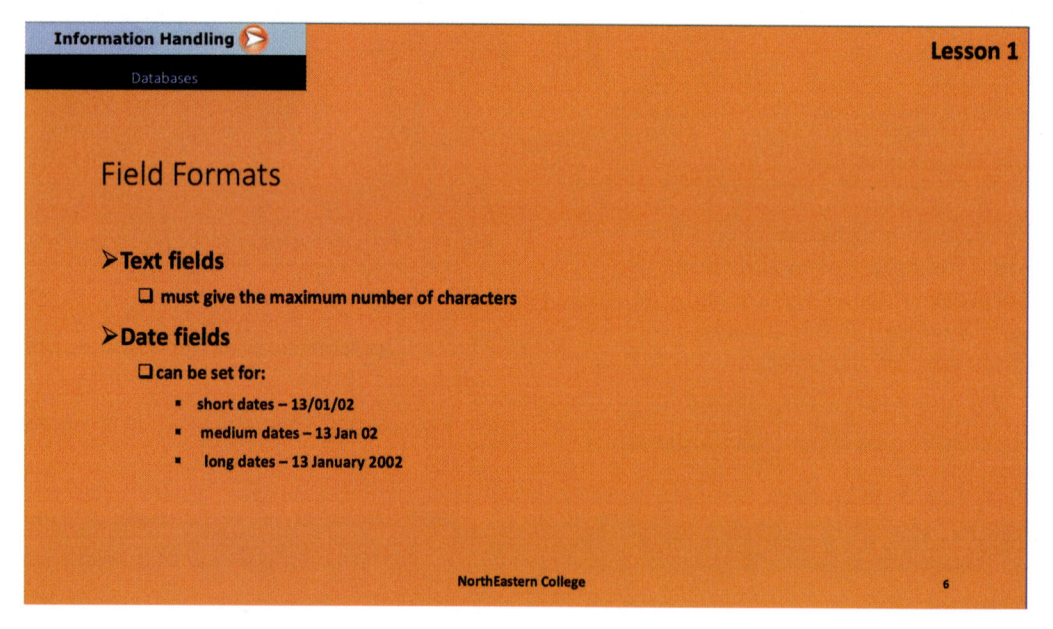

Figure 19.14: Practical task result

Challenge

6   Insert a fixed date at the left of the footer.

7   Change the 'Master title style' so that the text is red. Change the 'Master text styles' so that the text is white.

8   Save the presentation as *Task1_Challenge*.

Question

1 Define the following:
   - a text file
   - b presentation
   - c header and footer
   - d placeholder
   - e master slide.

ACTIVITY 19.1

You have been asked to draw some plans for a **presentation template** that all students will use to create their own presentations on 'Climate Change'.

Draw two slide plans for the title and the title and content slide masters. They should have:

- Placeholders for headings, sub-headings, logo, shapes, images, bulleted text, footer with automated slide numbering.
- Appropriate font styles, sizes and colours to match the theme of climate change.

Label the slide plans.

Swap with one of your class members and use their drawing plan to create a title and a content slide master in a presentation software package. You should avoid communicating with them during the time you create their presentation.

Peer assessment

When you have both completed creating each other's presentations, look at them and discuss if that was how you had hoped your presentation would look. Give each other critical feedback.

REFLECTION

Reflect on how much detail you included in your plans in Activity 19.1. Did you change anything between planning and creating the presentation? What would you do differently when doing drawing plans for future presentations?

The look of a presentation is not all that matters. Presentations must be effective. This means that the presentation should serve its intended purpose, regardless of what it looks like. The main reasons why presentations are used include:

- To help a speaker to remember all the main points of the speech. This means that presentations should not have a lot of sentences and text. A slide can only contain a limited amount of text; if the audience are expected to read a lot of the text from each slide, they would struggle to listen to what the speaker is saying at the same time.

- To highlight relevant information from a chart, graph or picture during a presentation.

- To use as a teaching tool during interactive **multimedia** presentations where students can drag and drop items into the correct blocks and receive immediate feedback to their responses.

- To display on a loop where information can be presented automatically without stopping and without a real-time speaker, such as in offline digital advertisements. This is a presentation mode called **carousel**, because it goes round and round.

KEY WORDS

presentation template: a frame upon which to build a presentation by simply filling in your own relevant information in the spaces provided

multimedia: a combination of graphics, text, audio, video and animations

carousel: a presentation mode that allows a slide presentation to repeatedly play until you stop it

Creating a presentation using a text file

A presentation can also be made directly by opening a formatted word processed file in the presentation software. The different styles applied to the document are interpreted as different levels by the presentation software.

CAMBRIDGE IGCSE™ ICT: COURSEBOOK

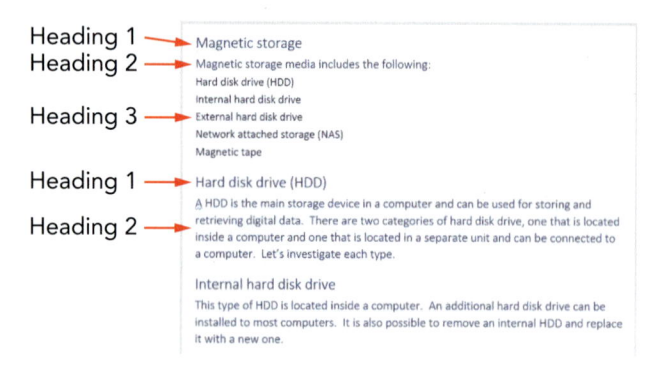

Figure 19.15: Word document

In the example text document in Figure 19.15:

- Where there is a new Heading 1, a new slide is created.
- Heading 2 creates a first level bulleted line.
- Heading 3 creates a second-level bulleted line.

A presentation created from a text document will be basic (Figure 19.16) and will need further editing.

19.2 Editing a presentation

Editing a presentation involves deciding on the layout, inserting new slides or **duplicating** an existing slide so that you can change a few aspects of it without having to recreate a similar slide. You can move slides around in a presentation by dragging and dropping them into position. If you wish to delete a slide, simply highlight it and press the delete button on your keyboard. This section looks at how to do these things.

> **KEY WORD**
>
> **duplicate:** make a copy of (verb) or a copy of something (noun)

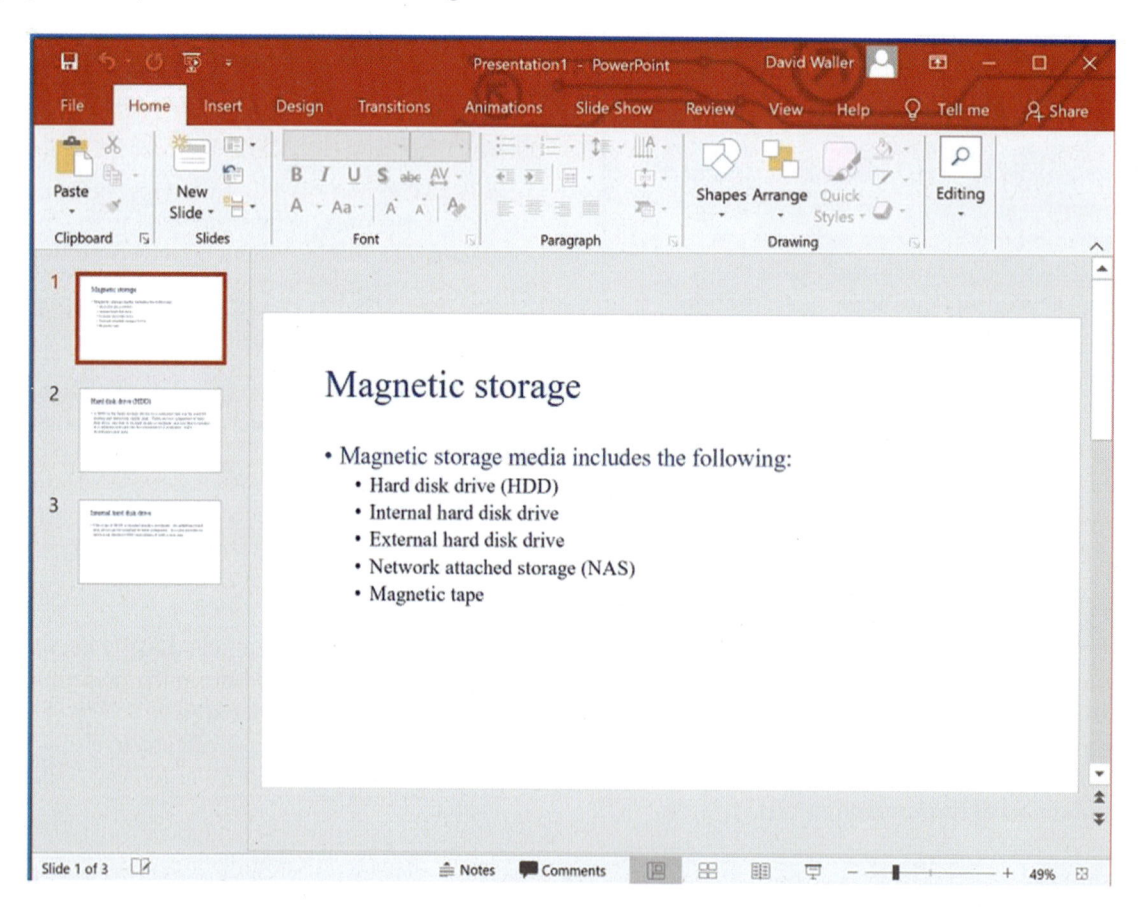

Figure 19.16: Presentation from the document shown in Figure 19.15

446

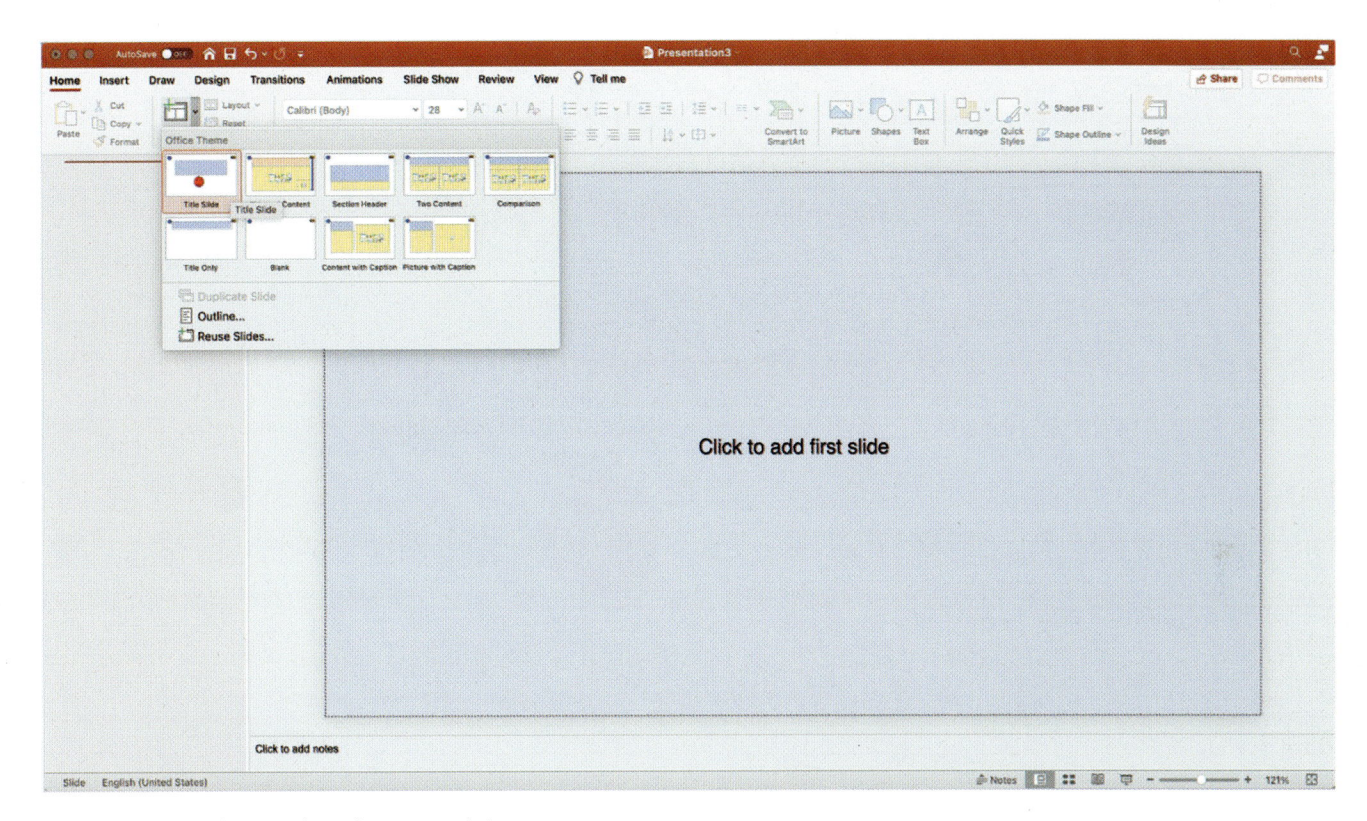

Figure 19.17: Selecting the title master slide

ICT IN CONTEXT

PowerPoint was first released in 1987 under the name Presenter for the Macintosh computer. The software was later sold to Microsoft for $14 million.

It has been estimated that every second, more than 350 PowerPoint presentations are started around the world. That is about 30 million a day!

Inserting and editing a new slide

A slide can be added or inserted by selecting New Slide from the Home menu and choosing the required layout master (see Figure 19.17).

If it is the first slide in a presentation, the title layout master should be selected. A suitable heading can then be inserted in the placeholder that was defined in the title layout master. This can be done by left-clicking in the placeholder to set the cursor and then typing using the keyboard (see Figure 19.18 on the next page).

After the title slide, a content slide can be added by selecting the title and content layout master (see Figure 19.19 on the next page). The content slide is used for the main content of the presentation.

Content slides have placeholders for headings, bulleted text and a video.

Text can be added into the heading and text placeholders and a suitable video can be selected (see Figure 19.20 on the following pages).

Items such as text boxes, images, videos, audio clips, charts, tables, shapes, call out boxes, symbols and animations can be inserted, in the usual way, by selecting objects from the Insert menu as you would in other software (see Chapter 13), or – for objects such as image, videos and audio clips – by dragging the items onto the slide from other folders on the computer and placing them on the slide (see Figure 19.21 on the following pages).

When an audio file is inserted, its playback can be formatted.

When the audio icon on the slide is highlighted, the Playback ribbon can be accessed (see Figure 19.22 on the following pages).

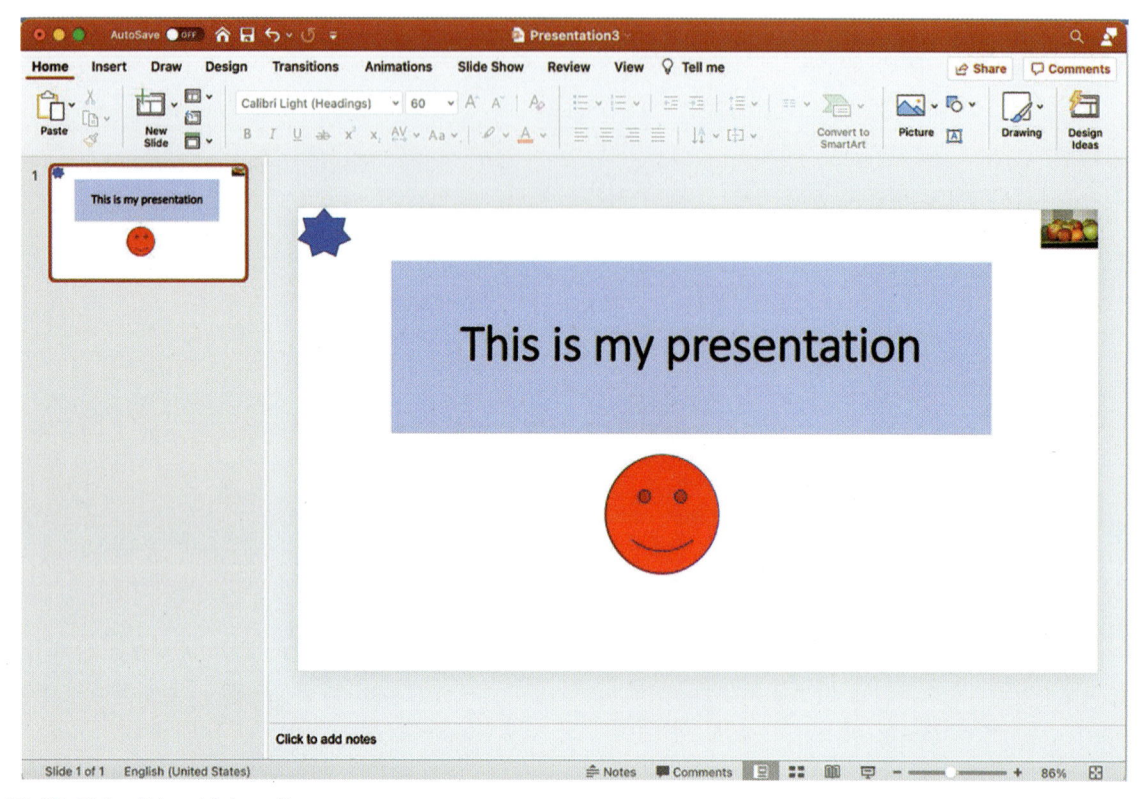

Figure 19.18: Title slide with heading

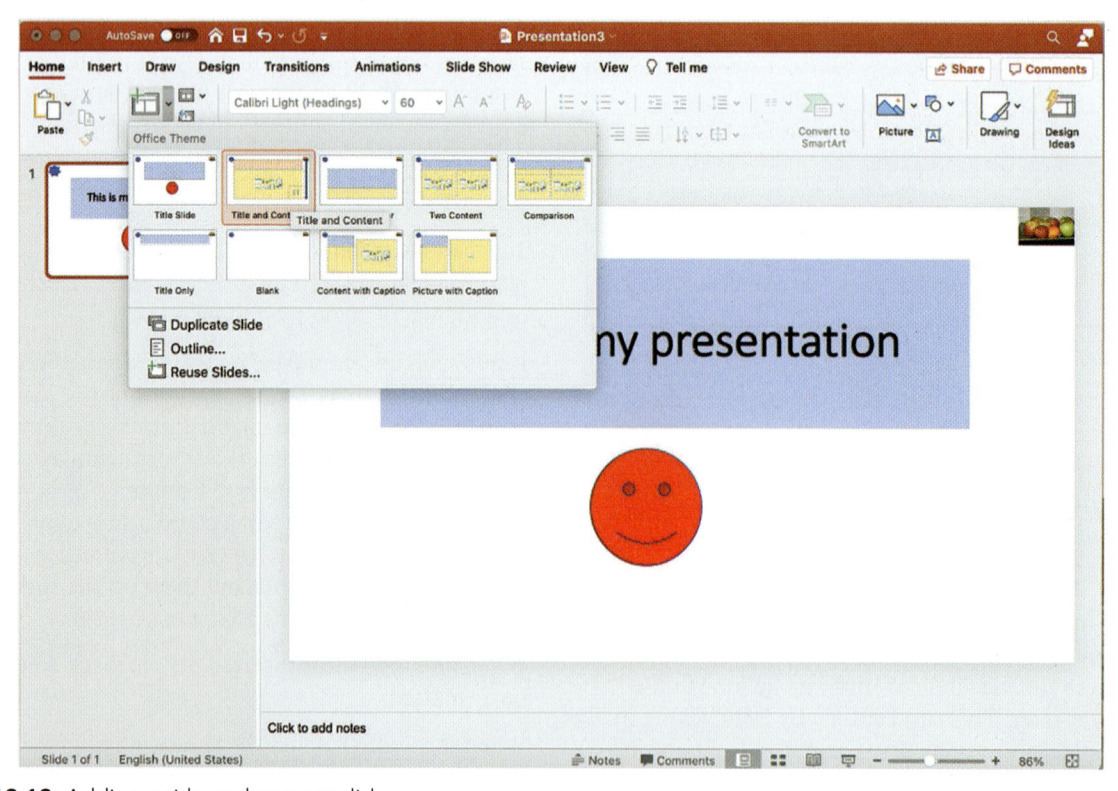

Figure 19.19: Adding a title and content slide

19 Presentations

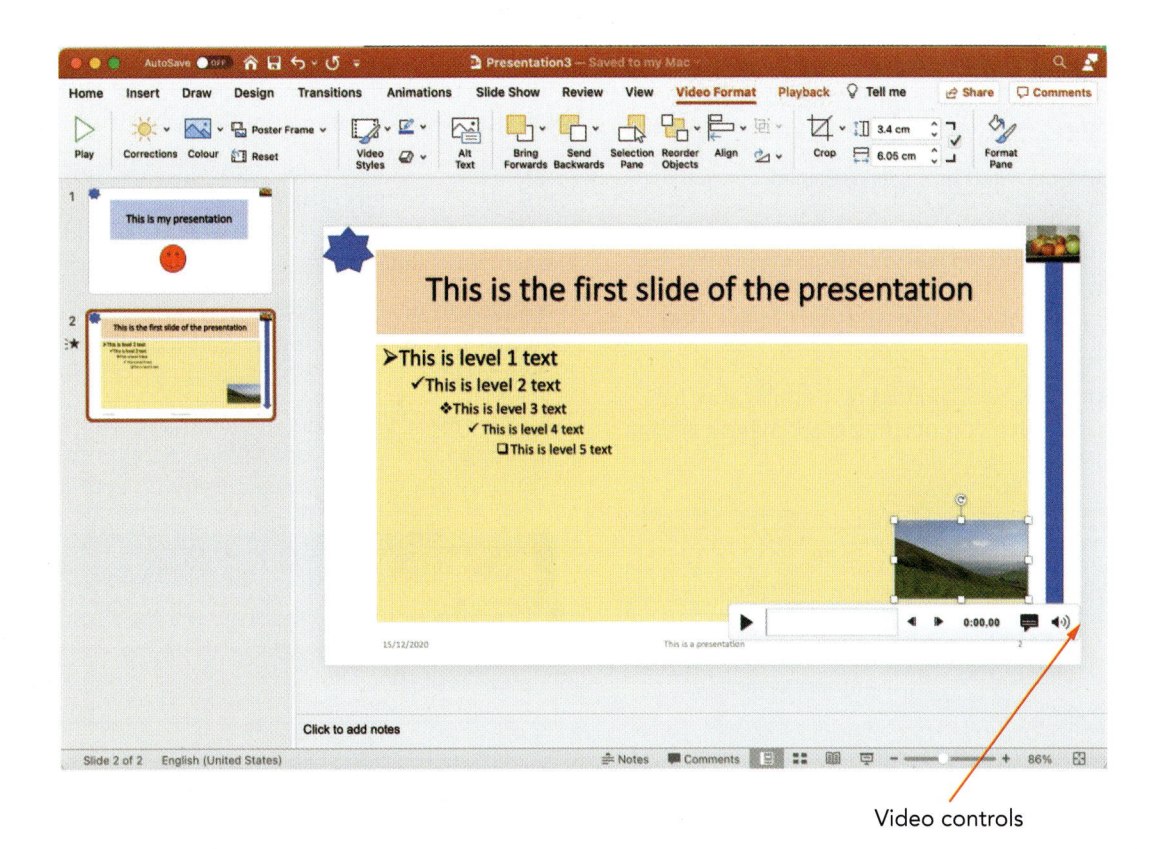

Figure 19.20: Adding text and video into the placeholders

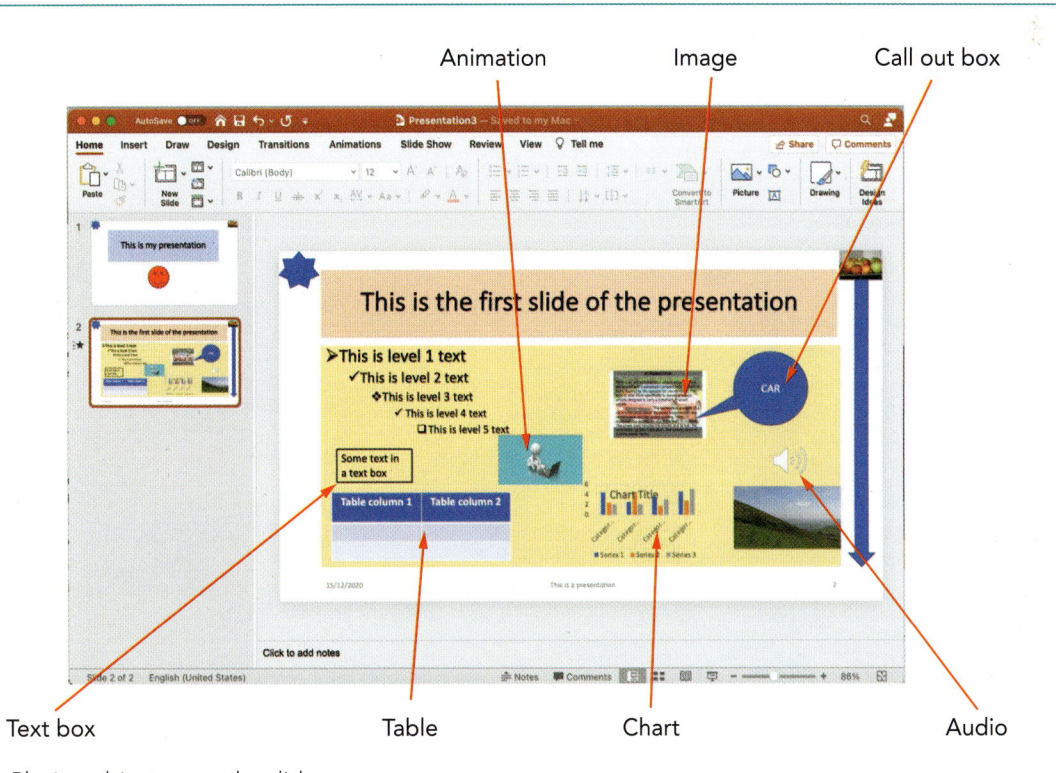

Figure 19.21: Placing objects onto the slide

449

Figure 19.22: Formatting the audio playback

Here there are ways of formatting the playback such as having a fade in and fade out, setting it to start playing automatically and making it loop if the presentation hasn't finished.

Video playback can be formatted in a similar way by highlighting the video and opening the Playback ribbon (see Figure 19.23).

Figure 19.23: Formatting video playback

Moving, deleting and duplicating slides

New slides can be added as above (see Figure 19.19, although any slide type can be chosen, not just the Content slide) or existing slides can be copied and pasted. This can be done by right-clicking on a slide thumbnail (see Figure 19.24) in the pane at the left and selecting copy or paste from the menu.

New slides can be placed anywhere in the presentation, not just at the start. To do this, select a slide, as in Figure 19.24, and a new slide will be inserted below it when New Slide is selected from the Home ribbon.

A slide can be moved into a new position by clicking on the slide and dragging it (see Figure 19.25 on the next page).

A slide can be deleted by right-clicking on it and selecting Delete Slide (see Figure 19.26 on the next page), or pressing the delete button on your keyboard.

ACTIVITY 19.2

Create a poster explaining how media such as images, audio and video can be inserted into a presentation.

Add presenter notes

Beneath the slide, there is an area where a user can add notes about the slide that they can use during the presentation (see Figure 19.27 on the following pages).

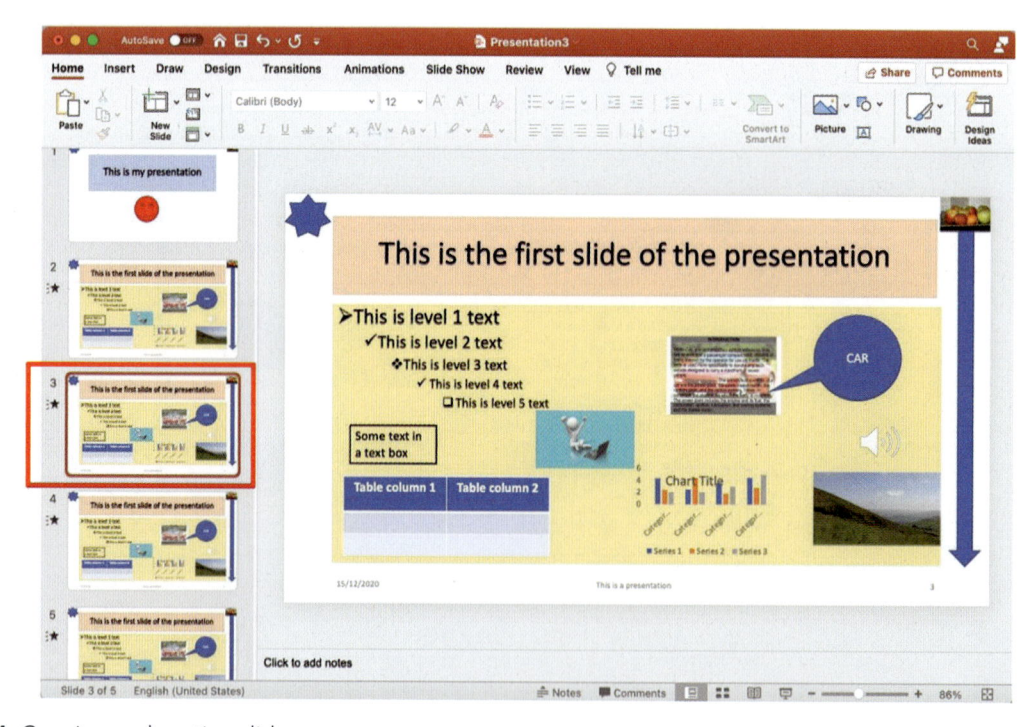

Figure 19.24: Copying and pasting slides

19   Presentations

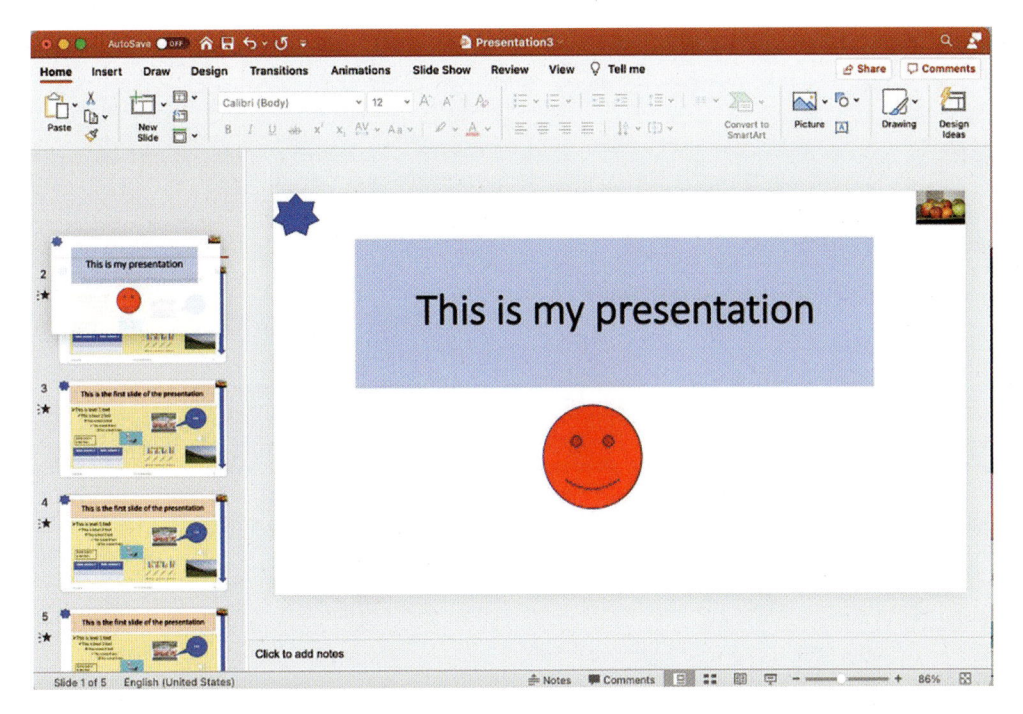

Figure 19.25: Dragging a slide into a new position

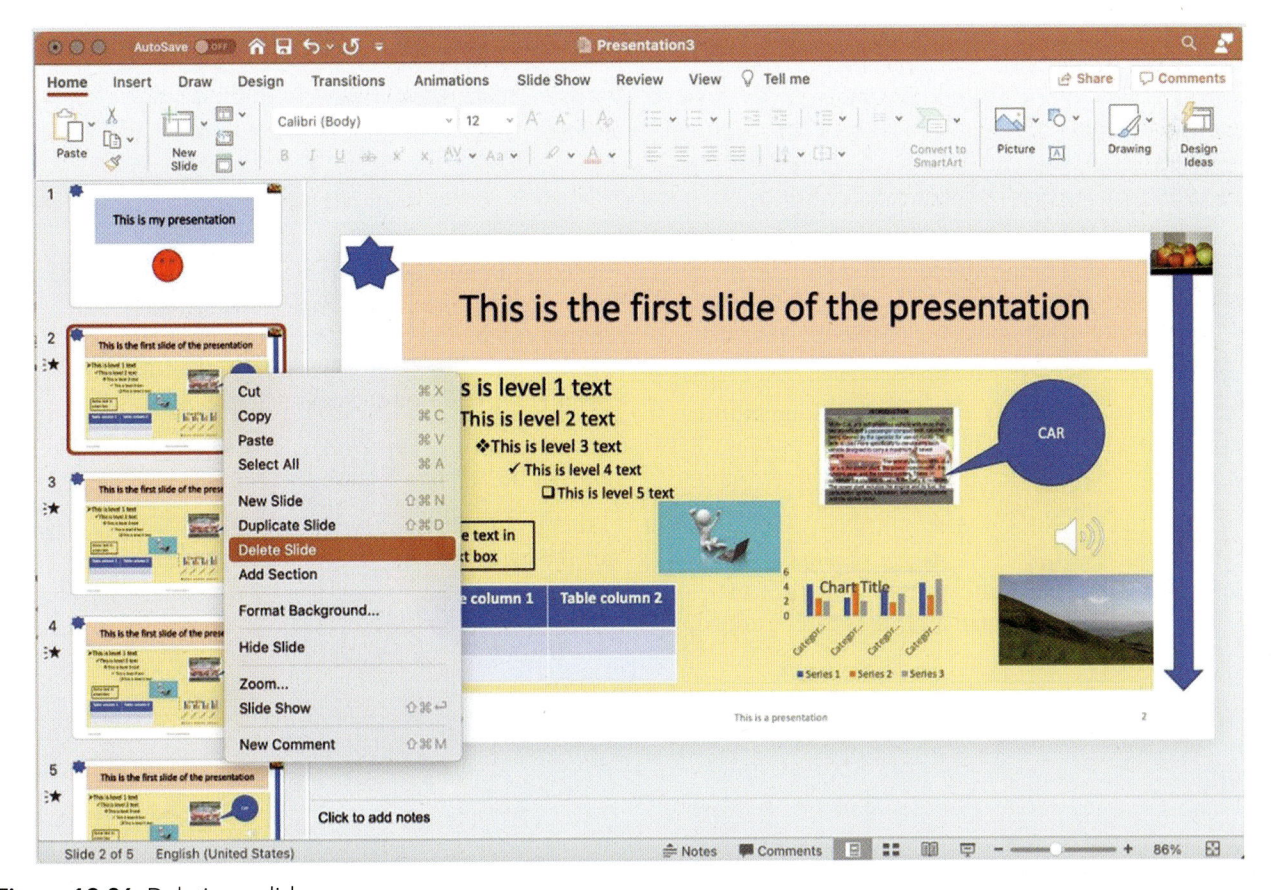

Figure 19.26: Deleting a slide

451

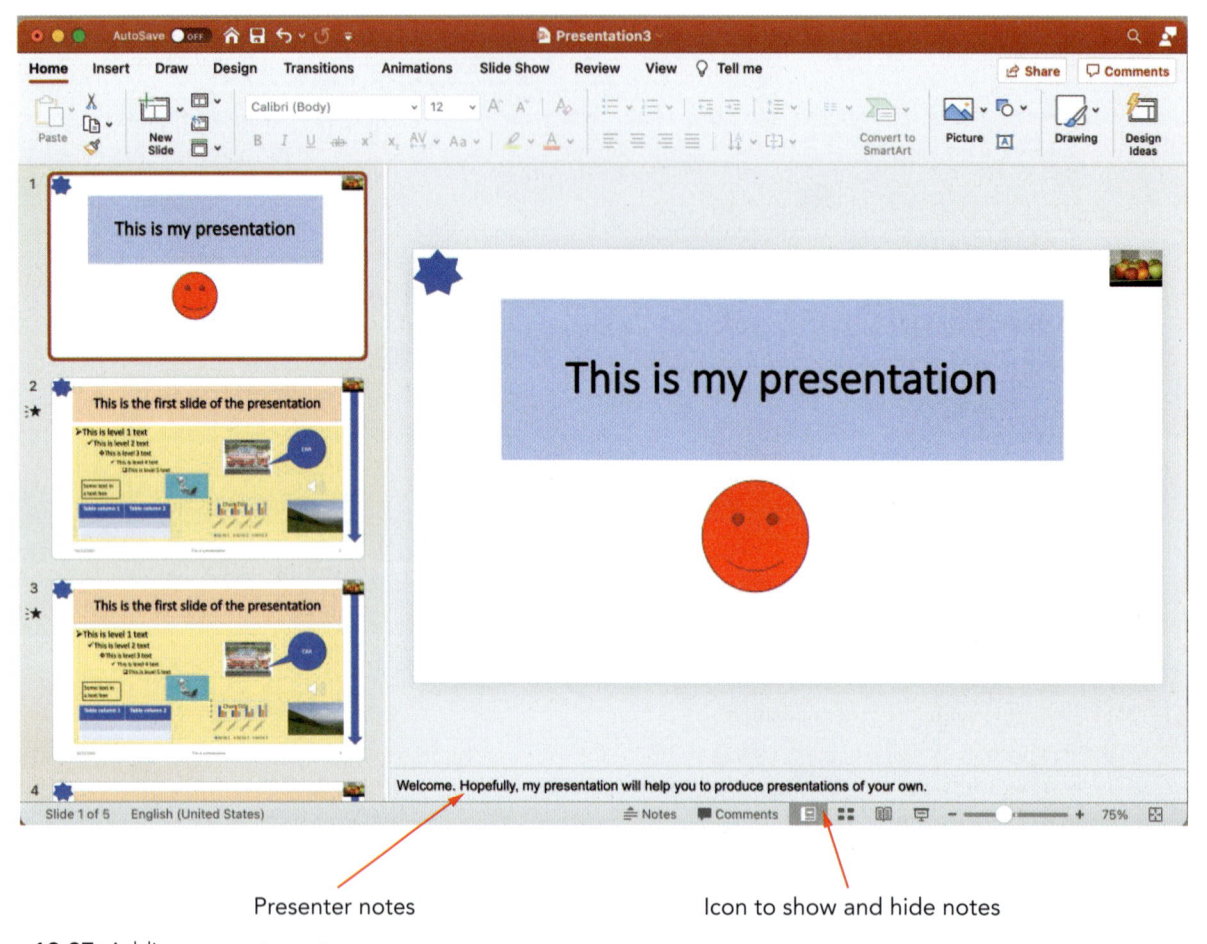

Figure 19.27: Adding presenter notes

These can be printed out, or there is an option on many presentation software programs to use Presenter view, which enables you to see your notes while the audience only sees the slides.

The notes area can also be accessed by selecting Notes Page from the View ribbon.

Hyperlinks

Hyperlinks to other slides, other presentations or files, and even to websites and email addresses can be added, edited and removed. In presentations, it's not just text that can be a hyperlink. Objects such as images or shapes can be hyperlinks too. Highlight the required text or object, and then select Link from the Insert ribbon (see Figure 19.28 on the next page).

The target of the hyperlink can be selected from the pane at the left (see Figure 19.29 on the next page).

Table 19.1 (on the following pages) shows other targets for the hyperlink.

19 Presentations

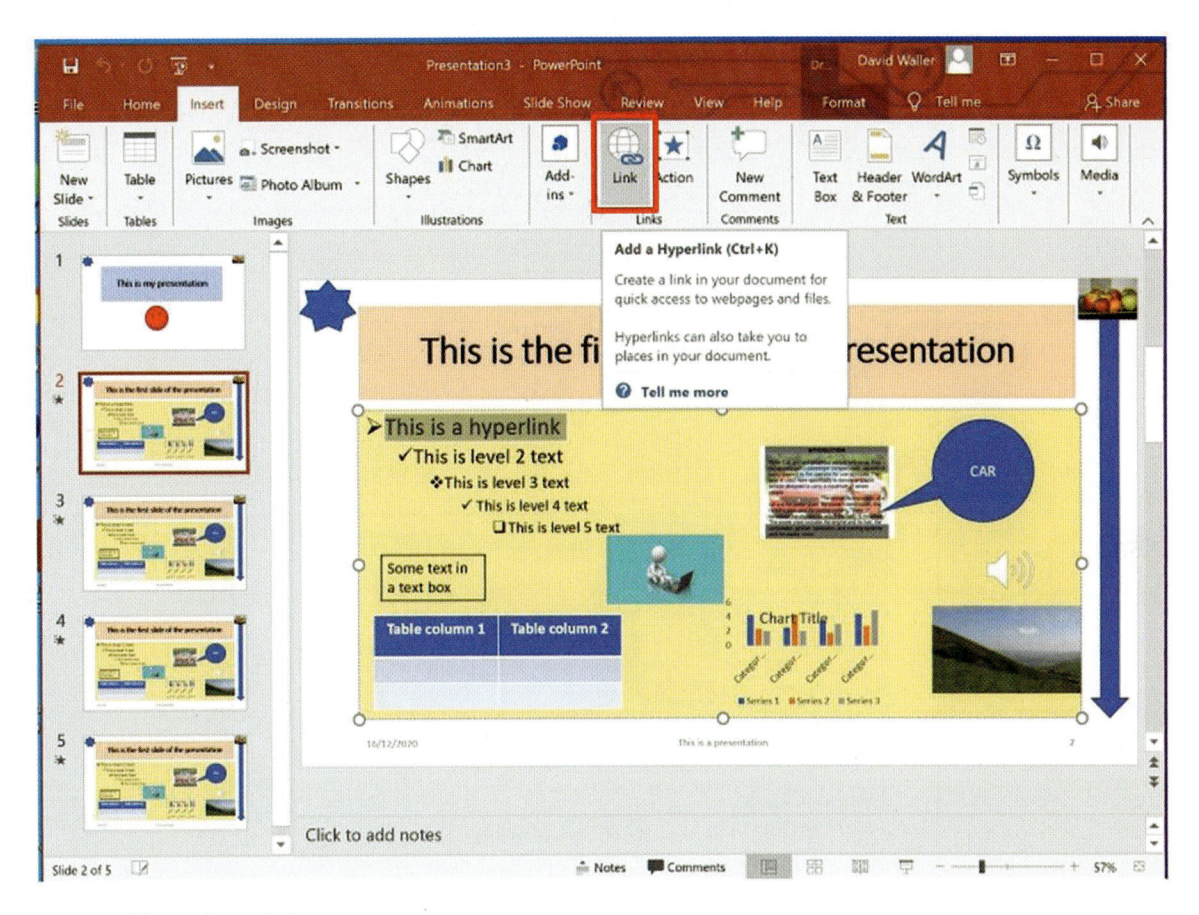

Figure 19.28: Adding a hyperlink

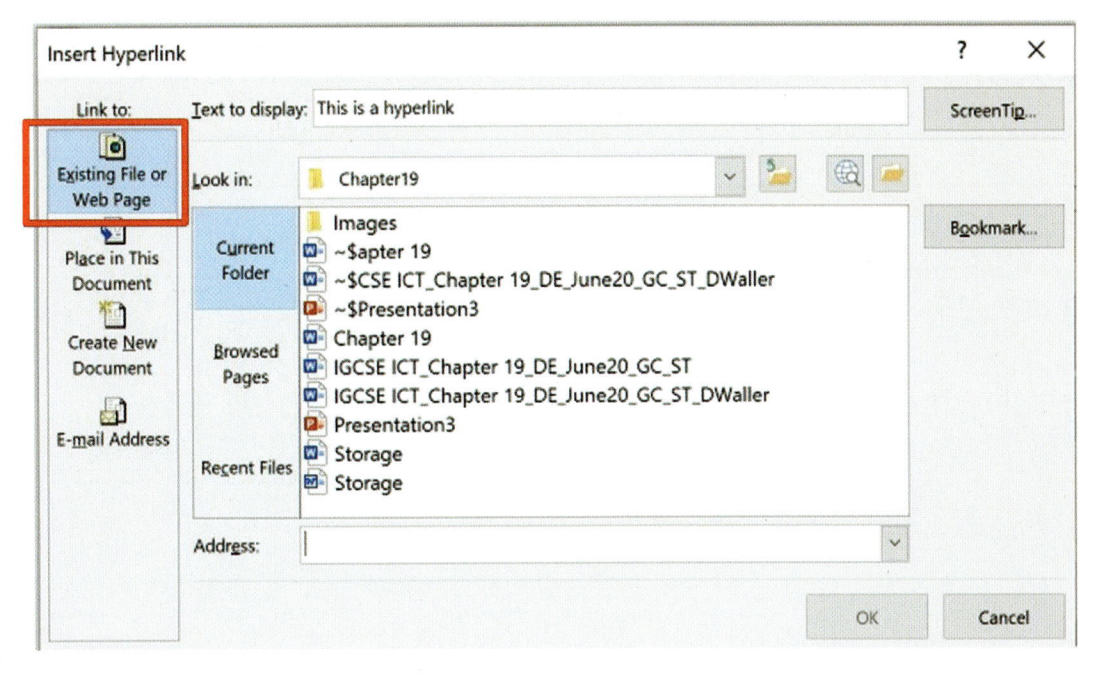

Figure 19.29: Selecting the hyperlink target

453

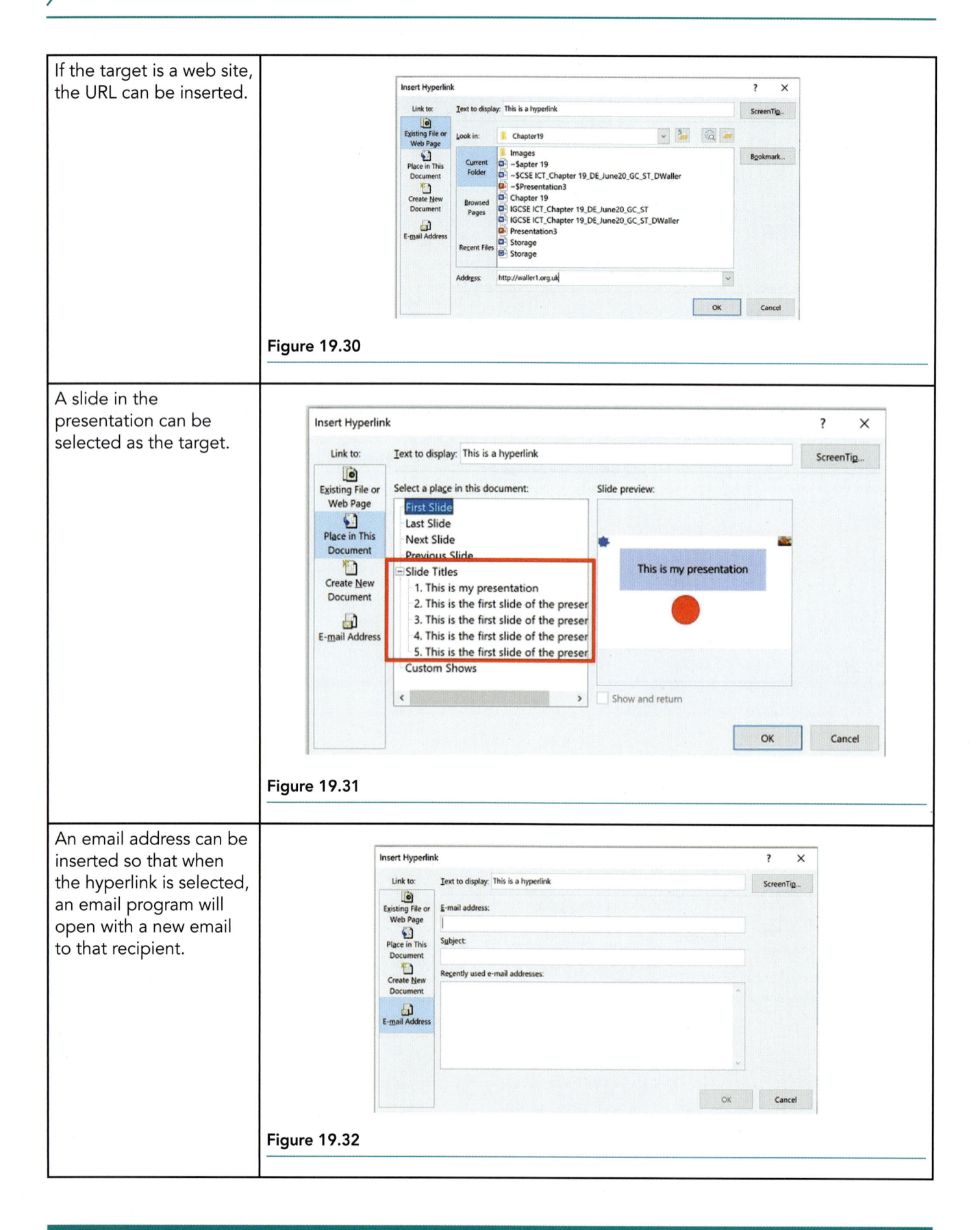

If the target is a web site, the URL can be inserted.	Figure 19.30
A slide in the presentation can be selected as the target.	Figure 19.31
An email address can be inserted so that when the hyperlink is selected, an email program will open with a new email to that recipient.	Figure 19.32

19 Presentations

Create New Document allows you to create a file name in the desired directory to create a new file.	Figure 19.33

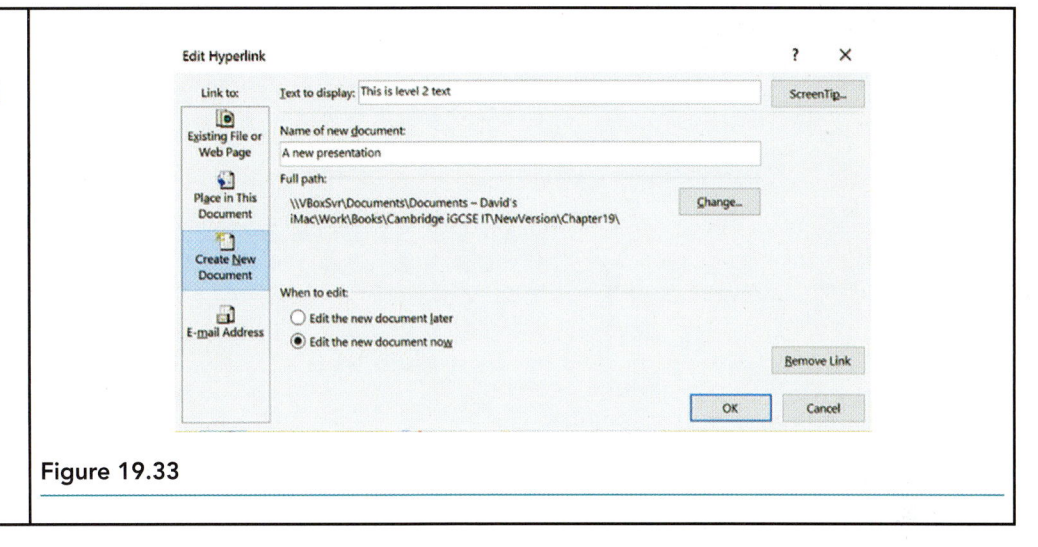

Table 19.1: Targets for the hyperlink

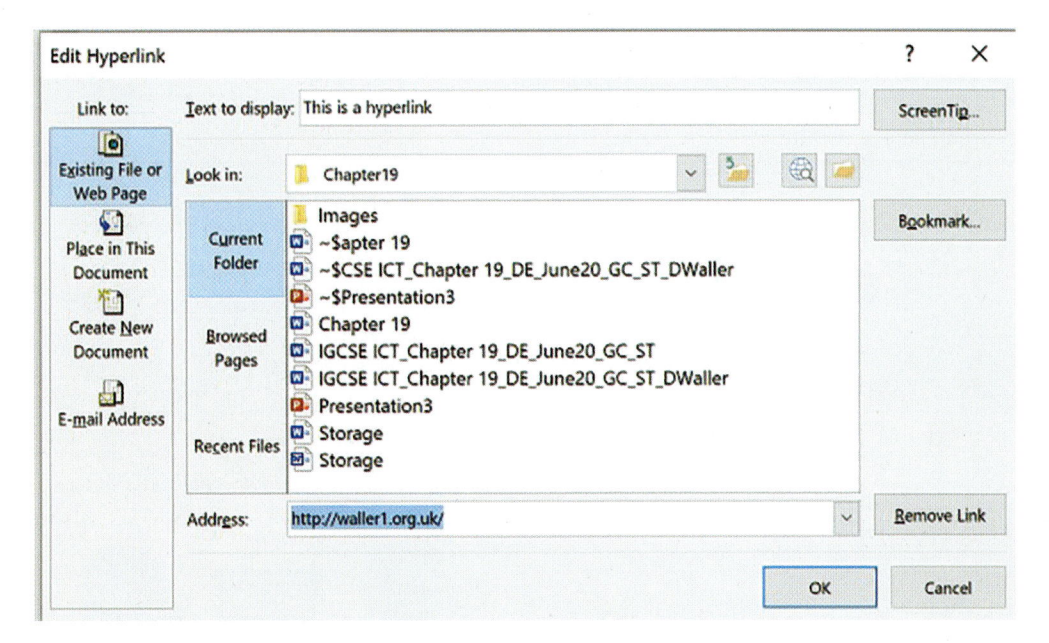

Figure 19.34: Editing a link

A hyperlink can be edited or deleted by highlighting and selecting Link on the Insert ribbon (See Figure 19.34).

Action buttons

Action buttons are icons that are already hyperlinked according to their name, for example, a 'Home' button which will take you back to your first slide. You can modify their settings to navigate to a specified slide, to a custom show or to a URL. Action buttons providing links to other slides (usually forward or backward, but they can jump to any slide in the presentation), and to web sites can be added edited and removed.

> **KEY WORD**
>
> **action buttons:** button shapes that cause an action to be performed, e.g. link to another slide or play a sound when it is clicked

455

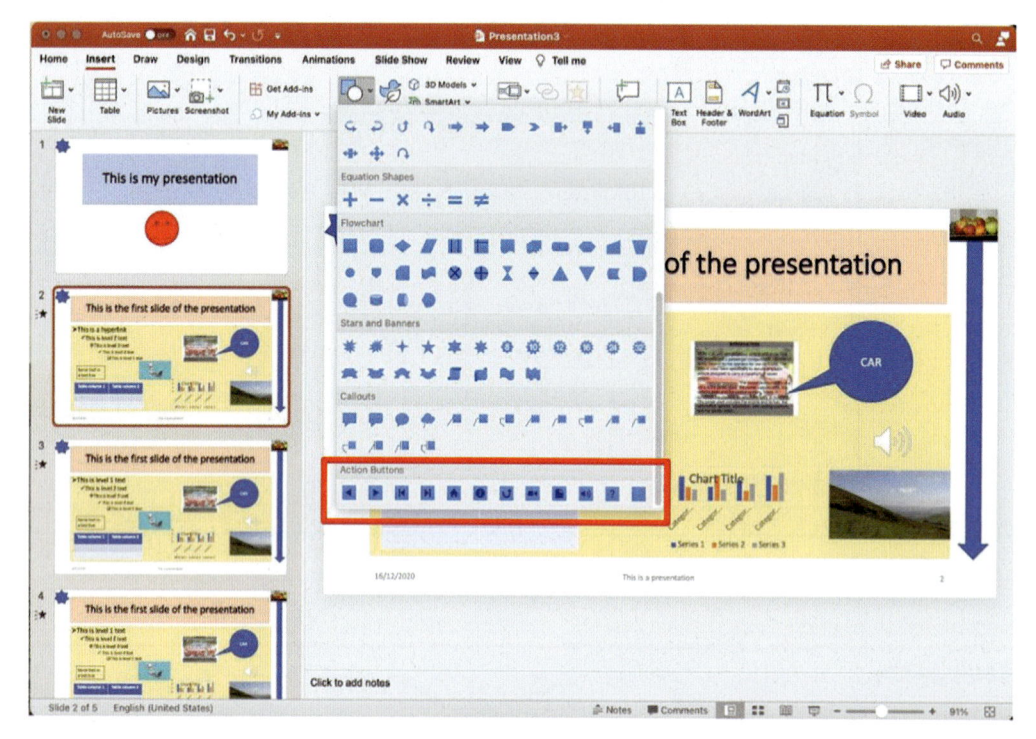

Figure 19.35: Inserting an action button

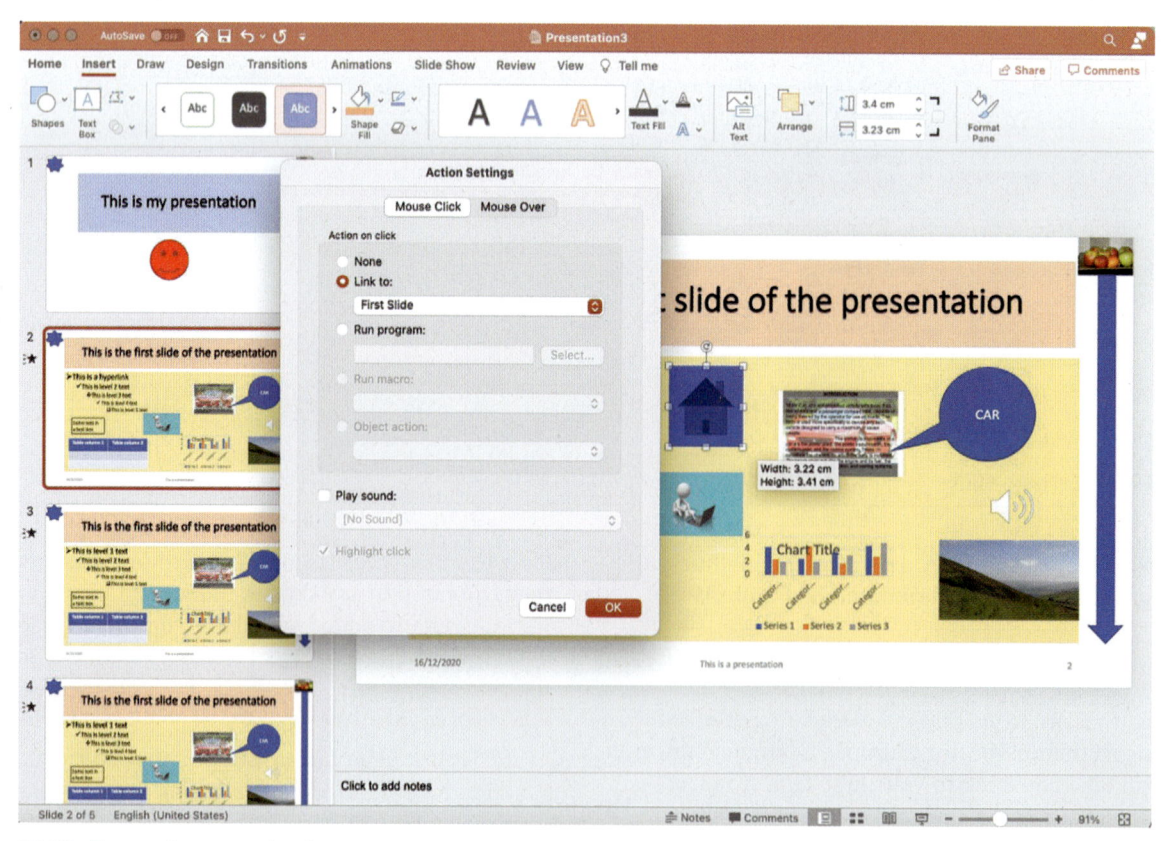

Figure 19.36: Formatting an action button

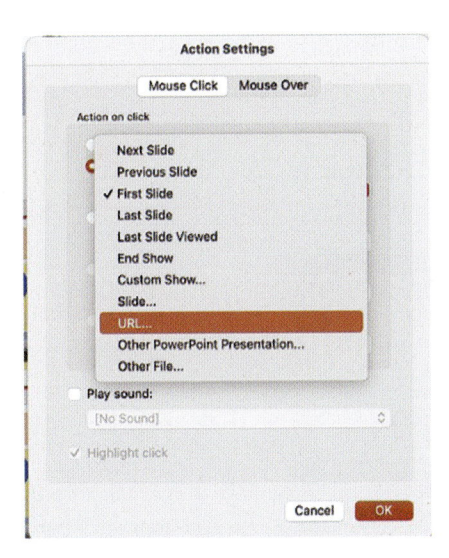

Figure 19.37: Selecting a destination for an action button

be **triggered** on a mouse click or merely by the mouse moving over it.

In the Link To drop-down menu (see Figure 19.37), a destination can be selected.

An action button can also be set to run a **Custom Show**. You can tag a subset of slides in a presentation file for the purpose of showing that subset to a particular audience. This allows you to adapt a presentation for different audiences. They can be created by selecting Custom Show from the Slide Show ribbon.

> **KEY WORDS**
>
> **trigger:** something that causes another event to occur
>
> **custom show:** an adaptation of an existing presentation that is suitable for a particular audience

Action buttons can be added by selecting Shapes from the Insert ribbon (see Figure 19.35 on the previous page).

A dialogue box is shown to format the action settings (see Figure 19.36 on the previous page). When you are running the presentation, the action button can

Actions can also be added to other objects such as images and text boxes by highlighting them and selecting Action from the Insert ribbon.

WORKED EXAMPLE 19.1

CREATING A PRESENTATION

1. Create a new presentation.
2. All slides should have a pale yellow background with black text.
3. The first slide should have title style of Arial, 60 pt, bold.
4. The other slides should have a title of Arial, 40 pt, bold.
5. Choose suitable bullets for first to fifth level text styles.
6. There should be a central footer of 'Validation'.
7. The image *Validation.png* should appear on each slide.
8. There should be a title slide.
9. The text and images in *Example_text.doc* should be used to produce five slides.
10. Create action button for slide navigation.

Step 1

A new presentation can be created using the File menu.

CONTINUED

Steps 2 and 3

The slide background and the font and style for the first slide can be set by going to Slide Master in the View menu (see Figure 19.38).

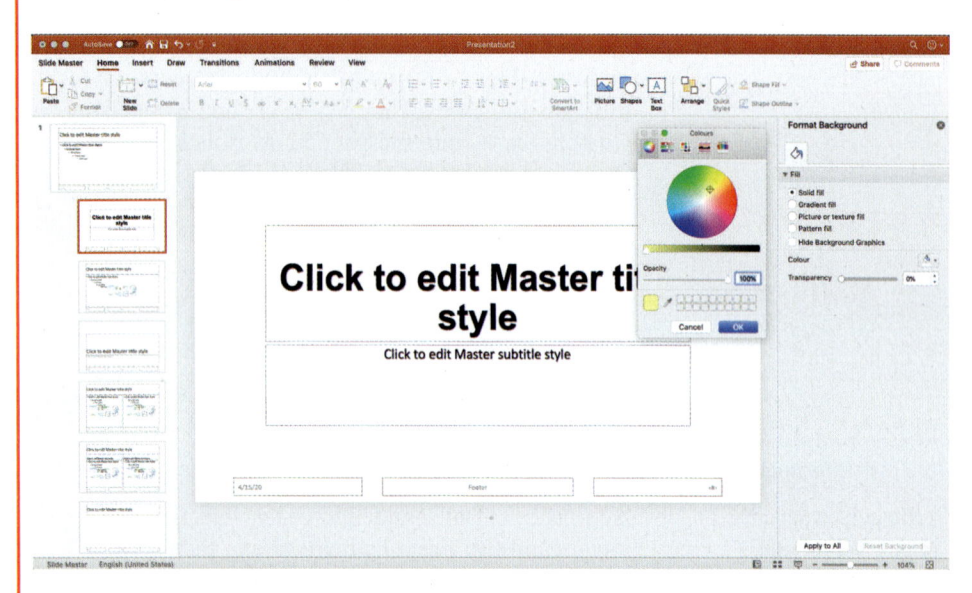

Figure 19.38: Formatting slide background

Steps 4 to 6

The styles for the other slides can be set using the master slide.

Suitable bullets can be selected (see Figure 19.39).

Figure 19.39: Selecting bullet styles

19 Presentations

> **CONTINUED**

Step 7

The image *Validation.png* can be added to the master slide (see Figure 19.40).

Figure 19.40: Inserting image to master slide

Step 8

The Slide Master view can be closed, and the title slide created (see Figure 19.41).

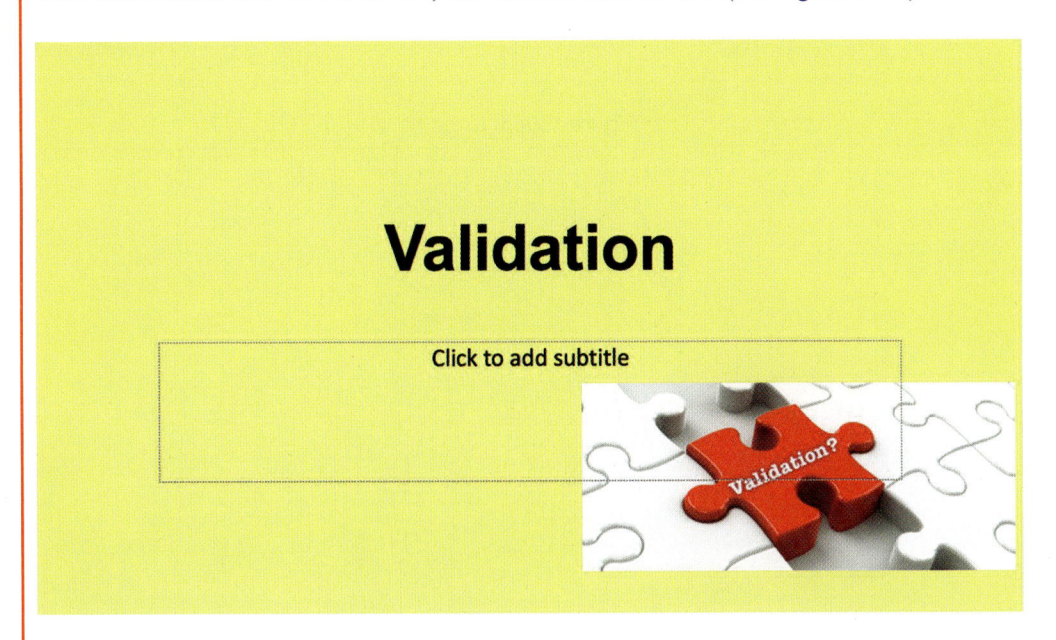

Figure 19.41: The title slide

> **CAMBRIDGE IGCSE™ ICT: COURSEBOOK**

CONTINUED

Step 9

The slides can be created using the text and images supplied (see Figures 19.42–19.45).

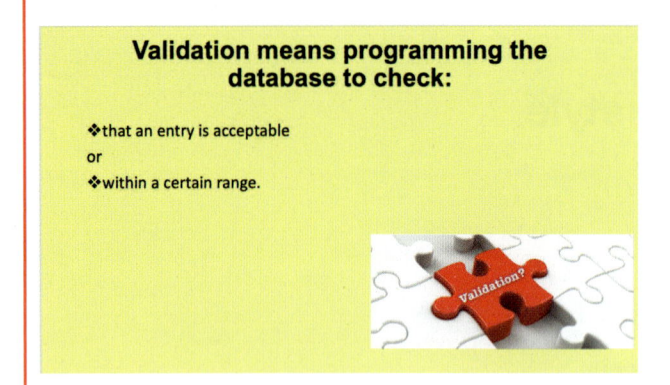

Figure 19.42: Creating slide 2

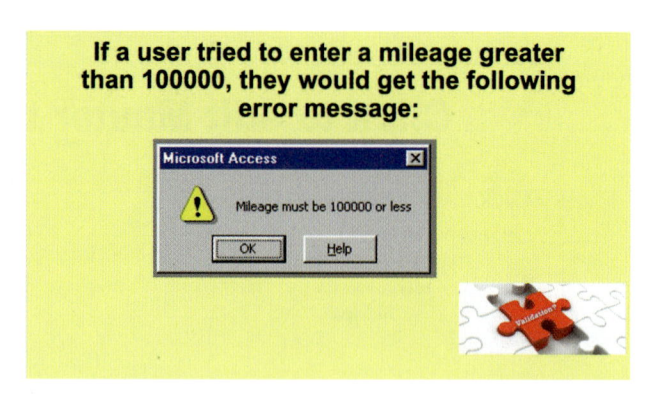

Validation means programming the database to check:
- that an entry is acceptable
or
- within a certain range.

Figure 19.43: Creating slide 3

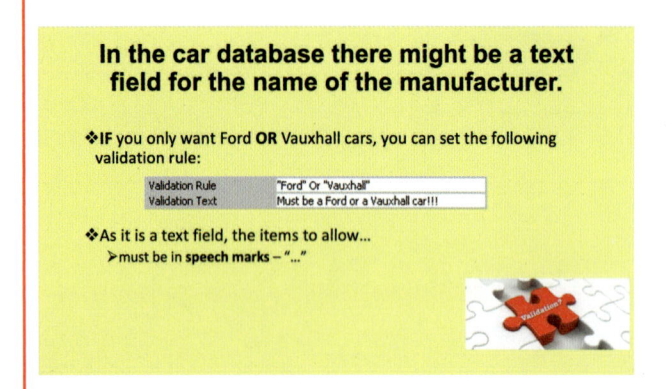

If a user tried to enter a mileage greater than 100000, they would get the following error message:

Microsoft Access: Mileage must be 100000 or less

Figure 19.44: Creating slide 4

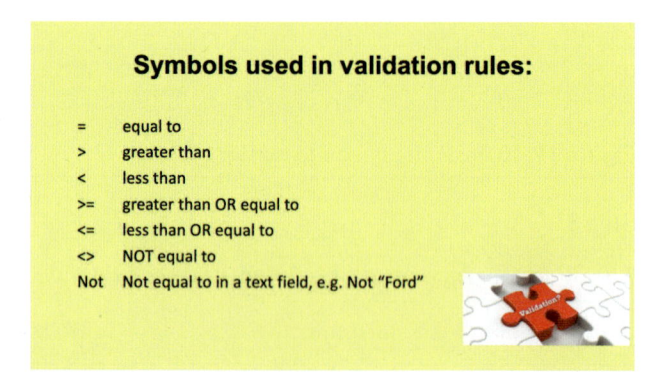

In the car database there might be a text field for the name of the manufacturer.
- IF you only want Ford OR Vauxhall cars, you can set the following validation rule:

| Validation Rule | "Ford" Or "Vauxhall" |
| Validation Text | Must be a Ford or a Vauxhall car!!! |

- As it is a text field, the items to allow…
  - must be in **speech marks** – "…"

Figure 19.45: Creating slide 5

Symbols used in validation rules:

=	equal to
>	greater than
<	less than
>=	greater than OR equal to
<=	less than OR equal to
<>	NOT equal to
Not	Not equal to in a text field, e.g. Not "Ford"

19 Presentations

CONTINUED

Step 10

Action buttons can be added to the slides (see Figures 19.46–19.48).

The first slide requires only a 'Next slide' button (see Figure 19.46).

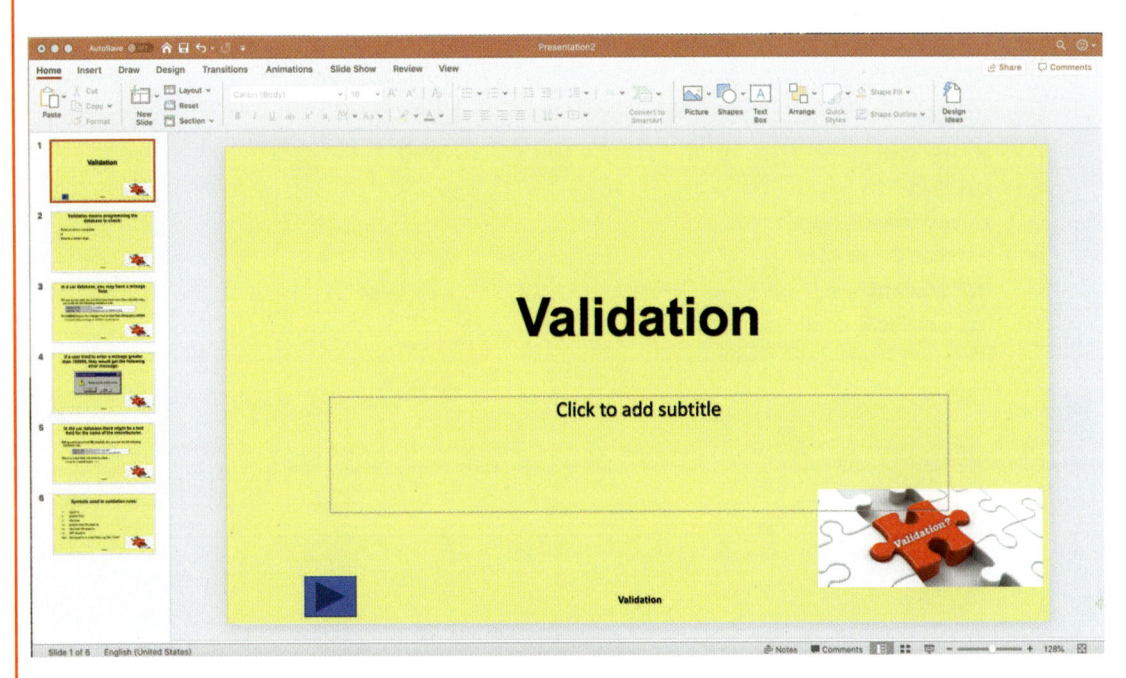

Figure 19.46: Next slide button added

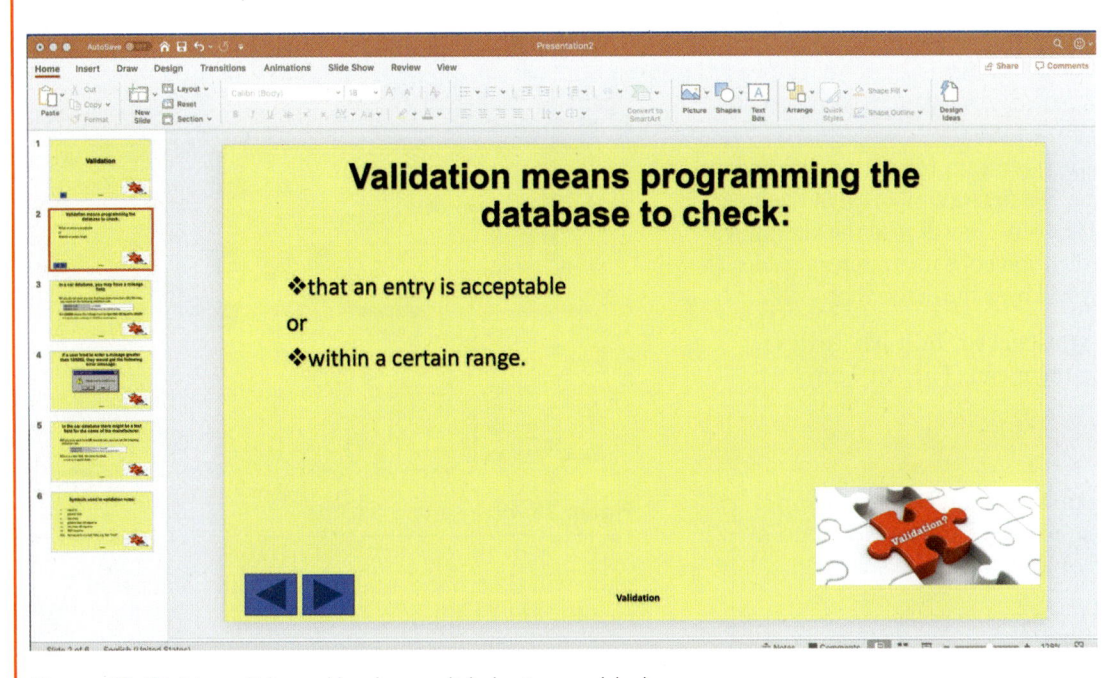

Figure 19.47: Next slide and back one slide buttons added

> CAMBRIDGE IGCSE™ ICT: COURSEBOOK

> CONTINUED

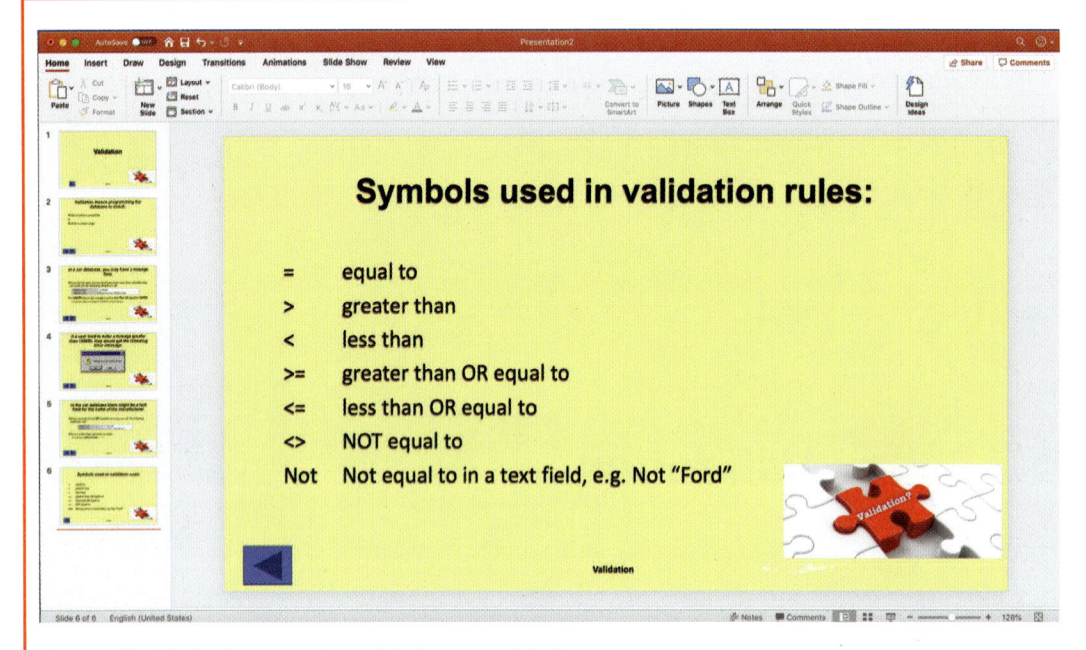

Figure 19.48: Back to previous slide button added

Questions

1. Create the presentation as instructed using the resources provided.
2. Show the slide number at the right of the footer. It should not appear on the first slide.

Adding alternative text and ScreenTips to an object

Alternative text (Alt Text) is meant to aid those with visual impairments. It is usually a description of what the image (or other object) is. The software will read the alternative text out aloud, and when someone uses a screen reader to view documents, they will hear the description.

When an object is right-clicked, Edit Alt Text can be selected from the menu. The Alt Text

> **KEY WORDS**
>
> **alternative text:** text that can be read aloud by screen readers, allowing them read aloud a description of an object, e.g. of an image
>
> **ScreenTip:** small windows, displaying descriptive text, that pop up when the mouse pointer is rested on them

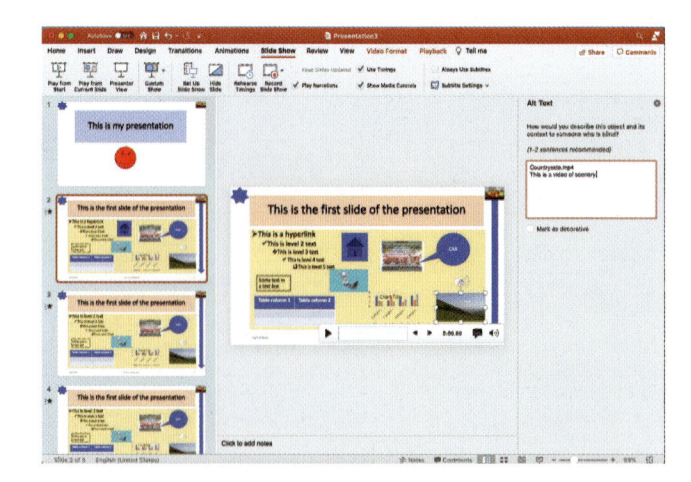

Figure 19.49: Inserting Alt Text

pane will then open, and the text can be inserted (see Figure 19.49).

A **ScreenTip** is a window with text that opens when the mouse is moved over an object, and it disappears when the mouse is moved away from it. A ScreenTip can be added to any shape or object.

Unfortunately, before a ScreenTip can be added to an object, a hyperlink must be added first.

But what if you don't want to have a hyperlink on the object? You don't want the object to send you off to another slide if it is clicked.

The answer is to set the hyperlink to itself (see Figure 19.50) – the slide that the object is on.

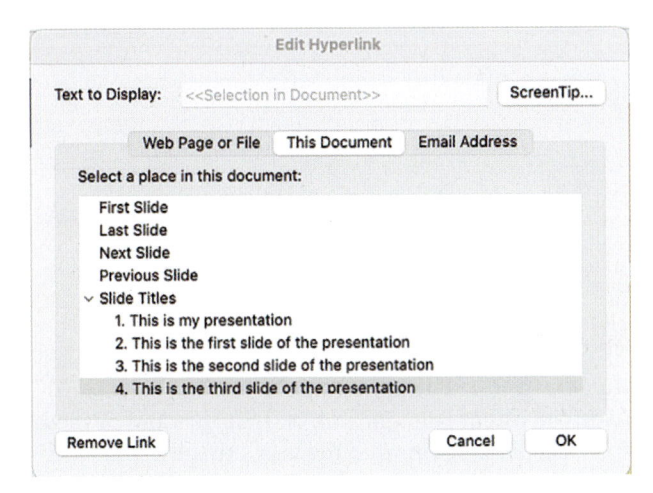

Figure 19.50: Setting a hyperlink to itself

As the object is on slide 4, the link is set for slide 4.

ScreenTip can then be selected and the tip can be inserted into the dialogue box (see Figure 19.51).

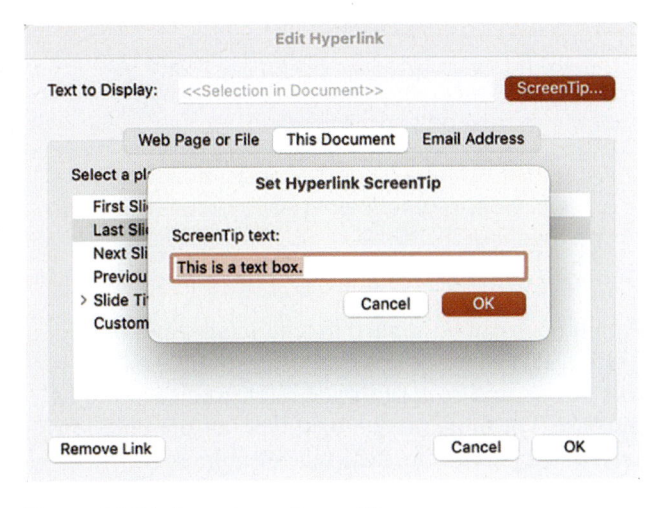

Figure 19.51: Inserting a ScreenTip

When the mouse pointer moves over the object, the pointer changes to a pointing finger and the ScreenTip is displayed (see Figure 19.52).

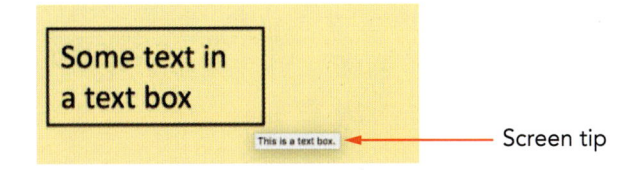

Figure 19.52: Displaying a ScreenTip

Creating and applying consistent transitions between slides

Transitions refer to the effects that occur as you move from one slide to the next, for example, the next slide flying in from the bottom left-hand side of the screen. It is best to make the transitions consistent so that they do not distract from the message of the presentation.

> **KEY WORD**
>
> **transition:** a visual effect that occurs when the presentation moves from one slide to another

Different transitions can be selected from the Transitions ribbon. The duration of the transition (how long it lasts) and its trigger can be set as indicated in Figure 19.53. For example, it can be set to occur on a mouse click or after a certain period of time. (Note that the 01.00 in the duration of transition box of figure 19.53 is 1 second and not 1 minute.) For 1 minute, you would need to type in 60.0, although a transition that takes 1 minute to complete is probably not a good idea!)

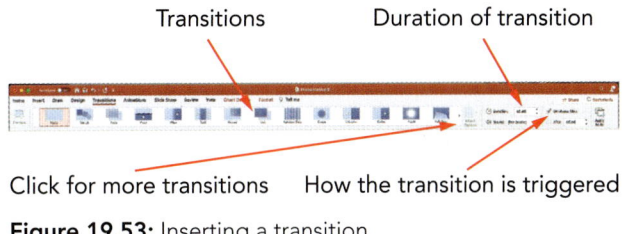

Figure 19.53: Inserting a transition

A transition is applied to the currently selected slide.

If a presenter is delivering a long speech, a set of transitions can provide interesting movements between slides to liven up the presentation. You can apply the same transition to all the slides for consistency or to only a select few slides, whichever is more appropriate. Transitions should be seamless and unobtrusive for

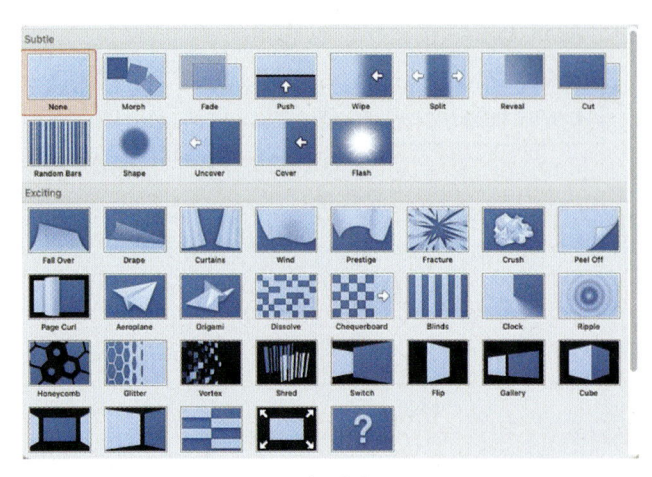

Figure 19.54: Some example slide transitions

also been set to 1 second. The transition can be applied to all slides if required.

Both mouse click and after a certain time can be set for the same slide. (Be aware that one second would probably be far too quick for most presentations.)

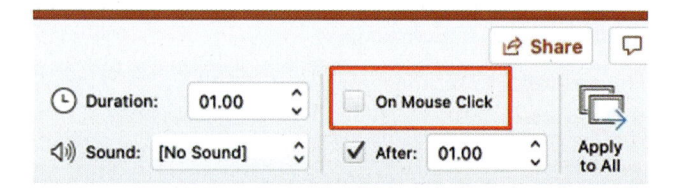

Figure 19.55: Applying a slide transition

mature or serious-natured adult audiences. Younger audiences may enjoy the more fun transitions such as the 'vortex' style (see examples in Figure 19.54 on the previous page). It also depends on the occasion at which the presentation is being delivered. An example where fun transitions may be appropriate could be at an end-of-year school prom party where a slide presentation could be looping photographs of students throughout the evening. However, a similar style of transition between slides would not be appropriate for a finance manager presenting his annual budget at a board meeting.

At times, you may wish to move to the next slide without having to use the mouse. In such a case, the slides can be set to move to the next slide automatically after a few seconds or minutes. This is very useful when a presentation is looping through a series of slides without a presenter – for example, the photographs at the end-of-year prom.

However, if you are delivering a presentation, you may have interruptions such as comments or questions that will extend the time of that section of the presentation to more than you have allowed. This could also cause you to rush through your speech so that it matches your slides more closely. If you think this is likely to happen, it might be better to use the '**On Mouse Click**' option. This allows you to move to the next slide when you are ready to move and not after a preset time, and can avoid confusing your audience if you rush through your slides and do not leave enough time for them to think about what you have said during your presentation. You may not always know beforehand how much time you will need to stay on each slide and therefore a set time is probably not always the best option to use.

The transition shown in Figure 19.55 has been set to occur after 1 second. The duration of the transition has

Creating consistent animation effects on text, images and other objects

After creating a slide presentation, you may have to create consistent **animation** on text, images and or media objects depending on what the user's requirements are. Animations on text are useful, for example, when you need to reveal each bullet point one at a time while you are delivering your presentation. You should select an animation to suit your target audience. For example, younger audiences may like objects, images and text whizzing in from different locations.

KEY WORDS

on mouse click: an action that occurs when one of the mouse buttons is pressed

animation: an effect used on individual elements on one slide, e.g. revealing each bullet point one at a time

Animations can be applied to text, images and other objects. It is worth noting that using animations in this way should be appropriate to the audience and its purpose. The more professional types of presentations tend to stick to a consistent type of animation, and use them more sparingly than those used for a younger audience.

There are many different animations that can be selected but 'Fly in' tends to be the most popular.

19 Presentations

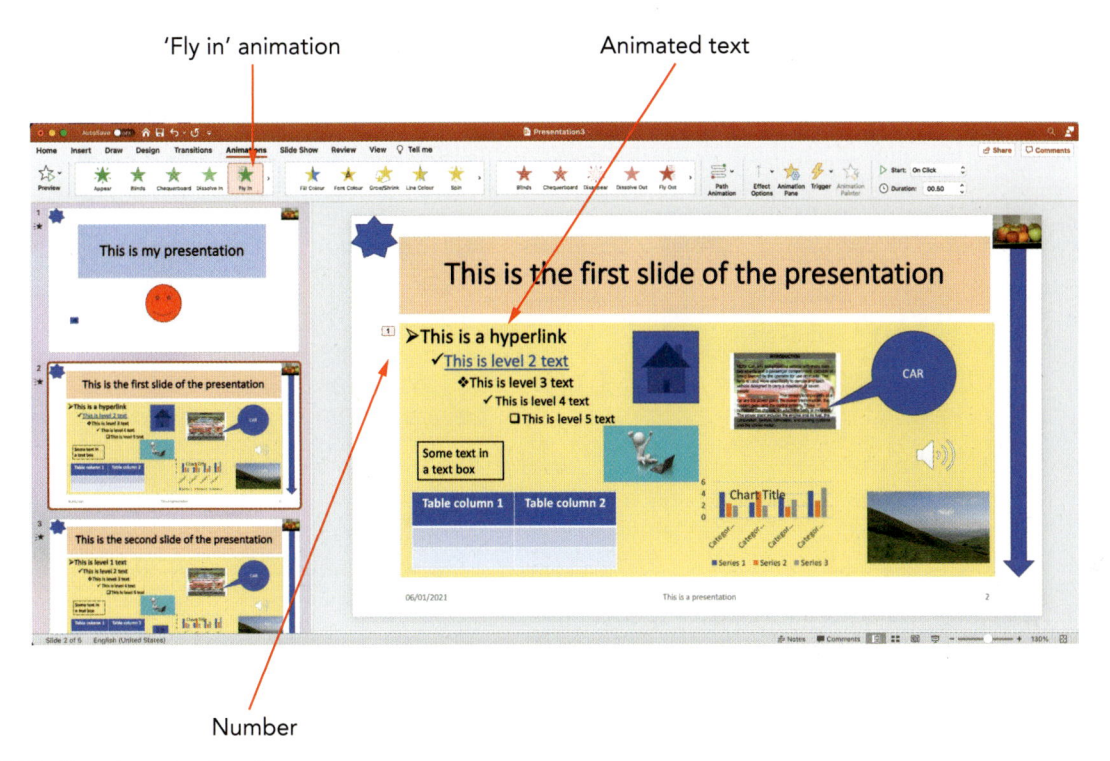

Figure 19.56: Creating an animation

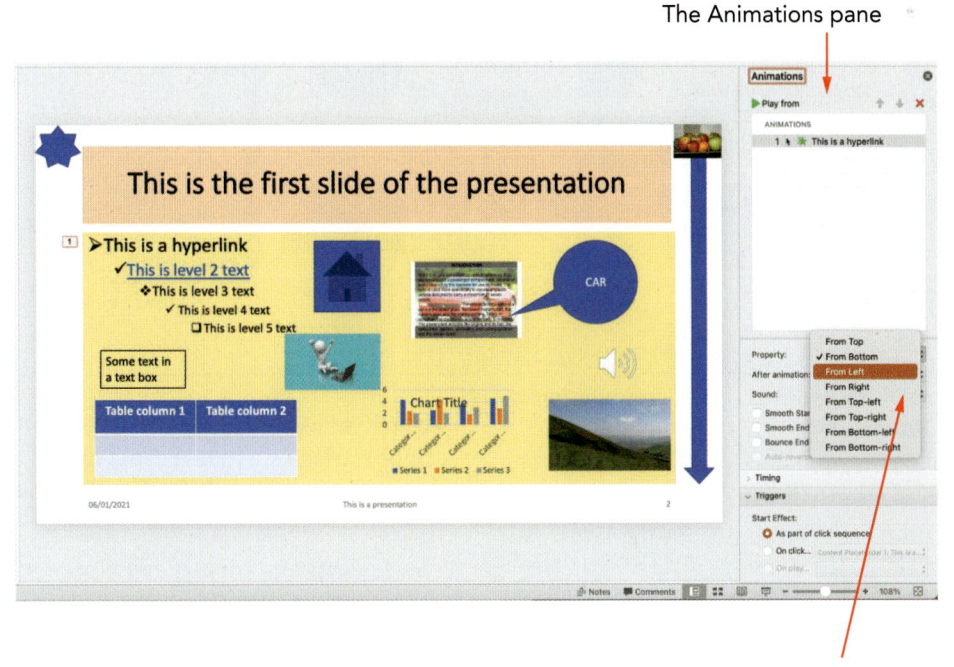

Figure 19.57: The Animations pane

465

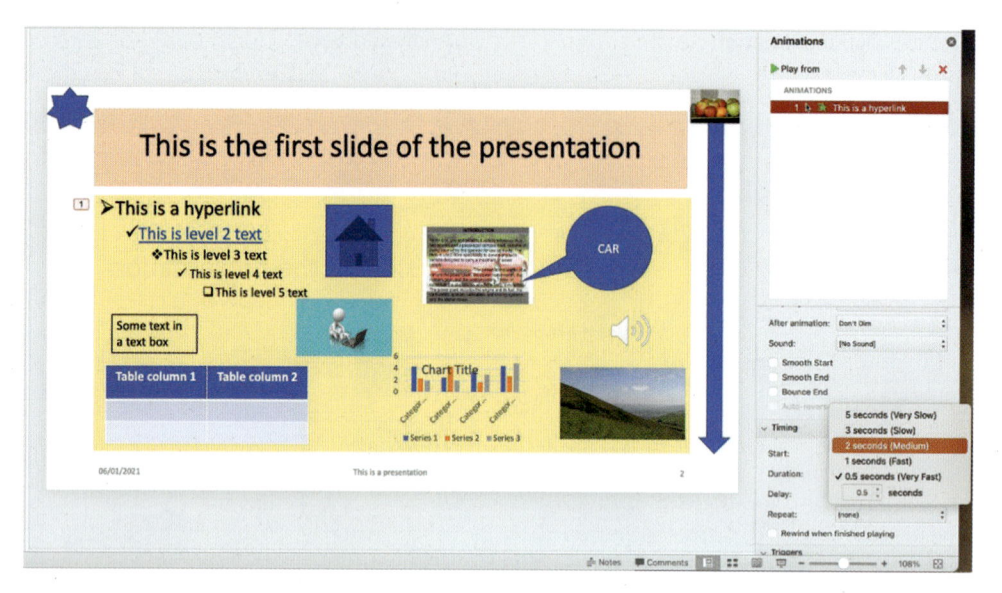

Figure 19.58: Setting the duration of an animation

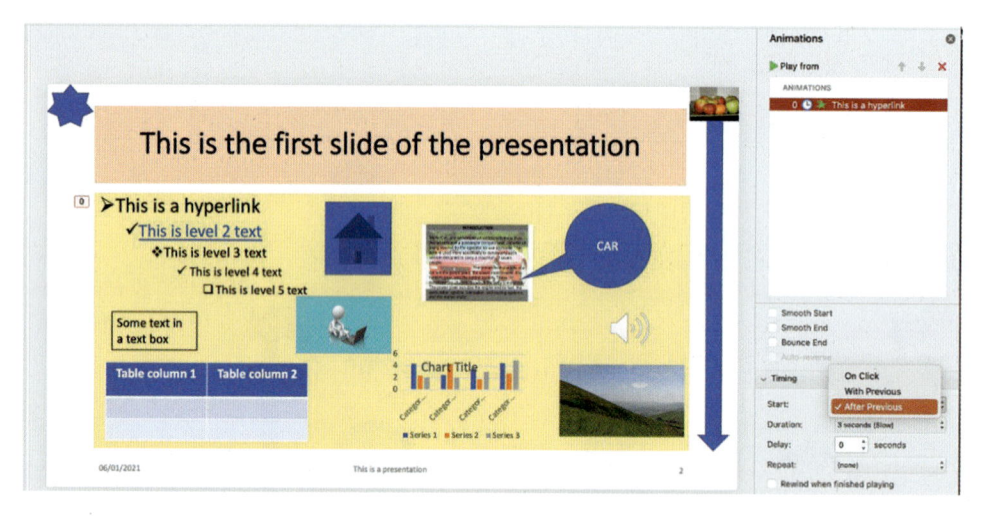

Figure 19.59: Setting when the animation will start

To set an animation, text, an object or an image must be selected and an animation chosen from the Animations ribbon.

The 'Fly in' animation has been chosen for the text 'This is a hyperlink'.

The animated item now has a number beside it. This shows whenever the Animations tab is selected.

If the number is clicked, the Animations Pane opens (see Figure 19.57 on the previous page) where the properties of the animation can be set.

The duration of the animation can be set (see Figure 19.58).

The trigger of the animation can be set – for example, it can be started by a mouse click, start at the same time as the previous event such as when the slide loading occurs or after the previous event (see Figure 19.59) has occurred.

These effects and timings can also be set from options on the Animations ribbon (see Figure 19.60).

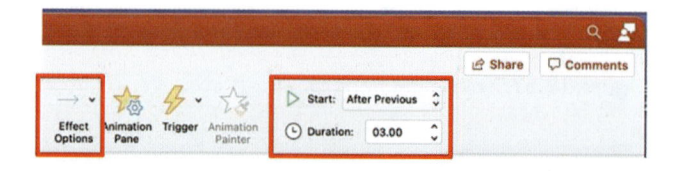

Figure 19.60: Using the Animations ribbon

19   Presentations

When an animation has been selected it can be edited. With some animations there are **Effect Options** which can be selected. With a 'Fly in' effect, any of those shown in Figure 19.61 could be selected.

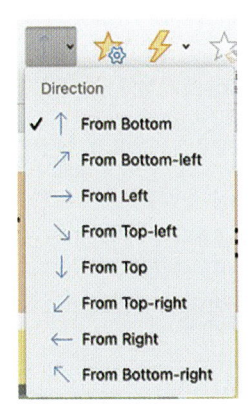

Figure 19.61: Some options for the 'Fly in' effect

> **KEY WORD**
>
> **effect options:** different ways that the animation can be modified, e.g. duration and direction of movement

The duration of the effect and how it is triggered can also be edited. It could be set to occur with a mouse click, when the previous animation occurs or a certain time after the previous animation or transition (see Figure 19.62).

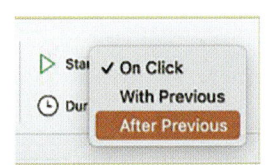

Figure 19.62: Setting when the animation occurs

> **ACTIVITY 19.3**
>
> Investigate the transitions and animations that are available in the presentation software you are using. Experiment with the effects and settings for the transitions and animations.

> **ACTIVITY 19.4**
>
> Set a timer for three minutes and then brainstorm everything that you think relates to the term 'consistency' in slide presentations. After the three minutes, compare your ideas and words with a partner and discuss why you chose the words you did.

Hiding slides in a presentation

Hiding slides in a presentation can be very useful if you want to use some slides from an existing presentation but not all, and you do not want to lose your initial slides. Hiding them saves you time by allowing you to simply hide slides and then 'unhide' them when you

Figure 19.63: A slide after it has been hidden

467

need your full version of that presentation again, rather than deleting them and having to recreate them again afterwards.

To hide a slide in a presentation, highlight the slide, right-click on it and select Hide from the options available. To 'unhide' it, right-click on the slide again and select Unhide. When a slide is hidden, it will still appear to be visible in the left-hand side panel; however, it will be faded out, and will not be visible in slide show mode (see Figure 19.63 on the previous page). This makes it possible for you to see which slide(s) has been hidden and so that you can know which ones to 'unhide' when you need to do so.

Questions

2   Define the following words relating to the topic of presentations:
    a   ScreenTip
    b   transition
    c   animation
    d   hyperlink.
3   Suggest objects that you might place in a presentation on how to play table tennis or any sport that you prefer. Your presentation should be aimed at primary school children.
4   Differentiate between an action button and a hyperlink.

PRACTICAL TASK 19.2

Getting started

Investigate your presentation software.

1   How many different slide transitions does it provide?
2   How many different ways of animating text or objects are there?

Practice

3   Open the *Task1* presentation that you created in the Practice session of Practical Task 19.1.
4   Set the transition for all slides to 'push upwards'. The transition should start after 5 seconds and last for 1 second.
5   Set the animation of Slides 1 and 2 so that the text moves up from the bottom of the slide.
6   Set the animation on Slide 3 so that the text just appears at 1-second intervals.
7   Set the animation on Slide 4 so that the text moves up from the bottom at 1-second intervals.
8   When viewing the presentation, the transitions may be too quick for some people. Therefore, add an action button on each slide, except the first one, that allows a user to go back to the previous slide.
9   Save the presentation as *Task2*.

Challenge

10   Hide Slides 4 to 6 so that they do not appear in the presentation.
11   Change the master slide so that all of the slide headings are red and the other text on the slide is white.
12   Save the presentation as *Task2_Challenge*.

19 Presentations

> **PRACTICAL TASK 19.3**
>
> **Getting started**
>
> Investigate your presentation software.
>
> 1   How many different media types can you insert into a slide?
>
> 2   How would you ensure that an image had to be placed in the same position on each slide?
>
> **Practice**
>
> 3   Create a new presentation named *Task3*.
>
> 4   Set the master slide so that there are the following placeholders:
>
>   - A pale blue slide background.
>   - Placeholders for title, text and an image.
>   - Bullets for first to fifth level text as shown.
>   - 'Holidays' as a central footer.
>
>   See example master slide in Figure 19.64.
>
> Figure 19.64: Example Practical Task master slide
>
> 5   There should be five slides in the presentation.
>
> 6   Slides 2 to 4 should use the images *Paris1.jpg*, *Paris2.jpg* and *Paris3.jpg* and the text from *Holidays.doc*. The images should be resized so that the complete images are shown in the placeholders. Add alternative text to each of the images.
>
> 7   Slide 5 should have the heading 'Countryside'. Insert the video *Countryside.mp4*.
>
> 8   Slide 1 should have a menu system with action buttons to select any of the other slides (see Figure 19.65 on the next page). Prevent slide transitions with a mouse click.
>
> 9   Slides 2 to 5 should have an action button to return to Slide 1.

469

> **CAMBRIDGE IGCSE™ ICT: COURSEBOOK**

> **CONTINUED**
>
> 10 Insert the audio *Opera.mp3* into slide 1 and format it so that:
>   - It starts automatically.
>   - It plays across all slides.
>   - It will loop until stopped.
>   - It will rewind after playing.
>
> **Figure 19.65:** Slide 1 with action buttons
>
> **Challenge**
>
> 11 Insert a 'Wipe' transition of 2-second duration for all of the slides.
>
> 12 Apply an animation of 'Dissolve in' of 1-second duration for the text on Slides 1 to 4.

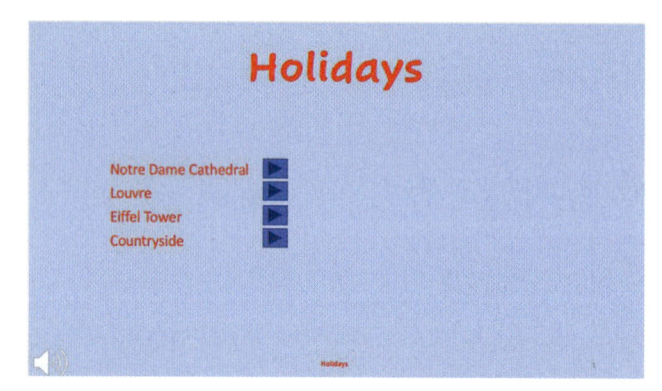

Question

5 Explain the relevance of applying consistency when applying transitions between slides and animated effects on text, images and other objects.

19.3 Outputting the presentation

Displaying a presentation in a variety of formats

The format that you should display your presentation in will depend on the purpose and aims of your whole presentation and on who your target audience is. If your presentation will be used for entertainment or marketing purposes, you could choose a looped, on-screen, carousel so that it plays indefinitely (see Figure 19.66). When you loop your presentation on-screen, you should set how long each slide should be displayed using the transition options mentioned above.

Settings can be made by selecting Set Up Slide Show from the Slide Show menu.

The show type option buttons allow a user to select the type of show:

- The default setting is 'Presented by a speaker (full screen)' where the speaker has full control over slide transitions and animations. This way of displaying a presentation is usually when a speaker is addressing an audience.

- To present the slide show in a window, where control over advancing the slides is available to the people watching, then '*Browsed by an individual (window)*' should be selected.

19 Presentations

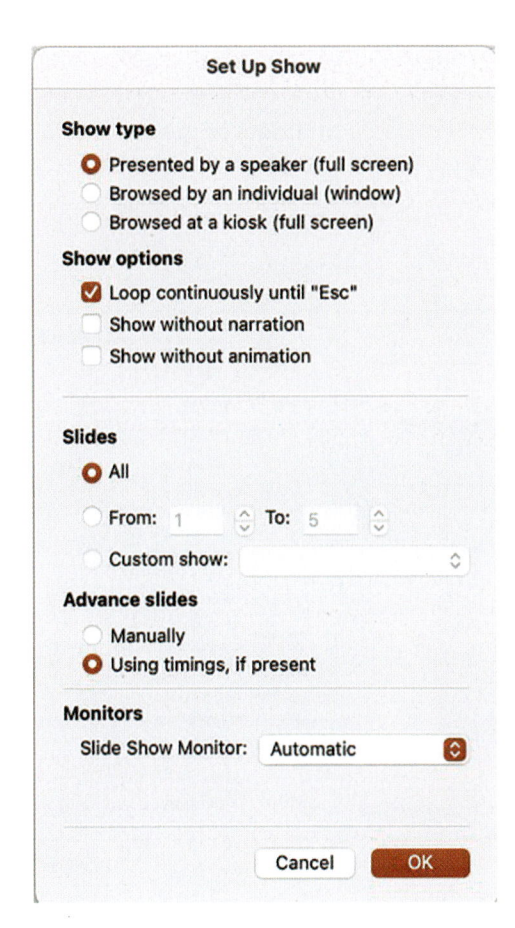

Figure 19.66: Setting a presentation to loop

- To loop the slide show, then 'Browsed at a kiosk (full screen)' should be selected. This mode will only stop when someone presses the Escape button.

ICT IN CONTEXT

Researchers at the University of Wilmington, USA carried out research and found that using animation in slides makes it harder for the viewer to remember the content than in slides with no animations. So, sometimes simpler may be better.

ACTIVITY 19.5

Discuss in small groups, how you could make your presentations more accessible to hearing-impaired individuals. Which objects and tools would you use to achieve this in your presentations?

Printing a variety of presentation layouts

You can also print presenter notes and audience notes in different layouts. You can print:

- full-page slides
- handouts
- presenter notes.

These options can be accessed by selecting Print from the file menu. To choose which layout you want, there will be a drop-down box with these options in. Depending on the software this may or may not have a label 'Layout'.

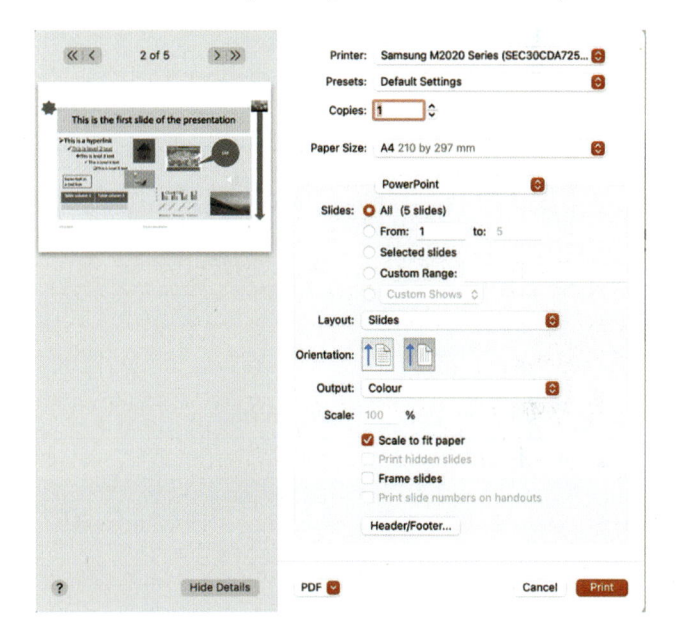

Figure 19.67: Printing out the slides

- **Full-page slides** could be used as posters or for any other display purposes (see Figure 19.67).
- **Handouts** allow the printing of the slides from two to nine slides per page. These can be given to the

KEY WORDS

full-page slides: one slide printed out on one page of paper

handouts: printed formats of a presentation which can be given to an audience. They can be printed in many formats depending on the audience and use

audience before the presentation to allow them to make notes or after to reinforce the message of the presentation. Some Handout layouts print lines next to the image of the slide for notes (see Figure 19.68).

- **Presenter notes** show the notes the speaker will follow when they deliver their presentation. These appear in the space below each slide (see Figure 19.69).

> **KEY WORD**
>
> **presenter notes:** printouts of the slides and notes that can be used by the presenter

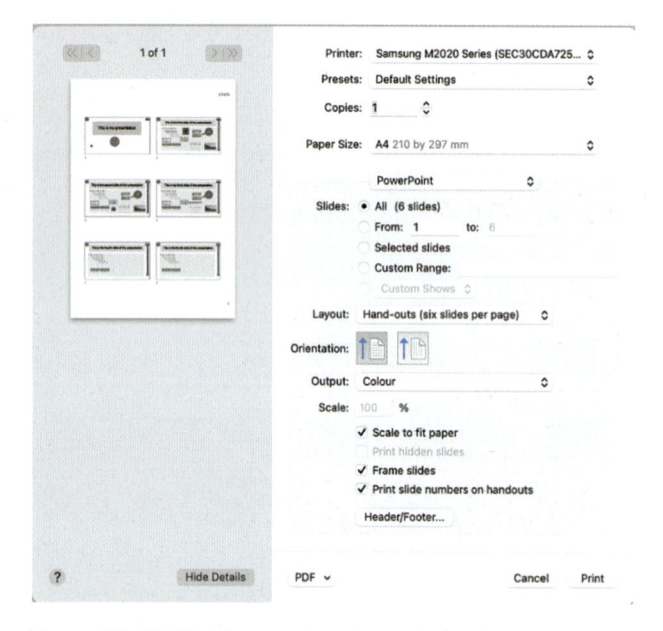

Figure 19.68: Handouts set at six per page

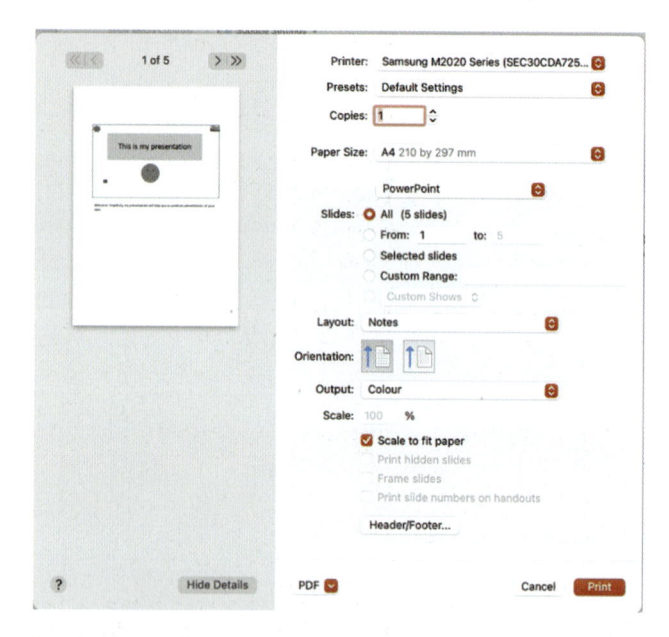

Figure 19.69: Printing presenter notes

PRACTICAL TASK 19.4

Getting started

1. Working with a partner, present a presentation you have done to each other. Think carefully about what you will say when each slide is shown. Do not just repeat what is on the slide.
2. When you are satisfied, add these as notes to each slide.

Practice

3. Open the *Task2* presentation that you created in the Practice session of Practical Task 19.2 and save it as *Task4*.
4. Read through the slides and then add teaching notes for each slide.
5. Print out as Handouts with three per page. Save to a PDF file named *Task4_1* by selecting 'Print to PDF' from the Print dialogue box.
6. Print out as Notes. Save as a PDF file named *Task4_2*.
7. Print as an Outline. Save as a PDF file named *Task4_3*.
8. Print the slides. Save as a PDF file named *Task4_4*.

CONTINUED

Challenge

9 Repeat Practice instruction 6 but set the program to print out only Slide 1. Save as a PDF file named *Task4_5*.

10 Print out as in Challenge Question 1 but change the orientation to portrait. Save as a PDF named *Task4_6*.

SUMMARY

Presentations can include many interactive and multimedia objects to make them interesting and engaging for the target audience.
Presentations can be edited by adding, moving and deleting: • new slides • objects such as shapes and images • hyperlinks • action buttons • video and audio clips.
Consistency is a key element of good quality presentations where the features used in the presentation do not distract the audience but are used effectively to engage and focus the minds of the target audience more sharply on the message within the presentation.
Master slides can be used to place objects consistently in a presentation, such as images, logos, slide headers and footers and numbering.
Presentations can be shown in a number of modes, such as presented by a speaker, browsed by an individual and browsed at a kiosk. Each of these modes is intended for a different audience type and purpose.
Presentations can move between slides using transitions, such as vortex.
Objects on a slide can be made to appear using animations.
Slides can be hidden within a presentation.
Presentations can be printed in a variety of layouts, including presenter notes and handouts.

EXAM-STYLE QUESTIONS

You have been requested to create a short presentation for a new garden centre in your neighbourhood. All slides must have a consistent layout and formatting, and each slide must display a title and a bulleted list, even those with objects, such as, images, etc.

1 Use the following information and images for your presentation.

Jambali's Garden Centre

Address: 8742 Bamboo Lane, Pine Village, Hockni, Malaysia

Tel: +60 7651 6592716

Fax: +60 7651 6592715

Email: office@jambali.co.my

Website: www.jambali.co.my

The following must appear on all slides:

- Slide Title Heading centred.
- The logo (Jambali Logo.jpg) should be placed in the top left-hand corner; size 3 cm by 3 cm retaining its aspect ratio.
- Footer with the name of the company, its address, tel, fax, email and website address: font size 12 pt on in the first slide and 8 pt on all others; centre aligned.
- Automatic slide numbering placed at the bottom right on the first slide and at the top right in all other slides.
- Background colours: gradient shades of your own choice of two colours.
- Consistent transitions between slides. [5]

Slide 1

Change the layout of Slide 1 so it displays a title, 'Jambali's Garden Centre' that is centred and has a sub-title beneath it, with your name in it, followed by the credentials, 'CEO'. [2]

Slide 2

- 'Monthly Discounts' as the title.
- Insert the four images of plants.
- Beneath the images in WORDART (not as a bullet point) '15% Discount'. [3]

Use images *Plants 1–4.jpg*.

Slide 3

- 'Monthly Events' as the title.
- Garden Tea Party – 7th – bring a friend with you and win a prize
- Unveiling of new saplings – 14th – Don't miss this special event by Prof. Shun
- Talk on how to look after your plants – 21st – RSVP by 16th as spaces are limited.
- Include appropriate image or animated image.
- Consistent animated effects on bulleted lists on Slide 3. [6]

Slide 4

'New Plants in Stock' as the title.

Change the layout of Slide 4 by adding New plants1.jpg and New plants2.jpg arranged as you would like to arrange them. [2]

| CONTINUED |

Slide 5

'Advice on how to look after your plants' as the title.

Step 1: Prepare the soil.

Step 2: Insert the seedlings in holes in the soil. Cover and water lightly.

Step 3: Water lightly as per instructions.

Step 4: Transfer to your garden where it will be for the longer period of time.

Step 5: Ensure there is enough sunlight.

Step 6: Trim and prune accordingly.

Place these steps in a flowchart. [3]

Slide 6

Change the layout of the slide so that the title is placed about a third downward of the slide.

Use the phrase, 'Thank you for your attention', as the title.

Add the file *Animated.gif* in the centre of the slide beneath the title. [2]

Save the presentation. [1]

2 Print out the presentation as handouts showing six slides on one page. [1]

[Total: 25]

| SELF-EVALUATION CHECKLIST |

After studying this chapter, think about how confident you are with the different topics.

This will help you to see any gaps in your knowledge and help you to learn more effectively.

You might find it helpful to rate how confident you are for each of these statements when you are revising. You should revisit any sections that you rated 'Needs more work' or 'Getting there'.

I can ...	See section	Needs more work	Getting there	Confident to move on
create a presentation using a text file	19.1			
use a master slide, placing objects consistently and formatting master slide objects	19.1			
edit a presentation by inserting, deleting and linking objects and applying transitions and animations in slides	19.2			
output the presentation to looped on-screen carousel or presenter-controlled displays	19.3			
print presentations as full-page slides, presenter notes or handouts	19.3			

# Chapter 20
Spreadsheets

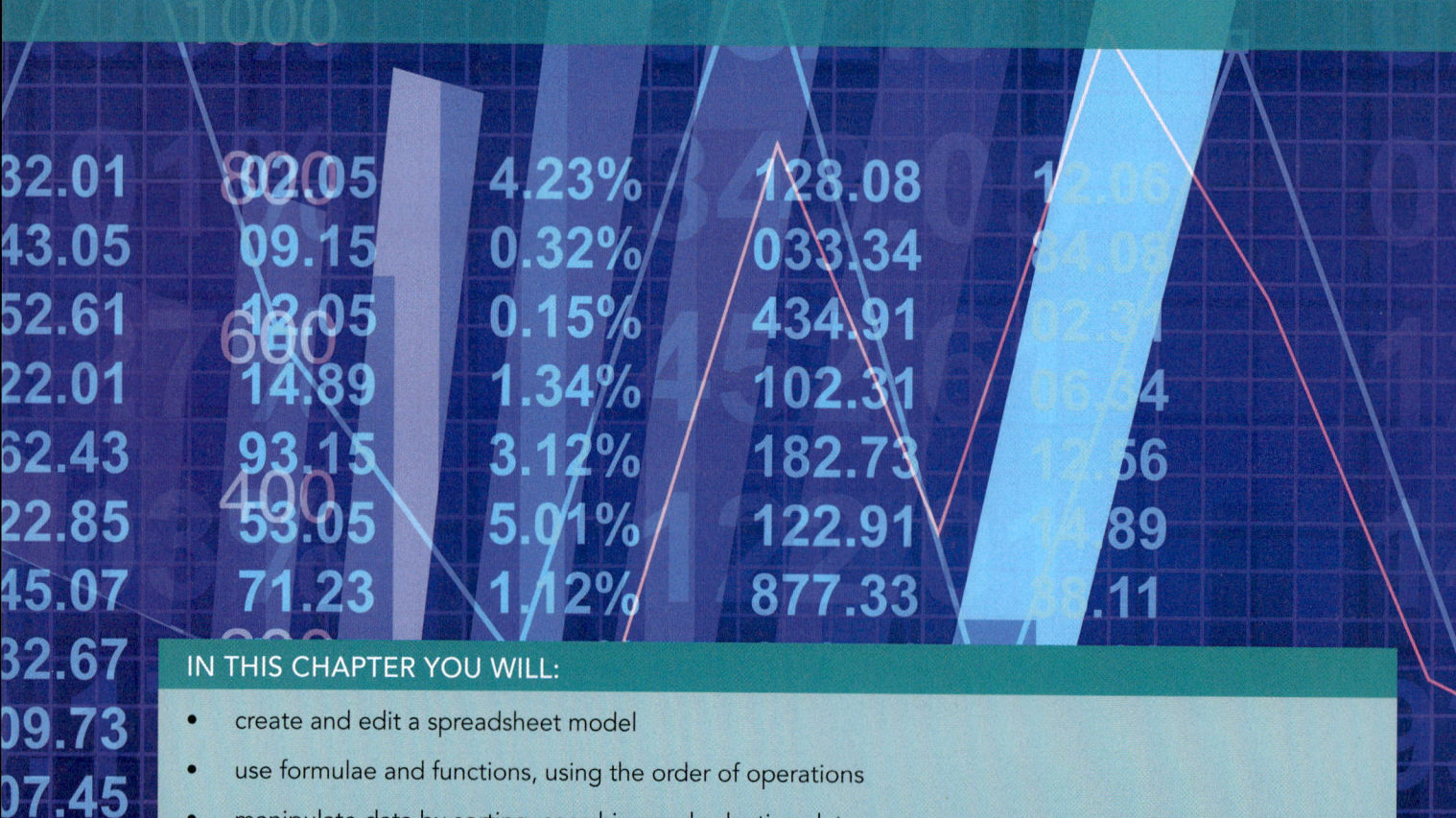

IN THIS CHAPTER YOU WILL:

- create and edit a spreadsheet model
- use formulae and functions, using the order of operations
- manipulate data by sorting, searching and selecting data
- present data by adjusting the display features and setting out page layout
- format a spreadsheet.

20 Spreadsheets

GETTING STARTED

Working with a partner, match the items relating to spreadsheets on the left with the correct definitions on the right.

1	=A3 + A4 + A5	a	A function.
2	Cell reference	b	Combination of column letter and row number.
3	Range	c	Collection of worksheets.
4	Rows	d	A formula.
5	Workbook	e	Changes when it is copied.
6	Relative reference	f	The currently selected cell.
7	Absolute reference	g	Does not change when it is copied.
8	=SUM(A3:15)	h	A selected group of cells.
9	Active cell	i	Used to copy data from one cell to adjoining ones.
10	Fill	j	Run horizontally.

BIRTH OF THE ELECTRONIC SPREADSHEET

In 1978, a student at Harvard Business School in the USA watched as the lecturer in accounting filled in a grid made of rows and columns on a blackboard. Whenever he changed a number, he had to go through all the others in the grid, erasing them and rewriting numbers so that everything still added up. In accounting, a table of this type, spread across two pages in a ledger was called a 'spreadsheet'. Everything had to be entered and recalculated manually.

The student, Dan Bricklin, had been a computer programmer and decided to write a program for the brand new Apple II computer and called it an 'electronic spreadsheet'.

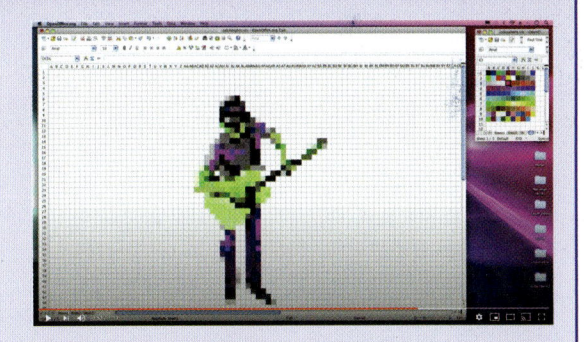

Figure 20.1: MysteryGuitarman's stop-go animations for his music

He named his program 'VisiCalc' – the first ever 'killer app', a program so brilliant that you had to buy a computer just to be able to use it. The program made the Apple II a huge success.

VisiCalc had 254 rows and 63 columns. Spreadsheets have rapidly improved in size and versatility and the latest Microsoft spreadsheet, Excel 365, has 1 048 576 rows and 16 384 columns!

Spreadsheets have revolutionised the ways in which businesses operate and are involved in all aspects of our daily lives. All organisations we buy products from use spreadsheets for financial and logistics planning; they are used in the design of cars and even in weather forecasting. The last two use spreadsheets to create computer models, which can be complex spreadsheets used to represent real-life situations. Data about a car's design, components and performance can be fed into the model.

> **CONTINUED**
>
> Designers can then carry out 'What if' scenarios, not just on costings (e.g. what if we change one component for another) but also for performance (e.g. 'What if we make a more rounded shape, how will it affect air flow and driving costs for the customer?'). This is all tested on a spreadsheet model without having to build a real-life, solid model. Far cheaper and also far safer as drivers not required.
>
> Spreadsheets have also been put to more unusual and artistic uses. They can be used to create interactive games and less obvious creations. For example, Tatsui Horiuchi uses spreadsheets to create artworks.
>
> Joe Penna creates stop-go animations for his music on YouTube under the name 'MysteryGuitarman' (Figure 20.1). He has almost 3 million subscribers.
>
> **Discussion questions**
>
> 1 How often do you use spreadsheets for your own tasks? List the ways in which spreadsheets could help you organise your life.
>
> 2 Can you think of any other creative uses for spreadsheets?

20.1 Create a data model

In this section, you will be asked to work on practical tasks using a spreadsheet as a **data model**. A data model is a way of representing the relationships in a real-life, complex system using text, diagrams, symbols or numbers and formulae.

> **KEY WORD**
>
> **data model:** a way of representing the relationships in a real-life, complex system using text, diagrams, symbols or numbers and formulae

Figure 20.2: Renaming, inserting or deleting a sheet

Setting up a new spreadsheet

As with all programs, a new spreadsheet can be created by clicking on New in the File menu.

When you create a new spreadsheet, you are actually creating a new workbook – which can have as many worksheets as you need. Each sheet has a tab at its bottom left corner stating its name. When the tab is right-clicked, it can be renamed (see Figure 20.2) or deleted or a new sheet can be inserted.

In some software, instead of Insert Sheet, it just says Insert. When you click on this, options to insert a variety of items are given (see Figure 20.3). Choose Worksheet and click OK.

Figure 20.3: Inserting a worksheet

Inserting and deleting cells, rows and columns, and merging cells

A spreadsheet consists of **rows** and **columns**, and where they intersect, they form **cells** (see Figure 20.4).

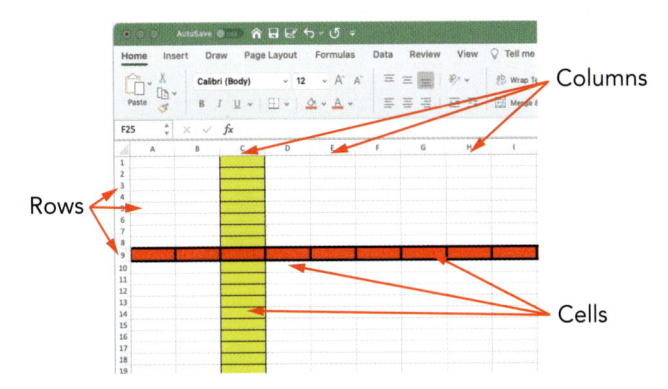

Figure 20.4: Columns, rows and cells

Columns are labelled A, B, C, etc. and rows are numbered 1, 2, 3, etc.

Each cell has an address – its column letter and row number. For example, the address of the cell where the yellow column and red row intersect in Figure 20.4 is C9.

Inserting rows and columns can be done by right-clicking on a row or column label (A, B, C or 1, 2, 3, etc.) and selecting the 'insert' option. Both columns and rows are inserted *before* the highlighted ones. Similarly, deleting rows and columns can be done by highlighting the row or column, right-clicking on it and selecting the delete option.

To **merge cells** (combine them) together, you can highlight the cells you want to merge, and select the correct option from the Merge & Centre menu on the Home ribbon (see Figures 20.5).

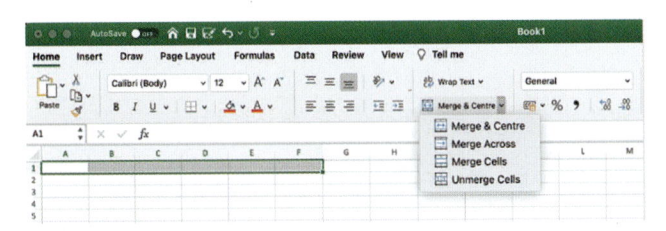

Figure 20.5: Merging cells A to F

They can be unmerged in the same way.

Create formulae using cell references

The basis of a data model in a spreadsheet are calculations made between the contents of different cells. In these calculations, the cell addresses – called **cell references** – are used rather than the contents of the cells. For example, a **formula** could be placed in cell C3 to add up the numbers in cells A1 to A6 (see the formula in Figure 20.6 and the result in Figure 20.7).

> ### KEY WORDS
>
> **rows:** made up of cells that are adjacent to each other and go from left to right or right to left horizontally
>
> **columns:** made up of cells that are adjacent to each other and go from top to bottom or bottom to top vertically
>
> **cells:** the small rectangular sections on spreadsheets used to enter data such as text, numbers or symbols and to perform calculations using formulae and functions
>
> **merged cells:** when more than one single cell has been joined to make a larger cell
>
> **cell references:** a way of pointing to a part of a spreadsheet using letters for columns and numbers for rows
>
> **formula:** arithmetical operations carried out on the contents of cells. The plural of formula is formulae

Figure 20.6: Formula to add up a series of numbers

A formula always has to start with an equals symbol '=' to inform the software that this is a formula and not just some text to display.

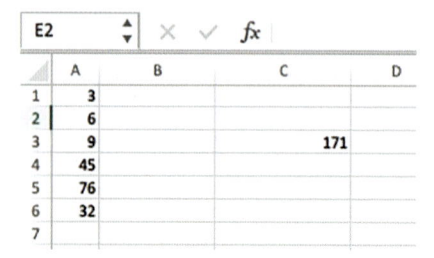

Figure 20.7: The result of the formula

The cell references are used in the formula rather than the contents of the cells. For example, in Figure 20.6, the formula in cell C3 could have been =3+6+9+45+76+32.

If the cell references are used (e.g. =A1+A2+A3+ A4+A5+A6), then the formula does not have to be changed if the numbers to be added together need changing. Using references, the formula is automatically recalculated if the numbers in any of the cells change. For example, if the value in cell A3 is changed to 19, the result shown in C3 will automatically change to 181 without you having to change the data in that cell as well.

Figure 20.8 shows columns of numbers in columns B to E. In cell B8, there is a formula to calculate the total of the numbers in the B column.

Figure 20.8: Columns of numbers

If the totals for columns C to E need to be found, the formulae do not have to be entered for each one as the formula in cell B8 can be copied across.

Copying, or replicating, be done by dragging the small box at the bottom, right corner of the highlighted cell (see Figure 20.9).

Once copied, the formulae to calculate the totals will now be in cells C8, D8 and E8 and the total for each of the columns will appear in the cells.

Note that as the formulae has been copied to the right, the cell references in the formula have changed from =A1+A2+A3, etc. to B1+B2+B3... and then C and D (see Figure 20.10).

Because the cell references changed from A to B to C to D, etc. as the formula was copied, the cell references

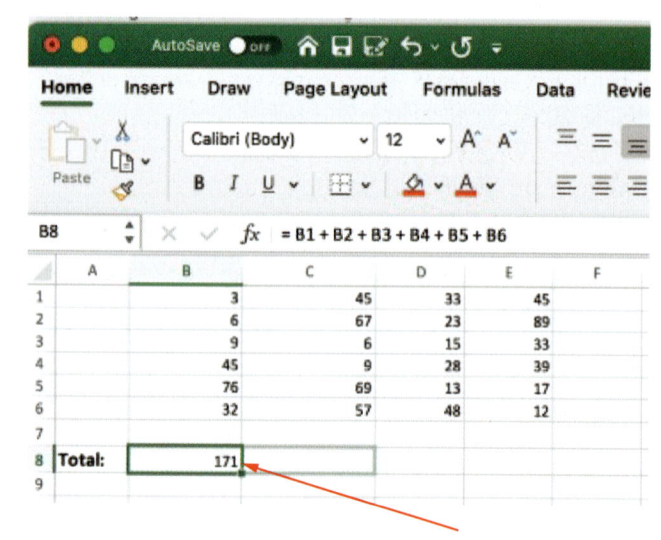

Figure 20.9: Copying a formula

Figure 20.10: Formulae to calculate totals

are said to be **relative references**. They are not fixed but change according to the columns they are in.

In Figure 20.11 there is a formula in cell C1 to calculate the result of multiplying the number in cell A1 with that in cell B1.

	A	B	C
1	3	4	=A1*B1
2		6	
3		9	
4		10	
5		12	
6			

Figure 20.11: Formulae using multiplication

If the same formula is needed in cells C2 to C5, it can be copied down.

When it is copied down in order to multiply all of the numbers in cells B2 to B5 by 3 (in A1), the totals shown are obviously incorrect.

If you look at the formulae in Figure 20.12, you can see where the problem is.

	A	B	C
1	3	4	=A1*B1
2		6	=A2*B2
3		9	=A3*B3
4		10	=A4*B4
5		12	=A5*B5
6			

Figure 20.12: The copied formulae

Just as the reference A changed to B, C and D when it was copied across, in this example the number 1 in =A1 * B1 has changed to =A2 * B2, B3 * C3, etc. as it is copied down.

In this example, the B1 should change to B2, B3, etc. but the A1 should stay at A1 as it is copied down.

To make it fixed and to prevent it from changing as it is copied, the $ sign should be placed in front of the row number in the cell reference It is now a fixed or **absolute reference**.

The original formula in cell C1 should be:

A$1 * B1.

When it is copied down, the expected results are returned (see Figure 20.13).

	A	B	C	D
1	3	4	12	
2		6	18	
3		9	27	
4		10	30	
5		12	36	
6				

Figure 20.13: The expected results

The position of the $ states which part of the reference remains absolute. In the example above, it keeps the reference to row 1. If the formula was $A1, then the reference to column A would remain the same as the formula was copied across the columns, but if it were copied down the rows, the formula would change to A2, A3, A4, etc. If the formula was A1, then the reference to cell A1 would remain the same when it was copied across the columns and down the rows.

> **KEY WORDS**
>
> **relative reference:** a cell reference that changes as it is copied down columns or across rows
>
> **absolute reference:** a cell reference that does not change as it is copied down columns or across rows

As well as formulae, data can also be copied down the rows and across the columns by dragging the box in the bottom right corner (see Figure 20.14). When the box is dragged, the data can just be copied (Figure 20.15) or it can create a series.

	A	B	C
1	1		
2			
3			
4			
5			
6			
7			
8			
9			
10	1		
11			
12			

Figure 20.14: The data in cell A1 being copied down the rows

Figure 20.15: The contents of cells A2 to A9 after cell A1 is copied down

If 1 is entered into cell A1 and 2 into cell A2 and they are both selected before copying, then a **series** will be produced. A series is a range of cells filled with values that increment. The first and second values are used as the starting values and the rest are added according to specified rules, e.g. if the first are 1 and 2 then the rest will be 3, 4, 5, 6, etc.

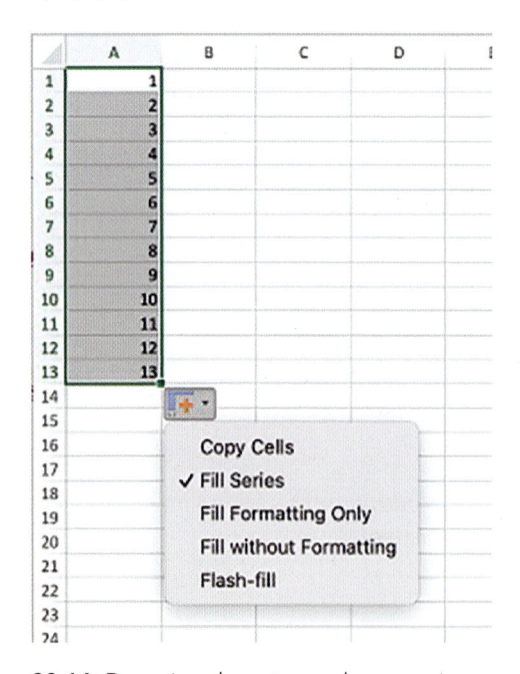

Figure 20.16: Dragging down to produce a series

When you drag down the values, an icon will appear – clicking on this will show a drop-down menu (see Figure 20.16). This menu allows a user to select a series or just copy the value. The Auto-fill Options icon appears when you release the mouse button to stop dragging.

Some text entries, such as months of the year or days of the week, can be copied to produce a series. If January is entered into cell A1, it can be copied down as January in every row, or used to create a series – January, February, March, etc.

Named cells

A cell or a **range** of cells can be given a name. This **named cell** can then be referred to in a formula. In the example above, cell A1 could have been given a name.

> **KEY WORDS**
>
> **series:** a range of cells filled with values that increment
>
> **range:** a group of cells in a spreadsheet where the cells are all adjacent to each other. Ranges can be used in formulae
>
> **named cell** or **named range:** a short text or name which is given to a cell or group of cells within a range by which they can be referenced in the spreadsheet model

In Figure 20.17, cell A1 is being named as 'Multiplier'.

Figure 20.17: Naming a cell

The name can be used in a formula (Figure 20.18).

Figure 20.18: Using a named cell in a formula

When it is copied down the name remains the same.

Arithmetic operators used in formulae

In the above examples, addition and multiplication were used. However, all operators can be used. These are shown in Table 20.1.

+	Addition
-	Subtraction
*	Multiplication
/	Division
^	To the power of, e.g. $3^2 = 3\wedge2 = 9$

Table 20.1: Arithmetic operations

Order of operations

When used in formulae, the arithmetic operators are applied in a particular order. This is called the order of operations. If the order of operations needs to be changed, parentheses (brackets) can be used and anything within them is calculated first.

The order is:

- **B** for brackets
- **I** for indices
- **D** for division
- **M** for multiplication
- **A** for addition
- **S** for subtraction

So all you have to remember is the name – BIDMAS.

The following equations $3^3 \times 6 + (16 - 7)$ would be evaluated in the following order:

- $3^3 \times 6 + 9$ (**Brackets:** $16 - 7 = 9$)
- $27 \times 6 + 9$ (**Indices:** $3^3 = 3 \times 3 \times 3 = 27$)
- $162 + 9$ (**Multiplication:** $27 \times 6 = 162$)
- 171 (**Addition:** $162 + 9 = 171$)

Question

1. A partially completed spreadsheet is shown. Copy the spreadsheet and then enter the formulae.

	A	B	C
1	27		
2	30		
3			

a. In cell C1 write a formula to add together the numbers in cells A1 and A2 and then multiply them by 3.

b. In cell C2 write a formula to subtract the number in cell A1 from the number in cell A2 and then subtract the result from the result of the number in cell A2 squared.

c. In cell C3 write a formula to deduct the result of the subtraction of the number in cell A1 from that in A2 from the result of adding the numbers together.

Functions

So far, we have looked at formulae written by a user using relative and absolute cell references to carry out calculations, but spreadsheets also provide predefined formulae, called **functions**, to perform calculations. These make it far quicker than having to type in long, complicated formulae. Most spreadsheet programs provide hundreds of these functions, but there are a few that are used more often than others.

> **KEY WORD**
>
> **function:** predefined formulae included in the spreadsheet

Sum

This function is used to add up a group of numbers.

Instead of writing a long formula such as =A1+A2+A3+A4+A5+A6, the far simpler SUM function can be applied.

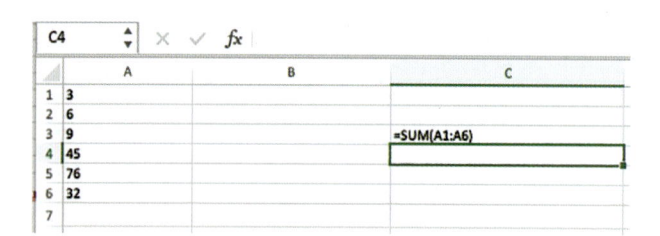

Figure 20.19: Using the SUM function

The function just needs to be told which cells are to be added – in the example in Figure 20.19, cells A1 to A6. It is written using a colon:

=SUM(A1:A6)

There is also an auto-sum icon that will automatically sum the values in the selected cells. You can find it in the Formulas menu (Figure 20.20), but, in many software, it is also in the Home menu.

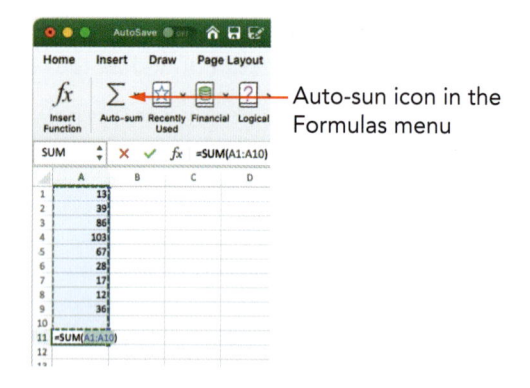

Figure 20.20: Using the auto-sum function

When the cells are selected, the auto-sum will sum the total of the values in the cells and place the answer in the cell below.

If you want to sum a range of numbers in a different part of the spreadsheet then you would click on the Auto-sum icon with the cursor in one cell and then select the range of cells manually.

Figure 20.21: Using the AVERAGE, MAXIMUM and MINIMUM functions

Average, maximum and minimum functions

Average, maximum and minimum functions are useful when analysing data (see Figure 20.21).

- The average function totals the average of the group of numbers:
  =AVERAGE(A1:A6)

- The maximum function displays the highest number in the group of numbers:
  =MAXIMUM(A1:A6)

- The minimum function displays the lowest number in the group of numbers:
  = MINIMUM(A1:A6)

They are used in the same way as the SUM function with the function name followed by the from and to cells separated by a colon.

Integer function

This function can be used when you want a whole number with no decimal places as the result. You write this function as =INT( ), with the number or calculation inside the brackets.

So =INT(6.45) would return 6.

In Figure 20.21, the AVERAGE function returns 28.5 as the result. If you did not want any decimal places, you could apply the INT function along with the AVERAGE function (see Figure 20.22).

Figure 20.22: Using the INT function

Figure 20.23: Using the ROUND function

The AVERAGE function is placed inside the INT function so that whatever is returned by the AVERAGE function will be converted to an integer. Using functions within other functions is called **nesting functions**.

> **KEY WORD**
>
> **nested function:** a function inserted as one of the arguments in another function

Note, when using nesting functions, always make sure you have closed all the brackets. In Figure 20.22, you can see the end of the Average function has two brackets, one closing (A1:A6) and the other closing the =INT() function.

The INT function always rounds down, so that 28.1, 28.5 and 28.9 would all be rounded down to 28.

Rounding function

ROUND is used to round a number to a particular number of decimal places. This function also rounds down. To use this function, you write: =ROUND( ), with the number or calculation inside the brackets (see Figure 20.23).

ROUND can also be used with negative numbers so that −9.7 rounded with no decimal places is rounded down to −10.

When the ROUND function is used, the number of decimal places has to be stated. In Figure 20.23, it is set to two decimal places (as specified by ', 2' in the function). If the number was 13.6372 and the number of decimal places was set to 1, then 13.6 would be returned but if it was 13.356, 13.3 would be returned.

There are two similar functions, ROUNDUP and ROUNDDOWN which obviously will round a number up or down.

With ROUNDUP, 3.2 with no decimal places would return 4.

With ROUNDDOWN, 3.9 with no decimal places would return 3.

COUNT function

The COUNT function counts the number of cells that contain numbers. This function is written as: =COUNT( ), with the cell range inside the brackets, similar to SUM( ) function.

In Figure 20.24, the COUNT function returns 4 as there are only four cells between A1 and A6 that contain numbers.

Figure 20.24: Using the COUNT function

LOOKUP function

The LOOKUP function allows the software to check a range of cells to see if it contains a particular value. A user has to insert the value being looked for and the range in which to check. The format of the function is shown in Figure 20.25.

The value to look up
=LOOKUP(A13,A2:A10)
The range to check

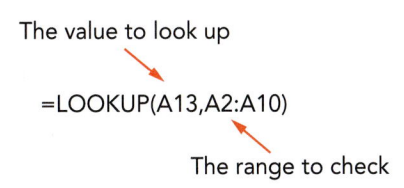

Figure 20.25: The LOOKUP function format

In cell B13 in Figure 20.26, the value to look up is in cell A13 and the range to check is A2:A10. These two conditions are separated by a comma.

The LOOKUP function will return an approximate match. As 35 is not in the range specified, the function returns the nearest match lower than that asked for. Therefore, when 35 is the target, 30 is returned.

```
    A25           fx
      A              B
1  Marks         Comment
2  0             Terrible
3  20            Not very good
4  30            Must try a lot harder
5  40            A bit more effort is needed
6  50            Just made it
7  60            satisfactory
8  70            Goog
9  80            very good
10 90            Excellent
11
12
13 35            =LOOKUP(A13,A2:A10)
```

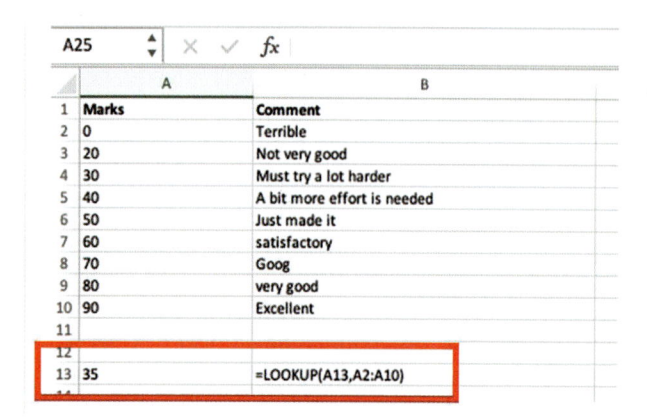

Figure 20.26: Using the LOOKUP function

The function will return more information. In column B, comments have been entered to correspond to the marks. The function can return the comment associated with the mark it returns. The format for this is shown in Figure 20.27

```
              The value to look
                    ↓
    =LOOKUP(A13, A2:A10, B2:B10)
                ↑            ↑
      The range to check   The range to check
        for the mark         for the comment
```

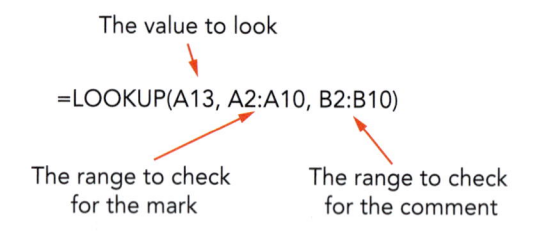

Figure 20.27: The extended LOOKUP function format

This will return the associated comment, as shown in Figure 20.28.

VLOOKUP

The 'V' in VLOOKUP stands for vertical, meaning the function will search up and down a column of values

```
    E11            fx
      A              B                        C
1  Marks         Comment
2  0             Terrible
3  20            Not very good
4  30            Must try a lot harder
5  40            A bit more effort is needed
6  50            Just made it
7  60            satisfactory
8  70            Goog
9  80            very good
10 90            Excellent
11
12
13 35            =LOOKUP(A13,A2:A10)      =LOOKUP(A13, A2:A10, B2:B10)
```

Figure 20.28: Using the LOOKUP function to return more information

```
    F9            fx
      A              B          C         D
1  Item Number  Descriptiopn   Price
2       1       Beans          $2.00
3       2       Bread          $1.50
4       3       Butter         $2.50
5       4       Flour          $1.00
6       5       Lemons         $0.75
7       6       Lentils        $1.25
8       7       Limes          $0.50
9       8       Milk           $0.25
10      9       Noodles        $1.00
11     10       Orange juice   $0.90
12     11       Pasta          $2.50
13     12       Peaches        $1.25
14     13       Peas           $2.00
15     14       Pomegranate    $1.90
16     15       Potatoes       $2.10
17     16       Rice           $2.50
18     17       Salt           $1.50
19     18       Sugar          $1.75
20     19       Tea            $2.60
21     20       Water          $1.00
22
23
```

Figure 20.29: List of items with descriptions and prices

that could be numbers or text. HLOOKUP searches along a row for a match. Which is used will depend on the structure of the table being searched.

Figure 20.29 shows a list of items for sale in a shop. Each item has an item number, description and price.

The number being looked for should be unique as the function stops after it finds the first one. The numbers should also be in ascending order (lowest to highest).

The VLOOKUP function can be used to display the description of an item and its price from a table by using its item number in column A if an item number is added.

```
    G19           fx
      A              B                    C
1  Marks         Comment
2       0        Terrible
3      20        Not very good
4      30        Must try a lot harder
5      40        A bit more effort is needed
6      50        Just made it
7      60        satisfactory
8      70        Goog
9      80        very good
10     90        Excellent
11
12
13     35        30   Must try a lot harder
```

For a description to be shown (from Column 2) when an item number is entered the function would be:

=VLOOKUP(F3, A1:C21, **2**)

- F3 is the cell where the item number is inputted.
- A1:C21 is the table where all of the items and their details are displayed.
- The 2 indicated the column containing the data to be returned.

So this function is saying, 'Look through the data in the table A1 to C21 and search for the value in cell F3. Return the information in the cell that is in the same row as the search value and in Column 2.' The function always looks down the left-hand column of the range specified but the range does not have to be the whole table. So if you wanted to find something in column B (e.g. bread) you would specify B1:C21.

For the price to be displayed (from Column 3), the function would be:

=VLOOKUP(F3, A1:C21, 3)

Indicating Column 3 instead of Column 2. These examples are shown in Figure 20.30.

If 3 is input into cell F3, the description 'Butter' and price '$2.50' are returned (Figure 20.31).

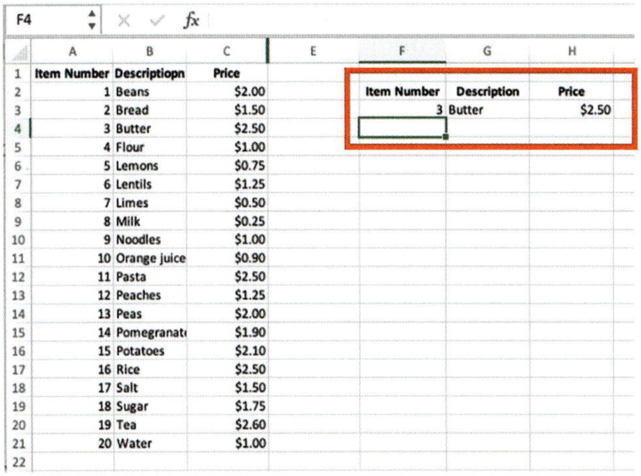

Figure 20.31: Description and price returned for an item

The VLOOKUP function goes down the first column looking for the number entered. If it can't find the exact one, it uses the nearest one below.

If a user entered 30 as the item number, then 'Water' would be returned as the description (Figure 20.32 on the next page).

But that is obviously incorrect.

To prevent this, the function can be extended by adding the word 'FALSE' at the end (see Figure 20.33 on the next page).

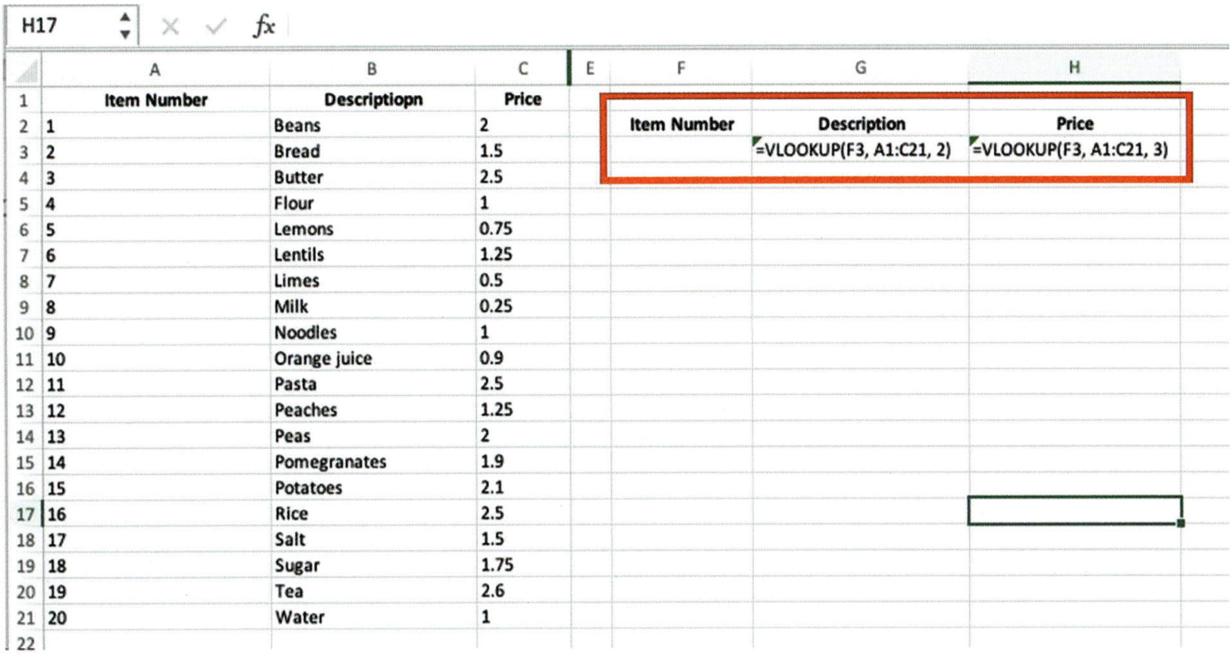

Figure 20.30: Functions to return a description and a price for an item

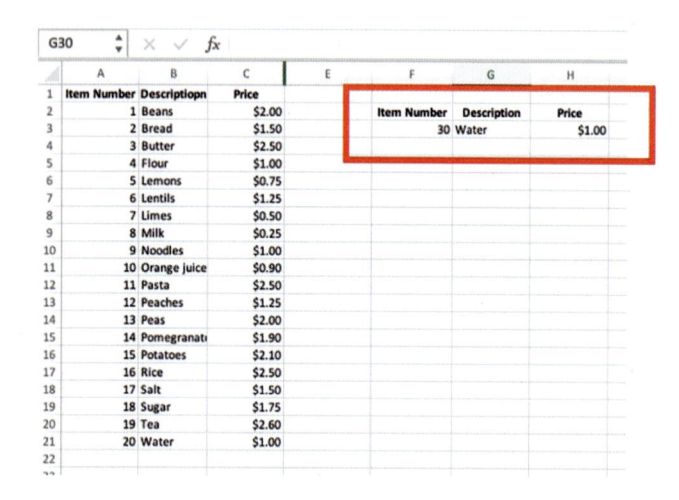

[Spreadsheet screenshot showing item list A1:C21 with Item Number, Description, Price columns; a lookup area in F1:H3 showing Item Number 30, Description "Water", Price $1.00]

Figure 20.32: Description and price returned for an item that doesn't exist

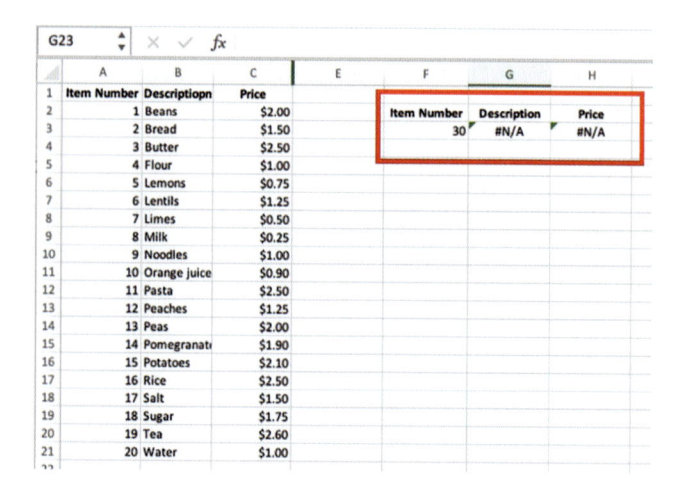

[Spreadsheet screenshot showing the same item list with a lookup area returning Item Number 30, Description #N/A, Price #N/A]

Figure 20.34: Error messages showing N/A or No Value Available

=VLOOKUP(F3, A1:C21, 2, **FALSE**)

So this function is saying, 'Look through the data in the table A1 to C21 and search for the value in cell F3. Return the information in the cell that is EITHER in the same row as the search value and in column 2 OR return an error message if the search value isn't in the table.' (See Figure 20.34)

HLOOKUP is exactly the same as VLOOKUP, except the search occurs along the top row of the specified range. This time, the final number (e.g. 2) refers to the row rather than the column.

We will enter =HLOOKUP(B6, A1:M2, 2) into our spreadsheet (see Figure 20.35). This function will search for the month entered in cell B6 and return the data that is held in the second row.

So in this example, if you typed 'July' in cell B6, the value returned in B7 would be 31.

XLOOKUP

The XLOOKUP function is a more modern replacement for VLOOKUP and HLOOKUP.

The XLOOKUP function can be used to find the year and the earnings for any movies that a user enters.

F	G	H
Item Number	Description	Price
30	=VLOOKUP(F3, A1:C21, 2, FALSE)	=VLOOKUP(F3, A1:C21, 3, FALSE)

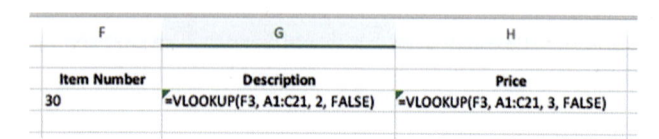

Figure 20.33: VLOOKUP to return an error message if item number is not found

VLOOKUP can also search text data in a column. The text items should be in alphabetical order.

HLOOKUP

As the V in VLOOKUP stands for vertical, then the H in HLOOKUP stands for horizontal.

The spreadsheet in Figure 20.36 on the next page shows the movies that earned the most money and the years they were released. The XLOOKUP functions take the name of the movie entered in cell F1 and search for it

	A	B	C	D	E	F	G	H	I	J	K	L	M
1	Month	January	February	March	April	May	June	July	August	September	October	November	December
2	Days	31	28	31	30	31	30	31	31	30	31	30	31
6	Enter Month:												
7	Number of days:	=HLOOKUP(B6, A1:M2, 2)											

Figure 20.35: The HLOOKUP function

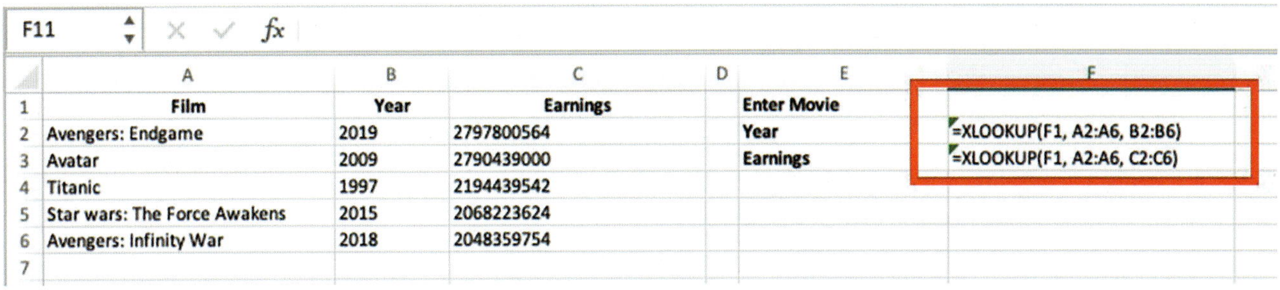

Figure 20.36: Using the XLOOKUP function

down column A. If it is found, the function will return the corresponding data from column B in row 2 and from column C in row 3.

If Avatar is entered as the movie, the year of its release and earnings are returned (Figure 20.37).

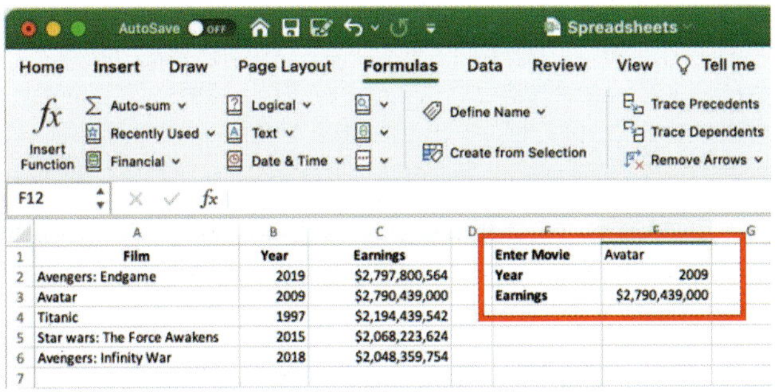

Figure 20.37: The values returned by the XLOOKUP functions

In the example in Figure 20.36, the function was used twice to return year end earnings, but it can also be configured so one function returns multiple values. In the example in Figure 20.38, the function will return all of the values associated with the movie entered. In this case, instead of specifying the single column, all of the columns are entered into the function in the one cell – i.e. instead of B2:B6 or C2:C6, B2:C6 is entered.

When Avatar is entered into cell E2 as the movie to search for, the function in cell F2 looks down column A until it finds the name of the movie, in this case Avatar. When it finds it, it returns the value in the same row of column B and the value in the same row of column C. The function is in F2, so the value in column B is placed in F2, and the value in column C is placed in G2 (see Figure 20.39 on the next page).

IF

The IF function is one of the most useful and widely used of the functions. It allows different decisions to be made depending on the circumstances.

An IF function has three parts to it. It first asks the question, 'Is a value equal to, greater than or smaller than this?' If the answer is 'yes' then do this, if it is 'no' then do something else.

The IF function is written like this:

=IF(Question, Yes, No)

1 **Question:** this is the question, 'Is a value equal to, greater than or smaller than this?'
2 **Yes:** this bit tells the function what to do if the answer to the question is 'yes'.
3 **No:** this bit tells the function what to do if the answer is 'no'.

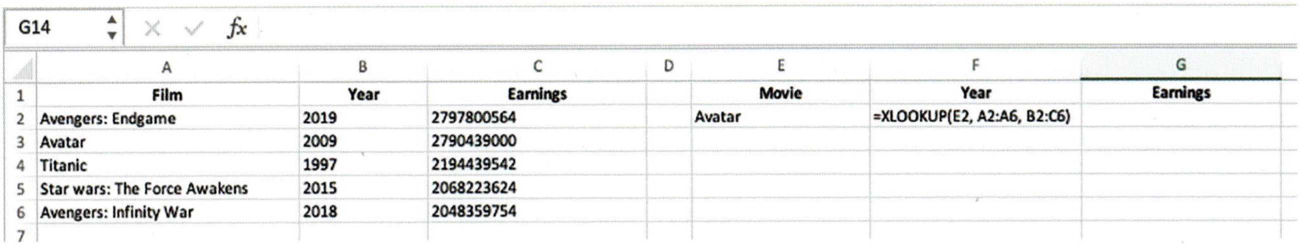

Figure 20.38: XLOOKUP to return multiple values

	A	B	C	D	E	F	G	H
1	Film	Year	Earnings		Movie	Year	Earnings	
2	Avengers: Endgam	2019	$2,797,800,564		Avatar	2009	$2,790,439,000	
3	Avatar	2009	$2,790,439,000					
4	Titanic	1997	$2,194,439,542					
5	Star wars: The For	2015	$2,068,223,624					
6	Avengers: Infinity	2018	$2,048,359,754					
7								

Figure 20.39: Multiple values returned by the XLOOKUP

	A	B	C	D	E	F	G	H	I
1	Pupil Number	Surname	First Name	Subject	Coursework	Examination	Total		
2	1036	Suparmanputra	Hasan	Science	60	70	130		
3	2872	Elmasry	Anat	History	56	82	138		
4	1725	Nasution	Abdul	Geography	90	80	170		
5	3916	Megat	Amina	Computing	82	69	151		
6	7321	Nababan	Annisa	Computing	73	67	140		
7	1328	Mansour	Hasina	Science	42	39	84		
8	1712	Zaky	Khalid	Maths	76	85	161		
9	2482	Sakura	Abe	Science	39	52	91		
10	2223	Mazur	Lucia	Languages	68	54	122		
11	3669	Sayid	Haziq	Technology	32	76	108		

Figure 20.40: Student results

I2 fx =IF(G2>100, "Good", "Poor")

	A	B	C	D	E	F	G	H	I	J
1	Pupil Number	Surname	First Name	Subject	Coursework	Examination	Total		Comment	
2	1036	Suparmanputra	Hasan	Science	60	70	130		Good	
3	2872	Elmasry	Anat	History	56	82	138		Good	
4	1725	Nasution	Abdul	Geography	90	80	170		Good	
5	3916	Megat	Amina	Computing	82	69	151		Good	
6	7321	Nababan	Annisa	Computing	73	67	140		Good	
7	1328	Mansour	Hasina	Science	42	39	84		Poor	
8	1712	Zaky	Khalid	Maths	76	85	161		Good	
9	2482	Sakura	Abe	Science	39	52	91		Poor	
10	2223	Mazur	Lucia	Languages	68	54	122		Good	
11	3669	Sayid	Haziq	Technology	32	76	108		Good	

Figure 20.41: Comments added using IF function

The spreadsheet in Figure 20.40 shows the results of some students.

An IF function can be used to insert a comment for each student.

=IF(G2>100, "Good", "Poor")

All text entered into a function must be surrounded by double quotation marks; this tells the function that it is text rather than function text. Numbers should not be in quotation marks.

The function asks if the total in cell G2 is greater than 100. If the answer is 'yes', the comment is 'Good' and if it is 'no', the comment is 'Poor'.

This function is then copied down to the other rows (see Figure 20.41) by dragging the little box, as before.

As mentioned previously, functions can be nested. More different comments can be added by nesting the IF functions. When the answer is 'no', instead of writing a comment, another IF function can be inserted.

If statement 1	Question: G2>160	Yes Excellent	No New IF statement				
If statement 2			Question: G2>140	Yes Good	No New IF statement		
If statement 3					Question: G2>100	Yes Satisfactory	No Poor

Table 20.2: Breaking down the IF statements

Figure 20.42: Result of using nested IF functions

The nested IF function:

=IF(G2>160,"Excellent",IF(G2>140," Good", IF(G2>100,"Satisfactory","Poor")))

asks the questions:

- Is the number greater than 160? If it is, the comment is 'Excellent'. If not, then go onto the next IF.
- Is the number greater than 140? If it is, the comment is 'Good'. If not, then go onto the next IF.
- Is the number greater than 100? If it is the comment is 'Satisfactory'. If not the comment is 'Poor'.

This is broken down in Table 20.2.

The results of using this nested IF example are shown in Figure 20.42.

Named ranges

Previously we looked at naming cells but ranges can also be named, simplifying their use in functions.

When we looked at using AVERAGE, MAX and MIN functions we set the range to check as A2:A6. But this range can be given a name, making it easier to refer to in functions. When the range is selected and right-clicked, a new name can be given to it by choosing Define Name from the menu (see Figure 20.43).

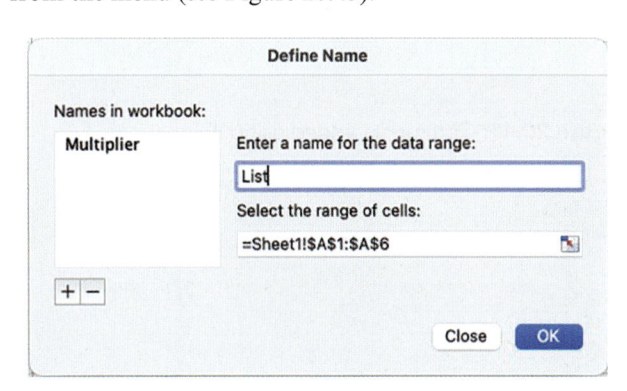

Figure 20.43: Naming a range

CAMBRIDGE IGCSE™ ICT: COURSEBOOK

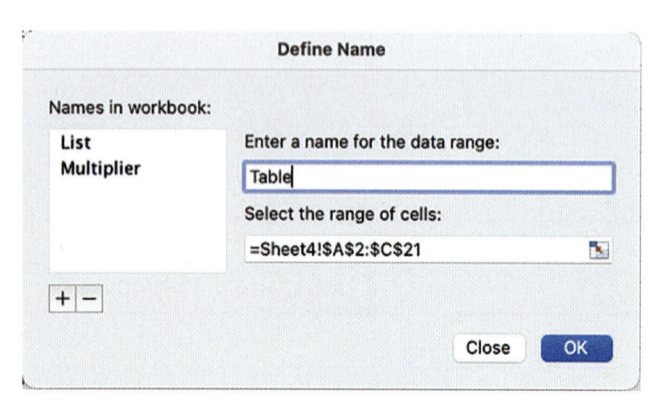

Figure 20.44: Naming a range in a VLOOKUP function

That name can then be used in the functions in cells D1, D3 and D5.

Similarly, a named range can be used in the VLOOKUP function we studied (see Figure 20.44).

The name can be used in the function instead of typing A2:C21 into the function, as shown in cells G3 and H3 in Figure 20.45.

When you are creating complicated formulae and functions, it is often better for the spreadsheet to display the formulae and functions rather than their results.

Displaying formulae

Often it is desirable to display the formulae in a spreadsheet rather than the values they produce, especially when it is being error checked (as has been shown in some of the figures in this chapter).

This can be done by selecting the Show Formulas icon in the Formulas menu (see Figure 20.46 on the next page). To change it back to the values, simply click on Show Formulas again.

> **ACTIVITY 20.1**
>
> Create a presentation, including screen prints, to teach other students how to use the following functions:
>
> SUM, IF and COUNT.

Figure 20.45: Using a named range in a VLOOKUP function

20 Spreadsheets

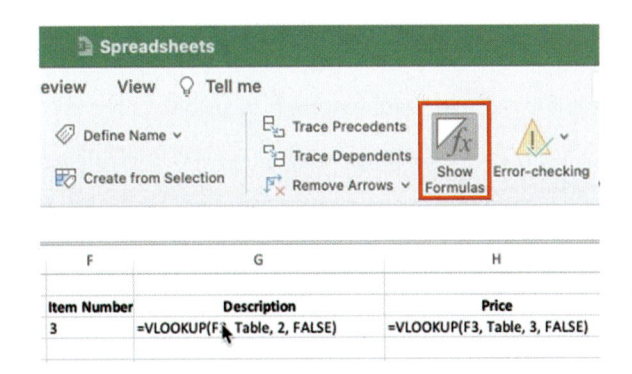

Figure 20.46: Displaying formulae

Using references on different sheets

When creating formulae and using functions, cells on different sheets can be used.

For example, the following formula would add up the values in cells A1 and A2 on the current sheet plus the value in cell A1 in sheet 2.

=A1+A2+Sheet2!A1

The name of the sheet is placed in front of the reference with an exclamation mark (!). This can also be achieved by clicking on the relevant cell in a different sheet while you are writing the function (i.e. after you have typed =), the same way you can click on a cell in the same sheet to reference a cell.

Functions and formulae can also use data from different workbooks in the same way. Once you have typed = , clicking on a cell in a different workbook can also reference that cell in the function. This will look like this:

= A1+A2+[Book1.xlsx]Sheet1!A1

The name of the workbook is *Book1.xlsx* is.

The name of the sheet sheet in *Book1* is Sheet1.

!A1 is the cell reference on Sheet1 of *Book1*.

ICT IN CONTEXT

In 2012, a formatting error on MI5's (the UK government security service) list of phones to be secretly monitored meant that the phones of people unrelated to the investigation were monitored instead.

A formatting error changed the last three digits of these phone numbers to 000 in the spreadsheet so that random British citizens had their phones monitored. The actual suspects weren't observed.

PRACTICAL TASK 20.1

Getting started

1 On paper, write a function that would find the total of the numbers in a spreadsheet between and including cells C1 to C13.

2 On paper, write a formula to add the contents of cells A3, A6 and A9 and divide the result by 3.

Practice

3 Open the *Students.xlsx* spreadsheet into your spreadsheet software. The spreadsheet shows the subjects that a class of students study and their examination marks.

4 Insert a row above row 1.

   Enter the heading 'Term 1 Results' with a font size of 20, bold and coloured red.

   Centre this heading between Rows A to M.

   Give the merged cells a light blue fill.

5 Make all of the column headings in the new row 2, bold.

6 In cell N2, add the following heading: 'Average Score'. Centre the title and adjust the column width so that it can all be read.

> **CONTINUED**
>
> 7   In cell N3, place a function that will find the average mark for the five tests for the first student. Format this cell so that it has one decimal place.
>
> 8   Copy this function down the entire column to the last student.
>
> 9   Change the heading in row 1 so that it is now centred between column A and column N.
>
> 10 Save the spreadsheet as *Task1.xlsx*.
>
> **Challenge**
>
> 11 Create a range name 'Average_Score' between and including cells N3 to N32.
>
> 12 In cell M34, enter the label 'Maximum' and in cell M35, 'Minimum'.
>
> 13 In cells N34 and N35, enter functions using the range name to find the maximum and minimum average marks.
>
> 14 Show the formulae in your spreadsheet and take a screenshot of column N.
>
>   Paste this into a document named *Task1.docx*.
>
>   Change back to showing the values and save the spreadsheet as *Task1_Challenge.xlsx*.

Questions

2   Explain the difference between a formula and a function.

3   Explain what the following functions are used for:
   - IF
   - SUM
   - VLOOKUP
   - INTEGER
   - AVG
   - HLOOKUP
   - ROUND
   - XLOOKUP

PRACTICAL TASK 20.2

Getting started

1. On paper, write a function to insert the comment 'Good' into cell C1 if the value in cell A1 is greater than 50 and 'Poor' if it less.

2. On paper, write a function to insert the comment 'Excellent' into cell C1 if the value in cell A1 is greater than or equal to 70, 'Good' if it greater than or equal to 50 and 'Poor' if it less than 50.

Practice

3. Open the *Task1_Challengex* spreadsheet you created in the Challenge section of Practical Task 20.1.

4. In cell O2 add the label 'Comment', bold and centred.

5. In cell P2 Add the heading 'Boundaries', bold and centred.

6. In cells P3 and P4 add the values 70 and 50.

7. In cell O3 write a function that will add one of the following comments:
   - 'Excellent' if the value in N3 is greater than or equal to the value in P3.
   - 'Good' if the value in N3 is greater than or equal to the value in P4.
   - 'Poor' if the value in N3 is less than the value in P4.

8. Copy the function down column O. Check your spreadsheet to see if the correct comments have been added.

9. Show the formulae in your spreadsheet, take a screenshot of column O to show the functions and paste it into a document named *Task2.docx* Change back to show the values.

10. Save the spreadsheet as *Task2.xlsx*.

Challenge

11. How many would obtain the 'Excellent' comment if the boundary was 65 instead of 70? Write your answer into *Task2.docx*. Change value back to 70.

12. How many would obtain the 'Poor' comment if the lower boundary was raised to 55? Write your answer into *Task2.docx*. Change value back to 50.

> CAMBRIDGE IGCSE™ ICT: COURSEBOOK

PRACTICAL TASK 20.3

This task asks you to combine the functions SUM, COUNT and IF to form the functions SUMIF and COUNTIF. They can be used to count or sum the number of cells that have a particular value or text.

Getting started

1   On paper, write a function to count all of the cells in the range A1 to A10 that contain a numerical value.

2   On paper, write a function that will count all of the cells in the range A1 to C13 that have the entry 'Entry'.

Practice

3   Open spreadsheet *Task2.xlsx* you created in Practice section of Practical Task 20.2.

4   In cells A36 to A44 are the names of the subjects shown in the table.

5   In cell B36, enter a function to count the total number of people studying Art as Subject1, Subject2 or Subject3.

6   Copy this function down the row to cell B44.

   Delete the functions in cells B37 and B42 as these will need different functions.

7   Add functions to cell B37 to count the number of students studying English and B42 to count the number of students studying Maths.

   (Note, these two cells may display a small triangle in the corner once you have done this; don't worry – this is just to warn you that the formula in these cells is different from the nearby cells.)

   You can count the number of cells that have an entry in each column.

8   Show the formulae in your spreadsheet. Take a screenshot of A35 to B44 to show the functions and paste it into a document named *Task3.docx*.

9   Save the spreadsheet as *Task3.xlsx*.

Challenge

10   In cells C36 to C44, create functions to find the total scores for each subject.

   The function should sum the marks for a subject entry in all of Subject1, for a subject entry in all of Subject2 and for a subject entry in all of Subject3.

11   In cells D36 to D44, enter formulae to calculate the average score for each subject. It should be formatted to one decimal place.

   Show the formulae in your spreadsheet; take a screenshot of A35 to D44 to show the functions and paste it into a document named *Task3.docx* Save the spreadsheet as *Task3_Challenge.docx*.

Self-assessment

How confident do you feel applying the correct formulae or function? (Rate it a 5 for very confident, down to a 1 for not at all confident.)

List the formulae or functions you still want to learn more about from the list below: add, subtract, multiply, divide, indices, sum, average, minimum, maximum, integer, rounding, counting. LOOKUP, VLOOKUP, XLOOKUP, IF.

> **REFLECTION**
>
> Which methods for learning how to use and apply a formula or function do you learn from most effectively? Online videos, online screenshots showing you step-by-step, the coursebook, from your teacher, from your peers? Explain why.

20.2 Manipulate data

Accurate data entry

Data entry has to be 100% accurate, because if there are any mistakes with data entry, the information taken from the processed data will also be inaccurate. The GIGO acronym means 'garbage in, garbage out': if you put any rubbish data into your data model, you can only expect rubbish results from it. For example, if you accidentally type someone's date of birth incorrectly and you update your data model automatically, you may end up with information that says someone is 200 years old, which is not possible (yet!).

In addition, data is often shared between organisations, and even bought and sold by many others. This is the main reason why data protection legislation (law) insists that data must be accurate and up to date. Organisations share information about you; sometimes you are aware of it, and sometimes they gain your permission in a way where you believe your data is safer than it actually is.

The data held in a spreadsheet can be **sorted** and searched.

Sort data

Quick sort

Select a cell in the column that is going to be sorted on, for example, Surname, and select either of the quick sort icons on the Data ribbon (see Figure 20.47). (It is also on the Home ribbon for some software.)

The A to Z icon sorts in **ascending order** (1 to 10 or A to Z) and Z to A in **descending order** (10 to 1 or Z to A).

The data in this spreadsheet will then be sorted according to Surname.

> **KEY WORDS**
>
> **sort:** arrange items into a particular order
>
> **ascending order:** arranged from smallest to largest or in alphabetical order
>
> **descending order:** arranged from largest to smallest or in reverse alphabetical order

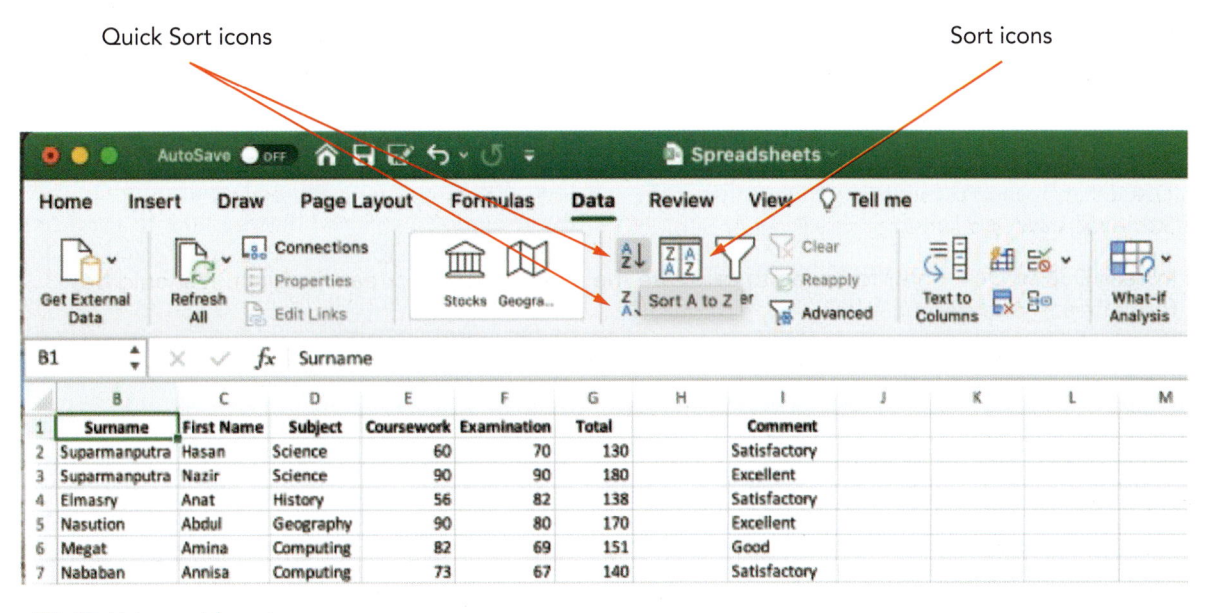

Figure 20.47: Using quick sort

Sort

Selecting the Sort icon allows the data to be sorted on more than one column.

When a cell in the table is selected and the Sort icon is clicked, a dialogue box opens (see Figure 20.48).

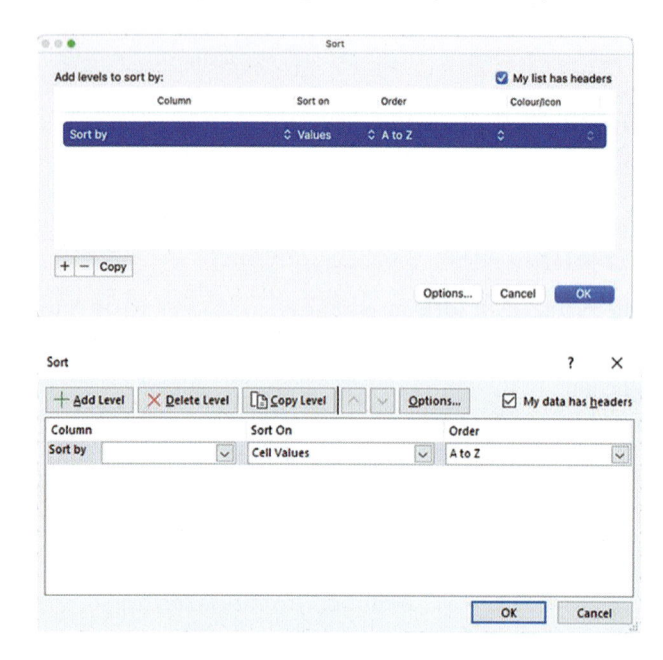

Figure 20.48: Dialogue box for entering sort criteria in different software

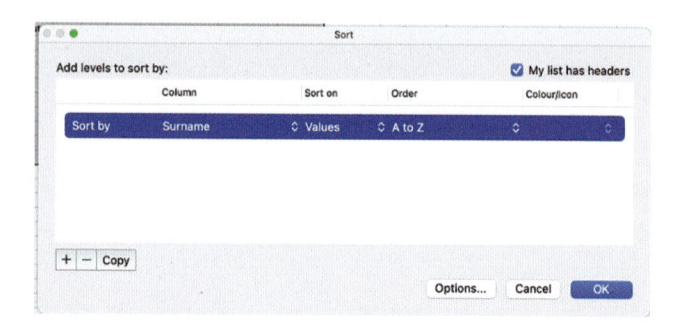

Figure 20.49: Set for sorting on the Surname column in alphabetical order

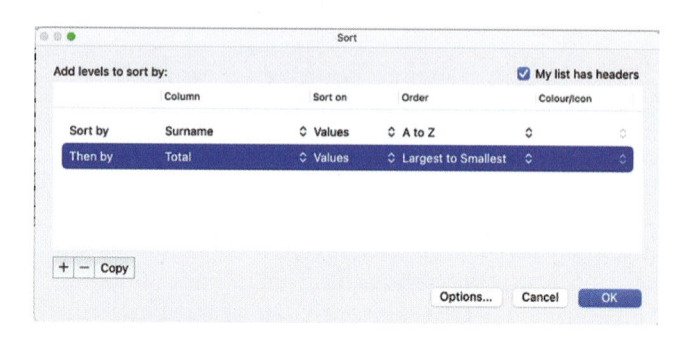

Figure 20.50: Adding a second column to sort on

At first it is empty.

Columns to sort on can be selected by clicking on 'Sort by' (see Figure 20.49), or the drop-down menu next to 'Sort by', depending on the software.

Another column can be added (see Figure 20.50) by clicking on the '+' icon at the bottom of the dialogue box, or the 'Add Level' at the top.

In this example, the data will be sorted by Surname into alphabetical order and then if there are several students with the same surname (for example, Supermanputra) they will be sorted by 'Total' from highest to lowest.

Search and select data

Simple searches can be carried out by **filtering** the data so that it displays only selected data.

With one of the cells in the table selected the Filter icon on the Home ribbon should be selected (see Figure 20.51 on the next page).

At the top of each column there is an arrow to display a drop-down dialogue box for setting a filter for that column. Figure 20.52 on the next page show a filter being set for the Total column.

It allows a user to select data that complies with the conditions shown in Figure 20.53 (on the following pages). (In some software, you have to click on the Number Filters option first before the drop-down menu appears.)

It can select data that is equal to or not equal to, greater than, less than, etc. an entered criterion. Figure 20.54 (on the following pages) shows a filter to select rows where there is a Total greater than or equal to 130.

The filter would return the subset shown in Figure 20.55 on the following pages.

The filter can be removed by clicking on 'Clear Filter' in the dialogue box.

Multiple criteria can be set by applying filters at several or all of the columns.

> **KEY WORD**
>
> **filtering:** to select and remove particular items from others

20 Spreadsheets

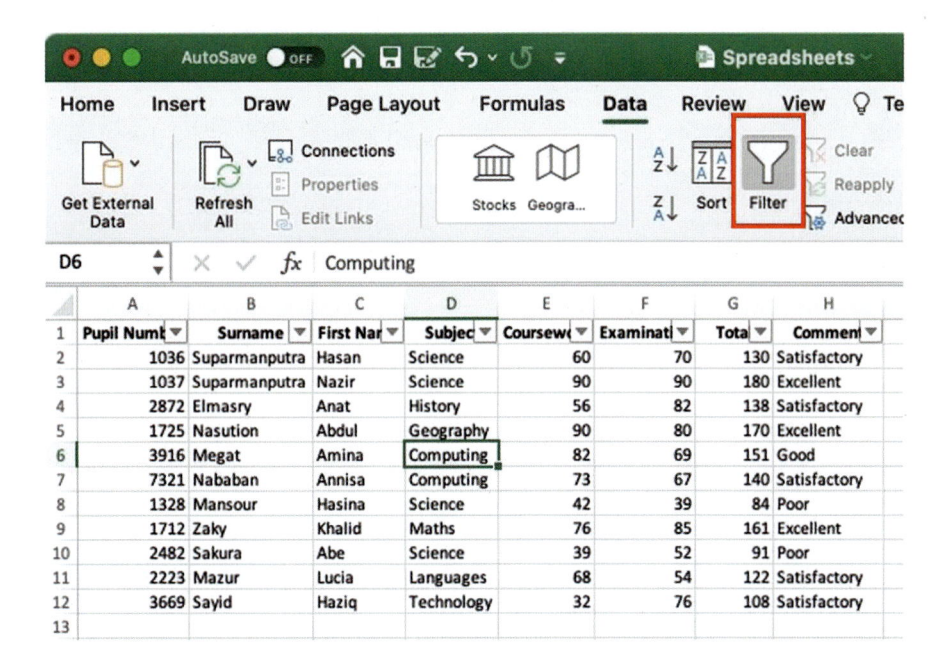

Figure 20.51: Filtering the records

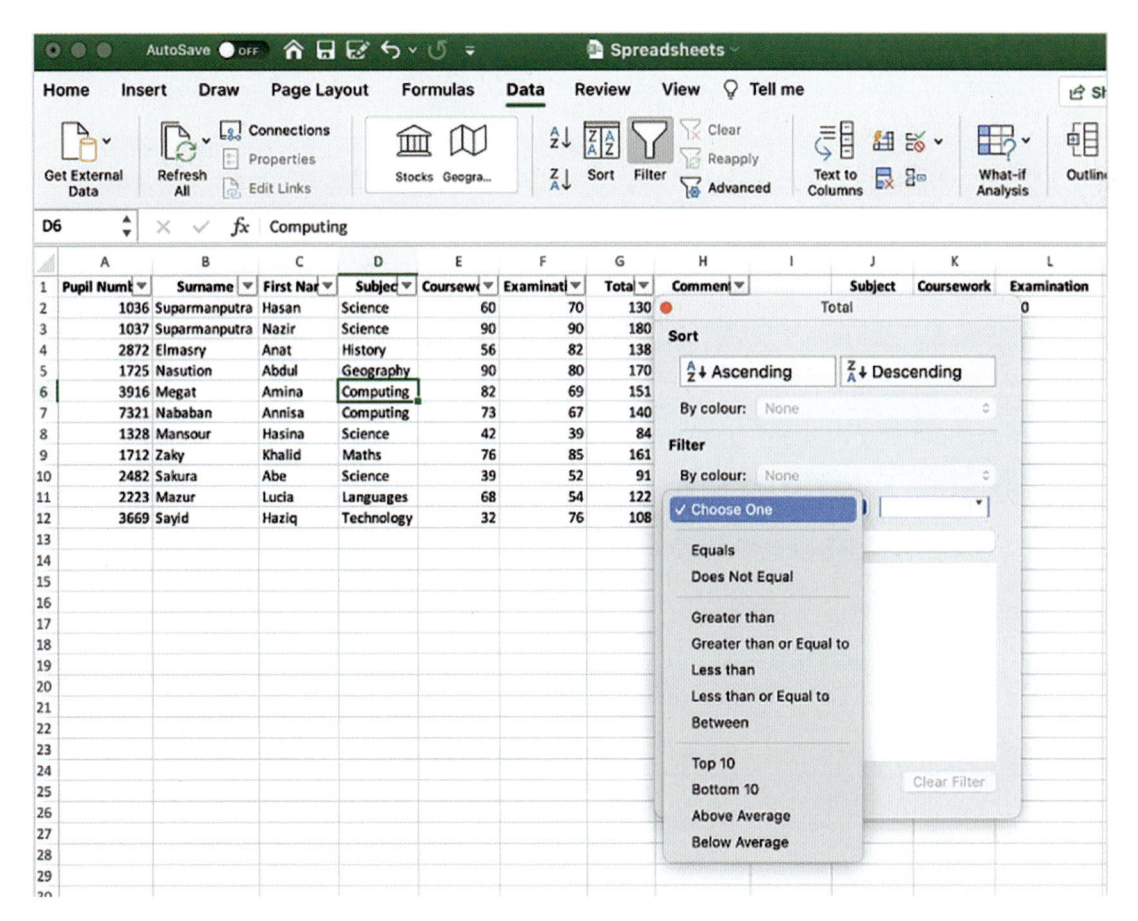

Figure 20.52: Setting a filter

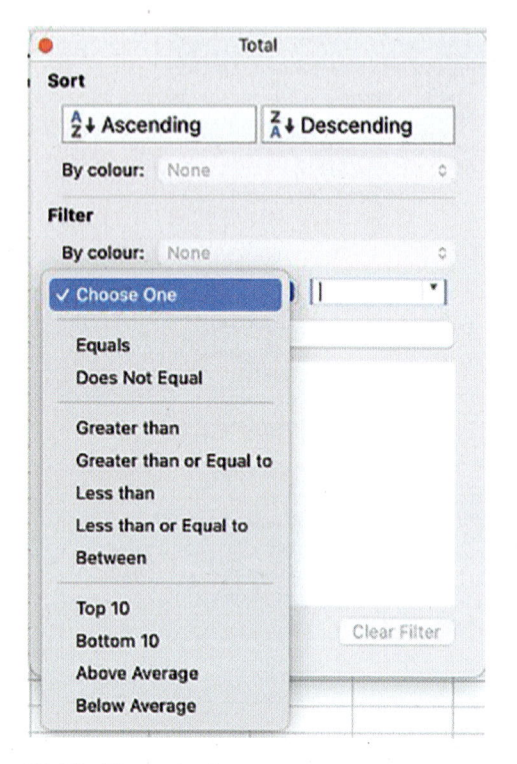

Figure 20.53: Filter criteria

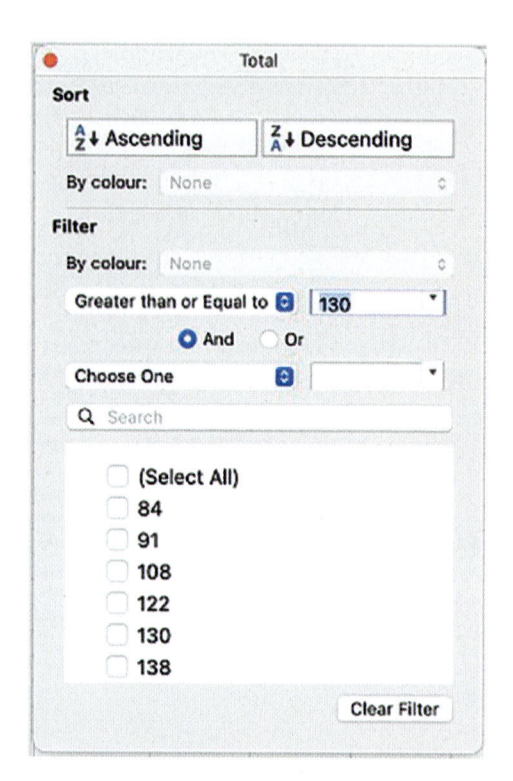

Figure 20.54: Filter to find Totals equal to or greater than 130

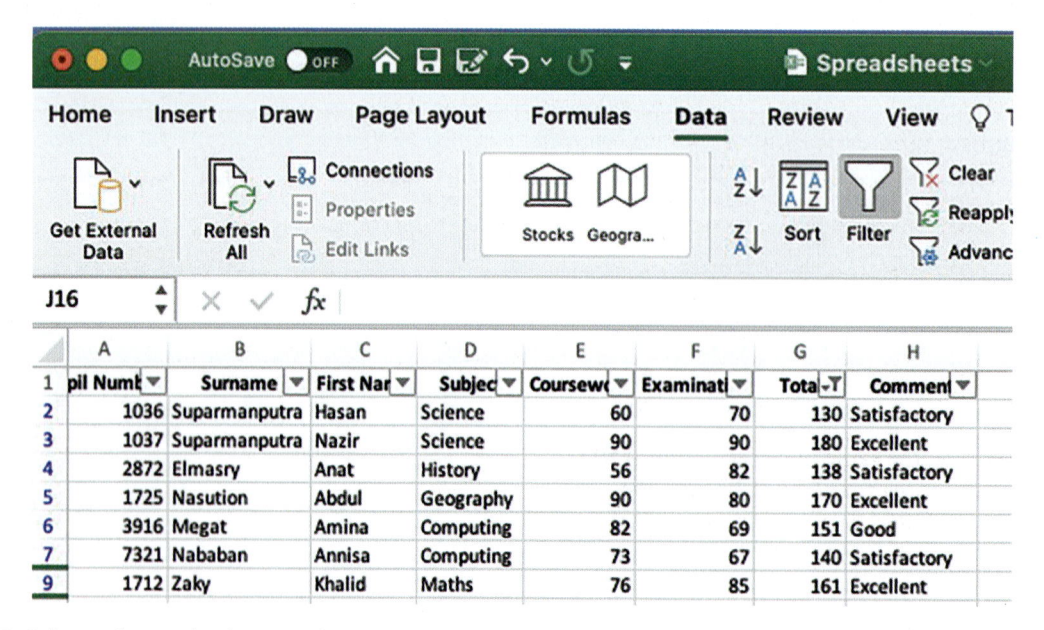

Figure 20.55: Subset of records where Total is equal to or greater than 130

20 Spreadsheets

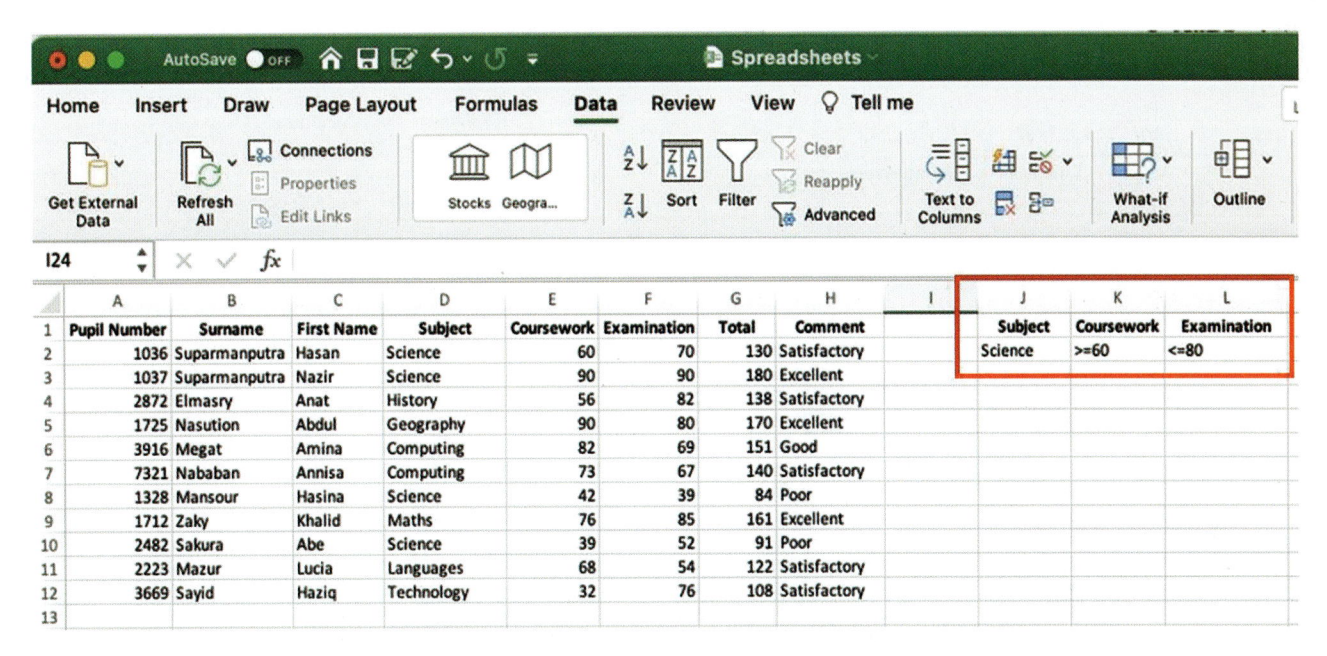

Figure 20.56: A criteria range

Advanced filters and searching

Selecting the Advanced icon on the Data ribbon allows a user to use another part of the spreadsheet to search the data for particular criteria. Figure 20.56 shows a search between J1 and L2. The criteria range is between 60 and 80, inclusive.

The criteria that have been set mean that rows will be selected where…

The Subject is equal to Science

AND

The Coursework mark is greater than or equal to 60

AND

The Examination mark is less than or equal to 80.

Placing the criteria on the same line specifies an AND query where two or more criteria must be met. We saw this in Chapter 18, Section 18.2 Manipulating data, when we were sorting and searching databases. Chapter 18, Tables 18.12 and 18.14 explain the logical operators needed to search data in spreadsheets too.

As with the Database searches, the operators that can be used in searches include:

AND, OR, NOT, >, <, =, >=, <=, <>

Once the criteria have been set and one of the cells in the table has been selected, the Advanced icon on the Data ribbon should be clicked.

The dialogue box often recognises the limits of the data table (see Figure 20.57); however, if it doesn't, they can be set by clicking at the end of the row and then highlighting the table. Criteria range must be set by clicking at the right of its area.

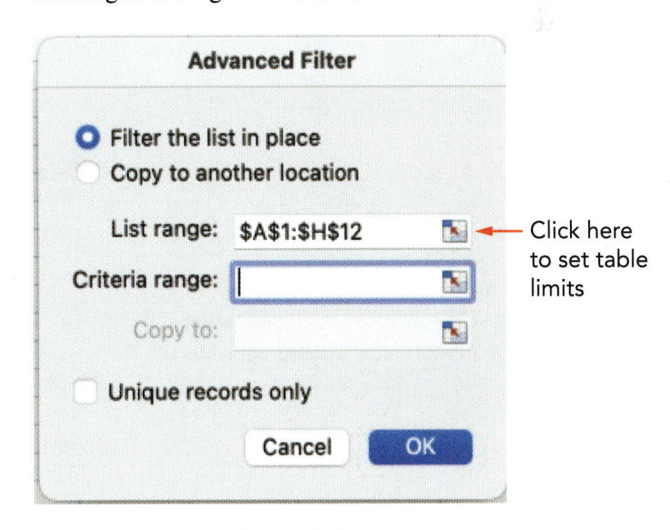

Figure 20.57: An advanced filter

The criteria range can then be selected and the box clicked again.

The criteria in Figures 20.58–59 would select only one row (the result is shown in Figure 20.60).

501

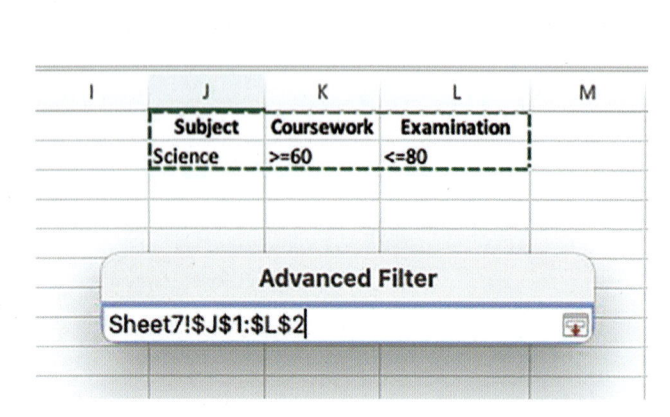

Figure 20.58: Setting the criteria range

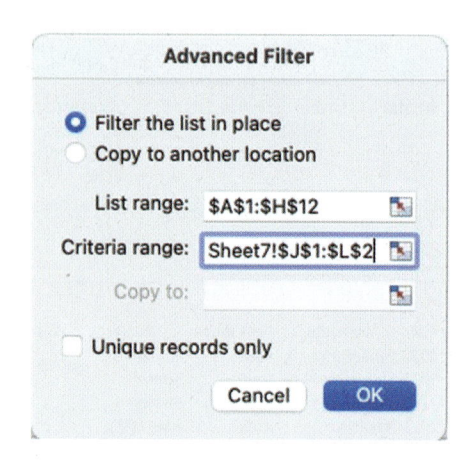

Figure 20.59: Criteria range set

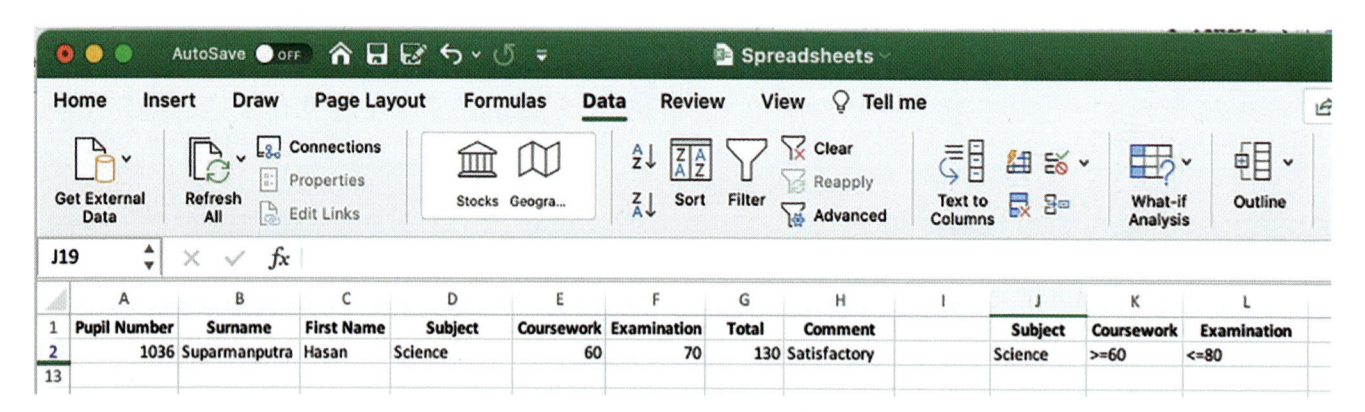

Figure 20.60: The result of the search

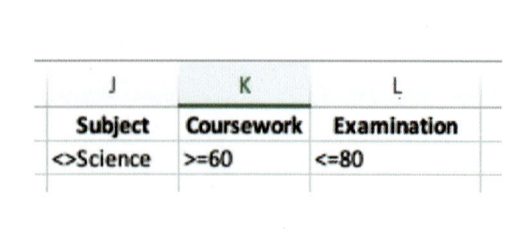

Figure 20.61: NOT Science

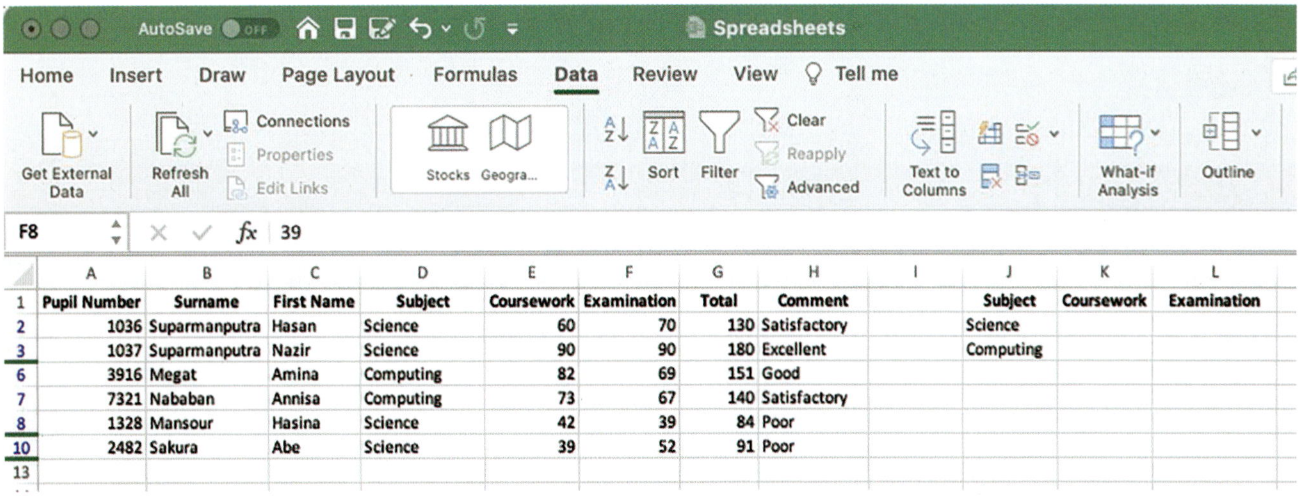

20 Spreadsheets

Figure 20.62: OR search

	A	B	C	D	E	F	G	H	I	J	K	L
1	Pupil Number	Surname	First Name	Subject	Coursework	Examination	Total	Comment		Subject	Coursework	Examination
2	1036	Suparmanputra	Hasan	Science	60	70	130	Satisfactory		Science		
3	1037	Suparmanputra	Nazir	Science	90	90	180	Excellent		Computing		
6	3916	Megat	Amina	Computing	82	69	151	Good				
7	7321	Nababan	Annisa	Computing	73	67	140	Satisfactory				
8	1328	Mansour	Hasina	Science	42	39	84	Poor				
10	2482	Sakura	Abe	Science	39	52	91	Poor				
13												

If an item is to be secluded, then the NOT operator (< >) should be used (see Figure 20.61).

If an OR search is required, then the criteria should be placed in different rows.

The criteria in Figure 20.62 find all rows with 'Science' OR 'Computing' in the Subject column.

Using wildcards

We looked at using wildcards in searches in Chapter 18, Section 18.2 Manipulating data on Databases.

They can also be used in spreadsheet searches. Table 20.3 shows the wild card symbols and how they are used.

? (Question mark)	Any single character.
* (Asterisk)	Any number of characters.

Table 20.3: Wildcards

Therefore, placing S* as a criterion in the Surname column would return all rows where the surname began with the letter 'S'.

ICT IN CONTEXT

The organising committee of the 2012 London Olympics had 10 000 tickets available for the synchronised swimming event. Unfortunately, an employee entered a '2' instead of a '1' and 20 000 tickets were offered. As a result, the committee oversold tickets and had to refund angry customers.

ACTIVITY 20.2

Working with a partner, each of you should draw a grid and write down five search criteria of your own. You should then ask your partner to explain what is being searched for – for example:

Surname	Age	Gender
L*	>=13	F

This would find all people with a surname beginning with L who are aged 13 and over and are female.

CAMBRIDGE IGCSE™ ICT: COURSEBOOK

PRACTICAL TASK 20.4

Getting started

1. On paper, write down the symbols you would use for the following operators: greater than, less than or equal to, greater than or equal to.

2. Write down the wildcard symbols you can use in a search and explain the function of each one.

Practice

3. Open the spreadsheet *Gym.xlsm* in your spreadsheet software. The spreadsheet shows some of the members of a gym and details about them and their membership.

4. Sort the data in the spreadsheet so that Surname is in alphabetical order.

   Take a screenshot of the spreadsheet and paste it into a document named *Task4.docx*.

5. Now sort the spreadsheet by Gender and then by SportName, both alphabetically.

   Take a screenshot of the spreadsheet and paste it into *Task4.docx*.

6. Filter the spreadsheet so that it shows only those whose sport is football.

   Take a screenshot of the spreadsheet and paste it into *Task4.docx*.

Challenge

7. Remove the filter so that all data is showing.

   Use an advanced filter to search for all members who are female and were born before the year 2000. Take a screenshot of the spreadsheet and paste it into *Task4.docx*.

8. Clear the filter and now use the advanced filter for all members who have the letter 'a' in their surname and play Lacrosse or any member with the letter 'b' in their surname.

   Take a screenshot of the spreadsheet and paste it into *Task4.docx*. Save this as *Task4_Challenge.docx*.

Questions

4. Explain the difference between a relative and an absolute cell reference.

5. Write down the following formula using absolute cell references.
   =A6*B9

6. Identify the symbols used within spreadsheet formulae for the following mathematical operators:
   a. multiply
   b. divide
   c. to the power of
   d. is not equal to.

20.3 Presenting data

The data in a spreadsheet can be presented on screen or as a hard-copy.

Adjust the display features

If you choose to present the data on screen, there are several things that can be adjusted: displaying the formulae, adjusting row height, column width and cell sizes, wrapping text and hiding rows and columns.

Adjusting row height, column width and cell sizes, and wrapping text were all covered in Chapter 13, Section 13.2 Tables.

Hiding rows and columns

Rows and columns can be hidden by selecting them, right-clicking and selecting Hide from the menu (see Figure 20.63).

To show them again, select the rows or columns on either side, right-click and select Unhide.

Format a spreadsheet

Spreadsheets can be formatted by adding text enhancements, aligning text and shading cells.

Colouring text and making it bold, underline or italic can be done by selecting the icons from the Home ribbon (see Figure 20.64), in the same way you would in any software.

Text can also be aligned Right, Left Centre and Justified by using icons on the Home ribbon.

Changing cell background colour was covered in Chapter 13.

Numeric data can be formatted by highlighting the cells, right-clicking and selecting Format Cells from the menu (see Figure 20.65).

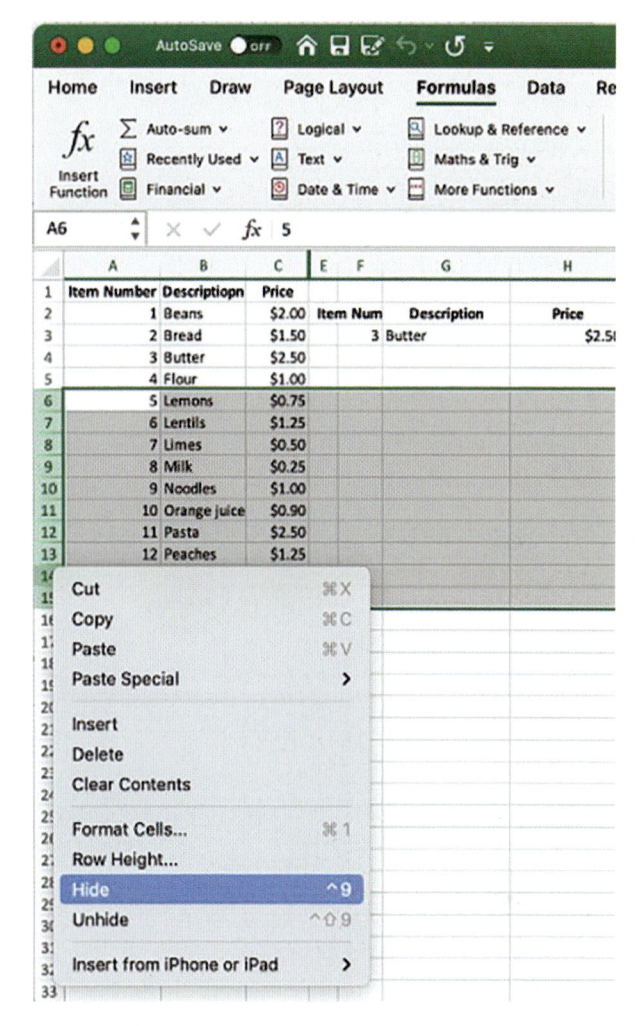

Figure 20.63: Hiding rows or columns

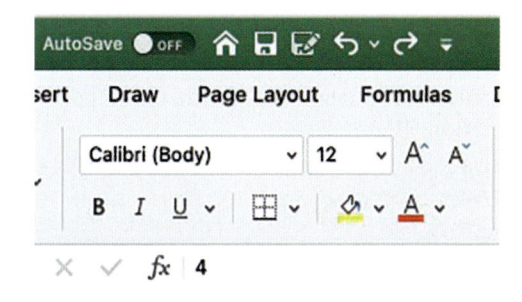

Figure 20.64: Formatting text

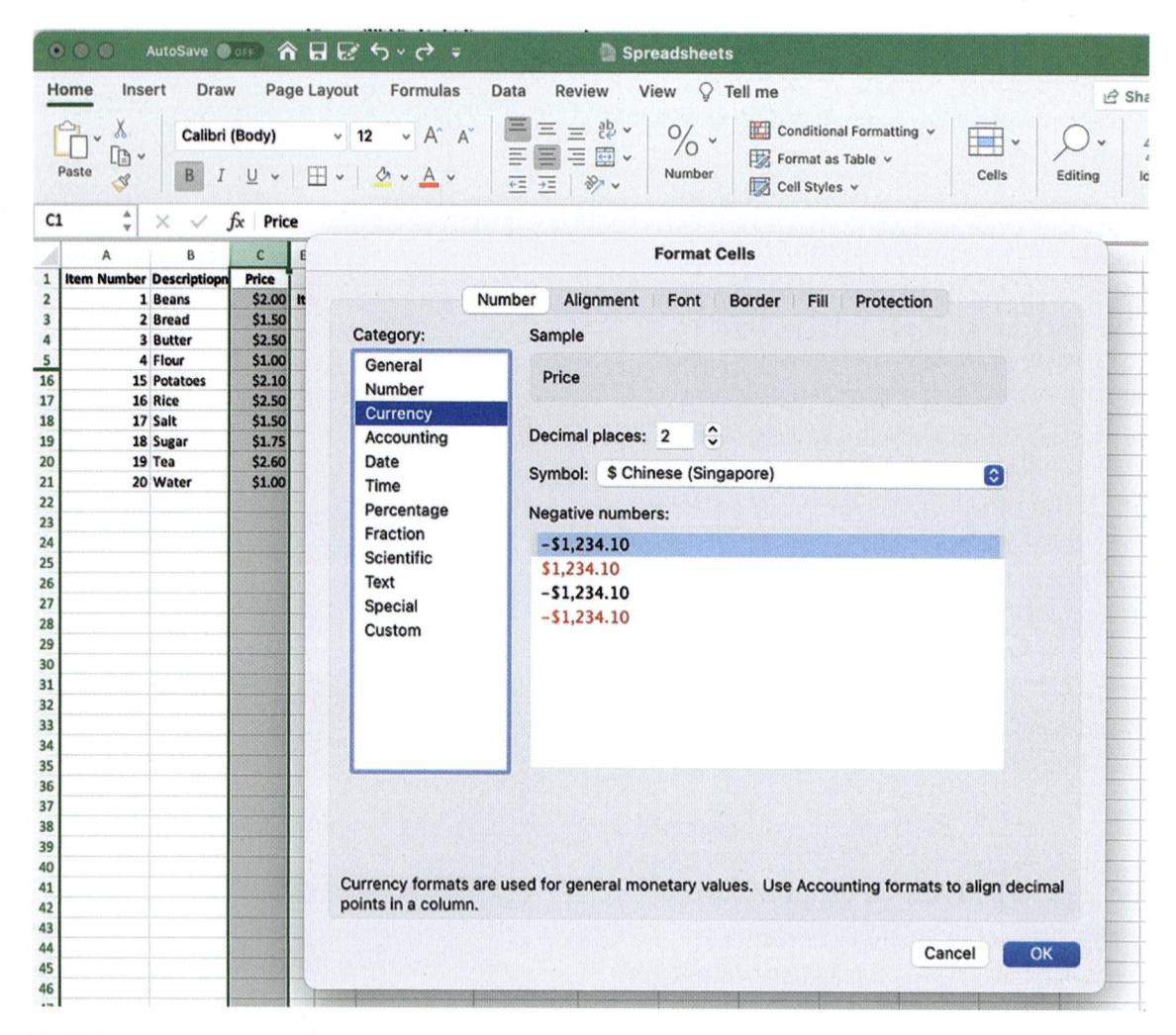

Figure 20.65: Formatting numeric data

The currency symbol, number of decimal places and percentages can be selected from the dialogue box. Some software also have icons for these on the Home ribbon (Figure 20.66).

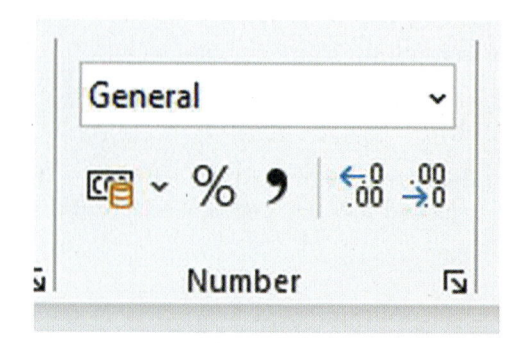

Figure 20.66: Numeric data options on the Home ribbon

20 Spreadsheets

> **ICT IN CONTEXT**
>
> Matt Parker created an algorithm to open digital photographs as spreadsheets. It involves placing all of the numbers that represent the colours in an image into the cells of a spreadsheet. An example is shown in Figures 20.67–68. 
>
> **Figure 20.67:** Digital image 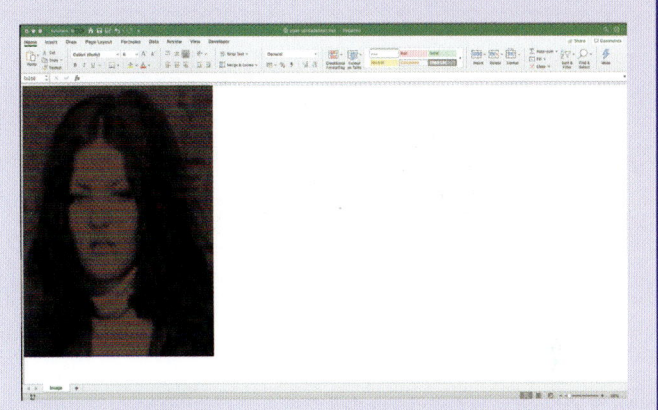
>
> **Figure 20.68:** Image placed in spreadsheet
>
> Upload an image to try it out. You can find the website by using 'Matt Parker spreadsheet' as search terms.

Conditional formatting

Conditional formatting is used to format cells that meet particular criteria. For example, cells with a value greater than a certain number could be given a particular fill.

After the range is highlighted and the Conditional Formatting icon on the Home ribbon is selected, different options for applying rules are given (see Figure 20.69).

The rule can be set. In the example in Figure 20.70 on the next page, cells with a cell value greater than or equal to 70 will be formatted with a light red fill with dark red text.

> **KEY WORD**
>
> **conditional formatting:** changing the appearance of a cell on the basis of specified conditions

Further rules can be applied. In the example in Figure 20.71 on the next page, a second rule to format cells with values greater than 80 is being set and the result of both rules is shown in Figure 20.72 (on the following pages).

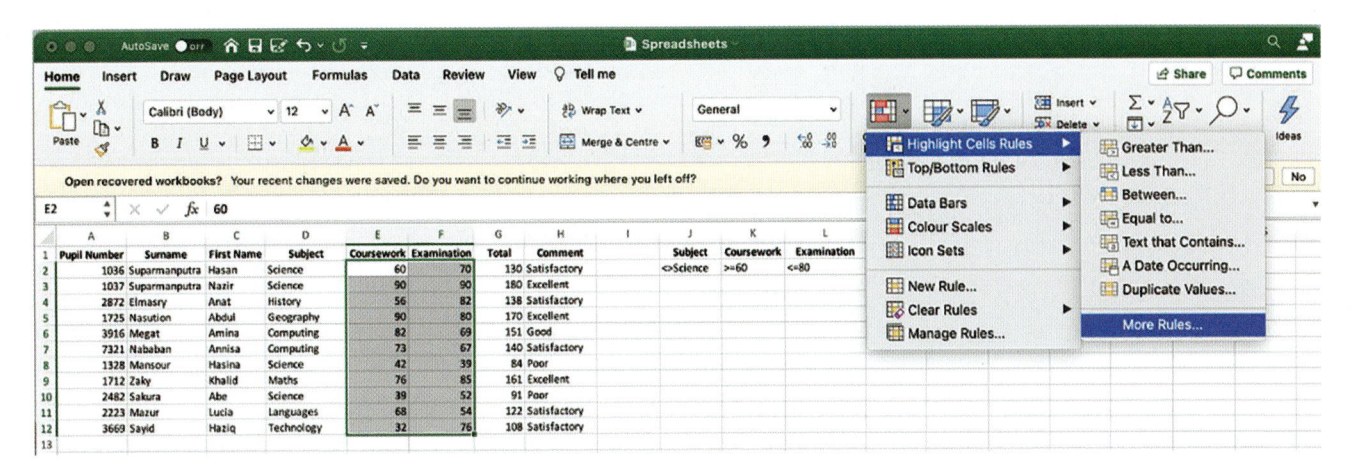

Figure 20.69: Applying conditional formatting

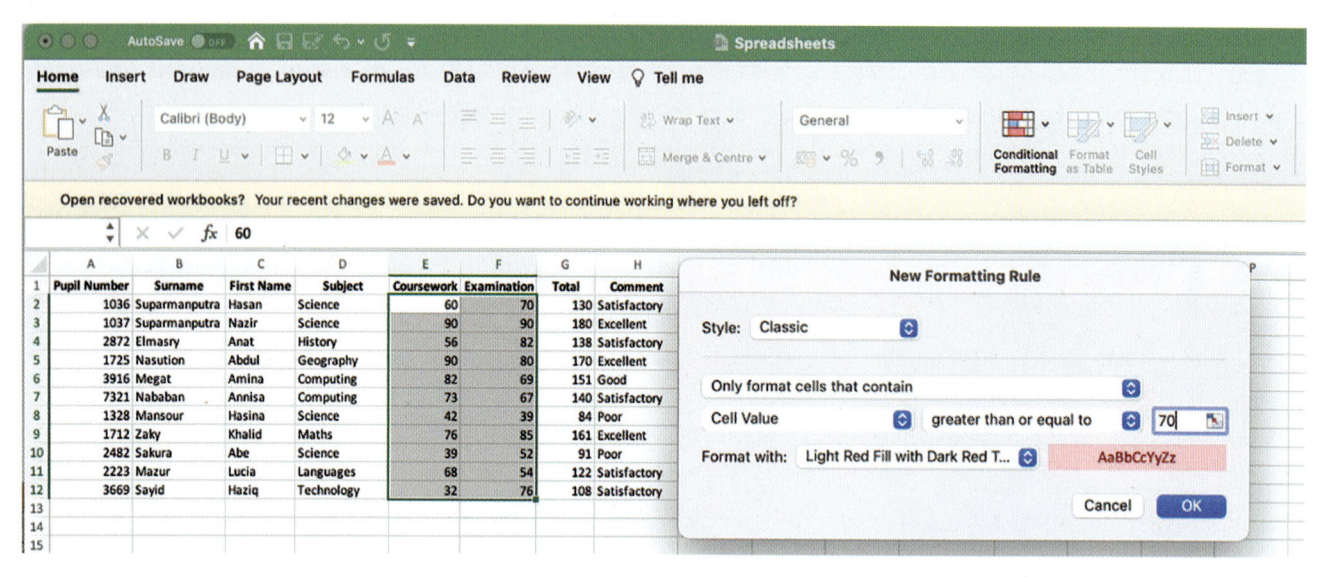

Figure 20.70: Formatting cells with values equal to or greater than 70

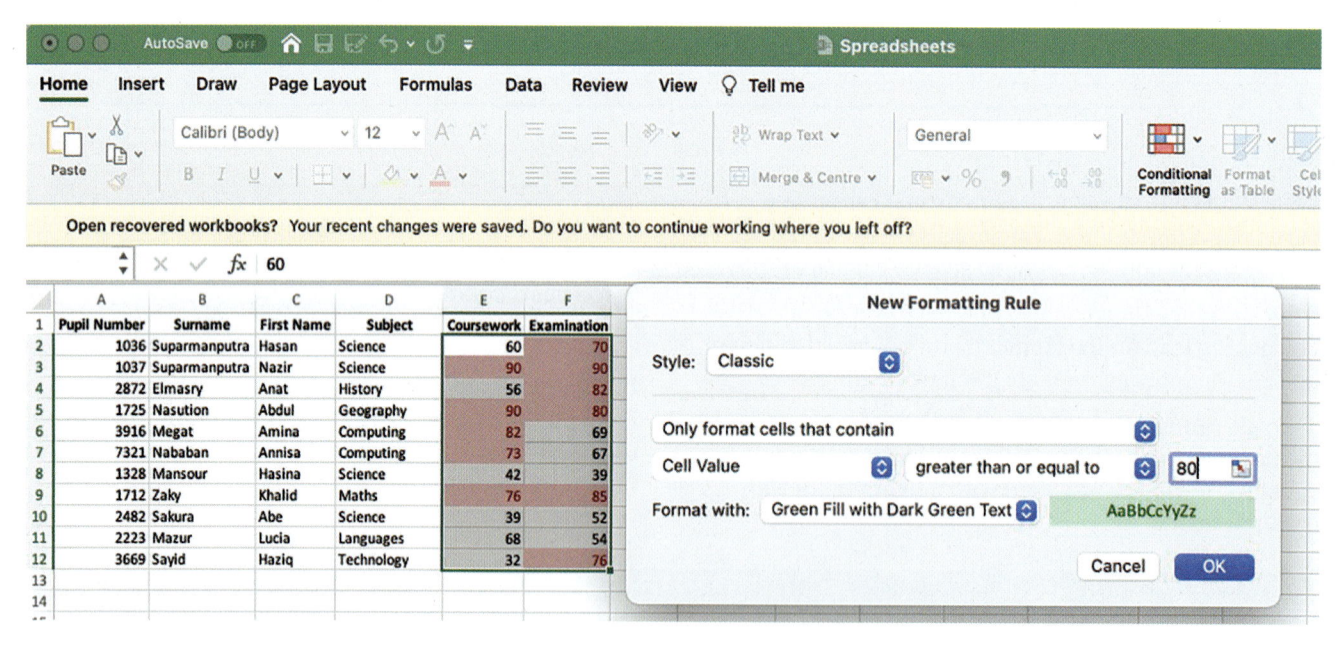

Figure 20.71: Creating a second rule

20 Spreadsheets

If the Managing Rules option is selected from the menu (see Figure 20.73), the rules can be viewed and altered.

The rules can be changed and deleted, and new ones can be added (Figure 20.74).

Set page layout

The page on which the spreadsheet will be printed can be set to a certain paper size and orientation using icons in the Page Layout ribbon (see Figure 20.75 on the next page).

Paper size can be chosen from the Paper Size icon; for information about the different paper sizes, see Chapter 17, Section 17.1 Organise page layout.

Often users will need a spreadsheet to be printed on a certain number of pages. This can be done by selecting the Page Setup icon in the Page Layout ribbon (see Figures 20.76 and 20.78 on the following pages).

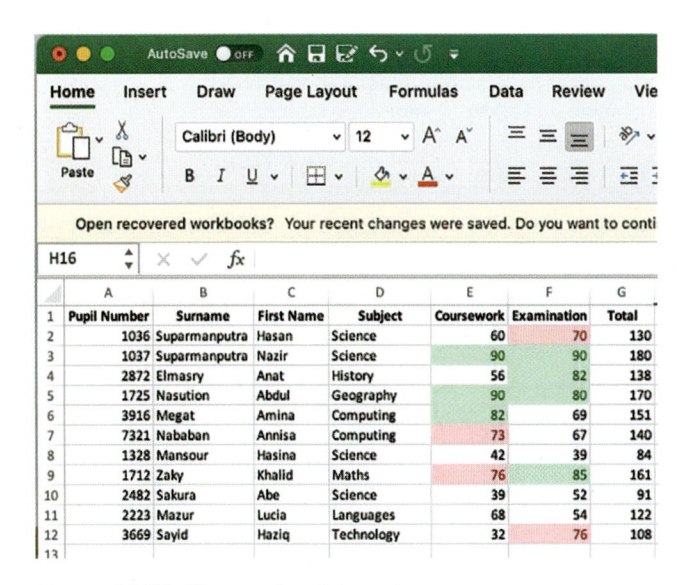

Figure 20.72: The results of the rules

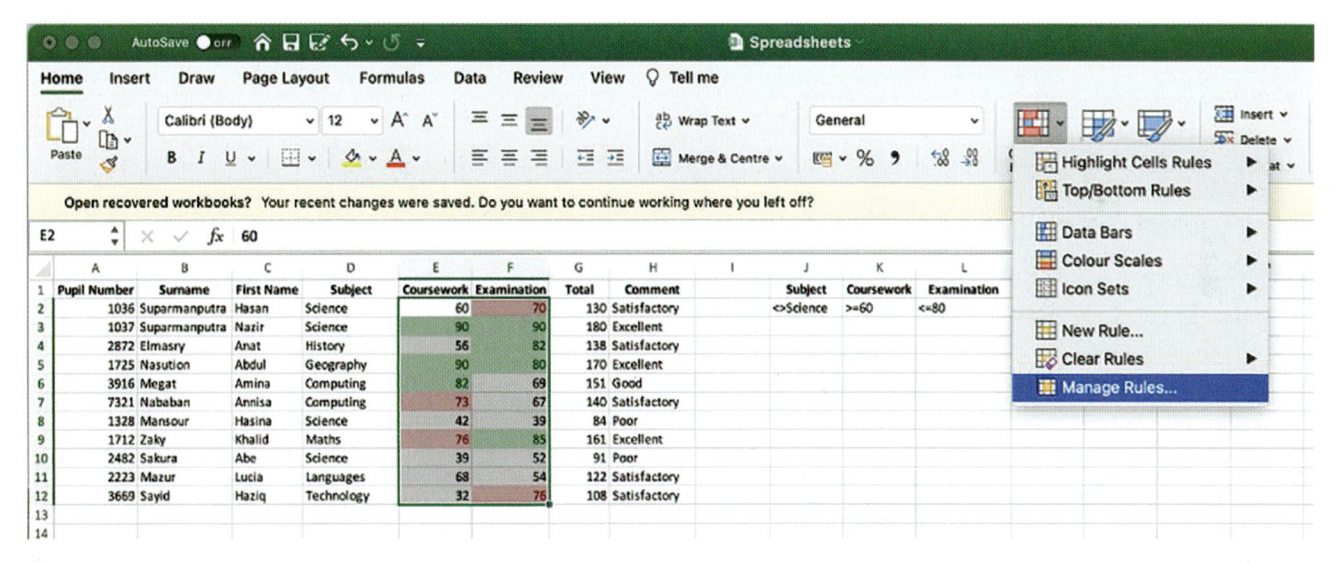

Figure 20.73: Managing the rules

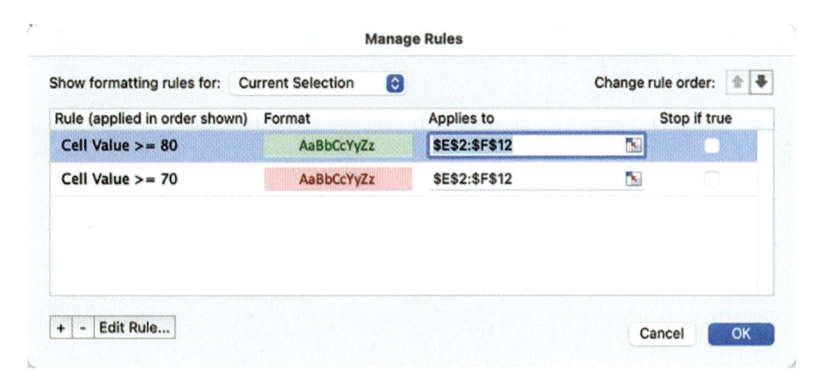

Figure 20.74: The rules that can be changed or deleted

509

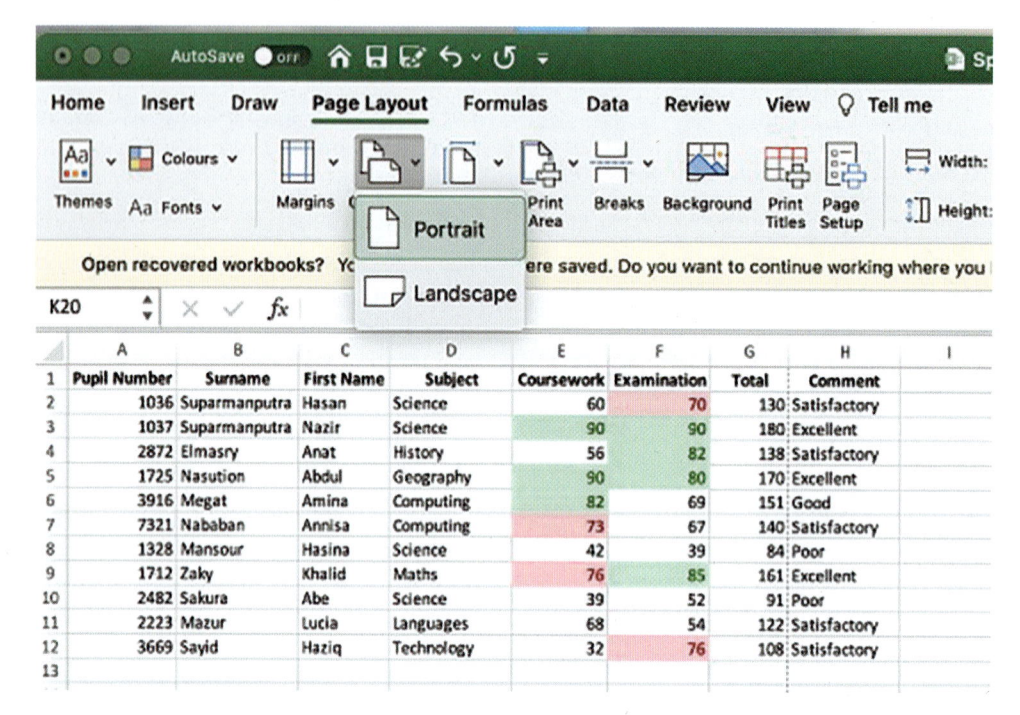

Figure 20.75: Setting page orientation

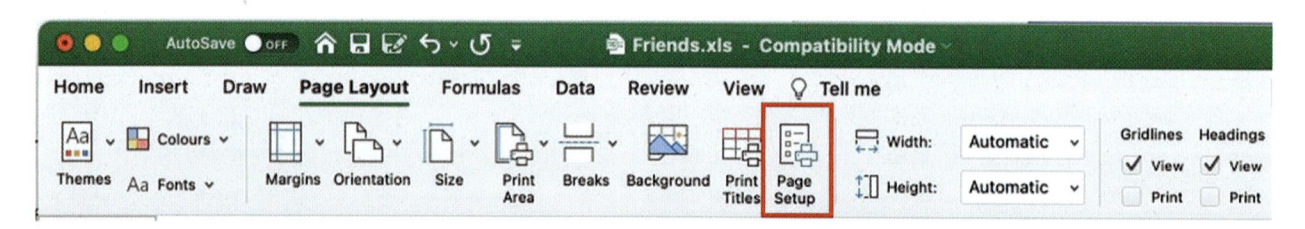

Figure 20.76: The Page Layout ribbon

In some software, there isn't a Page Setup icon, and you have to click on the arrow in the Page Setup area (see bottom right of Figure 20.77).

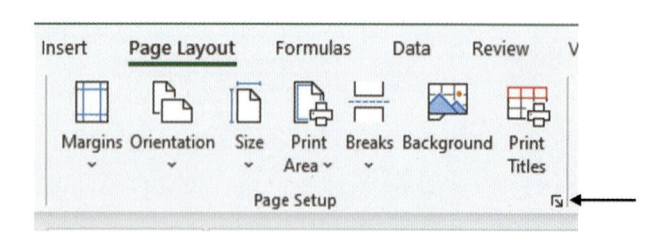

Figure 20.77: The Page Setup area arrow

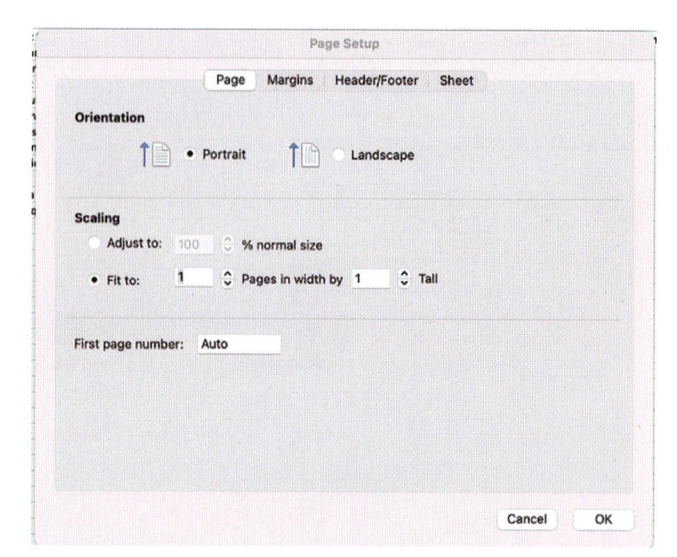

Figure 20.78: Setting the number of pages

The Page Setup dialogue box can also be used to set headers and footers (see Figure 20.79). Suggested ones can be chosen from a drop-down menu or custom ones can be designed.

Once the paper size has been selected, the spreadsheet will have dotted lines showing where page breaks will naturally occur because of the set paper size (see Figure 20.80).

If only a part of the spreadsheet needs to be printed, the print area can be set by highlighting the area and selecting Print Area from the Page Layout ribbon (see Figure 20.81 on the next page).

The row and column headings (Columns A, B, C, etc. and Rows 1, 2, 3, etc.) and gridlines can be turned on and off for both onscreen viewing and printing by selecting the required option from the Page Layout ribbon (see Figure 20.82 on the next page).

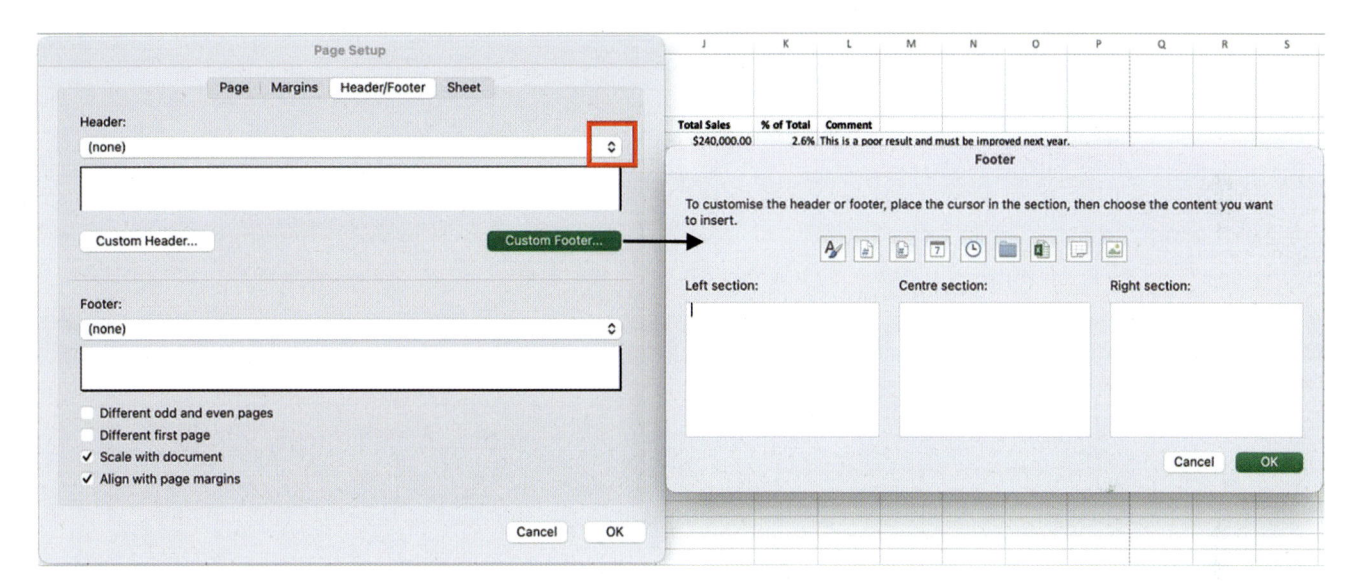

Figure 20.79: Adding headers and footers

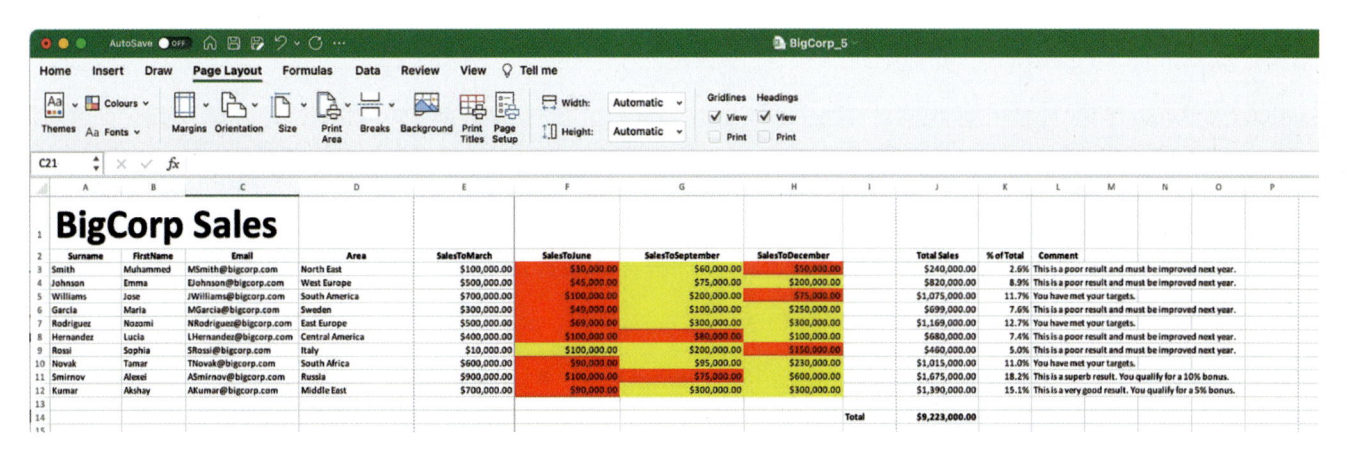

Figure 20.80: Lines showing where page breaks will occur

CAMBRIDGE IGCSE™ ICT: COURSEBOOK

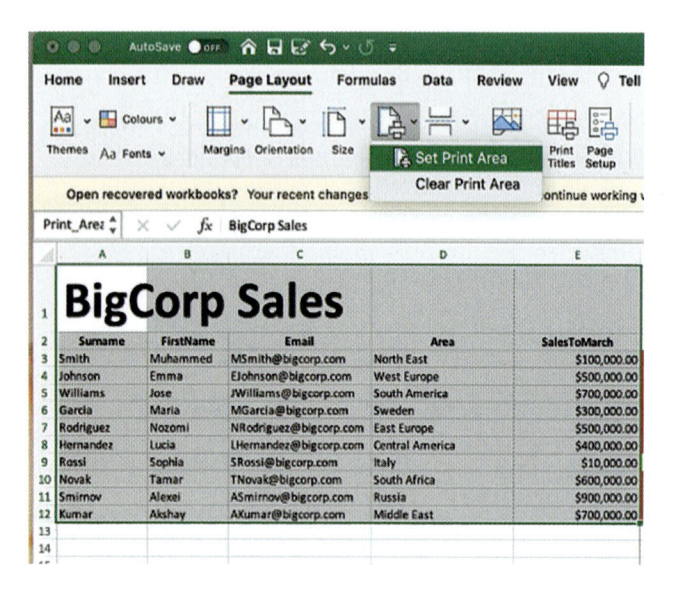

Figure 20.81: Setting the print area

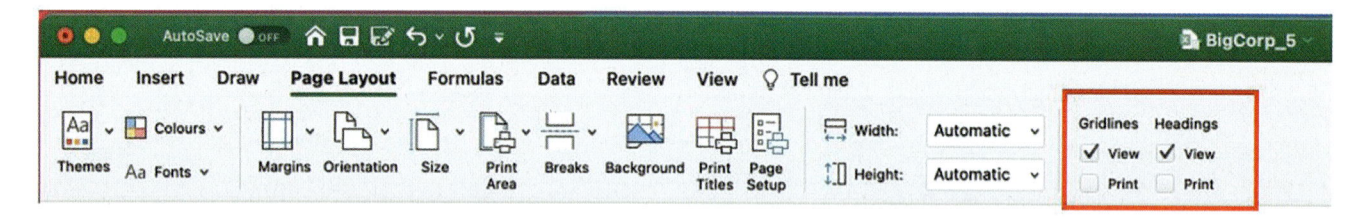

Figure 20.82: Showing and hiding gridlines and headings

> ### WORKED EXAMPLE 20.1
>
> ### SPREADSHEET FORMATTING AND FUNCTIONS
>
> Open *Sales.xlsx* in the spreadsheet software you are using. Edit the document as follows:
>
> 1. Insert a new row at the top of the spreadsheet and enter the title 'Sales for the Year'.
>
>   This should have a font size of 20 pt, be bold and centred across Columns A to I.
>
> 2. In column I add functions to calculate the total sales for each person.
>
> 3. In cell I14 enter a function to calculate the total.
>
> 4. In cell H15 enter the label 'Average' and in cell I15 enter a formula to calculate the average sales per person.
>
> 5. In column I apply formatting so that cells having a Total Sales over $1 000 000 are filled pale red and those below are filled pale blue.
>
> 6. In cells H16 and I16 enter the label 'Maximum' and a function to find the maximum Total Sales.
>
> 7. In cell J16 enter a function to return the Surname and FirstName of the salesperson achieving the maximum Total sales.
>
> 8. Save the spreadsheet as *WorkedExample.xlsx*.

CONTINUED

Step 1

A row can be inserted by selecting row 1, right-clicking and selecting 'Insert'.

The title can be entered, and the font size changed and emboldened.

It can be centred across the columns by using the 'Merge and Centre' command. (See Figure 20.83)

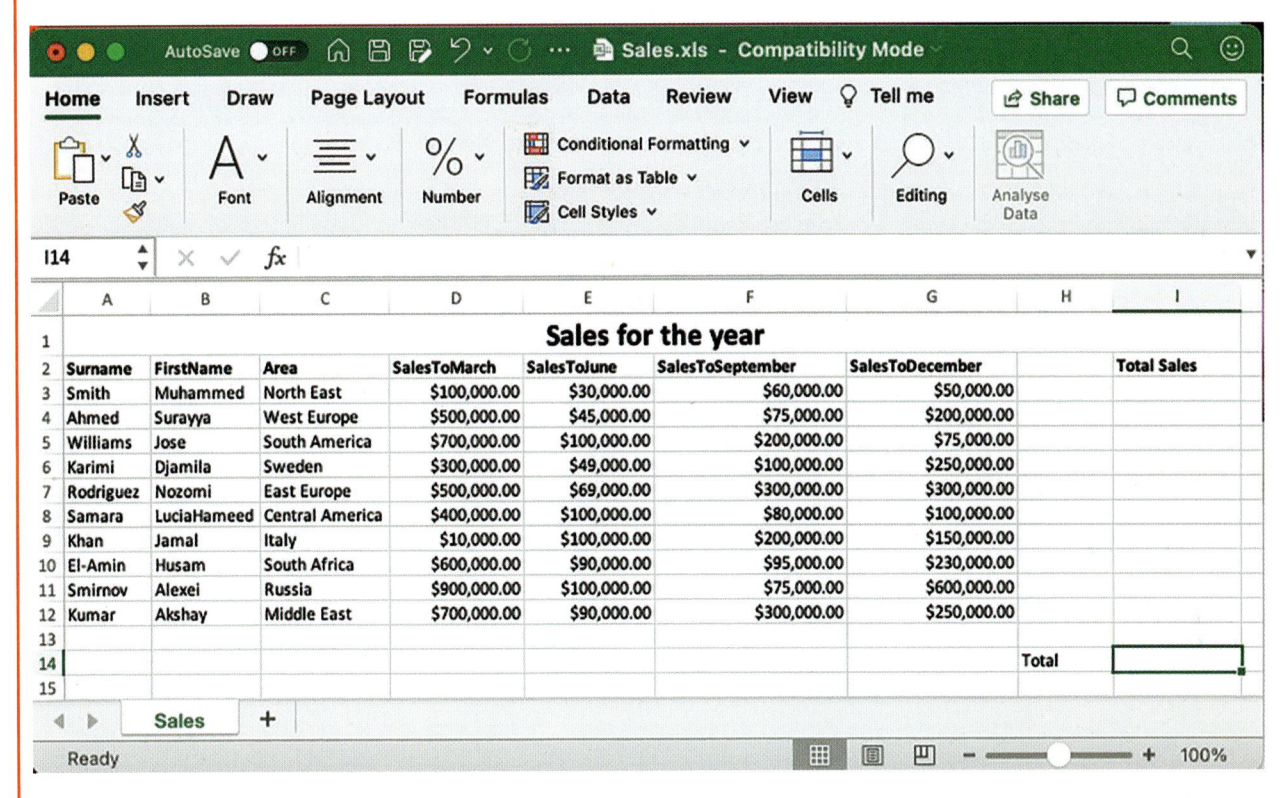

	A	B	C	D	E	F	G	H	I
1				Sales for the year					
2	Surname	FirstName	Area	SalesToMarch	SalesToJune	SalesToSeptember	SalesToDecember		Total Sales
3	Smith	Muhammed	North East	$100,000.00	$30,000.00	$60,000.00	$50,000.00		
4	Ahmed	Surayya	West Europe	$500,000.00	$45,000.00	$75,000.00	$200,000.00		
5	Williams	Jose	South America	$700,000.00	$100,000.00	$200,000.00	$75,000.00		
6	Karimi	Djamila	Sweden	$300,000.00	$49,000.00	$100,000.00	$250,000.00		
7	Rodriguez	Nozomi	East Europe	$500,000.00	$69,000.00	$300,000.00	$300,000.00		
8	Samara	LuciaHameed	Central America	$400,000.00	$100,000.00	$80,000.00	$100,000.00		
9	Khan	Jamal	Italy	$10,000.00	$100,000.00	$200,000.00	$150,000.00		
10	El-Amin	Husam	South Africa	$600,000.00	$90,000.00	$95,000.00	$230,000.00		
11	Smirnov	Alexei	Russia	$900,000.00	$100,000.00	$75,000.00	$600,000.00		
12	Kumar	Akshay	Middle East	$700,000.00	$90,000.00	$300,000.00	$250,000.00		
13									
14								Total	
15									

Figure 20.83: Merged and centred title row

> **CAMBRIDGE IGCSE™ ICT: COURSEBOOK**

CONTINUED

Step 2

In cell I3 a function to calculate the total for Muhammed Smith can be entered (see Figure 20.84).

This is the function, =SUM(D3:G3).

It can then be copied down the column (see Figure 20.98).

Column I should also be formatted for currency.

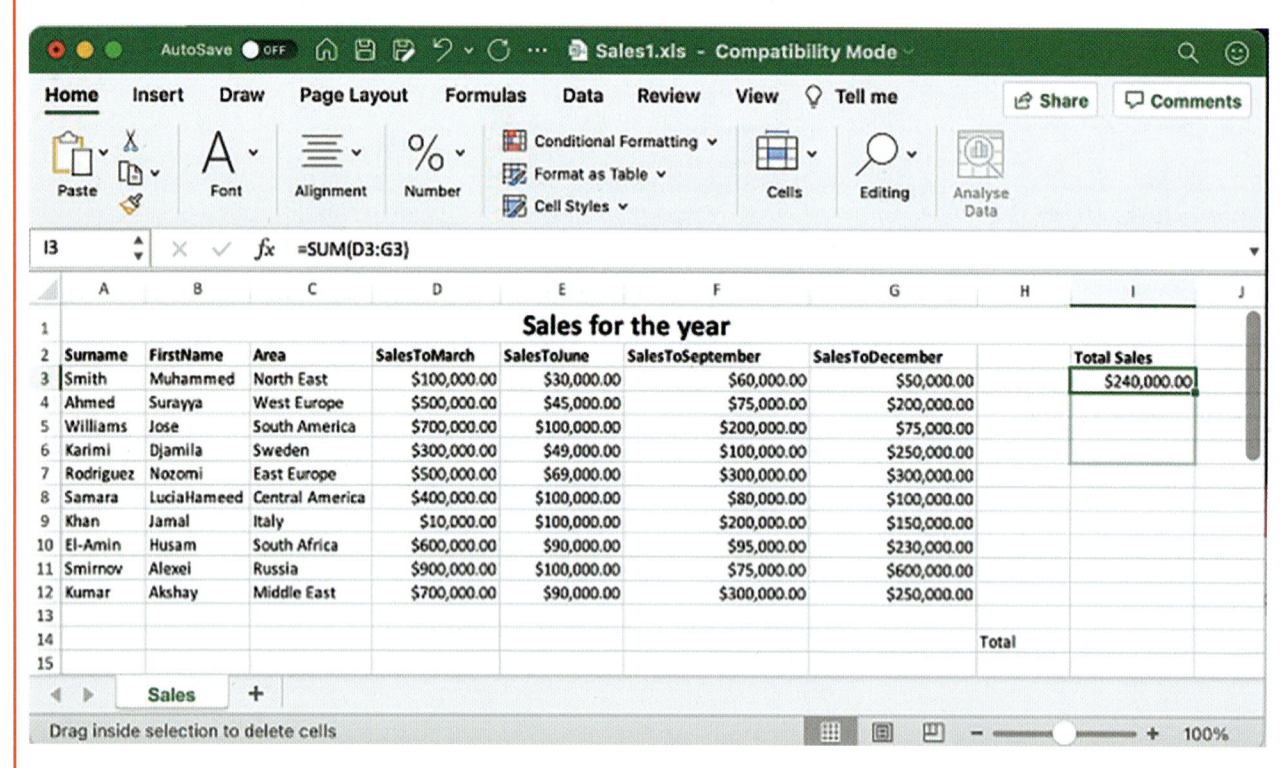

	A	B	C	D	E	F	G	H	I
1					Sales for the year				
2	Surname	FirstName	Area	SalesToMarch	SalesToJune	SalesToSeptember	SalesToDecember		Total Sales
3	Smith	Muhammed	North East	$100,000.00	$30,000.00	$60,000.00	$50,000.00		$240,000.00
4	Ahmed	Surayya	West Europe	$500,000.00	$45,000.00	$75,000.00	$200,000.00		
5	Williams	Jose	South America	$700,000.00	$100,000.00	$200,000.00	$75,000.00		
6	Karimi	Djamila	Sweden	$300,000.00	$49,000.00	$100,000.00	$250,000.00		
7	Rodriguez	Nozomi	East Europe	$500,000.00	$69,000.00	$300,000.00	$300,000.00		
8	Samara	LuciaHameed	Central America	$400,000.00	$100,000.00	$80,000.00	$100,000.00		
9	Khan	Jamal	Italy	$10,000.00	$100,000.00	$200,000.00	$150,000.00		
10	El-Amin	Husam	South Africa	$600,000.00	$90,000.00	$95,000.00	$230,000.00		
11	Smirnov	Alexei	Russia	$900,000.00	$100,000.00	$75,000.00	$600,000.00		
12	Kumar	Akshay	Middle East	$700,000.00	$90,000.00	$300,000.00	$250,000.00		
13									
14								Total	

Figure 20.84: SUM formula entered in cell I3

20 Spreadsheets

CONTINUED

Step 3

The function in cell I14 is =SUM(I3:I12).

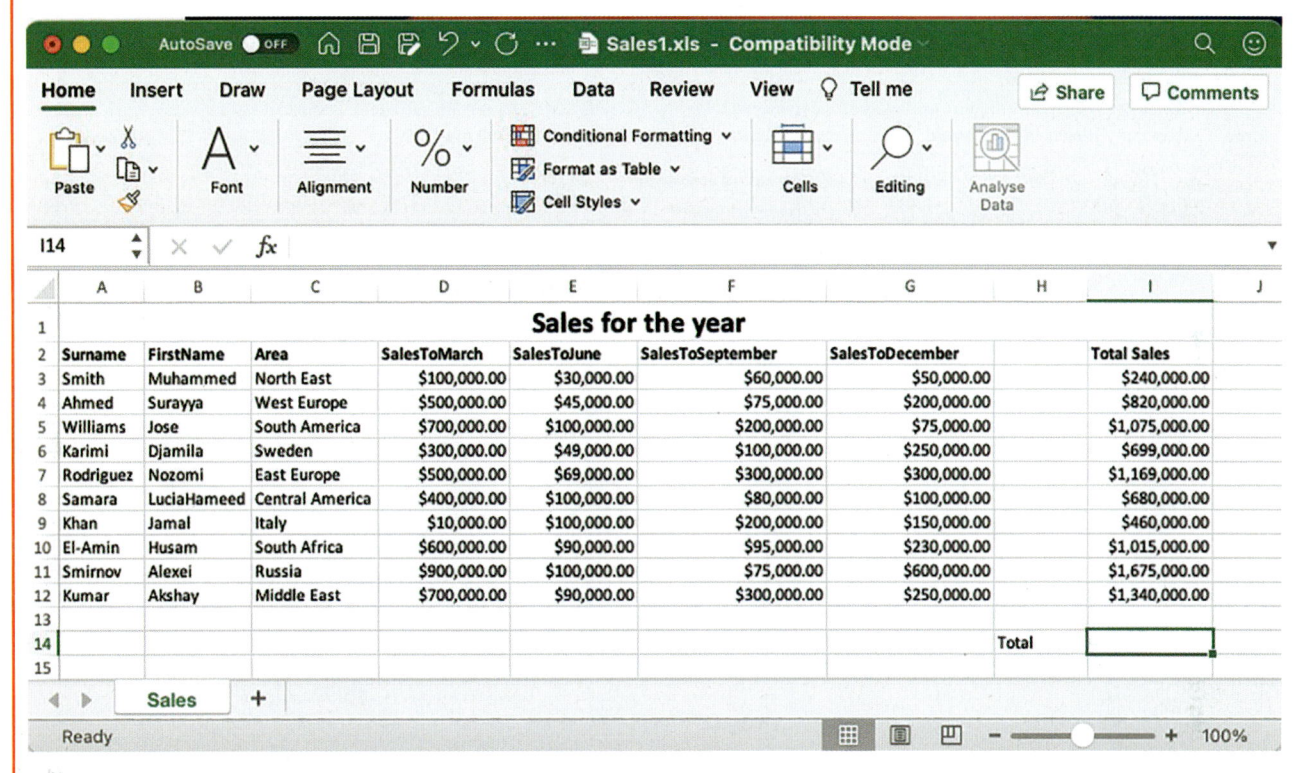

Figure 20.85: SUM formula copied down

CONTINUED

Step 4

The label and formula can be added to cells H15 and I15 (see Figure 20.86).

The formula is =I14/10

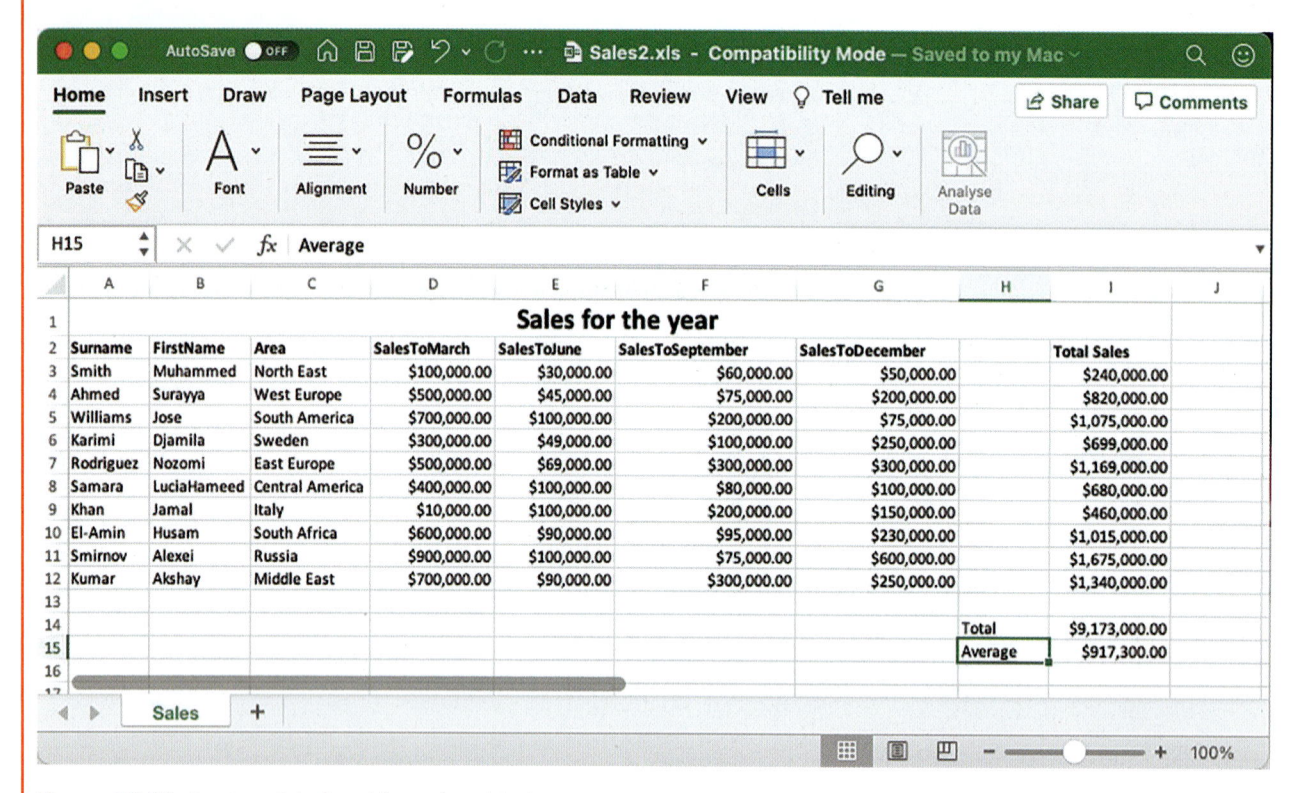

Figure 20.86: Average label and formula added

20 Spreadsheets

CONTINUED

Step 5

Conditional formatting can be applied to column I by setting a new rule (see Figures 20.87–88).

A rule to colour $1 000 000 and above with a pale red fill.

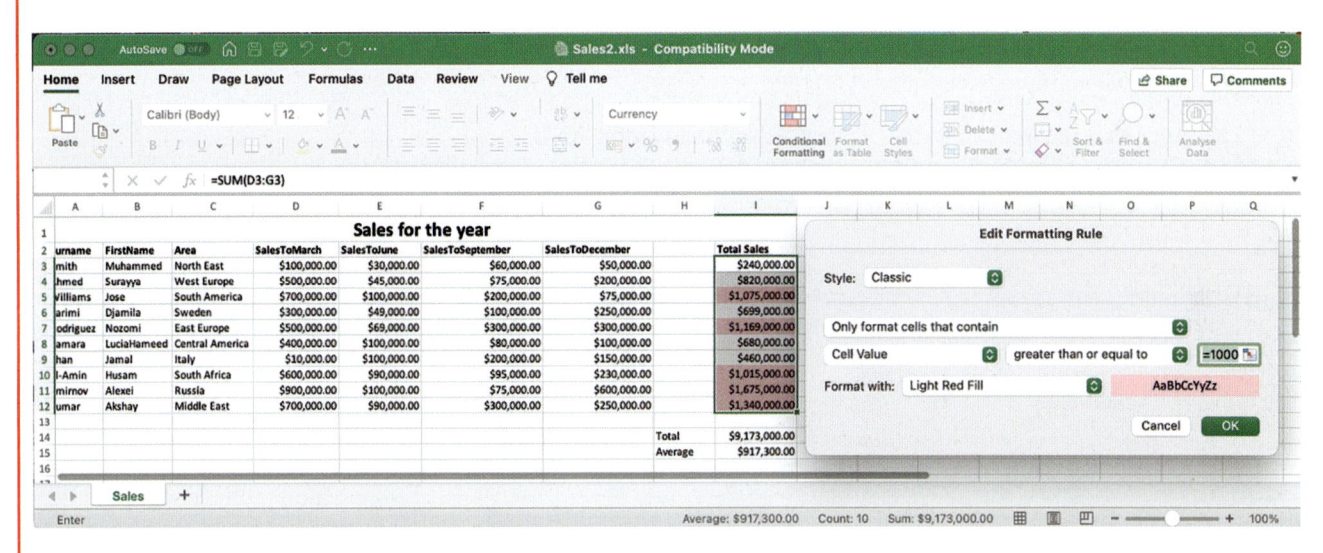

Figure 20.87: Applying conditional formatting

A rule to colour less than $1 000 000 with a pale blue fill.

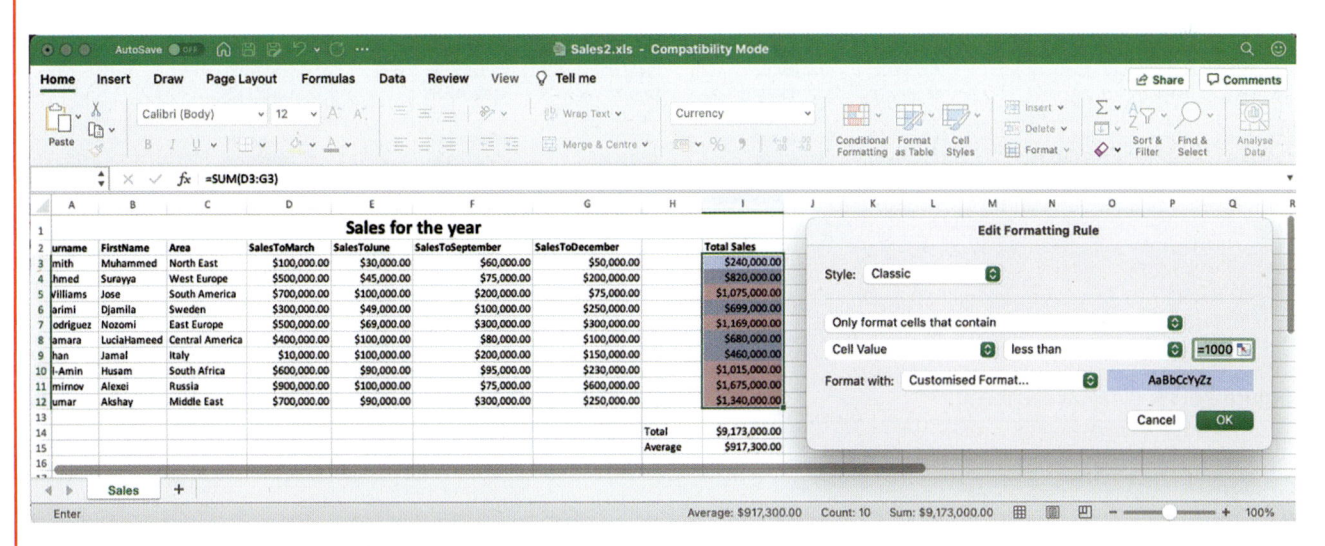

Figure 20.88: Applying second formatting condition

Step 6

The function in I16 will be =MAX(I3:I12).

CONTINUED

Step 7

This can be achieved using the XLOOKUP function.

This will contain:

- The cell with the value to be looked up: I16.
- The range where this can be found: I3: I12.
- The range that the matching rows have to be returned from: A3:B12.

This is =XLOOKUP(I16,I3:I12,A3:B12)

The final spreadsheet should look like Figure 20.89.

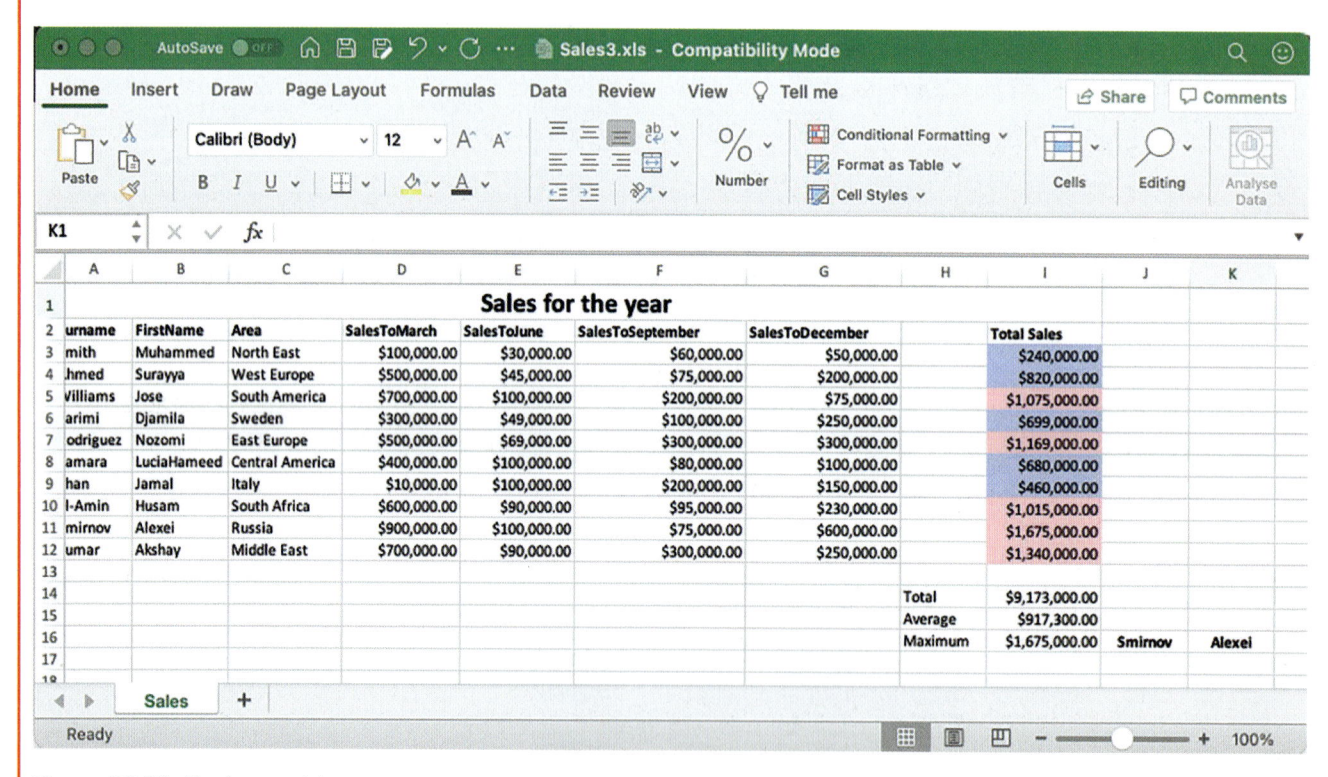

	A	B	C	D	E	F	G	H	I	J	K
1					Sales for the year						
2	urname	FirstName	Area	SalesToMarch	SalesToJune	SalesToSeptember	SalesToDecember		Total Sales		
3	mith	Muhammed	North East	$100,000.00	$30,000.00	$60,000.00	$50,000.00		$240,000.00		
4	hmed	Surayya	West Europe	$500,000.00	$45,000.00	$75,000.00	$200,000.00		$820,000.00		
5	villiams	Jose	South America	$700,000.00	$100,000.00	$200,000.00	$75,000.00		$1,075,000.00		
6	arimi	Djamila	Sweden	$300,000.00	$49,000.00	$100,000.00	$250,000.00		$699,000.00		
7	odriguez	Nozomi	East Europe	$500,000.00	$69,000.00	$300,000.00	$300,000.00		$1,169,000.00		
8	amara	LuciaHameed	Central America	$400,000.00	$100,000.00	$80,000.00	$100,000.00		$680,000.00		
9	han	Jamal	Italy	$10,000.00	$100,000.00	$200,000.00	$150,000.00		$460,000.00		
10	l-Amin	Husam	South Africa	$600,000.00	$90,000.00	$95,000.00	$230,000.00		$1,015,000.00		
11	mirnov	Alexei	Russia	$900,000.00	$100,000.00	$75,000.00	$600,000.00		$1,675,000.00		
12	umar	Akshay	Middle East	$700,000.00	$90,000.00	$300,000.00	$250,000.00		$1,340,000.00		
13											
14								Total	$9,173,000.00		
15								Average	$917,300.00		
16								Maximum	$1,675,000.00	Smirnov	Alexei

Figure 20.89: Final spreadsheet

Step 8

The spreadsheet can now be saved as *WorkedExample.xls*.

Questions

1. *Open Sales.xls* in the spreadsheet software you are using and carry out Tasks 1 to 8.
2. Create a border around range H14:K16.
    - Make all the text bold.
    - Apply a pale yellow fill.

PRACTICAL TASK 20.5

Getting started

1 Explain how you would display the formulae in a spreadsheet rather than their results.

2 With a partner, discuss what is meant by 'conditional formatting'.

Practice

3 Open the spreadsheet *Task3_Challenge.xlsx* you created in Challenge section of Practical Task 20.3.

4 Format the cells in the range F3:M32 so that:
   - They have a green background if the score is less than 55.
   - They have yellow background if the score is between 55 and 69.
   - They have a pink background if they have a value greater than or equal to 70.

5 Add 'Term1 Results 'as a page header.

6 Add the page number in the format page number of total number of pages, e.g. Page 1 of 3.

7 Change the left and right margins to 0.3 inches.

8 Print out your spreadsheet as a PDF file named *Task5*. (Change the printer to 'Print to PDF')

9 Save the spreadsheet as *Task5.xlsx*.

Challenge

10 The printout is not as user friendly as it could be as Subject1 and the Subject1 Scores are on different sheets. Investigate how you can set page breaks and assign them so that this does not happen.

11 Save the spreadsheet as *Task5_Challenge* and print out the spreadsheet as a PDF file named *Task5_Challenge*.

12 It is still not as user friendly as it could be as on Pages 2 and 3, it does not show who the marks are for. Investigate how you can change the settings so that columns B and C will be shown on Pages 2 and 3.

    Check that subjects and their scores have not been separated.

13 Print out the spreadsheet as a PDF file named *Task5_Challenge2*.

REFLECTION

What problems did you encounter when completing the practical tasks in this chapter?
How did you solve them?

> # CAMBRIDGE IGCSE™ ICT: COURSEBOOK

SUMMARY

Spreadsheet models can use formulae and functions to solve real-life problems.
Formulae can be created using cell references; these cell references can be absolute (fixed) or relative.
Arithmetic operators in spreadsheets use the same order of operation as in Mathematics: Brackets, Indices, Division, Multiplication, Addition and Subtraction.
Data can be manipulated using functions built into the spreadsheet software. These functions can also be nested.
Data in spreadsheet models can be sorted and searched using single and multiple criteria.
Data can be selected using a variety of operators, including AND, OR, NOT, >, <, =, <=, >= and < >.
The use of wildcards to represent single or multiple missing characters help to refine searches significantly.
The results from manipulating data in a spreadsheet model can be presented using various formats to make the results fully visible and clear using page orientation, conditional formatting and colour.

EXAM-STYLE QUESTIONS

1 Open spreadsheet *Friends.xls* in your spreadsheet software.

   This is a spreadsheet that Habibah has created to store details of her friends and contacts.

   Instead of looking through it each time she wants some information, she would like to enter first name and be shown all of the information about them.

   a Add a new sheet before the *Friends* worksheet and name it 'Lookup'. [2]

   b On the sheet named Lookup, write an XLOOKUP function to allow Habibah to enter the first name in cell B1 and be shown the person's other information in cells C4 to I4. [3]

   c With the cell with the XLOOKUP function as the active cell, take a screenshot of the worksheet and paste it into a document named *Question1.docx*. [1]

   d Two rows down from the XLOOKUP function, create VLOOKUP functions to achieve the same aim. [3]

   e At first, you may receive error messages. When you have solved the problem and both functions are returning the same results, take screenshots of:
   - The 'LOOKUP worksheet with the first cell with the LOOKUP function as the active cell.
   - The 'Friends' worksheet.
     Paste them into *Question1.docx*. [4]

   f In the 'Lookup' worksheet, when there is nothing entered in the lookup cell, these error messages 'N/A' appear in the cells with the LOOKUP functions.

   Carry out research to find a method to prevent this from happening.

   The cells should be blank when the lookup cell is empty.

   When you have done this, write down the new XLOOKUP function and the first of the VLOOKUP functions in *Question1.docx*. [6]

   g Resave the spreadsheet as *Question1.xlsx*. [1]

> **CONTINUED**
>
> 2 Open *Question2.xlsx* into your spreadsheet software. This spreadsheet was started by a student.
>
>   She has a part-time job selling cups of tea and coffee. The tea is $1.20 per cup and the coffee is $1.90 per cup.
>
>   She is supposed to keep a record of how many cups of each she sells but unfortunately she has been too busy and has lost count but knows that she did not sell more than 100 cups of each.
>
>   She has collected $285.
>
>   a Create and copy formulae to calculate the cost for all of the combinations – i.e. from 1 to 100 of each. [7]
>
>   b Use conditional formatting so that any cell containing $285 can be easily seen.
>
>   Save your completed spreadsheet as *Question2_Complete.xlsx*. [3]
>
>   [Total: 30]

> **SELF-EVALUATION CHECKLIST**
>
> After studying this chapter, think about how confident you are with the different topics.
>
> This will help you to see any gaps in your knowledge and help you to learn more effectively.
>
> You might find it helpful to rate how confident you are for each of these statements when you are revising. You should revisit any sections that you rated 'Needs more work' or 'Getting there'.
>
> | I can … | See section | Needs more work | Getting there | Confident to move on |
> |---|---|---|---|---|
> | create and edit a spreadsheet model | 20.1 | | | |
> | use formulae and functions, using the order of operations | 20.1 | | | |
> | manipulate data by sorting, searching and selecting data | 20.2 | | | |
> | present data by adjusting the display features and setting out page layout | 20.3 | | | |
> | format a spreadsheet | 20.3 | | | |

Chapter 21
Website authoring

IN THIS CHAPTER YOU WILL:

- use the three web development layers: the content, behaviour and presentation layers
- understand and use HTML to create the content layer of a web page
- understand the use of a script language in the behaviour layer of a web page
- understand and use CSS in the presentation layer of a web page.

21 Website authoring

GETTING STARTED

Figure 21.1 shows a simple HTML document layout.

Fit the following descriptions to the elements and tags.

- a   Contains the visible page content.
- b   Contains JavaScript code.
- c   Defines this document to be HTML5.
- d   Contains meta information about the document.
- e   The root element of an HTML page.
- f   Contains style information for the page.

```
 1  <!DOCTYPE html>
 2  <html>
 3
 4      <head>
 5
 6          <style>
 7
 8          </style>
 9
10          <script>
11
12          </script>
13
14      </head>
15
16      <body>
17
18
19      </body>
20
21  </html>
22
```

Figure 21.1: Simple HTML document layout

THE WORLD WIDE WEB

Whatever would we do without it? world wide web. The most important service on the internet. No more websites to browse, no more social media, no more videos and music to stream, no more information instantly at our fingertips. No more online games to play. No more browsing online shops.

The world wide web (www) has not been in existence for long, but it has completely transformed the lives of everyone on the planet. It was first proposed by Tim Berners-Lee in 1989 (see Figure 21.2). In 1990, he created the first successful communication between a computer and a server using HTTP. His first web page went live in 1991.

Figure 21.2: Tim Berners-Lee, the founder of the WWW

The www was designed as a huge resource of documents stored on computers across the world which could be accessed using links called hyperlinks.

He based this design on another brilliant invention – hypertext. This term was first used in 1963 by Ted Nelson and in 1967, Nelson developed the Hypertext Editing System. It was the origin of multimedia and interactivity – click on a link and zoom off to another document or see an image of something you are reading about. Groundbreaking!

Since the early 1990s, the www has developed at an incredible speed and the code in which content is written – HyperText Markup Language (HTML) is now onto its fifth version. Technological developments have also allowed the speed and volume of communications to vastly increase.

The www has had a huge effect on the social and working lives of everyone. These effects have mostly been beneficial. But like all areas of human endeavour, developments can be used for bad as well as good. There are always criminals waiting to exploit new opportunities. Online bullying on social media. Targeted, unwanted adverts. Online fraud. Hacking and data theft. Misinformation. Fake news. Cyber warfare.

> **CONTINUED**
>
> Disappointingly, misuse has happened with all new developments, but Tim Berners-Lee recently launched a global action plan to save the web. His Contract for the Web requires governments, companies and individuals to make real commitments to protect the web from abuse and ensure it benefits humanity and not just individual companies.
>
> **Discussion questions**
>
> Think about your experiences of navigating web pages.
>
> 1 List five attributes of a good web page.
> 2 List five attributes of a bad web page.

21.1 The three web development layers

Website development involves three separate **layers**, or areas of development (coding) that all contribute to the finished web pages and website. They are called layers because the commands or formatting provided by one layer influence those of the others.

Content layer

The **content layer** is what people see when they look at a web page. Content can consist of text, images, videos, tables and links. The function of the content layer is to enter the content and create the structure of a web page using **HTML**.

Behaviour layer

This layer, sometimes also called the **scripting** layer, refers to how web elements will behave when users interact with them. In the **behaviour layer**, users enter **code** to control elements in the web page and how users interact with them. Different **scripting languages** can be used, for example, JavaScript.

Presentation layer

The **presentation**, or style layer refers to the styles that have been applied to the elements of the web pages – how they will appear to users. The function of the presentation layer is to display and format elements within a web page – a little like setting styles in text documents (Chapter 14) or master slides for a presentation (Chapter 19). The styles are assigned using another scripting language called CSS, which stands for Cascading Stylesheets.

> **KEY WORDS**
>
> **layer:** an area of website design, e.g. content, style and behaviour
>
> **content layer:** the text, images, videos, tables and links in the web page
>
> **HTML:** Hyper Text Markup Language is the code you use to create web pages
>
> **script:** a set of computer programming instructions for a computer
>
> **behaviour layer:** an area of website design concerned with how elements interact with each other and with the user
>
> **code:** text written using the commands and syntax of a particular computer language
>
> **scripting language:** a programming language, such as JavaScript, used to create a script to control web elements in the behaviour layer of a web page
>
> **presentation layer:** this is responsible for the appearance or styling of objects on a webpage and is achieved using a cascading stylesheet

21 Website authoring

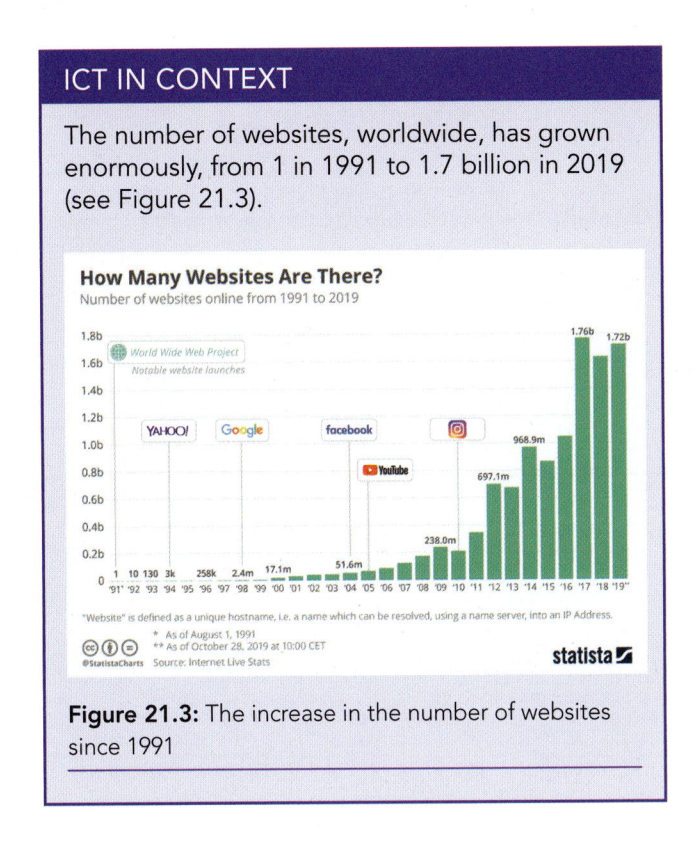

> **ICT IN CONTEXT**
>
> The number of websites, worldwide, has grown enormously, from 1 in 1991 to 1.7 billion in 2019 (see Figure 21.3).
>
> **Figure 21.3:** The increase in the number of websites since 1991

> **KEY WORDS**
>
> **source code editor:** a text editor that is specialised for writing code for software and websites. They use markup colouring, autocompletion and will often highlight if there is an error
>
> **tag:** words or phrases that describe the content of the section of a website

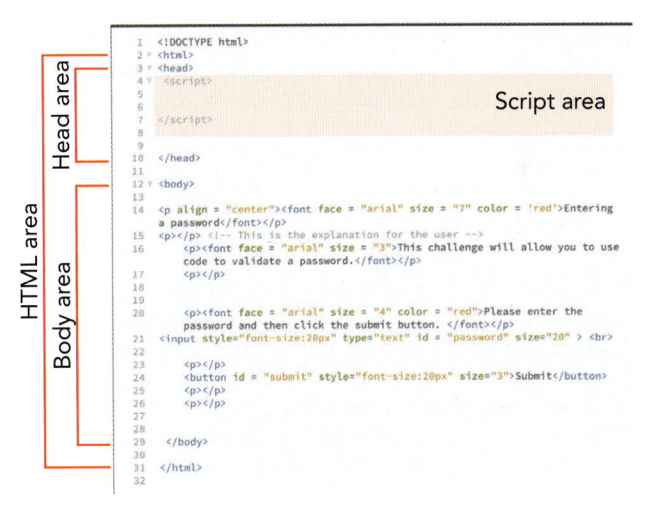

Figure 21.4: A web page in a source code editor

21.2 Creating a web page

When you create a web page, you might be working interchangeably on all three web development layers, but in a web design company, there will probably be different developers working on different ones.

A web page can be created in any type of text software, for example, a word processor or text editor. But there are specialist programs called **source code editors** that assist by making suggestions and highlighting where there is an error.

There are many free source code editors available online.

All web pages need to be saved with an .html extension to inform a browser how the data has to be interpreted.

Using HTML

HTML or Hypertext Markup Language is used to place and position elements on a web page, e.g. headings, text, tables and images. HTML is a type of code that uses **tags**, < >.

As shown in Figure 21.4, a web page design consists of separate sections. Each section is given a name or tag.

There are opening and closing tags – a bit like using brackets. The `<html>` tag tells the browser that the following text should be interpreted as HTML. At the end, at the bottom of the page, is the closing tag `</html>`. The forward slash in the second tag denotes the end of using that tag.

There is an order to get started in HTML. You should always begin with the following tags:

```
<!DOCTYPE html>
<html>
<head>
```

After you've entered the html codes for the head section of your web page, you must end the head section with:

```
</head>
```

It is worth noting that everything that is written in the head section of your html codes is invisible when you open your web page in the browser.

525

To start the second section, the body, of your web page, you should immediately start your next html code:

`<body>`

After you've entered all your html codes for your main body of the web page, you should close the tag with:

`</body>`
`</html>`

At the top of the page is a `<!DOCTYPE>` declaration. This is not an HTML tag but provides information to the browser about what document type to expect. In the latest version of HTML, HTML5, the declaration is `<!DOCTYPE html>`. In earlier versions of HTML, e.g. HTML4, the declaration was more complicated.

Within the head area there is data about the data in the web page such as the title of the document, the author's name and the **character set** to be used. This data, called **metadata**, is not displayed when viewed in a **browser**.

In Figure 21.4, there is an area denoted by `<script></script>`. This contains JavaScript code used to provide interaction and is placed within the head section.

Other areas can be placed within the head such as `<style></style>`, which provides information on styles such as fonts, font colours and font sizes, background colours and shading, etc.

The main area of the web page is contained within the `<body></body>` tags.

> ### ACTIVITY 21.1
>
> Carry out research online, to find a list of HTML tags. Create a poster listing the following tags and explaining their functions:
>
> `<b>`, `<br>`, `<H1>`, `<h2>`, `<hr>`, `<i>`, `<img>`, `<p>`, `<table>`.

The head section of a web page

Title and metadata

The **head** section of a webpage contains metadata, such as, the title of your web page, styles, character set, scripts, links and other data, such as the author's name (see Figure 21.5).

> ### KEY WORDS
>
> **character set:** a list of characters that are valid
>
> **metadata:** data about the HTML document. Metadata is not displayed in the web page
>
> **browser:** a type of software that allows you to go on the internet.
>
> **head:** a container for metadata and scripting language such as CSS

```
1.html
 1    <!DOCTYPE html>
 2    <html>
 3       <head>
 4          <title>A Sample Page</title>
 5          <meta charset = "UTF-8">
 6          <meta name = "keywords" content = "computer, ICT, databases, spreadsheets">
 7          <meta name = "description" content = "ICT, iGCSE">
 8          <meta name = "author" content = "A Person">
 9          <meta name = "viewport" content = "width=device-width, initial-scale=1.0">
10       </head>
11
12       <body>
13
14
15       </body>
16
17    </html>
```

Figure 21.5: Items in the head section

The `<title>` is used to define the title of the page (see Figure 21.6) and must be placed in the head of all HTML documents. The title web element has three important functions:

- They show up in search engines as the titles of web pages.
- They define the title in a web browser.
- When a web page is saved as a favourite, it provides a title for the web page.

Figure 21.6: The title in the tab of the browser window

The metadata is placed in `<meta>` tabs, with the extra text explaining what the metadata is. In Figure 21.5, these are:

- **Charset:** The character set is a list of characters (a, b, c, etc.) each defined by a number. Browsers make use of character sets in order to determine what should be displayed on a web page. There are many character sets but the most popular in HTML5 is UTF-8.

- **keywords:** These are used by search engines to determine what is in a document and return web pages that contain them.
- **description:** Provides information for search engines.
- **viewport:** This is the user's visible area of a web page and obviously it will be smaller on a mobile phone than on a computer. It gives instructions to the browser on how to control the scaling of the page. The first part 'width=device-width' sets the page width to that of the device and the second part 'initial-scale=1.0' sets the zoom level when the page is first loaded.

The head section can also include a command telling the browser how to open new web pages.

`<base target="_blank">` means open pages in new windows.

`<base target="_self">` means open pages in the same window.

The body section of a web page

The **body** section of the code is contained in `<body></body>` tags. This is the content layer discussed in Section 21.1. It contains all the information that will be visible on the web page, including any text, tables, images, videos and sound. All of these are enclosed in tags instructing the web browser on how to interpret or display them.

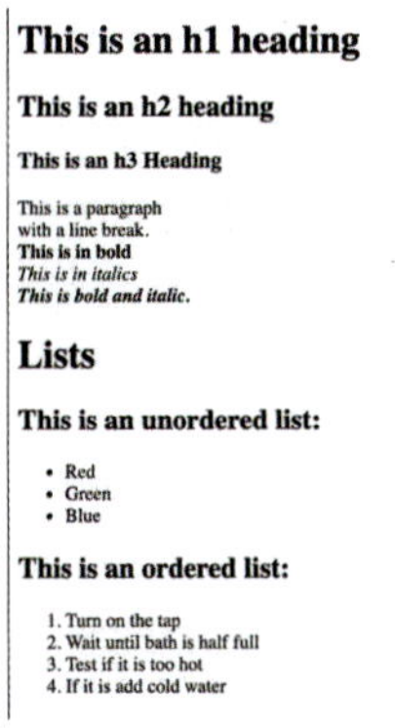

Figure 21.7: HTML in the body section and displayed in a browser

In the example in Figure 21.7, the `<h1>`, `<h2>` and `<h3>` tags have been used for different sized headings.

The `<p> </p>` tag has been used to designate a paragraph and `<br>` for a line break within a paragraph. The `<p> </p>` tags allow you to format different paragraphs in different ways. This is especially important when you are using CSS (see Section 21.3 later in this chapter). `<b> </b>` will give you bold text and `<i> </i>` will give you italics. As you can see in the **bold and italic line**, you can use as many text enhancements as you wish. Just remember to close each one when that section of text is finished.

The `<ul>` and `<ol>` tags have been used for *u*nordered *l*ists, which use bullets, and *o*rdered *l*ists, which use numbers. Each item in both of the lists has an `<li>` (*l*ist *i*tem) tag.

Hyperlinks, bookmarks and anchors

A **hyperlink** is any image, icon, text or item that, when clicked on, takes the user to another web page, an email link or a file on their computer. The user does not need to know the exact URL of each web page you want to see; the hyperlink has this web address in the background and will take you there if you click on it.

All hyperlinks have a source (where it will go from) and a destination (the place it will take you to).

Hyperlink sources can start on documents, such as a word processing document or a presentation you are working on, and take you to a destination within the same document or to somewhere on the web. Alternatively, they can start from the web and refer you to other documents.

A **bookmark** is a type of hyperlink. It is a quick link to another location on the same web page (especially if you have a very long web page that is not all visible on the screen at the time you might wish to view it). It can also link to another web page or to another file saved somewhere other than the same web page.

> ### KEY WORDS
>
> **body:** the content layer that defines the document's body
>
> **hyperlink:** either text, an image or part of an image that is a link to another item or web page
>
> **bookmark:** a named anchor at a specific place on a web page

An **anchor** helps a user navigate a website or between websites. It is a tag within a page's HTML that you can create a link to – like bookmarks in word documents we looked at in Chapter 17, Section 17.4 Navigation. You can use anchors if you want a user to go to another part of the page or to other pages.

Links

The basis of the **world wide web** are hyperlinks, which allow users to jump from one web page or website to another. Figure 21.8 shows the code for a web page with links.

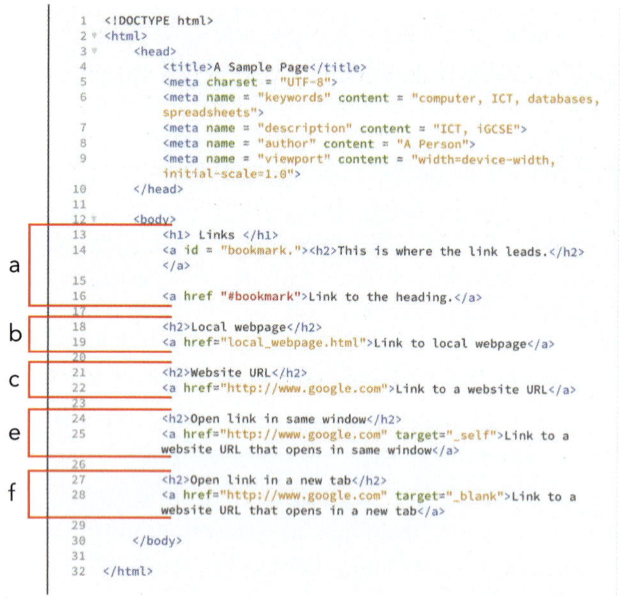

```
 1   <!DOCTYPE html>
 2   <html>
 3     <head>
 4       <title>A Sample Page</title>
 5       <meta charset = "UTF-8">
 6       <meta name = "keywords" content = "computer, ICT, databases,
             spreadsheets">
 7       <meta name = "description" content = "ICT, iGCSE">
 8       <meta name = "author" content = "A Person">
 9       <meta name = "viewport" content = "width=device-width,
             initial-scale=1.0">
10     </head>
11
12     <body>
13       <h1> Links </h1>
14       <a id = "bookmark."><h2>This is where the link leads.</h2>
15       </a>
16       <a href "#bookmark">Link to the heading.</a>
17
18       <h2>Local webpage</h2>
19       <a href="local_webpage.html">Link to local webpage</a>
20
21       <h2>Website URL</h2>
22       <a href="http://www.google.com">Link to a website URL</a>
23
24       <h2>Open link in same window</h2>
25       <a href="http://www.google.com" target="_self">Link to a
             website URL that opens in same window</a>
26
27       <h2>Open link in a new tab</h2>
28       <a href="http://www.google.com" target="_blank">Link to a
             website URL that opens in a new tab</a>
29
30     </body>
31
32   </html>
```

Figure 21.8: Hyperlinks

There are several different types of links in the HTML. All of them use the `<a></a>` tag (or anchor tag), which defines the target of the link.

a   Link to items on the same page

An element on the page must be formatted as a target. This is called the bookmark.

`<a id = "bookmark."><h2>This is where the link leads.</h2></a>`

The 'id' tag is used to identify the element to be jumped to. In this example the target is given the id "bookmark" but it could be any name.

The link to jump to the target is:

`<a href "#bookmark">Link to the heading.</a>`

A # symbol is placed in front of the target id.

b   Link to a locally stored web page

These links will find pages within the same folder as the page with the link (usually on the same website).

`<a href="local_webpage.html">Link to local webpage</a>`

c   Link to a website using its URL

This will link to a specific website **URL** (usually another website).

`<a href="http://www.google.com">Link to a website URL</a>`

> ### KEY WORDS
>
> **anchor:** a type of hyperlink that will take you to a specific part of a web page
>
> **world wide web:** a way of accessing information using the internet using HTTP
>
> **URL:** the unique web address of every page on the world wide web

Open in the same or a new window/tab

The 'target' option can be used to define whether the target will open in the same window/tab or in a new one.

d   In the same window/tab

`target = "_self"` is used.

`<a href="http://www.google.com" target="_self">Link to a website URL that opens in same window</a>`

e   In a new window/tab

`target="_blank"` is used.

`<a href="http://www.google.com" target="_blank">Link to a website URL that opens in a new tab</a>`

f   In a specified window/tab

The target can be made to open in a window/tab that is already open.

To do this the window/tab has to be given a name. This can be done using a scripting language such as JavaScript.

Link to send an email to a specified address

This isn't shown in Figure 21.8, but a link can be provided to send an email to a specified address.

`<a href = mailto:somebody@somewhere.com>Send me an email.</a>`

When a user clicks on this link, their email program will open with a new email already addressed.

Comments

If you want to make a comment, to explain what the HTML code is intended to do, you place it between <!-- at the start and --> at the end.

`<!--This is a comment-->`

> **ACTIVITY 21.2**
>
> In small groups, make a list of all the things you place in web pages. Categorise them into the following groups: text, images, media, links.

PRACTICAL TASK 21.1

Getting started

On paper:

1. Show how you would make 'My Document' the title of the web page and state the section in which it should be placed.

2. Show how you would create a paragraph with the following text:

   'This is the first paragraph'.

Practice

3. Create a new web page and save it as *Task1.html*.

4. Set the title of the document as 'Task one'.

5. Use the correct tags to show the content of Figure 21.9 at the start of the document.

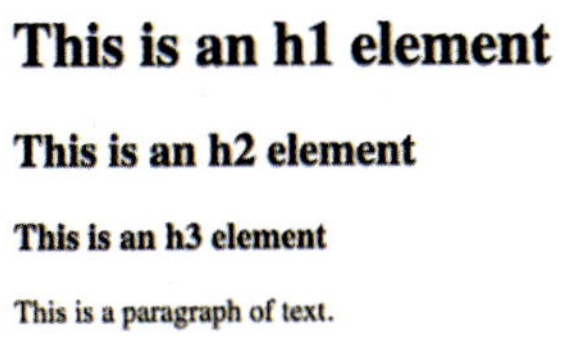

   # This is an h1 element
   ## This is an h2 element
   ### This is an h3 element
   This is a paragraph of text.

   Figure 21.9: Heading and paragraph text

6. Under this create the unordered and ordered lists shown in Figure 21.10.

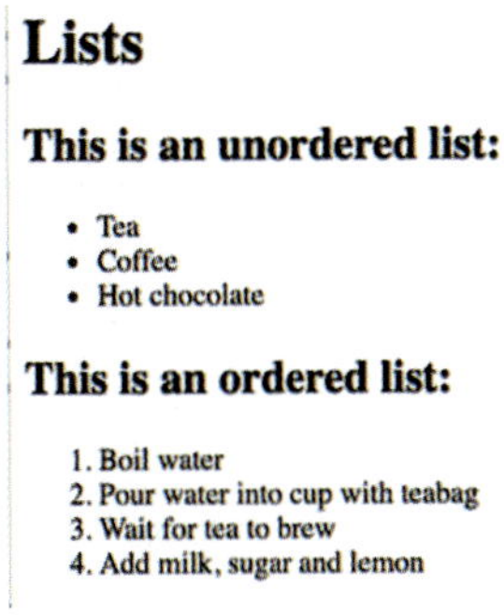

   ## Lists

   This is an unordered list:
   - Tea
   - Coffee
   - Hot chocolate

   This is an ordered list:
   1. Boil water
   2. Pour water into cup with teabag
   3. Wait for tea to brew
   4. Add milk, sugar and lemon

   Figure 21.10: Lists

CONTINUED

7 Add the heading 'Links' and create the types of links shown in Figure 21.11.

Links

Local webpage

Link to local webpage

Website URL

Link to a website URL

Open link in same window

Link to a website URL that opens in same window

Open link in a new tab

Link to a website URL that opens in a new tab

Figure 21.11: Links

The local webpage link should be to *local_webpage.html* which is supplied with this coursebook.

The external links should be to a website of your choice.

8 Save the file.

Challenge

At the end of a document add `<h2>Section 2</h2>`.

9 Bookmark this section.

10 In the Links section add a link to Section 2 (see Figure 21.12).

Bookmark

Jump to section 2

Figure 21.12: Bookmark

11 Add a link in Section 2 to jump back to the Links section.

12 Save the document as *Task1_Challenge.html*.

21 Website authoring

Tables

Tables are an excellent way of ordering and presenting information because they provide a structure into which elements can be placed. They are widely used in websites. The tag for defining a table is `<table> </table>`.

Within the table:

- The header of a group of table cells is defined by the `<th> </th>` tag.
- Rows are defined by the `<tr> </tr>` tag.
- Cells are defined by the `<td> </td>` tag.

Columns are defined by the number of cells in each row. There are usually the same number in each row although some cells can span more than one column.

The code shown in Figure 21.13 will create a simple table with four columns and three rows and Figure 21.14 shows how it will appear in a browser.

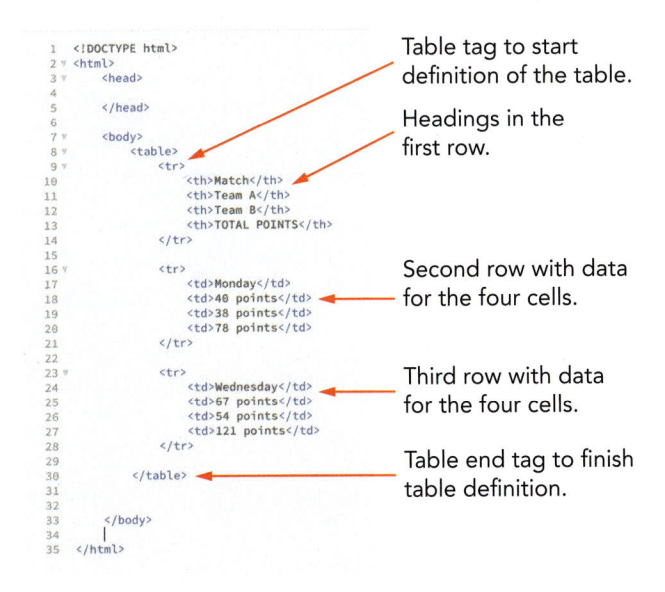

```
1  <!DOCTYPE html>
2  <html>
3    <head>
4
5    </head>
6
7    <body>
8      <table>
9        <tr>
10         <th>Match</th>
11         <th>Team A</th>
12         <th>Team B</th>
13         <th>TOTAL POINTS</th>
14       </tr>
15
16       <tr>
17         <td>Monday</td>
18         <td>40 points</td>
19         <td>38 points</td>
20         <td>78 points</td>
21       </tr>
22
23       <tr>
24         <td>Wednesday</td>
25         <td>67 points</td>
26         <td>54 points</td>
27         <td>121 points</td>
28       </tr>
29
30     </table>
31
32
33   </body>
34
35 </html>
```

- Table tag to start definition of the table.
- Headings in the first row.
- Second row with data for the four cells.
- Third row with data for the four cells.
- Table end tag to finish table definition.

Figure 21.13: HTML code for creating a table

Match	Team A	Team B	TOTAL POINTS
Monday	40 points	38 points	78 points
Wednesday	67 points	54 points	121 points

Figure 21.14: The code interpreted by a browser

As the code in Figure 21.13 illustrates, it is fairly easy to see the three separate rows (denoted by `<tr></tr>`) with the four cells that make up the columns.

This is a pretty basic table but it can be improved by using different **attributes** to improve its appearance.

KEY WORD

attributes: an attribute is an additional piece of information about an HTML element

These attributes are:

- Width of the table relative to the window:

  `width = "1"`

- Height of the rows and cells:

  `height = "1"`

- Borders around the table and the cells:

  `border = "1"`

- Alignment within cells:

  `alignment = ""`

  (NB you can insert left, centre or right for alignment)

- Spanning columns and rows:

  `colspan = "1"`

  `rowspan = "1"`

(Note: the number 1 can be replaced by any number in the examples above.)

Width and border

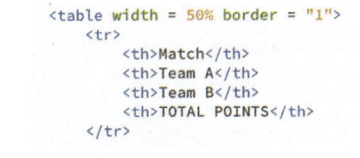

In the top line of the code in Figure 21.15, you can see that, in the `<table>` tag, the width of the table is set to 50% and the border is set to '1'. The greater the number of the border, the thicker it is.

```
<table width = 50% border = "1">
  <tr>
    <th>Match</th>
    <th>Team A</th>
    <th>Team B</th>
    <th>TOTAL POINTS</th>
  </tr>
```

Match	Team A	Team B	TOTAL POINTS
Monday	40 points	38 points	78 points
Wednesday	67 points	54 points	121 points

Figure 21.15: The attributes for width and border

In Figure 21.15, the table is half the size of the webpage, or 50%. The width can be set as a percentage of the whole or as a certain size. The units used are px which

531

stands for pixels. Therefore a width of 50px would be 50 pixels.

Tables aren't the tags that can contain size. Table cells can be defined by either px or percentage in the same way.

Row heights

Information about the height of the rows are placed in the `<tr>` tags (see Figure 21.16).

```
<table width = 50% border = "1">
    <tr height = "50px">
        <th>Match</th>
        <th>Team A</th>
        <th>Team B</th>
        <th>TOTAL POINTS</th>
    </tr>

    <tr height = "30px">
        <td>Monday</td>
        <td>40 points</td>
        <td>38 points</td>
        <td>78 points</td>
    </tr>

    <tr height = "20px">
        <td>Wednesday</td>
        <td>67 points</td>
        <td>54 points</td>
        <td>121 points</td>
    </tr>

</table>
```

Match	Team A	Team B	TOTAL POINTS
Monday	40 points	38 points	78 points
Wednesday	67 points	54 points	121 points

Figure 21.16: Rows of different heights

The units for the row heights are in pixels (px).

Alignment

In the code in Figure 21.17, the headings have been centre aligned (notice the spelling is 'center') and the numbers have been right-aligned. This information in Figure 21.17 has the alignment attribute in the `<th>` and the `<td>` tags. However, if you wanted the whole row to be aligned the same way (e.g. right), you could place align = "right" in the table row tag `<tr>`; if you wanted the whole table aligned the same way, you could place the attribute in the `<table>` tag.

```
<table width = 50% border = "1">
    <tr height = "50px">
        <th align = "center">Match</th>
        <th align = "center">Team A</th>
        <th align = "center">Team B</th>
        <th>TOTAL POINTS</th>
    </tr>

    <tr height = "30px">
        <td>Monday</td>
        <td align = "right">40 points</td>
        <td align = "right">38 points</td>
        <td align = "right">78 points</td>
    </tr>

    <tr height = "20px">
        <td>Wednesday</td>
        <td align = "right">67 points</td>
        <td align = "right">54 points</td>
        <td align = "right">121 points</td>
    </tr>

</table>
```

Match	Team A	Team B	TOTAL POINTS
Monday	40 points	38 points	78 points
Wednesday	67 points	54 points	121 points

Figure 21.17: Alignment within cells

Table headings in HTML are formatted to be bold and centred by default. But the align attribute can move the heading to be left or right.

Table header

A table can be given a header or caption using the `<caption>` tag.

```
<table>
    <caption> Match results and points
    </caption>
```

Would place 'Match results and points' above the table (see Figure 21.18).

Match results and points			
Match	Team A	Team B	TOTAL POINTS
Monday	40 points	38 points	78 points
Wednesday	67 points	54 points	121 points

Figure 21.18: The table with a caption

Spanning of columns and rows

Often a heading may need to span more than one column or more than one row.

The `rowspan` attribute allows the data to span a certain number of rows; for example:

`<td rowspan = "2">`

would create a cell that is two rows deep.

The `colspan` attribute allows data to span a certain number of columns; for example:

`<td colspan = "2">`

would create a cell that is two columns wide.

The code shown in Figure 21.19, shows how they are both used and Figure 21.20 shows how it would appear in a browser.

There are other style improvements that can be made to tables, but they cannot be done with HTML. They are done using CSS, which is covered in the next section.

```
1  <!DOCTYPE html>
2  <html>
3      <head>
4          <title>Task Two</title>
5
6      </head>
7      <body>
8          <table width=75% border="1">
9              <tr height=50px>
10                 <th align = "center"> Week</th>
11                 <th align = center>Day</th>
12                 <th align = center>Revenue</th>
13             </tr>
14
15             <tr>
16                 <td rowspan="5">Week 1</td>
17                 <td>Monday</td>
18                 <td> $300</td>
19             </tr>
20             <tr>
21                 <td> Tuesday</td>
22                 <td> $200 </td>
23             </tr>
24             <tr>
25                 <td> Wednesday</td>
26                 <td> $400 </td>
27             </tr>
28             <tr>
29                 <td> Thursday</td>
30                 <td> $100 </td>
31             </tr>
32             <tr>
33                 <td> Friday</td>
34                 <td> $300 </td>
35             </tr>
36             <tr>
37                 <td colspan = "2">Total</td>
38                 <td align = "center"> $1300</td>
39             </tr>
40         </table>
41     </body>
42  </html>
```

This rowspan attribute allows the first entry in column 1 to span 5 entries (or rows) in columns 2 and 3.

This colspan attribute allows the first entry in the last row to span the first two columns.

Figure 21.19: Using rowspan and colspan

Week	Day	Revenue
Week 1	Monday	$300
	Tuesday	$200
	Wednesday	$400
	Thursday	$100
	Friday	$300
Total		$1300

Figure 21.20: The code interpreted by a browser

PRACTICAL TASK 21.2

Getting started

On paper write down the purpose of the following tags.

1. `<table>`
2. `<tr>`
3. `<th>`
4. `<td>`

CONTINUED

Practice

5   Create a web page called *Task2.html* with a title of 'Task Two'.

6   Create a table with the following specifications:

- Width should be set to 75%.
- It should have a border and each cell should have a border.
- There should be at least nine rows and a heading.
- There should be three columns in all.
- Text should be entered into each cell as shown in Figure 21.21.

Country	City	# European Cups Won
Spain	Barcelona	5
	Madrid	13
United Kingdom	Birmingham	1
	Glasgow	1
	Liverpool	6
	London	1
	Manchester	3
	Nottingham	2
Total number of European Cups won		32

Figure 21.21: Table text for task

7   Save the page as *Task2.html*

Challenge

Improve the table (as in Figure 21.22) so that:

8   In the Country column there is only 1 row for each country.

9   In the bottom row, the 'Total number of European Cups won' spans the first two columns.

10 The number of wins and total should be centred.

11 Save the page as *Task2_Challenge.html*

21 Website authoring

> **CONTINUED**
>
> | Country | City | # European Cups Won |
> |---|---|---|
> | Spain | Barcelona | 5 |
> | | Madrid | 13 |
> | United Kingdom | Birmingham | 1 |
> | | Glasgow | 1 |
> | | Liverpool | 6 |
> | | London | 1 |
> | | Manchester | 3 |
> | | Nottingham | 2 |
> | Total number of European Cups won | | 32 |
>
> **Figure 21.22:** Improved table
>
> Tables are often used to structure web pages. Different elements can be placed in different rows, columns and cells. If no borders are used, then viewers do not realise that it is a table. This is particularly useful if you use the table to structure the elements within the web page.

Questions

1. List **four** appropriate HTML elements that can be placed in the head section of a web page.
2. Complete the following sentences in relation to metatags:
   a. Charset refers to …
   b. Keywords are useful for …
   c. Author would display …
   d. Viewport helps to …

> **ICT IN CONTEXT**
>
> The list changes over time but as of 16 April 2020, the most visited websites were:
> - Google
> - YouTube
> - Tmall
> - Facebook
> - Baidu.

Inserting images, videos and sound into a web page

Images

The `<img>` tag is used to insert images into a web page.

The code shown in Figure 21.23 on the next page will load an image that is in the same folder as the web page. The `<img>` tag has the source attribute (src) which tells the browser which image to display (in this case, *whitby2.jpg*):

`src="whitby2.jpg"`

Video and audio tags also use src to define which file to use.

Alternate text (alt) can be added. This text will be displayed (see Figure 21.24 on the next page) if the image cannot be found or it can be read by reading software if the user has a visual impairment.

`<img src="whitby2.jpg" alt = "Girl on seat">`

Attributes can be set, such as the width and height of the displayed image.

`<img src="whitby2.jpg" alt = "Girl on seat" width = "256">`
`<img src="whitby2.jpg" alt = "Girl on seat" height = "128">`

Figure 21.23: The code to display an image and the image in the browser

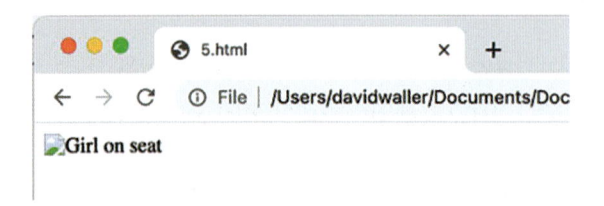

Figure 21.24: Alternate text displayed by the browser

In each example, either the width OR the height has been set; the browser will reset the other (Figure 21.25 shows how these would look in the browser). This is to automatically preserve the aspect ratio. If both were set in the code, then the aspect ratio would not be maintained and the image would become distorted.

However, you can specify both in the tag if you want to.

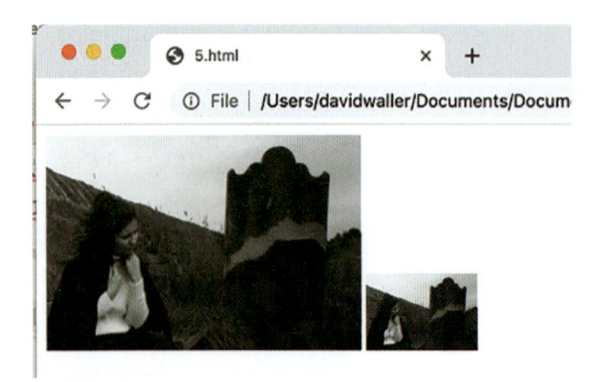

Figure 21.25: Resized images displayed in the browser

An image can also be used as a hyperlink.

The following code:

```
<a href="http://www.google.com">
    <img src="Whitby2.jpg" width="150"
    height="150"/>
</a>
```

would set the image as a hyperlink to google.com.

Video

The browser can be instructed to load a video and play it using the `<video>` tag:

```
<video width="320" autoplay>
    <source src="Country.mp4">
</video>
```

The size can be set by width and height attributes, but again only one has been used the preserve the aspect ratio. The `autoplay` attribute means that it will automatically start playing when the web page loads.

If the video controls need to be displayed then the 'control' attribute should be given (see Figure 21.26). This adds the controls such as, play, pause and the volume. If it is not given then the controls will not be shown.

```
<video width="320" controls>
    <source src="Country.mp4">
</video>
```

If you remove the controls from the HTML in the video element, you will only see an image of your video.

If you have video files saved in a different file format, HTML will accept these file formats and their accompanying attributes are as shown in Table 21.1.

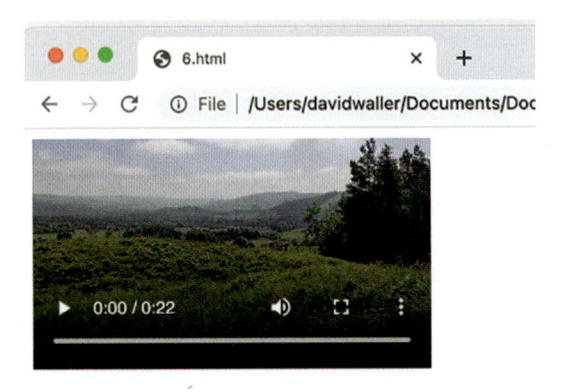

Figure 21.26: Video displayed with controls

Video file format	Video type attributes
.mp4	video/mp4
.webm	video/webm
.ogg	video/ogg

Table 21.1: File extensions for video objects

Audio

The `<audio>` tag is very similar to the video tag.

The code:

```
<audio controls>
    <source src="Singing.mp3">
</audio>
```

will cause the audio file to be loaded with the controls showing (see Figure 21.27).

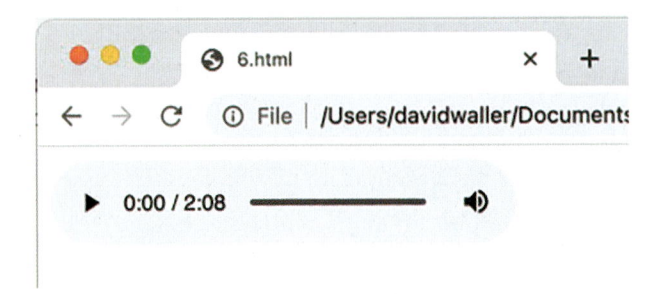

Figure 21.27: Audio controls

The following code will cause it to be loaded automatically and start playing because the `autoplay` attribute has been applied.

```
<audio controls autoplay>
    <source src="Singing.mp3">
</audio>
```

If you have sound files in a different file format, the acceptable file formats for HTML are as shown in Table 21.2.

Audio File Format	Audio Type Attributes
.mp3	audio/mpeg
.wav	video/wav
.ogg	audio/ogg

Table 21.2: File extensions for audio objects

However, be aware that not all browser types take all file formats. .mp3 is the most widely accepted.

Absolute and relative file paths

When you start creating your website, you should create a main (root) folder to store all your files. Sometimes you might wish to store the different types of data, such as images, audio or video files, in separate folders (possibly within the main folder). When files are placed in different folders, you need to specify the file location or path so that browsers can find them. HTML supports two kinds of paths: **relative** and **absolute file paths**.

> **KEY WORDS**
>
> **relative file path:** a route to a destination folder or file starting at the folder you are already in. It will work only if you are at this starting point
>
> **absolute file path:** a full file path to a precise location starting at the top of the computer's or website's folder structure, e.g. http://www.mysite.com/documents/homework/mypage.html or C:\documents\homework\IT\webpages.doc An absolute file path will work whatever the starting point

Absolute file path

An absolute file path specifies a file's precise location within a computer's entire folder structure or on another website; so if you wish to link to a URL on the web (outside of your site), use the http protocol, for example, http://wikipedia.com. A precise location in a computer's folder structure would look something like:

C:\Users\David\Website Folder\Images

Relative file path

A relative file path will refer you to a file in another place in relation to the file you are working on. If the file is in the same directory as the current file you are working on then it is not necessary to specify the folder name, just the file name.

```
         This PC
Up        |- Folder A
          |- Folder B
          |-Website Folder        ← Task1.html is in this folder
Down      |-Image Folder
```

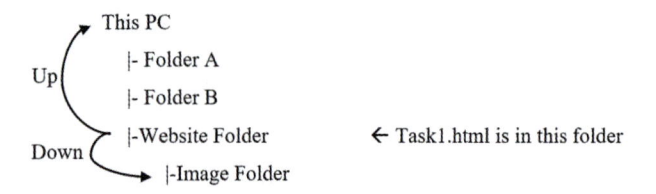

Figure 21.28: Directory structure for an html file

If you want to refer to any other file that is in the same folder, you just type the file name. For example, a link from *Task1.html* to *Task2.html*, would just write:

`<a href="Task2.html">Task2</a>`

If it is in another folder within the folder containing the current file then the path would be /*Task2.html*.

If you want to refer to a file that is up one level in the **folder hierarchy** (e.g. from Website Folder to a file in This PC in Figure 21.28), you must state the relative file path by starting with two full stops ('..') and a slash, followed by the file name, for example, '../filename':

`<a href="../Task2.html">Task2</a>`

If you want to refer to a file that is down one level in the folder hierarchy (e.g. from Website Folder to a file in Image Folder),you must start with the name of the subfolder followed by a slash, for example, 'Image Folder/filename':

`<a href="Image Folder/Task2.html">Task2</a>`

If you want to refer to a different folder within the same folder (this is called a **sibling folder**), you must first move up the folder hierarchy (using '..') slash and then move down the folder hierarchy by using the name of the sibling folder. So if you were in Website Folder and wanted to refer to something in Folder A, you would type '../Folder A/filename':

`a href="../Folder A/Task2.html">Task2</a>`

It is best practice to use relative file paths creating hyperlinks to **local web pages** (i.e. in the same folder as the .html file) because it makes it much easier to do something like change your domain name without having to change every hyperlink. It also means you can test your website while it's still saved on your own computer before you upload it to a server. If you use relative file paths, your site structure and all the links within it can remain the same, even if you decide you'd like to change the name or location of the site itself.

KEY WORDS

folder hierarchy: the organisation of folders in a computer

sibling folder: a folder that is inside the same parent folder as another folder

local web pages: a file in the same folder as the web page you are accessing or working on

ICT IN CONTEXT

By tracking the eye movements of people viewing websites, researchers have found:

- Text attracts more attention than pictures.
- People who read from left to right start viewing a website from the top left corner, and those who read from right to left start viewing a website from the top right corner.
- Readers ignore banners.
- Fancy fonts are ignored.
- Lists are better at keeping readers focused than large paragraphs. Some people even ignore large chunks of text.

21.3 Use CSS in the presentation layer

Development of HTML and CSS

Tim Berners-Lee created the world wide web in 1989 as a system based on hypertext written in HTML. This was used to describe the content of a web page with tags such as `<h1> </h1>` and `<p> </p>` to designate a heading or a paragraph.

But as web design developed people wanted to start adding style, such as coloured fonts of different sizes and types.

The `<font>` tag was introduced in 1996 as part of HTML3. It defined size, face type and colour; for example, `<font size=12>`. Soon the HTML code of a website didn't just have content, it had more and more code setting the style. And it had to be redefined every time a particular style was needed and it soon became a long and expensive process to design a web page.

To simplify the styling of web pages, **CSS** – or Cascading Stylesheets – were developed. HTML5 uses CSS instead.

CSS is a coding language that allows users to specify styles; for example:

- Fonts
- Colour of text and links
- Use colours in the text's background
- Where and how boxes within the content look and are placed

This code, specifying the styles of different elements, can be either internal (specified within the `<head>` section of a web page; they are coded between the `<style> </style>` tags) or external (on a separate document that can be shared by multiple web pages).

> **KEY WORD**
>
> **CSS:** Cascading Stylesheets is a simple way to add style such as fonts, colours or spacing to web pages

```
1   <!DOCTYPE html>
2   <html>
3       <head>
4
5           <style>
6
7               body {
8                   background-color: AliceBlue;
9               }
10
11
12              p {
13                  font-family:Times;
14                  font size: 12px;
15              }
16
17              h1 {font-family: Comic Sans MS, Comic Sans, cursive;
18                  font size: 20px;
19                  color: red;
20                  background-color: lightblue;
21                  align-content: center;
22              }
23
24
25          </style>
26
27      </head>
28
29      <body>
30          <h1>This is the heading</h1>
31
32          <p> This is some body text.</p>
33
34      </body>
35  </html>
```

- Style tags enclosing the CSS.
- Style to be applied to the `<body>` section.
- Style to be applied to paragraphs.
- Style to be applied any main `<h1>` headings.
- End Style tag.

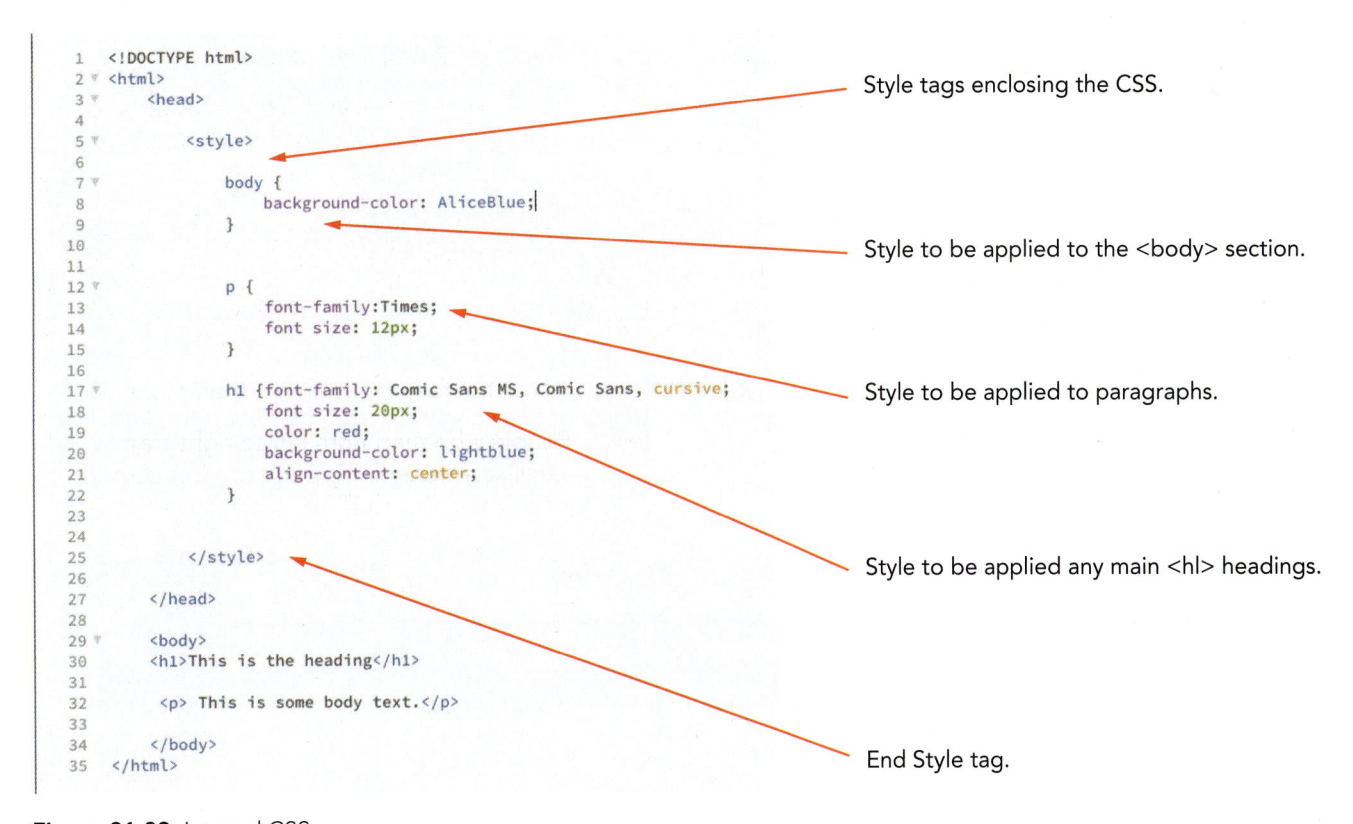

Figure 21.29: Internal CSS

These are called **external stylesheets**, and can be accessed by using the link element. The next section discusses external stylesheets.

CSS can also be applied in a third way, called **inline**, where it is used to apply a unique style for a single element. These are explained later in the chapter.

Like all languages, CSS has its own **key words** and **syntax** – the way in which it has to be written. Therefore for developing websites, you need to learn HTML and CSS.

Internal CSS

Internal CSS is placed in the web page itself, in a discrete section of the header.

It is contained within the `<style> </style>` tags (see Figure 21.29 and how it would look in a browser in Figure 21.30).

Notice how each style is written within brackets { } and with a semicolon at the end of each statement. The style type (e.g. font-family, font size, etc.) all have a colon after, which states that the next piece of information is what that style type should be. For example, font size: 20px tells the browser that the size of the font should be 20 pixels.

In the example in Figure 21.29, all the paragraphs enclosed by the `<p> </p>` tags would have the same styles applied. But what if you wanted paragraphs with different styles? CSS allows you to do this using an 'id' or '**classes**'.

Colours

Text, backgrounds and borders can be set to a particular colour.

The colour to be used can be given by name, e.g. DarkOrange, DeepPink or by a series of characters and numbers with a # symbol in front of them. These are called **hex codes**, and you can find these online or in the colour picker in most software.

AliceBlue = #F0F8FF

DarkOrange = #FF8C00

DeepPink = #FF1493

So if you wanted to change the text to AliceBlue, you could insert:

`background-color: AliceBlue;`

or

`background-color: #F0F8FF;`

> ### KEY WORDS
>
> **external stylesheet:** a document, outside the web page, containing the styles to be applied to the elements in the web page
>
> **inline:** style attributes placed within the HTML code
>
> **key word:** words used in a computer language to specify particular actions
>
> **syntax:** the combinations of symbols that are considered to be a correctly structured document or fragment in that language
>
> **class:** one or a group of attributes that can be applied to any element
>
> **hex codes:** hexadecimal is a number system that's based on 16s (instead of 10s); hex codes can be used to represent colours on web pages

Using ids

A style for a particular element, such as a paragraph can be given an id. This is done by placing a # before the style name when you are defining what it will look like. The attributes (font face, size alignment and colour – spelt color) are then placed between curly braces {}.

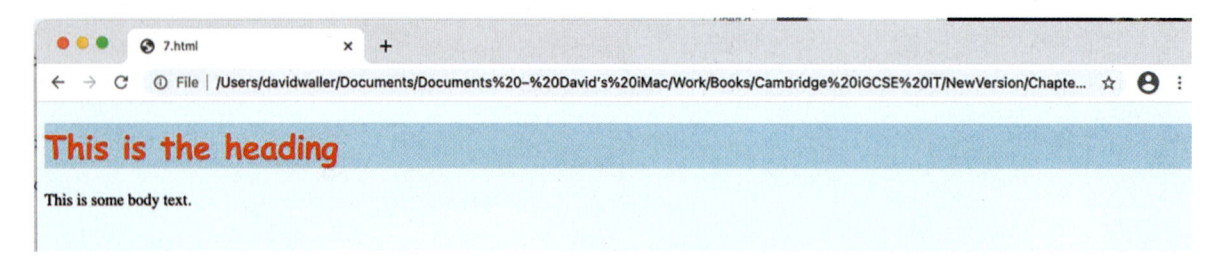

Figure 21.30: The code identified by a web browser

```
#para1 {
font-family: Arial;
font size: 17px;
color: red;
}
#para2 {
text-align: center;
color: black;
font-family: Times;
font size: 12px;
}
```

These two styles, both for paragraphs, have different ids – `#para1` and `#para2`. Then, when you define the paragraph using `<p></p>` tags, you place the id in the tag (Figure 21.31 and how it looks in a browser in Figure 21.32).

```
<p id = "para1"> This is some text with para1 style.</p>
<p id = "para2"> This is some text with para2 style.</p>
```

Figure 21.31: Applying the ids

This is the heading

This is some text with para1 style.

This is some text with para2 sty

Figure 21.32: Displayed in a web browser

These styles can then be applied as often as required in the web page.

Using classes

A class, like an id, is a set of style attributes but they can be applied to any element. A style defined by an id can be applied to only one element type. However, a class can be added to many elements within an .html document.

A class definition is written by placing a '.' before the style name when you are defining what it will look like. The attributes (font face, size alignment and colour – spelt 'color') are then placed between curly braces {}.

Here are two classes. `.myClass` and `.myOther`.

```
.myClass1 {
    color: red;
    font-size: 50px;
    text-align: center;
}
.myOther {
    color: blue;
}
```

They are being applied to the following elements.

```
<h1 class = "myOther">This is a main header with MyOther style.</h1>
<p class = "myClass1"> This is some text with myClass1 class.</p>
<p class = "myOther"> This is some text with myOther class.</p>
<p> This has no class style applied</p>
<h1 class = "myClass1"> This is a main header with myClass1 style</h1>
<h1> A header with no class applied.</h1>
```

In a web browser they will appear as shown in Figure 21.33.

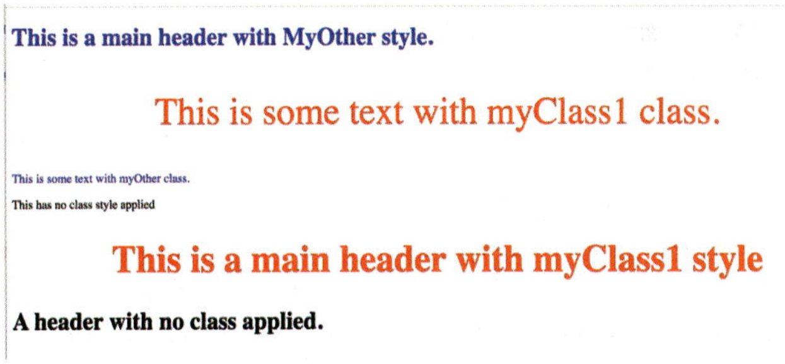

This is a main header with MyOther style.

This is some text with myClass1 class.

This is some text with myOther class.
This has no class style applied

This is a main header with myClass1 style

A header with no class applied.

Figure 21.33: The styles displayed by the browser

- The same class attributes can be applied to any element. In this case to both headings and paragraphs.
- If no style is applied, then the normal HTML ones are displayed.

In the above example, the several attributes have been set in the same class, for example, colour, font size and alignment in `.myClass1`. It is more efficient to set only one attribute in each class as many classes can be applied to each element. Therefore, a class specifying an attribute of a particular font colour could be added to any element requiring that font colour whatever other attributes they have.

For example:

```
<p class = "myClass1 myClass2"> This is a paragraph</>
```

Would apply both of the classes to the element.

Difference between a style and a class

- A style can only be used once whereas a class can be re-used.

- Class is used to style a group of elements and is used on several elements with the same class name.

Attaching comments to CSS

You can add comments to your CSS code to help explain what each section of the document is meant to be doing by using CSS comment tags.

```
/*This is a comment about my
stylesheet*/
```

Any comments placed between the /* */ tags will not be interpreted as CSS by a web browser. Comments are very helpful in long CSS documents as they help to explain what each section of the code is designed to do.

Images

CSS can be used to apply and format background images.

The CSS command:

```
background-image: url(Whitby2.jpg);
```

will use an image named *Whitby2.jpg* as a background image and, by default, it will repeat it. This is called '**tiling**' (see Figure 21.34).

> **KEY WORD**
>
> **tiling:** where an image is repeated to fill the available space

Figure 21.34: Background image repeated

To prevent the image from being repeated, the following command is used:

```
background-image: url(Whitby2.jpg);
background-repeat: no-repeat;
```

Then, only the first image in the top left corner will be displayed.

An image can be resized to cover as much of the background as required (see Figure 21.35).

```
body {
    background-image: url(Whitby2.jpg);
    background-repeat: no-repeat;
    background-size: 1300px, 1300px;
}
```

The width and height can also be given as a percentage of the window size.

```
background-size: 90%;
```

Figure 21.35: Background image resized

CSS and tables

When you use HTML5, you must use CSS styles for tables.

This includes:

- Background colour.
- Horizontal alignment and vertical alignment.
- Spacing.
- Padding.
- Borders (collapsed, border thickness and visible/invisible).

21 Website authoring

```html
1    <!DOCTYPE html>
2    <html>
3        <head>
4
5            <style>
6                table, th, td {
7                    border: 1px solid black;
8                }
9            </style>
10
11       </head>
12
13       <body>
14           <h1>This is a table heading</h1>
15
16           <table>
17               <tr>
18                   <th>Column 1</th>
19                   <th>Column 2</th>
20               </tr>
21               <tr>
22                   <td>Cell 1</td>
23                   <td>Cell 2</td>
24               </tr>
25               <tr>
26                   <td>cell 3</td>
27                   <td>Cell 4</td>
28               </tr>
29           </table>
30
31       </body>
32   </html>
```

Table styles defined. Notice that table, th and td are defined

Table definition in HTML

Figure 21.36: Table styles in html

In the code in Figure 21.36, the CSS is written to define table, th and td in one definition, so any time those tags are used in the body code, the browser will apply the style (see Figure 21.37).

This is a table heading

Column 1	Column 2
Cell 1	Cell 2
cell 3	Cell 4

Figure 21.37: Table in the browser

If table style is changed to:

```
Table, th, td {
    border: 1px solid black;
    border-collapse:collapse;
}
```

then only one line will be shown around the cells (Figure 21.38).

This is a table heading

Column 1	Column 2
Cell 1	Cell 2
cell 3	Cell 4

Figure 21.38: Using border-collapse

Borders of different thickness can be set by changing `border: 1px solid black;` to (for example) 5px or 10px.

There are more border styles than the solid used above, for example, dotted, dashed and double.

These can be applied in the same way, for example:

```
border: 1px dotted red;
border: 1px dashed blue;
border: 1px double green;
```

The colour attribute can also be added to `border:` command.

There are ways in which a border can be made invisible. For example:

```
border: transparent;
```

or

```
border: 0px;
```

A border is made visible by setting one of the styles listed above.

> **ACTIVITY 21.3**
>
> Carry out research to find all of the border options. Create a web page with tables displaying these options.

Table headings in HTML are formatted to be bold and centred by default. If you want to have a left-aligned or right-aligned heading you can use the CSS 'text-align' property. Here is an example:

```
th {
    text-align: right;
}
```

Other attributes that can be set using CSS include background colour, horizontal and vertical alignment, padding and border spacing.

Background colour

Adding the following to the style given in Figure 21.36:

```
Table, th, td {
    border: 1px solid black;
    border-collapse:collapse;
    background-color: aliceblue;
    }
```

will result in browser view shown in Figure 21.39.

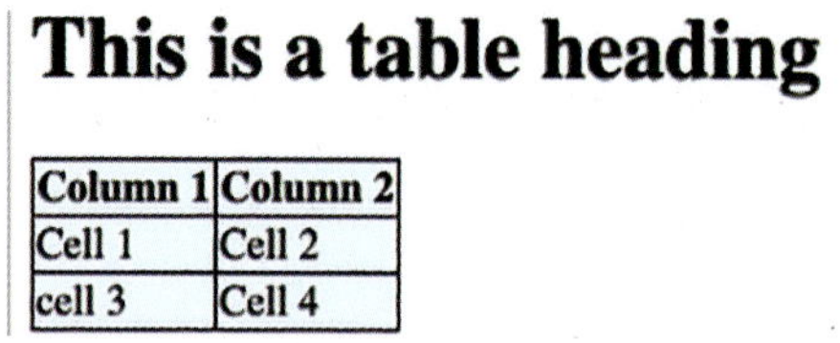

Figure 21.39: Using the background-color attribute

You can also create new classes for background colour and apply them to individual cells.

Adding the new class:

```
.a {background-color: red; }
```

and applying it to one particular cell (from the code in Figure 21.36):

```
<tr>
    <td class = "a">Cell 1</td>
    <td>Cell 2</td>
</tr>
```

would produce the browser view shown in Figure 21.40.

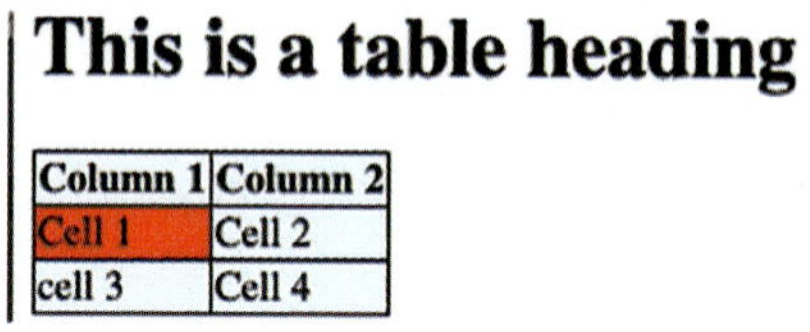

Figure 21.40: Applying a style to one cell

Horizontal and vertical alignment

Horizontal and vertical alignment was discussed in Chapter 13; however, they can also be set for tables using CSS. For horizontal alignment, the `text-align` command can be used.

The following classes can be designed:

```
.c {text-align: center;}
.r {text-align: right;}
```

and added to particular cells.

```
<tr>
    <td class = "c">cell 3</td>
    <td class = "r">Cell 4</td>
</tr>
```

These would produce the results shown in Figure 21.41 in cells 3 and 4. By default the alignment is left.

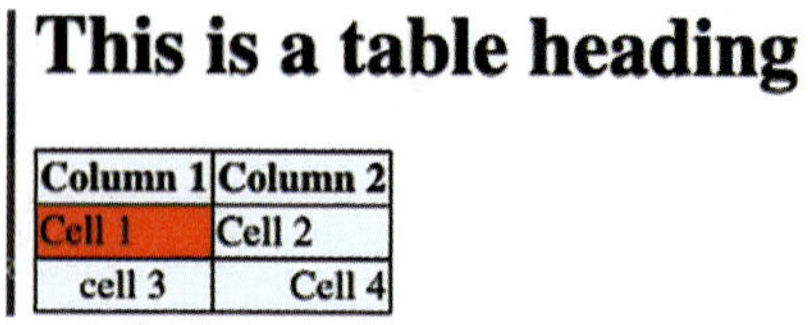

Figure 21.41: Aligning content in cells 3 and 4

The `vertical-align` property sets the vertical alignment as top, bottom or middle and different cells can be aligned independently.

If the following classes are created:

```
.vm {
    height: 50px;
    vertical-align: middle;
}
.vb {
    height: 50px;
    vertical-align: bottom;
}
```

and applied to cells 3 and 4

```
<tr>
    <td class = "c vm">
    cell 3</td>
    <td class = "r vb">
    Cell 4</td>
</tr>
```

Two separate classes have been applied to each of these cells.

what is shown in Figure 21.42 is displayed.

Figure 21.42: Vertical alignment of middle and bottom

Padding

Padding is the space between the border and the content of the table. It can be set using the `padding` property.

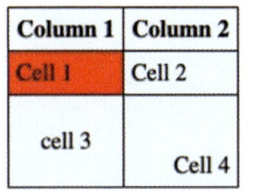

Figure 21.43: Padding added to the cells

If a padding property is added to the table style:

```
table, th, td {
    border: 1px solid black;
    border-collapse:collapse;
    background-color: aliceblue;
    padding: 5px;
}
```

padding of five pixels will be placed between the border and context.

The padding is more clearly seen in cells 1, 2 and 4.

Border spacing

The `border-spacing` property sets the distance between the borders of adjacent cells.

If border spacing is being used, the `border-collapse` property has to be set to 'separate'.

The following will produce a 15 pixel distance between the borders (and will display as shown in Figure 21.44).

```
Border-collapse: separate;
Border-spacing: 15px;
```

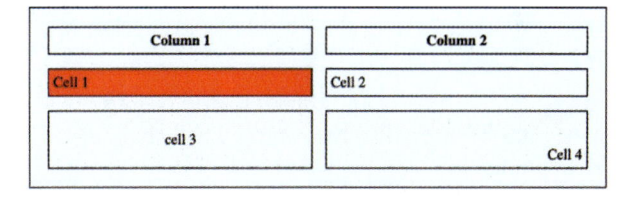

Figure 21.44: Border spacing between the cells

As mentioned previously, tables can be used to structure elements within a web page.

For example, the page layout may have been designed as shown in Table 21.3.

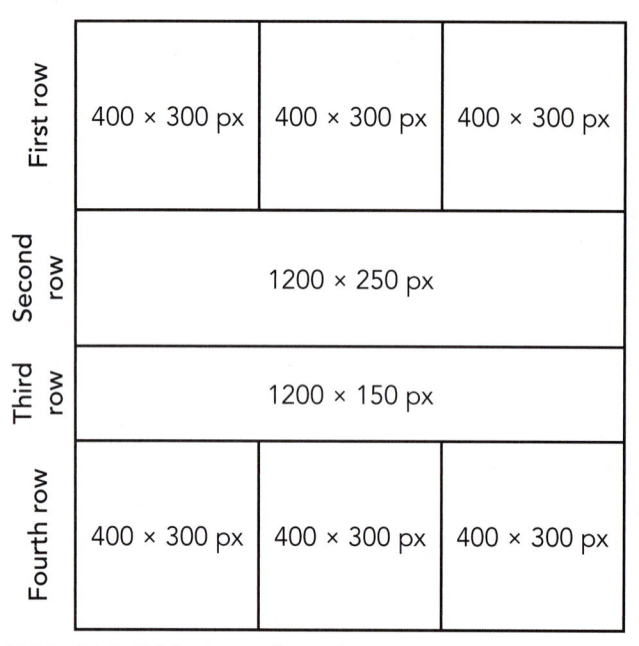

Table 21.3: Table design for code in Figure 21.45

```
1   <!DOCTYPE html>
2   <html>
3       <head>
4
5           <style>
6               table, th, td {
7                   border: 1px solid black;
8                   border-collapse:collapse;
9               }
10
11              .first {width: 400px;height: 300px}
12              .second{width: 1200px; height: 250px}
13              .third{ width: 1200px; height:150px;}
14              .fourth{ width:400px; height:300px}
15
16          </style>
17
18      </head>
19
20  <body>
21
22      <table>
23          <tr>
24              <td class = "first"></td>
25              <td class = "first"></td>
26              <td class = "first"></td>
27          </tr>
28      <tr>
29
30              <td class = "second" colspan = "3" ></td>
31
32          <tr>
33
34              <td class = "third" colspan = "3" ></td>
35          </tr>
36
37          <tr>
38              <td class = "fourth"></td>
39              <td class = "fourth"></td>
40              <td class = "fourth"></td>
41          </tr>
42      </table>
43  </body>
44  </html>
```

Figure 21.45: Code to create the table

This can be created using standard table properties as shown in Figure 21.45.

In rows 2 and 3 (second and third), the `colspan` property has been used so that one cell will span all three columns.

Table 21.4 is more difficult to produce:

It is more difficult because of row 4 as, unfortunately, a cell cannot be made to span 1.5 columns.

The way to solve this is to multiply the number of columns by 2. Therefore in row 1, each cell spans two columns and the cells in rows 2 and 3 span six columns. In row 4, each cell spans three columns. The code is shown in Figure 21.46.

External stylesheets

The CSS can be written on an external document, which is linked to the web page (see Figures 21.47–48).

An external stylesheet can be written in any text editor, and must be saved with a .css extension. It must not contain any HTML tags.

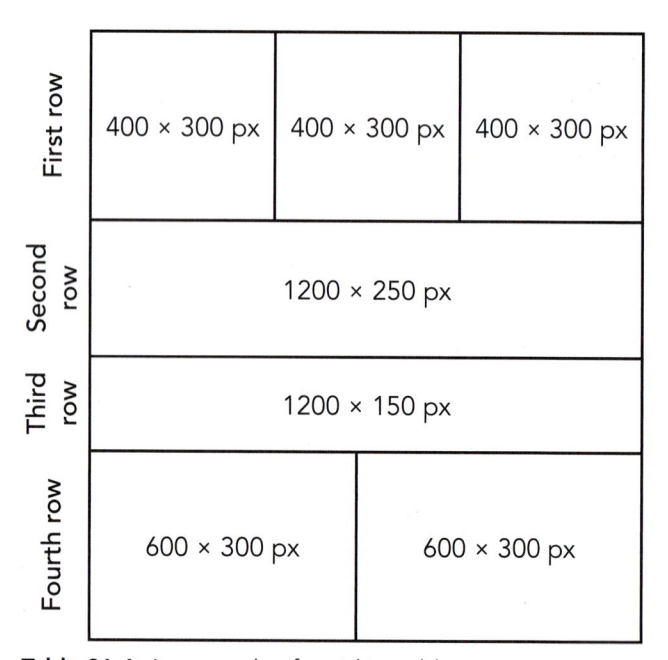

Table 21.4: An example of a trickier table

21 Website authoring

```
1   <!DOCTYPE html>
2   <html>
3       <head>
4
5           <style>
6               table, th, td {
7                   border: 1px solid black;
8                   border-collapse:collapse;
9               }
10
11              .first {width: 400px;height: 300px}
12              .second{width: 1200px; height: 250px}
13              .third{ width: 1200px; height:150px;}
14              .fourth{ width:400px; height:300px}
15
16          </style>
17
18      </head>
19
20      <body>
21
22          <table>
23              <tr>
24                  <td class = "first" colspan = "2"></td>
25                  <td class = "first" colspan = "2"></td>
26                  <td class = "first" colspan = "2"></td>
27              </tr>
28              <tr>
29
30                  <td class = "second" colspan = "6" ></td>
31
32              <tr>
33
34                  <td class = "third" colspan = "6" ></td>
35              </tr>
36
37              <tr>
38                  <td class = "fourth" colspan = "3"></td>
39                  <td class = "fourth" colspan = "3"></td>
40
41              </tr>
42          </table>
43      </body>
44  </html>
```

Figure 21.46: Code to create Table 21.4

```
h1 {
    color: red;
    background: blue;
    font-family: sans-serif;
    font-size: 36;
    font-weight: bold;
    text-align: center;
}

h2 {
    color: red;
    font-family: sans-serif;
    font-size: 17;
    text-align: left;
}

p {
    color: black;
    font-family: Times;
    font-size: 12;
    background: pink;
}
```

Figure 21.47: External stylesheet saved as Style.css

Link element

The HTML element, `<link>`, is used to link to external stylesheets and is represented as follows:

```
<link  rel="stylesheet"
href="myparagraphstyle.css">
```

```
1   <!DOCTYPE html>
2   <html>
3       <head>
4           <title>A Sample Page</title>
5           <link rel="stylesheet" href="Style.css">    ← The link to the stylesheet.
6
7       </head>
8
9       <body>
10          <h1> Using an external style sheet </h1>
11
12          <h2>Some example text</h2>
13
14
15          <p> This text should be in the style as defined by the external style
                sheet. <br> The style sheet can be reused with other web pages.</p>
16
17      </body>
18
19  </html>
```

Figure 21.48: The HTML code

This is a file that you will have stored in your web page folder with a .css file extension. It will have the formatting information such as background colours, heading colours, font types, font sizes and text enhancements that you want to apply to the text on your web page. This HTML link element connects this particular style to all the web pages that you type this line of code into. You then do not have to repeat the same style instruction for each web page of a website (see Figure 21.49).

The link to the stylesheet is relative and it must, therefore, be in the same directory or folder as the web page.

File paths to stylesheets should be relative so that they are not fixed to a particular URL which may change. Also the links will work on a local computer where the web page is being developed without connecting to the internet.

Inline styles

Using inline styles loses the advantages of using internal and external stylesheets. It mixes content with presentation and should be used sparingly. Inline styles place styles along with the content, which can cause confusion. Also, they can only be used once on this particular element.

The styles are set using the style attribute, as shown in Figure 21.50.

Usually, inline styles would not be used in this way; rather they are used to make a style change in one particular instance. For example, if the style for `<h1>` had been set in a stylesheet, an inline style could be used if it needed changing in one place only.

Using an external stylesheet

Some example text

This text should be in the style as defined by the external stylesheet.
The stylesheet can be reused with other web pages.

Figure 21.49: The styles applied from the external stylesheet

```
1   <!DOCTYPE html>
2   <html>
3       <head>
4           <title>A Sample Page</title>
5
6
7       </head>
8
9       <body>
10          <h1 style = "color: red; background: blue; font-family: sans-serif; font-
            size: 36; font-weight: bold;  text-align: center;"> Using inline styles
            </h1>
11
12          <h2 style = "color: red;font-family: sans-serif; font-size: 17; text-align:
            left; ">Some example text</h2>
13
14
15          <p style = "color: black; font-family: Times; font-size: 12; background:
            pink"> This text should be in the style as defined by the external style
            sheet. <br> The style sheet can be reused with other web pages.</p>
16
17      </body>
18
19  </html>
```

Figure 21.50: The styles shown in Figure 21.48 applied inline

The styles are applied in the order in which they are read. If an internal style is read after the style in an external stylesheet then the internal one will be applied. And vice versa.

So if you had (reading down the html document from top to bottom):

3   Internal styles (styles set between <style> tags in the head area).
2   THEN a link to an external stylesheet.
1   Then an inline style in the body.

The styles set in the external stylesheet would take precedence over the internal styles; however, if you had :

3   A link to an external stylesheet.
2   THEN Internal styles (styles set between <style> tags in the head area).
1   Then an inline style in the body.

The styles set in the internal styles would take precedence over the external stylesheet.

Obviously as an inline style is the last to be specified, then it will take precedence over the others.

WORKED EXAMPLE 21.1

CREATING A WEBPAGE

1   Create a webpage named *Travelhomepage.html*.

2   The web page must work in any browser and contain a table with the structure shown in Table 21.5.

   The width of the table is set in the stylesheet and the height of the rows by their contents.

Travel Anywhere Set in style h1	
Insert *Image1.png* here. Add appropriate alternative text for this image.	Insert the text in *Text1.txt* here. Set in style h2 Set as an ordered list
Insert *Image2.png* here. Add appropriate alternative text for this image	Insert *Text2.txt* here. Set in style h2.
Click here to contact us Link to http://travelanywhere.co.uk Set in style h3	

Table 21.5: Structure for web page

Insert the text shown in bold.

Save the web page.

3   Create a stylesheet named *TravelAnywhere.css* and attach it to *Travelhomepage.html*.

   Add the following styles to the stylesheet:

   Table

   - Centre aligned within the browser window.
   - Size 900 pixels wide.
   - No visible borders.
   - Cell padding 10 pixels.

> **CONTINUED**

h1
- Colour red.
- Background pale blue.
- Sans-serif font.
- 36 points.
- Bold.
- Centre aligned.

h2
- Colour red.
- Sans-serif font.
- 17 points.
- Left aligned.

h3
- Colour black.
- Sans-serif font.
- 13 points.
- Centre aligned.

Ordered list
- Colour blue.
- Sans-serif font.
- 15 points.
- Justified.

Save the web page and stylesheet.

4 Make the table header span both columns.

5 Insert *Image1.png* and *Text1.txt* into the first row.

6 Insert *Image2.png* and *Text2.txt* into the second row.

7 Make the final row span both columns.

8 Save the final web page and run it in a browser.

Step 1

The web page can be created and saved as *Travelhomepage.html*.

Step 2

In the `<head>` region a link to the stylesheet is inserted (see Figure 21.51).

```
1   <!DOCTYPE html>
2   <html>
3       <head>
4           <title>Travelhomepage</title>
5           <link rel="stylesheet" type="text/css" href="TravelAnywhere.css">
6       </head>
```

Figure 21.51: Code for head region

CONTINUED

Step 3

The specified styles can be defined on *TravelAnywhere.css* (see Figure 21.52).

```css
table {
    margin-left:auto;
    margin-right:auto;
    width: 900px;
    border: none;
    padding: 10px;
}

h1 {
    color: red;
    background: blue;
    font-family: sans-serif;
    font-size: 36;
    font-weight: bold;
    text-align: center;
}

h2 {
    color: red;
    font-family: sans-serif;
    font-size: 17;
    text-align: left;
}

h3 {
    color: black;
    font-family: sans-serif;
    font-size: 15;
    text-align: center;
}

ol {
    color: blue;
    font-family: sans-serif;
    font-size: 15;
    text-align: justify;
}
```

Figure 21.52: Styles for web page

Step 4

The table header can be created in the body section of *Travelhomepage.html*, spanning both columns (see Figure 21.53).

```html
<table>
    <tr>
        <td colspan="2"><h1>Travel Anywhere</h1></td>
    </tr>
```

Figure 21.53: Code for table header

CONTINUED

Step 5

The first image (*Image1.png*) and *Text1.txt* can be inserted into the first row (see Figure 21.54).

```html
<tr>
    <td><img src="Image1.png" alt="Louvre" /></td>
    <td>
        <h2>
            <ol>
                <li>Holiday planning</li>
                <li>Flight Booking</li>
                <li>Sea cruises</li>
                <li>River cruises</li>
                <li>Adventure holidays</li>
                <li>Trekking</li>
            </ol>
        </h2>
    </td>
</tr>
```

Figure 21.54: Code for *Image1* and *Text1*

Step 6

The second image (*Image2.png*) and *Text2.txt* can be inserted in the second row (see Figure 21.55).

```html
<tr>
    <td><img src="Image2.png" alt="Istanbul.png" /></td>
    <td>
        <h2>Travel Anywhere have been established for fifty years.</h2>
        <h2>We do not do packages. We plan individual holiday adventures with our clients.</h2>
        <h2>Anywhere in the world. Any activity.</h2>
        <h2>Just imagine and then come to us to fulfil your dreams.</h2>
    </td>
</tr>
```

Figure 21.55: Code for *Image2* and *Text2*

Step 7

The final row can be created (see Figure 21.56).

```html
<tr>
    <td colspan="2">
        <h3><a href="http://www.travelanywhere.co.uk">Click here to contact us</a></h3>
    </td>
</tr>
```

Figure 21.56: Code for final row

CONTINUED

Step 8

Save the final web page. It should look like Figure 21.57.

Figure 21.57: The final web page

Questions

1. Create the web page according to the specifications.
2. Create a border around the tab

Questions

3. Define the following terms:
   a. cascading stylesheets
   b. class
   c. style attributes
   d. relative file paths
   e. padding.
4. Explain how you would attach comments to an external stylesheet.
5. Examine the following:
   ```
   <h2 style="color: green">This is a blue sub-heading</h2>
   ```
   a. What colour is the sub-heading?
   b. What method is being used to apply a style to this HTML element: inline styling, internal stylesheet or external stylesheet? Give a reason for your choice.

PRACTICAL TASK 21.3

Getting started

Look at the following HTML. Two different methods are used to specify the font colour.

```
<html>
<p> <font color = "red">Hello</font></p>
<p style="color:red">Hello.</p>
</html>
```

1. Which method is recognised by HTML versions before HTML5?
2. Which method is recognised by HTML5?

Practice

3. Create a new web page and save it as *Task3.html*.
4. Set the title as 'Task Three – basic formatting'
5. Enter the following 'Formatting using HTML attributes' as a heading.
6. Enter 'Text formatting' as a second-level heading.
7. Add 'This text is bold.', 'This text is italic.' and 'This text is underlined.' in those styles as separate paragraphs.
8. Add a table with border style '1'. It should have two columns and two rows with 'Header1', 'Header2' and data1 and data2 as text.
9. Insert an image.
10. Insert an image as a link to Google.

The result should look like Figure 21.58.

Formatting using HTML attributes

Text formatting

This text is bold.

This text is italic.

This text is underlined.

Table with border=1

Header1	Header2
data1	data2

Image

Image as a link to Google

Figure 21.58: An example of Task3 web page

CONTINUED

Challenge

11 Add the heading 'Formatting using the style attribute'.

12 Using the style tag add the following paragraphs:

This text is bold

This text is italic.

This text is underlined.

This font is Arial.

This text is red.

Background colour is green.

13 Repeat the table above (in Practice question 6) but this time, using the style tag, give it a border of 1 pixel.

14 Save the document as *Task3_Challenge.html*. Your table should look like Figure 21.59.

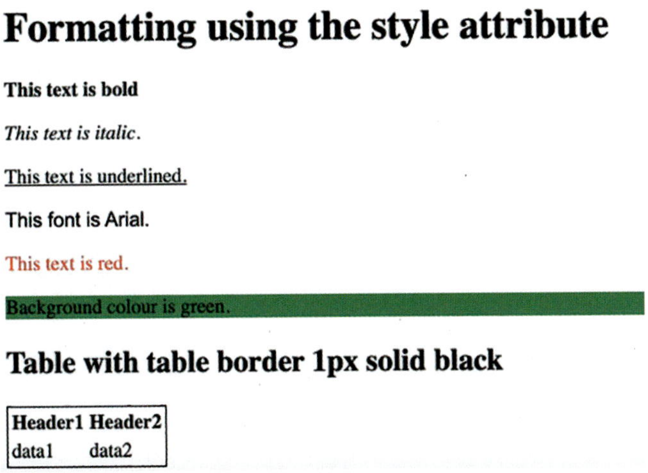

Formatting using the style attribute

This text is bold

This text is italic.

This text is underlined.

This font is Arial.

This text is red.

Background colour is green.

Table with table border 1px solid black

Header1	Header2
data1	data2

Figure 21.59: An example of Task3_Challenge web page

PRACTICAL TASK 21.4

Getting started

On paper, write down the purpose of the following tags:

1 `<p>`

2 `<h1>`

3 `<b>`

CONTINUED

Practice

4   Open *Task2_Challenge.html* that you saved in Practical Task 21.2.

5   Create the following inline style attributes:

- **For the table:**
  - San serif font.
  - Width of 100%.
  - A single border.

- **For the table and heading cells:**
  - A border colour of lavender.
  - A border thickness of 2px.
  - Padding of 10px.

- **For the heading cells only:**
  - Background colour of blue.
  - White text.
  - Top and bottom padding of 15px.
  - Text aligned to the left.

- All the even rows in the table should have a background colour of #F0FFFF.

- All cells containing countries and those in the bottom row should be defined as key fields and text in key fields should be set to bold.

  The styled table should look like Figure 21.60.

Country	City	# European Cups Won
Spain	Barcelona	5
	Madrid	13
United Kingdom	Birmingham	1
	Glasgow	1
	Liverpool	6
	London	1
	Manchester	3
	Nottingham	2
Total number of European Cups won		32

Figure 21.60: Styled table

6   Save the finished web page as *Task4.html*.

21 Website authoring

> **CONTINUED**
>
> **Challenge**
>
> 7 Open *Task2_Challenge* and save it as *Task4_Challenge.html*.
>
> 8 Create an external stylesheet named *table_styling.css* containing the internal styles used in *Task4.html*. Remove the internal styles from *Task4.html*.
>
> 9 Link the stylesheet to *Task4_Challenge/html*. Test the page to ensure the table is formatted exactly the same as in *Task4.html*.

Use the `<div>` tag

The `<div>` tag is an empty container that is used to define a section (or division) of a web page. It does not affect the content and is used to group HTML elements to be styled with CSS or manipulated with scripts.

In the code shown in Figure 21.61, the div is styled as well as being defined within the section. (Figure 21.62 shows how this looks in a browser.)

```html
<html>
<head>
    <title>The div Tag</title>

</head>
<body>

<h1> This is outside the div.</h1>

        <div style = "background-color:lightgreen; color:red; width:50%">
            <h1> The div Tag</h1>
            <p> The div tag is used to group elements so that they can be styled
                together. </p>
            <p> They are also used to structure the web page</p>
        </div>


    <h1>This is outside the div.</h1>


</body>
</html>
```

Figure 21.61: Using the `<div>` tag

The div is defined between the `<div>` `</div>` tags. The style attributes including background colour, font colour and width in relation to the page are given in the definition.

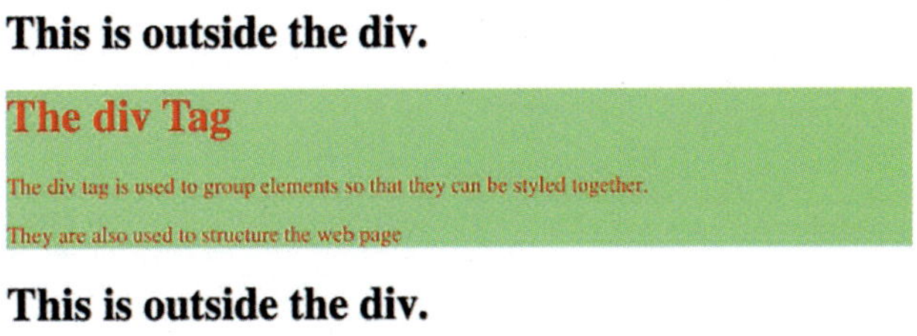

This is outside the div.

The div Tag

The div tag is used to group elements so that they can be styled together.

They are also used to structure the web page

This is outside the div.

Figure 21.62: The div shown in a web browser

The best way to apply styles to a div is to create a class. In the example in Figure 21.63, a class (`.mydiv`) has been created in the `<style>` section of the web page.

Divs can be placed within divs, like nesting functions in spreadsheets, so that areas with different styles and appearances can be created but allowing far more flexibility. Instead of creating a table to structure a web

```html
<html>
<head>
    <title>The div Tag</title>

    <style>

        .mydiv {

            background-color:lightgreen;
            color:red;
            width: 50%
        }

    </style>



</head>
<body>


        <div class = "mydiv">
            <h1> The div Tag </h1>
            <p>The div tag is used to group elements so that they can be styled
                together. </p>

            <p> They are also used to structure the web page</p>
        </div>
</body>
</html>
```

— Definition of a class named mydiv.

— Class applied to a div.

Figure 21.63: Styling a div by class

page, there could be an outer div with divs placed within it representing the cells of the table

These sections can be orientated to the left or right of the parent div by using the `float` attribute. This attribute is used for positioning and formatting content.

In the example in Figure 21.64, one div is set to float to the left of the parent div and the other to float to the right. Their margins and space between them is automatically calculated depending on their sizes and the size of the outer div. How this looks in a browser can be seen in Figure 21.65.

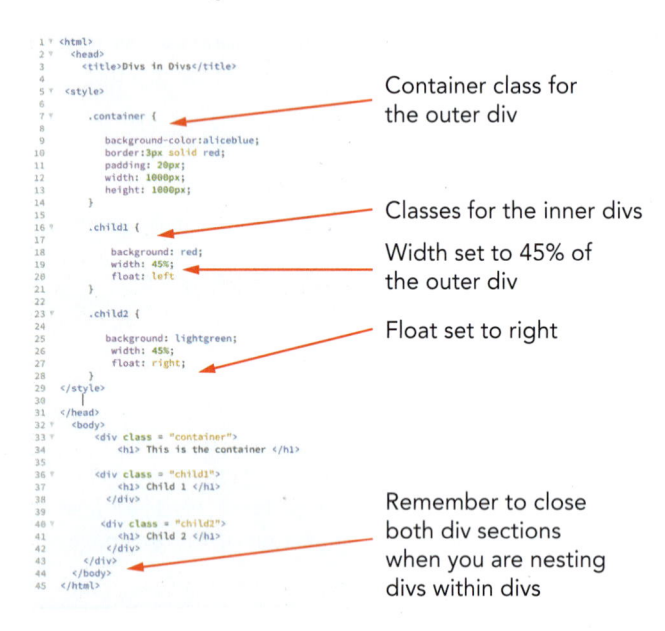

Figure 21.64: Nesting divs

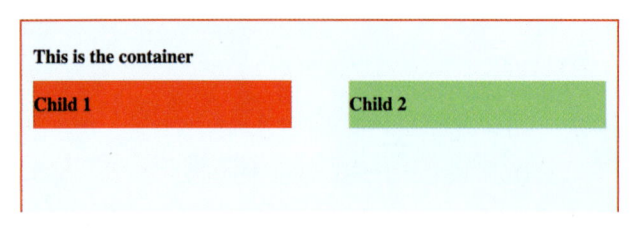

Figure 21.65: The nesting divs shown in a web browser

The float attribute can be applied to the outer container, to position it within the web page.

Another way to align divs within a container is to use the `flexbox` attributes.

If the following is added to the `.container` class:

```
flex-direction:row;
justify-content:space-around;
```

The child divs will be spaced evenly over the width and their height will be increased to fill the outer div (see Figure 21.66).

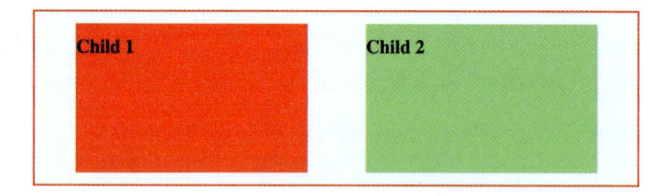

Figure 21.66: The effect of using flexbox properties

If flex direction is set to `column` the divs would be arranged vertically (see Figure 21.67).

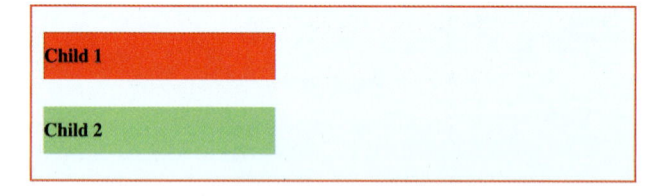

Figure 21.67: Flex direction set as column

ACTIVITY 21.4

Carry out research to find more 'justify-content' options and create web pages to display them. Take screen prints of the results of each option and insert them into a document named *Activity4.doc*.

Being able to use divs, and nest and position them provides a much better means of structuring a website than using tables, and is also used far more often.

PRACTICAL TASK 21.5

Getting started

On paper:

1. Write the HTML code for inserting an mp3 file named 'Sound' into a page.
2. Write the HTML code for inserting an mp4 file named 'Video' into a page.

Practice

3. Create a new web page named *Task5.html*.
4. It should have a title of 'Task Five – Audio and Video'.
5. Insert a second-level heading of 'Audio'.
6. Insert a heading of 'Audio and Video'.
7. Insert audio controls and the sound file *Opera.mp3*. It should be muted when it loads.
8. Insert a second-level heading of 'Video'.
9. Insert video controls and the video file *Countryside.mp4*. It should be muted when it loads.
10. Give alternative text for each.

Your finished page should look like Figure 21.68.

Figure 21.68: Task Five – Audio and Video web page

CONTINUED

Challenge

The page is a bit plain.

11 Use `<div>` tags to create two areas, side-by-side for the audio and the video (see Figure 21.69).

12 Set inline style.

13 The audio and video controls should be centred in their containers.

14 When the window is resized, the video should resize accordingly (see Figure 21.70).

15 Save the page as *Task5_Challenge.html*

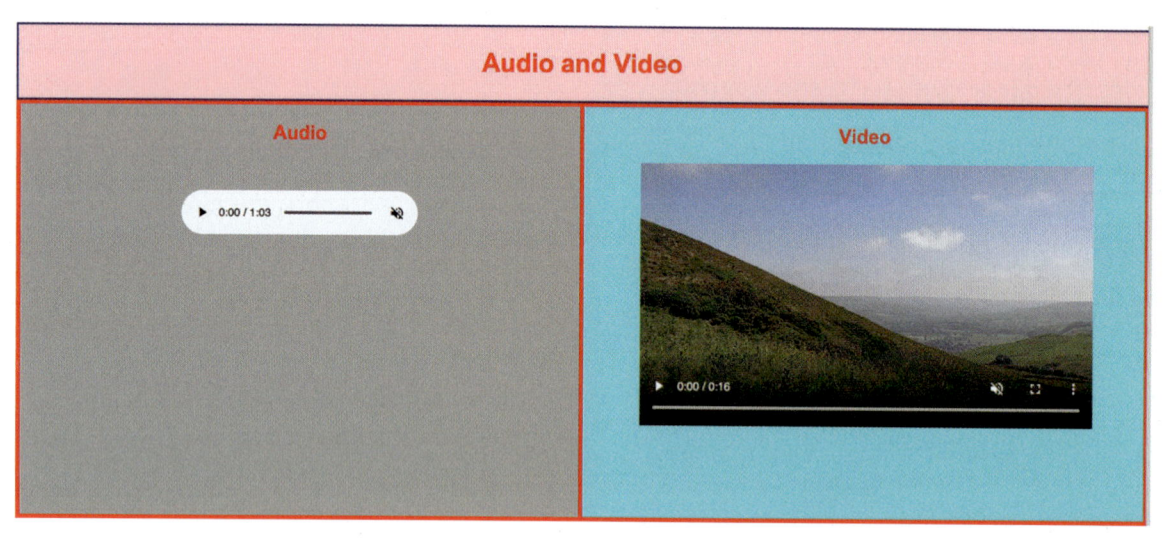

Figure 21.69: Side-by-side areas

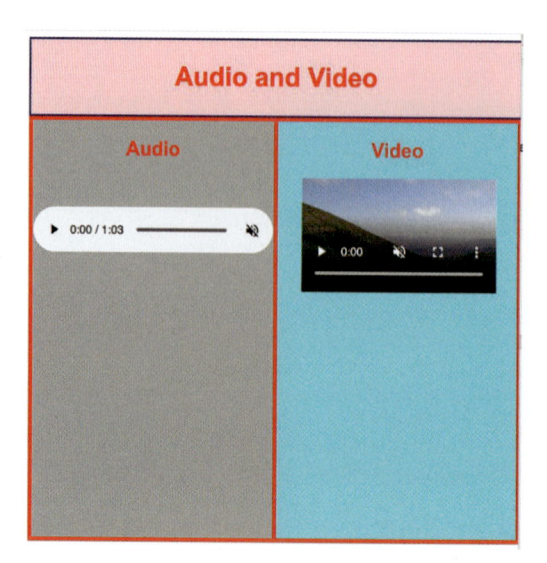

Figure 21.70: Resized page

CONTINUED

Peer assessment

Working with a partner, view each other's web pages and assess them according to the following criteria.

- Has the title 'Task Five – Audio and Video' being added?
- Have the headings been added?
- Have the audio and video files been inserted?
- Have the audio and video controls being added?
- Do the controls work for both audio and video?
- Has alternative text been added?
- For the challenge, have `<div>` tags been used?
- When the window is resized does the video resize accordingly?

ACTIVITY 21.5

Web pages and websites appear in many different styles. Write down a set of five questions relating to website styles and designs, one beginning with What? one beginning with Why? then When? Whom? How? Move around the room to ask your peers to help you answer each of your questions while you should answer their questions, too. You may only ask one student per question. You should be in contact with five other students – to ask them to answer your five questions and to answer their question, one at a time.

Questions

6 Explain what is meant by a `<div>` element.

7 Write a class definition for a div with the following properties:

It should have:
- A background colour of light blue.
- A width that takes up half of the width of the window.
- A double border with a red colour.
- Padding of 20px.

8 Explain why using divs is a suitable method of structuring web pages.

REFLECTION

In small groups, talk about what you each found difficult in this chapter, and come up with ideas to help each other learn the material.

SUMMARY

There are three web development layers: content, presentation and behaviour.
These three layers are linked together as follows: content layer with HTML, presentation layer with CSS and the behaviour layer with scripting languages.
The head section of a web page contains elements to define the page title, stylesheets, metatags and target windows.
The main content is defined in the body section of a page. There are predefined styles including headers, paragraphs and lists.
Tables are widely used for the purposes of structuring the web elements on a web page. Attributes to consider within a table include width in terms of pixels and % values, borders, background colour, horizontal and vertical alignment, all in order to meet the needs of the user.
Animation, sound clips and videos have attributes to view their controls and if they will play automatically.
HTML elements can be labelled with class names to apply styles to all of the elements with the same name.
CSS is used to set the style of elements using selectors and declarations.
CSS code can be used to create files that will cascade a style throughout the whole website by simply changing one file.
HTML can link to email addresses, bookmarks within a web page or on other web pages and to external websites.
Relative file paths must be used when attaching stylesheets because a relative file path specifies a file location in relation to the location of the current document.

EXAM-STYLE QUESTIONS

1 Are the following statements TRUE or FALSE?
   a Items in the head section of HTML do not appear on a web page.
   b A `<div>` tag is used for inserting an image.
   c The behaviour layer is for a scripting language to control the media elements in a web page.
   d Audio files cannot be included in web pages.
   e Hyperlinks from text and images can be linked to data within the same web page. [5]

CONTINUED

2 Examine this example containing an internal CSS section.

```
<!DOCTYPE html>
<html>
<head>
<style>
h1   {
    color: black;
    font-family: Times New Roman;
    font-size: 300%;
}
p   {
    color: green;
    font-family: calibri;
    font-size: 180%
}
</style>
</head>
<h1>Music Favourites</h1>
<p>Popular music is amazingly uplifting and makes me feel happy.</p>
</html>
```

   a **Identify** the CSS section by explaining how it is identifiable from the other HTML material. [1]

   b **State** what is an:

      i inline CSS

      ii internal CSS

      iii external CSS? [6]

   c Edit the internal CSS by adding a style for a sub-heading with h2, using the font type, 'Consolas' font-size of 160% and a blue font. [3]

   d Add a sub-heading in the body of the HTML document and use the text, 'Types of Music'. [1]

   e Add another sub-heading h3, Arial, Purple and use these three sub-headings: Pop Music, Classical Music, Folk Music. [4]

   f Save your edits from questions **2c**, **2d** and **2e** as an external CSS file. [1]

   g Screenshot your CSS file contents and screenshot your HTML document here also. [2]

> **COMMAND WORDS**
>
> **identify:** name / select / recognise
>
> **state:** express in clear terms

CONTINUED

3 There are several types of links found on web pages.
  a **Compare** by commenting on the similarities and differences between bookmarks and hyperlinks. **[5]**
  b **Describe** the methods of creating a bookmark within a webpage. **[3]**
4 The use of tables in web pages is mostly invisible yet it is an important consideration.
  a Why is using a table in a web page important? **[1]**
  b **Explain** how you can use table attributes where you would specify that you'd want to have three rows and two columns in a table. **[3]**

[Total: 35]

COMMAND WORDS

compare: identify / comment on similarities and / or differences

describe: state the points of a topic / give characteristics and main features

explain: set out purposes or reasons / between things evident / provide why and / or how and support with relevant evidence

SELF-EVALUATION CHECKLIST

After studying this chapter, think about how confident you are with the different topics.

This will help you to see any gaps in your knowledge and help you to learn more effectively.

You might find it helpful to rate how confident you are for each of these statements when you are revising. You should revisit any sections that you rated 'Needs more work' or 'Getting there'.

I can ...	See section	Needs more work	Getting there	Confident to move on
use the three web development layers: the content, behaviour and presentation layers	21.1			
understand and can use HTML to create the content layer of a web page	21.2			
understand the use of a script language in the behaviour layer of a web page	21.1			
understand and can use CSS in the presentation layer of a web page	21.3			

Glossary

Command words

The command words and definitions in this section are taken from the Cambridge International syllabuses (0417/0983) for examination from 2023. You should always refer to the appropriate syllabus document for the year of your examination to confirm the details and for more information. The syllabus document is available on the Cambridge International website www.cambridgeinternational.org.

analyse: examine in detail to show meaning, identify elements and the relationship between them

compare: identify / comment on similarities and / or differences

contrast: identify / comment on differences

define: give precise meaning

demonstrate: show how or give an example

describe: state the points of a topic / give characteristics and main features

discuss: write about issue(s) or topic(s) in depth in a structured way

evaluate: judge or calculate the quality, importance, amount, or value of something

explain: set out purposes or reasons / make the relationships between things evident / provide why and / or how and support with relevant evidence

give: produce an answer from a given source or recall / memory

identify: name / select / recognise

justify: support a case with evidence / argument

state: express in clear terms

suggest: apply knowledge and understanding to situations where there are a range of valid responses in order to make proposals / put forward considerations

Key words

3D printer: a printer that works by printing in layers on top of each other, eventually creating a 3D object

3D scanner: a device that takes multiple photographs of an object from all angles and combines them into a 3D representation or model of it

3G and 4G: communication protocols used by smartphones to connect to the internet, 4G being much faster than 3G

5G: the 5th generation of wireless technologies for digital cellular networks

abnormal data: data that should not normally be accepted by the system being tested because the values are invalid and should therefore be rejected

absolute file path: a full file path to a precise location starting at the top of the computer's or website's folder structure, e.g. http://www.mysite.com/documents/homework/mypage.html or C:\documents\homework\IT\webpages.doc An absolute file path will work whatever the starting point

absolute reference: a cell reference that does not change as it is copied down columns or across rows

action buttons: button shapes that cause an action to be performed, e.g. link to another slide or play a sound when it is clicked

actuator: a device that causes a machine or other device to operate

alignment: how text flows in relation to the rest of the page

alternative text: text that can be read aloud by screen readers, allowing them read aloud a description of an object, e.g. of an image

analogue: information represented by a quantity (e.g. an electric voltage or current) that is continuously variable. Changes in the information are indicated by changes in voltage

analysis: a detailed examination of something for a specific purpose, e.g. to see how it works or to improve it

anchor: a type of hyperlink that will take you to a specific part of a web page

animation: an effect used on individual elements on one slide, e.g. revealing each bullet point one at a time

anti-malware software: software used to prevent, detect and neutralise malware

antivirus software: software to prevent a virus from entering your computer and searching for it and destroying it if it already has

applications software: programs that carry out operations for specific applications, such as word processing, spreadsheets or presentations. Applications software cannot run on its own without system software

appropriateness: how suitable or fitting something is

arithmetic and logic unit: part of the CPU that performs arithmetical and logical operations such as addition, subtraction, or comparison

arithmetic operator: symbols to represent arithmetic operations such as addition, subtraction, multiplication and division

artificial intelligence: the ability of a digital computer or computer-controlled robot to perform tasks commonly associated with human intelligence such as learning, problem solving and pattern recognition

ascending order: arranged from smallest to largest or in alphabetical order

aspect ratio: relationship between the width and height of an image

asymmetric encryption: a method of encryption that uses two different keys

attributes: an attribute is an additional piece of information about an HTML element

audio communication: any form of transmission that is based on sound, speaking and hearing

audio-conference: people in different locations use technology to speak to each other

augmented reality: a combined virtual and real environment

authentication: the process or action of proving or showing something to be true, genuine or valid

autocorrect: automatic spelling correction

automated number plate recognition system (ANPR): a system capable of reading car number plates, with a high degree of accuracy, without human intervention

automated object: item that changes as the document develops, e.g. number of pages, file size

automated slide numbering: numbering slides in all the slides without having to number each slide individually and usually in the slide header or footer

automated software tool: software that works in the background as a user is working

automated teller machine (ATM): this is a machine that allows you to carry out banking services in locations other than inside a bank

autonomous vehicle: a vehicle capable of sensing its environment and operating without human involvement

axes titles: words describing the data represented on axes

backing storage device: a secondary storage device that will continue to hold data even after the computer has been turned off. Examples include hard drives, solid-state drives, memory sticks, memory cards and CDs and DVDs. Backing storage can be internal (inside the computer case) or external

bar chart: a chart where data are represented by horizontal rectangles

bar code: a set of short parallel lines in contrasting colours, often black and white, that stand for the digits 0 to 9. Bar code readers shine a laser at them and then read the reflection to tell how thick the lines are

base station: a fixed point of communication for cellular phones on a carrier network. The base station has an antenna (or multiple antennae) that receives and transmits the signals in the cellular network to customer phones and cellular devices

batch process: a group of jobs executed together, either sequentially or at the same time

bcc: short for 'blind carbon copy'. This is the field you type an address into if you don't want others to see who you have copied into the email

behaviour layer: an area of website design concerned with how elements interact with each other and with the user

bias: to favour or prefer one thing more than another unfairly

bio-ink: the material used to produce engineered (artificial) live tissue using 3D printing technology. It is usually composed only of cells, but in most cases, an additional carrier material is also added

biomaterials: substances used to support, enhance or replace damaged tissue. They may be natural or synthetic, e.g. plastic used in contact lenses

biometric data: records that are used to identify people by a physical attribute that doesn't change. An example of this would be a database of fingerprints of known criminals

Glossary

biometric methods: technologies that analyse unique personal characteristics such as fingerprints, eye retinas and irises, voice and facial patterns, and hand measurements as a form of identification

bioprinting: the process of producing tissues and organs similar to natural body parts and containing living cells, using 3D printing

bit: short for binary digit, is the smallest unit of data in a computer. It has a single binary value, either 1 or 0

blank pages: a page on which there is no text or images

blog: a website that you can use either as a diary of thoughts (a reflection), or to share ideas and opinions and links

Bluetooth: protocols for short-range wireless interconnection of mobile phones, computers and other electronic devices

Blu-ray disk: a plastic coated disc on which music digital information is written and read using a laser. Can store more data than a DVD

body: the content layer that defines the document's body

bookmark (layout): a means of navigation within a document

bookmark (web authoring): a named anchor at a specific place on a web page

Boolean: data indicating whether something is true or false

bottom-up design: the smallest sub-systems are designed first and then combined into progressively larger units

bridge: a device for linking separate segments of a local area network

brightness: the amount of light an image is emitting; an image with 0% brightness will be all black, an image with 100% brightness will be all white

browser: a type of software that allows you to go on the internet

bullet list: a list in which each item is on a new line, and each line starts with a symbol

bullets: a symbol used next to text, usually when outlining key points

calculated field: a field whose data is calculated from other fields

capacitive touch screen: a touch screen that is sensitive to the static electricity from your finger

CVV (card verification value): a 3-digit number on the back of a credit or debit card. Users have to give this number when they are ordering items online

carousel: a presentation mode that allows a slide presentation to repeatedly play until you stop it

category axis: displays labels for the items that the values represent

category axis labels: the labels on the category axis

category axis title: the title of the axis displaying labels for the items that the values represent

cc: short for 'carbon copy'. This is the field you type an address into if you want the person to see the email, but not necessarily respond to it

CD-ROMs and DVD-ROMs: CDs and DVDs that are read only

CD-Rs and DVD-Rs: blank CDs and DVDs which can be written to once only

CD-RWs and DVD-RWs: CDs and DVDs on which data can be written, erased and re-recorded

cell: a geographical area covered by one base station

cell: a box into which a single piece of data can be added

cell references: a way of pointing to a part of a spreadsheet using letters for columns and numbers for rows

cells: the small rectangular sections on spreadsheets used to enter data such as text, numbers or symbols and to perform calculations using formulae and functions

cellular network: a radio network distributed over land through cells where each cell includes a fixed base station

central processing unit (CPU): or processor, is the unit which performs most of the processing inside a computer

certificate authorities (CA): a trusted entity that issues digital certificates

challenge-response check: an authentication method used to identify a user who has to produce a piece of evidence, e.g. a password

character check: a validation rule to ensure that only certain characters are entered

character set: a list of characters that are valid

chart: information presented as a table, graph or diagram

chart title: the main heading of the chart or graph

charts: visual representations of sets of data

check box: a small box on a form into which a tick or other mark is entered

check digit: an extra value that is calculated from the entry made and is sometimes added to it

cheque: a written document that orders a bank to pay a specific amount of money from a person's account to the person in whose name the cheque has been issued

chip and PIN reader: device used to read the data stored in the silicon chip of a credit or debit card to verify the personal identification number (PIN) entered using a numeric keypad

cipher: a method of encrypting data

ciphertext: the encrypted plaintext

circuit board: a thin rigid board containing thin lines of metals on the surface to create electric circuits

class: one or a group of attributes that can be applied to any element

clock: a quartz crystal that sends pulses to control the rate at which the CPU processes instructions

cloning: making an exact copy of something

cloud computing: the delivery of computer services over the internet

cloud storage: the storage of digital data on remote servers

code: text written using the commands and syntax of a particular computer language

colour depth: the number of bits used to store colour data about each pixel

column break: a command to end the current column and start a new one

column chart: a chart where data are represented by vertical rectangles

columns (layout): a vertical area reserved for text

columns (spreadsheets): made up of cells that are adjacent to each other and go from top to bottom or bottom to top vertically

column width: how long or narrow the cells are

columnar form: a form that displays one record at a time

combo box: a control on a form that contains a drop-down list

comma separated values (CSV): this file format can be used on data saved in a table structured format, such as a spreadsheet or a database, where each value is separated by a comma

command button: a button that brings about an action when it is pressed

command line interface (CLI): a text-based interface that allows the user to interact with a computer using keyboard input at a prompt on the screen

compact disk (CD): a plastic coated disc on which (usually) music digital information is written and read using a laser

compilers: convert the program written by a human in a high-level language into code that the microprocessor can understand – a series of 1s and 0s

component: the parts that make up a whole machine. The internal parts are usually referred to as components and the external devices as 'peripherals'

compound key: a key consisting of two or more fields

compressed: any file that contains one or more files or directories that is smaller than their original file size

compression algorithm: a method to compress files, reducing their size and making them more portable

computer: a device that follows a set of instructions to carry out a series of arithmetical and logical operations

computer aided design (CAD): software that allows the creation, modification and analysis of a design

computer aided learning (CAL): the use of computer systems to aid the user in learning

computer modelling: an attempt to abstract the rules and mechanisms that control real-life systems and apply them in computer programs so that they can be used to simulate the behaviour of those systems

computer system: a computer combined with other equipment so that it can carry out desired functions

computer-generated environment: the use of software to create 3D images of scenery, buildings, etc. in which objects can move

conditional formatting: changing the appearance of a cell on the basis of specified conditions

consistent character spacing: using the same character spacing for particular elements throughout the document

consistent layout: when the placement and design of features on multiple documents are similar

consistent style: the use of the same colours, logo position, layout, images, etc. across documents

contactless payment: a transaction that require no physical contact between the consumer's payment device, e.g. credit card or smartphone, and the physical terminal

content layer: the text, images, videos, tables and links in the web page

contiguous data: data in columns and rows that are next to each other and easy to select together to make charts with

contrast: the difference between the highest and lowest light intensities in an image

control: parts of a form or report used to display and manipulate data

control signals: electrical signals that are sent out to all of the devices to check their status and give them instructions

Glossary

control unit: component of the central processing unit (CPU) that directs the operations of the processor

copy: make a copy (an identical version) of the highlighted text in the clipboard without removing it from the document

copyright: rights that prevent people using a piece of work without the creator's (the copyright holder's) permission

copyright acts: laws enacted to protect intellectual property

corporate branding: the promotion of a particular company or organisation through the advertising style it uses. The more people see the style the more they associate it with that particular company or organisation

corporate house style: a set of styles adopted by an organisation which specifies the formatting to use for their documents

credentials: pieces of information

credit card: a card that allows a customer to borrow funds to pay for goods and services

credit card fraud: theft or fraud that is committed using a payment card, such as a credit card or a debit card

criminal material: content that is illegal in the country where it is accessed

criterion: an expression used to query field values. Criteria is the plural form of criterion

cropping: to remove unwanted portions of an image by 'cutting off' or removing the sides. The crop tool is used to achieve this

CRT monitor: a monitor with a cathode ray tube; CRT was used in the traditional TV sets and monitors

CSS: Cascading Stylesheets is a simple way to add style such as fonts, colours or spacing to web pages

currency: numbers that have a currency symbol with them

custom show: an adaptation of an existing presentation that is suitable for a particular audience

customised medicine: (also called personalised medicine) a medicine that is specially formulated and created to meet the needs of one, unique person

cut: remove something from its current position and copy it to the computer's memory (often called 'the clipboard' when performing cut/copy and paste) so that it can be replaced in a new position

data: raw, unorganised items without any description or explanation, e.g. 69, 90, 30. Data values don't have any meaning until they are put into context

data capture form: a document used for capturing information

data entry form: a form through which data can be input into a particular table

data integrity: the maintenance of data accuracy and consistency

data label: label stating the name of the item represented in the chart

data model: a way of representing the relationships in a real-life, complex system using text, diagrams, symbols or numbers and formulae

data packet: one of the small parts into which network communications are broken

data redundancy: when the same piece of data is held in two separate places

data structure: a way of storing and managing data

data subject: the person whose personal data is being stored

data type: the different types of data that each field can hold, such as date/time, text, etc

data value labels: labels on a graph showing the value represented at each plot point or by each bar or column

database: an example of application software, used to store organised data electronically, so that data can easily be retrieved, managed or updated

database queries: searches made on the data held in a database to find ones with a particular specification, e.g. to find all of the female members of a gym

date/time: when date or time is written in the conventional time or date formats

debit card: a card allowing the holder to transfer money electronically from their bank account when making a purchase

decrypt: changing the ciphertext back into plaintext

decryption: the process of recovering the original text from the encrypted text

default setting: the standard setting or configuration

delete: remove something from a document

descending order: arranged from largest to smallest or in reverse alphabetical order

design: the process of defining the elements of a system, including software, the different interfaces, the data that goes through that system and the hardware required

design wizard: an online tool that takes a user through the steps of designing something, e.g. a form or a report

desktop computer: a computer system designed to be used at a desk in a fixed location

device drivers: part of the operating system. Device drivers allow the processor to communicate with devices such as the keyboard, mouse, monitor and printer

dialogue-based interface: an interface that allows a user to interact with a computer through the spoken word

digital: information represented by certain fixed values rather than as a continuous range. Usually data represented by the digits 1 and 0

digital camera: produces digital images that can be stored in a computer and displayed on a screen

digital certificate: a digital certificate is a method of guaranteeing that a website is genuine and that communication between you (the client computer) and the server is secure. A website with a digital certificate has a small padlock icon you see in the bottom right of your web browser

digital-to-analogue converter: a device used to convert digital signals into analogue ones

digital versatile disk (DVD): a plastic coated disc on which digital information is written and read using a laser. Can store more data than a compact disk

direct access: see random access

direct changeover: implementation where the old system is shut down and the new system is started up

documentation: official information about a system

documents: written or printed information such as a web page, presentation, spreadsheet, report or database, among others

domain name: the text equivalent of an IP address

dongle: a small device able to be connected to and used with a computer, especially to allow the use of protected software

dot matrix printer: a printer that uses a set of pins to press an inked ribbon against the paper, creating the output out of dots

double data entry: a proofing technique that uses the COUNTIF spreadsheet function together with conditional formatting to highlight the differences in two lists of items

dragging: moving a selected/highlighted object with the mouse

drive: a disk drive on which data is stored. The operating system gives it a logical name, e.g. drive A, drive C

driving wheel: also called a 'racing wheel'. Used as an input device in racing games and simulations where users control vehicles

drop-down menu: a menu that appears when the user clicks on a particular item

duplicate: make a copy of (verb) or a copy of something (noun)

dynamic: changes with different circumstances or as other things change

ease of use: how easy it is to use something to perform a task

effect options: different ways that the animation can be modified, e.g. duration and direction of movement

efficiency: the amount of work that has to be done to carry out a particular task

electrical overload: electrical circuit overloads are when too many electrical items are plugged into one socket causing more current to be put across an electrical wire or circuit than it can handle

electronic control unit (ECU): a device responsible for overseeing, regulating and altering the operation of a car's electronic systems

electronic fund transfer (EFT): this is the transfer of money electronically from one account to another

electronic fund transfers point of sale (EFTPOS): a POS with a chip and PIN reader

electronic tokens: also called cryptocurrencies. They function as a medium of exchange between people and businesses

electronic-conference: a meeting between individuals who are not in the same room or location using communications technology

email: short for electronic mail. Messages distributed by electronic means

email attachment: a computer file that is sent with an email message

email group: contact group or a mailing list

embedded object: an object created with one application and placed into a document created by another application so that it retains its format

encrypted: data that has been scrambled into a form that cannot be understood

encryption: the process of turning information (e.g. a message) into a form that only the intended recipient can decrypt and read

entity: a thing that is recognised as being capable of an independent existence, which can be uniquely identified, and about which data can be stored. It is usually a physical object (e.g. a gym member, car, person, book) or it can be a concept (e.g. a customer transaction storing details of the items that were purchased)

e-publications: digital materials published online such as e-books or digital magazines and e-newspapers

Glossary

e-readers: a device on which you can read e-publications

eSafety: being safe on the internet but it can also include the safe use of technology in general

expert system: a computerised system that attempts to reproduce the decision-making process of an expert human

explanation system: provides an explanation of the reasoning processes used to arrive at a particular decision

export: saving a file in a particular format in one application so that it can be opened in another, different application

expression: a combination of mathematical and arithmetic operators and fields used to evaluate a single value

extended reality: a virtual or a combined virtual and real environment

external stylesheet: a document, outside the web page, containing the styles to be applied to the elements in the web page

extranet: a communication system for a particular company or organisation that can be accessed from the internet by other parties or organisations who have been granted access. It is an extension of an intranet

extreme data: (also called boundary data) values at the minimum and maximum range of what should be accepted by the system

field: one item of information about an entity, e.g. Pupil Number, Surname, First Name

field name: also called a label or column heading, is the name for a column by which it can be identified. E.g. Name, Date Modified, Type, Size, etc.

file allocation table (FAT): maps the locations in which files and folders are stored on the disk

file extension: a short name at the end of a file which tells the computer what format the file is in and which program or application can be used to open that file

file format: the structure of a file that tells a program how to display its contents

file name: a unique identification for a file stored on a storage medium

file/data structures: the way in which the different data items will be stored

fill: add shading to the inside of the cell. It can have no fill of one of many different colours

filters: these restrict the type of results that will be supplied, e.g. images or videos or even websites

filtering: to select and remove particular items from others

final testing (or terminal testing): tests carried out on the whole system once it has been completely developed

find: a tool that finds words in a document

find and replace: software that will search for a word and replace it with the one suggested by the user

firewall: software or hardware devices that protect against unauthorised access to a network

fixed hard disk drives: drives permanently connected to the computer and are contained within the cases of both desktop and laptop computers. They are built in

flash memory: a non-volatile memory chip used for storage and for transferring data between digital devices. It has the ability to be electronically reprogrammed and erased

flash memory cards: similar to memory sticks as they are a form of portable memory but the device is flat and looks like a card. The card slots into a port which is a different shape. Such cards are also called computer flash (CF) cards, CFast cards, or secure digital (SD) cards

flat-file database: a database that has only one table. Each line of the table holds one record

floating gate transistors: transistors that keep their charge when the power is switched off

folder hierarchy: the organisation of folders in a computer

font face: also known as typeface. The specific characteristics of a font in a particular family, e.g. Helvetica Bold, Helvetica Italic, Helvetica Bold Italic. Bold and italic are the font faces or typefaces

font family: a set of fonts with a common design, e.g. Arial, Arial light, Arial bold, etc

font type: serif, sans-serif or script

footer: a small area at the bottom of a document

foreign key: a field in one table that refers to a primary key in another table

format check: a validation rule to ensure the characters entered are in a particular order or pattern

formula: arithmetical operations carried out on the contents of cells. The plural of formula is formulae

formulae: a mathematical relationship or rule expressed in symbols

forum: a website where groups of people can discuss topics that interest them

forwarding: re-sending an email message that you have received to another person's email address

FTP: File Transfer Protocol. Used to transfer files from one computer to another in a secure way

full-page slides: one slide printed out on one page of paper

function (database): a block of reusable code that can be used to perform an action

function (spreadsheet): predefined formulae included in the spreadsheet

functions (programs): a self-contained section of code, within a module, which is called by the main program to perform a particular task

generic file type: a file that can be opened on any operating system using a standard application

geographic information systems (GIS): geographic information systems capture, store, check and display data related to the surface of the Earth as a map

gesture-based interface: an interface that allows a user to interact with a computer at a distance by using movements of various parts of their body

global positioning systems (GPS): a navigation system that uses satellites to locate items on the ground

grammar check: checks for improper sentence structure and word usage

grammar check tool: a program that tries to check the grammatical correctness of text

graph: a type of chart showing the relationship of one variable with another one

graphical user interface (GUI): an interface that provides an intuitive way of interacting with a computer through a screen by clicking on icons, menus, buttons or windows using (for example) a mouse, touchpad or touch screen

graphics card: a printed circuit board that controls the output to a display screen or monitor

graphics tablet: an input device consisting of a flat pad which the user 'draws' on or points at with a special light pen or stylus

graphs: a chart that shows the relationship between sets of data

gridlines: information intended to advise people on how something should be done

group: combining images so that they can be selected and moved together

guidelines: a policy or rules to be followed

gutter margins: the extra margins created for documents that need to be bound into a book format, so that the binding doesn't obscure the text

hacker: a person who carries out hacking

hack: to gain of unauthorised access to data in a system or computer

handouts: printed formats of a presentation which can be given to an audience. They can be printed in many formats depending on the audience and use

handover: the automatic transfer of a user's connection to a base station to another base station which is nearer to the user

hanging paragraph: indentation of the second and subsequent lines of a paragraph that is further in than the first indentation of the paragraph

hard disk drive: a non-volatile memory hardware device that stores data on magnetic disks

hard page break: a page break inserted by the user

hard-copy: a document printed on paper (a soft-copy is a digital version)

hardware: the physical parts of a computer system, the parts you can touch. This includes the motherboard, CPU, keyboard, mouse, printer, and so on

hazard map: a map that highlights areas that are vulnerable to particular adverse conditions

head: a container for metadata and scripting language such as CSS

header: a small area at the top of a document

headphones: personal speakers that only the person wearing is intended to hear

hex codes: hexadecimal is a number system that's based on 16s (instead of 10s); hex codes can be used to represent colours on web pages

hierarchical structure: a file system that organises files in a top to bottom structure where files are saved in directories that have parent directories until the top of the structure is reached

highlight: select text in a document by dragging the cursor across it holding down the left mouse button

homophone: two words having the same pronunciation but different spellings

horizontal: parallel to the bottom edge

hosting: allocating space on a web server for people to create their own websites

HTML: HyperText Markup Language is the code you use to create web pages

HTTPS: HyperText Transfer Protocol Secure variant. HTTP using a secure encrypted link

hub: a device used for connecting computers to form a network. It broadcast data to all devices not just the one they are intended for

hyperlink: either text, an image or part of an image that is a link to another item or web page

Glossary

HyperText Markup Language (HTML): a way of tagging text files to achieve font, colour, graphic, and hyperlink effects on world wide web pages

HyperText Transfer Protocol (HTTP): used by the world wide web to define how a web page is formatted and transferred

identity theft: a type of fraud where personal information is stolen and used to impersonate that person

image colour depth: the number of bits used to store colour data about each pixel

image resolution: the number of pixels per unit area of resolution

implementation: the act of starting to use a new system

import: to start a file in an application of a different format so that it is ready to use, e.g. to open a spreadsheet in a word processing application

inappropriate material: content that is not suitable for the age of the person accessing it

indentation: space at the beginning of a line or paragraph

indented paragraph: a paragraph that begins its first line of text a few spaces away from the left-hand margin

inference engine: the program that can apply the rules to the data in order to get sensible judgements

information: data that has been put into context and is meaningful, e.g. exam results were 69%, 90% and 30%

information assets: valuable data that you wouldn't want to be stolen or corrupted

inheritance factor: a physical characteristic that someone can use for authentication, e.g. their fingerprint

inkjet printer: a printer that works by squirting ink at the page out of different nozzles for different coloured ink

inline: style attributes placed within the HTML code

input device: any hardware device that sends data to a computer

input format: how data is to be entered into the system and how it will be interpreted

input mask: a string of characters that indicates the format of valid input values

insert: place something between other things

integer: a whole number with no decimal places

intellectual property: the ideas and skills of other people that belong to them

intelligent transport system: the use of communications devices, computers, control and sensing devices to improve the safety and efficiency of traffic movement through transmitting real-time information

internal memory: data storage spaces that are accessible to the CPU

international data protection legislation: laws to govern the collection and storage of personal data

internet: a global, public system of interconnected computer networks that serves billions of users worldwide and is therefore a wide area network. The internet provides many services including email and the world wide web (www). The contents of the internet are not controlled

internet banking: a method of banking in which transactions are conducted electronically via the internet

internet of things (IOT): the interconnection via the internet of computing devices embedded in everyday objects, enabling them to send and receive data

internet protocol (IP): a set of rules that computers must follow when accessing the internet

Internet Service Provider (ISP): an organisation that provides services for accessing and using the internet

interview: a meeting in which someone asks questions to another person

intranet: a communication system, solely within a particular company or organisation

IP address: An IP address is a set of numbers used to identify one particular computer on the internet. The IP address is like a postal address and it will allow data and messages to be sent directly to the correct computer. It consists of a series of numbers e.g. 216.27.61.137

joystick: a joystick can carry out the same tasks as a mouse as well as other functions such as controlling movement

key: a piece of information that is used for encrypting and decrypting data

key field: a field that holds unique information

key logger: short for 'keystroke logger'; type of malware that records individual key strokes that are pressed on a computer's keyboard

key word: words used in a computer language to specify particular actions

keyboard: an input device that is used to enter fixed values, often characters, into the computer system

knowledge base: a database of related information about a particular subject

knowledge factor: something that a person knows that can be used for authentication

landscape: the document is wider than it is tall

laptop computer: a portable computer with the same functionality as a desktop computer

laser printer: a printer that works by using a laser to 'draw' the required outputs onto a drum and uses toner to print the output onto paper

layer (images): the term used to describe the different levels at which you can place an image

layer (web authoring): an area of website design, e.g. content, style and behaviour

layout: on a document or screen

layout master: a template for a particular layout based on the master slide

legend: a key at the side of a chart or graph that indicates what the symbols or colours and patterns represent in the chart or graph

legislation: a group of laws about something

length check: a validation rule to ensure the number of characters entered are a certain number, greater than a minimum number or less than a maximum number

licence key: a data string that, upon installation, unlocks a software product and makes it available for use

light pen: a specialised pen that works with a CRT monitor

light sensor: a device that measures light intensity and sends the data to a processor

limitations: restrictions that prevent something working correctly

line graph: a chart where values are connected by a line

line spacing: the space between one line and the next

linked object: a pasted object in a document that automatically updates when it is changed in the original document

linkers: take one or more of the files produced by the compiler and combines them into a program that the microprocessor can execute

live data: actual, real-life data that has been used while the old system was running

live streaming: when streamed video is sent over the internet in real time, without first being recorded and stored, e.g. many sporting events are live streamed

live system: a system that is being used in real life, not being tested

local area network (LAN): network used for data transmission by computing devices within one building or site, such as an office building or a school or university campus

local web pages: a file in the same folder as the web page you are accessing or working on

logical operator: operator such as AND, OR, NOT, which perform comparisons values in different fields

lossless compression: a method of compressing a file where no data is discarded

lossy compression: a method of compressing data where some data is discarded

machine learning: the ability of computers to learn without being explicitly programmed

magnetic polarity: the state of being a north pole or a south pole; similar to positive or negative charge for electricity

magnetic storage media: media that stores data magnetically by using local magnetic polarity to represent binary code

magnetic stripe reader: a device used to read a magnetic stripe of a card, which contains data, or to write to the stripe

magnetic tape: stores data in a long line on magnetic tape and read by a magnetic tape drive

magnetic tape drive: a device for collecting, backing up and archiving data on magnetic tape

malware: software designed to gain unauthorised access to a computer system in order to disrupt its functioning or collect information without the user's knowledge

margins: the edge or border of something

master page: a page used as a template for all pages within a document

master slide: a type of template where you can create the style and formatting that you wish to copy across all the other slides

match points: areas on a person that are compared with those on the stored data

mathematical formula: an expression or equation that expresses the relationship between particular quantities. (Plural is formulae)

maximum value: the largest value shown

media access control (MAC) address: a serial number that is unique to each device and is used to identify it on a network

media streaming: a method of transmitting or receiving data (especially video and audio material) over a computer network as a steady, continuous flow, allowing playback to start while the rest of the data is still being received

memory card: a type of storage device that is used for storing data files and media. They are often used in small, portable devices, such as cameras and phones

Glossary

memory sticks (USB flash drives)/pen drives: small storage devices with a lot of storage space that plug into a USB socket for reading/writing

merge: combine two or more cells to create a single, larger cell

merged cells: when more than one single cell has been joined to make a larger cell

metadata: data about the HTML document. Metadata is not displayed in the web page

microphone: a device that converts sound to an analogue electrical signal

microprocessor: an electronic circuit or chip that makes the computer or electronic device work by processing data, performing calculations and issuing instructions based on the results

minimum value: the smallest value shown

modelling software: programs used to create computer models

modules: part of a computer program that carries out a particular function of the program

money transfer: the act of transferring money electronically from one place to another. A money transfer agent carries this out, for example, VITTA or Western Union

monitor: an output device that visually displays the data output by a computer

motherboard: also called the system board. The main printed circuit board of the computer; it has connectors that other circuit boards can be slotted into

mouse: a hand-held device that is used with a computer to move the pointer/cursor on the screen. There are several different types of mouse such as mechanical and optical mouse. (note: the plural of mice is 'mice')

multi-factor authentication: a user has to produce several pieces of evidence in a challenge test

multimedia: a combination of graphics, text, audio, video and animations

multimedia presentation: a presentation that uses a mix of media, for example, text, sound, photos, animations, videos and interactive content

multimedia projector: device that can project an image from a computer onto as large a surface as is necessary, often used in presentations

named cell or **named range:** a short text or name which is given to a cell or group of cells within a range by which they can be referenced in the spreadsheet model

navigation: clicking on a link or hyperlink that will take you to another place on the same page, on another page in the same document or to an online place, such as a website

navigation controls: command buttons that allows a user to move between forms

near field communication (NFC): a short-range wireless method for devices to communicate with each other without needing a power supply

nested function: a function inserted as one of the arguments in another function

netiquette: a set of rules for acceptable online behaviour

network: two or more computers or other digital devices connected together in order to share data and resources

network interface card (NIC): a printed circuit board that allows the computer to communicate with other devices over a computer network

network switch: a device used for connecting computers to form a network. It transmits data only to the device for which it is intended

network traffic: the overall network usage caused by all of the data that is being transmitted at a given time

newsletter: news, updates and information issued periodically to the members of a society or other organisation

non-contiguous data: data where the columns and rows are not adjacent to each other

non-volatile: a state where data is retained when power is switched off

normal data: data that would normally be expected to be entered

numbered list: a list in which each item is on a new line, and each line starts with a number

numeric: are only numbers as a data type in a database

numeric keypad: a keyboard with a group of keys representing the digits from 0 to 9 arranged in a rectangle

observation: closely watching something

OCR: optical character recognition scans a typewritten or printed document and translates the images of the characters into digital text that can be used on the computer

OMR: optical mark recognition enables data marked by a human, by making marks to select options to be captured for processing by a computer

on mouse click: an action that occurs when one of the mouse buttons is pressed

one-to-many relationship: where the data in one row of a table can be linked to data in many rows of another table

online booking systems: systems that allow people to book tickets and make reservations over the internet

open: to start a file in its own application so that it is ready to read or use

operating system (OS): the operating system is a collection of programs to control and manage all of the software and hardware of the computer system

optical mouse: an optical mouse emits light and uses an optical sensor to detect changes in the reflected light to move the pointer on a computer screen

optical storage device: a device that writes data to or reads data from optical media using laser light

optical storage media: media that store data on their surface that can be read using a light source (usually a laser)

option group: a control on a form that displays a number of alternatives

orphan (databases): records that reference records in other tables that no longer exist

orphans (layout): when the first line of a paragraph appears as the last line of a page or column

output device: any device used to send data from a computer to another device or user

output format: how the results of processing are to be presented to the users

packet switching: when certain areas of the network are too busy to carry the packets, they are automatically switched to emptier circuits

page layout: the arrangement of text, images and other objects on a page

page orientation: the way you position your page: having the narrower width across the top of the page is called 'portrait' orientation; having the wider width across the top of the page is called 'landscape' orientation

page size: this differs depending on the type of document you are producing, such as A4

pagination: placing numbers or characters to indicate the sequence of pages in a document

parallel running: implementation that involves both the old and new systems running at the same time

parent directory: a directory in which another directory is placed

password: a secret word or phrase that must be used to gain admission to a place

paste: placing the copied text at a selected position in the document

paste special: a feature that gives a user more control of how content is displayed or functions when it is pasted from the clipboard

patient record system: a computer system used to keep an account of a patient's examinations and treatments

percentages: data value labels on a pie chart showing the relative contribution of each sector to the whole

peripherals: external devices that provide input and output for the computer

personal data: data relating to a living individual; it covers any information that relates to an identifiable, living individual

personal financial model: creating a plan to manage a person's budget

phablet: a smartphone with a screen size larger than most smartphones but smaller that a tablet

pharmacy records: details of medicines and drugs prescribed for each patient and the overall dispensed from a particular source

pharming: when a hacker installs a malicious program on a computer or a server. This program code causes any clicks that you make on a website to be redirected to another website without you knowing

phased implementation: implementation where one part of the system is changed but the rest of the system continues to use the old methods

phishing: a criminal activity trying to find sensitive information, such as passwords or banking details, by fraudulent means

physical token: a personal device that authenticates a person's identity

pie chart: a circular chart cut into sector representing the values of the data items

pilot running: the new system is trialled in just one part of the organisation

piracy: copying intellectual property that belongs to someone else

pixel: an individual point of light in a digital image. (It is a shortened version of '**pic**ture **el**ements')

placeholder positions: 'frames' or 'empty boxes' to insert items of text, images, sound, video, etc

plaintext: the text that is to be encrypted

plot point: a fixed point on a graph with a measured position on the x- and y-axes

podcast: a digital audio file made available on the internet for downloading to a computer or mobile device

Glossary

point: used for measuring the size of a font. One point is 1/72 of an inch and the standard size is 12 points

point of sale (POS): the place where you pay for goods or services, e.g. a cash register

portable hard disk drives: contained within their own cases and are separate from main computer systems to which they are connected by cable

portrait: the document is taller than it is wide

possession factor: something that a person owns that can be used for authentication

poster: a large printed sheet containing text and pictures which is displayed in a public space

predictive text: automatic word prediction when entering text

presence check: a validation rule to ensure that data is entered and that the field is not empty

presentation: a way of presenting something to an audience; can include a speaker showing slides, videos, sound and looped slides in an exhibition

presentation layer: this is responsible for the appearance or styling of objects on a webpage and is achieved using a cascading stylesheet

presentation template: a frame upon which to build a presentation by simply filling in your own relevant information in the spaces provided

presenter notes: printouts of the slides and notes that can be used by the presenter

pressure sensor: a device that measures pressure and sends the data to a processor

primary key: the key field used to identify each record

printers and plotters: devices that produce output onto paper and onto other materials

private key: a key that is known only to the person to decrypt messages encrypted by their public key

process: carry out or execute the instructions

production line: a line of machines and workers in a factory that a product moves along while it is being produced. Each machine or worker performs a particular job that must be finished before the product moves to the next position in the line

program code: the statements and commands written in a particular programming language

programming languages: sets of commands, instructions and the rules of how to use them, that are used to create software

proofing: the general term for checking documents for accuracy and correctness

proofread: to check a document for spelling and grammatical errors before it is released to its target audience

property sheet: a list of all of the settings for all of the items, e.g. field, label, heading on a form

prosthetics: an artificial body part

protocol: sets of rules governing how devices communicate with each other over networks

public key: a key that is freely available and is used to encrypt a message

QR code: quick response code – a type of two-dimensional barcode (in a square) that can store data such as URLs, geotags and links

QR scanner: a quick response scanner consists of software and hardware, such as a smartphone and an app used to read and respond to the data stored in a QR code. They are most conveniently used on smartphones which can be easily positioned in front of the QR code

quarantine: the placing of suspected malware into a specific area of a storage device

query: a method of interrogating the data held in a database

questionnaire: a set of questions with a choice of answers to carry out a survey

radio button: an icon representing one of a set of options

random access (also called direct access): accessing data in any order and not in a fixed sequence, regardless of its position in a list

random-access memory (RAM): memory that stores data and applications while they are being used. It only stores them while the computer is on, but when you turn the computer off, everything in the RAM is lost. This is known as being volatile

range: a group of cells in a spreadsheet where the cells are all adjacent to each other. Ranges can be used in formulae

range check: a validation rule to ensure the data is between a minimum and maximum value

read-only memory (ROM): memory that has data preinstalled onto it that cannot be removed. Unlike RAM, ROM keeps its contents when the computer is turned off. It is therefore known as being non-volatile

real-time: as things occur, with no delay. For example, the model would be updated with data as weather changed so everyone would know exactly what was happening at that moment

record: consists of all the fields about an individual instance of an entity in a database, e.g. all the details about one gym member

referential integrity: preventing orphan records – records that reference records in other tables that no longer exist

reflecting: to produce a mirror image of the original image

registers: memory storage locations within the CPU

relational database: a database with many linked tables

Relational Database Management System (RDMS): software to create and manage relational databases, e.g. Microsoft Access

relationship: fields in different tables with corresponding data

relative: considered where something is in relation to something else

relative file path: a route to a destination folder or file starting at the folder you are already in. It will work only if you are at this starting point

relative reference: a cell reference that changes as it is copied down columns or across rows

remedial action: steps taken to correct an error

remote control: a small, handheld device that can be used to operate equipment such as a TV or stereo

repetitive strain injury (RSI): pain felt in muscles, nerves and tendons caused by continuously making the same movements

reply to all: sending a reply to all of the people the email was sent to and not just to the sender

requirements specification: a document listing all of the functions the system is expected to perform and the data flow needed

resistive touch screen: a touch screen that is sensitive to pressure from your finger

RFID (radio-frequency identification): an RFID reader uses radio waves to identify and track special tags attached to objects

RFID tag: radio-frequency identification tag. Contains digital data that can be interrogated by and send the data to a reader device using radio waves

robot: a machine controlled by a computer that is used to perform jobs automatically

rotate: turn an image through an angle relative to its original position

router: a device for transmitting data between networks

row height: how tall or short the cells are

rows: made up of cells that are adjacent to each other and go from left to right or right to left horizontally

rules base: a set of rules that will be used to produce an output or decision by the expert system

sample: making a physical measurement of a wave at set time intervals and converting those measurements to digital values

sans-serif font: a font without the decorative strokes at corners or bases

satellite: an artificial body placed in orbit round the earth or moon or another planet in order to collect information or for communication

satellite dish: a bowl shaped aerial through which signals are transmitted to or received from a communications satellite

satellite phones: telephones that have the ability to connect to orbiting satellites

satellite systems: provide voice, data and broadcast services with global, coverage to mobile users as well as to fixed sites

satellite television: a service that delivers television programmes to viewers by relaying them from communications satellites orbiting the earth

scales: the units of measurement used on the axes of a chart or graph

scanner: a device that digitises text, diagrams and images

school management system: software designed to assist school administrative and educational tasks such as registration and predicting student progress

screenshot: an image of the data displayed on the screen

ScreenTip: small windows, displaying descriptive text, that pop up when the mouse pointer is rested on them

script: set of computer programming instructions for a computer

scripting language: a programming language, such as JavaScript, used to create a script to control web elements in the behaviour layer of a web page

search engine: a website through which users can search internet content

secondary axis: a vertical axis at the right-hand side of the graph or a horizontal axis at the top

second-level domain: the name directly to the left of the final dot

section break: a break between one section and another

sections: areas of a document with their own layouts and formatting

sector: a 'slice' of a pie chart

sector labels: a description of what each slice of a pie chart represents

Glossary

sensor: a device that detects and responds to some type on input from the environment, e.g. light, temperature, motion, pressure

sequential storage: data arranged and stored in a particular order, for example, alphabetical order or date order

serial storage: data stored in a line on a tape so it has to be read in order

series: a range of cells filled with values that increment

serif font: a font with decorative lines at corners or bases

server: a computer that provides services to other computers on a network

shapes: pre-drawn objects that can be inserted and manipulated

short message service (SMS): system where users can send short text messages to each other from one mobile phone to another or from a computer to a mobile phone

shoulder surfing: finding login names, passwords, credit card and PIN numbers by standing next to someone and watching as they enter them

sibling folder: a folder that is inside the same parent folder as another folder

Simple Mail Transfer Protocol (SMTP): a communication protocol for mail servers when they transmit data

simulate: to make something that looks and acts like a real object or situation but isn't real

slide: one screen of information in a presentation

slide show: a presentation made up of screens of information including digital images, text and audio viewed in a progression

smart card: a plastic card with a built-in processor

smart city: a city where sensor-driven data collection and powerful computers are used to automate and coordinate a wide range of services in the interests of better performance, lower costs and lessened environmental impact

smart device: as the name suggests, an electronic gadget that is able to connect, share and interact with its user and other smart devices

smartphone: a mobile phone that can perform many other functions, e.g. taking photographs and web browsing

smartphone sensor: a sensor in a smartphone for measuring such things as movement and rotation, pressure and light intensity

smishing: uses mobile phone text messages to lure people into returning their call or to click on a link in the text message

social networking site: a site that allows people to communicate and share news, views and events

social networking sites: types of websites or services that allow you to interact with friends and family online and to find other people online who have similar interests or hobbies

soft page break: a page break automatically inserted by the software

softcopy: an electronic copy of a document

software: programs or applications that give instructions to the computer to tell it what to do

software licence: proof that you have paid the owner for the right to use their software under specific terms and conditions, usually agreed when it is purchased

solid-state drive (SSD): a mass storage device similar to a hard drive but it doesn't have any moving parts and data is stored using flash memory

solid-state storage media: a method of storing data electronically. It has no moving parts

sort: arrange items into a particular order

sound card: a printed circuit board that controls output to speakers and headphones

source code editor: a text editor that is specialised for writing code for software and websites. They use markup colouring, autocompletion and will often highlight if there is an error

spam: junk email that involves nearly identical email messages being sent to lots of people. Usually sent to try and persuade you to buy something

spatial laser sensors: sensors which are used with lasers to detect, measure and analyse the space and objects in an environment, in real-time

speaker: a device to enable you to hear sounds or music on your computer system

specified data range: the highlighted data range to be used for the chart

spell check: checks the spelling in a document and make suggestions to correct them

spyware: malware that is designed to be installed secretly on a computer. It records private information as the user enters it and transmits it to the installer

static: does not change

stock control system: a computerised system to automatically maintain records of stock levels. They are automatically informed of the numbers sold to customers and delivered from suppliers. They can automatically order new items when they get below a certain level

storage device: this is the machine that lets you write data to and read data from the storage medium

storage location: a place in internal memory where a single piece of data can be stored until it is needed

storage media: the material on which the data is stored, e.g. magnetic tape or optical disk. (Note: media is the plural of medium)

strong password: a password that is difficult to detect by both humans and computer programs

style sheet: a document illustrating the house style of a particular organisation

style template: a design that serves as a starting point for a new presentation

stylus: a pen-shaped instrument whose tip position on a touchscreen or tablet can be detected

subscript: text printed below the line

superscript: text printed above the line

switch: a device used for connecting computers to form a network. It transmits data only to the device for which it is intended

symmetric encryption: the same key is used for encryption and decryption

syntax: the combinations of symbols that are considered to be a correctly structured document or fragment in that language

systems analyst: an IT specialist responsible for the life cycle of a new/modified IT system, from analysing the problem to implementing an entire system

system flowcharts: diagrams using symbols to display how data flows in a computer system

system manager: the person who oversees the system and is responsible for ensuring that it works correctly

system software: system software provides the services that the computer requires to operate. This may be classified as the operating system and utility software

system specification: a list of all of the software and hardware required by the new system

tab: a paragraph-formatting feature used to align text

tab key: the key used to advance the cursor to the next tab stop

tab stop: the location that the cursor stops at when the tab key is pressed

table: a collection of rows and columns forming cells that are used to store data in a structured and organised manner in a database

tablet: a thin, flat, portable computer with a touch screen, mobile operating system and battery

tabular form: a form that displays multiple records at the same time

tabulation: means arranging data in an orderly manner in rows and columns

tag: words or phrases that describe the content of the section of a website

TCP/IP: transmission control protocol/internet protocol. The protocols used by devices to connect to and communicate over the internet

technical documentation: documentation that includes details about the structure of the system and details of software and hardware needed by programmers and technicians

temperature sensor: a device that reads the temperature of its surroundings and sends the readings to the processor

test data: data that will be used for testing a system

test design: a detailed description of a particular task listing test data, expected results and actual results

test plan: a detailed and structured plan of how testing should be carried out

test strategy: a set of guidelines explaining how the testing will be carried out

testing: checking, using sample data, that all parts of the system function as expected

text: letters of the alphabet and numbers are both classified as a text data type

text alignment: text can be aligned left, right, centre or justified. The text is positioned next to the left margin, right margin, in the middle of each line or evenly along left and right margins respectively

text box: an area in which text can be entered and moved, formatted and manipulated independently of the main document text

text enhancement: text enhancements refer to making your text bold, underlined, italicised or highlighted. They are often applied on top of the existing text font

text wrapping: surrounding an image with text

thesaurus: a dictionary of synonyms or words having the same meaning as the one selected

thread: a series of messages that have been posted as replies to each other. A digital conversation about a topic

tiling: where an image is repeated to fill the available space

top-down design: an approach that starts with the design of complete system and then breaks it down into designs for the component parts or sub-systems

Glossary

top-level domain: the domain extension, e.g. .com, .net, .edu

touch screen: a display screen that is both an input and an output device and that can respond to a user interacting with a specific area

touchpad: a pointing device, often found on a laptop, that allows the user to use their finger to move the pointer on the screen

trackerball: a device to move a pointer where a ball is rolled around directly by the user rather than being moved by the whole mouse being pushed

track changes tool: a tool that highlights any changes that have been made to a document

traffic management: directing vehicles and pedestrians along certain routes to ensure optimal traffic flow with minimum traffic jams

traffic modelling: using mathematical and computer simulations of real-world traffic situations to ensure optimal (best or most desirable) traffic flow with minimum traffic jams

transcription: the transfer of data from one medium to another, e.g. from written data on a form to digital data in a database

transistor: a device that regulates current or voltage flow and acts as a switch for electronic signals

transition: a visual effect that occurs when the presentation moves from one slide to another

transmission: transferring something from one place to another

transparency: how see-through an image is

transpose: when two or more items have changed places

transposition error: when two digits or words in data entry have been accidentally reversed. A mistake made by transposing items

trigger: something that causes another event to occur

trilateration: a method of determining the relative positions of three points by treating them as the points of a triangle

two-factor authentication: a user has to produce **two** pieces of evidence in a challenge test

type check: a validation rule to ensure that the correct data type has been entered

typographical: relating to the accuracy, style or appearance of text

uncompressed: a compressed file returned to its original state

ungroup: separating the image group so that they all have to be selected and moved individually

Uniform Resource Locator (URL): the unique web address of every page on the world wide web

unique: something of which there is only one example

unique identifier: a characteristic or element that is found only on one particular item

units of memory: 8 bits = 1 byte; 1000 bytes = 1 kilobyte; 1000 kilobytes = 1 megabyte; 1000 megabytes = 1 gigabyte; 1000 gigabytes = 1 terabyte

user interface: the on-screen form through which the user interacts with the expert system

utility software (utilities): part of the system software that can analyse, configure, optimise and maintain a computer to keep it working as well as possible

valid: data that has passed a validation test

validation: a proofing technique whereby rules can be set up that prevent you from entering incorrect types of data

validation routines: routines to check that the data entered by a user or from a file meets specified requirements

validation rules: routines to check that the data entered by a user or from a file meets specified requirements

value axis: the axis that shows the values being measured or compared

value axis labels: the labels on the value axis

value axis title: the title of the axis that shows the values being measured or compared

variable: a section of computer memory used to store data about a particular element in a program. When writing a program, variables are given names, e.g. StudentNumber, FirstName. While a program is running the data stored in a variable can change

verification: a proofing technique to check that valid data is accurate

verify: to check, test or agree that something is true or correct and accurate

version control: the process by which different drafts and versions of a document or record are managed. For example, each time it is edited it could be 'Saved As' a new file with the version number added

vertical: at right angles to the horizontal

video camera: a camera to make a record of moving pictures that are stored electronically

video communication: any form of transmission that is based on moving pictures as well as sound

video-conference: a meeting where people at different locations can see and talk to each other while sitting in front of a camera and a microphone

virtual reality: a computer-generated environment

vishing: a combination of 'voice' and phishing, it is when fraudsters obtain personal details of a victim through their landline telephone

visual verification: a proofing technique whereby you visually check a document for accuracy and correctness

voice over internet protocol (VOIP): allows the use of the internet to carry voice data when making phone calls

volatile: a state where data is permanently lost when power is switched off

weather forecasting: predicting weather conditions over the next few days

web browser: an application used to access websites on the world wide web

web page: a document containing text, images, audio, video and links to other pages that can be viewed on a web browser

web server: the computer that the website is saved on

webcam: a special category of video camera that have no storage capacity but is connected directly to a computer

webcast: a one-way transmission which is non-interactive

web-conference: a live meeting held via the internet usually on a computer or smartphone

webinar: teaching session or other presentation that take places on the internet, allowing participants in different locations to see and hear the presenter and ask and answer questions

website: a collection of web pages

wide area network (WAN): a network of networks connecting local area networks over a large geographical area

widget: a self-contained mini program that performs a function for a user

widows: when the last line of a paragraph appears as the first line of a new page or column

Wi-Fi: one protocol allowing computers, smartphones, or other devices to connect to the internet or communicate with one another wirelessly within a particular area

wiki: a website that allows you to become a participant in its creation

wildcard: special characters that can stand for unknown characters

wireless local area network (WLAN): a local area network accessed using radio wave communications

wireless mouse : a mouse that is not connected to the computer by a cable but communicates with it using radio waves

world wide web: a way of accessing information using the internet using HTTP

wrap: text automatically forms a new line when it reaches the right margin

x-**axis:** the horizontal axis of a chart

y-**axis:** the vertical axis of a chart

z-**axis:** the third axis in a three-dimensional graph to represent vertical coordinates

zero login: a method of authentication not requiring a user to login. They are authenticated by their behaviour and the way they do things

Index

3D printers 41
   medical applications 111–13
3D scanners 41
3G, 4G, 5G 97

abnormal data 142
absolute file paths 537–8
absolute references 481
access levels 67
accuracy 302, 497, 503
action buttons 455–7, 461
actuators 8, 42
   autonomous vehicles 103
adaptive cruise control (ACC) 85
advanced filters 488–9
adware 74
Aibo (robot dog) 17
alarm systems 32
alignment of text 266, 271
   tables 245–6, 544–5
alternative text 462
Amazon 93–4
amps calculation 155
analogue data 7
analogue-to-digital conversion 7–8
analysis
   current system analysis 133–4
   research methods 132–3, 134
   system specification 134–5
Analytical Engine 2
anchors 528
AND 399, 400, 401–2, 501
Android 12
animal identification systems 115
animation effects 464–7, 471
anti-locking braking systems 85
anti-malware software 73–4
anti-spyware software 70–1
antivirus software 185
applets 6
applications software 5–6
appropriateness of solutions 149
apps (applications) 6, 15
arithmetic and logic unit (ALU) 8, 9
arithmetic operators 407, 419, 421, 483
artificial intelligence (AI) 17–18, 293–4

ascending order 497
aspect ratio 214
asymmetric encryption 70, 166–7
attributes 531–3
audience characteristics 173, 174–5, 182
audio communication 96
audio-conferencing 75
audio files
   insertion into a web page 537
   lossless compression 206
augmented reality 19–20
authentication 10, 70–3
   biometric 121–2, 165
   multi-factor 169
author of documents 253, 257
autocorrect 289–90, 291
automated number plate recognition (ANPR) 120–1
automated objects 252
automated slide numbering 441
automated software tools 288
automated teller machines (ATMs) 107–8
autonomous machines 18
autonomous vehicles 86, 103
auto-sum function 484
AVERAGE function 484
axis labels 315
axis scales 316
axis titles 314, 315

Babbage, Charles 2
back problems 88
backing storage devices 10–11
banking applications
   automated teller machines 107–8
   cheques 110
   credit/debit cards 109–10
   EFTPOS 118
   electronic fund transfer 108–9
   internet banking 110
bar charts 319
   worked example 329–31
bar codes 37, 38, 121
base stations 97
batch processes 117
bcc box, emails 183
behaviour layer (scripting layer) 524

behavioural biometrics 71, 73
Berners-Lee, Tim 523–4, 539
bias 190
BIDMAS 483
bio-inks 113
biomaterials 112
biometric authentication 10, 71, 121–2, 165
biometric data 71
bioprinting 112, 113
bits 7, 48
blank pages 303
blogs 186
Bluetooth 62
Blu-ray disks 51, 52–3
body section of a web page 527–9
bold 267, 351
   HTML 527
booking systems 106–7
bookmarks 356, 357, 361–3
   web pages 527
Boolean data type 376, 379–80
border spacing, tables 545
botnets 162
bottom-up design 136
Bricklin, Dan 477
bridge design 99
bridges 64
brightness of an image 219
browsers 526
building design 99, 100
bullet symbols 353–4
bullets 266, 270, 275, 352–4, 363–4
bytes 11

cables, safety issues 154
calculated fields 380–1
cameras 30–1
capacitive touch screens 29
car park sensors 24–5
card cloning 164
carousel presentations 445, 470
cars
   automated number plate recognition 120–1
   autonomous vehicles 86, 103
   data security 86–7
   driverless 18
   engine fault diagnostic systems 115
   vehicle safety 85
Cascading Stylesheets (CSS) 539–40
   classes 541–2
   colours 540, 544
   comments 542

   external 546–8
   ids 540–1
   images 542
   inline styles 548–9
   internal 540–6
   tables 542–7
   worked example 549–53
case, consistent use of 305
case changes 352
category axis 313
   titles and labels 315
catfishing 159
cave drawings 211
cc box, emails 183
CD ROMs 51
CD-R 51
CD-RWs 52
celebrity data breaches 60
cell references 479–81
   referencing different sheets 493
cells 97, 244
   merging 245, 479
   named 482
   spreadsheets 479
cellular networks 97, 125
central processing unit (CPU, processor) 3, 4, 8–9
certificate authorities (CAs) 167
challenge-response checks 169
chaos storage system 93–4
character checks 138–9
character sets 526
character spacing 305
chart titles 314
charts 310–11
   insertion into a document 238, 239, 260
   pie charts 320–2
   text wrapping 243
   types of 313, 319
   worked example 329–34
   see also graphs and charts
check boxes 376, 392, 393, 397
check digits 140
cheques 110
chess games 115
chip and PIN readers 34–5, 38
ciphers 165
ciphertext 165
circuit boards 4
classes, CSS 540, 541–2
clipboard 236
clock 8, 9
cloning 164

Index

cloud computing 67
cloud storage 68
    data security 168
Codd, Edgar F. 370
code 524
colour depth 228
colour representation 228
coloured fonts 268–9
colours, CSS 540, 544
column breaks 346
column charts 313, 319
    worked example 332–4
column insertion and deletion 244–5 479
column width 244
columnar forms 390
columns
    documents 342–3
    spreadsheets 479, 505
    tables 244, 342–3
combo boxes 392–4
command buttons 394, 396
command line interfaces (CLIs) 12–13
command words 21
comments
    in CSS 542
    in HTML 529
communication 173
    blogs 186
    forums 187–8
    mobile 97
    satellite systems 124–5
    social networking sites 188
    wikis 186–7
    see also email
communication media 94–6
compact disks (CDs) 51–2
compilers 6
components 3
    backing storage 10–11
    central processing unit 8–9
    input and output devices 10
    internal memory 9–10
compound keys 374
compressed files 205
    lossless compression 206
    lossy compression 206
compression algorithms 205
computer aided design (CAD) 112
computer aided learning (CAL) 104–5
computer-based exams (CBEs) 105
computer-controlled systems 100
    autonomous vehicles 103
    production line control 102
    robotics 101–2
computer-generated environments 18–19
computer modelling 98–100
computer systems 2, 3
    hardware 3–4
    software 5–6
computer vision syndrome (CVS) 88
computers 3
    types of 14–16
conditional formatting 507–9, 517
consistent style 266–7, 282, 304, 305
contact groups (email groups) 184
contactless smart cards 72, 118
content layer 524
contiguous data 311
contrast of an image 220
control signals 8
control unit (CU) 8
controls, forms 390
copy 236
copyright 176–8
copyright acts 176
corporate branding 282
corporate house style 268, 282
corporate images 95
COUNT function 485
creating a new document 235
credit card fraud 164–5
credit cards 109–10
credit/debit cards 34
criminal material 193
criteria (singular: criterion) 399–400
cropping an image 215
CRT (cathode ray tube) monitors 32
.css (cascading style sheet) files 204
    see also Cascading Stylesheets
CSV (comma separated variables) files 204, 384
    importing into a database 385–6
currency symbols 326–7
custom shows 457
customised medicines 113
cut 236, 259
CVV (card verification value) numbers 109
cyberbullying 159

data 311, 371
    analogue and digital 7–8
data breaches 60
data capture forms 136–7
data entry 144
    accuracy 302, 497, 503

double 306
data entry forms
    design features 392–7
    desirable characteristics 392
    form design wizard 390–1
data flow diagrams 133, 134
data integrity 372
data labels 239, 314, 315
data models 478
data packets 64–5
data protection/security 156–7, 161, 388
    biometrics 165
    card fraud 164–5
    in the cloud 168
    digital certificates 167–8
    encryption 165–7
    hacking 162
    pharming 163
    phishing 162–3
    smart devices 84
    threats to data 162
    transport systems 86–7
    viruses and malware 163–4
    vishing and smishing 163
data redundancy 372
data structures 136
data subjects 157
data types 137, 375–6
data value labels 319, 320
database queries 137
database reports 413–14
    fields 417–19
    formatting 421–2
    labels 415–17, 420
    output layouts 423
    page numbers 421
    performing calculations 419, 421
databases 312, 370
    entering and importing data 384–7
    insertion into a document 239–43
    linking to a spreadsheet 241–3
    queries 399–404
    relationships 383–4
    run-time calculations 407–11
    search operators 405
    sorting 400–1, 403–4
    structure 371–4
    tables, creation 374–81, 386
    worked example 425–34
date insertion, documents 253, 258
date/time data 376, 377
debit cards 34, 109–10

decimal places, setting 327, 333
decryption 70, 165
default settings 269, 270
deleting text 236
delimited data items 386
delivery route scheduling 115
descending order 497
design 135–6
    file/data structures 136, 137
    input formats 136–7
    output formats 137–8
    validation routines 138–40
design wizards 390
desktop computers 14
    advantages and disadvantages 16
device drivers 6
dialogue-based interfaces 12, 13
dictation software 42
dictionaries 288, 289
Difference Engine 2
digital cameras 30
digital certificates 167–8
digital data 7
digital footprints 160
digital-to-analogue converters (DACs) 8, 41
digital versatile disks (DVDs) 51–2, 53
direct access (random access) 49
direct changeover 144, 146
direct data-entry (DDE) devices 25, 34–8
    advantages and disadvantages 38
direct messaging 188
directories 199
distributed denial of service (DDoS) attacks 84
<div> tag 557–8
document examination 133, 134
document layout *see* layout
documentation 146
    technical 146–7
    user 147–8
documents 339
    find and replace text 354–5
    formatting text 346–54, 358–65
    inserting charts and graphs 312–15
    inserting spreadsheet and database extracts 239–43
    navigation 356–8
    page layout 340–6
    placing objects 236–9
domain names 188–9
dongles 177
dot-matrix printers 40–1
double data entry 306
dragging 235

Index

drinks, spillage of 154–5
driverless cars 18
drives 199
driving wheels 28
drop-down menus 392–4, 397
DVD ROMs 51
DVD-Rs 51
DVD-RWs 52
dynamic information 252
dyslexia 292

earpieces 42
ease of use 149
e-banking (internet banking) 110
editing a document 235–43
effect options 467
efficiency 148
electrical overload 155
electronic control units (ECUs) 85
electronic fund transfer (EFT) 108–9, 117
electronic fund transfers point of sale (EFTPOS) 117–18
electronic stability control (ESC) 85
electronic tokens 72–3
electronic-conferencing 75–7
email 182
    attachments 184
    eSafety 158
    forwarding 184
    history of 181–2
    netiquette 183–4
    phishing 162–3
    security issues 184–5
    Simple Mail Transfer Protocol 191
    spam 185
    use as evidence 183
    writing a message 182–3
email groups 184
embedded objects 239–40
    emerging technologies 17
    artificial intelligence 17–18
    augmented reality 19–20
    extended reality 18
    virtual reality 18–19
encryption 69–70, 165–7
energy use 68
entities 136, 371
e-publications 96
e-readers 96
error messages 488
    errors 287
    grammatical 290–1
    misspellings 288–90
    typographical 290
eSafety 158
    data protection 156–7
    online gaming 160–1
    personal data security 157–8
    using email 158
    using social media 159–60
    using the internet 158, 193
Ethernet 62
ethics, autonomous vehicles 86
evaluation of information 190–1
evaluation of systems 148–9
exams, computer-based 105
expert systems 113–15
explanation systems 114
exporting a file 203
expression building 381
extended reality (XR) 18
extension leads 155
external stylesheets 539–40, 546–8
extranets 66, 186
extreme data 142
eye strain 88

Federation Against Copyright Theft (FACT) 178
field names 137, 375
field properties 137
fields 136, 372
    controls 390
    database reports 417–19
file allocation tables (FATs) 49
file formats 202–5
file information, documents 253
file management 199
    saving and exporting formats 202–5
    saving and printing formats 202
    storage and location 199–200
file names 200
    version control 201
file size reduction 205
    images 221–2, 228
    lossless compression 206
    lossy compression 206
file structures 136, 137
File Transfer Protocol (FTP) 192
fill
    cells 246–7
    shapes 257
filters 190, 193, 498–503
final testing 141
financial planning 115
find and replace 291–2, 354–5

fingerprints *see* biometric authentication
firewalls 70, 73, 168
fitness, smart devices 83–4
fixed hard disk drives 49
flash drives 54
flash memory 53, 54
flat-file databases 372
flipping (reflecting) an image 216–17
floating gate transistors 53
flood water management 99
folder hierarchies 538
font colours 268–9
font face 268
font families 268
font type 267–8
fonts 267
footers 251–3, 258–9, 276
    database reports 414
foreign keys 373–4
form design wizard 390–1
formal documents 339
format checks 139
formatting a spreadsheet 505–6
    conditional formatting 507–9, 517
    page layout 509–12
    worked example 512–18
formatting text 269–72, 346–7
    case changes 352
    in database reports 421–2
    indented paragraphs 348–51
    tabulation 348
    text enhancement 267, 351
    worked example 358–65
formulae 407
    arithmetic operators 483
    order of operations 483
    spreadsheets 479–83, 492–3, 516
forums 187–8
forwarding emails 184
full-page slides 471
functions 141, 407, 408–11
    nested 484–5, 490–1
    spreadsheets 483–91, 514–15
    use in database reports 419, 421

Garbage In, Garbage Out (GIGO) principle 138, 497
generic file types 203–5
geographic information systems (GIS) 124
gesture-based interfaces 12, 14
gigabytes 11
global positioning systems (GPS) 123
grammar check 288, 290–1

graph databases 312
graphical user interfaces (GUIs) 12, 13
    file management 199
graphics cards 4
graphics interchange format (.gif) files 204
graphics tablets 33
graphs and charts 310–11
    adding a second data series 323
    adding a secondary axis 323–4
    axis scales 316
    formatting 326–7
    insertion into a document 239, 312–15
    line graphs 319
    misleading 321
    selecting data 311–12, 329–30
    worked example 329–34
gridlines 247
grouping images 220–1
guidelines 183
gutter margins 341–2

hacking 60, 67, 69, 70, 162
    smart devices 84
handouts 471–2
handover 97
hanging paragraphs 348, 351
hard-copy 29
hard disk drives 48
hard page breaks 344
hardware 3–4
hardware installation 144
hazard maps 99
hazards 153, 154–6
head section, web pages 526–7
headaches 88
headers 251–3, 257–8, 276, 345–6
    database reports 414, 415
headphones 42
health issues 87–9
    repetitive strain injury (RSI) 81
hex codes 540
hiding rows and columns 505
hiding slides 467–8
hierarchical structures 199
    folder hierarchies 538
highlighting data 311–12
highlighting text 235–6, 259
HLOOKUP function 488
home, smart devices 83
homophones 293
horizontal alignment 245–6
hosting 188

Index

house style 95
hubs 63
human error 287
hyperlinks 189, 356, 357–8, 527, 528–9
   in presentations 452–5
hypertext 523
HyperText Markup Language (HTML) 202, 203, 204, 524, 525–6, 539
   attributes 531–3
   comments 529
   `<div>` tag 557–8
   link element 547–8
   links 528–9
   see also web page creation
HyperText Transfer Protocol (HTTP) 186, 189, 192
HyperText Transfer Protocol Secure (HTTPS) 166, 167, 192

identity theft 162
IF function 489–91
image resolution 228
   images 211–12
   brightness adjustment 219
   contrast adjustment 220
   cropping 215
   in CSS 542
   file size reduction 221–2, 228
   grouping 220–1
   insertion into a web page 535–6
   layers 221
   precise placement 212–13
   reflecting (flipping) 216–17
   resizing 214
   rotating 215–16
   transparency 219
   worked example 225–7
implementation 143–6
importing a file 199
indentations 266, 270
   in lists 353
indented paragraphs 348–51
infographics 311
information 311
information assets 161
inheritance factors 169
inkjet printers 40
inline CSS 540, 548–9
input devices 4, 10, 25
   bar code readers 37
   cameras 30–1
   chip and PIN readers 34–5
   direct data entry 25, 34–8

driving wheels 28
joysticks 27–8
keyboards and keypads 25–6
light pens 32–3
magnetic stripe readers 34
manual devices 25–33
microphones 31
OCR and OMR 36
pointing devices 26–7
QR scanners 37–8
remote controls 27
RFID readers 35
scanners 29–30
sensors 24–5, 31–2
touch screens 28–9
input formats 136–7
input masks 139
instant messaging 188
INT (integer) function 484–5
integers 375
intellectual property (IP) 176
intelligent transport systems 85–6
   data security 86–7
internal CSS 539, 540–6
internal memory 4, 9–10, 11
international data protection legislation 156–7
internet 61, 66, 185
   access from mobile devices 97
   blogs 186
   cloud computing 67
   cloud storage 68
   domain names 188–9
   eSafety 158
   evaluating information 190–1
   forums 187–8
   routers 64
   safety issues 193
   search engines 190
   social networking sites 188
   Universal Resource Locators (URLs) 189
   uses of 186
   web browsers 189
   wikis 186–7
internet banking 108, 110
internet games, safety issues 160–1
internet of things (IOT) 82
   security issues 84
internet protocols (IPs) 188, 191–2
Internet Service Providers (ISPs) 188
   restriction of content 193
internet shopping 118–20
interviews 132–3, 134

intranets 66, 185–6
iOS 12
IP addresses 65, 188
italics 267, 351
    HTML 527

joint photographic expert group (.jpg) files 204
joysticks 27–8

key fields 373–4, 379–80
key fobs (physical tokens) 72
key logging 164–5
key words 540
keyboards and keypads 25–6
keys, encryption 70, 165–6, 177
keywords 527
kilobytes 11
knowledge bases 114
knowledge factors 169
knowledge graphs 312

labels, database reports 415–17, 420
lands, CDs and DVDs 51, 52
landscape orientation 341
laptops 14–15
    advantages and disadvantages 16
laser printers 40
layers, web development 524
layers of images 221
layout 234
    headers and footers 251–3
    margins 235
    page layout 340–6
    placing objects 236–9
    text manipulation 235–6
    worked example 255–61
layout masters 441–3
LCD (liquid crystal display) monitors 39
learning, computer-aided 104–5
LEDs (light-emitting diodes) 39
legends 314
legislation, copyright 176–7
leisure, smart devices 83
length checks 139
licence keys 177
light pens 32–3
light sensors 32
limitations 148
line graphs 319
line spacing 269, 270, 303
link element, HTML 547–8
linked objects 240–1

linked tables
    see also relational databases
linkers 6
lists 270, 352–4, 363–4
live data 143
live streaming 96
live systems 143
local area networks (LANs) 61
local web pages 538
logical operators 399
logistics 103
logos 266, 282–3
LOOKUP functions 485–9, 492
lossless compression 205, 206
lossy compression 205, 206
Lovelace, Ada 2
lower case 305, 352

MAC (media access control) addresses 63
machine learning 17, 18, 101, 293–4
macOS 11
magnetic polarity 48
magnetic storage media 48, 55
    hard disk drives 48–9
    magnetic tapes 47, 50
magnetic stripes 34, 38, 72
mailing lists (email groups) 184
malware 70–1, 73–4, 158, 162, 163–4
managers 11
margins 235, 255, 341–2, 359
master pages 267
master slides 441–3
match points 122
mathematical formulae 98
MAXIMUM function 484
maximum values 316, 333
media communication systems 124–5
media streaming 96
medical applications
    3D printing 111–13
    computer aided design 112
    customised medicines 113
    expert systems 114
    records systems 111
megabytes 11
memory 4, 9–10, 11
    units of 11
memory cards (SD cards) 30, 54
memory sticks 54
merging cells 245, 479
metadata 526
mice (singular: mouse) 26

Index

microphones 31
microprocessors 82
mineral prospecting, expert systems 114–15
MINIMUM function 484
minimum values 316
misspellings 287, 288, 292
    autocorrect 289–90
    see also spell check
mobile communication 97
mobile computers 14–15
mobile networks 97
mobile phones
    satellite systems 125
    see also smartphones
modelling 98–100
modelling software 98
modules 141
money transfers 108
monitors 32, 39
motherboard 4
MSDOS (Microsoft Disk Operating System) 13
multi-factor authentication (MFA) 169
multimedia presentations 95, 445

named cells 482
named ranges 491–2
navigation 356, 361–3
    bookmarks 357
    hyperlinks 357–8
navigation controls 394, 396
near field communication (NFC) 118
Nelson, Ted 523
nested functions 484–5, 490–1
netiquette 183–4
network devices 63–5
network environments 66
network interface cards (NICs) 4, 63
network switches 63–4
network traffic 63
networks 61
    electronic-conferencing 75–7
    mobile (cellular) 97
    security issues 69–75
    types 61–2
    Wi-Fi and Bluetooth 61–2
newsletters 94, 95
NHS National Program for IT 131
non-contiguous data 312
non-volatile memory 9
normal data 142
NOT 399, 502
numbered lists 352, 353

numeric data 376
numeric keypads 25, 26

observation 132, 134
one-to-many relationships 384
online banking 110
online booking systems 106–7
online gaming 160–1
online shopping 93
opening a file 199
operating systems (OS) 5, 11–12
optical character recognition (OCR) 36, 38, 120
optical mark recognition (OMR) 36, 38, 104, 120
optical mice 26
optical storage media 51, 55
option groups 394, 395
OR 399, 400, 402–3, 503
order of operations 483
orphan records 384
orphans 303–4
output devices 4, 10, 39
    actuators 42
    monitors 39
    multimedia projectors 39
    printers and plotters 40–1
    speakers 41–2
    touch screens 39
output formats 136, 137–8
output layouts, database reports 423

packet analysers (packet sniffers) 69
packet switching 65
packets 64
padding 545
page breaks 344, 359–60
page layout 340–6
    spreadsheets 509–12
page number total 253
page numbers 252, 259, 276
    database reports 421
page orientation 340, 341, 361
page size 340–1
pagination 344–6
paragraph styles 269–72, 303–4, 364
    indents 348–51
    worked example 273–6
parallel running 145, 146
parent directories 199
parental controls 193
Parker, Matt 507
passwords 70, 71, 161, 169
paste 236

Paste Special 240
patient record systems 111
pen drives 54
peripheral devices 2, 11
personal area networks (PANs) 61
personal data 157–8
personal finance
    expert systems 115
    modelling 98
personalised medicines 113
phablets 15
pharmacy records 111
pharming 163
phased implementation 144, 146
phishing 162–3
physical safety 153, 154–6
physical tokens 72, 169
pie charts 320–2
pilot running 145, 146
PINs (personal identification numbers) 35
piracy 176, 178
pits, CDs and DVDs 51, 52
pixels 30, 222, 228
placeholders 441, 443
placing an image 212–13
plaintext 165
plant identification systems 115
Playfair, William 310
plot points 319
plotters 40, 41
podcasts 96
point of sale (POS) terminals 116–17
point sizes 268
pointing devices 26–7
Pokémon Go 19–20
portable document format (.pdf) 204
portable hard disk drives 49
portable network graphics (.png) files 204
portrait orientation 341
possession factors 169
posters 94–5
posture 81, 87, 89
predictive text 290
presence checks 139
presentation layer 524
presentation templates 445
presentations 173, 439–40
    action buttons 455–7, 461
    alternative text 462
    animation effects 464–7, 471
    audience characteristics 174–5
    creation from a text file 445–6

    display formats 470–1
    editing 446–57
    hiding slides 467–8
    hyperlink targets 454–5
    hyperlinks 452–5
    inserting a new slide 447–9
    inserting audio files 447, 450
    inserting video files 450
    master slides 441–3
    moving, deleting and duplicating slides 450, 451
    presenter notes 450, 452
    printing layouts 471–2
    purpose of 174
    reasons for 445
    ScreenTips 462–3
    transitions 463–4
    worked example 457–62
presenter notes 472
pressure sensors 32
primary keys 373–4, 379–80
printers 40–1
privacy issues
    personal data security 157–8
    social media 159–60
private keys 70, 166
processing 7
production line control 102
program code 147
programming languages 147
proofing 288
    grammar check 290–1
    'Replace' tool 291
    spell check 288–90, 292–3
    typographical errors 290
    visual verification 304–6
proofreading 289, 302–4
property sheets 390
prosthetics 112
protocols 62
    IPs 188, 191–2
    TCP/IP 66
public keys 70, 166

QR (quick response) codes 37–8, 121
quarantine 73
queries 399–404
    run-time calculations 407–11
    search operators 405
    sorting results 400
    wildcards 405
questionnaires 133, 134
quick sort 497–8

Index

QWERTY keyboards 25

radio buttons 376, 394, 396, 397
random access (direct access) 49
random-access memory (RAM) 9, 11
range checks 138
ranges, spreadsheets 482
    naming 491–2
.rar (roshal archive) files 205, 206
read-only memory (ROM) 9–10
real-time models 99
rebranding 282–3
recognition systems
    automated number plate recognition 120–1
    bar codes, QR codes and RFID 121
    biometric 121–2
    OCR and OMR 36
    optical 120
records 136, 137, 372
redundant data 206
referential integrity 384
reflecting (flipping) an image 216–17
registers 8, 9
registration systems 104
Relational Database Management Systems (RDMS) 372
relational databases 312, 372–4
relationships 383–4
relative file paths 537–8
relative references 481
remedial action 142
remote controls 27
repetitive strain injury (RSI) 26, 81, 87, 89
'Replace' tool 291
reply to all, emails 184
reports 413–14
requirements specification 134
research methods 132–3, 134
resistive touch screens 29
resizing an image 214
retail applications
    electronic fund transfer 117–18
    internet shopping 118–20
    point of sale terminals 116–17
    stock control systems 117
RFID (radio-frequency identification) 35, 38, 121
rich text format (.rtf) files 204
robots 2, 17, 42
    use in manufacturing 101–2
rotating an image 215–16
ROUND functions 485
route scheduling 115
routers 64–5

routing tables 65
row height 244
rows
    insertion and deletion 244–5
    spreadsheets 479, 505
    tables 244
rules bases 114
run-time calculations 407–11

safety 153
    eSafety 156–61
    internet use 193
    physical 154–6
sampling 7–8
sans-serif fonts 267
satellite dishes 125
satellite navigation (satnav) 123–4
satellite phones 125
satellite systems 122
    geographic information systems 124
    global positioning systems 123
    media communication systems 124–5
satellite television 124–5
satellites 122
saving files 202–5
scales 316
scanners 29–30
    3D 41
school management systems 104–5
screen readers 41–2
screens *see* monitors
screenshots 202
ScreenTips 462–3
scripting languages 524
search engines 190
    eSafety 158
search operators 405
searches
    databases 399–405
    spreadsheets 498–503
    wildcards 405, 503
secondary axes 323–4
secondary storage devices 10–11
second-level domains (SLDs) 189
section breaks 344–5, 360
section headers 345–6
section orientation 345
sector labels 321
secure digital (SD) cards 30, 54
Secure Socket Layer (SSL) 168, 192
security 153
    anti-malware software 73

authentication 70–3
   data breaches 60
   databases 388
   emails 184–5
   encryption 69–70
   firewalls 70, 168
   of networks 69
   of patient records 111
   see also data security
security measures 73–5
security tokens (physical tokens) 72
self-driving vehicles 86
sensors 24–5, 31–2
   autonomous vehicles 103
sequential storage 50
serial storage 50
series 482
serif fonts 267
servers 64, 67, 68
   web servers 95
shapes, insertion into a document 237–8, 256
short message service (SMS) 97
shoulder surfing 164
sibling folders 538
Simple Mail Transfer Protocol (SMTP) 191
simulation 98
'skimming' 164
slide presentations *see* presentations
smart cards 72
smart cities 85
smart devices 82
   positive and negative effects 83–5
smart home systems 13
smartphone payments 73
smartphone sensors 32
smartphones 14, 15, 97
   advantages and disadvantages 16
   near field communication 118
   tethering 62
smishing 163
Snow, John 310–11
social networking sites (social media) 188
   eSafety 159–60
social interaction, impact of smart devices 84–5
soft page breaks 344
software 5–6
software licences 177
solid-state drives (SSDs) 53–4
solid-state storage media 53, 55
   flash memory cards 54
sorting data 400–1, 403–4, 497–8
sound cards 4

sound sampling 7–8
source code editors 525
spam 162, 185
spatial laser sensors 103
speakers 41–2
specified data range 311
speed of a computer 11
spell check 288–90
   AutoCorrect options 291
   limitations 292–3
spreadsheets 477–8
   cells, rows and columns 479
   computer modelling 98
   conditional formatting 507–9, 517
   copying down 480–2
   data entry 497
   display features 505
   displaying formulae 492–3
   filters 498–503
   formatting text 505–6
   formulae 479–83, 516
   functions 483–91, 514–15
   insertion into a document 239–43, 260
   linking to a database 241–3
   named cells 482
   named ranges 491–2
   page layout 509–12
   referencing different sheets 493
   series 482
   sorting data 497–8
   worked example 512–18
spyware 69, 70–1, 74, 163
SSL (Secure Sockets Layer) 168, 192
stacked layout 423
staff training 144
static information 252
stock control systems 117
storage
   backing storage devices 10–11
   cloud storage 68
storage devices 48
storage locations 9
storage media 48
   comparison of different types 55
   magnetic 47, 48–50
   optical 51–3
   solid-state 53–5
streaming 96
stream-ripping 178
stress 88
strong passwords 70
style 265–6

Index

consistency 266–7, 304
corporate house style 282
fonts 267–9
paragraph styles 269–72
tables 272
worked example 273–6
style sheets 282
style templates 441
styluses 33
subscript 351
SUM function 483–4
superscript 351
switches 63–4
symmetric encryption 165–6
syntax 540
system flowcharts 147
system managers 146
system specification 134–5
systems analysts 132
systems life cycle 131
    analysis 131–5
    design 135–40
    documentation 146–8
    evaluation 148–9
    implementation 143–6
    testing 141–3
systems software 5, 6

tab stops 348, 349
tables 136, 137, 371
    alignment of text 245–6, 544–5
    cell shading/colouring 246–7
    creation 247–8
    creation for databases 374–81, 386
    in CSS 542–7, 549–53
    gridlines 247
    inserting and deleting rows and columns 244–5
    insertion into a document 238–9
    linked 373
    merging cells 245
    proofing 304
    row height and column width 244
    style 272
    text wrap 246
    text wrapping 243
    web pages 531–3, 542–7
tablets 14, 15
    advantages and disadvantages 16
    tethering 62
tabular forms 390
tabulation (tabs) 347–8
tags 525

TCP/IP protocols 66
technical documentation 146–7
television, satellite systems 124–5
temperature sensors 31–2
templates 267
terabytes 11
terminal testing 141
test data 142
test design 142
test plans 142–3
test strategies 141
testing 141–3
tethering 62
text
    fonts 267–9
    insertion from another document 236–7
    point sizes 269
text alignment 266, 271
    tables 245–6
text boxes 237
text data type 376
text enhancement 266, 267, 351
    bullets and numbers 352–4
    HTML 527
text (.txt) files 204
text manipulation 235–6
text wrapping 213, 243, 261
    within a cell 246
TFT (thin film of transistors) monitors 39
thesaurus 293
tickets, online booking systems 106–7
tiling images 542
time insertion, documents 253
timetable creation 105
tissue engineering 113
title of a web page 526–7
TLS (Transport Layer Security) 168
Tomlinson, Raymond 181
top-down design 136
top-level domains (TLDs) 189
touch screens 28–9, 39
touchpads 26–7
track changes tool 303
trackerballs 27
traffic management 99
traffic modelling 99
training staff 144
transcription 137
transistors 7
    floating gate 53
transitions, slide presentations 463–4
transmission of files 205

transparency 219
transposition errors 305
triggers 457
trilateration 123
Trojans 74
two-factor authentication 169
type checks 139
typographical errors 290

ultrasonic sensors 25
uncompressed files 205
ungroup 220
unique data 373
unique identifiers 35
unit of memory 11
Universal Resource Locators (URLs) 189, 528
Unix 11
upper case 352
   consistent use of 305
USB tokens (physical tokens) 72
user documentation 147–8
user IDs 169
   see also authentication; passwords
user interfaces 12, 13, 114
   command line 12–13
   dialogue-based 13
   gesture-based 14
   graphical 13
utility software (utilities) 5, 6

validation 306
validation routines 138–40, 288, 294, 377–9
   worked example 294–8
validation rules 136
validity 138, 191
value axis 313
   titles and labels 315
variables 147
vehicle safety 85
verification 294, 304–6
version control 201
vertical alignment 245–6
video, insertion into a web page 536–7
video cameras 30
video communication 96
video-conferencing 30–1, 75–7
viewport 527
virtual personal assistants 18
virtual reality (VR) 18–19
viruses 74, 163–4
vishing 163
visual verification 304–6

VLOOKUP function 486–8, 492
voice over internet protocol (VOIP) 97
volatile memory 9

washing machines 31–2, 42
weather forecasting 98, 99–100
web browsers 95, 189
web development layers 524
web page creation 525
   HTML 525–6
web pages 95, 202, 203
   body section 527–9
   file paths 537–8
   head section 526–7
   inserting audio files 537
   inserting images 535–6
   inserting video files 536–7
   links 528–9
   tables 531–3
   worked example 549–53
web servers 95
webcams 30–1
webcasts 75
web-conferencing 75–7
webinars 75
websites 95
   increasing numbers 525
what3words 123–4
white space 397
wide area networks (WANs) 61
widgets 289
widows 303–4
Wi-Fi 62
wikis 186–7
wildcards 405, 503
WIMP interfaces 13
Windows 11
wireless local area networks (WLANs) 61
wireless mice 26
worksheets 478
   referencing different sheets 493
world wide web (www, web) 186, 523–4, 528
worms 74

x-axis 313
XLOOKUP function 490, 518

y-axis 313

z-axis 112
zero login 73
.zip files 205, 206

> Acknowledgements

The authors and publishers acknowledge the following sources of copyright material and are grateful for the permissions granted. While every effort has been made, it has not always been possible to identify the sources of all the material used, or to trace all copyright holders. If any omissions are brought to our notice, we will be happy to include the appropriate acknowledgements on reprinting.

Microsoft product screenshots are used with permission from Microsoft. Microsoft is a registered trademark of Microsoft Corporation.

Thanks to the following for permission to reproduce images:

Cover Image Xu Binf/GI; *Inside* **Unit 1:** Tek Image/Science Photo Library/GI; 1.1a PC Gamer Magazine/GI; 1.1b PC Plus Magazine/GI; 1.1c Tim Grist Photography/GI; 1.1e Membio/GI; Merznatalia/GI; 1.2 Phonlamaiphoto/GI; 1.3 S3studio/GI; 1.10 KAZUHIRO NOGI/AFP via GI; 1.11 John Macdougall/GI; 1.12 Bernhard Lang/GI; 1.13 Keongdagreat/GI; **Unit 2:** Francesco Cantone/GI; 2.1a Carol Yepes/GI; 2.1b Stephen Brashear/Stringer/GI; 2.1c Hispanolistic/GI; 2.1d Ron Levine/GI; 2.1e Izusek/GI; 2.3 Ligorko/GI; 2.4 Lumen-Digital/Shutterstock; 2.5 24K-Production/GI; 2.6 John Greim/GI; 2.8 John Keeble/GI; 2.9 Smith Collection/Gado/GI; 2.10 Dragomer Maria/Shutterstock; 2.11 Andreypopov/GI; 2.12 Xefstock/GI; 2.13 Brian A Jackson/Shutterstock; 2.14a Macformat Magazine/GI; 2.14b Macbrianmun/GI; 2.14c Burnel1/Shutterstock; 2.14d Will Ireland/T3 Magazine/GI; 2.15a Moreno Soppelsa/Shutterstock; 2.15b James Davies; Izusek/GI; **Unit 3:** Kyoshino/GI; 3.1a Ffolas/Shutterstock; 3.1b A&G Reporter/AGF/ Universal Images Group/GI; 3.1c Anton Starikov/Shutterstock; 3.1d Science & Society Picture Library/GI; 3.1e Ethamphoto/GI; 3.1f Sean Gladwell/GI; 3.2 Gregory Gerber/Shutterstock; 3.3 Be Good/Shutterstock; **Unit 4:** Yuji Sakai/GI; 4.1a Fotosearch/GI; 4.1b Yevgen Romanenko/GI; 4.1c Chatcharin Sombutpinyo/GI; 4.1d Powerbeephoto/GI; 4.1e thanks to Landis+Gyr AR; 4.7a Izusek/GI; 4.7b Krysteq/GI; 4.7c Drbimages/GI; 4.7d Hanis/GI; 4.7e Rolando Caponi/GI; 4.7f Luxizeng/GI; 4.7g Mikroman6/GI; 4.7h Edwardolive/GI; 4.8 Stephen Barnes/Technology/Alamy Stock Photo; 4.10 Rocketclips, Inc./Shutterstock; **Unit 5:** Monty Rakusen/GI; 5.1 Maanas/GI; 5.2 Jazzirt/GI; 5.3 Ullstein Bild/GI; 5.5 Maanas/GI; **Unit 6:** Hiroshi Watanabe/GI; 6.1 Jeff Spicer/GI; 6.4 NASA Earth Observatory/Science Photo Library; 6.7 Marin Tomas/GI; 6.9 Jeff Greenberg/GI; 6.11 Alexlmx/GI; 6.12 Miakievy/GI; 6.13 The Apple Pay name and mark are property of Apple; The Google Pay mark is property of Google; The Contactless Symbol is a Trademark owned by and used with Permission of Emvco, LLC.; 6.14 Xefstock/GI; 6.15 Tuul & Bruno Morandi/GI; 6.17 Used by permission of What3words; **Unit 7:** Cavan Images/GI; 7.1 Svetikd/GI; 7.2 Westend61/GI; 7.7 Whitemay/GI; **Unit 8:** Yuichiro Chino/GI; 8.2a P A Thompson/GI; 8.2b Mike Goldwater/Alamy Stock Photo; 8.3 Stockyme/GI; 8.5 Peter Dazeley/GI; **Unit 9:** Jovo Marjanovic/GI; 9.1a Graphic: The pathway by which plastic enters the world's oceans by Our World in Data https://ourworldindata.org/where-does-plastic-accumulate; 9.1b © Ruby Tuesday Books Ltd.; 9.2 Yoshiyoshi Hirokawa/GI; 9.3 Jlgutierrez/GI; **Unit 10:** Alengo/GI; 10.1 Getty Images; **Unit 11:** MF3d/GI; 11.5 © Cambridge University Press; **Unit 12:** Matthew Leete/GI; 12.2 Photography By Mangiwau/GI; **Unit 13:** Ijeab/GI; 13.2 Bgblue/GI; 13.4 The Washington Post/GI; Peter Cade/GI; **Unit 14:** Sky Noir Photography By Bill Dickinson/GI; 14.2 Delmaine Donson/GI; 14.3 G Fiume/GI; 14.6 Karen Bleier/GI; 14.35 Jim Steinfeldt/GI; 14.36 Nurphoto/GI; Cavan Images/GI; **Unit 15:** Lamaip/GI; 15.2 Education Images/GI; **Unit 16:** Phongphan Supphakankamjon/GI; 16.2 William Playfair/Wikimedia; Andreypopov/GI; **Unit 17:** Mapodile/GI; 17.2 DEA/G. Dagli Orti/GI; 17.27 Mcininch/GI; **Unit 18:** Andriy Onufriyenko/GI; 18.1 Canjoena/GI; **Unit 19:** DIPA/GI; 19.1a Westend61/GI; 19.1b Maanas/GI; 19.2 Filo/GI; 19.4 Photoquest/GI; **Unit 20:** Sean Gladwell/GI; 20.1 Mysteryguitarman's Stop-Go Animation, Reproduced with permission from Joe Penna (Author); **Unit 21:** Manoonpan Phantong/GI; 21.2 Rosdiana Ciaravolo/GI; **Answers:** 5.1 Alonzodesign/GI

In chapters 12 and 21 the photos within screenshots demonstrating how to manipulate images are property of the author, David Waller. Photos in Source Files are also property of the author, except for DataCentre (baranozdemir/GI), New plants 1 (Westend61/GI), New plants 2 (C Squared Studios/GI), Paris 1 (Julian Elliott Photography/GI) and Paris 2 (Ingenui/GI).

Key: GI= Getty Images